OCLC

U.S. FEDERAL DEPOSITORY 0401A
574-A
SEP 06 1988

Lougheed Library
St. Thomas Aquinas College

0574 A

D1205600

#22427819
y1985 v1

PUBLIC PAPERS OF THE PRESIDENTS
OF THE
UNITED STATES

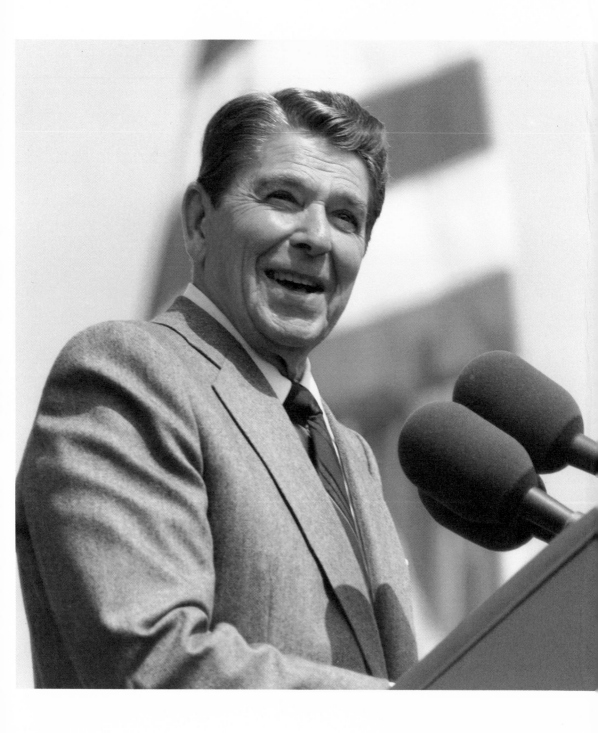

PUBLIC PAPERS OF THE PRESIDENTS
OF THE
UNITED STATES

Ronald Reagan

1985

(IN TWO BOOKS)

BOOK I—JANUARY 1 TO JUNE 28, 1985

UNITED STATES GOVERNMENT PRINTING OFFICE
WASHINGTON : 1988

ST. THOMAS AQUINAS COLLEGE
LOUGHEED LIBRARY
SPARKILL, NEW YORK 10976

Published by the
Office of the Federal Register
National Archives and Records Administration

For sale by the
Superintendent of Documents
U.S. Government Printing Office
Washington, DC 20402

Foreword

The first half of 1985 was a time of stability both at home and abroad, a time of confidence and of laying the foundation for future progress. By January our country had entered its 27th month of economic recovery. The gross national product was on the rise, while inflation remained low. Throughout the country, a spirit of enterprise flourished as new businesses were started and older businesses—with, in most cases, a significant contribution from labor—reinvigorated their operations and increased productivity.

The Federal Government, in the meantime, struggled with issues fundamental to the future economic well-being and security of our country. Reducing Federal deficit spending was high on the list of priorities. Meeting this challenge, first and foremost, meant getting control of the growth and size of the Federal budget. Many seemingly mundane skirmishes over spending proposals were, in actuality, part of an historic budget battle.

During this time I campaigned, publicly and privately, to build a bipartisan consensus to overhaul the Federal tax system, make it more fair, and bring down the rates. Progress on Capitol Hill was slow, and pessimists were convinced meaningful reform was impossible.

On the foreign front, the United States, bolstered by its economic success, used its influence and power to further the cause of human freedom, promote international economic growth, and preserve peace between the nations. The vitality and scope of cooperation among the Western democracies were reaffirmed on numerous occasions, especially at a highly successful economic summit that took place in Bonn, the Federal Republic of Germany. Other issues vital to our security, such as support for the freedom fighters battling the Communist regime in Nicaragua and America's Strategic Defense Initiative, continued to be the focus of much of the national debate.

The following pages reflect the workings of our great Republic. It is the unfolding history of a free people, a history in which each and every citizen is free to participate.

Ronald Reagan

Preface

This book contains the papers and speeches of the 40th President of the United States that were issued by the Office of the Press Secretary during the period January 1–June 28, 1985. The material has been compiled and published by the Office of the Federal Register, National Archives and Records Administration.

The material is presented in chronological order, and the dates shown in the headings are the dates of the documents or events. In instances when the release date differs from the date of the document itself, that fact is shown in the textnote. Every effort has been made to ensure accuracy: Remarks are checked against a tape recording, and signed documents are checked against the original. Textnotes, footnotes, and cross references have been provided by the editors for purposes of identification or clarity. Speeches were delivered in Washington, DC, unless indicated. The times noted are local times. All materials that are printed full-text in the book have been indexed in the subject and name indexes.

The Public Papers series was begun in 1957 in response to a recommendation of the National Historical Publications Commission. An extensive compilation of messages and papers of the Presidents covering the period 1789 to 1897 was assembled by James D. Richardson and published under congressional authority between 1896 and 1899. Since then, various private compilations have been issued, but there was no uniform publication comparable to the Congressional Record or the United States Supreme Court Reports. Many Presidential papers could be found only in the form of mimeographed White House releases or as reported in the press. The Commission therefore recommended the establishment of an official series in which Presidential writings, addresses, and remarks of a public nature could be made available.

The Commission's recommendation was incorporated in regulations of the Administrative Committee of the Federal Register, issued under section 6 of the Federal Register Act (44 U.S.C. 1506), which may be found in Title I, Part 10, of the Code of Federal Regulations.

A companion publication to the Public Papers series, the Weekly Compilation of Presidential Documents, was begun in 1965 to provide a broader range of Presidential materials on a more timely basis to meet the needs of the contemporary reader. Beginning with the administration of Jimmy Carter, the Public Papers series expanded its coverage to include all material as printed in the Weekly Compilation. That coverage provides a listing of the President's daily schedule and meetings, when announced, and other items of general interest issued by the Office of the Press Secretary. Also included are lists of the President's nominations submitted to the Senate, materials released by the Office of the Press Secretary that are not printed full-text in the book, and acts approved by the President. This information appears in the appendixes at the end of the book.

Volumes covering the administrations of Presidents Hoover, Truman, Eisenhower, Kennedy, Johnson, Nixon, Ford, and Carter are also available.

The Chief Editor of this book was William K. Banks.

White House liaison was provided by Marlin Fitzwater, Assistant to the President for Press Relations. The frontispiece and photographs used in the portfolio were supplied by the White House Photo Office.

John E. Byrne
Director of the Federal Register

Don W. Wilson
Archivist of the United States

Contents

Administration of Ronald Reagan

1985

Message to the Berliner Morgenpost
January 1, 1985

Berlin is a place and a people close to the American heart. It is a pleasure for me to write for the people of Berlin about this special city.

With the coming of the new year, it will be forty years since Berlin as a city under four-power administration was created. This special status has made Berlin the free and prosperous city we see today. This status and the determination of the Allies to insist on their rights and to fulfill their responsibilities is why Berlin stands today in such contrast to its surroundings.

Even today, the Western Allies are Berlin's trustees. They are also, in an important sense, the trustees of the German nation. They are in Berlin as sentinels and as reminders that the tragic division of Germany and Europe is not immutable.

Berliners can be confident that the Allied role in Berlin, with its roots in history long past, with its present complexities, is still the guarantor of Berlin's liberty. Building on this solid foundation, it has been possible to construct East-West arrangements to benefit the people of Berlin.

The close partnership that has grown up between the Western Allies and the Berliners, based on mutual respect and sensitivity, is also vital. We have been together through the Berlin airlift. Together we have celebrated successes such as the Quadripartite Agreement. These shared experiences have forged an unbreakable bond. Together we will work to create a bright future for Berlin. For the new year, I would like to renew to every Berliner our pledge: the American commitment to Berlin is unshakable.

Informal Exchange With Reporters in Los Angeles, California
January 2, 1985

Q. Mr. President, what about that Soviet cruise missile that was fired over Finland and Norway?

The President. Well, you know, I shouldn't be answering any questions, but on that particular one, let me just say we still have no absolute verification of that. So——

Q. Were they trying to send us a message of some kind in advance of the talks in Geneva?

The President. Well, I wouldn't know because, as I say, we don't have any verification yet.

Q. Why were you unable to keep Judge Clark, Mr. President?

The President. This is so current, and I haven't seen you and—forgive me, I will answer that, and then we won't have any more questions here in a photo opportunity.

I took him into public life for 18 years. He left his own pursuits in private life. And a couple of years ago, he was desirous of getting back, but at my request, he stayed on. Now, I just don't have any—I'm going to miss him very much—but I don't have any continued arguments to keep him on longer if he feels he must return to his own——

Q. Who are you going to replace him with, sir?

Q. Can you just say what kind of arguments you're going to use with the Prime Minister on the trade deficit?

The President. We won't argue. We're good friends.

1

Q. But what about the size of that trade deficit and the implications for our own economy?

The President. Our trade deficit, of course, is worldwide due to some of our own economic problems.

Q. Doesn't a lot of it have to do with Japan's barriers?

The President. What?

Q. Doesn't a lot of it have to do with Japan's barriers on certain——

The President. No, we've made great progress. But I'll be making a statement on that when the meetings are over.

Q. Who are you going to replace Judge Clark with, sir?

Mr. Hart. Thank you. Please proceed to your left.

The President. No decision yet.

Q. Isn't Mr. Laxalt, your other good, close personal friend, a candidate?

The President. Mr. Laxalt would be a— Senator Laxalt—a good man anywhere, but right now I think we need all the help we can get in the United States Senate.

Q. What about your Energy Secretary, Mr. Hodel?

Mr. Gray. Thank you.

Mr. Weinberg. Thank you.

The President. No decisions yet.

Q. Ms. Mitchell [Andrea Mitchell, NBC News], are you available? [Laughter]

Mr. Speakes. Thank you. Let's go.

Mr. Weinberg. Turn to your left.

Mr. Speakes. You've got two more groups to come behind you.

The President. Now, you witness I broke all my own rules here to answer your questions.

Q. Yes, sir. That's one reason that we love to keep asking—[laughter]——

Q. Is that a new tie?

Q. Is that a Christmas tie, Mr. President?

Q. We're admiring your new tie.

The President. Yep. It is.

Q. Do you like it?

The President. I think it's an answer to— does away with all the jokes about Christmas ties. I think it's beautiful.

Q. Who gave it to you?

The President. Just one of our friends.

Q. It wasn't Mrs. Reagan?

The President. No.

Q. Because I wouldn't say anything against one of her gifts.

The President. No. Then, you'll love the pickup.

Q. But if it wasn't her, sir, I must tell you there's divided opinion about your tie. [Laughter] You think it's beautiful. Others——

The President. Well, some have good taste and some don't. [Laughter]

Note: The exchange began at 11:10 a.m. in the library of the President's suite at the Century Plaza Hotel. The reporters were present to observe the beginning of the President's meeting with Prime Minister Yasuhiro Nakasone of Japan.

Stephen T. Hart was a member of the White House Press Advance staff. Robin C. Gray and Mark Weinberg were Assistant Press Secretaries. Larry M. Speakes was Principal Deputy Press Secretary to the President.

Remarks Following Discussions With Prime Minister Yasuhiro Nakasone of Japan in Los Angeles, California
January 2, 1985

The President. I was very pleased to welcome Prime Minister Nakasone and Foreign Minister Abe to Los Angeles for an official working visit at the start of both this new year and, I'm pleased to say, the second terms in office for two of us.

This visit has reconfirmed and strength-ened the vital relationship between the United States and Japan. When I visited Japan in November a year ago, I told Prime Minister Nakasone that there's no relationship that is more important to peace and prosperity in the world than that between the United States and Japan. The discussions that we've had today have convinced me once again of the truth of that statement.

The Prime Minister and I have discussed a number of key regional and international issues, with a special focus on our relations with the Soviet Union and the upcoming arms reduction talks in Geneva. I informed the Prime Minister of my intention to pursue effective arms reduction agreements with the Soviets seriously and zealously, while pointing out that we believe that some hard bargaining lies ahead.

I promised the Prime Minister that as we pursue these talks, we'll keep very much in mind the interests of our friends and allies in both Europe and Asia. I told Prime Minister Nakasone that if the Soviets are prepared to cooperate, then we will make progress. I'm grateful that the Prime Minister supported our approach to these negotiations.

We have reaffirmed the importance that our own defense efforts make to regional peace and stability, and we vowed to work together to strengthen our mutual security cooperation within the framework of the Treaty of Mutual Cooperation and Security.

Our economic relations, particularly our trading relations, have been at the top of the agenda today, and we've discussed very candidly those areas where we have problems. We agreed to work strenuously in the months ahead to open our markets fully and to resist protectionist pressures in both countries.

I believe that we both agree that there is an urgent need to work together to resolve the problems in our trade relationship. We both recognize, I believe, that failure to overcome these obstacles in trade will complicate our ability to fulfill the vision of international partnership between Japan and the United States that we both share.

I have also reiterated our view that the capital markets measures that Japan announced last May should be fully and promptly implemented. I outlined my belief that implementation of the Agreement on Energy Cooperation should be accelerated. And I also indicated that we're pleased to welcome increased Japanese investment in the United States, which already is providing over 150,000 jobs to American workers.

In their effort to strengthen our overall relations, we have agreed to put Secretary Shultz and Foreign Minister Abe in charge of overseeing an intensified cooperative effort to make progress in our economic relations, including special, urgent efforts in key sectors.

Now, underlying today's meeting is a reaffirmation of the close and friendly ties between our two great peoples and our shared democratic values. Prime Minister Nakasone and I have pledged that we shall work to strengthen further our relations and cooperation as bilateral, Pacific, and international partners. And with this in mind, we've agreed that the recent report of the United States-Japan advisory commission is an excellent starting point for charting the future course of our relationship. Officials of our two governments will come together soon to review the report and its many excellent recommendations.

And finally, Mr. Prime Minister, it's been an immense personal pleasure to see you again. In five meetings, we have helped strengthen the powerful partnership for good between the United States and Japan of which I spoke before your distinguished Diet.

We value deeply our close friendship with Japan. As economic powers and as democratic nations, we're committed to the search for peace and prosperity for our own people and for all people. As leaders of two great nations, we have the mutual responsibility to work together in partnership to help people throughout the world secure the blessings of freedom and prosperity that we enjoy.

The Prime Minister. President Reagan and I have just completed a very fruitful discussion.

I believe that there are three distinctive elements in the current Japan-U.S. relationship. They are trust, responsibility, and friendship. At the beginning of the new year, the President and I have set a framework for our two countries to work together, based on these three elements, for promoting dynamic cooperation in quest of the peace and prosperity of the world.

The President and I exchanged views on

the issue of peace and arms control. The negotiation on arms control will start next week in Geneva between Secretary Shultz and Foreign Minister Gromyko. I expressed my respect to the President's firm determination in pursuit of peace. I fully support his endeavor in launching this important negotiation.

The President and I reaffirmed the importance of maintaining close contact and unity among the industrial democracies on this issue. I earnestly hope that the historians of the future will mark 1985 as the year in which a great step forward was taken towards the consolidation of the world peace.

The President and I reconfirmed that the United States and Japan share heavy responsibilities for the sustained, noninflationary growth of the world economy and for the maintenance and development of the open and multilateral economic and trading system of the world. For this purpose, it is important to implement appropriate economic policies in our respective countries and to endeavor to maintain and expand the open market.

We also confirmed that Japan and the United States will cooperate even closer for launching the preparations for a new round of multilateral trade negotiations this year.

The President and I welcomed the advent of a new era characterized by the active cooperation in high technology, investment in capital exchanges, services, and other areas. We shared the determination of making serious efforts for a more balanced development of our trade and economic relations. To this end, Japan will promote economic policies that will enhance growth led by domestic private demand and will make further market-opening efforts.

To secure effectiveness of such mutual efforts, we will be engaged in an active joint followup effort and have designated Secretary Shultz and Foreign Minister Abe to oversee this cooperative process. Such work, needless to say, should be conducted with a view to strengthening our overall bilateral relationship.

The President and I shared the view that the report of the Japan-U.S. advisory commission was a valuable contribution and would merit a serious study by both sides. I expressed to the President that Japan intends to proceed further with its efforts at its own initiative to improve its self-defense capabilities, together with further strengthening the credibility of the Japan-U.S. security arrangements.

Mr. President, California has been a major gateway in the history of our trans-Pacific exchanges, and of course, California means a great deal for you, Mr. President. It was a great pleasure for me to meet with you here in California and to exchange views on our precious bilateral relationship in order to set the direction towards the 21st century. And there is no better place than California to talk about the importance of further promoting the dynamic development of the Asia and Pacific region.

Mr. President, it is indeed encouraging that I can continue to work with you as close partners in pursuit of our common objectives. Thank you very much for your kind hospitality.

Note: The President spoke at 1:48 p.m. in the Century Ballroom at the Century Plaza Hotel. The Prime Minister spoke in Japanese, and his remarks were translated by an interpreter. Earlier, the President and the Prime Minister met privately in the library of the President's suite at the Century Plaza Hotel. They then held a working luncheon with U.S. and Japanese officials, including Secretary of State George P. Shultz and Minister of Foreign Affairs Shintaro Abe. Following his remarks, the President returned to Washington, DC.

Foreword Written for a Report on the Strategic Defense Initiative
December 28, 1984

Since the advent of nuclear weapons, every President has sought to minimize the risk of nuclear destruction by maintaining effective forces to deter aggression and by pursuing complementary arms control agreements. This approach has worked. We and our allies have succeeded in preventing nuclear war while protecting Western security for nearly four decades.

Originally, we relied on balanced defensive and offensive forces to deter. But over the last twenty years, the United States has nearly abandoned efforts to develop and deploy defenses against nuclear weapons, relying instead almost exclusively on the threat of nuclear retaliation. We accepted the notion that if both we and the Soviet Union were able to retaliate with devastating power even after absorbing a first strike, that stable deterrence would endure. That rather novel concept seemed at the time to be sensible for two reasons. First, the Soviets stated that they believed that both sides should have roughly equal forces and neither side should seek to alter the balance to gain unilateral advantage. Second, there did not seem to be any alternative. The state of the art in defensive systems did not permit an effective defensive system.

Today both of these basic assumptions are being called into question. The pace of the Soviet offensive and defensive buildup has upset the balance in the areas of greatest importance during crises. Furthermore, new technologies are now at hand which may make possible a truly effective nonnuclear defense.

For these reasons and because of the awesome destructive potential of nuclear weapons, we must seek another means of deterring war. It is both militarily and morally necessary. Certainly, there should be a better way to strengthen peace and stability, a way to move away from a future that relies so heavily on the prospect of rapid and massive nuclear retaliation and toward greater reliance on defensive systems which threaten no one.

On March 23, 1983, I announced my decision to take an important first step toward this goal by directing the establishment of a comprehensive and intensive research program, the Strategic Defense Initiative, aimed at eventually eliminating the threat posed by nuclear armed ballistic missiles.

The Strategic Defense Initiative (SDI) is a program of vigorous research focused on advanced defensive technologies with the aim of finding ways to provide a better basis for deterring aggression, strengthening stability, and increasing the security of the United States and our allies. The SDI research program will provide to a future President and a future Congress the technical knowledge required to support a decision on whether to develop and later deploy advanced defensive systems.

At the same time, the United States is committed to the negotiation of equal and verifiable agreements which bring real reductions in the power of the nuclear arsenals of both sides. To this end, my Administration has proposed to the Soviet Union a comprehensive set of arms control proposals. We are working tirelessly for the success of these efforts, but we can and must go further in trying to strengthen the peace.

Our research under the Strategic Defense Initiative complements our arms reduction efforts and helps to pave the way for creating a more stable and secure world. The research that we are undertaking is consistent with all of our treaty obligations, including the 1972 Anti-Ballistic Missile Treaty.

In the near term, the SDI research program also responds to the ongoing and extensive Soviet anti-ballistic missile (ABM) effort, which includes actual deployments. It provides a powerful deterrent to any Soviet decision to expand its ballistic missile defense capability beyond that permitted by the ABM Treaty. And, in the long-term, we have confidence that SDI will be a crucial means by which both the United States and the Soviet Union can safely agree to very deep reductions, and eventually, even

5

the elimination of ballistic missiles and the nuclear weapons they carry.

Our vital interests and those of our allies are inextricably linked. Their safety and ours are one. They, too, rely upon our nuclear forces to deter attack against them. Therefore, as we pursue the promise offered by the Strategic Defense Initiative, we will continue to work closely with our friends and allies. We will ensure that, in the event of a future decision to develop and deploy defensive systems—a decision in which consultation with our allies will play an important part—allied, as well as U.S. security against aggression would be enhanced.

Through the SDI research program, I have called upon the great scientific talents of our country to turn to the cause of strengthening world peace by rendering ballistic missiles impotent and obsolete. In short, I propose to channel our technological prowess toward building a more secure and stable world. And I want to emphasize that in carrying out this research program, the United States seeks neither military superiority nor political advantage. Our only

purpose is to search for ways to reduce the danger of nuclear war.

As you review the following pages, I would ask you to remember that the quality of our future is at stake and to reflect on what we are trying to achieve—the strengthening of our ability to preserve the peace while shifting away from our current dependence upon the threat of nuclear retaliation. I would also ask you to consider the SDI research program in light of both the Soviet Union's extensive, ongoing efforts in this area and our own government's constitutional responsibility to provide for the common defense. I hope that you will conclude by lending your own strong and continuing support to this research effort—an effort which could prove to be critical to our nation's future.

RONALD REAGAN

December 28, 1984.

Note: The foreword was printed in the report entitled "The President's Strategic Defense Initiative—January 1985" (Government Printing Office, 10 pages), which was issued at the White House on January 3.

Statement Announcing an African Hunger Relief Initiative
January 3, 1985

Hunger and extreme malnutrition now threaten over 14 million people in Africa through the end of 1985. In response to this human catastrophe, America has responded as a government and as a people in a tremendous outpouring of aid. This fiscal year, the United States has already committed to Africa over 600,000 tons of emergency food, worth $250 million—this is in addition to our regular food aid program of about 1 million tons. The U.S. response has been far larger and faster than that of any other donor nation or institution.

The American people have also responded selflessly to this crisis, from the U.S. grain company that recently donated enough food to provide over 1 million meals to Ethiopian children to an elderly

woman who sent the Agency for International Development (AID) $2. Yet, even with all our country has already done to feed the starving, more—much more—must be accomplished by our nation in the months ahead to meet this challenge.

I am thus announcing today a comprehensive African hunger relief initiative. It addresses Africa's immediate emergency food needs, its pressing refugee problems, and its need to stimulate agricultural development on that continent.

Based on my discussions with African officials, congressional and private sector leaders, heads of voluntary organizations, and members of my administration, I am today directing that the U.S. Government's total commitment to Africa for fiscal year 1985 for emergency and regular food aid and disaster relief programs exceed $1 billion. This aid will provide over 1.5 million tons of emergency food. This overall $1 billion program will include resources already committed to Africa for the coming year, other AID resources, and a supplemental request on which I will ask the 99th Congress to take immediate action.

I have also today approved a $25 million drawdown from the United States Emergency Refugee and Migration Assistance Fund to finance urgent humanitarian assistance needs in Africa. This action is in response to appeals by the United Nations High Commissioner for Refugees and the International Committee for the Red Cross. This money will go to victims of the crises in Ethiopia, the Sudan, and other countries.

On the economic development side, efforts will continue on three fronts: policy reform, agricultural research, and human resource development.

This past March I directed a study to be undertaken to produce new, effective initiatives to address Third World hunger problems—emergency situations, such as the Ethiopian tragedy, and longer term problems. In July this food aid task force completed its work on emergency food crises. On July 10, the anniversary of the Food for Peace (P.L. 480) Program, I announced an initiative to help cut down the response time to Third World life-threatening food emergencies. This is being done by the creation of a central forecasting capability for impending food emergencies; by prepositioning food for quick response; by helping poor countries pay for the sea and inland transportation of food; by increasing coordination among the donor countries; and by seeking increased private sector participation.

Today's food emergency in Africa reemphasizes the need to tackle the underlying structural problems of agricultural stagnation in the Third World. Poor countries must become more productive in agriculture if they are to grow the food so needed to feed their people.

Socialist economic systems, prevalent in underdeveloped countries, have failed to achieve economic growth and have weakened agricultural production by not paying farmers a living wage. As a result of this, coupled with the failure of the Soviet Union to fulfill its promises of economic assistance, an increasing number of Third World countries once dominated by the socialist model are experimenting with free market approaches.

The United States Government will thus implement a new food aid policy to be called Food for Progress. This policy will emphasize use of America's agricultural abundance to support countries which have made commitments to agricultural policy reform during a period of economic hardship, including: (1) adequate price levels for agricultural production, based on market principles, and (2) improved rural infrastructure and private sector involvement.

Provisions of Food for Progress will be presented to Congress this year. We hope that this approach holds the promise to help prevent tragedies like Ethiopia from recurring in future years.

Last year the administration initiated a 5-year program intended to support economic reform and agricultural production. Important work in agricultural research is also going forward, research that shows great promise of breakthroughs in seed varieties that can usher in a new era of productivity for rain-short regions of Africa.

The underlying structures of policies, institutions, appropriate technology, and human knowledge are being built. Progress is being made. We will not lose sight of the ultimate goal of strengthened economies, food self-sufficiency, and human enlightenment for Africa. But for the present, much of sub-Saharan Africa suffers increasingly from severe hunger, malnutrition, and starvation. A timely American response can save many lives. This is what the African hunger relief initiative is designed to do.

Statement on Bombings at Abortion Clinics
January 3, 1985

During the past few months there has been a series of bombings at abortion clinics throughout the country. I condemn, in the strongest terms, those individuals who perpetrate these and all such violent, anarchist activities. As President of the United States, I will do all in my power to assure that the guilty are brought to justice. Therefore, I will request the Attorney General to see that all Federal agencies with jurisdiction pursue the investigation vigorously.

Statement by the Assistant to the President for National Security Affairs on the Upcoming Soviet-United States Arms Reduction Negotiations in Geneva, Switzerland
January 3, 1985

In the course of the past year, the President has directed and managed a review of the full family of United States arms control positions, covering the spectrum of separate negotiations which have gone on in the past and presumptively will be resumed in the future. More recently, he has chaired and now completed a review of preparations for the opening of talks with the Soviet Union to take place next Monday in Geneva.

The United States approaches the January 7th and 8th meetings with the Soviet Foreign Minister with a sense of determination and patience and with hope for a productive outcome. We fully recognize that this is the beginning of a long and complicated process. The issues involved go to the very heart of national security interests of both countries.

They're extremely complex from a technological standpoint. Furthermore, these talks are only a part, although a vital part, of the broader relationship between our two countries, a relationship involving regional issues, human rights, bilateral issues, as well.

While considerable time, therefore, may be needed to reach agreement on arms control outcomes, the U.S. is hopeful that the Geneva meetings will facilitate progress toward addressing the difficult arms control issues before us. We are realistic concerning the obstacles we face, but we are determined at the same time to do our part to make these efforts succeed and to establish a framework and a process for resuming the bilateral arms control dialog.

Both the U.S. and the Soviet Union have a special responsibility to the international community to make these efforts succeed. The United States, for its part, has constructive ideas to present in Geneva, and we will listen carefully to the Soviet presentations. Our negotiators will be flexible and patient.

With equal commitment and flexibility on the part of the Soviet Union, we are hopeful that these meetings will provide a start down the long road toward achieving equitable and verifiable reductions in nuclear forces, toward enhancing deterrence and ensuring the peace.

Note: Robert C. McFarlane read the statement to reporters at noon in Room 450 of the Old Executive Office Building.

Statement on the Resignation of Michael K. Deaver as Assistant to the President and Deputy Chief of Staff
January 3, 1985

I am today with deep regret accepting the resignation of Michael K. Deaver as Deputy Chief of the White House Staff. Mike plans to return to the private sector at a date to be subsequently determined, but in the general timeframe of March to May 1985.

Mike has rendered 18 years of loyal and outstanding service to me and to the First Lady both in California and in Washington.

Nancy and I will sorely miss him, as will the Nation. He has compiled an outstanding record during his 4 years of service to this administration. Mike has been an excellent public servant, and the Nation is fortunate to have had the benefit of his talent and vision. Much of the success we've enjoyed in the first term is directly attributable to him. His shoes will be difficult to fill, and he leaves with our best wishes and affection.

Nomination of Four Members of the National Advisory Council on Women's Educational Programs
January 3, 1985

The President today announced his intention to nominate the following individuals to be members of the National Advisory Council on Women's Educational Programs.

Mary Jo Arndt, of Lombard, IL., vice Eleanor Knee Rooks.

Lilli Dollinger Hausenfluck, of Arlington, VA (reappointment).

Marcilyn D. Leier, of Roseville, MN (reappointment).

Virginia Gillham Tinsley, of Tempe, AZ (reappointment).

Appointment of T. Burton Smith as Physician to the President
January 4, 1985

The President today announced the appointment of T. Burton Smith to be Physician to the President. Dr. Smith replaces Dr. Daniel Ruge, who has returned to the Veterans Administration central office as Director of its Spinal Cord Injury Service.

Dr. Smith is a specialist in urology and has been one of the President's physicians for many years. He has been in private practice in California since 1951. He earned his undergraduate degree at the University of California in 1937 and his graduate degree at the University of Southern California in 1941. He was an intern in 1942–1943 at Los Angeles County General Hospital and was a resident in urology from 1946

to 1949 at Jefferson Medical College Hospital in Philadelphia, PA.

He served as urological consultant at the United States Veterans Hospital in west Los Angeles from 1950 to 1967 and as an assistant professor of urology (clinical) at the University of California, Los Angeles Medical School, during the same period. He is a past chief of the department of urology at St. John's Hospital and Santa Monica Hospital, both in Santa Monica. He is also past chief of staff at St. John's Hospital.

Dr. Smith was born August 26, 1915, in Hermosa Beach, CA. He is married to the former Kathleen Hambly and has four children. They will reside in the District of Columbia.

Note: On the same day, the White House announced the names of two Assistant Phy- *sicians: Dr. John E. Hutton, Jr., a colonel in the U.S. Army, and Dr. Kenneth Lee, a commander in the U.S. Navy. The White House also announced that Dr. Smith's appointment became effective on January 2.*

Nomination of Two Members of the National Council on the Arts
January 4, 1985

The President today announced his intention to nominate the following individuals to be members of the National Council on the Arts, National Foundation on the Arts and the Humanities, for terms expiring September 9, 1990:

Lloyd George Richards will succeed Maureene Dees. He is dean of the Yale Drama School and presently serves as artistic director of the Yale Repertory and the Eugene O'Neill Theaters. Mr. Richards is married, has two children, and resides in New York City. He was born in Toronto, Canada.

James Nowell Wood will succeed Martin Friedman. He is director of the Art Institute of Chicago. Mr. Wood is also an author on the subject of modern art. He is married, has two children, and resides in Chicago, IL. Mr. Wood was born March 20, 1941, in Boston, MA.

Executive Order 12498—Regulatory Planning Process
January 4, 1985

By the authority vested in me as President by the Constitution and laws of the United States of America, and in order to create a coordinated process for developing on an annual basis the Administration's Regulatory Program, establish Administration regulatory priorities, increase the accountability of agency heads for the regulatory actions of their agencies, provide for Presidential oversight of the regulatory process, reduce the burdens of existing and future regulations, minimize duplication and conflict of regulations, and enhance public and Congressional understanding of the Administration's regulatory objectives, it is hereby ordered as follows:

Section 1. General Requirements. (a) There is hereby established a regulatory planning process by which the Administration will develop and publish a Regulatory Program for each year. To implement this process, each Executive agency subject to Executive Order No. 12291 shall submit to the Director of the Office of Management and Budget (OMB) each year, starting in 1985, a statement of its regulatory policies, goals, and objectives for the coming year and information concerning all significant regulatory actions underway or planned; however, the Director may exempt from this Order such agencies or activities as the Director may deem appropriate in order to achieve the effective implementation of this Order.

(b) The head of each Executive agency subject to this Order shall ensure that all regulatory actions are consistent with the goals of the agency and of the Administration, and will be appropriately implemented.

(c) This program is intended to complement the existing regulatory planning and review procedures of agencies and the Executive branch, including the procedures established by Executive Order No. 12291.

(d) To assure consistency with the goals of the Administration, the head of each agency subject to this Order shall adhere to the regulatory principles stated in Section 2 of Executive Order No. 12291, including those elaborated by the regulatory policy guidelines set forth in the August 11, 1983, Report of the Presidential Task Force on Regulatory Relief, "Reagan Administration Regulatory Achievements."

Sec. 2. Agency Submission of Draft Regulatory Program. (a) The head of each agency shall submit to the Director an overview of the agency's regulatory policies, goals, and objectives for the program year and such information concerning all significant regulatory actions of the agency, planned or underway, including actions taken to consider whether to initiate rulemaking; requests for public comment; and the development of documents that may influence, anticipate, or could lead to the commencement of rulemaking proceedings at a later date, as the Director deems necessary to develop the Administration's Regulatory Program. This submission shall constitute the agency's draft regulatory program. The draft regulatory program shall be submitted to the Director each year, on a date to be specified by the Director, and shall cover the period from April 1 through March 31 of the following year.

(b) The overview portion of the agency's submission should discuss the agency's broad regulatory purposes, explain how they are consistent with the Administration's regulatory principles, and include a discussion of the significant regulatory actions, as defined by the Director, that it will take. The overview should specifically discuss the significant regulatory actions of the agency to revise or rescind existing rules.

(c) Each agency head shall categorize and describe the regulatory actions described in subsection (a) in such format as the Director shall specify and provide such additional information as the Director may request; however, the Director shall, by Bulletin or Circular, exempt from the requirements of this Order any class or category of regulatory action that the Director determines is not necessary to review in order to achieve the effective implementation of the program.

Sec. 3. Review, Compilation, and Publication of the Administration's Regulatory Program. (a) In reviewing each agency's draft regulatory program, the Director shall (i) consider the consistency of the draft reg-

ulatory program with the Administration's policies and priorities and the draft regulatory programs submitted by other agencies; and (ii) identify such further regulatory or deregulatory actions as may, in his view, be necessary in order to achieve such consistency. In the event of disagreement over the content of the agency's draft regulatory program, the agency head or the Director may raise issues for further review by the President or by such appropriate Cabinet Council or other forum as the President may designate.

(b) Following the conclusion of the review process established by subsection (a), each agency head shall submit to the Director, by a date to be specified by the Director, the agency's final regulatory plan for compilation and publication as the Administration's Regulatory Program for that year. The Director shall circulate a draft of the Administration's Regulatory Program for agency comment, review, and interagency consideration, if necessary, before publication.

(c) After development of the Administration's Regulatory Program for the year, if the agency head proposes to take a regulatory action subject to the provisions of Section 2 and not previously submitted for review under this process, or if the agency head proposes to take a regulatory action that is materially different from the action described in the agency's final Regulatory Program, the agency head shall immediately advise the Director and submit the action to the Director for review in such format as the Director may specify. Except in the case of emergency situations, as defined by the Director, or statutory or judicial deadlines, the agency head shall refrain from taking the proposed regulatory action until the review of this submission by the Director is completed. As to those regulatory actions not also subject to Executive Order No. 12291, the Director shall be deemed to have concluded that the proposal is consistent with the purposes of this Order, unless he notifies the agency head to the contrary within 10 days of its submission. As to those regulatory actions subject to Executive Order No. 12291, the Director's review shall be governed by the provisions of Section 3(e) of that Order.

(d) Absent unusual circumstances, such as new statutory or judicial requirements or unanticipated emergency situations, the Director may, to the extent permitted by law, return for reconsideration any rule submitted for review under Executive Order No. 12291 that would be subject to Section 2 but was not included in the agency's final Regulatory Program for that year; or any other significant regulatory action that is materially different from those described in the Administration's Regulatory Program for that year.

Sec. 4. Office of Management and Budget. The Director of the Office of Management and Budget is authorized, to the extent permitted by law, to take such actions as may be necessary to carry out the provisions of this Order.

Sec. 5. Judicial Review. This Order is intended only to improve the internal management of the Federal government, and is not intended to create any right or benefit, substantive or procedural, enforceable at law by a party against the United States, its agencies, its officers or any person.

RONALD REAGAN

The White House,
January 4, 1985.

[*Filed with the Office of the Federal Register, 4:05 p.m., January 4, 1985*]

Memorandum on the Regulatory Planning Process
January 4, 1985

Memorandum for the Heads of Executive Departments and Agencies

Subject: Development of Administration's Regulatory Program

With your help and active support, this Administration has substantially reduced the burden and intrusiveness of Federal regulatory programs. In the past three years, we have eliminated many needless rules, revised ill-conceived ones, and held the number of new rules to the minimum necessary. The policies and procedures of Executive Order No. 12291 have imposed long needed discipline on the rulemaking process. As a result, Federal paperwork and the size of the *Federal Register* have declined for four consecutive years—for the first time ever. Our accomplishments so far have been substantial, and we can take pride in them.

Much more can and should be done, however. Regulation has become one of the most important and costly activities of government, yet it is managed far less systematically than direct government spending. Several statutes and Executive Order No. 12291 establish procedures for agency rulemaking, but this is only the final stage of the regulatory process. Developing a government rule often involves years of studies, hearings, and intermediate decisions before even a proposed rule is issued for public comment. Frequently, senior agency officials are involved only after these earlier activities have greatly narrowed the options for final action and precluded effective Administration policy review.

Today, I have signed an Executive Order to establish a regulatory planning process by which we will develop and publish the Administration's Regulatory Program for each year. Under this process, it will be the personal responsibility of the head of each agency to determine—at the beginning of the regulatory process, not at the end—whether a given regulatory venture is consistent with the goals of the Administration and whether agency resources should be committed to it. Each agency head will thus be accountable for the management of the regulatory process, to ensure that policy options are not narrowed prematurely and that each significant regulatory proposal will be considered in relation to others.

To do this, I am requesting each regulatory agency to draft its proposed regulatory policies at the beginning of each year and to set forth a statement of priority regulatory activities, including prerulemaking actions, that constitute the agency's regulatory program for the year. This document should explain how each new activity will carry out the regulatory policies of this Administration and specify the agency's plan for reviewing and revising existing regulatory programs to bring them into accord with Administration policies.

After approval by the head of the agency, the agency's draft regulatory program should be submitted for review by the Office of Management and Budget. This review should focus on consistency with general Administration policy, and with the draft regulatory programs submitted by other agencies. The Office of Management and Budget will circulate a draft of the Administration's Regulatory Program for agency comment, review, and interagency consideration if necessary before the document is put in final form for publication. Issues may be raised for further review by a Cabinet Council or by me or by such other group as I may designate. This review will not interfere with the exercise of authority committed by statute to heads of agencies.

The final regulatory programs of all agencies will be published by the Office of Management and Budget in May as the Administration's Regulatory Program for the twelve-month period beginning April 1, 1985. During the year, this document will be used as a basis for reviews of individual rules under Executive Order No. 12291. At the end of the year, it should be used to assess the agency's performance and to prepare the next year's program.

I am directing the Director of the Office of Management and Budget to implement this regulatory review process immediately and to establish the procedures under which these documents will be submitted to the Director and reviewed. For their first submission, agencies shall submit their draft regulatory program to the Director on the date specified by him. The Director will prepare for my consideration the goals and priorities for all agencies in a manner similar to the identification of significant issues in the fiscal budgetary process.

I am convinced that this process will result in substantial improvements in Federal regulatory policy. It will help ensure that each major step in the process of rule development is consistent with Administration policy. It will enable agency heads to manage agency regulatory actions more effectively, at the same time that it enables the President to hold agency heads more closely accountable for implementing Administration policy.

While ambitious, this program will build on our earlier efforts that have proven successful—the Executive Order No. 12291 review process, the reviews of inherited rules by the Task Force on Regulatory Relief, and the annual "paperwork budget" process.

I am confident that your wholehearted support will make this next stage of our regulatory reform program equally successful.

RONALD REAGAN

Message to the Congress Reporting Budget Deferrals
January 4, 1985

To the Congress of the United States:

In accordance with the Impoundment Control Act of 1974, I herewith report two new deferrals of budget authority for 1985 totaling $11,000,000 and five revised deferrals now totaling $5,405,581,139. The deferrals affect International Security Assistance, the Departments of Defense, Health and Human Services, State, Transportation, and the United States Institute of Peace.

The details of these deferrals are contained in the attached report.

RONALD REAGAN

The White House,
January 4, 1985.

Note: The attachment detailing the deferrals was printed in the Federal Register *of January 10.*

Message to the Senate Transmitting the 1983 Partial Revision of the Radio Regulations (Geneva, 1979)
January 4, 1985

To the Senate of the United States:

With a view to receiving the advice and consent of the Senate to ratification, I transmit herewith the 1983 Partial Revision of the Radio Regulations (Geneva, 1979) and a Final Protocol, signed on behalf of the United States at Geneva on March 18, 1983.

I transmit also, for the information of the Senate, the report of the Department of State with respect to the 1983 Partial Revision.

The 1983 Revision constitutes a partial revision of the Radio Regulations (Geneva, 1979) to which the United States is a party. The primary purpose of the present revision is to update the existing Regulations to take into account introduction of advanced techniques for maritime mobile, distress and safety communications. The Revision is consistent with the proposals of and positions taken by the United States at the 1983 World Administrative Radio Conference for the Mobile Services of the International Telecommunication Union.

At the time of signature, the United States Delegation submitted a statement countering an unfounded political allegation of Cuba. The specific statement, with reason, is given in the report of the Department of State.

The 1983 Partial Revision of the Radio Regulations will enter into force on January 15, 1985 for Governments that, by that date, have notified the Secretary General of the International Telecommunication Union of their approval thereof. I believe that the United States should become a party to the 1983 Partial Revision as soon as possible, and it is my hope that the Senate will take early action on this matter and give its advice and consent to ratification.

RONALD REAGAN

The White House,
January 4, 1985.

Appointment of Six Members of the Board of Trustees of the John F. Kennedy Center for the Performing Arts
January 7, 1985

The President today announced his intention to appoint the following individuals to be members of the Board of Trustees of the John F. Kennedy Center for the Performing Arts, Smithsonian Institution, for terms expiring September 1, 1994:

Melvin R. Laird, of Maryland. This is a reappointment.

Jean Kennedy Smith, of New York. This is a reappointment.

Caroline Hunt Schoelkopf will succeed Frank N. Ikard. She is involved in a variety of business enterprises and charitable organizations. Mrs. Schoelkopf is married, has five children, and resides in Dallas, TX. She was born January 8, 1923, in Eldorado, AR.

Roger B. Smith will succeed J. William Fulbright. He is chairman of the board of General Motors. Mr. Smith is married, has four children, and resides in Detroit, MI. He was born July 12, 1925, in Columbus, OH.

Leonard L. Silverstein will succeed Peter H.B. Frelinghuysen. He is a partner in the law firm of Silverstein & Mullens in Washington, DC.

Mr. Silverstein is married, has two children, and resides in Bethesda, MD. He was born January 21, 1922, in Scranton, PA.

Trammell Crow will succeed Donna J. Stone. He is founding partner of the Trammell Crow Real Estate Development Co. Mr. Crow is married, has six children, and resides in Dallas, TX. He was born June 10, 1914, in Dallas, TX.

Remarks Announcing the Nomination of James A. Baker III To Be Secretary of the Treasury and the Appointment of Donald T. Regan as Assistant to the President and Chief of Staff
January 8, 1985

I'm going to read a statement, and then, since there is a press conference tomorrow night, I want to tell you that we will not be taking any questions on the subject of the statement or anything else, and I'll see you tomorrow night.

But today I am announcing the following reassignment of responsibilities among two of my most senior advisers. I intend to nominate James A. Baker III to become Secretary of the Treasury. And I intend to appoint Donald T. Regan as Chief of Staff and Assistant to the President, effective upon the date of Jim Baker's confirmation by the Senate.

Upon confirmation as Treasury Secretary, Jim Baker would become chief economic spokesman for my administration and would remain a designated member of the National Security Council. And upon appointment as Chief of Staff, Don Regan would also be designated a member of the National Security Council and remain a member of my Cabinet.

Don Regan and Jim Baker have both served loyally and admirably as members of my team for the past 4 years. They've done so at considerable personal sacrifice for which I am deeply grateful. They both compiled outstanding records of achievement. Each has indicated to me that while willing to serve in whatever capacity I would wish, each would welcome an opportunity to assume new responsibilities and new challenges. After 4 grueling years in their current positions, their desire for change is completely understandable.

This particular change will allow them each to meet new challenges and will bring renewed vigor to their respective responsibilities, while it gives me and the public the benefit of the continued service of two extraordinarily talented individuals.

While both men are admirably suited for their current positions, each is extremely well suited for his new assignment. Don Regan is a proven successful administrator. He has broad domestic and international experience. He has now gained extensive Washington experience, and he enjoys the respect of Members of the Congress and the Cabinet.

Jim Baker is a proven, successful member of our national security, legislative, and economic policymaking teams, and he would bring to Treasury not only his extensive Washington experience but also more than two decades of private sector experience with corporate law and finance. I'm confident that this change can be effected smoothly and that it will contribute substantially to the success of our second term.

And now, I will conclude by saying I'll see you tomorrow night.

Note: The President spoke to reporters at 9:45 a.m. in the Briefing Room at the White House.

15

Nomination of James A. Baker III To Be Secretary of the Treasury
January 8, 1985

The President today announced his intention to nominate James A. Baker III to be Secretary of the Treasury. Mr. Baker has been Chief of the White House staff since January 1981. Previously he served as deputy director of the Reagan-Bush transition and as a senior adviser to the 1980 Reagan-Bush Committee.

A 1952 graduate of Princeton University, Mr. Baker served 2 years on active duty with the U.S. Marine Corps from 1952 to 1954. He received his law degree from the University of Texas at Austin with honors in 1957. He practiced law with the Houston, TX, law firm of Andrews, Kurth, Campbell and Jones from 1957 until August 1975, when he was appointed Under Secretary of Commerce by President Ford. Mr. Baker was active in President Ford's campaign in

1976, serving as its national chairman during the general election. After returning to Andrews, Kurth, Campbell and Jones in late 1976, he ran in 1978 as the Republican nominee for attorney general of Texas. From January 1979 until May 1980, he was the national chairman of the George Bush for President Committee.

Active in numerous civic endeavors, Mr. Baker has served on the governing bodies of Texas Childrens Hospital in Houston, the M.D. Anderson Hospital and Tumor Institute, and the Woodrow Wilson International Center for Scholars at the Smithsonian Institution.

Mr. Baker and his wife, the former Susan Garrett, reside in Washington, DC. They have eight children. Mr. Baker was born April 28, 1930, in Houston, TX.

Appointment of Donald T. Regan as Assistant to the President and Chief of Staff
January 8, 1985

The President today announced his intention to appoint Donald T. Regan to be Chief of the White House staff. He has been serving as Secretary of the Treasury since January 1981. Previously he was chairman and chief executive officer of Merrill Lynch and Co., Inc., the holding company formed in May 1973 by Merrill Lynch, Pierce, Fenner and Smith, Inc.

Secretary Regan was born December 21, 1918, and graduated from Harvard University with a B.A. in 1940. He joined the U.S. Marine Corps and retired at the end of World War II as a lieutenant colonel. In 1946 Secretary Regan joined Merrill Lynch as an account executive trainee. Following his training, he worked as an account executive in Washington, DC. In early 1952 he was named manager of the Over-the-Counter Department in New York, and in

1954 he became a general partner in Merrill Lynch. From 1955 to 1960, Secretary Regan served as manager of the Merrill Lynch office in Philadelphia and as administrative division director in New York. In 1964 he was elected executive vice president of Merrill Lynch, and in 1968 he became president. He was named chairman and chief executive officer in January 1971.

Secretary Regan has served as a member of the Policy Committee of the Business Roundtable, as a member of the Council on Foreign Relations, and as a trustee of the Committee for Economic Development. He has also served as chairman of the trustees of the University of Pennsylvania. He holds honorary degrees from four universities and has served as a trustee of the Charles E. Merrill Trust, a charitable foundation.

He is married to the former Ann Buchanan, and they have four children.

Letter to the Speaker of the House and the Chairman of the Senate Foreign Relations Committee Reporting on the Cyprus Conflict
January 8, 1985

Dear Mr. Speaker: (Dear Mr. Chairman:)

In accordance with Public Law 95–384, I am submitting herewith a bimonthly report on progress toward a negotiated settlement of the Cyprus question.

Since my last report to you, leaders of the two Cypriot communities have completed a series of proximity talks with United Nations Secretary General Perez de Cuellar in New York. Those talks resulted in the Secretary General's announcement on December 12, 1984, that the differences between the parties' positions have been narrowed sufficiently to permit the scheduling of a summit meeting. President Kyprianou and Turkish Cypriot leader Denktash are now scheduled to meet January 17 in New York. The Secretary General has said he expects the two, at that time, to conclude an agreement containing the elements necessary for a solution to the Cyprus problem. While a great deal remains to be done, we view the staging of the summit as a very positive step, one which can bring closer the day when all Cypriots can live together in a reunified country.

On December 14, 1984, the U.N. Security Council renewed the peacekeeping mandate of the U.N. Forces in Cyprus (UNFI-CYP) for another six months. The Secretary General's report to the Council on the occasion of that vote includes his description of the progress made under his good offices mandate as well as the status of U.N. forces on the island. I am enclosing with this letter a copy of the Secretary General's informative report.

We have worked closely with the Secretary General and with all parties to the Cyprus question during the period, urging their cooperation and encouraging them to make progress. The Administration is pleased with the statesmanlike approach of both Cypriot parties that led to the announcement of the summit. We will continue to consult closely with Secretary General Perez de Cuellar, offering him any assistance we can to assure a successful meeting in January and continuing progress toward a fair and lasting Cyprus settlement.

Sincerely,

RONALD REAGAN

Note: Identical letters were sent to Thomas P. O'Neill, Jr., Speaker of the House of Representatives, and Richard G. Lugar, chairman of the Senate Foreign Relations Committee.

Interview With Burl Osborne and Carl Leubsdorf of the Dallas Morning News
January 8, 1985

U.S.-Soviet Talks in Geneva

Q. Can we ask you, since our time is limited, if you can tell us anything about what's been going on in Geneva? Because that's what I think everyone is the most interested in.

The President. Well, let me just say there isn't too much I can tell you right at the moment. But I have just finished talking to George Shultz, and the meetings are concluded. And in 45 minutes, by our time, George will be addressing the press over there, making a statement to the press and probably taking some of their questions.

And then he will be home. Some of the others are going to stop by other heads of state, like Bud McFarlane's going to go to see Mrs. Thatcher and, I think, also in France and Italy and brief others of our allies on what took place. And George will

17

be here to brief me tomorrow afternoon. And then I'll know more when they start asking questions at the press conference tomorrow night.

Q. Are you pleased with what's happened? I mean, has it met what you expected?

The President. It sounds very good. I don't want to go any further than calling attention to what George is going to say, but I think we're going to see meetings that will be arranged shortly, meetings to negotiate nuclear weapons and space and all.

Q. But this would really meet what you had hoped? Have we gotten from this what we had hoped to get?

The President. Yes, this is all this meeting was supposed to do is to establish procedures for negotiations. I'm afraid some of the people overlook that. And I'd flinch a little when I would see references, and particularly on the air, as if this was supposed to be the arms negotiation. No, this was to set up the procedures.

Q. But there was always a question whether it would, in fact, set up the procedures.

The President. That's right, yes.

Q. From what you're saying, the announcement will tell us that it, in fact, has.

The President. I think that's what George will be telling people in 45 minutes.

Federal Budget

Q. Okay. I guess we'll switch it to domestic issues. The Senate Republicans are planning to put out a budget several days before you put out your budget. And there has been information from White House officials in recent days that they don't think you'll be able to reach the targets that had been established about a month or so ago for deficit reduction. Do you think that this process is moving away from the White House? Do you think there's some danger you may be dealt out of this process?

The President. No, not at all. As a matter of fact, I'm perfectly willing to have the Senate do that. I think that in working together they may have some ideas we didn't have. But, no, what our goal is, and what we hope to present to the Congress in our budget proposal is one in which the overall spending will be no greater in '86 than it

was in '85. Now, that means that because some things are inflexible, such as the interest on the debt, that there will be some particular parts of government that will be getting less money. There may be some that we think ought to be eliminated. And so it won't be a freeze in the sense of freezing every item of spending in the budget at its previous level—some will be increased; some will be decreased; some will be eliminated. But the total we're aiming at will be no increase in overall spending.

Defense Spending and Social Security

Q. Many people on the Hill—and many Republicans as well as Democrats—are saying this: They're saying that because of your feeling that defense spending has to grow at the rate, or close to the rate intended, and because of what you've said about Social Security and other things like that, that it's impossible to reach even that goal.

The President. No. Let me take two items: defense to begin with. For 1986, the Defense Department itself has come in with a bigger cut than had been asked in the original plan that came over from OMB. The difficulty there, however, is in the out years. And I think that Defense has a legitimate argument about not setting figures. Now, you know we're required anymore by Congress—and I have to tell you, having been 8 years in the budgeting process in California, I do not look with great favor upon this idea that you're supposed to project for the next 5 years what your budgets are going to be.

And with Defense, their argument is that no one, with regard to defense spending, can tell you what the necessities are going to be down the road or in years ahead. What if a potential adversary does something in the coming year that forces your hand to have to meet, in some way, with an additional defense capability or whatever? So Defense has done it for this year, and then has expressed the inability—they have to project some figures, but those figures are meaningless for the out years. But they've done that.

Now, as for Social Security, here again I'd like to point out with regard to Social Security that while Social Security is included in the unified budget—and that, again, by an edict of Congress—Social Security is totally funded by a payroll tax. And that payroll tax cannot be used for any other part of government. In other words, if you somehow reduced Social Security—actually, Social Security's running a surplus over and above its present income, but that surplus goes into their trust fund. It cannot be used to fund some other department of government.

Q. There's been some indication that an administration official who met with a group of reporters yesterday indicated that you might be willing to accept some kind of freeze on cost-of-living adjustments for Social Security recipients if Congress gets together on the idea.

The President. No, I think whoever that individual was referring to was someplace here in our own meetings—and there have been hours of them on the budget thing. My own remark on one occasion that, obviously, if Congress was—because there were stories that Congress was targeting and said something should be done about that—that if Congress, en masse came down on the side of, say, reducing or holding off on the COLA, the cost-of-living increase, you know, what would I be able to do about that?

Now, a veto is only possible if there's a chance that your veto would be upheld. And I never remark about possible vetoes until whatever legislation we're talking about comes down to my desk and I see it. But that was the only remark. But again, as I say, you can't blame any of the deficit on Social Security.

Q. Are you saying that they would have to be able to pass it over your veto in order for that to happen? Or that——

The President. Well, I'm saying I'm waiting to see what is Congress' attitude about that.

Q. But you might be willing to change your previous position on that if it looked like an overwhelming number of Congressmen really felt this was necessary?

The President. No, I feel committed to what I said about Social Security before: That this attempt during the campaign, as they did in 1982, to charge that I had secret plans for reducing Social Security—I had no

such plans, I have no such plans, and I see no reason to target Social Security when it plays no part in the deficit.

Q. So that in fact, you're basically not encouraging this idea very much?

The President. No, no.

Personnel Changes in the White House and the Cabinet

Q. Some of the conservatives in town have been watching what's been going on with your administration, especially since the election, and they see Bill Clark is going to go back to California, and they see that Ed Meese is going to go to the Justice Department, and from their initial comments, they're not going to be any much more happy with Don Regan than they are with Jim Baker. And they're afraid that there are not going to be any true believers in this White House in the second term. Should they be concerned?

The President. No, I don't think so, because the true believer in the White House is sitting here in the Oval Office. And no one has been whittling at me or trying to change my philosophy since I've been here.

But now, the case, for example, of Ed Meese going over to Justice. Well, he's been a Counsellor to me, and we've been together for a great many years, as you well know. Well, being my Attorney General—[*laughing*]—does not remove him from my being able to seek his counsel whenever I feel like doing so.

As for Don Regan coming over here, I don't know how anyone can complain about him, ideologically or philosophically. He has been as loyal to everything that I've wanted to do as anyone that I could name.

Q. So you think that this is not something they should worry so much about?

The President. No. And sometimes I wonder if some of those very vocal conservatives are really conservatives in conservatives' eyes. They're not in mine.

Q. One of the people they would like to see you find a place for is Mrs. Kirkpatrick.

The President. I want to find a place for Mrs. Kirkpatrick.

Q. Have you found one yet?

The President. We'll be talking again after the Inaugural. I could quite understand.

She's been longer in her post at the U.N. than anyone who ever held that job. And it is a job in which you can find yourself saying, "Enough, already." But I am hoping that I can keep her in the administration.

Q. With all these changes, how do you feel about this? You're going to enter your second term with a rather changed cast of characters around here. And a lot of people you've dealt for with a long time, really, like——

The President. Yes.

Q. ——Ed and Mike are not going to be here.

The President. Well, Ed's going to be here. As I say, he's within reach. He'll still be a member of the Cabinet. He'll just be sitting in a different chair. And Mike, I can understand his wanting to leave now for the private sector. But this isn't as many changes as some administrations have had.

Q. It's been remarkably stable up till now.

The President. Yes. And I have been gratified by that, because everyone that I asked to serve, I told them, as I told the public, that I recognize that they—many of them, most of them—would be coming at a great personal sacrifice. And I could not expect them to contract in for the run of the show. And so they've all known that when the time came that they felt they had to return to their own lives, I would understand, and I'd try to replace them with someone equally qualified. And I'm just gratified that we have so many still here. And some of the moves are just, as I say, changing slots, but still here in government.

Q. Let me ask you about this latest change. Is this correct that you didn't know what was going on till they came to you yesterday?

The President. [*Laughing*] They weren't ready to come to me until yesterday.

All I know is that it was—originally, it was Don Regan's idea, and he'd talked to Jim. Jim has always—and has let me know—he has always wanted, if something opened up, a Cabinet post. And he's been on a long stretch, 4 full years here in that job.

Q. You don't think he encouraged the Secretary with this idea?

The President. No, as a matter of fact, it was Don's idea. And Don himself felt that

he'd had enough of what he was doing, that he wanted a change. So I was——

Q. Were you easily convinced?

The President. What?

Q. Were you easily convinced?

The President. Well, Don came and we had a talk about it, and then I had a talk with Jim. I wanted to make sure that this was something that both of them were very happy about and wanted to do. And frankly, I thought it was a great idea. It sure beat having them decide to go back to private life.

Tax Reform Program

Q. Now that you have Mr.—we're going to have Don Regan over here, are you going to have his tax plan over here, too? Are you going to——

The President. [*Laughing*] No, that'll be Jim's to sell up on the Hill. But I'm quite sure that Don will be most helpful on that because——

Q. Are you going to endorse it, basically, in your State of the Union speech?

The President. I'm going to speak of the need for simplifying taxes. I'm not going to get into great details, as I will in the subsequent State of the Union Address. But the tax program—and incidentally, some of your colleagues in the press and particularly columnists have been sniping that I'm dangling in the wind here, and all the momentum has stopped because we haven't been doing anything with that. That's not true.

We realized, all of us agreed, that the first priority had to be the budget. And we've been spending hours and hours— we've had no time to go on to something else. When that's done, then we go at the tax program. And that's one that—just like the budget—we're going to have to look at everything that has been recommended, treat some of them, I'm sure, as options, and then decide what form we want to take. I think it's been one of the best tax studies that's ever been made.

Q. But you're not ready to endorse a lot of the specifics in it yet?

The President. Well, we haven't had time to do as we've done with the budget, to sit down with it and say, "All right, point by point, let's go through it." I haven't even done that. I have a copy of the plan on my desk. And while I've read a summary, I haven't been able to do that because my mind is too filled with the budget.

Federal Budget

Q. Could you tell us the level of your confidence that you can enact a plan along the lines you describe and meet the deficit reduction targets that you've set?

The President. Yes, I think we can. Yes. And the goal is one thing that I will be saying publicly is that—there's never been any thought on the part of any of us that after 50 years of built-in, structural deficit spending, with only a few exceptional years when it didn't take place—there's no way that you can gear segments of the society to government doing many of these things and then just pull the rug out from them all at once and say, "We're going to balance the budget in 1 year." It just couldn't be done.

It's only fair to do as we will with some programs and say to the people, "Look, this program is going to either disappear down here or be reduced down sizably in the years ahead," to give people a chance to adjust to this.

So, yes, we have hit upon a plan of putting us on a declining path as far as the deficits are concerned to the point that we will be able to project a date certain at which the budget will be balanced. And then I would hope—and before then—I would hope that we would make it constitutionally impossible for the Government to run another deficit.

Q. Burl, you had a question you wanted——

The President's Views on the Media

Q. I was going to ask, given the fairly widespread view, perception, that you don't think too highly of the media, however one defines it—I wonder if you would tell us what you do think of—not the media, but newspapers and television, specifically, and what their faults are, and what the——

The President. I've never had any complaints about the paper you represent. [*Laughing*]

Q. Well, that's very kind.

The President. No, I think inside the beltline here, in Washington, is a kind of a company town. And the great search for leaks, and the premature billing of something as a fact when many times it isn't a fact, this can become a problem. It can become a problem, for example, on the international scene to take a leak, some information from someone who won't let their name be used, and to take this as valid enough to print on the front page of a paper, and then leave us with having to mend fences with some friendly government that is offended by this misinformation. And there have been cases of that kind.

I guess all that I would like to say is that I wish that the media that does so much of that—that portion of the media—I wish that they would have an ethic in which they would check that out with us to see whether it, in some way, might be harmful to our national security, and take our word for it if we said that it would be. And we'd be willing to explain why it would be. Then we might not have so many incidents that do cause us problems and set back, sometimes, programs that have been going forward.

Q. Thank you, Mr. President.

The President's Views on Astrology

Q. Mr. President, is it true that, as I've heard, that you have some interest in astrology? Someone told me that recently.

The President. [*Laughing*] No. No, I'll tell you, we knew personally, Nancy and I, the gentleman out in California that did this for the Los Angeles Times. And so, knowing him and all, it used to be fun in the morning, in the morning with the paper—and it's easy for me, because I always read the comics, and they put it on the same page as the comics—that I would take delight in telling Nancy what her day was going to be, and—[*laughing*]—and what mine was supposed to be, and so forth.

Q. Do you know what the signs are for your Inauguration?

The President. No. No, I haven't done things like——

Q. I looked it up. It looked pretty good——

The President. It did?

Q. ——if you're an Aquarian.

The President. I'm an Aquarian, yes. And of course I do believe that part of astrology since I found out that there are more Aquarians in the, recorded up there in New York someplace, in the well-known citizen's list of—[*laughing*]——

Q. Hall of Fame or——

The President. ——yes, the Hall of Fame, so I said, "Well, that must be true, then."

Q. Thank you very much, Mr. President.

We appreciate the time.

The President. You bet.

Note: The interview began at 4:17 p.m. in the Oval Office at the White House. It was released by the Office of the Press Secretary on January 9.

Appointment of Two Members of the National Advisory Committee on Oceans and Atmosphere
January 9, 1985

The President today announced his intention to appoint the following individuals to be members of the National Advisory Committee on Oceans and Atmosphere:

Carl Franklin Brady, Sr., of Anchorage, AK, is with Carl Brady Investments. He is married and has three children. He was born October 29, 1919, in Chelsea, OK.

FitzGerald Bemiss, of Richmond, VA, is president of FitzGerald & Co. He is married and has two children. He was born October 2, 1922, in Richmond, VA.

Appointment of William D. Mounger as a Member of the Board of Visitors of the United States Military Academy
January 9, 1985

The President today announced his intention to appoint William D. Mounger to be a member of the Board of Visitors to the United States Military Academy for a term expiring December 30, 1986. He will succeed Shirley Hufstedler.

Mr. Mounger is an independent oil and gas producer in Jackson, MS. He graduated from the United States Military Academy (B.S., 1948). He is married, has two children, and resides in Jackson, MS. He was born March 31, 1926, in Jackson.

Appointment of Edward R. Borcherdt, Jr., as a Member of the Board of Visitors of the United States Naval Academy
January 9, 1985

The President today announced his intention to appoint Edward R. Borcherdt, Jr., to be a member of the Board of Visitors to the United States Naval Academy for a term expiring December 30, 1987. This is a reappointment.

He is president of Borcherdt & Co., financial consultants, in Washington, DC. He graduated from Stanford University (A.B., 1953; M.B.A., 1957). He is married, has two children, and resides in Washington, DC. He was born July 12, 1930, in Butte, MT.

Appointment of Two Members of the Board of Visitors of the United States Air Force Academy
January 9, 1985

The President today announced his intention to appoint the following individuals to be members of the Board of Visitors to the United States Air Force Academy for terms expiring December 30, 1987. These are reappointments.

Terrence O'Donnell is an attorney with the firm of Williams & Connolly in Washington, DC. He graduated from the United States Air Force Academy (B.S., 1966) and Georgetown University (J.D., 1971). He is married, has three children, and resides in Bethesda, MD. He was born March 3, 1944, in New York, NY.

Henry B. Sayler is president of Henry Sayler & Co. in St. Petersburg, FL. He graduated from the United States Military Academy in 1943. He is married, has four children, and resides in St. Petersburg, FL. He was born January 16, 1921, in Savannah, GA.

The President's News Conference
January 9, 1985

U.S.-Soviet Relations

The President. Good evening. I have an opening statement.

Earlier today on his return from Geneva, Secretary Shultz reported to me on the full details of his discussions with Soviet Foreign Minister Gromyko over this past January 7th and 8th. As you're aware, his meeting with Mr. Gromyko has resulted in agreement between our two nations to begin new negotiations on nuclear and space arms. Our objective in these talks will be the reduction of nuclear arms and the strengthening of strategic stability. Our ultimate goal, of course, is the complete elimination of nuclear weapons.

I want to take this opportunity to congratulate George Shultz, Bud McFarlane, and the rest of our delegation for a job well done. Their teamwork in Geneva was American diplomacy at its best.

Our differences with the Soviets are many and profound. And these new negotiations will be difficult as we grapple with the issues so central to peace and security for ourselves, our allies, and the world. But we will persevere. And while we must continue to resist actions by the Soviet Union that threaten our freedom and vital interests or those of other nations, we must also be prepared to work together wherever possible to strengthen the peace.

When I spoke before the United Nations General Assembly this past September, I set out my objective and proposals for a more stable and constructive relationship between East and West. Today it's my hope that this week's meeting in Geneva, while only a single step, is the beginning of a new dialog between the United States and the Soviet Union. It's also my hope that as 1985 unfolds, this year will emerge as one of dialog and negotiations, a year that leads to better relations between the United States and the Soviet Union.

I believe a more stable peace is achievable through these negotiations, and I urge all Americans to join us in supporting this search for a more stable peace. But it takes two sides to have constructive negotiations; one side alone cannot do it. We've made clear our intentions and expectations for progress in U.S.-Soviet relations. Secretary Shultz has reinforced that message in his lengthy sessions with Mr. Gromyko. For our part we'll be flexible, patient, and determined, and we now look to the Soviet Union to help give new life and positive results to that process of dialog.

Now, Helen [Helen Thomas, United Press International]?

Strategic Defense Initiative

Q. Mr. President, if you are flexible, are you willing to trade off research on "Star Wars" technology for deep cuts in the Soviet nuclear arsenal, or are you set in concrete, as your advisers say, against any negotiations on "Star Wars"?

The President. Well, let me say, what has been called "Star Wars"—and, Helen, I wish whoever coined that expression would take it back again——

Q. Well, Strategic Defense——

The President. ——because it gives a false impression of what it is we're talking about—but that will be on the table with everything else, of course. There are no preconditions with regard to the talks that we're going to have.

But this is research, a research program, and it is within the provisions of the ABM treaty. So, all that we've made clear is that we're going forward on the research, but we've also made it clear that if that research does come up, as we hope, with something that could be the defensive weapon we're talking about, nonnuclear, then we would be willing to go into negotiations and discussions with the other nations of the world, and with our allies, about what to do about that and whether and how to deploy.

Q. May I ask you, then, if "Star Wars"— even if you don't like the term, it's quite popular—is on the table for negotiations at some point where the technology might be developed?

The President. Well, as I say, it's on the table only because we made it very clear——

Q. But I mean it's not just a bargaining chip——

The President. No. Oh, no.

Q. ——that could not be bargained?

The President. No, no.

U.S.-Soviet Arms Agreements

Q. Mr. President, in the past you have characterized the Soviet Union as an evil empire, and you have said that they have repeatedly violated the arms agreements that they have made with the United States. Some of your advisers today doubt that the technology exists to adequately verify any agreement. Do you believe verification is possible, or do you think the Soviets will try to violate any agreement you might make?

The President. Well, we know that they have had a past record of violating agreements. We know also that absolute verification is impossible, but verification to the extent possible is going to be a very necessary feature in our negotiations. And I would like to also point out that because they themselves have expressed the desire to totally eliminate nuclear weapons, zero nuclear weapons is far easier to verify than if you're simply reducing the numbers. To have to continue trying to count numbers is much more difficult.

Gary [Gary F. Schuster, Detroit News]?

Social Security Program

Q. Mr. President, thank you. Senate Republicans and the leadership and one of your top advisers both have said Social Security cost-of-living allowances are not necessarily untouchable in the effort to reduce the budget deficit. Is the Social Security COLA off limits, as you promised during the campaign, or is it negotiable?

The President. Well, Gary, I never specifically mentioned that. I did say, however, that I would resist anything that would reduce the payments and the benefits which, it had been intimated in the campaign—you will remember I was responding to charges that I had some secret plot and plan to do that. I had no such plan, and I am resisting of this.

I think what someone has taken is a comment in one of our own meetings about the present budget, based on some news reports that up on the Hill there was widespread feeling about freezing the COLA's in Social Security. And all I commented on was that we might be faced with an overwhelming bipartisan majority in both Houses in support of that. Well, I don't talk about what I would or would not veto until something reaches my desk, but I think I would have to look at that situation and what I was faced with, with regard to a possible congressional mandate.

On the other hand, I have to say this about Social Security and the COLA's—and I think some of those who are calling for that on the Hill should recognize—Social

Security is running a surplus. Social Security is not a part of the deficit problem. It is totally financed by a payroll tax, and that tax is totally dedicated to that one program. If Social Security's spending were reduced, you could not take that money saved and use it to fund some other program in the deficit. It would simply go back into the Social Security trust fund.

So, I think it far more profitable—the idea of balancing a budget—to turn to the programs that are really causing the deficit.

Sam [Sam Donaldson, ABC News]?

Bernhard Goetz

Q. Mr. President, a man in a subway in New York City took a gun and shot four youths who apparently were trying to shake him down. Without reference to that specific case, since it is in the courts, what do you think of the use of deadly force in trying to defend oneself against attack?

The President. Sam, I'm glad that you said that about it being a case now before the courts, because that does prohibit me from commenting on that particular case.

In general, I think we all can understand the frustration of people who are constantly threatened by crime and feel that law and order is not particularly protecting them. On the other hand, I think we all realize there is a breakdown of civilization if people start taking the law in their own hands. So, while we may feel understanding or sympathy for someone who was tested beyond his control, his ability to control himself, at the same time, we have to abide by the law and stand for law and order.

Q. If I may, sir, many Americans feel that there is no law and order, that the police either are unable or not sufficiently in force to do their job. What then is the alternative for Americans?

The President. Well, there apparently are some centers of crime and places where criminals have found happy hunting more than others. But, actually, we've been making sizable progress in the last few years with regard to law enforcement. For the first time, I think, since the crime statistics have been kept, in the last 2 years, they have gone down, 2 years in a row in regard to serious crime. So, a lot of it, I think, depends on all of us in our insisting on law

and order.

I don't blame the police so much for what we've seen over the years as a kind of an attitude in the whole structure of judicial and everyplace else in crime in which it seemed that we got overzealous in protecting the criminals' rights and forgot about the victim. And I think if we have stricter enforcement and stricter punishment, we'll continue to see decline in crime.

Bill [Bill Plante, CBS News]?

Federal Budget

Q. Mr. President, have you painted yourself into a corner with your campaign promises to raise taxes only over your dead body, not to cut Social Security, and to keep up defense spending? The majority leader in your own party in the Senate is talking about writing his own budget, and it appears to many people that you have walked away from the deficit problem and the budget problem and are going to leave it to Congress.

The President. No, in the first few days of February, we will be submitting our budget to the Congress. And I don't mind if they want to do what they're doing and have some plans of their own or suggesting some. Maybe they've got some ideas we hadn't thought of. And I'd be very happy to look at theirs as well as ours.

But it is my responsibility to submit a budget. I'm going to submit it. And our target is to have a budget that in overall spending will be no greater in '86 than the spending in '85.

Q. But, sir, the consensus even within your own party seems to be that if you keep all your promises, there's no way that you can accomplish that goal.

The President. I just don't believe them.

First of all, I think that the risk of a tax increase, of slowing down the economy, and putting us right back in a pattern that we've had since World War II, eight recessions in a row, and every recession led to the next one being worse and inflation higher and unemployment greater and so forth. We have made a great start on a recovery that is based on sound principles and not on artificially stimulating the economy. We're going to stay with a plan of that kind.

I think that a tax increase would be counterproductive. And I think also that today—even though you all had to report that there was a fraction of a percent of increase in the unemployment rate for December over November, I'd like to point out that—and the statisticians always do puzzle me—however, there were 340,000 more people employed in the United States in December than were employed in November. But, evidently, there were more new entrants to the job market. But we have more people employed today.

But just as one figure—the only reason I brought that up is to point out there are 340,000 more people in December—unanticipated, I'm sure, by many—who are now taxpayers and who'll be contributing to government's revenues.

And the best way to increase government's revenues is not by increasing the rates. The best way is by keeping the rates down but increasing the economic upsurge.

Presidential Advisers

Q. Mr. President, you said after your reelection you did not want to break up a winning team. Yet your three top assistants are leaving the White House, and Mr. Deaver and Mr. Clark are leaving the administration entirely. Are you going into your second term with a second-string team, and aren't you going to feel a little lonely without your longtime California aides?

The President. Well, of course. I'll miss any one of those—we've been a fine team—and any that feel they have to leave. But it was no great surprise to me. I said from the beginning that I wanted people to take these positions in government, but I was not setting any time limit as to how long they had to stay. I know that some people can only stay a short time, and then they have to return to their own private lives and careers. And I said that I would then go out and find someone to replace them when that time came.

So, I'd like to point out that Secretary Clark, at my behest, was in public life longer than I was, because between being Governor of California and being President, I had a few years as a civilian. He didn't.

Due to me, he was on the California State Supreme Court. He's given 18 years to public life, away from his private life, and he told me a couple of years ago, and he stayed on at—when I urged him at that particular time to do so, for a while. But I've understood that he was coming to the point that he wanted to—and would—return.

Mike Deaver—I knew that if there was a second term that he didn't feel that he could go for 8 years. He'll be very much missed.

But some of the other people you mention, they're just changing chairs at the Cabinet table. They'll still be around. And I don't care which side of the table they're talking from. I'll be listening.

Chris [Chris Wallace, NBC News]?

Strategic Defense Initiative

Q. Yes, sir. I'm a little confused by your original answer on, if you'll forgive me, "Star Wars"—if we can continue to use that term. You say that you're willing to negotiate about it now, but you also said that you want to go forward with research and only really discuss limits after it proves out whether the plan is feasible or not, which is sometime, perhaps, beyond your term—into 1990 or so. The question is now, in the talks that are going to begin this year, would you consider setting limits on the deployment and the testing of "Star Wars"?

The President. Chris, I think that would be way ahead of ourselves. We don't even know what kind of a weapon—if we're able to come up with one—that this would be. Now, I think maybe some of you have been looking at those drawings on your TV news programs at night in which you've already got a picture of the weapon—and I can see it shooting missiles down, and it looks so easy. We don't know. That's why when I said "Star Wars" and criticized it, I never mentioned space or anything. I don't know. I'm not a scientist.

I said, all through history we've always been able to come up with a defensive weapon. Isn't it worth researching to see if there isn't some weapon that is more humane and moral than saying that the only defense we have in the nuclear age is that if they kill tens of millions of our people, we'll kill tens of millions of theirs?

We're searching for a weapon that might destroy nuclear weapons, not be nuclear itself—destroy weapons, not people. And if we come up with such a thing, then is a time to turn to the world, to our allies, possibly even our adversaries, and say, "Look, we now have this." And if we haven't by that time eliminated nuclear weapons entirely, this could be a big contributing factor to bringing that about.

Q. But aren't you running the risk of letting these arms talks break down over this issue? The Soviets say that's their top priority.

The President. No, no. One of the three phases that has been agreed upon in what I think is a most successful meeting in Geneva is that we will be talking in three groups about strategic nuclear weapons—these are offensive weapons—about strategic intermediate-range weapons—again offensive—and there will be a third sector where we will be talking about defense and space, whether it has to do with weapons shooting things down that are in space or whether it's weapons in space shooting down.

And, as I say, what we're doing with this research—and the Soviets had no argument about that, they couldn't argue about it—is to research, continue researching—is within the provisions of the ABM treaty.

Yes.

Federal Budget

Q. Mr. President, in response to Gary's question, you indicated that you might accept a freeze in Social Security COLA's if it were forced on you by Congress. Would you also accept cuts in military spending and a tax increase if Congress pressed you on that?

The President. No. I feel that a tax increase, as I say, would be counterproductive and would set us back in the very thing that we have accomplished in these first 4 years and intend to carry on, and that is an economic expansion.

With regard to defense, here again I have to say, defense is not a program in which we can determine what we want to spend. That is dictated by outside influences,

things outside our country. And I would like to point out that the Defense Department has come in on its own, voluntarily, with a bigger cut than had been asked of it for the first year, for 1986.

Now, they point out—and I think I support them in this—very logically that it is impossible to make a projection over 3 or 5 years as to what you will spend in those outyears. What if some development on the other side of the ocean absolutely makes it necessary for us to do something that we can't even contemplate now with regard to national security? So, all Defense has asked is do not pin them down to the outyears, but to accept that here, in good faith, they have come up with, as I say, a bigger increase [decrease] than was asked.

And may I call your attention to something else—and maybe you'd like to rally around and help with a few editorials. I think this policy sometime ago of the Congress demanding that the President submit a budget and then, based on that budget, submit projections for what the government budgets are going to be for the next 5 years—there isn't any economist in the world who can do that and accurately tell you what you're going to need down the road. And I'd like to point out that all of the projections that we inherited went out the window. They didn't match what we're doing now, and I think it is enough—I know that most of the States get along just fine with constitutional provisions that they can't have deficits and with the Governors having to present a budget for that year, and a budget then when the next year comes around. And those projections, frankly, I pay no attention to them.

Q. But, sir, by putting forth a budget that doesn't even meet your own goals for deficit reduction, aren't you really begging Congress to do these things?

The President. No, we're going to reach our goal. We're going to submit a budget that sets us on that declining path. And, as I say, our aim is a budget that is based on—that will be no more than the money spent in 1985. And that's our target, and we intend to meet that target.

There are a couple of things we can't control—for example, the interest on the debt. So, we have to make allowances in other areas and find cuts that we can make there. It would be very simple if the budget was of such a nature that you could simply say everybody spend the same amount of money next year. We can't. Some are going to spend more, some are going to spend less, and some we're just going to wipe out entirely.

U.S.-Soviet Summit Meetings

Q. Mr. President, given the progress that you indicated made with the Soviets in these recent talks, do you feel that this might be the time now to have a summit with Soviet leaders, Chernenko?

The President. Well, to have a meeting, as I said before, just to have a meeting doesn't make any sense. Now, in this next month or so, we're all supposed to get together and find out when the negotiations can start and where. If, at any time, a reason arises in which a summit could be helpful in that or in other matters, and a carefully planned agenda created which they, themselves, have said is necessary, I'm perfectly willing, and have been all this time, to go to a summit meeting.

I don't think it would make much sense simply to say, "Well, now that we're going to talk about these other things, let's have a meeting just to get acquainted." That builds up people's hopes. And some previous Presidents have done that and found that the letdown was very terrible.

Jerry?

Q. Could you tell us if that summit conference was broached at all by Secretary Shultz to Foreign Minister Gromyko?

The President. About a summit?

Q. Was it brought up in these talks?

The President. No, they had a very carefully planned agenda. And, incidentally, there was no infighting among our group, and 15 people that went over there as the total delegation were in complete unanimity in their support of what we arrived at. And they were, all of them, experts in their fields. And there has been no infighting, as some have suggested, about what we were going to talk about there.

And there was very careful planning, and my last meeting with George and Bud McFarlane was just a few hours before they

got on the plane to go over there. But we had agreed upon what our agenda was going to be and what our demands were.

Jerry [Jeremiah O'Leary, Washington Times]?

Central America

Q. Mr. President, the time is drawing near when you will have to certify to Congress whether there's a need to continue supplying aid to the rebel forces inside Nicaragua. And I'd like to ask if you intend to press on with this program when that date comes, or do you see any reason or any developments that have occurred, that would permit the United States to drop this covert aid program.

The President. Well, Jerry, as you know, I shouldn't be talking about anything that is supposed to be covert, but I will say this: that our plans, we have no plans for abandoning the overall ideas of help such as were created by the Kissinger commission down there—program proposed for over about the next 5 years to help those nations that are trying to become democracies to be democracies, and to support the people of Nicaragua, who, I have to point out, are governed by a group that took over by force—ousted others that had been fighting for a revolution. And I think that—and they are supporting the guerrillas that are trying to overthrow the duly elected Government of El Salvador. And, no, we're not retreating from what we feel are obligations there in Central America at all.

Q. Mr. President——

The President. No, no—I was—yes, you.

Nuclear Arms Levels

Q. Thank you, Mr. President. By the end of the year, if the United States continues to deploy its strategic submarines as planned, it will exceed the limits for strategic missiles under the SALT II agreement, Mr. President. What is your intention with respect to that agreement? Are you going to decrease the number of ICBM's and outmoded submarine missiles in order to keep that SALT II agreement alive, even though it's not ratified?

The President. Well, we have been holding to that and thought that it would be helpful in now what we're planning and going forward with. We have been eliminating some of the older missiles and taking out of service some of the submarines. We will continue on that ground.

The development of the Trident is not so much in the sense of adding to the nuclear force as it is in modernizing it, replacing older, less accurate missiles and submarines with not quite the capacity of the Trident. So, yes, we feel that we can live within it.

Remember, the SALT II is nothing but a limitation on how fast you increase weapons, which is one of the reasons why I was in support of a Senate—even though I wasn't here at the time—that refused to ratify it. And that's why my belief is that the type of negotiations we're suggesting are the only ones that make sense. Don't just limit the rate of increase; reduce the number of weapons.

Q. Well, Mr. President, your aides have said that they have some innovative, interesting ideas if the negotiations are resumed. What are your ideas? Defensive weapons aside, what are your ideas for reducing offensive systems, ideas that were not put forward in the negotiations that were aborted and that could offer some hope for progress in this new round of negotiations?

The President. Well, I don't want to give away anything in advance, the things that belong at the negotiating table. But, yes, one of the things that we've made clear to the Soviets is that we recognize there may be differences with regard to the mix of weapons on both sides. And we're prepared to deal with that problem, and where, perhaps, we have something that is an advantage to us, they have something that's an advantage to them, to discuss tradeoffs in that area.

It is true that when we first went into the strategic missile negotiations, we believed that the top priority should be land-based missiles. But the Soviets made it plain that they weren't following our pattern of mix of missiles, that they placed more reliance than we did on the land-based. And they didn't wait for us when we told them that we were willing to—okay, to deal with them on that problem. They went home anyway and didn't come back.

But these are new negotiations. Both sides rule that they're new negotiations.

Q. Mr. President——

The President. No, no. I'm sorry. I want to——

Q. Oh, I'm sorry.

The President. No, right there.

Q. Wake up!

The President. Put your pen down. [*Laughter*] I thought you had your hand up.

Presidential Appointments

Q. I'm sorry, Mr. President. I didn't know you recognized me.

Mr. President, you started the workweek with a number of surprises and changes in your staff. I'm wondering, now that you have the opportunity, if you wouldn't like to get any other personnel changes off your chest, such as the change in—a replacement for Mr. Clark. Is it true, for example, that Mr. Hodel is going to replace him?

The President. I ain't talking. [*Laughter*] I'll tell you when we've made a decision.

Oh, then there's a young lady over here who I understand is new among us.

U.S.-Soviet Relations

Q. Thank you, Mr. President. Do you think that the Geneva meetings this week and the resumption of arms negotiations in the near future might lead to the new era of détente that Mr. Chernenko called for last November?

The President. I think that there will be other things talked about other than just weapons. And, yes. But let me make it plain about détente. That is a word that—been a little abused in the past in some ways.

Yes, we would welcome such a thing as long as it was a two-way street. Our problem in the past has been that it has too much been a one-way street, and we were going the wrong way on that. So, we very definitely are trying to arrive at a position in which we can settle some of the other bilateral and regional issues that—and trade matters that are at odds between us.

Q. What about other matters like Afghanistan, Southeast Asia—problems there. Would they come up as well?

The President. We did not and I—well, I can't say whether we voiced our opinion of those in these meetings. They very well could have in the long hours of those meetings. But, no, all of those things—and we've made it very clear to them what our opinion is of some of those practices.

Richard M. Nixon

Q. Mr. President, are you about to name former President Richard Nixon to a post in your administration, perhaps as a roving ambassador of some sort, or perhaps somehow involved in the upcoming arms negotiations?

The President. Well, he has never suggested, himself, that he had any interest in such a thing. And, no, we have no such plans.

Jerry, did you——

Q. Have you been consulting——

The President. What?

Q. Have you been consulting with him on the arms talks, or do you plan to?

The President. I feel that, and we do keep all the former Presidents briefed and bring them up to date on things that we've done and so forth. So, I talk to him every once in a while—like today, to say "Happy Birthday."

Jerry [Gerald M. Boyd, New York Times]?

Tax Simplification

Q. Thank you, Mr. President. In light of the changes in jobs between Mr. Regan and Mr. Baker, do you now plan to make a greater push on simplifying the tax system, and do you think it has a better chance of getting congressional approval?

The President. Oh, Jerry, whether that will help or not, all of us—and the two that are changing jobs and myself, as well as others—are totally dedicated to trying for the tax simplification.

Now, I know that some have suggested that maybe we're putting that on a back burner. No. We have been so busy, and we put top priority on getting the budget ready. And with regard to that tax study made by the Treasury Department, they now are also getting input from various sectors of the business world out there in society and also dealing with people on the Hill. I believe that there are—they recognize that there are things in there that may be options to choose or not to accept.

And as soon as we get the budget in shape and presented, then we will go into the same lengthy process we've been in on the budget, only this time on the tax simplification, because we're determined that we're going forward on these tracks. But it is a two-track approach. We're not sending them up there as a package that somehow people can begin trading between one and the other.

Ms. Thomas. Thank you, Mr. President.

The President. Helen? Thank you. I'm sorry. Why don't you all get together and find some way in which I don't have to leave so many hands in the air? [*Laughter*]

Q. Would you ride unarmed on a New York subway, Mr. President? [*Inaudible*]

The President. Security wouldn't allow me. [*Laughter*]

Q. Are you going to be back next month?

Q. Will we see you soon?

The President. What?

Q. Are you going to be back next month?

The President. Probably.

Q. What?

The President. Probably.

Note: The President's 27th news conference began at 8 p.m. in the East Room at the White House. It was broadcast live on nationwide radio and television.

Statement by Principal Deputy Press Secretary Speakes on the Nomination of Three Department Secretaries and One Deputy Secretary
January 10, 1985

The President is today announcing his intention to nominate four distinguished members of the administration to new positions. The nominations are Donald P. Hodel to be Secretary of the Interior, John S. Herrington to be Secretary of Energy, William J. Bennett to be Secretary of Education, and Richard G. Darman to be Deputy Secretary of the Treasury. The nominations will be transmitted to the Senate at an early date.

The President believes these nominees will provide exceptionally strong leadership in the second term of his administration. They are men of proven ability who have served in key positions within the Government. They will make a strong team even stronger.

In conjunction with these nominations, the President has directed Mr. Hodel and Mr. Herrington, once confirmed, to commence a study of their respective departments and to propose reorganizational options to the President. These options should be designed to recognize the interrelationship of energy, natural resource, and defense policies. The President is committed to maximizing effective management and efficiency in the natural resource area.

The President has also directed Mr. Bennett, following confirmation, to conduct a study of the Education Department's functions to determine the proper organizational structure and role of the Federal Government in education.

Note: Larry M. Speakes read the statement to reporters at 3:30 p.m. in the Briefing Room at the White House.

Nomination of Donald P. Hodel To Be Secretary of the Interior
January 10, 1985

The President today announced his intention to nominate Donald P. Hodel to be Secretary of the Interior. He would succeed William P. Clark.

Mr. Hodel is currently serving as Secretary of Energy. From February 1981 until November 1982, he was Under Secretary of the Department of the Interior. Prior to this he was president of Hodel Associates, Inc., an energy consulting firm in Oregon. Mr. Hodel graduated from Harvard College (B.A., 1957) and the University of Oregon School of Law (J.D., 1960). He is married and resides in Arlington, VA. He was born May 23, 1935.

Nomination of John S. Herrington To Be Secretary of Energy
January 10, 1985

The President today announced his intention to nominate John S. Herrington to be Secretary of Energy. He would succeed Donald P. Hodel.

Since June 1983 Mr. Herrington has been Assistant to the President for Presidential Personnel. From February until May 1983, he was Special Assistant to the Chief of

31

Staff, the White House. Previously he was Assistant Secretary of the Navy (Manpower and Reserve Affairs) from October 1981 until February 1983. He also served as Deputy Assistant to the President and Director of Presidential Personnel from January 1981 until September 1981.

Mr. Herrington graduated from Stanford University (A.B., 1961) and the University of California, Hastings College of Law (LL.B., J.D., 1964). Mr. Herrington is married, has two children, and resides in McLean, VA. He was born in Los Angeles on May 31, 1939.

Nomination of William J. Bennett To Be Secretary of Education
January 10, 1985

The President today announced his intention to nominate William J. Bennett to be Secretary of Education. He would succeed Terrel H. Bell.

Since November of 1981, Dr. Bennett has been serving as Chairman of the National Endowment of the Humanities. Prior to this he was president and director of the National Humanities Center, Research Triangle Park, North Carolina. He graduated from Williams College, Williamstown, MA (B.A., 1965), the University of Texas, Austin, TX (Ph.D., 1967), and Harvard Law School (J.D., 1971). He resides in Chapel Hill, NC, and was born July 31, 1943.

Nomination of Richard G. Darman To Be Deputy Secretary of the Treasury
January 10, 1985

The President today announced his intention to nominate Richard G. Darman to be the Deputy Secretary of the Treasury.

Mr. Darman now serves as Assistant to the President and Deputy to the Chief of Staff, a position he has held since 1981. Prior to joining the White House staff, Mr. Darman was a member of the faculty of Harvard's Graduate School of Government and a partner in ICF Inc., a management and economic consulting company. He served previously in government from 1970 to 1977, in policy positions in five Cabinet Departments (HEW, Defense, Justice, Commerce, and State). His prior service included service as Assistant Secretary of Commerce for Policy, a position for which he was nominated by President Ford and confirmed by the Senate.

Mr. Darman, 41, is an honors graduate of Harvard College and Harvard Business School. He is married to Kathleen Emmet (Darman), Ph.D. They have two sons and reside in Virginia.

Appointment of Four Members of the National Advisory Council on Continuing Education
January 10, 1985

The President today announced his intention to appoint the following individuals to be members of the National Advisory Council on Continuing Education for terms expiring September 30, 1987. These are reappointments.

Mary Fenske Buestrin is active in Republican Party politics in Ozaukee County, WI. She graduated from Valparaiso University (B.A., 1960). She is married, has two children, and resides in Mequon, WI. She was born August 9, 1939, in Oak Park, IL.

Sylvia Bernstein Hermann is chairman of the committee for public service and community involvement, Montgomery County Federation of Republican Women. She has two children and resides in Bethesda, MD. She was born March 2, 1914, in Newark, NJ.

Bonnie Blackman McClure is a member of the board of Los Angeles Orphanage Guild Juniors-Volunteer support group. She is also an active fundraiser, volunteer, and member of the board of directors for the Children's Hospital of Los Angeles. She is married, has one child, and resides in Beverly Hills, CA. She was born April 17, 1939, in Los Angeles, CA.

Hilary Paterson Cleveland is a professor of history and political science at Colby-Sawyer College in New London, NH. She graduated from Vassar College (B.A., 1948) and the Institute of International Relations in Geneva, Switzerland (M.A., 1950). She is married, has five children, and resides in New London, NH. She was born December 7, 1927, in Orange, NJ.

Appointment of Two Members of the Board of Trustees of the Woodrow Wilson International Center for Scholars
January 10, 1985

The President today announced his intention to appoint the following individuals to be members of the Board of Trustees of the Woodrow Wilson International Center for Scholars in the Smithsonian Institution for terms expiring October 23, 1990:

Max M. Kampelman is a reappointment. Since 1955 he has been an attorney with the law firm of Fried, Frank, Harris, Shriver & Kampelman in Washington, DC. He graduated from New York University (A.B., 1950), New York University School of Law (J.D., 1945), and the University of Minnesota (M.A., 1946; Ph.D., 1951). He is married, has five children, and resides in Washington, DC. He was born November 7, 1920, in New York, NY.

Gertrude Himmelfarb will succeed Anne Firor Scott. She has been a distinguished professor of history at the Graduate School of City University in New York, NY, since 1965. She graduated from Brooklyn College (B.A., 1942), the University of Chicago (M.A., 1944; Ph.D., 1950), Rhode Island College (L.H.D., 1976), and Smith College (Litt.D., 1977). She is married, has two children, and resides in New York, NY. She was born August 8, 1922, in New York, NY.

Appointment of Richard Bender Abell as a Member of the Board of Directors of Federal Prison Industries, Incorporated
January 10, 1985

The President today announced his intention to appoint Richard Bender Abell to be a member of the Board of Directors, Federal Prison Industries, Incorporated, Department of Justice. He will succeed Peter D. Bensinger.

Mr. Abell is Deputy Assistant Attorney General for Justice Assistance. Previously he was an associate with the law offices of Reilly, Fogwell & Lachall in West Chester, PA. He was assistant district attorney, police legal coordinator, in Chester County, PA, in 1974–1979.

He graduated from the George Washington University (B.A., 1966) and the George Washington University Law School (J.D., 1974). He also attended the Instituto Politecnico Colombiano in 1967. He is married, has three children, and resides in Alexandria, VA. He was born December 2, 1943, in Philadelphia, PA.

Appointment of Gerhard Casper as a Member of the Permanent Committee for the Oliver Wendell Holmes Devise
January 11, 1985

The President today announced his intention to appoint Gerhard Casper to be a member of the Permanent Committee for the Oliver Wendell Holmes Devise for a term of 8 years. He will succeed Charles Alan Wright.

Mr. Casper joined the faculty of the University of Chicago Law School in 1966. He served as Max Pam Professor of Law in 1976–1980, when he was appointed William B. Graham Professor of Law. He has been dean of the law school since 1979. He is a member of the American Law Institute and its council and was a fellow of the American Academy of Arts and Sciences.

He received his first law degree in 1961 from the University of Hamburg. He also received a master of laws degree from Yale University in 1962 and the *doctor iuris utriusque* from the University of Freiburg (1964). He is married, has one child, and resides in Chicago, IL. He was born December 25, 1937, in Hamburg, Germany.

Appointment of Three Members of the National Highway Safety Advisory Committee
January 11, 1985

The President today announced his intention to appoint the following individuals to be members of the National Highway Safety Advisory Committee for terms expiring March 15, 1987:

Stuart J. Northrop will succeed Matthew J. Binder. Mr. Northrop is chairman of the board of the Huffy Corp. in Dayton, OH. He was founding vice president and general manager of the Singer Co., Water Resource Division, in 1969–1972. He is married, has two children, and resides in Haverford, PA. He was born October 21, 1925, in New Haven, CT.

William H. Taggart will succeed James H. Brennan. He is retired senior vice president and director of public affairs for the Home Federal Savings and Loan Association of San Diego. He is married, has four children, and resides in La Jolla, CA. He was born October 8, 1920, in Seattle, WA.

Larry Zarian will succeed Richard L. Berkley. He is owner and president of Anthony's Home

and Auto Center Department Store in Bell Gardens, CA. He has three children and resides in Glendale, CA. He was born October 20, 1937, in Iran and became a United States citizen in 1956.

Written Responses to Questions Submitted by La Libre Belgique of Belgium
January 11, 1985

Intermediate-Range Nuclear Force Deployment

Q. Given its delicate political situation regarding INF deployment, why should the Belgian Government proceed with deployment if these new negotiations might make such a move unnecessary?

The President. Because Belgium, like the United States, is a member of NATO. Belgium has long been an important member and played a prominent role in the NATO alliance. As an alliance member, Belgium committed itself in 1979 to go forward with NATO's two-track approach to deployment and arms control regarding intermediate-range nuclear forces. This major decision was necessitated by the new and unprovoked threat to the West represented by the Soviet Union's buildup in SS–20 missiles, a buildup which is still going on. The deployment of cruise missiles in Belgium is a sovereign question for the Government and people of your country to decide. But it was alliance solidarity behind NATO's two-track decision that helped to bring the Soviets back to negotiations, and alliance solidarity behind the dual track approach is crucial to our prospects for success in renewed negotiations. We hope Belgium will act with its commitments under NATO's 1979 decision in mind.

NATO Solidarity

Q. What does the United States expect its European allies like Belgium to do to strengthen the U.S. position in the upcoming arms control negotiations with the Soviets?

The President. As I said, alliance solidarity in proceeding with deployment is a major

reason why the Soviets decided to return to Geneva. Our European allies fully appreciate this relationship between deployment and arms control. Our negotiating prospects would be seriously weakened if the Soviets believe they can get what they want in some other way than engaging seriously in a negotiating process leading to a balanced and verifiable arms control agreement.

This brings us to the question of public opinion in Belgium and throughout Europe. I can understand why some European polls, including the recent one that you published, suggest public concern about the deployments. The fact is that most people don't fully take into account the Soviet missile buildup in which the Soviets have more than a thousand warheads aimed at Western Europe. They launched an enormous disinformation campaign to persuade the people of Europe that somehow NATO is at fault for beginning to redress the balance in Europe. Our allies can help by standing firm and by making sure their publics understand the truth in this situation.

European Defense Spending

Q. Is the United States now satisfied with current levels of European defense expenditures?

The President. The share of the common defense burden our European allies are shouldering varies. The United States is certainly doing its fair share for alliance security, although assessing national defense contributions is not nearly as simple as adding up money spent. One thing is clear—massive and growing Soviet military capabilities threaten the credibility of NATO's deterrent. That's why we must all do more.

Strategic Defense Initiative

Q. What reassurance can you give Europeans that your Strategic Defense Initiative will not lead to decoupling of Europe from the protection of American strategic forces?

The President. Well, first let me explain that this program is one of vigorous research focused on advanced defensive technologies with the aim of finding ways to provide a better basis for deterring aggression, strengthen strategic stability, and increasing the security of the United States and our allies.

In March 1983 I made clear in my original speech on the Strategic Defense Initiative, which we call SDI, that no change in technology can or will alter our commitments to our allies. I have repeatedly stated our commitment to NATO, and I am pleased to reaffirm that commitment here. And from the beginning I have directed that the SDI research program look at the entire ballistic missile threat, not just those which can reach the United States.

In 1979 NATO agreed that the best way to resolve any doubts about "decoupling" was to go forward with a two-track approach of deployments and arms control of intermediate-range nuclear forces. Alliance solidarity on all issues of deterrence is essential, both for our collective security and for arms control prospects.

We look forward in the coming weeks to the opportunities presented by the recent Geneva meeting. First, we have a renewed opportunity to reduce the level of offensive nuclear weapons. Second, we can open a serious exchange with the Soviet Union on what role ought to be played by defensive systems in improving stability of deterrence.

In the course of these exchanges we hope that it will be possible to make clear how nonnuclear systems may, over time, offer us the chance to move away from reliance upon offensive forces which threaten massive destruction and, perhaps one day, move closer to reliance upon nonnuclear defense systems. We are very conscious in the United States that this will not occur overnight; that perhaps by the turn of the century, however, this evolution may be possible. Between now and then, we will have to rely upon existing forces on both sides. But perhaps in the process we can come to an understanding of how these forces can be reduced and, over time, nonnuclear, nonthreatening defensive elements can be introduced.

Export Controls

Q. In light of the new dialog and warming East-West relations, can we expect some relaxation of present export controls?

The President. We understand the importance of exports, especially to countries like Belgium, and fully support the lowering of trade barriers. In this regard we are working hard to cooperate on a number of export requests from Belgian firms involving U.S. technology.

With regard to the broader question, we remain concerned about the Soviets acquiring advanced technology with potential military application. It simply doesn't make sense to give our adversaries technology that they could then use to threaten the West.

Note: The questions and answers were released by the Office of the Press Secretary on January 13.

Appointment of Rick J. Neal as a Member of the National Advisory Committee on Oceans and Atmosphere
January 14, 1985

The President today announced his intention to appoint Rick J. Neal to be a member of the National Advisory Committee on Oceans and Atmosphere for a term expiring July 1, 1987. He will succeed Vernon E. Scheid.

Mr. Neal is presently serving as manager of State government affairs for MAPCO,

Inc., in Tulsa, OK. He served at the White House as Deputy Assistant to the President for Intergovernmental Affairs (1983–1985) and Special Assistant to the President for Intergovernmental Affairs (1981–1983). Prior to joining the White House staff, he ran his own consulting firm, Rick Neal Co.

In 1976–1978 he was administrative assistant to Congressman Mickey Edwards (R–OK).

He graduated from Southwestern State University in Oklahoma (B.A., 1970). He is married and resides in Tulsa, OK. He was born June 23, 1947, in Downey, CA.

Remarks Following Discussions With Prime Minister Wilfried Martens of Belgium
January 14, 1985

The President. It was a great pleasure to meet Prime Minister Martens today and to discuss with him a number of matters of mutual concern. As befitting the traditionally close relations between our two free countries, our talks were both friendly and productive.

Belgium is one of our oldest, closest, and most valuable allies. The Prime Minister and I devoted considerable attention to the current state of East-West relations, focusing on the importance of continued allied solidarity and resolve. We agreed on the value of improving East-West relations and achieving meaningful arms reductions. In this regard, I was pleased to review with the Prime Minister the results of the recent Geneva talks and to discuss the prospects for future progress.

We recognize that the progress that we're now enjoying in arms control discussions is linked to the alliance's commitment to modernize our defenses and the steps we've taken to maintain a balance of nuclear forces in Europe. And that's why we give special emphasis to an issue of central concern to the NATO alliance—the deployment of intermediate-range nuclear forces in Western Europe to counter Soviet SS–20 deployments. At the same time, we both place a high priority on finding a responsible means of reducing the arsenals of nuclear weapons that now threaten humankind.

In a related question, the Prime Minister and I examined the problem of transfer of technology from the West to potential adversaries. We reaffirmed our willingness to work closely together and with our other allies to establish guidelines consistent with our security interests in this vital area.

And finally, I'd like to note the high level of respect and affection that is apparent in our meetings today. The Prime Minister and the people of Belgium are good friends and solid allies, and we're grateful for this chance to exchange ideas. It was a pleasure to have Prime Minister Martens, Foreign Minister Tindemans, and all the official party here.

The Prime Minister and Mrs. Martens will be visiting Boston and New York prior to returning to Belgium, and I would like to wish them a pleasant stay for the remainder of their visit to the United States and a smooth journey home.

The Prime Minister. I am very happy to have the opportunity to meet once again with President Reagan, and I am most satisfied with the talks that Foreign Minister Tindemans and myself had here in Washington. Our talks were based on the common values we share and in which we believe, and they were held in an atmosphere of frankness and friendship.

For my part, I want to stress five points: First, the outcome of the recent talks in Geneva is a first, positive step towards arms reduction negotiations, aiming at establishing a balance of forces at the lowest possible level. I especially value the fact that according to the preoccupations we expressed, the INF problem was given full consideration during these negotiations.

Second, in the course of the negotiations, which may be lengthy, it is important that the allies will be kept fully informed and consulted whenever their security interests are at stake.

Three, I reaffirmed our commitment to the objectives of the alliance. The security of Western Europe depends essentially on the solidarity and the joint efforts of the American and European allies. Concerning INF, I confirmed our attachment to the dual track decision which is an expression of firmness in defense and of openness for dialog.

Four, the smaller NATO countries contribute in an important way to our common defense. I feel that Belgium made the substantial effort in order to bring about the resumption of the Geneva dialog. In this regard, I refer to Mr. Tindemans' and my own contacts with East European countries and to the early suggestions we made there on how to restart negotiations on arms control and disarmament.

Five, in the economic field, the cohesion of the alliance would be strengthened by further eliminating protectionism in our trade relations and by perfecting the procedures of our common approach towards East-West trade.

I thank you.

Reporter. Mr. President, will the Belgians take the cruise missile, sir? Will the Belgians take the cruise?

The President. He has just announced that they are consistent with the whole NATO program.

Q. Well, he said that he reconfirmed his attachment to the dual track system. Does that mean that in March he will accept the first of the cruises? Consultation is allowed.

Mr. Secretary, will he take the cruise, sir?

Secretary of State Shultz. I meet and greet, and I say goodbye.

Note: The President spoke at 1:27 p.m. at the South Portico of the White House. Earlier, the President and the Prime Minister met in the Oval Office. They then held a working luncheon, together with U.S. and Belgian officials, in the State Dining Room.

Proclamation 5292—National Sanctity of Human Life Day, 1985
January 14, 1985

By the President of the United States of America

A Proclamation

America was founded by men and women who shared a vision of the value of each and every individual. Our forebears strove to build a nation in which the dignity of every person was respected and the rights of all were secure. Our laws have sought to foster and protect human life at all its stages.

Legal acceptance of abortion imperils this cherished tradition. By permitting the destruction of unborn children throughout the term of pregnancy, our laws have brought about an inestimable loss of human life and potential. Yet the tragedy of abortion extends beyond the loss of the nearly 17 million children who have been robbed of the gift of life. This tragedy is multifaceted—inflicting emotional harm on women, deny-

ing prospective adoptive couples the joy of sharing their loving homes with children, and eroding respect for the most fundamental of rights, the right to life.

No cause is more important than restoring respect for this right because the freedoms we hold so dear cannot endure as long as some lives are regarded as unworthy of protection. Nor can our commitment to defend the dignity of all persons survive if we remain indifferent to the destruction of 1.5 million children each year in the United States.

I do not believe that Americans will continue to tolerate this practice. Respect for the sanctity of human life remains too deeply engrained in the hearts of our people to remain forever suppressed. This respect for life is evident in communities throughout our Nation where people are reaching out, in a spirit of understanding and helping, to women with crisis pregnancies and to those who bear the spiritual and emotional scars of abortion. Such efforts strengthen the bonds of affection and obligation that unite us and assure that the family, the primary guardian of life and human values, will continue to be the foundation of our society.

If America is to remain what God, in His wisdom, intended for it to be—a refuge, a safe haven for those seeking human rights—then we must once again extend the most basic human right to the most vulnerable members of the human family. We must commit ourselves to a future in which the right to life of every human being—no matter how weak, no matter how small, no matter how defenseless—is protected by our laws and public policy.

Now, Therefore, I, Ronald Reagan, Presi-dent of the United States of America, do hereby proclaim Sunday, January 20, 1985, as National Sanctity of Human Life Day. I call upon the citizens of this blessed land to gather on that day in homes and places of worship to give thanks for the gift of life, and to reaffirm our commitment to the dignity of every human being and the sanctity of each human life.

In Witness Whereof, I have hereunto set my hand this 14th day of January, in the year of our Lord nineteen hundred and eighty-five, and of the Independence of the United States of America the two hundred and ninth.

RONALD REAGAN

[*Filed with the Office of the Federal Register, 11:47 a.m., January 15, 1985*]

Remarks at the Opening of the Michael Evans Portrait Exhibit at the Corcoran Gallery of Art
January 14, 1985

Thank you very much. And thank you, Michael, and good evening, everyone. It's a pleasure for Nancy and me to join all of you here at the Corcoran for the opening of an exhibition of portraits by our good friend, Michael Evans.

And by the way, Mike, I was relieved to see that the exhibition's title is "Portraits of Power." Last time we talked it over, he was thinking of naming it "The Michael Evans Gallery of Rogues." [*Laughter*]

For the past 4 years Michael Evans has been our official White House photographer, snapping the parade of events at the Executive Mansion and traveling with us around the world. Mike has captured everything from Cabinet meetings to Easter egg rolls, and his thousands of pictures provide a full and fascinating record of the hard work, exhilaration, and pageantry of American government.

And yet, in the course of his duties, Mike saw the need for another kind of record—one that would focus entirely on individuals. In these pictures there would be no seals of office, no shots of executives behind their desks or journalists at their typewriters. There would be no flags, no gardens, no tall, white pillars. Each subject would simply stand before a backdrop of plain gray. Michael would snap, and in the picture that resulted, nothing would matter but the individual—the way he or she stood, the way they held their hands, the look on his or her face.

Mike worked on this project for 3 years, and tonight we celebrate the results—600 portraits of Washington character and characters.

Taken together, these portraits say something fundamental about the greatness or openness of American democracy, for they show men and women of all backgrounds and walks of life. And although these people are helping to govern the most prosperous and powerful nation in history, you can examine all 600 pictures without once finding an arrogant or imperial gaze.

In the words of George Will, "Representative governments are, well, awfully representative, at least in this sense: They are made up of folks who look like and are like most other folks. The portraits testify, I think, to democracies' pleasantness." End of George Will quote.

Consider, for example, the portrait of the senior Senator from Mississippi. John Stennis first came to the Congress when the family that lived in the White House was named Truman and before half the Americans now alive were even born. For almost four decades he has played a central role in all the great events of our national life. Yet his portrait shows, despite all those years of exercising power, John Stennis has remained what he was at the outset—a man of gentleness, courage, and conviction.

The Senator has many friends here tonight. And I know that we all wish him well as he continues to recover from his surgery.

Look, if you will, at the portrait of Helen Thomas. For 24 years Helen has been a member of the White House press corps, keeping six Presidents and scores of fellow reporters on their toes by putting in some hours—or more hours, writing more dispatches, and asking more questions than just about anybody else. Helen's portrait suggests that she's a woman of great charm, and that's true. It also suggests that she's a woman of immense determination, and believe me that, too, is true. [*Laughter*]

Pause for a moment before the portrait of Barbara Bush. During the first 4 years of our administration Barbara traveled with her husband some 600,000 miles. She's been a staunch supporter of a great Vice President and our administration, and in her portrait we see Barbara Bush as she always is—intelligent, charming, gracious.

Consider, finally, the portraits of two skilled and dedicated government servants. Although they have hectic schedules, both are nevertheless looking into the camera calmly, even perhaps with a twinkle in their eyes. Secretary of the Treasury Donald Regan and Chief of Staff James Baker—or is it the other way around? [*Laughter*]

So, there we have it—a comprehensive portrait of the men and women involved in the government of our great Republic during this fleeting but crucial moment in our history. Tonight we will enjoy these pictures; future generations will treasure them.

Michael Evans, well done. Congratulations, and God bless you.

And now it is my honor to declare this exhibit officially open. Thank you.

Note: The President spoke at 7:30 p.m. The exhibit was entitled "People and Power: Portraits From the Federal Village."

Statement on the Birthday of Martin Luther King, Jr.
January 15, 1985

When Dr. Martin Luther King, Jr., began his career, the principles of social justice for which he stood were very controversial. But by the end of his career, he was a deeply respected leader of international stature who helped lead an extraordinary revolution in America's laws and customs. His moving example of dignity in the face of threats and hatred gave the whole Nation a new hero to admire and emulate.

Martin Luther King knew that America's democracy was imperfect, but he also knew

that America's conscience was a powerful force for reform. His unique combination of moral leadership and practical political wisdom enlisted America's conscience on the side of peaceful change.

The memory of Martin Luther King is engraved in the hearts and minds of his fellow Americans. It is appropriate that we remember him today and that we remember and honor the values for which he stood.

Message to the Congress Transmitting the Annual Reports on Highway, Traffic, and Motor Vehicle Safety Programs
January 15, 1985

To the Congress of the United States:

The Highway Safety Act and the National Traffic and Motor Vehicle Safety Act, both enacted in 1966, initiated a national effort to reduce traffic deaths and injuries and require annual reports on the administration of the Acts. This is the 16th year that these reports have been prepared for your review.

The report on motor vehicle safety includes the annual reporting requirement in Title I of the Motor Vehicle Information and Cost Savings Act of 1972 (bumper standards). An annual report also is required by the Energy Policy and Conservation Act of 1975, which amended the Motor Vehicle Information and Cost Savings Act and directed the Secretary of Transportation to set, adjust, and enforce motor vehicle fuel economy standards. Similar reporting requirements are contained in the Department of Energy Act of 1978 with respect to the use of advanced technology by the automobile industry. These requirements have been met in the Seventh Annual Fuel Economy Report, the highlights of which are summarized in the motor vehicle safety report.

In the Highway Safety Acts of 1973, 1976, and 1978, the Congress expressed its special interest in certain aspects of traffic safety, which are addressed in the volume on highway safety.

For the second year in a row, traffic fatalities have dropped significantly. The 43,945 fatalities recorded in 1982, while still unacceptably high and a tragedy to the Nation both in terms of lives lost and the economic consequences of the deaths, represent an 11 percent decrease from the preceding year.

In addition, despite large increases in drivers, vehicles, and traffic, the Federal standards and programs for motor vehicle and highway safety instituted since 1966

have contributed to a significant reduction in the fatality rate per 100 million miles of travel. The rate has decreased from 5.5 in the mid-60's to the 1982 level of 2.76. This means that motorists can drive more miles today with less risk. If the 1966 fatality rate had been experienced in 1982, more than 87,586 persons would have lost their lives in traffic accidents.

Achieving even greater reductions in the annual traffic death toll will not be easy, but it is a challenge we readily accept and intend to actively pursue. Motorists today are better informed and driving in safer vehicles and on safer roads. But they are still victims of habit and of human nature. They choose not to wear safety belts because they do not expect to be in an accident. They drive after drinking too much, because alcohol is part of our social mores. And they sometimes speed and take unnecessary chances, because being in a hurry is an unfortunate fact of modern life. Changing these ingrained behaviors is the traditional and most challenging obstacle to improving traffic safety.

The answer lies in widespread public education efforts, and a continuing national traffic safety commitment that involves government, the private sector, and the individual motorist. We will also consider new regulations, but only when there is no practical alternative, and when we are certain that doing so will result in a clear and beneficial improvement in safety.

While we can be justifiably proud of the accomplishments to date, we are convinced that this approach will bring about even more progress, and that American motorists and pedestrians will ultimately enjoy a greater level of personal safety as a result.

RONALD REAGAN

The White House,
January 15, 1985.

Appointment of Anne Crellin Seggerman as a Member of the President's Committee on Mental Retardation
January 15, 1985

The President today announced his intention to appoint Anne Crellin Seggerman to be a member of the President's Committee on Mental Retardation for a term expiring May 11, 1987. This is a reappointment.

She is president and founder of the Fourth World Foundation, Inc., in Fairfield, CT. She is also chairman of the board and founder of the Huxley Institute for Biosocial Research, Fairfield County chapter. She is a member of the board of directors of the Easter Seal Rehabilitation Center in Fairfield, CT.

She is married, has six children, and resides in Fairfield, CT. She was born May 13, 1931, in Los Angeles, CA.

Appointment of Michael W. Grebe as a Member of the Board of Visitors of the United States Military Academy
January 16, 1985

The President today announced his intention to appoint Michael W. Grebe to be a member of the Board of Visitors to the United States Military Academy for a term expiring December 30, 1987. He will succeed Bernard J. Lasker.

Mr. Grebe is a partner in the law firm of Foley & Lardner in Milwaukee, WI. He serves as a member of the Greater Milwaukee Committee and is chairman of the board of the Curative Rehabilitation Center, Inc.

He graduated from the United States Military Academy (B.S., 1962) and the University of Michigan (J.D., 1970). He is married, has two children, and resides in Mequon, WI. He was born October 25, 1940, in Peoria, IL.

Statement Following a Meeting With the United States Delegation to the Arms Reduction Negotiations With the Soviet Union
January 16, 1985

Today I met with the Vice President, Secretaries Shultz and Weinberger, and the members of the U.S. delegation which recently conducted the 2 days of tough but successful talks with their Soviet counterparts in Geneva. I invited our team members to the White House so that I could personally express to them my recognition of their extremely hard work and my gratitude for the successful outcome.

I also expressed my appreciation to our team for the unity and the discipline they demonstrated in Geneva and in the deliberative process leading up to the talks. As I indicated in my report to the Nation at the beginning of last week's press conference, the work performed by the delegation and its staff members represents an example of American diplomacy at its finest.

I took this occasion to emphasize my satisfaction that we have succeeded in getting the U.S.-Soviet arms control process back on track. I emphasized my determination to reach agreements which bring about deep and verifiable reductions in nuclear forces and which enhance strategic stability.

I am keenly aware of the hard work and long hours ahead for these dedicated people in carrying out the analyses needed to support American negotiating positions. But I am confident that with the expertise and dedication each member of our team brings

to this work, the United States will do its part to make the coming negotiations succeed.

Appointment of Two Members of the Advisory Commission on Intergovernmental Relations
January 16, 1985

The President today announced his intention to appoint the following individuals to be members of the Advisory Commission on Intergovernmental Relations for terms of 2 years:

David Nething, senate majority leader for the State of North Dakota. This is a reappointment. He graduated from Jamestown University (B.A., 1956) and the University of South Dakota

(J.D., 1963). He is married, has three children, and resides in Jamestown, ND. He was born June 29, 1933, in Valley City, ND.

Joseph P. Riley, Jr., mayor of Charleston, SC. This is a reappointment. He graduated from The Citadel (1964) and the University of South Carolina (J.D., 1967). He is married, has two children, and resides in Charleston, SC. He was born June 19, 1943, in Charleston, SC.

Statement on the 40th Anniversary of the Disappearance of Swedish Diplomat Raoul Wallenberg
January 17, 1985

Forty years ago today, a brave young man named Raoul Wallenberg disappeared from the streets of war-torn Budapest. This young Swedish diplomat had been assigned to his country's legation in Hungary in March 1944, where he undertook a humanitarian mission to save the lives of as many Hungarian Jews as possible.

Heedless of personal danger, Wallenberg pulled people out of death marches, boarded deportation trains, handed out Swedish papers to thousands of innocent people on the way to death camps and insisted to the Nazi occupation authorities that anyone holding Swedish papers be released in his custody. Altogether, Wallenberg is responsible for saving the lives of nearly 100,000 Jewish men, women, and children from certain death in Nazi extermination camps. Some of the people whom he saved are now prominent citizens of our own country.

On January 17, 1945, Raoul Wallenberg was taken by Soviet soldiers to the Provi-

sional Hungarian Government in southern Hungary, ostensibly to discuss relief efforts. He never returned. It has been 40 years.

It is written in Holy Scriptures: "Greater love hath no man than this, that a man lay down his life for his friends." Raoul Wallenberg's friends were any and all who suffered injustice. Each day he willingly jeopardized his own life so that others might live. In the face of horror and evil, this noble young man stood tall and unflinching.

In 1981, as a reflection of the debt of gratitude which all Americans owe to Raoul Wallenberg, I signed into law legislation making him an honorary United States citizen. He is the only non-American, other than Winston Churchill, ever to be honored in this way. To be true to our own values, this was the least that we—as Americans—could do to underscore our unbounded admiration for Wallenberg's courage and dedication to humanity and the abhorrence with which we view his unjust and illegal imprisonment by the Soviet Government.

The U.S. Government has repeatedly raised Raoul Wallenberg's case with the Soviet Government, and has requested a full and satisfactory clarification of his fate. But the only Soviet explanation of Wallenberg's fate was a statement in 1957 that he died 10 years earlier in a Soviet prison. No explanation has been given of the circumstances of his arrest and subsequent disappearance. Furthermore, over the years, there have been numerous reports from survivors of the Gulag that Wallenberg may be alive.

In the depths of the horrors of World War II, Raoul Wallenberg was one shining light of inspiration, upholding the honor of the human race. The world owes a tremendous and eternal debt to this great man. And the Soviet Union owes the world a full and complete accounting of his fate.

Statement Following a Meeting With the United States Representative to the Conference on Confidence and Security Building Measures and Disarmament in Europe
January 17, 1985

I met today with Ambassador James E. Goodby, the U.S. Representative to the Conference on Confidence and Security Building Measures and Disarmament in Europe—commonly known as CDE, or the Stockholm Conference. The Ambassador briefed me on the recently concluded fourth round of this Conference, involving the U.S., Canada, and 33 European nations, and on the prospects for the fifth round, beginning on January 29.

I took this occasion to assure Ambassador Goodby of my continuing strong support for the efforts of the U.S. delegation, working with our NATO allies, to search for an outcome in Stockholm which will enhance confidence and reduce the risk of war in Europe. Earlier in the Conference, the West put forward a package of concrete proposals designed to achieve these goals.

As it enters its second year, the Stockholm Conference is entering a new phase of its work. During the previous round, the Conference finally succeeded in adopting a new working structure which should encourage more detailed discussions and comparison of the proposals before it. We hope that this new arrangement will foster the beginning of productive negotiations on the substance of a final agreement.

The Stockholm Conference has a unique role to play in East-West relations. Its resumption comes shortly after the agreement reached in Geneva between Secretary of State Shultz and Soviet Foreign Minister Gromyko calling for renewed U.S.-Soviet negotiations. Complementing those arms control efforts which seek to reduce force levels, the Stockholm Conference addresses the proximate causes of war—miscalculation and misinterpretation—and seeks to ensure that those forces are never used.

One year ago, I said that, in dealing with the Soviet Union: "We are prepared to discuss the problems which divide us, and to work for practical, fair solutions on the basis of mutual compromise." We have brought this spirit of practicality, fairness and compromise to the Stockholm Conference. It was in this spirit that I addressed the Irish Parliament last June and offered to meet the Soviets' concerns in Stockholm halfway. We agreed to discuss their declared interest in the principle of renunciation of force if this would lead them to negotiate seriously on concrete measures to give effect to that principle.

The Soviet response to our invitation to negotiate has not been forthcoming. The Soviets have yet to demonstrate a willingness to put aside those ideas which are more rhetorical than substantive; they have yet to join the majority of participants who favor a serious, practical approach to developing meaningful confidence-building measures.

At Stockholm, 35 nations are being offered the opportunity to seek solutions to security problems through cooperation rather than confrontation. The U.S. and our allies look for a successful outcome to this Conference, one which will further the goals of the Helsinki process to which it belongs, by lowering the artificial barriers which divide Europe and encouraging more constructive, cooperative relationships among individuals as well as among nations.

Even with good will on all sides, the Stockholm Conference faces a difficult task. The issues are complex and important, touching the vital interests of the participants. Nonetheless, meaningful progress can be achieved this year in Stockholm if all participants work seriously and in a constructive spirit.

Appointment of the Membership of Emergency Board No. 207 To Investigate a Railroad Labor Dispute
January 17, 1985

The President today announced his intention to appoint the following individuals to be members of the Presidential Emergency Board No. 207, created by Executive Order 12495 of December 21, 1984:

Harold M. Weston, of New York, to serve as Chairman. He is an arbitrator in private practice and been appointed to dockets of cases with the National Railroad Adjustment Board, arbitration boards, Emergency Board No. 200, special boards of adjustment and public law boards. He was born June 4, 1912, in New York City and now resides in Hastings-on-Hudson, NY.

Irving T. Bergman, of New York. He is an attorney and a member of the National Academy of Arbitrators. He is regularly selected by Railroad Carriers and Brotherhoods as a Referee on public law boards and special boards of adjustment. He was born May 30, 1910, in Brooklyn, NY, and now resides in Lawrence, NY.

Peter Florey, of New Jersey. He is an attorney and arbitrator. He is a member of the National Academy of Arbitrators and has served on public law boards and special boards of adjustment. He was born April 25, 1925, in Plauen, Germany.

Interview With Ann Devroy and Johanna Neuman of USA Today
January 17, 1985

President's Second Term

Ms. Devroy. Well, we really want to do something sort of—a little reflective, as you prepare to be—for your second term here.

The President. All right.

Ms. Devroy. And we're going to start with some domestic things.

There seem to be some signs that you intend to stay on the sidelines and let Congress wrestle with a lot of the touchy things like the budget, Social Security COLA's, and that sort of thing, at least in the beginning of this second term. Is that your intent?

The President. No, and how that story has been concocted or what it's based on, I don't know. We're been putting in long and bloody hours on this budget matter, and in a few weeks, we will be ready. But we've keeping our people up there in the Congress posted on this, keeping them as well informed as we can of where we are, the type of things that we're talking about doing. And in a short time, as I say, in just a matter of a few weeks, we will be delivering to Congress our proposal, and we think it'll be on target with what we're trying to do for 1986.

Ms. Devroy. Well, you seem content to have the Senate Republicans write a budget, which is very different from the way you acted your first year.

The President. Well, except that those same leaders have been—we've been in touch with them. They know what we're talking about, and, frankly, we're glad to have that as a—and if they've got any ideas that we haven't had. But this is their version, but it's based on what we've been doing.

Ms. Neuman. And you don't feel in any sense that you have abdicated your leadership responsibility?

The President. Oh, no, no. All these lines as if, well, when the election was over I sat back and disappeared or something—I disappeared into the Cabinet Room, where we've been having these meetings for endless hours. There wasn't anything to go out and wave a flag about until we have it put together. And then after you have it put together, you've got to allow your Cabinet officers and department heads to come in on their own and present their views as to whether we can do better or whether we've done too much.

Federal Budget and the Economy

Ms. Devroy. Despite the work that you've been doing on the budget, it seems likely from what David Stockman has said and others have said that you will go out of office as a President who presided over the biggest deficits in history. Are you resigned to that?

The President. Well, I almost have to be, although if I also go out of office with having put us for the first time in 50 years on a declining deficit pattern to where we can target a date certain that the budget will be balanced and have put us on a program that is of a permanent nature, so that that's the end of deficit spending.

You have to realize how much this has been built in. This increase is not anything that we created. This was the built-in pattern. From 1965 to 1980, this was when the War on Poverty and the Great Society really got under way and came into effect. Well, in those 15 years, the budget increased to almost 5 times what it was 15 years before. But the deficit increased to 38 times what it was before.

Nineteen seventy-four—the Congress came up with a whole new budget plan. They were going to—they had a new proce-

dure. And since they did that, I don't think we've had a budget. All they do is tear apart the budget that you send up. But in those several years, from 1974 on up to past 1980, there were more than $500 billion in deficits. The pattern was set.

Ms. Devroy. Back to the first part of your—you said if you go out of office with a date certain when the budget will be balanced, that would mitigate somewhat against all the red ink.

The President. Yes.

Ms. Devroy. What is that date? My understanding is it doesn't show up in any of the documents I've seen, not 1989 and——

The President. Well, what we're aiming at right now is a program in which we can project—in other words, a 3-year program, '86 through '88, which is about all that I can be responsible for. And as I say, you can't be too certain about projections. As a matter of fact, most of the projections that we inherited were far more pessimistic than they turned out to be. We've——

Ms. Devroy. You are no fan of economic projections, I know.

The President. No, not at all.

Ms. Neuman. Well, in this struggle to balance or reduce the deficit, how much are you thinking about your role in history?

The President. Actually—I know I get that question an awful lot, as if you sit over here and that's all you think about is what are they going to write in the history books. You know, the truth of the matter is, I don't think about it at all. I think about trying to get the job done. And I came here with an idea in mind of what I felt should be done, that it was time that something should be done, both on the international scene but also domestically. I'd been out on the mashed-potato circuit talking about it for three or four decades.

And so, we started in with the plan. And, as you know, the only thing that has remained constant are the pessimists. They're still around. They said the plan wouldn't work. And now that it's working, they say it won't last. Well, they were wrong the first time, and they're wrong the second time.

This is the first recovery in eight recessions since World War II that has been a real recovery based on solid principles in which unemployment has come down at the same time inflation has come down, the same time the interest rates have come down. If you'll look back in the history of previous recessions, you'll find that usually they brought about what they said was a recovery artificially. And you'd have—well, if unemployment came down some, inflation went up. This is a recovery based on solid principles, where all these things are happening.

There were 3 years before we got here of double-digit inflation. We've now had, the last 3 years of inflation, down in the 4-percent range. The interest rate, prime rate, was 21 percent. It's now 10½. So, we're down to half of what that was. And I think we're going to see it continue to go lower. Unemployment—3.3 million people got jobs just in the last year. There are more people, close to 108 million people, working, more people employed than ever in the history of our country.

So, all of these, I think, are solid gains that show that what we came into office to do has been accomplished, except that it takes time. It'll have to continue.

Ms. Devroy. In referring to those, those are—a lot of your legislative success in the beginnings of those kind of successes occurred early in your first term and then picked up, particularly the legislative area. Historically, second terms for Presidents have not been roaring successes; they sort of trickle off. What are your expectations? Do you expect to be as successful legislatively as you were the first term?

The President. I think there's a very good chance of it, because I think that the very thing you were talking about, the size of the deficits, has finally caught everybody's attention. And I think that there's a possibility that we'll see one of those moments when we forget we're Democrats and Republicans and realize that we're citizens of this country and we've got a job to do. But in other words, it's of crisis proportions. And it is based on built-in spending increases that must be altered and altered permanently.

Black Americans

Ms. Neuman. Mr. President, some people say that recovery has benefited primarily white people, that the "We the People Inaugural" we are about to witness is a "We the White People Inaugural." Given your meeting this week with some black representatives, do you have any thoughts about how to reach out to the majority of blacks, who were not in your column?

The President. Well, I know that there are a number of leaders of various organizations that are coming forth all the time with reports that build this idea, that somehow we've relegated the black community to a second-class status. Well, that's not our intent, and that's not our practice.

First of all, of the people, since we came here, who got jobs, more than a million of them are blacks who have left the unemployment ranks. It's true, they've got farther to go. There was no question of that, that based on some of our past history and all, they're on an upward climb, but, as I say, they have further to go.

What we have done—we have some things before the Congress that we haven't gotten yet that would be further of benefit to them. The enterprise zones program would benefit them disproportionately to others. It's been there 3 years, and we haven't been able to get it through the House. The very fact of reducing inflation has been of benefit to people who are in the lower earning scale, because it means a lot more to them. In education the number of blacks who are now getting college and university educations is far higher than it has ever been in our history.

There must be specific things. This is what we talked about with this group of very fine people who came in—these black leaders from every kind of calling you can imagine. We have done more than has ever been done with regard to stimulating, in the small business community, entrepreneurship, businesses that are black owned. We have—in aiding that—we have made sure that government contracts definitely are aimed to make sure that minority-owned businesses get a fair crack at those.

Now, all of this is aimed at a problem that has been ignored by too many people in the various ethnic communities in our country—and we have them, as you know, the Irish in south Boston and so forth. You find that their standard of living, their prosperity is based on how many times a dollar that comes in to that community by way of pay. The individual goes out to work and brings home his paycheck—how many times that dollar turns over before it gets back out into the general economy, out of that community.

Now, in most communities, that can be up seven or eight times. And that means that's the equivalent of seven or eight dollars in the economy that it produces. In the black communities, it has been barely one. In other words, they have, in the past, been behind with having professionals and businesses that are owned and performed by blacks within their own community. When they go down to buy groceries in their own neighborhood, they're buying them from—have been buying them from a white-owned business. Well, that is changing. And that's what we're aiming at, is to get them into this same framework——

Ms. Devroy. They don't seem to——

The President. ——of being able to turn the dollars over.

Ms. Devroy. They don't seem to, in general——

The President. They what?

Ms. Devroy. They don't seem, in general, to accept the idea that you're aiming at helping them at all.

The President. I know.

Ms. Devroy. Your—in terms of the election, 9 out of 10, I think, black voters voted for your opposition.

The President. Mm-hmm, well——

Ms. Devroy. Do you think—how would you rate that in terms of disappointments? You had said during the end of the first term that you were going to make a major effort to reach out to black voters and all voters, and it didn't seem to work.

The President. Well, maybe because they weren't told very much by some of those leaders we're talking about of what we've accomplished and what we have done.

I don't think that the rank-and-file know about minority-owned businesses and how far we've gone with that. I don't think they know about legislation that we have sent up to the Hill—like the enterprise zones—that has not been passed. Legislation that—in other areas that has to do with improving

their status. I don't think they know about the fair-housing proposals that we have sent up there and that, again, a Democratic majority has not dealt with.

Ms. Devroy. Have you, in recent times, or plan to sit down with some of the black leaders—not like the ones you've been talking to—and say, "Why can't we communicate better? Why don't you like my policies? Why won't blacks vote Republican? What is the problem here?"

The President. I tried that in the very beginning, and I found out, very frankly, that they are so committed politically to the opposite party that they don't want to hear. And I have to come to the conclusion that maybe some of those leaders are protecting some rather good positions that they have, and they can protect them better if they can keep their constituency aggrieved and believing that they have a legitimate complaint. If they ever become aware of the opportunities that are improving, they might wonder whether they need some of those organizations.

Presidential Advisers and the Second Term

Ms. Devroy. On a personal level, as you start another 4 years with the distinction of being the oldest President in history——

The President. Yeah.

Ms. Devroy. ——are you getting tired of this job? Are you getting weary of it? Is the excitement gone?

The President. No, not at all.

Ms. Devroy. Well, it seems it is to most of your chief staff, who are all sort of going off and being replaced. The old gang is leaving——

The President. Oh, no, I can understand that. I can understand when you come into government, it's a little different than the private sector. Someone gives up a great deal to take an appointment in government, whether it's a Cabinet position or whatever it is. And, unlike a business, where there's the continued challenge of the profit motive and growth and so forth, yes, after a time, I can see where some of the excitement is gone in that particular job. But what we've found out here is that it doesn't mean that it's just—that it's gone for being—continuing to work in government or they wouldn't be taking other jobs.

When you start listing the people that are leaving, yes, a few have left, and for legitimate reasons that they—they knew when they came that they were not going to stay endlessly. And I said in appointing them, from the very first, I said, "If these people that I've selected and want to come to government, if they can only come for a year or two, fine, I'll take them and then get someone else if they have to return to their private lives."

But when you have someone that goes from one position to another—we found that out in California when I was Governor, even with some of the permanent staff of government, that we took people that had been 20 years in jobs, and we did switch them with other people. And you'd be surprised. The first protest was, "I'm—this is my—I've been doing this for 20 years. What do you mean I've got to go over here?" You'd be surprised: Before the next 6 months was over, after those changes, you never saw happier people in your life, more excited, where they'd found a new challenge. They were asking questions in the new position, of saying, "Well, why are you doing it this way?" And when someone— "Well, we've always done—" Well, they say, "Well, why don't we do it this way?" Well, the same thing happens with these appointees.

Ms. Neuman. But, Mr. President, the question is——

Ms. Devroy. But that's not going to happen with you.

Ms. Neuman. ——are you still excited?

Ms. Devroy. I don't think they're going to let you switch with George Bush, for example, and I don't think you want to. So——

The President. No, not as long as I stay healthy. [*Laughter*]

Ms. Devroy. And you expect to, I presume.

The President. Yes. No, I think the difference is in here, as I say, I had a reason that compelled me to do this. And as long as the challenge is still there—and it still is—as I said earlier, the job isn't finished. So, no, I'm just——

Ms. Devroy. You must have a different feeling starting a second term, though, compared to the excitement of the first one.

You brought a Republican Senate with you. There were all these signs of major changes. During the second campaign, it was, "I'm going to keep doing what I'm doing." and that——

The President. Yeah.

Ms. Devroy. Can that be as exciting?

The President. Yes, it is, because, as I say, we've got a great start. If you really look at the whole tone of government today and what was being debated in government up until 4 years ago, about cost—or programs, and this new program, and let's spend money over here in doing this—the whole debate now has turned around to how much should the rate of cutting be and what should we cut. No one's talking about new programs and spending more money by government. No one's talking about more authority in the Federal Government. We're adjusting and giving back to local government and to State governments authority that the Federal Government should never have taken from them in the first place.

And then I have an experience, a previous experience that makes this exciting. As Governor of California, most of our great accomplishments came in the second term. The great welfare reform that was different than anything that's ever been accomplished in this Nation took place in the second term.

Ms. Neuman. But having conquered the agenda, you don't feel a little of the thrill of the chase is gone?

The President. Oh, no, no, because, as I say, it's—no, if you walked away now and someone else came in with a different view, all of this could be unraveled. The idea is to get it clinched and in place, that we can then have an amendment to the Constitution that says hereafter the Federal Government cannot borrow money, it must stay within its means, have an economic recovery that is based on sound principles to where the people have accepted that if the government takes too much money from the private sector, you have these recessions that we've been having for 50 years.

Ms. Devroy. Let me jump to foreign policy quick before——

Principal Deputy Press Secretary Speakes.

Yes, let's make this—one more because——

Ms. Devroy. Oh.

Mr. Speakes. ——we've got the Vice President coming in, Mr. President, to join you for lunch.

The President. Oh.

Strategic Defense Initiative

Ms. Devroy. Quick on foreign policy, then. At this point are you so committed to the Star Wars defense or the—I'm sorry, the SDI initiative, that you'd be willing to go out of office not having achieved any arms control if the Soviets won't move on the other two?

The President. Well, I don't think—I don't look at it as that—that that is a possibility. I think when they actually see this—and the very fact that at Geneva we successfully put it there as one of the things that's going to be negotiated—you see, when they're talking space wars and so forth, they're talking about some things where they're even ahead of us, and that is having nuclear weapons in space that can shoot down at us. We're not talking about anything of that kind.

We're talking about research to see if there is not a defense that can be built that doesn't kill people, kills weapons, that can keep the weapons from coming to your shores, if there is such a thing. And I would hope that they would work on such a thing. If you can have that, then the very thing that they themselves have said they want, an elimination of these weapons, becomes more than just possible.

Ms. Devroy. How important is actually signing an arms control agreement with the Soviets to you, in the sense of an accomplishment, a record-book accomplishment?

The President. I don't believe, since research is contained in the ABM treaty today, I don't think that this is going to cause a walk-away from the table. And if it is, then they never meant to come to the table to begin with.

But let me point out something that they'd have to consider. Suppose we could succeed in getting down to the point of elimination of nuclear weapons. But we know how to make nuclear weapons, and if down someplace in the future there should come a time of strain and stress, who would know if somebody—they would have to think maybe we were doing—we could think that they were doing—somebody say, "Hey, maybe let's get a few of these things ready for use," and who would know that they were doing it? But, if in the meantime, our technology has made it plain that there is a defense against such things, then you have guarded against that ever happening in the future.

It's the same thing, in other words, as when at Geneva, after World War I, we outlawed chemical weapons, gas, poison gas, but our soldiers on both sides—all sides— were also still equipped with gas masks. And we find today—because why? Because people have, knowing how to make it, have continued to make it or started in to make it again. Well, the same thing with the nuclear weapons.

You see, the point is, all we're asking for is the research. And we have said to them that if such a weapon—if that research is fruitful and if such a weapon is developed, we're not going to keep it a secret. And we'd be very happy, then, to sit down with them and say, "Hey, now let's look at the situation here."

Mrs. Reagan

Ms. Neuman. Mr. President, I wanted to ask you a quick question about——

Mr. Speakes. Mr. President——

Ms. Neuman. ——the influence——

The President. Yes.

Ms. Neuman. ——of your wife on your policies.

Ms. Devroy. You've got to answer Nancy questions. [*Laughter*]

The President. The influence that I think any wife has on a husband, if you've got a happy marriage, and we do have one. This whole thing as if—you know, that's one thing—may I just say—may I voice a frustration?

Ms. Neuman. Please.

The President. It's not only my wife, it's everyone—this picture that is being created that I sit at the desk and wait to see who's going to grab this arm and pull me this way or grab this one and pull me that way. You know something?

Ms. Neuman. What?

The President. I'm too old and stubborn to put up with that. I make up my mind, and I do—I listen for counsel and advice. I want to get expertise from people that are expert in various fields. But I haven't changed my views since I've been here.

And with Nancy, yes, we've been married for 30-odd years, and of course we talk, and of course she has opinions. And I listen to her opinions. And sometimes we argue about them, and I don't listen. But sometimes—well, as I say, we get along, and I find myself going home and, I think like every other happy husband, telling them what the day was like and what we did and all.

Ms. Neuman. What'd you last fight about? [*Laughter*]

The President. No, not "fight."

Ms. Neuman. Argue, I mean.

The President. Argue. Maybe I should have put that, "discuss and debate." [*Laughter*]

Ms. Neuman. Okay.

The President. I just want to point that we, you know, like any other human beings, we don't always see eye to eye on something of that kind. But it doesn't make any dents in the marriage.

Ms. Neuman. Thank you, Mr. President.

Ms. Devroy. So they're going to let Reagan be Reagan this second term?

The President. They've never done——

Ms. Devroy. You must be tired of that phrase.

The President. Yes. They've never done anything else.

Ms. Devroy. Thank you for spending the time with us, Mr. President.

Ms. Neuman. It was a pleasure.

The President. I think part of that is that I don't think there's ever been a Cabinet system here like we have. I may be wrong, but my impression of previous Cabinets is that they'd meet periodically in regular meetings, and they would report to the President what they were doing in their departments. Well, in California, I decided to—[*inaudible*]—system and brought it here. They're like a board of directors meeting, and they don't have to keep their mouths shut about somebody else's area or agency's department.

The only difference between them and a board of directors is you don't take a vote. When I've heard on all sides the discussion and debate, I make the decision.

Note: The interview began at 11:31 a.m. in the Oval Office at the White House. The interview was released by the Office of the Press Secretary on January 18.

Statement Announcing the United States Negotiators and Special Advisers for the Nuclear and Space Arms Negotiations With the Soviet Union
January 18, 1985

Today I have asked three highly capable Americans to be the head negotiators of each of three groups making up the U.S. delegation to the negotiations on nuclear and space arms. These negotiations will take place in accordance with the agreement reached at Geneva on January 8 between Secretary of State George P. Shultz and Foreign Minister Andrey A. Gromyko of the Soviet Union.

Senator John Tower of Texas will be nominated to serve as U.S. negotiator on strategic nuclear arms. Ambassador Maynard W. Glitman, a minister-counselor of the Foreign Service of the United States, will be nominated as U.S. negotiator on intermediate-range nuclear arms. Ambassador Max M. Kampelman will be nominated as U.S. negotiator on space and defensive arms. Ambassador Kampelman would also serve as Head of the U.S. delegation.

Ambassador Paul H. Nitze and Ambassador Edward L. Rowny will serve as special advisers to the President and to the Secretary of State on arms reduction negotiations.

I am pleased that these distinguished Americans have agreed to serve in these positions of great importance to the United States.

Note: Secretary of State George P. Shultz read the President's statement to reporters at 3 p.m. in the Briefing Room at the White House.

Executive Order 12499—President's Blue Ribbon Task Group on Nuclear Weapons Program Management
January 18, 1985

By the authority vested in me as President by the Constitution and laws of the United States of America, and in order to establish, in accordance with the provisions of Section 1632 of the Department of Defense Authorization Act, 1985 (Public Law 98–525) ("the Act"), and of the Federal Advisory Committee Act, as amended (5 U.S.C. App. I), a Blue Ribbon Task Group on Nuclear Weapons Program Management, it is hereby ordered as follows:

Section 1. Establishment. (a) There is established the President's Blue Ribbon Task Group on Nuclear Weapons Program Management. The Task Group shall consist of seven members qualified for service by reasons of experience and education. The President shall appoint three members and shall designate one of those members to act as chairman of the Task Group. The chairman and ranking minority members of the Committees on Armed Services of the Senate and House of Representatives will each appoint one member.

(b) None of the members of the Task Group may be an employee of the Department of Defense or the Department of Energy.

Sec. 2. Functions. (a) The Task Group shall examine the procedures used by the Department of Defense and the Department of Energy in establishing requirements for, and in providing resources for, the research, development, testing, production, surveillance, and retirement of nuclear weapons and shall recommend any needed change in such procedures.

(b) The Task Group shall report to the President and the Committees on Armed Services of the Senate and the House of

Representatives as specified in its charter but not later than July 15, 1985. The Task Group's report shall contain recommendations in the areas specified in Section 1632(e) of the Act.

Sec. 3. Administration. (a) The heads of Executive agencies shall, to the extent permitted by law, provide the Task Group such information as it may require for purposes of carrying out its functions.

(b) Members of the Task Group shall serve without compensation for their work on the Task Group. To the extent funds are available therefore, all members of the Task Group performing duties away from their home or regular place of business, or designated post of duty, may be allowed travel expenses, as authorized by law, including per diem in lieu of subsistence for persons serving intermittently in the government service, as provided under 5 U.S.C. 5701–5707.

(c) The Secretary of Defense shall provide the Task Group with such administrative services, facilities, staff, and other support services as may be necessary. Any expenses of the Task Group shall be paid from such funds as may be available to the Secretary of Defense.

Sec. 4. General. (a) Notwithstanding any other Executive order, the functions of the President under the Federal Advisory Committee Act, as amended, except that of reporting to the Congress, which are applicable to the Task Group, shall be performed by the Secretary of Defense, in accordance with guidelines established by the Administrator of General Services.

(b) The Task Group shall terminate on September 30, 1985, unless its existence is sooner extended in accordance with the Federal Advisory Committee Act.

RONALD REAGAN

The White House,
January 18, 1985.

[*Filed with the Office of the Federal Register, 10:53 a.m., January 22, 1985*]

Oaths of Office Taken by the President and the Vice President at the White House Swearing-in Ceremony
January 20, 1985

Oath Administered to the Vice President by Potter Stewart, Associate Justice of the Supreme Court of the United States:

I, George Herbert Walker Bush, do solemnly swear that I will support and defend the Constitution of the United States against all enemies, foreign and domestic, that I will bear true faith and allegiance to the same, that I take this obligation freely, without any mental reservation or purpose of evasion, and that I will well and faithfully discharge the duties of the office on which I am about to enter, so help me God.

Oath Administered to the President by Warren E. Burger, Chief Justice of the United States:

I, Ronald Reagan, do solemnly swear that I will faithfully execute the Office of President of the United States, and will to the best of my ability, preserve, protect and defend the Constitution of the United States, so help me God.

Note: The private swearing-in ceremony began at 11:50 a.m. on the landing of the Grand Staircase on the State Floor at the White House. The ceremony was attended by immediate members of the Reagan and Bush families, members of the Cabinet and the senior White House staff, and bipartisan congressional leaders.

The 20th amendment to the Constitution requires that the President be sworn in on January 20; however, because the date fell on a Sunday, the public inauguration ceremony was held at the Capitol on the following day.

Remarks of the President and Coach Bill Walsh of the Championship San Francisco 49'ers Following Super Bowl XIX
January 20, 1985

The President. Coach Walsh, there ought to be a bigger word than "congratulations" for all that we saw tonight and what you and that team of yours have accomplished. But that's the word to use, and I just want to say congratulations to you and, of course, congratulations to Joe Montana for his being picked and for the performance. But for all of that team—I guess as a coach you couldn't have asked for anything greater than they gave you tonight. So——

Mr. Walsh. Well, they——

The President. Yes?

Mr. Walsh. Well, I tell you, they've given it all year, Mr. President. This is the greatest football team and the greatest group of people I've ever been around. And I hope we've added to today's festivities.

The President. You certainly did. And, you know, if now that the season's over and you fellows haven't anything to do for a while, I have to go up on the Hill and deal with Congress in a few days—how would you like to come back and I could use a

53

front-line four?

Mr. Walsh. Well, I think we'll stick to football, Mr. President. You're equipped for your job. We'll just try to deal with this one.

Congratulations to you on your election. We're all behind you, and we're praying for you.

The President. Thank you very much. And again, God bless you all, and it was just great.

Note: The President spoke at 9:40 p.m. from the Map Room at the White House. In his opening remarks, the President referred to 49'ers quarterback Joe Montana, who was chosen as the most valuable player of the game. The exchange was broadcast live on the ABC network.

Earlier, the President participated in a pregame ceremony via a special video hookup between Stanford Stadium in California and the Map Room. At approximately 6:15 p.m., he tossed the coin to start the game.

Statement on the Decision To Hold the Official Inaugural Ceremony in the Capitol Rotunda and the Cancellation of the Inaugural Parade
January 20, 1985

I have this evening accepted the recommendation of the Committee for the 50th American Presidential Inaugural to cancel the Inaugural Parade. And the Joint Congressional Inaugural Committee has, at my request, agreed to move the official Inaugural ceremony to the Rotunda of the United States Capitol. I have directed the Committee for the 50th American Presidential Inaugural to make every effort to develop an alternate event for tomorrow afternoon— one which would allow those who have traveled so far and have given so unselfishly an opportunity to be a part of this historic occasion.

Nancy and I are disappointed that the weather in Washington caused this change, but the health and safety of those attending and working at these outdoor events must come before any celebrations. Medical and military experts have warned that tomorrow's weather—which could see temperatures with a windchill factor as low as 30 degrees below zero—would pose significant risks to the well-being of the many thousands of persons who planned to attend and

work at these events. Under such conditions, exposed flesh can freeze within 5–10 minutes, triggering considerable danger to many of the parade and ceremony participants, spectators, and the general public. In addition, equipment would not be operable.

We are deeply grateful for the enthusiasm and patriotism which has been the hallmark of so many persons from all 50 States who have given so much to make this Inaugural a success. We look forward to seeing many of them Monday night at the Inaugural balls, which will be held as scheduled. It may be cold outside, but our hearts will always be warmed by the many wonderful memories of thousands of our fellow citizens coming to Washington this weekend to join us as we continue our work to make America great again.

Note: Earlier in the day, the White House announced that the Committee for the 50th American Presidential Inaugural had canceled that evening's National Pageant of Young Americans, which would have included musical entertainment and fireworks displays at the Jefferson Memorial.

Inaugural Address
January 21, 1985

Senator Mathias, Chief Justice Burger, Vice President Bush, Speaker O'Neill, Senator Dole, reverend clergy, and members of my family and friends and my fellow citizens:

This day has been made brighter with the presence here of one who, for a time, has been absent. Senator John Stennis, God bless you and welcome back.

There is, however, one who is not with us today. Representative Gillis Long of Louisiana left us last night. And I wonder if we could all join in a moment of silent prayer.

[*The President resumed speaking after a moment of silence.*]

Amen.

There are no words adequate to express my thanks for the great honor that you've bestowed on me. I'll do my utmost to be deserving of your trust.

This is, as Senator Mathias told us, the 50th time that we, the people, have celebrated this historic occasion. When the first President, George Washington, placed his hand upon the Bible, he stood less than a single day's journey by horseback from raw, untamed wilderness. There were 4 million Americans in a union of 13 States. Today, we are 60 times as many in a union of 50 States. We've lighted the world with our inventions, gone to the aid of mankind wherever in the world there was a cry for help, journeyed to the Moon and safely returned. So much has changed, and yet we stand together as we did two centuries ago.

When I took this oath 4 years ago, I did so in a time of economic stress. Voices were raised saying that we had to look to our past for the greatness and glory. But we, the present-day Americans, are not given to looking backward. In this blessed land, there is always a better tomorrow.

Four years ago, I spoke to you of a New Beginning, and we have accomplished that. But in another sense, our New Beginning is a continuation of that beginning created two centuries ago when, for the first time in history, government, the people said, was not our master, it is our servant; its only power that which we the people allow it to have.

That system has never failed us, but for a time we failed the system. We asked things of government that government was not equipped to give. We yielded authority to the National Government that properly belonged to States or to local governments or to the people themselves. We allowed taxes and inflation to rob us of our earnings and savings and watched the great industrial machine that had made us the most productive people on Earth slow down and the number of unemployed increase.

By 1980 we knew it was time to renew our faith, to strive with all our strength toward the ultimate in individual freedom, consistent with an orderly society.

We believed then and now: There are no limits to growth and human progress when men and women are free to follow their dreams. And we were right to believe that. Tax rates have been reduced, inflation cut dramatically, and more people are employed than ever before in our history.

We are creating a nation once again vibrant, robust, and alive. But there are many mountains yet to climb. We will not rest until every American enjoys the fullness of freedom, dignity, and opportunity as our birthright. It is our birthright as citizens of this great Republic.

And if we meet this challenge, these will be years when Americans have restored their confidence and tradition of progress; when our values of faith, family, work, and neighborhood were restated for a modern age; when our economy was finally freed from government's grip; when we made sincere efforts at meaningful arms reductions and by rebuilding our defenses, our economy, and developing new technologies, helped preserve peace in a troubled world; when America courageously supported the struggle for individual liberty, self-government, and free enterprise throughout the world and turned the tide of history away from totalitarian darkness and into the warm sunlight of human freedom.

My fellow citizens, our nation is poised for greatness. We must do what we know is right, and do it with all our might. Let history say of us: "These were golden years—when the American Revolution was reborn, when freedom gained new life, and America reached for her best.

Our two-party system has solved us—served us, I should say, well over the years, but never better than in those times of great challenge when we came together not as Democrats or Republicans, but as Americans united in a common cause.

Two of our Founding Fathers, a Boston lawyer named Adams and a Virginia planter named Jefferson, members of that remarkable group who met in Independence Hall and dared to think they could start the world over again, left us an important lesson. They had become, in the years then in government, bitter political rivals in the Presidential election of 1800. Then, years later, when both were retired and age had softened their anger, they began to speak to each other again through letters. A bond was reestablished between those two who had helped create this government of ours.

In 1826, the 50th anniversary of the Declaration of Independence, they both died. They died on the same day, within a few hours of each other, and that day was the Fourth of July.

In one of those letters exchanged in the sunset of their lives, Jefferson wrote: "It carries me back to the times when, beset with difficulties and dangers, we were fellow laborers in the same cause, struggling for what is most valuable to man, his right of self-government. Laboring always at the same oar, with some wave ever ahead threatening to overwhelm us, and yet passing harmless . . . we rode through the storm with heart and hand."

Well, with heart and hand let us stand as one today—one people under God, determined that our future shall be worthy of our past. As we do, we must not repeat the well-intentioned errors of our past. We must never again abuse the trust of working men and women by sending their earnings on a futile chase after the spiraling demands of a bloated Federal Establishment. You elected us in 1980 to end this prescription for disaster, and I don't believe you

reelected us in 1984 to reverse course.

At the heart of our efforts is one idea vindicated by 25 straight months of economic growth: Freedom and incentives unleash the drive and entrepreneurial genius that are the core of human progress. We have begun to increase the rewards for work, savings, and investment; reduce the increase in the cost and size of government and its interference in people's lives.

We must simplify our tax system, make it more fair and bring the rates down for all who work and earn. We must think anew and move with a new boldness, so every American who seeks work can find work, so the least among us shall have an equal chance to achieve the greatest things—to be heroes who heal our sick, feed the hungry, protect peace among nations, and leave this world a better place.

The time has come for a new American emancipation—a great national drive to tear down economic barriers and liberate the spirit of enterprise in the most distressed areas of our country. My friends, together we can do this, and do it we must, so help me God.

From new freedom will spring new opportunities for growth, a more productive, fulfilled, and united people, and a stronger America—an America that will lead the technological revolution and also open its mind and heart and soul to the treasures of literature, music, and poetry, and the values of faith, courage, and love.

A dynamic economy, with more citizens working and paying taxes, will be our strongest tool to bring down budget deficits. But an almost unbroken 50 years of deficit spending has finally brought us to a time of reckoning. We've come to a turning point, a moment for hard decisions. I have asked the Cabinet and my staff a question and now I put the same question to all of you. If not us, who? And if not now, when? It must be done by all of us going forward with a program aimed at reaching a balanced budget. We can then begin reducing the national debt.

I will shortly submit a budget to the Congress aimed at freezing government program spending for the next year. Beyond this, we must take further steps to permanently control government's power to tax and spend. We must act now to protect future generations from government's desire to spend its citizens' money and tax them into servitude when the bills come due. Let us make it unconstitutional for the Federal Government to spend more than the Federal Government takes in.

We have already started returning to the people and to State and local governments responsibilities better handled by them. Now, there is a place for the Federal Government in matters of social compassion. But our fundamental goals must be to reduce dependency and upgrade the dignity of those who are infirm or disadvantaged. And here, a growing economy and support from family and community offer our best chance for a society where compassion is a way of life, where the old and infirm are cared for, the young and, yes, the unborn protected, and the unfortunate looked after and made self-sufficient.

Now, there is another area where the Federal Government can play a part. As an older American, I remember a time when people of different race, creed, or ethnic origin in our land found hatred and prejudice installed in social custom and, yes, in law. There's no story more heartening in our history than the progress that we've made toward the brotherhood of man that God intended for us. Let us resolve there will be no turning back or hesitation on the road to an America rich in dignity and abundant with opportunity for all our citizens.

Let us resolve that we, the people, will build an American opportunity society in which all of us—white and black, rich and poor, young and old—will go forward together, arm in arm. Again, let us remember that though our heritage is one of blood lines from every corner of the Earth, we are all Americans, pledged to carry on this last, best hope of man on Earth.

I've spoken of our domestic goals and the limitations we should put on our National Government. Now let me turn to a task that is the primary responsibility of National Government—the safety and security of our people.

Today, we utter no prayer more fervently than the ancient prayer for peace on Earth.

Yet history has shown that peace does not come, nor will our freedom be preserved, by good will alone. There are those in the world who scorn our vision of human dignity and freedom. One nation, the Soviet Union, has conducted the greatest military buildup in the history of man, building arsenals of awesome offensive weapons.

We've made progress in restoring our defense capability. But much remains to be done. There must be no wavering by us, nor any doubts by others, that America will meet her responsibilities to remain free, secure, and at peace.

There is only one way safely and legitimately to reduce the cost of national security, and that is to reduce the need for it. And this we're trying to do in negotiations with the Soviet Union. We're not just discussing limits on a further increase of nuclear weapons; we seek, instead, to reduce their number. We seek the total elimination one day of nuclear weapons from the face of the Earth.

Now, for decades, we and the Soviets have lived under the threat of mutual assured destruction—if either resorted to the use of nuclear weapons, the other could retaliate and destroy the one who had started it. Is there either logic or morality in believing that if one side threatens to kill tens of millions of our people our only recourse is to threaten killing tens of millions of theirs?

I have approved a research program to find, if we can, a security shield that will destroy nuclear missiles before they reach their target. It wouldn't kill people; it would destroy weapons. It wouldn't militarize space; it would help demilitarize the arsenals of Earth. It would render nuclear weapons obsolete. We will meet with the Soviets, hoping that we can agree on a way to rid the world of the threat of nuclear destruction.

We strive for peace and security, heartened by the changes all around us. Since the turn of the century, the number of democracies in the world has grown fourfold. Human freedom is on the march, and nowhere more so than in our own hemisphere. Freedom is one of the deepest and noblest aspirations of the human spirit. People, worldwide, hunger for the right of self-determination, for those inalienable rights that make for human dignity and progress.

America must remain freedom's staunchest friend, for freedom is our best ally and it is the world's only hope to conquer poverty and preserve peace. Every blow we inflict against poverty will be a blow against its dark allies of oppression and war. Every victory for human freedom will be a victory for world peace.

So, we go forward today, a nation still mighty in its youth and powerful in its purpose. With our alliances strengthened, with our economy leading the world to a new age of economic expansion, we look to a future rich in possibilities. And all of this is because we worked and acted together, not as members of political parties but as Americans.

My friends, we live in a world that's lit by lightning. So much is changing and will change, but so much endures and transcends time.

History is a ribbon, always unfurling. History is a journey. And as we continue our journey, we think of those who traveled before us. We stand again at the steps of this symbol of our democracy—well, we would have been standing at the steps if it hadn't gotten so cold. [*Laughter*] Now we're standing inside this symbol of our democracy, and we see and hear again the echoes of our past: a general falls to his knees in the hard snow of Valley Forge; a lonely President paces the darkened halls and ponders his struggle to preserve the Union; the men of the Alamo call out encouragement to each other; a settler pushes west and sings a song, and the song echoes out forever and fills the unknowing air.

It is the American sound. It is hopeful, big-hearted, idealistic, daring, decent, and fair. That's our heritage, that's our song. We sing it still. For all our problems, our differences, we are together as of old. We raise our voices to the God who is the Author of this most tender music. And may He continue to hold us close as we fill the world with our sound—in unity, affection, and love—one people under God, dedicated to the dream of freedom that He has placed in the human heart, called upon now to pass that dream on to a waiting and hopeful world.

God bless you, and God bless America.

Note: The President spoke at 11:49 a.m. in the Rotunda of the Capitol. Prior to his address, the President repeated the oath of office, again administered by Chief Justice Warren E. Burger, which he had taken on January 20. The Inaugural ceremony was originally scheduled to take place on the West Portico of the Capitol, but was held inside due to the extremely cold weather in Washington.

Remarks at the Inaugural Luncheon at the Capitol
January 21, 1985

The President. I'm not trying to play Dean Martin. [*Laughter*]

Senator Mathias, honorable Members of the House, and distinguished guests, and Members of the Senate, of course.

This has been an historic day, and it's not over yet. Together, we mark the end of one term and the beginning of another. And I want each of you to know how grateful I am for all that you've done—all the energy and personal commitment that you have mustered in these last 4 years to make our system work.

In the shifting alliances of a free government, we in this room have been intense allies on some issues, while disagreeing on others. But I think the level of respect and courtesy with which we've treated each other speaks well for us and confirms the viability of this great democratic system which is now in our care.

There's been quite a few Inaugurations in my lifetime. I missed Abe Lincoln's but—[*laughter*]—I do remember Calvin Coolidge's. [*Laughter*] Even though I was of the other party at the time, he was much loved and respected. I was a Democrat in those days.

His Inaugural Address said: "Our Congress represents the people and the States. In all legislative affairs, they are the natural collaborator with the President. In spite of all the criticism which often falls to its lot, I do not hesitate to say that there is no more independent and effective legislative body in the world. It is, and should be, jealous of its prerogatives. I welcome the cooperation and expect to share with it not only the responsibility but the credit for our common effort to secure beneficial legislation." Calvin Coolidge.

Well, I hope we can work together in that same spirit. I have a plaque on my desk in the office that says what I firmly believe, and that is there is no limit to what a man can accomplish if he doesn't—what he can do and where he can go if he doesn't care who gets the credit.

So, I hope in the days and the years to come that we can move ahead, meet the challenges of our day, thinking only of how much we can accomplish if we maintain our good will and cooperation.

We're very grateful to you for these gifts. And may I offer a toast to all of you here, the Members of the Congress, all the guests who are here with you, and to the best Vice President this country has ever had, George Bush, and to the next 4 years.

Thank you very much.

Senator Mathias. The distinguished Republican leader of the House of Representatives, Bob Michel.

Representative Michel. Thank you, Mac. Mr. President, Mr. Vice President, Mr. Speaker, and Mr. Chief Justice, your wives, and ladies and gentlemen:

Four years ago, we presented to the President one of the letter openers that was used in opening the Electoral College ballots that came in from the State.

We'd like to do that again this year, in addition to give the Vice President one,

but, Mr. Speaker, we're going to spare you any—we're just going to spare you by not reading the inscription on the plaque because of the number on the Electoral College vote. [*Laughter*]

There's one other here that I'd like to present to the President on behalf of the leadership of both the House and Senate, Republican and Democrat alike.

Mr. President, you've been very good to come up here to the Hill every once in awhile, not only with official messages, but when you just had an informal word to say from time to time. As you know, beyond this beautiful picture here is a normal route to the House of Representatives. When this Chamber was once the old Chamber, and then as we developed the new Chamber beyond it, there were a set of beautiful bronze doors that were between the two, that are now down in the East Portico of the Capitol.

We have here for you, Mr. President, a likeness prepared by one of our craftsmen here in the Capitol, and also a very special key to those doors, because, as you know, the Speaker pretty well controls this side of the Capitol over here. [*Laughter*] In the event you want to come up sometime for some reason, for whatever—[*laughter*]—here's the key to the Capitol and to the House of Representatives. [*Laughter*]

The President. I've just been told we should get out of here. [*Laughter*] They said I could do anything I wanted on the way out, so I just want to express a very heartfelt thanks. These are wonderful things to have in celebration of this day. And, Tip, do you have a key, too? [*Laughter*] If you don't, feel free to borrow it anytime. [*Laughter*]

All right, thank you all very much.

Note: The President spoke at 1:50 p.m. at the luncheon for congressional leaders and invited guests which was held in Statuary Hall at the Capitol. Following the luncheon, the President and Mrs. Reagan returned to the White House.

Remarks at the Inaugural Band Concert at the Capital Centre in Landover, Maryland
January 21, 1985

Well, good afternoon. I'm told that this is the coldest day in Inauguration history. But looking out at all of you, I somehow feel there's a lot of warmth inside this building.

Who would ever have thought that I'd be the one standing up and talking, while all of you were—well, almost all of you—were sitting down and listening. It just goes to show here in Washington things have a way of turning out the opposite of how we intend.

I know you didn't get your chance to salute all of us, but I just want you to know how happy and how important it was for Nancy, myself, and the Vice President and Mrs. Bush to come here to salute all of you.

You know, we and all America were so looking forward to seeing each one of you perform and delight us with your wonderful talents and exuberance. And what a great American family you are. Because whether you come from as far away as Hawaii, California, Texas, Florida, New York or Mississippi, or Washington or Alaska, or—I'm told the team from Alaska was the only one that came here and really was and could have gone through with the parade because they came with a team of huskies. I can't go on naming all your States, because I know all 50 are represented here, and the territories, and you represent America at its best. And you would have given America the greatest show on Earth.

Now, we were all anticipating the parade. And I was looking forward to every unit. I'd heard about all of you. And particularly, there was one that—someplace in here, I think, is a band from my home, or the town where I was born, Tampico, Illinois. And with that band was going to be the pompom girls from the high school in Dixon, Illinois, where I graduated.

I want to tell you, I have a little knowledge and understanding of some of your problems. I was the drum major of the Dixon YMCA Boys Band, and I had a brief career, because we were asked to head up the parade in a nearby town on Decoration Day. And I know that everyone was briefed

about the parade course and everything, but I had also been told that a fellow on a white horse was going to be out in front, and I figured I'll just follow the man on the white horse. Who can go wrong doing that? And I was going down the street, making with the baton, and pretty soon I thought the music was beginning to sound a little faint. [*Laughter*] I looked over my shoulder. Everybody had turned the corner. I was going down the wrong street all by myself. [*Laughter*] I kept right on walking—right out of a musical career. [*Laughter*]

Well, we know the tremendous time and personal dedication that each of you put into your preparations—everything from bake sales to getting church and civic groups to help you raise the money to pay your way, to the long, long hours of rehearsal so that you perform at your very best.

I don't want to forget to mention one other very important group of participants who are here with us, too—our United States military personnel.

You know, all of them and most of you are about pretty much the same age group. I just want to say something. Back in World War II, General George Marshall was asked by someone what he thought was our secret weapon. And General Marshall said, "The best damn kids in the world." And do you know something? If he were here today, he could say the same thing, because you are.

Our military, led by Paul Miller, the director of ceremonies and special events for the Military District of Washington; deputy parade chairman, Marine Lieutenant Colonel Frank Turner—they were a tremendously effective organizational team, and they would have been there to line your parade route down Pennsylvania Avenue.

And let me tell you, I and all of us up here, George and Barbara and Nancy, we were raring to go. I went searching into the closet—I had a pair of long johns—I was going to put them on. [*Laughter*] The last time I wore them was the 1980 primary campaign in New Hampshire.

But it would have been a magical moment to tuck away and cherish with your loved ones during all your later years. But it was not to be. And I just hope you understand that we only made this decision after we were convinced that it was absolutely necessary to protect your own health, as well as the health of the thousands who would be lining the parade to watch you. Believe me, we had professional medical advice in making that decision.

But I pledge one thing to all of you today, and that is to serve with the very best of my abilities and to try, during these next 4 years, to live up to the spirits of unity and pride that you have brought to Washington, because that's what makes America the greatest country on Earth.

There's another thought that I'd like to leave with you, and that is that your trip here, despite the cancellation of the parade, is still very worthwhile and important, because all of us together have been participants in a great miracle of modern history—the simple, peaceful continuation of power ratifying the sovereignty of we, the people. There has never been a transfer of power by bayonet in America and, God willing, there never will be.

Thomas Jefferson once said: "How little do my countrymen know what precious blessings they are in possession of and which no other people on Earth enjoy."

Well, today we can rejoice that more and more people on Earth are moving toward democracy, and we can rejoice that America, a nation still young compared to so many others, is the oldest, most successful republic on Earth.

In 2 years, we will celebrate together the 200th anniversary of our Constitution. And what a day that will be for parades, not only in Washington, DC, but all across our land. So, while we could not go through with today's festivities, we can celebrate in our hearts the continuation of this wonderful experiment in individual liberty and self-government. And we can give thanks that we remain today, as Abraham Lincoln said over a hundred years ago, "The last, best hope of man on Earth."

God bless you all. Thank you all again. Have a safe journey home. Thank you.

Note: The President spoke at 3:18 p.m. following remarks and an introduction by the First Lady. The audience was mainly composed of high school band members from across the country who had been scheduled to participate in the traditional Inaugural Parade down Pennsylvania Avenue. Several of the bands performed while the President and Mrs. Reagan and the Vice President and Mrs. Bush were seated on what was to have been a float in the parade. The parade was canceled due to the extremely cold weather in Washington.

Statement on the 1984 Gross National Product and Inflation Figures
January 22, 1985

I am delighted by today's reports that the gross national product in 1984 increased by 6.8 percent—the biggest increase in 34 years—and that inflation, as measured by the price deflator, increased only 3.7 percent. We are succeeding in building strong and lasting economic growth without inflation. And I believe these results demonstrate, once again, that our economic program, given a chance to work, has worked beautifully in spite of the naysayers. Credit for this must go to the hard-working people of the United States.

Yesterday I pledged a new America, an opportunity society in which all would benefit from economic freedom. We are pushing closer than ever to that great goal, but we cannot rest on our laurels. Further economic progress can and will be made for all Americans once we simplify taxes and lower tax rates, create enterprise zones to stimulate economic activity in our cities, and permanently limit the ability of the Federal Government to spend, so that less money will go to the Federal Establishment and more will stay in the hands of the people, who are the creators of the prosperity we enjoy.

Remarks to Participants in the 1985 March for Life Rally
January 22, 1985

The President. Hello, Nellie, am I speaking to you?

Ms. Gray. Yes, Mr. President, you're speaking to me. And you're speaking to thousands of your pro-life Americans, who are here to tell you that we appreciate your being in the White House so very, very much.

The President. Well, thank you. And thank all of the participants in this 1985 March for Life for coming here and demonstrating your overwhelming support for the right to life of the unborn.

I feel a great sense of solidarity with all of you. And I'm convinced, as I know you are, that our response to the 12th anniversary of *Roe* vs. *Wade* and *Doe* vs. *Bolton* must be to rededicate ourselves to ending the terrible national tragedy of abortion.

A year ago, in my State of the Union Address, I called on everyone in our country to rise above bitterness and reproach and seek a greater understanding of this issue. I believe that spirit of understanding begins with the recognition of the reality of life before birth and the reality of death by abortion.

But the spirit of understanding also includes, as all of you know, a complete rejection of violence as a means of settling this issue. We cannot condone the threatening or taking of human life to protest the taking of human life by way of abortion.

And I want you to know that I feel these days, as never before, the momentum is with us. Surely, recent advances in medical technology have changed the debate. Surgeons now speak of the "patient in the womb." We now know more than ever before about the unborn. Doctors have invented procedures that can give blood transfusions to the fetus and even administer medication. For the first time, through the new technique of real-time ultrasound imaging, we're able to see with our own eyes, on film, the abortion of a 12-week-old unborn child.

The film—which, as you know, I'm sure, is narrated by a former director of the world's largest abortion clinic—provides chilling documentation of the horror of abortion during the first 3 months of life. It's been said that if every Member of the Congress could see this film of an early abortion, the Congress would move quickly to end the tragedy of abortion. And I pray that they will.

I will continue to work with all of those—in the Congress and out—who believe, as I do, that abortion is taking the life of a living human being; that the right to abortion is not secured by the Constitution; and the state has a compelling interest in protecting the life of each person before birth.

I've spoken here of the evidence today that establishes that the unborn is a living human being. We must not forget that in reality, if there is any justice in the abortionist position, it would require that they establish beyond a doubt that there is not life in the unborn—and they can't do that.

It's been a long, hard struggle the past dozen years. But I know all of us are feeling hopeful about a positive resolution of this issue, and I don't think our feeling of hope is inappropriate. There are already signs that we've changed the public attitude on abortion. The number performed each year is finally leveling off. The general feeling that abortion is just a small, harmless medical procedure that's simply a matter of choice has almost disappeared.

We're making a lot of progress, and partly because a dozen years ago people like yourselves who were told that banning abortion was a losing battle said, "Fine, that's the only kind of battle worth fighting."

62

God bless you for your courage and commitment, and thank you for your wonderful work. And I'm proud to stand with you in the long march for the right to life.

Ms. Gray. Mr. President?

The President. Yes, Nellie.

Ms. Gray. Mr. President, before you leave us, you know, many times we have been in the White House and you have said to us that we must come together. And I want you to know that we have had, maybe, some of our differences before. But now this grassroots, pro-life, American, whole movement is united. We want the paramount human life amendment with no compromises, Mr. President.

The President. Good for you, and I support you.

Ms. Gray. And, Mr. President, we want to work with you this year because we know that there are some things that we can do right now. One is, we can stop the funding of abortions in the District of Columbia, and we, as pro-life Americans, want to work with you to get that bill through. There are

things that we can do, and we want to work with you.

And before you leave us, we just want to give you a resounding "Thank you, Mr. President" from all of us here who are standing with you.

Goodbye, Mr. President.

The President. Goodbye, and thank you.

Ms. Gray. God bless you, Mr. President.

The President. Thank you very much, Nellie, and thank everyone.

Note: The President spoke at 12:01 p.m. from the Oval Office via a loudspeaker hookup with the rally site. Participants had gathered on the Ellipse for a march to the Supreme Court on the occasion of the 12th anniversary of the Supreme Court's decision on the abortion issue. Nellie Gray was president of March for Life.

In response to the President's comment, "I support you," Principal Deputy Press Secretary Larry M. Speakes issued the following statement: "There is no change in the President's position on abortion. He believes that abortion should be prohibited except when the life of the mother is endangered."

Statement on the Soviet-United States Nuclear and Space Arms Negotiations
January 22, 1985

I have just met with Secretaries Shultz and Weinberger, General Vessey, Bud McFarlane, Ken Adelman, and our new arms control negotiators. I am very pleased that the three distinguished Americans who will be our representatives have agreed to serve our country in these important new arms control negotiations.

Max Kampelman, John Tower, and Mike Glitman bring to their new assignments broad experience and deep knowledge. With the strong support of Paul Nitze and Ed Rowny, I am confident that our new team will represent the United States very effectively.

I view the negotiating commitments we undertook 2 weeks ago with the Soviets in Geneva with the utmost seriousness. I have no more important goal than reducing and, ultimately, eliminating nuclear weapons. The United States will have concrete ideas to put on the negotiating table. We hope the Soviet Union will follow a similarly constructive approach.

I also want to emphasize that we are determined to achieve a good agreement—an agreement which meets the interests of both countries, which increases the security of our allies, and which enhances international stability. Our new negotiators share this important goal. I look forward to working closely with our negotiating team in the months ahead. In this effort, I have charged Max and his colleagues with the responsibil-ity of keeping appropriate Members of the Congress fully informed. With the patience and support of the American people, Congress, and our allies, I am confident that we will succeed.

Appointment of Two Members of the Commission on Executive, Legislative, and Judicial Salaries
January 22, 1985

The President today announced his intention to appoint the following individuals to be members of the Commission on Executive, Legislative, and Judicial Salaries for the period of the 1985 fiscal year of the Federal Government:

Lloyd Norton Cutler will succeed Martha W. Griffiths. He is a partner in the law firm of Wilmer, Cutler & Pickering in Washington, DC. He served as Counsel to the President of the United States in 1979–1981. Previously he was with Wilmer, Cutler & Pickering in 1962–1979. He graduated from Yale University (A.B., 1936; LL.B., 1939). Mr. Cutler is married, has four children, and resides in Chevy Chase, MD. He was born November 10, 1917, in New York, NY.

Alexander B. Trowbridge will succeed Joseph Howard McDonnell. He is president of the National Association of Manufacturers in Washington, DC. Previously he was vice chairman of Allied Chemical Corp. in 1976–1978. He served as Secretary of Commerce in 1967–1968. Mr. Trowbridge graduated from Princeton University (B.A., 1951). He is married, has six children, and resides in Washington, DC. He was born December 12, 1929, in Englewood, NJ.

Memorandum Directing a Review of Federal Advisory Committees
January 22, 1985

Memorandum for the Heads of Executive Departments and Agencies

Subject: Reform of Federal Advisory Committees

Federal agencies receive outside advice, information, and assistance from some 900 advisory committees, councils, boards, and commissions. They include a total of about 20,000 members, at a combined annual cost of approximately $74 million. About two-thirds are established by statute.

A recent analysis found that 284 advisory committees reported no significant accomplishments during the last reporting period, and of these, 161 reported no activity whatever. The study also found that in many cases agencies failed to give serious consideration to the policy recommendations of committees.

It is evident that many advisory committees are not serving a useful purpose, and should be eliminated. It is also obvious that valuable committees are not receiving proper support and attention from agency leadership. Elimination of needless committees and improved management of the remainder will result in increased committee credibility and better advice and information at lower cost to the government.

Therefore, you should undertake a thorough review of your agency's committees and achieve the following objectives:

1. Assure that all committees are effectively managed, that they are provided adequate policy guidance, that recommendations are evaluated, and cost savings achieved wherever possible.

2. Eliminate all committees not produc-

ing significant results, or whose advice is no longer needed by the government. Legislation would be required to abolish committees established by statute.

The Office of Management and Budget and the General Services Administration will assist you in this effort and will report overall progress, consistent with the annual review required by the Federal Advisory Committee Act.

In the interest of good management, I urge your continued attention to this matter.

RONALD REAGAN

Appointment of Two Members of the National Advisory Committee on Oceans and Atmosphere, and Designation of the Chairman
January 23, 1985

The President today announced his intention to appoint the following individuals to be members of the National Advisory Committee on Oceans and Atmosphere for terms expiring July 1, 1987. The President intends to designate John E. Flipse as Chairman upon his appointment.

S. Fred Singer is a reappointment. He is a visiting professor at George Mason University in Fairfax, VA. He served as Deputy Administrator of the Environmental Protection Agency (1970–1971) and as Deputy Assistant Secretary for Scientific Programs at the Department of the Interior in 1967–1970. He received a Ph.D. from Princeton University in 1948. He was

born September 27, 1924, in Vienna, Austria, and now resides in Arlington, VA.

John E. Flipse will succeed John A. Knauss. He is associate vice chancellor of the Texas A&M system and associate dean of engineering of the college of engineering at Texas A&M University. Prior to joining the faculty of Texas A&M University in 1978, he was founder, chairman, president, and chief executive officer of Deepsea Ventures, Inc. (1968–1977). He graduated from the Massachusetts Institute of Technology (B.S., 1942) and New York University (M.M.E., 1948). He is married, has four children, and resides in College Station, TX. He was born February 4, 1921, in Montville, NJ.

Proclamation 5293—National Jerome Kern Day, 1985
January 23, 1985

By the President of the United States of America

A Proclamation

Musical theater is an American art form that has been part of our lives for over a century. The songs are a true expression of the era in which they were written, but they also evoke something eternal in the American ethos—echoing our joy in good years, reflecting our sadness in difficult ones, and lifting our spirits in times of challenge.

Jerome D. Kern, one of the founding fathers of the American musical theater, whose centenary we observe this year, is

widely honored for his many contributions to this uniquely American art form. His prodigious body of work—over 1,000 songs and 108 complete scores for Broadway shows and Hollywood films—forms a major part of the core of musical theater as we know it in America and as it has spread throughout the world.

Jerome Kern is remembered for individual songs, such as "Lovely to Look At," "They Didn't Believe Me," "All the Things You Are," and "Look for the Silver Lining," as well as entire film and stage scores, most notably the classic *Show Boat*.

He collaborated with other great talents

like Oscar Hammerstein II, Johnny Mercer, and Ira Gershwin and wrote with the elegance, wit, and sophistication that characterize the best American popular music. He was esteemed by his peers, who twice voted to honor him with Academy Awards—for "The Way You Look Tonight" and "The Last Time I Saw Paris." New generations of audiences of all ages and backgrounds have taken his melodies to heart and given them a permanent place in our American musical heritage.

In recognition of the many contributions of Jerome Kern in enriching the American musical theater and in celebration of the one hundredth anniversary of his birth, the Congress, by House Joint Resolution 583, has designated January 27, 1985, as "National Jerome Kern Day."

Now, Therefore, I, Ronald Reagan, President of the United States of America, do hereby proclaim January 27, 1985, as National Jerome Kern Day. I encourage the people of the United States to observe the day with appropriate ceremonies, programs, and activities throughout the country, and in particular, by enjoying the music of this renowned American composer.

In Witness Whereof, I have hereunto set my hand this twenty-third day of January, in the year of our Lord nineteen hundred and eighty-five, and of the Independence of the United States of America the two hundred and ninth.

RONALD REAGAN

[*Filed with the Office of the Federal Register, 12:42 p.m., January 24, 1985*]

Note: The proclamation was released by the Office of the Press Secretary on January 24.

Remarks at the Western Hemisphere Legislative Leaders Forum
January 24, 1985

I know that many of you come from somewhat warmer climates and aren't accustomed to this Washington deep freeze, but I'll hope that the warmth of our hospitality has helped make up for the temperature outside.

I think it's particularly fitting that your visit coincides with our Inaugural time, when the mantle of power here in the United States is passed to the choice of the electorate. Wherever we are, no matter what our political agenda, those who believe in democracy and human rights should rejoice in times like this. Believing in the peaceful transfer of power through democratic elections and a solid respect for human rights unites all of us here today with millions of people across the globe. Recognizing that bond is what this gathering and this Center for Democracy are all about.

I want to take this opportunity to thank the Democratic and Republican Members of the United States Congress, Professor Allen Weinstein, Dr. John Silber, Peter Kelly, and Frank Fahrenkopf for all they've done to ensure the success of this conference.

Being from democratic countries, you know it's difficult to get opposing political parties together, even in worthwhile endeavors like this. Well, the bipartisan support behind this effort reflects the value we place on enhancing long-range hemispheric collaboration among the free and democratic countries of the Americas. Building and reinforcing these ties has been of the utmost importance to this administration and will continue to be so during the next 4 years.

Our efforts are guided by three consistent and mutually reinforcing goals: We seek to promote the development of democratic political institutions; we want to encourage economic growth, which will increase opportunity and improve the standard of living for people throughout the hemisphere; we're willing to help our friends defend themselves against Soviet bloc, Cuban, and Nicaraguan sponsored subversion.

I like to think that the first of these goals is simply a reaffirmation of something in which our Forefathers believed so firmly, and that is that free and democratic government is the birthright of every citizen of this hemisphere. The Americas should be, and by right of heritage, ought to be populated by free and independent people.

As you know, not long after our own War of Independence, Simón Bolivar led the people of Latin America in a courageous struggle for independence. Bolivar, like Washington, a giant in the annals of human freedom, pointed out in his later years: "It is harder to maintain the balance of liberty than to endure the weight of tyranny."

The Great Liberator lamented that mankind is all too willing to rest unconcerned and accept things as they are. And that's why we who are committed to free government and democratic institutions must maintain a sense of fraternity between ourselves and other freedom-loving peoples.

Today, there are many reasons for optimism. Despite economic problems and the threat of well-armed, anti-democratic forces, we Americans—and by that I mean all of us, all Americans, from the North Slope of Alaska to the tip of Tierra del Fuego—are enjoying a rising tide of democracy.

Of the 34 countries in Latin America, 27, with about 90 percent of the region's population, are either democratic or in transition to democracy. A decade ago, less than 40 percent of Latin America's population was so fortunate.

I'd like to take this opportunity to offer my heartfelt best wishes to the representatives who are with us from the hemisphere's newest democratic governments— Uruguay and Brazil. And I'd like also to offer my congratulations to the people in political leadership of Argentina who, I understand, have been chosen by the Center for the 1985 International Democracy Prize.

The trend to democracy not only underscores the desire of people to be free but also suggests a new recognition that free government is the surest path to economic progress. This was pointed out long ago by Andres Bello, one of the hemisphere's intellectual giants. "Liberty," he noted, "gives wings to the spirit of enterprise wherever it meets it."

Well, today, as never before, we need this spirit of enterprise to overcome the economic challenges of the hemisphere. The leap in energy prices, the onset of global recession in 1979 and 1980 brought serious hardship throughout the world.

Here in the United States we countered the economic downturn with economic reforms that lowered tax rates, eliminated counterproductive government regulations, and brought down the rate of increase in government spending. We concentrated on promoting growth and opportunity, on encouraging business enterprise and investment. And this formula worked well for us. Last year we had a growth rate of 6.8 percent. And that was the best since 1951. And the inflation rate was only 4 percent. In fact, it has only averaged 3.9 percent over the last 3 years.

While putting our own economic house in order, we've tried to help our hemispheric neighbors and friends. We increased by over 50 percent the level of bilateral economic assistance over the previous administration. We've continued to support the World Bank, the Inter-American Bank, and the IMF programs. We've worked with leaders in government and the private sector to encourage the refinancing of international debt. Your cooperation has been indispensable in this effort.

And last year a dramatic and innovative approach to progress in Central America and the Caribbean went into effect. It took considerable effort to pass the Caribbean Basin Initiative, and we're anxious to work with you to see that its benefits are enjoyed by all concerned.

A few moments ago, I expressed optimism about the course of political developments in the Americas. I'd like to add that I'm equally optimistic that our economic problems, which today seem so menacing, will be overcome. Free people, given time, will find a way to solve what may appear to be unsolvable. I can assure you, the people of the United States are anxious to work with your people to build a prosperous and opportunity-filled future. Our cooperation

ST. THOMAS AQUINAS COLLEGE
LOUGHEED LIBRARY
SPARKILL, NEW YORK 10976

will enhance our chance for economic progress and help us meet some serious challenges to our security as well.

The transition to democracy, especially in Central America, has been accompanied by a concerted and well-financed effort by the Soviet bloc and Cuba to undermine democratic institutions and to seize power from those who believe in democracy. This is nothing new. Venezuelans who struggled so long and hard for freedom faced this same threat as they transformed their country into a democracy. Similar subversion—financed, armed, and supported by the outside—has plagued Colombia and other countries, as well.

A new danger we see in Central America is the support being given the Sandinistas by Colonel Qadhafi's Libya, the PLO, and, most recently, the Ayatollah Khomeini's Iran.

The subversion we're talking about violates international law. The Organization of American States, in the past, has enacted sanctions against Cuba for such aggression. The Sandinistas have been attacking their neighbors through armed subversion since August of 1979. Countering this by supporting Nicaraguan freedom fighters is essentially acting in self-defense and is certainly consistent with the United Nations and OAS Charter provisions for individual and collective security.

Two centuries ago, when our Forefathers in the United States were risking all to establish our democracy, one of our Founding Fathers said, "We must all hang together, or assuredly we shall all hang separately."

Well, I think it behooves all of us who believe in democratic government, in free elections, in the respect for human rights, to stand side by side with those who share our ideals, especially in Central America. We must not permit those heavily armed by a faraway dictatorship to undermine their neighbors and to stamp out democratic alternatives at home. We must have the same solidarity with those who struggle for democracy as our adversaries do with those

who would impose Communist dictatorship.

It was just 1 year ago when the Bipartisan Commission on Central America, of which John Silber was a member, issued their report. These distinguished citizens concluded that there is indeed a threat to Central America. As they recommended, I have asked the United States Congress to provide $8 billion in aid over the next 5 years for economic and social help. We're also taking steps, including active diplomacy, to defuse a potential crisis. We support, for example, all 21 objectives of the Contadora process, including the implementation of the democratic commitments made by the Sandinistas to the Organization of American States in 1979.

I believe that the answer lies in democracy. There's never been a war between two free countries. If we're for democracy, we're for peace, domestically and internationally. Today, with democracy on the rise, we have it within our power to recapture Simón Bolívar's dream. We can have a united hemisphere, living in peace, opportunity, and freedom.

The ideals we share have come of age. And now is the time; we are the people; democracy is the way. There are some 600 million of us from that tip of Tierra del Fuego up to that north coast of Alaska, bound together by a common heritage and history, all of us Americans, all of us worshiping the same God. What a power for good in the world we can be if we strengthen our neighborliness and the contact and the cooperation between us.

Thank you for being here, and God bless you all.

Note: The President spoke at 11:47 a.m. in Room 450 of the Old Executive Office Building. The Western Hemisphere Legislative Leaders Forum was cosponsored by the Western Hemisphere Affairs Subcommittee of the House Foreign Affairs Committee, Boston University, and the Center for Democracy.

Executive Order 12500—Delegation to the Secretary of State and the Director of the International Development Cooperation Agency Concerning Foreign Assistance
January 24, 1985

By the authority vested in me as President by the Constitution and statutes of the United States of America, including section 621 of the Foreign Assistance Act of 1961, as amended (22 U.S.C. 2381), and section 301 of title 3 of the United States Code, and in order to delegate certain functions concerning foreign assistance to the Secretary of State and the Director of the International Development Cooperation Agency, it is hereby ordered as follows:

Section 1. Section 1-201(a) of Executive Order No. 12163, as amended, is further amended by inserting the following new paragraphs at the end thereof:

"(26) title III of the Foreign Assistance and Related Programs Appropriations Act, 1985 (as enacted in Public Law 98–473) under the unnumbered paragraph entitled "Military Assistance" insofar as they relate to El Salvador, Turkey and Honduras;

"(27) section 540 of the Foreign Assistance and Related Programs Appropriations Act, 1985;

"(28) section 1540 of the Department of Defense Authorization Act, 1985 (Public Law 98–525), which shall be exercised in consultation with the Secretary of Defense".

Sec. 2. Section 1-102(a) of Executive Order No. 12163, as amended, is further amended by inserting the following new paragraph at the end thereof:

"(6) Section 533 of the Foreign Assistance and Related Programs Appropriations Act, 1985, which shall be exercised in consultation with the Secretary of State".

Sec. 3. Section 1-701(d) of Executive Order No. 12163, as amended, is further amended by deleting "481(a)" and inserting in lieu thereof "481(h)".

Sec. 4. Section 1-902(c) of Executive Order No. 12163, as amended, is amended to read as follows:

"References in this order to provisions of any Act, and references in any other Executive order or in any memorandum delegation to provisions of any Act related to the subject of this order shall be deemed to include references to any hereafter-enacted provision of law that is the same or substantially the same as such provisions, respectively."

RONALD REAGAN

The White House,
January 24, 1985.

[*Filed with the Office of the Federal Register, 4:51 p.m., January 24, 1985*]

Statement by Principal Deputy Press Secretary Speakes on a Bill Prohibiting Discrimination by Educational Institutions Receiving Federal Financial Assistance
January 24, 1985

I have been advised that legislation has been introduced in the Senate to effectively overturn the Supreme Court's decision in the *Grove City College* case. Majority Leader Bob Dole has introduced the legislation as S. 272. This bill reflects the compromise reached after long and arduous efforts between Members of the Senate and the administration at the end of the 98th Congress. Regrettably, the press of time prevented the 98th Congress from adopting the approach embodied in this bill.

S. 272 accomplishes the stated intention of proponents of legislation to overturn the

Supreme Court's decision in the *Grove City College* case and, at the same time, avoids the problem created by the overly broad proposals which were introduced in the last Congress. In *Grove City,* the Supreme Court held that the statutory prohibition against sex discrimination (Title IX of the Education Amendments of 1972) applies only to the "specific programs" to which Federal financial assistance is actually extended. The bill introduced today would amend not only that law but also the three major parallel civil rights statutes (Title VI of the Civil Rights Act of 1964; Section 504 of the Rehabilitation Act of 1973; and the Age Discrimination Act) so that extension of Federal financial assistance to any program or activity of an educational institution covers all of its educational programs and

activities, subjecting them to the prohibitions in these Federal laws against discrimination on the basis of sex, race, handicap, and age.

The administration fully supports S. 272 and will work to see the legislation enacted in the Congress. The 98th Congress almost completed the task of developing an acceptable response to the *Grove City College* decision, and there is no good reason why the 99th Congress cannot finish this work by enacting the legislation introduced today. I am confident that this will happen so long as no efforts are made to alter the legislation's fundamental purpose or add to it needless and crippling amendments that go beyond the careful reversal of *Grove City* contained in S. 272.

Remarks at the 1985 Reagan Administration Executive Forum
January 25, 1985

Again, thank you.

I was thinking as George [Bush] was speaking that I've been truly blessed these past 4 years to have been surrounded by some of the most capable and talented executives and leaders the White House has ever seen. This is truly—and this is not hyperbole—this is truly a history-making team.

I believe the historians will recognize George Bush as a great Vice President. And I've had the help for 4 years of the fine men and women that you see up here with me—the whole Cabinet. And I'll try not to take a nap. [*Laughter*]

These are the people who quietly and with complete commitment have worked with you to change the realities in our country.

It's been a tremendous 4 years. And I'm feeling absolutely bullish on the next 4. I was just thinking the other day that in our first administration, we made history, and in the second, we can change history forever.

Four years ago we came here knowing what was wrong, but in truth, as conservatives who'd been out of power for a great

many years, some of us had limited practical experience in how exactly to right all the wrongs that had preceded us. But we had a philosophy, and we had a vision.

Our philosophy could be boiled down to one word: freedom. Freedom was at the heart of our plans for our economy, for individuals, for our country, and for all the nation states of the world. And so we pulled up our sleeves and went to work.

We lowered tax rates for individuals in businesses; we instituted tax indexing; we slowed the growth of government; we slowed the number of regulatory edicts emanating from Washington; we began to return power to the States and counties and towns and cities; and we began to return power to the people.

You know the results of our efforts: an economy come alive again, a nation come alive again. You know the facts about inflation, about how more people are employed than ever before in our history. But I think the most eloquent testimony about the success of our program and how we were right to stand firm in the face of the pessimists and doom-and-gloomers is in the numbers that came out Tuesday: the biggest increase in the gross national product since the Truman administration and the smallest increase in inflation since 1967.

We've taken control of the ship of state and changed direction. And what are we going to do now? Well, the way I see it, it's all ahead full, no turning back.

Now, that term, if you haven't heard it before, "all ahead full," that's a Navy command that has to do with guiding or directing a ship. The last time I used that I was in an entirely different career. [*Laughter*] I was playing the captain of a submarine. [*Laughter*] And we were taking the sub out the harbor at San Diego to get some shots at sea, and the director just thought he could get some extra footage that might come in handy. So he told me to replace Commander Kelly of the submarine who stepped out of camera range, standing above the open hatch in the conning tower, so that he could then say to me the commands that I was actually to give to get us out of the harbor. And I would repeat those commands down below. And it was, you know, "half speed," and it was "hard right," and it was all those commands. And I was repeating them, and the enlisted man down below, in the open hatch down there, would repeat back the order that I had given.

And finally, we came with the clear sea ahead of us to "all ahead full." And I said, "All ahead full." And it was repeated up, "All ahead full." And then the director— I've often thought that I got at this point a great—really a great review of my acting— because the director said to me, "Give that last one again." So I said, "All ahead full." There was a pause, and a very aggrieved voice from below said, "Sir, it *is* all ahead full." [*Laughter*] So—I won't say it again; you got the idea. [*Laughter*]

In the next 4 years, all of us together are going to transform America. We're going to lower tax rates further by instituting for the first time since the income tax began real tax reform to make the entire system more simple, more fair, and more efficient. And by lowering tax rates, we're going to encourage greater productivity and the creation of wealth for all.

We're going to continue to trim the size of government. Think a moment how remarkable and truly revolutionary it is that hundreds of people who came to Washington to assume positions of governmental authority actually succeeded in diminishing the government's authority. Now this is not the normal bureaucratic way of things. Normally, people say, "Put me in power, and I'll return more power to you." But they get into power, and they find they kind of like it and figure ways to get some more. Well, we've been the administration that didn't do that. And this alone is cause for great pride.

In the next 4 years, we're going to go for economic growth. Now, "growth" can sound like some kind of a buzzword, as if all kinds of growth are always good in and of themselves. But when we talk about growth, we mean letting the free marketplace of the freest country in the world expand to its ultimate, and thereby give complete opportunity to every person in our country. We've made great strides in civil rights in our history, but blacks and Hispanics and all minority group members won't have full and equal power until they have full economic power. And that begins with the jobs that are created by growth. We want opportunity for all. And if we have to say goodbye to needless regulations and turn an unfair tax structure on its ear to give opportunity to all, well, that's what we'll do.

We're going to continue to speak out in support of the other great change—the return to traditional values that was sparked in 1980. We're for prayer in the schools; we're against abortion. We support the return to basics. We'll continue, under our next Secretary of Education Bill Bennett, the policies that already have resulted in renewed excellence in education. We support the family and oppose anything that would take from it its power and its moral authority. We recognize that the family is the center of our society, and as the family goes, so goes civilization.

In our international relations, we'll continue to be what we set out to be 4 years ago—a reliable friend to our allies and to our neighbors and a leader to those who care about human liberty. We're a friend of peace first, last, and always. But the American soul was forged in freedom. And we will be a friend of freedom everywhere, and the foes of freedom will be our foes. We must assure the survival and success of freedom in Central America. We cannot break faith with freedom anywhere. This is our heritage and our moral obligation.

I think there's an understandable tendency when a second term begins to think that all the great work is behind us; that the big battles have been fought, and all the rest is anticlimax. Well, that's not true. What's gone before is prolog. Our greatest battles lie ahead—all is newness now, and the possibility of great and fundamental change. We can change America forever. And that's some great and beautiful music we've been playing these past 4 years, but the way I see it, from here on, it's shake, rattle, and roll.

I'm aware of how hard you've all worked. These past 4 years have been rough and demanding. Governing isn't easy. And some of you, I know, feel an understandable fatigue. There have been bureaucratic disagreements and tensions. Well, this weekend, I want you to put up your feet and

relax. And Monday—don't think too much about the job—Monday when you come in, sit down at the desk and breathe deep, because Monday the world starts all over again. It's the beginning of a brand new administration, and we're going to make new history together from here on in.

I think you sense, as I do, an ebullience in our country, and our joy is not inappropriate to the times. Our joy is an engine that is going to move our nation into a great promised land of freedom, dignity, and happiness. We've only just begun. We're here together as we were 4 years ago. We share a covenant, a public trust.

I rely on you, for you are the Reagan administration. And I look forward to the next 4 years. I'm excited about what we have the potential to do and about what kind of America we can leave behind us.

And so, once again, I thank you all so very much. And God bless you all.

Note: The President spoke at 11:35 a.m. at DAR Constitution Hall at the 4th annual Executive Forum for political appointees of the administration.

Nomination of Richard T. McCormack To Be Permanent United States Representative to the Organization of American States
January 25, 1985

The President today announced his intention to nominate Richard T. McCormack to be the Permanent Representative of the United States of America to the Organization of American States, with the rank of Ambassador. He would succeed J. William Middendorf II.

Since 1982 he has been serving as Assistant Secretary of State (Bureau of Economic and Business Affairs). Previously he was a consultant for international economics at the Department of State, representing the Department at a number of functions abroad. In 1979–1981 he served as a legisla-

tive assistant to Senator Jesse Helms. He was at the American Enterprise Institute in 1975–1977 and Deputy to the Assistant Secretary of the Treasury for International Economic Affairs in 1974.

He is the author of "Asians in Kenya," and a number of other articles and monographs on foreign affairs. He graduated from Georgetown University (B.A., 1963) and the University of Fribourg in Switzerland (Ph.D., 1966). He is married, has one child, and resides in Washington, DC. He was born March 6, 1941, in Bradford, PA.

Nomination of J. William Middendorf II To Be United States Representative to the European Communities
January 25, 1985

The President today announced his intention to nominate J. William Middendorf II to be the Representative of the United States of America to the European Communities with the rank and status of Ambassador. He would succeed George Southall Vest.

Since 1981 he has been serving as Permanent Representative of the United States of America to the Organization of American States, with the rank of Ambassador. Previously he was chairman of the finance committee of the Presidential Inaugural Committee. He was president and chief executive officer of Financial General Bankshares, Inc., in 1977–1981. He served as Under Secretary, then Secretary of the Navy in 1974–1977. In 1969–1973 he was the United States Ambassador to the Netherlands.

He received a bachelor of naval science from Holy Cross College in 1945 and a bachelor of arts degree from Harvard University in 1947. He also graduated from New York University Graduate School of Business Administration (M.B.A., 1954). He is married and has four children. He was born September 22, 1924, in Baltimore, MD.

Nomination of George Southall Vest To Be Director General of the Foreign Service
January 25, 1985

The President today announced his intention to nominate George Southall Vest, a Career Member of the Senior Foreign Service, Class of Career Minister, to be Director General of the Foreign Service, Department of State. He would succeed Alfred L. Atherton, Jr.

Since 1981 he has been serving as Representative of the United States of America to the European Communities, with the rank and status of Ambassador Extraordinary and Plenipotentiary. Previously, he served in the State Department as Assistant Secretary for European Affairs in 1977–1981; Director of the Bureau of Politico-Military Affairs in 1974–1976; Deputy Assistant Secretary for Press Relations in 1973–1974; and Special Assistant to the Secretary for negotiations on CSCE in Helsinki and Geneva (1972–1973). He was Deputy Chief of Mission in Brussels (USEC, 1967–1979) and NATO (1969–1971).

He graduated from the University of Virginia (B.A., 1941; M.A., 1947). He served in the U.S. Army in 1941–1946. He is married, has three children, and resides in Bethesda, MD. He was born December 25, 1918, in Columbia, VA.

Appointment of Six Members of the National Afro-American History and Culture Commission
January 25, 1985

The President today announced his intention to appoint the following individuals to be members of the National Afro-American History and Culture Commission:

Aletha Odom-Foxworth for a term expiring January 18, 1987. She will succeed Alan Pifer. She is a science teacher at North Miami Beach Senior High School. She graduated from Fisk University (B.A., 1967) and the University of Miami (M.B.A., 1976). She was born April 27, 1939, in Miami, FL, where she now resides.

Dorothy B. Parker for a term expiring January 18, 1987. She will succeed Leon Litwack. She is special assistant to the associate director of the National Institute of Education in Washington, DC. She graduated from Cheyney State College (B.S., 1964), Temple University (Ed.M., 1970), and Peabody College of Vanderbilt University (Ed.D., 1981). She was born January 28, 1933, in Philadelphia, PA, and now resides in Alexandria, VA.

James E. Stratten for a term expiring January 18, 1987. He will succeed C.J. McLin. He is owner of R&J Futuristic, Inc., land developers in San Francisco, CA. He graduated from Talladega College (B.A., 1936) and Columbia University (M.A., 1939). He was born November 20, 1913, in Cedartown, GA, and now resides in San Francisco, CA.

Ronald J. Crutcher for a term expiring January 18, 1989. He will succeed James Alfred Joseph. He is chief bailiff of the Dayton Municipal Court in Dayton, OH. He is also a general partner in R&D Associates in Dayton. He graduated from Wright State University (B.A.). He was born September 30, 1954, in Detroit, MI and now resides in Dayton, OH.

Theophilus W. Mungen, Jr., for a term expiring January 18, 1989. He will succeed Karen Zuniga. He is a sales associate with Skagits Land and Home Realty in Mount Vernon, WA. He graduated from Volusia County Community College (A.A., 1963), Florida A&M University (B.S., 1965) and the University of Idaho (M.S., 1971). He was born March 24, 1943, in St. Augustine, FL, and now resides in Mount Vernon, WA.

Lucy Phelps Patterson for a term expiring January 18, 1989. She will succeed Topper Carew. She is Branham professor and director of the Social Work Program at Bishop College in Dallas, TX. She graduated from Howard University (A.B., 1950) and the University of Denver School of Social Work (M.A., 1963). She was born June 21, 1931, in Dallas, TX, where she now resides.

Announcement of the Beginning of the Soviet-United States Nuclear and Space Arms Negotiations
January 26, 1985

The United States and the Soviet Union have agreed to begin negotiations on nuclear and space arms on March 12, 1985, in Geneva, Switzerland.

The U.S. delegation will be headed by Ambassador Max Kampelman, who at the same time will represent the United States in one of the groups at the negotiations; in the two other groups, the American side will be represented by Senator John Tower and Ambassador Maynard Glitman. The U.S.S.R. delegation will be headed by Ambassador V.P. Karpov; in the two other groups, the Soviet side will be represented by Ambassador Y.A. Kvitsinskiy and Ambassador A.A. Obukhov.

Radio Address to the Nation on Economic Growth
January 26, 1985

My fellow Americans:

Hello again. This is my first radio talk since last November's election, and I'm glad to be back. There was some question if this show would be continued, but I guess the ratings were pretty good, so they took up my option.

As you know, it was so cold here in Washington this week, we had to hold the inaugural ceremonies inside. It was a great disappointment to many who planned to attend, but I'm sure it was a good idea. An outside event would have given new meaning to our planned "freeze" on the Federal Government.

The inauguration ceremony is simple and unpretentious, but sitting there next to Nancy, waiting to take the oath of office, I was deeply stirred. In that short ceremony, our nation comes together to reaffirm our faith in individual liberty and celebrate the democratic institutions that have preserved and protected our freedom for over 200 years. To place one's hand on the Bible and solemnly swear to defend the Constitution of the United States is to be reminded of how strong the will of our free people, guided by faith, can be.

Not only has our nation withstood and triumphed over the trials of history, the principles and values embodied in our Constitution have inspired the spread of democracy throughout the world. From times of hardship, we've always emerged with a renewed sense of confidence and a determination to meet and to conquer whatever challenges lie ahead.

We start out the new year with good news. The fundamental strength and vitality of our economy is unquestionable. In 1984 we grew stronger and faster than we have in over 30 years, while inflation stayed lower than any time since 1967. Last month 340,000 people found new jobs in an economy that now employs more people than ever before in history. Like a sapling in springtime, our economy sprang back after a long winter and reached for the Sun. Once we began to remove the crushing weight of high taxes and overregulation, nothing could hold us back.

Our challenge in 1985 is to build on the momentum of progress, to carry the economic expansion forward so that its opportunities and benefits touch every American. Let's make 1985 the year of opportunity. Let's use our economy, America's tremendous engine of prosperity, to break down the barriers and obstacles on the road to achievement.

Our goal must be an open society in which hope is nourished and effort rewarded, where the promise of tomorrow is found in opportunity today. The entrepreneurial genius of the American people transformed a continent covered by wilderness into the leading industrial power in the world today.

We in government should learn to look at our country with the eyes of the entrepreneur, seeing possibilities where others see only problems. That way, instead of the unemployed, we'd see a resource of potential workers waiting to add their labors, their ingenuity, their creativity to an expanding marketplace. And instead of ghettos, we'd see potential enterprise zones, where increased incentives to work and invest could produce a renaissance of business activity and community involvement.

It's my great hope that, in the months ahead, forward-looking Members from both sides of the aisle in the Congress will join with us in this important work. We must follow through on the policies that have given us 25 months of economic growth by simplifying our cumbersome tax codes and lowering rates still further, while making sure that the overall burden of government on our private economy grows no bigger.

After we've come so far, we must never turn back to the old destructive habits of taxing and spending. With a future beckoning so brightly, we must move forward on the optimistic path of economic growth and expanding opportunity. Don't let anyone underestimate America.

I'm reminded of a remark attributed to Thomas Watson, the chairman of the board of IBM back in 1943, to the effect that there was a world market for about five computers. Well today, of course, there are millions of computers in homes and businesses, schools and hospitals across the country and around the world. But even an expert in the field couldn't predict the explosive growth of technology that we've seen recently. That's why we shouldn't hesitate to dream big.

We must ask of ourselves only the best.

We must challenge ourselves to hurdle the accepted limits of the past, to draw a new map of possibilities, and give new meaning to the word "success." Isn't that, after all, what it means to be Americans?

Until next week, thanks for listening. God bless you.

Note: The President spoke at 12:06 p.m. from the Oval Office at the White House.

Interview With Representatives of Independent Radio Networks
January 26, 1985

Q. Live from the Roosevelt Room of the White House, welcome to a conversation with President Reagan, an unrehearsed interview with representatives of seven radio networks.

Mr. President, thank you for being with us today.

The President. It's a pleasure.

Q. The correspondents who'll be questioning the President are Candy Crowley of the AP Radio Network, Nelson Benton of the Mutual Radio Network, Jim Angle of National Public Radio, Joe Ewalt of the RKO Radio Networks, Bob Ellison of the Sheridan Radio Network, Gene Gibbons of the UPI Radio Network, and Philomena Jurey from Voice of America.

The first question is from Candy Crowley of AP Radio.

Q. Thank you.

U.S.-Soviet Negotiations on Nuclear and Space Arms

Mr. President, shortly before today's announcement that U.S.-Soviet negotiators would meet in Geneva March 12th, one of your top advisers to those talks, Ambassador Nitze, said that he could not say that chances for an agreement are very good. Is that so?

The President. I think when people like— [*inaudible*]—Dr. Nitze, who have been engaged in negotiations back over the years, the many negotiations, they are aware of the difficulties and how tedious and long they can be, how patient you must be, and

how many times we've gone to the table and come away without anything that was of really any great importance. So, I can understand that.

I, on the other hand, tend to be a little more optimistic, not euphoric. I, too, know how tough this is going to be. But, at least, it is the first time that I can recall the Soviet Union openly, themselves, saying that they wanted to see the number of weapons reduced, and have even gone so far as to say what we have said, that they would like to see the elimination of nuclear weapons entirely.

Q. So, if I could just ask you, you do think there's a chance for an agreement in your second term?

The President. Well, we're certainly going to try. I know that I wouldn't try to confine it to 4 years, because I know how long some negotiations have taken with them. But we're going to stay there at the table, with the hope that this time we can arrive at an actual reduction of weapons.

Q. Thank you. Now to Nelson Benton.

Q. Mr. President, there are persistent reports from Western capitals about the health of President Chernenko. Some reports even say he has had a stroke. Can you add to that or subtract? And can you say, sir, what effect his longevity and apparent infirmity may have on the talks?

The President. Well, on the first part of that I can only say that we know no more than you have just said about this—that there are voices, and some from within Russia, that have indicated to others in conversation that perhaps his illness is quite serious. I don't know whether that would have an effect on these talks or not. The very fact that they're going forward with them, that after 17 days of the month that was given to setting a date and so forth, they've come forth with a date and named their negotiators, would lead me to believe that, no, they intend to go forward.

Q. Thank you, Mr. President. Jim Angle?

Federal Budget

Q. Mr. President, you've said that even though you support a balanced budget amendment to the Constitution, you couldn't submit a budget, a balanced budget, yourself, because cutting that much suddenly would hurt too many people. But you'll leave your successor—possibly a Republican—deficits of more than a hundred billion dollars a year. Wouldn't a constitutional amendment require him or her to make cuts so large that they would do what you don't want to do, which is hurt many people?

The President. Well, in all this talk and during the campaign, when I was accused of never having submitted a balanced budget since I'd been here, I had to wonder how they had the nerve to say that. The President has no right to spend money. The Constitution doesn't give the President the right to spend a nickel. That's up there on the Hill. And every budget that we have submitted since I've been here has been smaller than the one that Congress would finally agree to. So, in fixing the blame for why we haven't done more than we've done in reducing spending seems to be pretty evident.

Now, the thing about the constitutional amendment—after 50 years of this deficit spending, and much of it simply accepted as a standard policy, we forget that over these 50 years the Government has just said, "Yes, deficit spending is kind of good for us. It helps maintain prosperity." I've never believed that myself. But you can't now pull the rug out from under people who have maybe directed their business practices or agriculture, things of that kind, and say to them, "We're pulling the rug out

right now. The whole game has changed."

So, I've always believed that the constitutional amendment, if adopted, would set a target date, that based on a declining path of deficits, then you could foresee and say by such and such a date we must achieve a balanced budget, and from then on, the Government spend no more than it takes in. And this is one of the reasons why our own plan, here, of getting the deficit down to 4 percent of the gross national product and then 3 percent and then 2 percent would give us a pattern in which we could then pick that date and say that's when it should be effected.

Q. Well, Mr. President, if there's a specific date, do you have a specific date in mind that you will propose when you propose the balanced budget amendment?

The President. No, because we're still trying now to get started on this path, with the budget that we'll be taking up to the Congress. But we think we're going to meet our goal with regard to a $50 billion reduction and the 4 percent figure. And, having once started that, I think we can keep on the other track.

I don't believe that I'll be leaving a budget deficit quite as large as some of the prognostications. And I would just like to qualify that by saying that if you will look back over these last 4 years, most of the projections have been greater, as to deficit and so forth, than we have achieved.

Q. Mr. President, Joe Ewalt.

Defense Spending

Q. Mr. President, Senate Majority Leader Bob Dole—the man you're depending on to shepherd many of your programs through Congress—said yesterday that any deficit reduction plan is going to be in real trouble unless you hold down the growth in defense spending. The Pentagon responded by saying that those who try to lower military spending want to weaken the security of the country. Now, how are you going to possibly get meaningful deficit reduction plans through Congress when there's such a big gap between your administration and the Republican allies in Congress?

The President. Well, I saw Bob on television saying some of those things. And I think sometimes the shading, and then quoting him later in the printed media, has not been reviewing the bidding with the same inflection. I think he was calling attention to what could be a fact within the Congress—that consistently, over the years, the Congress have, when they've needed money for some other program, they have thought, well, defense is the place we can get it.

I think what's being ignored right now on the part of many of them who haven't seen the budget that we're presenting is that they aren't aware of the cuts the Defense Department has already made. In fact, the cut for 1986, volunteered by the Department of Defense, is a greater cut than had been asked by the Office of Management and Budget in laying out our program for this '86 budget. And I think, there, that cut was based on the Department of Defense saying, "We can achieve this much of a reduction and still not seriously set back our need for national security."

Now, to go beyond that and just simply say, on a matter of dollars, "We're going to take more dollars regardless," is very risky, because the Defense Department—that's the budget, the one budget that is dictated by people outside the United States. You can't ignore what other people are doing, other possible adversaries, with regard to your own defense spending.

And so, I think when they see, and when we have a chance to explain, how much the Department of Defense has come down from its original projections for this period and for '86, I think, they're going to see that there isn't much more to get there. We've squeezed that apple pretty good.

Q. But, sir, Senator Dole has been down here once or twice a week meeting with you or your aides on the budget. How could he not know what you're proposing?

The President. Well, that's what I meant in the beginning about the inflection. What he was talking about, I think, was the attitude of Congress and that if there's any appearance to Congress that we're not putting the Defense Department on the table along with everything else in the negotiations, that we wouldn't get anyplace with them. It is going to be there, but then we're actually going to show where the cuts

are.

But beyond that, if there's reluctance, as there has been for 4 years now—the Congress—to go as far as we want to go in reducing the growth in Federal spending, then I've said we'd take our case to the people and explain to the people what it is we're trying to do and why we have to do it.

Q. Sir, your next question is from Bob Ellison.

Black Americans

Q. Mr. President, last week you indicated that America's black leaders had misled their constituents about your administration's performance. Would you address the suggestion, in your remarks, that black Americans who voted against you, by a margin of 9 to 1, did so based solely on the statements made by the leaders?

The President. I don't know that they did that entirely, but I do think that there is a lack of understanding of what our policies are and what we've been trying to achieve in these 4 years. In fact, one very well-known leader of a black organization confirmed what I said. I wasn't speaking about all leaders. I've been working with a great many leaders.

But it isn't just leaders of black organizations. I think there is a tendency of some individuals who have positions in organizations that have been created for whatever purpose, but for some purpose—to rectify some ill—that then, once that gets going, they're reluctant to admit how much they've achieved, because it might reveal then that there's no longer a need for that particular organization, which would mean no longer a need for their job.

And so, there's a tendency to keep the people stirred up as if the cause still exists. And I think that there's some of this that's been going on, because if you look at the accomplishments and the achievements that we've made in this field—from the very beginning I ordered a program of aid to the historic black colleges and universities because of their great tradition and what they have done in the field of making education possible at the time when, without them, it wouldn't have been possible;

small business and the efforts that we have made to lead to entrepreneurship and the ability in the minority communities for them to create businesses; the directing of some of our subcontracting, defense and other government areas—that a percentage of that is going to go to minority-owned businesses; the things like the enterprise zones bill, that we've been trying now for 2 or 3 years and can't get it out of committee in the House of Congress. Here is a bill that is aimed directly at inner city areas which would be heavily minority, and it would provide jobs and opportunity in those areas for those people.

Such accomplishments as the lowering of inflation is of greater benefit to minorities who have not brought themselves up to the level of income of the rest of society. All of these things right now—the youth opportunity pay scale, we want a lower minimum wage for teenagers that are out there looking for their first jobs. And the heaviest segment of unemployment in the United States is among black teenagers. The Black Mayors' Council endorses this bill, and yet it's being opposed in the Congress. We haven't been able to get it yet because what we've done with the minimum wage right now is price out of the job market young people without job training who are out there looking for their first job.

Q. If I may, were you suggesting that there's no longer a need for organizations like the NAACP, Urban League, or Southern Christian Leadership Conference?

The President. I'm not going to name the organizations, but I'm going to say something about redirecting their efforts—a number of the organizations. I'm a little older than the rest of you, and I can remember before there was a civil rights movement. I can remember very clearly the injustices in this country—and they weren't confined to one section of the country—the prejudice that prevailed, the things that were just accepted, even by people who maybe felt no prejudice themselves. And I think there is a need for us to focus more on what has been accomplished and less on creating an ill will and a feeling that all the grievances still remain.

No, we haven't done the job completely. There is still further to go, but let's not forget what has been accomplished. And one of the things that a black leader referred to the other day was his protest that some leaders in this cause are actually striving to build, for whatever reason, two Americas: a black America and a white America. That isn't good enough. That isn't what we need or what we want. That would be very destructive to the very things that these people say they're striving to attain.

What we need, what my goal is, is an America where something or anything that is done to or for anyone is done neither because of nor in spite of any difference between them racially, religiously, or ethnic origin-wise.

Q. Thank you. Gene Gibbons asks the next question.

Nicaragua and the Middle East

Q. Sir, I would like to move on to the issue of Central America. You said the other day Nicaragua is receiving support from Iran's Khomeini regime. Can you elaborate? What kind of support and how serious a security threat is it for us?

The President. Well, as far as I want to go here is to say that it's very evident that they have sought their advice. I believe that very possibly there has been some help in training and in certain types of munitions now that have come to them from Iran. The whole problem also is this: That we know that Iran has backed and supported certain terrorist activities. We also know that there are representatives of most of the prominent terrorist groups, worldwide, in Nicaragua giving advice and training and help to the Sandinista government.

Q. Are you saying, sir, that we face, now, an imminent threat of terrorism here as a result of what's going on in Nicaragua?

The President. Oh, I think the United States faces an imminent threat of terrorism from a number of groups not only for that reason but for other reasons that have to do with our relations with the Communist bloc, our activities in the Middle East. We know that our people, worldwide, have been targeted and American institutions targeted. And we're doing everything we can to minimize that threat and to work with our allies and the other democratic nations to try and exchange intelligence information, to see if we can't treat with those criminals the way we treat with other criminals, by way of Interpol.

Q. Sir, the next question from Philomena Jurey.

Q. Mr. President, are you going to try to revive your Middle East peace initiative when Saudi Arabia's Prince Fahd and Egyptian President Mubarak come to see you in the next 2 months?

The President. Well, let me just hasten to say, lest there's some misinterpretation of your question there—there is no relationship between those two visits happening to come together at the time. That's just coincidence. But I'm quite sure that that will be part of the discussion that we have.

I've never retreated from the belief that the peace proposal that we made is the best way to go. It is based on a continuation of the Camp David accords and the United Nations 442 [242]. And what it requires is the getting together of moderate Arab nations, agreeing that Israel does have a right to exist as a nation, and Israel coming together—with regard to the whole matter of lands still occupied by Israel, that they took in armed conflict—and to see if we cannot create more Egypts, more countries willing to arrive at peace agreements with Israel, bring peace to that very troubled region. And I would think that both those leaders would be very important ones to talk about this subject.

Q. Thank you. The next question from Candy Crowley.

Q. Let me get back to the subject of terrorism for a moment here and remind you that 4 years ago tomorrow was when you welcomed to the South Lawn the American hostages home from Iran. During that ceremony, you said, "Let terrorists be aware that when international law is broken, American policy will be one of swift and effective retribution." Obviously, since that time some awful things have happened——

The President. Yes.

Q. We've had attacks on our Embassies and our marines and our diplomats, and our citizens have been kidnaped. I wonder, sir, there's been no public sign of American retaliation that you spoke of 4 years ago, and

has it been over the past 4 years that you've found that it's actually somewhat impossible for us to deal out swift and effective retribution?

The President. Well, Candy, let me just say that it's—I referred to them as criminals a little while ago. They are criminals. They may think they've got a noble cause or something—they're criminals, committing the worst and most despicable kind of crimes. Now, you have the same problem that you have with crime. They act surreptitiously; they come out of hiding; they're anonymous; they disappear again. You have to track them down; you've got to find them. You try to prevent their crimes by crime prevention measures, defensive measures, the best you can. You try to track them down. Then you hope that you can punish.

Right now the terrorists—one of the things that has kept us from retaliation is the difficulty in getting definite information enough as to who they are and where they are that you do not risk killing—doing the same thing they're doing—killing innocent people in an effort to get at them. And this is why we have moved up our relationship with our allies and our democratic friends, so that we can exchange intelligence information and try to locate.

The other thing is, I can't go much beyond that because, I mean in talking about specifically what we're doing, because then that's like the policeman warning the—[*laughter*]—the killers that he's on his way. So, I can only tell you that it is very much a problem for us that is being dealt with, and that we are not just sitting back saying, "Isn't it too bad."

Q. Well, if I could just quickly ask you then, are you suggesting—I understand your inability to talk of specifics—but are you suggesting that the case is not closed in Beirut and what happened to our marines and our Embassies, that's still a very active search for those responsible and will there then still be swift and—retribution?

The President. Yes. The answer is yes to all of that.

Jeane Kirkpatrick

Q. Mr. President, your communications

with Ambassador Kirkpatrick about her future in the administration at least has created the perception that those communications are either through intermediaries or through the press. You're meeting with her Wednesday—is this like a summit meeting—you don't plan a summit until you are assured of some reasonable amount of success?

The President. [*Laughing*] No. And I have to tell you those press stories that I've been reading are driving me right up the wall, because they're not based on fact or anything. She and I will be having a talk. I need to know what she might be interested in doing. I have to present what might be the opportunities at this end. But I hear and have read all these things, and they're not being helpful at all—these stories. And I don't know where the leaks are coming from.

Q. Well, have you communicated with her directly about her future, recently?

The President. No. We had an earlier meeting and agreed to come back after the inauguration and talk about this.

Q. You wouldn't like to tell us what job you're going to offer her, would you?

The President. No. But, as I said, the press is trying to pretend that they know what jobs I'm going to offer. No—and I haven't said anything to her or to anyone else about that particular subject. So, I'm as amazed at the stories that are appearing as I can be.

Trident Submarines

Q. Mr. President, you've said twice in recent days that the U.S. would abide by the unratified SALT II agreement. But, your Navy Secretary says he's waiting for a decision from you on the next action required to stay within SALT limits regarding Trident submarines. Have you made that decision, and has it been communicated to the Defense Department?

The President. No. What he's talking about is the fact that, as we continue with our Trident submarines, we are approaching a point at which, if we abide completely by the SALT II agreement, we would then have to find other weapons to eliminate. We have eliminated some in going forward with this, and we've run out of, I think, of the particular weapon that we were elimi-

nating—that we'll have to do that, or discuss whether we actually go above. And, in that regard, we have to take into consideration that the Soviet Union has, we believe, not stayed within the limits.

Now, do we want to join them in that and forget the whole idea, or do we want to talk to them about going forward. But we haven't made a decision because, and I say, that's down the road aways, and it's a few Trident submarines away from where we are now.

Q. Mr. President, we have about 4 minutes left, and Joe Ewalt has our next question.

Black Americans

Q. Sir, I'd like to go back to your relationship with black voters in the United States. While there obviously have been some gains, it's still a fact that black unemployment is about 2½ times what it is for whites. And there are virtually no blacks holding visible jobs in the executive branch. And we keep seeing these reports saying that your programs are hurting poor people, many of whom are black, and that just doesn't square with the statement that it's a misperception, that all the problems are a misperception.

The President. Well, there is a black in our Cabinet, and I had a meeting not too long ago with some 200 blacks in executive positions in our administration. And as Governor of California, I appointed more blacks to executive and policymaking positions than all the previous Governors of California put together.

So, I think that there is a lack of understanding or communication, for some, because there are many black groups and individuals who know what we're doing and who are highly supportive of us and of what we're doing. So, again, as I say, I hope we can get the message to the others what it is we're trying to accomplish.

With regard to unemployment, it is better than it has been in the past, and of the more than six million people who have obtained jobs in the last 4 years, over a million of them are black.

Q. Bob Ellison?

South African Apartheid Policy

Q. Mr. President, South African President P.W. Botha has indicated plans to change some aspects of the Government's apartheid policy. For example, limited political participation for blacks living outside the so-called homeland areas. What is your reaction to this? Do you consider this a major, minor, or no step at all toward freedom for the black majority?

The President. Bob, we feel that we are making some progress there. They know of our feeling about the repugnance of apartheid, and we think that there are many people in South Africa who want that system changed. And we think that we are giving them encouragement in our support of that position. And we are working steadily and quietly with them and are going to continue to do that.

Nicaragua

Q. Mr. President, I'd like to go back to your answer about Nicaragua being a base for terrorism. You've said that American troops would not be involved in Central America, but if we started facing a terrorist threat from Nicaragua, couldn't you have a situation where you'd have to send in American troops?

The President. Well, a President should never say never, but I can tell you right now that we've never had any plans at all. We've realized that that would be counterproductive, even with regard to our friends in Latin America. So, we're continuing to work with the Contadora, we're continuing to work with the other Central American nations down there to be helpful. The Kissinger commission report, that called for aid that would be mainly social aid and economic aid and only military help in the line of training and arms and so forth and equipment. And that's still going to be our policy.

Visit to West Germany

Q. Mr. President, since you'll be in Bonn just before V–E Day, would you like to stay over in Europe to observe the anniversary and possibly observe it with the Soviets?

The President. No. I have agreed to stay beyond the summit meeting for a couple of days for a state visit, official state visit to Germany, to Western Germany. And that will be close enough to the time that, I think, that if there's any observance, it would be there and with our hosts, the German Government. And I have to tell you that I hope that, worldwide, the observance this time, of the end of World War II, will not be the rejoicing of a victory and recalling all of the hatred that went on at the time. I hope we'll recognize it now as the day that democracy and freedom and peace began, and friendship between erstwhile enemies.

Q. Mr. President, on that note, our time is just about up. Thanks for joining us today.

The President. Well, thank all of you.

Q. You've been listening to a conversation with President Reagan, an interview with correspondents from seven radio networks. This program has come to you live from the Roosevelt Room of the White House.

Note: The interview began at 12:30 p.m. in the Roosevelt Room at the White House.

Statement on the 132d Anniversary of the Birth of José Marti
January 28, 1985

I am pleased to note that today, January 28, is the 132d anniversary of the birth of the great Cuban patriot and author, José Marti. Nancy and I want to join with all those celebrating this important and inspiring event.

Throughout the struggle for freedom and democracy, men and women of extraordinary dedication have emerged to lead others in the pursuit of human dignity. José Marti was one of those heroes, and today we are proud to honor his numerous accomplishments on behalf of his fellow Cubans. His lifelong desire to see an independent Cuba, free from the tyranny of colonial domination, is an ideal that remains alive today for Cuban-Americans and all those who love freedom.

"Man loves liberty," he wrote, "even if he does not know he loves it. He is driven by it and flees from where it does not exist." It is because of Marti's lifelong commitment to freedom—of speech, of the press, and of political pluralism—that he is a symbol of the need for the unfettered flow of ideas. It

is for this reason that his name was chosen for the radio service that will broadcast to the people of Cuba, beginning in the near future.

José Marti was one of those giants who possessed numerous talents. As an orator, journalist, lawyer, novelist, and literary critic he was able to do much to enhance and further his people's rich cultural heritage. It is certain that he will be remembered by the freedom-loving people of our world as a pioneer and leader in the movement for true human liberation.

Designation of Senator William S. Cohen of Maine as an Alternate United States Member of the Roosevelt Campobello International Park Commission
January 28, 1985

The President today announced his intention to designate William S. Cohen, United States Senator from the State of Maine, to be an alternate member on the part of the United States on the Roosevelt Campobello International Park Commission. He will succeed James H. Rowe, Jr.

Senator Cohen was first elected to the U.S. House of Representatives in 1972, where he served until his election to the United States Senate in 1978. He is currently a member of the Senate Armed Services Committee and is chairman of the Subcom-

mittee on Seapower and Force Projection. He is a member of the Governmental Affairs Committee and chairman of the Subcommittee on the Oversight of Government Management. Additionally, he is a member of the Select Committee on Intelligence.

He graduated from Bowdoin College (B.A., 1962) and Boston University Law School (LL.B., 1965). He is married, has two children, and resides in McLean, VA. He was born August 28, 1940, in Bangor, ME.

Proclamation 5294—Import Quotas on Certain Sugar Containing Articles
January 28, 1985

By the President of the United States of America

A Proclamation

1. By Proclamation No. 5071 of June 28, 1983, I imposed, on an emergency basis, import quotas on certain sugars, blended sirups, and sugars mixed with other ingredients. These quotas were to be effective pending my further action after receipt of

the report and recommendations of the United States International Trade Commission (hereinafter "Commission") on this matter pursuant to Section 22 of the Agricultural Adjustment Act of 1933, as amended (7 U.S.C. 624) (hereinafter "Section 22"). The Commission has made its investigation and reported its findings to me.

2. The Secretary of Agriculture has ad-

vised me that he has reason to believe that certain other sugar containing articles, not covered by Proclamation No. 5071, are practically certain to be imported into the United States under such conditions and in such quantities as to materially interfere with the price support operations being conducted by the Department of Agriculture for sugar cane and sugar beets.

3. I agree that there is reason for such belief by the Secretary of Agriculture and, therefore, I am requesting the Commission to make an investigation with respect to this matter pursuant to Section 22, and report its findings and recommendations to me as soon as possible.

4. The Secretary of Agriculture has also determined and reported to me with regard to the sugar containing articles described in paragraph (B) below that a condition exists which requires emergency treatment and that the import quotas hereinafter proclaimed should be imposed without awaiting the report and recommendations of the Commission.

5. On the basis of the information submitted to me, I find and declare that:

(a) On the basis of the report and recommendations of the Commission, the articles described in items 958.10 and 958.15 of Part 3 of the Appendix to the Tariff Schedules of the United States (TSUS) are practically certain to be imported into the United States under such conditions and in such quantities as to materially interfere with the price support operations of the Department of Agriculture for sugar cane and sugar beets;

(b) A condition exists requiring the imposition, on an emergency basis, of the import quotas hereinafter proclaimed with regard to the sugar containing articles described in paragraph (B) below; and

(c) The representative period within the meaning of the first proviso to subsection (b) of Section 22 is, for imports of the articles described in TSUS items 958.10 and 958.15, the years 1978–81, during which there were no imports of the articles described in TSUS items 958.10 and 958.15; and for imports described in paragraph (B) below, the years 1978–81.

Now, Therefore, I, Ronald Reagan, President of the United States of America, by the authority vested in me by Section 22 of the Agricultural Adjustment Act of 1933, as amended, and the Constitution and Statutes of the United States, do hereby proclaim as follows:

(A) TSUS items 958.10 and 958.15 of Part 3 of the Appendix to the Tariff Schedules of the United States are continued in effect subject to the provisions of paragraph (C) below;

(B) Part 3 of the Appendix to the Tariff Schedules of the United States is amended by inserting in numerical sequence following TSUS item 958.15 the following items:

Item	Articles	Quota quantity	Effective period

During the period beginning on the effective date of this proclamation through September 30, 1985, if the respective aggregate quantity specified below for one of the numbered classes of articles has been entered no article in such class may be entered during the remainder of such period:

Articles containing sugars derived from sugar cane or sugar beets, whether or not mixed with other ingredients, except articles within the scope of TSUS items 958.10, 958.15 or other import restrictions provided for in part 3 of the Appendix to the Tariff Schedules of the United States:

958.16	Provided for in TSUS item 156.45	1,000 short tons....................................	Until 10/1/85
958.17	Provided for in TSUS item 183.01	2,500 short tons....................................	Until 10/1/85
958.18	Provided for in TSUS item 183.05	28,000 short tons	Until 10/1/85

Beginning October 1, 1985, whenever, in any 12-month period beginning October 1 in any year, the respective aggregate quantity specified below for one of the numbered classes of articles has been entered, no article in such class may be entered, during the remainder of such period:

Item	Articles	Quota quantity	Effective period

Articles containing sugars derived from sugar cane or sugar beets, whether or not mixed with other ingredients, except articles within the scope of TSUS items 958.10, 958.15 or other import restrictions provided for in part 3 of the Appendix to the Tariff Schedules of the United States:

958.20	Provided for in TSUS item 156.45		3,000 short tons
958.25	Provided for in TSUS item 183.01		7,000 short tons
958.30	Provided for in TSUS item 183.05		84,000 short tons

(C) The provisions of this proclamation shall terminate upon the filing of a notice in the *Federal Register* by the Secretary of Agriculture that the Department of Agriculture is no longer conducting a price support program for sugar cane and sugar beets.

(D) Pending Presidential action upon receipt of the report and recommendations of the Commission referenced in paragraph 3 above, the quotas established by paragraph (B) of this proclamation shall apply to articles entered, or withdrawn from warehouse, for consumption on or after the effective date of this proclamation. However, those quotas shall not apply to articles entered, or withdrawn from warehouse, for consumption if application of those quotas would prevent the entry, or withdrawal from warehouse, for consumption of the articles and if the articles were (1) exported from the country of origin prior to the effective date of this proclamation and (2) imported directly into the United States, as determined by the appropriate customs officials, in accordance with the criteria set forth at 19 CFR 10.174, 10.175 (1984).

(E) This proclamation shall be effective as of 12:01 a.m. Eastern Standard Time on the day following the date of its signing.

In Witness Whereof, I have hereunto set my hand this 28th day of Jan., in the year of our Lord nineteen hundred and eighty-five, and of the Independence of the United States of America the two hundred and ninth.

RONALD REAGAN

[*Filed with the Office of the Federal Register, 4:19 p.m., January 28, 1985*]

Executive Order 12501—Arctic Research
January 28, 1985

By the authority vested in me as President by the Constitution and laws of the United States of America, including the Arctic Research and Policy Act of 1984 (Title I of Public Law 98–373) ("the Act"), it is hereby ordered as follows:

Section 1. Establishment of Arctic Research Commission. There is established the Arctic Research Commission.

Sec. 2. Membership of the Commission.

(a) The Commission shall be composed of five members appointed by the President, as follows:

(1) three members appointed from among individuals from academic or other research institutions with expertise in areas of research relating to the Arctic, including the physical, biological, health, environmental, social, and behavioral sciences;

(2) one member appointed from among indigenous residents of the Arctic who are representative of the needs and interests of Arctic residents and who live in areas directly affected by Arctic resources development; and

(3) one member appointed from individuals familiar with the Arctic and representative of the needs and interests of private industry undertaking resource development in the Arctic.

The Director of the National Science Foundation shall serve as a nonvoting *ex officio* member of the Commission. The President shall designate a Chairperson from among the five voting members of the Commission.

(b) In making initial appointments to the Commission, the President shall designate one member to serve for a term of two years, two members to serve for terms of three years, and two members to serve for terms of four years as provided by Section 103(c) of the Act. Upon the expiration of these initial terms of office, the term of office of each member of the Commission shall be four years.

(c) Each of the Federal agencies represented on the Interagency Committee established by Section 7 of this Order may designate a representative to participate as an observer with the Commission. These representatives shall report to and advise the Commission on the activities of their agencies relating to Arctic research.

Sec. 3. Meetings of the Commission.

The Commission shall meet at the call of the Chairman or a majority of its members. The Commission annually shall conduct at least one public meeting in the State of Alaska.

Sec. 4. Functions of the Commission.

(a) The Commission shall:

(1) develop and recommend an integrated national Arctic research policy;

(2) assist, in cooperation with the Interagency Arctic Research Policy Committee established by Section 7 of this Order, in establishing a national Arctic research program plan to implement the Arctic research policy;

(3) facilitate cooperation between the Federal government and State and local governments with respect to Arctic research;

(4) review Federal research programs in the Arctic and suggest improvements in coordination among programs;

(5) recommend methods to improve logistical planning and support for Arctic research as may be appropriate;

(6) suggest methods for improving efficient sharing and dissemination of data and information on the Arctic among interested public and private institutions;

(7) offer other recommendations and advice to the Interagency Arctic Research Policy Committee as it may find appropriate; and

(8) cooperate with the Governor of the State of Alaska, and with agencies and organizations of that State which the Governor may designate, with respect to the formulation of Arctic research policy.

(b) Not later than January 31 of each year, the Commission shall:

(1) submit to the President and Congress a report describing the activities and accomplishments of the Commission during the immediately preceding fiscal year; and

(2) publish a statement of goals and objectives with respect to Arctic research to guide the Interagency Arctic Research Policy Committee in the performance of its duties.

Sec. 5. Responsibilities of Federal Agencies.

(a) The heads of Executive agencies shall, to the extent permitted by law, and in accordance with Section 105 of the Act, provide the Commission such information as it may require for purposes of carrying out its functions.

(b) The heads of Executive agencies shall, upon reimbursement to be agreed upon by the Commission and the agency head, permit the Commission to utilize their facilities and services to the extent that the facilities and services are needed for the establishment and development of an Arctic research policy. The Commission shall take every feasible step to avoid duplication of effort.

(c) All Federal agencies shall consult with the Commission before undertaking major Federal actions relating to Arctic research.

Sec. 6. Administration of the Commission.

Members of the Commission who are otherwise employed for compensation shall serve without compensation for their work on the Commission, but may be allowed travel expenses, including per diem in lieu of subsistence, as authorized by law for persons serving intermittently in the government service. Members of the Commission who are not otherwise employed for compensation shall be compensated for each day the member is engaged in actual performance of duties as a member, not to exceed 90 days of service each calendar year, at a rate equal to the daily equivalent of the rate for GS–16 of the General Schedule.

Sec. 7. Establishment of Interagency Arctic Research Policy Committee. There is established the Interagency Arctic Research Policy Committee (the "Interagency Committee"). The National Science Foundation shall serve as lead agency on the Interagency Committee and shall be responsible for implementing Arctic research policy.

Sec. 8. Membership of the Interagency Committee.

The Interagency Committee shall be composed of representatives of the following Federal agencies or their designees:

(a) National Science Foundation;
(b) Department of Commerce;
(c) Department of Defense;
(d) Department of Energy;
(e) Department of the Interior;
(f) Department of State;
(g) Department of Transportation;
(h) Department of Health and Human Services;
(i) National Aeronautics and Space Administration;
(j) Environmental Protection Agency;
(k) Office of Science and Technology Policy; and
(l) any other Executive agency that the Director of the National Science Foundation shall deem appropriate. The Director of the National Science Foundation or his designee shall serve as Chairperson of the Interagency Committee.

Sec. 9. Functions of the Interagency Committee. (a) The Interagency Committee shall:

(1) survey Arctic research conducted by Federal, State, and local agencies, universities, and other public and private institutions to help determine priorities for future Arctic research, including natural resources and materials, physical and biological sciences, and social and behavioral sciences;

(2) work with the Commission to develop and establish an integrated national Arctic research policy that will guide Federal agencies in developing and implementing their research programs in the Arctic;

(3) consult with the Commission on:
(a) the development of the national Arctic

research policy and the 5-year plan implementing the policy;

(b) Arctic research programs of Federal agencies;

(c) recommendations of the Commission on future Arctic research; and

(d) guidelines for Federal agencies for awarding and administering Arctic research grants;

(4) develop a 5-year plan to implement the national policy, as provided in section 109 of the Act;

(5) provide the necessary coordination, data, and assistance for the preparation of a single integrated, coherent, and multiagency budget request for Arctic research, as provided in section 110 of the Act;

(6) facilitate cooperation between the Federal government and State and local governments in Arctic research, and recommend the undertaking of neglected areas of research;

(7) coordinate and promote cooperative Arctic scientific research programs with other nations, subject to the foreign policy guidance of the Secretary of State;

(8) cooperate with the Governor of the State of Alaska in fulfilling its responsibilities under the Act; and

(9) promote Federal interagency coordination of all Arctic research activities, including:

(a) logistical planning and coordination; and

(b) the sharing of data and information associated with Arctic research, subject to section 552 of title 5, United States Code.

(b) Not later than January 31, 1986, and biennially thereafter, the Interagency Committee shall submit to the Congress through the President a report concerning:

(1) its activities and accomplishments since its last report; and

(2) the activities of the Commission, detailing with particularity the recommendations of the Commission with respect to Federal activities in Arctic research.

Sec. 10. Public Participation. The Interagency Committee will provide public notice of its meetings and an opportunity for the public to participate in the development and implementation of national Arctic research policy.

Sec. 11. Administration of Interagency Committee.

Each agency represented on the Committee shall, to the extent permitted by law and subject to the availability of funds, provide the Committee with such administrative services, facilities, staff, and other support services as may be necessary for effective performance of its functions.

RONALD REAGAN

The White House,
January 28, 1985.

[Filed with the Office of the Federal Register, 4:20 p.m., January 28, 1985]

Executive Order 12502—Chemical Warfare Review Commission
January 28, 1985

By the authority vested in me as President by the Constitution and the laws of the United States of America, and in order to establish, in accordance with the provisions of Section 1511 of the Department of Defense Authorization Act, 1985 (Public Law 98–525), and of the Federal Advisory Committee Act, as amended (5 U.S.C. App. I), a Chemical Warfare Review Commission, it is hereby ordered as follows:

Section 1. Establishment. (a) There is established the Chemical Warfare Review Commission. The Commission shall be composed of no more than nine members appointed or designated by the President. The membership shall be bipartisan.

(b) The President shall designate a Chairman from among the members of the Commission.

Sec. 2. Functions. (a) The Commission shall review the overall adequacy of the chemical warfare posture of the United States with particular emphasis on the question of whether the United States should produce binary chemical munitions. In conducting its review, the Commission shall take account of the considerations specified in Section 1511 of Public Law 98–525.

(b) The Commission shall make sequential reports to the President on its findings and recommendations, by February 15, 1985, as to the need to maintain a chemical retaliatory stockpile; by March 1, 1985, as to the adequacy of the current stockpile if one has been determined to be needed; and by March 15, 1985, as to whether the United States should produce binary chemical munitions or undertake other actions.

Sec. 3. Administration. (a) The heads of Executive agencies shall, to the extent permitted by law, provide the Commission such information as it may require for purposes of carrying out its functions.

(b) Members of the Commission shall serve without any additional compensation for their work on the Commission. However, members appointed from among private citizens may be allowed travel expenses, including per diem in lieu of subsistence, as authorized by law for persons serving intermittently in the government service (5 U.S.C. 5701–5707), to the extent funds are available therefor.

(c) The Secretary of Defense shall provide the Commission with such administrative services, facilities, staff and other support services as may be necessary. Any expenses of the Commission shall be paid from such funds as may be available to the Secretary of Defense.

Sec. 4. General. (a) Notwithstanding any other Executive order, the functions of the President under the Federal Advisory Committee Act, as amended, except that of reporting to the Congress, which are applicable to the Commission, shall be performed by the Secretary of Defense, in accordance with guidelines and procedures established by the Administrator of General Services.

(b) The Commission shall terminate 30 days after submission of its report, or on September 30, 1985, whichever date is earlier.

RONALD REAGAN

The White House,
January 28, 1985.

[Filed with the Office of the Federal Register, 4:21 p.m., January 28, 1985]

Executive Order 12503—Presidential Commission on Outdoor Recreation Resources Review
January 28, 1985

By the authority vested in me as President by the Constitution and statutes of the United States of America, including the Federal Advisory Committee Act, as amended (5 U.S.C. App. I), and in order to create an advisory commission to review outdoor recreation resources, it is hereby ordered as follows:

Section 1. Establishment. (a) There is hereby established the Presidential Commission on Outdoor Recreation Resources Review.

(b) The Commission shall be composed of not more than 15 members appointed or designated by the President from among the private sector, the Legislative branch of the Federal government, recreational and other service organizations, and State and local governments. The President shall designate a Chairman and Vice Chairman from among the members of the Commission.

Sec. 2. Functions. (a) The Commission shall review existing public outdoor recreation policies, programs, and opportunities provided by the Federal government, State and local governments, and private organizations and entities and shall review privately provided outdoor recreation resources to the extent that they affect the demand for public outdoor recreation resources. The Commission shall, consistent with the need for fiscal economy at all levels of government, make recommendations to the President concerning the outdoor recreation resources, programs, and opportunities that will ensure the future availability of outdoor recreation for the American people. In making its recommendations, the Commission shall assess the budgetary and regulatory cost increases or cost savings of its proposals, and shall, to the extent possible, utilize such studies, data, and reports previously prepared or under

preparation by Federal agencies, States, private organizations or other entities.

(b) In conducting its review, the Commission shall examine:

(1) existing outdoor recreation lands and resources and the land and resource base necessary for future outdoor recreation;

(2) the roles of the Federal, State, county, and municipal governments in providing outdoor recreation opportunities, protecting outdoor recreation resources, and meeting anticipated outdoor recreation conditions;

(3) the role of the private sector in meeting present and future outdoor recreation needs, and assess the potential for cooperation between the private sector and government in providing outdoor recreation opportunities and protecting outdoor recreation resources;

(4) the relationship between outdoor recreation and personal and public health, the economy, and the environment;

(5) the future needs of outdoor recreation management systems, including qualified personnel, technical information, and anticipated financial needs;

(6) the relationship of outdoor recreation to the broader range of recreation pursuits and its implications for the supply of and demand for outdoor recreation resources and opportunities;

(7) underlying social, economic, and technological factors that are likely to affect the demand for and supply of outdoor recreation resources, including trends in disposable income and demographic characteristics of the United States;

(8) the findings and recommendations of the National Urban Recreation Study (1978), the Third Nationwide Outdoor Recreation Plan (1979), the Forest and Rangeland Renewable Resources Planning Act—Assessment Supplement (1984), and

other relevant Federal survey and planning activities.

(c) The Commission may conduct public hearings and otherwise secure information and expressions of public opinion on recreation issues, policies and programs, and anticipated national, regional, State, and local recreation needs and concerns.

(d) The Commission shall submit its report and recommendations to the President not later than twelve months after the date of this Order.

Sec. 3. Administration. (a) The heads of Executive agencies shall, to the extent permitted by law, provide the Commission with such information as may be necessary for the effective performance of its functions.

(b) Members of the Commission shall serve without compensation for their work on the Commission. Members appointed from among private citizens of the United States may be allowed travel expenses, including per diem in lieu of subsistence, as authorized by law for persons serving intermittently in the government service (5 U.S.C. 5701–5707).

(c) The Secretary of the Interior shall, to

the extent permitted by law, provide the Commission with such administrative services, facilities, staff, and other support services as may be necessary for the effective performance of its functions.

Sec. 4. General. (a) Notwithstanding any other Executive order, the functions of the President under the Federal Advisory Committee Act, as amended, which are applicable to the Commission, except that of reporting annually to the Congress, shall be performed by the Secretary of the Interior, in accordance with guidelines and procedures established by the Administrator of General Services.

(b) The Commission shall terminate 30 days after submission of its report, or March 1, 1986, whichever sooner occurs.

RONALD REAGAN

The White House,
January 28, 1985.

[Filed with the Office of the Federal Register, 3:37 p.m., January 29, 1985]

Note: The Executive order was released by the Office of the Press Secretary on January 29.

Remarks by Telephone to the Annual Convention of the National Association of Home Builders in Houston, Texas
January 29, 1985

The President. Hello, Peter Herder.

Mr. Herder. Good morning, Mr. President. We have—*[applause]*. That's our 1,500-member board of directors, and most of them are very optimistic.

The President. Well, I'm glad to hear that. And, Peter, it's good to talk to you, and greetings to all of you members of the National Association of Home Builders.

I'm glad that Sam Pierce represented me at your meeting yesterday, and I hope he brought you my very best wishes.

Mr. Herder. Yes, he did, did a great job.

The President. Good.

Well, last year was a good year for America, and I know it was for housing. In fact, 1984 was, as I understand it, the best year

for builders since 1979.

Mr. Herder. That's right. It was a very good year for us.

The President. Well, your industry played an integral part in the national economy. Your contributions to the revitalization of America's fundamental values of personal initiative and perseverance have been especially significant.

And today, our economy is showing solid growth. Just as of about 55 minutes ago, here in Washington, we released some figures that over the past four quarters productivity has increased at the highest rate since 1971, and manufacturing productivity in those same four quarters was at the highest rate since 1973.

More people are working now than at any time in our history, and those people are keeping more of what they earn. And I think that's good news for your industry.

Our efforts to lower taxes, cut government spending, and rid our economy of inflation have paid off. And I really appreciate the role that your association, the National Association of Home Builders, played to make our program succeed.

And, Pete, I want to give a special thanks to you for your leadership and support. And I appreciate your participation in the Housing commission. We're implementing those recommendations.

And, also, I send greetings and congratulations to your new incoming president, John Koelemij, who met yesterday—I met with him here at a meeting on the deficit. John, we have a full platter of issues this year, and we're looking forward to your help and support.

Our primary goal for the second term is to ensure continuation of strong economc growth with low inflation and lower inter-

est rates. And to achieve this, we have to cut Federal spending to control the deficit.

We got into this deficit mess not because government collects too little in taxes, but because government spends too much. And this year we're planning to take bold steps to remedy the situation and to start a trend of declining deficits as a percentage of gross national product.

You've helped us in the past, and I'm sure that we can count on you again. Let's finish the job we started in 1981, building an economy that keeps America strong.

Thank you for giving me this chance to be with you. I wish it could have been in person.

Mr. Herder. Thank you, Mr. President. Thank you for your commitment to homeownership. Thank you, and goodbye.

The President. Well, thank all of you. God bless you all. Goodbye.

Note: The President spoke at 10:55 a.m. from the Oval Office at the White House. In his remarks, the President referred to Secretary of Housing and Urban Development Samuel R. Pierce, Jr.

Proclamation 5295—American Heart Month, 1985
January 29, 1985

By the President of the United States of America

A Proclamation

Despite progress in many areas, cardiovascular disease remains this Nation's number one cause of death. The sad fact is that more than 40 million Americans have one or more forms of heart or blood vessel disease. Strokes afflict almost two million people annually. As many as 1.5 million persons will have a heart attack this year, and approximately 550,000 of them will die. In all, diseases of the heart and blood vessels will take the lives of almost one million of our fellow citizens—some of whom may be our family members, our friends and our co-workers.

Almost as many people will die from cardiovascular disease during 1985 as from

cancer, accidents, and all other causes combined. Economic losses will also run high. This Nation will spend an estimated $72 billion in 1985 for medical treatment, lost salaries, rehiring and training, and insurance and disability claims resulting from heart and blood vessel disease.

The American Heart Association, a not-for-profit volunteer health agency, and the Federal government, primarily through the National Heart, Lung and Blood Institute, are providing hope. In 1948, those two organizations joined forces to seek ways to reduce early death and disability from heart disease, stroke, and related disorders. Since then, much has been accomplished through research, professional and public education, and community service programs.

We have learned, for example, that maintaining proper nutrition, not smoking, and controlling high blood pressure can make a significant difference in the rate of incidence of these diseases. As a result, the death rates for heart attacks and strokes are much lower today than they were in 1948.

Even more progress should result from efforts by the Federal government and the American Heart Association to make everyone more aware of the dangers of smoking. Tougher labeling laws for cigarette packaging and advertising enacted last year by Congress will help. Research projects, such as the Coronary Primary Prevention Trials concluded in 1984, have given new impetus to the American Heart Association's longstanding finding that control of blood cholesterol decreases risk for heart attacks and strokes. The American Heart Association has taken major steps to inform the public about the significance of those test results, to influence Americans to adopt a prudent diet, and to encourage the efforts of scientists who are unlocking the mysteries of heart and blood vessel diseases.

Recognizing the need for all Americans to help in the continuing battle against cardiovascular disease, the Congress, by joint resolution approved December 30, 1963 (77 Stat. 843; 36 U.S.C. 169b), has requested the President to issue annually a proclamation designating February as American Heart Month.

Now, Therefore, I, Ronald Reagan, President of the United States of America, do hereby proclaim the month of February 1985 as American Heart Month. I invite the Governors of the States, the Commonwealth of Puerto Rico, the officials of other areas subject to the jurisdiction of the United States, and the American people to join me in reaffirming our commitment to the resolution of the nationwide problem of cardiovascular disease.

In Witness Whereof, I have hereunto set my hand this twenty-ninth day of January, in the year of our Lord nineteen hundred and eighty-five, and of the Independence of the United States of America the two hundred and ninth.

RONALD REAGAN

[*Filed with the Office of the Federal Register, 12:16 p.m., January 30, 1985*]

Note: The proclamation was released by the Office of the Press Secretary on January 30.

Proclamation 5296—National Day of Prayer, 1985
January 29, 1985

By the President of the United States of America

A Proclamation

The history of the American Nation is one of conviction in the face of tyranny, courage in the midst of turmoil and faith despite the roils of doubt and defeatism. Throughout our 208 years of freedom, the people of the United States have drawn upon the lessons learned at the dawn of our liberty by acting "with a firm reliance on Divine Providence" and expressing gratitude for the many blessings a loving God has showered upon us.

These lessons have not been learned and honored without difficulty. During the Revolutionary War, the Continental Congress proclaimed a National Day of Prayer each year for eight years, a practice that ended with the winning of the peace in 1783. Decades later, while the Civil War raged, this observance was renewed by Abraham Lincoln. Responding to a Senate Resolution requesting the President to designate and set apart a day for prayer and humiliation, Lincoln said that "intoxicated with unbroken success, we have become too self-sufficient to feel the necessity of redeeming and preserving grace, too proud to pray to the God that made us." He then called the Nation to prayer.

Our very existence as a free Nation, then, has provided potent witness to the efficacy of prayer. Grover Cleveland, in his First

Inaugural Address, said, "Above all, I know that there is a Supreme Being who rules the affairs of men and whose goodness and mercy have always followed the American people, and I know He will not turn from us now if we humbly and reverently seek His powerful aid." Franklin D. Roosevelt, in his Fourth Inaugural Address, expressed the same thought, "The Almighty God has blessed our land in many ways . . . So we pray to Him now for the vision to see our way clearly—to see the way that leads to a better life for ourselves and for all our fellow men—to the achievement of His will, to peace on earth."

Today our Nation is at peace and is enjoying prosperity, but our need for prayer is even greater. We can give thanks to God for the ever-increasing abundance He has bestowed on us, and we can remember all those in our society who are in need of help, whether it be material assistance in the form of charity or simply a friendly word of encouragement. We are all God's handiwork, and it is appropriate for us as individuals and as a Nation to call to Him in prayer.

By joint resolution of the Congress ap-proved April 17, 1952, the recognition of a particular day set aside each year as a National Day of Prayer has become a cherished national tradition. Since that time, every President has proclaimed an annual National Day of Prayer, resuming the tradition begun by the Continental Congress.

Now, Therefore, I, Ronald Reagan, President of the United States of America, do hereby proclaim May 2, 1985, as a National Day of Prayer. I call upon the citizens of this great Nation to gather together on that day in homes and places of worship to pray, each after his or her own manner, for unity of the hearts of all mankind.

In Witness Whereof, I have hereunto set my hand this twenty-ninth day of January, in the year of our Lord nineteen hundred and eighty-five, and of the Independence of the United States of America the two hundred and ninth.

RONALD REAGAN

[*Filed with the Office of the Federal Register, 12:17 p.m., January 30, 1985*]

Note: The proclamation was released by the Office of the Press Secretary on January 30.

Appointment of Alfred H. Kingon as Cabinet Secretary and Deputy Assistant to the President
January 30, 1985

The President today announced his intention to appoint Alfred H. Kingon to be Cabinet Secretary and Deputy Assistant to the President. Mr. Kingon will succeed Craig L. Fuller, who will assist the Chief of Staff in coordinating the transition for the next few months before returning to the private sector.

Mr. Kingon has been serving as Assistant Secretary of the Treasury for Policy Planning and Communications since March 1984. Prior to that, he served as Assistant Secretary of Commerce for International Economic Policy (1983–1984).

Previously he was with Macro Communications, Inc., in New York City, serving as editor in chief of Financial World (1973–1983) and Saturday Review (1980–1982) and editor of Money & Credit (1970–1973). He was portfolio manager for the Businessman's Fund in 1969–1971; security analyst, vice president, and director of research for Scheinman, Hochstin & Trotta in 1967–1969; and investment adviser with Burnham & Co. in 1963–1967. He was a member of the executive committee of the President's Private Sector Survey for Cost Control Task Force (1983–1984) and the President's National Productivity Advisory Committee (1982–1983).

Mr. Kingon graduated from Union College (B.S., 1953) and attended New York University Graduate School of Business Administration in 1956–1961. He is married, has one child, and resides in Washington, DC. He was born May 11, 1931, in Brooklyn, NY.

Appointment of Thomas C. Dawson as Executive Assistant to the Chief of Staff and Deputy Assistant to the President
January 30, 1985

The President today announced his intention to appoint Thomas C. Dawson to be Executive Assistant to the Chief of Staff and Deputy Assistant to the President.

Mr. Dawson was appointed Assistant Secretary of the Treasury for Business and Consumer Affairs in January 1984. In this position he serves as the Secretary's principal adviser on Treasury issues effecting business, trade and professional organizations and groups. Prior to becoming Assistant Secretary he served, since 1981, as the Deputy Assistant Secretary for Developing Nations, with responsibility for economic and financial relations with developing countries, including debt rescheduling and International Monetary Fund programs.

Before joining the Treasury Department, Mr. Dawson was active in the Reagan/Bush campaign, working with the planning task force on examination of government organization. From November 1980 to February 1981, he was executive assistant to Transition and White House Personnel Director E. Pendleton James, where he assisted in the screening, evaluation, and selection of Cabinet and sub-Cabinet appointees.

From 1978 to 1980, Mr. Dawson was affiliated with McKinsey & Co., focusing on international business operations for corporate clients.

Mr. Dawson was a Foreign Service officer for 5 years in the Office of Investment Affairs as staff assistant to the Under Secretary of State for Economic Affairs, William Casey, and with the U.S. Embassy in Brazil, where he was responsible for analysis of Brazilian foreign trade performance and prospects.

Mr. Dawson earned his M.B.A. from the Stanford University Graduate School of Business, graduating in the top 5 percent of his class. He has a bachelor's degree, with honors, in economics from Stanford University and has done graduate work in economics at Woodrow Wilson School of Public and International Affairs at Princeton University.

Mr. Dawson is married to the former Moira Haley. They have three children, Thomas, Andrew, and Catherine.

Appointment of David L. Chew as Staff Secretary and Deputy Assistant to the President
January 30, 1985

The President today announced his intention to appoint David L. Chew to be Staff Secretary and Deputy Assistant to the President.

Mr. Chew has been serving as Senior Deputy Comptroller of the Currency for Policy and Planning since April 1984. In that capacity he has been responsible for OCC's analysis of the economic, structural, and deregulatory policy issues affecting the national banking system. In addition, he has overseen the Office's bank chartering and licensing functions, including applications for national bank charters, branches, mergers, and other banking activities. He has been responsible for the Office's financial management, strategic planning, and the computer and systems modernization programs. From 1981 to April 1984, Mr. Chew served as Executive Assistant to the Secretary of the Treasury. He previously was vice president of Citizen's Choice, a public interest organization affiliated with the U.S. Chamber of Commerce.

In 1979 Mr. Chew served as administrative assistant to Senator Robert Dole, and prior to that, he was director of research for Timmons and Co., a consulting firm in Washington, DC.

Mr. Chew received a B.S.F.S. in Foreign Service from Georgetown University in 1974. He resides with his wife, Sheila Burke, in Washington, DC.

Appointment of Christopher Hicks as Deputy Assistant to the President for Administration
January 30, 1985

The President today announced his intention to appoint Christopher Hicks to be Deputy Assistant to the President for Administration.

Mr. Hicks has served since April 1984 as the Executive Assistant to the Secretary of the Treasury and as Executive Secretary for the Treasury Department. He joined the Department in December 1983 as Executive Secretary. Previously Mr. Hicks, 34, was the Associate Director (Economic and Transportation Group) of the Office of Presidential Personnel at the White House. From March 1981 to May 1982, he was Associate Counsel in the Office of the Counsel to the President.

Prior to joining the Reagan administration, Mr. Hicks was a trial attorney with the firm of Fulbright & Jaworski in Houston, TX. He also served for a year as a law clerk to the Supreme Court of Texas. During the 1980 Presidential campaign, Mr. Hicks was an advanceman for the Reagan/Bush campaign.

Mr. Hicks received his bachelor of arts degree from Colorado College in Colorado Springs, CO, in 1972 and earned his J.D. from Southern Methodist University in 1977. At SMU he was an editor of the law review, an officer of the student government, and a member of Barristers (an honorary scholastic/service organization).

Mr. Hicks resides in Maryland with his wife, Elizabeth Bellamy Hicks, and son, Austin Bellamy Hicks.

Nomination of John F.W. Rogers To Be an Assistant Secretary of the Treasury
January 30, 1985

The President today announced his intention to nominate John F.W. Rogers as Assistant Secretary of the Treasury for Management. This is a new position created by Public Law 98–594. The position of Assistant Secretary of the Treasury for Administration (an SES position) is currently held by Terrence C. Golden. Mr. Golden has been recommended for a Presidential appointment.

Mr. Rogers has been a member of the White House staff since 1981 and now serves as Assistant to the President for Management and Administration and Director, Office of Administration. In addition to his present responsibilities, he recently served as director and general manager of the Committee for the 50th American Presidential Inaugural.

Prior to joining the White House staff, he was executive assistant to the director of the White House transition team, and prior to the transition served as assistant to the president for administration at the American Enterprise Institute for Public Policy Research (AEI). He previously worked as a researcher in the White House during the Ford administration.

Mr. Rogers is a graduate of George Washington University. He is a member of the board of trustees of the National Building Museum and represents the President on the board of the United States Capitol Historical Society. He is also a member of the Advisory Council on Historic Preservation. He was born in Seneca Falls, NY, on April 15, 1956.

Nomination of Margaret DeBardeleben Tutwiler To Be an Assistant Secretary of the Treasury
January 30, 1985

The President today announced his intention to nominate Margaret DeBardeleben Tutwiler as Assistant Secretary of the Treasury for Public Affairs and Public Liaison.

Miss Tutwiler has served as a member of the White House staff since 1981 and is now Deputy Assistant to the President for Political Affairs. In addition to her White House responsibilities, she recently served as director of public liaison of the Committee for the 50th American Presidential Inaugural.

Prior to joining the White House staff, Miss Tutwiler was director of scheduling for Vice President Bush in the election campaigns of 1979–1980. In 1977–1978 she was a public affairs representative for the National Association of Manufacturers. She participated in the 1976 Presidential campaign as executive director of the President Ford Committee of Alabama.

Miss Tutwiler was born in Birmingham, AL, on December 28, 1950, and received her bachelor of arts degree in political science from the University of Alabama in 1973.

Appointment of Mervin J. Flander as a Member of the Committee for Purchase from the Blind and Other Severely Handicapped
January 30, 1985

The President today announced his intention to appoint Mervin J. Flander to be a member of the Committee for Purchase from the Blind and Other Severely Handicapped for a term expiring December 21, 1989. This is a reappointment.

Mr. Flander is chief of the Bureau of Services to the Blind for the State of Nevada in Carson City, NV. He graduated from Drake University (B.A.; J.D., 1953).

He is married, has four children, and resides in Carson City, NV. He was born April 25, 1926, in Sigourney, IA.

Remarks at the Annual National Prayer Breakfast
January 31, 1985

Thank you, ladies and gentlemen. It's very good to be here again. I look forward to this meeting every year more than any other. And I want to personally welcome our guests from other countries to Washington, our Capital. We're happy to have you here with us.

I would like to say something more about this National Prayer Breakfast and how it came about. We've already heard some of the history from representatives of the two Houses. But I think some of the story may be unknown, even to a few of our hosts from the Congress here today. Back in 1942, at the height of World War II, a handful of Senators and Congressmen discussed how they might be of personal and spiritual support to one another. If they could gather now and then to pray together, they might discover an added resource, which would be of sustaining value. And so, very informally, they began to meet.

In time, in both the House and Senate groups, some informal rules evolved. The members would meet in the spirit of peace and in the spirit of Christ, but they need not be Christians. All members would be welcome, regardless of their political or religious affiliation. Sincere seekers, as well as the deeply devoted, all on a common journey to understand the place of faith in their lives and to discover how to love God and one's fellow man.

They wouldn't publicize the meetings, nor would they use them for any kind of political gain. The meetings would be off the record. No one would repeat what was said. And, above all, the members could talk about any personal problem on which they needed guidance, any sadness for which they needed prayers.

Well, the two groups met quietly and with no fanfare for 10 years. And then President Eisenhower, as we've been told, came into the story. In 1952, when he was running for President, one of his most important strategists, and a fine man—was a fine man, a Senator named Frank Carlson. I guess he was kind of Ike's Paul Laxalt. [*Laughter*] One night, out on the campaign trail, Eisenhower confided to Senator Carlson that during the war, when he was commanding the Allied forces in Europe, he had had a spiritual experience. He had felt the hand of God guiding him and felt the presence of God. And he spoke of how his friends had provided real spiritual strength in the days before D-day. Senator Carlson

said he understood, that he himself was getting spiritual strength from members of a little prayer group in the Senate.

A few months later, just a few days after he was sworn in as President, Eisenhower invited Frank Carlson over to the White House. He said, "Frank, this is the loneliest house I've ever been in. What can I do?" And Carlson said, "I think this may be a good time for you to come and meet with our prayer group." And Eisenhower did. In 1953 he attended the first combined Prayer Breakfast. And Presidents have been coming here for help ever since. And here I am.

The prayer meetings in the House and Senate are not widely known by the public. Members of the media know, but they have, with great understanding and dignity, generally kept it quiet. I've had my moments with the press, but I commend them this day, for the way they've worked to maintain the integrity of this movement.

Some wonderful things have come out of this fellowship. A number of public figures have changed as human beings, changed in ways I'd like to talk about, but it might reveal too much about the membership. Fellowships have begun to spring up throughout the Capitol. They exist now in all three branches of the Government, and they have spread throughout the capitals of the world, to parliaments and congresses far away.

Since we met last year, members of the fellowship throughout the world have begun meeting with each other. Members of our Congress have met with leaders and officials from other countries, approaching them and speaking to them, not on a political level, but a spiritual level.

I wish I could say more about it, but it's working precisely because it is private. In some of the most troubled parts of the world, political figures who are old enemies are meeting with each other in a spirit of peace and brotherhood. And some who've been involved in such meetings are here today.

There are many wars in the world and much strife, but these meetings build relationships which build trust, and trust brings hope and courage.

97

I think we often forget in the daily rush of events the importance in all human dealings of the spiritual dimension. There are such diversities in the world, such terrible and passionate divisions between men, but prayer and fellowship among the great universe of God's believers are the beginning of understanding and reconciliation. They remind us of the great, over-arching things that really unite us.

In this job of mine, you meet with so many people, deal with so many of the problems of man, you can't help being moved by the quiet, unknown heroism of all kinds of people—the Prime Minister of another country who makes the bravest of brave decisions that's right, but may not be too popular with his constituency; or the fellow from Indiana who writes to me about some problems he's been having and what he did to solve them.

You see the heroism and the goodness of man and know in a special way that we are all God's children. The clerk and the king and the Communist were made in His image. We all have souls, and we all have the same problems. I'm convinced, more than ever, that man finds liberation only when he binds himself to God and commits himself to his fellow man.

Will you forgive me if I repeat a story that I told here last year? It's a story that goes back to the fourth century. There was an Asian monk living in a little remote village, tending his garden, spending much of his time in prayer. And then one day, he thought he heard the voice of God telling him to go to Rome. Well, he obeyed the Lord's command, and he set out on foot. And many weary weeks later, he arrived in the capital city of the Roman Empire at the time of a great festival that was going on in Rome. And the little monk followed the crowd that was surging down the streets into the Colosseum. He saw the gladiators come forth, stand before the Emperor, and say, "We who are about to die salute you." And, then, he realized these men were going to fight to the death for the entertainment of the crowd. And he cried out, "In the name of Christ, stop!" And as the games began, he fought his way down through the crowd, climbed over the wall and dropped to the floor of the arena. And when the crowd saw this tiny figure making his way out to the gladiators, saying, "In the name of Christ, stop," they thought it was part of the entertainment. And they began laughing. But when they realized it wasn't, then their laughter turned to anger. And as he was pleading with the gladiators to stop, one of them plunged a sword into his body, and he fell to the sand of the arena, and as he was dying, his last words were, "In the name of Christ, stop." Then a strange thing began to happen. The gladiator stood looking at the tiny figure lying there in the sand. A hush fell over the Colosseum. Way up in the upper tiers, a man stood and made his way to the exit. Others began to follow. In dead silence, everyone left the Colosseum. And that was the last battle to the death between gladiators in the Roman Colosseum. Never again in the great stadium did men kill each other for the entertainment of the crowd. And all because of one tiny voice that could hardly be heard above the tumult. One voice that spoke the truth in God's name.

I believe we witness here this morning that that voice is alive today. May it continue to rise above the tumult and be heard.

Thank you so much. And God bless you.

Note: The President spoke at 9:00 a.m. in the International Ballroom at the Washington Hilton Hotel. He was introduced by Representative Ralph Regula of Ohio.

Nomination of Donna M. Alvarado To Be Director of ACTION
January 31, 1985

The President today announced his intention to nominate Donna M. Alvarado to be Director of the ACTION agency. She would succeed Thomas W. Pauken.

Since 1983 she has been serving as Deputy Assistant Secretary of Defense (Equal Opportunity and Safety Policy) in the Office of the Assistant Secretary of Defense for Manpower, Installations and Logistics. Previously, she was counsel to the United States Senate Committee on the Judiciary, Subcommittee on Immigration and Refugee Policy, in 1981–1983; assistant director, Office of Policy Coordination, Office of the President-elect (1980–1981); and research associate for the United States Select Commission on Immigration and Refugee Policy in 1980–1981.

She is a member of the President's Task Force on Legal Equity for Women and serves as executive vice president of the Mexican-American Women's Association. She is also a member of the Republican National Hispanic Assembly.

She graduated from Ohio State University (B.A., 1969; M.A., 1970) and the University of Oklahoma (Ph.D., 1980). She was born November 8, 1948, in Washington, DC, and now resides in Alexandria, VA.

Statement on the Mutual and Balanced Force Reduction Negotiations
January 31, 1985

Today in Vienna, members of NATO and the Warsaw Pact will resume their efforts to negotiate reductions of conventional forces in central Europe. These talks on mutual and balanced force reductions (MBFR) are an integral and important part of our commitment to achieve genuine progress in arms reductions—conventional, chemical, and nuclear.

It is clear that a militarily significant, verifiable MBFR agreement is possible. Last April, the NATO participants tabled a major initiative designed to break the East-West deadlock. We remain hopeful of a constructive reply from the Warsaw Pact participants.

Last month, the NATO alliance in its ministerial communique expressed the continuing Western commitment to do everything possible to achieve a verifiable agreement reducing conventional forces to parity at lower levels. Such an agreement would enhance confidence, improve military stability, and reduce the risk of war in Europe. On its return to Vienna, the United States delegation will continue to do its part to achieve such an agreement.

Appointment of Joseph W. Canzeri as a Member of the American Battle Monuments Commission
January 31, 1985

The President today announced his intention to appoint Joseph W. Canzeri to be a member of the American Battle Monuments Commission. He will succeed Lawrence A. Wright.

Mr. Canzeri is president of the Canzeri Co. in Washington, DC. He served at the White House as Assistant to the President and Assistant to the Deputy Chief of Staff in 1981–1982. Previously, he was tour director of the 1980 Reagan Presidential campaign; personal assistant to Nelson A. Rockefeller in 1976–1979; assistant to Vice President Rockefeller for special events in 1974–1976; and assistant to the Governor of New York in 1966–1972.

He received a degree in hotel administration from Paul Smith's College in 1953. He served in the United States Army in 1949–1951. He is married, has one child, and resides in Washington, DC. He was born May 16, 1930, in Schuylerville, NY.

Nomination of Two Members of the Mississippi River Commission
January 31, 1985

The President today announced his intention to nominate the following individuals to be members of the Mississippi River Commission. Brig. Gen. Thomas Allen Sands will be President of the Commission.

Thomas Allen Sands, Brigadier General, United States Army, would succeed Maj. Gen. William Edgar Read. He is Commanding General of the U.S. Army Engineering Division, Lower Mississippi Valley, in Vicksburg, MS. He graduated from the United States Military Academy (B.S.) and Texas A&M University (M.S.). He is married, has two children, and resides in Vicksburg, MS. He was born June 7, 1935, in Columbia, TN.

Robert Joseph Dacey, Brigadier General, United States Army, would succeed Maj. Gen. Richard Samuel Kem. He is Commanding General of the United States Army Engineer Division, Southwestern, Dallas, TX. He graduated from Norwich University (B.S.), the University of Missouri (B.S.), and George Washington University (M.A.). He is married, has two children, and resides in Dallas, TX. He was born May 15, 1935, in Watertown, NY.

Nomination of Two Members of the National Council on the Handicapped
January 31, 1985

The President today announced his intention to nominate the following individuals to be members of the National Council on the Handicapped:

Justin W. Dart, Jr., for a term expiring September 17, 1987. This is a reappointment. Mr. Dart is active as a volunteer with the National League of Disabled. In 1966–1981 he was involved in an independent living program involving teaching, guidance, and career planning for more than 45 disadvantaged and disabled persons. He graduated from the University of Houston (B.S., 1953; M.A., 1954). He is married, has five children, and resides in Fort Davis, TX. He was born August 29, 1930, in Chicago, IL.

Jeremiah Milbank, for a term expiring September 17, 1986. He would succeed Carmine R. Lavieri. Mr. Milbank is president of ICD International Center for the Disabled in New York City. He graduated from Yale University (B.A., 1942) and Harvard Business School (M.B.A., 1948). He has four children and resides in Greenwich, CT. He was born March 24, 1920, in New York, NY.

Message on the Observance of National Afro-American (Black) History Month, February 1985
January 31, 1985

On February 1st we begin the Fifty-Ninth Annual Black History Month, a national celebration of the role of Black Americans in all segments of life in this nation and of Black culture around the globe.

This year's Black History Month theme, "The Afro-American Family: Historical Strengths for the New Century" reflects my belief that if families are strengthened, other social ills will be lessened. It is in the home that we learn respect for authority, the importance of protecting the weak, a sense of honor, and justice.

If families are the building blocks of society—then society has a great stake in sound families. That is why black families throughout this great nation can be a powerful, organizing theme for America's social policies.

It is a very special privilege for me to call on the people of the United States to join in this important time of exploring, learning, appreciating, and saluting all that Black Americans have done to help build our country.

RONALD REAGAN

Executive Order 12504—Protection of Semiconductor Chip Products
January 31, 1985

By the authority vested in me as President by the Constitution and laws of the United States of America, including the Semiconductor Chip Protection Act of 1984 (17 U.S.C. 901 *et seq.*) and in order to provide for the orderly implementation of that Act, it is hereby ordered that, subject to the authority of the Director of the Office of Management and Budget under Executive Order No. 11030, as amended, requests for issuance by the President of a proclamation extending the protection of Chapter 9 of title 17 of the United States Code against unauthorized duplication of semiconductor chip products to foreign nationals, domiciliaries, and sovereign authorities shall be presented to the President through the Secretary of Commerce in accordance with such regulations as the Secretary may, after consultation with the Secretary of State, prescribe and cause to be published in the *Federal Register*.

RONALD REAGAN

The White House,
January 31, 1985.

[*Filed with the Office of the Federal Register, 11:03 a.m., February 1, 1985*]

Proclamation 5297—Modification of Tariffs on Certain Sugars, Sirups, and Molasses
January 31, 1985

By the President of the United States of America

A Proclamation

1. Headnote 2 of Subpart A, Part 10, Schedule 1 of the Tariff Schedules of the United States (10 U.S.C. 1202), hereinafter referred to as the "TSUS," provides, in relevant part, as follows:

"(i) . . . if the President finds that a particular rate not lower than such January 1, 1968, rate, limited by a particular quota, may be established for any articles provided for in items 155.20 or 155.30, which will give due consideration to the interests in the United States sugar market of domestic producers and materially affected contracting parties to the General Agreement on Tariffs and Trade, he shall proclaim such particular rate and such quota limitation, . . ."

"(ii) . . . any rate and quota limitation so established shall be modified if the President finds and proclaims that such modification is required or appropriate to give effect to the above considerations; . . ."

2. I find that the modifications hereinafter proclaimed of the rates of duty applicable to items 155.20 and 155.30 of the TSUS give due consideration to the interests in the United States sugar market of domestic producers and materially affected contracting parties to the General Agreement on Tariffs and Trade.

Now, Therefore, I, Ronald Reagan, President of the United States of America, by authority vested in me by the Constitution and Statutes of the United States, including section 201 of the Trade Expansion Act of 1962, and pursuant to General Headnote 4 and Headnote 2 of Subpart A, Part 10, Schedule 1 of the TSUS, do hereby proclaim until otherwise superseded:

A. The rates of duty in rate columns 1 and 2 for items 155.20 and 155.30 of Subpart A, Part 10, Schedule 1 of the TSUS are modified and the following rates are established:

	Rates of duty	
	1	2
155.20	0.6625¢ per lb. less 0.009375¢ per lb. for each degree under 100 degrees (and fractions of a degree in proportion) but not less than 0.428125¢ per lb.	1.9875¢ per lb. less 0.028125¢ per lb. for each degree under 100 degrees (and fractions of a degree in proportion) but not less than 1.284375¢ per lb.
155.30	Dutiable on total sugars at the rate per lb. applicable under Item 155.20 to sugar testing 100 degrees..	Dutiable on total sugars at the rate per lb. applicable under Item 155.20 to sugar testing 100 degrees.

B. The provisions of this Proclamation shall apply to articles entered, or withdrawn from warehouse, for consumption on and after the date of this Proclamation.

In Witness Whereof, I have hereunto set my hand this 31st day of January, in the year of our Lord nineteen hundred and eighty-five, and of the Independence of the United States of America the two hundred and ninth.

RONALD REAGAN

[*Filed with the Office of the Federal Register, 11:02 a.m., February 1, 1985*]

Message to the Congress Transmitting a Report on Soviet Noncompliance With Arms Control Agreements
February 1, 1985

To the Congress of the United States:

During 1984, at the request of the Congress, I forwarded two reports to the Congress on arms control compliance. The first, forwarded last January, was an in-depth analysis of seven specific issues of violations or probable violations by the Soviet Union of arms control obligations and commitments. The second report, forwarded in October, was an advisory study prepared independently by the General Advisory Committee on Arms Control and Disarmament.

These reports indicate that there is cause for serious concern regarding the Soviet Union's conduct with respect to observance of arms control agreements.

In the FY-1985 Defense Authorization Act and the Conference Report on that Act, the Congress called for additional classified and unclassified reports regarding a wide range of questions concerning the Soviet Union's compliance with arms control commitments. The Administration is responding to these requests by providing both classified and unclassified reports which update the seven issues initially analyzed in the January 1984 report, and analyze a number of additional issues.

In this unclassified report the United States Government reaffirms the conclusions of its January 1984 report that the USSR has violated the Helsinki Final Act, the Geneva Protocol on Chemical Weapons, the Biological and Toxin Weapons Convention, and two provisions of SALT II: telemetry encryption and ICBM modernization. The United States Government also reaffirms its previous conclusions that the USSR has probably violated the SS–16 deployment prohibition of SALT II and is likely to have violated the nuclear testing yield limit of the Threshold Test Ban Treaty. In addition, the United States Government has determined that the USSR has violated the ABM Treaty (through the siting, orientation and capability of the Krasnoyarsk Radar), violated the Limited Test Ban Treaty, and violated the SALT II provision prohibiting more than one new type of ICBM, and probably violated the ABM Treaty restriction on concurrent testing of SAM and ABM components. Evidence regarding the USSR's compliance with the ABM Treaty provision on component mobility was determined to be ambiguous. In addition, the United States Government is concerned about Soviet preparations for a prohibited territorial ABM defense. Further, the USSR was determined to be currently in compliance with those provisions of the SALT I Interim Agreement and its implementing procedures that deal with reuse of dismantled ICBM sites and with the reconfiguration of dismantled ballistic missile launching submarines.

Beyond the issues that are treated in the unclassified report released today, there are other compliance issues that will not be publicly disclosed at this time but which remain under review. As we continue to work on these issues, we will brief and consult with the Congress in detail and will, to the maximum extent possible, keep the public informed on our findings.

In order for arms control to have meaning and credibly contribute to national security and to global or regional stability, it is essential that all parties to agreements fully comply with them. Strict compliance with all provisions of arms control agreements is fundamental, and this Administration will not accept anything less. To do so would undermine the arms control process and damage the chances for establishing a more constructive US-Soviet relationship.

As I stated last January, Soviet noncompliance is a serious matter. It calls into question important security benefits from arms control, and could create new security risks. It undermines the confidence essential to an effective arms control process in the future. With regard to the issues analyzed in the January 1984 report, the Soviet Union has thus far not provided satisfactory explanations nor undertaken corrective actions sufficient to alleviate our concerns. The United States Government has vigorously pressed, and will continue to press, these compliance issues with the Soviet Union through diplomatic channels.

Our approach in pursuing these issues with the Soviet Union is to ensure that both the letter and intent of treaty obligations and commitments will be fulfilled. To this end the Administration is: analyzing further issues of possible noncompliance; as noted above, seeking from the Soviet Union through diplomatic channels explanations, clarifications, and, where necessary, corrective actions; reporting on such issues to the Congress; and taking into account in our defense modernization plans the security implications of arms control violations. At the same time, the United States is continuing to carry out its own obligations and commitments under relevant agreements. Our objectives in the new negotiations which begin in March are to reverse the erosion of the ABM Treaty and to seek equitable, effectively verifiable arms control agreements which will result in real reductions and enhance stability. While all of these steps can help, however, it is fundamentally important that the Soviet Union take a constructive attitude toward full compliance with all arms control obligations and commitments.

The Administration and the Congress have a shared interest in supporting the arms control process. For this reason, increased understanding of Soviet violations or probable violations, and a strong Congressional consensus on the importance of compliance to achieving effective arms control, will strengthen our efforts both in the new negotiations and in seeking corrective actions from the Soviet Union.

I look forward to continued close consultation with the Congress as we seek to make progress in resolving compliance issues and in negotiating sound arms control agreements.

RONALD REAGAN

The White House,
February 1, 1985.

Note: The text of the President's unclassified report was included in the White House press release.

Radio Address to the Nation on the Fiscal Year 1986 Budget
February 2, 1985

My fellow Americans:

On Monday morning we will submit to the Congress our budget for fiscal year 1986. It is a budget that carries an enormous investment of human time and effort; indeed, I believe, the most exhaustive effort ever made to rein in government's chronic overspending. Every proposal is based on a careful review of what government should and should not do, what's worked and what hasn't, what we can and can no longer afford. Collectively, the more than 50 proposals we are making can stop the excessive growth of Federal spending in its tracks and put budget deficits on a permanent downward path.

We'll be going into details on Monday and asking Congress to join us in a strong bipartisan effort. But today I want to lay a few facts on the table, so you understand why some so-called solutions you will hear aren't solutions at all and also what all of us must do to cure government's overspending once and for all.

First, as surely as night follows day, you'll hear that we can't make lasting progress bringing deficits down until we agree to a tax increase. Wrong. Our problem isn't that you're paying too little taxes; it's that government is spending too much money. In the past 10 years, your tax revenues have grown by more than $400 billion, but spending by government has grown by almost 600 billion—40 percent more than revenues. And government spending has grown more than one-third faster than the growth of our economy. In other words, Washington's policy is: "Heads, I win; tails, you lose."

When your families do well, government spends and borrows. When you don't do well, government spends and borrows. Our future economic success depends on the economy growing faster than government spending. That's why raising taxes would boomerang. Economic growth would slow, revenues would decline, and the budget deficit would swell.

The second so-called solution you will hear is that lasting progress won't be made without deep cuts in defense. Wrong again. Defense spending accounts for less than 30 percent of our budget today—far less than 20 years ago. We've cut our planned defense buildup 3 years in a row and cut it again this year—and all this while our adversaries have raced ahead with the greatest military buildup in the history of man.

It's time everyone faced up to why government, for nearly 50 years, has been heading down a one-way street of overspending and rising public debt. Part of the spending is understandable—improved Social Security benefits for a growing elderly population, for example. But much of it results from the combination of special interest groups and flawed budget procedures. Our system of budgetmaking in the Congress practically guarantees spending growth, and this unsettles financial markets and helps keep interest rates from falling.

When government makes redistributing

income more important than producing it, people reallocate their energies from economic to political action. The growth in special interests, which many in Congress lament, parallels a pattern of government taking from some to give to others. It parallels the ability of special interests to lobby for benefits and override the national interest by concentrating great power on a small group of legislators. So, spending and taxes rise, and growth declines. That's why we have a rising national debt and a growing burden of paying interest on that debt.

Our challenge is to strive for the strongest possible level of economic growth while making sure spending by government remains well below that. To accomplish this, we're proposing three long-term reforms.

First, we want to reform the tax system, make it more fair and simple for all, so we can bring down tax rates for individuals and businesses, provide incentives for stronger growth, and thereby increase revenues to government.

Second, we want the Congress to pass a constitutional amendment mandating government spend no more than government takes in. I will urge the House of Representatives to follow the positive actions of the Senate and pass this long-overdue reform.

Third, we need passage of a line-item veto, so Presidents would have the power 43 Governors now have to veto individual items of wasteful overspending in appropriation bills.

We're doing a lot to bring down spending growth and keep our economy growing. We could do a lot more if we keep our eyes on the facts and work together.

Until next week, thanks for listening, and God bless you.

Note: The President spoke at 12:06 p.m. from Camp David, MD.

Letter Accepting the Resignation of James A. Baker III as Assistant to the President and Chief of Staff
February 1, 1985

Dear Jim:

It is with the deepest possible regret that I accept your resignation as Chief of Staff, effective February 3, 1985.

I've read that there are no indispensable men in politics but, during the past four years, you've come as close to being indispensable here in the White House as anyone I can imagine. In fact, I would not be inclined to let you leave at all if it weren't for the fact that you'll be just a short walk away dealing with some of the most crucial issues we will confront during the second term.

I'd like to make a list of the major decisions you've been involved in during the past four years, but what would I leave off? You've been deeply involved in the planning and presentation of all the major initiatives of my Administration, and it is due in great measure to your efforts that so many of them have been enacted into law. You've fought many battles on behalf of our principles, but even those who have opposed us offer willing testimony to your intelligence, your fairness and your integrity.

It's hard to believe—in view of the immense respect in which you are held in Washington—that you occupied your first high-level Federal job less than ten years ago. You have mastered the art of Washington politics, but your roots are still deep in the soil of Texas, and it was there that you learned the fundamental values that you and I share. You know that life can be hard and is always unpredictable, but you also know that Americans are a people who look forward to the future with optimism. That sense of optimism is the most important thing we have tried to restore to America during the past four years, and it has helped me more than I can say to have someone by my side who understands that bedrock faith in our nation's future as well as you do.

But this letter is starting to sound like you're leaving public service. Fortunately

105

for me, you're just moving across the street to be Secretary of the Treasury. I'll warn you right now that I'm going to keep on asking your advice on any and every issue that comes up during the next four years. So don't plan any long vacations until you check with me.

Nancy and I send you and Susan our warmest wishes for every future happiness.

Sincerely,

/S/RONALD REAGAN

February 1, 1985

Dear Mr. President:

I respectfully submit this letter of resignation as Chief of Staff and Assistant to the President, effective February 3, 1985.

You have accorded me the greatest privilege of my life: the honor of serving as your Chief of Staff over the past four years—years which historians will undoubtedly view as a period of much-needed and striking accomplishment. I know you are fond of saying that such achievements are a team effort, but if that is so, it is also true that rarely in our Nation's history has a team been so ably led and inspired.

In 1981, the spirit and the confidence of the American people were in decline. Our economy was stagnant, our defenses deteriorating, our values under siege at home, and our national prestige trampled abroad. Your leadership and courage have brought about a remarkable reversal of every one of those situations. Today, our economy is reinvigorated, and our defenses restored. We are also seeing new faith in our traditional values, and renewed respect for an America which again has the strength of will to uphold its interests. You have restored America's pride and confidence in itself.

Such were your tangible achievements. Yet there is one other, less tangible, but no less important point: by your success and personal example you have restored the potency, purpose and effectiveness of the Presidency. And now, by virtue of your overwhelming reelection victory last year, you are positioned to be the first President since Eisenhower to complete two successful terms.

I hope to contribute to a successful second term as your new Secretary of the Treasury. I am grateful that you saw fit to honor my desire to serve you in this capacity and I look forward to the challenges of the future with confidence and optimism.

Susan and the rest of my family agree that you have given us many fine and fond memories. In the years ahead, we will look back on this special time in our lives with a deep sense of appreciation and pride. You have my heartfelt thanks and my pledge of continued loyalty and service to you and your Administration.

With best wishes to you and Nancy,

Sincerely,

/S/JIM

Note: The letters were released by the Office of the Press Secretary on February 4.

Letter Accepting the Resignation of Richard G. Darman as Assistant to the President and Deputy to the Chief of Staff
February 1, 1985

Dear Dick:

It is with great regret, and a deep sense of personal gratitude for your four years' of service in the White House, that I accept your resignation as Assistant to the President, effective February 3, 1985.

Your abilities, your intelligence, and your willingness to work long hours are well-known in Washington because they have been your trademark for many years. With such an extraordinary combination of talents, there is no question in my mind that you could have been a success in any career you chose. But, while you have been successful in both the business and academic worlds, you have chosen to devote yourself instead to a career that has chiefly been oriented toward public service. Knowing you as I do, I know that it is your deep love of America, and your strong belief in its future greatness, that has impelled you to make this choice.

Like you, I can remember well the period in the late fifties and early sixties when America's self-confidence and optimism were almost palpable. We thought then that we could do anything we set our minds to. The years that followed brought pain, national division, and an uncharacteristic pessimism. They also brought a corrosive cynicism and despair in many quarters.

But I believe that we have made great progress during the past four years in bringing America back to its traditional optimism. And one of the reasons for our progress is the success we have had in reinvigorating the Presidency and once again offering a clear banner of leadership. Yet I'm not taking credit for this because I know how many of our policy decisions and legislative victories were crafted by groups of people working long hours—groups so many of which benefitted from your extraordinary personal contributions.

You designed and implemented the internal management systems which have helped to restore the efficiency and professionalism of the White House. That was an impressive accomplishment but you are probably better known for initiating and coordinating the White House Legislative Strategy Group, which helped achieve some of the most remarkable legislative victories of the first term. You contributed to virtually every central White House activity from communications planning and scheduling to preparing for Economic Summits; from overseeing Speechwriting and Research to coordinating the work of the Budget Review Board; from negotiating with the Congress to accompanying me on every major foreign and campaign trip of the first term. Last, but not least, you managed the seemingly endless flow of paper (alas) in and out of my office.

For these and many, many other contributions, I want to say a very warm "Thanks!" I'd like to tell you also that as

you assume the position of Deputy Secretary of the Treasury—serving in what will be your sixth Cabinet Department—you can lay off the 80-hour weeks you've been working for four years (without vacations). But I gave you that advice four years ago (when Jonathan was born), and you did not follow it—so I have no reason to believe you would follow it this time!

Instead, I'll just say that Nancy and I send you, Kath, Willy and Jonathan our very best wishes for every future success and happiness.

/S/RONALD REAGAN

January 31, 1985

Dear Mr. President,

The Senate has just voted to confirm your nomination of me to serve as Deputy Secretary of the Treasury. I am, of course, extremely pleased. I look forward to continued service in your Administration—and to the opportunity to try to help meet such exciting challenges as: improving the domestic tax system; strengthening the international economic system; and, in these and other ways, advancing the technological and economic growth that can contribute to creative human development. Please accept my thanks for affording me this outstanding opportunity.

But while I am grateful to have exciting new challenges, it is with an inescapable sense of at least partial regret that I resign from my current position. Like most Americans, I have a special respect for both you and the office of the Presidency. Unlike most, I have had, for the past four years, the privilege and opportunity to try to serve both you and the office directly. For that special privilege and rare opportunity I shall always be deeply grateful.

After countless hours and countless issues and countless wonderful moments, there is what seems an almost infinite range of points I might reflect upon. Trying to step back from it all—and sparing you the burden of my reflections!—I take the liberty of sharing but one general line of personal thought:

I was a seventeen year old freshman at Harvard when John F. Kennedy assumed the Presidency. For those of us who were the first of the "baby-boom" generation, it was a time of hope—and enormous confidence in both America's and humanity's potential. Yes, there was some of the naivety of youth. But even adjusting for that, it seemed entirely reasonable to think that America should reach for the stars—indeed, that America and Americans were specially destined to do so.

At the start of my senior year, President Kennedy was shot. We did not realize it quite then, but the shots that cracked the fall air shattered more than a young President's life. They halted the flow toward America's special destiny. Vietnam and Watergate followed. Confidence plummeted. America's sense of itself—and of the possible—contracted. And the Carter Presidency compounded the problems of eroding confidence and shrinking dreams.

Yet now, the words you made resonant ring true: "America is back." And the sense of *America* is no small thing. You are right to talk again of a "revolution of hope." And as important: you are believed. America *is* back. There is a renewed sense of her spe-cial mission—as a beacon of hope, a land of opportunity, a protector of freedom, a pioneer of new frontiers. Millions and millions of people feel again that wonderful sense of hope and promise that I felt years ago as a seventeen year old freshman.

You have given America back the best of her youthfulness—which in some sense we hope may be eternal. You have renewed America on the path toward her special destiny—giving all our lives the possibility of an extra dimension of meaning.

It is inconceivable to me how we could thank you enough for your historic contribution. And yet I must find a way not only to do that, but also to thank you for your having permitted me to play a small part in this process. I do not have words which seem adequate. I can only promise to serve with renewed dedication—and to hope that, by my actions, I may repay the debt I feel I owe, and prove to merit the trust you have reposed in me.

Yours, with deepest appreciation and respect,

/s/DICK

Note: The letters were released by the Office of the Press Secretary on February 4.

Proclamation 5298—Red Cross Month, 1985
February 2, 1985

By the President of the United States of America

A Proclamation

Whenever disaster strikes, Americans everywhere count on the American Red Cross for immediate response.

This past year, Red Cross volunteers aided victims of fires, tornadoes, floods, hurricanes, and other tragedies on more than 50,000 occasions. In the last six months, the American Red Cross has faced a special challenge. It mobilized its resources to help provide food and medical relief to 14 African nations suffering from a famine of mammoth proportions. By providing funds contributed by generous Americans and seeing to it that they are converted into food for the hungry, the Red Cross is fulfilling its humanitarian mission of helping those in distress.

The American Red Cross has handled this unprecedented challenge without sacrificing any of its ongoing responsibilities. Annually, Red Cross teaches millions of our fellow citizens vital lifesaving techniques in CPR, first aid, small craft operation, and water safety. Its thousands of volunteer donors provide blood to more than half of the Nation's medical facilities. Red Cross also serves the men and women of our Armed Forces and their families, furnishing financial assistance and handling emergency requests through its worldwide communications network.

What all this adds up to is an organization of Americans who have volunteered their money, their time, and their hearts to ensuring that all of us are provided with the most efficient and effective health and human services possible.

Now, Therefore, I, Ronald Reagan, President of the United States of America, and Honorary Chairman of the American National Red Cross, do hereby designate March 1985 as Red Cross Month, and I urge all Americans to give generous support to the work of their local Red Cross Chapter.

In Witness Whereof, I have hereunto set my hand this second day of February, in the year of our Lord nineteen hundred and eighty-five, and of the Independence of the United States of America the two hundred and ninth.

RONALD REAGAN

[*Filed with the Office of the Federal Register, 2:51 p.m., February 4, 1985*]

Note: The proclamation was released by the Office of the Press Secretary on February 4.

Memorandum Urging Support of the American National Red Cross
February 2, 1985

Memorandum for Heads of Executive Departments and Agencies
Subject: Red Cross Month, 1985

I have just issued a proclamation that designates March as Red Cross Month.

This has been an especially tragic year for hundreds of thousands of our fellow countrymen left destitute by disasters. To assist these victims, the Red Cross has spent a record amount of money for help and for disaster preparedness. As a recipient of blood voluntarily donated through the Red Cross, I know the value of its Blood Services and its efforts to ensure that we constantly have adequate supplies for the sick and injured. The Red Cross also provides help for men and women serving in our country's military forces, their families, and veterans. Millions of Americans are trained in first aid, water and boating safety, and health care through programs sponsored by the Red Cross. Our Nation's young people,

through Red Cross school programs, acquire leadership skills and learn the value of giving service to their communities.

Within the Federal government, the Red Cross is part of the Combined Federal Campaign. During the month of March, more than one-half of the Red Cross chapters nationwide will raise funds, while others will use this observance to inform the public about Red Cross services and to recruit new blood donors.

As President of the United States and Honorary Chairman of the American National Red Cross, I urge all civilian employees of the Federal government and members of the Armed Forces to support in every way possible this vital voluntary effort.

RONALD REAGAN

Note: The memorandum was released by the Office of the Press Secretary on February 4.

Message to the Congress Transmitting the Fiscal Year 1986 Budget
February 4, 1985

To the Congress of the United States:

In the past 2 years we have experienced one of the strongest economic recoveries of the post-war period. The prospect of a substantially brighter future for America lies before us. As 1985 begins, the economy is growing robustly and shows considerable upward momentum. Favorable financial conditions presage a continuation of the expansion. Production, productivity, and employment gains have been impressive, and inflation remains well under control. I am proud of the state of our economy. Let me highlight a few points:

• The economy expanded at a 6.8% rate in 1984 and at a 6% annual rate over the 2 years since the recession trough at the end of 1982—faster than any other upturn since 1951.

• Confidence in the economy has prompted business firms to expand their capital facilities. Real investment in new plant and equipment has grown 15.4% annually since the end of 1982—faster than in any other post-war recovery.

• The ratio of real investment to real GNP has reached its highest level in the post-war period.

• Industrial production is 23% above its level at the recession trough in November 1982—a greater advance than in any other recovery since 1958.

• Corporate profits have risen nearly 90% since the recession trough in 1982—the fastest 8-quarter increase in 37 years.

• Civilian employment has grown 7.2 million over the past 25 months and the number of unemployed has fallen by 3.7 million. In the last 4 months alone, more than 1.1 million Americans have found jobs.

• Inflation remains well under control. The December 1984 CPI was 4% higher than a year earlier, about a third of the rate of inflation this administration inherited. The GNP deflator, the broadest measure of inflation, increased only 3.5% last year and at only a 2.4% annual rate in the fourth quarter.

• The prime rate of interest is now only half of what it was when I took office.

Contrast our current circumstances with the situation we faced just 4 years ago. Inflation was raging at double-digit rates. Oil prices had soared. The prime rate of interest was over 20%. The economy was stagnating. Unemployment had risen sharply and was to rise further. America's standing in world opinion was at low ebb.

All that, mercifully, is behind us now. The tremendous turnaround in our fortunes did not just happen. In February 1981, I presented the four fundamentals of my economic program. They were:

• Reducing the growth of overall Federal spending by eliminating activities that are beyond the proper sphere of Federal Government responsibilities and by restraining the growth of spending for other activities.

• Limiting tax burdens to the minimum levels necessary to finance only essential government services, thereby strengthening incentives for saving, investment, work, productivity, and economic growth.

• Reducing the Federal regulatory burden where the Federal Government intrudes unnecessarily into our private lives, the efficient conduct of private business, or the operations of State and local governments.

• Supporting a sound and steady monetary policy, to encourage economic growth and bring inflation under control.

Four Years of Accomplishment

These policies were designed to restore economic growth and stability. They succeeded.

The past 4 years have also seen the beginning of a quiet but profound revolution in the conduct of our Federal Government. We have halted what seemed at the time an inexorable set of trends toward greater and greater Government intrusiveness, more and more regulation, higher and higher taxes, more and more spending, higher and higher inflation, and weaker and weaker defense. We have halted these trends in our first 4 years.

• The rate of Federal spending growth was out of control at 17.4% a year in 1980. Under my budget proposals the growth of programmatic spending—that is, total Federal spending except for debt service—will be zero next year—frozen at this year's levels.

• Further, spending will grow only 30% over the 4 years from 1982 to 1986, compared to its record pace of 66% between 1977 and 1981, and this despite legislated additions to my program and the needed rebuilding of our defense capabilities.

• The Federal tax system was changed for the better—marginal tax rates were reduced and depreciation reform introduced. These reforms were designed to increase incentives for work, training and education, saving, business growth, and capital expansion. Tax loopholes have been closed, improving the equity of the system.

• Domestic spending, which previously grew faster than any other major part of the budget (nearly four-fold in real terms between 1960 and 1980), will have been virtually frozen from 1981 to 1985.

• Our defense capabilities are now getting back to a level where we can protect our citizens, honor our commitments to our allies, and participate in the long-awaited arms control talks from a position of respected strength.

• Federal credit programs, which had also grown out of control, have been cut back, and their management has been vastly improved.

• The rapid growth of regulations and red tape has also been halted. The number of Federal rules published by agencies has fallen by over 35% during the past 4 years, and many unnecessary old rules have been eliminated. For the first time, the Federal Register of new regulatory actions has grown shorter for 4 consecutive years; it is now 41% shorter than it was in 1980.

• Major management improvement initiatives are underway that will fundamentally change the way the Federal Government operates. The President's Private Sector Survey on Cost Control has completed its report, and many of its recommendations are included in this budget. The President's Council on Integrity and Efficiency has reported $46 billion in improved use of funds through reduction of waste and fraud.

• The Federal nondefense work force has been reduced by over 78,000.

The proposals contained in this budget will build on the accomplishments of the last 4 years and put into action a philosophy of government that is working and that has received the overwhelming endorsement of the American people.

The 1986 Budget Program

If we took no action to curb the growth of spending, Federal outlays would rise to over a trillion dollars in 1986. This would result in deficits exceeding $200 billion in each of the next 5 years. This is unacceptable. The budget I propose, therefore, will reduce spending by $51 billion in 1986, $83 billion in 1987, and $105 billion in 1988. Enactment of these measures would reduce the deficit projected for 1988 to $144 billion—still a far cry from our goal of a balanced budget, but a significant step in the right direction and a 42% reduction from the current services level projected for that year.

Last year my administration worked with Congress to come up with a downpayment on reducing the deficit. This budget commits the Government to a second installment. With comparable commitments to further reductions in the next two budgets, and, I hope, other spending reduction ideas advanced by the Congress, we can achieve our goal in an orderly fashion.

The budget proposes a 1-year freeze in total spending other than debt service. This will be achieved through a combination of freezes, reforms, terminations, cutbacks, and management improvements in individual programs. For a number of reasons, a line-by-line budget freeze is not possible or desirable. Further, such an approach would assume that all programs are of equal importance. Taken together, the specific proposals in this budget hold total Federal spending excluding debt service constant in 1986 at its 1985 level.

The budget proposals provide for substantial cost savings in the medicare program, in Federal payroll costs, in agricultural and other subsidies to business and upper-income groups, in numerous programs providing grants to State and local governments, and in credit programs. A freeze is proposed in the level of some entitlement program benefits, other than social security, means-tested programs, and programs for the disabled, that have hitherto received automatic "cost-of-living adjustments" every year. The budget proposes further reductions in defense spending below previously reduced mid-year levels.

Despite the reforms of the past 4 years, our Federal tax system remains complex and inequitable. Tax rates are still so high that they distort economic decisions, and this reduces economic growth from what it otherwise could be. I will propose, after further consultation with the Congress, further tax simplification and reform. The proposals will not be a scheme to raise taxes—only to distribute their burden more fairly and to simplify the entire system. By broadening the base, we can lower rates.

THE BUDGET TOTALS

[In billions of dollars]

	1984 actual	1985 estimate	1986 estimate	1987 estimate	1988 estimate
Receipts	666.5	736.9	793.7	861.7	950.4
Outlays	851.8	959.1	973.7	1,026.6	1,094.8
Deficit (−)	−185.3	−222.2	−180.0	−164.9	−144.4

Note: Totals include outlays that are off-budget under current law, proposed to be included on-budget.

There will be substantial political resistance to every deficit reduction measure proposed in this budget. Every dollar of current Federal spending benefits someone, and that person has a vested self-interest in seeing these benefits perpetuated and expanded.

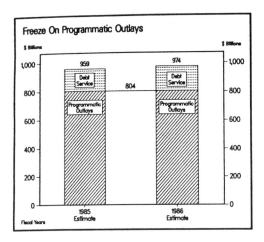

Prior to my administration, such interests

had been dominant and their expectations and demands had been met, time and time again.

At some point, however, the question must be raised: "Where is the political logrolling going to stop?" At some point, the collective demands upon the public Treasury of all the special interests combined exceed the public's ability and willingness to pay. The single most difficult word for a politician to utter is a simple, flat "No." The patience of the American people has been stretched as far as it will go. They want action; they have demanded it.

We said "no" frequently in 1981, and real spending for discretionary domestic programs dropped sharply. But we did not accomplish enough. We now have no choice but to renew our efforts with redoubled vigor. The profusion of Federal domestic spending programs must be reduced to an acceptable, appropriate, and supportable size.

It will require political courage of a high order to carry this program forward in the halls of Congress, but I believe that with good faith and goodwill on all sides, we can succeed. If we fail to reduce excessive Federal benefits to special interest groups, we will be saddled either with larger budget deficits or with higher taxes—either of which would be of greater harm to the American economy and people.

1986 Management and Regulatory Program

Not only must both the scope and scale of Federal spending be drastically cut back to reduce the deficit: we must also institute comprehensive management improvements and administrative reforms to make sure that we use available funds as efficiently as possible.

Tough but necessary steps are being taken throughout the Federal Government to reduce the costs of management and administration. Substantial savings in overhead costs have been achieved under provisions of the Deficit Reduction Act of 1984. A 5% Federal civilian employee salary cut has been proposed; a 10% reduction in administrative overhead has been ordered; termination of programs that have outlived their usefulness is proposed; outmoded, inefficient agency field structures that have evolved over the past half-century are being consolidated and streamlined to take advantage of efficiencies made possible by modern transportation, communication, and information technology.

Administration of Federal agencies is being made more efficient through the adoption of staffing standards, automation of manual processes, consolidation of similar functions, and reduction of administrative overhead costs. A program to increase productivity by 20% by 1992 in all appropriate Government functions is being instituted, as are improved cash and credit management systems and error rate reduction programs.

This management improvement program will result in a leaner and more efficient Federal structure and will be described in a management report that I am submitting to the Congress for the first time shortly after my annual budget submission.

We have also made a great deal of progress in reducing the costs imposed on businesses and State and local governments by Federal regulations. These savings are estimated to total $150 billion over a 10-year period. We have reduced the number of new regulations in every year of my first term and have eliminated or reduced paperwork requirements by over 300 million hours each year. In addition, the regulations are more carefully crafted to achieve the greatest protection for the least cost, and wherever possible to use market forces instead of working against them.

A recent Executive Order will strengthen the executive branch coordination that has made these accomplishments possible. For the first time, we will publish an annual program of the most significant regulatory activities, including those that precede the publication of a proposed rule. This will give Congress and the public an earlier opportunity to understand the administration's regulatory policies and priorities.

Conclusion

The key elements of the program I set out 4 years ago are in place and working well. Our national security is being restored; so, I am happy to report, is our economy. Growth and investment are healthy; and inflation, interest rates, tax rates, and unemployment are down and can be reduced further. The proliferation of unnecessary regulations that stifled both economic growth and our individual freedoms has been halted. Progress has been made toward the reduction of unwarranted and excessive growth in domestic spending programs.

But we cannot rest on these accomplishments. If we are to attain a new era of sustained peace, prosperity, growth, and freedom, Federal domestic spending must be brought firmly under control. This budget presents the steps that I believe must be taken. I do not exclude other economies that Congress may devise, so long as they do not imperil my fundamental constitutional responsibilities to look after the national defense and the general welfare of the American people.

Let us get on with the job. The time for action is now.

RONALD REAGAN

February 4, 1985.

Note: The President's message was printed in the report entitled "Budget of the United

States Government, Fiscal Year 1986—Executive Office of the President, Office of

Management and Budget" (Government Printing Office).

Remarks to Congressional Leaders During a White House Briefing on the Fiscal Year 1986 Budget
February 4, 1985

Well, thank you very much and good morning and welcome to the White House. And thank you for all joining us.

In a moment, you're going to hear from Treasury Secretary Baker and OMB Director Stockman. And by the way, Jim, this will be the first chance I'll have had to introduce you by your new title. Congratulations, Mr. Secretary.

But Jim and Dave will fill you in on the specifics. But before they do, permit me to give you a brief overview.

I think we can all agree that our number one priority is a growing and vibrant economy which creates jobs and offers increasing opportunity for all Americans. We've seen the remarkable potential for growth in our economy, that had for too long been held down by the heavy hand of government— by high taxation, excessive Federal spending, and overregulation.

It's time to follow through with the policies that have brought us success. We must now build on our accomplishments to secure a more permanent and far-reaching prosperity, and that means we must work together to continue to liberate the creative energies of our nation by cutting the tax rates still further, while making our tax system fairer and simpler and less susceptible to abuse.

And it also means that we can't wait a moment longer to get our Federal budget under control. If we lose the budget battle, if we allow all the lessons of all the decades of unchecked government spending to go unheeded, then, I believe, we'll consign ourselves and our children to the tyranny of a government that respects no boundaries and knows no limits. But if we win, we'll show ourselves and the world that in America the Government is still the servant of the people, not their master.

And, thus, the budget that I'm sending to the Congress this year is $974 billion, including debt service costs—only about 1½ percent higher than the fiscal year '85 level. The fiscal year '86 budget calls for an absolute freeze on overall government program spending. However, some programs cannot be frozen, so we must find savings in other areas. First, I'm proposing structural reforms and other economies in a wide range of programs, from entitlements to government lending. And second, there are a number of areas of discretionary spending, such as Federal overhead costs, where I'm confident the Government can get by on less next year. And the third, we're requesting cancellation of a long list of programs that, I believe, the taxpayers should not be subsidizing. I'm confident that many of these activities currently being subsidized could be efficiently provided in the private sector, without government assistance.

The defense of our nation is the one budget item which cannot be dictated solely by domestic considerations. Despite severe constraints on our budget, we must respond to the unprecedented military buildup of the Soviet Union, the largest military buildup in world history. And, unfortunately, we've had to start from a weakened position, brought on by long years of neglect and underfunding, and we still have a ways to go.

Ultimately, our security and our hopes for success at the arms reduction talks hinge on the determination that we show here, to continue our program to rebuild and refortify our defenses. In all my years in public office, both as Governor of California and now as President, I don't think I've ever submitted a budget that wasn't controversial, and I'm sure this one will be no exception. Nevertheless, I believe it's possible that working together, in a spirit of compromise and cooperation, we can bring our budget under control without damaging our economy or endangering our national security.

As we lighten government's burden on our private sector through budget control, we should remember that no amount of cutting and no paring will help if we, at the same time, add to the burden by raising taxes. All we should be doing is shifting the load from one saddlebag to another.

Raising taxes would be an admission of failure. It would announce to the country that we didn't have the political will and courage to do what we know is right to get our economic house in order. We've come to recognize an essential truth about our economy: that incentives are the key that unlocks prosperity.

When the Government takes away incentives to work and save, the economy goes flat—millions are thrown out of work and government revenues plunge. But when we restore incentives, as we did with our cuts in personal income tax rates, the economy comes back to life and government revenues rise.

It's no accident that during fiscal year 1984, the first full year that all three installments of our income tax cuts were in place, Federal revenues actually rose 7 percent in

real terms. So, we already have dramatic revenue increases, and the last thing we want to do is derail this impressive engine of economic growth.

Later during this session of the Congress, we'll be submitting to you our plan for tax reform. And I'm confident that, once again, lower rates and new incentives for the American people will keep us on the track of vigorous economic growth and, therefore, expand government revenues.

We have a truly exciting chance to change the course of our nation's history, to return our country to the optimism and prosperity that we knew two decades ago. There's a lot of hard work before you, the Members of the 99th Congress. But in taking the positive steps necessary to keep the economy on the road to progress on the all-important issues of budget control and tax reform, you have the overwhelming support of the American people, and that's all that really matters.

So, good luck. Thank you. God bless you. And I will turn the meeting over to those who are going to give you more detailed briefings on our budget.

Note: The President spoke at 10:32 a.m. in the East Room at the White House. Prior to the briefing, the President signed and presented copies of the budget to the bipartisan congressional leadership in the Oval Office.

Remarks to Business and Trade Representatives During a White House Briefing on the Fiscal Year 1986 Budget
February 4, 1985

Good afternoon, and welcome to the White House.

I have to tell you, with the South Lawn out here alternately being white and then green—and I'm so desperate to see it green permanently—that if it doesn't stop snowing that way, I'm going to have the House painted green—[*laughter*]—have a different welcome here.

Well, I want to start by thanking all of you for the support that you've given us

over the last 4 years. Back in the beginning of our first term, it was in large measure the support from the business community, from other groups such as yours that enabled us to pass the dramatic tax cuts of '81 and the budget cuts, which lifted the pall of malaise from our economy and put us back in the path of strong, noninflationary growth.

We need your help again. We have before us an historic opportunity to build on the achievements of our first term and secure the foundation of economic prosperity. The American economy is growing faster and stronger than many ever dreamed possible. The resilience with which we snapped back from more than a decade of overtaxation, excessive spending, and stifling regulation demonstrates the tremendous vitality of the American community—or the American economy, I should say. I guess both are all right.

We must continue to lift the burdens of wasteful government and tap the energy that still lies dormant in our economy. We must move ahead with a comprehensive tax reform that would liberate incentives by cutting rates still further, while making the tax system fairer and simpler for every American. And we must finally, once and for all, gain control of our runaway budget.

If we deal successfully with those major tasks—budget and tax reform—I'm convinced that economic growth in the second half of the eighties will exceed the record of strong, sustained expansion sparked by the Kennedy tax cuts two decades ago.

Earlier today, I presented our new fiscal '86 budget to the Congress, many of them sitting right here where you're sitting. And I had my brand new Treasury Secretary, Jim Baker, and David Stockman[1] behind me, as well as my Secret Service detail, so I wasn't too worried. [*Laughter*]

Needless to say, I didn't expect immediate and unanimous approval from Congress. But I believe that working together we have what it takes to get our budget under control, without either damaging the economy or endangering the national security.

Basically, we're proposing a freeze for the overall budget, excluding uncontrollable debt service costs. Our budget is $974 billion. That's only about 1½ percent higher than the fiscal '86 ['85] level.

We've asked for structural reforms and other economies in a wide range of programs, from entitlements to government lending. We've requested real cuts in certain areas of discretionary spending, such as Federal overhead costs, where I'm sure the

Government can get by on less next year. And there are a number of programs that we suggest canceling entirely. Some of these, such as Amtrak, could be run much more efficiently in the private sector.

The defense of our nation is the one budget item which cannot be dictated by domestic considerations. Despite severe constraints on our budget, we must respond to the unprecedented military buildup of the Soviet Union, the largest military buildup in world history. Unfortunately, we had to start from a weakened position, brought on by long years of neglect and underfunding, and we still have a ways to go.

You might be interested to know that the Scriptures are on our side in this—Luke 14:31, in which Jesus in talking to the disciples spoke about a king who might be contemplating going to war against another king, with his 10,000 men. But he sits down and counsels how good he's going to do against the other fellow's 20,000 and then says he may have to send a delegation to talk peace terms. Well, I don't think we ever want to be in a position of only being half as strong and having to send a delegation to negotiate under those circumstances—peace terms—with the Soviet Union. So, ultimately, our security and our hopes for success at the arms reduction talks hinge on the determination that we show here to continue our program to rebuild and refortify our defenses.

In this session of the Congress, we'll also be presenting our bill for an historic, comprehensive reform of our tax structure. Although we'll be pursuing budget reform and tax reform separately, they're each vital and necessary complements of the other. They're the twin elements of our program to keep our economy growing, creating jobs, and spreading opportunity.

We've seen how high taxes will choke off incentive and drive the economy into a downward spiral of disinvestment and unemployment. The mirror image of that is the expanding cycle of prosperity that lowering taxes brings, where more investment brings more growth; and more growth brings more jobs, which means more people paying taxes.

We've already seen this work. It's no acci-

---

[1] *Director of the Office of Management and Budget.*

dent that during fiscal 1984, the first full year that all three installments of our income tax cuts were finally in place, Federal revenues actually rose 7 percent in full terms.

Now is the time to get control of our budget, cut tax rates still further, and keep the cycle of prosperity going. Budget and tax reform won't be easy, and we're going to need every ounce of support that you can give us in the months ahead to move this through the Congress. We're counting on you. And with your help, we can make the frustration, the stagnation, and the de-

cline of only 4 years ago a distant memory.

Together, we can open the way to a bright future of continuing prosperity. Together, we can really make history. We can get back to a principle of government not spending more than government takes in.

So, I thank you, and God bless you all. And I wish I were just saying, permanently, thank you and that we've done the job, but thank you and stay with us. Thank you.

Note: The President spoke at 2:03 p.m. in the East Room at the White House.

Remarks at the Annual Convention of the National Religious Broadcasters
February 4, 1985

The President. Thank you very much. Thank you very much. Brandt Gustavson, Dr. Ben Armstrong, and all of you distinguished ladies and gentlemen, it's good to be here.

I've been coming to this annual convention since 1982, and it's always been one of the high spots of the year. This year, with the inaugural and the State of the Union and our arms control preparations and our work on reforming the tax system, I had to discipline myself and say no to a few things that I enjoy, but I didn't like—or learn to like my decision.

So, the other day I reversed myself. [*Laughter*] I was so mad I almost fired myself. [*Laughter*] I've decided to give myself another chance, and I hope you will, too. [*Laughter*]

There is a real and a heartfelt reason why I'm here today. I just sent the budget to the Congress. [*Laughter*] And I hope that, at least in spirit, sort of figuratively, we can all from here on have our hands joined in prayer.

Audience members. Amen.

The President. The next few days, and maybe weeks, will probably be dominated, in terms of the news, by talk of economic matters—budgets and the tax structure and so forth. But I want you to know that as we

begin the great work ahead of us, I've been thinking very much about Divine Providence and turning to our Lord and asking for His guidance. I have found myself, as Abraham Lincoln did once, driven to my knees more than ever because there was no place else to go.

But I'm also aware, as never before, that what the polls show is true: In virtually every public survey, there are indications that the importance of spiritual faith has grown stronger among the people of our country. Recent Gallup surveys show 64 percent of Americans—adults—express a great deal or quite a lot of confidence in the church of organized religion. Fifty-six percent of Americans believe that religion can answer all or most of today's problems. In fact, only one in five doubts the relevance of religion in the modern world. And we'll get them, too. [*Laughter*]

As a resident of 1600 Pennsylvania Avenue, I may have a special vantage point from which to judge these things. In December, when I looked north from the White House, I would see the huge menorah, celebrating the Passover [Hanukkah] season in Lafayette Park. And when I looked south from the Truman Balcony, I could see the Pageant of Peace and the creche symbolizing the birth of Christ.

117

Showing the symbols of our beliefs in this way and what it is, for many of us, the holiest time of the year, is good—good for all of us, for Christians and Jews and any others who wish to share the joy of our holidays.

The other day I was at the National Prayer Breakfast here in Washington, and I spoke, as so many others did, of the central place of faith in our lives and how belief in something bigger than ourselves is probably a necessary precondition to peace. And I mentioned that after 4 years in this job, I know as never before that we are all God's children, that the clerk, the king, and, yes, the Communist were made in His image.

And I've often wondered about one individual there, because when I said that, a fellow in the back of the room—and I heard him say, "Amen." There were more than 3,000 people in that room, from almost every country in the globe—African chiefs, Central American businessmen, people from Australia and Europe and the Middle East. And the room seemed to hum with agreement that faith and belief are the key to man's salvation and the only way we'll learn to live with each other in peace.

All of you, all of the people in this room are doing your part to fill the world with God's work and make more gentle man's life on Earth. Like St. Peter and his brother, St. Andrew, you've been good and faithful fishermen, and you've fought the good fight—for prayer in the schools and against abortion and for freedom in the world. You know, perhaps better than I, that you have never let us down.

And I'm not shy today about asking you for your continued support in many areas, including our economic program. It occurs to me that the doctrine of election means one thing to some of you and quite another to those of us who hold public office. [*Laughter*] When I was reelected in November, I didn't figure I was being sent back to the White House to turn back to the policies of the past.

Audience members. Amen.

The President. I still believe the government is the servant of the people and not the other way around.

We're trying to get government spending down, to hold down the huge cost of gov-

ernment, to keep it from taking the money you deserve to keep for your family and your future and for God's work. We mean to ensure greater possibility for the production of wealth by lowering tax rates through tax reform. We mean to maintain a strong defense, because only with a strong defense can we preserve the peace we cherish.

And I found myself wanting to remind you of what Jesus said in Luke 14:31: "Oh, what king, when he sets out to meet another king in battle will not first sit down and take counsel whether he is strong enough with 10,000 men to encounter the one coming against him with 20,000. Or else, while the other is still far away, sends a delegation and asks the terms of peace." I don't think the Lord that blessed this country, as no other country has ever been blessed, intends for us to have to someday negotiate because of our weakness.

But all of these things I've mentioned are pretty revolutionary. All of these things—learning to control the government, limiting the amount of money it can take from us, protecting our country through a strong defense—all of these things revolve around one word, and that word is "freedom." And as Jefferson said, "The Lord who gave us life, the God who gave us life gave us liberty also."

That's what we stand for here and everywhere. And that's what I need for your continued help in preserving and promoting. And every voice counts. These are crucial days ahead of us, in terms of the budget and taxes and keeping our commitment to rebuild our defenses.

I need all of you as never before. And we need Him as never before. And we mustn't doubt at all that He will give us help and support and encouragement and guidance. You've given me these things time and again. And for all of this, I am truly thankful.

And I thank all of you now for your wonderful warmth. I bask in this and will all the way back to the White House. [*Laughter*] God bless you all.

Note: The President spoke at 4:39 p.m. in the Washington Ballroom at the Sheraton

Washington Hotel. In his opening remarks, the President referred to the president and *executive director, respectively, of the National Religious Broadcasters.*

Statement on the 40th Anniversary of the Yalta Conference
February 5, 1985

Forty years ago this week, the leaders of the United States, Great Britain, and the Soviet Union met at Yalta, to confer on the approaching end of World War II and on the outlines of the postwar world. The agreements they reached, including the Declaration on Liberated Europe, committed all three governments to the reconstruction of a democratic continent.

Since that time, Yalta has had a double meaning. It recalls an episode of cooperation between the Soviet Union and free nations, in a great common cause. But it also recalls the reasons that this cooperation could not continue—the Soviet promises that were not kept, the elections that were not held, the two halves of Europe that have remained apart.

Why is Yalta important today? Not because we in the West want to reopen old disputes over boundaries; far from it. The reason Yalta remains important is that the freedom of Europe is unfinished business.

Those who claim the issue is boundaries or territory are hoping that the real issues—democracy and independence—will somehow go away. They will not.

There is one boundary which Yalta symbolizes that can never be made legitimate, and that is the dividing line between freedom and repression. I do not hesitate to say that we wish to undo this boundary. In so doing, we seek no military advantage for ourselves or for the Western alliance. We do not deny any nation's legitimate interest in security. But protecting the security of one nation by robbing another of its national independence and national traditions is not legitimate. In the long run, it is not even secure.

Long after Yalta, this much remains clear: The most significant way of making all Europe more secure is to make it more free. Our 40-year pledge is to the goal of a restored community of free European nations. To this work we recommit ourselves today.

Appointment of Patrick J. Buchanan as Assistant to the President and Director of Communications
February 5, 1985

The President today announced his intention to appoint Patrick J. Buchanan to be Assistant to the President and Director of Communications.

A journalist by profession, Mr. Buchanan has for 10 years written a thrice-weekly column of political and social commentary, distributed by Tribune Media Services to 125 newspapers in the United States. He has also been, for almost 3 years, cohost of "Crossfire," a nightly interview program on the Cable News Network, and a weekly

panelist on "The McLaughlin Group," a public affairs show distributed locally by WRC–NBC and nationally by PBS.

Mr. Buchanan cohosted the "Buchanan-Braden Program," a 3-hour daily radio show on WRC, and delivered daily commentary on the NBC radio network from 1978 to 1984.

In 1965 Mr. Buchanan became the first full-time staff member of the Nixon, Mudge, Rose, Guthrie, Alexander & Mitchell law offices in New York City. For 3 years, between January 1966 and January 1969, he served as press aide, executive assistant, and speechwriter and traveled with former Vice President Nixon throughout the campaigns of 1966 and 1968. In 1967 he accompanied Mr. Nixon to West Europe, Africa, and the Middle East in the immediate aftermath of the Six-Day War.

On January 20, 1969, Mr. Buchanan was named Special Assistant to the President and served throughout the Nixon Presidency, resigning from the Ford White House in November 1974. During the near-6 years of the Nixon Presidency, he wrote speeches both for the President and the Vice President, developed political strategy, published the President's daily news summary, and prepared the foreign and domestic briefing books for Presidential news conferences.

Mr. Buchanan was a member of the 15-person official delegation to the People's Republic of China in 1972 and accompanied President Nixon to the final summit in Moscow, Yalta, and Minsk in the summer of 1974.

In addition to his syndicated column, Mr. Buchanan has authored two books, "The New Majority" and "Conservative Votes, Liberal Victories," and written over two decades for The Nation, Rolling Stone, National Review, Conservative Digest, Skeptic, and The American Spectator. He is an honors graduate in English and philosophy from Georgetown University.

Mr. Buchanan was born November 2, 1938, in Washington, DC. He is married and resides in McLean, VA.

Appointment of Max Friedersdorf as Assistant to the President and Legislative Strategy Coordinator
February 5, 1985

The President today announced his intention to appoint Max Friedersdorf as Assistant to the President and Legislative Strategy Coordinator.

Mr. Friedersdorf has been serving as Vice President for Pepsico, Inc., of Purchase, NY, since September 19, 1983.

Mr. Friedersdorf was Assistant to President Reagan for Legislative Affairs in 1981. He subsequently was consul general to Bermuda for nearly 2 years before joining Pepsico. He was a member of the Federal Election Commission in 1979 and 1980.

Prior to joining the Commission, he was staff director for the U.S. Senate Republican Policy Committee. In 1971–1977 he served at the White House as Congressional Liaison. In 1961–1970 he was administrative assistant for former U.S. Representative Richard L. Roudebush (R–IN). He is also a former reporter for the Louisville Times, the Indianapolis News, and the Chicago Daily News.

Mr. Friedersdorf is a graduate of Franklin (IN) College and The American University. He is married and has two children. He was born July 7, 1929, in Grammer, IN.

Appointment of Edward J. Rollins as Assistant to the President for Political and Governmental Affairs
February 5, 1985

The President today announced his intention to appoint Edward J. Rollins as Assistant to the President for Political and Governmental Affairs.

Mr. Rollins was the national director of the President's reelection campaign, Reagan-Bush '84. Prior to his appointment to head the campaign in October of 1983, he served as Assistant to the President for Political Affairs and, before that, as Deputy Assistant to the President for Political Affairs.

Immediately before accepting his first White House appointment in January 1981, Mr. Rollins was Republican chief of staff for the State of California Assembly.

From 1973 to 1977, he was at the Department of Transportation, where he had responsibility for the Department's liaison with the Congress and State and local governments. Prior to that, Mr. Rollins served as principal assistant to the Republican leader and speaker of the California Assembly. In addition, he has managed numerous political campaigns in the West.

From 1969 to 1973, Mr. Rollins was assistant vice chancellor for student affairs at Washington University in St. Louis, where he also taught political science and public administration. In 1968 he served as assistant to the president of California State University, Chico.

He is a graduate of the California State University system, where he also completed graduate studies in political science. He was born March 19, 1943, in Boston, MA, and now resides in Arlington, VA.

Remarks on Signing the Annual Economic Report of the President
February 5, 1985

The President. I think I have a few words here and a little ceremony to go through with. I'm pleased to sign this Economic Report, and I want to commend Bill Niskanen and his staff, here, for the fine job that they have done.

I think we can take pride in the very significant progress that, to our—that it's hard work and sticking to our principles that transformed a sick economy to one of healthy growth with much lower inflation and interest rates. Now is the time for recommitment. We need the full support of the Congress to end nearly 50 years of deliberate deficit spending by the Federal Government.

Well, one sure path to a balanced budget is to keep the rate of growth spending below the growth of the economy. So, we've submitted a budget that will freeze over all government program spending, while ensuring that the funds crucial to our defense rebuilding program are there.

If the Congress cooperates and helps us reform our tax system and continue reducing unneeded regulation, we can end the burden of overspending and borrowing and leave our children a much stronger future.

And now I'm going to sign the Economic Report.

[The President signed the report.]

The President. For the Senate. For the House of Representatives. And for Dr. Niskanen. There you are.

Dr. Niskanen. Mr. President, the American economy is once again the envy of the world, and you deserve a lot of the credit. And only as a minor compensation for that, we'd like—*[laughter]*—to award you honorary membership in the Council of Economic Advisers and give you something to chop wood in back at the ranch.

[*The President was presented with a T-shirt with a copy of the report cover printed on it.*]

The President. Well, thank you very much. All right. I appreciate that.

Reporter. Where do you plan to wear it, sir? [*Laughter*]

The President. He's just told you when I have to wear it—at the ranch, chopping wood. [*Laughter*]

Q. Mr. President, you're a realist, and you're listening to what Capitol Hill is saying. How far are you willing to give on the defense budget, because you must know that you're going to have to?

The President. Why is it that everybody, including so many of you, continue to say that no cuts in the defense budget—when there've been cuts in the neighborhood of around $30 billion in what was the projected budget for the Defense Department?

I just think that the mistake we made was in making the cuts in advance. We should have sent it up the way it was and let the Congress make the cuts. And then they'd have been happy.

Q. Well, then, has Congress got your bottom line on military spending?

The President. Well, I'm quite sure that we'll be discussing this, going at this. But I think it is unfair to say that there has been no cut. As a matter of fact, the defense budget for 1986, as it's submitted now, is just about where the projected budget of President Carter was when he left office and made his 5-year projections as to what

should be spent on national defense.

Q. Mr. President, are you going to take this case to the country soon?

The President. Yes, I think the people have a right to express themselves on this, and they need to have the facts. So, I'm going to try to give them the facts.

Q. How are you going to do that?

The President. What?

Q. How are you going to do that? Are you going to go out and make some speeches and make some appearances on television——

The President. I really haven't made any specific plans yet.

Thank you all very much. Thank you.

Q. Mr. Reagan, do you have any reaction to the vote on Mr. Meese today?

The President. Yes—a happy one. I'm pleased that—so far, I think there are three or four others of our nominees that were approved also today by the committees.

Q. Any special plans for your birthday tomorrow?

The President. Birthday? [*Laughter*] Oh, you mean the 35th anniversary of my 39th birthday? [*Laughter*] No, I've gotten used to that. I just treat it as any other day. It makes me feel better to do it that way. [*Laughter*]

Note: The President spoke at 1:50 p.m. in the Roosevelt Room at the White House. Attending the ceremony were Dr. William A. Niskanen and other members of the Council of Economic Advisers.

Message to the Congress Transmitting the Annual Economic Report of the President
February 5, 1985

To the Congress of the United States:

In 1981, when I first assumed the duties of the Presidency, our Nation was suffering from declining productivity and the highest inflation in the postwar period—the legacy of years of government overspending, overtaxing, and overregulation.

We bent all of our efforts to correct these

problems, not by unsustainable short-run measures, but by measures that would increase long-term growth without renewed inflation. We removed unnecessary regulations, cut taxes, and slowed the growth of Federal spending, freeing the private sector to develop markets, create jobs, and increase productivity. With conviction in our principles, with patience and hard work, we restored the economy to a condition of healthy growth without substantial inflation.

Although employment is now rising, business opportunities are expanding, and interest rates and inflation are under control, we cannot relax our economic vigilance. A return to the policies of excessive government spending and control that led to the economic "malaise" of the late seventies would quickly draw us back into that same disastrous pattern of inflation and recession. Now is the time to recommit ourselves to the policies that broke that awful pattern: policies of reduced Federal spending, lower tax rates, and less regulation to free the creative energy of our people and lead us to an even better economic future through strong and sustained economic growth.

Major Economic Developments 1981–1984

The Program for Economic Recovery that we initiated in February 1981 had four key elements:

- Budget reform to cut the rate of growth in Federal spending,
- Reductions in personal and business taxes,
- A far-reaching program of regulatory relief, and
- Restoration of a stable currency and a healthy financial market through sound monetary policy.

The success of this program is now obvious—the U.S. economy is experiencing the strongest recovery in 30 years:

• Real business fixed investment in plant and equipment is higher, relative to real gross national product, than at any time in the postwar period.

• Productivity growth in the business sector has averaged 2.2 percent since the fourth quarter of 1980, compared with a rate of less than 0.3 percent over the prior 4 years.

• The inflation rate is now about one-third the rate in 1980, and short-term interest rates are less than one-half their peak 1981 levels.

But the quantitative record alone does not tell the full story. Four years ago, there was a widespread and growing anxiety about the economy. Many thought that the Nation had entered a condition of perma-nent economic decline, and that we would have to live with permanent double-digit inflation unless we were willing to suffer massive long-term unemployment.

We did not share this pessimism. It was clear to us that the Nation's economic problems were not the product of the economic system, but of the onerous influence of government on that system. The creative potential of the American people, choosing their own economic futures, was more constrained than helped by the increasingly heavy hand of government. Nor did we share the negative views that a reduction of inflation would increase long-term unemployment; that economic growth, by itself, would increase inflation; and that the government had to protect a "fragile" market system by regulating oil prices and interest rates.

The primary economic responsibility of the Federal Government is not to make choices for people, but to provide an environment in which people can make their own choices. The performance of the economy in the past 2 years under our Program for Economic Recovery fully justifies our faith in the Nation's basic economic health. In 1983 and 1984 the economy generated about 300,000 new jobs per month without an increase in inflation. Real gross national product increased 5.6 percent during 1984, and the unemployment rate declined from 8.1 percent to 7.1 percent. Inflation was steady at its lowest level in more than a decade, and most interest rates are now lower than a year ago. Yet while the U.S. economy grew rapidly in 1984, it maintains the potential for continued strong growth. The inventory/sales ratio is low by historical standards, and capacity utilization rates in most industries are well below prior peak rates.

Economic conditions in 1984 were more favorable than during the second year of a typical recovery, and we see none of the warning signs that usually precede the end of an expansion. The temporary showing of economic growth starting in July—reflecting the combination of a minor adjustment of consumer spending and inventories and little growth of the basic money supply—seems to have ended in November. These conditions, plus an expectation that the Federal Reserve System will maintain sufficient money growth, support our forecast that the present recovery will continue. *The thriving venture capital market is financing a new American revolution of entrepreneurship and technological change. The American economy is once again the envy of the world.*

The Economic Outlook

For the years 1985 through 1988, we assume real gross national product growth of 4 percent per year, slowing slightly in 1989–90. We know that economic recoveries have not been stable in either duration or magnitude, in part because monetary and fiscal policies have often been erratic. We may not be able to eliminate recessions entirely, but a sustained commitment to policies that promote long-term growth and stability can reduce their frequency and severity. Our forecast that the unemployment rate, the inflation rate, and interest rates will decline gradually in the years ahead reflects this commitment to sound, sustainable, and predictable policies.

The Task Ahead: A Program for Growth and Opportunity

Our 1981 Program for Economic Recovery was designed for the long run with priority attention to the major problems we faced at that time. Our second-term Program for Growth and Opportunity represents a continuation and expansion of the earlier program, with priority attention to the major problems we face in 1985 and beyond. Our objectives—economic growth, stability of the general price level, and increased individual economic opportunity— have not changed. Federal economic policy will continue to be guided by the four key elements of the earlier program. Our progress in solving the most important economic problems we inherited in 1981, however, has allowed us to refocus our attention on the remaining problems and to shift our priorities and resources toward their solution.

Several significant problems remain to be addressed. The rate of growth of Federal spending has been substantially reduced from the rate projected in the budget we

inherited in fiscal 1981, but spending growth continues to outpace the economy. Spending too much has left us with a large budget deficit that must and will be reduced. In our efforts to reduce the deficit, we must not forget that the cause of the deficit is increased spending and insufficient growth, not decreased taxes. Federal tax receipts are now almost the same share of gross national product as in the late 1970s, even after the substantial reduction in tax rates that we initiated in 1981.

Another economic problem demanding resolution is unemployment and its effects on the Nation's workers and families. Despite significant progress, much remains to be done. More than 6 million more Americans are now employed than in January 1981, but the unemployment rate is still too high. We will not be satisfied until every American who wants a job is employed at a wage that reflects the market value of his or her skills. Another aspect of this problem is that the poverty rate remains stubbornly high, despite a strong recovery and a continued increase in government assistance. Also, although the inflation rate has been reduced substantially, it is still higher than during most of our peacetime history prior to 1965. We will not be satisfied until we have totally and permanently wrung inflation out of our economy.

Work also remains to be done in the areas of regulatory and monetary policy. Many Federal regulations still impose a substantial cost to the economy. In addition, we need to strengthen the commitment to a sound monetary policy that never again retards economic growth, or reaccelerates inflation.

Our trade deficit, another area of concern, has been caused in large part by a strong dollar. Investors around the world have bid up the dollar as they have become increasingly confident in our economy. That confidence is an asset and not a liability. However, the conditions that have led to the trade deficit have increased the obstacles faced by some important industries. Agriculture, one of our most productive export sectors, has been harmed by a combination of rigid and outdated Federal agricultural policies and subsidized foreign competition as well as by the strong dollar. Some of our import-competing industries, such as steel, have also been hurt by subsidized foreign competition and the strong dollar. In one respect the trade deficit is like the budget deficit; both are too large to be sustained, but there are both beneficial and detrimental ways to reduce them. Our goal is a system of free and fair trade in goods, services, and capital. We will work toward this goal through both bilateral and multilateral agreements.

Economic conditions during the past 4 years are best characterized as transitional—from a period of low productivity growth to a period of high productivity growth; from a period of high inflation and interest rates to a period of much lower inflation and interest rates; from a period of economic "malaise" to a period of economic opportunity. Our task is to consolidate and extend these gains.

Federal Spending and the Deficit

The rate of growth of Federal spending has been reduced from 14.8 percent in fiscal 1981 to an average rate of 9.1 percent in fiscal years 1982 through 1985. During this period, however, current dollar gross national product has increased at an average rate of 7.6 percent. The continued growth of the Federal spending share of gross national product and lost revenues from the recession are the main reasons we are now faced with such large Federal deficits.

The projected Federal deficits are much too large, and they must be reduced. As explained in the accompanying report, however, the economic consequences of reducing these deficits depend critically on how they are reduced. A sustained reduction of the growth of Federal spending will contribute to economic growth, while an increase in tax rates would constrain economic growth. Federal spending on many programs is far larger than necessary, and far larger than desired by most Americans.

My fiscal 1986 budget proposal will protect the social safety net and essential programs, such as defense, for which the Federal Government has a clear constitutional responsibility, and will reform or eliminate many programs that have proven ineffective or nonessential. With no resort to a tax increase, this budget will reduce the deficit to about 4 percent of gross national product in fiscal 1986 and to a steadily lower percentage in future years. Additional spending reductions will probably be necessary in future years to achieve a balanced budget by the end of the decade.

The problems of excessive spending and deficits are not new. In the absence of fundamental reform, they may recur again and again in the future. I therefore support two important measures—one to authorize the President to veto individual line items in comprehensive spending bills, and another to constrain the Federal authority to borrow or to increase spending in the absence of broad congressional support. These structural changes are *not* substitutes for the hard fiscal choices that will be necessary in 1985 and beyond, nor for the need to simplify our tax system to stimulate greater growth; but they are important to provide the mechanisms and discipline for longer term fiscal health.

The case for a line-item veto should by now be obvious. The Governors of 43 States have used this authority effectively, and such authority has only once been withdrawn, only later to be reinstated. For over a century, Presidents of both parties have requested such authority.

The proposed constitutional amendment providing for a balanced budget and a tax limitation would constrain the long-run growth of Federal spending and the national debt. In 1982 a proposed amendment to constrain Federal authority to spend and borrow was approved by more than two-thirds of the Senate and by more than a majority of the House of Representatives; a balanced budget amendment has also been endorsed by the legislatures of 32 States. Approval of the proposed balanced budget/tax limitation amendment would ensure that fiscal decisions by future Presidents and Members of Congress are more responsive to the broad interests of the American population.

Federal Taxation

The Economic Recovery Tax Act of 1981 was one of the most important accomplishments of my first term. Individual income tax rates were reduced by nearly 25 percent, effective tax rates on the income from new investment were substantially reduced, and beginning this year tax brackets are adjusted for inflation.

But more needs to be done. Personal tax rates should be reduced further to encourage stronger economic growth which, in itself, is our best tool for putting deficits on a steady downward path. Our tax system needs basic reform. It is extraordinarily complicated; it leads to substantial economic inefficiency; and it is widely perceived to be unfair.

At my request, the Treasury Department has developed a comprehensive proposal to simplify and reform the Federal tax system, one that for expected economic conditions would yield about the same revenues as the present system. This proposal, by substantially broadening the tax base, would permit a significant further reduction of marginal tax rates. Shortly, I will be submitting my own proposal for tax simplification, and will urge the Congress to give serious sustained attention to tax simplification—in order to enact a program that will increase fairness and stimulate future savings, investment, and growth.

Federal Regulation

We have made major efforts in the past 4 years to reduce and eliminate Federal regulation of economic activity. Executive Office review of new regulations was streamlined. Oil prices were deregulated by Executive authority early in 1981. New legislation was approved to reduce regulation of banking and to largely eliminate regulation of interstate bus travel.

Regulatory reform, however, has been painfully slow. The Congress failed to approve our proposals to further deregulate banking and natural gas prices, and to reform the regulation of private pensions. In addition, the reauthorization of several major environmental laws has been delayed for several years.

I urge the Congress to consider further deregulation efforts in several areas. The experience with deregulation of oil prices makes clear that continued regulation of natural gas prices is not appropriate. Reform of nuclear licensing requirements also deserves attention. Further deregulation of the banking system should be paired with a major reform of the deposit insurance systems. Some changes in the single-employer pension law and an increased premium are necessary to preserve the pension insurance system. We should also seriously consider eliminating the remaining Federal regulation of trucking and railroads. Finally, I remain hopeful that the Administration and the Congress can work together to reauthorize the major environmental laws in a way that serves our common environmental and economic goals.

Monetary Policy

The Constitution authorizes the Congress "To coin Money (and) regulate the Value thereof," and Congress has delegated this authority to the Federal Reserve System. The role of the executive branch is restricted to advising the Congress and the Federal Reserve about the conduct of monetary policy, and to nominating members of the Board of Governors as positions become vacant.

During my first term, the Federal Reserve reduced the rate of money growth relative to the high rates of the late 1970s. This change in policy, assisted by the related strong increase in the exchange value of the dollar, helped produce a substantial reduction of inflation and market interest rates. On occasion, however, the rate of money growth has been quite volatile, contributing to instability in interest rates and a decline in economic activity. The sharp reduction in money growth through mid-1982, for example, undoubtedly added to the length and severity of the 1981–1982 recession. And a similar reduction in money growth in the second half of 1984 contributed to the temporary slowing of economic growth late in the year.

We reaffirm our support for a sound monetary policy that contributes to strong, steady economic growth and price stability. Moreover, we expect to cooperate closely with the Federal Reserve in defining and carrying out a prudent and predictable monetary policy.

Conclusion

The Federal Government has only a few important economic responsibilities. Given a proper conduct of these important roles, additional Federal intervention is more often a part of the problem than a part of the solution. We should continue to reduce the many less-important economic activities of the Federal Government so that individuals, private institutions, and State and local governments will have more resources and more freedom to pursue their own interests. Good stewardship of our constitutional responsibilities and the creative energies of the American people will ensure a future of continued economic growth and opportunity.

RONALD REAGAN

February 5, 1985.

Note: The President's message was printed in the report entitled "Economic Report of the President, Transmitted to the Congress, February 1985—Together With the Annual Report of the Council of Economic Advisers" (Government Printing Office, 356 pages).

Appointment of Frederick J. Ryan, Jr., as Deputy Assistant to the President
February 6, 1985

The President today announced the appointment of Frederick J. Ryan, Jr., to be Deputy Assistant to the President. He will be responsible for the White House Office of Private Sector Initiatives, as well as continuing to serve in his current position as Director of Presidential Appointments and Scheduling.

Mr. Ryan began serving at the White House in February 1982 as Deputy Director of Presidential Appointments and Scheduling. In February 1983 he was appointed Special Assistant to the President and Director of Presidential Appointments and Scheduling.

Mr. Ryan was previously an attorney with the Los Angeles law firm of Hill, Farrer, and Burrill. While engaged in his practice, he published several articles on various aspects of the law.

During the 1980 Presidential campaign, Mr. Ryan was active in the Reagan-Bush Committee. While residing in California, he was involved in several State, local, and congressional races.

Mr. Ryan graduated from the University of Southern California (B.A., 1977) and the University of Southern California Law Center (J.D., 1980). He was born April 12, 1955, in Tampa, FL.

Nomination of John E. Krings To Be Director of Operational Test and Evaluation of the Department of Defense
February 6, 1985

The President today announced his intention to nominate John E. Krings to be Director of Operational Test and Evaluation, Department of Defense. This is a new position.

Mr. Krings has been with the McDonnell Aircraft Co. since 1956 and is presently serving as Director of the United States Navy–United States Marine Corps Group Program. Previously he was Director of Flight Operations (1980–1983) and a test pilot (1956–1980). He served in the United States Air Force in 1952–1956 and in the Air National Guard in 1956–1960.

127

He graduated from Louisiana State University (B.S., 1952). He was born April 2, 1930, in Pittsburgh, PA, and now resides in Arlington, VA.

Message to the Congress Reporting Budget Rescissions and Deferrals
February 6, 1985

To the Congress of the United States:

In accordance with the Impoundment Control Act of 1974, I herewith report sixteen new rescission proposals totaling $1,047,089,569, nine revised rescission proposals totaling $386,829,000, twenty-one new deferrals of budget authority totaling $1,249,016,539, and eight revised deferrals of budget authority totaling $443,179,221.

The rescissions affect programs in the Departments of Agriculture, Commerce, Education, Housing and Urban Development, Interior, Justice, and Labor, and the Appalachian Regional Commission.

The deferrals affect programs in the Departments of Commerce, Energy, Interior, Health and Human Services, Justice, and Transportation, the African Development Foundation, the National Science Foundation, and the Railroad Retirement Board.

The details of the rescission proposals and deferrals are contained in the attached report.

RONALD REAGAN

The White House,
February 6, 1985.

Note: The attachment detailing the proposed rescissions and deferrals was printed in the Federal Register *of February 14.*

Message to the Congress Reporting Budget Rescissions
February 6, 1985

To the Congress of the United States:

In accordance with the Impoundment Control Act of 1974, I herewith report 226 rescission proposals totaling $371,994,000.

These rescissions are proposed pursuant to the Deficit Reduction Act of 1984, and affect International Development Assistance programs, Peace Corps programs, Overseas Private Investment Corporation programs, programs in the Departments of Agriculture, Commerce, Defense-Civil, Education, Energy, Health and Human Services, Housing and Urban Development, Interior, Justice, Labor, State, Transportation, and Treasury, as well as programs in the Environmental Protection Agency, General Services Administration, National Aeronautics and Space Administration, Office of Personnel Management, Small Business Administration, Veterans Administration, ACTION, Federal Emergency Management Agency, National Archives and Records Administration, National Labor Relations Board, National Science Foundation, Nuclear Regulatory Commission, Tennessee Valley Authority and the United States Information Agency.

The details of the rescission proposals are contained in the attached reports.

RONALD REAGAN

The White House,
February 6, 1985.

Note: The attachments detailing the proposed rescissions were printed in the Federal Register *of February 14.*

Proclamation 5299—International Youth Year, 1985
February 6, 1985

By the President of the United States of America

A Proclamation

America rejoices in the energy, the imagination, and the promise of her young people. Whether in voluntary service, athletics, education, music, military service or within the family, young Americans display an enthusiasm, creativity, idealism, and dedication that have accomplished so much for our society and the world. Their patriotism and commitment to peace with freedom ensure a vigorous American democracy and a safer world in the years ahead.

In 1985 the United States joins the celebration of United Nations' International Youth Year. If we are to honor the potential of America's youth, we must remember that the most powerful force for progress comes not from governments or public programs, but from the vital traditions of a free people. Parents, youth organizations, and teachers deserve our support, encouragement, and thanks for the indispensable role they play in fostering and strengthening these traditions.

History makes clear that progress is swiftest when people are free to worship, create, and build—when they can determine their own destiny and benefit from their own initiative. The dream of human progress through freedom is still the most revolutionary idea in the world, and it is still the most successful. It is the priceless heritage America bestows on each new generation, with the hope that succeeding generations the world over will come to better know its fruits.

In the coming months, I urge American youth to reflect on our precious freedoms, to exchange ideas among themselves and with young people around the world, and to join with others in efforts to increase mutual understanding, enhance the observance of human rights, and promote world peace. In short, I urge our youth to be what they have been for many generations: America's proudest ambassadors of goodwill and our national values. One such opportunity is being offered by the people of Jamaica as they host the first-ever International Youth Conference in early April. The Conference will enable young Americans to discuss with their peers in other countries ways in which they can help shape the world of tomorrow.

Let all of us approach this year dedicated to youth by resolving to use our God-given talents and freedom to elevate our ideals, deepen our understanding, and strengthen our determination to make this world a better place for ourselves and for the generations of young people who will follow.

Now, Therefore, I, Ronald Reagan, President of the United States of America, do hereby proclaim 1985 as International Youth Year in the United States. I invite the Governors of the several States, the chief officials of local governments, and all Americans to observe this year with appropriate ceremonies and activities.

In Witness Whereof, I have hereunto set my hand this sixth day of February, in the year of our Lord nineteen hundred and eighty-five, and of the Independence of the United States of America the two hundred and ninth.

RONALD REAGAN

[*Filed with the Office of the Federal Register, 4:16 p.m., February 6, 1985*]

Address Before a Joint Session of the Congress on the State of the Union
February 6, 1985

Mr. Speaker, Mr. President, distinguished Members of the Congress, honored guests, and fellow citizens:

I come before you to report on the state of our Union, and I'm pleased to report that after 4 years of united effort, the American people have brought forth a nation renewed, stronger, freer, and more secure than before.

Four years ago we began to change, forever I hope, our assumptions about government and its place in our lives. Out of that change has come great and robust growth—in our confidence, our economy, and our role in the world.

Tonight America is stronger because of the values that we hold dear. We believe faith and freedom must be our guiding stars, for they show us truth, they make us brave, give us hope, and leave us wiser than we were. Our progress began not in Washington, DC, but in the hearts of our families, communities, workplaces, and voluntary groups which, together, are unleashing the invincible spirit of one great nation under God.

Four years ago we said we would invigorate our economy by giving people greater freedom and incentives to take risks and letting them keep more of what they earned. We did what we promised, and a great industrial giant is reborn.

Tonight we can take pride in 25 straight months of economic growth, the strongest in 34 years; a 3-year inflation average of 3.9 percent, the lowest in 17 years; and 7.3 million new jobs in 2 years, with more of our citizens working than ever before.

New freedom in our lives has planted the rich seeds for future success:

For an America of wisdom that honors the family, knowing that if [as] the family goes, so goes our civilization;

For an America of vision that sees tomorrow's dreams in the learning and hard work we do today;

For an America of courage whose service men and women, even as we meet, proudly stand watch on the frontiers of freedom;

For an America of compassion that opens its heart to those who cry out for help.

We have begun well. But it's only a beginning. We're not here to congratulate ourselves on what we have done but to challenge ourselves to finish what has not yet been done.

We're here to speak for millions in our inner cities who long for real jobs, safe neighborhoods, and schools that truly teach. We're here to speak for the American farmer, the entrepreneur, and every worker in industries fighting to modernize and compete. And, yes, we're here to stand, and proudly so, for all who struggle to break free from totalitarianism, for all who know in their hearts that freedom is the one true path to peace and human happiness.

Proverbs tell us, without a vision the people perish. When asked what great principle holds our Union together, Abraham Lincoln said: "Something in [the] Declaration giving liberty, not alone to the people of this country, but hope to the world for all future time."

We honor the giants of our history not by going back but forward to the dreams their vision foresaw. My fellow citizens, this nation is poised for greatness. The time has come to proceed toward a great new challenge—a second American Revolution of hope and opportunity; a revolution carrying us to new heights of progress by pushing back frontiers of knowledge and space; a revolution of spirit that taps the soul of America, enabling us to summon greater strength than we've ever known; and a revolution that carries beyond our shores the golden promise of human freedom in a world of peace.

Let us begin by challenging our conventional wisdom. There are no constraints on the human mind, no walls around the human spirit, no barriers to our progress except those we ourselves erect. Already, pushing down tax rates has freed our economy to vault forward to record growth.

In Europe, they're calling it "the American Miracle." Day by day, we're shattering accepted notions of what is possible. When I was growing up, we failed to see how a new thing called radio would transform our marketplace. Well, today, many have not yet seen how advances in technology are transforming our lives.

In the late 1950's workers at the AT&T semiconductor plant in Pennsylvania produced five transistors a day for $7.50 apiece. They now produce over a million for less than a penny apiece.

New laser techniques could revolutionize heart bypass surgery, cut diagnosis time for viruses linked to cancer from weeks to minutes, reduce hospital costs dramatically, and hold out new promise for saving human lives.

Our automobile industry has overhauled assembly lines, increased worker productivity, and is competitive once again.

We stand on the threshold of a great ability to produce more, do more, be more. Our economy is not getting older and weaker; it's getting younger and stronger. It doesn't need rest and supervision; it needs new challenge, greater freedom. And that word "freedom" is the key to the second American revolution that we need to bring about.

Let us move together with an historic reform of tax simplification for fairness and growth. Last year I asked Treasury Secretary—then—Regan to develop a plan to simplify the tax code, so all taxpayers would be treated more fairly and personal tax rates could come further down.

We have cut tax rates by almost 25 percent, yet the tax system remains unfair and limits our potential for growth. Exclusions and exemptions cause similar incomes to be taxed at different levels. Low-income families face steep tax barriers that make hard lives even harder. The Treasury Department has produced an excellent reform plan, whose principles will guide the final proposal that we will ask you to enact.

One thing that tax reform will not be is a tax increase in disguise. We will not jeopardize the mortgage interest deduction that families need. We will reduce personal tax rates as low as possible by removing many

tax preferences. We will propose a top rate of no more than 35 percent, and possibly lower. And we will propose reducing corporate rates, while maintaining incentives for capital formation.

To encourage opportunity and jobs rather than dependency and welfare, we will propose that individuals living at or near the poverty line be totally exempt from Federal income tax. To restore fairness to families, we will propose increasing significantly the personal exemption.

And tonight, I am instructing Treasury Secretary James Baker—I have to get used to saying that—to begin working with congressional authors and committees for bipartisan legislation conforming to these principles. We will call upon the American people for support and upon every man and woman in this Chamber. Together, we can pass, this year, a tax bill for fairness, simplicity, and growth, making this economy the engine of our dreams and America the investment capital of the world. So let us begin.

Tax simplification will be a giant step toward unleashing the tremendous pent-up power of our economy. But a second American revolution must carry the promise of opportunity for all. It is time to liberate the spirit of enterprise in the most distressed areas of our country.

This government will meet its responsibility to help those in need. But policies that increase dependency, break up families, and destroy self-respect are not progressive; they're reactionary. Despite our strides in civil rights, blacks, Hispanics, and all minorities will not have full and equal power until they have full economic power.

We have repeatedly sought passage of enterprise zones to help those in the abandoned corners of our land find jobs, learn skills, and build better lives. This legislation is supported by a majority of you.

Mr. Speaker, I know we agree that there must be no forgotten Americans. Let us place new dreams in a million hearts and create a new generation of entrepreneurs by passing enterprise zones this year. And, Tip, you could make that a birthday present. [*Laughter*]

Nor must we lose the chance to pass our

youth employment opportunity wage proposal. We can help teenagers, who have the highest unemployment rate, find summer jobs, so they can know the pride of work and have confidence in their futures.

We'll continue to support the Job Training Partnership Act, which has a nearly two-thirds job placement rate. Credits in education and health care vouchers will help working families shop for services that they need.

Our administration is already encouraging certain low-income public housing residents to own and manage their own dwellings. It's time that all public housing residents have that opportunity of ownership.

The Federal Government can help create a new atmosphere of freedom. But States and localities, many of which enjoy surpluses from the recovery, must not permit their tax and regulatory policies to stand as barriers to growth.

Let us resolve that we will stop spreading dependency and start spreading opportunity; that we will stop spreading bondage and start spreading freedom.

There are some who say that growth initiatives must await final action on deficit reductions. Well, the best way to reduce deficits *is* through economic growth. More businesses will be started, more investments made, more jobs created, and more people will be on payrolls paying taxes. The best way to reduce government spending is to reduce the need for spending by increasing prosperity. Each added percentage point per year of real GNP growth will lead to cumulative reduction in deficits of nearly $200 billion over 5 years.

To move steadily toward a balanced budget, we must also lighten government's claim on our total economy. We will not do this by raising taxes. We must make sure that our economy grows faster than the growth in spending by the Federal Government. In our fiscal year 1986 budget, overall government program spending will be frozen at the current level. It must not be one dime higher than fiscal year 1985, and three points are key.

First, the social safety net for the elderly, the needy, the disabled, and unemployed will be left intact. Growth of our major health care programs, Medicare and Medic-

aid, will be slowed, but protections for the elderly and needy will be preserved.

Second, we must not relax our efforts to restore military strength just as we near our goal of a fully equipped, trained, and ready professional corps. National security is government's first responsibility; so in past years defense spending took about half the Federal budget. Today it takes less than a third. We've already reduced our planned defense expenditures by nearly a hundred billion dollars over the past 4 years and reduced projected spending again this year.

You know, we only have a military-industrial complex until a time of danger, and then it becomes the arsenal of democracy. Spending for defense is investing in things that are priceless—peace and freedom.

Third, we must reduce or eliminate costly government subsidies. For example, deregulation of the airline industry has led to cheaper airfares, but on Amtrak taxpayers pay about $35 per passenger every time an Amtrak train leaves the station. It's time we ended this huge Federal subsidy.

Our farm program costs have quadrupled in recent years. Yet I know from visiting farmers, many in great financial distress, that we need an orderly transition to a market-oriented farm economy. We can help farmers best not by expanding Federal payments but by making fundamental reforms, keeping interest rates heading down, and knocking down foreign trade barriers to American farm exports.

We're moving ahead with Grace commission reforms to eliminate waste and improve government's management practices. In the long run, we must protect the taxpayers from government. And I ask again that you pass, as 32 States have now called for, an amendment mandating the Federal Government spend no more than it takes in. And I ask for the authority, used responsibly by 43 Governors, to veto individual items in appropriation bills. Senator Mattingly has introduced a bill permitting a 2-year trial run of the line-item veto. I hope you'll pass and send that legislation to my desk.

Nearly 50 years of government living beyond its means has brought us to a time of reckoning. Ours is but a moment in history. But one moment of courage, idealism, and bipartisan unity can change American history forever.

Sound monetary policy is key to long-running economic strength and stability. We will continue to cooperate with the Federal Reserve Board, seeking a steady policy that ensures price stability without keeping interest rates artificially high or needlessly holding down growth.

Reducing unneeded redtape and regulations, and deregulating the energy, transportation, and financial industries have unleashed new competition, giving consumers more choices, better services, and lower prices. In just one set of grant programs we have reduced 905 pages of regulations to 31. We seek to fully deregulate natural gas to bring on new supplies and bring us closer to energy independence. Consistent with safety standards, we will continue removing restraints on the bus and railroad industries, we will soon end up legislation—or send up legislation, I should say—to return Conrail to the private sector where it belongs, and we will support further deregulation of the trucking industry.

Every dollar the Federal Government does not take from us, every decision it does not make for us will make our economy stronger, our lives more abundant, our future more free.

Our second American revolution will push on to new possibilities not only on Earth but in the next frontier of space. Despite budget restraints, we will seek record funding for research and development.

We've seen the success of the space shuttle. Now we're going to develop a permanently manned space station and new opportunities for free enterprise, because in the next decade Americans and our friends around the world will be living and working together in space.

In the zero gravity of space, we could manufacture in 30 days lifesaving medicines it would take 30 years to make on Earth. We can make crystals of exceptional purity to produce super computers, creating jobs, technologies, and medical breakthroughs beyond anything we ever dreamed possible.

As we do all this, we'll continue to protect our natural resources. We will seek reauthorization and expanded funding for the Superfund program to continue cleaning up hazardous waste sites which threaten human health and the environment.

Now, there's another great heritage to speak of this evening. Of all the changes that have swept America the past 4 years, none brings greater promise than our rediscovery of the values of faith, freedom, family, work, and neighborhood.

We see signs of renewal in increased attendance in places of worship; renewed optimism and faith in our future; love of country rediscovered by our young, who are leading the way. We've rediscovered that work is good in and of itself, that it ennobles us to create and contribute no matter how seemingly humble our jobs. We've seen a powerful new current from an old and honorable tradition—American generosity.

From thousands answering Peace Corps appeals to help boost food production in Africa, to millions volunteering time, corporations adopting schools, and communities pulling together to help the neediest among us at home, we have refound our values. Private sector initiatives are crucial to our future.

I thank the Congress for passing equal access legislation giving religious groups the same right to use classrooms after school that other groups enjoy. But no citizen need tremble, nor the world shudder, if a child stands in a classroom and breathes a prayer. We ask you again, give children back a right they had for a century and a half or more in this country.

The question of abortion grips our nation. Abortion is either the taking of a human life or it isn't. And if it is—and medical technology is increasingly showing it is—it must be stopped. It is a terrible irony that while some turn to abortion, so many others who cannot become parents cry out for children to adopt. We have room for these children. We can fill the cradles of those who want a child to love. And tonight I ask you in the Congress to move this year on legislation to protect the unborn.

In the area of education, we're returning to excellence, and again, the heroes are our people, not government. We're stressing basics of discipline, rigorous testing, and homework, while helping children become computer-smart as well. For 20 years scholastic aptitude test scores of our high school students went down, but now they have gone up 2 of the last 3 years. We must go forward in our commitment to the new basics, giving parents greater authority and making sure good teachers are rewarded for hard work and achievement through merit pay.

Of all the changes in the past 20 years, none has more threatened our sense of national well-being than the explosion of violent crime. One does not have to be attacked to be a victim. The woman who must run to her car after shopping at night is a victim. The couple draping their door with locks and chains are victims; as is the tired, decent cleaning woman who can't ride a subway home without being afraid.

We do not seek to violate the rights of defendants. But shouldn't we feel more compassion for the victims of crime than for those who commit crime? For the first time in 20 years, the crime index has fallen 2 years in a row. We've convicted over 7,400 drug offenders and put them, as well as leaders of organized crime, behind bars in record numbers.

But we must do more. I urge the House to follow the Senate and enact proposals permitting use of all reliable evidence that police officers acquire in good faith. These proposals would also reform the habeas corpus laws and allow, in keeping with the will of the overwhelming majority of Americans, the use of the death penalty where necessary.

There can be no economic revival in ghettos when the most violent among us are allowed to roam free. It's time we restored domestic tranquility. And we mean to do just that.

Just as we're positioned as never before to secure justice in our economy, we're poised as never before to create a safer, freer, more peaceful world. Our alliances are stronger than ever. Our economy is stronger than ever. We have resumed our historic role as a leader of the free world. And all of these together are a great force for peace.

Since 1981 we've been committed to seeking fair and verifiable arms agreements that would lower the risk of war and reduce the size of nuclear arsenals. Now our determination to maintain a strong defense has influenced the Soviet Union to return to the bargaining table. Our negotiators must be able to go to that table with the united support of the American people. All of us have no greater dream than to see the day when nuclear weapons are banned from this Earth forever.

Each Member of the Congress has a role to play in modernizing our defenses, thus supporting our chances for a meaningful arms agreement. Your vote this spring on the Peacekeeper missile will be a critical test of our resolve to maintain the strength we need and move toward mutual and verifiable arms reductions.

For the past 20 years we've believed that no war will be launched as long as each side knows it can retaliate with a deadly counterstrike. Well, I believe there's a better way of eliminating the threat of nuclear war. It is a Strategic Defense Initiative aimed ultimately at finding a nonnuclear defense against ballistic missiles. It's the most hopeful possibility of the nuclear age. But it's not very well understood.

Some say it will bring war to the heavens, but its purpose is to deter war in the heavens and on Earth. Now, some say the research would be expensive. Perhaps, but it could save millions of lives, indeed humanity itself. And some say if we build such a system, the Soviets will build a defense system of their own. Well, they already have strategic defenses that surpass ours; a civil defense system, where we have almost none; and a research program covering roughly the same areas of technology that we're now exploring. And finally some say the research will take a long time. Well, the answer to that is: Let's get started.

Harry Truman once said that, ultimately, our security and the world's hopes for peace and human progress "lie not in measures of defense or in the control of weapons, but in the growth and expansion of freedom and self-government."

And tonight, we declare anew to our fellow citizens of the world: Freedom is not the sole prerogative of a chosen few; it is the universal right of all God's children.

Look to where peace and prosperity flourish today. It is in homes that freedom built. Victories against poverty are greatest and peace most secure where people live by laws that ensure free press, free speech, and freedom to worship, vote, and create wealth.

Our mission is to nourish and defend freedom and democracy, and to communicate these ideals everywhere we can. America's economic success is freedom's success; it can be repeated a hundred times in a hundred different nations. Many countries in east Asia and the Pacific have few resources other than the enterprise of their own people. But through low tax rates and free markets they've soared ahead of centralized economies. And now China is opening up its economy to meet its needs.

We need a stronger and simpler approach to the process of making and implementing trade policy, and we'll be studying potential changes in that process in the next few weeks. We've seen the benefits of free trade and lived through the disasters of protectionism. Tonight I ask all our trading partners, developed and developing alike, to join us in a new round of trade negotiations to expand trade and competition and strengthen the global economy—and to begin it in this next year.

There are more than 3 billion human beings living in Third World countries with an average per capita income of $650 a year. Many are victims of dictatorships that impoverished them with taxation and corruption. Let us ask our allies to join us in a practical program of trade and assistance that fosters economic development through personal incentives to help these people climb from poverty on their own.

We cannot play innocents abroad in a world that's not innocent; nor can we be passive when freedom is under seige. Without resources, diplomacy cannot succeed. Our security assistance programs help friendly governments defend themselves and give them confidence to work for peace. And I hope that you in the Congress will understand that, dollar for dollar, security assistance contributes as much to global security as our own defense budget.

We must stand by all our democratic allies. And we must not break faith with those who are risking their lives—on every continent, from Afghanistan to Nicaragua—to defy Soviet-supported aggression and secure rights which have been ours from birth.

The Sandinista dictatorship of Nicaragua, with full Cuban-Soviet bloc support, not only persecutes its people, the church, and denies a free press, but arms and provides bases for Communist terrorists attacking neighboring states. Support for freedom fighters is self-defense and totally consistent with the OAS and U.N. Charters. It is essential that the Congress continue all facets of our assistance to Central America. I want to work with you to support the democratic forces whose struggle is tied to our own security.

And tonight, I've spoken of great plans and great dreams. They're dreams we can make come true. Two hundred years of American history should have taught us that nothing is impossible.

Ten years ago a young girl left Vietnam with her family, part of the exodus that followed the fall of Saigon. They came to the United States with no possessions and not knowing a word of English. Ten years ago—the young girl studied hard, learned English, and finished high school in the top of her class. And this May, May 22d to be exact, is a big date on her calendar. Just 10 years from the time she left Vietnam, she will graduate from the United States Military Academy at West Point. I thought you might like to meet an American hero named Jean Nguyen.

Now, there's someone else here tonight, born 79 years ago. She lives in the inner city, where she cares for infants born of mothers who are heroin addicts. The children, born in withdrawal, are sometimes even dropped on her doorstep. She helps them with love. Go to her house some night, and maybe you'll see her silhouette against the window as she walks the floor talking softly, soothing a child in her arms— Mother Hale of Harlem, and she, too, is an American hero.

Jean, Mother Hale, your lives tell us that the oldest American saying is new again: Anything is possible in America if we have the faith, the will, and the heart. History is

135

asking us once again to be a force for good in the world. Let us begin in unity, with justice, and love.

Thank you, and God bless you.

Note: The President spoke at 9:05 p.m. in *the House Chamber of the Capitol. He was* *introduced by Thomas P. O'Neill, Jr., Speak-* *er of the House of Representatives. The ad-* *dress was broadcast live on nationwide* *radio and television.*

Informal Exchange With Reporters Prior to a Meeting With Prime Minister Robert Hawke of Australia
February 7, 1985

Q. Mr. President, does the ANZUS alliance have any future, given the lack of cooperation we've been getting from our South Pacific allies?

The President. Well, the only thing that has happened that disturbs that is the New Zealand position on our vessels there and the right of entry at the ports. But, other than that, I think our ANZUS alliance is very sound and very solid. And I think the presence here of the first head of state, in the new term, the Prime Minister of Australia, is evidence of that.

Q. Doesn't the announcement yesterday of a change of plans on the MX test give you any reason for concern, Mr. President?

The President. No, because that was pretty much our own idea. We had several alternatives, and we made a choice.

Q. Are you concerned at all about a ripple effect throughout the other allies?

The President. No.

Q. What does the U.S. intend to do, sir, about the New Zealand position on our vessels?

The President. About what?

Q. What does the U.S. intend to do? Will we be considering economic sanctions or reviewing our relationship with New Zealand?

The President. Oh, this is I don't think any time to discuss that.

Q. Will you be talking to your guest about a separate alliance between the U.S. and Australia and excluding New Zealand?

The President. No. As I say, we feel the ANZUS alliance is very much alive and working.

Q. How do you feel about the reaction to your speech last night, sir?

The President. Well, that's a whole different subject. I only answered those other questions, because I thought that I couldn't avoid them on the subject they were on. But I've been pleased, yes.

Note: The exchange began at 11:35 a.m. in *the Oval Office at the White House.*

Appointment of Robert H. Tuttle as Deputy Assistant to the President and Director of Presidential Personnel
February 7, 1985

The President today announced the appointment of Robert H. Tuttle as Deputy Assistant to the President and Director of Presidential Personnel.

Mr. Tuttle has served as Special Assistant to the President in the Office of Presidential Personnel since December 1982.

A successful west coast business executive for the past 15 years, Mr. Tuttle served as president of three automobile dealerships in Los Angeles and Tucson prior to accepting his position on the White House staff.

An active member of the California Republican Party, Mr. Tuttle served as chairman of the budget and expenditures committee and deputy finance chairman and was a member of the executive committee. In 1980 he was cochairman of the California Reagan for President Committee.

Mr. Tuttle's civic and community involvement include service as a member of the national board of directors of the Boys Clubs of America, chairman of the board of Curtis School, and a member of the board of directors of the Los Angeles Red Cross and the Los Angeles Motor Car Dealers Association.

Mr. Tuttle, 41, holds a bachelor of arts degree from Stanford University and a master's of business administration from the University of Southern California. He is married to the former Donna Frame. They have two daughters, Tiffany and Alexandra, and reside in Washington, DC.

Remarks Following Discussions With Prime Minister Robert Hawke of Australia
February 7, 1985

The President. Prime Minister Bob Hawke, it was a pleasure to meet with you today, the first head of state to visit us since the inauguration. And this, I understand, is also your first trip abroad since your own reelection. We're each getting our new terms started by sitting down and talking with a good friend.

I cannot overstate the value America places on our friendship with Australia. We share a commitment to democratic ideals. In fact, at the heart of our election process is the secret ballot, which, by no coincidence, was referred to as the Australian ballot when it was first introduced into our country.

Australia is a reliable ally, an important trading partner, a trusted friend, and a fellow democracy. We've stood together through trials and tribulations. We've rejoiced together in triumph. And now, as Australia approaches its bicentennial in 1988, the United States Government and private sector will play an active part in that historic event.

As a key ally and a vital voice in world affairs, Australia makes a significant contribution to the way that we approach international challenges. My conversations with Prime Minister Hawke today reflected the serious consideration with which we take Australia's views in national interest.

Much of our consultation was focused on arms control. Prime Minister Hawke made clear the importance of this issue to the Australian people, and it is no less so for us. I reiterated my sincere desire to achieve deep reductions in nuclear arms, as a giant first step toward eliminating them altogether.

As allies, we've always consulted closely on foreign policy issues. And now that Australia has been named a member of the U.N. Security Council, new weight will be added to our consultations.

On regional issues, we reaffirmed our strong belief in cooperation among Pacific States to maintain secure, prosperous, and democratic societies. Prime Minister Hawke and I agreed that strength and unity of purpose will give the West the leverage it needs to achieve effective and verifiable arms reductions with the Soviet Union.

We consider that close and comprehensive interaction among ANZUS members on political, economic, and defense matters is central to the continued effectiveness of the ANZUS alliance. In particular, continued military cooperation is essential to maintenance of the alliance's integrity and strength.

We deeply regret the decision by the New Zealand Government to deny port access to our ships. We consider New Zealand a friend. It's our deepest hope that New Zealand will restore the traditional cooperation that has existed between our two countries. Allies must work together as partners to meet their shared responsibilities. The security which we derive from these arrangements is at the foundation of the growing prosperity we share.

Prime Minister Hawke and I were very pleased to discuss the economic good news coming from both our countries and many others around the world. The global economy is picking up steam, and we're happy to have played a part in that recovery.

This is our second meeting, Bob. It's still a long way from Australia to the United States, but modern technology and good old-fashioned friendship are bringing us closer than ever before.

I'm grateful for your visit, and I'm looking forward to working together with you in the coming years to make the world a safer and a better place. And Godspeed now on your way home.

The Prime Minister. Thank you very much.

Mr. President, I greatly appreciate the warmth and the friendliness of your statement and of the consultations we have just concluded with you and with the members of your administration.

But this is my first overseas visit since our elections, and that we have the honor to be the first official visitors here since your second inauguration point up the prime importance of our personal relationship and those between our governments and between our countries.

The timing of our talks has not just been of symbolic significance but has added greatly to their substantive value. We have again found an extensive coincidence of preoccupations and of priorities in managing our respective foreign and domestic affairs.

You have just launched a budgetary process which will have great significance for the international community. Both our governments face the task of maintaining the strong growth that both the United States and Australia have recently enjoyed. And we shall both be tackling this on a number of fronts during 1985.

We're looking also to increasing trade flows to sustain economic recovery fully and widely. We seek to resist protectionism and to preserve and to strengthen the multilateral trading system. And, Mr. President, we

look to and we know we will receive from you strong leadership in that direction.

One aspect—an important one—of the ANZUS relationship has become a matter of close concern to us both and will require continuing consultation. Let me say, first, that the relationship between Australia and the United States under the ANZUS treaty and the rights and obligations assumed by us under the treaty are undiminished by recent events. Your statement accurately reflects the position. The ANZUS treaty remains; the fundamental importance of cooperation within it has been reaffirmed here today.

Similarly, we have reaffirmed the need for solidarity and common purpose in pursuit of arms reductions. I congratulate you again on reaching agreement with the Soviet Union to enter into the forthcoming round of negotiations and on the approach you have taken to that agreement. You will have our continuing support in what is bound to be a difficult and protracted process.

We will remain closely in touch as that process moves forward. And we will continue to offer counsel, while maintaining our own direct participation with you in multilateral disarmament work.

We will continue both nationally and in the established pattern of partnership with you to make our contribution to Western security in every way open and acceptable to us. We will do so against the basic criteria that a situation of stable deterrence, despite its defects, is necessary in order to produce progress on disarmament.

We have a fundamental interest in that starting point of stable deterrence, in the final goal of disarmament, and in an intermediate and, hopefully, early stage of substantial arms reductions.

I said, Mr. President, at the outset that the timing of our talks was important. I believe we have been successful in bringing steady consideration to the issues before us. In the process, we have once more tested and proved our ability to work closely together.

One of the continuing strengths of a mature relationship is that neither seeks from the other a complete conformity of views and actions. But we have shown, once again, the capacity to respond to each other's needs in the pursuit of major objectives on which we have the widest measure of agreement.

Mr. President, I thank you for your hospitality and for your warm references to our bicentennial celebrations, in which we look forward to active United States participation.

I thank you, also, Mr. President, for the kind reception which you and Mrs. Reagan have given to me and to my wife. I look forward to continued meetings with you and members of your administration, whether up here or down under.

Note: The President spoke at 1:22 p.m. at the South Portico of the White House following a meeting in the Oval Office and a luncheon in the Residence.

Nomination of Lynda Anne Barness To Be a Member of the Board of Directors of the Inter-American Foundation
February 7, 1985

The President today announced his intention to nominate Lynda Anne Barness to be a member of the Board of Directors of the Inter-American Foundation for a term expiring October 6, 1990. She would succeed Doris B. Holleb.

In 1983 she was the eastern finance director for the Arlen Specter for U.S. Senate Committee. Previously she was in the office of Senator Arlen Specter in 1982. She was with the Barness Organization in 1979–1982.

She graduated from Tufts University (B.A., 1971) and the University of Pennsylvania (M.A., 1972). She has two children and resides in Ambler, PA. She was born April 22, 1929, in Philadelphia, PA.

Appointment of Seven Members of the National Council on Vocational Education
February 7, 1985

The President today announced his intention to appoint the following individuals to be members of the National Council on Vocational Education. These are new positions.

The following individuals to serve for terms expiring January 17, 1988:

Marva Nettles Collins is founder and director of the Westside Preparatory School in Chicago, IL. She is married, has three children, and resides in Chicago, IL. She was born August 31, 1936, in Monroeville, AL.

Mary B. Liu is an educational consultant for the San Francisco Unified School District. She was born May 1, 1914, in China, and now resides in San Francisco, CA.

Gertrude McDonald is retired director of special education for Fremont Unified School District in Fremont, CA. She is married and resides in Fremont, CA. She was born July 21, 1923, in the Irvington District of Fremont, CA.

Joyce Newman is a travel consultant in Cedarhurst, NY. She is married, has three children, and resides in North Woodmere, NY. She was born January 29, 1936, in Bronx, NY.

J. Fernando Niebla is president of INFOTEC Development, Inc., a high technology aerospace firm in Costa Mesa, CA. He is married, has three children, and resides in Cypress, CA. He was born October 2, 1939, in Nogales, Mexico.

Patricia Glaser Silversmith is a teacher at Community School in St. Louis County, MO. She is married and resides in St. Louis, MO. She was born February 16, 1931, in St. Louis.

139

The following individual to serve for a term expiring January 17, 1987:

Christine Valmy is president of Christine Valmy,

Inc., manufacturer of skin care products, in New York City. She is married and resides in New York City. She was born October 25, 1926, in Bucharest, Romania.

Interview With a Group of Senior Executives and Staff Members From the Wall Street Journal
February 7, 1985

Tax Simplification

Q. Last night, you enthusiastically endorsed the tax simplification concept and said you've instructed the Treasury to fashion a final bill. The word from some parts of the business community is that one part of that deal has already been struck; namely, that you will change the Treasury proposals and continue favorable capital gains tax treatment and accelerated depreciation and in return that you would continue the present taxation of dividends. Is that the general direction you wish to head?

The President. Well, let me just say about that that I'm hard put to answer a specific question of that kind. We were faced with the two problems: the one of what we want, the tax reform; the other with the necessity of coming in with the budget. We have been long hours around that Cabinet table on the budget matter and, finally, have now submitted it. We have not yet begun that process on the tax program.

I think, as I've said before, I think that Treasury study was probably the finest and broadest study that's been made of the tax structure that I can ever remember. And I hesitate to give any opinion on any single thing until—again, those of us who've sat around the table on the budget are going to sit around that same table now on the tax program and go at every facet of it. I think we recognize that in that study—I don't think anyone has said, "Why, buy this entirely as it is"—we recognize there are things in there that are options.

And so, I don't think that I could or should give an answer on a specific of that kind.

Q. Well, apart from the specifics, sir, it's been argued that venture capital has helped fuel the American economy in

recent years.

The President. Yeah.

Q. I think you agree with that. Does it worry you that by eliminating the special treatment given to capital gains that that might kill the goose that's laying the golden eggs?

The President. Well, this is going to be a consideration. This is one of the things that——

Q. Is that a real word?

The President. Yes. And, so, I think that this'll be one of the points that will be very much discussed, because the whole aim of both of these things—well, in addition to the tax reform being necessary to eliminate a lot of unfairness—and the biggest unfairness of all is the complexity of the present tax system—but, in addition to that, we're looking to these both as things necessary for economic growth. And, therefore, we're going to look at this tax proposal and at anything as to whether it could contribute to economic growth or whether it could set economic growth back.

Q. Is that a suggestion—you'd like to keep the current capital gains tax treatment?

The President. No, you're getting me to— [*laughter*]—to give an opinion on it. No. [*Laughter*]

Q. Try us. [*Laughter*]

The President. What I'm saying is, we will be giving each of these things consideration on that basis that I just outlined.

Q. Well, let me ask another concept question, then. You said last night that the individual tax rates would be no higher than 35 percent, perhaps even lower. Well, the way the Treasury proposal lowers individual tax rates is by increasing corporate taxes by 37 percent. Again, as a concept, do you generally favor that approach of individual versus corporate taxes?

The President. Oh, wait a minute. The corporate tax is given a ceiling of lower than the——

Q. No, but overall corporate taxes would go up about 37 percent. Not the rates, but overall corporate taxes would go up about 37 percent under the Treasury proposal while individual taxes would come down. Is that a general approach that you endorse?

The President. I, as I say, I haven't even made an attempt to study that bill in detail that much to know that. I assume that that would mean things that would be taken away from them that are present deductions. No. I would have to be convinced of the need to do that, because I'm a believer that one day we must recognize that only people pay taxes. And someday I would hope that we could arrive at a tax structure that would recognize that you can't tax things; you only tax people.

Q. Well, you also said last night that this was not going to be a tax increase under any disguise. Let me turn that around and ask: If the bill is modified to meet the objections of some critics, whether it's from the business community or elsewhere, could it be that the bill would be a revenue loser? And would that be acceptable to you?

The President. Well, no. I think what we're talking about here is a tax reform, and you're striving for neutrality in this. Now, in that kind of a reform, I'm also sure that there are going to be some people, obviously, who are going to pay more tax than they're paying now.

But, then, you're talking about people who are unfairly not paying a share of the tax today. And if you—the aim of this kind of a tax program, and I think this is true of all three of the proposals that are now before us—the two that are up in the Congress now, plus this Treasury report—I think it is true that one of the targets there is the large amount of tax that is not being paid, many times legally, by virtue of the complexities of the present tax laws, in which some who fairly should be paying a share are avoiding it. And with the simplification comes a straightening out of that kind of a problem.

Q. But you want your final bill to be rev-enue neutral?

The President. Yes. And if it is revenue neutral, it will end up actually providing more revenues from the simple reason that you will broaden the base of the economy.

Q. Let me try one more tax question, sir. You also spoke favorably about the notion of lowering rates and, as you just said, broadening the base by eliminating many exemptions. But right after you did that, you then called for two new exemptions; namely, enterprise zones and tuition tax credits. Doesn't that just encourage others to try to carve out their own special places for their own pet writeoffs and threaten to unravel that whole concept of lowering the base by broadening—or lowering the rates by broadening the base?

The President. Well, if you're trying to make a tax program more fair, which is also part of this proposal—take the issue you've raised of tuition tax credits. Here you have, I think, a very broad—based on fairness in the country—you've got people who are compelled to send their children to school under the law, because we believe that a democracy can only exist if you have a literate citizenry. And yet these people who, if they choose or feel they can get a better education for their children, choose a private or parochial school, independent school of some kind, they pay the full cost of sending their child to that school. But at the same time, they're paying the full cost that parents of children are paying—they're paying that in taxes to support the public school system.

Now, if you stop and think what the additional cost to public schools would be if suddenly the independent schools closed and all those students were turned over to the educational market—and it would not mean an increase in revenues for public education, because already they're getting the money from those parents—you could see what a burden this would be.

Well, it seems to me that it's only fair that some parent—as a matter of fact, the ultimate fairness would be educational vouchers. Does government properly support a school system, or does it provide the funds directly to the students to get an education? And there would be public schools

141

available; there would be independent schools available. They could take that voucher and go where they want, and you put competition back into education.

Q. Mr. President, on the politics of tax simplification, the general idea doesn't seem to have a lot of support among the Senate Republican leadership, and the business community has its problems with some of the provisions. What can you do, personally, to turn around the opposition from these kinds of people who are normally in your corner on things?

The President. I'm—at the beginning, you said at the beginning what——

Q. The Senate—on tax simplification.

The President. Oh. Well, I think that there are some people, simply on the basis of what was revealed of the Treasury Department study, that read into it things they thought were inimical to their interests and immediately took off. But I think in many instances, when you sat down with those people and pointed out what the change in rates did, some of their hostility disappeared.

I think the most important thing that we're going to face is, once we have settled on and agreed on a package that we believe is fair and is the reform that is needed, is then to make sure there's no misunderstanding or lack of understanding of what it will actually mean to the taxpayer.

Basically, we found that the overwhelming majority of people were going to get a sizable decrease in taxes, based roughly on this setup, and that those that weren't were going to get an increase were people who, as I say, are not presently paying their fair share.

Federal Reserve System

Q. More generally on the economy, you've made it pretty clear that you believe that we're on the brink of a sustained economic boom. Are you worried that this might be cut short by the Federal Reserve? And would you like to have a greater say in Federal Reserve policy?

The President. Well, we try to work very closely, as closely as we can, with the Federal Reserve on this. And they know what it is that we feel is the sound policy. And so far, I must say, right now they're on

target—and that is we need a money supply that is commensurate to the growth in the economy and to continue that growth without inflation. And that provides two lines between which you must stay. And so far, as I say, right now they're right on target with that.

Q. You're comfortable right now. Were you comfortable back in July and August?

The President. I think there were some times when it fluctuated widely and when they got well below their target and all. But, as I say, we're trying to stay in close touch with them. And I think we've made it plain what we believe.

I also recognize that there are times the tools are not that accurate. There are times when it isn't an outright decision of theirs that sees the money supply fluctuating, and the fluctuations can be caused from other and outside forces. But I think we're pretty much in agreement on——

Nicaragua

Q. If we could shift to foreign policy for a moment. Your administration is obviously headed into a battle with Congress over the aid to the *contra* forces in Nicaragua. Last night, you said that aid was necessary to our own self-defense. What I keep wondering is, would you like to see the *contras* actually overthrow the Sandinista government? And, if not, what's the purpose of aiding them?

The President. The purpose of aiding them is to aid literally the people of Nicaragua, who are striving to get the government that the revolution promised them. If you'll recall during the revolution, the revolutionary forces appealed to the Organization of American States for help. And they asked the Organization if they would please try to persuade Somoza to step down and, thus, end the bloodshed. And, in return for this, they gave the Organization of American States the declaration of principles of what it was they were seeking in the revolution. And this was pure democracy. This was all the civil rights and human rights, freedom of speech, freedom of labor unions, freedom of religion, and all of these things.

Now, what happened we saw happen once before with Castro's coming to power in Cuba. He had other allies that wanted a democracy, and he never admitted to his true leanings until that revolution was over.

Well, what happened was the faction known as the Sandinistas took over. They ousted a number of other revolutionary leaders; some of them were exiled; some, I think, were done away with; some imprisoned.

But they have set up a totalitarian government. They've made it plain: Their allies are Cuba, the Soviet Union, the Communist bloc, even Mr. Qadhafi, and now Iran is getting into the picture. But they've set up a totalitarian government. They have betrayed the principles that the people of Nicaragua were fighting for. And what we think is that we should be on the side of those people who actually are only asking for the democracy that they'd fought a revolution to get.

Q. It sounds as though you are saying that the objective is an entirely new government in Nicaragua. Would that be fair to conclude?

The President. Well, when you answer a question that simply, though, and you come back, then, you see, you get into the thing—well, are you talking about individuals or are you talking—you're talking about the governmental form. Now, if that governmental form can come by way of the people who are presently in that government and who then will be willing to stand for elections at appropriate times, that's fine. But that's what it's really all about, is getting the revolution the people fought for.

Terrorism

Q. On a similar kind of question, Secretary Shultz has been giving speeches about the need to retaliate against terrorism. But, in fact, there hasn't been any U.S. retaliation for the attacks on our Embassies and our Marines, and five Americans right now are being held hostage——

The President. Yes.

Q. ——in Lebanon. Is your policy on using force against terrorism really any different from the Carter administration's?

The President. Well, I think you're putting some apples and oranges together there. The Carter situation was not dealing with unknown, hidden terrorists. They were

dealing with a legitimate government, and not a very good government, but—[laughter]—at least it was the government of the nation. You knew who you were dealing with; you were dealing with a national entity.

The problem with terrorism so far and why, as I've said, much of the answer lies in what we're going forward with now, and that is better relationships with all the other democracies to where we'll make extradition easy, we'll exchange intelligence information. There are two ways you could deal with terrorism, and one of them is terrorism itself.

Suppose in revenge, just on the basis that you think some people of a certain group or sect or belief did this, and then you strike back and perform the same kind of brutal crimes against some of those people, without any knowledge or assurance that you're getting the people who perpetrated the first crime. Well, that's no way to fight, and we don't believe in that.

The thing is, you have to find an ability to locate the source, if possible; obviously, the best way is if you can infiltrate and then get some advanced information on when they're going to strike—be prepared for them.

Our problem with the worst terrorist act—the big one, of course, was our Marines in the Embassy, was nothing but some suspicion of a certain locale in Lebanon, and yet there was no way to sort that out or separate it out from a community of other people and no way to strike back without causing a lot of innocents to die.

And what we now, I think, are looking at is the possibility that some terrorists actually do have national support and backing. Then, with that established, then you can let that government know that there is going to be redress against that government if these acts continue.

U.S.-Soviet Negotiations on Nuclear and Space Arms

Q. On the broad question of arms control and the U.S.-Soviet relationship, you talk about arms control agreements with deep cuts and offensive weapons and extensive verification. When you do that—aren't you really asking the Soviet Union to become an entirely different kind of country? And can we really expect that in our lifetimes?

The President. Well, I'm not going to be euphoric about this, but I do think that one of the things we have going for us at this time, that hasn't been present in much of our previous negotiations, is that we go to the table now in a situation in which you're not going there looking at the Soviets as if, "Well, they're people just like us, and maybe if we talk sweetly enough, why they will be conned into being nice, too." No. The only way you're ever going to succeed in negotiations is if you can go there with a situation in which it is to their practical interest also, that their interests are served by coming to an agreement.

And I think the fact that we go there now with our own military buildup, with them seeing that the alternative to legitimate arms reduction could very well be an arms race with an industrial power that they know they cannot match; in other words, we're saying to them, "We're not going to let you get a monopoly on power to the point that you can start winning by simple ultimatums—threats of, 'Surrender, or die'—so make up your mind. You either join in a legitimate reduction in which both of us will reduce in such a way that neither one of us represents a threat to the other, or you face that kind of a race."

It was all summed up in a cartoon. I know your paper doesn't have cartoons, but——

Q. Sort of—[*Laughter*]

The President. Sort of—all right. But a cartoon one day and it—right back early on in our military rebuilding—and it was two Russian generals, and one of them was saying to the other, "I liked the arms race better when we were the only ones in it." And I think that's been the situation over a number of years.

Q. On the military buildup, one of the prominent things is the Strategic Defense Initiative. And would you continue to favor this, even if your own scientists concluded that it could never be leak-proof and that even a few missiles would always get through and destroy cities?

The President. Oh, I've never asked for 100 percent. That would be a fine goal, but you can have a most effective defensive weapon even if it isn't 100 percent, because what you would have is the knowledge that—or that the other fellow would have the knowledge that if they launched a first strike, that it might be such that not enough of their missiles could get through, and in return we could launch the retaliatory strike.

Now, that isn't really the goal of the Strategic Defense Initiative. I tie that to what I think is the goal of these arms negotiations. The Soviet Union—Chernenko and Gromyko both have publicly stated that they would like to see the elimination, ultimately, of nuclear weapons. All right, they've said it. That's what our goal is.

Now, if they really mean it, we can go to a table and sit down and start negotiating reductions, aiming toward the elimination of those weapons. If they don't mean it—or either way—I think that to go forward with this research on a strategic weapon is hand in hand with that goal, that ultimate goal. If you could have that kind of a defense in which they would have to say: "Well, wait a minute. How many missiles would we have to build to get enough through on a first attack that we wouldn't be threatened with, then, the retaliation?" And then they will see the value that this is what I mean by making nuclear weapons obsolete—they'll see that this defensive weapon could be a contributing factor to eliminating such weapons.

If we come up with such a weapon, we're not going to stand there and say: "Okay, now we've got you. We can launch the first attack." I don't think this country is ever in a position where it wants to do that. We don't start wars. We have no intention of starting one now. But what we would then be able to say to them is: "Look, we're willing to join you. We'll do away with ours. You do away with yours. We've got this thing here now, this defensive weapon, and we're very willing to use this, not to enable us to fight you, but to simply do what we both want, and that is get rid of the weapons."

Q. Mr. President, let me bring you back if I may——

Principal Deputy Press Secretary Speakes.

You're about 10 minutes into your next appointment, so—

Farm Credit Programs

Q. Just a quick one. Leaving aside David Stockman's indelicate remarks about the military caring more about their pensions than the security, for which he's apologized, do you agree with the substance of his remarks that the system of military retirement benefits is bloated and the taxpayers shouldn't be bailing out farmers who took out bad loans?

The President. Well, right now, we're offering a program in which we're hopeful that we can salvage some of those farmers. The situation we're facing today with those farmers is one other people in other lines of work have faced, and it's the result of ending an era of building your business on expected inflation. And farmland, unfortunately, was one of those things that, in an inflationary world, zoomed in value. And then they borrowed on the basis of that as security. And when we were successful in bringing down inflation, one of the first things that happened was the nose-diving of that land.

Military Retirement Benefits

Q. How about the other part of his criticism—the military pensions are bloated? Is he right?

The President. No. I have to think this is a little different than any other pension program you want to name—the military. They go into a profession or a business—profession is the word; I guess it should be used—in which they know that, say, in a matter of a certain number of years, even though in any other line of activity they would be literally at their prime—your business or mine or anything else—but they know that the physical requirements are such that they're going to be out.

Now, there is that coupled with the sacrifice that is made by the military. I talked to a retired military man—in this case he was an officer and reached high rank—and he had retired, and then he had found other employment. But he told me that one of the reasons—retiring was that in 31 years of his marriage—they sat one night and totted it up—20 years of the 31, they had been separated from each other, that he, in the call of duty, for 20 of his 31 married years had not been—he and his wife had not been together. He was out there in the world someplace. And you——

Q. That's worse than someone running for President.

The President. What?

Q. That's worse than someone running for President. [*Laughter*]

Sir, Larry Speakes would not forgive me if I didn't ask at least one question about the budget deficit before we leave.

The President. All right.

Mr. Speakes. The last one.

Budget Deficit

Q. Okay. I will. I knew you'd be mad if I didn't get that in, though.

You know, in fiscal years '83, '84, and '85 we'll have budget deficits of about $600 billion. At the same time, unemployment's coming down, inflation is staying around 4 percent, interest rates have actually come down a little bit. Could it be that maybe these budget deficits really don't matter?

The President. Yes, they come to a point where they matter. I've been saying that for about 30 years.

Q. I know. And yet you've run these——

The President. Yes.

Q. ——huge deficits, and you're doing so well.

The President. I think just one of the most wonderful things to see and to hear is to hear my own words coming back at me from over those years by a few Democrats right now, who suddenly have discovered deficits. And yet for 50 years, with the exception of about 4 years in that 50, they have controlled the Congress of the United States.

Q. But why don't they affect inflation and interest rates and unemployment now, if they're so bad?

Mr. Speakes. Last——

The President. No, what they can do is get to a point in which the total debt—and remember, with all their moaning and crying, the national debt was about a trillion dollars when I came into office. And the first of those major big deficit increases occurred after I was in office. However, it was not my responsibility, because your first 8 months in office, you're on the other fellow's budget. I don't come into office and declare how much we can spend. The budget is there until the following October. In fact, when the bottom fell out of the economy in July of '81, not one facet of my economic program had been passed as yet. So, it couldn't have had anything to do with that deficit.

But what is happening now indicates the danger that over the 50 years, the situation keeps getting worse. And let me give you one. When we put into effect the War on Poverty, which started in the last half of the sixties and ran through the seventies—and poverty won, because the rate of increase in people in poverty increased in spite of the War on Poverty and all those great programs—but in the 15 years from 1965 to 1980, the budgets multiplied to 5 times what they were; the deficit went to 38 times what it had been.

So, you've got a built-in, structural deficit. And the President—to call it the President's budget—the President is responsible for submitting to the Congress what they have required in the programs they have legislated. And the Congress, in turn, when the President—and this is the situation a President's in—when the President submits and says, "We can run this program for this amount of money," and it's less than what the Congress thinks you should, the Congress insists that you spend more money. And they even tell you that if at the end of the year there's any money left, you're going to have to spend it before the end of the year. This is a structural problem.

And, of course, it's multiplied, and it's gotten worse. And a large part of this had to do with the great fall into recession that occurred in '81 and through '82. And so, there's no question that we're going to be better off and there's not going to be inflation on the things that bother us if we get government back to where 43 States or so have it, and that is that you can't spend more than government takes in.

Q. Thank you.

Note: The interview began at 2:48 p.m. in the Oval Office at the White House.

Remarks at a White House Luncheon Commemorating the 75th Anniversary of the Boy Scouts of America
February 8, 1985

Good afternoon and welcome. And forgive me for interrupting our lunch.

I'm delighted to be able to help celebrate the 75th anniversary of the Boy Scouts of America. I'm delighted to celebrate anything that's older than I am—[*laughter*]—but 75 years of unparalleled service to the youth and the families and the communities of our nation.

As you might imagine, in my job there's some things I must do and some I want to do and a few special things that I just can't wait to do. And this celebration is one of those special moments.

On Inauguration Day I spoke of the American sound—those symbols of our democracy and echoes of our past that give us purpose and guide us forward. And I said that sound—our heritage, our song—is hopeful, big-hearted, idealistic, daring, decent, and fair. And you know, come to think of it, I could have added trustworthy, loyal, helpful, friendly, courteous, kind, and the rest of the Scout law, because the Boy Scouts of America and the values that you hold close are an important part of the American sound and have been for 75 proud years.

And it was in the early days of scouting that the life of a young New Yorker was changed forever. Manhattan's Lower East Side was a very tough neighborhood, and far too many young men were drawn into the turmoil and the violence there and never recovered.

But this particular youngster from the

Lower East Side found the Boy Scouts. He was challenged to learn positive values—leadership, camping, fitness. Aaron took up the challenge and gained in moral strength, confidence, and ambition. He became a successful attorney. And his son became the second Eagle Scout in the family.

But Aaron never forgot his roots and, in 1943, left the practice of law to give more of his time to Boy Scout fundraising.

And his son? Well, during our first term, Ken Duberstein served here in the White House as my Assistant for Legislative Affairs. So, I'm very pleased that they're both here today.

You know, America sure turns out winners. And much of the credit belongs to organizations like the Boy Scouts. And so it's not surprising that yesterday's Scouts have helped to shape our today—in business, government, the media, science, medicine, education, show business, and—well, the list goes on and on.

Former Scouts have walked on the Moon, become President, and won the Heisman Trophy. Today they serve as Cabinet Secretaries, as my Press Secretary, and in the Congress. In fact, about two-thirds of the Members of the Congress have been in the Boy Scouts. I can't help but think, two-thirds of them Boy Scouts—[*laughter*]—how nice it would have been if the Boy Scouts had a merit badge for a balanced budget amendment. [*Laughter*]

But you can be certain that today's Scouts will help shape America. And when they do, I'll bet there'll be Scouts like the ones who are with us today, like Randy Reed of nearby Vienna, Virginia. Two days ago Randy received the Boy Scouts highest and rarest award—the Honor Medal for Lifesaving with Crossed Palms for extraordinary heroism.

And he's not alone. I've just been sitting beside a young man here, Freddie Hill, who also is wearing that medal very proudly. But Randy, also, at the extreme risk of his own life, rescued a young man who had slipped, who had struck his head and fell unconscious, wedged between rocks in 14 feet of murky water. With great bravery and skill, Randy did everything his Scout training would tell him to do and more. And, Randy, congratulations and God bless you.

Let me ask: Freddie, how many others in here are wearing that medal also? Which Scouts? Look at you, too. Freddie is wearing the medal.

Thank you. Well, it's easy to understand why the Boy Scout badge, the American eagle superimposed on the north sign of the mariners compass, means Follow me, I know the way. The Boy Scouts of America do know the way, the way to set high standards and how to live by them, and the way to build character, train in citizenship, and foster fitness of mind and body.

And here's one last thought: Without the thousands of adult leaders, corporate sponsors, and other caring Americans, it would not be possible for young Americans to capture the Scouting spirit and the special joys of camping, fellowship, service, and love of country.

So, thank all of you for what you're doing for our young people and for America's future. We're in good hands. So, God bless you all, and God bless the Boy Scouts of America.

Note: The President spoke at 12:53 p.m. in the State Dining Room at the White House.

Nomination of Vernon A. Walters To Be United States Representative to the United Nations
February 8, 1985

The President today announced his intention to nominate Vernon A. Walters to be the Representative of the United States of America to the United Nations, with the rank and status of Ambassador Extraordinary and Plenipotentiary, and the Representative of the United States of America in the Security Council of the United Nations, with Cabinet rank. He would succeed Jeane J. Kirkpatrick. Since July 18, 1981, he has been serving as Ambassador at Large.

Ambassador Walters was in the United States Army from 1941 to 1976, when he retired as lieutenant general. His special assignments included serving directly under Presidents Truman, Eisenhower, and Nixon; as aide to Averell Harriman at the Marshall plan in Paris; Assistant to General Eisenhower, to set up SHAPE headquarters in Paris; Staff Assistant to President Eisenhower on all his foreign trips; accompanied Vice President Nixon on his trip to South Amer-

ica in 1957; military attaché in Italy, Brazil, and France. He conducted negotiations with the North Vietnamese and Chinese in Paris from 1969 to 1972. In 1972–1976 he was Deputy Director of the Central Intelligence Agency. In 1976–1981 he was a consultant, lecturer, and author. In 1981 he was Senior Adviser to the Secretary of State.

Ambassador Walters was born January 3, 1917, in New York, NY. He attended the St. Louis de Gonzague in Paris and Stoneyhurst College (United Kingdom). His languages are French, Spanish, Portuguese, Italian, German, Dutch, and Russian.

Nomination of Daniel H. Carter To Be a Member of the National Commission on Libraries and Information Science
February 8, 1985

The President today announced his intention to nominate Daniel H. Carter to be a member of the National Commission on Libraries and Information Science for a term expiring July 19, 1989. He would succeed Margaret S. Warden.

Mr. Carter is vice president for strategic business services at Walter Ulrich Consulting, a management and technology consult-

ing firm, in Houston, TX. He was with Texas Instruments in 1966–1985, serving most recently as director of business relations for the data systems group.

He graduated from the University of Oklahoma (B.S., 1943 and 1949). He is married, has three children, and resides in Houston, TX. He was born October 4, 1922, in El Reno, OK.

Nomination of Two Members of the Board of Directors of the National Institute of Building Sciences
February 8, 1985

The President today announced his intention to nominate the following individuals to be members of the Board of Directors of the National Institute of Building Sciences for terms expiring September 7, 1987. These are reappointments.

MacDonald G. Becket is chairman of the board of the Becket Group of companies, including Welton Becket Associates, an architectural/engineering firm. He is a founding contributor to the Architectural and Design Endowment for the Museum of Contemporary Art in Los An-

geles and a fellow of the American Institute of Architects. He also served on the U.S. Capitol Architect's Long-Range Planning Committee and has been admitted to the National Council on Architectural Registration Boards. He is married, has four children, and resides in Los Angeles, CA. He was born November 2, 1928, in Seattle, WA.

Kyle Clayton Boone has been proprietor of Boone: Hunton Associates (architects, planners, interior designers) since 1968. Previously, he was an architect with Six Associates architectural firm in Asheville, NC, in 1963–1968; an architect with Echols-Sparger architectural firm in Marion, VA, in 1962–1963. He received the Reynolds Aluminum prize for architectural

students in 1962. He is married, has four children, and resides in Weaverville, NC. He was born December 16, 1932, in Washington, DC.

Appointment of Charles R. Hauser as a Member of the Architectural and Transportation Barriers Compliance Board
February 8, 1985

The President today announced his intention to appoint Charles R. Hauser to be a member of the Architectural and Transportation Barriers Compliance Board for a term expiring December 3, 1987. This is a reappointment.

Mr. Hauser is president of Hauser Associates, a design consulting firm he helped es-

tablish in 1966, in Atlanta, GA. He attended Washington University, School of Architecture, and graduated from Rhode Island School of Design in 1964.

He has four children and resides in Atlanta, GA. He was born February 17, 1941, in Litchfield, IL.

Radio Address to the Nation on Economic Growth
February 9, 1985

My fellow Americans:

Last Wednesday night I spoke to you about the great days that lie ahead for America if we do what we must to continue our economic expansion, creating new freedom and opportunities for people and uniting across party lines to keep bringing government spending growth down.

Since the beginning of 1983, when all the elements of our tax program were finally in place, our economy has burst ahead with 2 straight years of economic growth, leaving inflation and all the experts' pessimistic predictions in the dust. America did not win such a dramatic victory just to declare defeat.

Today we're poised on the launching pad of the future. We can make these next 4 years the greatest victories for growth, opportunity, and freedom America has ever known. Let me repeat what you know in your hearts and what has been the great guiding force of our philosophy from the very beginning: There are no limits to growth, no constraints on how strong America can become if all of you are set free.

You elected us to get results, and we, as

leaders, must show courage and imagination worthy of you: leadership for a growth economy that provides new and greater incentives and keeps inflation and interest rates heading down; leadership to bring forth economic opportunity in the inner cities, resurgence in our industrial heartland, new productivity and technological breakthroughs, and help for farmers in distress from past government failures in this time of transition to a market-oriented economy.

Already we're hearing old, familiar voices telling us to slow down, prepare to slash the defense budget, and raise taxes—all in the name of reducing projected budget deficits. Well, those arguments were rejected on November 6th. The single best deficit program is an all-out push for economic growth.

As I said Wednesday night, each added percentage point per year of real gross national product growth will lead to a cumulative reduction in deficits of nearly $200 billion over 5 years.

So, let's make one thing plain at the outset of the new term. We're raring to go. We have no intention of sitting at the starting gate. We're going to begin working now and pushing hard, in the Congress and across the country, for initiatives like tax simplification, enterprise zones, and the youth employment opportunity wage to help America reach her full potential.

As we lift America onto a stronger growth path, with more businesses starting up, more investments made, and more people employed and paying taxes, we will reduce the need for government spending on many of today's support programs.

But we must do more. We must also face up to the legacy of some 50 years of overspending, born of a deliberate policy that told us planned deficits and inflation would be good for us.

The budget I've sent to the Congress this year calls for an absolute freeze on overall government program spending at the fiscal 1985 level of approximately $804 billion, excluding debt service costs. Now, I know that there'll be differences of opinion on how to achieve this freeze. But if the Congress will work with us in a spirit of cooperation and compromise, then together we can bring our budget under control without damaging the economy or endangering national security. I urge the Congress to move quickly on a spending cut package that will reduce overall government spending growth. I hope our energies will be spent finding ways that we can reduce spending, rather than finding reasons why we cannot.

Other reforms are needed. I've often mentioned a constitutional amendment mandating a balanced budget and a line-item veto to cut individual items in overall appropriation bills. But elsewhere, our efforts to reduce bureaucracy through efficiencies and reductions in unnecessary personnel have been thwarted by congressionally mandated employment levels for certain programs. Our managers could get the job done just as well with fewer employees, but their hands are tied.

The executive branch has also been thwarted by legislative restraints from having its commercial-type activities—cafeterias and the like—handled by private businesses, which can run them less expensively than government.

And a President's power to limit spending himself is also restricted to the Congress. Once an appropriations bill has been signed into law, the President must spend all that money, even if he believes certain items are unnecessary. I continue to urge the Congress to give me the authority for line-item vetoes.

This week we've begun a new journey. If Congress works with us, we can accomplish great things for America. But the time to act is now.

Till next week, thanks for listening. God bless you.

Note: The President spoke at 12:06 p.m. from Camp David, MD.

Remarks at the Welcoming Ceremony for King Fahd bin 'Abd al-'Aziz Al Sa'ud of Saudi Arabia
February 11, 1985

The President. Ahlan wa Sahlan [Welcome]. It's a great privilege to welcome a world statesman, a leader of Arab and Muslim people, and a good friend of the United States, His Majesty King Fahd bin 'Abd al-'Aziz Al Sa'ud.

Although he is no stranger to our shores, it's been almost 8 years since he has paid an official visit to the United States. And I'm honored to welcome him back again today.

King Fahd's visit is in keeping with the warm, personal relations enjoyed between the leaders of our two countries, a tradition which began 40 years ago this week when King Fahd's father and President Franklin Roosevelt met to exchange views. The good will that emerged from that meeting of two great men has enormously benefited both our peoples in the last four decades.

The friendship and cooperation between

our governments and people are precious jewels whose value we should never underestimate. The positive nature of our relations demonstrates that cultural differences, as distinct as our own, need not separate or alienate peoples from one another.

As the guardians of Mecca and the protectors of your faith, you rightfully exert a strong moral influence in the world of Islam, and the people of the United States are proud of their leadership role among the democratic nations.

King Fahd, I hope that we can work together to seek a new rapprochement between the Islamic world and the Western democracies. Destiny has given us different political and social systems, yet with respect and good will, as our two countries have demonstrated, so much can be accomplished.

I firmly believe that in the years ahead, there should be and will be a more powerful recognition of the common interests shared by these two significant world forces. Already, the bonds of commerce are strong, especially between our two countries. Petroleum from Saudi wells helps drive the engines of progress in the United States, while at the same moment, American technology and know-how help in the construction of Saudi roads, hospitals, and communications systems.

Saudi Arabia has grown into one of America's largest trading partners. The commercial and economic power that we exert in the world spurs enterprise and bolsters stability.

I'd like to take this opportunity to express admiration for the responsible manner in which Saudi Arabia has conducted its economic affairs. King Fahd and other Saudi leaders, conscious of the global impact of their financial and economic decisions, have earned our respect and gratitude.

Their many humanitarian contributions touch us deeply, as well. Saudi aid to refugees uprooted from their homes in Afghanistan has not gone unnoticed here, Your Majesty. The people of the United States share with the people of Saudi Arabia a deep moral outrage over the continuing aggression and butchery taking place in Afghanistan. The citizens of the Western democracies and the Muslim world, by all that they believe to be true and just, should stand together in opposition to those who would impose dictatorship on all of mankind.

Marxist tyranny already has its grip on the religious freedom of the world's fifth largest Muslim population. This same grip strangles the prayers of Christians, Jews, and Muslims alike. We all worship the same God. Standing up to this onslaught, the people of Afghanistan, with their blood, courage, and faith, are an inspiration to the cause of freedom everywhere.

Afghanistan, of course, is not the only conflict in the region. We're also concerned about the tragic war between two of Saudi Arabia's neighbors—Iran and Iraq—a conflict that is raging only a few minutes by air from Saudi territory. This bloodshed has dragged on far too long and threatens peace throughout the region. The United States will do what we can, diplomatically, to end the fighting. And we will cooperate with Saudi Arabia to ensure the integrity of your borders.

Your Majesty, I look forward to our discussions about these and other serious problems which continue to plague the Middle East. Together, our considerable influence and our moral suasion can, at the very least, decrease the threat of war.

If the Saudi and American Governments focus their energies, progress can be made, especially in the lingering dispute between Israel and her neighbors.

I continue to believe that a just and lasting settlement, based on United Nations Security Council Resolution 242, is within reach. The security of Israel and other nations of the region and the legitimate rights of the Palestinian people can and should be addressed in direct negotiations. It is time to put this tragedy to rest and turn the page to a new and happier chapter.

Bringing about a better and more peaceful world will require courage, integrity, and wisdom. King Fahd and others in his family before him have been admired for just these traits.

I look forward to our discussions, King Fahd, and welcome to the United States.

The King. [*In English*] President, Mrs. Reagan, the people—thank you very much,

Mr. Reagan. I'm very sorry because my English is not good. I try to speak English, but I can't speak English good. Now I speak Arabic—very sorry.

[*In Arabic*] Mr. President, I should like to express my happiness on the occasion of my first meeting with you on the soil of the United States and express my satisfaction with the steady growth of relations between our two countries. I look forward to a fruitful exchange of views for the benefit of our two countries and peoples in the interest of peace in our region.

Mr. President, since the historic meeting between His Majesty the late King 'Abd al-'Aziz Al Sa'ud and the late President Franklin Roosevelt 40 years ago this month, the leaders of our two countries have continued to meet from time to time to discuss ways of promoting friendship and cooperation between our two countries and to consult and exchange views on international matters of mutual interest. This visit to your friendly country takes place in this same context.

Permit me, Mr. President, to turn back the pages of history to the period following the First World War, to the time when the majority of the Arab countries were suffering under the yoke of colonialism; when your country affirmed the principles that advocated the right of peoples to freedom, independence, and self-determination.

At that time, when the name of the United States stood for freedom, justice, and independence, the aspirations of the Arab peoples were directed toward your country as the defender of truth and justice. Now we are in a new era in which the United States reaffirms those principles, this time under your leadership, Mr. President.

Mr. President, the majority of the Arab countries gained their freedom and independence, with the exception of one people—the Palestinian people, who committed no wrong that could justify what has befallen them. The Palestinians, who were never aggressors or invaders, found themselves, through no fault of their own, the victims of unjust aggression.

The Palestinian question is the single problem that is of paramount concern to the whole Arab nation and affects the relations of its peoples and countries with the outside world. It is the one problem that is the root cause of instability and turmoil in the region. I hope, Mr. President, that your administration will support the just cause of the Palestinian people.

We only ask for a just position that conforms with the history and ideals of your great country, a position that is consonant with its role of leadership in the international community. Such a position will earn the United States the respect and appreciation not only of the Arab and Muslim worlds but also of freedom-loving peoples everywhere.

Similarly, the problem of Lebanon needs to be addressed in such a way that would guarantee the withdrawal of Israel from Lebanese territory and the achievement of Lebanon's sovereignty, territorial integrity, and full independence.

Mr. President, I share your view that Saudi Arabia, with its Islamic beliefs and principles, and the United States, with its ideals and values, can together find a common ground against aggression, injustice, and oppression.

Mr. President, as far as the people of Afghanistan are concerned, this people who want nothing but freedom against oppression, freedom from killing women and children—this people deserve our help.

Mr. President, I do not wish to be long, but I would like to say in conclusion that it is, indeed, a pleasure to have this opportunity to congratulate you on the full confidence that your people have placed in you by supporting your Presidency for a second term. This clearly demonstrates the extent of the confidence your people have in your wise leadership and your farsightedness.

And, in conclusion, Mr. President, I would like to thank you very much and to thank the American people and all the officials of the U.S. Government. And I wish you progress and good health. And I would like to thank God for giving us a beautiful sunny day today. [*Laughter*]

[*In English*] Thank you very much. I come again in the United States. I see many people, my close friends. And next time, I come just like anybody. Thank you very much. [*Laughter*]

Note: The President spoke at 10:10 a.m. at the South Portico of the White House, where the King was accorded a formal welcome with full military honors. The King's remarks in Arabic were translated by an in-terpreter. Following the ceremony, the President and King Fahd met in the Oval Office. They then joined U.S. and Saudi officials for a meeting in the Cabinet Room.

Message to the Congress Transmitting the Annual Report of the United States Arms Control and Disarmament Agency
February 11, 1985

To the Congress of the United States:

The security of our people, the primary responsibility of the Federal government, is accomplished through the complementary objectives of a strong defense capability and unambiguous and credible arms control agreements. While we have made substantial progress in rebuilding our defenses during the past four years, progress in arms control has not kept pace.

It is my intention in the next four years to do everything possible to find practical arrangements with the Soviet Union that will sharply reduce nuclear weapons. Arms control negotiations are surely the best way for pursuing such important objectives, and thus, I view with the utmost seriousness the negotiating commitments made with the Soviet Union four weeks ago in Geneva. We are now prepared to address not only nuclear offensive systems, but also strategic defenses and the essential improvements in

verification.

In addition to these new bilateral arms control efforts, a number of multilateral activities play significant roles in our comprehensive arms control program. For example, discussions are being directed to banning chemical weapons and to reaching agreement on measures that will build confidence in understanding the activities and intentions of adversaries. This 24th Annual Report of the United States Arms Control and Disarmament Agency describes these and all the many facets of the Administration's 1984 program. I am pleased to forward it to the Congress.

RONALD REAGAN

The White House,
February 11, 1985.

Note: The report was entitled "United States Arms Control and Disarmament Agency—1984 Annual Report."

Toasts at the State Dinner for King Fahd bin 'Abd al-'Aziz Al Sa'ud of Saudi Arabia
February 11, 1985

The President. Your Majesty and distinguished guests, ladies and gentlemen, welcome to the White House.

It was my honor today to renew my friendship with King Fahd. And when we last met in Cancún, it was a bit warmer, but, Your Majesty, I only hope the warmth of our hospitality helps make up for the coldness outside.

I'd like to take this opportunity, Your Majesty, to thank you for a piece of cutlery. It's a fine, jeweled saber that I received as a gift from the Saudi Boy Scouts who visited the White House last year. And with the budget battle about to commence in Washington, it's going to come in very handy. [*Laughter*]

King Fahd and the Saudi Royal Family,

153

reflecting the values at the heart of their society, have been sharing and generous leaders. In addition to their humanitarian aid throughout the world, they contribute to such cultural and educational institutions as the American University in Beirut, for example. And closer to home, when fire destroyed a major cultural facility at Wolf Trap here in Washington, threatening to short-circuit an entire theatrical season, the Saudi Embassy quickly located a huge tent and had it flown to Washington, and the show went on. In 1977 Terraset Elementary School in Reston, Virginia, received a solar heating system dedicated by none other than our guest of honor this evening.

King Fahd's exuberance for getting involved is well known. He's maintained the rich tradition of the *majlis* [council], meeting directly with his people, listening to their ideas as often as not to their problems.

His personal identification with his people has manifested itself in his avid support for Saudi Arabia's soccer team. And, Your Majesty, I understand that you have, on occasion, gone so far as to call the coach and offer suggestions. [*Laughter*] Being a former radio sportscaster, I'd love to do that. However, in this country, they only permit me to call them after the game is over. [*Laughter*]

But there's an Arab saying: The sands are blowing. And I submit to you, King Fahd, that if the sands of time give us any hint of the future, it is that in the days ahead the friendship between the Saudi Arabian and American people will be a strong and vital force in the world and that the future of the Middle East is one of peace.

Your Majesty, it's been an honor for us to have you as our guest. I look forward to building on what we've accomplished today.

The King. Mr. President, dear friends, I am pleased indeed this evening to hear these valuable words, these precious words from my good friend, His Excellency, President Reagan.

And on this good occasion, I would like to give my greetings to Mrs. Reagan and all the friends that are assembled here once again.

I was indeed happy when I heard the President is following the news of sports in the Kingdom of Saudi Arabia. [*Laughter*] As a matter of fact, just exactly as the President said, this is true, because I follow the news of sports in my country, and, therefore, the Saudi soccer team was first among all the Asian countries and became the only candidate as far as a candidate for the Olympics in Los Angeles this past summer. The Saudi soccer team came to Los Angeles, but it was not lucky enough in order to win any medals. But the most important thing is that the team participated in Los Angeles, and it showed the world that Saudi Arabia cares about athletics and sports. And the team found all kinds of reception and greetings from this good people in the United States.

And, also, a couple of months ago, the team won the Asian Cup among some Asian countries that have had soccer and practiced the game of soccer for 100 years before Saudi Arabia. [*Laughter*] The Kingdom of Saudi Arabia took up soccer only about 20 years ago, or maybe less, and won the Asian Cup, rightfully so. [*Laughter*] And, of course, in such matches nobody takes into consideration the good feelings of the other. You play to win—[*laughter*]—so much so that one of the Asian countries that played against Saudi Arabia said that their team was going to win the cup. As a matter of fact, they even reserved a special desk on the plane for that cup. [*Laughter*] We did not claim that we were going to win the cup, but the Saudi team won two cups instead of one—[*laughter*]—the African Cup and also the goalie won the cup for the most valuable player or the best goalie in those games and tournaments.

Of course, in the past, only 5 years ago, we were defeated. As a matter of fact, I have adopted sports in my country, not only soccer but many other sports and athletics. Now we have 125 athletic clubs. Those clubs practice all kinds of sports, including soccer. And we also hope that we will be able to participate in many international tournaments in the future.

The day before yesterday, the Saudi youth group, those who are under 16, won the cup for the youth under 16 years old. And the tournament for the Asian and African games will be held in China next year.

And the Saudi team is going to go in order to play. And, of course, we think this is a very good thing that it has already defeated the similar teams in Asia and now it is going to China in order to defeat other, more powerful teams. [*Laughter*]

Furthermore, there is another soccer team for those who are 18- or 19-year-olds. It has won all the tournaments, and there are only four countries left that it is going to face. And we believe that we are going to defeat those also. [*Laughter*] When this takes place in Abu Dhabi, in the United Arab Emirates, and faces those four countries, it will go to Moscow. We don't know whether the members of the team will come back as Communists to us or not. [*Laughter*] But I believe that our team will meet millions of Muslims there in the Soviet Union, so I don't know whether the Soviets will allow the Saudi flag to flutter and to be raised, because the wordings on the flag says, "There is no God but the God and Mohammed is His only Prophet." What is important, that we are going to have matches in China and in Moscow. If this proves anything, it proves that the level of sports in Saudi Arabia is rather good.

And in conclusion, before I finish what I have to say with these limited remarks, I would like to thank His Excellency, my friend, President Reagan, and Mrs. Reagan and all my dear friends assembled here.

I don't know whether His Excellency, the President, realizes that at the present there are some 500 American companies working in Saudi Arabia, doing business. If this is of any indication, it also indicates the close ties of friendship that exist between our two countries. And furthermore, the Saudi-American Commission [U.S.-Saudi Joint Economic Commission] did its duty, and it holds its meetings regularly, once in Saudi Arabia and once in the United States in a regular manner. I would like to take this opportunity to express my gratitude for the officials in this Commission, be they Americans or Saudis, because they have accomplished many of the important projects, and also those companies that contributed greatly to our progress, and among them, many American companies.

Therefore, what I would like to say, that there are many levels of relationships be-

tween our two countries. Be they political, economic, or social, they all indicate the strong ties of friendship between our two countries.

When we are in need of any product that is produced by the United States, be it in the field of technology or otherwise, that means we are in need of this, and we will work to get it. The reason we try to acquire these things, because we consider ourselves as friends of the United States. Our aim, of course, is we want peace and stability for our region in the Middle East, and we want for all people to live in peace.

I forgot to mention something important earlier, and that is that we have about 13,000 of our sons that are studying in American colleges and universities. And they all find very good treatment. I am sure that some of them are probably—who have study in the United States, and they are here this evening. My sons studied in the United States, four of them. And they received their B.A. degrees from American universities. And I have now my young Aziz, Prince 'Abd al 'Aziz. When he is older, he will go to a university. Therefore, I have an interest here in the United States, because my sons graduated from American colleges and universities.

I hope that this friendship will continue, because it was built on firm and sound foundations.

And in conclusion, I would like to thank President Reagan and Mrs. Reagan, again, and all my friends here. And I would like for anybody who wishes to visit Saudi Arabia—you are all welcome to come and see my country. And at this moment, I would like to invite President Reagan and Mrs. Reagan. For any time they wish to come and visit Saudi Arabia, they will find a friendly people there to welcome them.

Thank you very much.

Note: The President spoke at approximately 10 p.m. in the State Dining Room at the White House. King Fahd spoke in Arabic, and his remarks were translated by an interpreter. The following morning, the President and King Fahd, together with U.S. and Saudi officials, including Secretary of State George P. Shultz, Assistant to the President for National Security Affairs Robert C. McFarlane, Saudi Minister of Foreign Affairs Sa'ud al-Faysal Al Sa'ud, and Ambas- *sador Bandar bin Sultan bin 'Abd al-'Aziz Al Sa'ud, met in the Residence for a breakfast meeting.*

Interview With Bernard Weinraub and Gerald Boyd of the New York Times
February 11, 1985

Q. We just wanted to start off with some foreign policy questions first. Okay?

The President. All right.

Arms Control

Q. And a question on arms control: Are we going into negotiations in a position of inferiority?

The President. That we are not up to a strength level of the Soviet Union——

Q. Right.

The President. ——militarily?

Q. Yes.

The President. Oh, I don't think there's any question of that, and we have been for quite some time. We have fewer—for example, in nuclear weapons—we have fewer warheads than we had in 1967. But I think, in one way, we're going in in a stronger sense than we have in recent years, because over recent years, we followed a policy of kind of unilaterally disarming and the idea that maybe the others would follow suit.

This time, with the refurbishing of our military defenses that we've been undergoing for these 4 years, we're going to the table, and they have the knowledge that not only are we stronger than we were, even though we have not caught up with them as yet, but they have the awareness that we're determined to not allow them to have a superiority over us to the extent that our forces wouldn't be a deterrent. And I think in that regard, we sit down to the table with a little more realism than there's been in the past.

Q. Isn't there a—statements by yourself during the campaign, Mr. President, and by Secretary of State George Shultz, to the effect that we have been able to reestablish the military balance in the few years and that otherwise we could not negotiate on an even basis?

The President. Well, I was trying to be completely accurate here that, obviously, we have not completely caught up with the imbalance between us. For example, we have in uniform in the military 17 divisions. Well, they've got more than that on the Chinese border. So, we have not caught up with the naval buildup. But the fact that we are doing that, the fact that we have 24 more ships, I believe, out there scheduled for addition to the fleet; that is what I think brings us to the table. They know our industrial power. They know what we've been able to achieve when we set our minds to it.

So, they know that there's been a change of attitude, that we are not canceling weapons systems without getting anything in return. And, from that standpoint, I think this is what they mean—that our whole attitude is different now, and they can look down the road and see that there's a point at which they won't have any margin of superiority.

Q. Can you——

The President. And they don't have enough of a margin today to tempt them into a first strike.

Q. On the subject of arms control treaty violations, you and your administration have said for several years that the Soviets are violating these treaties. A, what do you intend to do about that, and B, would you sign treaties in the future without clearing up those matters?

The President. Well, I think all of that is part of what has to be negotiated and probably under the cap of—or the part of the negotiations that'll deal with verifiability. In other words, it's not enough to have an agreement; it's got to be a verifiable agreement.

And some of the violations that they're doing are violations of what had previously been negotiated as the right of each one of us to know about the other. The encrypting of the signals that some of their nuclear tests—ordinarily that we would be able, simply electronically, to have the facts that it was agreed upon we should have, both sides should have. But then they have been encrypting so that we don't get that full information from a test. And all of these will be part of the negotiations.

Q. Do those violations block the possibility of another agreement until they are cleared up?

The President. Now we get into the area of the actual negotiating, and I don't think that I should be discussing those particular facets of what are we going to do, what are we going to offer, what are we going to trade. I don't think that should be voiced in advance.

Situation in the Philippines

Q. Mr. President, to shift to another subject, there are people in Congress who are talking about the situation in the Philippines with the opposition parties in turmoil there, with the Communist insurrection. They're saying that the Philippines is our next Iran. Do you see the Philippines that way? Do you agree?

The President. I certainly hope not. We're trying to be as helpful as we can in their situation. The Philippines and the United States certainly have a close relationship and alliance over the years, and we've had a good relationship with President Marcos.

Now, we realize there is an opposition party that, we believe, is also pledged to democracy. We also are aware that there is another element in the Philippines that has Communist support and backing. What we're hopeful of is that the democratic processes will take place and, even if there is a change of party there, it would be that opposition faction which is still democratic in its principles. I think it would be a disaster for all of us if, out of the friction between those two parties, the third element, the Communist element, should get in, because we know their result is always totalitarian.

Q. Do you feel there are certain steps that should be taken in order to prevent that from happening, either by the government or by the opposition?

The President. Well, I hope that both parties are aware of this over there and are going to, neither one of them, look to that third element for any kind of help or alliance. And, as I say, we're going to do, continue to do, everything we can as a long-time friend to see that the Philippines remain a democracy.

South Korea

Q. Sir, on South Korea, let me just ask you: Given today's news, do you think that some of these Americans who were accompanying the opposition leader there were, in fact, meddling as——

The President. Let's just say that I think there was bad judgment on both sides.

Q. You mean the Americans as well as the Korean officials?

The President. Yes. And certainly here in the treatment of this, it's tended to hide the fact that Korea, South Korea, has made great strides in democracy, that they have a prosperity that is far above that of a great many of their neighbors in that part of the world. Their democracy is working. And I think there was some bad judgment there on both sides.

Nicaragua

Q. Could we talk about Nicaragua, I guess, Mr. President? There seems to be a real stalemate there. You're not providing aid to the *contras* now. There are no negotiations that are going on now. What are you planning to do in the way of policy to try to get something going that might bring about the kind of Nicaragua that you would like?

The President. Well, I'm going to continue to ask the Congress to let us, in all of Latin America, go forward with the kind of program that was born of the Kissinger-led commission down there in which 75 percent of the help we offer is going to be in social and economic aid to try and make these countries more self-sufficient, to eliminate the great poverty in so many of those countries by simply helping them become more viable economically and, at the same time, giving them help for security, so that they're not victims of subversion, particularly from outside their own countries.

With regard to Nicaragua, I think that we should continue to offer support to the people of Nicaragua who have been betrayed in the revolution that they, themselves, supported.

That revolution was supposed to result in democracy. And assurances were given by the people who were fighting the revolution and leading it. Then the Sandinistas did what Castro before them had done in Cuba. Once the revolution was successful, they ousted from the government, or any participation in government, all the other factions that were dedicated to democracy and have instituted a totalitarian regime.

And what the Nicaraguan people want is the revolution they fought for. And I think they're entitled to have it.

Q. So, support to the people of Nicaragua is support to the *contras?* Or what?

The President. Well, they certainly are part of the people, and they were part of the revolution in many instances. The thing that so many people that are arguing against this don't seem to be aware of a difference between, for example, Nicaragua and El Salvador. El Salvador now, after several elections, is a government that is striving for democracy, that was chosen by the people. And the people trying to overthrow it, the guerrillas in El Salvador, are trying to overthrow a government that the majority of the people elected.

In Nicaragua, the so-called Sandinista government is a government that seized power out of the barrel of a gun; it's never been chosen by the people. And it has directly contravened the principles of the revolution that they were fighting. And I think there's every reason for the *contras* to be representing those who continue to strive for the democracy that they fought a revolution to get.

Q. Well, are you talking about a fundamental change in the Nicaraguan Government, or can they do things incrementally? Can they, for example, ease up on press freedom, or can they provide more press freedom, or can they provide certain steps that you might think would be acceptable

without making a fundamental change in their government?

The President. Well, Jerry, I don't know what—when we talk about this, are we talking about the people that are in the government or the form of government? If it's the people, obviously those who have grabbed power are not going to want to give it up; that's typical of totalitarianism. But as to the other part—all the Sandinistas would have to do is go back to what they, themselves, participated in promising to the Organization of American States—that they wanted democracy, they wanted free voting, they wanted free labor unions, they wanted a free press and all—and subject themselves—or submit themselves, I should say, and anyone else who chooses to, to the will of the people by way of the elections and voting.

Q. Sir, let me ask you—on the *contras* question—what form of aid should this take, in terms of helping the *contras?* I mean, how do we propose to help the *contras?*

The President. Well, I still believe in covert programs where they're necessary and where they're desirable. And so, once you say that, then there are some limits as to what you can specify.

Q. Right. I understand.

Strategic Defense Initiative

Q. Mr. President, to go back to the issue of arms control and, particularly, to your Strategic Defense Initiative—if, in the Geneva negotiations, the Soviets were to agree to go along with the deep reductions in offensive weapons that you've proposed, would you still want to proceed with this Strategic Defense Initiative, or would you be ready to call it off in return for that?

The President. No. I would want to proceed with what we're doing, which is research to discover whether there is such a weapon and whether it is practical and feasible. And then I, myself, have said that my own view would be that if that is determined and we can produce such a weapon, that then before deployment I'd be willing to sit down and, in a sense, internationalize.

In other words, to negotiate then, before there would be any deployment or anything, to make sure that they understood that we weren't trying to create the ability of a first strike ourselves, that our goal was still the elimination of nuclear weapons; and that I would see that defensive weapon as another step in attaining that goal; that if we could say that this virtually makes those weapons, if not obsolete, certainly most ineffective—the nuclear weapons—then we've got a real reason for saying, "Now, let's all do away with them, because we've come up with this defensive weapon." That would eliminate any of the protests that some of the people on the Soviet side have made that we're seeking a first-strike capability.

I don't think anyone in the world can honestly believe that the United States is interested in such a thing or ever would put itself in that position.

Q. So, proceeding with the Strategic Defense is independent of whatever agreement is reached——

The President. That's right——

Q. ——on offensive weapons.

The President. ——because it's not in violation of the ABM treaty, and they have been conducting—you know, who are they kidding? They've been conducting research in this sort of thing for a long time. And they already have—far beyond anything we have—and we believe, in violation of the ABM treaty, that kind of defense.

And we're seeking a nonnuclear weapon that could render these weapons obsolete.

U.S.-Cuba Relations

Q. Sir, just—excuse me—back on Latin America—Fidel Castro said recently that he saw possibilities for improving relations with the U.S. Do you see any possibility of you or the Government improving relations with Castro?

The President. Well, I'm not greatly optimistic, because we've heard this before. Early in my administration there were signals sent of this kind, and we took them up on it. And we tried to have some meetings with them, and nothing came of it. Their words are never backed by deeds. There are very simple things that they could do that would indicate that they were ready for a change.

The Middle East

Q. On the Middle East, Mr. President, do you expect a current review of the arms sale policy to result in some kind of change in U.S. policy in the region?

The President. Well, now, you're asking about——

Q. The Middle East.

The President. In arms policies, though.

Q. Yes, you're conducting a review of arms——

The President. Yes.

Q. ——policy.

The President. I'm still dedicated to that September 1st, 1982, provision of a negotiated peace. I don't believe it can be achieved without King Hussein of Jordan and with—or at least with the permission of the Palestinians, representing them in direct negotiations with the Israelis. And we are prepared to be of whatever help we can be. We're not seeking to impose a settlement on anyone; we haven't got some plan of how it must be worked out.

But I feel that we have to make the moderate Arab States recognize that we can be their friend as well as the friend of Israel and that this could be helpful in our trying to be of help in peace negotiations. And part of this would be—because they're under threat—there's a war going on just minutes away from them by air. The Soviet Union, with its invasion of Afghanistan, has made it evident that the Middle East can't rule out the possibility of expansionism on the part of the Soviets there. And, therefore, we think that they're entitled to some defensive weapons also.

At the same time, we have ensured Israel that we will never see them lose their qualitative edge to the point that they're endangered by anything we do.

Q. Do you see an opportunity, at this point, to push that peace initiative of yours once again? With the Fahd visit and other developments, is this the time to make another move?

The President. We have another meeting coming tomorrow morning. I'm going to talk to him, definitely, so that he knows that we haven't retreated. The events in Lebanon and so forth kind of put the plan on ice.

It was not only that. If you'll remember, there was a very definite breaking off of relations between the PLO and King Hussein. Hussein was going forward, trying to work with them, and then suddenly they parted company.

Now, there have been talks resumed, because anyone who talks for the Arab side is going to have to be able to represent the Palestinian problem in those negotiations. You can't write them off or ignore their right to some claims. And so what we're trying to talk about is hoping that this can now come to the point that there can be direct negotiations.

Q. Do you put any limit on who can represent the Palestinians?

The President. Well, it more or less has to be worked out between them and King Hussein——

Q. But if——

The President. ——as to whether they will permit him or whether they will want direct representation, and then, then I think with the Israelis the issue comes up, then—will whoever represents the Palestinians be willing to say that they recognize the right of Israel to exist as a nation. This is a great sticking point. It's why we cannot enter into any discussions with the Palestinians, the PLO. As long as they say that, how do you talk to a country and say to a country, "You should negotiate with these people," when these people say, "We don't recognize that country's right to exist."

Q. As part of the comprehensive review that you're doing on the Middle East, are you thinking of connecting arms sales to the peace process?

The President. Well, we have—you know, there have been—we have made some arms sales in a number of instances. Actually, what I feel is necessary is—this is a part of convincing the Arabs that we do sincerely intend to be their friends also, that we're not in any way an opponent.

Black Americans

Q. Mr. President, on the question of black leaders—you've criticized black leaders, recently, as representing a special interest and being concerned about their own jobs and positions. Assuming that that might be true, how do you then plan to keep in touch with the black community in general, if you're not doing it through these black leaders?

The President. Very willing to do it through those, and tried. And there were meetings here, and they came to naught. What I said there is a general thing that I was saying—not about all—because there are leaders of quite prominent black groups, like Roy Innis of CORE [Congress of Racial Equality], who agrees completely with what I said.

But I think it's something that happens even in government bureaucracies that are set up to solve a certain problem. But once the bureaucracy is set up, it never quite wants to admit that the problem has been solved, because there's no longer any need for the bureaucracy. And I think that there is some element of this. See, I've just lived longer than the rest of you. [*Laughter*] I remember when things were very much different—not from reading about them, from seeing them. And I think that there is an unwillingness on the part of some leaders to bring to the attention or remind the people they represent how much progress has been made, because—and again, as I say, because if you do, they might then say, well, then, what are we still organized for?

Now, granted, we have not totally eliminated all the problems. There are a lot of us that are still heart and soul for continuing. But the progress that we've made is such that there is no reason anymore to try to keep a group in existence on the basis of animus, anger, and others.

Q. Well, how do you really get that message through to the black community if you don't deal with black leaders? How do you——

The President. Now, what constitutes black leaders? I've been meeting with an awful lot of people that have, I think, achieved quite some prominence in their work in that field. And, as I say, Roy Innis, of CORE—he sees this exactly the same way.

I'm perfectly willing to try and say these same things to the people that are in the organizations where a few of the leaders have seemed to be, well, very frankly, more interested in some political differences than they are in resolving the problem.

Poland

Q. Mr. President, shift to a totally different area—Poland. Does the trial and the conviction of those four police officers and the murder of that Catholic priest constitute any kind of a step on the part of the Polish Government that justified, in your mind, relaxing any of our sanctions or making any moves towards Poland to ease the situation, improve it?

The President. I honestly don't think that it reflects any change. I think it reflects something that went wrong. And the Government doesn't mind throwing somebody to the wolves in order to keep the sleigh going ahead of the wolfpack.

Q. No fundamental change internally, therefore no reason for us to change our policy?

The President. No.

Strategic Defense Initiative

Q. Mr. President, taking it back to the question of your Strategic Defense Initiative. Throughout history there's always been a question of offensive being able to overcome defense, and it always has in the past. Here we're about to embark on the expenditure of a lot of money to test this proposition again. Why do you think this time the defense might be able to prevail over the offense?

The President. Well, all right, let me give you a parallel that I've used here among our own people. World War I—poison gas came into being for the first time, and it was horrible. Nineteen twenty-five—all the nations of the world met in Geneva and ruled out poison gas in the future for war. But by that time the gas mask had been developed, and gas mask has been standard soldier equipment in just about every army in the world ever since 1925. We haven't thrown the masks away.

Now, we're talking about a weapon that has been developed for which there is no defense whatsoever. The only program we have is MAD, mutual assured destruction. Why don't we have MAS instead, mutual assured security?

Now, we all know how to make that weapon. Suppose that we were so successful at the arms talks that we all agreed to do away with them, just as we agreed to do away with poison gas. And the years go by, but we all know how to make them. You can't take out of your mind the knowledge that we now have. And sometime, in a time of stress and, whether it's the two great countries or some other countries, somebody is going to say, just as they have in recent years, maybe it would be handy for us to produce a few of these things. And you wouldn't be able to tell if they had or not. But at least your security would be your own kind of gas mask—that if somebody does cheat after you've tried to eliminate them, and comes up with those, you'd have a weapon in which you could knock them down, just as today, you could put on the gas mask if somebody cheats and decides to use poison gas.

So, I think it would be well worth having. And then, of course, there's the possibility that you can't get everybody to eliminate those weapons as we're seeking to do, and, therefore, you have made it through defense. You've changed the whole ratio—the opponent that might want to be expansionist and resort to war has to say in the face of that defensive weapon: How many of these things do I have to have before I can be sure that enough get through that they won't be able to blow me out of the water?

Q. Mr. President, you've talked at times of two different kinds of a defense—one, defending cities, the whole population. Somebody referred to it as an "Astrodome" defense, so to speak. And you seem now to be talking about a defense that would be around our missiles. Which is it you want—a limited defense or a total defense?

The President. I want a defense that simply says that if somebody starts pushing the button on those weapons, we've got a good chance of keeping all or at least the bulk of them from getting to the target. Because, even if it's around missile sites, that's the type of weapon anymore in which there's no way to restrain that from killing any number of people, or now, as a great many reputable scientists are telling us, that such a war could just end up in no victory for anyone, because we would wipe out the Earth as we know it. And if you think back to a couple of natural calamities, back in the last century, in the 1800's, just natural phenomena from earthquakes—or, I mean, volcanoes, we saw the weather so changed that there was snow in July in many temperate countries. And they've called it the year in which there was no summer. Well, if one volcano can do that, what are we talking about with a whole nuclear exchange: the nuclear winter that scientists have been talking about? It's possible.

So, I think if you have a defensive weapon, I don't think of it in terms of let's put it around this place or that place. Let's put it in such a way that those missiles aren't going to get to their target.

George Bush

Q. One last question, if I might, Mr. President. Won't you have to support George Bush in '88? Won't you have to endorse him or support him?

The President. Well, now, you have me between a rock and a hard place here, because I have to tell you I think that—as I have said—he has been the finest Vice President that I ever have any recollection of. He has been an integral part of everything that we're doing.

I have always had the feeling—I had it about a Lieutenant Governor in California when I was Governor—that the Vice President shouldn't be just someone standing by waiting to be called off the bench. He should be like an executive vice president in the corporation or business; you use him. And he's been all of those things.

But, at the same time, in this job, you are titular head of the party and as such you've kind of got a responsibility to let the party function and make its decisions. Now, it's not an easy thing for me to think about, but I have to keep that in mind.

Q. So, you won't support him under any circumstances?

The President. What?

Q. You won't endorse him under any circumstance?

The President. Let me just say it's a decision I have said—I know must be made, and I'm just not going to think about it. I'll be like Scarlett O'Hara, I'll think about it tomorrow. [*Laughter*]

Q. Don't your comments almost make him a logical successor to you?

The President. What?

Q. I mean, your praise of him and the performance of the office, doesn't that make him a logical successor?

The President. Well, I have to say that, if anyone was a voter, in considering, they would have to recognize who's had the most contact with what's going on.

Q. Thank you.

Note: The interview began at 2:38 p.m. in the Oval Office at the White House. The transcript was released by the Office of the Press Secretary on February 12.

Proclamation 5300—National Big Brothers and Big Sisters Week, 1985
February 11, 1985

By the President of the United States of America

A Proclamation

No task is more important to the future of our society than raising the next generation. And few volunteer organizations have done more over the years to help our Nation perform that task successfully than the Big Brothers and Big Sisters of America. These are men and women who take time from their own responsibilities and families to offer a helping hand to young people in need. Big Brothers and Big Sisters offer youngsters support, counseling, and—most important of all—friendship.

The spirit of voluntarism exemplified by this organization is the foundation of our way of life. Americans have always been a compassionate and decent people, and they have never waited for directions from government before devoting their time and energy to helping their neighbors. The Big Brothers and Big Sisters of America are adding new luster to this old tradition.

The Congress, by House Joint Resolution 594, has designated the week of February 17 through February 23, 1985, as a time to recognize the contributions of volunteers who give their time to become Big Brothers and Big Sisters to youths in need of adult companionship and authorized and requested the President to issue a proclamation in observance of this week.

Now, Therefore, I, Ronald Reagan, President of the United States of America, do hereby proclaim the period from February 17 through February 23, 1985, as "National Big Brothers and Big Sisters Week." I call

upon the people of the United States and local and national governmental officials to observe this day with appropriate ceremonies.

In Witness Whereof, I have hereunto set my hand this eleventh day of February, in the year of our Lord nineteen hundred and eighty-five, and of the Independence of the United States of America the two hundred and ninth.

RONALD REAGAN

[Filed with the Office of the Federal Register, 12:06 p.m., February 12, 1985]

Note: The proclamation was released by the Office of the Press Secretary on February 12.

Message to the Congress Transmitting the Annual Report on Nuclear Nonproliferation
February 12, 1985

To the Congress of the United States:

I have reviewed the activities of United States Government departments and agencies during the calendar year 1984 related to preventing nuclear proliferation, and I am pleased to submit my annual report on this subject pursuant to section 601(a) of the Nuclear Non-Proliferation Act of 1978 (Public Law 95–242).

The Report concludes that the United States during 1984 continued to make important progress in its efforts to achieve its non-proliferation goals.

It is my firm conviction that preventing

the spread of nuclear explosives to additional countries is essential to world peace and stability. It forms an indispensable complement to the efforts we have undertaken to bring about deep reductions in strategic and intermediate-range nuclear weapons. It is no exaggeration to say that the future of mankind may well depend on the achievement of these goals, and I intend to pursue them with unflagging determination and a deep sense of personal commitment.

RONALD REAGAN

The White House,
February 12, 1985.

Message to the Senate Transmitting the Canada-United States Pacific Salmon Fishery Treaty
February 12, 1985

To the Senate of the United States:

I transmit herewith, for the advice and consent of the Senate to ratification, the

Treaty between the Government of the United States of America and the Government of Canada Concerning Pacific Salmon,

163

with annexes and a related Memorandum of Understanding, signed at Ottawa January 28, 1985. I also transmit for the information of the Senate the report of the Department of State. This treaty would establish a basis for bilateral cooperation in salmon management, research, and enhancement on the west coast of North America. It will enter into force upon exchange of instruments of ratification.

The treaty would establish a bilateral commission with coastwide responsibilities for management of "intercepting" salmon fisheries, fisheries of one Party that harvest fish which spawn in the waters of the other Party. These responsibilities would include management of the fisheries on Fraser River sockeye and pink salmon, now governed by the Convention for the Protection, Preservation, and Extension of the Salmon Fishery of the Fraser River System, signed at Washington May 26, 1930, entered into force July 28, 1937, as amended. That convention would be superseded by this treaty. An annex to this treaty would prescribe specific fishery regimes, establish-

ing allocations, annual catch levels, and broad regulations by time, area, or gear for (1) transboundary rivers, (2) the northern boundary area, (3) chinook, (4) Fraser River pink and sockeye, (5) southern coho, and (6) southern chum.

This treaty represents the culmination of fourteen years of negotiations on this issue. It establishes a basis for bilateral cooperation on management, research, and enhancement of salmon stocks throughout the west coast of North America. This treaty provides a framework that will enable us to conserve this precious resource. The increases in salmon production made possible by this treaty will inure to the benefit of fishermen of both the United States and Canada.

I recommend that the Senate give early consideration to the treaty and give its advice and consent to ratification of the treaty, including its annexes and related Memorandum of Understanding.

RONALD REAGAN

The White House,
February 12, 1985.

Remarks at a White House Luncheon for the New Pioneers
February 12, 1985

Thank you for being here, and welcome to the White House. To paraphrase an earlier President: This must be one of the most extraordinary collections of talent and human intelligence that is ever to come together in one room in the White House, with the possible exception of when Thomas Jefferson dined alone. [*Laughter*]

To tell you the truth, I was a little nervous in the face of so much accumulated brainpower. As President, I'm often being awarded honorary degrees, which always, as I've said on a number of occasions, complicate—or increases a sense of guilt that I have nursed for more than a half a century, because I always figured the first one they gave me was honorary. [*Laughter*]

So I was nervous, but then I realized that I was about to eat lunch with a group of

people who spend their time doing things like investigating quarks, measuring the curve of space, engineering genes, and proving the existence of two different kinds of infinity. And that reminded me of a story—[*laughter*]—something always reminds me of a story. [*Laughter*]

This was an occasion when three gentlemen arrived at the gates of heaven, and St. Peter told them that there were certain limitations on who could get in, due to crowding. And he said they had decided that whichever one of the three practiced the oldest profession or avocation would be admitted.

And one stepped forward and said, "Well, I think that's me." He said, "I am a doctor." He said, "We know that the Lord made Adam, and then He created Eve from a rib of Adam—that required surgery. And so I guess that's the oldest."

But before he could move on in, the second one said, "Wait a minute. I'm an engineer, and," he said, "before the Lord made Adam, all was chaos. And He spent 6 days and on the seventh day rested, after eliminating the chaos. So, I think engineering—I go in."

And before he could advance, the third one said, "I'm an economist. Where do you think they got all that chaos?" [*Laughter*]

Now, I can tell that story because my degree, that dishonest degree, was in economics. [*Laughter*]

I sometimes feel that the journalists who cover our everyday political affairs here in Washington have a tendency to miss the real news, the transforming discoveries and achievements that you and your colleagues are making every day. I remember just a little over 4 years ago, all the headlines were of shortages. Every morning it seemed that we read that there was some new scare story telling us that the Earth's resources were about to run out for good, leaving our world poorer and shrinking our hopes for the future.

But at the same time, largely unheralded, scientists, inventors, and entrepreneurs in the computer field were molding silicon chips from sand—one of the commonest substances known to man—and in the process revolutionizing our lives.

It's been pioneering, such as you who have discovered new universes on a blackboard, have charted new continents inside the living cell and extended the boundaries of human mortality. Today space is just one more laboratory, and the idea that there are material limits on the mind of man has been shattered once and for all.

You understand that freedom is not a luxury, but a necessity; not a privilege, but the source of our life's bread. In science, just as in our economy, our object must be to maximize freedom, to open up new avenues of inquiry and new areas of experimentation.

I've asked Congress to approve funding for a permanently funded, manned space station. Despite the constraints of a freeze in program spending, there are few genuine cuts in our budget for basic science

items. We're requesting a 6.7-percent increase for basic research in the physical sciences for fiscal year '86. And we're asking for increased funding for science and technology and basic research through the end of the decade.

I believe that our nuclear dilemma presents us with some of the major unfinished business of science. And we have begun research on a nonnuclear defense against nuclear attack. You, on the cutting edge of technology, have already made yesterday's impossibilities the commonplace realities of today. Why should we start thinking small now? In protecting mankind from the peril of nuclear destruction, I think we must be ambitious. We can't lock ourselves into a fatalistic acceptance of a world held in jeopardy.

In this area, most especially, we must approach the future with such vision and hope that reach for the greatest possibilities. Only if we try can we succeed.

Back in 1842—I was just a lad at the time—[*laughter*]—the royal astronomer in Great Britain studied Charles Babbage's new "analytical engine"—the forerunner of the modern computer, and pronounced it worthless. His foresight was almost equaled a half century later, when the head of the U.S. Patent Office advised President McKinley to abolish the Patent Office, because "we had," he said, "everything that can be invented had already been invented." [*Laughter*]

Well, if science has taught us anything, it's taught us that—well, it's not to be modest in our aspirations. That fact, I have to confess, is my secret agenda for bringing you all here today. After lunch is over, I'm going to ask all of you to turn your attention to the budget problem. [*Laughter*] Until then and while you're doing that, why thank you all again for being here. God bless all of you.

I have to take orders, and I think that I was told that my schedule called for me to run like a deer when I finished talking here—that would prevent any of you from asking me any questions. [*Laughter*] But I think they have me scheduled that way. I've read some of these things that—articles about the supposed power of the Presidency—but I have to tell you, there's somebody here in the administration—I haven't found out yet—that every day puts a thing on my desk that tells me what I'm going to be doing every 15 minutes for the rest— [*laughter*]—for the entire day.

But thank you all again for being here now. Please excuse me.

Note: The President spoke at 1:02 p.m. in the State Dining Room at the White House at the luncheon for leaders in the fields of science, medicine, mathematics, engineering, and education.

Proclamation 5301—National DECA Week, 1985
February 12, 1985

By the President of the United States of America

A Proclamation

The value of the free enterprise system in America is confirmed when the products of our research, our industry, and our agriculture improve the quality of people's lives not only in America, but throughout the world. And the genius of American business has been to make the wealth of its factories and farms accessible to all.

For thirty-eight years, the Distributive Education Clubs of America have introduced high school and college students to the challenges, skills, and responsibilities of delivering the products of our free enterprise system to those who use them. Now numbering some 150,000 members in all 50 States, the District of Columbia, and Puerto Rico, the Distributive Education Clubs of America are helping to prepare a cadre of professionals with the spirit of enterprise, the civic responsibility, and the complex skills needed to assure that America's strength in marketing keeps pace with the vast expansion of technology and the increasingly sophisticated needs of people in all parts of the world.

To give special recognition to the valuable contribution the Distributive Education Clubs of America are making to maintaining our Nation's economic strength and to introducing young Americans to the opportunities and rewards of free enterprise, the Congress, by Senate Joint Resolution 36, has designated the week of February 10, 1985, through February 16, 1985, as "National DECA Week" and authorized and requested the President to issue a proclamation in observance of that week.

Now, Therefore, I, Ronald Reagan, President of the United States of America, do hereby proclaim the week beginning February 10 through February 16, 1985, as National DECA Week, and I call upon all government agencies, interested organizations, community groups, and the people of the United States to observe this week with appropriate programs, ceremonies, and activities.

In Witness Whereof, I have hereunto set my hand this twelfth day of February, in the year of our Lord nineteen hundred and eighty-five, and of the Independence of the United States of America the two hundred and ninth.

RONALD REAGAN

[*Filed with the Office of the Federal Register, 11:11 a.m., February 13, 1985*]

Executive Order 12505—Conversion of Appointments in the Office of Management and Budget
February 12, 1985

By the authority vested in me as President by the laws of the United States of America, including Section 3301 and 3302 of Title 5, and Section 521 of Title 31 of the United States Code, it is hereby ordered as follows:

Section 1. No later than April 1, 1985, any employee of the Office of Management and Budget serving under an appointment under Schedule A in a position not limited to one year or less, concerned with implementation of the President's paperwork reduction and regulatory review and planning programs, may have his or her appointment converted to a career or career-conditional appointment if the Director of the Office of Management and Budget determines that:

(a) The employee has completed at least one year of full-time continuous service in a position concerned with the paperwork reduction and regulatory program;

(b) There is a continuing need for the position filled by the employee;

(c) The employee's past performance has been satisfactory and the employee possesses the qualifications necessary to continue in the position; and

(d) The employee meets the citizenship requirements and qualification standards appropriate for the position.

Sec. 2. If the Director determines not to convert an employee's appointment to career or career-conditional status under the preceding Section, the employee shall be separated not later than the date of expiration of the current appointment.

Sec. 3. Employees whose appointments are converted under this Order shall become career-conditional employees, or career employees if they have completed the service requirements for career tenure, and all converted employees shall acquire a competitive status.

RONALD REAGAN

The White House,
February 12, 1985.

[*Filed with the Office of the Federal Register, 11:12 a.m., February 13, 1985*]

Informal Exchange With Reporters
February 13, 1985

Q. What about Chernenko?

The President. Maybe I should ask you. We have no other information than you have with regard to his still not being seen in public.

Q. ——this might affect the arms talks?

The President. I wouldn't think so, no. I think those are well on their way, and there's been no problem about meeting.

Q. ——Arafat-Hussein——

The President. What's that?

Q. What do you think of the Arafat-Hussein agreement?

Principal Deputy Press Secretary Speakes. Arafat-Hussein agreement?

The President. Oh, well, the little we know about it, it seems as if some progress has been made. That's where the first break in the progress began—came after our first proposal in '82. So, we're being optimistic about it.

Q. Are they encouraging you, Mr. President, to get more involved right now in the Middle East?

The President. Well, we've never been uninvolved. And, yes, we want to push the same thing that we proposed 2 years ago: the peace proposal there between the Arab States and Israel.

Q. What do you hope to get from the talks in Vienna with the Soviets?

The President. Well, there are a number

of things that I think are of interest to both countries, and I think we'll—there's some reason to believe that we can straighten out some things, matters.

Q. ——Fahd——

The President. Helen [Helen Thomas, United Press International], I've got a problem with you and the helicopter.

Q. ——the Fahd visit?

Mr. Speakes. Results of the Fahd visit?

Q. The meeting with King Fahd?

The President. ——what?

Mr. Speakes. Results of the Fahd visit?

The President. Oh. Well, we think it was a very worthwhile visit for both countries and for both heads of state.

Q. ——the Israelis express any concern about the Russians becoming involved in the Mideast negotiations or the Vienna talks?

The President. No. We very definitely are not in support of an idea of a great international conference on the Middle East.

Q. Have you invited Mr. Peres to come back and talk with you after Mr. Mubarak? Is Peres coming back after Mubarak to talk again?

The President. I don't know exactly what the schedule is of visitors now, but he's coming here on issues that have to do between them—and I don't know whether there'd be a reason for another visit.

Q. Mr. President, what about the strength of the U.S. dollar overseas? Is there anything the Government can or should do about that?

The President. The main problem is not the strength of the American dollar; it's the weakness of foreign currency, because our recovery has progressed beyond theirs. We hope that we can help their recovery to where their currency comes up in relation to ours.

I have to get on that thing now.

Q. What are you getting Mrs. Reagan for Valentine's Day?

The President. A valentine. [*Laughter*]

Q. How many?

The President. Oh, about five.

Note: The exchange began at 10:26 a.m. on the South Lawn of the White House as the President prepared to board Marine One, which was waiting to take him to Andrews Air Force Base for a trip to Rancho del Cielo, his ranch near Santa Barbara, CA.

Joint Saudi Arabia-United States Communique
February 13, 1985

The State visit of His Majesty King Fahd bin 'Abd al-'Aziz Al Sa'ud has reaffirmed the long-standing bonds of friendship and mutually beneficial cooperation that have existed between the United States and Saudi Arabia for over fifty years. In their meetings on February 11 and 12, President Reagan and King Fahd concentrated on the search for a just, stable and lasting solution to the Arab-Israel conflict, which the two leaders agreed was their primary concern.

The King expressed his belief that the Arab consensus defined in the communique issued at Fez in September 1982 provided a just basis for negotiations leading to a comprehensive peace. The President expressed his appreciation for the Fez consensus, positive elements of which have been recognized by the United States. He reaffirmed his continuing commitment to the positions for peace which he announced on September 1, 1982, and renewed his pledge that the United States will support those positions in direct negotiations involving the parties most concerned.

In their discussions, the President and the King stressed that a stable peace must provide security for all states in the area and for the exercise of the legitimate rights of the Palestinian people. Both agreed to maintain their dialogue on this urgent issue.

The two leaders discussed the situation in Lebanon and agreed on the need for rapid restoration of its sovereignty, independence and territorial integrity.

The President and the King discussed the continuing war between Iran and Iraq. They deplored the tragic loss of life and destruction it has brought and the threat to regional stability and peace which it poses. They pledged to continue to support efforts to bring the fighting to a speedy end.

The discussions between the President and the King, to which cabinet members and ministers contributed, charted the course for continued development of U.S.-Saudi relations. In this regard, Saudi Arabia's emergence as an exporter of industrial goods, as well as of crude oil, was examined in the light of the United States' traditional commitment to open markets for goods and investment. The delegations of the two countries foresaw growth and rising mutual benefit from a sustained partnership in trade, development and regional cooperation that joins Saudi resources and aspirations with American technological leadership.

Nomination of George D. Hart To Be a Member of the National Council on the Humanities
February 13, 1985

The President today announced his intention to nominate George D. Hart to be a member of the National Council on the Humanities, National Foundation on the Arts and the Humanities, for a term expiring January 26, 1990. He would succeed Jacob Neusner.

Mr. Hart is president of Farnsworth & Ruggles in San Francisco, CA. He is also president and owner of Farnsworth & Ruggles, Draying and Warehousing and Inglewood Realty Corp. He is chairman of the Associated Investors of Northern California.

He serves as a member of the boards of trustees of Boston University, the San Francisco Fine Arts Museums Foundation, and the Institutes of Medical Sciences. He is a member of the board of overseers of the Museum of Fine Arts in Boston and the board of fellows of Boston University. In 1962–1974 he served on the board of trustees of the California State University and Colleges by appointment of the Governor of California.

He graduated from Stanford University (A.B., 1931), the University of San Francisco (LL.D., 1974), the University of the Redlands (D.B.A., 1974), and Boston University (LL.D., 1980). He is married, has four children, and resides in Ross, CA. He was born January 25, 1908, in San Francisco, CA.

Appointment of Gertrude Catherine McDonald as a Member of the National Commission for Employment Policy, and Designation as Chairman
February 13, 1985

The President today announced his intention to appoint Gertrude Catherine McDonald to be a member of the National Commission for Employment Policy for a term of 1 year. This is a new position. Upon her appointment, she will be designated Chairman.

Mrs. McDonald was recently announced

to be appointed as a member of the National Council on Vocational Education. She is retired director of special education for Fremont Unified School District in Fremont, CA.

She is married and resides in Fremont, CA. She was born July 21, 1923, in the Irvington District of Fremont, CA.

Appointment of Five Members of the Northern Mariana Islands Commission on Federal Laws, and Designation of the Chairman
February 13, 1985

The President today announced his intention to appoint the following individuals to be members of the Northern Mariana Islands Commission on Federal Laws. Benigno R. Fitial will be appointed as Chairman.

Joel J. Bergsma will succeed Agnes Manglona McPhetres. He is Chief Legal Counsel to the House of Representatives, Fourth Northern Marianas Commonwealth Legislature. He is married and resides in Saipan in the Commonwealth of the Northern Mariana Islands. He was born December 16, 1954, in Grand Rapids, MI.

Dewey Lawes Falcone will succeed Myron Bennet Thompson. He is an attorney with the firm of Falcone & Falcone in Los Angeles, CA. He is married, has four children, and resides in Redondo Beach, CA. He was born June 27, 1931, in Hermosa Beach, CA.

Benigno R. Fitial will succeed James A. Joseph. He is a member of the House of Representatives of the Fourth Northern Marianas Commonwealth Legislature. He was born November 27, 1945, in Saipan in the Commonwealth of the Northern Mariana Islands, where he now resides.

Edward DLG. Pangelinan is a reappointment. He is a consultant to the Northern Mariana Islands Government. He is married, has five children, and resides in Olney, MD. He was born October 24, 1941, in Saipan in the Commonwealth of the Northern Mariana Islands.

Pedro Agulto Tenorio is a reappointment. He is Lieutenant Governor of the Commonwealth of the Northern Mariana Islands. He was born August 8, 1941, in Saipan in the Commonwealth of the Northern Mariana Islands, where he now resides.

Nomination of Roxanne S. Vierra To Be a Member of the National Council on the Handicapped
February 14, 1985

The President today announced his intention to nominate Roxanne S. Vierra to be a member of the National Council on the Handicapped for a term expiring September 17, 1987. This is a reappointment.

Mrs. Vierra is currently a broker associate for the Devonshire Co. Additionally, she is executive vice president of Introducing Denver, Inc., which assists spouses being moved with the problems of becoming acclimated in a new environment. In 1970 she founded Retardates Unlimited, Inc., an organization designed to establish business ventures owned and operated by the mentally retarded.

Mrs. Vierra attended Ohio State University and the University of Colorado. She is married, has two children, and resides in Littleton, CO. She was born May 29, 1930, in Chanel, OH.

Nomination of Two Members of the National Council on Educational Research
February 14, 1985

The President today announced his intention to nominate the following individuals to be members of the National Council on Educational Research.

Elaine Y. Schadler, for a term expiring September 30, 1987. This is a reappointment. Mrs. Schadler is currently professional liaison for Children's Hospital of Philadelphia. Previously she was a proofreader and copyeditor for The Intercollegiate Review, The Political Science Reviewer, and The Academic Reviewer (1975–1979) and was an assistant buyer for Kaufman's

Department Store (1967–1969). Mrs. Schadler is married, has one child, and resides in Bryn Mawr, PA. She was born December 1, 1944, in Pittsburgh, PA.

Gwyneth Gayman, for a term expiring September 30, 1987. This is a reappointment. Mrs. Gayman is a former teacher, counselor, and department head at Sun Valley Junior High School in Sun Valley, CA. She is also a former member of the Board of Education of Los Angeles. Mrs. Gayman has one child and resides in LaCanada, CA. She was born March 24, 1914, in Vancouver, BC, Canada.

Appointment of Truman H. Cline as a Member of the Architectural and Transportation Barriers Compliance Board
February 14, 1985

The President today announced his intention to appoint Truman H. Cline to be a member of the Architectural and Transportation Barriers Compliance Board for a term expiring December 3, 1987. He will succeed Scott Moore Duncan.

Beginning in 1937 Mr. Cline has been an industrial engineer serving with several different companies including Sears, Roebuck Manufacturing Divisions. Mr. Cline graduated from Purdue University (B.S.E.E., 1930; M.S.E.E., 1933). He is married, has four children, and resides in Kansas City, MO. He was born October 31, 1909, in Camden, IN.

Appointment of Frederick William Mario Guardabassi as a Member of the Christopher Columbus Quincentenary Jubilee Commission
February 14, 1985

The President today announced his intention to appoint Frederick William Mario Guardabassi to be a member of the Christopher Columbus Quincentenary Jubilee Commission. This is a new position.

Mr. Guardabassi is currently president of Guardabassi Investments. He also serves as chairman of the Broward Citizens Committee. He has served on the board of directors for Gulfstream Bank Holding Co., the American National Bank and Trust Co., and Sunrise American National Bank and Trust Co.

Mr. Guardabassi graduated from Georgetown University (B.S., 1956). He is married, has three children, and resides in Fort Lauderdale, FL. He was born April 3, 1929, in Los Angeles, CA.

171

Message on the Observance of Brotherhood/Sisterhood Week, February 17–23, 1985
February 14, 1985

Brotherhood/Sisterhood Week affords us the opportunity to celebrate the rich diversity of cultures that comprise our great Republic. This year's theme, "America is many, count me in," reminds us that ours is a nation of immigrants built by men and women who came here seeking liberty, opportunity and equality.

Those who arrived on our shores soon learned that enjoyment of these rights entailed the responsibilities of citizenship. Above all, they learned that we remain free only for so long as we remain tolerant of the rights of others.

This spirit of tolerance has helped make America an open society, a nation whose strength is derived from its tapestry of cultures. Our ability to meet the complex challenges of an uncertain future depends on our willingness to nurture the spirit of brotherhood and sisterhood that for so long has been characteristic of our people. Working together in that spirit, we can build an opportunity society in which every American is encouraged to attain his or her fullest potential.

RONALD REAGAN

Designation of Jon R. Thomas as United States Representative on the United Nations Commission on Narcotic Drugs
February 14, 1985

The President today announced the designation of Jon R. Thomas as the Representative of the United States of America on the Commission on Narcotic Drugs of the Economic and Social Council of the United Nations. He will continue to serve as Assistant Secretary of State for International Narcotics Matters at the Department of State. He would succeed Dominick L. DiCarlo.

Since October 1984, Mr. Thomas has been serving as Assistant Secretary of State. Beginning in 1982 he served as Deputy Assistant Secretary of State for International Narcotics Matters. Previously he was senior staff member of the policy planning staff at the Department of State in 1980–1982. In 1977–1981 he was president of TURFAID, a Midsouth-based equipment distributorship. Mr. Thomas joined the Department of State in 1971 and served as a Foreign Service reserve officer in Spain and Switzerland until 1977. He served in the U.S. Special Forces (Green Berets) in 1966–1969 and received several decorations, including the Silver Star, Bronze Star, and Purple Heart.

He graduated from the University of Minnesota (B.A., 1970). He is married, has two children, and resides in McLean, VA. He was born January 7, 1946, in Minneapolis, MN.

Radio Address to the Nation on Central America
February 16, 1985

My fellow Americans:

One of the most inspiring developments of recent years is the move against communism and toward freedom that is sweeping the world. In the Soviet Union and Eastern Europe, we see the dissidents; in Poland, the Solidarity movement. We see freedom fighters in Afghanistan, Ethiopia, Cambodia, and Angola. These brave men and women are fighting to undo the infamous Brezhnev doctrine, which says that once a nation falls into the darkness of Communist tyranny, it can never again see the light of freedom.

Nowhere do we see this more than in Nicaragua, whose Sandinista government is a Marxist-Leninist clique that broke the hearts of the freedom-loving people of their country by imposing a brutal dictatorship soon after taking control in 1979. Functioning as a satellite of the Soviet Union and Cuba, they moved quickly to suppress internal dissent, clamp down on a free press, persecute the church and labor unions, and betray their pledge to hold free elections. Now they're exporting drugs to poison our youth and linking up with the terrorists of Iran, Libya, the Red Brigades, and the PLO. The Sandinistas aren't democrats, but Communists; not lovers of freedom, but of power; not builders of a peaceful nation, but creators of a fortress Nicaragua that intends to export communism beyond its borders.

The true heroes of the Nicaraguan struggle—non-Communist, democracy-loving revolutionaries—saw their revolution betrayed and took up arms against the betrayer. These men and women are today the democratic resistance fighters some call the *contras.* We should call them freedom fighters.

Sandinista propaganda denounces them as mercenaries and former National Guardsmen of the Somoza dictatorship; but this is a lie. The freedom fighters are led by those who oppose Somoza, and their soldiers are peasants, farmers, shopkeepers, and students—the people of Nicaragua. These brave men and women deserve our help. They do not ask for troops, but only for our technical and financial support and supplies. We cannot turn from them in their moment of need; to do so would be to betray our centuries-old dedication to supporting those who struggle for freedom. This is not only legal, it's totally consistent with our history.

Time and again in the course of our history, we've aided those around the world struggling for freedom, democracy, independence, and liberation from tyranny. In the 19th century, we supported Simón Bolivar, the Great Liberator. We supported the Polish patriots, the French Resistance, and others seeking freedom. We well remembered how other nations, like France, had come to our aid during our own Revolution. It's not in the American tradition to turn away. And lucky for us that those who loved democracy 200 years ago didn't turn away from us.

Most of us know of the heroism of Lafayette, who chose to be a brother to those who fought for American independence. But he did more than fight in the field for the Continental Army. He went to France during the war and pleaded with his government for financial aid for the American rebels. And he returned to General Washington with a promise that France would send support, including a large contingent of troops to help in the crucial last campaign. It was those French troops and Lafayette, himself, who helped defeat General Cornwallis and assure the British surrender at Yorktown.

America may never have been born without the help and support of the freedom-loving people of Europe, of Lafayette and Von Steuben and Kosciusko. And America did not forget. More than a century after our Revolution, American soldiers went to France to help them resist tyranny in World War I. And they said, in words that will live forever in the history of gratitude, "Lafayette, we are here."

This is not a story from some romantic past. This is how democracy was built: with one country, one people helping another in their hour of greatest peril.

And now the free people of El Salvador, Honduras, and, yes, of Nicaragua ask for our help. There are over 15,000 freedom fighters struggling for liberty and democracy in Nicaragua and helping to stem subversion in El Salvador. They're fighting for an end to tyranny and its only reliable product: cruelty. They are our brothers. How can we ignore them? How can we refuse them assistance when we know that, ultimately, their fight is our fight? We must remember that if the Sandinistas are not stopped now, they will, as they have sworn, attempt to spread communism to El Salvador, Costa Rica, Honduras, and elsewhere.

The freedom fighters are putting pressure on the Sandinistas to change their ways and live, not as Communist puppets, but as peaceful democrats. We must help. Congress must understand that the American people support the struggle for democracy in Central America. We can save them, as we were once saved, but only if we act and *now.*

Until next week, thanks for listening, and God bless you.

Note: The President spoke at 9:06 a.m. from Rancho del Cielo, his ranch near Santa Barbara, CA.

Interview With Jerry Rankin of the Santa Barbara News-Press
February 13, 1985

Rancho del Cielo

Q. Well, we appreciate your taking the time to, in effect, chat with your neighbors through us. That's a very nice thing to do.

The President. Well, please do it.

Q. I was pleased to see in the bulkhead back there that the temperature in Santa Barbara is 74 degrees, and we were joking that with the wind chill factor, it's 78 degrees. [*Laughter*]

So, now that you've got the houses built for your guests and for Lee Clearwater, and I guess the irrigation ditch is either finished or almost done, what's your next big project at the ranch? Or is there one?

The President. Well, it's been quite a time since the last one. Yes, we finished the irrigation project, and right now I can't think of anything else to fence in. There are always some little things to do around there. But there's always firewood. And the last 2 years there has been, I must say, an ongoing project which can fill in any time that we don't have a special thing like the irrigation to do.

A couple of years ago in April, you'll remember, there was a freak snowstorm up in that area.

Q. Yes, indeed.

The President. And that was about an 8-inch wet snowfall at our ranch. And during the night, Lee told me that it sounded like an artillery barrage—with those live oak trees, the limbs breaking off. So, wherever you go in the woods, to this day, I think we could spend the rest of our lives—there are these downed limbs all over. And so when there's nothing else to do, why, we pick another spot—go in, clear it out, and cut the brush off, stack that for burning in the winter; and then whatever's usable, make into firewood.

We're trying to clear it up, because it really—it was just—you can't imagine—I've got some 8 by 10 photos for an album from the ranch—what it looked like, scenes of some of them. But it was just, well, it was a disaster.

Q. We tried to leave your privacy alone as much as we can. But under the circumstances, I remember that morning when I heard about snow, I called Lee up at the ranch, and I said, "Lee, did you get any of that snow, because we can see it from downtown." He said, "We got 8 inches of snow up here, 9 inches." And I said, "Come on, you've got to be kidding me." "No," he says, "8 inches outside the President's side door there."

And so I ran a little piece in the paper, and——

The President. Not only downed, but then there's some that, you know, that the lumberjacks call widow makers—and that's the limbs that have broken off, and they're still hanging up there. We never know when one of them is going to come in.

Q. Right. What is it exactly that keeps pulling you back to the ranch? I mean, what do you get from attacking all that innocent wood? [*Laughter*]

The President. Well now, remember though, the environmentalists, I am sure, will be happy to know we don't cut down trees for firewood. We have to cut the fire-wood, because the only heat we have are—come from firewood and such. But, no, we don't cut down trees. We've done it by things that are down, and there's always—in as much woods as we have—there's always trees that come down by themselves, that nature takes care of. And those we cut up, and sometimes some judicious pruning, where we think we can improve the tree with a little pruning.

Q. Is it the sheer physical enjoyment of doing it? I mean, when you're doing this, are you really thinking about anything else, like the Mideast, or are you really thinking about that log there?

The President. No, it's a real change. And it isn't always that; I think part of it also is that there's always a kick into building something. And we did a lot of work—all those wood fences that we put in that weren't there, a lot of work on the house itself. It was a little, old adobe that was built in 1872, and we did most of the work our-selves there, fixing it up—the fences. You get a good feeling out of what you've ac-complished there. But the riding, of course, we like.

But I'll tell you, I think that particular place casts a spell on you. Maybe it's the fact that you have to turn into a kind of private road that just serves a few ranches; unlike the previous ranch we had down south where the highway went within 250 feet of the house.

Q. At Malibu.

The President. Yes.

Q. Yes, I was there one time.

The President. Well, in this one, when you get in there, the world is gone.

Q. I was lucky enough one time in the '76 campaign—you took Frank Reynolds and Walt Zaboski and a couple of other people up there, and I went along, and so we got the tour of the house and a couple of things we've seen.

We know that there's mountain lions and bears up there. Have you ever actually seen them?

The President. I have not—*[knocking on wood]*—*[laughter]*—seen a bear yet. I've seen the evidence—tracks and so forth from the bear. And it's usually just a bear; they're pretty territorial. And the same with the mountain lions. Now, I saw one young one. Bobcats you see frequently. But the closest adventure that we had with a mountain lion was one day, early on—they had Secret Service, and there was a big—one station up on the hill above the house, looking down the pasture to where they could survey everything. And the fellows would take turns up there—and with a camp stool—sitting and watching.

And one day one of the agents came down, and his eyes were as big as saucers. And he didn't know whether what he saw was just to be expected or whether it was unusual. But he had sat there, motionless, while a mountain lion strolled by about 30 feet away. *[Laughter]*

Q. Wise. *[Laughter]*

The President. And he was wise to stay motionless. But that was the closest contact any of us have had with one.

Q. Someone told me that I ought to ask you about snakes, because they heard that awhile back, maybe right after you bought it, you and Lee Clearwater bagged, I guess, some rattlesnakes and dumped them in some place called Snake Lake?

The President. We named it Snake Lake after what we'd done. No, they weren't rat-tlesnakes. We had some—these rattlesnakes. In California and that kind of country, you're going to.

We had a pond there that——

Q. The one next to the house?

The President. ——that used to be tempo-rary. It would go dry in the summer, and we fixed it so that now it catches the drain-age, and we have a year-round pond. And all of a sudden, there must have been a hatch of snake eggs of the kind that—I don't know what you call them—it was a kind of a gray snake with black and red vertical stripes on it, and it seemed to be a water snake. They headed for the water.

But this hatch—they were all about 12, 14 inches long. And if you'd come out the door, they'd scatter across the lawn; you'd see them going. And to the women on the place, that was not very attractive.

So one day, Barney, Lee, and I—I said, "I've got an idea." Now, I've never liked to pick up a snake. I've always heard that people who handle them—herpetologists—

will tell you that if you ever do, you will lose any of that feeling about a snake—that once you've picked it up—it's firm and a cool body; it isn't slimy or anything of that kind.

But I headed down—I got some big paper bags like they use, the markets use—and we put on gloves, and then we went out. We started catching them, putting them in the bags. Well, pretty soon—we missed too many. We'd grab, and with those clumsy work gloves on—so I peeled off the gloves, and I found out the herpetologists were right. After picking up a few, well, we'd pick them up and stuff them in; we had a bagful. And then I didn't want to go around, you know, slaughtering them and—bloody, awful bloody to do that.

So, we put them in a jeep, and down we'd go. Way back down the back corner, there is a pond just off the—our border, the ranch of our border. So, we dumped these snakes there—and kept wanting to get the big ones, because I figured they have to do this every year if we didn't—and eventually came upon the two adults. And we captured them the same way and dumped them down there.

But one day when we were getting them pretty well, we kept count. It was over 120, 120-odd snakes that we picked up and dumped. But the last half-sackful, we were—this was before the helicopter, still had agents—I had a half a sackful and no time—we were leaving the ranch that day—to go down to Snake Lake. It was the wrong direction. So, I just put it in the car.

And we started down the hill—[laughter]—and two agents in the front. And you cross a stream about three times on the road down. So, at the first crossing, I said, "Pull up, stop." And they tried to—stopped. And I got my sack and got out—[laughter]—and dumped the snakes. [Laughter] And I came back, and three people were just staring at me—[laughter]—those were in the car all the time. [Laughter]

Q. Was that while you were campaigning or while you were President?

The President. It had to be from the campaigning because, the other—I was—we have the helicopter now.

Q. You were talking about shooting a rattlesnake one time.

The President. Which story do you want?

Q. The one where you shot the rattlesnake.

The President. Oh, well, I was still Governor when we took over the ranch. And some of the people, my staff—they loved to come up there with us on a weekend, come down from Sacramento. And they'd come up, and they'd pitch in. We were doing all this work. And one of them—he's now an architect—he and I got in the jeep and went down the back country looking for some type rocks—there's rock everyplace up there, but a lot of rugged kind—but one of those rounded things for something we were doing up on the lawn; then we didn't locate any. And we started back, and he said, "There's a snake." There was a kind of a ditch beside the road and then a bank going up, and then rocks are all up on the bank. And I stopped, and I got out and started around the front of the jeep. And I said—I don't like to go around killing things, but—I said, "If that's a rattler, I'm going to have to."

And he had started to get down on his side, the side where the snake was. And all of a sudden, he was backing up right onto the jeep. [Laughter] And he says, "Kill it! Kill it!" And sure enough, it was about 4 feet long, and it was a rattler. And it was trying to get up the bank.

I looked and I couldn't find anything to get it. And there was a rock about the size of a lime—nice, oval, smooth rock—there in the road. And I picked it up, and just desperately I let go. I hit it right on the head, and it was—just squashed. I never said a word. I just came back around, got in the jeep. We started back down.

When we got to the house, I went in where Nancy was, and I heard him outside telling: "And then," he says, "then he picked up this stone, and he threw the stone, and he hit that snake right on the head." And Nancy's listening to this, too. And I turned to Nancy and I said, "And he will never see me throw a stone again as long as I live." [Laughter]

Q. Is there something on the ranch that you call the hanging tree?

The President. Yes.

Q. What is that?

The President. Well, there's a great history about that ranch.

Q. Yes, I'm familiar with a lot of it.

The President. It goes back to the old Refugio Pass. Originally part of it went right through our ranch. Now it goes around the——

Q. Yes.

The President. But the trail is still there, the evidence of the trail. And all of this history—and you know the bandit——

Q. Oh, yes.

The President. The famous romantic bandit——

Q. I know the one you mean, with the Spanish name.

The President. He traveled it. And when we came there, when I first saw the place before we actually bought it—down this canyon, a friend of—Ray Cornelius, who had the ranch—Ray showed us this big oak tree. Now, on one side of the tree was a face carved on the side of the bark. And it looked like the pictures that you see of Jesus. It's gone now. The bark, you know, got old and peeled away. Only a little sliver shows a part of it——

Q. Right.

The President. But on the other side, not gone, is a cross, and then some notches. And Ray thought it was a clue to some kind of treasure. And he used to go down there trying to figure out these notches—what do they mean?

Well, I took one look after we—and I said, "I know what that is." Got to doing some reading of the history of the area—there's a great big limb comes out of there—and I said, "That's a hanging tree." That must have been where they did their own justice in those days. So, we've just named the canyon "Hanging Tree Canyon." But there—those notches—are, how many? About 9, 10 of them.

Q. Do you still run cattle on the ranch for the agricultural preserve status, or is that not the case anymore?

The President. No. Well, I did run—when we got up there, it was what they had done before me, and they had grazers. Bring them in at the beginning of the grazing season—yearlings—keep them, and then sell them for the increase in weight. And, naturally, that would not meet the cost of the ranch. And then something in the Treasury Department happened where they began naming ranches "hobby ranches," and there were no longer deductible. And—[*laughter*]—but, also, this move—why there was just no way to keep on doing that, being away as much as we are. So, I quit.

But what I do do is bring in a few yearlings now and then and butcher them for our meat and so on——

Q. Well, you still qualify for the California—the Williamson Act Ag Preserve status?

The President. Well, yes, because we are not subdividing or anything else of the land——

Q. Right.

The President. So, yes, this meets those terms.

Q. There's been some criticism by people saying that, "Gee, on the one hand President Ronald Reagan may get some significant cutbacks and some Federal tax breaks that are enjoyed, but son of a gun, he's still taking that California tax break."

The President. Well, that's the only break we have. But that was on there 10 years before we came there—from the time that the act went in. The County Board of Supervisors in California can designate certain land, that if you will sign a contract—I think they're in 10-year stretches—sign a contract that you will not develop that land, you will not, you know, sell it for tracts and that sort of thing, and keep it in its present condition, then it will be taxed on that basis, not on its best potential value.

The truth is, I don't think very many people could afford to do this without that act. I think it was one of the great land preservation things that's ever been done in California. It was there in effect when we came, but——

Q. It's been very successful, certainly in our county. There's half a million acres in Ag Preserve, and yours is just a little——

The President. Yes. And I love it the way it is, and I don't want to change it. But I wouldn't be able to afford to stay there if somebody said, "Oh, how much would it be worth if it was a subdivision?"

Presidential Security

Q. Right. Real value. It sort of brings up security. You made clear that you wanted as little security as possible commensurate with your new position when you became President. You've still got the guy sitting outside at night on the vehicle, and you've got dogs around—you know, the whole bit. Down at Point Mugu, when you come and go, there's some personnel, you know, you wave to who are across the street. And then there's a little disgruntlement. They say, "Well, gee, we've got all the super secret clearance,"—you know, they do the missile work and that kind of stuff, and yet now they've got buses parked there, so it's very difficult for them to see—you know, they say, "Why is all that really necessary?"

The President. Well, I'll tell you, I've never intervened in any of the security things that are done. And when we land at a military base, not only that but some kind of other ones, sometimes the families of the personnel are turned out, and I say a few words to them; and sometimes not. And I've never asked who does that, or who determines that. But today I have been told that there is going to be a whole turnout there at the base—all the families and everything—going to be——

Q. Maybe they'll let them back in closer to, say, where the press is.

The President. I've never even inquired or intervened in anything like that or who makes those decisions.

Q. You leave it to the pros?

The President. Yes. Or whether it's the local base.

Rancho del Cielo

Q. Your home is about the size of a Goleta tract home. It is—what, 1,500 square feet? Other places you live, such as the White House and down at Pacific Palisades, that are a bit larger—do you ever miss any of the amenities at Rancho del Cielo in that very modest house?

The President. It was very wonderful to get in that size house. It is—you've said it; I think I heard you say—it's about 1,500 square feet. Well, this is one of the benefits of going up to Camp David. There you go to a—and you spend a weekend in a normal size house, where you can open a door and go out in the backyard and things of that kind.

No, the White House—there's no question about the luxury and all of that, but you can get a kind of a bird-in-a-gilded-cage feeling out of it also.

Q. So, you like rattling around, obviously, in that small house?

The President. Yes.

Q. The house itself, of the ranch, I guess, may be possibly the most isolated, geographically, retreat of any President in modern times. I gather you don't feel the isolation?

The President. No, no, not at all.

Q. You don't feel out of touch at all?

The President. I cite the passage: "And I look to the hills from whence cometh my strength."

The President's Retirement Plans

Q. I assume that you and Mrs. Reagan have given some thought to what happens in that glorious day when you return to California after the second term. What are your current plans about retirement? I remember you told Barbara Walters that you didn't think the ranch would be your full-time retirement home.

The President. No, I've never thought that. I think then that would be too secluded and so forth. No, we've always loved living in Los Angeles, and we just assume that we'll find ourselves a home in Los Angeles and then, just as we did before, go to the ranch and——

Q. So, somewhere in the L.A. area?

The President. Yes.

Q. Did you give any thought to Palm Springs?

The President. No, no, that's nice to go to at certain times, but I've never been a——

Q. Gets a little hot out there.

The President. ——I've never been a great aficionado of the desert.

Q. Well, are you and Mrs. Reagan actually looking for a house at this point, or is that something that's far in the——

The President. No, I think we'll wait for awhile, closer to the time when——

Presidential Vacations

Q. Occasionally we run a letter to the

editor, wondering why does President Reagan have to come out to California so often at substantial cost of the flights and all of that. And some of them say, "Well, we understand that, but couldn't it be once or twice a year, instead of five or six?" So, this is your chance to give a direct reply to those letters to the editor.

The President. Yes, and I would like to very much. Let's look back over the history of previous Presidents. I don't know of any of them that didn't have some place, sometimes even more than one, that they liked to go. I remember the same criticism of Jerry Ford because of Vail, Colorado, and his wanting to ski. Certainly my immediate predecessor seemed to get back to——

Q. Georgia—[*laughter*]—a lot——

The President. ——Georgia quite a bit. But before them, there was President Eisenhower in Augusta, Georgia; there was Nixon and his home in Biscayne Bay, Florida, in addition to the California——

Q. Right——

The President. ——house out there. No, I have to say that, first of all, I think Nancy put it once better than anyone else: "Presidents don't get vacations; they just get a change of scenery." And you're still President. The job goes with you.

Now, an awful lot of this cost is a cost that would go on anyway, if you stop to think about it. This plane—now it's been many, many weeks since we've been on this plane—but this plane doesn't just sit there. This plane has to get so many hours that it's put in flying. And this just takes the place of those. The salaries of the people and so forth, those would go on—the staff who're going along—whether they do that or not. Yes, there is some cost of—while they're away, out there—living expense and all.

But as I say, the job goes with you. And I find, and I guess every President before me has found—with Franklin D. Roosevelt it was Warm Springs—you find that there is, there's something that you need. And I look at it in another way: At my age, how many more years do I have to go to the ranch and enjoy the ranch? You give up an awful lot in privacy and so forth in these positions, and I think you're entitled, as long as you're still President, are still faced with the problems that—I've spent some days at that

ranch, the better part of the day, on the telephone.

California Offshore Oil Drilling

Q. Well, let me ask you a couple of questions about oil, which is of some interest to us out in Santa Barbara. Is there any spot from your property that you can actually see the oil platforms out in the ocean?

The President. Oh, yes, because those that are up, further up—I'm always tempted to say north, but actually it's west, as the coastline there runs——

Q. Right, exactly. A true Santa Barbara resident knows the directions.

The President. But, we can see them, because from our ranch—and that's one of the reasons why, when you asked a little while ago about Palm Springs—no, I couldn't get that far from the ocean. There are spots on our ranch for riding when we can see both the Santa Barbara Channel and the Santa Ynez Valley at the same time. We just have to turn our heads.

Q. Can you see as far as Goleta? Like Storke Tower on the campus? Or is that a little too far down?

The President. No, we can't see that, never see that, but we see all the way to Anacapa, out to the Anacapa rocks——

Q. That's very good——

The President. ——the coastal islands. We're at—we're about 2,400 feet at the ranch. But we see those derricks.

Q. When you see those, obviously, you must think about this business of the drilling in the channel. Some people in Santa Barbara, including some businessmen, say, "Well, let's explore—find out where the oil is, but not drill, not actually put it out. Let's hold it in reserve, because of the danger to the economy if there were another spill." Obviously, do you think that's possible, or realistic?

The President. I think they're ignoring one thing we found out at the time of the spill, because I was Governor at that time. And we sent—incidentally, that was a Federal lease that leaked. And we found out at that time and they, themselves, told us that had they known the regulations on State leases, had followed the same regulations, there never would have been a spill. So, the

179

Federal Government at that time—the Nixon administration—they adopted for Federal leasing—we still do—the same standards and requirements the State imposes.

Now the Federal Government has about 16 platforms off the coast of California, as increasing by some—and they seem, we seem now, the Federal Government, to be getting all the attention and abuse. But there are several hundred wells that are State leases that have been there for quite some time. But when we sent the experts in—and they weren't buddies of ours—we sent scientists from the university campuses of California in to study this whole area and the problem. And they came back with one unanimous recommendation—drill, get the oil out. They said the bottom of the channel is badly fractured. There are 16 permanent oil slicks that have been there as long as the memory of man.

Q. Yes.

The President. And they said the safest thing you can do is get that oil pumped out of there because there could be a natural disaster—I'm sure they were speaking of an earthquake at that fractured bottom—that would create a disaster of such dimensions that you could never get a—the previous oil strike, or leak, as far as I can learn, was only about 790 barrels of oil. Now we're taking out tens of thousands of barrels. But their recommendation was drill, get it out, and remove that permanent threat that lies off the coast.

Q. But also, it's, of course, the policy of the administration to go after the off-shore oil, even though—which reminds me that we've got a glut now in the world of oil that doesn't show any signs of slacking off. It may happen. And so a lot of people say—and, again, we get letters to the editor——

The President. But we don't——

Q. ——"Why drill with this glut?"

The President. Well, we've offered oil lands for lease, and they've turned it down. There have been no takers.

But here's another thing. The same people can't scream about the trade deficit, the imbalance of trade, when 50 percent of that is the oil that we have to import.

Now, wouldn't it make more sense for us—we've already reduced considerably the amount of oil that we have to import, making ourselves closer to self-sufficient. But from a security standpoint, from even the balance in trade, it would make much more sense for us to be producing the oil ourselves than having to go out and buy it.

Q. There's an ongoing debate, I guess, perpetual in Santa Barbara—some people say, "Oh, those platforms are ugly as sin." Other people say, "Well, they're not. Jeez, at night, they're beautiful." What do you think about them? Which side of the debate do you come down on?

The President. I have to say, you know, I think this is really reaching to say that some structure out there that far out in the ocean—when you've got that whole expanse of ocean—it isn't as if you were looking at the ocean through a little frame, and now somebody put something in the way.

And I once said to people that were complaining, I said, "You know, we've got a lot of freighters, those liberty freighters, up in mothball. Why don't we bring down some and anchor them between the shore and the oil derrick? And then the people would see a ship, and they wouldn't find anything wrong with that at all." Or they don't mind seeing piers that go out a half or a quarter mile into the ocean. And why, I don't find them—and then, as you say, at night—I know one lovely old lady there who automatically complained in the daytime because she could see this derrick from her place. And then it was one of them that I guess they—no, it was when they were drilling, and then, when they evidently didn't find oil, then they left. Then, she said, "I miss the lights at night." [*Laughter*]

Q. Of course, the great solution would be to drill—the rigs underneath the water, so we wouldn't have to see the platforms.

The President. Yes.

Q. But, of course, the expenses of that are——

The President. I know that there have been times when——

Q. ——outrageous.

The President. There have been times when some people in the business have talked about the possibility of submerged parts. Of course, there, you look at it in another way, too, what if you have—nothing's perfect—what if you have an accident there and then how do you deal——

Q. How do you—exactly.

The President. Hundreds of feet down in the ocean.

Rancho del Cielo

Q. Tell me about the first time you saw the ranch.

The President. Well, you come in that private road. And now, you come down about a half a mile or so, and then you turn in the entrance road that was built before we got the ranch. But when we first looked at it, the entrance was way up here, right near that—after you go through that gate.

Q. Right.

The President. Then you come in on a road. And you come in through the trees and everything. Well, Bill Wilson and his wife, knowing that—see, we had to sell the ranch in order to be Governor because there wasn't a Williamson Act and the property taxes on that ranch—there's no way I could be Governor and keep that. But we always knew we would want one.

So, as we were coming to the end of the second term, we started looking for a ranch. And Bill knew us very well, and they had a dude ranch down at the bottom of the——

Q. ——uh-huh.

The President. ——pass. And they knew the kind of thing that I was looking for. So, one day we were up visiting them. And Nancy and Betty got in the back seat, and he and I got in the front seat, and up the mountain we went, up Refugio Pass.

Of course, pretty soon, you know, all you're going through is that chaparral and——

Q. Yes.

The President. ——goat land.

Q. Right.

The President. And I was kind of thinking, gee, you know, maybe somebody's got a house up here on the mountain with a view and calls it a ranch. But it doesn't look like there's any space up here for a ranch. And Betty had never been up the road before. And Betty was saying, "Bill, turn around. There can't be anything up here." He just silently kept driving.

And all of a sudden, as we came up close to the gate, suddenly here is a kind of a

meadow of smoke trees beside the road—and I think, well, then, maybe he does know what he's doing. And then we came to the gate where we turned in at the private road. And we came in through that second gate, now, and we're winding on this little gravel road through all of these trees. But it is, you know, kind of looking like rolling land and heavily wooded—and suddenly you come out of those trees, and there is this saucer.

Q. Right.

The President. Down there you could see the house and the barn and so forth, and then you could see this thing. It's a 600 and some acres of meadows and oak and the—forests and rolling hills. And there are some very steep canyons and so forth also.

But I just took one look, and I said, "Let's buy it." [*Laughter*] And Bill said, "Hey, don't talk that way. We've got to talk with the couple that's selling here." He says, "Quiet down."

But then we got down there, and—Ray Cornelius and I—they had horses, and we got on the horses. And we took a ride and——

Q. That did it.

The President. And I tell you, it's just unbelievable. It really is.

Q. Well, it's a fabulous place, and, you know, you're very fortunate to have it. And I think you got a pretty good deal on it, too, myself.

The President. I do, too.

Q. I went back, and I looked at the deed at the courthouse to see what was on it.

The President. The ranch at Malibu. Bob Taylor is alive. Bob, Ursula, and their son, Terry. And they came up to the ranch, and Bob and I—I've always liked to plink—and I'm not a great hunter. I've never killed a deer or anything. But I don't mind killing rodents.

And ground squirrels in California are an official, you know, pest. In other words, you can call the State, and they'll come in to eliminate them.

Q. Absolutely.

The President. And with the horses—I mean, we were infested at that other ranch. So, Bob and I—because he was a hunter—well, we decided we'd go down—and Terry, his son, came with us to a place where I knew there was a colony and where we could lie in wait. And all of a sudden the boy, Terry, was wandering around, came running back in, "Snake! Snake!" So, we went over, and sure enough it was a rattler. And it was heading toward the rocks also.

Well, I looked around, and there was a stick. And I grabbed the stick, and I swung at it, and the stick broke. And it was almost to the rocks and getting away. Well, now, I always at the ranch wore boots and britches, English-type boots, and I knew you can be pretty brave about snakes with those boots on. There's no way they're going to get through those boots, and they're not going to strike that high to get above. So, the stick broke, and he was almost getting away. I stomped on his head with my heel and then looked down. I had sneakers on. [*Laughter*]

Q. Oh, my God. [*Laughter*]

The President. Just entertaining them—hadn't ridden that day or anything, waiting for them to come up. I'd forgotten all about it that that day. I just put on sneakers and a pair of jeans. And I'm looking down at my heel—snake's head just—if I'd missed him——

Q. But you nailed him, huh?

The President. ——that was the end of——

Q. Between your sneakers and the rock, you know, the Pentagon might be interested in a new weapons system, it seems to me. [*Laughter*]

Q. Thank you very much.

Note: The interview began at 11 a.m. on board Air Force One en route to California. A tape was not available for verification of the content of this interview, which was released by the Office of the Press Secretary on February 17.

Proclamation 5302—Lithuanian Independence Day, 1985
February 16, 1985

By the President of the United States of America

A Proclamation

Sixty-seven years ago, a small nation achieved freedom in the aftermath of World War I. Proclaiming the Lithuanian Republic, its founders stepped forward on February 16, 1918, to assert their country's independence and commitment to a government based on justice, democracy, and the rights of individuals. Twenty-two years later, Soviet tyranny imposed itself on Lithuania and denied the Lithuanian people their just right of national self-determination as well as basic human freedoms.

Among the freedoms most consistently attacked by Soviet authorities is the freedom of religion. The victims of these attacks have often been Catholic Church figures, such as Father Alfonsas Svarinskas, Father Sigitas Tamkevicius, and, most recently, Father Jonas-Kastytis Matulionis. Their crimes: administering to the spiritual needs

of the faithful.

Yet the people of Lithuania refuse to submit quietly. Hundreds of thousands of people have signed petitions demanding the release of priests and other human and civil rights leaders. Underground publications such as the sixty-fourth issue of the "Chronicle of the Catholic Church in Lithuania" and forty-first issue of "The Dawn," which have recently come to the West, continue to inform the world of ongoing persecutions.

Americans are united in an enduring belief in the right of peoples to live in freedom. The United States has refused to recognize the forcible incorporation of Lithuania into the Soviet Union. We must be vigilant in the protection of this ideal because we know that as long as freedom is denied to others, it is not truly secure here.

We mark this anniversary of Lithuanian Independence with a renewed hope that the blessings of liberty will be restored to Lithuania.

The Congress of the United States, by House Joint Resolution 655, has designated February 16, 1985, as Lithuanian Independence Day and authorized and requested the President to issue a proclamation in observance of this event.

Now, Therefore, I, Ronald Reagan, President of the United States of America, do hereby proclaim February 16, 1985, as Lithuanian Independence Day. I invite the people of the United States to observe this day with appropriate ceremonies and to reaffirm their dedication to the ideals which unite us and inspire others.

In Witness Whereof, I have hereunto set my hand this sixteenth day of February, in the year of our Lord nineteen hundred and eighty-five, and of the Independence of the United States of America the two hundred and ninth.

RONALD REAGAN

[*Filed with the Office of the Federal Register, 11:06 a.m., February 19, 1985*]

Note: The proclamation was released by the Office of the Press Secretary on February 19.

Remarks at the Presentation Ceremony for the National Technology Awards
February 19, 1985

The President. Thank you very much. I hope you haven't said everything. [*Laughter*]

Secretary Baldrige. No, I haven't. [*Laughter*]

The President. All right.

Well, Secretary Baldrige and ladies and gentlemen, good afternoon and welcome to the White House.

You know, one of the last times that this grand old mansion played host to an event concerning technology was back in '76—1876. President Rutherford B. Hayes was shown a recently invented device. "That's an amazing invention," he said, "but who would ever want to use one of them?" He was talking about a telephone. I thought at the time that he might be mistaken. [*Laughter*]

But in those days, most Americans were tied to the land. And the most familiar means of transportation were the sailing ship and the horse. Then, advances like the telephone and the electric light, the internal combustion engine, transformed our nation, enabling us to achieve the highest standard of living in the world; to lead longer, richer, and fuller lives; and to share our bounty with millions beyond our borders.

Today we see all around us the beginnings of a second transformation, a quantum technological leap that's making possible still greater prosperity and individual fulfillment than we've ever known. This new technology is affecting every aspect of our lives. In manufacturing, lightweight and inexpensive materials like fiber composites and ceramics are taking the place of costly metals. In transportation, cars and airplanes are being equipped with inexpensive microchips that keep track of maintenance needs and enable engines to run better on less fuel. In the home, computers are putting art, literature, and vast sums of information at families' fingertips.

Perhaps the most exciting advances are taking place in medicine. A diagnostic process, for example, has been made faster, safer, and more accurate by the advent of technologies like cat scanning and the use of soundwaves. Biotechnology is enabling us to produce human growth hormones more easily and inexpensively—a godsend to children whose growth might otherwise be impaired. Research is advancing against cancer, and new drugs are combating high blood pressure, diabetes, and heart disease. Countless medical breakthroughs have meant that, for the past decade, the life expectancy of Americans has gone up.

As technology goes on providing new

goods, services, and techniques of production, our entire economy is expanding and worker productivity is up. At one semiconductor plant in Pennsylvania in 1957, workers produced five transistors a day for $7.50 apiece. And they now produce over a million for less than a penny apiece.

Perhaps the best news of all concerns new job formation. Employment in the computer industry has skyrocketed. Computers and robotics are also bringing new efficiency to our older industries, helping them modernize their plants and compete better. And today American cars are once again as advanced as those built anywhere on Earth.

Economic growth is our most powerful tool for reducing poverty and fostering vigor and self-esteem among the millions in America's work force. I expect today's burgeoning technology to work hand in hand with the incentives in our tax reform plan to keep our economy growing and creating ever-wider opportunities for all Americans.

Our administration has made a firm commitment to technological progress. Both of them are probably true, but one we view as nothing less than a commitment to human creativity and imagination. While we're cutting back, wherever possible, unnecessary government spending, we're continuing our strong commitment to basic research and development.

We have cut personal income tax rates; we plan to cut them again. This could spur savings, and higher savings could, in turn, boost the capital formation so important in funding new high-technology ventures. And we've rolled back needless government regulations to help provide the freedom needed by those at the frontiers of technology to experiment with new hypotheses and techniques.

In space, we're opening the way to private enterprise; the space shuttle program is already working closely with private industry. And in 1985 NASA is scheduled to deploy eight commercial communications satellites. Space technology will continue to grow even more rapidly as we pursue our plans to launch a permanently manned space station—and to do so within a decade.

In defense, we're putting technology at the service of a decade's old dream: the elimination of nuclear weapons. Our Strategic Defense Initiative represents, perhaps, the most dramatic and wide-reaching research effort to explore the means for making nuclear weapons obsolete.

Let me make one thing plain: The Strategic Defense Initiative is not a bargaining chip. It's an historic effort on behalf of our national defense and peace throughout the world, and we intend to see it through.

The story of American technology is long and proud. It might be said to have begun with a blacksmith at his bellows, hammering out fine tools, and the Yankee craftsman using simple wood planes, saws, and mallets to fashion the fastest sailing ships on the ocean. And then came the railroad men, driving spikes across our country.

And today the story continues with the workers who built the computer in a child's room; the engineers who designed the communications satellite that silently rotates with the Earth, shining in the sunlight against the blackness of space; and the men and women of skill and determination who helped to put American footprints on the Moon.

In a few moments, 14 Americans will become the first recipients of the National Technology Awards, and you are heroes, each one of you, just as surely as were Thomas Edison and Alexander Graham Bell. You sing the songs of a people using their hands and minds in freedom, the songs of Americans at work making their lives even more full. And it's only fitting that our nation should pay you honor. And on behalf of the American people, I congratulate you.

Thank you, and God bless you. And, Mac, you take over.

Note: The President spoke at 1:33 p.m. in the East Room at the White House. Following his remarks, the President and Secretary of Commerce Malcolm Baldrige presented the awards to Joseph F. Sutter of Boeing Commercial Airplane Co.; Bob O. Evans, Frederick P. Brooks, Jr., and Erich Bloch, formerly of IBM Corp.; Allen E. Puckett and Harold A. Rosen of Hughes Aircraft Co.; Marvin M. Johnson of Phillips Petroleum Co.; John T. Parsons and Frank L.

Stulen of John T. Parsons Co.; Steven P. Jobs and Stephen G. Wozniak of Apple Computer, Inc.; Ralph Landau, formerly with *Halson S.D. Group, Inc.; and Ian Ross and William O. Baker of AT&T Bell Laboratories, Inc.*

Remarks to Veterans of the Battle of Iwo Jima
February 19, 1985

Thank you very much. That's quite a reception for a horse cavalryman and a Navy flyboy. [*Laughter*]

Well, at dawn, 40 years ago today, 450 United States Navy ships stood off a tiny island in the Pacific. Few Americans had heard of the place. It measured 4⅔ miles by 2½ miles, ash-covered beaches and one extinct, unknown volcano. And at 7 o'clock, 0700 hours to you, a command was passed to the ships: Land the landing force!

No one, not even you, the marines and the Navy corpsmen who stepped ashore from the Amtracs at 2 minutes after 9, knew that what you were about to do would forever enshrine the island, Iwo Jima, and the volcano, Mount Suribachi, in American history.

Today Iwo Jima is remembered with other names like Saratoga, the Alamo, Gettysburg—remembered, not simply because Americans were again conspicuously gallant in battle, but because our sons were called upon to endure unspeakable hardship for the sake of freedom.

Every one of you present today, and all of you 40 years ago, have a special place in our nation's heart, reserved only for the few in every generation called upon to sacrifice themselves so that a great nation's ideals of freedom and peace may live and prosper and endure. The manner of your performance—as captured in Joe Rosenthal's photo of your flag-raising at Mount Suribachi—remains a beacon, indeed a birthright, for America's young people and for every future American.

The other day, I came across a description of Iwo written by the then-Private First Class Russell Werts. And it ended in the following note: ". . . our troopship started to pull away from Iwo and head for Guam. As I stood by the rail and watched the little island fade in the distance, a feeling of loneliness came over me. It was as if a part of me was left behind, as if an Iowa farm boy was waving goodbye. We would never meet again. Somewhere in that jagged jungle of rocks, he forever walked with the ghosts of Iwo. . . ."

Well, I would like to say to Russell, and to each of you who willingly gave your youth to the Nation, that you receive in kind a place in the American heart and the national memory that endures so long as this nation and the ideals for which it stands endure. We're very grateful to you.

And we're deeply honored to have you here today. The White House really belongs to the American people. And I couldn't help but reflect today that seldom in history has any President been in the company of more deserving Americans.

I hope that each of you enjoyed being here as much as Nancy and I am delighted to have you. And on behalf of all Americans, we salute today, you, the men of Iwo. God bless all of you.

Note: The President spoke to former members of the 28th Marine Regiment at 4:45 p.m. in the East Room at the White House. In his opening remarks, the President referred to his own and the Vice President's military service.

Nomination of Four Members of the Advisory Board for Radio Broadcasting to Cuba
February 20, 1985

The President today announced his intention to nominate the following individuals to be members of the Advisory Board for Radio Broadcasting to Cuba. These are all new positions.

Anne Elizabeth Brunsdale, for a term of 2 years. This is a new position. Since 1967 she has been at the American Enterprise Institute and is presently serving as managing editor of Regulation, a bimonthly magazine dealing with regulatory matters. She was director of publications at the AEI in 1970–1977. She graduated from the University of Minnesota (B.A., 1945; M.A., 1946) and Yale University (M.A., 1949). She was born October 1, 1923, in Minneapolis, MN, and now resides in Washington, DC.

Joseph Francis Glennon, for a term of 3 years. In 1960–1980 he served as counselor for host country relations at the U.S. Mission to the United Nations in New York. Previously he was attaché at the American Embassy in Ankara, Turkey. He graduated from Seton Hall University (B.S., 1947). He is married, has six children,

and resides in Boynton Beach, FL. He was born December 12, 1919.

Jose Luis Rodriguez, for a term of 2 years. Since 1970 he has been president and owner of M & R Farms, Inc., in Boynton Beach, FL. He has also been serving as chief executive officer of Corky Foods Corp. in Boynton Beach, FL, since 1979. In addition, he serves as treasurer and director of CBI Corp. (Caribbean Basin Investment Corp.) in Miami, FL. He is married, has three children, and resides in Boynton Beach, FL. He was born November 11, 1946, in Havana, Cuba.

Danford L. Sawyer, Jr., for a term of 3 years. He is vice president and director of management services for R.R. Donnelly & Sons in Chicago, IL. Previously he was president of Sawyer & Associates Advertising, Inc., and president of Area Guides, Inc., in Sarasota, FL. He is a founding director of Presidential Savings & Loan Association in Sarasota. He is married, has three children, and resides in Lincolnshire, IL. He was born November 11, 1939, in New York, NY.

Informal Exchange With Reporters Prior to a Meeting With Prime Minister Margaret Thatcher of the United Kingdom
February 20, 1985

Q. Mr. President, did you hear the Prime Minister speak today?

The President. No. I was just saying I didn't get a chance to, but some of our people did——

Q. She handles the teleprompter now as well as you do. [*Laughter*]

The Prime Minister. Not quite. Not quite. No, we were just comparing notes, because I'm not so used to it. And there's always a little worry that one of them, you know, might stop working.

Q. And did you have a text to back you up?

The Prime Minister. I have a text always—yes, of course. I went into one speech—it was a speech to young Conservatives, as a matter of fact—intending to use

the teleprompter, and the lights behind it were so strong that you could not see a word on the teleprompter itself.

The President. That has to be worked out. Yes, that can happen.

The Prime Minister. So, you have to have always your speech with you.

The President. Yes, that can happen.

The Prime Minister. If the worst comes to the worst, we could always ad lib, you know, but not for great diplomatic speeches.

Q. What did you think of the reaction to your speech?

The Prime Minister. Oh, it was very thrilling, because it's a great ordeal to speak in the greatest forum, the greatest free people.

Q. Mr. President, what will you tell the Prime Minister about our deficit and about the strength of the dollar? She'll be concerned, won't she?

The President. Let me just answer that by saying I am quite sure that will be a subject of discussion when we have our meeting.

The Prime Minister. I endorse that approach. [*Laughter*]

Q. Is it true that you're going to drop the quotas, the voluntary quotas on the autos—Japanese?

The President. No decision to be announced on that yet.

Q. Well, we're trying.

Q. Are you going to talk to the Prime Minister about New Zealand? About New Zealand?

The President. Oh, I wouldn't be surprised if that's mentioned.

The Prime Minister. I'm only, I think, about 2½ to 3 hours. [*Laughter*] There's a lot to discuss.

Q. You can cover a lot of ground——

Q. What's on the top of your list?

The Prime Minister. What?

Q. What's on the top of your list?

The Prime Minister. Well, obviously, we will talk about East-West matters, with the arms control things coming up. I hope we'll have a word about Middle East, and I hope we'll have a word about general economic matters. And then there are lots of other particular things as well.

Q. And you agree on all matters?

The Prime Minister. Yes, I think we agree on most matters. But more than agree, I think we discuss things through, because even though you agree on your fundamental approach—we're often in the same summit meetings. It may be an economic forum, it may be various other summits, but you've got to discuss how you handle things. Your strategy may be the same, but the tactics require a great deal of discussion. And the way of achieving your goals require a great deal of discussion.

We're now quite old hands at economic summits, aren't we? [*Laughter*] The President's chaired the economic summit—Williamsburg. I have done one in London. And I think the next one is in Bonn. And that, too, will be a very important one.

The President. Yes. In May.

Q. You two now have met almost a dozen times or so——

The Prime Minister. Oh, at least——

Q. ——good friends——

The Prime Minister. ——because we used to meet from time to time before we held these august offices. We had a similar fight to the top, I think, didn't we?

The President. Yes.

Q. Well, if you're his greatest fan, what does the President say about you?

The President. It's mutual.

Note: The exchange began at 12:03 p.m. in the Oval Office at the White House. The first question referred to the Prime Minister's address before a joint session of the United States Congress earlier in the day.

Remarks Following Discussions With Prime Minister Margaret Thatcher of the United Kingdom
February 20, 1985

The President. It's always a pleasure to exchange views with Prime Minister Thatcher, a dear friend and the respected leader of one of America's closest allies. We've had a cordial discussion on a wide range of matters. Our conversations reflected the excellent relationship which exists between our two countries, as well as the warm friendship between Mrs. Thatcher and myself.

We discussed East-West relations, and in particular the preparations for the upcoming Geneva talks with the Soviets. We fully agree that the unity, patience, and determination of the North Atlantic alliance are essential if arms control negotiations are to succeed.

What we're seeking are significant reductions in the numbers of nuclear weapons through fair and verifiable agreements. Prime Minister Thatcher and I agree that it's absolutely necessary to continue NATO's INF deployments on schedule, in accord with the alliance's 1979 decision.

We're both hopeful that the dialog opening in Geneva will result in progress. And while that progress continues, however, we will be steadfast in the modernization of our forces and in our determination to promote full adherence to existing arms control agreements. These are crucial incentives to any real progress.

Prime Minister Thatcher and I also discussed the current situation in the Middle East and agreed on the need for parties in that region to take concrete steps toward peace.

We reviewed the situation in Central America, and I assured the Prime Minister of our determination to preserve democracy and to seek peaceful solutions to the problems of that area.

We also discussed the threat of international terrorism, and we agreed that increased international cooperation is called for to combat this evil. We expressed our willingness to work together and with other governments to fight terrorism and deter those who give support to terrorists.

We discussed the situation in Northern Ireland, and I told the Prime Minister that the United States applauds the continuation of her dialog with Irish Prime Minister Fitz-Gerald and assured her of our support of all those working for peaceful solutions and reconciliation.

Prime Minister Thatcher and I reviewed the current economic situation and the prospects for our economies in the future.

And in closing, I wish to note that 1985 marks the 200th anniversary of the establishment of diplomatic relations between the United States and Great Britain.

Over the years these relations have taken on a very special quality. In fact, they're quite extraordinary. We, as Americans, are proud of our relations with our allies the British. And I am personally proud of my close collaboration with my friend Margaret Thatcher.

The Prime Minister. Mr. President, may I say how very grateful I am to you for inviting me for this brief visit, the first official one in your second term, although I paid an unofficial working visit to Camp David in December. Our talks are always particularly valuable, because we see so many things in the same way, and you can speak of a real meeting of minds.

As the President pointed out, this meeting is a special one because 1985 marks the 200th anniversary of diplomatic relations between Britain and the United States. And I think I can safely say that our relations now are better than when John Adams presented his credentials to King George III. Indeed, I feel no inhibitions about describing the relations as very, very special.

And it is a particular honor that President Reagan and Mrs. Reagan have accepted an invitation to dinner at the British Embassy tonight to mark this very special diplomatic anniversary.

The President has given you an account of the discussions we had today. We had some very thorough ones, especially about the prospects for arms control negotiations. Those negotiations carry our hopes with them. They will, as I indicated this morning, be complex, but those who are negotiating on the part of the West know of our fundamental, sincere wish to get down the number of nuclear weapons in the world in a way which is still balanced and which still keeps our security. We believe our negotiators will strive to that end, and they will carry our good wishes with them.

We also spent some time discussing the Middle East, and both agreed that the moment is propitious for a fresh effort to achieve progress towards a Middle Eastern settlement. And I told the President of my support for the statement issued following King Fahd's recent visit to Washington. And we both endorsed King Hussein's efforts to arrive at a joint Arab position, which would allow direct negotiations with Israel to take place.

We also, as you'd expect, had a thorough discussion on economic matters. The record of the American economy and its success in creating new jobs is enviable. And such is the scale of your economy that your decisions affect all of us.

We discussed how important it is to keep down public spending. We have a different problem with the deficit, but we both share similar problems of how to keep down public spending so that people may be able to keep a bigger proportion of their own money in their own pockets. And I think we're at one in resisting any moves towards protectionism.

We also touched on a number of other issues, perhaps the most important of which was the Northern Irish and Republic of Ireland talks—always to try to secure an agreement which will respect both communities in Northern Ireland and always recognizing that any change must come about by consent of the people concerned.

It was, as always, Mr. President, a very friendly visit. You always make them friendly and warm by your own very welcome reception of us. But we do have just a very special ease in talking about these things, an ease which comes because we share common goals and common political philosophies. A very happy and successful visit.

Thank you very much, Mr. President, for your hospitality.

Note: The President spoke to reporters at 2:37 p.m. at the South Portico of the White House. Earlier, the President and the Prime Minister met in the Oval Office and then attended a working luncheon in the State Dining Room, followed by a meeting in the Blue Room.

Proclamation 5303—National Safe Boating Week, 1985
February 20, 1985

By the President of the United States of America

A Proclamation

Americans increasingly look to the water for recreation and relaxation. This year, approximately one-quarter of us will enjoy boating in one or more of its many and varied forms. Therefore, it is important that all those involved in recreational boating observe proper safety practices, know and obey rules of safe boating, and show courtesy and consideration on the water.

In addition, all boaters should wear personal flotation devices while on the water. According to the United States Coast Guard, seventy-five percent of those who died in boating accidents last year might have been saved had they worn these devices.

The theme of this year's National Safe Boating Week emphasizes the dangers of combining alcohol consumption with operating a boat. The use of alcohol and other intoxicating substances is a major factor in boating accidents and fatalities. Boat operators who drink often cannot react promptly to hazards and thereby endanger not only themselves but also others on the water.

The use of even small amounts of alcohol can significantly impair an operator's judgment and boat-handling skills. This is particularly true as fatigue caused by sun, glare, noise, wind, and boat motion intensifies the effects of alcohol. Through the observance of National Safe Boating Week, 1985, all Americans should be alerted to these dangers.

In recognition of the need for boating safety, the Congress, by joint resolution approved June 4, 1958, as amended (36 U.S.C. 161), authorized and requested the President to proclaim annually the week commencing on the first Sunday in June as National Safe Boating Week.

Now, Therefore, I, Ronald Reagan, President of the United States of America, do hereby proclaim the week beginning June 2, 1985, as National Safe Boating Week. I invite the Governors of the States, Puerto Rico, the Northern Mariana Islands, the Virgin Islands, Guam, and American Samoa, and the Mayor of the District of Columbia to provide for the observance of this week.

In Witness Whereof, I have hereunto set my hand this twentieth day of February, in the year of our Lord nineteen hundred and eighty-five, and of the Independence of the United States of America the two hundred and ninth.

[*Filed with the Office of the Federal Register, 3:36 p.m., February 20, 1985*]

RONALD REAGAN

Message to the Congress Transmitting Proposed Legislation To Approve the Compact of Free Association With the Marshall Islands and Micronesia
February 20, 1985

To the Congress of the United States:

There is attached a draft of a Joint Resolution to approve the "Compact of Free Association," the negotiated instrument setting forth the future political relationship between the United States and two political jurisdictions of the Trust Territory of the Pacific Islands.

The Compact of Free Association is the result of more than fourteen years of continuous and comprehensive negotiations, spanning the administrations of four Presidents. The transmission of the proposed Joint Resolution today, and Congressional enactment of it, marks the last step in the Compact approval process.

The full text of the Compact is part of the draft Joint Resolution, which I request be introduced, referred to the appropriate committees, and enacted. I also request that the Congress note the agreements subsidiary to the Compact. Also attached is a section-by-section analysis to facilitate your consideration of the Compact.

I originally submitted this same draft Joint Resolution to the 98th Congress on March 30, 1984. Before their adjournment, both Houses held extensive hearings on the Joint Resolution. The Administration stands by the policies it outlined during these hearings and hopes that they will serve to expedite consideration and approval of the Compact in this new Congress.

The defense and land use provisions of the Compact extend indefinitely the right of the United States to foreclose access to the area to third countries for military purposes. These provisions are of great importance to our strategic position in the Pacific and enable us to continue preserving regional security and peace.

Since 1947, the islands of the Trust Territory have been administered by the United States under a Trusteeship Agreement with the United Nations Security Council. This Compact of Free Association with the governments of the Marshall Islands and the Federated States of Micronesia would fulfill our commitment under that Agreement to bring about self-government in accordance with the freely expressed wishes of the peoples concerned. Upon termination of the Trusteeship Agreement, another political jurisdiction of the Trust Territory—the Northern Mariana Islands—will become a commonwealth of the United States.

The Compact was signed for the United States by Ambassador Fred M. Zeder, II, on October 1, 1982, with the Federated States of Micronesia, and on June 25, 1983, with the Republic of the Marshall Islands. It is the result of negotiations between the United States and broadly representative groups of delegates from the prospective freely associated states.

In 1983, United Nations-observed plebiscites produced high voter participation, and the Compact was approved by impressive majorities. In addition to approval in the plebiscites, the Compact has been approved by the governments of the Marshall Islands and the Federated States of Micronesia in accordance with their constitutional processes.

Enactment of the draft Joint Resolution approving the Compact of Free Association would be a major step leading to the termination of the Trusteeship Agreement with the United Nations Security Council, which the United States entered into by Joint Resolution on July 18, 1947. Therefore, I urge the Congress to approve the Compact of Free Association.

RONALD REAGAN

The White House,
February 20, 1985.

Toasts of the President and Prime Minister Margaret Thatcher of the United Kingdom at a Dinner at the British Embassy
February 20, 1985

The Prime Minister. Mr. President, Mr. Vice President, ladies and gentlemen, it's a very special occasion, indeed, and a great honor to Britain when the President of the United States and the First Lady, together with such a glittering company, come to dinner at Her Majesty's Ambassador's residence. We welcome you here this evening, sir.

In this year 1985, it adds splendor to an important anniversary in our relations. In 1785 John Adams, the first American Envoy to Britain, was formally received by King George III and thus opened 200 years of diplomatic relations between our two countries.

Of course, there have been a few changes in diplomacy since then. [*Laughter*] And I'm told there is a memorandum surviving in the Smithsonian from President Jefferson to his Secretary of State in which he wrote as follows: "We haven't heard anything from our Ambassador to France for three years." [*Laughter*] "If we don't hear from him this year"—[*laughter*]—"let us write him a letter." [*Laughter*]

Of course, American Ambassadors in London have been much more communicative than American Ambassadors in Paris. But, no doubt, Charles Price, who is such a good Ambassador to London, and Oliver Wright, who I believe is such a good Ambassador here, sometimes wish they still lived in such an easygoing world.

I've discovered another interesting fact. American Ambassadors to London tend to go places. Five of them, including John Adams and his son, became Presidents of the United States. And eight became Secre-

taries of State. Well, Charlie, we'll be watching you. [*Laughter*] But for the avoidance of doubt, Geoffrey Howe[1] and I would like to remind Oliver Wright that there is no such tradition with ours. [*Laughter*]

Perhaps I should also mention that 1985 marks the 200th anniversary of a famous British institution—the Times newspaper. And one of the first reports carried by The Times, shortly after its launching, was of the reception given to John Adams when he presented his credentials, not that John Adams himself found that an exactly comfortable occasion. What worried him most was that he would have to make a complimentary speech about King George III, and that wasn't calculated to endear him to the folks at home at that time. [*Laughter*]

But this evening, Mr. President, I've no such inhibitions about being complimentary about everything about the United States. We in Britain think you are a wonderful President. And from one old hand to another, welcome to a second term. [*Laughter*]

And Dennis will be saying exactly the same to Nancy. And neither of us could have done what we've done without them.

I remember with pride and with gratitude many occasions we've shared during your first term: the Williamsburg summit, with all its pageantry and history; your powerful and moving address to the assembled Lords and Commons in London in the Royal Gallery; your visit to us last year for

---

[1] *Secretary of State for Foreign and Commonwealth Affairs.*

191

the London Economic Summit; and most recently, my expedition to Camp David.

We've always found it easy to discuss great matters together. We see so many things in the same way. We share so many of the same goals and a determination to achieve them, which you summed up so well—and, alas, I cannot imitate this wonderful American English accent—"You ain't seen nothin' yet." [*Laughter*]

Mr. President, over the 200 years that our countries have dealt with each other, it's not always been plain sailing. But one thing has not changed: The joint common sense, which is an essential part of our common heritage, has led the two Governments to resolve their differences and to work constructively together for our common purpose. Our joint interests prevailed, and I know they will continue to prevail.

There's a union of mind and purpose between our peoples, which is remarkable and which makes our relationship truly a special one. I'm often asked if it's special and why. And I say it is special—it just is—and that's that. As Winston once said—Winston Churchill—"The experience of a long life and the promptings of my blood have wrought in me the conviction that there is nothing more important for the future of the world than the fraternal association of our two peoples in righteous work both in war and peace." No one could put it better than that.

Let us look forward with confidence to the next 200 years of Anglo-American friendship, to an enduring and confident alliance, and to peace and freedom for today's and future generations.

May I ask you to rise and drink a toast—the President of the United States of America—the President.

The President.

The President. Prime Minister, Vice President Bush, Secretary of State, Defense Secretary, Saint Oliver—or Sir Oliver. Saint Oliver? No, Sir Oliver—[*laughter*]—and Lady Wright, and ladies and gentlemen. Tonight, as we've just been told—and I have to preface this by saying, based on the career that I once had before this one, you are a very tough act to follow. [*Laughter*] Tonight we celebrate, as we've been told, 200 years of diplomatic relations between Great Britain and the United States.

For two centuries, we've been trading partners. We've stood together through two great world conflicts. Forty years ago last summer, Americans and Englishmen joined together in an invasion launched from Britain, the greatest invasion in all of man's history; together, we fought on the sands of Normandy. And together we reclaimed a continent to liberty.

Prime Minister, the United States and the United Kingdom are bound together by inseparable ties of ancient history and present friendship. Our language, our law—even though you do use our language with an accent—[*laughter*]—our law, our democratic system of government, and our fierce belief in the God-given right of all men to be free—all of these the United States shares with your proud island.

We share a deep affection for one another. But then, there've been a few moments in our history when relations were not so smooth. I remember being tempted to recall one of those at the summit conference at Williamsburg, where the opening meeting was a dinner in what had been the British Colonial Governor's residence. And I thought that I was all set to open the summit because when we were seated around the table—the heads of seven states—I was going to say to Margaret Thatcher that had one of her predecessors been a little more clever she would have been hosting the gathering. [*Laughter*]

And, so, with my well-thought-out line, I opened—that if one of her predecessors had been a little more clever, and she turned to me and said, "I know. I would have been the host." [*Laughter*] So, I'm careful. But, anyway, Margaret, welcome back to America.

In our discussions, I have, as always, been delighted by the vigor, the clarity, and the directness of your views. And I've wanted to tell you that when I ran for office in 1980 I was greatly encouraged by the victory that you won in 1979. And it was very thoughtful of you to set me another good example in 1983. [*Laughter*] We've been inspired by your leadership.

Sir Oliver and Lady Wright, thank you for hosting this splendid event. Nancy and I are honored to be here. We celebrate tonight our past and our future. Great challenges loom ahead, and we must do all that we can to expand human freedom and unleash the great potential for economic growth both in our countries and throughout the world.

In our own countries we've already done much to free our economies from the dead hand of government control. But we can do more. Here in America, we're determined to reduce spending growth and significantly reduce tax rates further by simplifying our entire tax structure. In international commerce, our task is to knock down barriers to trade and foreign investment and to the free movement of capital. And I look forward to working with you on these matters, as we prepare for the 11th Economic Summit of Industrialized Nations in Bonn.

In foreign affairs we and our NATO allies have stayed strong, while demonstrating our openness to genuine arms reductions. And Prime Minister Thatcher, I know you share my satisfaction that the Soviets have agreed to return to the bargaining table. And now we must press on together for success in mutual and verifiable arms reductions and a more secure peace.

We believe that our Strategic Defense Initiative represents the most hopeful possibility of the nuclear age. And we greatly appreciate your support. In many areas of this research, technical progress appears very promising. And we're eager to be joined in this research by our allies and look forward to collaborating with you.

It's hard to be here on this candlelit evening and your stately Embassy without thinking of the great men and women—British and American—who've gone before us and who've worked together as we do today. I think of F.D.R. and Churchill conferring in the rain. Roosevelt deeply admired his friend, Winston. And many of us remember the warmth John Kennedy felt for Harold Macmillan and Macmillan's grief after Kennedy's tragic death. There's been something very special about the friendships between the leaders of our two countries. And may I say to my friend the Prime Minister, I'd like to add two more names to this list of affection—Thatcher and Reagan.

Prime Minister, ladies and gentlemen, mindful of the two centuries of diplomatic relations that our two nations have enjoyed and grateful for our common heritage of liberty and in a spirit of celebration, please join me in a toast to your gracious Sovereign, to Her Majesty the Queen.

Note: Prime Minister Thatcher spoke at approximately 9:33 p.m.

Statement on the Nation's Economy
February 21, 1985

I am delighted by today's report that the gross national product increased at a 4.9-percent rate in the fourth quarter. The great American expansion is rolling forward, carrying us from a banner year in 1984 toward continued success of high growth, more jobs, and low inflation in 1985.

The United States economy grew by 6.9 percent in 1984, exceeding by better than half the consensus of leading blue chip forecasters. This strength, together with inflation, as measured by the price deflator, of only 3.8 percent, gave us our best economic performance since 1951. And growth of real final sales at an 8.5-percent rate in the fourth quarter indicates that this will be an excellent spring for the American economy.

Today's harvest of good news sprang from the seeds of new policies for greater economic freedom—lower spending growth by government and greater incentives for individuals—that we planted in our first term. Now is the time to ensure that our future harvests will be even more bountiful. I ask the Congress to move quickly to pass a package of urgently needed spending restraints and to begin working with us to draft and pass legislation for tax simplification this year.

Nomination of Beryl W. Sprinkel To Be a Member of the Council of Economic Advisers, and Designation as Chairman
February 21, 1985

The President today announced his intention to nominate Dr. Beryl W. Sprinkel to be a member of the Council of Economic Advisers. Upon his appointment the President intends to designate him Chairman of the Council. He will be economic adviser to the President. Dr. Sprinkel will succeed Dr. Martin Feldstein, who returned to his tenured position at Harvard University.

Since March 1981 Dr. Sprinkel has been serving as Under Secretary of the Treasury for Monetary Affairs. Previously he was executive vice president and economist at Harris Trust and Savings Bank in Chicago, IL, where he worked for 28 years. He was director of Harris Economics, an economic and financial forecasting service published by the bank; a member of Time magazine's board of economists; chairman of the economic advisory committee of the American Bankers Association; and member of the board of directors of the U.S. Chamber of Commerce. He also served as a consultant to various government agencies and congressional committees.

Before joining Harris Trust and Savings, he taught economics and finance at the University of Chicago (1949–1952) and at the University of Missouri School of Business and Public Administration (1948–1949). He is the author of two books, and coauthor of a third, on the effects of monetary policy on financial markets and the economy and has written numerous articles.

Dr. Sprinkel received his B.S. degree in public administration from the University of Missouri in 1947, M.B.A. degree from the University of Chicago in 1948, and Ph.D. in economics and finance from the University of Chicago in 1952. He was a founding member of the Shadow Open Market Committee. He holds a chartered financial analyst degree from the Institute of Chartered Financial Analysts, an honorary doctor of humane letters degree from DePaul University, and an honorary doctor of laws degree from St. Michael's College.

He was born November 20, 1923, on a farm near Richmond, MO. He is married to the former Barbara Angus. They have four children and reside in McLean, VA.

Proclamation 5304—Save Your Vision Week, 1985
February 21, 1985

By the President of the United States of America

A Proclamation

Good vision is a priceless treasure. Our ability to see the print in a book, the beauty of a sunset, and the faces of our loved ones is a gift that should be cherished and protected. Yet each year many Americans lose vision that could have been saved. To halt this tragic waste, we must make more people aware of the steps that all of us can take to safeguard our vision.

Of all sight-saving precautions, the most important is to have regular eye examinations by an eye care professional. Such check-ups are more valuable today than ever before. Thanks to vision research, effective treatment is now available to many people whose sight is threatened by eye disorders. But the greatest medical benefits generally go to those who get the earliest warning of serious eye disease. For them, there may be an opportunity to stop the disease before it has caused significant visual loss.

Middle age is a particularly good time for a person to take advantage of the protection that regular eye examinations can offer. This is because glaucoma, diabetic retinal disease, and several other disorders that are major causes of blindness tend to strike during the middle years of life.

Older Americans, too, should have regular eye check-ups. Cataract, macular disease, and a number of other age-related conditions that can rob elderly people of their vision are detectable by means of a routine eye examination. For many older Americans, learning of the existence of a visual problem is the first step toward obtaining the medical treatment or special visual aids that will allow them to go on leading active, independent lives.

Children also have much to gain from eye examinations. Even very young babies can benefit from discovery of an unsuspected eye problem that should be corrected while the child is still small. Some childhood eye problems, if left untreated, can cause a child to be needlessly handicapped at school and play or even lead to permanent visual loss.

An important concern for people of all ages in protecting the eye from injury. By wearing safety glasses, goggles, or face shields in all hazardous work situations and recreational activities, we can dramatically reduce the toll of visual loss caused by injuries.

There is yet another way for citizens to help improve the eye health of our Nation. Each of us can sign an organ donation card and carry it all times to insure that after death our eyes are used for vision research and for people who must have a cornea transplant in order to see again.

To encourage people to consider how important their eyesight is and what they can do to preserve it, the Congress, by joint resolution approved December 20, 1963 (77 Stat. 629, 36 U.S.C. 169a), has requested the President to proclaim the first week in March of each year as "Save Your Vision Week."

Now, Therefore, I, Ronald Reagan, President of the United States of America, do hereby designate the week beginning March 3, 1985, as Save Your Vision Week. I urge all Americans to participate in this observance by making eye care and eye safety an important part of their lives. Also, I invite eye care professionals, the communications media, and all public and private organizations committed to the goal of sight conservation to join in activities that will make Americans more aware of the steps they can take to protect their vision.

In Witness Whereof, I have hereunto set my hand this twenty-first day of February, in the year of our Lord nineteen hundred and eighty-five, and of the Independence of the United States of America the two hundred and ninth.

RONALD REAGAN

[*Filed with the Office of the Federal Register, 11:41 a.m., February 21, 1985*]

Appointment of 11 Members of the President's Advisory Committee on Mediation and Conciliation
February 21, 1985

The President today announced his intention to appoint the following individuals to be members of the President's Advisory Committee on Mediation and Conciliation. These are all new positions.

Norman L. Benjamin is vice president, human

resources, for Lockheed Corp. in Burbank CA. He is married, has four children, and resides in Calabasas, CA. He was born April 27, 1928, in Salt Lake City, UT.

Owen Bieber is president of the International Union of United Auto Workers in Detroit, MI. He is married, has five children, and resides in

Southfield, MI. He was born December 28, 1929, in North Dorr, MI.

Merlin P. Breaux is vice president, industrial relations, for Gulf Oil Co. in Houston, TX. He is married, has five children, and resides in Sour Lake, TX. He was born January 15, 1932, in Edgerly, LA.

Fred A. Hardin is chairman of the Railway Labor Executives Association and international president of the United Transportation Union in Cleveland, OH. He is married, has three children, and resides in Hilton Head Island, SC. He was born February 21, 1918, in Greenville, SC.

John T. Joyce is president of the International Union of Bricklayers and Allied Craftsmen in Washington, DC. He is married and resides in Washington, DC. He was born December 6, 1935, in Chicago, IL.

Peter J. Pestillo is vice president, labor relations, for Ford Motor Co. in Dearborn, MI. He is married, has three children, and resides in Grosse Pointe Farms, MI. He was born March 22, 1938, in Bristol, CT.

J.A. Sage is vice president of Southern Pacific Transportation Co. in San Francisco, CA. He is married, has three children, and resides in Tiburon, CA. He was born January 9, 1935, in North Bay, Ontario.

John J. Sweeney is president of the Service Employees International Union in Washington, DC. He is married, has two children, and resides in Bethesda, MD. He was born May 5, 1934, in New York, NY.

David L. Trezise is vice president for industrial relations of Westinghouse Electric Corp. in Pittsburgh, PA. He is married, has five children, and resides in Pittsburgh, PA. He was born October 17, 1926, in Wakefield, MI.

Raymond Earl Williams is corporate vice president, labor relations, at American Telephone & Telegraph Co. in New York, NY. He is married, has four children, and resides in Madison, NJ. He was born June 21, 1927, in Utica, NY.

William H. Wynn is international president of the United Food Workers & Commercial Workers International Union in Washington, DC. He is married, has two children, and resides in Alexandria, VA. He was born July 17, 1931, in South Bend, IN.

Proclamation 5305—Duty Reductions on High Technology Products
February 21, 1985

By the President of the United States of America

A Proclamation

1. Pursuant to section 308 of the Trade and Tariff Act of 1984 (Pub. L. 98–573; 98 Stat. 2948, 3013) and section 128 of the Trade Act of 1974 (19 U.S.C. 2138), I have, through my duly empowered representative, entered into an agreement with Japan to achieve the negotiating objectives under section 104A(c) of the Trade Act of 1974 (19 U.S.C. 2114A). In order to obtain those objectives, in particular the maximum openness with respect to international trade and investment in high technology products, I have determined that the reduction to zero of existing column 1 duties provided for in the items of the Tariff Schedules of the United States (TSUS) (19 U.S.C. 1202) listed in section 128 is appropriate.

2. Accordingly, I have determined that the agreement should be implemented and duty-free treatment should be afforded to certain articles enumerated in section 128, effective on or after March 1, 1985. Furthermore, I authorize the United States Trade Representative (USTR), or his designee, on behalf of the United States of America, to modify the TSUS in order to make duty-free treatment effective for the remaining articles set forth in section 128.

3. Pursuant to section 604 of the Trade Act of 1974 (19 U.S.C. 2483), I have determined that technical corrections are necessary in order to implement modifications to the TSUS made by Proclamation 5291 of December 28, 1984 (50 F.R. 223), modifying duties on certain articles used in civil aircraft and on globes. Certain new items in the TSUS created in the Annex to that Proclamation must be redesignated to eliminate numbering conflicts resulting from the redesignation of other provisions by the Trade and Tariff Act of 1984.

Now, Therefore, I, Ronald Reagan, President of the United States of America, acting under the authority vested in me by the Constitution and the statutes of the United States, including but not limited to sections 128 and 604 of the Trade Act of 1974 and section 308 of the Trade and Tariff Act of 1984, do proclaim that:

(1) Items 687.72, 687.74, 687.77, 687.81, and 687.85 in part 5 of schedule 6 of the TSUS are modified by striking out, from the column entitled "Rates of Duty 1" for each item, the duty rate "4.2% ad val." and inserting in such column for each item the duty rate "Free". These modifications shall be effective with respect to articles entered, or withdrawn from warehouse for consumption, on or after March 1, 1985.

(2) Item 687.70 in part 5 of schedule 6 of the TSUS is modified by striking out, from the column entitled "Rates of Duty 1" for such item, the duty rate "4.2% ad val." and inserting in such column for such item the duty rate "Free". This modification shall be effective with respect to articles entered, or withdrawn from warehouse for consumption, on or after a date determined by the USTR and published in the *Federal Register* which is after the effective date of legislation making technical corrections in section

128 of the Trade and Tariff Act of 1984.

(3) The USTR is hereby authorized to make any other modifications of the TSUS in order to make duty-free treatment effective for the remaining articles covered by section 128.

(4) The Annex to Proclamation 5291 is modified—

(a) by striking out, in the modification numbered 16, the item numbers "708.09" and "708.10" and inserting in lieu thereof "708.10" and "708.12", respectively; and

(b) by striking out, in the modification numbered 17, the item numbers "708.29" and "708.30" and inserting in lieu thereof "708.30" and "708.32", respectively.

These modifications are effective on or after December 28, 1984.

In Witness Whereof, I have hereunto set my hand this 21st day of February, in the year of our Lord nineteen hundred and eighty-five, and of the Independence of the United States of America the two hundred and ninth.

RONALD REAGAN

[*Filed with the Office of the Federal Register, 10:50 a.m., February 22, 1985*]

The President's News Conference
February 21, 1985

The Nation's Economy

The President. Good evening. I have a brief statement here.

The final economic figures are in for 1984 and the news is even better than anticipated. The U.S. economy grew at a rate of almost 5 percent in the fourth quarter, and final sales increased at a rate of 8½ percent. Economic growth for calendar year 1984 measured just a shade under 7 percent. It was the strongest performance in a single year by the American economy since 1951. Our recovery is now well into its 27th month. It's the strongest expansion since the Korean war, and ours is a peacetime expansion, rooted not in a military buildup for overseas conflict but in a broadening

prosperity when America is at peace.

We intend to prolong and to protect this expansion, and we'll work with Congress for a sweeping program of tax simplification and reform, and we're convinced this historic legislation can and should be passed this year. America has rediscovered that the key to greater economic growth, opportunity, and prosperity for all is to unharness the energies of free enterprise.

The American miracle of which the world now speaks is a triumph of free people and their private institutions, not government. It was individual workers, business people, entrepreneurs, not government, who created virtually every one of our 7 million new jobs over the past 2 years.

But protecting recovery will require political courage. A Federal Government that collects nearly 20 percent of the gross national product in taxes must cease spending nearly 25 percent of the gross national product in Federal programs. Our administration proposes to freeze overall Federal program spending at last year's level, to cut $51 billion out of programs in need of restraint, to reduce spending by half-a-trillion dollars over the next 5 years; and these proposals are rooted both in economic necessity and common sense.

To cite one example: revenue sharing. It doesn't make sense for a Federal Government running a deficit to be borrowing money to be spent by State and local governments that are now running surpluses, thanks to our economic recovery. As for those who tell us that growth and expansion are not enough, that spending restraint is politically impossible, that higher taxes are necessary, our answer is simple: That issue was debated and decided on November 6th. We intend to proceed with the mandate that we've been given by the people.

All right, Mike [Michael Putzel, Associated Press]?

Farm Credit Programs

Q. Mr. President, budget director David Stockman says the taxpayers of this country shouldn't be responsible for the bad debts of farmers. Do you agree with Mr. Stockman? And if you do, why use Federal funds to extend emergency credits to family farmers?

The President. I think that Mr. Stockman's made it plain that—in fact, has apologized for some of his remarks, because after 3 hours of what was an appearance before a committee in which, I think, there was a certain amount of harassment and heckling going on, he himself has said that he got a little upset.

No, I think the farm problem is the result of things that have been done in the past. It's the result of the inflationary economy that we had for some time. There are a number of farmers now who—their main problem is they borrowed on the basis of inflated land values, and then when we brought inflation down, that left them with loans, and the collateral did not have the same value.

And we have—making a proposal, and we'll be talking tomorrow with the Congressmen about a proposal for this short-term problem that will include loans and loan guarantees—some $650 million in that—and then, subsequently, we will be taking up proposals for, hopefully, getting the farm economy back into the free marketplace and government out of the agricultural business.

Q. May I follow up, Mr. President? Do you see a contradiction between giving farmers emergency aid now, while proposing to phase out price supports and crop restrictions that they've lived with for half a century?

The President. And that's the problem. We won't pull the rug out from under anyone instantly who has geared themselves to these government programs, but the Government programs didn't succeed. Many of the problems they face today are the result of government's involvement. And I think you'll find that a great majority of farmers believe that the answer to their problems *is* out in the free market. And then if government is to help, then we should help by opening up world markets for them, by holding trade negotiations, because much of the farming elsewhere in the world is government subsidized. And we intend to do all that we can. In fact, that was one of the things I talked to the Prime Minister about, and we both agreed that we should be discussing, in the coming months, with our trading partners and friends, the reopening of trade negotiations as much as we can to have free trade, and both ways, in the world at large.

U.S.-Soviet Arms Agreements

Q. Mr. President, Jack Anderson said in his column today that in 1981 you passed the word to Moscow that even if the Senate ratified SALT II, you would not sign it; that in 1982, Moscow told you that they are no longer bound by the SALT II treaty, and they began to build up their arsenal over the limit. Is that true? And I'd like to follow up.

The President. Helen, [Helen Thomas, United Press International], I read that myself this morning, and I went into the office and I said, "Where is all this coming from?" I do not remember any statement from the Soviet Union of that kind.

Both countries had been involved with obeying the restraints or staying within the restraints mainly because of our efforts toward what we're now approaching, arms reduction talks; that we felt that if we were going to engage in those talks, it would be even better if we did abide by an agreement—one that had been signed, but never been ratified by our government.

And I don't recall that at all. And I have to say that we know that the Soviet Union, we're sure, has violated some of the restraints now. And we know that we're coming to a point at which we have, up until now, been biding by it. And as we replace older weapons with new, we have destroyed the older ones.

The Soviet Union—one of the violations of theirs has been that they were taking nuclear missile submarines out of action, but they were cutting them down and rebuilding them as cruise missiles carrying submarines——

Q. Well, is your mood now to stay with the treaties that we have negotiated, like, even, ABM, while the new negotiations go on?

The President. Well, we're going to stay with the treaties that are in effect, that have been ratified and are in power. We'll have a——

Q. And SALT II?

The President. We'll have a decision several months from now to make with regard to whether we join them in violating the restraints.

Andrea [Andrea Mitchell, NBC News]?

Tax Reform

Q. Mr. President, you have said that you would need to be convinced of shifting the tax burden from individuals to corporations, as the Treasury tax plan suggests doing. But in the State of the Union speech, you committed yourself to lowering individual tax rates to 35 percent or lower. Now, where would you make up that revenue if not to get it from corporations?

The President. Well, Andrea, where we're going with reducing the rates and where we're going to achieve what we call tax neutrality, or revenue neutrality, will be in the elimination of a number of exemptions that have existed and that sometimes have—well, they've been unfair in the sense that some are entitled to them and others are not. When I answered that question the other day, I misunderstood. I thought they were telling me that the plan was actually going to get a great higher percentage from business. And I mentioned the fact that I did not want to do something that would interfere with our recovery or keep business from being able to expand. And then I found out that, no, there'd been a misunderstanding about that question.

What we're talking about, as to more revenue from business, is from those elements of business that have not been paying taxes. Now, it hasn't been cheating. It's been legal in that that's just the way some of the exemptions had worked out. And we want to change that so there will be a reduction in rates for everyone. And where the difference will be made up is some who are not now paying taxes at all, or paying very low taxes, will be paying their fair share.

Q. But are you saying, sir, that there would be no increase in the corporate share for those businesses that are now paying taxes, that only those corporations that are not paying their fair share would be affected? And, again, how would you make up the difference, since just the things that you committed yourself to in the State of the Union would amount to $132 billion under the Treasury plan by 1990, when they are phased in?

The President. Well, the Treasury plan as it is now, and while we're still going to have to review that plan, and there are some options in there that we may find aren't suitable to put into operation, but the plan works out to revenue neutral and with a reduction in rates and the, you know, the business rate and the corporation rate is going to come down from 46 percent to 33 percent under that plan.

Ralph [Ralph Harris, Reuters]?

Middle East

Q. Mr. President, this week in Vienna, American and Soviet officials held 2 days of talks on the Middle East, apparently their most intensive on this issue for 7 years. Can you tell us anything about them? And, also, Mr. President, do these talks fit into any other recent development, such as King Hussein's recent move and your talks with King Fahd last week?

The President. No, Ralph. These talks had nothing to do with negotiations or anything of that kind. We simply felt that it was time to exchange views with each other and make sure that there couldn't be any miscalculations that could lead to some kind of confrontation or problem.

We brought them up to date on our own views and what we thought, and they were talking on their own, and that's all.

Q. May I have a followup, Mr. President? Is the Soviet Government still pushing for a direct negotiating role in Middle East diplomacy?

The President. I haven't had a full report enough to say whether they mentioned some specific things. They have tended to support the idea of a great international meeting. We don't favor that. We don't believe that there should be that many hands in the pot, just as we're not envisioning any participation in negotiations. We have said we'll stand by and we'll help in any way we can, but these negotiations must be between the Arabs and the Palestinians and the Israelis.

Let me come over here for a minute—Sam [Sam Donaldson, ABC News]?

Nicaragua

Q. Mr. President, on Capitol Hill—on Capitol Hill the other day, Secretary Shultz suggested that a goal of your policy now is to remove the Sandinista government in Nicaragua. Is that your goal?

The President. Well, remove in the sense of its present structure, in which it is a Communist totalitarian state, and it is not a government chosen by the people. So, you wonder sometimes about those who make such claims as to its legitimacy. We believe, just as I said Saturday morning, that we have an obligation to be of help where we can to freedom fighters and lovers of freedom and democracy, from Afghanistan to Nicaragua and wherever there are people of that kind who are striving for that freedom.

And we're going to try to persuade the Congress that we can legitimately go forward and, hopefully, go forward on a multiyear basis with the Scoop Jackson plan for trying to bring development and help to all of Central America.

Q. Well, sir, when you say remove it in the sense of its present structure, aren't you then saying that you advocate the overthrow of the present government of Nicaragua?

The President. Well, what I'm saying is that this present government was one element of the revolution against Somoza. The freedom fighters are other elements of that revolution. And once victory was attained, the Sandinistas did what Castro had done, prior to their time, in Cuba. They ousted and managed to rid themselves of the other elements of the revolution and violated their own promise to the Organization of American States—as a result of which they had received support from the Organization—that their revolutionary goal was for democracy, free press, free speech, free labor unions, and elections, and so forth, and they have violated that.

And the people that are fighting them, the freedom fighters opposing them, are Nicaraguan people who want the goals of the revolution restored. And we're going to try to help.

Q. Is the answer yes, sir? Is the answer yes, then?

The President. To what?

Q. To the question, aren't you advocating the overthrow of the present government? If——

The President. Not if the present——

Q. ——you substitute another form of what you say was the revolution?

The President. Not if the present government would turn around and say, all right, if they'd say: "Uncle. All right, come on back into the revolutionary government, and let's straighten this out and institute the goals."

President's Religious Views

Q. Mr. President, theologians recently criticized you for saying, in defending your military budget, that the Scriptures are on our side. I wonder, do you think it's appropriate to use the Bible in defending a political argument?

The President. Well, I was actually speaking to some clergymen, and I checked that with a few theologians—if it was appropriate and—well, what I meant about appropriate, was I interpreting it correctly? Was it a warning that you should be prepared and otherwise ask for peace because you were outnumbered and out—well, now, we would say outgunned—on the other side. And they seemed to think that it was perfectly fitting, yes. It was a caution to those people in our own country who would, if given the opportunity, unilaterally disarm us.

Q. To follow up, you don't have any problem with using the Bible in a political context?

The President. Well, I don't think I've ever used the Bible to further political ends or not, but I've found that the Bible contains an answer to just about everything and every problem that confronts us, and I wonder sometimes why we don't recognize that one book could solve a lot of problems for us.

Yes?

Farm Credit Programs

Q. Mr. President, I'd like to come back to the problem of the farmers. You met with some State legislators today. Afterwards they said you're not really doing enough for the farmers; in fact, you're cutting back too much too soon. You mentioned $650 million in aid. Up on Capitol Hill they're trying to provide another billion. Where does the compromise lie, in your mind?

The President. Well, I think that what we're doing can go a long way toward meeting this problem. I think we've been encouraging some of the banks, and if you've noticed lately some of the banks, themselves, out in the farming area have voluntarily reduced the interest rates on some of those outstanding loans because they want to contribute and want to help.

We have spent over $50 billion on agriculture in the last 3 years. We have in the budget for this year some $15 billion, and it'll be a pretty sizable amount—close to that next year. And that is in the long-range

thing of the type of permanent programs that we're trying to phase out over a period of time.

But I think that we are proposing measures and guarantees of loans and so forth that will meet this present crisis. And I think, because I didn't explain that this morning in my remarks—they weren't on that subject—I think maybe they're looking at the news and they don't exactly know what we have in mind and what we're going to do.

Q. Could I follow, sir? You own a ranch. Perhaps it's a sort of a gentleman rancher situation—I understand you don't raise cattle anymore. But you do get a tax break for one reason or another. How would you explain to the farmer in Iowa or Nebraska who can't find a break right now that kind of difference which seems to exist in the system?

The President. The only tax break that applies to my ranch was in effect a long time before I bought the ranch. It is a law in California, and it is a law brought about in environmental interests, and that is that formerly property tax—and that's a local tax—property tax on agricultural land or just open land was based on the highest potential use of that land. And it was literally driving some farmers into sale of land, giving up farming, because they could no longer afford to use as farm land, or maintain as open space, land that was being taxed as if it were a subdivision.

And this was in place, as I say, when we bought that ranch. It is still in place. California has found that program very successful. It taxes it on that use as long as you sign a contract that you are not going to subdivide, that you are going to maintain that open land. I get no income tax deductions whatsoever with regard to the ranch because the Treasury Department decided that, since I couldn't be there to run cattle or anything, that it was a hobby ranch, and I couldn't argue with them on that.

Bill [Bill Plante, CBS News]?

Nicaragua

Q. Mr. President, I wonder if we might return to Nicaragua. In answer to Sam's question, when he pressed you, you said that you—or you seemed to be saying that you wouldn't advocate the overthrow of the government, not if the present government would turn around and say, "Uncle." Well, aren't you really saying that you want the present government out, and secondly, sir, should the United States be trying to influence a government of another nation in this hemisphere?

The President. I think that what we're doing and what we have proposed doing is within the U.N. Charter and within the OAS Charter and the right of people to do what the freedom fighters are doing. You can say it's like saying, is the glass half full or half empty? You can say we're trying to oust the Sandinistas by what we're saying.

We're saying we're trying to give those who fought a revolution to escape a dictatorship, to have democracy, and then had it taken away from them by some of their fellow revolutionaries—we're saying we want them to have a chance to have that democracy that they fought for. And I don't think the Sandinistas have a decent leg to stand on.

What they have done is totalitarian. It is brutal, cruel. And they have no argument against what the rest of the people in Nicaragua want.

Q. Well, sir, what about the specific prohibitions by the United States Congress against the kind of conduct which would overthrow their government or provide money to do so?

The President. The what?

Q. I'm referring to the Boland amendment, sir—the specific prohibitions of the Congress.

The President. I think that some of the proposals that have been made in Congress have lacked a complete understanding of what is at stake there and what we're trying to do.

Trade with Japan

Q. Mr. President, you will soon be making a decision on how to handle the March 31st expiration of Japanese auto import quotas. If Japanese auto sales do increase in this country, will you demand that the Japanese allow more American-made goods to be sold in their country?

The President. Let me just say that—com-menting on anything of that kind—we have been in communication with the Japanese, we have discussions going forward now on open markets both ways, in improving the situation between our two countries.

A deal of progress has been made. We've got a long way to go yet. But everything that we're going to decide is going to be in that context of the two of us as trading partners having fair trade and free trade between us.

Q. Let me just follow up. With no restraints, your special trade representatives predicted a sales increase of 750,000 vehicles in this country. Will the benefits of that for consumers outweigh the adverse or the presumed adverse effects on the U.S. auto industry?

The President. Well, the agreement that is being discussed is a voluntary agreement that the Japanese themselves instituted. And we've had a Cabinet Council that has—I know some of you've gotten information before I did on this—that is going to be coming to me with a recommendation. They have not done so as yet. But I will hear all their arguments, and I will consider them in the context of the negotiations and the communication—or discussion that is going on between us and the Japanese.

Yes.

David Stockman

Q. Mr. President, back, if I may, to David Stockman for a moment, even his mother thought that his comments on farmers were a bit heartless. He managed to alienate in almost the next breath almost every veterans group in the country. Admittedly, his is kind of a thankless job. But some have suggested that you could find someone who could accomplish that job with a little less rancor. What do you think, sir?

The President. Well, as I told you, I think he's expressed some regret. And at the same time, I know the circumstances at the time that he made some of those statements. And I know also that under the guise of a committee hearing—some of the harassment that he'd been subjected to. And I could understand a fellow blowing his cool.

I think he feels, as we all do, and I certainly feel myself, yes, the farmers have a very real problem, and a lot of it has to do with policies that led to the runaway double-digit inflation that we had, in which their land became a haven for those who were seeking hedges against inflation. All of these, plus the government programs, have left them with a very real problem. And we're going to do our utmost to help them find a solution to it.

Q. But, if I may, sir, you want Mr. Stockman to stay on the job?

The President. Did I say—Yes! [*Laughter*]

Devaluation of the Dollar

Q. Mr. President, a number of the questions have been on our economic problems abroad. The farmers' problem, part of it is, sir, that they're priced out of the market in the international trade because of the overvalued dollar. I think that's part of our problem in the auto sales abroad, and in this country—we're at a disadvantage because our dollar is so valuable compared to other currencies. I wonder, sir, if you have discussed this with Mr. Baker and some of your other economic advisers, and if you have studied the possibility of taking any action by this country to try to reduce the value of the dollar against other currencies, both in Europe and in Asia?

The President. Jim, I think that the problem—I can remember when our dollar was devalued, and there weren't very many people happy about that. I think the problem of the dollar today is that our trading partners in the world have not caught up with us in economic recovery.

I think they have a ways to go in changing some rigidities in their customs and their methods of doing business and in industry. And what we really need is their recovery to bring their money up in value comparable to ours.

There are two sides to this problem, as we find with the trade deficit, for example, because of our inability, with the price of our dollar, to sell some of our goods abroad—they are too high priced. But at the same time, you turn to the other hand and see the people in this country that are benefitting by the purchase of products which are cheap by our standards—cheap in price, not quality—in our imports, and

how that has managed to hold down inflation.

I think if you start toying around with trying to reduce the value of the dollar without curing this other side of the issue, we put ourselves back into the inflation spiral, and that we don't want.

Yes, ma'am?

NATO Alliance

Q. Mr. President, do you see any weakening signs in the region of the southeastern flank of NATO in the light of the last Greek attitude? And according to Washington Post there was a story saying that the United States bases will be moved out of Athens. Do you intend to do so?

The President. We have no plans about any moves of any kind. But all I can say about the other, and I don't think I should go farther than this, is to say that, yes, we're very concerned about some of the bilateral problems between countries there at our southern flank of NATO and the effect that they can have on the whole security of the alliance.

Gary [Gary Schuster, Detroit News]?

Strategic Defense Initiative

Q. Mr. President, if you and Mrs. Thatcher are correct that the Soviets plan to hold hostage any progress on intermediate-range and strategic weapons in the talks in Geneva in return for concessions on your part on your space defense program, how far are you willing to go in getting concessions to get an arms agreement?

The President. We believe if the Soviets are sincere in the statements they've made about actually wanting a reduction and even the elimination of nuclear weapons, they'll stay at the table and negotiate with us. All that we have proposed and all that we're doing is engaging in research, which is legal within the ABM treaty—we're not violating that treaty.

And I have said repeatedly, and Prime Minister Thatcher is aware of this, that if our research does produce the possibility of such a weapon, a defensive weapon that could alter the balance, then I would be willing to come forth before any deployment and negotiate and discuss the deployment and the use of that weapon in such a way that it would be used to rid the world of the nuclear threat, not to give us any particular advantage over anyone else.

We just think that the ABM treaty itself—this is one part that has been violated—the ABM treaty in being passed, being a defensive weapon treaty, expressed the belief that this should then be accompanied by realistic reductions of nuclear weapons. And all there has been since the treaty was passed was a tremendous increase in those weapons.

Tax Reform

Q. Mr. President, back to the tax reform for a minute. The Republican chairman of the Senate Finance Committee has floated a proposal to impose a consumption tax, and he says, "preferably on energy." Does this fall within the bounds of forbidden territory in your pledge for no new taxes?

The President. Well, I would have great difficulty accepting such a proposal. I imagine that he's talking about a tax in the nature of a value-added tax. First of all, this appears to be increasing taxes, which I've said we wouldn't do. But a value-added tax actually gives a government a chance to blindfold the people and grow in stature and size. First of all, you are kind of interfering with one of the principal sources of local government levels and State governments in their use of the sales tax, since the

Federal Government had so—you might say, confiscated the area of the income tax. But the other thing with that tax is, it's hidden in the price of a product. And that tax can quietly be increased, and all the people know is that the price went up, and they don't know whether the price went up because somebody got a raise, or whether the company wanted to increase profits, or whether it was government.

And I just am not enthused about it. I think I've said before, taxes should hurt in the sense that people should be able to see them and know what they're paying.

Q. If I may follow up, sir. Would you put an import tax on oil or on oil-refined products in that same category?

The President. I'm just not considering a tax of that kind.

Q. Thank you, Mr. President.

The President. Oh, all right. Good night.

Q. Will you be back next month? Come back next month, sir?

Q. Are you considering steps against Mexico for not cooperating with us?

The President. We're cooperating with them.

Q. Will you be back next month?

Q. We'll be here, same time, same place.

Note: The President's 28th news conference began at 8 p.m. in the East Room at the White House. It was broadcast live on nationwide radio and television.

Remarks on the March of Dimes Campaign
February 22, 1985

The President. Ladies and gentlemen, this little gathering here is because this is Kristen Ellis, the March of Dimes Poster Girl, who was here on December 6th with her mother and father, who I think are probably around—there they are. Well, they brought us the gift of Lucky [1] at the same time.

Well, shortly after that meeting "Dear Abby" wrote a column in which she sug-

gested that just as in 1938, Franklin Delano Roosevelt had asked people to send him dimes for the March of Dimes that he would turn over to that program—now that a dollar is worth only what a dime was then, "Dear Abby" wrote a column and suggested that on my birthday people might do the same thing with a dollar instead of a dime.

And the evidence is in front of you. They've been coming in at the rate of about 2,000 a day, and there are now more than

---

[1] *A black sheepdog.*

$41,000 in the bags for the March of Dimes that came here as a result of her column.

And we're deeply grateful to her. And it's a great pleasure again to see Kristen, who has had a little accident. She broke a leg. But the doctor—whoops. [*Laughter*]

Mrs. Reagan. She's saying hello.

The President. He's saying hello—she's saying hello.

But the doctor tells me she'll soon be out of that cast and everything will be all right.

I had a broken leg, myself. I know what it's like. We have that in common now. All right.

Well, thank you all. And thank you, Kristen, for coming. And, Abby, thank you.

Note: The President spoke at 2:33 p.m. in the Rose Garden at the White House. In his remarks, the President referred to syndicated columnist Abigail Van Buren.

Statement on Proposed Superfund Reauthorization Legislation
February 22, 1985

Today I am sending to the Congress legislation which will expand and strengthen the Comprehensive Environmental Response, Compensation, and Liability Act of 1980, better known as Superfund, which is currently scheduled to expire on September 30, 1985.

The Superfund was enacted in 1980 to provide for the cleanup of abandoned hazardous waste sites, which pose a threat to the public health and the environment. EPA currently has an inventory of 18,000 potential sites that require investigation. Additionally, the National Priorities List, which includes those sites requiring long-term cleanup, has already been expanded from the statutorily mandated minimum of 400 sites to 756 sites. Ultimately, EPA estimates that the number of sites requiring long-term cleanup could total between 1,500 and 2,000. These sites represent the legacy of decades of neglect. We, as a society, must address these serious health threats.

This legislation will more than triple the size of the existing Superfund program, from $1.6 billion to $5.3 billion, which will allow us to substantially increase the size and pace of the Superfund program. In order to fund this threefold increase, we will ask the Congress to extend for another 5 years the existing tax imposed on the manufacture of certain chemicals and to enact a fee, which will go into a dedicated trust fund, on the disposal and treatment of hazardous waste. These taxes and fees will raise approximately $1 billion per year over the next 5 years. I strongly believe that the funds used to pay for the program should be generated entirely through these dedicated sources, not the general Treasury. In addition to the expansion of the Superfund, we have requested increased enforcement authority to ensure that responsible parties either conduct or pay for the cleanup of hazardous waste sites that endanger public health or the environment. We will also seek to guarantee a larger role for affected citizens and the States, and expand authority to respond to emergencies.

In my 1984 and 1985 State of the Union Addresses and in the campaign, I promised that this administration would seek reauthorization of Superfund. This bill fulfills our commitment to the American people to address the legacy of abandoned hazardous waste sites in an expeditious manner. It will allow us to move aggressively forward to eliminate the health and environmental risks associated with past waste disposal practices.

To help ensure prompt enactment of responsible legislation, I have instructed Lee Thomas, Administrator of the Environmental Protection Agency, to make reauthorization of this important legislation his highest priority.

Letter to the Speaker of the House and the President of the Senate Transmitting Proposed Superfund Reauthorization Legislation
February 22, 1985

Dear Mr. Speaker: (Dear Mr. President:)

I am pleased to send you proposed legislation of critical importance to every American, the Administration's proposal for improving the Comprehensive Environmental Response, Compensation, and Liability Act of 1980 (better known as Superfund) and for extending the taxing authorities which support it, now due to expire on September 30, 1985.

My Administration has been moving forcefully to implement the Superfund program, expanding the national priorities list from the statutorily mandated minimum of 400 sites to 756 sites, greatly augmenting the money available for the program, and, most importantly, beginning the cleanup process at an ever increasing number of sites. The danger to public health and the environment presented by releases and threatened releases of hazardous substances from inactive waste sites persists, however, and we must not lose the momentum we have achieved.

The Administration's proposed legislation will more than triple the size of the existing program, from $1.6 billion to $5.3 billion. In order to fund this three-fold increase, we are requesting the Congress to extend for another five years the existing tax imposed on the manufacture of certain chemicals and to enact a fee, which will go into the dedicated trust fund, on the disposal and treatment of hazardous waste. These taxes and fees will raise approximately $1 billion per year over the next five years, which should provide adequate, stable, and equitable financing for the program. I strongly believe that funds used to pay for the program should be generated entirely through these dedicated sources, not the general treasury.

In addition to the expansion of the Superfund, we are requesting other authorities which will allow us to build on our momentum and will strengthen our ability to respond to the health and environmental threats emanating from abandoned hazardous waste sites. These authorities will allow us to:

• continue a comprehensive but focused Federal response program;

• strengthen our existing enforcement tools to ensure that responsible parties undertake or pay the costs of cleanup;

• enhance the Federal-State partnership needed for effective response action; and

• actively involve citizens in the cleanup decisions that will affect them.

To help ensure prompt enactment of responsible legislation, I have instructed Lee Thomas, Administrator of the Environmental Protection Agency, to make reauthorization of this important legislation his highest priority.

Sincerely,

RONALD REAGAN

Note: Identical letters were sent to Thomas P. O'Neill, Speaker of the House of Representatives, and George Bush, President of the Senate. A copy of the proposed legislation and a section-by-section analysis was made available by the Office of the Press Secretary.

Radio Address to the Nation on Farm Credit Programs
February 23, 1985

My fellow Americans:

I'd like to expand today on what I said in my Thursday night news conference about our farmers' financial plight and what must be done to hasten the return of their prosperity.

It's important to note that about two-thirds of today's farmers have no debt problems and only a minority of the remainder are in severe financial distress. Now, that's not to minimize one bit the difficulties all farmers face following the shocks of the 1970's: two grain embargoes, double-digit inflation, and record interest rates at 21 percent.

As farmers' land values shot up, some borrowed large sums of money and, yes, sometimes exorbitant sums, based on that inflated land value. Then, as we brought inflation down—and believe me, we're determined to keep it down—those farmers have been left with declining land values to cover their loans, making them harder to repay.

These problems have been worsened by the inflexible farm programs under which we operate. Designed to help agriculture, they have increased dependency upon the Federal Government, weakening incentives for self-reliance.

For example, between 1973 and 1983, the Federal Government went from purchasing 1.9 percent to 12 percent of all dairy products—the equivalent of 17 billion pounds of butter, cheese, and dried milk piled up in cold storage. The cost to taxpayers soared from $117 million to well over $2 billion. Other programs leading to surpluses in corn and wheat depressed prices, sent false signals to the markets, and drove more farmers toward bankruptcy.

The same government which played a part in this unhappy drama must not turn away from those who are the backbone of our nation, who gave America the highest standard of living in the world, and who preserved the blessing of life for millions of the world's hungry.

Last September we announced a $650 million debt restructuring initiative. Yesterday Agriculture Secretary Block announced a modification of Federal regulations so that banks will have an incentive to work out lower payments for farmers having trouble paying off their loans. We're providing loan guarantees for eligible farmers whose local banks fail and who can't find a new private lender without such a guarantee. Our program will ease further the farmers' requirement for participation in it, so more of them can take advantage of our credit offer. This administration is moving forward with its credit program because spring planting cannot wait.

Let me make one thing very plain: Yes, we are sympathetic, and we will extend support. But American taxpayers must not be asked to bail out every farmer hopelessly in debt, some by hundreds of thousands of dollars, or be asked to bail out the banks who also bet on higher inflation. We have already extended a tremendous amount of assistance. It's time for others to pitch in and do more, from officials at the State level to banks, private groups, and individuals in our communities—all joining in partnership to help farmers.

Over the long haul, there's only one sure solution. We have the ability to change, the opportunity to act, and we're going to begin now working our way back to a free market economy. What farmers need and we're determined to provide is less dependence on politicians to supply their incomes and greater independence to supply their own incomes.

Yesterday Secretary Block outlined our proposals when we sent the agricultural adjustment act of 1985 to the Congress. The 1985 farm bill will create stability for the future through policies that permit U.S. agriculture to realize its full potential and be more competitive in world markets.

Our package will be market-oriented, enabling farmers during a transition period to become more independent and make their own decisions in the marketplace again. Government will stop purchasing commodities, stop trying to manipulate supply and demand, refrain from quick fixes and extravagant new farm legislation, and move aggressively to expand markets for American farm products.

The time is now for a fresh start for American agriculture. And if we combine passage of our farm legislation with spending restraints to reduce Federal borrowing so interest rates can come down further and tax simplification to lower tax rates so we can reach greater growth, then farmers can finally reap a real prosperity every bit as bountiful as their own harvests.

Until next week, thanks for listening, and God bless you.

Note: The President spoke at 12:06 p.m. from Camp David, MD.

Toast at a White House Dinner Honoring the Nation's Governors
February 24, 1985

Well, I certainly appreciate this opportunity to be with all of you, and thank you very much for being here tonight.

When I was Governor of California, I especially enjoyed the camaraderie of other Governors. And I've changed jobs since those days, yet I still feel that as chief executives there is a special bond between us.

In the early days of the Republic, those holding our jobs weren't so certain of what our relationship should be. They knew that every decision they made would set precedents, especially concerning the sovereignty of State government in relation to the Federal Government. And Frank Chodorov, a man of liberating insight, wrote of the time when George Washington was to make his first visit as President to Massachusetts. And according to Chodorov, Governor Hancock of Massachusetts was beside himself over a matter of protocol. Would it be proper to meet President Washington on his arrival? Or would it be more appropriate for the President to call at the State capitol? What Hancock did, he thought, might be taken as an acknowledgment of the supremacy of the Federal Government or simply as a matter of courtesy.

It was a difficult decision, and finally the day of Washington's arrival was at hand. And Hancock boldly made the decision: He pleaded illness. [*Laughter*] Wouldn't it be nice if feigning illness would substitute for making some of the hard decisions that we face?

Today, of course, that's not an alternative. The challenges before us, especially concerning tax simplification and spending restraint, will require great courage and effort and extraordinary cooperation between us. I hope that I can count on you to continue to work with me in a spirit of good will in the months ahead. I've sought and appreci-

ated your advice and will continue to do so.

The Federal-State relationship should strive to maximize the benefits of limited resources, to eliminate waste, to further reduce the Federal regulatory burden, and to preserve the strength and vitality of our nation's economy. A vigorous and expanding economy must be priority number one. As Governors you know that better than most. Low inflation and high growth have cut your costs and increased your tax base. No Federal program is more important to the viability of State government than economic expansion.

Today the people no longer look to Washington as an Emerald City with magic solutions to every problem. I've been here going on 5 years now, and I can tell you it's more like the Twilight Zone than the Land of Oz. [*Laughter*] But this new view of the Federal Government, a more realistic understanding of its limitations as well as its potentials, has been a great boon to our country.

Now, all over America we hear stories of the success of innovative and creative State and local enterprises. Only a few years ago people were waiting for the Federal Government to act. Well, today they're taking the initiative, taking the future in their hands, and in doing so, accomplishing things that would never have happened if encumbered by Federal redtape and another layer of bureaucratic entanglement.

We in this room, as chief executives, are lucky to be holding office during a period of great change. It's a difficult time, and what we do will lay the foundation for a better future. Let us not be afraid to make these historic decisions—consulting openly and honestly, one with another.

All of us seek the same goal: America, as our God and our forefathers intended her to be, a land of limited government and unlimited opportunity, a land of prosperity and freedom. And you know—just to convince you that I do understand, having been there where you presently are—I remember once as Governor, shortly after I'd taken office, and on the way to the office—and the problems seemed to be multiplying as the days went by—and then, on the way in, the car radio was on. And I heard a disc jockey in Sacramento, who became my instant hero, because, for whatever reason he said it—I don't know—but all of a sudden

between records, he said: "Every man should take unto himself a wife, because sooner or later something is bound to happen that you can't blame on the Governor." [*Laughter*]

So, I offer you a toast: To the Governors of the sovereign States of this federation of United States.

Thank you.

Note: The President spoke at 9:30 p.m. in the State Dining Room at the White House.

Remarks at a White House Meeting With Members of the National Governors' Association
February 25, 1985

Thank you all for coming today. I want you to know I can sympathize with what you're thinking. I was once a Governor visiting the White House. And I can remember sitting where you're sitting and looking around and thinking I could be happy here. [*Laughter*] But it isn't always roses. [*Laughter*]

Washington can get pretty cold, and sometimes I really do miss California—California's sandy beaches and the California sunshine and the California surplus. [*Laughter*]

If I might be serious for a moment, I do want you to know that we've asked you here because I do welcome your advice on the three major questions that currently confront me: what must be done to keep our economy strong, what is needed to keep our nation secure, and what went wrong in Minnesota. [*Laughter*]

Really now, I do want to be serious. I noted last week in my press conference that we're enjoying the strongest economic expansion since the Korean war and that our first duty now is to prolong and protect this expansion. We intend to do this by carrying out the mandate delivered November 6th by the American people, the terms of which I think were quite clear. We seek the full cooperation of the Congress in moving forward *now* on this agenda and keeping

our promises.

First, our administration proposes to freeze overall Federal program spending at last year's level, to cut $51 billion out of programs in need of restraint, to reduce spending by half a trillion dollars over the next 5 years.

And these proposals are rooted both in economic necessity and common sense. There's simply no justification, for example, for the Federal Government, which is running a deficit, to be borrowing money to be spent by State and local governments, some of which are now running surpluses—surpluses resulting from your leadership and a recovery that was brought on by this administration—its recovery plan, I should say.

I ask here particularly for your help and understanding, not as a Republican or a Democrat, but in a spirit of partnership, as one chief executive to another.

I know the States still have their problems. Those of you from the farm States know what I mean. I was Governor of a State with a huge agricultural industry, not to mention the fact that I was born in farm country and got my first job in a farm State. I know what you're going through; things are very tough for you and your farmers. And together, we have to do something about that.

But it's also true that many of your States are in better fiscal shape today because of the courage that you showed and the hard decisions you made during the recent recession. I hope you can understand that these tough calls have to be made now at the Federal level.

And it's up to us to show the same kind of fortitude many of you have shown in the past. And this I intend to do. And I need your help in making the Congress and the public understand that the time has come for budgetary restraint and deficit reduction.

Second, we want to solidify the gains we've already made by institutionalizing reforms against government excess, reforms that will prevent the burden of government from falling so heavily on future generations. We want to take a lesson in federalism and give the Presidency that same powerful tool that 43 of you Governors use to fight pork-barrel items in catchall appropriations—the line-item veto.

We also want to do what 49 States have done in some form. We want to adopt the wisdom understood in every American household: that government shouldn't live beyond its means, that it shouldn't spend more than it takes in. We need that balanced budget amendment. And I'm pleased to see that your executive committee yesterday included language calling for both a balanced budget amendment and a line-item veto authority.

It's especially pleasing for me to see Republicans and Democrats working together. In that same spirit, we can achieve our mutual goals of continued economic growth and declining deficits.

Third is tax simplification. We want it this year; so do the American people. The present tax code burdens some of our citizens too heavily while permitting others to avoid paying their fair share. It makes honest people feel like cheats, and it makes cheats pose as honest citizens. It allows the underground economy to thrive and wastes millions of man-hours on needless paperwork and regulations. It drives money needed for growth, investment, and jobs into unproductive tax shelters. It acts as the single biggest obstacle to enterprise and economic expansion.

To put it simply, our tax system is unfair, inequitable, counterproductive, and all but incomprehensible. I've mentioned before, and this is absolutely a fact, that even Albert Einstein had to write to the IRS for help with his Form 1040. We want to end the trauma and tangle of April 15th, and let's do it this year.

Something else to keep in mind: In 1981, during the debate over our tax bill, we pointed out that the most important effects of reducing tax rates were sometimes not easily quantified or immediately apparent; that its very passage could send out a subtle message and create long-term changes in a political or economic culture that are infinitely more important. So, we have before us a tremendous opportunity to further the spirit of enterprise and growth, to accomplish the greatest deregulatory task of them all, and to haul ourselves out of the morass that is the Federal tax code. Let's get started.

Lots of people told you a few years ago that passing our budget cuts, or tax cut bills, would mean less revenue for you in the States, and some were even saying the States would go bankrupt. Well, all of you know how much truth there was to that. Growth begets growth; hope begets hope. If we can get on with phase two—those budget cuts, so we can steadily shrink the deficit; the line-item veto and constitutional amendment on balancing the budget; and that tax simplification plan—we will be sending out a message of hope and growth, whose potential for good is incalculable.

And let me conclude with an aside about another subject that's very dear to my heart—that of private sector initiatives. We've seen a real surge in them during the last few years. Businessmen are adopting schools, corporations are supporting nonprofit organizations, and record numbers of volunteers are providing for community needs. This growing public-private partnership strengthens our State-Federal partnership.

In closing, I would like to compliment you, the Governors, and especially Governors Carlin and Alexander, for providing the leadership for this enhanced bipartisan partnership. Thank you.

Note: The President spoke at 11:32 a.m. in the East Room at the White House. In his remarks, the President referred to Gover-nors John Carlin of Kansas and Lamar Alexander of Tennessee, chairman and vice chairman, respectively, of the association.

Remarks at a White House Meeting With Members of the President's Private Sector Survey on Cost Control in the Federal Government
February 25, 1985

Well, as you know, we have our share of meetings and visitors in this room, but believe me, there's no group that I'd rather see coming my way than all of you; no subject more dear to my heart than the one to which you've so generously dedicated your time and talent during the past few years.

I hope you'll let me reminisce here for a moment. I remember back during the campaign of 1980, I used to bring up the subject of waste, fraud, and abuse in the National Government and even mentioned the idea of a commission such as yours. Out there on the campaign trail, it was an issue that really hit home. But somehow back here in Washington, it didn't play as well. To the permanent establishment, waste and fraud are a little bit like the issue of higher taxes. It was all okay for politicians to talk about it now and then, but it was never really considered proper to go out and talk about it as if you meant it. And come to think of it, we did do something about higher taxes, also.

And then, just when the Washington establishment was getting over the shock from that one, we came up with this little number called the Grace commission. And that put some of them right back in intensive care. [*Laughter*]

The impact that you've had in this city is testimony to your own dedication and to that of your leadership. Now, right here somebody suggested that I mention that when I asked Peter Grace to take on the responsibility of running this commission, I had no idea the kind of energetic, but healthy, troublemaking I was contracting for. [*Laughter*]

I'm sure they must have been kidding. I mean, anybody who knows Peter Grace for more than 5 minutes knows that he is not a man who—let me see how I can phrase this—he's not a man who dislikes taking things to their logical conclusion. [*Laughter*] And that's exactly what Peter and all of you have done. With dedication and selflessness, you've succeeded where others failed. You provided clear, concise, and practical recommendations to enormously complicated problems. And instead of stopping there, you went out to build a groundswell of support for the Grace commission recommendations throughout this country.

Recently, I know you've participated in the House Budget Committee hearings held at various points around the country. You must have been quite a disappointment to some of them in those commissions. They didn't go out there to hear the kind of things you were saying.

And now, Peter Grace and Jack Anderson[1]—and if that isn't an unusual, but high octane team—[*laughter*]—you've created a group called Citizens Against Waste. It's a group that will be a focus for citizens action, a truly bipartisan organization whose only loyalty is to the one special interest group that we should all support, because we all belong to it—the 77 million United States taxpayers who, with their work, patriotism, and, may I say, immense patience, finance the Federal Government.

I think this kind of grassroots, educational program will, like the Grace commission itself, focus on the abuse of taxpayer dollars

---

[1] *Nationally syndicated newspaper columnist.*

and hold elected and appointed officials accountable. In doing this, Citizens Against Waste will not just help reduce our national deficit, without increasing taxes, but spark a much needed increase in citizen involvement in the workings of government and a long-overdue renewal of confidence in our democratic system.

But in addition to congratulating and thanking you today for this and other efforts, I also want to give you a progress report on where we stand with the Grace commission recommendations. The statistics are impressive. Already 1,148 of your recommendations are being implemented or have been proposed for implementation. And the dollar savings are impressive: $112 billion over 3 years in prior budgets and $56 billion proposed in the budget that I have just sent to the Hill. And I'm proud to say that we discussed these fine results in our first-ever management report to the Congress that we sent to the Hill last week.

We've come a long way together, this far. That's a record to be proud of, but something else needs to be said here. Some people have the odd idea that it's fine while you're a political candidate or during the first year or so in office to talk about waste and fraud. You may remember, in my first speech to the Congress, I called waste and fraud an unrelenting national scandal. But they warned that after a certain period of time, the political danger tends to grow. After all, if the headlines about government boondoggles like $400 hammers or millions in benefits to the ineligible recipients start appearing on your watch, the public might just decide to start blaming you.

Well, look, let's be realistic. In the 15 years before my administration came to Washington, Federal expenditures increased 400 percent. Now, thanks to you and others like you, we've worked hard on this problem for 4 years, and we've made progress in reducing the growth in spending. But we know no problem of this size could ever have been solved in one year or one term of office.

And no matter what some of the political pros might say, I think the public knows this. And I think they know we're trying and succeeding. And I think they're smart enough to understand that all those stories about waste and fraud are a direct result of a fight that we're proud to say we started in the first place.

So, let's forget political angles. Let's just trust the uncommon wisdom of the common people. I'm not worried about political angles anymore. I haven't got a political future anymore. [*Laughter*]

But keep up your good work. Bring on the headlines about waste and fraud. The Grace commission has led the way, and now it's everybody's fight.

Beyond this, the impact of your work is incalculable. Even if nothing else gets done—and I can assure you a lot more is going to get done—you have permanently changed the mood of the country. From frustration and despair over a spendthrift, irresponsible bureaucracy, the public now knows some hope and optimism that government can at last be made lean, cost-effective, and responsive to the people. That's why they're behind the Grace commission's work, and that's why they're behind our plan for deficit reduction.

Another project I know you'll be out there helping us fight for—I speak for myself when I say I owe you all a personal debt of thanks, but I also speak for the Nation and for many future generations of Americans when I say that, in making government more responsive to the wishes of the people, you have reached back to make contact with the very principle of government that began this nation: the belief that government is here to serve the people and not the other way around.

In doing this, you're helping to restore faith in the democratic process and make our cherished way of life more secure. And for that, I thank you and salute you, as do all your fellow Americans.

God bless you all, and thank you for what you've done and the tools that you have given us that are going to rewrite an awful lot of economic textbooks in the next few years; some have been rewritten already. Thank you very much.

Note: The President spoke at 2 p.m. in Room 450 of the Old Executive Office Building.

Message to the Senate Transmitting the Barbados-United States Convention on Taxation and Fiscal Evasion
February 25, 1985

To the Senate of the United States:

I transmit herewith, for Senate advice and consent to ratification, the Convention between the United States of America and Barbados for the Avoidance of Double Taxation and the Prevention of Fiscal Evasion with Respect to Taxes on Income ("the Convention"), together with an exchange of notes, signed at Bridgetown on December 31, 1984. I also transmit the report of the Department of State on the Convention.

The Convention, in general, follows the pattern of other United States income tax treaties and the current draft United States Model Income Tax Convention, but deviates from the model in certain respects to reflect Barbados' status as a developing country.

Among the principal features of the Convention are provisions to prevent third-country residents from taking unwarranted advantage of the treaty. The Convention also establishes maximum rates of tax at source on payments of dividends, interest, and royalties.

The exchange of notes indicates the willingness of the United States Government to reopen discussions, should circumstances change, which would permit the inclusion of additional provisions to create incentives to promote the flow of United States investment to Barbados.

I recommend that the Senate give early and favorable consideration to this matter, and give advice and consent to ratification of the Convention, together with the related exchange of notes.

RONALD REAGAN

The White House,
February 25, 1985.

Appointment of William P. Longmire, Jr., as a Member of the President's Cancer Panel
February 25, 1985

The President today announced his intention to appoint William P. Longmire, Jr., to be a member of the President's Cancer Panel for a term expiring February 20, 1988. This is a reappointment.

Dr. Longmire is a physician and surgeon. In addition he is professor emeritus at the University of California School of Medicine in Los Angeles. He is a consultant in surgery at the Los Angeles County Harbor General Hospital. He has been civilian consultant to the Surgeon General, U.S. Army, since 1960. Previously, he was a consultant, general surgery, Special Medical Advisory Group, Veterans Administration (1963–1968 and 1977–1981); chairman of the department of surgery at the University of California School of Medicine (1948–1976); and national consultant in general surgery to the Office of the Surgeon General, U.S. Air Force (1954–1976).

Dr. Longmire graduated from the University of Oklahoma (A.B., 1934) and the Johns Hopkins Medical School (M.D., 1938). He is married, has two children, and resides in Los Angeles, CA. He was born September 14, 1913, in Sapulpa, OK.

213

Appointment of Five Members of the Arctic Research Commission, and Designation of the Chairperson
February 26, 1985

The President today announced his intention to appoint the following individuals to be members of the Arctic Research Commission. These are new positions.

Oliver Leavitt, for a term of 4 years. Mr. Leavitt is currently first vice president of Arctic Slope Regional Corp. He is a graduate of the RCA Institute (1965). He is married, has two children, and resides in Barrow, AK. He was born October 11, 1943, in Barrow.

Elmer Edwin Rasmuson, for a term of 3 years. Mr. Rasmuson is currently director of the National Bank of Alaska. He graduated from Harvard University (S.B., 1930; M.A., 1935). He is married, has three children, and resides in Anchorage, AK. He was born February 15, 1909, in Yakutat, AK.

Juan Gualterio Roederer, for a term of 2 years. Mr. Roederer is currently director of the Geophysical Institute at the University of Alaska.

He graduated from the University of Buenos Aires (Ph.D., 1952). He is married, has four children, and resides in Fairbanks, AK. He was born September 2, 1929, in Priest, Italy.

Albert Lincoln Washburn, for a term of 3 years. Mr. Washburn is currently professor emeritus of geology at the University of Washington, Quaternary Research Center, in Seattle, WA. He graduated from Dartmouth College (B.A., 1935) and Yale University (Ph.D., 1942). He is married, has three children, and resides in Mercer Island, WA. He was born June 15, 1911, in New York, NY.

James Herbert Zumberge, for a term of 4 years. Upon his appointment the President intends to designate him as the Chairperson. Mr. Zumberge is currently president of the University of Southern California. He graduated from the University of Minnesota (Ph.D., 1959). He is married, has four children, and resides in San Marino, CA. He was born December 27, 1923, in Minneapolis, MN.

Remarks at the Presentation Ceremony for the National Medal of Science
February 27, 1985

I'm delighted to welcome all of you here today. In a few minutes, it'll be my privilege to present the National Medal of Science to 19 Americans who have made outstanding contributions to our way of life and to our future.

Recently, I was told that all those scientists don't want it generally known, most enjoy their work so much that they almost feel guilty getting paid for it. [*Laughter*] I was told this either by Jay Keyworth, reminiscing about his previous job—[*laughter*]—or by Dave Stockman, reminiscing about his present one. [*Laughter*]

Well, we're not here to take up a collection. [*Laughter*] In fact, despite the constraints in Federal spending, our budget for the next fiscal year calls for a 6.7-percent increase for basic research in the physical

sciences. I should add that we're also planning for increased funding for science and technology and basic research through the end of the decade, and that's because what you do is that important. The ultimate source of innovation, of new technology, of human progress itself, is knowledge; and that's the business of science.

Now, there's no nation on Earth that can match our scientific capability, but, of course, no nation depends as much as we do on the science base. Our enviable standard of living, our national security, our ability to create millions of new jobs—more than 7 million over the last 2 years, in what the Europeans are calling an American miracle—all depend on new talent, knowledge, and our talent for making use of it.

And there's no doubt that the measure of

America's future safety, progress, and greatness depends on how well scientists keep pushing back new frontiers. That's why I'm so pleased that today's ceremony is the third White House event this month honoring the people whose work will determine that future.

Last week we presented the first National Technology Awards for exceptional achievements in developing and using technology for industrial advances. Technology last week; science this week. Isn't that just like the Government? Getting the cart before the horse. [*Laughter*]

Jay Keyworth tells me that there have been times, not too long ago, when scientists and technologists barely spoke to each other. Well, I believe that one of today's real strengths is the enthusiasm with which scientists and technologists explore each other's interests. In fact, it occurs to me that if we could have brought together last week's doers with today's thinkers in a single ceremony, we might have seen the formation of several new companies before—[*laughter*]—the medals were even presented. Maybe we should keep that in mind for next year and invite a few venture capitalists. [*Laughter*]

But at least this year, today is the day for the National Medal of Science. And I know Einstein once remarked that, "The whole of science is nothing more than a refinement of everyday thinking." Well, that was easy for him to say. [*Laughter*] As for me, I'm still trying to decide—or decode energy equals mass times the speed of light squared. And I must tell you that when I looked over the briefing materials for this event and saw phrases like "discovery of the free neutrino" and the "central role of neuropeptides" and "spectroscopic investigations," I thought they were mentioning some of the questions left over from [Attorney General] Ed Meese's confirmation hearings. [*Laughter*]

But today's awards honor a remarkable group of American scientists. The National Medals of Science are a tribute from your fellow—well, from a group of—why should I pause right here when it's right in front of me and all I have to do is look at it?—from your fellow scientists. I started to say just from your fellow Americans, but I think that would have been proper, too, because I'm sure they share our gratitude and appreciation for all you do.

Each of you has devoted your energies not to truth as understood, but to the search for truth not yet understood. You had faith that you'd come to understand the unknown, and you did. You had faith that your discoveries would bring progress, and they did. And because of your achievements and those of your colleagues, we stand on the verge of greater advances than mankind has ever known.

Your work is proof that there are no limits to discovery and human progress when men and women are free to follow their dreams. You've proven time and again that freedom plus science equals opportunity and progress and that America's future can be determined by our dreams and our visions.

On behalf of the American people in whose names these medals are presented, I extend my congratulations to all of you, to your families, and your coworkers. We deeply appreciate what you've done, and we thank you. And God bless you all.

And now I'm going to ask Jay Keyworth to help me present the medals.

Note: The President spoke at 11:29 a.m. in the East Room at the White House. In his remarks, the President referred to George A. Keyworth II, Science Adviser to the President and Director of the Office of Science and Technology Policy, and David A. Stockman, Director of the Office of Management and Budget.

Recipients of the medal were Howard L. Bachrach, Paul Berg, E. Margaret Burbidge, Maurice Goldhaber, Herman H. Goldstine, William R. Hewlett, Roald Hoffmann, Helmut E. Landsberg, George M. Low, Walter H. Munk, George C. Pimentel, Frederick Reines, Wendell L. Roelofs, Bruno B. Rossi, Berta Scharrer, J. Robert Schrieffer, Isadore M. Singer, John G. Trump, and Richard N. Zare.

Memorandum on Uniform Relocation Assistance and Real Property Acquisition
February 27, 1985

Memorandum for the Heads of Executive Departments and Agencies

The purpose of this Memorandum is to improve administration and implementation of the Uniform Relocation Assistance and Real Property Acquisition Policies Act of 1970.

Specifically, I hereby direct the following actions:

1. The Presidential Memorandum of September 6, 1973 on this subject is superseded.

2. As with other Administration management improvement initiatives, a lead agency, the Department of Transportation (DOT), is designated to coordinate and monitor implementation of the Act, and consult periodically with State and local governments and other organizations and interest groups affected by administration of the Act.

3. DOT, jointly with the Department of Housing and Urban Development, shall interact with the principal executive departments and agencies affected by the Act in developing Administration policy.

4. Within 90 days of the date of this Memorandum, all affected executive departments and agencies shall propose common regulations under the Act. Within one year of the date of this Memorandum, such departments and agencies shall issue common regulations under the Act. Such regulations shall be consistent with the model policy promulgated by DOT, in consultation and coordination with other affected agencies, and published in final form in the *Federal Register* simultaneously with this Memorandum.

5. DOT shall report annually to the President's Council on Management Improvement, through the Office of Management and Budget, on implementation of the Act.

RONALD REAGAN

[*Filed with the Office of the Federal Register, 4:14 p.m., February 28, 1985*]

Remarks at the Annual Meeting of the National Association of Independent Schools
February 28, 1985

Secretary Bennett, ladies and gentlemen, I'm delighted to have this opportunity to speak to your National Association of Independent Schools.

America has a long heritage of educational diversity, of public schools working alongside our independent schools, and this tradition has done much to contribute to our nation's greatness. You and the schools you represent have helped keep our educational standards high. You've earned the deep respect and appreciation of the American people, and I thank you.

And let me just say how proud I am to appear here with our new Secretary of Education, Bill Bennett. Whether as a student in his undergraduate days or studying for his doctorate or, later, as a teacher, author, or Chairman for the National Endowment for the Humanities, Bill Bennett has spent a lifetime taking serious ideas seriously.

He's also an authority on rock and roll—[*laughter*]—as well as the fortunes of the Dixon, Illinois, high school football team, and that makes him A–OK in my book—[*laughter*]—because that's where I played my football.

But, Bill, I know that in your new post you're working passionately to improve

American education. And you have my enthusiastic support. And so far, I have only one complaint: I've been following those press reports of your interviews, and I just wish you'd stop mincing your words. [*Laughter*]

When our administration began its first term in 1981, we had to clean up the mess we'd inherited. And today we're creating a new nation. Our economy is growing, our spirit is renewed, our country is stronger, and America is at peace.

As Prime Minister Thatcher told the Congress this month, it wasn't Soviet good will that brought the Soviets back to the bargaining table; it was American strength. So it is that, as we begin this second term, I believe we face an historic challenge. We have the chance to prepare America, not just for the next 4 years or the next decade, but for the 21st century. And together, we can keep America moving toward that first shining vision—a land of golden opportunity, where achievement is limited only by how big we dream, how hard we work, and how well we learn.

And we know the path to that vision is through economic growth and new technologies and renewed excellence in American education. Today we're making history with the most sustained, far-reaching economic expansion since the end of World War II. More than 7 million jobs have been created over the last 2 years, and more Americans are now working than ever before in our history. And we're determined to go on creating more jobs until every American can share in the self-esteem that comes from the honest work of hands and mind.

A stronger economy is leading us into a technological revolution that's offering dazzling progress for the future. During the past couple of weeks, it so happens that I have presented the first National Technology Awards, awarded the National Medals of Science, and had lunch with a group of futurists. I've heard about the fiber composites and ceramics that are taking the place of costly metals in manufacturing, about new medical techniques like the use of lasers and sound waves. And I've learned more about the miracles of microchips, about the practical benefits of the space station that we plan to have in orbit by the

mid-1990's, and the home computers that are putting our literature and vast sums of information at families' fingertips.

Albert Einstein once said that science is nothing but everyday thinking carefully applied. Well, that's easy for him to say. [*Laughter*] Yet, even laymen like us can see that in coming decades technology promises to make life in America longer, healthier, and fuller.

Yet as important as technology and economic growth are to our future, education is more important still. Without education, economic growth and technological innovation will be limited. Without education, we could even lose our most fundamental values—our beliefs in a just and loving God, in freedom, in hard work. Yet if we do educate our children well, grounding them in our values, sharpening their minds, teaching them greatness of spirit, then the coming decades will be the best that America has ever seen.

Secretary Bennett has said that education is the architecture of the soul. Well, with the very soul of our nation at stake, let us consider the future of education in America. This spring we mark the second anniversary of a Department of Education report that was entitled "A Nation at Risk." Now, that report concluded that if an unfriendly foreign power had attempted to impose on America the mediocre educational performance that exists today, we might well have viewed it as an act of war.

Well, from 1963 to 1980, scholastic aptitude test scores showed a virtually unbroken decline. Science achievement scores showed a similar drop. Most shocking, the report stated that more than one-tenth of our 17-year-olds could be considered functionally illiterate.

And so Americans decided to put an end to educational decline. Across the land, parents, teachers, school officials, and State and local officeholders began to improve the fundamentals of American education. I don't mean they went to work on budget-busting proposals of new frills in the curriculum. They went to work as you have— on teaching and learning.

When we took office, only a handful of States had task forces on education. Today they all do. Since 1981, 43 States have raised their graduation requirements; 5 more have higher requirements under consideration. Perhaps the most telling figure is this: scholastic aptitude test scores have risen in 2 of the last 3 years, the best record in the last 20 years. And we've only begun.

States and localities, which quite properly bear the main responsibility for our schools, have taken an active part in this movement for educational reform. But we've made certain that the Federal Government has also played a leading role. Our administration has replaced 28 narrow educational programs with one block grant to give State and local officials greater leeway in spending Federal aid.

We've rolled back regulations that were hampering educators with needless paperwork. We've taken steps to promote discipline in our schools, including the establishment of the National School Safety Center. And we've launched Partnerships in Education, a program in which businesses, labor unions, and other groups of working people are pitching in to help schools in their communities. Today there are more than 40,000 such partnerships in operation. In Philadelphia, for example, business leaders have raised $26 million to support the Catholic schools that educqte one-third of the city's children. I should add that one of the most effective Federal actions has been the growth of the economy, that I mentioned a moment ago.

Private contributions to schools, especially colleges and universities, are up. Indeed, in 1983 the colleges and universities that responded to a survey conducted by the Council for Financial Aid to Education reported endowments totaling some $29.6 billion, the largest 1-year figure since the council began conducting its surveys in 1966.

Under the previous administration, even though Federal education budgets soared, overall spending on education throughout America, adjusted for inflation, actually declined by $17 billion, dragged down by the weakening economy. But with inflation down and the economy now growing again, education spending throughout the country, despite restraint at the Federal level, has actually gone up by almost $18 billion. And today many States are running a surplus and are in a better position to help fund our public schools and universities.

From the State university that has new funds for research to the community that can afford a new school bus, economic growth is giving education throughout America a powerful lift. Continuing this economic growth will prove invaluable during the 4 years to come. And that's why we intend to provide more incentives, cut personal income tax rates further, and keep America the investment capital of the world. And that's why we can and must bring Federal spending under control.

Now, in recent weeks, there's been a certain amount of confusion regarding our budget proposals on education. Let me take this opportunity to make matters clear. In our proposal, we have recommended reserving aid for the needy, limiting aid per student to a level we can afford, closing loopholes that lead to abuse and error, and cutting excessive subsidies to banks and others.

Regarding student loans, as things stand now, our nation provides some aid to college students from the highest income families; some to students who come from families with incomes higher than $100,000. This defies common sense, insults simple justice, and must stop. Government has no right to force the least affluent to subsidize the sons and daughters of the wealthy. And under our proposal, this will change. Those whose family incomes are too high to qualify for guaranteed loans with heavy interest subsidies will still have access to guaranteed, but unsubsidized loans of up to $4,000. And every qualified student who wants to go to college will still be able to do so.

Yes, our proposal may cause some families to make difficult adjustments. But by bringing the budget under control, we will avoid the far more painful adjustment of living in a wrecked economy. And that's what we're absolutely determined to do.

Our budget proposal is prudent; it's reasonable and just. I consider it fully deserving of the support for it that I'm asking you and all Americans to give.

State task forces on education, college entrance scores growing—or edging up, a growing economy providing schools with more resources—yes, education has taken its first steps on the long, hard road to excellence. And as we continue our journey during the next 4 years and beyond, Secretary Bennett and I believe there are five aspects of education to which we must give our full attention, five guideposts, if you will, to lead us on our way: choice, teachers, curriculum, setting, and parents. And let me touch briefly on each of them for you now.

The first, choice: Parents should have greater freedom to send their children to the schools they desire and to do so without interference by local, State, or Federal levels of government. Diversity and competition among schools should be encouraged, not discouraged.

At the State level, efforts to encourage parental choice might involve both legislation to permit parents to choose from any public schools within their districts and efforts to eliminate redtape surrounding within-district transfers.

At the Federal level, our administration has made two proposals to expand parental choice. Tuition tax credits would provide some support to middle and lower income parents with children in independent schools. And this would be only fair, since these parents are also paying their full share of taxes to support our public schools.

Education vouchers would deliver aid for educationally disadvantaged children, not to schools but directly to the parents. And under our plan, each year, selected parents would receive one voucher worth several hundred dollars per child. These parents would then be free to use their vouchers at any schools they chose.

Tuition tax credits and education vouchers would foster greater diversity and, hence, higher standards throughout our system of education. These proposals have the support of the American people. And make no mistake, Secretary Bennett and I intend to see them through to their enactment.

Our second guidepost, teachers: Studies indicate that by the end of this decade America will need more than a million new teachers and that by 1990 almost two-thirds of our teachers will have been hired since 1980. Today America boasts thousands of fine teachers, but in too many cases teaching has become a resting place for the unmotivated and the unqualified. And this we can no longer allow.

We must give our teachers greater honor and respect. We must sweep away laws and regulations, such as unduly restrictive certification requirements, that prevent good people from entering this profession, and we must pay and promote our teachers according to merit. Hard-earned tax dollars have no business rewarding mediocrity; they must be used to encourage excellence.

And third, curriculum: deciding what we want our children to learn. This is, to be sure, a difficult question. But this much we already know: We cannot allow our curricula to be divided by narrow interest groups. They must be determined by the intellectual, moral, and civic needs of our students themselves.

We must also know certain basic subjects must not be neglected. Too many students today are allowed to abandon vocational and college prep courses for courses of doubtful value, that prepare them neither for work nor higher education. Compared to other industrialized countries, moreover, we have fallen behind in the sciences and math.

In Japan advanced coursework in mathematics and science starts in elementary school. So Japan, with a population only about half the size of ours, graduates about as many engineers as we do. In the Soviet Union students learn the basic concepts of algebra and geometry in elementary school. Compared to the United States, the Soviet Union graduates from college more than three times as many specialists in engineering. It's time to put an end to this learning gap by insisting that all American students become fully conversant with science and math, as well as history, reading, and writing.

But students should not only learn basic subjects but basic values. We must teach the importance of justice, equality, religion, liberty, and standards of right and wrong. And we must give them a picture of America that is balanced and full, containing our virtues along with our faults.

New York University Dean, Dr. Herbert London, learned this the hard way. One day his 13-year-old daughter came home from school with tears in her eyes to say, "I don't have a future." She showed her father a paper she'd been given in school. It listed horrors that it claimed awaited her generation, including air pollution so bad that everyone would have to wear a gas mask.

Well, as a result of that incident, London wrote a book called, "Why Are They Lying To Our Children?" It documents the myths that are taught in so many of our schools. Our children should know, London argues, that because our society decided to do something about pollution, our environment is getting better, not worse. Emissions of most conventional air pollutants, for example, have decreased significantly, while trout and other fish are returning to streams where they haven't been seen for decades.

Our children should know that because Americans abhor discrimination, the number of black families living in our suburbs has grown more than three times the rate of white families living in suburbs and that between 1960 and 1982, the number of black Americans in our colleges more than quadrupled.

By any objective measure, we live in the freest, most prosperous nation in the history of the world, and our children should know that. As Jeane Kirkpatrick once put it, "We must learn to bear the truth about our society no matter how pleasant it is." [*Laughter*]

You know, our fourth guidepost is setting in schools throughout—in setting, I should say: In schools throughout America, learning has been crowded out by alcohol, drugs, and crime. In 1983, for example, a distinguished panel reported on one of our major urban school systems and found that during the prior year fully one-half of the high school teachers who responded to the survey had fallen victim to robbery, larceny, or assault on school property. Of the high school students surveyed, nearly four-tenths had likewise been victimized. And the panel found, moreover, that during the prior year 17 percent of the female students and 37 percent of the male students

surveyed had carried weapons to school. In the name of our children, this must stop. In the courts, for too long, we've concentrated on the rights of the few disruptive students and allowed simple matters of discipline to become major legal proceedings.

Supreme Court Justice Powell has criticized the "indiscriminate reliance upon the judiciary and the adversary process as the means of resolving many of the most routine problems arising in the classroom." It's high time we return common sense to the process and paid attention to the rights of the great majority of students who want to learn.

I'm proud to say that our Justice Department participated in the recent Supreme Court case that restored the authority of school officials to conduct reasonable searches. There's no need to call in a grand jury every time a principal needs to check a student locker. And today I'm directing our outstanding new Attorney General, Ed Meese, to work with Secretary Bennett in examining possible modifications of Federal law to avoid undercutting the authority of State and local school officials to maintain effective discipline.

Discipline is important, not for its own sake, but as a way of instilling a virtue that is central to life in our democracy—self-discipline. And if it is sometimes difficult to assert rightful authority, we must ask: Who better to correct the student's arithmetic—his math teacher or, years later, his boss? Who better to teach the student respect for rules—his principal or, someday, the police?

Let's teach our sons and daughters to view academic standards, codes of civilized behavior, and knowledge itself with reverence. And let us do so not for the sake of those standards, those codes, or that knowledge, but for the sake of those young human beings.

Now, our fifth and perhaps most important guidepost is parents. Parents care about their children's education with an intensity central authorities do not share. A widely respected educator, Dr. Eileen Gardner, has written: "The record shows that when control of education is placed in Federal hands it is not control by the people, but by small, yet powerful lobbies motivated by self-interest or dogma. When centralized in this way, it is beyond the control of the parents and local communities it is designed to serve. It becomes impervious to feedback."

Well, the answer is to restore State and local governments and, above all, parents to their rightful place in the educational process. Parents know that they cannot educate their children on their own. We must recognize, in turn, that schools cannot educate students without the personal involvement of parents.

Choice, teachers, curriculum, setting, parents—if we concentrate on these five guideposts, then I know American education will enjoy a great renaissance of excellence and enable us to achieve new strength, freedom, and prosperity in the century to come.

You know, this month we celebrate the hundredth anniversary of the publication of an American classic. It's a book I read in school myself. My guess is that most of you read it in school, too, and that most of your children and their children will as well. Its title: "The Adventures of Huckleberry Finn."

You remember the story: Huck and Jim, an escaped slave, float on a raft down the Mississippi. They seemed to have an adventure every time they drift ashore. And they become entangled with townsfolk, two colorful con artists, and members of feuding clans. Huck works hard to keep Jim free, and in the end he succeeds.

In this work, Mark Twain presents the humor, the openness, and purity of hearts so characteristic of the American spirit. I believe the book says much about the moral aims of education, about the qualities of heart that we seek to impart to our children.

At one point in the book, Huck talks about evenings on the raft. He says: "We catched fish and talked, and we took a swim now and then to keep off sleepiness. It was

kind of solemn, drifting down the big, still river, laying on our backs looking up at the stars, and we didn't ever feel like talking loud, and it warn't often that we laughed— only a low kind of chuckle . . .

"Every night we passed towns, some of them away up on black hillsides, nothing but just a shining bed of lights . . . The fifth night we passed St. Louis, and it was like the whole world lit up. In St. Petersburg, they used to say there was 20,000 or 30,000 people in St. Louis, but I never believed it till I see that wonderful spread of lights at two o'clock that still night."

Well, in the decades to come, may our schools give to our children the skills to navigate through life as gracefully as Huck navigated the Mississippi. And may they teach our students the same hatred of bigotry and love of their fellow men that Huck showed on every page, and especially in his love for his big friend, Jim. And may they equip them to be as thankful for the gift of life in America in the 21st century as was one Huckleberry Finn in the 19th.

And may I just say something also, too, about getting a little overboard and using something—prestige—or getting it out of education. It's a story about the author of Huckleberry Finn, Mark Twain. He was on an ocean voyage. And one day in the dining salon on the ship, one of his tablemates asked him if he would pass the sugar. And then, knowing that he was speaking to Mark Twain, he thought he would impress him a little bit with his knowledge. And he said, "Mr. Twain, isn't it interesting that the only two words in the English language in which the 'su' has the 'shu' sound are sumac and sugar?" Twain said, "Are you sure?" [*Laughter*]

Thank you all. God bless you all.

Note: The President spoke at 11:21 a.m. in the International Ballroom at the Washington Hilton Hotel.

Appointment of William French Smith as a Member of the President's Foreign Intelligence Advisory Board
February 28, 1985

The President today announced his intention to appoint William French Smith to be a member of the President's Foreign Intelligence Advisory Board.

Mr. Smith is a partner of Gibson, Dunn & Crutcher of Los Angeles. Previously, he served as Attorney General of the United States (1981–1985); senior partner of Gibson, Dunn & Crutcher (1946–1981); director of Pacific Lighting Corp. of Los Angeles (1967–1981) and San Francisco (1969–1981); director of Jorgensen Steel Co. (1974–1981); and director of Pullman, Inc., of Chicago (1979–1980).

He has served as a member of the U.S. Advisory Commission on International, Educational, and Cultural Affairs in Washington (1971–1978); a member of the board of directors of the Los Angeles World Affairs Council since 1970 and its president since 1975; a member of the Los Angeles Committee on Foreign Relations (1954–1974); and a member of the Harvard University School of Government since 1971. He has also served as a member of the Advisory Board of the Center for Strategic and International Studies, Georgetown University, since 1978 and as a member of the Stanton Panel on International Information, Education and Cultural Relations, Washington (1974–1975).

He was a member of the California delegation to the Republican National Convention in 1968, 1972, and 1976, serving as chairman of the delegation in 1968 and vice chairman of the delegation in 1972 and 1976.

Mr. Smith graduated from the University of California (A.B., 1939) and Harvard University (LL.B., 1942). He served in the United States Naval Reserve from 1942 to 1946 and attained the rank of lieutenant. Mr. Smith is married to the former Jean Webb, and they have four children. He was born August 26, 1917, in Wilton, NH.

Statement on the Death of Henry Cabot Lodge
February 28, 1985

Nancy and I were saddened, as were all Americans, by the recent death of Henry Cabot Lodge. Few men have played a more prominent role in the events of the last 50 years. Senator, soldier, diplomat, and political figure, former Ambassador Lodge served his country long and selflessly. Henry Cabot Lodge was celebrated for his eloquence on behalf of the American cause. At a crisis point in the cold war, he spoke for honesty and human freedom in the United Nations; as a Senator and Vice Presidential candidate, he often inspired his countrymen with words of vision and uplift. Yet perhaps the best measure of his dedication to this nation and the ideals for which it stands was his willingness to forsake high political office to defend his country in time of war. His service in uniform was like that of his public career: long, valorous, dedicated.

Henry Cabot Lodge's sense of personal honor and his devotion to country remain an inspiration to those of us who knew him and will remain so for many generations of Americans to come. Massachusetts has lost a loyal son, and America has lost a distinguished public servant and symbol of America's quest for decency in a tumultuous era. On behalf of all Americans, Nancy and I extend our deepest sympathy to the Lodge family.

Designation of Theodore J. Garrish as an Acting Assistant Secretary of Energy
February 28, 1985

The President today designated Theodore J. Garrish, General Counsel of the Department of Energy, to be Acting Assistant Secretary for Congressional, Intergovernmental, and Public Affairs of the Department of Energy, effective March 1, 1985.

Mr. Garrish has been serving as General Counsel since May 1983 and was previously a special assistant to the Secretary of Energy in 1982. He was legislative counsel at the Department of the Interior in 1981–1982; partner in the Washington, DC, law firm of Deane, Snowdon, Shutler, Garrish, and Gherardi in 1978–1981; General Coun-

sel at the U.S. Consumer Product Safety Commission in 1976–1978; assistant to the Secretary of the Interior in 1976 and 1974–1975; assistant to the Special Counsel, the White House, in 1974; and senior trial attorney and chief of the advertising evaluation section at the Federal Trade Commission in 1973–1974.

He graduated from the University of Michigan (A.B., 1964) and Wayne State University (J.D., 1968). He has two children and resides in Alexandria, VA. He was born January 6, 1943, in Detroit, MI.

Nomination of Donald E. Shasteen To Be an Assistant Secretary of Labor
March 1, 1985

The President today announced his intention to nominate Donald E. Shasteen to be Assistant Secretary of Labor for Veteran's Employment. He would succeed William Plowden, Jr.

Mr. Shasteen is currently Deputy Assistant Secretary for Veteran's Employment and Training. Previously, he was Deputy Under Secretary for Legislation and Intergovernmental Relations (1981–1982); codirector, Senate transition assistance, Republican Conference of the U.S. Senate (1980–

1981); administrative assistant to Senator Gordon J. Humphrey of New Hampshire (1979–1980); and executive assistant (1966–1973) and then administrative assistant to Senator Carl T. Curtis of Nebraska (1973–1978). He was a candidate for United States Senator in Nebraska in 1978.

Mr. Shasteen graduated from the University of Colorado at Boulder (B.A., 1950). He is married, has four children, and resides in Potomac, MD. He was born December 3, 1928, in Englewood, CO.

Nomination of John H. Moore To Be Deputy Director of the National Science Foundation
March 1, 1985

The President today announced his intention to nominate John H. Moore to be Deputy Director of the National Science Foundation. He would succeed Donald Newton Langenberg.

Mr. Moore is currently associate director and senior fellow at the Hoover Institution at Stanford University. Previously, he was associate director of the Law and Economics Center, Emory University (1981), and associate director of the Law and Economics Center, University of Miami (1977–1981). He was at the University of Virginia for 14 years, serving as research assistant (1963–1965), teaching assistant (1965–1966), assistant professor (1966–1970), and associate professor (1970–1977).

Mr. Moore graduated from the University of Michigan (B.S.E., 1958; M.B.A. 1959) and the University of Virginia (Ph.D., 1966). He is married, has two children, and resides in Palo Alto, CA. He was born April 19, 1935, in Grand Forks, ND.

Statement on Japanese Automobile Export Restraints
March 1, 1985

I have today concluded a review of a number of elements of the U.S.-Japan trade relationship, including Japanese restraints on the export of its automobiles and other market access issues. I have concluded this review believing in the wisdom of maintaining the principle of free and fair trade for the benefit of the world's consumers, and I will continue to actively support further liberalization of the global trading system.

In this context, it is my decision not to urge the Japanese to extend their voluntary export restraints on automobiles to the United States. I take this position in the spirit of the common understanding reached between me and Prime Minister Nakasone during our January 2 meetings in Los Angeles. As a separate matter, I would like to commend the improved performance of our own automobile manufacturers. In taking this action, I hope that we can look forward to reciprocal treatment by Japan concerning the high-level discussions underway between our countries in the weeks and months ahead.

Message to the Congress Reporting Budget Deferrals
March 1, 1985

To the Congress of the United States:

In accordance with the Impoundment Control Act of 1974, I herewith report six new deferrals of budget authority for 1985 totaling $58,900,000 and four revised deferrals now totaling $110,566,481. The deferrals affect the Departments of Agriculture, Health and Human Services, Justice, and Labor.

The details of these deferrals are contained in the attached report.

RONALD REAGAN

The White House,
March 1, 1985.

Note: The attachment detailing the deferrals was printed in the Federal Register *of March 7.*

Letter Accepting the Resignation of William A. Niskanen as a Member and Acting Chairman of the Council of Economic Advisers
March 1, 1985

Dear Bill:

It is with regret that I accept your resignation as a Member and Acting Chairman of the Council of Economic Advisers, effective at the end of this month.

The past four years have seen great changes not only in the substance of economic policy but, more importantly, in its direction. You have been an important and valued adviser throughout this period when we have been turning once more to the creative energies of individuals in the marketplace to provide our Nation with stable, long-term growth.

As a distinguished professional economist who advised me even before I became President and as a longtime defender of the principles of a free society, you have done an outstanding job of helping me to craft sound economic policies. I believe that the change in direction we have instituted during the past four years will continue even beyond this Administration, and I want to thank you personally for the excellent job you have done as one of my principal advisers.

Nancy joins me in sending you our best wishes for every future success and happiness.

Sincerely,

RONALD REAGAN

[The Honorable William A. Niskanen, member, Council of Economic Advisers, Washington, D.C. 20506]

March 1, 1985

Dear Mr. President:

I hereby submit my resignation as a Member and Acting Chairman of the Council of Economic Advisers, effective at the end of this month.

I have been honored to serve you as an economic adviser over the years since you first recruited me as a member of the group to draft Proposition 1. Your consistent support of the principles of a free society has changed the debate about the economic role of the government. Stay the course.

Sincerely,

WILLIAM A. NISKANEN
Member

[The President, The White House, Washington, D.C.]

Appointment of Three Members of the President's Blue Ribbon Task Group on Nuclear Weapons Program Management
March 1, 1985

The President today announced his intention to appoint the following individuals to be members of the President's Blue Ribbon Task Group on Nuclear Weapons Program Management.

William P. Clark most recently served as Secretary of the Interior (1983–1985). Previously, he was Assistant to the President for National Security Affairs (1982–1983) and Deputy Secretary of State (1981–1982). From 1973 to 1981, Mr. Clark was an associate justice on the California State Supreme Court. Following World War II he served in the United States Army Counter Intelligence Corps in Western Europe. Mr. Clark attended Stanford and Santa Clara Universities and Loyola Night Law School. He was born October 23, 1931, in California.

Jeane J. Kirkpatrick is currently the United States Permanent Representative to the United Nations. Previously, she was associate professor (1967–1973), professor (1973–1978), and then Leavey Professor in the Foundations of American Freedom (1978-on leave) at the Georgetown University. She is also the author of several scholarly works and has contributed to the New Republic, the American Political Science Review, and other publications. She graduated from Barnard College (B.A., 1946) and Columbia University (M.A., 1950). She was born November 19, 1926, in Duncan, OK.

Alan C. Furth has been with the Southern Pacific Co. since 1950, serving as general counsel (1963–1966), executive vice president (1976–

1979), and president (1979–present). He is also director and member of the executive committee of the Southern Pacific Co. Mr. Furth graduated from the University of California at Berkeley (A.B., 1944; LL.B., 1949). He is also a graduate of the advanced management program at Harvard University (1959). He was born September 16, 1922, in Oakland, CA.

Remarks at the Annual Dinner of the Conservative Political Action Conference
March 1, 1985

Thank you, Vice Chairman Linen, for those very kind words. I'm grateful to the American Conservative Union, Young Americans for Freedom, National Review, Human Events, for organizing this wonderful evening. When you work in the White House, you don't get to see your old friends as much as you'd like. And I always see the CPAC speech as my opportunity to "dance with the one that brung ya."

There's so much I want to talk about tonight. I've been thinking, in the weeks since the inauguration, that we are at an especially dramatic turning point in American history. And just putting it all together in my mind, I've been reviewing the elements that have led to this moment.

Ever since F.D.R. and the New Deal, the opposition party, and particularly those of a liberal persuasion, have dominated the political debate. Their ideas were new; they had momentum; they captured the imagination of the American people. The left held sway for a good long time. There was a right, but it was, by the forties and fifties, diffuse and scattered, without a unifying voice.

But in 1964 came a voice in the wilderness—Barry Goldwater; the great Barry Goldwater, the first major party candidate of our time who was a true-blue, undiluted conservative. He spoke from principle, and he offered vision. Freedom—he spoke of freedom: freedom from the Government's increasing demands on the family purse, freedom from the Government's increasing usurpation of individual rights and responsi-

bilities, freedom from the leaders who told us the price of world peace is continued acquiescence to totalitarianism. He was ahead of his time. When he ran for President, he won 6 States and lost 44. But his candidacy worked as a precursor of things to come.

A new movement was stirring. And in the 1960's Young Americans for Freedom is born; National Review gains readership and prestige in the intellectual community; Human Events becomes a major voice on the cutting edge. In the seventies the antitax movement begins. Actually, it was much more than an antitax movement, just as the Boston Tea Party was much more than antitax initiative. [*Laughter*] In the late seventies Proposition 13 and the Sagebrush Rebellion; in 1980, for the first time in 28 years, a Republican Senate is elected; so, may I say, is a conservative President. In 1984 that conservative administration is reelected in a 49-State sweep. And the day the votes came in, I thought of Walt Whitman: "I hear America singing." [*Laughter*]

This great turn from left to right was not just a case of the pendulum swinging—first, the left hold sway and then the right, and here comes the left again. The truth is, conservative thought is no longer over here on the right; it's the mainstream now.

And the tide of history is moving irresistibly in our direction. Why? Because the other side is virtually bankrupt of ideas. It has nothing more to say, nothing to add to the debate. It has spent its intellectual capital, such as it was—[*laughter*]—and it has done its deeds.

Now, we're not in power now because they failed to gain electoral support over the past 50 years. They did win support. And the result was chaos, weakness, and drift. Ultimately, though, their failures yielded one great thing—us guys. [*Laughter*] We in this room are not simply profiting from their bankruptcy; we are where we are because we're winning the contest of ideas. In fact, in the past decade, all of a sudden, quietly, mysteriously, the Republican Party has become the party of ideas.

We became the party of the most brilliant and dynamic young minds. I remember them, just a few years ago, running around scrawling Laffer curves on table napkins—[*laughter*]—going to symposia and talking about how social programs did not eradicate poverty, but entrenched it; writing studies on why the latest weird and unnatural idea from the social engineers is weird and unnatural. [*Laughter*] You were there. They were your ideas, your symposia, your books, and usually somebody else's table napkins. [*Laughter*]

All of a sudden, Republicans were not defenders of the status quo but creators of the future. They were looking at tomorrow with all the single-mindedness of an inventor. In fact, they reminded me of the American inventors of the 19th and 20th centuries who filled the world with light and recorded sound.

The new conservatives made anew the connection between economic justice and economic growth. Growth in the economy would not only create jobs and paychecks, they said; it would enhance familial stability and encourage a healthy optimism about the future. Lower those tax rates, they said, and let the economy become the engine of our dreams. Pull back regulations, and encourage free and open competition. Let the men and women of the marketplace decide what they want.

But along with that, perhaps the greatest triumph of modern conservatism has been to stop allowing the left to put the average American on the moral defensive. By average American I mean the good, decent, rambunctious, and creative people who raise the families, go to church, and help

out when the local library holds a fundraiser; people who have a stake in the community because they are the community.

These people had held true to certain beliefs and principles that for 20 years the intelligentsia were telling us were hopelessly out of date, utterly trite, and reactionary. You want prayer in the schools? How primitive, they said. You oppose abortion? How oppressive, how antimodern. The normal was portrayed as eccentric, and only the abnormal was worthy of emulation. The irreverent was celebrated, but only irreverence about certain things: irreverence toward, say, organized religion, yes; irreverence toward establishment liberalism, not too much of that. They celebrated their courage in taking on safe targets and patted each other on the back for slinging stones at a confused Goliath, who was too demoralized and really too good to fight back.

But now one simply senses it. The American people are no longer on the defensive. I believe the conservative movement deserves some credit for this. You spoke for the permanent against the merely prevalent, and ultimately you prevailed.

I believe we conservatives have captured the moment, captured the imagination of the American people. And what now? What are we to do with our success? Well, right now, with conservative thought accepted as mainstream thought and with the people of our country leading the fight to freedom, now we must move.

You remember your Shakespeare: "There is a tide in the affairs of men which, taken at the flood, leads on to fortune. Omitted, all the voyage of their life is bound in shallows and in miseries. On such a full sea are we now afloat. And we must take the current when it serves, or lose our ventures." I spoke in the—[*applause*]. It's typical, isn't it? I just quoted a great writer, but as an actor, I get the bow. [*Laughter*]

I spoke in the State of the Union of a second American revolution, and now is the time to launch that revolution and see that it takes hold. If we move decisively, these years will not be just a passing era of good feeling, not just a few good years, but a true golden age of freedom.

The moment is ours, and we must seize

it. There's work to do. We must prolong and protect our growing prosperity so that it doesn't become just a passing phase, a natural adjustment between periods of recession. We must move further to provide incentive and make America the investment capital of the world.

We must institute a fair tax system and turn the current one on its ear. I believe there is natural support in our country for a simplified tax system, with still lower tax rates but a broader base, with everyone paying their fair share and no more. We must eliminate unproductive tax shelters. Again, there is natural support among Americans, because Americans are a fair-minded people.

We must institute enterprise zones and a lower youth minimum wage so we can revitalize distressed areas and teenagers can get jobs. We're going to take our revolution to the people, all of the people. We're going to go to black Americans and members of all minority groups, and we're going to make our case.

Part of being a revolutionary is knowing that you don't have to acquiesce to the tired, old ideas of the past. One such idea is that the opposition party has black America and minority America locked up, that they own black America. Well, let me tell you, they own nothing but the past. The old alignments are no longer legitimate, if they ever were.

We're going to reach out, and we need your help. Conservatives were brought up to hate deficits, and justifiably so. We've long thought there are two things in Washington that are unbalanced—the budget and the liberals. [*Laughter*]

But we cannot reduce the deficit by raising taxes. And just so that every "i" is dotted and every "t" is crossed, let me repeat tonight for the benefit of those who never seem to get the message: We will not reduce the deficit by raising taxes. We need more taxes like John McLaughlin [1] needs assertiveness training. [*Laughter*]

Now, whether government borrows or increases taxes, it will be taking the same

---

[1] *Washington executive editor, National Review magazine.*

amount of money from the private economy, and either way, that's too much. We must bring down government spending. We need a constitutional amendment requiring a balanced budget. It's something that 49 States already require—no reason the Federal Government should be any different.

We need the line-item veto, which 43 Governors have—no reason that the President shouldn't. And we have to cut waste. The Grace commission has identified billions of dollars that are wasted and that we can save.

But the domestic side isn't the only area where we need your help. All of us in this room grew up, or came to adulthood, in a time when the doctrine of Marx and Lenin was coming to divide the world. Ultimately, it came to dominate remorselessly whole parts of it. The Soviet attempt to give legitimacy to its tyranny is expressed in the infamous Brezhnev doctrine, which contends that once a country has fallen into Communist darkness, it can never again be allowed to see the light of freedom.

Well, it occurs to me that history has already begun to repeal that doctrine. It started one day in Grenada. We only did our duty, as a responsible neighbor and a lover of peace, the day we went in and returned the government to the people and rescued our own students. We restored that island to liberty. Yes, it's only a small island, but that's what the world is made of—small islands yearning for freedom.

There's much more to do. Throughout the world the Soviet Union and its agents, client states, and satellites are on the defensive—on the moral defensive, the intellectual defensive, and the political and economic defensive. Freedom movements arise and assert themselves. They're doing so on almost every continent populated by man—in the hills of Afghanistan, in Angola, in Kampuchea, in Central America. In making mention of freedom fighters, all of us are privileged to have in our midst tonight one of the brave commanders who lead the Afghan freedom fighters—Abdul Haq. Abdul Haq, we are with you.

They are our brothers, these freedom fighters, and we owe them our help. I've spoken recently of the freedom fighters of

Nicaragua. You know the truth about them. You know who they're fighting and why. They are the moral equal of our Founding Fathers and the brave men and women of the French Resistance. We cannot turn away from them, for the struggle here is not right versus left; it is right versus wrong.

Now, I am against sending troops to Central America. They are simply not needed. Given a chance and the resources, the people of the area can fight their own fight. They have the men and women. They're capable of doing it. They have the people of their country behind them. All they need is our support. All they need is proof that we care as much about the fight for freedom 700 miles from our shores as the Soviets care about the fight against freedom 5,000 miles from theirs. And they need to know that the U.S. supports them with more than just pretty words and good wishes. We need your help on this, and I mean each of you—involved, active, strong, and vocal. And we need more.

All of you know that we're researching nonnuclear technologies that may enable us to prevent nuclear ballistic missiles from reaching U.S. soil or that of our allies. I happen to believe—logic forces me to believe—that this new defense system, the Strategic Defense Initiative, is the most hopeful possibility of our time. Its primary virtue is clear. If anyone ever attacked us, Strategic Defense would be there to protect us. It could conceivably save millions of lives.

SDI has been criticized on the grounds that it might upset any chance of an arms control agreement with the Soviets. But SDI is arms control. If SDI is, say, 80 percent effective, then it will make any Soviet attack folly. Even partial success in SDI would strengthen deterrence and keep the peace. And if our SDI research is successful, the prospects for real reduction in U.S. and Soviet offensive nuclear forces will be greatly enhanced.

It is said that SDI would deal a blow to the so-called East-West balance of power. Well, let's think about that. The Soviets already are investing roughly as much on strategic defenses as they are on their offensive nuclear forces. This could quickly tip

the East-West balance if we had no defense of our own. Would a situation of comparable defenses threaten us? No, for we're not planning on being the first to use force.

As we strive for our goal of eventual elimination of nuclear weapons, each side would retain a certain amount of defensive—or of, I should say, destructive power—a certain number of missiles. But it would not be in our interest, or theirs, to build more and more of them.

Now, one would think our critics on the left would quickly embrace, or at least be openminded about a system that promises to reduce the size of nuclear missile forces on both sides and to greatly enhance the prospects for real arms reductions. And yet we hear SDI belittled by some with nicknames, or demagogued with charges that it will bring war to the heavens.

They complain that it won't work, which is odd from people who profess to believe in the perfectability of man—machines after all. [*Laughter*] And man—machines are so much easier to manipulate. They say it won't be 100 percent effective, which is odd, since they don't ask for 100 percent effectiveness in their social experiments. [*Laughter*] They say SDI is only in the research stage and won't be realized in time to change things. To which, as I said last month, the only reply is: Then let's get started.

Now, my point here is not to question the motives of others. But it's difficult to understand how critics can object to exploring the possibility of moving away from exclusive reliance upon nuclear weapons. The truth is, I believe that they find it difficult to embrace any idea that breaks with the past, that breaks with consensus thinking and the common establishment wisdom. In short, they find it difficult and frightening to alter the status quo.

And what are we to do when these so-called opinion leaders of an outworn philosophy are out there on television and in the newspapers with their steady drumbeat of doubt and distaste? Well, when all you have to do to win is rely on the good judgment of the American people, then you're in good shape, because the American people have good judgment. I know it isn't becoming of me, but I like to think that maybe 49 of our 50 States displayed that judgment just a few months ago. [*Laughter*]

What we have to do, all of us in this room, is get out there and talk about SDI. Explain it, debate it, tell the American people the facts. It may well be the most important work we do in the next few years. And if we try, we'll succeed. So, we have great work ahead of us, big work. But if we do it together and with complete commitment, we can change our country and history forever.

Once during the campaign, I said, "This is a wonderful time to be alive." And I meant that. I meant that we're lucky not to live in pale and timid times. We've been blessed with the opportunity to stand for something—for liberty and freedom and fairness. And these are things worth fighting for, worth devoting our lives to. And we have good reason to be hopeful and optimistic.

We've made much progress already. So, let us go forth with good cheer and stout hearts—happy warriors out to seize back a country and a world to freedom.

Thank you, and God bless you.

Note: The President spoke at 9:35 p.m. in the main ballroom at the Sheraton Washington Hotel. He was introduced by James A. Linen IV, vice chairman of the American Conservative Union.

Radio Address to the Nation on the Fiscal Year 1986 Budget
March 2, 1985

My fellow Americans:

Perhaps you've noticed, as I have, an interesting change in the country in recent weeks. All last year, right through the election and into January, we witnessed a nonstop barrage in speeches, commentaries, and editorials about the dangers of deficits and what must be done to reduce them. I was actually becoming hopeful that new courage was taking root, hopeful that a new consensus to cut Federal spending growth was even emerging among those who've labored a lifetime to expand government size and power.

That was a hasty judgment. For just 1 month ago, the mood of the born-again budget balancers abruptly changed. Now they're suffering from a crisis of faith.

What caused this sudden change of heart? We submitted our budget to Congress, a budget designed to do just what we pledged during the election: tackle the deficits by cutting spending where it's wasteful, where it is not urgent, and where it subsidizes some people at everyone else's expense.

Many of its proposals follow the spirit of recommendations by the Grace commission, some 2,000 citizens who compiled a report on how to cut spending growth without harming the needy or impairing any essential purpose of government. For example, the Small Business Administration has made subsidized loans to only a fraction of the small business community, while the remainder relied on commercial rate financing. Yet, at a time when small business is thriving, many of these subsidized loans are in or near default. We propose ending such subsidies for the benefit of taxpayers at large.

Subsidizing Amtrak costs taxpayers $35 per passenger every time a train leaves a station. But that's not the only unwise transportation subsidy. Why, for instance, should the Federal Government be forcing taxpayers in, say, Colorado to subsidize subway fares in New York? Why should any taxpayer subsidize the operating costs of the Washington, DC, transit system, an area with the second highest per capita income in America?

Yet these and other proposed budget savings have been greeted by a chorus of boos from guess who?—the very people who told us again and again that tough action on deficits couldn't wait. Today they say now is not the time.

Consider the political spectacle of recent days. The House Budget Committee, with its members insisting the deficit must be reduced, travels the country inviting special interest groups to resist every proposal for budget savings. The president of the U.S. Conference of Mayors accuses us of abandoning the Federal Government's commitment to urban America, when the growing noninflationary economy has been creating almost 300,000 jobs a month and record revenues for State and local governments.

Leaders of four higher education associations shiver outside the Department of Education to symbolize, as they put it, that higher education is being frozen out of the budget. Their word "frozen" is meant to describe a proposal that would spend more than $7 billion more than in 1982 and '83 and nearly three times what it was just 10 years ago.

Members of the business community oppose the end of subsidies from the Export-Import Bank. Farm State Senators push multibillion-dollar bailouts for banks and farmers, and one Member even rebukes proposed cutbacks in spending on opera and music in our budget for the National Endowment for the Arts.

This past week the Nation's Governors were in Washington. To their credit, they urged Congress to pass the line-item veto and the balanced budget amendment. But they adopted a resolution that would disallow cost-of-living increases for Social Security recipients and rule out any real increases in defense, yet, as California's Governor Deukmejian pointed out, still leave a higher deficit while paving the way for tax increases.

I won't deny all the groups I mentioned represent valid interests, which may seem compelling. But there is a larger interest to represent, more compelling and urgent than all the rest—the freedom and security of American taxpayers who must not only work, save, and invest to pull our economy forward but also pay all the bills for everything this government does.

Well, as long as I'm President, we're not going back to the days when America was fast becoming an impotent democracy, too weak to meet defense commitments or to resist Communist takeovers and, yes, too weak to stop a Federal spending machine from impoverishing families and destroying our economy with runaway taxes and inflation.

We're asking Congress to have the political courage to cut $50 billion by Easter. If there isn't enough courage to approve these cuts, then at least give me the authority to veto line-items in the Federal budget. I'll take the political responsibility. I'll make the cuts, and I'll take the heat.

Until next week, thanks for listening, and God bless you.

Note: The President spoke at 12:06 p.m. from the Oval Office at the White House.

Message to the Congress Transmitting a Report on the MX Missile
March 4, 1985

To the Congress of the United States:

The attached report on the Peacekeeper missile contains my assessment of the requirement for Peacekeeper and my anticipated impact of the continued procurement of Peacekeeper missiles, pursuant to the provisions of Public Law 98–525, Section 110 of October 19, 1984.

My report concludes that the continued procurement and deployment of the Peacekeeper are essential to national security.

The recommendations of the Scowcroft Commission are still valid. One hundred Peacekeeper missiles should be deployed in existing Minuteman silos as soon as possible.

My report also concludes that Peacekeeper is an essential element of our arms control strategy. Without the Peacekeeper our chances of reaching an equitable agreement with the Soviet Union to reduce significantly the size of our nuclear arsenals are substantially lowered. Indeed, should Congress delay or eliminate the Peacekeeper program, it would send an unmistakable signal to the Soviet Union that we do not possess the resolve required, nor the continuity of purpose, to maintain a viable strategic triad and the policy of deterrence the triad represents.

The time has come to place this issue behind us. While we have debated the merits of the Peacekeeper program, the Soviets have deployed over 600 Peacekeeper type missiles. If we are to move towards an equitable treaty in Geneva, procurement of 100 Peacekeeper missiles must continue.

I urge each member of Congress to approve the Peacekeeper and join me in a bipartisan and united effort in Geneva. With your support, and the support of the American people, our efforts at the negotiation table could lead to the more stable world we all seek, and lead to that day when mankind is free of the terrible threat of nuclear weapons.

RONALD REAGAN

The White House,
March 4, 1985.

Note: The 18-page report was entitled "The President's Report on Continuing the Acquisition of the Peacekeeper (MX) Missile— March 1985."

Statement by Principal Deputy Press Secretary Speakes on the MX Missile Report
March 4, 1985

The President has submitted to the Congress his report on continuing the acquisition of the Peacekeeper missiles as mandated in the fiscal year 1985 defense appropriation and authorization acts.

The report strongly emphasizes the need for continued congressional funding of the MX/Peacekeeper missile, especially the 21 missiles from the FY 85 Defense Department request to be considered by Congress later this month. Congress already approved funding for production of 21 missiles in FY 84, and these missiles are in production, at this time, in preparation for deployment at F.E. Warren AFB in Wyoming beginning in 1986. The full complement of 100 missiles is scheduled to be operational by December 1989. Total cost of the program is $21.5 billion, with approximately half of the funding approved at this time.

The report describes Peacekeeper as ". . . a necessary part of our concerted effort both to improve deterrence and strategic stability and to enhance our ability to achieve deep meaningful arms reductions."

The report also details the buildup in new Soviet strategic weapons, including two new ICBM's, three new bombers, and additions to its submarine missile force. The pace of the Soviet strategic force improvements has given no indication of slackening over the past year.

The President is concerned that a perception may develop in the minds of the Soviets that the United States is unable or unwilling to take the steps necessary to offset their growing strategic power, giving the Soviet leadership confidence it can use its political and military leverage to exert influence against other nations in the world. Furthermore, a growing risk of direct confrontation with the Soviet Union could cause regional powers to become more inclined to accept a greater level of Soviet interference in their affairs. And most dangerously, this perception, the President believes, could over time suggest to the Soviet leadership that the threat or actual use of military force, including nuclear weapons, against the United States or its allies could result in significant military advantages for them.

The report describes all facets of the President's strategic modernization program: the deployment of B–52 bombers with the air-launched cruise missile, continued production of the B–1B strategic bomber, operational deployment of new Trident submarines, initial deployment of the sea-launched cruise missile, new communication systems, preliminary research and development efforts for the new small ICBM, and the successful flight test for the MX/Peacekeeper ICBM.

This final and cornerstone system of the President's strategic program is described as being on cost, on schedule, and as meeting or exceeding every performance goal set for it. The Peacekeeper's superior performance has been verified by seven consecutive successful flight tests of the missile, during which it met or exceeded performance goals. The report points out, however, that a strong modern triad and maintaining deterrence requires more than Peacekeeper flight testing; continued production and deployment of this missile is essential.

The President makes clear the vital role of the Peacekeeper in the forthcoming arms reduction negotiations in Geneva with the Soviet Union. He believes continued procurement and deployment of Peacekeeper is necessary to show U.S. national resolve to modernize the strategic forces, which un-derpin our national policy of deterrence. The President points out that if we fail, on the eve of these new negotiations in Geneva, to proceed with Peacekeeper production and deployment, the impact of our lack of resolve may not be limited to failure of the strategic negotiations, but may affect the broader East-West relationship as well.

In this respect, the President believes a cancellation or slowdown of Peacekeeper deployment in existing Minuteman silos would give the unmistakable appearance of a lack of national resolve on the part of the United States. There would be little reason for the Soviets to engage in meaningful arms reduction initiatives without Peacekeeper because they will have achieved their desired goal with no concessions on their part whatsoever.

The President believes the strategic modernization program to be vital for the defense of the United States, necessary for meaningful arms reductions negotiations, and vital to our continued deterrent posture. He urges the Congress to continue funding the Peacekeeper missile system, the cornerstone of the strategic modernization program.

Remarks at the Annual Legislative Conference of the National Association of Counties
March 4, 1985

Well, thank you very much. I'm delighted to have another chance to talk to NACo. Before I say anything else, I want to thank you for the solid support that you've given us during these past 4 years. It's been a pleasure working with Phil Elfstrom and with all of you, and congratulations on 50 years of service to America's 3,106 counties, and a special welcome to the 7 past presidents of your outstanding association who are with us here today.

You stood with us when the going was rough, and I'll never forget your encouragement here in Washington and in counties all across America. Just before I came over here, I had the chance to look at your association's statement on our budget proposal. As you know, last week we met with our nation's Governors and with State legislative leaders, and I couldn't help thinking that if the definition of a good budget proposal is to distribute dissatisfaction evenly, ours is a real winner. [*Laughter*]

Seriously, I know that you're facing tough problems and tough decisions in many of your counties. In fact, I'm reminded of a story about a local official—or local officials who were planning to build a new bridge, and they discussed location and design and construction and timing and cost, and then they got around to financing. And part should be paid by the city, part by the county, they said, and part by the suburbs, and part by the State. The tough question was how much by each. And there were strong differences of opinion because no matter how it was divided up, it meant more State, county, and local taxes. And there was no solution in sight until one eager fellow at the end of the table stood up and said, "Hold it, we're wasting our time. Let's just get the money from Washington, then nobody'll have to pay for it." [*Laughter*]

And, you know, because of wrongheaded thinking like that, when we met during your 1981 legislative conference, there wasn't much good news to report. Our national economy was near the breaking point, and so were our local communities. We'd paid a steep price for years of good intentions badly misdirected. Families were desperate in the face of double-digit inflation, 21½-percent interest rates—the prime rate—and high taxes, all of which sent the economic growth into a tailspin. And local governments didn't escape the punishment.

High inflation and low growth hit your counties with a double whammy, increasing your costs and squeezing your tax base. Your cost-revenue gap widened. Labor costs increased, and services had to be cut. Dramatic increases in bond rates knocked many of you out of the bond market, and there was no choice but to delay infrastructure projects.

As you know too well, Federal programs provided no magic solution. In fact, years of compulsive spending had taken a heavy toll. It was almost as if some economic medicine man had the idea that since money could buy anything, and Federal programs could provide everything, then more money and more programs were the answer to all our problems. But the dramatic increase of Federal participation in local government only complicated your problems.

To make matters worse, the shift of power toward Washington moved us away from the very principles that had kept our country on a sound footing for most of our history. Calvin Coolidge, one of our most underrated Presidents, put it well: "Our country," he said, "was conceived in the theory of local self-government. It has been dedicated by long practice to that wise and beneficient policy. It is the foundation principle of our system of liberty."

When Cal Coolidge was President, taxes—Federal, State, and local—were taking a dime out of every dollar earned, and two-thirds of that dime went to State and local government. By 1980 taxes were up to 35 cents of every dollar, and three-fifths of that came to Washington.

No wonder communities had lost control of some of the most basic decisions affecting everyday life. As the Federal Government grew more intrusive, you became less able to respond to community needs. And to top it off, Federal oversight—a fancy term that usually means burdensome regulations and unnecessary paperwork—did little more than put you in handcuffs.

We knew that America could not move forward until local communities were back on their feet again. And that's why, back in March of 1981, we asked for your support to embark on a new course. It's been 4 years, and we've begun well, but it's only a beginning. I believe that in lifting your communities toward a new era of lasting prosperity and stability there are four keys to success.

First, we must continue working to return power to levels of government closer to the people. We believe that when it comes to running county government, county officials will always do better from the county seat than bureaucrats could ever do from Washington.

From the first days of our administration, I heard over and over from local officials that you wanted regulatory relief and reform. We agreed and have been reducing cumbersome and unnecessary Federal oversight regulations. The cut in wasteful overhead has been dramatic: 647 pages of regulations have been eliminated, and the paperwork burden at State and local levels has been cut by 90 percent. We estimate that local governments have been spared at least $2 billion in annual costs and between $4 billion and $6 billion in startup costs. And we're still looking for ways to save you more.

Now, the second key to success is a revitalized public-private partnership, pooling our resources to harness the power and creativity of the marketplace for the benefit of all Americans. No single sector of our nation—government, business, labor, or nonprofit organizations—can solve our problems alone. But by working together, pooling our resources, and building our strengths, we can accomplish great things.

Partnerships produce jobs. The Job Training Partnership Act gives local governments new flexibility, and by using private industry councils it matches local needs with sensible training. Now, that's a genuine partnership for real jobs with a bright future.

And there are more genuine partnerships that can be ours, if only the Congress would give our enterprise zones and our youth employment opportunity wage bill a full hearing. We want hope and opportunity to reach every nook and cranny of our great land, and these initiatives deserve your support.

The third key to our nation's prosperity is strengthening traditional values for a modern age, promoting a renewal of community life, and reviving the social fabric of our society—safety on the streets, excellence in education, voluntarism, and a sense of responsibility.

People coming together in a spirit of community and neighborhood is what makes the smallest rural hamlet or the largest urban center worth living in. It's what keeps businesses in your counties and attracts new ones, and it's what keeps faith with the fine traditions of the past, as we turn to build the future.

For too many years, crime and the fear of crime robbed our communities of their vitality, threatened our sense of well-being, and frightened away new investment.

Well, common sense is beginning to pay off. For the first time in 20 years, the crime index has fallen for 2 years in a row. We've convicted 7,400 drug offenders and put them, as well as leaders of organized crime, behind bars in record numbers. And as you've read and seen recently, we are stepping up the pressure, and we're not going to stop until we wipe out organized crime in America.

In the area of education, we're seeing a strong, new commitment to excellence, stressing the basics of discipline, learning, rigorous testing, and homework. And that commitment, too, is also paying off. For 20 years scholastic aptitude test scores of our

high school students went down. But now they've gone up 2 of the last 3 years.

And this spirit of renewal, from Lincoln County, Maine, to Oakland County, Michigan, on out to Orange County, California, is the American spirit at its best. And we see it everywhere we look, from the record rise in corporate and private giving to thousands of exciting and important private sector initiatives, from neighborhood watch programs to increased attendance in places of worship, and from love of country rediscovered by our young people who've led the way to the millions of Americans who, in their quiet, caring way, are pulling together to move us forward and upward.

The fourth and most important key to success is strong and steady economic growth. A vibrant economy is our single most powerful tool for revitalizing every county in America. In fact, I believe that our economic expansion is the most important county improvement program, urban renewal program, and rural recovery program in America today.

The final economic figures for 1984 are in, and they're even better than anticipated. The U.S. economy grew at a rate of almost 5 percent in the fourth quarter, and final sales increased at a rate of 8½ percent. Overall economic growth for the calendar year measured just a shade under 7 percent. Inflation was under 4 percent for the second year in a row, and that's the lowest in 17 years. And when you add it up, 1984 gave America its strongest economic performance since 1951.

As our recovery enters its 28th month, with more than 7 million new jobs created during the past 2 years, Americans have good reason to look to the future with pride and confidence.

We intend to prolong and protect this wonderful expansion with a sweeping program of tax reform and with a Federal budget that reflects the reality that our economic recovery is a triumph of free people and their institutions, not government.

Tax reform and simplification will be a giant step toward lasting prosperity. I believe our tax system currently acts as the single, biggest threat to stronger enterprise and lasting economic expansion. Many of our citizens are required to pay more than their fair share of the tax bill, while others are permitted to pay far less. Today's tax code drives money needed for investment and future growth and unproductive tax shelters—or into unproductive tax shelters. And hundreds of millions of dollars are wasted in needless paperwork. Plain and simple, the tax code is unfair, inequitable, counterproductive, and all but incomprehensible.

And there's something else to keep in mind, something I told our nation's Governors just last week. During the debate of our 1981 tax bill, we pointed out that the most important effects of substantially reducing tax rates just might be the intangibles: the feeling of a positive political and economic climate for enterprise and growth and the message that government wants the people and business to succeed.

Well, it's time to send out another message—one of determined commitment to lasting growth and a secure future—by making the system more fair and easier to understand, so we can bring personal and corporate income tax rates further down.

Now, in speaking of our fiscal 1986 Federal budget, let me remind you of an observation by Thomas Jefferson: The principle of spending money to be paid by posterity, under the name of funding, is but swindling futurity on a large scale.

Ray Larson, chairman of the Cass County Board of Commissioners in North Dakota, and one of your contemporaries, said to us: "We know that many political subdivisions will have to scramble to meet current program expenses if federal monies are lost; however, if these programs are important on a local level, they should be subject to the scrutiny of a local electorate . . . No federal program is more important than the economic security of the country."

There's great wisdom in those words. Over the past 10 years, while Federal tax revenues grew by $400 billion, Federal spending grew by $600 billion—50 percent faster. And during that same decade, government spending grew one-third faster than the growth of our economy.

If there's to be a secure economic future for our children, we must make sure that those days never return. The public treasury is a trust, not a gift shop. And we must move toward a budget that spends no more than government takes in. Either we move in that direction or we will never be able to pass on a legacy of economic security.

We cannot and will not do this by raising taxes—period! We must ensure that the economy grows faster than the growth in Federal spending.

The fiscal 1986 budget stops the built-in momentum of spending increases dead in its tracks. Our proposal will freeze overall Federal program spending at the fiscal 1985 level, cut $51 billion out of programs in need of restraint, and reduce spending growth by half a trillion dollars over the next 5 years.

Now, these tough but essential measures are driven by economic necessity and plain old common sense. Now, I understand that every budget dollar saved is a dollar someone expected to receive. And I know that your counties face difficult problems.

Less than 3 months ago I met with Earl Baker, the chairman of your tax and finance committee, to discuss the unique problems facing local government. And over the past few weeks, many of you've taken the time to write to me about our plans for general revenue sharing. I appreciate your comments, and I was aware that nearly $2 billion of the $4.6 billion in annual funds went directly to your counties. Indeed, I've been one of the strongest boosters for general revenue sharing, as you've been quick to point out. General revenue sharing has served us well.

But the fundamental question remains: How can we afford revenue sharing when we have no revenues to share? How can the Federal Government justify, strapped as it is with a deficit, borrowing money to be spent by State, county, and local governments, some of which are running surpluses?

I sympathize with your position on this issue, but the Federal spending dollar is not magic, and it certainly isn't free. It comes straight out of your pockets, and I just have to believe that over the long haul you'll be a lot better off with the Federal Government's hands out of your pockets.

On another front, the time is long overdue to end what have become indefensible subsidies. Because when you look at some of them, you just shake your head.

Every time a passenger boards an Amtrak train, the American taxpayer pays about $35. But on the New York to Chicago train, it's much higher. In fact, on that run it would cost the taxpayer less for the Government to pass out free plane tickets.

The mass transit Federal subsidy is another headshaker. In Miami the $1 billion subsidy helped build a system that serves less than 10,000 daily riders. That comes to $100,000 a passenger. It would have been a lot cheaper to buy everyone a limousine.

And then there's the air carrier subsidy, started in 1978 for communities thought to be hurt by airline deregulation. At one time the General Accounting Office found that the subsidy for one round trip airline ticket from Blythe, California, to Los Angeles cost $1,096. For that money the air traveler could have flown to Hawaii, stayed a week on the beach, and returned with money left over. And with due apologies to Los Angeles, I'll bet he or she would have had a better time. [*Laughter*]

Nearly 50 years of government living beyond its means has brought us to this time, to this budget, to this day of reckoning. It's up to us to have the courage to make sure that the American taxpayer is protected from the Government.

And, as usual, it's the people outside of Washington who are providing leadership. 32 States and, as of last week, the National Governors' Association as well, have called for an amendment long overdue, an amendment mandating the Federal Government spend no more than it takes in.

It seems incredible that the chief executives of 43 States and many of your own county executives have line-item veto authority, but the President of the United States does not. I've told the Congress that this is a time for political courage. We're asking for $50 billion in spending cuts by Easter. If that courage is lacking, then let them at least give me the line-item veto. I'll take the responsibility, I'll make the cuts, and I'll take the heat.

While you're here in town and up on Capitol Hill, I'd appreciate your reinforcing that message for me. Tell them it serves me

right. [*Laughter*]

But let me turn briefly to another matter, a matter of overriding importance. In a few days American negotiators will leave for Geneva for the most important set of arms discussions this nation will likely conduct in this decade. As talks begin, each House of Congress will cast a vote that will directly, perhaps dramatically, affect the outcome at Geneva. Now, that vote is on release of the funds for the Peacekeeper missile, or MX— a vital component of a long-overdue modernization of America's deterrent, the deterrent that has kept the West free, independent, and secure for nearly 40 years.

Just as a strong bipartisan congressional vote to move ahead with Peacekeeper would send a signal that America comes to Geneva united and resolute, so a negative vote in either House would undercut our negotiators and send a message to Moscow that America is an irresolute and divided nation, whose divisions can be exploited at Geneva. That must not happen. When it comes to standing up for a national defense that is second to none, there should be no Democrats, no Republicans, only Americans.

You and I know that reaching a new era of lasting prosperity and stability will take much effort and patience and great cooperation between us. I just hope that I can count on NACo to continue to work with us in a spirit of good will in the months ahead. I've sought and appreciated your advice and will continue to do so.

We all want what is best for the American people. We can make it happen. And with your leadership and our partnership, it will happen.

And let me just say one more thing. I have felt for a long time, and felt especially as a Governor in one of our States, that many of the problems that had come to local government had to do with that shift from two-thirds of the tax dollar going to local and State government, instead of almost two-thirds going to the Federal Government. And I believe that one of the things in this partnership I've mentioned that I can do—or we can do for you is continue to bring down the Federal Government's share of the tax burden, instead of preempting and confiscating so much of the tax source that when you're faced with a problem, there's no place left for you to turn, except to ask for money from the Federal Government. I think it would be a lot better if we get back to only taxing what should be our fair share and leaving you tax sources out there that you can use for problems which you see at your own level and have decided to do something about.

Thank you, and best wishes for a most successful conference, and God bless you all.

Note: The President spoke at 1:29 p.m. in the International Ballroom at the Washington Hilton Hotel. In his opening remarks, the President referred to Philip B. Elfstrom, president of the association.

Nomination of William L. Ball III To Be an Assistant Secretary of State
March 4, 1985

The President today announced his intention to nominate William L. Ball III to be an Assistant Secretary of State (Legislative and Intergovernmental Affairs). He will succeed W. Tapley Bennett, Jr.

Mr. Ball most recently served as administrative assistant to Senator John Tower (R-TX). Previously, he served as administrative assistant to Senator Herman Talmadge (D-GA) (1978–1980); staff assistant with the Senate Armed Services Committee (1977–

1978); and legislative assistant to Senator John Tower (1975–1977). From 1969 to 1975, he served as a commissioned officer in the U.S. Navy (active duty). He is currently a lieutenant commander with the Naval Reserve.

Mr. Ball graduated from the Georgia Institute of Technology (B.S., 1969). He is married and resides in Washington, DC. He was born June 10, 1948, in Belton, SC.

Proclamation 5306—National Consumers Week, 1985
March 4, 1985

By the President of the United States of America

A Proclamation

America's economy has been revitalized by the highest level of consumer confidence in nearly twenty years. Our free enterprise system and the high productivity of American workers have made such economic growth possible, providing the American consumer with an unprecedented choice of goods and services.

As the range of consumer choice increases, competition compels our businesses to provide even greater value for consumer dollars. Increasingly, business leaders respond to consumer expectations by improv-

ing the quality, safety, and effectiveness of their products. Competition also generates reliable servicing.

This year's slogan for National Consumers Week, "Consumers Should Know," highlights the right of consumers to information about the products offered them. Knowledgeable, selective consumers make their dollars count. In that way, families not only enjoy better products but are able to put more money aside for future needs. Those savings translate into business investments, and that means growth for our Nation's economy.

Buyers and sellers alike should recognize the basic rights of consumers: the right to choice among products and services; the right to information enabling them to make sound purchases; the right to healthful and safe products; the right to be heard when products do not meet standards. Government at all levels will continue its responsible stewardship of consumer safety as well as its vigorous prosecution of illegal and deceptive practices. But in the final analysis it is the knowledgeable consumer and the responsible business person whose decisions will determine the success or failure of products and services in the competitive marketplace.

In celebration of National Consumers Week, I encourage schools, community organizations, labor unions, businesses, the media, and consumers themselves to help further public awareness of consumer issues and services. I urge American consumers to take advantage of this opportunity to seek and use the wealth of information available to all.

Now, Therefore, I, Ronald Reagan, President of the United States of America, do hereby proclaim the week beginning April 21, 1985, as National Consumers Week.

In Witness Whereof, I have hereunto set my hand this fourth day of March, in the year of our Lord nineteen hundred and eighty-five, and of the Independence of the United States of America the two hundred and ninth.

RONALD REAGAN

[*Filed with the Office of the Federal Register, 11:10 a.m., March 5, 1985*]

Letter to the Speaker of the House and the President of the Senate on Nuclear Cooperation With EURATOM
March 4, 1985

Dear Mr. Speaker: (Dear Mr. President:)

The United States has been engaged in nuclear cooperation with the European Community for many years. This cooperation was initiated under agreements concluded over two decades ago between the United States and the European Atomic Energy Community (EURATOM) which extend until December 31, 1995. Since the inception of this cooperation, the Community has adhered to all its obligations under those agreements.

The Nuclear Non-Proliferation Act of 1978 amended the Atomic Energy Act to establish new nuclear export criteria, including a requirement that the United States have the right to consent to the reprocessing of fuel exported from the United States. Our present agreements for cooperation with EURATOM do not contain such a right. To avoid disrupting cooperation with EURATOM, a proviso was included in the law to enable continued cooperation until March 10, 1980, if EURATOM agreed to negotiations concerning our cooperation agreement, which it did.

The law provides that nuclear cooperation with EURATOM can be extended on an annual basis after March 10, 1980, upon determination by the President that failure to cooperate would seriously prejudice the achievement of United States non-proliferation objectives or otherwise jeopardize the common defense and security and after notification to the Congress. President Carter made such a determination five years ago and signed Executive Order 12193, permitting continued nuclear cooperation with EURATOM until March 10, 1981. I made such determinations in 1981, 1982, 1983 and 1984 and signed Executive Orders 12295, 12351, 12409 and 12463, permitting continued nuclear cooperation through March 10, 1985.

In addition to numerous informal contacts, the United States has engaged in six rounds of talks with EURATOM regarding the renegotiation of the U.S.-EURATOM agreements for cooperation. These were conducted in November 1978, September 1979, April 1980, January 1982, November 1983 and March 1984. The European Com-

239

munity is now considering U.S. proposals relating to our cooperation agreements, and further progress in the talks is anticipated this year.

I believe that it is essential that cooperation between the United States and the Community continue and, likewise, that we work closely with our Allies to counter the threat of nuclear explosives proliferation. A disruption of nuclear cooperation would not only eliminate any chance of progress in our talks with EURATOM related to our agreements, it would also cause serious problems in our overall relationships. Accordingly, I have determined that failure to continue peaceful nuclear cooperation with

EURATOM would be seriously prejudicial to the achievement of United States nonproliferation objectives and would jeopardize the common defense and security of the United States. I intend to sign an Executive Order to extend the waiver of the application of the relevant export criterion of the Nuclear Non-Proliferation Act for an additional twelve months from March 10, 1985.

Sincerely,

RONALD REAGAN

Note: Identical letters were sent to Thomas P. O'Neill, Jr., Speaker of the House of Representatives, and George Bush, President of the Senate.

Executive Order 12506—Nuclear Cooperation With EURATOM
March 4, 1985

By the authority vested in me as President by the Constitution and statutes of the United States of America, including Section 126a(2) of the Atomic Energy Act of 1954, as amended (42 U.S.C. 2155(a)(2)), and having determined that, upon the expiration of the period specified in the first proviso to Section 126a(2) of such Act and extended by Executive Orders No. 12193, 12295, 12351, 12409 and 12463, failure to continue peaceful nuclear cooperation with the European Atomic Energy Community would be seriously prejudicial to the achievement of the United States nonprolif-

eration objectives and would otherwise jeopardize the common defense and security of the United States, and having notified the Congress of this determination, I hereby extend the duration of that period to March 10, 1986.

RONALD REAGAN

The White House,
March 4, 1985.

[*Filed with the Office of the Federal Register, 11:11 a.m., March 5, 1985*]

Memorandum Urging Support of the Federal Management Improvement Program
March 4, 1985

Memorandum for the Heads of Executive Departments and Agencies

Subject: Management of the Federal Government

We came to Washington in 1981 pledged to reduce the size, cost, and inefficiency of the government. Much has been achieved

in only four years, but this huge task is not completed. In 1984, we promised renewed commitment to the full and lasting achievement of our management goals. Now, it is time to redouble our efforts.

We have made great progress in reducing waste and fraud through the efforts of our

President's Council on Integrity and Efficiency. Forty-six billion dollars have been put to better use in the past four years.

And we have also made a good start on the massive task of improving the management of the Federal government by reducing the size of the Federal work force in civilian agencies, controlling administrative overhead costs, developing effective cash and credit management systems, improving the delivery of services, reducing program error rates, enhancing Federal productivity, and making more effective use of modern computer and communications technology. It is an evolving success story and one in which we can all take pride.

Last month, as a companion document to the FY 1986 Budget, the first annual management report was transmitted to the Congress. This new report, *The Management of the U.S. Government,* is a description of comprehensive interagency efforts including Reform '88, the President's Private Sector Survey on Cost Control in the Federal Government, and other initiatives being implemented as part of this Administration's Management Improvement Program.

However, we cannot rest in our efforts to reform, revitalize, and restructure the U.S. Government. The implementation of a massive management improvement program like this requires your personal support. Therefore, I am asking you, as the head of your agency, to commit to an increased effort to implement the initiatives in our new management report to improve the management efficiency and effectiveness of your agency.

Only through your continued commitment, the enthusiastic support of your staff, and a redoubling of our efforts can we leave the American public with a permanent legacy of a more efficient and effective Federal government.

RONALD REAGAN

Nomination of John R. Norton III To Be Deputy Secretary of Agriculture
March 5, 1985

The President today announced his intention to nominate John R. Norton III to be Deputy Secretary of Agriculture. He would succeed Richard E. Lyng.

Mr. Norton is currently president and chief executive officer of J.R. Norton Co., an agricultural production company which he founded in 1955. He is involved in numerous business and civic organizations, holding various positions including director and past chairman of the United Fresh Fruit and Vegetable Association; director of the Arizona Public Service Co.; director and member of the executive committee of the Central Arizona Project Association; and director and past chairman of the Western Growers Association.

Mr. Norton graduated from the University of Arizona (B.S., 1950). He served in the Air Force as a first lieutenant from 1953 to 1955. He is married, has three children, and resides in Paradise Valley, AZ. He was born April 10, 1929, in Glendale, AZ.

Message to the Congress Transmitting the Italy-United States Social Security Agreement
March 5, 1985

To the Congress of the United States:

Pursuant to section 233(e)(1) of the Social Security Act, as amended by the Social Security Amendments of 1977 (P.L. 95–216;

42 U.S.C. 433(e)(1)), I transmit herewith the Supplementary Agreement between the United States of America and the Italian Republic on the matter of social security, signed at Rome April 17, 1984.

The U.S.-Italy social security agreement is similar in objective to the social security agreements in force with Belgium, Canada, the Federal Republic of Germany, Norway, Switzerland, and the United Kingdom. Such bilateral agreements, which are generally known as totalization agreements, provide for limited coordination between the United States and foreign social security systems to overcome the problems of gaps in protection and of dual coverage and taxation for workers who move from one country to the other. The present Supplementary Agreement with Italy would amend the original agreement to update and simplify

several of its provisions which have caused both countries unforeseen and unnecessary administrative difficulties.

I also transmit for the information of the Congress a comprehensive report prepared by the Department of Health and Human Services, which explains the provisions of the Supplementary Agreement, as well as the effect on social security financing as required by the same provision of the Social Security Act.

The Department of State and the Department of Health and Human Services join with me in commending the U.S.-Italy Supplementary Social Security Agreement and related documents.

RONALD REAGAN

The White House,
March 5, 1985.

Remarks Following Discussions With Prime Minister Bettino Craxi of Italy
March 5, 1985

The President. I'm honored today to welcome Prime Minister Craxi back to the United States. Since your visit in October of 1983, Mr. Prime Minister, you've taken on a new responsibility—assuming the Presidency of the European Community.

We're pleased to have had this opportunity to meet with you as a friend, as a leader of a great nation, and as the representative of the European peoples. Cooperation between Italy and the United States is at a level unsurpassed in our history.

Your country, Mr. Prime Minister, is an ally second to none. Our efforts have kept the peace in Europe for almost 40 years. Italy has played an active role in the cause of peace. It continues to do so today in the Middle East, an area which, as Prime Minister Craxi explained, is of special importance to Italy.

And today the Prime Minister and I also discussed East-West relations and arms control. We reviewed the approach the United States will take in the coming Geneva talks.

And the Prime Minister reconfirmed Italy's continued steadfastness on INF development—deployment, I should say.

We also discussed the Strategic Defense Initiative. The Prime Minister assured me of Italy's full understanding of the program's objectives, and we agreed on the great potential benefits this research effort could provide. We firmly agree that now is the time for alliance solidarity. And our goal remains the reduction and eventual elimination of the means of aggression, nuclear and conventional.

In another area of cooperation, we look forward to a productive Bonn summit. I affirmed to the Prime Minister the high priority we place on undertaking a new round of trade negotiations by early 1986. These talks are necessary, not just to forestall a possible slide back toward protectionism, but to take new steps for freer and more open trade and a stronger world economy.

The United States and Italy are two of the world's great democracies. Our bilateral relations, reflecting our shared values, are on a high plane. When the Prime Minister last visited, we decided to improve our coordination and cooperation against narcotics. And I'm happy to report that our initiative has now yielded an effective new instrument to combat this scourge—our Binational Working Group on Narcotics and Organized Crime.

Our common fight against terrorism is another area of close cooperation, and Italy deserves accolades for its courageous struggle against terrorism. I know I speak for all Americans in thanking you publicly, Mr. Prime Minister, for Italy's successful thwarting last November of a potential bomb attack against our Embassy in Rome.

As the head of a vital, vibrant democracy, nurtured by statesmen like yourself and your illustrious predecessors, you and your coalition partners have put Italy in the forefront of the world's functioning democracies. You've demonstrated your unequivocal and compelling commitment to Western values. We're grateful to the Italian people as our friends and allies. And we're also proud, Mr. Prime Minister, to welcome your historic address to the Congress tomorrow. It will, I'm certain, be another milestone in the numerous and long-lasting ties between our two countries.

Mr. Prime Minister, America welcomes you with her warmest friendship, and we salute you and your partners and wish you continued success.

The Prime Minister. I wish to thank President Reagan for the warm welcome he has extended to me. My visit to this great, friendly nation has a particular importance in view of the responsibilities which fall upon Italy now that it is holding the Presidency of the European Community. Our talks have been extensive, open, and very constructive.

I have renewed to President Reagan the heartfelt congratulations of the Italian Government and my own personal ones for the great consensus received at the recent Presidential elections. I have also congratulated him for his success in expanding the American economy which has resulted in greater employment.

The United States has succeeded in the hard task of combining modernization of productivity with the creation of new jobs. Europe and the United States should work together to achieve coordinated action and initiatives which are necessary to improve transatlantic economic cooperation to mutual benefit.

I have expressed to President Reagan my assessment of the issues which Italy follows with the utmost attention: first of all, those of peace, security, development, and the safeguarding of the rights of peoples. And while also illustrating the programs and prospects of the Ten [European Community member nations] for a wider community integration, I have stressed that our willingness to proceed towards European unity is consonant with the framework of constant strengthening of the European-American partnership through a balanced relationship and more effective mutual responsibility.

Again, on this occasion, I have realized how deep and strong are the bonds of friendship, alliance, and cooperation between Italy and the United States. It is our firm intention to continue to strengthen them. I have particularly appreciated the special consideration shown by President Reagan and his administration for Italy and for the development of Italian-American relations. I consider this attention as a recognition of the consistency and the commitment shown by the Italian Government in making a positive contribution to the search of more stable international equilibria in the field of defense, as well as in the economic and political ones.

Our exchange of views confirmed the existence of broad and encouraging convergence, since I am convinced that the basic goals of the United States policy remain defense and peace based on a balance of forces. The President has assured me that these same goals will be pursued through the SDI, from whose research program we will draw mutual advantages in the scientific and technological field.

We attach a fundamental importance to the success of the forthcoming Geneva negotiations. We are firmly convinced that a substantial, balanced, and verifiable reduction of armaments is the essential condition for a stabler and safer peace. We will work hard to strengthen confidence so that this negotiation and those which are taking place in other fora may develop under the best possible circumstances.

There are no substitutes for the negotiation process. An agreement on a gradual and balanced elimination of armaments and on the organization of peace based on an accepted and recognized balance is in the interest of all.

We have discussed the Middle East situation and noted with satisfaction the emergence of positive signs indicating that there is a possibility of reactivating the negotiation process towards a political solution of the Arab-Israeli crisis. We both noted with interest the recent Jordanian-Palestinian dialog. We hope that this agreement will shortly allow for a joint Arab stand on the opening of realistic negotiations with Israel.

We agreed to keep in constant contact in order to effectively support all positive steps towards a just, global, and lasting peace in the Middle East.

In my talks here in Washington, we also examined the international economic situation and exchanged views on ways and means to consolidate and strengthen economic recovery within the context of greater stability. We must harmonize our national efforts so that the beneficial results of recovery will be fully reflected on the occupational levels.

However, we cannot pay attention only to our own economic prosperity. The increasing serious problems in the Third World are a matter of great concern. We must help in seeking solutions to them. We agreed to hold effective consultations between our governments on these issues in order to ensure the success of the summit conference of the industrialized nations,

which will take place in Bonn on May 2d through the 4th.

Having just visited Latin America, I also emphasized, in my talks here, the great importance of the return of democracy in the highly civilized nations of that continent and drew attention to the expectations for the democratic solidarity of the peoples living there who aspire to a regime based on freedom.

Last year I worked out with President Reagan a program for a more effective bilateral cooperation in the fight against drug traffic and organized crime. The results have been positive and significant. Our cooperation has been carried out with mutual satisfaction. We will continue these efforts, while trying at the same time to improve bilateral and multilateral agreements so as to defend our democratic system against any rise of the threat of international terrorism.

I wish to thank President Reagan for this fruitful exchange of views. It was, for me, a confirmation of how much the sharing of values and aspirations, in a context of long-standing friendship, makes it easier to reach mutual understanding and agreement on how to cope with and solve problems for which we have responsibilities not only as governments but for which we have responsibilities to our own peoples.

Note: The President spoke to reporters at 1:28 p.m. at the South Portico of the White House. Prime Minister Craxi spoke in Italian, and his remarks were translated by an interpreter. Earlier, the President and the Prime Minister met in the Oval Office and then attended a luncheon in the State Dining Room.

Appointment of Henry R. Beasley as a United States Commissioner on the Inter-American Tropical Tuna Commission
March 6, 1985

The President today announced his intention to appoint Henry R. Beasley, of the National Marine Fisheries Services, Department of Commerce, to be a United States

Commissioner on the Inter-American Tropical Tuna Commission. He would succeed Gerald V. Howard.

Since 1971 Mr. Beasley has been with the

National Marine Fisheries Services and is currently serving as the Acting Director. Previously he served as foreign affairs officer in the National Marine Fisheries Services and its predecessor agency, the Bureau of Commercial Fisheries (1967–1971). He was involved in the collection, analysis, and editing of information for various publications of the Bureau of Commercial Fisheries from 1957 to 1967.

Mr. Beasley graduated from Emory University (B.A., 1949) and Emory University Law School (LL.B., 1952). He is married, has one child, and resides in Washington, DC. He was born October 4, 1929, in Thomasville, GA.

Nomination of George S. Rosborough, Jr., To Be a Member of the National Museum Services Board
March 6, 1985

The President today announced his intention to nominate George S. Rosborough, Jr., to be a member of the National Museum Services Board, National Foundation on the Arts and the Humanities, for a term expiring December 6, 1988. He would succeed C. Douglas Dillon.

Mr. Rosborough is currently chairman of the St. Louis Community Foundation. He is also president emeritus of the St. Louis Art Museum. He has served as the director of the Business Committee for the Arts, a member of the board of the Associated Council for the Arts, and as a member of the trustees committee of the American Association of Museums.

Mr. Rosborough graduated from Grinnell College (B.A., 1940). He is married, has two children, and resides in Clayton, MO. He was born September 27, 1918, in St. Louis, MO.

Remarks to Private Sector Leaders During a White House Briefing on the MX Missile
March 6, 1985

I appreciate this opportunity to speak with all of you today. I learned early on that if an issue was important enough, the best thing is to go directly to the people and enlist their help. And once the people are mobilized, they don't have to make politicians see the light, they just make them feel the heat. [*Laughter*]

So, of course, asking for help suggests a certain degree of trust, which reminds me of a story. It has to do with a fellow that fell off a cliff, and he grabbed a limb on the way down and there he hung, dangling above the rocky canyon. And he looked up and didn't see anyone. And he finally shouted out, "Oh, Lord, if you're up there, tell me what to do!" And a moment later, a voice came booming down from the heavens that said, "If you have faith, let go!" Well, he took another look down at those rocks 200 feet below and then looked up again and says, "Is there anyone else up there?" [*Laughter*]

Well, we can be thankful that we're not in that kind of situation, but we as a people do face a decision that's vital to the safety of our country. And that's why I've asked you here today. One of the most sacred duties of any President is keeping America secure and at peace. And peace and security are not free commodities; they're precious, and like everything of great value, there's a price to pay.

During the 1970's, perhaps as a reaction to the confusion and the division over the

245

Vietnam war, the strength of our conventional and strategic forces was permitted to erode; and by 1980 it was clear that a weaker America was not a safer America and that it was time to get down to the business of strengthening our defenses.

I was elected in 1980 and reelected a few months ago, pledging to put our economy back on track and to rebuild our defenses. Modernizing our strategic forces was vital. We unilaterally refrained from deploying many new strategic systems in the 1970's—unilaterally refrained, even as the Soviets rushed forward to expand and upgrade their nuclear capability, testing and deploying at least three new intercontinental ballistic missile systems and stationing them in the hardened silos. More than 800 new missiles with some 5,000 warheads were added to their arsenal.

Nuclear war would be the greatest tragedy, I think, ever experienced by mankind, in the history of mankind. And we've avoided that tragedy because we've maintained a credible deterrent force. We can't afford to play political games with the delicate balance of deterrence. No room should be left for doubt about a nuclear exchange; no one would win.

That reality has worked well for 30 years. And yet if we're not willing to modernize our forces to keep our systems current, the credibility of deterrence will vanish. Knowing this, we began immediately to make up for the irresponsibility of the seventies and to revitalize the three legs of our nuclear triad. We've had some success—the Trident submarine and the B-1 bomber will go a long way toward filling the gap—but you can't sit on a three-legged stool if there's only two legs. The third leg means the Peacekeeper missile, as we call it, the MX. Our current, aging land-based missiles are suffering from attrition. The 22-year-old Titan missiles are being retired, leaving our land-based missile force with less and less punch with which to deter aggression. And that's one of the reasons we need the Peacekeeper. It's the most reliable and accurate land-based missile America has ever produced. It'll bring our deterrent to a state-of-the-art level and reinforce the futility of attack on [by] any potential adversary.

Whether or not that message is sent now

depends on the Congress. We've proposed the production and deployment of 100 Peacekeeper missiles, a minimum investment needed for the security of our country. A blue-ribbon bipartisan commission, the Scowcroft commission, studied the security requirements of the United States and agreed; prominent Democrats, like the late Senator Henry "Scoop" Jackson, also agreed. "If America maintains a strong deterrent, and only if it does," Scoop Jackson said, "this nation will continue to be a leader in the crucial quest for enduring peace among nations."

Well, the Senator knew the price of living free, secure, and at peace. Senator Jackson—well, I can assure you—I might as well say—I don't enjoy spending money, that might have struck you already that that's—if it wasn't absolutely essential to the security of our country, my conservative philosophy would rebel at taxing money away from those who've worked hard to earn it. I grew up in the age of Coolidge. Some people think it was McKinley, but, no, it was—[laughter]—it was Coolidge. [Laughter] And he was a champion of thrift and economy in government, and yet even he knew the importance of strength—there we were in that postwar period immediately after the war to end all wars when, I think, most of us felt that we had ended all wars.

But in his 1925 inaugural address, Coolidge said: "Our country represents nothing but peaceful intentions toward all the Earth, but it ought not to fail to maintain such a military force as comports with the dignity and security of a great people. It ought to be a balanced force, intensely modern, capable of defense by sea and land—beneath the surface and in the air. But it should be so conducted that all the world may see in it, not a menace, but an instrument of security and peace."

Well, that's the spirit with which we must move forward in this debate. We've requested a minimum number of Peacekeepers—only 100. This number is far too few for any first strike, and it underscores the purely defensive nature of our proposal. The missile is now in production, and the costs are reasonable and under control, and funding would not add to the deficit, because it's already been appropriated in the fiscal '85 budget. What's more, we've had seven excellent test launches.

Of course, there are those who will continue to search for any reason to vote "No." If the decisions were determined that way, our military could have no weapons at all; and this would be fine, except that the Soviets would not be suffering from the same handicap. Our goal is to negotiate with the Soviets, to reach agreements which will permit us to reduce the number of weapons threatening mankind, both nuclear and conventional.

And as you are aware, next week we will begin negotiations in Geneva. The vote on the Peacekeeper is also a vote on Geneva, and the Soviets are watching this with intense interest. So, let no one misjudge what is at stake.

Rejecting the Peacekeeper will knock the legs out from under the negotiating table, leaving the Soviets no conclusion but that America lacks unity and resolve. I can think of no greater disaster for the negotiating position of the United States; weakness does not make for good negotiations.

This isn't a new revelation. President Teddy Roosevelt said it a long time ago: "We need to keep in a condition of preparedness," he said, "not because we want war, but because we desire to stand with those whose plea for peace is listened to with respectful attention." The success we've had in getting the Soviets to the negotiating table or getting their "respectful attention," as Teddy would say, can be traced not to vacillation, but to firmness and sense of purpose.

We pledged that if the Soviets would not work with us to reduce the number of their intermediate-range missiles aimed at Europe, we would deploy our cruise and Pershings to balance the threat. Our courage and that of our allies let the Kremlin know that we will not compromise our security and that we have the political will to stick with it. We mean no threat to them, but we'll not permit them to pose a threat to us.

There should be no mistake—a rejection of the Peacekeeper will diminish our chance of reaching a fair and equitable arms reduction agreement now or in the future. Without the Peacekeeper, the Soviets will have little incentive to discontinue their buildup or to reach agreements with us.

Years ago I was a negotiator for my union. When we picked a team and sent them to the bargaining table, we stood behind them; unity was the key to success— then we were seeking higher wages and better working conditions. The team we're sending to Geneva will be seeking peace and security for our country and the free world. It's the American team, and I need your help in backing them up.

I hope that we can count on you to get the message out that *now* is not the time to cancel a major weapons system or undercut our allies or to reward Soviet belligerence. Now is the time for American courage, unity, and resolve—time to stand together behind our team in Geneva so they can represent us with all the vigor and confidence that they can muster.

The Soviets respect this kind of resolve. Andrei Sakharov, a courageous voice for peace in the Soviet Union, understands this. He won the Nobel Peace Prize, and he holds the respect of the world for his struggle for peace and human rights. Well, he wrote to a friend in the West that arms control talks with the Soviets would be easier if the U.S. were to have the MX. He knew the risk of sending a message like that.

Peace is not easy to maintain; it'll take hard work and diligence. It'll take unity and sense of purpose, and yes, it will cost money. This generation of Americans must meet the test. That's up to us.

And I hope I can count on you, all of you, to give us help in this. There have been four wars in my lifetime. And I've said before, I don't know of a single war—one of those four—that was fought because the United States was too strong. The truth of the matter is, the two World Wars were because people on the other side looked at us, looked at our military weakness, and decided we wouldn't fight.

I don't think we should ever have to fight a third time under those circumstances. And I don't want us to ever have to fight at all.

So, thank you for joining us today, and God bless you all.

And I'm going to place you in the capable hands of Secretary Weinberger. I don't think he'll argue with any of the points that I just made. [*Laughter*] Thank you all very much.

Note: The President spoke at 2:04 p.m. in *the East Room at the White House. Attending the briefing were leaders from various business, labor, ethnic, and other interest groups. Following the President's remarks, Secretary of Defense Caspar W. Weinberger and Robert C. McFarlane, Assistant to the President for National Security Affairs, addressed the group.*

Remarks and a Question-and-Answer Session With Reporters on Signing the Veto Message for the Farm Credit and African Famine Relief Bill
March 6, 1985

The President. I am not signing the piece of legislation that came down to me today. I am signing a veto.

[*At this point, the President signed the veto message to the House of Representatives.*]

And I would like to make a statement with regard to that to my fellow Americans. And they all know some of our farmers are facing severe financial problems. They're living with the results of a generation of failed policies that drove down farm prices, drove up the cost of their land, seed, and equipment. And then in the late 1970's, they were hit again by runaway inflation and interest rates, grain embargoes that robbed them of long-term markets.

Farmers who've toiled to make America productive, growing food and fiber for all of us and millions beyond our shores, deserve our sympathy and our support. And the Federal Government mustn't shirk its responsibility to help undo some of the damage that it created. And with spring planting upon us, we're meeting that responsibility.

Last September we initiated a carefully targeted effort to direct special help to farmers with credit problems. And just last month we modified this new program to ensure its effectiveness.

This year, under plans that I approved, the Federal Government will make nearly $4½ billion in credit available to farmers. We will also spend just over $15 billion to support the price of farm commodities. We're doing a great deal to help farmers. But I've pleaded and warned repeatedly that, just as your families don't have a blank check for whatever your needs may be, neither can government—and that means taxpayers—bail out every farmer hopelessly in debt or every bank which made imprudent or speculative loans and bet on higher inflation. I asked for help. I asked Congress, which just days ago was bemoaning the size of deficits, to demonstrate courage—hold the line and match rhetoric with deeds. Congress failed. In the first major bill since convening in January, a majority proved itself incapable of resisting the very tax and spend philosophy that brought America to its knees and wrecked our economy.

So, today I have vetoed this massive new bailout that would add billions to the deficit over the next several years. And let's be clear on one thing: The bill I vetoed would not really help farmers; it's too late in the season for that. This bill is merely designed to convey the impression of helping farmers.

But if Congress wants to help, it will help us reduce unnecessary spending and increase incentives for greater real economic growth, which will provide confidence to the markets and help interest rates come further down.

Let me add that my veto will not interfere with the African relief effort now underway. Using authority and existing law, we can maintain the flow of emergency assistance.

The bottom line is that someone in Washington must be responsible. Someone must be willing to stand up for those who pay America's bills. And someone must stand up to those who say, "Here's the key, there's the Treasury, just take as many of those hard-earned tax dollars as you want."

I applaud and thank the 35 Senators and 168 Members of the House who courageously stood with me on this issue. And now that I've vetoed this bill, I hope the Congress will get the message and work with me to reduce spending in a responsible way that does not threaten our national security. If it doesn't, then I'll do what must be done. I will veto again and again until spending is brought under control. So, please help me by telling your representatives to stop talking about deficits and to start helping me bring them down.

Thank you. God bless you.

Q. Mr. President, are you confident that this veto will stand up in Congress?

The President. Well, I believe if those in Congress vote as they voted for the piece of legislation and if they vote that same way with regard to a veto, yes, it will be upheld.

Q. The Democrats say that the farmers who voted for you are going to feel betrayed and are going to take this out on other Republicans. What do you think the political fallout of this will be? Aren't you hurting Republicans?

The President. Well, the thing is, if the farmers would only consider this, they would recognize that we are helping. I've just given the figures there—$4½ billion that's already planned for their help, plus $15 billion. We have spent $50 billion on aid to farmers in the last 4 years. More than that in the last 3 years, as a matter of fact.

And what I said in there with regard to figures doesn't touch on the additional program that in September—Secretary Block initiated several new issues: a 5-year set-aside of up to 25 percent to a maximum of $200,000 of a FmHA borrower's interest payments; $650 million in guarantees for refinancing up to 90 percent of the restructured commercial loans, provided the private sector lender writes off 10 percent of

the principal or interest on the loan. Now, up till now, only about $25 million of that 650 has been used—has anyone sought it.

And then on February 6th, Secretary Block initiated additional measures to build upon the September initiatives: The Farm Credit Coordinating Group, chaired by him, will make sure that all Federal credit agencies work closely together to solve the farm liquidity problems; modified Federal regulations will make it possible for banks to work out lower payments for farmers having liquidity problems; and guarantees of up to 90 percent of operating loans will be provided for eligible farmers whose local banks fail and who can't find a new private lender without such a guarantee. Now, some lenders have been unwilling to participate in this program, but that was due to the uncertainty about whether something better might come out of the Congress. But these are the things we're doing.

The truth of the matter is: In need of immediate help are less than 4 percent, or around 4 percent at best, of all the farmers in the United States; 96 percent do not have any liquidity problems.

Q. Well, the Democrats seem to think they have a pretty hot political issue. Do they?

The President. Well, I would rather treat with the issue as it relates to our own financial problems with the Federal Government and not as a political issue.

Q. Do you think they're playing politics with it, sir?

The President. You'll have to ask them. But I certainly don't think that tying this to a bill on food aid for the starving people in Africa was exactly the way to go in this kind of legislation. As a matter of fact, it emphasized the real need for a line-item veto.

Q. Mr. President, would you sign the food aid bill if the farm provision was stripped away?

The President. Yes. But again, let me reiterate what I've said that as of right now there is going to be no interruption of the aid that we're giving because of funds that are already available.

Q. The Senate Budget Committee yesterday voted to cut your defense budget by $11 billion. Doesn't that show a lack of support for your defense program just as we're going to Geneva?

The President. Well now, Chris [Chris Wallace, NBC News], I took your questions here that had to do with the issue of the day, and I'd rather limit it to that. And I think I should, rather than we get into a general press conference. There'll be time coming up for us to talk about those other things.

Q. Well, it is Congress.

The President. What?

Q. It is Congress.

The President. Yes, but I've been meeting and—with a great many of them on both sides of the aisle—and there's evidence of some willingness to stand together on these other matters. So, if you don't mind, I'll make my way out the door now, all right.

Q. Mr. President, do you think it's appropriate for Mr. Deaver and the others to have taken a discount on those cars?

The President. Now, that's another question that doesn't have to deal with the farm problem.

Q. Well, would you nod or shake your head?

The President. But you're talking about something that has gone on for a great many years, that exists in our Embassies in all other countries. It's a standard practice that's been used for many, many years.

Q. So, you see nothing wrong with what he did, sir?

The President. No.

Reporter. Thank you.

The President. Yes, thank all of you.

Note: The President spoke at 4:16 p.m. in the Oval Office at the White House. Michael K. Deaver was former Deputy Chief of Staff and Assistant to the President.

Message to the House of Representatives Returning Without Approval the Farm Credit and African Famine Relief Bill
March 6, 1985

To the House of Representatives:

I am returning without my approval H.R. 1096, a bill to authorize emergency relief for victims of famine in Africa and to establish additional farm credit programs that would add a minimum of $2.5 billion to the deficit over the next several years.

I should note at the outset that my veto of this bill will not interfere with the African relief effort now under way. Using authority in existing law, we can continue to provide relief in the near term, but I urge the Congress to act expeditiously on the request for additional relief authority I submitted earlier this year.

My disapproval of this bill is based on objections to the farm credit provisions, which are completely unacceptable and unnecessary in view of measures already instituted by my Administration.

Title II of the bill would alter the regulations governing the special Debt Adjustment Program that I announced last September. The bill would institute a series of changes that would primarily benefit banks at the expense of farmers and taxpayers. Another of its provisions would establish a new program to pay banks to reduce the interest rate on loans to certain farmers. This program, although initially limited to $100 million, would soon grow into an uncontrollable, multi-billion dollar annual spending spree. A third section of this title would require bank regulatory agencies to refrain, under a vaguely delineated standard, from classifying adversely delinquent loans to farmers and ranchers. This provision would inject uncertainty into the authority of the regulatory agencies charged with ensuring the soundness of our banking system, provoke needless litigation, and possibly jeopardize the interests of depositors in banks that have made agricultural loans.

Title III of the bill would require establishment of a program of "advance loans" from the Commodity Credit Corporation of up to $50,000 per farmer. This provision would have added a minimum of $7 billion to fiscal year 1985 outlays, only part of which would be returned in 1986. By distorting the purpose of the basic Federal mechanism for stabilizing farm prices, this provision risks serious disruption at harvest time as well as long-term damage to the soundness of Federal farm programs.

I share the concern for problems facing certain of our farmers this year. That is why I have taken a number of steps to strengthen existing programs and to institute a new Debt Adjustment Program to help financially strapped farmers refinance their existing

debt.

It is time to get on with the job of making these programs work. That will require the cooperation of all concerned, but most important of all, it will require an end to the uncertainty that would be created by hasty legislation requiring massive changes in rules just as the planting season begins.

RONALD REAGAN

The White House,
March 6, 1985.

Remarks at a White House Meeting With Members of the National Newspaper Association
March 7, 1985

Well, I want you all to know how delighted I am that you're here with us again. This is the fifth year now that we've had the privilege of having you as our guests, and I feel as though we've sort of grown up together. [*Laughter*] I hope that doesn't offend anyone. Actually, as far as I'm concerned, none of us is really any older. We're just better. [*Laughter*] You know, as Cardinal Spellman used to say: There are three ages in life—there's youth, middle age, and "Hey, you're looking great." [*Laughter*] Always spoken with a little surprise.

Well, that brings up the story about a cub reporter who went out to interview a 65-year-old man who'd just won the local marathon. And the fast-paced gentleman explained that vitality was a part of his family heritage. "After all," he boasted, "my father's 90 years old and he's still swimming a mile every day." He said, "and my grandfather is 110, just got married for the third time." And the young reporter asked why he would want to do that. And the runner said, "Who said he wanted to?" [*Laughter*]

All this talk about age is not really accidental; I'm aware that you're celebrating your 100th anniversary. And here at the White House we do issue our share of messages and congratulations, yet yours was and is very special. As the message of congratulations suggests, community newspapers had their origins in the early days of our nation in the struggle for independence and liberty. As our political parties grew and democracy flourished, the newspaper business also came of age. And today, with enormous advances made in technology, you're even more capable than in the past of bringing to your hometowns timely, provocative, and comprehensive coverage of what concerns and affects your readers.

I know that local news—what's happening in your communities—is one of the real important focuses for your newspapers. I think it's interesting that the new technology, leading to such mass developments as newspaper chains and television networks, is now being put to use by many of you to strengthen the very thing that so many people said the modern age would help to eliminate, and that is the sense of community—the rich diversity and the difference that exists in America's towns and cities.

I think you also know that at the Federal level we're trying to do the same thing. The administration has always believed that the real source of America's economic and social progress is not national edicts and mandates that are issued from Washington, but the toil and creativity of her people working at the local level through their own private institutions and associations.

And that's why we are trying to shrink

the cost and the size of the Federal Government, bring its expenditures under control, transfer as much of its power as we can back to the States and localities, where it will be subject to more control by the people themselves and, I might add, to more scrutiny by their watchdogs, those of you of the local press.

It hasn't been all that easy. Federal expenditures during the 15 years before we took office went up 400 percent, and the number of Federal programs escalated beyond belief, so much so—and I think this is interesting—no one's been able to come up with a way of counting exactly how many such programs currently exist in our government. Government and regulations were America's biggest growth industry.

And now, at last, we're putting a stop to that. I won't go through all the statistics about how we're cutting the number of programs and regulations, the rate of growth in spending, or elaborate on the amount of power that we're returning to the people in the local communities. I think the best measure of our success is the change in the climate here in Washington.

All of you can remember that a few years ago the surest way to headlines and success for Washington politicians was to propose another Federal initiative in spending extravaganza, to laugh at the deficit and claim that we could spend our way to prosperity. Well, now, at least, our elected officials publicly acknowledge that deficit spending is a serious problem and that spending yourself rich is a little bit like drinking yourself sober. But they still have a ways to go from talking about bringing deficits down to bringing deficits down.

And you know one additional point here is important. Perhaps you've noticed that when some newspapers start to lose their impact, they do it by trying to cover everything on the international and national scale but lose their real focus—what's important to the people in their local community. Well, it's always fascinated me that as government grows larger and larger and started to do more and more things it was neither intended to do or competent enough to handle, it grew less capable of carrying out its traditional and far more important functions: maintaining civil order and pro-

tecting our national security.

Even as we fought to get the Federal behemoth under control during these past few years, we were emphasizing these traditional and most important duties of government. I think many of you have been reading and writing about our success against crime, much of it the result of a sweeping organized crime initiative that we announced a few years ago.

So far, we've also been moving against the dangers to our national security. We've come a long way from the days when the growth of totalitarianism was unchecked and America was routinely held up to world humiliation.

But all the work of the past few years—the rebuilding of our military strength and our international stature—depends on the continued support of the American people and the Congress. And very shortly, one critical vote will be held on the Hill on one of the mainstays of our strategic defenses: the MX missile. And, oh, how I wish they had listened to Barry Goldwater when that thing started a few years ago, because he said, "Why don't we just call it Minute Man IV and no one will raise a fuss of any kind." [*Laughter*] Because in reality, it is a modernization of what we have in the silos now—the II and the III are out-dated and way behind the state of the art.

And I'm very grateful for the editorial support that all of you've given us in the past on so many issues, but let me emphasize this morning that MX is one of the most critical items on the national agenda. I know I don't have to tell you it just isn't those of us at home who will be watching the vote—the world is watching too, and especially those with whom we're now trying to negotiate arms control and reduction measures in Geneva. A vote now against the MX would be interpreted as a sign of weakness, a symbol of disunity; and it could be interpreted by some as a signal to exploit rather than seriously negotiate the arms reduction process.

We need passage of the MX program; we need it now. We need it for the success of our arms reduction efforts, and we need it for the sake of our future. And there we are again talking about the future and the passage of time. I know that many of you during these past few years have gone through the business of hiring young reporters and executives in your business, and I know that sometimes you must reflect on how young they are and counsel them on the work and adventures that await them.

And that's what it really is all about. Passing on to another generation and the generations after them this thing called the American dream—making sure it remains a beacon of hope to a troubled but waiting world. You've been doing that now through this association for a hundred years. And during the past 4 years, especially, all of us together have come a long way toward bringing back excitement and energy to that dream.

So, this morning I want to thank you all for your editorial support in the past and ask your support for the future, particularly on that crucial MX vote, and wish you, at the same time, all a very happy birthday.

I would like to just point out because I know that there's kind of an image created with regard to defense spending—would you be interested to know with relation to the gross national product, defense spending is considerably lower than it has been over the past, back in the fifties and back in the Kennedy days, and as a percentage of gross national product. We tend to overlook that. It isn't the great stupendous increase that everyone thinks it is; it's actually a lower percentage. In Kennedy's years, it was almost 50 percent of the budget; here it isn't 30 percent, and it is a smaller percent of the gross national product at the same time.

But before I—and, incidentally, also, our negotiators will leave this weekend for Geneva. And I can't tell you that passing the MX will guarantee a good arms reduction treaty with the Soviet Union; but I can guarantee you that a vote against it and not passing it will make that kind of a treaty much more difficult, if not impossible. The fellows on the other side of the table aren't there out of good will; they're there for the reason that Margaret Thatcher said to our Congress just a few days ago: They're there because of our strength; that's why they've

come back to the table. And they see a determination on our side to maintain that strength.

Well, before I close, I want to speak to you just briefly about a great power for public service that you possess. I'd like to suggest one especially tragic area where your newspapers can do a great deal of good: the problem of missing children.

Well over a million American children disappear from their homes or neighborhoods every year causing, as we can all understand, heartbreaking anguish. Parents cry out for help, many through letters to me. For example, I learned about Jonelle Matthews of Greeley, Colorado, who would have celebrated a happy 13th birthday with her family just last month. But 5 days before Christmas, Jonelle disappeared from her home.

Letters like these touch us deeply, and we've tried our best to help. Last June we opened the National Center for Missing and Exploited Children, which runs a toll-free hotline and gives other aid as well. But a President can only do so much. So, today I'd like to ask for your help.

We saw how reaction to the television program "Adam" led to recovery of at least 36 missing children. We also know how milk carton manufacturers have begun putting photos of missing children on milk cartons. If your newspapers—and forgive me for sticking my nose into your business—but if you could publish, as a regular feature, pictures and descriptions of children missing in or near your circulation areas, I know that you would give the police a welcome new source of leads that could solve some of these cases. So, I'm asking you to enlist your newspapers in this mission of mercy. Even if it only finds one missing child, it's worth it.

So, I'll thank you for what you can do to help. And I'll thank you also for coming, and God bless you all, and a happy birthday.

Note: The President spoke at 11:55 a.m. in Room 450 of the Old Executive Office Building.

Remarks to the United States Negotiating Team for the Nuclear and Space Arms Negotiations With the Soviet Union
March 8, 1985

The challenge of statesmanship is to have the vision to dream of a better, safer world and the courage, persistence, and patience to turn that dream into reality. Since the dawn of the nuclear era, all God's children have lived with the fear of nuclear war and the danger of nuclear devastation. Our moral imperative is to work with all our power for that day when the children of the world can grow up without the fear of nuclear war.

So, today we reaffirm that vision: a world dedicated to the elimination of nuclear weapons, a world in which technology provides ever greater safety rather than greater fear. Today we set out on a new path toward agreements which radically reduce the size and destructive power of existing nuclear missiles.

Soviet leader Konstantin Chernenko said last month: "Our ultimate objective here is the complete elimination of nuclear weapons everywhere on this planet, the complete removal of the threat of nuclear war." Well, I welcome that statement and assure Mr. Chernenko that the elimination of nuclear weapons is also the ultimate objective of the American government and the American people.

It's now our task and responsibility to take practical steps to turn this vision into reality. We should have no illusions that this will be easy, since any venture of this magnitude will take time. And since the most vital security interests of both sides are at stake, this will clearly be long and difficult. We're realistic because we know that our differences with the Soviet Union are great. Patience, strength, and unity—Western unity—will, therefore, be required if we're to have a successful outcome.

Next week the United States and the Soviet Union meet in Geneva to begin a new dialog on these issues. And above all, we seek agreement as soon as possible on real and verifiable reductions in American and Soviet offensive nuclear arms. For our part, the United States is ready with firmness, patience, and understanding to negotiate fair and equitable agreements reducing the dangers of nuclear war and enhancing strategic stability.

I've just concluded a very good meeting with our three negotiators—Ambassadors Max Kampelman, John Tower, and Mike Glitman—which culminates an extensive round of preparations. In the meeting I gave my instructions for the first round of talks. These instructions enabled our negotiators to explore every promising avenue for progress. And they have my personal support.

Like Americans everywhere, I want these negotiations to succeed and will do everything I can to ensure that this happens. And I pray that the Soviet leadership is prepared to make the same commitment.

I want to thank our team for the fine work that they've already done in getting ready for this endeavor. As all of you prepare to leave for Geneva, I can't think of a more welcome message than an unmistakable vote of confidence from the American people and the Congress.

Ambassadors Kampelman, Tower, and Glitman and all the members of our negotiating team, I know that all of our fellow Americans wish you every success. And I know from my conversations with the bipartisan leadership of the Congress that the Congress of the United States joins in supporting you.

So, to all of you—those who will be at Geneva and those who will be supporting this crucial effort from Washington—best wishes, and God bless you.

Note: The President spoke at 10:11 a.m. in the Roosevelt Room at the White House. Earlier, the President met with the U.S. negotiators in the Oval Office.

Nomination of Donald J. Devine To Be Director of the Office of Personnel Management
March 8, 1985

The President today announced his intention to nominate Donald J. Devine to be Director of the Office of Personnel Management for a term of 4 years. This is a reappointment.

Dr. Devine has served as the Director of the Office of Personnel Management since 1981. He was given the United Negro College Fund's Humanitarian Award for his efforts in conducting the Government's annual charity drive, the Combined Federal Campaign. An award given by AMVETS recognized his efforts on behalf of veterans employed as civilian government employees. The District of Columbia Rehabilitation Association presented him with their Employer of the Year Award in 1984 in recognition of the fact that OPM hired the largest number of handicapped individuals of any Federal Agency or private sector firm in the Washington area during 1983. A former professor of government and politics at the University of Maryland (1967–1981), Dr. Devine has authored a number of books, including The Political Culture of the United States; The Attentive Public; Does Freedom Work?; and most recently Reagan Electionomics, 1976–1984. In 1978 he was the Republican nominee for State comptroller of Maryland.

Dr. Devine graduated from St. John's University (B.B.A., 1959), City University of New York (M.A., 1965), and Syracuse University (Ph.D., 1967). He is married, has four children, and resides in Wheaton, MD. He was born April 14, 1937, in Bronxville, NY.

Appointment of Warren B. French, Jr., as a Member of the President's National Security Telecommunications Advisory Committee
March 8, 1985

The President today announced his intention to appoint Warren B. French, Jr., to be a member of the President's National Security Telecommunications Advisory Committee. He would succeed Robert H. Snedaker, Jr.

Mr. French is currently chairman of the United States Telephone Association and president of the Shenandoah Telecommunications Co. He is also vice chairman, National Exchange Carrier Association; director and past president of Virginia Exchange Carrier Association; director of Southern Net, Inc.; director and chairman of the board of SouthernTel of Virginia, Inc.; and director of the First National Bank of Strasburg.

Mr. French graduated from the University of Virginia (B.S., 1947). He is married, has three children, and resides in Edinburg, VA. He was born April 14, 1923, in Woodstock, VA.

Nomination of Jacob Neusner To Be a Member of the National Council on the Arts
March 8, 1985

The President today announced his intention to nominate Jacob Neusner to be a member of the National Council on the Arts, National Foundation on the Arts and the Humanities, for a term expiring September 3, 1990. He would succeed Jessie A. Woods.

Mr. Neusner has been at Brown University since 1968, serving as a professor of religious studies, university professor, and Ungerleider Distinguished Scholar of Judaic

Studies (since 1982). Previously, he was assistant professor (1964–1966) and associate professor (1966–1968); research associate at Brandeis University (1962–1964); and assistant professor of Hebrew at the University of Wisconsin (1961–1962).

Mr. Neusner graduated from Harvard College (A.B., 1954) and Columbia University (Ph.D., 1960). He is married, has four children, and resides in Providence, RI. He was born July 28, 1932, in Hartford, CT.

Designation of Paul E. Thornbrugh as United States Commissioner on the Kansas-Oklahoma-Arkansas River Commission
March 8, 1985

The President today announced his intention to designate Paul E. Thornbrugh as United States Commissioner on the Kansas-Oklahoma-Arkansas River Commission. He would succeed Richard W. Soudriette.

Mr. Thornbrugh has been corporate coordinator for governmental affairs for MAPCO since 1966. Previously he was divi-

sion manager for tax, insurance, and claims with Phillips Petroleum Co. in Wichita, KS.

Mr. Thornbrugh attended the University of Kansas and Tulsa University. He is married, has four children, and resides in Tulsa, OK. He was born April 15, 1921, in Olathe, KS.

Radio Address to the Nation on the MX Missile
March 9, 1985

My fellow Americans:

I'd like to talk to you today about the deep desire we all share to keep America free, secure, and at peace. In 3 days' time, American and Soviet negotiators will meet in Geneva to explore ways to reduce nuclear arsenals and lower the risks of war.

No issue concerns me more and none has taken up more of my time than our quest for a breakthrough on arms reductions. I do so willingly because as your President and as a husband, a father, and a grandfather, I know what's at stake for everyone. And I'm pleased that the Soviets, after staying away

for more than a year, have agreed to return to the bargaining table. The renewal of these negotiations is an important step in the right direction, and America will be ready to move forward on all promising avenues for progress.

As I speak to you, our team is in Geneva. I cannot think of a more welcome message to give them than a strong vote of confidence from you the people and the Congress. I know that all Americans stand foursquare behind our negotiating team and wish them every success. In fact, you're the reason that the Soviet Union returned to the negotiating table. The Soviet leadership has seen your patience and your determination to keep America strong. They've seen the renewal of your spirit and the rebuilding of a robust and expanding American economy. They know we're going to continue moving forward to protect our freedom and our way of life.

I want to believe the Congress will follow your lead, but that's not yet certain, and I need your help. Each House of Congress will soon vote on an issue that will directly and, perhaps, dramatically affect the outcome at Geneva—that vote concerns the modernization of our strategic forces with the MX Peacekeeper missile.

Let me take a moment to explain what that vote is all about. Nearly 2 years ago after a decade of indecision, confusion, and endless debate over the merits of modernizing our aging land-based strategic missiles, our political process forged a bipartisan consensus that united us in our common search for ways to protect our country, reduce the risks of war, and work for dramatically reduced levels of nuclear arms.

The MX Peacekeeper missile has been part of the consensus and with good reason: Time and again, America exercised unilateral restraint, good will, and a sincere commitment to arms reductions. As a result, many of the missiles protecting our security at this very moment are older than the Air Force men and women taking care of them. They're missiles of the sixties, originally equipped with 1950's aerotechnology. It's sort of like a 1963 jalopy with some new parts. You know as well as I do that in many States automobiles that old will soon qualify as antiques, but the Soviets don't deal in antiques. Their response was the same as it's always been: no restraint, just build, build, and build. While we debated and delayed, they developed three new types of land-based intercontinental missiles, and they've added to their arsenal 800 new missiles with more than 5,000 nuclear warheads.

It took us too long to realize there is no easy, cheap way to buy security. In 1983, based on the recommendations of a distinguished blue-ribbon panel, the Scowcroft commission, the Congress joined with us to approve the MX Peacekeeper program— 100 up-to-date missiles that will replace aging Minuteman missiles. Since that time, the MX Peacekeeper has finished seven successful flight tests, and the Soviets are back at the bargaining table.

Well, once again, the moment of truth is at hand. As I mentioned a few minutes ago, each House of Congress will soon vote on whether to release the MX funds they approved last year and continue production of the missile. The Soviet leadership views the current debate on the MX as a key test of American resolve.

If the Congress acts responsibly, our negotiators will have a chance to succeed, but if we don't have the courage to modernize our land-based strategic missile systems, the Soviets will have little reason to negotiate meaningful reductions. And why should they? We would be signaling to them that they can gain more through propaganda and stonewalling than through serious negotiations. The time is now to send a signal loud and clear that a united and resolute America backs our negotiators at Geneva, and that could be the real key to a successful outcome.

My fellow Americans, the stakes are so very high. The vote on the MX Peacekeeper isn't a budget issue; it's about our nation's security. And when it comes to protecting America's security, we can't afford to divide ourselves as Democrats or Republicans—we must stand together as Americans. It's up to you to let your feelings be known. Your voice matters; let it be heard.

Until next week, thanks for listening, and God bless you.

Note: The President spoke at 12:06 p.m. from Camp David, MD.

Interview With Morton Kondracke and Richard H. Smith of Newsweek Magazine
March 4, 1985

Strategic Defense Initiative

Q. We've come to talk as much about the SDI as possible today. And one of the concerns that we have is that, by your own admission, this is a 20-, 30-year process before it really bears fruit. Why so much publicity, so much investment in terms of political and financial resources so early on this?

The President. Well, the only thing I can say about technology and science is that, yes, it could take that long. But how many times have we seen the breakthroughs once you embark on a program of this kind, where suddenly you have it at hand?

But however long it takes, the possibility that there can be a defensive weapon—there's never been an offensive weapon until the nuclear missile that has not given birth to a defense against it. And now the only defense that we have are two sides sitting here with increasing numbers of these weapons saying that our defense is that if you blow our people up, we'll blow your people up. Well, there's certain immorality about this.

I can remember when the rules of warfare, usually negotiated in Geneva, protected noncombatants against war and against the threat of it, that war would take place between the armed forces. And we've departed a long way from that now, when the principal weapon is one whose main characteristic is it would be wiping out populations.

But to go on and think, all right, suppose it takes 20 years? But then suppose for the next 20 years the world is sitting here with ever-mounting piles of nuclear missiles aimed at each other—isn't it worth it to see if we can't come up with a nonnuclear weapon that won't destroy people, will prevent those weapons from reaching their targets, and the goal would be to nullify them, to destroy them before their warheads were separated out—and in a nonnuclear way—so that there wouldn't be any nuclear explosion.

Q. Right. There's been a lot of talk about when you first thought about or heard about this idea. When was that?

The President. I know and it kind of amuses me that everybody is so sure I must have heard about it, that I never thought of it myself. And the truth is, I did. Oh, there's been talk—I think there's a general conversational talk about things of this kind—about what I said earlier that every weapon has a defensive weapon—and then, of course, the antiballistic missile, some years ago, came on the scene and was ruled out.

I know, too, that some of our scientists were thinking in terms of a nuclear response in which nuclear explosions from here that would then prevent the others from coming through. And in one of my regular meetings with the Chiefs of Staff, I brought up this subject about a defensive weapon and that every other weapon had always—there had been a defensive weapon. And I asked them—I said: Isn't it possible that our modern technology today and all that we have been able to develop, that it would be worthwhile to see if we could not develop a weapon that could perhaps take out, as they left their silos, those nuclear missiles? And the Joint Chiefs said that such an idea, they believed, was worth researching.

Q. Yes. But you had supposedly been thinking about this before you became President, even when you were Governor of California?

The President. No. This idea—this latter idea came after I'd heard the other things and, as I say, had been called upon by some of the scientists who were thinking in terms of nuclear explosions to destroy a nuclear explosion. And this came to me—actually, the first time I ever voiced it, I think, was in that room—in the Cabinet Room in there—after we'd had the meeting—it was coming toward the end of the meeting. And when they so much did not, you know, look aghast at the idea and instead said yes, they believed that such a thing offered possibility and should be researched, and I gave the order—I said go.

Q. Mr. President, when the first public announcement of the SDI——

The President. 1983.

Q. ——program——

The President. Yes?

Q. ——came in a speech that was particularly harsh on Soviet behavior and recent Soviet behavior. Are you at all concerned that this will be read as a bargaining chip to be used in the current negotiations with the Soviet Union and future negotiations?

The President. They will find out very quickly that it isn't because—no, what we're doing is not prevented by any treaty—research, there it is. And even Mr. Gromyko himself admitted not too long ago that research—that there's no one who could know whether you're researching or not—there's no way to prevent that. We know that they've been on this kind of research themselves; they've probably been at it for a while longer than we have.

But when I made that speech was when I—by that time, they hadn't wasted any time over at Defense. They had started the research on this and had enough hopeful signs that they were optimistic and were continuing, and so I thought the people ought to know about it.

Q. Again, going back to the long time frame for the development of these weapons, many people have suggested that in this interval the Soviets will take every advantage of the time to build up offensive weaponry to defeat such a system and that perhaps it will be destabilizing in the development period.

The President. Yes. You know, all of this reminds me—all these things, I hear them and these protests about them. And it reminds me of that wonderful cartoon, not too long ago, where the man was sitting watching the TV screen and from the TV the voice was coming out saying that it would never work, that it was too expensive, that you couldn't do it. And his wife was just leaving the room, passing through behind him, and she said, "Well, then why don't the Russians want us to have it?"

Q. [*Inaudible*]

The President. Well, no, and let me say—and this ties in with my previous answer

also—first of all, I thought in speaking as quickly as I knew that actually research was going forward—and there were legitimate scientists saying, "Yes, there is a potential here," that the people ought to be given the hope, that our people ought to know that there may be an answer other than just saying, "Well, if they slaughter us, somebody will slaughter them." Both sides will blow each other up. And I felt it very necessary that they know that.

On this other thing, first of all, I've made it plain that if this research could develop or bring us to the knowledge that we had such a weapon that then I think it ought to be internationalized. There's no intention for this ever to be viewed as giving us a first-strike capacity. I'd be the first one to say, if we had such a weapon, we don't need the offensive weapons. And I would think that it would be very worthwhile if the other side of the world has this—if the potential for the weapon is there and that the research reveals that—but I wouldn't want them to think that we were ever trying for a first strike. I don't think there's an American alive that ever believes that this country would for some reason want to be the first to use nuclear weapons on them.

Q. But they're not Americans, the Soviets, and——

The President. No.

Q. ——they don't have our sensibilities. Then why wouldn't they look at this and look at the technological, perhaps, superiority of the United States and be scared that we were going to use it for that reason and build up as many offensive weapons as they could in the meantime?

The President. Because there's another and a better answer, and they themselves have voiced it. We're going to Geneva and both Gromyko and Chernenko—maybe others, I don't know about them; but at least these two on several occasions lately have said that their purpose, their goal is the total elimination of nuclear weapons. Now, we'll accept that goal and strive with them to meet that goal. And it seems to me that this, if it developed, could be an aid in bringing that about.

Just suppose today that we were able to

say, "We have discovered a thing that now can make it very difficult, if not impossible, to get a nuclear weapon through to the target." Well, then, wouldn't you sit down in Geneva and say, "Well, there's just another reason why we ought to do away with these things."

MX Missile

Q. Well, let's go to Geneva a second. If SDI research is not negotiable and is not a bargaining chip, is the MX a bargaining chip? Is that why you're appealing to Congress and the country to give you the MX?

The President. No, the MX is not a bargaining chip in the sense of we'd need something to give away—not at all. This is a long-overdue modernization, and modernization in all of the treaties, including the one not signed, SALT II, has been recognized. We are sitting here with our land-based missiles outdated by anything and any comparison with the Soviet Union. They have come up with at least four new weapon systems, all superior in accuracy and megatonnage than our Minuteman missiles. And, as you know, some years ago we even shut down the Minuteman assembly line. We don't even have anything with which to build them. So, here is a weapon that is very definitely needed until and unless we come to a total elimination of weapons.

Even if we came to a build-down, which we're going to optimistically hope we will on the way to the other elimination, this modernization would certainly be in keeping with everything they've done. They say they've come up with at least four systems; they're now testing a couple of additional ones. So, modernizing—that is valid until we decide we don't need weapons at all. So, in the sense of a bargaining chip—no. But where it is valuable at Geneva is if suddenly we're told by the Congress, for example, that we can't have this modernized weapon. The fellows on the other side of the table who have already done their research, who already have all these new weapon systems and some of them bigger, more powerful, and certainly just as accurate and with as many warheads as the MX—they sit there and say, "Why do we have to give up anything?" They have such

a superiority.

Q. So, you would build the MX regardless of any agreement at Geneva?

The President. Oh, yes, and the weapons that you would take out in reducing is just the same as they would do—you'd take out the oldest one first.

Q. Why so much confusion on this? And people within your administration and certainly a lot of people up on the Hill seem absolutely convinced that the MX is a bargaining chip.

The President. Oh, no. I just say this about the MX: I can't guarantee that if we build the MX we will get the kind of a reduction agreement that we want, but I believe I can guarantee you that if we don't get it, we won't get an agreement.

Q. What is the incentive for the Soviet Union to destroy forces that they have in being if they can't trade—if we're going to go ahead with the MX no matter what and we're not willing to trade Star Wars research or Star Wars deployment? What are we willing to trade for a build-down on their side?

The President. Well, as I say, we're talking nothing but research. And I have made it plain, come deployment time if the research yields such a weapon, come deployment, then you sit down. You don't hoard it and say, "Ah, we're stronger than they are." No, you sit down and see how you can internationalize it and use it to further get rid of whatever nuclear weapons might remain.

Strategic Defense Initiative

Q. Why not research it with them from the beginning so that they have confidence that we're not concealing something from them?

The President. Well, they're already doing research and, as I say, probably have gone further than we have in particle-beam weapons, lasers and that sort of thing, and have been very active at it.

Isn't there the possibility that—I don't know, I'm not a scientist—but what if they would use that research then, instead, to find out how to make offensive weapons impervious, that could defeat your defensive weapon?

They are the force that has revealed itself as expansionist; we haven't shown any tendency to be that way. We know, Americans know, that however they may fear us over there, they may think that we're the other—you know that we don't have any aggressive intentions of suddenly going after them with a weapon of this kind. But on the other hand, we have to look at their whole expansionist policy and say they constitute the threat.

As a matter of fact, their own words—there hasn't been a Russian leader yet who has not at some time or other confirmed that he is committed, as they have always been, to the world revolution—the idea of the one world Communist state. Now, can they blame us for sitting here saying we have to protect ourselves against you?

Q. At various times in your speeches you have talked, on the one hand about the Soviet Union as the evil empire, on the other hand that the Soviet Union will end up on the ash heap of history. Are there any contradictions there or——

The President. No, because I've never thought of that from the standpoint of destroying them and leaving them in rubble. No, I have thought of it that the desire and the soul of man—more than any other, as long as man has lived on this Earth—has been for freedom. And I just can't believe that a system such as theirs can continue to hold its people and to hold other peoples in subjugation, and that someday, the people are going to say, hey, there's a better way to do things.

This is my reference to—that their system has been tried and failed. And the other things of calling them evil empire and everything, that wasn't just done for words, the sake of words. I felt, after all of the years of pursuing détente, and détente was usually a one-way street, it never really became a two-way street; unilateral disarmament—hoping they would follow suit and they didn't, they just grew stronger. I thought it was necessary to let them know we were looking at them realistically; that we didn't have any illusions about that they would suddenly take off the wolf's clothing and put on sheepskins. Then—and I think that it maybe has played a part in their willingness to come now and negotiate—

they know—for once, maybe for the first time—they know that we're not going to sit here and let them go on piling up a massive advantage over us.

Q. Do you think that Star Wars or—you don't like the term Star Wars, do you?

The President. Well, no, and I guess because it was first used in an effort to denigrate the whole idea. But again, Star Wars has a sound of—brings an image, maybe from too many television shows or something—but an image of destruction back and forth. And I'm talking about a weapon, nonnuclear, that is, as I say—only destroys other weapons, doesn't kill people.

Q. Right. Do you suppose that the expenditure that they would have to go through in order to build a defensive system of their own would be so onerous on their tottering economy that it could hasten the day of putting them on the ash heap of history?

The President. Well, no, because, as I said, I've never thought of using this weapon offensively, in an offense against them. If their goal is really what they've said it was, we'll meet their goal of the elimination of the nuclear weapons.

Q. But I think what Mort was trying to get at is, are we using this as an economic and a technological weapon as much as a military device——

The President. Oh.

Q. ——that by forcing them to respond with a similar program, that it could create serious economic problems for the Soviet Union?

The President. Well, as I say, there's the potential of them not having to create it. What if the weapon is such and so complete that you'd say, look—because you remember this—we all know how to make nuclear missiles. Now, if you eliminate them by treaty, you always have to wonder is someone sequestering a few away, or since we know how to meet them, could there come a day down the road, possible confrontation, some time of strain, when somebody says, "Hey, let's turn out a few of these?"

Now, if you have the defense weapon, even though the others are supposed to be gone, you don't have to fear whether your verification has been complete or whether someone down the road—a latter-day Qadhafi or someone—is going to say there's a weapon. And if we make it, we can—you know, the mouse that roared—we can rule the world. You've got a proof against that, and I like to draw the parallel—I mentioned gas, earlier—1925, after World War I, everybody met in Geneva and decided to outlaw poison gas; no more poison gas in war.

But isn't it funny. Everybody kept their gas masks; they remained standard issue on all sides as military equipment. And now today, what has happened? We have found that some countries do have it and have used it. So that's, I feel, a little bit—if such a weapon as we're talking about can be developed—that it would be like the gas mask. It'd just be nice to have in case somebody got out the textbook—how you build a nuclear missile—and built one someday.

Q. Is there anything in your experience in dealing with the Soviet Union that suggests to you that they will not try to build up offensively while we are researching Star Wars or that they will not try to match the SDI program?

The President. Oh, I think they're trying to match it, and, as I say, I think they started ahead of us on that, which would be all the more reason, then, why we should have it. If we're right in our suspicions that they are expansionist and—they already outnumber us greatly in the offensive weapons, and then they alone developed a defensive weapon before us, then they wouldn't have to worry about our deterrent—a retaliatory strike. Then they could issue the ultimatum to the world.

So, if there's any thought of that, then it would make it all the more necessary that we have a defensive weapon, too.

Q. How optimistic are you that this Geneva process is actually going to lead to an agreement?

The President. It's hard to be optimistic when you look back at the record. There have been some 19 offers and efforts by ourselves since World War II to seek control of this, including at one time to totally internationalize it and give it to everybody, put it in the hands of an international group.

The open skies proposal of Eisenhower to open both countries up to complete inspection—and all of these things and always the Soviet Union has resisted, even when they didn't have it and when we had the monopoly. But they evidently had seen what it could mean to them, so they were going forward.

So, it's hard to be optimistic. On the other hand, there are a couple of things that lead me to believe there's a possibility. Number one are their own words about voicing—before they even get to the table—this desire to rid ourselves. One of them said to me, just between the two of us, he said, "Can we go on forever sitting on these ever-rising mountains of weapons?" And I said, "No, why don't we start reducing the mountains?" And if we do it evenly and are still sitting on them when we get down here, the mountains aren't so big and we still are safe from each other.

So, what leads me to believe there's hope is not the idea, as I said before, that too often in the past when we've said, well, if they understand how nice we are, maybe they'll be nice, too. No, you'll get an agreement when it is to their practical interest also. All right, we have announced our determination to not let them have the monopoly of power that they've been building.

They know they cannot match us industrially. They sat there in World War II taking the horrible losses that they took before victory, and they saw us—two oceans and two sides of the world—fighting a war. And we even had the one line that—contrary to things they've said since—when Stalin after the war said that without our industrial might, without our help, victory could not have been theirs.

Well, they've never admitted anything like that since. But I think now that that could be the way in which they can say, look, if we're faced with an ongoing arms race with the United States—and they're already pretty much up to full capacity with how far down their people's subsistence level is and all—that they could now see the practical value in saying, well, there is another way—if we start reducing them instead of increasing them.

And this leads me to believe that possibly they can see the practicality of this and do it. This brings to mind—there's another cartoon about this one, and that was some time ago, when the cartoon appeared of the two Russian generals, and the one of them was saying to the other, "I liked the arms race better when we were the only ones in it." [*Laughter*]

Q. We're out of time.

Nicaragua

Q. We're out of time? Do you want to— can we shoo one in on Nicaragua?

Q. Fire away, and see if you can sneak it by.

Q. This will be the last one. If you say that you want them to say "Uncle," doesn't that practically mean that they should give up power, do it our way, and get themselves out of office? I mean, if you were the President of—you are the President of a country—and somebody said that they wanted you to say "Uncle," you'd think that they wanted to take you over. Why shouldn't they think that we want to topple them?

The President. Well, maybe that was an unfortunate choice of words for what I was trying to say, because it inevitably has created a different image than I had in mind. The questions had to do and was dealing with the military pressure from the *contras,* which is certainly affecting their economy. And we know that there is widespread dissatisfaction among the people.

We know that their new increase in the draft has driven the families that can do it to getting their young men—their sons out of the country. There's quite a traffic to Panama and from there then on to other places—of these young men—so that pressure, and then with the Contadora and what they've been trying to impose on them or persuade them to adopt.

What I meant by the term was that—and it was also in a refutation of saying that we want the overthrow of the government as such—like a coup—that throws them out and treats them as they've treated others. That, no, what we want is that they finally give in to saying we will restore the original goals of the revolution, because the *contras* are made up and led by revolutionaries who fought against Somoza. And all they're saying is: "This isn't what we fought the revolution for." And the total revolution, put in writing to the Organization of American States—when they asked for their help, they asked the OAS to persuade Somoza to step down and end the bloodshed. And the OAS said: "What are your goals? What do you want? Why should we help?'

And they gave them the statement, and it was pure democracy: elections, a pluralistic society, free press, free labor unions, all of these things. And the OAS asked Somoza to step down, and Somoza did. Whatever else anyone may think of him, he said, "If it will stop the bloodshed, yes." And he stepped down. The revolution was over, except that the Sandinistas then kept on with their own kind of revolution and gradually got rid of—gradually—almost suddenly—got rid of the other elements in the revolution that really wanted the democracy, because the Sandinistas were Communist to begin with. And now they have a totalitarian government.

Now, here are the *contras*—here's a funny situation. Here in El Salvador is a democratic, elected government that has tried repeatedly to negotiate with its guerrillas and say, come in and participate in the elections—be a part of the democratic process. And the guerrillas won't.

Over here in Nicaragua are the guerrillas, and I prefer to call them freedom fighters, who are saying to the government, "Let us participate. Let us get back into the democratic process." And it's the Sandinista government—the totalitarian government says "No, we won't talk to you." And that's all I meant by, "Uncle." [*Laughter*]

Reporters. Thank you.

Note: The interview began at 4:34 p.m. in the Oval Office at the White House. The transcript was released by the Office of the Press Secretary on March 11.

Written Responses to Questions Submitted by Maclean's Magazine of Canada
March 6, 1985

U.S.-Canada Relations

Q. Canadians long have suffered from a national inferiority complex in regard to our great neighbor to the south. How do you think of Canada, and what do you see as Canada's importance to the United States?

The President. No other country in the world is more important to the United States than Canada, and we are blessed to have such a nation on our northern border. Canada is a friend, a neighbor, and a trusted ally. We may have a larger population and a larger GNP, but we're also dependent on you. Canada consumes a fifth of our exports, and that's more than any other nation. You use more of our capital than other nations, and, of course, our mutual security interests are closely intertwined. It's up to both of us to make this partnership continue to work in both our interests.

Canada's Role in International Affairs

Q. How do you see Canada's role—as a smaller power—in international affairs? For instance, External Affairs Minister Joe Clark will be in Moscow next month as arms control negotiations resume in Geneva. Is there a part we can play in conjunction with that or with the Contadora process in Central America?

The President. Canada has played a significant role in international affairs ever since World War II, a role which has reflected the talents of Canadian statesmen and the democratic values of its peoples. It has been an activist in the United Nations—indeed, Canadians were amongst the founders in San Francisco 40 years ago—and has shown time and time again that it is prepared to back up its convictions on peaceful settlement of disputes with courageous participation in peacekeeping operations in such hotspots as Cyprus and the Middle East. But I also note that your Prime Minister recently quoted Dante to the effect that the "hottest place in hell is reserved for those who in times of moral crisis strive to maintain their neutrality." Canadians are not neutral—they believe in democracy and work hard to protect it.

To get down to specifics, I am convinced that the unity and solid support of Western leaders on arms control were the principal factors that brought the Soviets back to the negotiating table. Prime Minister Mulroney has been very helpful, and we feel certain that Mr. Clark will convey to the Soviet leaders our continuing resolve to achieve significant, verifiable, and equitable arms reductions. With regard to the Contadora process, we value Canadian assistance, and I would note that Canadian suggestions on the verification process have been most helpful.

Canada's Defense Policy

Q. What do you see as Canada's role in defense? How did you feel when the new government had to cut $154 million from military spending, for example, contrary to what they had promised during the election campaign? Is Canada doing its fair share in NATO, and will you be pressuring us to do more?

The President. When Prime Minister Mulroney was here last September, he expressed his personal commitment to enhancing Canada's role in the Atlantic alliance and to carry its full share of the allied defense burden. But he and I recognized then and now that domestic political pressures affect outcomes. I believe Brian Mulroney shares my conviction that there is no reasonable alternative but to work to protect freedom and democracy.

I understand Canada is now conducting a major review of its defense policy, and I believe that the review will conclude that the only meaningful defense question facing both our nations is how to meet the challenge now before us. And that challenge has nothing to do with pressure from Canada's allies, but rather, how best to defend freedom and democracy.

Nuclear Weapons Deployment

Q. In recent weeks, there has been an uproar over the news that contingency plans exist to deploy nuclear weapons—specifically B–57 nuclear depth charges—in Canada in case of an emergency. In your view, is Canada bound to accept these weapons, especially when the government never was notified of such plans? And what sort of emergency would prompt such a deployment?

The President. I know that stories have recently appeared concerning wartime contingency plans. There have also been allegations that America is pressuring its allies to accept nuclear weapons. I have two comments to make on these reports. First, over the years NATO has worked out various defense plans designed to strengthen deterrence, but under these plans any deployments would be carried out only, let me repeat only, with the prior agreement of the states involved.

Second, it is contrary to the interest of the alliance and to the individual member states to talk publicly about confidential contingency planning. Such discussion would not serve our shared security interests.

Allied Defense Cooperation

Q. If Canada suddenly balked at going along with such contingency plans—or refused to allow the further testing of cruise missiles or barred an American battleship from our ports as New Zealand recently did—would the United States respond in the same way that it did to New Zealand, that is, threatening a broad range of countermeasures, including economic sanctions?

The President. Let me start by stressing that United States defense cooperation with our allies begins with a common understanding of our shared security interests and a determination to protect those interests against any threat. Each of us entered into our alliances—whether ANZUS or NATO or NORAD—as fully sovereign nations, not because we were pressured to do so.

Let me point out that we are not taking economic sanctions against New Zealand. Rather, we are reviewing our cooperation in security matters in light of New Zealand's decision to reduce cooperation with us in the ANZUS alliance.

Our longstanding and excellent defense cooperation with Canada is grounded in our partnership in NORAD and our joint membership in NATO. Clearly, we share common objectives. For example, Canada's cooperation in the testing of cruise missiles, which we greatly value and appreciate, was, I am sure, a recognition by the Canadian Government that this missile plays an important role in NATO's deterrent posture and is directly related to Canada's own security.

Strategic Defense Initiative

Q. The Canadian Government has said it supports the Strategic Defense Initiative, but there has been an uproar each time it has been suggested that defense cooperation could lead to our actual involvement in the program. In your view, should Canada have a role in SDI research, and why?

The President. We have absolutely no intention of pressing any of our allies to participate in this program. It will be entirely up to Canada to decide the extent to which, if at all, it wishes to share in the research efforts. Should Canada decide such participation is in its interests, we would be delighted to work with you in this important undertaking.

But let's get this straight about the Strategic Defense Initiative: For more than a generation, we have believed that no war will begin as long as each side knows the other can retaliate with devastating results. Well, I believe there could be a better way to keep the peace. The Strategic Defense Initiative is a research effort aimed at finding a nonnuclear defense against ballistic missiles. It is the most hopeful possibility of the nuclear age. Nuclear weapons threaten entire populations; the SDI seeks to end that possibility forever. I was extremely heartened by the understanding and support for this research effort by Prime Minister Mulroney and External Affairs Minister Clark. It may take a long time, but now we have started.

Acid Rain

Q. The Federal and Provincial governments have just taken substantial measures to control the contributions to acid rain on our side of the border. What is the United States prepared to do for its part?

The President. The United States is a world leader for a cleaner environment. We take pride that our Clean Air and Clean Water Acts and our other comprehensive environmental legislation have helped to set international standards. We have invested $150 billion—yes, that's billions—under our Clean Air Act, and as a result the air today is cleaner than in many years. Emissions of sulphur dioxide, a major concern, are down nearly 30 percent in the last decade. This trend is continuing: down 10 percent since I became President, including 2½ percent in 1983. We strictly control nitrogen oxides, which come mainly from auto emissions, and their level has also been dropping in recent years. For the future, I believe it is a question of doing what is reasonable and responsible after getting all the facts.

U.S.-Canada Free Trade Agreement

Q. What do you think the prospects are for negotiating a free trade agreement with Canada during your second term? Will the obstacles come from Congress or from Canadian nationalists?

The President. As I understand it, the Canadian Government is reviewing its trade policy right now and hasn't yet decided whether to propose any negotiations. In our Congress, I believe there is a deep-seated appreciation that trade between the United States and Canada—the largest trade volume between any two countries on Earth—is beneficial to both countries and should be fostered. Of course, there are sensitive trade areas, and the Congress would want to be sure that any new bilateral understanding is in the interest of the United States—so would I, and I'm sure Canada would do the same.

What is important is that we continue to work together to reduce trade barriers. Perhaps we can set an exmple for others to follow. We are not interested in building a North American island; rather, we would like to establish a trend toward trade liberalization that others can emulate.

U.S.-Canada Relations

Q. Much has been made of the warmer relations that now exist between Canada and the United States. What particularly irked you about the previous government's actions? Now, having made concessions to Canada to signal the warmer relationship, what do you expect of Canada in return? And what would you tell Canadian nationalists who fear that a warmer relationship means that we sell out our independence?

The President. You're right to suggest that relations between our two countries are in good shape. But rather than talk about concessions, I believe that what has happened is that we've come to recognize that warm close relations serve both our interests. As a result, we both have become a lot more attentive to each other's concerns; we talk with each other more often. And I don't believe that means either nation becomes less independent.

Q. How important is a warm personal relationship among leaders? And what aspects of Mr. Mulroney's personality contribute to the chemistry reported between the two of you?

The President. People respond more warmly to some than to others. We're all human. And I confess that I like Brian Mulroney a lot. He is a true Canadian patriot. He is honest, hardworking, intelligent, and articulate—in two languages at that! So, let's just say that the chemistry is good.

Note: The questions and answers were released by the Office of the Press Secretary on March 11.

Proclamation 5307—Women's History Week, 1985
March 9, 1985

*By the President of the United States
of America*

A Proclamation

The history of the United States is the history of women and men working together to realize their dreams. In times of war and peace, of hardship and prosperity, we have shared disappointments and achievements.

Today there are more opportunities open to women than at any time in our history, and women are using these opportunities to excel in every field. But even before our own era, courageous and persevering women had achieved leading roles in all walks of life. Women led reform movements, including the movement for women's suffrage; they ran businesses, entered the professions, and pioneered in activities such as art, literature, and science. These achievements have not always received the recognition they deserve, and one of the purposes of Women's History Week is to encourage all Americans to remember this sometimes forgotten part of our heritage. By doing so, we will encourage the women of today to pursue their dreams wherever they lead—even to the stars, as our women astronauts have done.

But in remembering the achievements of especially talented individuals, we should not forget the immense contribution made to our Nation by millions of women whose names we will never know. These women raised families, worked part-time or full-time to support them, and passed on their love, hopes, and dreams to the next generation. They crossed deserts and mountains alongside their families and in times of national emergency, such as war, they undertook vital work in factories and on farms which enabled our Nation to survive and prosper. They were known only to their families, friends, and neighbors, but their influence on their communities was enormous. Whatever greatness our Nation has achieved, we owe in very large measure to them, and we should never overlook or forget their contribution.

In recognition of the many vital contributions of women to our Nation's history, the Congress, by House Joint Resolution 50, has designated the week beginning March 3, 1985, as "Women's History Week" and authorized and requested the President to issue a proclamation in observance of this week.

Now, Therefore, I, Ronald Reagan, President of the United States of America, do hereby proclaim the week beginning March 3, 1985, as Women's History Week. I invite the Governors of the States, the chief officials of local governments, the scholars of our institutions of education, and Americans everywhere to mark this occasion with appropriate ceremonies and activities recognizing the contributions of women to our Nation and our culture.

In Witness Whereof, I have hereunto set my hand this ninth day of March, in the year of our Lord nineteen hundred and eighty-five, and of the Independence of the United States of America the two hundred and ninth.

RONALD REAGAN

[Filed with the Office of the Federal Register, 11:36 a.m., March 12, 1985]

Note: *The proclamation was released by the Office of the Press Secretary on March 11.*

Remarks and a Question-and-Answer Session With Regional Editors and Broadcasters
March 11, 1985

The President. Good afternoon, and welcome to the White House. It's an honor to have you join us today. And if I may say so, it's also refreshing. You are the editors and broadcasters who shape and reflect concerns in the place that is most important to every citizen—not far-off Washington, but hometown America. I welcome this opportunity to get to know you, to thank you for your service to our country and through you to speak to your readers and listeners—the people who live beyond the Potomac, in what I still can't help thinking of as the real America.

By the way, our administration has quite a few members who've spent part of their careers working with you on regional stations and newspapers, among them is our new Communications Director, Pat Buchanan, who was an editorial writer for the St. Louis Globe Democrat. There's another fellow who—one who started as a sports announcer on radio station WOC back in Davenport, Iowa, who remembers his broadcasting days as some of the happiest in his life. I think you know his name, and—[*laughter*]—as an old radio man, I view welcoming you here as an honor.

Today we've learned of the death of the head of state, Konstantin Chernenko, and I've sent my condolences to the Soviet leadership and people. I want them to know that we will deal with Chairman Chernenko's successor with an open mind and will continue our efforts to improve relations between our two nations—to settle our differences fairly and, particularly, to lower the levels of nuclear arms.

Tomorrow in Geneva, American negotiators will sit down with their Soviet counterparts to begin the most important arms talks in which our nation is likely to participate for the rest of this decade. I'm pleased that negotiations will begin as scheduled. Weeks of painstaking preparation have now been completed, and although in the interest of confidentiality I can't go into the details of our negotiating positions, let me assure you of this: Our team stands ready to put forward concrete and constructive proposals. And they will in turn respond to good-faith Soviet proposals with flexibility and an active interest. We earnestly hope that the Soviets are equally prepared for serious give-and-take.

Our short-term goal at Geneva will be to reduce American and Soviet offensive nuclear forces, systems which are already in place, whose use would prove a calamity to tens of millions of people.

Our goal for the medium term, if research goes as we expect, is to discuss how the United States and the Soviet Union can move away from sole reliance on the threat of nuclear retaliation toward greater reliance on defenses which threaten no one.

Our long-term goal: the complete elimination of nuclear arms.

As our negotiators begin their work in Geneva, we at home must remain firm in our resolve to maintain an adequate deterrent to war. Our negotiating flexibility must be coupled with firmness and resolve if it is to be effective in producing the outcome we all desire: radical reductions in nuclear weapons, as a step toward the ultimate goal of eliminating them.

We're realistic about the differences between ourselves and the Soviets. As we pursue arms control, we will at the same time press forward on a worldwide respect for the dignity of man.

In Geneva we face a long and difficult road. To travel it, we'll need strength, patience, and allied unity. The effort will be great, and the final destination, which will so heavily depend on the Soviet intentions, is uncertain. But the road before us is the road of peace, and on that we dare not hesitate or falter.

So, I'd just like to close by saying: Let us travel it together, Americans united as never before. We have sent a congressional delegation, Members of the Senate and the House over there of both parties, for the sole purpose of impressing on the Soviet

Union that when it comes to the water's edge—we aren't Democrats or Republicans, we're Americans.

So, thank you, God bless you, and——

Soviet Government

Q. Mr. President——

The President. Yes?

Q. ——what changes do you foresee under Gorbachev? [1]

The President. I think it's very hard to predict anything of the kind when you realize that the Soviet policy is really determined by a dozen or so individuals in the Politburo. They are the ones who chose him. It is a collective government. And while an individual once chosen by them can, undoubtedly, influence or persuade them to certain things that might be particular theories or policies of his, the government basically remains the same group of individuals.

Cuba

Q. Mr. President, the question of Nicaragua and Cuba is in the minds very much of people from south Florida, as I am. If, for any reason, sir, if in Cuba there would be a change of that leadership, for instance, try to change the leadership of the regime of Cuba by overthrowing Castro, would the United States help that new government to give freedom a chance in Cuba?

The President. Well, I think all of us dream of a Cuba that will one day recognize that it should be once again a member of the American states in the Western Hemisphere and not a satellite of the Soviet Union.

Now, there have been statements by Castro at one time or another to the effect that he wanted to talk better relations with us. We followed up on those every time, and every time there's been no substance, only sound.

So, we'll continue to hope. I don't know what the result would be. I'm rather hesitant in my position now to say something that might—if you're looking far afield—

---

[1] *Mikhail Gorbachev, a member of the Politburo who became General Secretary of the Communist Party upon the death of Konstantin U. Chernenko on March 10.*

might bring about some abortive undertaking that would cause great tragedy to a lot of people. But just let me say that we believe that Cuba belongs back in the Organization of American States, and it can only get there by becoming a democracy instead of the totalitarian government that it is.

Funeral for Soviet President Chernenko

Q. Mr. President, we were told this morning, sir, that you considered going to the funeral of Chernenko and then you decided that the Vice President should go. What were the pluses and minuses of you going personally, and why did you decide not to, sir?

The President. Well, no, as of 4 a.m. this morning, I started thinking about it after the phone call came. And no, I had a feeling—first of all, there's an awful lot on my plate right now that would have to be set aside. I didn't see that anything could be achieved by so going. And we discussed it in the office this morning. But, no, I leaned the other way, that we have heads of state coming here; I have at the end of the week—I'll be leaving for Canada for a meeting that's been set up for a long time there, things of that kind. And I didn't see where I could do it. And the Vice President is already in Europe, so that it would seem very logical for him to do that.

Nicaragua

Q. I thank you very much for this opportunity. Under the new Soviet leadership, do you think the Nicaraguans will say uncle at this point? Will there be any shifts, do you think, in Nicaragua's situation as it relates to us?

The President. Well, we have to believe that there will be a change. And this is one of the reasons why we're hoping we can still persuade the Congress to support us in our desire to support the *contras* that I call freedom fighters there, because these are people who are participants in the revolution that overthrew Somoza. And then they were thrown out of the revolution that they had helped bring about.

They did much as Castro did in Cuba in the beginning—the Sandinistas, I mean. They simply took over that revolution, and they have violated their promise to the Organization of American States. They asked for help from the Organization in getting Somoza to step down. And he did step down at the request of the Organization, and that ended the bloodshed. And in doing that, they had promised the Organization of American States that their goal was democracy: free elections, free labor unions, freedom of the press, observance of human rights, as should be in a democracy. And they have violated every one of those promises with a totalitarian form of government.

Now, I believe that it is our place to lend help to those people of Nicaragua who still want the original revolution and want a democracy there. And we're going to continue to try to help them.

Q. Mr. President——

The President. I thought I would go a little further afield—I'm kind of concentrated here.

U.S.-Soviet Relations

Q. Mr. President, are you anxious perhaps to meet with the new Soviet leader to get to know him a little bit?

The President. Am I anxious to meet——

Q. Anxious to meet with him?

The President. Very much so, and I was with the previous three also. [*Laughter*] I was ready to have a meeting—and as they themselves said, at such a time as you could have a legitimate agenda and not just have a meeting to get acquainted.

But I'm looking forward to this, and—I can give you one figure that would kind of spell out what my problem has been, because there have been some who've wanted to criticize me in contrast with previous Presidents.

In 48 years, of 8 Presidencies prior to mine, there were only 3 leaders over that span of 48 years and 8 Presidents of the Soviet Union. Well, we're coming up the fourth in mine, and I've just started my fifth year, and there were 3 of them in a little over 3 years.

So, you know, you have to wait for a new man now to get in place and establish his regime, and then I'll be more than ready because I think there's a great mutual suspicion between the two countries; I think that ours is more justified than theirs. And I—at my own table here I spoke of—reminded of the fact that when World War II ended and we had the monopoly of the nuclear weapon and our industry was intact and had never been bombed into rubble as it had in most of Europe, if we really were the aggressor the Soviets accused us of being, we could have taken anything in the world then, and no one could have stopped us. And we didn't do it, instead we went abroad with the Marshall plan to help everyone, including our erstwhile enemies.

And, on the other hand, we see their expansionism—we see it in Afghanistan and Ethiopia and Angola and yes, in Cuba and Nicaragua. So, I'd like to have a talk and see if some way we can't some day have a meeting of minds and recognize that we—well, that delegation that's just going home from here—I asked the leader of that delegation when they were going to go to Texas and California to see if they couldn't look at the American people—the people around them, the working people of this country—and ask themselves if they thought there was any way that Americans would rather be in a war than living the way we live. And they didn't get much time to look at that.

Q. One more?

Terrorism

Q. Mr. President, what is the government doing, if anything, to regain release of the hostages in Beirut?

The President. I can't tell you in detail what we're doing, obviously, because those four lives are at stake. So, everything we're doing is trying to find where they're located. We have appealed to others that we believe have some influence with the terrorists who kidnaped them to begin with, and particularly since the one escaped. And we're doing, as I say, everything that we can. We can't give details on that. We must not do anything to endanger their lives. But terrorism is a new form of warfare, and all we can do is try to meet it with intelligence efforts—to find out, if we can, where retaliation can take place, but, also, to work closely with our allies and other countries in the world because it's becoming more and more evident that there are some sovereign governments who are backing this terrorism. And if that's the case, then we would know exactly where to retaliate for terrorist deeds.

I've just been told that I can't take any more questions here, and you thought that I was the most powerful fellow here, didn't you? [*Laughter*] No, I'm sorry. It's just like a press conference. But I want to tell you, your questions were great, and I appreciated them very much. And if any of you had one particular one and you wanted to get it—drop a line and we'll send it to you in writing. But what she means is I've got another hundred people from State legislatures that are waiting for me over in the Executive Office Building. So, I'd better run and get there.

Thank you all very much.

Note: The President spoke at 1:06 p.m. at a luncheon for the editors and broadcasters in the State Dining Room at the White House.

Message to Vasiliy V. Kuznetsov on the Death of General Secretary Konstantin U. Chernenko of the Soviet Union
March 11, 1985

Please accept my condolences on the death of the Chairman of the Presidium of the Supreme Soviet, Konstantin Ustinovich Chernenko.

At this solemn time, I wish to reiterate the strong desire of the American people for world peace. Although the problems which divide our countries are many and complex, we can and must resolve our differences through dialog and negotiation. Our two delegations are sitting down in Geneva to begin negotiation on how to reduce and eliminate nuclear weapons. We must seize the opportunities for peace. We need to find ways to reduce the threat and use of force in solving international disputes. We must also establish a working relationship that builds greater trust and cooperation between us. I hope that the Soviet leadership will join with me with renewed dedication to create a firm and durable basis for better relations between our two countries.

Note: Vasiliy V. Kuznetsov is First Deputy Chairman of the Presidium of the Supreme Soviet of the Soviet Union.

Nomination of Marshall B. Babson To Be a Member of the National Labor Relations Board
March 11, 1985

The President today announced his intention to nominate Marshall B. Babson to be a member of the National Labor Relations Board for a term expiring December 16, 1989.

Since 1977 Mr. Babson has been a partner with Wiggin and Dana in New Haven, CT. Previously, he was an associate with Littler, Mendelson, Fastiff and Tichy in San Francisco (1975–1977); a law clerk with Palmer and Dodge in Boston, MA (summer, 1974); and a law clerk with Surrey, Karasik, Morse and Seham in New York (summer, 1973).

Mr. Babson graduated from the University of Pennsylvania (B.A., 1968) and the Columbia Law School (J.D., 1975). He is married, has two children, and resides in New Haven, CT. He was born November 27, 1945, in Boston, MA.

Nomination of Wilford W. Johansen To Be a Member of the National Labor Relations Board
March 11, 1985

The President today announced his intention to nominate Wilford W. Johansen to be a member of the National Labor Relations Board for a term expiring August 27, 1988. He would succeed Howard Jenkins, Jr.

Mr. Johansen has been the National Labor Relations Board Regional Director of region 21 since 1971. Previously, he was Acting General Counsel of NLRB (1984);

Deputy Assistant General Counsel of NLRB (1961–1971); and field attorney for NLRB in region 21 (1959–1961).

Mr. Johansen graduated from Idaho State College (B.A., 1951) and George Washington University Law School (LL.B., 1957). He is married, has two children, and resides in Rancho Palos Verdes, CA. He was born April 15, 1928, in Salt Lake City, UT.

Appointment of Four Members of the Council of the Administrative Conference of the United States
March 11, 1985

The President today announced his intention to appoint the following individuals to be members of the Council of the Administrative Conference of the United States for terms of 3 years. These are reappointments.

Walter Gellhorn has been on the faculty of the Columbia Law School since 1933, serving as a Betts professor (1957–1973); university professor (1973–1974); and currently as professor emeritus (since 1974). He graduated from Amherst College (A.B., 1927; L.H.D., 1952), Columbia University (LL.B., 1931), and the University of Pennsylvania (LL.D., 1963). He is married, has two children, and resides in New York, NY. He was born September 18, 1906, in St. Louis, MO.

Edith Dinneen Hakola is currently general counsel, treasurer, and vice president of the National Right To Work Legal Defense Foundation. Previously, she was assistant professor of law at Delaware Law School (1973–1975) and administrative assistant at the National Right To Work Committee (1962–1966). She graduated from George Washington University (B.A., 1966) and the University of Richmond (J.D., 1968). She is married, has two children, and

resides in Springfield, VA. She was born August 2, 1938, in Washington, DC.

Otis M. Smith is currently an attorney with Lewis, White & Clay in Detroit, MI. He was a member of the legal staff of the General Motors Corp. for 17 years, serving as assistant general counsel (1973–1974); associate general counsel (1974–1977); general counsel (1977–1984); and vice president (1974–1984). He graduated from Catholic University (J.D., 1950). He is married, has four children, and resides in Detroit, MI. He was born February 20, 1922, in Memphis, TN.

Edward L. Weidenfeld is currently a partner with the firm of McKenna, Conner & Cuneo in Washington, DC. Previously, he was senior member and managing partner with Hall, Estill & Weidenfeld, P.C. (1974–1979); attorney with Fried, Frank, Harris, Shriver & Kampelman (1973–1974); and counsel on energy matters and director of the energy staff, Committee on Interior and Insular Affairs, House of Representatives (1971–1973). He graduated from the University of Wisconsin (B.S., 1965) and the Columbia University School of Law (J.D., 1968). He is married, has one child, and resides in Washington, DC. He was born July 15, 1943, in Akron, OH.

Statement by Principal Deputy Press Secretary Speakes on the Death of General Secretary Konstantin U. Chernenko of the Soviet Union
March 11, 1985

The President has sent a message of condolence to Acting Head of State, Vasiliy Vasil'yevich Kuznetsov, on the death of Chairman and General Secretary Konstantin Ustinovich Chernenko. In his message the President reaffirmed his commitment to peace and to working for a cooperative relationship with the peoples of the Soviet Union and the Soviet Government. The President called upon the Soviet leadership to seize the opportunity offered by the negotiations about to begin in Geneva to make progress toward our shared goal of eliminating nuclear weapons from the face of the Earth.

In our relations with the Soviet Union, the United States has three basic goals: to reduce significantly the unacceptably high numbers of weapons which now exist; to eliminate the use and the threat of force in international relations; and to develop greater trust and confidence in our relations with the Soviet Union overall. Our nations share an interest in the development of stable and constructive relations for the long term.

We believe that the problems which exist in U.S.-Soviet relations can be resolved and that progress is possible in the near term. We cannot achieve progress singlehandedly, but we will do our part to bring it about. The United States hopes to work with the Soviet leadership to build on common interests in order to help create a better and safer world.

Note: Larry M. Speakes read the statement to reporters at 4:07 p.m. in the Briefing Room at the White House.

Appointment of Eight Members of the Chemical Warfare Review Commission, and Designation of the Chairman
March 11, 1985

The President today announced his intention to appoint the following individuals to be members of the Chemical Warfare Review Commission. These are new positions. The President intends to designate Walter J. Stoessel, Jr., as Chairman upon his appointment.

Philip John Bakes, Jr., is president and chief operating officer of Continental Airlines in Houston, TX. He is married, has two children, and resides in Houston. He was born March 6, 1946, in Little Rock, AR.

Zbigniew Brzezinski is senior adviser at the Georgetown University Center for Strategic and International Studies. He is married, has three children, and resides in McLean, VA. He was born March 28, 1928, in Warsaw, Poland.

Gen. Richard E. Cavazos, United States Army, retired. He is married, has four children, and resides in Leander, TX. He was born January 31, 1929, in Kingsville, TX.

Barber B. Conable, Jr., is a senior fellow at the American Enterprise Institute. He is married, has four children, and resides in Washington, DC. He was born November 2, 1922, in Warsaw, NY.

John N. Erlenborn is a partner in the law firm of Seyferth, Shaw, Fairweather & Geraldson in Washington, DC. He is married, has three children, and resides in Fairfax, VA. He was born February 8, 1927, in Chicago, IL.

Alexander Meigs Haig, Jr., is president of Worldwide Consultants, Inc., in Washington, DC. He is married, has three children, and resides in McLean, VA. He was born December 2, 1924, in Philadelphia, PA.

John G. Kester is an attorney with the law firm of Williams & Connolly in Washington, DC. He is

273

married, has two children, and resides in Washington, DC. He was born June 18, 1938, in Oshkosh, WI.

Walter J. Stoessel, Jr., has served in the past as U.S. Ambassador to Poland (1968–1972), the Union of Soviet Socialist Republics (1974–1976), and the Federal Republic of Germany (1976–1978). He is married, has three children, and resides in Washington, DC. He was born January 24, 1920, in Manhattan, KS.

Appointment of Carlton E. Turner as Deputy Assistant to the President for Drug Abuse Policy
March 12, 1985

The President today appointed Carlton E. Turner, Ph.D., to be Deputy Assistant to the President for Drug Abuse Policy. Dr. Turner is currently serving as Special Assistant to the President.

Dr. Turner will continue to be the President's adviser for drug abuse policy and provide assistance to the First Lady with her drug abuse education projects, both domestic and international.

Dr. Turner came to the White House in July 1981 as the senior policy adviser for drug policy. Prior to joining the administration, he was the director of the Research Institute of Pharmaceutical Sciences, School of Pharmacy, University of Mississippi. He has served as a consultant for various government agencies and private firms in the United States, Mexico, and Canada, as well as for the United Nations.

Dr. Turner is the past president of the American Council on Marijuana's Scientific Advisory Board and was the 1982 Harry G. Armstrong lecturer at the Aerospace Medical Association's scientific meeting. He has published over 100 scientific papers, patents, chapters in books, and is coauthor of "Marijuana, An Annotated Bibliography," volumes I and II. In addition to extensive drug research, Dr. Turner has been involved in the training of Federal, State, and local narcotics agents since 1971.

He graduated from the University of Southern Mississippi (B.S., M.S., Ph.D.). He is married and has two daughters. He was born September 13, 1940, in Choctaw County, AL.

Remarks Following Discussions With President Mohammed Hosni Mubarak of Egypt
March 12, 1985

President Reagan. I have enjoyed this opportunity to host President Mubarak and to exchange views with him on issues of mutual interest and importance to Egypt and the United States.

As close friends and partners in peace, we've had a good discussion, including a thorough review of developments in the Middle East area. The substantial economic and military assistance that we're requesting for Egypt reflects our strong commitment to Egypt's security and economic well-being.

Earlier this morning our representatives signed agreements which will result in $215 million in U.S. assistance to support rehabilitation of Egypt's infrastructure, $300 million in balance-of-payments support which will enable Egypt to buy needed goods from the United States. Egypt faces economic difficulties, and as your friend and full partner in the Middle East peace process, we'll be giving careful and sympathetic consideration to what we might do to help.

A major focus of our talks today was how to broaden the historic Middle East peace process. And Egypt's experience as peacemaker and your leadership in the region uniquely suits you to help build new bridges of understanding, confidence, hope, and trust.

Recently, President Mubarak, you've made suggestions which have helped renew interest in the peace process. I regard them as a positive contribution, and I appreciate the constructive spirit in which you offered them. We note particularly your realistic assessment that the path to peace between Israel and its Arab neighbors is through direct negotiations.

The United States continues to believe that such negotiations should take place on the basis of United Nations Security Council Resolution 242, which provides both for the restoration of Arab land and the right of Israel, as all states in the region, to live in peace within secure and recognized borders. As reaffirmed in my initiative of September 1st, 1982, the United States also believes that the outcome of this process must recognize the legitimate rights of the Palestinian people.

Let us hope that the positive trends that have recently begun in the region will be strengthened and, that with Egypt's valued help, they will open the path to direct negotiations. In the full knowledge that the parties are still a long way from the negotiating table, the United States takes an active interest in these developments, and we'll support the parties' efforts to build on this promising beginning.

The road to peace in the Middle East has been long, frustrating, and marked by great tragedy. Fortunately there have also been great achievements, such as the Egyptian-Israeli peace treaty, which reminds us that success is possible—it's not only possible, it's imperative.

I reassured President Mubarak of the commitment of the United States and my personal commitment to work with Egypt and our other friends in the area to achieve a just and lasting peace.

I thank you, and God bless you.

President Mubarak. President Reagan, it was a great pleasure to meet with you once again, in the spirit of friendship and the fraternity which characterizes our relations.

As ever, I found the conversations were most constructive and rewarding. Our friendly meeting today reaffirmed my belief that you are a man of honor and vision. It's a good omen that our meeting today coincides with the 150th anniversary of the establishment of relations between our two countries. Throughout these years we have endeavored to set up a model for cooperation among nations. Our bilateral relations are moving from good to excellent. We encounter no problems in setting the stage for more cooperation, which is equally profitable.

We conduct our relations on the basis of mutual respect and profound understanding. Your appreciation of the efforts the Egyptian people are exerting on the road of economic development and reform is recognized by every Egyptian. On the other hand, your commitment to peace and justice in our part of the world is unwavering. I am pleased to note that we agree, together, on the centrality of the Palestinian question to the situation in the Middle East. It is the key to progress and the source of despair and tension. Hence, we should devote ourselves to reaching a just and honorable solution, therefore, without delay.

I believe that no nation is more qualified than America to support the Palestinian peoples' right to self-determination. This is a stand that is consistent with the American heritage and values. This country was founded on the principle that all men are equal and were created by God Almighty to live in freedom and dignity.

I also believe that no leader is more equipped to play an historic role and fulfill a sacred mission in the Middle East. Destiny has chosen you to lead this great nation at a time when a golden opportunity for peace is emerging.

The Jordanian-Palestinian agreement to pursue a peaceful settlement is a major development that should not be discounted or discarded. We cannot afford another missed opportunity for peace, and not during your Presidency. I'm confident that the United States will act without delay in order to keep the momentum going and to pave the way for further progress. We have discussed the variety of available options for following up this move.

In the months ahead we shall work together as faithful partners on the road to peace. We shall persevere in our drive which aims at bridging the gap existing between the positions of the parts and ushering in a new era of peace and reconciliation.

We realize that the task is difficult and the challenge is great, but the cause is greater. President Reagan, during the past few years you offered your help to African countries suffering from the drought and famine; this has been appreciated by fellow Africans. May I suggest that the United States champions a worldwide effort to cope with the problem on a long-term basis.

May I also express our confidence that the United States will spare no effort in order to help end the plight of our brothers in southern Africa and secure the immediate independence of Namibia.

Again, Mr. President, thank you, dear friend, and I'm looking forward to meeting with you again in pursuit of our common goals, and thank you.

Note: The President spoke to reporters at 1:24 p.m. at the South Portico of the White House. Earlier, the two Presidents met in the Oval Office and then attended a luncheon in the Residence.

Toasts at the State Department Dinner for President Mohammed Hosni Mubarak of Egypt
March 12, 1985

President Reagan. My, it's quiet in here. [*Laughter*]

Well, distinguished friends, we are privileged indeed to honor tonight President and Mrs. Mubarak.

Now, I bring you the regrets of Mrs. Reagan, but she can't be here, as she said to me on a phone call from Arizona, where she is tonight.

As you all know, Vice President Bush could not be here tonight, and it's a pleasure to serve as his stand-in. [*Laughter*] Come to think of it, he's doing that for me right now. [*Laughter*]

President Mubarak's visit here underscores the special bonds of friendship that have developed over many years between Egypt and the United States. Our two countries are partners in a broad range of endeavors, most notably as full partners in the search for a lasting Middle East peace. Today there's a renewal of hope that the peace process can be broadened and invigorated.

Egypt's indispensable leadership position in the area is reflected in its important dialogs with two key countries—Israel and Jordan. And, after all, we're engaged in a process that can only advance with the support of those directly concerned. In this respect, Egypt is uniquely equipped to help reconcile differing points of view and build the solid bridge of confidence necessary for progress.

Mr. President, as you recently emphasized, the path to a peace that recognizes the legitimate rights of the Palestinian people is through direct negotiations. The inescapable basis for such negotiations is U.N. Security Council Resolution 242, which provides both for the restoration of Arab land and for the right of Israel and all states to live in peace within secure and recognized borders. The challenge now is to clear the way so that negotiations can begin. We shouldn't underestimate the obstacles—we never have—but we shouldn't be daunted by them either.

One question that we must address forthrightly is how the Palestinians should be represented. And, Mr. President, you've wisely stressed the need for practicality. In our quest for peace, we reaffirm with you that in all stages of the negotiating process there should be Palestinian participation. As we've said many times before, these Palestinians should include representatives from the West Bank and Gaza and other Palestinians as mutually agreed to by the parties.

Now, these are wide parameters; they provide ample scope, and they should be put to use. And in this context we especially welcome the improvement in the Egyptian-Israeli dialog. And the integrity of this relationship is the cornerstone of the peace process.

With realism as our guide, let us seize this moment to rededicate ourselves to the task of peace. And with your continued help and commitment, Mr. President, I feel sure that we will make great progress.

In this spirit, ladies and gentlemen, please join me in a toast to President Mubarak and Mrs. Mubarak and to a broadening of the process of peace to which Egypt has so courageously contributed.

President Mubarak. Mr. President, dear friends, really, I'm very touched by your kind words, Mr. President. And we are very happy to be with you tonight, again.

Today we had a working session and a working lunch. I pursued the work by having two sessions in the Congress, where I met with friends in both the Senate and the House. It was a full working day, and I take it that you thought that we deserve to have this dinner and to see this magnificent, newly redecorated quarters in the State Department—another good piece of work of my friend, George Shultz.

President Reagan, in my remarks today, as we departed after lunch, I referred to the establishment of formal Egyptian-American relations 150 years ago. There is, however, another aspect to this event: the role of individual Americans who began to visit Egypt since the early years of last century. Most of them were fascinated by the history of our people and of our land. They wanted to unravel the mystery of all the Egyptian civilizations. They sailed down the Nile. They lived by the monuments. They recorded their observations in articles and in letters. Some of them returned home with samples of antiquities, and some even remained and were employed by the Egyptian Government. The Washington Monument, which stands marvelously in your capital, was inspired by those early Americans who came to admire Egyptian obelisks. Thus, many achievements in American-Egyptian relations took place particularly on the human and the cultural levels.

The movement has not been confined to Americans traveling to Egypt; but Egyptians also traveled and even settled in America. In fact, a new phenomenon was born: the immigrant Egyptian settling in America. I am happy and proud to see many of them, all walks of American life: university professors, doctors, scientists, engineers, workers, et cetera. I am sure, Mr. President, that you would agree with me that it was the pure individual initiative which brought about these achievements.

There is also something else to it that brings our peoples together. It could be a certain sense of optimism about life whose root is faith in God. I was touched during this visit by a distinguished Congressman who told me that he noticed the warmest friendly relations between the Americans and the Egyptian peoples even when our former relations were under strain for a brief period in the past.

Today Egyptian-American relations provide in their intensity an ever-greater example of solid friendship, based on mutual respect and whose objective is nothing more noble than strengthening the cause of peace in our part of the world. We both share an irreversible commitment to bring total peace to an area whose peoples have long suffered from conflicts and violence. Nothing is more worthwhile than an investment in peace. In the interdependent world in which we live, such an investment becomes even more precious, if not indispensable. It is in that sense that the American-Egyptian partnership is a partnership for peace in the Middle East and, as such, offers the greatest contribution to the world peace.

Mr. President, let me once again congratulate you on the fact that you have been reelected the President of the great Nation by such an impressive majority of the American people. What stands behind that are great American values: faith in God, faith in human ingenuity, courage, and enlightened patriotism.

Let me also express our admiration for Vice President George Bush, who I know did all the best and planned his travels in such a way that he would have made it possible for us to meet with him here during the trip. But, as the saying goes in Arabic, "Man plans and God determines."

Dear President and dear friends, may I ask you to rise in a tribute of admiration and respect for the President of the United States, President Ronald Reagan, and for his great country, the United States, and the great American people. And thank you.

Note: The President spoke at 9:30 p.m. in the Thomas Jefferson Room at the Department of State.

Nomination of Midge Decter To Be a Member of the Advisory Board for Radio Broadcasting to Cuba
March 13, 1985

The President today announced his intention to nominate Midge Decter to be a member of the Advisory Board for Radio Broadcasting to Cuba for a term of 1 year. This is a new position.

She is an author and editor whose essays and reviews have, over the past two decades, appeared in a number of periodicals including Harper's, the Atlantic, Esquire, and the Saturday Review. She has been a regular contributor to Commentary and is the author of three books.

As an editor she has served in various positions, beginning with the Hudson Institute and CBS Legacy Books. She has been the acting managing editor of Commentary, the executive editor of Harper's, and the managing editor of the Saturday Review. Most recently she has been a senior editor at Basic Books.

She was one of the founders of the Coalition for a Democratic Majority, of which she is a past national chairman, and a cochairman of the Advisory Committee on European Democracy and Security. She is presently the executive director of the Committee for the Free World.

She attended the University of Minnesota. She is married, has four children, and resides in New York City. She was born July 25, 1926, in St. Paul, MN.

Remarks at a White House Meeting With Members of the American Business Conference
March 13, 1985

Thank you very much, and good afternoon, and welcome to the White House.

It's good to be meeting with you again. In the last 4 years, the American Business Conference has been a staunch and much-appreciated ally in the battle to liberate our economy from the old ideas of overtaxation, overspending, and government control. But as we've been seeing recently in Congress, old habits die hard, very hard.

I've been thinking of starting a new counseling group up in Congress along the lines of Overeaters Anonymous. [*Laughter*] We'd call it Big-Spenders Anonymous. It could meet every week or so, and the members would get together and talk about how, try as they might, they just can't stop squandering the people's money. [*Laughter*]

The scene in the Senate Budget Committee this past week was a disappointing one, I think, for the American people. They seem to be in full-scale retreat from spending cuts and are talking about raising people's taxes again. When push comes to shove, I guess it's always easier to let the taxpayer take the fall. Well, let them be forewarned: No matter how well intentioned they might be, no matter what their illusions might be, I have my veto pen drawn and ready for any tax increase that Congress might even think of sending up. And I have only one thing to say to the tax increasers: Go ahead, make my day. [*Laughter*]

The defense budget has also become a convenient scapegoat for those in Congress who aren't willing to face up to the tough budget decisions. The fact is, however, that the recent growth in the deficit has nothing to do with defense spending. I know that's going to be hard for some to believe in view of all that you're hearing and that has been printed. But in the last 2 years the projected defense spending we had projected for the fiscal year 1985 has decreased by $26 billion in real terms. Now, this wasn't waiting for someone up on the Hill to do it. We ourselves and the Defense Department found that we could reduce that much by differences in management and inflation and things that had happened. And during that same period, while that was going down $26 billion, expected total revenues for this year have increased $30 billion in real terms.

But projected nondefense, nondebt service spending has increased about double that amount—around $60 billion. It seems that despite all the rhetoric about the deficit, Congress has been carrying on its old pork-barreling politics as usual. We're now seeing dramatic growth in our economy, the kind of growth that used to be called impossible. Revised figures for '84 show a 6.9-percent increase in the gross national product, but no economy can grow faster than Congress can write a check.

While I'm on the subject, let me say that we just need your support for our strategic modernization program, especially the Peacekeeper-MX. The Peacekeeper's already included in the budget. It's shortsighted in the extreme to try to make savings by cutting out a program so essential to our national security and to the success of our arms reduction talks that are now underway in Geneva. The effort of some to cut the Peacekeeper is just another example of scapegoating by those who are unwilling to face up to their budget responsibilities.

If special interest group pressures on Congress are too great for them to get spending under control, let's do as Senator Mack Mattingly has proposed and give the Presidential line-item veto a 2-year trial run. That's all that he's asking for. Let's try it for a couple of years; see if it works. Somebody's got to stop this spending splurge, and I'm willing to take the political heat. To tell you the truth, I'll enjoy it. [*Laughter*] Somebody has to start looking out for the long-term interests of the American people as a whole.

Later in this session of Congress, we'll be presenting our proposals for tax reform that will lower tax rates, broaden the tax base, and make the tax code simpler and fairer. We're looking at a top rate on personal income taxes of 35 percent, very possibly less. And we'll be sure that incentives for capital formation are maintained. And I just want to reemphasize one thing: Tax reform will not be a tax increase in disguise. We're also moving forward on the new GATT negotiations—a series of trade liberalization talks with our trading partners, developed and developing alike.

These three initiatives—tax reform, budget control, and trade liberalization—are the heart of our economic program. And taken together, they can produce an economic renaissance in this country. With the political will to carry these programs through, I'm convinced that we can grow stronger and faster than even the most optimistic economists are predicting.

We can look back to the midsixties to see another period of dramatic growth liberated by tax cuts and trade liberalization at that time. But we have an advantage they didn't have back then. Today's economy is being powered by a high-tech explosion whose effects are only beginning to be felt. The face of American industry is being transformed daily by revolutionary new inventions and breakthroughs in productivity.

But we should keep in mind as we work to reform our tax code that misguided tax policies back in the seventies almost destroyed America's position as the leader of the high-tech revolution. Exorbitant tax rates together with a high rate of inflation almost wiped out the venture capital markets in this country, forcing American entrepreneurs to look abroad for financing.

One such case is the story of Gene Amdahl, the inventor of what many consider the most successful computer ever built. Back in the seventies he decided to start his own company, but he couldn't find the venture capital that he needed in this country, and he was forced to go to Japan, to a large, high-tech competitor in Japan. They gave him the money in return for his ideas.

High tax rates were literally producing an exodus of American high-tech to foreign countries. We were creating tax refugees out of our best minds and talents and most successful entrepreneurs. But when tax rates were cut, the dollars committed to venture capital exploded—from barely 39 million in 1977 to over 4 billion last year.

One of the first rules of economics is if you tax something, you get less of it. High tax rates discourage work, risk-taking, initiative, and imagination. And they're really a tax on hope, optimism, and our faith in the future. And they penalize the very people that give the most—the risk-takers, the entrepreneurs who create whole new businesses and industries, often out of no more than a dream and some hard work.

Bob Swiggett, a member of ABC, started the Kollmorgen Corporation in his garage. George Hatsopoulos, founder of Thermo Electron, and Dermot Dunphy, chief executive officer of Sealed Air Corporation, came to this country as immigrants. Entrepreneurs such as these may have started with very little, but they have added immeasurably to the wealth and the prosperity of our nation. They took hold of the opportunity that America offers, and they used it to create opportunity for others.

I got a letter from one such entrepreneur a few days ago—well, let's say it's a week or so ago—and they'd mentioned—he and his partner mentioned what a pleasure it would be if someday they could come in and say hello. And I turned some people loose on this, found out that they had a business trip planned—those two partners—to Richmond, and so I had Kathy [1] get on the

---

[1] *Kathleen Osborne, Personal Secretary to the President.*

phone and tell them that if it was possible for them to come by way of Washington, I'd be very happy to see them. I was kind of curious to see them, two very bright young fellows and their lovely young wives. They came in, and the reason I was intrigued was that the fellow's name who wrote to me was Cain. And he told me that he and his partner started a business in 1981 with $1,000 capital between them. And everybody told them they could never make it. Last year they did a million and a half in business and are expecting to do $2.5 million this year. And isn't this typical of entrepreneurs in America? The White House operators were kind of awestruck when they called me back to tell me that I had them on the phone, that they were there to talk to me, because their business is now known as Cain and Able. [*Laughter*] He found a fellow named Able and—[*laughter*]. Cain and Able, an electric company—[*laughter*]—have 35 employees.

Well, the entrepreneurial, high-growth firms of the American Business Conference created new jobs 10 times faster than the overall economy and more than 10 times faster than the Fortune 500. America's entrepreneurs are this country's lifeblood. We must allow them the wherewithal to follow through on their dreams and to build a great future for our country.

Taxes are simply the price of government, and democratic governments just like businesses exist in a highly competitive environment. Individuals are constantly making choices about the quality and extent of their participation in the taxed economy. Do high taxes make hard work less rewarding and increased leisure more attractive? Do they make investment less profitable and competition relatively cheaper? Do they channel the remaining investment out of the productive sector into tax shelters and nontaxable assets? And, finally, does the taxed economy begin to lose out altogether to an expanding underground economy?

This was the story of the high-taxed decade of the seventies when more and more Americans decided that the price of government was simply too high. But just as businesses can increase profits by cutting prices and expanding their share of the market, governments can increase revenues by cutting tax rates and expanding the tax base.

This is what Japan did between 1954 and '74 when they cut effective tax rates practically every year. These were, of course, years of unparalleled prosperity for Japan that catapulted them out of the league of underdeveloped nations and into the front ranks of the world's leading economic powers.

Our historic tax cut in '81 gave the United States the same kind of upward push. It's no accident that revenues increased by 11 percent in 1984, which was the first full year when all three elements of our tax cut were in place. There's no better time than now to follow through with a tax reform that will continue to stimulate the entrepreneurial genius of the American people.

You know, it's sometimes been said—and I can tell this. I can't tell ethnic stories anymore, but—[laughter]—present job. But

having gotten my degree in economics, I can tell stories about economists. [*Laughter*] It's been said that if you line a thousand economists up end to end, they still won't reach a conclusion. [*Laughter*]

But the American Business Conference and other companies that are on the cutting edge of our economy know the importance of the growth scenario of tax reform, budget control, and trade liberalization. We're poised on the threshold of an era of unrivaled prosperity, and we'll be looking to you for your support in the crucial months ahead to make it happen.

I thank you very much, and God bless all of you.

Note: The President spoke at 1:19 p.m. in Room 450 of the Old Executive Office Building. At the conclusion of the President's remarks, Arthur Levitt, Jr., chairman and founder of the American Business Conference, presented the President with an award commending his efforts in promoting entrepreneurship in America.

Statement on Signing the Interstate and Defense Highway Funding Bill
March 13, 1985

I am pleased to sign today H.R. 1251, which will release over $7 billion in urgently needed highway and transit construction funds. States can now move forward with projects to close the remaining gaps in the interstate system, and our goal of completing the interstate system by the early 1990's is once again attainable.

H.R. 1251 does not increase our deficit projections because expenditure of these funds is already anticipated in the 1985 and 1986 budgets. Furthermore, this spending is backed by fees paid by highway users who will benefit from highway improvements.

I recognize that many Members of Congress were faced with some hard decisions in supporting this legislation. I am pleased with the courage they showed in laying aside numerous provisions of considerable importance to them in order not to further delay release of these funds. It was a truly bipartisan effort, and I especially thank the leadership on both sides of the aisle in the Senate and House whose efforts made this possible.

Note: H.R. 1251, approved March 13, was assigned Public Law No. 99–4.

Remarks and a Question-and-Answer Session During a White House Briefing for Members of the Magazine Publishers Association
March 14, 1985

The President. Thank you very much, and I want to thank all of you for coming by today and tell you it's a pleasure to have you here.

You know, I've been accused, I know, of being a believer in Norman Rockwell's America; and that's one charge that, as a smalltown boy and a reader of the old Saturday Evening Post, I've always willingly pled guilty to that charge. But looking over your membership leads me to think that many of you are also among the guilty parties. The interests and the readerships that you represent are as wide and ranging as the makeup of our nation itself. That's just another indication of the diversity and the excellence that is so characteristic not only of America but especially her journalistic past and present—another sign that where freedom prospers, many good things happen.

You know, I'm supposed, I know, to do a little serious business here. And you're probably all expecting me to tie in this point about the benefits of a free press to the benefits of a free market and make a pitch for our budget savings and tax simplification. Now, when did I get so predictable? Well, right after inflation went down, interest rates went down, employment went up, and they didn't call it Reaganomics anymore. [*Laughter*]

But actually, though, I've noticed that some stories recently suggesting some remarks of mine on taxes, defense, and freedom in our hemisphere have been, well, shall we say, plain and direct. And as I said at the start of my last press conference, we have an obligation now to be as candid as we were last fall when these issues were very clearly debated and, I think, emphatically decided by the people.

And then, too, I think those of you in the press like a little candor now and then, especially if it's emanating from Washington. Seems that 25 of San Francisco's top bootleggers—this is a little story to illustrate what I've just said about candor—they were arrested back there in those days of the Volstead Act. And as they were being arraigned, the judge asked the usual question, of course, about their occupation. And the first 24 were all engaged in the same professional activity. Each claimed he was a realtor. [*Laughter*] And then he got to the last one, the 25th, and says, "And what are you?" he asked the last prisoner. And the fellow says, "Your Honor, I'm a bootlegger." And the judge was surprised, but he laughed and he said, "Well, how's business?" He said, "It'd be a lot better if there weren't so many realtors around." [*Laughter*]

Well, just like that bootlegger, this administration can make a pretty strong claim to being straightforward about its aims and views. And business is good because, unlike those realtors, we haven't been shy about where we stand. I think this has something to do with the mandate that we received last November.

You may remember a few years back, all of us were very much in need of some straight talk and decisive action. The economic pie was shrinking, and everybody was arguing about how to cut up and distribute a pie that was getting smaller everyday.

Government had grown too big, intrusive; and it seemed that government was subjecting everything we did to more rules, regulations, codes, and legal or quasi-legal proceedings. We were headed for a society where people spent more time getting around things than they did accomplishing them; where achievements were rare, but complaints many; where nothing functioned, but everything was discussed. Merit and excellence, enterprise and innovation, hard work and reward were being replaced by grievance and litigation, chatter and procedure, and gab and process.

Our whole society was in danger of becoming one massive talk show, an all-day seminar, or an unending court battle. And this was causing havoc within the economy.

Business frequently reacted to competition not by devising a better mousetrap but by filing a lawsuit. In fact, we lived in an era in which if you built a better mousetrap, the Government came along with a better mouse. [*Laughter*] And some businesses tended to concentrate not on their customers and how to improve for them its products and services but how to manipulate their cash flow or take advantage of inflation or the tax laws and report short-term profits and, ultimately, illusory gains.

Well, much of this is disappearing. But even today, too many businesses don't make decisions on the basis of what the public wants but what the tax code will permit or reward.

On this point, let me mention that during the debate over the Kemp-Roth bill in 1981, we pointed out that a piece of legislation's most important effects were sometimes not easily recognized or quantified, didn't become immediately apparent, that sometimes its very passage, however, can send out a subtle message and create long-term changes in a political or economic culture that are infinitely more important. We said then that in adopting our economic recovery program, especially the tax rate cuts, we would be setting loose forces whose power could not be fully estimated at the time. I borrowed a phrase from George Gilder and called it the X factor: That spirit of enterprise and creativity that is sparked by the knowledge that government was no longer going to monopolize the future and rob hard-working people of their just rewards—a spirit that could spark not just an economic recovery but an exciting economic expansion.

Well, we saw the X factor do just that. And I hope that you'll keep this in mind as we move ahead during the next few months with the second phase of our economic reforms, especially tax simplification. I also hope that as you see the special interests concentrating on the short-term effects and asking for special dispensations, you'll keep in mind the importance of keeping tax simplification simple. We need to take the long view, to keep in mind what we might call X Factor II or the Son of X Factor—that long-term change in economic climate that tax simplification would cause and the creative

forces it would release.

Just think, for example, what it will mean if that whole army of very talented and shrewd tax lobbyists, lawyers, and accountants suddenly turn its talents and energy to more productive work. Talk about upgrading the work force. [*Laughter*]

So, I think we have before us in tax simplification a tremendous opportunity to further the spirit of enterprise and growth as well as to complete the greatest deregulatory task of them all: to haul ourselves out of the morass that is the Federal tax code. And believe me, this administration intends to push for passage of tax simplification this year.

I'd like to believe, too, that in our foreign policy we've shown steadiness and consistency. I remember that early in the last term some people were a little bit critical of our emphasis on the danger posed to freedom by totalitarian expansion. But if you'll look at the record, you'll see that, while we didn't underestimate the dangers before us, we were taking very early on a view of things that was basically optimistic.

When Prime Minister Thatcher first visited us in February of '81, I mentioned then that totalitarianism had spent its moral energy and that perhaps, like Churchill at the height of World War II, he could sometimes turn our thoughts to a time of "bright, sunlit uplands." Well, when totalitarianism then was only a distant and tragic memory, I can remember, too, a few months later the reaction of the students at Notre Dame when I suggested that, in a sense, the struggle between freedom and totalitarianism was always biased in favor of the democratic side—democratic with a small "d"—that the moral worth and elementary appeal of freedom appeals to everything that's great about the human spirit; communism does not.

The tides are running again in the cause of freedom, but this doesn't necessarily mean the whole world has grown less dangerous. And that's why our position in the arms talks in Geneva is critically important. So, too, our defense buildup and Secretary Weinberger's budget proposals are critical to the success of those talks, indeed, to the safety of the world. Nothing could endanger us more than a perception in the East that America, after making so much progress, was suddenly losing her will to keep the peace and negotiate from strength. And that, in a few words, is the importance of the upcoming MX vote.

The Soviets will be following the vote on the MX with keen interest. And the signal to them will be unmistakable. America will be seen as united and ready to negotiate if the MX moves forward or returning again to vacillation and weakness if the MX fails.

And, so, too, our commitment is to those who are struggling for freedom around the world. That's particularly true in Central America where a democratic revolution in Nicaragua was hijacked by a small cadre of Marxist-Leninists. They are totalitarians. They share an all too familiar obsession with personal power, and they hold to a prideful and corrupt desire to rule and dominate the lives of others. We owe those who oppose these totalitarians the best assistance that we can give them.

Freedom is on the march. It's an exciting time to live and to live here in Norman Rockwell's America and all across the world.

And I'm going to quit with the monolog because they've told me that if I do, I can have a few minutes to take a few of your questions which I would like to do very well. I may be sorry after saying that but— [*laughter*]——

Q. Mr. President, Mr. Stockman said this morning that he found a lot of good things in the package passed by the Republicans on the Senate Budget Committee last night. Would you be willing to accept some moderation in the defense increases as part of a total package that came out of Congress?

The President. I've seen the general statement made in the press. I have not yet had time to look at the—in detail—what it was the Senate Committee came up with. So, I don't know what it is they've called for with regard to the defense budget. But I'd like to call your attention to just one thing about the defense budget, where it is different than anything else. I know over the years we've been accustomed to seeing Congress, anytime they needed money for another program or some favorite of theirs, to say, "We can get it from the defense budget."

And that's how we got to the position we were in in 1980, where half our airplanes on any given day couldn't fly for lack of spare parts or pilots, where ships couldn't leave port in the Navy because they didn't have enough noncommissioned officers left on board. And we started out to do something.

Defense budget isn't something that you sit down, as you do with some other programs, and say, "Well, here, let's spend so much or let's reduce so much." It's determined by what the other fellow's doing. What do you need? And you can't look at the dollars; you have to look and say, "Okay, if we must reduce, which of these things can we do without? What should we do away with, and what will that do to our national security?"

But I'd also like to point out that we have been conscious of the elimination of waste and fraud in the Federal Government, undue extravagance. Because right now our request for the 1986 budget is $26 billion less than our own projection for that budget 2 years ago. Congress didn't do that, we've done it.

We've done it with management improvements; we have done it with the reducing of inflation. And when you see those stories or even print some about $400 hammers, let me point something out that hasn't been noticed. Those figures were true. But that's what has been going on. We're the ones that are providing those figures because we're the ones that are finding the $400 hammers and doing something about it. And there have been hundreds of indictments, some imprisonments. There have been millions and millions of dollars, hundreds of millions of dollars in rebates made to us because we have been finding these things. And that's why, right now, our projected budgets are lower than the 5-year projected budgets of the previous administration.

And, so, I want to look very critically at what it is that someone there in the Budget Committee thinks we can do without. Have they actually specified something or are they just saying you can't spend as much money as you have listed?

Q. Mr. President, Secretary Gorbachev is

of a different generation than his immediate predecessors, perhaps more pragmatic and worldly and less theological. You see all those private, high-level reports that, of course, we don't see. Do you have any reason to believe that he is fundamentally different from his immediate predecessors?

The President. Well, I don't think there's any evidence that he is less dominated by their system and their philosophy than any of the others. But it isn't true that I don't trust anyone under 70. [*Laughter*]

I think he has spoken out there to his own people about improvements in the economy there, particularly is he noted for advocating, you might say, more private venture in the agricultural section than the present system of government farms. And I look forward to dealing with him.

I think what is most evident, and I believe that this will be reflected in him, is that the Soviet Union is in a different frame of mind than they've been in the past: That they are back at the negotiating table on arms reductions because they recognize a hard, cold fact, and that is that the United States isn't going to unilaterally disarm in the face of their military buildup.

And now that they know that they have to compete with us with regard to security needs, I think they've got a healthy respect for our technology and our industrial capacity and that they, I believe, are really going to try and, with us, negotiate a reduction of armaments.

That has never been done before. There have been agreements like the SALT agreements that only limited how fast you could increase. But this is the first time that they, themselves, have said they would like to see the elimination of nuclear weapons.

Ms. Mathis. One more quick question.

The President. Oh, dear. I should come over to this side. I'm on that side all the way.

Don Hanrahan, of Sport magazine. I have two questions, Mr. President. Georgetown going to repeat, and what are the chances of the Chicago Cubs making it to the Series? [*Laughter*]

The President. Well, now, I have to tell you I have a healthy respect for Georgetown because I remember when one of your magazines came and asked for a cover picture of me standing between their coach and Ewing, their star player. And I looked at that cover. It looked like I was sitting down. [*Laughter*]

And then one of your people said to me while I was holding a basketball between these two—one of them said, "Why don't you act like you're taking a shot and he's pretending to block you?" And I said, "What do you mean, pretend?" [*Laughter*] But I wouldn't count them out. But then, I was a sports announcer too long to make predictions.

In that sports announcing, I also broadcast the Chicago Cubs games. And I was broadcasting something that still lives in the record books. It's never been equalled since. And that was when the Chicago Cubs only had one mathematical chance of winning the pennant, and they had to win the last 21 games of the season to do it. And the final series was with the team they had to beat for the pennant, and they did it. They came through straight, all 21 games. And it was quite an exciting experience. And then they lost 4 straight to Detroit. [*Laughter*] I've always said that I think, having been in athletics myself, it was the letdown after that other achievement that they couldn't get back up there. But it's also led me to hesitate to predict when they'll win a series. [*Laughter*]

Well, you tell me that's all I can do. Well, I'm sorry. I should have cut the other remarks short. But thank you all very much.

Note: The President spoke at 11:32 a.m. in Room 450 of the Old Executive Office Building. Susan K. Mathis was Deputy Director of Media Relations.

Appointment of Denny E. Brisley as Staff Assistant to the Press Secretary
March 14, 1985

The President today announced the appointment of Denny E. Brisley to be Staff Assistant to the Press Secretary. She will serve as the administration coordinator for television interviews.

Since October 1982 Miss Brisley had been public affairs specialist with the Office of Management and Budget. While attending Stanford University, she served as an aide to the director of the Hoover Institution for War, Revolution and Peace at Stanford, CA, in 1980–1982.

Miss Brisley received her B.A. in international relations from Stanford University in 1982. She was born May 31, 1960, in Lebanon, MO, and now resides in Arlington, VA.

Message to the Senate Transmitting a Protocol to the International Convention for the Conservation of Atlantic Tunas
March 14, 1985

To the Senate of the United States:

I transmit herewith, for the advice and consent of the Senate to ratification, the Protocol agreed upon July 10, 1984 by the Conference of Plenipotentiaries of the Contracting Parties to the International Convention for the Conservation of Atlantic Tunas (ICCAT). The Protocol was signed by the United States on September 10, 1984. It will enter into force following ratification by all Contracting Parties of the ICCAT. Also transmitted for the information of the Senate is the report of the Department of State with respect to the Protocol.

The Protocol would amend the ICCAT to permit intergovernmental economic integration organizations, such as the European Economic Community (EEC), to become Contracting Parties to the ICCAT on behalf of their member States. The ICCAT, which seeks to promote the conservation of tuna and tuna-like fish in the Atlantic Ocean, now provides only for the accession of individual States as Contracting Parties.

Once the Protocol has entered into force, it is anticipated that the EEC will take the necessary steps to become a Contracting Party. At that time France will withdraw from the ICCAT. These actions are intended to recognize the competence of the EEC over fisheries matters on behalf of its member States and is consistent with the long-standing support of the United States for the process of European integration embodied by the EEC. Ratification by the United States will be necessary before the Protocol can enter into force, as the Protocol stipulates that all Contracting Parties must ratify the agreement in order for its provisions to take effect.

I recommend that the Senate give early consideration to the Protocol and give its advice and consent to ratification.

RONALD REAGAN

The White House,
March 14, 1985.

Letter to the Speaker of the House and the President of the Senate on the Designation of the Bahamas as a Caribbean Basin Economic Recovery Act Beneficiary
March 14, 1985

Dear Mr. Speaker: (Dear Mr. President:)

Pursuant to Section 212 of the Caribbean Basin Economic Recovery Act (CBERA), I wish to inform you of my intent to designate the Bahamas as a beneficiary of the trade-liberalizing measures provided for in this Act. Designation will entitle the products of the Bahamas to duty-free treatment until September 30, 1995, except for products statutorily excluded. As a beneficiary, this country will have the opportunity to become eligible for the convention expense tax deduction under Section 274(h) and to become an eligible domicile for the establishment of foreign sales corporations under Section 927(e)(3)(A) of the Internal Revenue Code of 1954, by entering into an exchange of information agreement with the United States on tax matters.

Designation is an important step for the Bahamas in its effort to strengthen its economy. Designation is also significant because it is further tangible evidence of the constructive cooperation between the United States and the peoples and governments of the Caribbean Basin.

My decision to designate the Bahamas flows out of discussions held between this Administration and that nation regarding the designation criteria set forth in Section 212 of the CBERA. Our discussions with the Bahamas were concluded this past month.

The Bahamas have demonstrated to my satisfaction that its laws, practices, and policies are in conformity with the designation criteria of the CBERA. The government of the Bahamas has communicated on these matters by letter with Secretary of State Shultz and Ambassador Brock and in so doing has indicated its desire to be designated as a beneficiary (copies of the letters are enclosed). On the basis of the statements and assurances in this letter, and taking into account information developed by the United States Embassy and through other sources, I have concluded that the objectives of the Administration and the Congress with respect to the statutory designation criteria of the CBERA have been met.

I am mindful that under Section 213(B)(2) of the CBERA, I retain the authority to suspend or withdraw CBERA benefits from any designated beneficiary country if a beneficiary's laws, policies, or practices are no longer in conformity with the designation criteria. The United States will keep abreast of developments in the Bahamas and other beneficiary countries and entities which are pertinent to the designation criteria.

This Administration has been and will continue to work closely with its fellow governments in the Caribbean Basin and with the private sectors of the United States and the Basin countries to ensure that the wide-ranging opportunities opened by the CBERA are fully utilized.

Sincerely,

RONALD REAGAN

Note: Identical letters were sent to Thomas P. O'Neill, Jr., Speaker of the House of Representatives, and George Bush, President of the Senate. The letters were released by the Office of the Press Secretary on March 15.

Proclamation 5308—Designation of the Bahamas as a Caribbean Basin Economic Recovery Act Beneficiary
March 14, 1985

To Amend Proclamation 5133 Implementing the Caribbean Basin Economic Recovery Act

By the President of the United States of America

A Proclamation

1. Section 212 of the Caribbean Basin Economic Recovery Act (the Act) (19 U.S.C. 2702) authorizes the President to designate certain countries and territories or successor political entities as "beneficiary countries" under the Act. In Proclamation 5133 of November 30, 1983, and Proclamation 5142 of December 29, 1983, I have designated 20 countries and territories as "beneficiary countries." I am now adding the Bahamas to the list of "beneficiary countries." I have notified the House of Representatives and the Senate of my intention to designate this country and given the considerations entering into my decision.

2. In order to add this country to the list of beneficiary countries, I am amending the Annex to Proclamation 5133.

3. Section 213(a)(2) of the Act directs the Secretary of the Treasury to prescribe regulations implementing the provisions of the Act relating to articles eligible for duty-free treatment. Section 213(a)(2) also sets out certain specific provisions that Congress sought to have included in the eventual amendments to the Tariff Schedules of the United States. Proclamation 5133 is to be amended in order to bring the language of its Annex into direct conformity with the express intent of the Congress and to eliminate language no longer applicable to the duty-free entry of eligible articles by virtue of recent amendments to the implementing regulations.

Now, Therefore, I, Ronald Reagan, President of the United States of America, acting under the authority vested in me by the Constitution and the statutes of the United States, including but not limited to Section 212 of the Act, do proclaim that:

(1) The list of countries in the Annex to Proclamation 5133 of November 30, 1983, is hereby amended by adding the Bahamas.

(2) The Annex to Proclamation 5133 is further amended to strike the phrase "manufacturer or exporter of the article accompanied by an endorsement thereof by the importer or consignee" in Paragraph A of the Annex amending language in general headnote 3(g)(ii)(B) of the Tariff Schedules of the United States and to replace it with the phrase "appropriate party."

In Witness Whereof, I have hereunto set my hand this 14th day of March, in the year of our Lord nineteen hundred and eighty-five, and of the Independence of the United States of America the two hundred and ninth.

Ronald Reagan

[*Filed with the Office of the Federal Register, 3:59 p.m., March 15, 1985*]

Note: The proclamation was released by the Office of the Press Secretary on March 15.

Nomination of D. Lowell Jensen To Be Deputy Attorney General
March 15, 1985

The President today announced his intention to nominate D. Lowell Jensen to be Deputy Attorney General, Department of Justice. He would succeed Carol E. Dinkins.

Since July 1983 he has been serving as Associate Attorney General at the Department of Justice. Previously he was Assistant Attorney General in charge of the Criminal Division in 1981–1983. He served as district attorney of Alameda County, CA, in 1969–

1980; assistant district attorney of Alameda County in 1966–1969; and deputy district attorney of Alameda County in 1955–1966.

He served as president of the California District Attorneys Association in 1979–1980; member of the board of directors of the California Crime Technological Research Foundation in 1970–1974; and chairman of the California Peace Officers Association's law and legislative committee in 1969–1977.

He graduated from the University of California at Berkeley (A.B., 1949) and the University of California School of Law, Boalt (LL.B., 1952). He is married, has three children, and resides in Arlington, VA. He was born June 3, 1928, in Brigham, UT.

Nomination of William Bradford Reynolds To Be Associate Attorney General
March 15, 1985

The President today announced his intention to nominate William Bradford Reynolds to be Associate Attorney General, Department of Justice. He would succeed D. Lowell Jensen.

Since July 1981 he has been serving as Assistant Attorney General in charge of the Civil Rights Division. Previously, he was a litigation partner with the law firm of Shaw, Pittman, Potts & Trowbridge in Washington, DC (1973–1981); assistant to the Solicitor General of the United States in 1970–1973; associate with the law firm of Sullivan & Cromwell in New York City (1967–1970); and assistant to the U.S. Attorney for the Eastern District of Tennessee in 1966.

Mr. Reynolds graduated from Yale University (B.A., 1964) and Vanderbilt University School of Law (J.D., 1967). He is married, has four children, and resides in Potomac, MD. He was born June 21, 1942, in Bridgeport, CT.

Appointment of Alan Michael Kranowitz as Deputy Assistant to the President for Legislative Affairs
March 15, 1985

The President today announced the appointment of Alan Michael Kranowitz as Deputy Assistant to the President for Legislative Affairs. His primary responsibility will be liaison with the House of Representatives. He will join the White House in mid-March to effect a transition with Dennis Thomas, who will leave that post on April 5.

Mr. Kranowitz has served since January 1979 as chief of staff to Congressman Tom Loeffler (R-TX). Prior to joining Congressman Loeffler's staff, Kranowitz was a professional staff member on the Senate Republican Policy Committee. In 1975–1976 he served as Assistant to the Director for Legislative Affairs at the Office of Management and Budget.

In 1971–1975 Kranowitz served as Director of Legislative Affairs at the Department of Housing and Urban Development under Secretaries George Romney, James Lynn, and Carla Hills.

He graduated from Yale University (B.A., 1963). He is married, has two children, and resides in Bethesda, MD. He was born March 19, 1941, in New Britain, CT.

Appointment of Bryce L. Harlow as Special Assistant to the President for Legislative Affairs
March 15, 1985

The President today announced the appointment of Bryce L. Harlow as a Special Assistant to the President for Legislative Affairs. He will succeed Nancy Mohr Kennedy, who has joined the staff of Max L. Friedersdorf, Assistant to the President, and Legislative Strategy Coordinator.

Mr. Harlow has been Director of the Office of Congressional Relations at the Federal Trade Commission since October 1981. Previously he was Special Assistant to the Administrator and Acting Director of the Office of Legislation of the Environmental Protection Agency from January

1981 until joining the Federal Trade Commission. He was director of governmental relations for the Grocery Manufacturers of America, Inc., in 1976–1981. Mr. Harlow also has handled State legislative liaison for the Environmental Protection Agency at the Denver regional office (1972–1976) and worked for Senator Howard Baker while attending college.

He graduated from George Washington University (B.A., 1971). He is married, has two children, and resides in Vienna, VA. He was born January 21, 1949, in Oklahoma City, OK.

Appointment of Frederick D. McClure as Special Assistant to the President for Legislative Affairs
March 15, 1985

The President today announced the appointment of Frederick D. McClure to be a Special Assistant to the President for Legislative Affairs (Senate). He will succeed Robert J. Kabel.

Mr. McClure most recently served as Associate Deputy Attorney General at the Department of Justice. Previously he served as legislative director to Senator John Tower (R-TX) in 1983–1984 and as State director

and legislative assistant to Senator Tower (1977–1979). In 1981–1983 he was a commercial trial attorney associated with Reynolds, Allen and Cook in Houston, TX.

He graduated from Texas A&M University (B.S., 1976) and Baylor University School of Law (J.D., 1981). He is married, has two children, and resides in Arlington, VA. He was born February 2, 1954, in Fort Worth, TX.

Appointment of Four Members of the Advisory Committee for Trade Negotiations
March 15, 1985

The President today announced his intention to appoint the following individuals to be members of the Advisory Committee for Trade Negotiations for terms of 2 years.

Stephen I. Danzansky will succeed James Dutt. He is a partner in the law firm of Wilkie, Farr & Gallagher in Washington, DC. Previously he

was a partner in the law firm of Danzansky, Dickey, Tydings, Quint & Gordon in Washington, DC (1971–1981, 1964–1970). He served as general counsel and operations coordinator for the White House Conference on Children and Youth in 1970–1971. He graduated from Washington & Lee University (A.B., 1961) and George Washington University (J.D., 1964). He is married, has two children, and resides in Washington, DC. He was born July 31, 1939, in Washington, DC.

Loyd Hackler is a reappointment. Since 1975 he has been president of the American Retail Federation in Washington, DC. Previously, he was administrative assistant to Senator Lloyd Bentsen (1971–1975); president of his own firm, Management Consultants, Inc., in 1969–1971; and Assistant Press Secretary to the President in 1966–1969. He graduated from Oklahoma State University (1949). He is married, has three children, and resides in Del Rio, TX. He was born March 23, 1926, in Cloud Chief, OK.

Linda Wachner will succeed John G. Hutchens. She is a partner in the firm of Adler & Shaykin in Encino, CA. Previously she was president and chief executive officer of Max Factor & Co. and before that served as vice president of the Warner Division of Warnaco. She serves as a board member of the Los Angeles Area Chamber of Commerce and the Mayor's Business Advisory Board of the City of Los Angeles. She graduated from the University of Buffalo (B.S., 1966). She was born February 3, 1946, in New York, NY, and now resides in Los Angeles, CA.

Virginia S. Weinman will succeed William Agee. She is president of SYMBIOSIS in Menlo Park, CA. She also serves as a financial and technical adviser to the Educational Support Corp. in Portola Valley, CA. She is cofounder and chief executive officer of Venture Equity Technology Corp. in Menlo Park, CA. In 1971–1978 she was cofounder and chief executive officer of Interactive Applications, Inc., in Palo Alto, CA. She graduated from Stanford University Graduate School of Business (M.Sc., 1983). She is married and resides in Menlo Park, CA. She was born November 20, 1938, in Edmonton, Alberta, Canada.

Remarks of the President and Irish Ambassador Tadhg F. O'Sullivan at a St. Patrick's Day Ceremony
March 15, 1985

The Ambassador. Mr. President, it's an old established tradition that a shamrock is presented to the President of the United States on St. Patrick's Day—I hope I can get this pin out. [*Laughter*] And this reflects the ties of kinship between the Irish in our island and the Irish here in the United States of whom you, sir, are the great representative. Thank you. And St. Patrick's Day is a day which reminds us all of these ties of kinship and affection. This year, in particular, we recall with special pleasure your own visit to Ireland, your visit to Galway, my own hometown, sir, where you were given the freedom of the city, and your stay in Ashford Castle.

This year is also the 800th anniversary of the city of Cork, an ancient seaport town in the south of Ireland with a long tradition of silvermaking. Indeed, it is said—a legend has it that Saint Finbarr, the patron of Cork and in a way the founder of the original settlement there, was himself a silversmith.

And to commemorate the 800th anniversary of the city of Cork, I present to you, sir, on behalf of all citizens of Cork and all Irish people, this silver dish.

Thank you.

The President. Well, thank you very much. And I would like in return to present to you, before my remarks, this letter. And you will notice that there is a very special letterhead on this White House stationery.

The Ambassador. [*Spoke in Gaelic.*]

The President. Well, I'm pleased that we could get together since on St. Patrick's Day we will be out of town; as a matter of fact, we'll be out of the country. But I'm always happy to spend St. Patrick's Day with great Irishmen, who reciprocate the warm hospitality that greeted us on our trip to Ireland last year.

And concerning Northern Ireland, I applaud and encourage the active Anglo-Irish dialog and support all those who are working for peaceful reconciliation there. And among them very prominently is Ambassador Tadhg O'Sullivan, who's working for that reconciliation.

I'm honored to receive this shamrock and will wear it as an expression of my hope for peace and good will in the year ahead.

Friendship with Ireland and the Irish people is deep and enduring.

I understand that this bowl here has, as we've been told, a special historical meaning for the city of Cork. It has a little historical meaning for me also because I understand that the Clan Reagan is very prominent in Cork and in that city.

To add some special flavor now, I would like to have a presentation made to the Ambassador: Girl Scout cookies are world famous, and here in emerald uniform are some representatives of the Girl Scouts. And one of them is going to present Girl Scout cookies to the Ambassador.

The Ambassador. Thank you.

The President. You have done it already. [*Laughter*] Well——

The Ambassador. Stand there, and we'll do it again—[*laughter*]——

The President. The—yes, just put——

[*At this point, the presentation was made.*]

The President. There.

The Ambassador. Thank you.

The President. Now—because I'm afraid that those people with the cameras didn't see you. Well, thank you very much, and thank you all for being here.

The Ambassador. Thank you, girls.

Girl Scouts. Thank you.

The Ambassador. Appreciate it; you're very kind.

The President. I didn't—are those special uniforms for the day? [*Laughter*] Well, thank you all for being here, and thank you, Mr. Ambassador.

The Ambassador. Thank you, sir.

The President. I'm very proud to have this.

The Ambassador. Thank you. Thank you very much.

Reporter. Mr. President, when's Gorbachev coming here? [*Laughter*]

The President. This is an Irish day. We're only talking about Irish who are already here.

Q. Well, Mr. President, are you going to use your shillelagh on Republican Senators who don't support you? [*Laughter*]

The President. I hadn't thought of it, but it's an idea. [*Laughter*]

Note: Ambassador O'Sullivan spoke at 10:53 a.m. in the Rose Garden at the White House.

Remarks Congratulating the Championship Spingarn High School Basketball Team
March 15, 1985

The President. The way I see it, there's no more fitting way to mark the coming of St. Patrick's Day than by greeting the Green Wave. So, welcome to the White House, all of you.

Students. Thank you.

The President. Well, we're very happy to see and meet our champions, the members of the City High School Basketball Championship Team of 1985 and we congratulate you.

And I can tell you that I know a little more about your victory than you think I do. I've heard about how Anthony Duckett, Emmanuel Jones, and Ernest Hall got together to control the boards; and I know that Robert Smith played with the flu; and I know that Sherman Douglas got 14 points; and I know Melvin Middleton played in spite of an injury that he received in the first play of the game. And I know that you faced a really strong and fine team in DeMatha—do I have the name right on that?

Coach Wood. You're right.

The President. All right, and that you had to work hard to win. I know all this because Kathy Reid, the wife of Joe Reid, your English teacher, is an assistant to Don Regan here in the White House. And Kathy gave us no peace. We couldn't get any work done in the White House until Spingarn won. So, believe me, on behalf of a grateful nation, I thank you.

We really are proud of you and of all the

people who've helped you. I think you ought to be proud of your coach, John Wood, who, himself, graduated from Spingarn. And I hope you thank your assistant coach, Robert Burrell. This ceremony is part of a plot to wean him from his lollipops. [*Laughter*] We're going to get him on jelly beans. [*Laughter*] And I congratulate your principal, Clemmie Strayhorn.

You know, the past few years the Spingarn concert choir has sung at the White House during Christmas tours. And the graduates of Spingarn include Michael Graham and Elgin Baylor, Earl Jones and Dave Bing—that's quite a powerhouse that you've been running, Clemmie.

Spingarn has brought honor to this city. And even though Nancy and I came here just a few years ago—we liked it enough to ask for a few more, as you know—we feel like citizens or members of the city of Washington, and we personally feel that you've done us all proud here in this city.

So, thanks, and God bless to all of you, and thank you for coming by to say hello.

Coach Wood. Mr. President, we would like to thank you for the generous invitation that you have extended to the Spingarn basketball team and also the cheerleading staff.

At this particular time, we would like for you to sign a basketball for us, and we will treasure it, this basketball, for a great deal of time.

The President. Any place in particular on here? I've got a pen.

Coach Wood. That will be fine, wherever your signature—wherever you put it.

The President. Looks like there's room under there.

[*At this point, the President signed the basketball.*]

Coach Wood. Also, Mr. President, we would like to give to you something we would like for you to cherish—a picture of the Spingarn basketball team——

The President. Thank you very much.

Coach Wood. ——and also we would like for you to have a basketball, the basketball that we used to beat DeMatha, and we are extending that to you.

Thank you.

The President. You mean I get the game ball? [*Laughter*]

Coach Wood. You get the game ball.

The President. Well, thank you very much.

Coach Wood. Thank you.

The President. I'm very pleased with all of this and to have this picture. It's a beautiful—isn't that the Lincoln Memorial?

Coach Wood. Yes, it is.

The President. Well, that's great.

Coach Wood. It exemplifies academic excellence.

The President. Well, I'm glad to hear that that goes along with basketball.

I must say, I'm glad there's still some here that are along about my height—[*laughter*]—but you all are growing bigger these days. [*Laughter*] But I'm pleased to have you all come down today.

I had hoped that there was going to be an opportunity—you could have a little visit—and I was reading about Reverend Jackson's appearance before your student body the other day, and I thought it was a very wonderful thing that he did with regard to drugs. I thought that was just great.

I did, though, then think that maybe he didn't quite understand our program with regard to aid to education, for college aid. We're not really cutting that back; we're redirecting it a little.

We found out, and we don't think that people with incomes of a hundred thousand dollars a year need your parents and others like them paying taxes to help put their kids through college. They ought to be able to do that themselves. And so what we've done is redirect the aid to people who really can claim a need for having help.

And we've set a cap so we can increase the numbers of—$4,000 of student aid in the form of jobs, grants, so forth, which is the average across the country, total thing of tuition and fees and room and board and so forth—all the State colleges and universities in the country.

And, in addition, students would be eligible for guaranteed loans of another $4,000. And we actually will be spending—I think the figure's around $13 billion on that.

So, I was glad that he suggested that you ask, but I'm sorry that we didn't have the chance to ask, so I just decided to answer it right here for you.

But, again, God bless you, and congratulations. You've really—31 straight; that's quite a record. Good luck to all of you.

Students. Thank you.

Reporter. Mr. President, what about [Secretary of Labor] Ray Donovan?

The President. We'll be releasing a statement later on.

Q. Is he leaving, sir?

The President. We'll be releasing a statement later on, Andrea [Andrea Mitchell, CBS News].

Q. What are your feelings about it?

The President. I still have faith and confidence in Ray Donovan.

Note: The President spoke at 2:06 p.m. in the Rose Garden at the White House.

Statement on the Observance of St. Patrick's Day
March 15, 1985

This year I will be celebrating St. Patrick's Day with Irishmen from north of our border—in a city more generally thought of for its French, not Irish, customs. Brian Mulroney, a great Irishman and Canadian, has invited me to participate in St. Patrick's Day festivities in Quebec City, and I look forward to sharing our Canadian friends' celebration of this very special day.

As you may know, our planned meeting in Quebec has been dubbed the "Shamrock Summit." I think this is only fitting—yet another indication of the far-reaching influence of the Emerald Isle. As we, all Irishmen, pay tribute to and revel in our shared heritage today, let us remember our kinsmen in the poetic "land across the Irish Sea" and reflect on how we can ensure that they too share fully in the blessings this great heritage has helped bring to us.

Is there a lovelier place on Earth? As a recent visitor, I must answer no. The whole island, from the glens of Antrim to the rugged coast of Cork, has a lyrical welcoming beauty, the memory of which a visitor will retain in his heart forever. Millions of Americans like me already know this; I hope that millions more will discover it.

Yet the tranquil beauty of the land itself is not sufficient to drown out the discord. We in America must make every effort to ensure that, whether knowingly or unknowingly, no material, financial, or psychological help originates from this side of the Atlantic for those who advocate and practice violence. As I have said on many occasions, such persons will find no welcome here. On the contrary, we have intensified our efforts to ensure that the United States is not the source of guns and money for such activities.

We encourage those who strive to peacefully resolve problems underlying the conflict. I also encourage Americans to let their foreign investment and vacation dollars find a profitable haven in the island, an approach that would benefit all. Indeed, we firmly believe that foreign investments, and the employment opportunities that would accompany such investments, can play an increasingly significant role in promoting peaceful change. In this regard, I urge that serious consideration be given to all economic as well as political proposals evolving from a spirit of consensus and reconciliation. We in the United States can be counted on to do our part to ensure that proposals which can be of assistance in promoting this process receive due consideration.

We applaud the increased political interchange in the last year regarding the Irish situation and hope that it leads to forward movement so that soon all Irishmen, whether on the green island or abroad, can share equally in the joy brought by a day like today in the United States, where it is marked by peace, friendship, and harmony.

I wish you all a very happy St. Patrick's Day.

Appointment of Two Members of the Federal Service Impasses Panel
March 15, 1985

The President today announced his intention to appoint the following individuals to be members of the Federal Service Impasses Panel, Federal Labor Relations Authority, for terms expiring January 10, 1990. These are reappointments.

Thomas A. Farr has been an associate with the law firm of Maupin, Taylor & Ellis in Raleigh, NC, since 1983. Previously, he was a law clerk to Frank W. Bullock, Jr., United States Judge for the Middle District of North Carolina, in 1983; attorney adviser, Office of the General Counsel, Office of Personnel Management, in 1982–1983; labor counsel to the United States Senate Labor and Human Resources Committee in 1981–1982; and staff attorney for the National Right To Work Legal Defense Foundation, Inc., in 1979–1981. He graduated from Hillsdale College (B.A., 1976), Emory University School of Law (J.D., 1979), and Georgetown University Law Center (LL.M., 1983). He is married and resides in Raleigh, NC. He was born October 24, 1954, in Cincinnati, OH.

Jean T. McKelvey has been a professor at the Cornell School of Industrial and Labor Relations since 1946. She is on the Panel of Arbitrators for the State of New York. She serves at the American Arbitration Association as a member of the Mediation Advisory Committee and the Advisory Council for the Arbitration Journal. She is also a member of the U.S. Postal Service Expedited Arbitration Panels and the executive board of the International Society for Labor Law and Social Legislation. She graduated from Wellesley College (A.B., 1929) and Radcliffe College (M.A., 1931; Ph.D., 1933). She is married and resides in Rochester, NY. She was born February 9, 1908, in St. Louis, MO.

Statement on the Resignation of Raymond J. Donovan as Secretary of Labor
March 15, 1985

It is with deep regret that I accept the resignation of Raymond Donovan as Secretary of Labor. Ray Donovan has not been convicted of anything; and, no less than any other American, he is entitled to the benefit of a presumption of innocence. While I agree with Ray that his need to devote himself fully to his defense now precludes his continuing in office, he leaves the Cabinet with my friendship and heartfelt gratitude for all of his efforts on behalf of this administration.

Note: Larry M. Speakes, Principal Deputy Press Secretary to the President, read the President's statement to reporters at 4:15 p.m. in the Briefing Room at the White House.

Letter Accepting the Resignation of Raymond J. Donovan as Secretary of Labor
March 15, 1985

Dear Ray:

It is with deep personal regret that I am today accepting your resignation as Secretary of Labor. While I understand and appreciate your desire to devote yourself fully to your defense, I want you to know that you leave the Cabinet with my friendship and gratitude for the years of service you have given to this Administration—and for the tireless efforts you have made in my campaigns. Nancy and I are aware of the sacrifices you made to serve your country as Secretary of Labor, and the difficulties you and your family have endured. Know that in the days ahead, you and Cathy will be in our thoughts, and in our prayers.

Sincerely,

RON

[The Honorable Raymond J. Donovan, 1333 Skipwith Road, McLean, Virginia 22102]

Dear Mr. President:

It is with a profound mixture of regret and pride that I submit to you my resignation as Secretary of Labor.

It has been the greatest privilege of my life to have served for four years in the Cabinet of the best President this country has ever elected. Under your leadership, we have renewed the vitality of our economy and restored our citizens' faith in this great Nation. I know your second Administration will continue on the path to ensure the economic and spiritual growth of America.

I will be forever indebted to you for the opportunity to have served you and our country, and for your unwavering support and friendship.

Godspeed in your continued efforts.

Respectfully,

RAY
RAYMOND J. DONOVAN

[The President, The White House, Washington, D.C. 20500]

Radio Address to the Nation on the Upcoming Trip to Canada
March 16, 1985

My fellow Americans:

Tomorrow, in our first trip outside the States in this second term, Nancy and I will be heading north to visit our good neighbors in Canada. We're going at the invitation of Canada's Prime Minister Brian Mulroney, who is an articulate and effective defender of Canadian interests, a strong friend of the United States, and the best votegetter in his nation's history.

We're delighted that Brian Mulroney has chosen Quebec City, capital of his home Province, as the site of our meeting. With its old streets and charming ways, Quebec is one of the most intriguing corners of North America, right on our northeastern doorstep. Quebec is modern, too, supplying the United States with everything from electric power to aerospace parts for our defense industries.

We're going to Canada now for one simple reason: No country is more important to the United States. Sometimes we overlook that fact. Sometimes our friendship and cooperation may not seem to warrant as much attention as the serious problems we're dealing with in other areas. But certain facts about our Canadian neighbors, with whom we share the world's longest undefended boundary, must never be overlooked.

Canada and the United States are each other's most important trading partner. There is greater volume of trade between our two countries than between any other two countries in the world. We sold $45 billion in goods to Canada in 1984, which supported hundreds of thousands of jobs in the United States. Canada is our principal foreign supplier of natural gas and electricity, and Canada is the most important locale for our foreign investment. Walk around our cities and towns today, and you can see increased Canadian investment in real estate and many other parts of our economy.

Most important, the national security of the United States and of Canada are very closely interrelated. The commander in chief of the North American Aerospace Defense Command in Colorado Springs is from the States; his deputy is Canadian; and their staff is divided among U.S. and Canadian officers.

Four years ago some problems had developed in relations between the United States and Canada. But we've been working hard on both sides of the border to set things right. Today Canadian-American relations are good, as good as they've ever been. And during this trip, the Prime Minister and I are determined to do all we can to make them even better.

We will seek to strengthen our economic relations: Market-oriented policies without government interference hold out the best opportunities for our two countries to prosper as economic partners. So, we welcome Canadian investment in the United States and the Mulroney government's legislation to loosen restrictions on foreign investment in Canada, which is an important first step toward liberalizing Canada's own investment policies. It's the firm policy of this administration to resist protectionist pressures. So, we would like Canada and other countries to join us in a new round of multilateral trade talks in 1986.

We will encourage the sharing of our mutual defense responsibilities. Canada is a founding member of NATO, with a proud military history stretching from Vimy Ridge in France during the First World War to the skies over Germany in the Second, to the seas off Korea during that conflict. We're pleased with the commitment of Brian Mulroney's government to increase significantly Canada's overall contribution to our shared defense responsibilities.

On the quest for arms reductions and on other global problems, Canada's counsel will be a source of great wisdom and strength. The Prime Minister and I will exchange views on developments throughout the world, including the Geneva arms reduction talks and our own efforts to protect freedom, democracy, and peace in this hemisphere.

The United States is a pioneer in environmental protection, and we share with Canada a special responsibility for protecting our shared North American environment. The problem of acid rain concerns both our countries, and I'm anxious to hear the Prime Minister's views on that subject.

In 1939 Winston Churchill, describing the 5,000-mile peaceful border dividing Canada and the United States, said: "That long frontier from the Atlantic to the Pacific Oceans, guarded only by neighborly respect and honorable obligations, is an example to every country and a pattern for the future of the world."

Today, more than ever, our progress, our partnership, and our friendship can be a model for others and a pattern for the future. Working together, Canada and the United States can accomplish great things for the cause of a safer, freer, and more prosperous world. And that's what our trip is all about.

Until next week, thanks for listening. God bless you.

Note: The President spoke at 12:06 p.m. from the Oval Office at the White House.

Remarks at the Welcoming Ceremony in Quebec City, Canada
March 17, 1985

Prime Minister, Mrs. Mulroney, thank you very much. Premier and Mrs. Levesque, distinguished ladies and gentlemen, and my friends, the people of Canada, it's a great pleasure to be here, for to be on Canadian soil is to be among friends, and Nancy and I are happy to return here.

Et nous sommes heureux que notre voyage nous permette de venir dans cette

belle ville de Quebec. [And we are happy that our trip takes us to this beautiful city of Quebec.] Quebec is one of the most intriguing spots on the continent. Here New France was founded. Here French is the language of commerce, the arts, and everyday life. Here English Canadians and French Canadians came together over a century ago to set the foundations for a country in whose Parliament both French and English would be spoken. And here the Citadel and the walls of the old city remind us that Canadians and Americans long ago put aside their differences to become friends. In fact, we're more than friends and neighbors and allies; we are kin, who together have built the most productive relationship between any two countries in the world today.

This is my first trip outside the United States since I was sworn into a second term. Four years ago I took my first trip as President, and then, too, I came to Canada. And this is not a coincidence. For the United States there is no more important relationship than our tie with Canada. We're each other's most important economic partner. We each play an important role in world affairs. We share a responsibility for the protection of the continent that we peacefully share. We have a joint stake in its environment. And we're partners in space and in the technologies of the future.

Between two such independent and sovereign countries there will always be some differences, as there will always be opportunities for agreement. We can still use what Franklin D. Roosevelt, our last American President to visit Quebec City while serving

at the White House, called for between us. He asked for frank dealing, cooperation, and a spirit of give-and-take. That's precisely what your Prime Minister and I will be engaged in here in Quebec. We will discuss many matters pertaining to the environment, economic growth, and our mutual security. We will discuss global affairs, including arms control.

We will also be celebrating St. Patrick's Day. For two fellows named Reagan and Mulroney, this would seem to be appropriate. I know a number of people today, including myself, are wearing green ties. But I will really make my contribution this evening at dinner. I'm going to think of the Prime Minister's majority in Parliament and turn green with envy. [*Laughter*]

It's wonderful to be here. Thank you. *Merci beaucoup.*

Note: The President spoke at 3:15 p.m. in Gouvernement du Quebec Hangar, L'Anceinne Lorette Airport, where he was accorded a formal welcome with full military honors. In his opening remarks, the President referred to Premier René Levesque of Quebec Province. Following his remarks, the President went to the Chateau Frontenac Hotel, where he met with Prime Minister Brian Mulroney.

Remarks of the President and Prime Minister Brian Mulroney in Quebec City, Canada, Announcing the Appointment of Special Envoys on Acid Rain
March 17, 1985

The Prime Minister. [*In English*] The President and I have had what I believe to be a very important discussion on the problem of acid rain. We have made a significant step forward, in that a matter that has been on the back burner really for the last 3 years has now been brought up forward, and I think on both sides we acknowledge that our problem is common in nature and requires a joint solution.

So, the President and I will be talking about this again tomorrow and in the future. But I think that we have managed

to break a deadlock, which has prevented some common action on this.

From the Canadian point of view, as you know, I've taken the position that it's important that we clean up our own act, and Canada has begun that process with a comprehensive national program. And so there will be a document released—I suppose within the next half-hour or so.

But to ensure that this matter—this matter that the President and I both agree is of such great importance to our respective countries—to ensure that this never finds its way again onto the back burner, we have agreed today to the appointment of two special envoys of great excellence and influence and uncommon access to us as leaders. They will carry the matters forward and I think help us achieve real results. They'll report to us on a regular basis. And I appreciate the President's commitment, as demonstrated by the caliber of his appointment, which he will announce momentarily.

For our part, the Government of Canada is particularly pleased to announce the appointment of the Honorable William G. Davis, former Prime Minister of Ontario, as our special Ambassador in this vital area.

[*In French*] I think that we've taken a very important step today—a very important step forward in this whole matter of acid rain. The process has thus begun, and we're going to look after our side of the problem as well, and I think that we're going to reach a common solution. Both sides have recognized the fact that there is a common origin to this problem—that one cannot act unilaterally, that the very fate of both our countries are very closely tied, the one to the other.

So, therefore, the Canadian Government has already started its own national program in this respect. And it is with a great deal of delight that, in order that we ensure that this very vital question is no longer to be the poor one of the pack, both of us have designated personal Ambassadors, people of exceptional quality, to ensure that the matters be brought back to us at an opportune moment and on a regular basis. Therefore, I take great pleasure in confirming to the President of the United States the appointment of the Honorable William G. Davis, a former Premier of the Province of Ontario, as our Ambassador.

I thank you, Mr. President. And now would you say a few words?

The President. Well, I'll only take a second here simply to endorse what the Prime Minister has told you. We're very pleased with the outcome of the discussion. We touched upon a number of things of interest, and we'll be dealing with those in the meetings to come tomorrow. But of particular concern to us was this issue of acid rain. And I'm very pleased with the envoys that have been chosen. The Prime Minister has named a man that—I'm sure you all know his access to him—and has a standing that will make him capable of carrying out what has to be a joint undertaking as the Prime Minister has said. And for our own part, my nominee—and he has accepted—is Drew Lewis, the former Secretary of Transportation, who has agreed to take on this task.

And, so, together we'll find an answer to this problem. And I couldn't be happier about getting this underway and off dead center.

Q. What are they supposed to do?

The President. We've agreed there'll be no questions, so I can't take it, your question there. But we shall go forward with finding an answer to what is a problem that belongs to both of us.

I think that it's very significant that our two countries should work together on all matters of environment, because entrusted to us is the care of a very unique continent and a very beautiful continent. And I think all of us share the desire to protect this for generations of Canadians and Americans yet to come.

Thank you.

Note: The Prime Minister spoke at 4:47 p.m. in Le Frontenac Room at the Chateau Frontenac Hotel, following a private meeting with the President. In the evening, the President and Mrs. Reagan attended a private dinner hosted by the Prime Minister and Mrs. Mulroney at the hotel. Later they attended a gala performance at the Grand Theatre of Quebec.

Joint Canada-United States Statement on Acid Rain
March 17, 1985

During their tête-à-tête, the President and the Prime Minister discussed environmental matters at some length. They took note of the 75-year history of environmental cooperation between the two countries as exemplified by the Boundary Waters Treaty, the Great Lakes Water Quality Agreement and the recent Skagit River-Ross Dam Treaty. The President and the Prime Minister expressed their determination to continue to deal with U.S.-Canadian environmental issues in a responsible and cooperative spirit.

In the spirit of cooperation, and in recognition that the actions of one country are of concern to the other, there was agreement that a high level Special Envoy would be appointed by each government to examine the acid rain issue and report to the President and Prime Minister by their next meeting. The Envoys will:

(a) pursue consultation on laws and regulations that bear on pollutants thought to be linked to acid rain;

(b) enhance cooperation in research efforts, including that for clean fuel technology and smelter controls;

(c) pursue means to increase exchange of relevant scientific information, and

(d) identify efforts to improve the U.S. and Canadian environment.

The President announced that the U.S. Special Envoy will be Andrew L. Lewis, former Secretary of Transportation.

The Prime Minister announced that his Special Envoy will be William G. Davis, former Premier of Ontario.

Appointment of Andrew Lindsay Lewis, Jr., as the President's Special Envoy for the Acid Rain Consultations with Canada
March 17, 1985

The President today announced his intention to appoint Andrew Lindsay Lewis, Jr., to be his Special Envoy.

Mr. Lewis is chairman of the board of Warner Amex Cable Communications, a position he has held since February 1983. Previously he was Secretary of Transportation in 1981–1983. He was deputy chairman of the Republican National Committee in 1980–1981 and served as deputy director of the office of the President-elect. He was associated with the firm of Lewis & Associates, financial and management consultants, in Plymouth Meeting, PA, in 1974–1980. He was president and chief executive officer of Snelling & Snelling, Inc., 1970–1974. In 1970 he joined the Simplex Wire & Cable Co. in Boston as president and chief executive officer and served as its chairman until 1972. He was assistant to the chairman of National Gypsum Co. in Buffalo, NY, in 1969–1970; vice president for sales and director of the American Olean Tile Co., Inc., in 1960–1968; and foreman, job superintendent, production manager, and director of Henkels & McCoy, Inc., of Blue Bell, PA, in 1955–1960.

He presently serves as a director of Campbell Soup Co., Equitable Life Insurance Co., and Smith, Kline & Beckman. He is also chairman of MTV Networks, Inc.

He graduated from Haverford College (B.S., 1953) and Harvard University (M.B.A., 1955). He did postgraduate work at the Massachusetts Institute of Technology in 1968. He is married, has three children, and resides in Philadelphia, PA. He was born November 3, 1931, in Philadelphia.

Informal Exchange With Reporters in Quebec City, Canada
March 18, 1985

Q. Mr. President, the Secretary of Defense was talking about putting missiles here in Canada this morning.

The President. Well, you know, Bill [Bill Plante, CBS News] that I'm not taking questions at a photo opportunity like this. But the only thing I know is the Secretary of Defense said it wasn't true. [*Laughter*]

Q. What wasn't true, sir—that he was going to put missiles in Canada?

Q. Thank you very much.

Q. He ought to know.

Q. Well, is it true or is it not true, sir?

Q. Ladies and gentlemen, thank you.

Principal Deputy Press Secretary Speakes. You're obviously misquoting the Secretary.

Q. Sir, I can't hear you, sir.

Mr. Speakes. You're obviously misquoting the Secretary.

Secretary Weinberger. Sadly, not for the first time.

Q. No, I'm quoting Bill, who was quoting the Secretary.

Note: The exchange began at 9:35 a.m. in Le Petit Frontenac Room at the Chateau Frontenac Hotel. A tape was not available for verification of the content of this exchange.

Toast at a Luncheon With Provincial and Community Leaders in Quebec City, Canada
March 18, 1985

Thank you very much. Mr. Prime Minister, Mrs. Mulroney, Mayor Pelletier, and all of you very distinguished ladies and gentleman:

Nancy et moi desirons vous remercier du fond du coeur de votre chaleureuse hospitalité. [Nancy and I wish to thank you from the bottom of our hearts for your warm hospitality.] Just as 4 years ago, it is an honor and a privilege to make our first visit of the term a visit to Canada, our close neighbor, our strong ally, and yes, our dear friend.

To have come to the heart of old Quebec, to this chateau that, for us, will forever be a memory of beauty—looking down on beauty all around—and still more, to have been joined by one who shares my roots on St. Patrick's Day—[*laughter*]—well, it's almost too much for this son of an Irishman to bear. [*Laughter*] As you might say in your native tongue, *c'est formidable.* [*Laughter*] And this might be enough to convince you that French is not my native tongue. [*Laughter*] Actually, I was told a long time ago: "Don't worry about your accent. It's not how well you speak French," the gentleman said, "but how well you appreciate our people and culture." And ever since Jacques Cartier told me that—[*laughter*]—I've been a great admirer of all things French-Canadian. [*Laughter*]

As we begin anew, we come again to be with friends. We come to share great dreams in a land where "big" is a word too small to describe the sweep of Laurentian peaks and prairie plains or the strength of Canadian spirit that tamed a giant continent and now looks to a future rich with promise.

Flying over Canada yesterday afternoon, I thought of your Commander Marc Garneau. He's the first of what we hope will be many Canadian astronauts on joint space shuttle missions. And aboard the space shuttle *Challenger*, at a moment high above Quebec, Commander Garneau said: "My country is very fantastic. We are lucky to be Canadian, to have such a big and wonderful country." To which I would only add: And are we not lucky to be neighbors in these good, free lands that God has blessed as none others have ever been blessed?

When we look around the world today, when we see a scar of shame dividing families in Europe, east from west, and in Korea, north from south, see the anguish that aggression has wrought upon so many innocent lives across our planet, then, yes, we would do well to give thanks for the principles of democracy and human dignity that have cradled us with peace and showered us with abundance since the birth of our two nations.

Victor Hugo once observed: No army can stop an idea whose time has come. Well, today the tide of freedom is up, lifting our economies ever higher on new currents of imagination, discovery, and hope for our future.

There is a leader who personifies this new spirit, who has said: "Canadians in the mid-eighties have a renewed sense of confidence in themselves as a nation." There is "a role for government that is less interventionist," he said, "a role that creates a climate in which the entrepreneurial genius of the private sector can do what it does best—namely, create new wealth, new possibilities of employment."

We take a friendly neighbor's quiet pride in your campaign [Canadian] revival, and we share your great respect for the man doing so much to carry it forward, your Prime Minister and my friend, Brian Mulroney.

Canadians live at the top of North America, and sometimes we think of you as fellow homedwellers inhabiting the upper floors of the house. And we who live downstairs have heard some rumbling up here in that portion that we know to be Quebec. The changes in French Canada during the past 25 years, your *revolution tranquille*, propelled the transformation of Quebec into a modern community while emphasizing all along its French-speaking character.

In a unique referendum, the people of Quebec declared themselves Canadian and Québécois. Now your long history as a French-speaking North American community is entering an exciting phase—Quebec entrepreneurs competing across the continent, spreading business know-how with a French face.

We see and feel your progress. And we value highly the friendship of a people unafraid to embrace the challenge of change, yet unwilling to forsake your oldest, most trusted companions—Canadian traditions, values, and roots.

There's a saying I've always liked: One should keep old roads and old friends. You have not strayed from the road of Canadian culture, from those good and graceful virtues that enrich your lives and keep you free to be kind and true, free to strive for progress and greatness, without surrendering your souls to a mad and mindless pursuit of the material.

Mes amis, the eyes of all America are on Canada. In our universities new programs for Canadian studies have been created, in our government new importance given to the Canadian-American relationship, and in our economy we feel Canada's heightened presence in our daily lives—from Quebec electrical power to Alberta's oil and natural gas, and from your help in building our telecommunications industry to what many believe is the best beer in the world. [*Laughter*] We're with you, Mr. Prime Minister. We feel mighty grateful for Canada, and we always will.

At the heart of my nation's policies is one conviction, and please hear it well: No relationship is more important to the United States than our ties with Canada. We are by far each other's most important trading partner. Our two-way trade, the largest in the world, is valued at over $100 billion. We're allies. In North America and across the North Atlantic, we're proud to stand watch with you, and together we shall keep our people free, secure, and at peace. Above all, we're friends, and friends we shall always be.

The question is, having righted ourselves and regained our optimism, where do we go from here? Well, I believe your Prime Minister and I agree: Canada and America can invest together, grow together, and lead together. And leaders we shall be in a new partnership pointing toward the 21st century. That new partnership begins with our being more mindful of our need for close cooperation and constant communication, each of us carefully respecting the other's interests and sovereignty.

For our part, the United States has begun a great change in direction—away from years of creeping socialism and ever-greater dependency that slowed our progress toward a new American revolution—a peaceful revolution to be sure, rising from our conviction that successful action must begin with a vision of hope and opportunity for all.

The evidence is clear: Freedom works, incentives are key, and nations ignoring these principles will lose out in the economic competition in the 1980's and beyond. Japan, a devastated country after World War II, cut tax rates almost every year for two decades, producing an explosive, noninflationary expansion, making them a world economic power, and leaving Europe and North America falling behind. Other Pacific nations have also become champions for growth.

Let us, then, set our sights on a new vision: a renaissance of growth in a world come alive with entrepreneurial vigor; each nation trading freely with its neighbors; all of us together a mighty freedom tide carrying hope and opportunity to the farthest corners of the globe.

We in the States have tried to learn from our mistakes and show once again that nothing succeeds like freedom. Since our tax rate reductions took effect, we have enjoyed 27 straight months of economic growth and a record 7 million jobs, producing a dramatic increase in our purchases from other nations—starting with Canada.

We know we must do much more to restrain the growth of government, break down barriers of trade, and become more competitive. And since tax rates, functioning as prices for producing, saving, and investing, are the keys to economic growth or decline, we're committed to an historic reform of our tax code, making America's aftertax rewards the brightest light for growth and stability in the industrialized world.

Protecting the environment is one of paramount concern to us both. The United States has the strictest auto emissions standards in the world, and during the last decade we spent over $150 billion to comply with our Clean Air Act. Emissions of sulphur dioxide are down nearly 30 per-

cent, and nitrogen oxides are declining as well. But we must make further progress, and by acting reasonably and responsibly, we can and we will. Yesterday the Prime Minister and I issued a statement on our agreement to address together the problem of acid rain.

In all that we do, we seek to go forward with Canada as our partner, two leaders for progress through shared vision and enlightened cooperation. This afternoon at the Citadel, Prime Minister Mulroney and I will take further steps together to put our new partnership to work. We will issue a declaration on international security and sign a memorandum on the modernization of our North American air defense system. We will exchange the instruments of ratification that will bring the Pacific salmon treaty into effect, as he told you. We will sign a mutual legal assistance treaty which will aid law enforcement authorities in both our countries. And we will issue a declaration on trade.

The prosperity of Canada and the United States depends upon freer flowing trade within this continent and across the seas. We stand ready to improve further the Canada-U.S. trading relationship and to work with you to initiate a new multilateral trade round in early 1986.

Mr. Prime Minister, I'm confident there isn't an area where you and I cannot reach an agreement for the good of our two countries. Come to think of it, maybe there is one. I know it's a great concern to you, but I don't think I have the authority to send Gary Carter back to the Expos. [*Laughter*]

But more powerful in our economies, more powerful in our friendship, the United States and Canada can meet together the challenge of defending freedom and leaving a safer world for those who will follow. For more than 35 years, we and our European friends have joined together in history's most successful alliance—the North Atlantic Treaty Organization. The world will not forget that Canada was in the forefront of the nations that formed and armed NATO.

Upgrading NATO's conventional forces is essential to deterrence. The greater our ability to resist Soviet aggression with conventional forces, the less likely such aggression will ever occur. NATO is engaged in a rebuilding program, and today I want to thank publicly Prime Minister Mulroney and the Canadian people for your commitment to enhance your contribution to NATO's conventional forces and our overall defenses.

Your deficit as a percentage of gross national product is bigger than ours, but you understand that protecting freedom is government's primary responsibility. And we salute Canadian wisdom and Canadian courage.

The United States will continue to pursue the arms control talks in Geneva with determination, flexibility, and patience. It is our deepest conviction that a nuclear war cannot be won and must never be fought. We must not rest in our search for a safer world dedicated to eliminating nuclear weapons, with technology providing ever greater safety, not ever greater fear.

We're enthusiastic about the research done so far on our Strategic Defense Initiative. The possibility of developing and sharing with you technology that could provide a security shield and someday eliminate the threat of nuclear attack—it is, for us, the most hopeful possibility of the nuclear age, and we very much appreciate Canada's support on SDI research.

You know, it puzzles me to hear the Soviets describe research to protect humanity as a threat to peace. Their protests ring a little hollow. I did some research of my own and found that in 1967 former Soviet Premier Aleksei Kosygin said, "The antimissile system is not a weapon of aggression or attack, it is a defensive system." And the Soviets took his words to heart and began investing heavily in strategic defense.

Let us all acknowledge that humanity will be far better served by moving away from offensive nuclear systems that kill people to nonnuclear defensive systems that protect people. We will be consulting closely with your government during these negotiations. And I have told the Prime Minister that I'm never more than a phone call away. As allies, we must maintain our unity and insist on agreements that are equitable and verifiable.

As much as we may hope for greater stability through arms control, we must re-

member that the Soviet record of compliance with past agreements has been poor. The Soviet Union signed the Yalta accord, pledging free elections, then proceeded to dominate Eastern Europe. They signed the Geneva Convention, banning use of chemical weapons; SALT II, limiting development of new weapons; and the ABM treaty—but are now violating all three. And they signed the Helsinki accord, solemnly pledging respect for human rights, but then jailed the individuals trying to monitor it in the U.S.S.R.

Arms control is not the only issue on the East-West agenda, and the opening of the Geneva talks is not the only development in East-West relations. In most of our Western countries, our peoples can look forward to continued strong, stable governments, and our alliances are in good shape. We have demonstrated unity and firmness in our dealings with the East. We're ready to work with the Soviet Union for more constructive relations. We all want to hope that last week's change of leadership in Moscow will open up new possibilities for doing this.

There's plenty to talk about—in arms control, on regional issues, on human rights, and in our bilateral relations. My representatives in Moscow had good talks with Mr. Gorbachev, and Prime Minister Mulroney has given me his own assessment of the new Soviet leadership. If the Soviets are as ready as we are to take the other side's concerns into account, it should be possible to resolve problems and reduce international tensions.

Let us always remain idealists but never blind to history. Each of us—I suspect that our lives grow richer and fuller as we help make other lives more secure and more free. We must never doubt the great good that Canada and the United States can accomplish together, never doubt for a moment our journey toward a world where someday all may live under freedom's star—free to worship as they please, to speak their thoughts, to come and go as they will, to achieve the fullness of their potential, and yes, reach out to comfort those who have fallen with the godly gift of human love.

This is the idealist within us whose heart

is pure and can power our journey with faith and courage. But the realist must be there, too—our navigator at the helm whose eagle eyes discern each movement of the sky above and waves below. We must never stop trying to reach a better world, but we'll never make it if we don't see our world as it truly is.

We cannot look the other way when treaties are violated, human beings persecuted, religions banned, and entire democracies crushed. We cannot ignore that while Canadians and Americans have donated nearly $100 million from their own pockets to help feed starving Ethiopians, the Soviets and all their satellites have given almost no aid. But they continue to provide more than a half a billion dollars a year in military supplies that the Ethiopian Government is using against its own people.

These are painful realities, but history may well remember them as the birth pangs of a new, much brighter era. Brave men and women are challenging the Brezhnev doctrine that insists once a country has been taken from the family of free nations, it may never return.

Freedom movements are rising up—from Afghanistan to Cambodia, Angola, Ethiopia, and Nicaragua. More than twice as many people are fighting in the field right now against the Nicaraguan Communist regime as fought against Somoza. The weight of the world is struggling to shift away from the dreary failures of Communist oppression into the warm sunlight of genuine democracy and human rights.

Will history speak of freedom victorious? May we someday salute new heroes from nations reborn—sons and daughters who might grow up to be like a Marc Garneau or Roberta Bondar, bringing honor to science and their nations; or perhaps like Andre Viger, who lost the use of his legs, but with his will of steel in a land of the free could keep on going to open six stores employing more than 40 people, many of them handicapped, and even win our Boston Marathon as well?

History's verdict will depend on us—on our courage and our faith, on our wisdom and our love. It'll depend on what we do or fail to do for the cause of millions who carry just one dream in their hearts: to live lives like ours, in this special land between the seas, where each day a new adventure begins in a revolution of hope that never ends.

You know, Prime Minister Mulroney once suggested that Americans and their President should be grateful for Canada. How can we not be grateful for the greatness of Banting and Best, of Mike Pearson, of young Steve Fonyo, and of so many we never knew. For the inspiration you give, for the success that you enjoy, and for the friend of America and friend of freedom that you will always be, yes, we say, thank God for Canada.

And I ask you now to raise your glass with me, to the Queen of Canada, and to my good friend, the Prime Minister, Brian Mulroney.

Thank you, and God bless you.

Note: The President spoke at 12:20 p.m. in the Salle De Bal at the Chateau Frontenac Hotel. In his opening remarks, the President referred to Jean Pelletier, mayor of Quebec City. Earlier, the President and Prime Minister Mulroney met with American and Canadian officials.

Remarks at the Signing Ceremony for the Joint Canada-United States Declarations in Quebec City, Canada
March 18, 1985

The Citadel of Quebec says so much about Canada and about the relations between our two countries. On this rock once flew the flag of France and then the flag of Britain. And today, the maple leaf flag symbolizes a united Canada.

Over two centuries ago Canadians and Americans battled one another in this city.

But the walls surrounding us today were erected later for a war which never came. Canada and the United States put aside suspicion to build not only a lasting and permanent friendship but a great and productive relationship. Today the Citadel and other places like it in both our countries stand as monuments to a history of peace, good will, and cooperation.

Earlier today I suggested that Canada and the United States are forging a new partnership. This afternoon Prime Minister Mulroney and I have put that new partnership to work. The relationship between our two countries is complex and varied. The agreements we announced this afternoon reflect that variety.

We share the world's longest undefended border and the world's longest water boundary. Yet, more fundamentally, we share Earth's most bountiful continent. We're responsible for managing and preserving that common environment. We have a long history of cooperating in doing so. I'm personally committed to continuing this proud tradition. I know that our two governments share this commitment.

And I know that the issue of acid rain has received a great deal of attention in Canada. Let me simply say, cooperation on this issue is possible, and the appointment by the Prime Minister and by me of special envoys is another step forward. So difficult a problem deserves the best talent that our two governments can enlist.

For almost three decades the Distant Early Warning Line—known as the DEW Line—has been the northernmost edge of our early warning capability. It's been a vital part of the deterrent system which protects both our countries from attack, serving as a watchtower for NORAD. The technology of the DEW Line is now almost obsolete, but the need for an early warning line remains. Accordingly, the Prime Minister and I issued an agreement to modernize the North American air defense system.

The mutual legal assistance treaty which we signed will facilitate cooperation between Canadian and American law enforcement officials.

Protecting the environment, defending our people, and ensuring that justice is done—these are all special roles for government. Economic prosperity, however, requires the enterprise, work, and investment of the private sector. As each other's largest trading partner, Canada and the United States have long enjoyed profitable economic and commercial ties. And today Prime Minister Mulroney and I are issuing an important declaration which we expect will facilitate expanded trade.

We also exchanged the instruments of ratification for a U.S.-Canada Pacific salmon treaty. This brings a 15-year-old undertaking to a successful and mutually beneficial conclusion, as you've been told. The treaty will be a boon to our citizens along the Pacific coast. It symbolizes how we're able, with a combination of hard work and high-level attention, to turn an irritant in our relations into a form of cooperation.

The poet Rupert Brooke wrote: "And high and grey and serene above the morning lay the citadel of Quebec. Is there any city in the world that stands so nobly as Quebec?" Nancy and I have deeply appreciated your hospitality. We'll always remember the beauty of your city. *Nous garderons toujours un excellent souvenir de notre séjour à Quebec et de vous.* [We will always have the best of memories of our stay in Quebec and all of you.] We will always remember Quebec; we will always remember you.

Mila and Brian, we look forward to seeing both of you in the United States next year.

Note: The President spoke at 2:44 p.m. in the ballroom at the Citadel. Following the ceremony, the President returned to Washington, DC.

Joint Canada-United States Declarations on Trade and International Security
March 18, 1985

Declaration by the Prime Minister of Canada and the President of the United States of America Regarding Trade in Goods and Services

We embark today on a joint effort to establish a climate of greater predictability and confidence for Canadians and Americans alike to plan, invest, grow and compete more effectively with one another and in the global market.

We are convinced that an improved and more secure climate for bilateral trade relations will encourage market forces to achieve a more rational and competitive production and distribution of goods and services.

We remain committed to the principles of the multilateral trading system embodied in the General Agreement on Tariffs and Trade as the cornerstone of our respective trade policies. We are determined to exercise the political will to make the open, multilateral trading system work better and to strengthen and extend the disciplines governing international commerce.

We will work jointly to strengthen the effectiveness of GATT rules and establish new disciplines. We call on all nations to join with us in establishing a preparatory committee this summer for a new round of multilateral trade negotiations to ensure that negotiations commence in early 1986.

We believe that the challenge to our two countries is to invigorate our unique economic relationship. We intend to build on our success in resolving a number of disputes and achieve something of lasting significance to provide a model to other nations of the way in which two modern societies can work in harmony.

We have today *agreed* to give the highest priority to finding mutually-acceptable means to reduce and eliminate existing barriers to trade in order to secure and facilitate trade and investment flows.

As a first step, we commit ourselves to halt protectionism in cross-border trade in goods and services.

We have *charged* Ambassador Brock, the United States Trade Representative, and the Honorable James Kelleher, Minister for International Trade, to establish immediately a bilateral mechanism to chart all possible ways to reduce and eliminate existing barriers to trade and to report to us within six months.

We have also *directed* that action be undertaken over the next twelve months to resolve specific impediments to trade in a manner consistent with our international obligations and our legislative requirements. Such action will proceed on the basis of full consultation with the private sector and other levels of government and will concentrate initially on:

• national treatment, on a contractual, equitable and mutually advantageous basis, with respect to *government procurement and funding programs;*

• *standardization, reduction or simplification of regulatory requirements* which would facilitate trade in goods and services;

• improvement in the Canada-United States *Air Transport Agreement* aimed at facilitating transborder travel and commerce by expanding the number of available services and reducing obstacles to the introduction of innovative and competitive new services;

• strengthening our market approach to Canada-United States *energy trade* by reducing restrictions, particularly those on petroleum imports and exports, and by maintaining and extending open access to each other's energy markets, including oil, natural gas, electricity and coal;

• improving access for traders on both sides of the border through reduction in *tariff barriers;*

• facilitation of *travel* for business and commercial purposes;

• elimination or reduction of tariff and non-tariff barriers to trade in *high-technology goods and related services,* such as computers, data flow and computer-assisted design and manufacturing technology; and

• cooperation to protect *intellectual property rights* from trade in counterfeit goods and other abuses of copyright and patent law.

We urge our respective private sectors to expand their contacts and continue to provide advice on the future of our trading relationship.

We are confident that these undertakings will facilitate trade and investment flows between our two countries and act as catalysts for broader international cooperation.

Declaration by the Prime Minister of Canada and the President of the United States of America Regarding International Security

We are neighbours and allies dedicated to the defence and nourishment of peace and freedom. The security of Canada and the United States are inextricably linked.

We have committed ourselves at Quebec to reinvigorate the defence and security partnership between the two countries. To reinforce deterrence and to reduce the risk posed by threat of nuclear attack, we agreed to strengthen continental defence, with particular reference to our joint participation in the North American Aerospace Defence Command. Accordingly, we concluded an agreement to modernize the North American Air Defence Surveillance and Warning System. We agreed that in implementing this program, as in all of our defence relations, we shall be guided by the principle of mutual respect for the sovereignty of our two countries.

In the spirit of mutual trust and confidence between our countries, we have committed ourselves to consult fully, frankly, and regularly on defence and arms control matters.

To permit systematic consultation and overall review, at the most senior levels, of arrangements bearing on the security of Canada and the United States, we resolved that the responsible ministers of our governments will meet together on a regular basis. We have also agreed to make greater use of the Permanent Joint Board on Defence, established at the historic meeting of Prime Minister Mackenzie King and President Franklin Delano Roosevelt at Ogdensburg forty-five years ago.

To provide for an effective use of resources and to aid both of our countries in bearing our share of the Allied defence burden, we reaffirm the Canada/United States Defence Development and Production Sharing Arrangements and agree to strengthen our North American defence industrial base. Recognizing the importance of access to, and participation of, Canadian firms in the U.S. defence market, we will work to reduce barriers, and to stimulate the flow in defence goods. We will seek to improve our joint access to information relating to defence procurement; we will explore ways to establish a separate designation for mobilization base suppliers for U.S. and Canadian firms, and we will seek to take greater advantage of flexibility inherent in second source suppliers. We will also undertake to establish a freer exchange between both countries of technical knowledge and skills involved in defence production, in order to facilitate defence economic and trade cooperation and joint participation in major defence programs. In this connection, we agree to strengthen our cooperation to ensure that transfers of strategic technology to our potential adversaries are effectively controlled. We have directed the responsible Ministers to give priority attention to all these issues and to provide a progress report within four months.

The security of Canada and the United States is inseparable from that of the European members of the North Atlantic Alliance. We remain fully dedicated to preserving the security of the Alliance as a whole through the maintenance of adequate military strength, an effective deterrent posture, and a stable balance of forces. We attach great importance to our continuing commitment to station Canadian and United States forces in Europe. We think it is essential to strengthen NATO's conventional capabilities and accordingly reiterate our determination to continue substantial real growth in expenditures for defence.

We share a commitment to deepening the dialogue among the Allies. Our Alliance draws strength from the unique and individual contributions of its sovereign members in the pursuit of our common goal of peace with freedom. The cohesion and political solidarity of the Alliance, maintained through frequent and timely consultations, remain the foundation for the protection of our common interests and values.

Significant, equitable, durable and verifiable arms control measures can play a role in strengthening strategic stability, maintaining our security at a lower level of force and armament, building trust and confidence between East and West, and reducing the risk of war. We have agreed to consider joint research efforts to strengthen our capacity to verify agreements on the control of armaments. We will work to gain agreement on effective measures in the international negotiations in Vienna, Geneva, and Stockholm, and we will strive, with the countries of Europe, to progress towards the aims enshrined in the Helsinki Final Act.

We further agreed that we can have no higher goal than the reduction and eventual elimination of the threat to peace, whether by nuclear or conventional means. Our aim is not to achieve superiority, but to enhance deterrence of armed aggression and bring about significant arms reductions between East and West. We seek a more stable world, with greatly reduced levels of nuclear arms. The prospect of an enhanced ability to deter war based upon an increasing

contribution of non-nuclear defences against offensive nuclear arms has prompted the U.S. research effort embodied in the President's strategic defence initiative. We are agreed that this effort is prudent and is in conformity with the ABM Treaty. In this regard, we agree that steps beyond research would, in view of the ABM treaty, be matters for discussion and negotiation.

Dialogue and negotiation between the United States and the Soviet Union at Geneva provide a historic opportunity to set East-West relations on a more secure foundation. We hope that these negotiations will lead to major steps toward the prevention of an arms race in space and to terminating it on earth, limiting and reducing nuclear arms, and, ultimately, eliminating them everywhere.

The security of Canada and the United States is linked increasingly with that of other regions in the world. We will therefore encourage and support the strengthening of multilateral and international mechanisms for the control and peaceful resolution of disputes. We will vigorously oppose the exploitation of regional instability, and promote at the same time, each by our distinctive contributions, the social, economic, and political development essential to the achievement of a stable and enduring peace.

Our one truly strategic aim is human freedom in a world at peace.

Nomination of Fernando Enrique Rondon To Be United States Ambassador to Ecuador
March 18, 1985

The President today announced his intention to nominate Fernando Enrique Rondon, of Virginia, a career member of the Senior Foreign Service, Class of Minister-Counselor, as Ambassador to Ecuador. He would succeed Samuel Friedlander Hart.

Mr. Rondon entered the Foreign Service in 1961 and was vice consul in Tehran in 1962–1964. He attended French language training at the Foreign Service Institute in

1964–1965 and Arabic language training in Tangier in 1965–1966. He was principal officer in Constantine (1966–1967), consular officer in Algiers (1967–1968), and political officer in Antananarivo (1968–1970). He served on the National Security Council at the White House in 1970–1973. He attended the National War College in 1975–1976 and was Alternate Director of the Office of East Coast Affairs in the Department in 1976–1978. He was deputy chief of mission

309

in Tegucigalpa in 1978–1980. In 1980–1983 he served as Ambassador to the Democratic Republic of Madagascar. Since that time he has been Director, Office of Andean Affairs.

He graduated from the University of California at Berkeley (B.S., 1960). His foreign languages are Spanish, French, Arabic, and Persian. He is married, has three children, and resides in Falls Church, VA. He was born May 6, 1936, in Los Angeles, CA.

Nomination of Faith Ryan Whittlesey To Be United States Ambassador to Switzerland
March 18, 1985

The President today announced his intention to nominate Faith Ryan Whittlesey, of Pennsylvania, as Ambassador to Switzerland. She would succeed John Davis Lodge.

Mrs. Whittlesey was a substitute teacher in the Philadelphia School District in Pennsylvania in 1962–1964. She was with the Pennsylvania Department of Justice as special assistant attorney general (1964–1965) and as special assistant attorney general in the Department of Public Welfare (1967–1970). In 1965 she was law clerk to the Honorable Francis L. Van Dusen of the United States District Court (Eastern District of Pennsylvania). In 1972–1976 she was a member of the Pennsylvania House of Representatives, serving on the committees of judiciary, consumer protection, education, health and welfare, and urban affairs.

She was a member of the Delaware County Council in Media, PA, in 1980–1981 having been elected as chairman and vice chairman (1976–1981). She was an attorney in the law firm of Wolf, Block, Schorr and Solis-Cohen of Philadelphia (1980–1981). Mrs. Whittlesey served as Ambassador to Switzerland in 1981–1983. And from 1983 to the present, she has been Assistant to the President for Public Liaison.

Mrs. Whittlesey graduated cum laude (B.A.) in 1960 from Wells College and received her J.D. in 1963 from the University of Pennsylvania Law School. In 1962 she attended the Academy of International Law at The Hague, Netherlands. She has three children and resides in Washington, DC. She was born February 21, 1939, in Jersey City, NJ.

Appointment of Jack L. Courtemanche as Executive Director of the National White House Conference on Small Business
March 18, 1985

The President today announced his intention to appoint Jack L. Courtemanche to be executive director of the National White House Conference on Small Business. This is a new position.

Since October 1983 Mr. Courtemanche has been serving as Deputy Assistant to the President for Public Liaison. Previously he was executive director of the White House Conference on Productivity. Prior to joining the White House staff, he served as president of Crown Coach Corp. in Los Angeles, CA. In 1970–1975 he was vice president of Mack Trucks, Inc., Allentown, PA, in charge of the western region. In 1961–1970 he was president of Automotive Equipment Co. in Portland, OR, and Los Angeles, CA.

Mr. Courtemanche attended the University of Oregon. He served in the United States Army in 1956–1958. He is married, has six children, and resides in Washington, DC. He was born March 9, 1935, in McMinnville, OR.

Remarks at the Welcoming Ceremony for President Raúl Alfonsin of Argentina
March 19, 1985

President Reagan. President Alfonsin, it is an honor today to welcome you to the United States. It was 26 years ago when the last Argentine President came to Washington on a state visit. I certainly hope that what we accomplish today will clear the path for increased good will and cooperation between our peoples in many more such visits, and let's make certain it's not another 26 years.

Argentina and the United States, though at different ends of the hemisphere, have much in common. The spirit of freedom and independence that freed the people of the United States, only a short time later, spread to Argentina. And your country is one of the oldest democracies of the hemisphere. The flame of liberty burned red hot in Argentina. And your country was the first on the continent to ban slavery. This was no mere coincidence, Mr. President; the Argentine people are the heirs of a great legacy. Similar to our own experience, Argentina was a frontier society, a land where people came from many parts of the world to better themselves and to live in freedom, an undeveloped land, yet one blessed by God with a richness of soil and resources. Our forefathers, here and in your country, shared the challenge of turning a wilderness into a modern nation.

Today we continue to share the challenge of maintaining the economic growth and development so vital to the well-being of our peoples. Keeping a national economy vital and robust requires hard work, vision, and commitment. It requires tough decisions today in order to make a better tomorrow. We appreciate here, Mr. President, the severe economic problems that you inherited. A few years ago I, too, assumed the Presidency during a time of great economic uncertainty. Inflation and economic decline sapped our strength. Had we challenged our efforts into finding easy and short-term answers, had we looked to redistribution of existing wealth—rather than creating more—we would still be trapped in a seemingly endless morass. Instead, by focusing efforts on economic growth, increasing productivity, creating new incentives that encouraged citizens to work and save and invest, we unleashed a ground swell of economy-building activity in the private sector that turned decline into progress, inflation into stability, and national doubt into optimism and growth.

President Alfonsin, every country must make its own way and walk its own path, yet friends can and should help one another. The United States will do what we can to assist you in your efforts to improve the economic conditions of your country. Argentina, like the United States, is a land of few limits. Your people, educated and strong in spirit, have enormous potential. I can assure you in the strongest terms that the people of the United States want you and the people of Argentina to succeed and to prosper.

This prospect is made even more likely now that Argentina has returned to the ranks of democratic nations. As we've seen throughout the world, there was a strong relationship between freedom and economic development. Democracy frees the spirit of man to achieve, to build, and to create. It's the only system consistent with the decent and humane values at the heart of our societies.

Democracy means government derives its just powers from the consent of the governed. It means freedom of speech and religion, the freedom of assembly, and the rule of law. It's more than a form of government; it's a way of life, an ideal which seems to be a process, yet is an end in itself. It's not the easiest system, but it is the most just, and it brings a better and a freer life for all. The spirit of democracy is not found in great halls or in marching armies but is enshrined in the hearts of the people.

Juan Bautista Alberdi, the father of the Argentine Constitution, said it well: "The Constitution, liberty, authority are not written. They are realized. They are not decreed. They are created. They are made by education. They are not made in the Congress. They are made in the home. They don't live on paper. They live in the man."

Well, today is an exciting time to be an American—and I mean all of us. From the North Slope of Alaska to the tip of Tierra del Fuego, more people here are living in democracy than ever before. Ninety percent of this hemisphere's population lives in democracies or in countries in transition to democracy. This trend, however, is threatened by Marxist-Leninists who continue, with the heavy support of the Soviet Union and Cuba, to undermine freely elected governments and democratic movements.

In Nicaragua Communists, who were just one faction in the broad coalition that pledged to replace their former dictatorship with democracy, quickly seized control of the organs of power. The vast majority of those fighting for true democracy in Nicaragua—for freedom of speech, religion, and press—actively opposed the former dictatorship. And the Nicaraguan people are joining the ranks of the freedom fighters. Nearly three times as many men are fighting the Communists right now as the Sandinistas had fighting Somoza before they seized power.

The free people of this hemisphere must not stand by and watch the Communist tyranny imposed on Nicaragua spread to the free lands of the Americas. We, like you, support the search for peace through the efforts of the Contadora group, strongly believing that if all 21 objectives were implemented, including the genuine democratization of Nicaragua, the Central American nations could live in peace and democracy.

Mr. President, as leaders of two great nations dedicated to democracy and committed to human rights, we are concerned not only with our own freedom but also the cause of freedom throughout our hemisphere. San Martin, a great freedom fighter of his day, once said, "In the last corner of the earth that I might find myself, I will be ready to sacrifice my existence for liberty."

Today democracy draws the people of the United States and Argentina, and all other Americans, closer in a bond of friendship and shared ideals. I welcome you, President Alfonsin, as an elected representative of

your people and as a man committed to the political liberty we cherish so deeply.

President Alfonsin. Mr. President, I wish to begin my statement by expressing my gratitude to you for the warm reception you are granting to the President of all Argentines.

As you have said, it's very important that we meet at this historical time when a real wave of democracy is going through Latin America. This is our hope, Mr. President: that the peoples of Latin America actually live in that respect and actually enjoy the prerogatives and the liberty that the people of the United States enjoy.

That's, on the other hand, what our Founding Fathers wanted for us—both the Founding Fathers of the United States and those of Argentina. That's precisely what the men that gave us independence fought for, starting with General Washington in the North and General San Martin in Argentina.

As you know, as you said, Mr. President, it is necessary that these democracies actually achieve tangible economic results, so necessary to also achieve social democracy. That's why right next to hope, fear is also there in Latin America—the fear that arises from nonsatisfied expectations of our peoples, our democracies having inherited very difficult charges in the economic order.

It's a debt that in my country reaches the $40 billion and that in Latin America reaches the $400 billion. That, of course, conspires against the democratic systems. That, Mr. President, is no doubt one of the big differences between our two countries.

For us, the philosophy you just mentioned—the philosophy of the state of law, the respect of human rights—that is equal to both of us. But a man, Mr. President, to be called such thing, not only has to have just the right to exercise his fundamental liberties; he also has to have the possibility of living a dignified life.

That's why, Mr. President, in Latin America we are ready to govern with the austerity that our times are demanding. We are making the necessary adjustments to suppress the obstacles of our economy, but we cannot make adjustments that will actually impose sacrifices on those who have less.

It's different from those developed countries in which the entire GNP is received by only 50 percent; in our countries, it doesn't reach even the 40 percent. And to ask from our peoples in that precise sector a bigger effort is no doubt to condemn them to marginality, to extreme poverty, to misery.

Of course, then we would mean that the demagogues that are always there would find in the arms those simple satisfactions that democracy couldn't grant. That's why, Mr. President, it has been very important for me to listen to your welcoming remarks, because you've shown a deep understanding of our problems. I am indeed persuaded that it couldn't be otherwise.

I am indeed persuaded that the United States understands the development of democracy is, of course, entrenched in our country. That's why there's been great expectations about the dialog that we will start today.

We will talk about the present, and we will talk about the future. We, two Presidents elected by the will of the people, will get together. We will, of course, talk about bilateral subjects and also those items that regard the continent as a whole. And, of course, in our dialogs the subject of Nicaragua and Central America will not be absent.

I am convinced that it's through dialog that we will be able to reach peace. And on the basis of the principle—a long-standing principle of international law in Latin America—of nonintervention, that will give us, of course, the possibility of democracy and pluralism in democracy to succeed without extracontinental interventions and affirming, of course, the freedom of man.

We will talk about all this, Mr. President, and as I said, there will be two men freely elected by the will of our peoples. So, Mr. President, it will be a dialog of both our peoples. That way and because of them we will try to reach solutions. We will work for them, for our peoples. We will try to build the future that our peoples deserve.

Note: President Reagan spoke at 10:13 a.m. at the South Portico of the White House. President Alfonsin spoke in Spanish, and his remarks were translated by an interpreter.

Joint Argentina-United States Declaration on Democracy
March 19, 1985

Presidents Alfonsin and Reagan expressed their gratification and support for the spread and strengthening of democracy and individual freedom in the western hemisphere. They said the foreign policies of both countries are driven by the goals of peace, democracy, individual liberty, and the rule of law. They affirmed that the most just and lasting resolution of the major problems facing nations comes from leadership democratically chosen by the people in periodic free and fair elections, through the actions of independent legislatures and judiciaries and by close cooperation among democratic countries. Victories against poverty are more certain and peace most secure where people live by laws that ensure political and economic freedom. Both presidents confirmed that relations are warmest and cooperation closest with those countries which practice effective democracy with full regard for the fundamental social, political, economic and human rights for each individual. President Alfonsin said Argentina has instituted a new era of stable and strengthened democracy guaranteeing full protection of human rights. President Reagan reiterated that the United States attaches the highest priority to sustaining that democracy in Argentina.

Remarks at a Senate Republican Policy Committee Luncheon
March 19, 1985

Thank you very much. Thank you all for inviting me here today. And my greetings to Bill Armstrong, your chairman, to Bob Dole, your leader. And, Bob, I don't suppose I could begin to count the times that I've relied on your efforts and counsel, and I want you to know that you have my heartfelt thanks. And before I forget, you called this morning to make sure I'd bring something with me. Here it is—15 percent for the tip. [*Laughter*]

And it's good to see Jake here. I know that all of us wish him luck on the upcoming space shuttle. To all of you, it's a pleasure to be here. Your reception has been so warm that I might even say you have made my day. [*Laughter*]

But after lunch I'd like us to have a give-and-take. But before we eat, permit me to touch briefly on two issues: the budget and the Peacekeeper missiles. You knew I'd mention a couple of things like that.

On the budget, all of us agree, I think, that the Government has spent too much, borrowed too much for too long. And this year the deficit must be cut, and there are three options for doing it.

Option one is a tax increase. Throughout the seventies, however, it was, in a large part, rising taxes that punished savings and investment and dragged our economy down. Then when our cuts in personal income tax rates restored simple economic incentives, the economy recovered, began the strongest expansion in more than three decades. And last year Federal revenues actually rose 11 percent.

The tax hike would squander our hard-won progress. The American people know it, and on November 6th they said so, I think, in 49 States. So, higher taxes are out.

Option two is a radical cut in defense spending. Yet already during the past 4 years, defense spending has been reduced by more than $150 billion below the 5-year plan that we produced in 1981. Indeed, our projected defense expenditures for 1985 are already almost $16 billion less than the figure the last administration had projected for 1985.

National security is not just another category on the budget; it's the first duty of the Federal Government to the American people. We must see through to completion our carefully laid plans to strengthen the national defense.

And that brings us to option three—the cuts in domestic spending. And it's here that I think we must meet the needed reductions. It will be tough, yes. The record suggests that in a democracy the scaling back of domestic spending may well be the most politically difficult act a government can undertake. Yet when we succeed, we'll know that we fought the good fight with intelligence and skill and that we put our nation on a course of prosperity for decades to come.

We Republicans have not been entrusted with the White House and the Senate to make easy decisions but because the American people want us to wean our nation away from decades of growing dependency and political quick fixes. Together we can make the GOP the true majority party, the centerpiece for decades to come of a governing coalition based on liberty, limited government, and economic growth. To do so, however, this spring we must prove to the country that we can produce a sound and responsible budget, one that cuts the deficit and fosters continued economic vitality. So let us not shrink from this task or be seen to approach it with doubts and hesitations. Let us, instead, unite and rise to the challenge with vigor.

On the Peacekeeper missile, the votes cast this week will bear directly on the outcome of the arms talks in Geneva and, hence, on the prospects for peace throughout the world.

In 1981, as you know, I announced our strategic modernization program. This program was designed to redress the strategic imbalance that had been created during the 1970's, when our defense efforts went slack while the Soviets conducted the biggest military buildup in the history of mankind.

Although far from complete, the strategic modernization program is proving effective. The development of our new bomber, the B–1B, is on track. Our new submarines, the Tridents, are on patrol in growing numbers. Before the decade ends, the Tridents will have improved missiles.

Despite these advances in the air and on the sea, however, there remains one important step: our strategic forces on the land. And today our land-based intercontinental ballistic missiles, or ICBM's, are technologically out of date. They're older, in many cases, than the Air Force men and women who are attending them. So, the Ford administrations—four administrations, I should say, both Republican and Democrat, have proposed replacing our obsolete missiles with the MX. But political controversy has held up the actual installation of MX missiles for more than a decade.

While we debated, the Soviets deployed. Indeed, the number of MX-caliber missiles they have already in place is now higher than 600. Deployment of the Peacekeeper at this point, I believe, represents a simple necessity.

Our proposal calls for the deployment of a hundred Peacekeeper missiles. It was made in consultation with the bipartisan Scowcroft commission, and it has the support of Members of the Congress on both sides of the aisle. Just last month, as prominent a Democrat as former Defense Secretary Harold Brown argued, "We have to proceed with the modernization program of

offensive forces, including the MX."

There's another point I must add here. Some of your colleagues have come up with the idea of simply putting a hold or a limit on MX production. Well, I strongly oppose those ideas, as the Soviets will see them for just what they are—a collapse of American resolve.

On the Peacekeeper you have a clear choice. A no vote will gravely weaken our national defenses, waste the billions already spent on the Peacekeeper program, undercut our allies who have already stood firm in accepting new Pershing and cruise missiles, cripple the position of our negotiators in Geneva, and show the Soviets that, despite the progress our country has made, at a moment of historical importance, a majority in the Congress of the United States still lacks resolve. In the wake of world peace, that must not happen.

If you vote yes, you'll show the Soviets that America today is united and resolute and, thereby, advance the cause of the peace for us and our children. With all my heart, I ask for your support.

I thank you all very much. And now the two words you've really been waiting for for about the last six pages: Let's eat.

Note: The President spoke at 12:36 p.m. in Room S–207 at the Capitol. In his remarks, the President referred to Senator Jake Garn of Utah, who was selected to be a crewmember on the space shuttle mission scheduled for mid-April.

Toasts at the State Dinner for President Raúl Alfonsin of Argentina
March 19, 1985

President Reagan. President Alfonsin and distinguished guests and ladies and gentlemen, it's a great pleasure for me to welcome you to the White House. And I thoroughly enjoyed meeting with President Alfonsin today.

Our discussions were cordial and productive, and of course today was not the first meeting that we've had. Last September we met just before attending the United

Nations General Assembly. That was in the midst of our Presidential campaign last September, and I remember that you remarked that although being President is a hard job, sometimes getting there is even harder. [*Laughter*]

President Alfonsin and I have much in common. We both have gone through many campaigns and asked for votes from many different kinds of people. Down in Texas during the 1976 primary, they had me out knocking on doors. And I remember one kind of rural area—I'd been Governor of California, but I wasn't all that well known in Texas—and I knocked on the door, and an old fellow in his undershirt and jeans came to the door. And I told him I was running for President. And having been in the occupation I'd been in for a number of years, I was kind of surprised when he asked me what I'd done for a living. [*Laughter*] And I told him I'd been an actor. And then he asked me what my name was. And I thought, well, maybe if I give him a hint. So I said, "Well, my initials were RR." And with that his face lit up, and he turned, and he ran back into the house, and he was yelling, "Ma, Ma, come on out here quick—Roy Rogers is outside." [*Laughter*]

But, seriously though, as I mentioned at our ceremony this morning, the people of our two countries have so much in common, not the least of which is the spirit of the frontier exemplified by the gaucho and the cowboy. More significant, however, is the bond of democracy, the love of freedom that's found in the hearts of our people. I'd like to take this opportunity to congratulate President Alfonsin, who is, on behalf of the Argentine people, accepting the international democracy prize from the Center for Democracy. And I can think of no finer example to others than Argentina's inspiring return to democracy. Congratulations, Mr. President.

This generation of Argentinians is laying the foundation for what will be enjoyed by your fellow countrymen hundreds of years hence. And this is in keeping with the tradition of San Martin, an heroic individual significant not only in your history but in that of the entire hemisphere. I think it's interesting to note that once San Martin was successful in freeing half a continent, he assumed the title of protector.

And that, perhaps, captures the essence of our responsibility. Those of us who enjoy the freedom and independence passed to us by brave and noble individuals like San Martin, Washington, and others, especially those of us in elected office, must be the protectors of liberty. This is our trust, our obligation. San Martin once said: "You will

be what you must be. If not, you are nothing."

President Alfonsin, you've already demonstrated to your countrymen and to all the world that you're willing to live up to the enormous trust that you hold in your hands. I look forward to working closely with you in the years ahead. I salute you. And I ask all of you to join me in a toast to President Alfonsin, Mrs. Alfonsin, and the free people of Argentina.

President Alfonsin. Mr. President and Mrs. Reagan, ladies and gentlemen, we have ended a day of intense, frank, cordial, and mutually enriching consultations. The success of this day, characterized from the beginning by exceptional American hospitality, is due in great part to your warmth, Mrs. Reagan, as well as to the informal and friendly atmosphere that you, Mr. President, imparted to our meetings. My wife and my friends are sincerely grateful for this hospitality, and I sincerely thank both of you.

In discussing the different aspects of international affairs, we have discovered that on many points our views converge. And if we also discovered a few differences in our analysis, it should neither surprise us nor alarm us. As I imagine it, the relationship between Washington and Buenos Aires presupposes—and I said that when I arrived—that we assume the defense of our respective national interests from a perspective of cooperation, foresight, and mutual sincerity.

It seems to me that within this framework we should explore with a certain amount of audacity, imagination, and good will the profiles of a realistic and enduring relationship between Latin America and the United States.

Mr. President, in your Inaugural Address—I mean your last Inaugural Address—I was moved by a suggestive evocation you made of the revolutionary past of the United States, and I quote you: "For the first time in history they said government is not our master, but rather our servant, and the only power of government—the government will be that which we, the people, allow it to have."

How can we not link these words to the

basic grounds that explain what the forces of democracy have achieved in Argentina to reestablish the sovereignty of our people. Why should two peoples whose convictions are nourished by such principles not be able to understand one another in fundamental matters?

And I am also aware of the fact that you and I share an intense concern about peace in the world. Of course, no doubt, our responsibilities are different. But in our area, we've made, I think, a great contribution to peace, because in the southern cone we've settled peacefully a century-old dispute with Chile.

Mr. President, Mrs. Reagan, as I toast for your personal well-being and that of all of you here tonight, I do so having specially in mind the American people. To your people we also offer this deeply felt tribute: They are a people who are the architects of the civilization where material achievements have always been united to a great spiritual force. Thank you very much.

Note: President Reagan spoke at approximately 9:45 p.m. in the State Dining Room at the White House. President Alfonsin spoke in Spanish, and his remarks were translated by an interpreter.

Statement on Senate Approval of MX Missile Production
March 19, 1985

I am pleased that the Senate today voted to support the MX Peacekeeper missile and to send a message of American resolve to the world. And I look forward to continuing to work with the Congress to build upon the consensus we achieved today.

As we continue to move forward to maintain the modern forces necessary for effective deterrence, let us remember that deterrence alone is not sufficient. The MX Peacekeeper will strengthen our national security and our negotiating position at

Geneva. Deterrence and arms reductions go hand in hand, and our negotiators are working hard—flexibly and with an open mind—to achieve agreements leading to deep reductions in nuclear arsenals.

It is critically important that the second Senate vote and next week's votes in the House reaffirm this demonstration of America's determination to achieve effective deterrence and significant nuclear arms reductions.

Remarks Announcing the Nomination of William E. Brock To Be Secretary of Labor
March 20, 1985

The President. And to add to that announcement, my nominee as the new Secretary of Labor: Bill Brock. He was our top choice from a blue-ribbon list of candidates, I have to say. He has an outstanding government background—6 years as a United States Senator from Tennessee, 4 years now at Cabinet level—and he was no stranger to politics. He was chairman of the GOP, helped rebuild the Republican Party from 1976 to 1980, and I think laid the ground-

work for what was one of the great Republican Party victories of quite some number of decades. And he has been a trade negotiator, and anyone who's spent 4 years dealing with international trade can negotiate with almost anyone.

Among his primary interest is rebuilding and maintaining the ties with labor—organized and unorganized—attacking the serious endemic problem of youth unemployment, in particular minority youth. And I know he looks forward to working with our job partnership plan that has been working fairly successfully now for some time in finding work particularly for the untrained, training them, and then placing them.

And so, I'm very pleased and proud to announce that Bill has agreed to accept the nomination for this Cabinet post. And having said that, I'm going to——

Q. We understand he didn't want the job.

The President. What?

Q. We understand he didn't want the job.

The President. Well, you know, you just can't believe everything you read, can you? [*Laughter*]

Q. This clears the way for you to move the Trade Representative right into Commerce, doesn't it, Mr. President?

The President. What?

Q. This clears the way for you to move the Trade Representative's job right into Commerce, right?

The President. That seems like a long way around, doesn't it?

Ambassador Brock. It sure does. Thank you.

The President. I'm not going to take any more questions. You're going to have at me tomorrow night.

Q. ——your reaction——

The President. What?

Q. ——to the MX vote? The House Appropriations——

The President. No, I'm not going——

Q. ——Committee voted against it today.

The President. ——to change the subject here. I'm going to leave you in the hands of the nominee for Secretary of Labor——

Q. When did you decide?

The President. ——William Brock.

Q. Did you make the decision this morning?

Ambassador Brock. Thank you, Mr. President, very much.

The President. We'd been talking about it for several days and——

Q. Mr. President, do you think this will help improve your ties——

Q. Do you think he will at least be able to——

Q. ——with organized labor, Mr. President?

Q. Do you think he will at least be able to meet and talk with [AFL–CIO president] Lane Kirkland, since your former Labor Secretary never did?

The President. I'm going to let you answer that.

Ambassador Brock. I'll be happy to answer that——

The President. All right.

Ambassador Brock. ——if I may.

Q. See you tomorrow.

The President. See you tomorrow.

Q. I'll be there. [*Laughter*]

Note: The President spoke to reporters at 12:14 p.m. in the Briefing Room at the White House.

Nomination of William E. Brock To Be Secretary of Labor
March 20, 1985

The President today announced his intention to nominate William E. Brock to be Secretary of Labor. He would succeed Raymond J. Donovan.

Since 1981 Ambassador Brock has been serving as United States Trade Representative. Previously he was chairman of the Republican National Committee in 1977–1981. He was United States Senator from Tennessee in 1971–1977 and represented the Third Congressional District of Tennessee in the United States House of Representatives in 1963–1971.

Ambassador Brock was born in Chattanooga, TN, on November 23, 1930. He attended Washington and Lee University, where he earned a B.S. in 1953. Following his service as an officer in the United States Navy, he became associated with the Brock Candy Co. as a marketing executive.

He was elected to the Congress in 1962 and throughout his service was active in Republican Party building efforts, serving as head of the National Young Voters Programs in 1972. In 1974 he was elected to head the Republican Senatorial Campaign Committee.

Ambassador Brock is married to the former Laura (Muffet) Handly, and they have four children.

Message to the Senate Transmitting a Protocol to the Interim Convention on Conservation of North Pacific Fur Seals
March 20, 1985

To the Senate of the United States:

I am pleased to transmit herewith, for Senate advice and consent to ratification, the Protocol Amending the Interim Convention on Conservation of North Pacific Fur Seals between the United States, Canada, Japan, and the Soviet Union, signed at Washington on October 12, 1984. I am also transmitting for the information of the Senate (1) a related statement of concerns, and (2) the report of the Department of State on the Protocol.

The Interim Convention was signed in 1957 and replaced an earlier convention concerning fur seals dating back to 1911. Under these conventions, the herds were protected and managed, and though there

has been a decrease in recent years, the population has increased significantly from 300,000 seals at the turn of the century to approximately 1.2 million presently. The Interim Convention has been extended previously in 1963, 1969, 1976, and 1980. This Protocol provides for the extension of the Interim Convention for four years until 1988. Accompanying the Protocol for purposes of information is a statement of concerns signed by the four Governments.

I urge the Senate to consider this matter at an early date and give its advice and consent to ratification of the Protocol.

RONALD REAGAN

The White House,
March 20, 1985.

Message to the Congress Transmitting the Annual Report on International Activities in Science and Technology
March 20, 1985

To the Congress of the United States:

In accordance with Title V of the Foreign Relations Authorization Act for Fiscal Year 1979 (Public Law 95–426), I am transmitting the Administration's annual report on international activities in the fields of science and technology for Fiscal Year 1984. The report was prepared by the Department of State in cooperation with other relevant agencies, consistent with the intent of the legislation.

This Administration has recognized from the outset that the achievement of our most essential national goals—enhanced national

security, increased industrial competitiveness, better health and quality of life for all our citizens—depends upon a strong and vital science and technology enterprise. In view of the impressive scientific and technological capabilities of many other countries, we are increasingly aware of the importance of international cooperation as a means of augmenting our strengths in these areas. The generation of new knowledge and progress in technology offer benefits to all nations committed to realistic and sustained economic growth. Indeed, the future of the world depends largely on science, technology, and the willingness of nations

319

to marshal their greatest resources—human creativity and talent—to work together to solve the problems that challenge mankind. We in the United States are determined to help make that future a bright one.

Substantial efforts were made during 1984 to implement the Title V legislation. In June, Secretary of State Shultz addressed a message to all our embassies abroad stressing the central importance of science and technology as a critical element of our foreign policy. In September, he followed that with a request for detailed descriptions of each mission's specific plans to better integrate science and technology into the conduct of our foreign affairs.

Consistent with our foreign policy objectives, we continue to emphasize government-to-government scientific cooperation in our bilateral and multilateral relations, in particular, fostering our cooperative relationships with the nations of Western Europe, with Japan and other democratic nations of the Pacific Basin, with India and the People's Republic of China, and with friends in our own hemisphere.

During 1984, we continued to participate in several cooperative scientific projects agreed upon at the Williamsburg Economic Summit in June 1983 and endorsed at the London Economic Summit in June 1984. As in the past years, we stressed the ability of cooperative efforts in science and technology to enhance the economic and military strength of the Western Alliance. We continue to support the NATO Science Committee's activities to stimulate collaborative research in significant frontier fields of science and to facilitate the exchange among member countries of their most promising young scientists and engineers. The importance the United States places on the NATO Science Committee was highlighted last Spring when we hosted the Committee's meeting in Washington.

During 1984, we continued to review our science and technology relationship with Japan. The U.S.-Japan Advisory Commission submitted a report to Prime Minister Nakasone and me entitled "Challenges and Opportunities in United States-Japan Relations." It suggested in particular that ". . . the time has come for a high-level review to determine possible improvements and

new directions for mutually beneficial cooperation." Such review was launched in April, and I expect to be able to highlight its conclusions in my message accompanying next year's Title V report.

Last January, we reviewed the range of activities that have been carried out during the first five years of our Bilateral Cooperative Agreement in Science and Technology with the People's Republic of China, and took particular pleasure in extending that agreement for five more years. Cooperative research is now being conducted under twenty-three separate protocols within the broad auspices of that agreement, and accords in several new areas, including fossil energy, and space cooperation, are in the final stages of negotiation.

Significant strides were made in the special cooperative programs with India—in health, agriculture, and monsoon research—that emerged from my discussions with Prime Minister Indira Gandhi in July 1982. The government of India continues its support of these initiatives under the new leadership of Prime Minister Rajiv Gandhi.

Special reference must be made to our bilateral science and technology relationship with the Soviet Union. In past reports, I have stressed that cooperation with that country depends upon steps taken by its government to comply with recognized standards of international behavior. While that behavior is often far from constructive, I have approved during 1984 renewed cooperative efforts in carefully selected areas such as agriculture, health, and environmental protection and safety, that recognize complementary strengths and ensure mutual benefits. I took this action to convince Soviet officials of our desire for peace and our willingness to explore whatever roads might be open to take us there together.

We recognize that there are important opportunities to address science and technology issues within the technical agencies of the United Nations system, but such opportunities should be pursued only where there are realistic expectations of shared benefit and success. Where success proves beyond our grasp, we must reevaluate our position and find more effective alternatives. Such is the case with our participation in UNESCO. I stated at the end of 1983 our intention to withdraw from that agency should acceptable reforms not be undertaken within a year. That period expired on December 31, 1984, and we have withdrawn as planned. Despite U.S. withdrawal, we remain committed to the belief that genuine reform of UNESCO is a worthwhile goal, and in the coming year, we will work with all countries, individuals, and private organizations who seek improvement in UNESCO to achieve that purpose. When UNESCO returns to its original mission and principles, we will rejoin UNESCO and participate in the full range of its multilateral scientific programs.

In conclusion, I want to stress again the importance of cooperative scientific and technological arrangements in our assist-

ance to developing countries. On November 22, 1984, in an address to members of an international association for research and development in nuclear energy, His Holiness John Paul II emphasized the importance he perceives in such arrangements. "Cooperation in the fields of science and technology is one of the most effective means not only for contributing to the physical welfare of people, but also of fostering the dignity and worth of every person."

The United States is committed to a role for scientific and technological cooperation in international affairs, and we will pursue this goal to the benefit of all nations willing to join us.

RONALD REAGAN

The White House,
March 20, 1985.

Nomination of Terence C. Golden To Be Administrator of General Services
March 20, 1985

The President today announced his intention to nominate Terence C. Golden to be Administrator of General Services. He would succeed Gerald P. Carmen.

Since 1984 Mr. Golden has been serving at the Department of the Treasury as Assistant Secretary for Administration. Previously, he was a managing partner of Trammell Crow Residential Companies in 1976–1984; president and chairman of the board of Palmas Del Mar Co. in Puerto Rico (1973–1976); in the nuclear energy division of Babcock & Wilcox Co. in 1970–1973; man-

ager for marketing and business planning of Babcock Brown Boveri Reaktor GMBH in Mannheim, Germany (1971–1973); and manager, systems and controls, for B&W Commercial Nuclear Fuel Plant in 1970.

He graduated from the University of Notre Dame (B.S., 1966), Massachusetts Institute of Technology (M.S., 1968), and Harvard Graduate School of Business Administration (M.B.A., 1970). He is married, has two children, and resides in Washington, DC. He was born August 1, 1944, in Honesdale, PA.

Nomination of Peter C. Myers To Be an Assistant Secretary of Agriculture
March 20, 1985

The President today announced his intention to nominate Peter C. Myers to be an

Assistant Secretary of Agriculture (Natural Resources and Environment). He would succeed John B. Crowell, Jr.

Mr. Myers has been serving as Chief of the United States Department of Agriculture's Soil Conservation Service since April 1982. Previously he was a full-time farmer, operating his own row crop and livestock farm in the Mississippi Delta area of southern Missouri (1955–1982). During that period, he was active in natural resource management and agricultural activities and served as commissioner of the Missouri Department of Conservation; adviser to the Governor of Missouri's Soil and Water Commission; director of the Missouri Cattleman's Association; and a member of the Missouri Farm Bureau.

He graduated from the University of Wisconsin (B.S., 1953). He served in the United States Army in 1953–1955. He is married, has five children, and resides in Annandale, VA. He was born January 4, 1931, in Racine, WI.

Nomination of Robert L. Thompson To Be an Assistant Secretary of Agriculture
March 20, 1985

The President today announced his intention to nominate Robert L. Thompson to be an Assistant Secretary of Agriculture (Economics). He would succeed William Gene Lesher.

Dr. Thompson has been on the staff of the department of agricultural economics at Purdue University since 1974. He is on leave from Purdue and currently serves on the Council of Economic Advisers as Senior Staff Economist for Food and Agriculture. He has been assistant professor (1974–1979), associate professor (1979–1983), and professor (1983–present) at Purdue University. He was visiting professor in economics, statistics, and cooperatives service to the U.S. Department of Agriculture in 1979–1980.

He is a member of the editorial council of the American Journal of Agricultural Economics, the American Agricultural Economics Association, the American Economic Association, and the International Association of Agricultural Economists. He was a member of the task force on domestic agricultural policy alternatives, National Agricultural Forum, in 1983–1984.

Dr. Thompson graduated from Cornell University (B.S., 1967) and Purdue University (M.S., 1969; Ph.D., 1974). He is married, has two children, and resides in Springfield, VA. He was born April 25, 1945, in Canton, NY.

Nomination of A. James Barnes To Be Deputy Administrator of the Environmental Protection Agency
March 20, 1985

The President today announced his intention to nominate A. James Barnes to be Deputy Administrator of the Environmental Protection Agency. He would succeed Alvin L. Alm.

Since 1983 Mr. Barnes has been serving as General Counsel of the Environmental Protection Agency. Previously, he was General Counsel of the Department of Agriculture in 1981–1983; partner in the law firm of Beveridge, Fairbanks & Diamond in Washington, DC, in 1973–1981; assistant to the Deputy Attorney General in 1973; Assistant Administrator of the Environmental Protection Agency in 1970–1973; trial attorney and special assistant to the Assistant Attorney General, Civil Division, in 1969–1970; and assistant professor in the Graduate School of Business at Indiana University in 1967–1969.

He graduated from Michigan State University (B.A., 1964) and Harvard Law School (J.D., 1967). He is married, has one child, and resides in Washington, DC. He was born August 30, 1942, in Napoleon, OH.

Appointment of General Andrew L. Goodpaster as a Member of the American Battle Monuments Commission
March 20, 1985

The President today announced his intention to appoint Gen. Andrew L. Goodpaster, United States Army, ret., to be a member of the American Battle Monuments Commission. He would succeed Gen. Mark Wayne Clark.

Since 1983 he has been serving as president of the Institute for Defense Analyses in Alexandria, VA.

General Goodpaster served in Italy, commanding the 48th Engineer Combat Battalion, in 1943–1944. He was then assigned to the Operations Division of the General Staff of the War Department, where he served until 1947. In 1950–1954 he was special assistant to the Chiefs of Staff, Supreme Headquarters of the Allied Powers, in Europe. He served at the White House as defense liaison officer and staff secretary to the President in 1954–1961. He was division commander of the 8th Infantry Division in 1961–1962, assistant to the Chairman of the Joint Chiefs of Staff in 1962–1966, and Director of the Joint Chiefs of Staff in 1967.

In 1967–1968 he was Commandant of the National War College. He was Deputy Commander of the U.S. forces in Vietnam in 1968–1969. He became Supreme Commander of the Allied Powers in Europe in 1969 and served there until 1974. He was Superintendent of the U.S. Military Academy in 1977–1981.

General Goodpaster received the Medal of Freedom in 1984. He graduated from the U.S. Military Academy (B.S., 1939), Princeton University (M.S.E., M.A., 1949; Ph.D., 1950). He is married, has two children, and resides in Alexandria, VA. He was born February 12, 1915, in Granite City, IL.

Nomination of Stephen L. Hammerman To Be a Director of the Securities Investor Protection Corporation
March 20, 1985

The President today announced his intention to nominate Stephen L. Hammerman to be a Director of the Securities Investor Protection Corporation for a term expiring December 31, 1985. He would succeed Ralph D. DeNunzio.

Since 1981 Mr. Hammerman has been assistant to the president of Merrill Lynch & Co. and vice president and general counsel of Merrill Lynch, Pierce, Fenner & Smith, Inc. Previously, he was the New York Regional Administrator of the Securities and Exchange Commission in 1979–1981; managing director and general counsel of Merrill Lynch White Weld Capital Markets Group in 1978–1979; and deputy chief operating officer, senior vice president and general counsel, director and vice chairman of the executive committee of White Weld & Co., Inc., in 1969–1978.

He was an associate with the firm of Paul, Weiss, Goldberg, Rifkind, Wharton & Garrison in 1968–1969 and Assistant United States Attorney in the United States Attorney's Office, Southern District of New York (Criminal Division), in 1964–1968.

He graduated from the University of Pennsylvania Wharton School of Finance and Commerce (1959) and New York Uni-

versity School of Law (1962). He is married, has four children, and resides in Atlantic Beach, NY. He was born April 18, 1938, in Brooklyn, NY.

Message to the Congress Transmitting the Annual Reports on Highway, Traffic, and Motor Vehicle Safety Programs
March 21, 1985

To the Congress of the United States:

The Highway Safety Act and the National Traffic and Motor Vehicle Safety Act, both enacted in 1966, initiated a national effort to reduce traffic deaths and injuries and require annual reports on the administration of the Acts. This is the 17th year that these reports have been prepared for your review.

The report on motor vehicle safety includes the annual reporting requirement in Title I of the Motor Vehicle Information and Cost Savings Act of 1972 (bumper standards). An annual report also is required by the Energy Policy and Conservation Act of 1975, which amended the Motor Vehicle Information and Cost Savings Act and directed the Secretary of Transportation to set, adjust, and enforce motor vehicle fuel economy standards. Similar reporting requirements are contained in the Department of Energy Act of 1978 with respect to the use of advanced technology by the automobile industry. These requirements have been met in the Eighth Annual Fuel Economy Report, the highlights of which are summarized in the motor vehicle safety report.

In the Highway Safety Acts of 1973, 1976, and 1978, the Congress expressed its special interest in certain aspects of traffic safety, which are addressed in the volume on highway safety.

I am pleased to report that traffic fatalities have dropped for the third year in a row. The 42,584 fatalities recorded in 1983, while still unacceptably high and a tragedy to the Nation both in terms of lives lost and the economic consequences of the deaths, represent a 3 percent decrease from the preceding year, and a 17 percent decrease

from as recently as 1980 when 51,091 people died in traffic accidents.

In addition, despite large increases in the number of drivers and vehicles, the Federal standards and programs for motor vehicle and highway safety instituted since 1966 have contributed to a significant reduction in the fatality rate per 100 million miles of travel. The fatality rate is a measure of the risk of death that a person is exposed to when travelling. The rate has decreased from 5.5 in the mid-60's to the present level of 2.57, the lowest rate ever recorded. This means that motorists can drive more miles today with less risk. If the 1966 fatality rate had been experienced in 1983, more than 91,000 persons would have lost their lives in traffic accidents.

A substantial number of deaths and injuries on our roadways can be traced in part to some human factor: the driver or passenger who was not wearing a safety belt; the drinking driver who continues to be involved in more than half of the Nation's traffic fatalities; speeding; or the habitual offenders whose privileges to drive have been revoked, but who continue to drive irresponsibly.

I am especially proud that in 1983 we had the safest Christmas holiday season since the late 1940's. The national outrage over drunk driving, combined with tougher State laws and stepped-up enforcement, apparently have caused some people to refrain from driving after they have been drinking.

We will continue to pursue highway and motor vehicle safety programs that are most effective in reducing deaths and injuries. We are placing greater emphasis on the human aspects of traffic safety, reflecting the national concern that emphasis be on those activities that have the most realistic prospect of success, and which yield the maximum safety gain per dollar invested.

I am encouraged by the significant fatality reduction this Nation has experienced over the past three years and am convinced that even more progress can be made to ensure that American motorists and pedestrians will enjoy the greatest level of personal safety possible.

RONALD REAGAN

The White House,
March 21, 1985.

Nomination of Martha Graham To Be a Member of the National Council on the Arts
March 21, 1985

The President today announced his intention to nominate Martha Graham to be a member of the National Council on the Arts, National Foundation on the Arts and the Humanities, for the remainder of the term expiring September 3, 1986. She would succeed Erich Leinsdorf.

She is founder and director of the Martha Graham Dance Company in New York, NY. She is the recipient of many awards for her contributions to the arts, including the Distinguished Service to the Arts Award of the National Institute of Arts and Letters in 1970, the New York State Council on the Arts Award in 1973, the Presidential Medal of Freedom in 1976, and the Kennedy Center Achievement Honor in 1979.

She was born May 11, 1894, in Pittsburgh, PA, and now resides in New York, NY.

Proclamation 5309—Afghanistan Day, 1985
March 21, 1985

By the President of the United States of America

A Proclamation

In a time of prosperity, we do not think of hunger and hardship. In a time of peace, we do not think of suffering and war. In a time when our families are together and healthy, we do not think of the pain we would feel if they were pulled apart. Yet, for the people of Afghanistan, it is impossible to escape such thoughts, because terror, hardship, and suffering have become an everyday way of life ever since the Soviet Union brutally invaded and occupied their country over five years ago.

March 21 is the start of a New Year for the Afghan people. It is traditionally a holiday when they bring their families together to celebrate life's new beginnings and to rejoice and give thanks for God's many gifts.

But in Afghanistan today it may be hard to remember the days when their country had peace, when there was enough food to eat, and when their homes were safe, for the overwhelming majority of Afghans are engaged in a fierce struggle to end the Soviet occupation of their country and the rule of the puppet regime headed by Babrak Karmal.

The year 1984 was an especially hard one for the Afghans. The Soviets have become frustrated with their inability to crush the spirit of the Afghan Freedom Fighters and are increasingly turning their military might against the civilian population of the country, forcing hundreds of thousands more innocent people into exile away from their homeland.

Reports of Soviet atrocities and human rights violations are increasingly gaining the attention of the world's public. Respected organizations such as the United Nations Commission on Human Rights, Amnesty International, and Helsinki Watch have recently released studies detailing the terror that the Soviets and the Karmal regime regularly inflict on the people of Afghanistan. Karmal's tenuous, and brutal, hold on power continues only because his rule is supported by more than 100,000 Soviet occupation troops.

All Americans are outraged by this growing Soviet brutality against the proud and freedom-loving people of Afghanistan. Moreover, the entire world community has condemned the outside occupation of Afghanistan. Six times, in fact, the UN General Assembly has passed strong resolutions—supported by the overwhelming majority of the world's nations—which have:

—called for the immediate withdrawal of foreign troops from Afghanistan;

—reaffirmed the right of the Afghan people to determine their own form of government and choose their economic, political, and social systems;

—reiterated that the preservation of the sovereignty, territorial integrity, political independence, and nonaligned character of Afghanistan is essential for a peaceful solution of the problem; and

—called for the creation of conditions that would enable the Afghan refugees to return voluntarily to their homes in safety and honor.

All Americans are united on the goal of freedom for Afghanistan. I ask the American people, at the time when we are blessed with prosperity and security, to remember the Afghan struggle against tyranny and the rule of government-by-terror. We stand in admiration of the indomitable courage of the Afghan people who are an inspiration to all freedom-loving nations around the globe.

Afghanistan Day will serve to recall the fundamental principles involved when people struggle for the freedom to determine their own future and the right to govern themselves without foreign interference. Let us, therefore, resolve to pay tribute to the brave Afghan people by observing March 21, 1985, as Afghanistan Day. Let us pledge our continuing admiration for their cause and their perseverance and continue to do everything we can to provide humanitarian support to the brave Afghan people, including the millions of Afghan refugees who have been forced to flee their own country.

Now, Therefore, I, Ronald Reagan, President of the United States of America, do hereby proclaim March 21, 1985, as Afghanistan Day.

In Witness Whereof, I have hereunto set my hand this twenty-first day of March, in the year of our Lord nineteen hundred and eighty-five, and of the Independence of the United States of America the two hundred and ninth.

RONALD REAGAN

[*Filed with the Office of the Federal Register, 12:32 p.m., March 22, 1985*]

The President's News Conference
March 21, 1985

MX Missile

The President. Good evening. I have just a few words first.

Let me commend again the Senate of the United States for having approved production of 21 more MX/Peacekeeper missiles. The Senate has endorsed the decision of four Presidents that the Peacekeeper is a vital component of the American deterrent. Now is the testing time for the House of Representatives. The votes there will answer the question of whether we stand united at Geneva or whether America will face the Soviet Union as a nation divided over the most fundamental questions of her national security.

For more than a decade we've debated the MX, and while we were debating, the Soviets were deploying more than 600 such missiles and targeting them upon the United States. Now they're on the verge of deploying two new strategic land-based systems, and we're still debating.

Not long ago the parliaments of four NATO countries courageously voted to accept deployment of Pershing II's and cruise missiles. And these NATO countries are now looking to see if the American Congress is possessed of equal courage—or resolve, I should say.

No request by an American President for a major strategic system deemed vital to the national security has ever been denied by an American Congress. It is that tradition of bipartisan unity on national defense that brought the Soviets back to Geneva. And unless that tradition is maintained next week in the House, there's little prospect of success at Geneva.

Meeting With Soviet Leader Mikhail Gorbachev

And now, Helen [Helen Thomas, United Press International], I know that Nancy upstairs would die—she's watching on television—if I didn't call on you in that pretty red dress. [*Laughter*]

Q. That's why I wore it. I wanted you to be sure to do that. [*Laughter*]

Mr. President, can you give us your thinking on the summit: why you think it would be good to meet with Gorbachev, what you think can be accomplished, and why you've been rebuffed so far?

The President. Well, I don't really consider it being rebuffed, Helen, because the man has only been in office for a few days, and I have some idea of what is confronting him now. But I've felt the same way about each of the three previous leaders there and then things intervened that made it impossible—that there are a number of things—bilateral situations between our two countries, other things to talk about that we're negotiating or talking to each other on a ministerial level, and that some of those could probably be further advanced if we met at a summit.

And so, what I always meant by an agenda, a planned meeting—not just one to get acquainted—is one in which—just as when we go in a meeting, even to Canada, we have announced things that we want to talk about, and they have an agenda of things they want to talk about—mutual problems that confront us—and I think it's high time that we did this.

Q. Well, what are the prospects for having it soon?

The President. Well, I have to think that they should be good. I think in some of our people, we've had about an hour and a half conversation—the Vice President, the Secretary of State did with him when they were there. And, so, I think there is a good chance of that.

The reason that I issued the invitation was because under the kind of protocol that exists—and you look back over the history of such meetings—why, it's our turn to be the host. So, that's why I proposed it, that if he would, the invitation was extended for whenever he found it convenient.

Where's your red tie? [*Laughter*]

Middle East

Q. Doesn't always work. May I say, sir, that it's nice to have you back again so soon.

Mr. President, in your first term you proposed your own Middle East peace plan. You dispatched special envoys to the region to seek solutions, you even sent in marines to try to stabilize Lebanon. These days we hardly ever even hear you mention the Middle East, and last week President Mubarak went home disappointed when he asked for your help in getting peace talks started again.

I wonder if you could tell us tonight, sir, what you expect to gain from the new policy of disengagement, and what do you expect to be achieved over there?

The President. Well, it isn't disengagement, and let me point out, I believe it's a misapprehension that President Mubarak left disappointed. He made no requests. He told us what he was doing, and certainly we complimented him highly upon what he's doing, and I think it's great.

But our proposal, in the very beginning, was that we did not want to participate in the negotiations. It wouldn't be any of our business to do so but that we'd do whatever we could to help bring the warring parties together and, in effect, you might say, continue the Camp David process and continue trying to find more countries that would do as Egypt did and make peace.

And we haven't been idle. We've not only have had President Mubarak here but—and a short time before that we had King Fahd of Saudi Arabia—Masri, the Foreign Minister, is now here. And we still feel the same way. We have been trying to build up a relationship with the Arab nations, as well as the relationship that we've always had with Israel. And we discussed with President Mubarak the—yes, the things that he has proposed, and the idea of the Palestinians—we did have to make it clear that we couldn't meet if it was the PLO. They still refuse to recognize the U.N. Resolutions 242 and 338, and they refuse to agree or admit that Israel has a right to exist as a nation. But we have said Palestinian representatives—yes. There's a large Palestinian community, and I'm sure that there are people that do not consider themselves represented by the PLO.

Q. Do you see a direct role for the United States in any talks over there?

The President. Well, not the direct role in sitting at the table and negotiating, that must be done in direct negotiations between the Arab States and Israel. And I think that King Hussein—the position he's taken—that was the one that we had hoped, and he did take 2 years ago, when we suggested all of this, and then things broke down with the Lebanese conflict. And now, thanks to Mubarak pushing ahead and Hussein, I think that there is a reasonable chance, and we have another traveling Ambassador on his way back there in a few weeks.

Yes, Jerry [Jeremiah O'Leary, Washington Times]?

Trade With Japan

Q. Mr. President, you now need a new U.S. Representative for Trade to replace Ambassador Brock. Are you looking for someone who will more sharply convey to other nations, especially Japan, the need for fairer trading conditions between the two countries? And are voluntary quotas ever going to work on automobile sales?

The President. Well, Jerry, we're just going to have to see what restraint might be used by the Japanese in this. But I have to say I couldn't fault Bill Brock and what he has done. He's been as forceful as anyone could be. And we are still leaning on our friends and trading partners, including Japan, for continued lifting of restraints that they have, particularly with regard to their own markets. And in the talks in Europe that will begin in May, I am going to propose again another round of trade negotiations to further get us back to completely free trade.

And we've made some progress. I have to say that Prime Minister Nakasone of Japan had been very forthcoming on this. He has some political problems that—just like me, he can't just give an order and have it happen. But he's working very hard on this. And Bill did a great job, and I'm quite sure that who we'll finally get to replace him will be equally forceful in those negotiations.

Lebanon

Yes?

Q. Mr. President, back to—[*inaudible*]— as you know, three Lebanese who were working for CBS News, taking pictures——

The President. Yes.

Q. ——during some hostilities, were shot at by the Israeli Army today—two were killed and one was critically wounded. I was wondering if you have a reaction to the incident and if you plan to lodge any protests with the Israeli Government?

The President. Well, first of all, I'd like to know all the details of this. I'm quite sure in combat of that kind this was not a deliberate killing. They were engaged in gunfire with armed persons who were in civilian, not uniformed as they would be in a war. So, these things can happen. And it is a tragedy. And all I can say is that I think all of us have a great feeling of sorrow about the tragedy that is going on there in Lebanon, and particularly in south Lebanon now as the Israelis try to withdraw. And whichever side, the acts of terror, the retaliation—both of them are leading to tragedies that just seem to be so needless.

Q. So, you're saying that the Israelis were engaged in gunfire with other people at the time, because one report said that they just opened fire on the newsmen who were obviously taking pictures and covering the story?

The President. My goodness, your own news program tonight showed an awful lot of gunfire with very sophisticated weapons, including grenade launchers, and they were obviously being used by civilians, at least people in civilian uniform; they weren't Israelis. So, yes, this is one of the things that happens in this kind of warfare, where you're not fighting another country's army.

There's a girl in a red dress just over your shoulder, started the whole thing. [*Laughter*]

Job Training Programs

Q. On March 31st, 340,000 Americans are going to lose their unemployment benefits when the Federal Supplemental Unemployment Compensation project expires. Are you going to let this happen, or do you plan to take some action to extend the program?

The President. No, we believe that it is time. It has been extended, you know, for quite some time through the emergency of the recession. But now we have about 300,000 people going back to work every month in new jobs. We believe that the place now is, for people who are having problems, is our job training program, particularly job training directed at those who have to be relocated because something has happened to the industries that they formally worked in. But we don't believe that we should continue with this program indefinitely.

Now—Sam [Sam Donaldson, ABC News]?

Violence in South Africa

Q. Sir, 17 blacks were shot to death in South Africa today by government authorities in what appears to be a continuing wave of violence by the white minority government against the black majority population. Are you considering changing your policy to put more pressure on the South African Government to mend its ways?

The President. No, Sam, I know the pressure that we are putting on them, and I

know the gains that we've made. But we know there's still a long way to go. But I think to put it that way—that they were simply killed and that the violence was coming totally from the law and order side ignores the fact that there was rioting going on in behalf of others there. And it is tragic, and, again, we hope that this can be corrected. But I think also it is significant that on the officer's side—or the police side—whichever—whether they were military police, I think they were police—it is significant that some of those enforcing the law and using the guns were also black policemen.

Q. Sir, then is it your estimate of the situation that the blacks posed a threat to the whites who had the guns when the blacks didn't?

The President. No. I say that there has been increasing violence, and there is an element in South Africa that do not want a peaceful settlement of this, who want a violent settlement, who want trouble in the streets. And this is what's going on. I don't hold with what has happened, and, as I say, I think all of us find the system there repugnant, but we're going to keep on trying to contribute to a peaceful solution if we can.

Chris [Chris Wallace, NBC News]?

The President's Views on the Media

Q. Yes, sir. Conservative groups have been talking recently about trying to take over one of the three major television networks, charging that our coverage is biased politically. You have occasionally been critical yourself of network news coverage, and I wonder what you think about a possible conservative takeover of a network?

The President. Well, I don't know what to comment on that. [*Laughter*] Boone Pickens—was that who you're talking about—[*laughter*]—is it, he's—? I know a merger is suggested for one. And no, this is often talked about. It's even been talked about for some of the print media, too, at times by people that find themselves unhappy with what they think is a bias. I don't have any comments on that. I just turn it on, look, and every once in awhile scream a little, but to myself. [*Laughter*]

Q. Lets get back to the problem for a minute though, sir. Do you have any concerns about major sources of information, like news networks, being taken over by political activists, or do you think they already have been?

The President. You just answered the question yourself.

No. Maybe the whole thing is a new school of what's called objective reporting, that in all of the media, in which the old rules when I took journalism—and I did, actually—you were supposed to tell the story based on who, what, where, when—putting first whichever one was the newsiest and have no opinions of your own. So, there's a——

Patricia [Patricia Wilson, Reuters]?

Strategic Defense Initiative

Q. Britain's Foreign Secretary, Sir Geoffrey Howe, has raised a long list of concerns and questions about your Strategic Defense Initiative, which conjured a public rebuke from Assistant Secretary of Defense Richard Perle. Was Mr. Perle speaking for the administration, and if not, how do you feel about an allied official publicly questioning SDI just as arms talks were starting in Geneva?

The President. Well, I haven't seen either the speech that Perle was answering or his remarks. I have simply heard that this happened. I'm interested in finding out what the exact words were about it. I do know that we have the support of Prime Minister Thatcher and, therefore, the English Government in our research for the Strategic Defense Initiative, and so I'm satisfied with that. I don't know what the other critic——

Q. Were you surprised by it?

The President. What?

Q. Were you surprised by Sir Geoffrey's words?

The President. Well, I was just surprised when I heard about it, yes. But I'm going to try and find out exactly what was said. Yes?

Arms Control

Q. Mr. President, at your last news conference you accused the Soviet Union of violating SALT II limitations on building new missiles, and you said you'd have to

decide in the next few months whether to join them in violating the agreement. Since the Soviets are insisting that all they're doing are making allowable upgrades of older missiles, won't an open violation by the United States run the risk of just dashing hopes for arms control and leading us into a real upward spiraling arms race?

The President. Well, I can assure you we're not going to do anything that's going to undercut the negotiations that are going on. We're hopeful that, for the first time, we really have an opportunity to get a reduction of missiles. I have said repeatedly—and continue it, and I really mean it—we're going to wait and deal with that problem when we come to that point—and it has to do with some of our submarine missiles—as to what our conduct's going to be.

Sam?

Q. But, sir, if I may follow up. That's this fall, and it's unlikely you're going to have any major arms control agreement before this fall.

The President. No, that's right, we don't know. But on the other hand, our record as compared to theirs with regard to observing all the niceties of all the treaties is so much superior that I don't think we're in a position to cause any great trouble.

Commemoration of V–E Day

Q. Mr. President, can you tell us why your decision not to visit a Nazi concentration camp site when you make your trip to Germany in May is commemorating V–E Day?

The President. Yes, I'll tell you. I feel very strongly that this time in commemorating the end of that great war, that instead of reawakening the memories and so forth and the passions of the time, that maybe we should observe this day as the day when, 40 years ago, peace began and friendship. Because we now find ourselves allied and friends of the countries that we once fought against. And that it be almost a celebration of the end of an era and the coming into what has now been some 40 years of peace for us.

And I felt that since the German people—and very few alive that remember even the war, and certainly none of them who were adults and participating in any way—and they have a feeling, and a guilt feeling that's been imposed upon them, and I just think it's unnecessary. I think they should be recognized for the democracy that they've created and the democratic principles they now espouse.

Q. If I can just follow that up—has the West German Government asked you to take one position or another on it?

The President. No, but in talking just informally some time ago with Chancellor Kohl and others, they all felt the same way—that if we could observe this as the beginning of peace and friendship between us.

All right.

Republican Party Unity

Q. Mr. President, there have been signals from the White House in recent days that you were, perhaps, somewhat dissatisfied with the level of loyalty of some Members of Congress on particular issues of importance to you. Could you tell us what you think is the responsibility of a Senator or a House Member who finds himself faced on an issue deciding between what he thinks his constituents want and his President wants?

The President. Well, I suppose this comes from the suggestion that I am supposed to penalize some Members in the coming campaign. No, I've never done that. I am a charter member of the California-born 11th commandment: Thou shalt not speak ill of another Republican. And, therefore, I'm dedicated to doing my best to see if we can't maintain the majority we have in the Senate and someday get ourselves a majority in the House, which we haven't had for more than 26 years. So, no, I'm not going to hold a grudge on anyone.

Federal Budget

Q. Mr. President, what about those Senate Republicans who want to come down and talk to you, and I think they're going to tomorrow—Senator Dole, Senator Domenici—who've pushed through a budget of their own that is not exactly yours. Are you prepared to look at that budget and make some compromise?

The President. Oh, yes! We've put togeth-er a budget—and after long, bloody hours—that we think does the job. But we recognize that others may have other ideas. But now they've got something that we can sit down and talk about—theirs and ours—see where we come out. The thing that we must recognize: Both of us have the same idea. We want to reduce spending and start ourselves on a path toward eliminating the deficit.

Social Security

Q. Mr. President, does that include Social Security? Are you willing to compromise on that, too, now?

The President. Social Security, I still feel, even though I did not refer to the COLA's in my statements during the campaign—I was answering what I thought were some demagogic falsehoods that I had some kind of a secret yen to destroy Social Security. And I didn't mean it, but it was interpreted as meaning that. And, actually, I think we're wasting a lot of time talking about it. Social Security is running on a surplus. And it is totally funded by a tax that can only be used for that purpose. So, when we talk about Social Security, we're not really getting at the deficit problem at all.

No, you had your hand up and——

Ohio Banking Crisis

Q. Mr. President, there's been some criticism that the Federal Government has not done enough in the Ohio banking crisis. Granted, these are State-regulated institutions. But on the other hand, there is some fear that what's happening in Ohio could quickly and easily threaten the entire national financial system. What is your view of the Federal Government's role in such matters? And at what point would you take action?

The President. Well, I'm pleased to say that this is a matter of a group of savings and loans that had taken out either private or State insurance, had not availed themselves of the Federal insurance program. And it is limited to Ohio. This is not a major threat to the banking system. There is no other problem of that kind anyplace else in the country that we're aware of. And the Federal Reserve has stepped in and said

331

that they will keep the window open for loans to those banks—or those savings and loans—any of them that meet the requirements of collateral and so forth, and the loans will be available for them when they reopen.

So, that situation, I think, is being taken care of by the Federal Government. There isn't anything else for the Federal Government to do.

Q. I realize this was somewhat of a hypothetical question, but at what point does the Federal Government play a role? Is there some breakpoint at which you believe that the Federal Government should step in?

The President. No, I can't see it as that kind of a crisis at all. We're perfectly ready to insure with Federal insurance any of the banks—there are just a half of dozen States that allow this other kind of insuring instead of getting into the Federal system. But——

The President's Views on the Media

Q. Mr. President, I would like to go back to Chris' question and ask you about reporting standards. Some of your friends and political allies have been suggesting recently that members of the news media are somehow unpatriotic. Senator Jesse Helms, for example, has charged that members of the press have what he says is a smug contempt for American values and principles. Do you subscribe to that, sir?

The President. No, but I'll tell you, I think I'll leave that argument to others. I won't even get into it. I don't see any point in that. And I guess I've done as much criticizing as anyone. As I say, I just wish sometime you'd drop me a hint of who some of those unidentified sources are in the White House. [*Laughter*]

Andrea [Andrea Mitchell, NBC News]?

Middle East

Q. Mr. President, back talking about the Middle East, you've been told by King Hussein, I believe, or at least King Hussein has said it publicly that his agreement with Yasser Arafat does include recognition of Israel's right to exist and renunciation of the use of force. Under those conditions would you, then, at least consider the possibility of inviting a joint Palestinian-Jordani-

an delegation for meetings if you thought they would lead to direct talks and if they did not include any members of the PLO?

The President. Well, as I say, we're willing to meet with a joint group—Palestinian and Jordanian. But at the moment not the PLO because we have not had any statement from them that they do recognize Israel and that they will recognize 242 and so forth. But there are many Palestinians who don't feel that they're represented by the PLO. And any delegation of them—for example, many of those who are living and holding local offices on the West Bank—but——

Q. Do you think, then, that it would be possible? Would you consider the Mubarak approach, which is for the United States to invite a joint delegation, if you had an understanding about the composition of the Palestinians?

The President. Well, this is what President Mubarak was talking about and that they're putting together. It's a case of their inviting us, not the other way around. And we've said that we'd be happy to discuss with them. But they've got to understand we are not getting into the direct negotiations. That's none of our business. We're only to do what we can to help.

Nicaragua

Q. Question about Central America: Are you giving any thought, sir, to recognizing the *contras*, who are fighting the Sandinistas in Nicaragua, as a government-in-exile?

The President. No, we haven't thought about that at all. And yet I must say that this matter that's before the Congress of whether it's $14 million or whatever—that isn't the issue.

The issue is the United States is trying to help people who had a Communist tyranny imposed on them by force, deception, and fraud. And either we continue with that tradition, which has always been ours, or we give that up entirely. And I don't think we should give that up. I think our position is clear.

Q. Mr. President, I'm sorry——

The President. Next.

Defense Spending

Q. Returning to the budget for just a moment, it's true you answered a question on the Social Security aspect of it, but two other issues in the budget compromise that Senator Dole was able to work in the Senate involved deeper cuts in defense spending than you would have liked, on the one hand, and lesser cuts in domestic spending than you had recommended. If Senator Dole takes Social Security cap on COLA off the table and you can agree with the deeper defense cut and a lesser domestic cut, do you see the makings of an agreement there, or do you think you're too far apart to resolve that issue without the Social Security element in it?

The President. Well, I hate to predict in advance what might happen when we discuss, but I will have to say this. One of the objections that I've had in all of the discussions with many Members of Congress with regard to defense spending and the other is: Those who advocate more cuts in defense spending don't add those to the cuts already made in domestic so that the reduction in spending is bigger. No, they use the cuts in defense to augment spending in domestic affairs. And I think that in the discussion of defense spending, we've got to quit talking about how many dollars do we want to or not want to spend. We've got to talk there about: All right, what is it you can see that would be eliminated by cuts in spending, and what would that do to our national security.

And I would like to call your attention to something that no one seems to be aware of: that we, ourselves, have cut the defense budgets over the last 4 years. Our own proposed—or projected 5-year defense spending—we have to date reduced those by more than $150 billion. And today the 1985 budget is $16 billion less than the 1985 budget that had been projected by the Carter administration. So, we think that we have made sizable cuts already. The trouble is if we cut it in half, there are people on the Hill who would still think that it had to be cut more than that. And I think that we've made some progress, and we have a defense program that any further cuts are actually going to run the risk of lowering our capability at preserving national security.

Tax Increases

Q. Sir, one followup, you answered this many times. If it comes down to resolving this issue as a last extreme, would you accept a tax increase as a means of reducing the deficit?

The President. I have said repeatedly that when we have finally reduced spending to the point that we say: All right, here it is. This is the best that can be obtained if government is to perform the services it should. And then that percentage of gross national product or earnings of the people that the Government is taking is bigger than what the tax revenues are bringing in then is the time to look at bringing the tax level up to that level. We're nowhere near that on the spending side yet.

And to start talking taxes now is to take the heat off the backs of those who don't want to cut spending.

Yes?

Ohio Banking Crisis

Q. Mr. President, going back to the Ohio banking situation, what measures are being taken to protect the commercial banks and the stockholder—big, large banks owned by the stockholders, that they don't get involved in that, in particular, because many of them have correspondent banking relationships with the savings and loan. And what could start out in Ohio as a little virus could become a national epidemic, which could involve some of our major, largest banks. I'd like to know just what legislation is being proposed and what Federal accountants are doing to check these things so that this situation cannot ever happen again anywhere else.

The President. Well, I don't know of any legislation that's being proposed for that, and I know that our people are looking at this situation and don't feel that there is any emergency that warrants Federal interference at this time in there.

Q. As a followup, Mr. President, have you had any discussions with Secretary of the Treasury Baker, Paul Volcker, and the Chairman of the FDIC about this situation?

The President. I have not talked to Chairman Volcker about this, but I do know that he, himself, has put the Fed in there. And as I've told you what they are prepared to do and which they believe is pretty much the proper answer to this situation.

Q. Thank you, Mr. President.

The President. Oh, well, all right, Helen.

Well, thank you all. Sam, I thought you were waiting until the meeting was over.

Q. How's the balance?

Note: The President's 29th news conference began at 8 p.m. in the East Room at the White House. It was broadcast live on nationwide radio and television.

Letter to the Speaker of the House and the President of the Senate on Soil and Water Conservation Programs
March 22, 1985

Dear Mr. Speaker: (Dear Mr. President:)

I am pleased to transmit this report on the relationship of my 1986 budget proposals to the policies enunciated in the Statement of Policy and recommended program for soil and water programs sent to the Congress in December 1982, pursuant to the Soil and Water Resources Conservation Act of 1977 (16 U.S.C. 2006).

My Fiscal Year 1986 budget seeks to foster strong economic growth, lower interest rates, and expansion of export markets. These objectives are especially important for the long-term well-being of the agricultural sector of the economy.

The 1986 budget sets forth a vigorous and concerted effort to reduce the annual deficit built into the Federal budget structure. With no action to curb spending, deficits would exceed $200 billion for each of the next five years and the ratio of Federal debt to gross national product would continue to increase to intolerably high levels. Deficit reduction, without additional taxes, is absolutely necessary to meet our national economic goals.

Therefore, my 1986 budget proposes significant reductions in spending from projected current service levels in many programs and complete termination of some. In total by 1988, the budget recommendations would reduce spending growth by $105 billion and reduce the budget deficit by 42 percent. Achieving these savings will require cutbacks, terminations, reforms, and management improvement in many activities. It will require realignments of financial

responsibilities among the Federal government, State and local governments, and beneficiary groups in many program areas. Soil conservation activities are no exception.

The 1982 Statement of Policy called for a greater role for State and local governments in working with private landowners to solve their individual resource conservation problems. It called for more efficient use of Federal resources by targeting assistance to critical problem areas, by improving management efficiency, and by eliminating program overlap and conflicting objectives. It called for focusing our efforts on those areas with critical erosion problems and pointed out that stewardship of the land is primarily the responsibility of the private landowner. All these themes are reflected in my 1986 budget.

The 1982 Statement of Policy anticipated future conservation budget levels within the range projected by the Program unless the demands placed on our financial resources by other competing national goals and interests made it necessary to propose lower amounts. The 1986 budget does envision reduced funding levels for Federal conservation programs.

The budget will continue the basic technical assistance program at a reduced level that permits the Soil Conservation Service to establish national priorities and to continue to provide Federal leadership for a national conservation program. In addition, the Soil Conservation Service will continue a reduced soil survey information program and will continue to develop plant materials for erosion control. Basic research and extension activities will also be maintained. Resource data collection, analysis, and program development activities can be funded on an "as needed" basis rather than as continuous activities.

Other programs such as direct Federal payments to landowners for installing conservation practices and to local units of government for flood control projects and for local resource and economic development activities are proposed to be discontinued. For the most part, these activities are well within the financial capabilities of State and local governments and private landowners if they act together to deal with local resource problems. Many are already doing so. In addition, our market-oriented farm program proposals will reduce the econom-

ic incentives to devote marginal, erosion-prone land to row crops.

These changes will produce a budget savings for the five-year period 1986–1990 of $2.8 billion and still provide the Federal leadership and technical assistance needed in the soil and water conservation area.

I look forward to working with the Congress as you consider resource conservation programs in the context of our national economic needs in the months ahead.

Sincerely,

RONALD REAGAN

Note: Identical letters were sent to Thomas P. O'Neill, Jr., Speaker of the House of Representatives, and George Bush, President of the Senate.

Message to the Congress Reporting Budget Deferrals
March 22, 1985

To the Congress of the United States:

In accordance with the Impoundment Control Act of 1974, I herewith report five new deferrals of budget authority for 1985 totaling $121,544,000 and three revised deferrals now totaling $162,677,884. The deferrals affect the Departments of Energy, Health and Human Services, Interior, and Transportation.

The details of these deferrals are con-

tained in the attached report.

RONALD REAGAN

The White House,
March 22, 1985.

Note: The attachment detailing the deferrals was printed in the Federal Register *of March 28.*

Executive Order 12507—Continuance of the President's Commission on Organized Crime
March 22, 1985

By the authority vested in me as President by the Constitution and laws of the United States of America, including the Federal Advisory Committee Act, as amended (5 U.S.C. App. I), it is hereby ordered that Section 4(b) of Executive Order No. 12435, establishing the President's Commission on Organized Crime, is amended to provide as follows:

"(b) The Commission shall terminate on April 1, 1986, or thirty days after it submits its final report, whichever occurs first."

RONALD REAGAN

The White House,
March 22, 1985.

[Filed with the Office of the Federal Register, 11:11 a.m., March 25, 1985]

Executive Order 12508—World Tourism Organization
March 22, 1985

By the authority vested in me as President by the Constitution and laws of the United States of America, including Section 1 of the International Organizations Immunities Act (59 Stat. 669; 22 U.S.C. 288), and having found that the United States participates in the World Tourism Organization as a party to the Statutes of the World Tourism Organization (27 UST 2211, TIAS 8307), I hereby designate the World Tourism Organization as a public international organization entitled to enjoy the privileges, exemptions, and immunities conferred by the International Organizations Immunities Act. This designation is not intended to abridge in any respect privileges, exemptions or immunities that such organization may have acquired or may acquire by international agreements or by Congressional action.

RONALD REAGAN

The White House,
March 22, 1985.

[*Filed with the Office of the Federal Register, 11:12 a.m., March 25, 1985*]

Proclamation 5310—National Skin Cancer Prevention and Detection Week, 1985
March 22, 1985

By the President of the United States of America

A Proclamation

Skin cancer is the most common cancer in the United States. It accounts for between 30 and 40 percent of all cancers and is increasing at a significant rate. Approximately 18,000 Americans will develop a primary melanoma and over 500,000 Americans will develop nonmelanoma skin cancer this year. Epidemiological studies show that the incidence of melanoma has doubled every decade since the 1930s and is now increasing at a faster rate than any other cancer, except lung cancer in women.

Melanoma has a mortality rate of 25 percent and causes 5,000 deaths per year, and nonmelanoma skin cancer causes another 2,000 deaths per year. The 1983 National Institutes of Health Consensus Conference on Precursors to Malignant Melanoma found that the incidence of melanoma and the number of deaths from melanoma are increasing in many areas of the world and found evidence that early recognition and surgical removal of melanoma make it a highly curable cancer.

Patients with increased risk of developing melanoma and nonmelanoma skin cancers can be identified, and early treatment of melanoma and nonmelanoma skin cancers results in high cure rates.

Sun exposure is an undisputed cause of nonmelanoma skin cancer and is an important factor in the development of melanoma. The number of skin cancers can be reduced through sun protection measures such as the use of sunscreening lotions and simple changes in lifestyle. The American Academy of Dermatology and State and local dermatologic organizations are committed to heightening the awareness and understanding of melanoma and nonmelanoma skin cancers among members of the general public and the health care community.

The first Melanoma and Skin Cancer Prevention and Detection Program, a coordinated national voluntary effort of professional dermatological organizations to reduce the increasing incidence of melanoma and nonmelanoma skin cancers and to better control such cancers, will be conducted in March 1985.

The Congress, by House Joint Resolution 85, has designated the week of March 24, 1985, through March 30, 1985, as "National Skin Cancer Prevention and Detection Week" and authorized and requested the President to issue a proclamation in observance of this event.

Now, Therefore, I, Ronald Reagan, President of the United States of America, do hereby proclaim the week of March 24, 1985, through March 30, 1985, as National Skin Cancer Prevention and Detection Week, and I urge health care professionals and all other interested persons and groups to assist efforts to advance the prevention and detection of skin cancer.

In Witness Whereof, I have hereunto set my hand this 22nd day of March, in the year of our Lord nineteen hundred and eighty-five, and of the Independence of the United States of America the two hundred and ninth.

RONALD REAGAN

[*Filed with the Office of the Federal Register, 11:09 a.m., March 25, 1985*]

Proclamation 5311—Cancer Control Month, 1985
March 22, 1985

By the President of the United States of America

A Proclamation

The past year has witnessed steady, encouraging progress against cancer. The latest data show that 49 percent of all patients diagnosed with cancer survive five years or more. This compares with 48 percent last year and 46 percent the year before. And because of the lag time in collecting data, we believe the true five-year survival rate is better than 50 percent. For some of the major cancers, more than two-thirds of patients will survive beyond this five-year mark.

In addition, we are seeing steady gains in survival for patients with a number of specific cancers: melanoma, Hodgkin's disease, and cancers of the lung, colon, prostate, and testis. For children under age 15 who develop cancer, the five-year survival rate has risen to 60 percent, up from 53 percent last year.

This record of continuing, steady gains assures us that we can meet our national goal for the year 2000: to reduce the 1980 cancer death rate in this country by one-half.

This is a realistic and achievable goal, built on the deeper understanding of cancer that we have derived from our research over the past decade and a half. We now have evidence, for example, that an individual can reduce personal cancer risk by a number of lifestyle choices. Quitting smoking is the single most important step an individual can take to reduce cancer risk. There are also a number of choices we can make in our daily diets that may help to reduce cancer risk, such as increasing the amount of fiber-rich foods, including fruits, vegetables, peas and beans, and whole-grain cereals. Another is to reduce the amount of fat in our diet.

Research designed to answer questions about ways to halt or prevent cancer is ongoing, including twenty-five studies concerning diet interventions. New community cancer programs have been formed to bring the latest in cancer care to patients in their own communities. A new computerized data base for physicians provides the latest information on cancer treatment. Trials of new therapies continue to seek better ways to help the cancer patient, and research to understand the nature of cancer at the cellular level continues to break new ground. We can look into the future with hope and optimism.

In 1938, the Congress of the United States passed a joint resolution (52 Stat. 148; 36 U.S.C. 150) requesting the President to issue an annual proclamation setting aside the month of April as "Cancer Control Month."

Now, Therefore, I, Ronald Reagan, President of the United States of America, do hereby proclaim the month of April 1985 as Cancer Control Month. I invite the Governors of the fifty States and the Commonwealth of Puerto Rico, and the appropriate officials of all other areas under the United States flag, to issue similar proclamations. I also ask health care professionals, the communications industry, and all other interested persons and groups to reaffirm our Nation's continuing commitment to control cancer.

In Witness Whereof, I have hereunto set my hand this 22nd day of March, in the year of our Lord nineteen hundred and eighty-five, and of the Independence of the United States of America the two hundred and ninth.

RONALD REAGAN

[*Filed with the Office of the Federal Register, 11:10 a.m., March 25, 1985*]

Radio Address to the Nation on the Federal Budget and Tax Reform
March 23, 1985

My fellow Americans:

April 15th is fast approaching—that dreaded deadline each year when we must turn our attention from jobs, finances, and families to the business of government and the taxes we pay to cover its bills.

I'm sorry to tell you that many of those you elected to keep watch over government's expenditures and to keep your taxes down have been hard at work since we submitted our budget doing something else: They've been promising special interest groups—not to save your tax dollars, but their spending programs.

Let me give you some cold, hard facts. If Congress doesn't enact the level of budget savings we've proposed, we'll add nearly three-quarters of a trillion dollars in additional red ink over the next 3 years—a crushing mortgage on America's future. But that ocean of red ink will not result from a deficit of tax payments. Even after cutting your personal tax rates, the Federal Government still takes away about 19 cents of every dollar America earns and produces—the same as before we came into office.

Moreover, reducing those rates has stimulated economic output and led to a bigger tax base and greater tax revenues than almost anyone anticipated. So, if Congress wants to increase revenues further, it must put aside all talk of tax increases, put tax reform on the front burner, and reduce personal tax rates as low as possible so we can free America to challenge the limits of growth.

With revenues rising faster than expected, it's clear that the deficit problem is not a problem of taxes, but of spending. But don't believe the drumbeat of propaganda that blames defense spending for government living beyond its means.

Our bipartisan effort to rebuild America's defenses only began 3 years ago after more than a decade of neglect, while the Soviets surged ahead with the greatest military buildup in history, adding countries to their empire with the ease of a thief plucking apples off a tree.

Fifteen years ago our combined domestic and defense spending amounted to only 20 cents on every dollar of gross national product—one-fifth less than today. Had spending not then soared out of control, today we would have nearly a balanced budget, far less national debt, and no threat to our current prosperity. But Federal spending didn't get off the track because of defense. We're spending less on defense this year than my predecessor predicted he would spend in his last budget. We're spending less on defense as a percentage of the Federal budget and our total economy than we did 15 years ago. And our budget calls for us to spend 2 cents less per dollar of the gross national product next year than we did in 1970.

Spending is zooming for only one reason: The domestic budget is still bloated with waste and unnecessary programs. Even after adjustment for inflation, nondefense program spending has almost doubled since 1970. Maybe it's time you asked Congress some questions of your own; for example: Why won't the Congress stop or cut back its $4.6 billion revenue sharing program that disburses money to communities, when the Federal Government has no revenues to share and local governments are in better fiscal shape? Why won't Congress stop subsidizing Amtrak, which costs taxpayers $35 per passenger every time a train leaves the station? Why won't the Congress stop subsidizing wealthy families earning up to $100,000 a year with thousands of dollars in annual student loan subsidies? Why won't the Congress stop subsidizing a few restaurants, bars, country clubs, and similar businesses with half a billion dollars in loans,

when every other small business has to pay the full market rate of interest? And why won't the Congress stop its export subsidies to a handful of corporations which account for less than 2 percent of U.S. exports?

Yesterday I invited the Senate leadership to the White House. We had a candid and constructive meeting, and I'm confident that we're coming closer to a meeting of the minds. We agreed that uncontrolled spending poses a threat to our expansion, and we agreed that we must face that threat together and face it now.

For my part, I made clear that in further reduction in defense, vital weapons systems—either conventional or strategic— must not be touched, period. The deficit can and will be brought down, but not by raising taxes, which would just torpedo growth and make the deficit worse, or by gambling with America's security when the Soviet Union is every bit as aggressive, expansionist, and dangerous as before.

Until next week, thanks for listening. God bless you.

Note: The President spoke at 12:06 p.m. from the Oval Office at the White House.

Remarks at a White House Ceremony for Participants in the Special Olympics From the Washington Metropolitan Area
March 23, 1985

The President. Thank you all, and good afternoon, and welcome to the White House.

We're just delighted that all of you, the Special Olympians from Metropolitan Washington, were able to stop by on your way to Park City and Salt Lake City, Utah. Nancy and I share the pride of your families, friends, and countrymen for your hard work and dedication in getting ready for the third International Winter Special Olympics.

Let me take a moment to mention the uncelebrated story behind the Special Olympics. It's the grace and goodness of Eunice and Sargent Shriver and of all the volunteers and coaches, mothers and fa-

thers, and private corporations, which stand behind our very special Olympians and who prove time and again that America is the most generous country in the world.

Sports have always been an important part of my life. Although my competitive playing days are over, except when it comes to arm-wrestling with Congress— [*laughter*]—I can appreciate what these games mean to all of you. There'll be the thrill of competition, the joy of meeting other athletes who love sports as much as you do. And I know that you'll have a glorious time in Utah and that each one of you will represent the American ideal, not necessarily by winning, but by doing the very best that you can.

A little over a year ago, another group of winter Olympians just back from Sarajevo—Scott Hamilton, Debbie Armstrong, Rosalyn Sumners, the Mahre brothers, the rest of America's 1984 team—made a very special visit to the White House. There was quite a feeling of excitement that day.

All of us relived the way Bill Johnson smoked 'em on the downhill and the grace and beauty of Kitty and Peter Carruthers in the pairs competition. Then there was the memory of Scott Hamilton's final Olympic moment and the way he battled back from a severe childhood illness to win three world championships and to top it all off with the Olympic Gold.

And Scott Hamilton's story points to the most important lesson of that day: The mark of greatness in sports is the quality of personal commitment, drive, and determination that all Olympians share. The athletes who competed in Sarajevo may have posted faster times or combined more spins into their routines, but sports has less to do with things like times and double toe loops than with courage of the human heart.

When it comes to heart, the athletes from Sarajevo and from everywhere will have to tip their caps to you. By competing in the Utah games you are proving that a disability doesn't have to stand in the way of a full and active life, and you're showing all of us just how far individuals can go if only they set their minds to it.

Thank you all for being such fine representatives of our country. And thank you for being here today. We'll be cheering for you no matter what—win, lose, or draw. In fact, no matter where you place in the competition, you'll soon be a part of that very elite group of Americans who have represented our country in Olympic competition, and that's a distinction that will be yours for the rest of your lives.

All of you are truly special. You and the more than 800 other athletes from 14 nations are a testimony to young people all over the world that no one should ever be afraid to dream big dreams or doubt his or her ability to try and make those dreams come true. You've warmed our hearts, and we wish you the very best.

And God bless you all.

[*At this point, the President was presented with an enlargement of a Special Olympics 22-cent stamp and a blue banner bearing the emblem of the Special Olympics.*]

The President. Thank you very much. Oh, that's great! Commemorates what you're doing. We'd be very proud to have that.

Reporter. I'm sorry to interrupt you, sir, but since you raised the subject of arm-wrestling with Congress, how persuasive do you think Mr. Kampelman will be in helping you with the MX missile in the House on Monday?

The President. Well, now, normally I don't take questions at a photo opportunity. But I have to say with regard to this one, I think that it is very meaningful that Max Kampelman—who is himself a Democrat, who is also an expert in that field, is heading up our negotiations over there in Geneva—would take 2 days off and make the arduous trip back here just, for those 2 days, to tell them what it means to our negotiations to have an approval of this weapon system and how much it'll help them in the negotiations.

Q. So, is it going to help your chances in the House, do you think?

The President. I would think if there's the common sense I think is there—yes.

Q. How do you rate your chances now in the House?

The President. You know me, I'm always just cautiously optimistic. [*Laughter*]

Q. Will the President of the United States help the Falashas get out of Sudan?

The President. No comment.

Note: The President spoke at 12:14 p.m. in the Roosevelt Room at the White House.

Remarks at a White House Briefing for Central American Leaders
March 25, 1985

Q. We all love you!

Q. We love you!

The President. Thank you very much. I don't think I can say anything that's going to top that. [*Laughter*]

Well, welcome all of you to the White House. And I want to express my deepest appreciation to you, the Concerned Citizens for Democracy; to Carlos Perez, who helped you organize your Spirit of Freedom Flight; and to the Jefferson Educational Foundation, your hosts here in Washington. We welcome you as neighbors, and we welcome you as fellow Americans. You represent the countries of Colombia, Costa Rica, El Salvador, Guatemala, Honduras, Nicaragua, Panama, and Venezuela. And you've come to Washington at your own expense to share with us and our Congress the most compelling truth of our time: the dream of a bright future for democracy, economic progress, and stability in this hemisphere. And it's all within our grasp. But that dream can quickly become a nightmare if we don't stand behind the brave men who are putting their lives on the line for the cause of freedom in Nicaragua.

We, the people of the Americas, share a common language; it's the language of freedom. Words like *democracia, justicia*— [*laughter*]—I didn't do that right—and liberty were handed down to us by the heroes that we share and honor together, Simón Bolivar and George Washington. And they gave us values that we cherish and strive to live by today: faith in a God of truth, love, and mercy; belief in the family as the center of our society; recognition of the unalienable rights of man; and a conviction that government must derive its legitimacy from the consent of the governed.

And so it is that the United States has a noble commitment to Central America. We're committed by geography, by treaty, and by moral obligation to stand with you, our American neighbors, in defense of liberty.

But the Soviet Union has its own plan for Central America, a region which Soviet Foreign Minister Gromyko described as "boiling like a cauldron." In the last 5 years, the Soviets have provided more military assistance to Cuba and Nicaragua alone than the United States has provided to all of Latin America. The Soviets' plan is designed to crush self-determination of free people, to crush democracy in Costa Rica, Honduras, El Salvador, Guatemala, and Panama. It's a plan to turn Central America into a Soviet beachhead of aggression that could spread terror and instability north and south, disrupt our vital sealanes, cripple our ability to carry out our commitments to our European allies, and send tens of millions of refugees streaming in a human tidal wave across all our borders.

Already the Nicaraguan people are fleeing the Sandinista tyranny, escaping into your neighboring countries. In just the last few weeks, thousands of Nicaraguans have fled to Costa Rica. They tell of rising resistance to the Sandinista dictatorship, a dictatorship that speaks reassuring words of peace to the outside world, even as it has moved to crush personal freedoms, attack the church, nearly wipe out an entire culture—the Miskito Indians—summarily execute suspected dissidents, drive leading democrats into exile, and force young boys to defend the revolution while Soviet-bloc advisers sit in Managua living off the people.

Just last week the Sandinistas started the forced movement of tens of thousands of people from Jinotega and Murra in order to create "free fire zones." And they're using Stalin's tactic of Gulag relocation for those who do not support their tyrannical regime.

How many times have we seen this pattern of forced relocation repeated—in the Ukraine, in Vietnam, in Cambodia, Afghanistan, Angola, Ethiopia, Cuba, and elsewhere? And yet because we're such a trusting people, anxious to believe others and believe that they share our hopes and our dreams, some still find it hard to look reality in the eye or to rouse themselves even when our most vital interests are threatened.

The United States was on the side of democracy during the fight against Somoza, and we're on the side of democracy today. When the Sandinistas came to power promising democracy, we gave them more aid than any other developed country—$119 million from 1979 to 1981, plus support for $244 million more from the Inter-American Development Bank. How did they respond to America's outstretched hand of friendship, trust, and generosity?

Well, the Sandinistas became, as they had always planned, eager puppets for the Soviets and the Cubans. They created their own Karl Marx postage stamps. They sang an anthem that called the United States the enemy of all mankind. They brought in East Germans to organize their state security. They became a rubber stamp for the Communist bloc in the U.N., voting against the democracies on virtually every crucial issue, from refusing to condemn Vietnam's invasion of Cambodia to not accepting Israel's credentials.

While the United States was offering friendship and providing unprecedented sums of aid, the Sandinistas were building up an army that dwarfed and bullied their neighbors. While Americans were debating the Sandinistas true intentions, Tomás Borge, the Sandinista Minister of the Interior, who received his training from the Soviets, Cubans, and PLO, was saying, "You cannot be a true revolutionary in Latin America without being Marxist-Leninist." Well, while we were bending over backward to be friendly and helpful, the Sandinistas were already conspiring to bring Communist revolution to all of Central America.

As far back as 1969, they pledged to "struggle for a true union of the Central American peoples within one country, beginning with support for national liberation movements in neighboring states." Once in power in Nicaragua, they began working for their revolution, without frontiers, in which small, democratic, unarmed Costa Rica would be—and I quote their words—"the dessert." Well, today the PLO is honored with an Embassy in Managua. And, in addition to their close ties with the Soviets, Cubans, and East Germans, the Sandinistas

receive support from Bulgaria, Vietnam, and North Korea. The radical states of Iran and Libya also have established military ties with the Sandinistas in a "new" Nicaragua, which also harbors members of the Red Brigades, the ETA, and other terrorist organizations.

And all this is taking place only a few hundred miles from our shores. The Sandinistas are masking these deeds behind well-rehearsed rhetoric of disinformation intended to lull the world in the weeks ahead. But you know their true intentions. You know what happened when a broad coalition of exiled Nicaraguan democrats recently met in San José and offered to lay down their weapons, if only the Sandinistas would accept democracy and free elections. The Sandinistas not only refused, but their state security rounded up the editor of La Prensa, the president of the Private Enterprise Council, and other leading democrats in Managua and threatened: If you meet with the members of the San José group, then "you will suffer the consequences."

Well, hasn't the time come for all freedom-loving people to unite in demanding an end to the Sandinistas intimidation?

And, you know—look, Nicaraguan freedom fighters don't ask us to send troops; indeed, none are needed, for the Nicaraguan people are coming over to their side in ever-greater numbers. The freedom fighters have grown to a force more than two times bigger than the Sandinistas were before they seized power. Their freedom fighters are people of the land; they're the true revolutionaries. They are the hope for a future of democracy, and with our help, democracy can and will be restored.

There are two among you here today—Señor Alberto Suhr and Señor Carlos Garcia—who have personally suffered the full range of Sandinista insults, persecution, and imprisonment. Alberto Suhr was jailed for helping to identify missing persons the Sandinistas had hidden in prisons. Carlos Garcia, a leading figure in the international world of baseball, was imprisoned for 1,640 days on totally trumped-up charges.

Their story, just like your journey, is a profile in courage. We can only be thankful for all of you who care enough to speak the truth. And we can only pray that all who hold the fate of freedom in their hands will heed your words before it is too late. Let it never be said that we were not told, that we were not warned, that we did not know.

Thank you all for being here. God bless you all.

[*At this point, the President was presented with a statement of appreciation and a recording of "America Immortal." Mr. Suhr and Mr. Garcia made the presentations on behalf of Concerned Citizens for Democracy.*]

Thank you all. I'm greatly honored, and I appreciate this more than I can say. And your words there—I'm just going to take a second and tell you a little experience—a few years ago when I made my trip down into your countries, in Costa Rica. And I was invited to speak, and I think mainly the audience was made up of the legislature there. And before I could start to speak, a gentleman rose and started making a

speech at me. And I wasn't familiar enough with the language to know just what was going on. And your statement about peasants and the poor and the people who really are on the side of freedom, when we hear so much from some others—that they represent those people.

I stepped back and asked the President, and he told me that this man was a member of the legislature, he was a Communist member of the legislature, and that he was making a Communist speech. Well, in the pride and democracy that so characterizes Costa Ricans, they resisted any effort to, by force, keep him from speaking. But I also thought it was interesting that the President told me he was the only member of their legislature that drove a Mercedes. [*Laughter*]

Thank you all very much. Thank you.

Note: The President spoke at 1:17 p.m. in Room 450 of the Old Executive Office Building.

Remarks at a White House Meeting on Proposed Youth Employment Opportunity Wage Legislation
March 25, 1985

The President. [*Inaudible*]—try and get around the table, but I extend a warm welcome to all of you for being here. And I'm pleased to see so many of the various groups that are represented here today. I know that Mayor Barry is due here in a few minutes. I guess we'll proceed and let him present an excuse when he comes in. [*Laughter*]

We've made real progress in bringing down unemployment—creating over 7 million new jobs in the last 3 years, and over 300,000 of those in the last month alone. But we can't rest until everyone who wants a job can find one.

And today I'm resubmitting legislation to establish a summer youth employment opportunity wage. And I want to thank Orrin Hatch, Trent Lott, Jerry Denton, Charlie Stenholm, who couldn't be here today, in advance for their work and leadership on

this.

A minimum wage differential would allow business to create an additional 400,000 jobs, we believe, for our young people and would have plenty of protection in there. But it wouldn't—no one could substitute, really, youth at the lower wage for legitimate wage earners.

Under the current Federal minimum wage, many inexperienced and disadvantaged young people are priced out of the labor market. There are jobs that, if you make them too expensive, there will be people who just figure they don't need to do those particular jobs.

This legislation will help provide the first job, with real work experience, for many of these young people. And it's experience that might never occur. I remember my first job. Do you remember yours?

And, you know, with all the best of intentions, today I look back and realize that we have passed various social reforms that would make it impossible for anyone to do this. I was 14 years old, found myself on a job where I was laying hardwood floor. Before the summer was over, I had shingled roof; I even painted. And so many of these things that just wouldn't be allowed today.

And, of course, I've often said that one of my better jobs, when I then got back to school and was continuing to work my way through school, is one of the better jobs I've ever had—I was washing dishes in the girls dormitory. [*Laughter*]

Summer is quickly approaching, and we can't afford to waste another opportunity to provide work and that work experience for so many of America's young people.

So, I think if we all work together, we can get this past Congress. And we know where the greatest numbers contributing to the unemployment figures are today, and they're among our young people, and particularly those who we want to help the most—those in our minority communities. And it's been too long coming—them shut out, in effect, of the summer job market. So, let's all go after it!

Note: The President spoke at 1:43 p.m. in the Cabinet Room at the White House. In his remarks, the President referred to Mayor Marion Barry of the District of Columbia.

Exchange With Reporters on the Death of Major Arthur D. Nicholson, Jr., in the German Democratic Republic
March 25, 1985

Q. Mr. President, the Soviets say that the soldier that they killed was a spy—was taking pictures. Can you comment on that?

The President. This is a tragedy that never should have happened, and we challenge that. But we have already registered our protest for the tragic death of this man.

Q. Have you protested personally, or has it been done by the State Department, sir?

The President. No. What's done there is done in my name.

Q. Was he a spy, Mr. President?

The President. No. I know that we can't go on with this other subject, and I don't want to take it up here. We've got another subject in our minds. But I think if you'll check, you'll find that each country, the Soviets and the United States, are permitted under the terms of the Four Power Agreement—we each have 14 military personnel. We have them in East Germany; they have them in West Germany. And what they can

do and the areas that they can go into are all delineated, and he was doing nothing except what we're entitled to do under the agreements.

Q. Was he taking pictures?

The President. What?

Q. Was he taking pictures of military installations?

The President. I'm still waiting for a lot of details on this, but that is permitted in both areas.

Q. There seems to be a lack of outrage on your part, sir.

The President. A lack of outrage? No, you can't print what I'm thinking. [*Laughter*]

Q. Would something like that prevent a summit meeting?

The President. No, it would make me more anxious to go to one.

Q. Thank you.

Note: The exchange began at 1:46 p.m. in the Cabinet Room at the White House.

Statement on Proposed Youth Employment Opportunity Wage Legislation
March 25, 1985

One of the Nation's most serious and longstanding problems is providing adequate employment opportunities for our young people. Even in times of great economic prosperity, unemployment remains a significant problem for young people, particularly young blacks and Hispanics. The purpose of the draft youth employment opportunity wage act of 1985 is to make it possible for employers to expand job opportunities for young people during a period of special need—when young people are looking for summer jobs.

The proposal would permit employers to pay young people under 20 years of age, from May 1 through September 30, a wage of no less than either 75 percent of the otherwise applicable minimum wage or $2.50 per hour, whichever is less. The bill also provides explicit protections for adult workers and previously hired youth to ensure that they will not be adversely affected by the summer wage differential.

Studies over the past decade have repeatedly demonstrated that the minimum wage has reduced job opportunities for large numbers of our unskilled young people by pricing them out of the job market. This is particularly true for jobs that involve initial training. There is a growing consensus that summer job opportunities for youth, especially minority youth, will be greatly expanded if the summer wage differential can be implemented. This will allow more young people than ever to find jobs, earn money, and gain the experience and skills needed for future work and higher wages. The bill would in no way diminish the opportunities for higher wages for those with job skills.

Many organizations, large and small, including the National Conference of Black Mayors, the National Association for Equal Opportunity in Higher Education, representing the presidents of America's historically black colleges, and the Boys Clubs of America, have formally endorsed the concept of a youth employment opportunity wage. I am grateful for their support.

I urge the Congress to enact this legislation soon. We cannot afford to waste another summer that would otherwise produce jobs, including that important first job experience, for our young people.

Message to the Congress Transmitting Proposed Youth Employment Opportunity Wage Legislation
March 25, 1985

To the Congress of the United States:

I am pleased to transmit to you proposed legislation entitled the "Youth Employment Opportunity Wage Act of 1985."

One of the Nation's most serious and long-standing problems is providing adequate employment opportunities for our young people. Even in times of great economic prosperity, unemployment remains a significant problem for young people, particularly young Blacks and Hispanics. The purpose of the draft bill is to make it possible for employers to expand job opportunities for young people during a period of special need—when young people are looking for summer jobs.

The proposal would permit employers to pay young people under 20 years of age, from May 1 through September 30, a wage of no less than either 75 percent of the otherwise applicable minimum wage or $2.50 per hour, whichever is less. This bill provides protections so that adult workers or previously hired youth will not be adversely affected by the proposal. It prohibits the discharge, transfer, or demotion of any employee because of ineligibility for the youth wage and for the purpose of hiring an eligible youth and it provides penalties to assist in enforcement of this provision.

For many businesses, the existing minimum wage prices unskilled young people out of the job market. While some businesses can afford to hire unskilled youth and provide the training and experience expected to pay off in future productivity, such expectations are often unreasonable over a short summer employment span.

Studies over the past decade have repeatedly demonstrated that the minimum wage has reduced job opportunities for large numbers of our youth. This is particularly true for jobs involving considerable initial training. The restricted job opportunities for youth, especially minority youth, due to the minimum wage have contributed to the growing consensus on the value of a lower minimum wage for youth as a means of expanding their employment.

The concept of a youth employment opportunity wage has attracted a broad coalition of support. It has been endorsed by many organizations, including the National Conference of Black Mayors and organizations representing businesses that would provide jobs for these youth.

The proposal would enable employers to expand job opportunities for youth during the summer months. It would enable many young people to find jobs, earn money, and gain the experience and skills needed for future work and higher wages. The bill would not diminish the opportunities for higher wages for those with job skills.

Because it provides for a demonstration period and an evaluation of the program, the bill should allay any doubts as to the ameliorative impact of the youth employment opportunity wage.

I urge the Congress to enact this legislation speedily.

RONALD REAGAN

The White House,
March 25, 1985.

Nomination of John Dimitri Negroponte To Be an Assistant Secretary of State
March 25, 1985

The President today announced his intention to nominate John Dimitri Negroponte, a career member of the Senior Foreign Service, Class of Minister-Counselor, to be Assistant Secretary of State for Oceans and International Environmental and Scientific Affairs. He would succeed James L. Malone.

Ambassador Negroponte entered the Foreign Service in 1960 and served in Hong Kong as consular officer (1960–1961) and commercial officer (1961–1963). In the Department he was administrative assistant in the Bureau of African Affairs (1963) and studied the Vietnamese language at the Foreign Service Institute (1963–1964). In 1964–1968 he was political officer in Saigon and a member of the Paris peace talks on Vietnam in 1968–1969. He attended Stan-

ford University in 1969–1970 and was a member of the staff at the National Security Council in 1970–1973. In 1973 he studied the Spanish language at the Foreign Service Institute. He was counselor for political affairs in Quito (1973–1975) and consul general in Thessaloniki (1975–1977). In the Department he was Deputy Assistant Secretary of State for Oceans and Fisheries Affairs, with the rank of Ambassador, in 1977–1979. He was Deputy Assistant Secretary of State for East Asian and Pacific Affairs in 1980–1981. Since 1981 he has been serving as United States Ambassador to Honduras.

He graduated from Yale University (B.A., 1960). His foreign languages are French, Spanish, and Vietnamese. He was born July 21, 1939, in London, England.

Nomination of Lee L. Verstandig To Be Under Secretary of Housing and Urban Development
March 25, 1985

The President today announced his intention to nominate Lee L. Verstandig to be Under Secretary of Housing and Urban Development. He would succeed Philip Abrams.

Since June 1, 1983, Dr. Verstandig has been serving as Assistant to the President for Intergovernmental Affairs. Previously he served at the Environmental Protection Agency as Acting Administrator and Acting Assistant Administrator for Legislation. He was Assistant Secretary for Governmental Affairs at the Department of Transportation in 1981–1983. He served as a member of the board of directors of Amtrak in 1982.

He was administrative assistant and legislative director to Senator John H. Chafee in 1977–1981; associate dean of academic affairs and dean of political affairs for special studies at Brown University in 1970–1977; professor of history and political science at Roger Williams College in 1963–1970 and served as its department chairman in 1965–1967. He is the author of numerous articles and books on government, political history, education, and public policy.

Dr. Verstandig graduated from Franklin and Marshall College (A.B., 1959), the University of Tennessee (M.A., 1961), and Brown University (Ph.D., 1970). He is married, has one child, and resides in Washington, DC. He was born September 11, 1937, in Memphis, TN.

Statement on the Death of Major Arthur D. Nicholson, Jr., in the German Democratic Republic
March 25, 1985

All Americans are shocked and saddened to learn of the shooting death of Maj. Arthur D. Nicholson, a U.S. Army officer assigned to the U.S. military liaison mission which serves as a point of contact for our government with Soviet forces in East Germany. The precise details are being investigated by our Embassy in East Germany, and we do not have full information, but it is clear that this violence was unjustified. We have protested this unwarranted act of violence and have asked Soviet authorities for a full explanation.

The Soviets have expressed their regret over Major Nicholson's death. We have no further comment at this time.

Note: Larry M. Speakes, Principal Deputy Press Secretary to the President, read the President's statement to reporters at 2:25 p.m. in the Briefing Room at the White House.

Remarks to Members of Congress During a White House Briefing on the MX Missile and the Soviet-United States Nuclear and Space Arms Negotiations
March 25, 1985

The President. Thank you very much. Let me just take a moment and say first why I want you to know why I feel that support for the Peacekeeper is so very important, not only for our national security but for the solidity of our NATO alliance and for our successful arms reductions talks in Geneva as well. Afterward, Ambassador Max Kampelman, who's flown in from Geneva, will discuss arms control with you and take your questions. Max has been meeting with Mr. Karpov, his Soviet counterpart, for almost 2 weeks now—too short a time, of course, to expect any dramatic breakthrough.

But I think we've already gotten a flavor of what those talks are going to be like. We have some tough negotiating ahead, but we expected that. The Soviets aren't going to compromise out of the goodness of their hearts, but only if they calculate that an agreement is in their immediate self-interest. We'd be doing the American people a disservice if we imagined otherwise.

We do, of course, have much common ground on which to negotiate. But if history is any guide, we can be sure that the Soviets are not going to simply give up their tremendous advantage in the MX-type missiles without some incentive, and without the MX that incentive is lacking.

For years, when the Soviets were planning an ABM system and we weren't, you'll remember we were trying to get negotiations on that. Only when you in the Congress appropriated funds for our own ABM system, the Soviets suddenly decided they wanted to talk seriously; and soon we had an ABM treaty. After staying away for more than a year now, they have returned to the bargaining table.

But let's not delude ourselves. The Soviets returned to the table only because they've recognized the failure of their efforts to divide us from our allies and weaken our determination to rebuild our national defense. Now, if we don't want to see our hopes evaporate, we must continue to demonstrate the resolve to carry the negotiations to a successful conclusion on a sound basis.

I join three previous Presidents, Republican and Democratic, who have urged that we deploy the Peacekeeper. Each is convinced that the missile is absolutely essential to our national security and our hopes for peace. The bipartisan Scowcroft commission, a study group made up of our country's finest strategic thinkers, endorsed the Peacekeeper. Secretary Weinberger and all our Chiefs of Staff, as you know, are unanimous in their support of this weapons system.

Just last month, former Defense Secretary Harold Brown said, "We have to proceed with the modernization program of offensive forces, including the MX." But while we've been debating, the Soviets have been deploying—over 600 MX-class missiles in the last decade. As our land-based deterrence slips slowly but surely toward obsolescence, the Soviets are upgrading, modernizing their systems every day. And they're busy developing two new mobile ICBM systems in addition to the 600 MX-class missiles. Our own mobile system, the Midgetman, is still on the drawing board and at least 7 years from deployment.

The Soviets have seen our restraint only as an opportunity to gain the advantage. The modernization of our land-based deterrent must no longer be delayed in the vain hope that they will simply follow suit. For us to back down now on Peacekeeper deployment will deliver a telling blow to our allies' confidence in us. They stood firm in the deployment of Pershing II and cruise missiles in Europe. We asked them to walk through fire and brave a storm of Soviet propaganda and not-so-veiled threats, and they did.

And I believe that not only the Soviets but our European allies view the current debate in the Peacekeeper as a key test of our resolve. If we fail, we'll be signaling to the world that on this key issue we are irresolute and divided. And the Soviet Union will see that, in dealing with the United States, propaganda and stonewalling are much more profitable than good-faith negotiations. And our allies may wonder how much confidence they can place in an alliance whose largest member cannot even show the determination and fortitude of its smallest.

Tomorrow's vote in the House could very well spell the difference between success or defeat in our arms reduction efforts. It's important that together we send a message—loud and clear—that a united and resolute America backs our negotiators in their efforts to reverse the arms race and bring us closer to a stable, secure, and lasting peace, without fear for us and our children.

And now, I've talked too long. I'm going to ask Max Kampelman, Ambassador Kampelman, to come up here and speak to you. And I have to tell you, he has, as you know, just flown in, and he's due at a meeting back in Geneva tomorrow morning. And I think that's service almost above and beyond.

Ambassador Kampelman. Thank you, Mr. President. Mr. Vice President, Mr. Secretary of State, Mr. McFarlane,[1] Members of Congress, it is true that I do have a meeting tomorrow morning at 11 a.m. Our negotiating in Geneva is now moving into the stage where our three negotiating groups have agreed to meet separately, one with another, so that we could get down to the serious business of negotiating. We've been making statements at each other and by each other, but now I hope we'll have an opportunity to begin talking to each other. And I didn't want to be in a position of missing that first of those sessions tomorrow morning at 11 o'clock.

The whole issue of arms control is, of course, intimately related, for a democratic society, with the issue of public opinion. We don't live in governments where policies are made just by dictate and by fiat. We

---

[1] *Robert C. McFarlane, Assistant to the President for National Security Affairs.*

live in a government where policy is made as a result of healthy democratic discussion and debate. The task is to try to see to it that following that healthy debate and discussion, that we end up with resolve; that we end up with dedication, with determination, and with a broad unity of purpose which reflects American values and American security interests.

Many of you here are people I've known for a long period of time, and you know that I'm a Democrat. But I operate out of the assumption that we have only one President at a time, and that when he is President, he is my President, as he is your President, and he's the President of the American people. And when he speaks and when he gives instructions to his negotiators to speak on behalf of the United States, I think it is essential that we do what we can to communicate to the world, and particularly to the other negotiating partner, that he speaks for a united country.

I am not speaking about a unanimous country; we're much too large to think in terms of unanimity. But I do believe that the American governmental system is facing a challenge today, which is to try to provide a kind of consensus—obviously, short of unanimity—behind these issues of American values and behind these issues of American national interests. And this is why I am very happy to serve as our President's representative in Geneva and pleased to return here in order to highlight one important aspect of the negotiation that is of particular interest to those of us who are negotiating now at this stage of the negotiation.

Our task is a difficult one of communicating with each other. We don't trust each other. We don't fully understand one another. One of the important first tasks that our delegation undertook was to suggest a procedure whereby we don't talk to the press about the substance of these negotiations. And I will not talk today about the substance of those negotiations in the few moments that I stand here.

But one of the reasons for that, as I explained to our Soviet colleagues, is I want to be talking to them about issues, about seeking understanding, and not necessarily engaging in a propaganda mechanism and in a propaganda device. And I hoped that they would respond.

Similarly, we have to communicate to them that we're serious about our objectives. I've learned, in many years of observing the Soviet Union and participating myself in negotiations with them, that they respect strength and determination, but that they also respect a trading position. Acts of good will, which we might do, for example, in negotiating with the Canadians, making a gesture of good will and then expecting something in return to reciprocate and foster that spirit, in my view, is not effective. It is looked upon, rather, as an absence of will, rather than an act of good will. And to negotiate successfully, we must have will and determination.

I, therefore, have long operated on the assumption, and I think the United States and the free world must operate on the assumption, that if the Soviets want something from us and if we feel it's in our national interest to weigh what they want, we must insist on getting something in return for it. The extent to which they receive something from us, without the necessity for them to give anything in return— we are seriously interfering with the negotiating process, because as they enjoy the apple that falls from the tree that they did not have to pay for, they quite understandably wonder what other fruit will fall from that tree that they do not have to pay for.

And the extent to which they don't know the answer to that question, they will wait for the answer to that question. And they are prepared to wait. And I am convinced—or I would not have returned from Geneva here—I am convinced that were the MX decision made in a manner which made it unnecessary for them to be concerned about it anymore, that this would inevitably delay the negotiations as they would, I think quite correctly and understandably, ask themselves: What else might we obtain through this understandable debate and discussion that we will not have to pay for?

I want to make something clear as a result of spending some time today on the Hill. People who differ with me on this MX issue include some very dear friends of mine, people whom I've worked with for a long period of time. I think they are wrong. But at no stretch of the imagination can we permit this debate to get to the point of saying that those who are wrong are necessarily unpatriotic or less interested in the success of the negotiations. I want to make that clear.

But as much as I feel that, I feel equally the obligation to say to my friends: You are wrong. And that I do without any hesitation here as I speak to you this afternoon.

I think America's resolve at the negotiating table and elsewhere outside of the table, in the multifaceted approach we have in dealing with the Soviet Union, must be one of strength, and that must include important military strength; a willingness to talk and to negotiate, but to have strength behind that talking and that negotiating; a willingness to resolve issues.

And I want to say one thing as a pledge to you here today: If there is an agreement to come out of Geneva—and I can't answer that question in all honesty; I can't answer it because I can only speak for our resolve, I cannot speak for anybody else's resolve— but if there is an agreement to come out of Geneva, your negotiators will find the means of coming out with that agreement and recommending it to the President of the United States.

I conclude by urging the President and the Secretary of State and the Vice President and others who represent the executive branch of our government to urge the urgency, the importance of bipartisan consultations and deliberations at all stages of policy development. And I also want to associate that by making a plea to my Democratic friends in this audience that you must respond to such an initiative constructively, because the best interests of the United States depend on it, our values depend on it, and the strength and integrity of the United States of America depend on it.

And I know that all of you will give this very important decision the careful attention and prayers that it deserves. And I can ask no more from any Member of Congress. But I would also have been derelict in my responsibility if I did not return here to tell you my judgment as to the effect of your decision on the vital, indispensable negotiations that are now taking place.

Thank you very much.

The President. Now, if you'll all be just patient for just a few moments, I will have to ask our friends of the press—I hope they have another engagement—[*laughter*]—to move on in order to have some time there for discussion between us, but to preserve also the position of our negotiators, that we don't go public with anything having to do with the negotiations. So, that is the reason why we have to ask you to depart.

Note: The President spoke at 5:08 p.m. in the East Room at the White House.

Appointment of Mitchell Daniels, Jr., as Deputy Assistant to the President and Director of the Office of Intergovernmental Affairs
March 26, 1985

The President today announced his intention to appoint Mitchell Daniels, Jr., as Deputy Assistant to the President and Director, Office of Intergovernmental Affairs.

Mr. Daniels served as executive director of the National Republican Senatorial Committee in 1983–1985. Previously, he was administrative assistant to Senator Richard Lugar of Indiana (1977–1982) and chief aide to then Mayor Richard Lugar of Indianapolis (1974–1976).

He graduated from the Woodrow Wilson School of Public and International Affairs at Princeton University in 1971 and received a J.D. degree from the Georgetown University Law Center in 1979.

He is married, has three children, and resides in Fairfax Station, VA. He was born April 7, 1949, in Monongahela, PA.

Nomination of Donald S. Lowitz for the Rank of Ambassador While Serving as United States Representative to the Conference on Disarmament
March 26, 1985

The President today announced his intention to nominate Donald S. Lowitz, of Illinois, for the rank of Ambassador while serving as United States Representative to the Conference on Disarmament.

Mr. Lowitz has been serving as the U.S. Representative to the Conference on Disarmament with the personal rank of Ambassador since December of last year. Prior to that time, he was engaged in the private practice of law in Chicago, IL, in the firms of Lowitz and Lowitz (1952–1954); Lowitz, Vihon, Lowitz and Stone (1959–1969); and Lowitz, Stone, Kipnis, and Goodman (1971–1974). He was a partner in the firm of Aaron, Schimberg, Hess, and Gilbert in 1974–1984.

He served as Assistant United States Attorney for the Northern District of Illinois in Chicago (1954–1959) and was general counsel of the Office of Economic Opportunity in Washington, DC (1969–1971). In 1972–1978 he was a member and then Chairman of the Board of Foreign Scholarships and served as a consultant in the Executive Office of the President in 1974–1975 and with the Department of Defense in 1975.

Mr. Lowitz received a bachelor of legal science in 1950 from the Northwestern University School of Commerce and a J.D. in

1952 from the Northwestern University School of Law. He is married, has three children, and resides in Chicago, IL. He was born April 16, 1929, in Chicago, IL.

Appointment of Michael P. Castine as a Member of the President's Advisory Council on Private Sector Initiatives
March 26, 1985

The President today announced his intention to appoint Michael P. Castine to be a member of the President's Advisory Council on Private Sector Initiatives. This is a new position.

Mr. Castine is attending the John F. Kennedy School of Government at Harvard University. He is the first recipient of the George S. Dively fellowship at Harvard to study the impact of public/private partnerships on the business community. Previous-ly, he served in the White House as Deputy Director of the Office of Private Sector Initiatives (1981–1984) and staff assistant in the Office of Presidential Appointments and Scheduling (1981). He was a legislative staff assistant to Congressman Jack Kemp (R–NY) in 1978–1981.

He graduated from the State University of New York (B.A., 1976). He was born April 29, 1954, in Buffalo, NY, and now resides in Boston, MA.

Statement on House of Representatives Approval of MX Missile Production
March 26, 1985

I am very pleased that the House of Representatives has approved the continued production of the MX Peacekeeper missile. And I want to thank everyone who helped us in our efforts to modernize our strategic nuclear forces.

Today's vote is an important and unmistakable signal of American unity and resolve. By building upon the consensus achieved last week in the Senate, the House of Representatives has affirmed—in a clear demonstration of American strength and determination—our commitment to maintain the modern forces necessary for effective deterrence and to do everything possible to achieve significant arms reductions.

I know this issue was difficult for many Members of the Congress. But I am pleased that a majority of Members understood that protecting the peace and working for a more secure and stable future must begin with a strong America.

And I sincerely believe that America—with the House of Representatives now standing with their Senate colleagues and the administration—has taken an important step forward in our efforts to build a lasting peace for our children and all the children of the world.

America has sent a message, loud and clear, that we back our negotiators, and we will continue to do so. Today's vote was a vote for peace, for a safer future, and for success in Geneva. And it is now essential that the House reaffirm today's vote for the MX Peacekeeper by a second positive vote to release appropriations.

Nomination of J. Michael Farrell To Be General Counsel of the Department of Energy
March 27, 1985

The President today announced his intention to nominate J. Michael Farrell to be General Counsel of the Department of Energy. He would succeed Theodore J. Garrish.

Since 1983 Mr. Farrell has been vice president of Global USA, Inc. He also serves as counsel to the law firm of Glynn & Graham and legislative counsel to the firm of Nofziger & Bragg. In 1982–1983 he was at the Department of State as a coordinator of the Carribean Basin Initiative. He served at the White House as Deputy Director of Presidential Personnel (1981–1982) and As-sistant Counsel in the Office of the Counsel to the President (1981). Prior to this time he was a member of the law firms of O'Connor & Farrell (1968–1977; 1979–1981) and Farrell & Daly (1978). He was Assistant Counsel, Office of the General Counsel, at the Federal Home Loan Bank Board in 1966–1967.

He graduated from Georgetown University (B.S., 1963) and Georgetown University Law Center (J.D., 1966). He is married, has three children, and resides in Washington, DC. He was born March 30, 1941, in Washington, DC.

Nomination of Theodore J. Garrish To Be an Assistant Secretary of Energy
March 27, 1985

The President today announced his intention to nominate Theodore J. Garrish to be an Assistant Secretary of Energy (Congressional, Intergovernmental, and Public Affairs). He would succeed Robert C. Odle, Jr.

Since 1983 Mr. Garrish has been serving as General Counsel of the Department of Energy. Previously, he was special assistant to the Secretary of Energy in 1983; legislative counsel at the Department of the Interior in 1981–1982; partner in the law firm of Deane, Snowdon, Shutler, Garrish and Gherardi; General Counsel of the Consumer Product Safety Commission in 1976–1978; assistant to the Secretary of the Interior in 1976; Deputy General Counsel in the Office of Consumer Affairs, Department of Health, Education, and Welfare, in 1975–1976; and assistant to the Special Counsel at the White House in 1974.

He graduated from Wayne State University (A.B., 1964; J.D., 1968). He has two children and resides in Alexandria, VA. He was born January 6, 1943, in Detroit, MI.

Nomination of Susan Meredith Phillips To Be a Member and the Chairman of the Commodity Futures Trading Commission
March 27, 1985

The President today announced his intention to nominate Susan Meredith Phillips to be a Commissioner of the Commodity Futures Trading Commission for the term expiring April 13, 1990, and to be Chairman of the Commodity Futures Trading Commission. These are reappointments.

Since November 1981 she has been serving as a Commissioner of the Commodity Futures Trading Commission. She served as

Acting Chairman of the Commission from May to November 1983 and has been Chairman since November 1983.

Dr. Phillips was associate vice president of finance and university services at the University of Iowa in 1979–1981. She was a Brookings economic policy fellow in 1976–1977 and an economic fellow with the Securities and Exchange Commission in 1977–

1978. She served as assistant professor in the department of business administration at the University of Iowa in 1974–1978 (on leave from 1976 to 1978).

She graduated from Agnes Scott College (B.A., 1967) and Louisiana State University (M.S., 1971; Ph.D., 1973). She was born December 23, 1944, in Richmond, VA, and now resides in Washington, DC.

Proclamation 5312—Small Business Week, 1985
March 27, 1985

By the President of the United States of America

A Proclamation

The history of America is the history of a nation at work—a nation of farmers, manufacturers, and merchants joining together to build a better society. The dedication and commitment of these early citizens provided the foundation for a growing and prosperous America—an America built on individual initiative, a competitive spirit, and an intense pride in the achievements of a new nation.

Today, this enterprising determination to work and to prosper is embodied in more than 14 million small businesses, which provide the technology to keep the economy growing, the manufacturing and marketing skills to keep the nation competitive, and the innovation to guide us into a better future. It is this enterprising genius that has helped small business create most of our news jobs and provide economic opportunities unsurpassed by any nation in the world.

Our sustained economic expansion is encouraging young Americans to form their own businesses. These aspiring entrepreneurs have always been on the leading edge of invention and progress in our society, and their confidence in the future has led to the creation not only of new jobs but of whole new industries. We all benefit from the contributions of small businesses and those who create them.

Now, Therefore, I, Ronald Reagan, President of the United States of America, do hereby proclaim the week of May 5 through May 11, 1985, as Small Business Week and ask that all Americans join with me in saluting our small business men and women by observing that week with appropriate activities.

In Witness Whereof, I have hereunto set my hand this twenty-seventh day of March, in the year of our Lord nineteen hundred and eighty-five, and of the Independence of the United States of America the two hundred and ninth.

RONALD REAGAN

[*Filed with the Office of the Federal Register, 11:44 a.m., March 28, 1985*]

Remarks to Brokers and Staff of the New York Stock Exchange in New York, New York
March 28, 1985

The President. Thank you all very much.

Audience member. 8 more years!

The President. This is a great view from up here. It's kind of like being at a Saturday night, tag team wrestling match at the Garden. [*Laughter*]

But in a few minutes I'll ring the bell so trading can begin.

Audience. Boo-o-o!

The President. Well, I know that if I don't, it'll ring itself, anyway, so—*[laughter]*—but in this lull before the storm, I'd like to say a few words about where this country's been and where we'll be going from here. The last time I visited the New York Stock Exchange was in 1980, and the mood sure was different then.

But in the last 5 years, we've moved from malaise to hope, confidence, and opportunity. We knew that malaise for what it really was: Government, with its high taxes, excessive spending and overregulation, had thrown a wrench in the works of our free markets. In essence government was trying to run the economy, but was ruining it instead.

So, we cut tax rates and counterproductive regulations and moved to limit spending growth. On those regulations, our estimate is that we have eliminated enough regulations to save 300 million man-hours a year that the public and local and State governments used in filling out government forms to meet the regulations.

And I think we've seen some healthy results on this trading floor. Those tax cuts helped reenergize the stock market, with the volume of shares traded hitting record highs and more Americans than ever before participating in the market. An enormous rush of new equity issues, venture capital, and new investment became the driving force behind an economic expansion as strong as any we'd seen in more than 20 years.

And for all those who say we can't repeat the dramatic growth or record of the past 2 years, I can only paraphrase my Chief of Staff: We're bullish on the American economy.

The American economy is like a race horse that's begun to gallop out in front of the field. Other nations, hobbled by high tax rates and weighed down by oversized government spending, have been slow to catch up. And this has caused some painful dislocations, especially for America's exporting industries. But the answer is hardly to hamstring the American economy to make it drop back with the others. The solution is for our trading partners to throw off the dead weight of government—cut their own tax rates, spending, and overregulation and join us in opening up their markets to foreign competition so they can catch up with us in our race to the future.

There's one sure method to cut the expense and price of American-made goods and increase our export sales. The surest way to make American products more competitive is to spur innovation, enterprise, and productivity by cutting tax rates again. And that's exactly what we intend to do.

It's time, too, that government got off its present spending spree before it squanders our future prosperity. Senate Republicans are trying to put together a package of genuine spending reductions, and they're going to need all of our support and encouragement in the coming weeks. And let me repeat again, if the political heat of budget cutting is too much for Congress, then they should give the President what 43 Governors have—a line-item veto. And if Congress can't cut, I will. And let me tell you it really would make my day.

With tax reform and budget control, our economy will be free to expand to its full potential, driving the bears back into permanent hibernation. That's our economic program for the next 4 years. We're going to turn the bull loose.

Audience. Ronnie! Ronnie! Ronnie!

[*At this point, the President rang the bell opening the trading session.*]

The President. Okay. Thank you all very much. Thank you. What you have done for me is better than a hot tip.

Note: The President spoke at 9:53 a.m. from the New York Stock Exchange trading floor rostrum. Following his remarks, the President met with members of the stock exchange and financial executives in the boardroom.

Remarks to the Students and Faculty at St. John's University in New York, New York
March 28, 1985

The President. Thank you all very much. Well, all of you, members of the administration, the faculty, students of St. John's—my fraters—and all of you, I can't tell you how deeply honored I am, and I bring the very sincere regrets of Nancy who——

Audience. Ahhh.

The President. ——who was invited, yes. But I have to tell you, I found out that I'm the only one in the family that gets paid, but the Government gets another employee free—Nancy. They've got her working, too. [*Laughter*]

But I think I should tell you why I've come here today and why I'm so honored by this degree. Now, it's true that I've heard about a rare and exotic flower that grows only in Queens. I think you call it the mulberry. And I wanted to see it. [*Laughter*] And it's true that I'm ever in search for candidates for our diplomatic staff—[*laughter*]—and so I wanted to meet a gentleman named Louis Carnesecca. I know he's elsewhere on a very important engagement right now. And it's also true that I wanted to see the school that some people are saying is just A–number one, top of the heap, king of the hill. And I know that right now that's being said in connection with college basketball, but from what I've learned of your university, the honor extends to a great many other areas as well. But there is more. For some time I've been hearing about a university in New York that boasts among its alumni the Governors of our two biggest States: Governor Mario Cuomo of New York and Governor George Deukmejian of California.

·I've heard that this university has the highest bar exam pass ratio in the Nation; that it attracts more than a thousand students a year from 88 countries on six continents of the Earth; and that among its alumni are a third of one State legislature and more than 250 judges. So, naturally, I wanted to see the new Harvard. [*Laughter*] And thanks, St. John's, for inviting me.

Audience members. We love you, Ronnie!

The President. Thank you.

I've come here today to talk about where our country has been for the past few years and where it's going. And I want to talk to you about our vision of the future and the kind of America that we now have a dazzling opportunity to create.

When I took office 4 years ago, many of you were in high school. But in spite of your youth, I know you were aware that America at that time was in a crisis. Inflation was over 12 percent, the prime interest rate was over 21 percent, unemployment was growing, and recent graduates were having trouble finding jobs. Government was weighing all of our people down with excessive personal taxes, with business taxes, and meddlesome regulations.

In 1981 we rolled up our sleeves and applied new thinking to these by now old problems. We cut tax rates for all individuals and businesses. We passed tax indexing so that inflation wouldn't force your parents into ever higher brackets as their income increased. We drove inflation down to below 4 percent. We got the economy moving again. And in truth, we can't take complete credit for the ideas that reignited our current economic growth. After all, John Kennedy had done what we had done, and great growth followed; and Japan had done what we had done, and became the economic dynamo of the East.

By 1984, last year, our economy was growing stronger and faster than it had in over 30 years, while inflation stayed lower than at any time since 1967. Civilian employment has grown by 7½ million new jobs over the past 2 years, and the number of unemployed has fallen by more than 3 million in the past 5 months alone. And that is more than a million-and-a-half Americans—what is more, I should say, have found jobs.

We have made great progress the past 4 years, but it's what we do in the next 4 years that will determine whether the American economy really lasts. Now is the time, now is the key moment, to make dramatic change. I'm speaking of a change so fundamental that I could really call it radical—radical as in reaching down to the roots.

The revolution that I'm talking about involves three things. One is taxes—the amount you and your parents and friends pay to the Government that demands your money. Another is spending—what the Government spends your money on and what effect that has on your life. But taxes and spending are like the foundation of a big house called growth. If our tax and spending policies are sound and balanced, the foundation will be rock solid, and the house of growth will stand and endure.

Our administration has reduced tax rates, as I've noted, but that's only the beginning. We have to do better. I believe we have to tear down our present tax structure and build a new one. We will propose a tax simplification plan. Tax simplification will make the rate structure simpler and more fair—that will limit deductions and that will lower tax rates further.

With a simplified tax system, we would have a top rate far lower than the current top personal tax rate of 50 percent. A side benefit of this is that it will move us away from the whole strange world of unproductive tax shelters. For once, all Americans will know that their neighbors, as well as they, are paying their fair share and not hiding behind loopholes and shelters. We want to make the tax system simpler and more fair, and we want to push tax rates down still further. This is economic justice;

it is economic sense and the key to America's economic future.

I want to talk a little here about how tax rates impinge directly on you. If you were a senior majoring in business, you'll get out of school and go into the job market in June. Let's say you have the good fortune to be hired as a salesperson for a firm with a starting salary of $20,000 a year. That's enough to live on with some comfort, but not luxurious by any means in these days.

Now, you're young and single. You share a small apartment in Manhattan, and your share of the—[*laughter*]. I mean that "share" in a certainly—[*laughter*]—different way than you reacted. And your share of the rent is, say, $500 a month.

Audience. Boo-o-o!

The President. When you make out your taxes, you claim one exemption for yourself. And you find that once you've worked for a year, that between Federal taxes, State taxes, city taxes, Social Security, and sales taxes you're giving over 30 percent of your entire $20,000 salary to taxes—more than $6,000.

Now, I could argue the morality of this— of your paying so much and involuntarily finding yourself in a condition of something approaching servitude. And I will. But I wish right now to speak of broader practical purposes.

If you were allowed to keep more of your money, you'd likely do one of three things with it. You could spend it on a portable computer, say, or—[*laughter*]—clothing or entertainment, and thereby stimulate the economy to hire more computer, clothing, and entertainment makers—[*laughter*]— thus creating jobs. Or you could save it and add to the pool of capital from which banks lend money, thereby stimulating the economy by making capital available for businesses to grow. Or you could be very creative and invest your money in a private enterprise.

Now, some of you are only a generation or two removed from the immigrant experience. Some of you are the grandsons and granddaughters of sharecroppers who came north for jobs. Many of you are the first in your family to go to college. I was the first in mine, and I, too, am a grandson of immigrants. All of you come from hardy, risk-taking stock, and you're very much the sort of people who would, in a few years, take the few thousand you'd gain from a tax cut and pool it with friends and acquaintances in order to invest it.

Twenty of you might put up as much as $5,000 each and start a business—a local newspaper, a small record company, a service industry, a small computer firm—whatever. And that expands the economy, creating new businesses, new jobs, and new wealth. This is the magic that is and always has been at the heart of America's economic strength.

We have lived through the age of big industry and the age of the giant corporation. But I believe that this is the age of the entrepreneur, the age of the individual.

That's where American prosperity is coming from now, and that's where it's going to come from in the future. Could I just pause here for a second and tell you about a couple of fellows who came to see me the other day—young men, 1981, just 4 years ago they started a business with only a thousand between them, and everyone told them they were crazy. Last year their business did $1½ million, and they expect to do $2½ million this year. And part of it was because they had the wit to use their names productively. Their business is using their names—the Cane and Able Electric Business. [*Laughter*]

The technological revolution has seen to some of the things that I'm talking about. We have to recognize that and encourage the brave men and women who are taking risks in investing in the future. They ought to be honored. But to invest your time and money and concern is a leap of faith: a profoundly hopeful act that says, yes, I have faith in the future; I am the future; the future is what I make it.

Economic growth and economic freedom are the economic answer. But we cannot stop at reforming our tax structure; we must also reform our spending policies. You may remember what I said last summer: that we could compare the big spenders in Congress with a drunken sailor out on a spree—but that would really be unfair to the sailor, because at least he's spending his own money.

We have to be frank about the Federal budget and deficit spending. Our problem is simple: Your Federal Government is now, and long has been, spending too much of your money. In the past 10 years tax revenues have grown by more than $400 billion, but spending by government has grown by almost $600 billion. That's about 50 percent more than the revenue. Government spending has grown more than one-third faster than the growth of our economy. Even our economy, the strongest in the world, hasn't been able to keep up with government's incessant demands.

Now, I've recommended a freeze on overall domestic spending for the recently submitted Federal budget, and I need your help in supporting these efforts. There's all sorts of ways for waste to be cut. There are many entitlements to be reexamined. We can and must do this, because if we don't get the size and weight of government down, then it will simply flatten the economy like a steamroller and make economic vitality an impossible dream.

I have asked for the support of Congress in getting spending down, and we're making some headway. But it takes a lot of courage for some Senators and Congressmen and women to support us, because there's always more of a constituency for spending than for cutting. They'll have to make some brave decisions. And when they make them, they will deserve the support and the thanks of our country.

I want to mention, by the way, that I know that some of you are concerned about our proposed limits on financial aid for students. All right, well, we're trying to ensure an aid system that helps all those who need it. Now, you know that spending on higher education is still more than $7 billion—as much as it was in 1982 and 1983, and more than double what it was 10 years ago. As Education Secretary Bill Bennett has pointed out, our student aid program is big, and our commitment to it will continue, and its primary purpose will be to provide the vital assistance to those who couldn't get an education without it.

Now, there are some Members of Congress who make a great show of concern about the problem of deficit spending. But they know that it's in the nature of a peaceful democracy not to want to spend money on weapons for defense but to prefer spending that money on social programs. If you really want to control spending, they say, if you really want to control spending, then cut defense. Well——

Audience. Boo-o-o!

Audience. [*Applause*]

The President. All right, I see you're divided in that, and I can understand, because you've been treated to a drumbeat of demagogic propaganda with regard to that.

Let's look at the facts. Defense spending accounts for less than 7 percent of our gross national product. That's far less than it was in the 1950's and 60's, when the threat facing us was not nearly so great. And since we first took office, we have cut $150 billion out of our own proposals for defense spending. In fact, right now, we're running almost $16 billion less than the Carter administration had projected would be their 1985 budget if they were still in office.

Now, at this point, it's a simple necessity to continue to bring our Armed Forces up to date. I've told the Senate leadership that I'm willing to consider more defense savings in noncritical areas, but I cannot compromise on the defense programs that are vital to our security.

The first responsibility of an American President is to see that this country is securely defended in a world in which trouble is, unfortunately, not the exception but the rule. All the great leaders of our time, from Winston Churchill to John Kennedy, have understood that to maintain the peace we must maintain our strength. If we don't, our adversaries will be inspired to wild action by our weakness.

Well, we can maintain the peace, and we will. We can maintain economic growth, and we must. Our economy is in good shape now, but we've got to make sure this isn't just a passing phase, a temporary pause in cycles of recession. We've got to see to it that economic growth becomes an unbreaking cycle of its own. And we can do that through getting tax rates down and spending down.

Now, back to that moral equation that I mentioned. It has to do with one word, and that word is freedom.

We live in difficult times; it's been a difficult century. Perhaps the biggest mistake mankind has made in this century is to think that the big answer is how difficult life is. Well, the big thing that will fill the void of the spiritual values that some of us rejected is the state—that's their idea—the state, with a capital "S"—well, the political edifice that man has built to govern himself.

Some have said that this is the thing from which all blessings come. But if we've discovered anything these past few decades, it is that our salvation is not in the state. Our salvation is in ourselves and what we do with our lives and the choices that we make. It is in the things that we choose to worship.

If we've learned anything, it is that government that is big enough to give you everything you want is more likely to simply take everything you've got. And that's not freedom, that's servitude. That isn't the way Americans were meant to live.

We will always take care of the poor and the helpless among us, because that's the kind of people we are and have always been. But we're a people who've discovered anew what a deep fountain freedom is and how we cannot live without drinking deep from it.

I am no longer young. You might have suspected that. [*Laughter*] The house we hope to build is one that is not for my generation, but for yours. It is your future that matters. And I hope that when you're my age, you'll be able to say as I have been able to say: We lived in freedom, we lived lives that were a statement, not an apology.

And so, if you can help us, we welcome your support. And either way, we welcome your interest in how our country is governed and how together we can secure justice for our people. When I ask for your help, it's very simple. You are the citizens; government works for you. And it doesn't hurt if sometimes you decide to be the boss and tell 'em.

I have said very many times that those elected in office who sit there in our Capitol Hill building, in the halls of Congress— it isn't necessary that you make them see the light; sometimes you have to make them feel the heat. [*Laughter*]

I've enjoyed being here very much. You've greatly honored me. And I thank you, and I love you, too.

I know you have an exciting weekend coming up. And knowing your faith, you may have considered how far you would go in trying for victory. Well, can I just tell you something? When I was playing college football—and I did—I found out one night in a chalk-talk that was going on with the coach up in front, and I don't know how the conversation got around to prayer, but it did.

Now, I had never gone into a game in all those 4 years that I hadn't said a prayer. And I was surprised and amazed to learn—I never told anyone that—that everybody else on the team did, too. But, now, the subject was: What do you pray, and what do you ask for? And believe it or not, all of us had figured out for ourselves you can't ask God to help you win. How can He favor you over others of His children that are on the other team? And what we'd figured out for ourselves was that there be no injuries, that everyone, everyone do their best, that the best team win, and that, thus, we have no regrets when the game is over.

Audience. Let's go Reagan! Let's go

Reagan! Let's go Reagan!

The President. Well, if you don't mind—[*laughter*]—I can say that prayer for the Redmen. God bless you all. Thank you very much.

[*At this point, the President was given a replica of the university basketball team's lucky sweater and the university's gold medal.*]

The President. Thank you very much. I can't tell you how deeply honored I am. I'd like to tell you also that during World War II, playing on a post basketball team, one of my teammates was an alumnus of St. John's and a great basketball player. Just so that I can even make it feel a little closer, in that school where I was playing football, we were called the Red Devils. Thank you very much. Thank you all.

Note: The President spoke at 12:07 p.m. at the university's Athletic Center. Prior to his remarks, he was awarded an honorary doctor of laws degree by Rev. Joseph I. Dirvin, vice president for university relations. Earlier, the President attended a reception with members of the university's board of trustees. Following his remarks, the President returned to Washington, DC.

Statement on House of Representatives Approval of MX Missile Production
March 28, 1985

Nearly 2 years have passed since the Scowcroft commission forged a bipartisan consensus that united us in our common search for ways to protect our country, reduce the risk of war, and ultimately and dramatically reduce the level of nuclear arms. And the American political process has tested that consensus ever since.

The latest test ended today. Thankfully, today's positive vote by the House of Representatives—the fourth congressional vote on the MX Peacekeeper during the past 2 weeks—sustained a key element of the Scowcroft commission recommendations, and production of the Peacekeeper missile will continue.

I want to thank everyone who helped us sustain the bipartisan consensus so essential for our security and our future. I will not soon forget those who chose the road of political courage and vision.

That road ahead will not be easy. We can expect tough bargaining in Geneva, and further tests of American resolve and unity will surely follow. But if we ensure American strength and determination and if we and the Soviet Union negotiate wisely and in good faith, we can reach agreements that will deeply reduce the level of nuclear arms and pass on a safer and more hopeful world to all of God's children. And I will do everything in my power to achieve that goal.

Notice of the Continuation of the National Emergency Concerning Export Control Regulations
March 28, 1985

On March 30, 1984, by Executive Order No. 12470, I declared a national emergency to deal with an unusual and extraordinary threat to the national security, foreign policy, and economy of the United States in light of the expiration of the Export Administration Act of 1979. Because the Export Administration Act has not been replaced by the Congress, the national emergency declared on March 30, 1984, must continue in effect beyond March 30, 1985. Therefore, in accordance with Section 202(d) of the National Emergencies Act (50 U.S.C. 1622(d)), I am continuing the national emergency in order to deal with the threat posed by the unrestricted access of foreign parties to United States commercial goods, technology, and technical data and by certain boycott practices of foreign nations. This notice shall be published in the *Federal Register* and transmitted to the Congress.

RONALD REAGAN

The White House,
March 28, 1985.

[Filed with the Office of the Federal Register, 11:02 a.m., March 28, 1985]

Message to the Congress on the Continuation of the National Emergency Concerning Export Control Regulations
March 28, 1985

To the Congress of the United States:

On March 30, 1984, in light of the expiration of the Export Administration Act of 1979, I issued Executive Order No. 12470 declaring a national emergency and continuing export regulations under the International Emergency Economic Powers Act (50 U.S.C. 1701 *et seq.*). Under Section 202(d) of the National Emergencies Act (50 U.S.C. 1622(d)), the national emergency terminates on the anniversary date of its declaration unless I publish in the *Federal Regis-* ter and transmit to the Congress notice of its continuation.

I am hereby advising the Congress that I have extended the emergency concerning the continuation in effect of export regulations. Attached is a copy of the notice of extension.

RONALD REAGAN

The White House,
March 28, 1985.

Appointment of 14 Members of the National Commission on Space, and Designation of the Chairman and Vice Chairman
March 29, 1985

The President today appointed the following individuals to be members of the National Commission on Space. These are new positions. He also designated Thomas

O. Paine as Chairman and Laurel L. Wilkening as Vice Chairman.

Thomas O. Paine, Chairman, is chairman of Thomas Paine Associates, consultants in high-technology enterprises. Previously he was president, chief operating officer, and director of the Northrop Corp. in Los Angeles, CA. He was Deputy Administrator, then Administrator, of NASA in 1968–1970. He graduated from Brown University (A.B., 1942) and Stanford University (M.S., 1947; Ph.D., 1949). He was born November 9, 1921, in Berkeley, CA, and now resides in Los Angeles, CA.

Laurel L. Wilkening, Vice Chairman, has been on the staff of the University of Arizona since 1973 and is now serving as vice provost. In 1980 she was division scientist, Planetary Division, NASA headquarters. She has served on several commissions and working groups at NASA from 1976 to the present. She graduated from Reed College (B.A., 1960) and the University of California (Ph.D., 1970). She was born November 23, 1944, in Richland, WA, and now resides in Tucson, AZ.

Luis W. Alvarez is currently a physicist at Lawrence Berkeley Laboratory and a professor emeritus at Berkeley. He was a founding member of the Massachusetts Institute of Technology Radiation Laboratory. He was born June 13, 1911, in San Francisco, CA, and now resides in Berkeley, CA.

Neil A. Armstrong is currently chairman of the board of Computer Technology Aviation, Inc. He was an astronaut at the Manned Spacecraft Center, NASA, Houston (1962–1970), and was command pilot of Gemini 8, commander of Apollo II, and the first man to walk on the Moon. He was born August 5, 1930, in Wapakoneta, OH, and now resides in Lebanon, OH.

Paul Jerome Coleman is currently president of the Space Research Association and professor of geophysics and space at the University of California at Los Angeles. He is also assistant director of Los Alamos National Laboratory. He was born March 17, 1932, in Evanston, IL, and now resides in Pacific Palisades, CA.

George Brooks Field is a senior physicist at the Smithsonian Astrophysical Observatory and a Robert Wheeler Willson professor of applied astronomy at Harvard University. He also serves as the chairman of the Space Telescope Advisory Committee at the Space Telescope Science Institute. He was born October 25, 1929, in Providence, RI, and now resides in Cambridge, MA.

Lt. Gen. William H. Fitch, USMC, Ret., most recently served as Deputy Chief of Staff, Aviation, at the headquarters of the U.S. Marine Corps in 1982–1984. He was born November 6, 1929, in Chattanooga, TN, and now resides in McLean, VA.

Charles M. Herzfeld has been with ITT Corp. since 1967 and currently serves as vice president and director of research and technology. He was born June 29, 1925, in Vienna, Austria, and now resides in Westfield, NJ.

J.L. Kerrebrock is Richard Cockburn Maclaurin professor and head of the department of aeronautics and astronautics at the Massachusetts Institute of Technology. He was born February 6, 1928, in Los Angeles, CA, and now resides in Lincoln, MA.

Jeane J. Kirkpatrick has been serving as Representative of the United States to the United Nations since January 1981. She is also a member of the President's Blue Ribbon Task Group on Nuclear Weapons Program Management. She has been the Thomas and Dorothy Leavey professor at Georgetown University since 1978 (currently on leave). She was born November 19, 1926, in Duncan, OK, and now resides in Bethesda, MD.

Gerard K. O'Neill is president, chairman, and chief executive officer of Geostar Corp. in Princeton, NJ. He was born February 6, 1927, in Brooklyn, NY, and now resides in Princeton, NJ.

Kathryn D. Sullivan is an astronaut at the NASA's Johnson Space Center in Houston, TX, and was the first woman to walk in space. She was born October 3, 1951, in Paterson, NJ, and now resides in Houston, TX.

David C. Webb is a consultant in the field of space development and chairman and founding member of the National Coordinating Committee for Space. He was born November 20, 1928, in County Tipperary, Ireland, and now resides in Arlington, VA.

Brig. Gen. Charles E. Yeager, USAF, Ret., was the first man to cross the sound barrier and the first to fly at a speed of more than 1,600 miles an hour, which he achieved in December 1953. He currently serves as a consultant to many corporations, including Northrop, Lear-Signon, and Piper. He was born February 13, 1923, in Myra, WV, and now resides in Cedar Ridge, CA.

Remarks at the National Space Club Luncheon
March 29, 1985

Thank you. Chuck and distinguished guests, ladies and gentlemen, I would like to express my appreciation to the Board of Governors for honoring me with this magnificent trophy.

One of the fun things about my current job is being able to get personally involved in history-making endeavors like the American space program. Nancy and I have watched space shuttles take off and land, as you all have, and we've spoken with the astronauts. I've learned that space has some interesting characteristics. For example, sound doesn't travel in space. I'm not really going to believe that until I see Sam Donaldson [of ABC News] up there. [*Laughter*]

But seriously, though, I'm proud to have been selected as the recipient of this coveted award. I accept it with thanks and on behalf of those tens of thousands of individuals across our great country who, with their hard work, creativity, and faith in the future, have built the American space program and laid the foundation for a better tomorrow.

Robert Goddard, our American rocket pioneer for whom this award is named, exemplified the ingenuity, the perseverance of individuals who make lasting contributions to their fellow countrymen and to mankind. Dr. Goddard persevered for decades of intense research and development. And as so often happens, his genius was not apparent to many until after his success.

Arthur C. Clarke, distinguished author of science and fiction, says ideas often have three stages of reaction: First, "It's crazy and don't waste my time." Second, "It's possible, but it's not worth doing." And finally, "I've always said it was a good idea." [*Laughter*]

In Dr. Goddard's case, the New York Times claiming rockets would never work in the vacuum of space ridiculed his effort. "He only seems to lack the knowledge ladled out daily in high schools," the Times editorialized.

I seem to remember when they were saying the same thing about Reaganomics.

[*Laughter*]

But due to the efforts of Dr. Goddard and other individuals of vision and tenacity, America is now on the edge of a new era. By standing on the shoulders of giants like Robert Goddard, this generation is moving forward to harness the enormity of space in the preservation of peace, in increasing our economic well-being, and in expanding the horizons of human freedom beyond the greatest dreams of our Founding Fathers.

American freedom was once protected by musket and ball. Today scientific advancements are changing the way we think about our security. Two years ago, I challenged our scientific community to use their talents and energies to find a way that we might eventually rid ourselves of the need for nuclear weapons—starting with ICBM's. We seek to render obsolete the balance of terror—or mutual assured destruction, as it's called—and replace it with a system incapable of initiating armed conflict or causing mass destruction, yet effective in preventing war. Now, this is not and should never be misconstrued as just another method of protecting missile silos.

The Strategic Defense Initiative has been labeled "Star Wars," but it isn't about war; it's about peace. It isn't about retaliation; it's about prevention. It isn't about fear; it's about hope. And in that struggle, if you'll pardon my stealing a film line: The force is with us.

Technology is with us as well. Twenty years ago, we simply could not build systems which would prevent ballistic missiles from reaching their targets; because of new advances in technology, that may no longer be true. That's why we've embarked on a vigorous research program, a program that does not violate treaties or threaten world stability.

The means to intercept ballistic missiles during their early-on boost phase of trajectory would enable us to fundamentally change our strategic assumptions, permitting us to shift our emphasis from offense to defense. What could be more moral than a system designed to save lives rather than to avenge them? What could be more peaceful than moving away from reliance on our ability to threaten global annihilation and toward reliance on systems which are incapable of threatening anyone?

We're not discussing a concept just to enhance deterrence, but rather a new kind of deterrence; not just an addition to our offensive forces, but research to determine the feasibility of a comprehensive nonnuclear defensive system—a shield that could prevent nuclear weapons from reaching their targets.

And SDI research is not aimed only at protecting the United States. Our security is inextricably linked with other free peoples. An essential element of SDI research is the eventual ability to defend the United States and our allies from both long- and short-range ballistic missiles. Thus, we will not be consulting with our allies on SDI research, but working actively with them. In fact, we have extended formal invitations to those allied nations which want to join us in making SDI a fully cooperative research effort. The Secretary of Defense will be coordinating these bilateral programs of cooperation with our allies.

Our activities in space are already helping keep the peace, providing us early warning and enabling us to verify arms agreements. And far from being a violation of existing arms agreements, once our adversaries fully understand the goal of our research program, it will add new incentives to both sides in Geneva to actually reduce the number of nuclear weapons threatening mankind. By making missiles less effective, we make these weapons more negotiable. If we're successful, the arms spiral will be a downward spiral, hopefully, to the elimination of them.

We must, as SDI research would permit, expand the opportunities, the options, for peace and arms reduction. At the same time, through our strategic modernization program, we must ensure that our current weapons remain capable of performing their essential task, until we reach that day that they may be replaced by a defensive system.

Let history record that in our day America's best scientific minds sought to develop technology that helped mankind ease away from the nuclear parapet. Let us move on to a happier chapter in the history of man. And I would think any scientist would be proud to help turn that page.

We have used and will continue to use space to make ours a safer world. Space is also making this a more prosperous world; and in this endeavor, we've only scratched the surface. Space technology has already revolutionized communications and is assisting everyone from farmers to navigators. Industries that seem far removed from any direct tie with the space program have benefited beyond expectation.

Recently, the Presidential Commission on Industrial Competitiveness—composed of leaders from business, labor, government, and academia—reported that America's leadership in science and technology is the key to future U.S. competitiveness. Space can give America the edge. And this is true not only for high-tech industries like computers and biotechnology but for mature ones as well. Innovation—often spurred on, if not inspired, by the space program—is vital to the modernization of our steel, automobile, and textile industries.

The grandeur of the space shuttle taking off and then landing after a successful mission has been a source of inspiration to America. We can't put a price tag on this. And we cannot take our achievements in space for granted.

Just 15 years ago, the first two Americans landed on the Moon and captured the imagination of the world. In 1969 the space program had momentum, and we seemed on the verge of moving permanently into space. Instead, in the 1970's America hesitated.

Luckily, however, we did invest in the shuttle program, and today we have an operating fleet of three—soon to be four—space shuttles. And I have asked NASA and the Department of Defense to study the next generation of space transportation systems for use in the 1990's.

As you are aware, last year we took the next step toward future achievements in space: a permanently manned space station. The space station will serve as an orbiting laboratory for scientific and industrial research. It will give us vital new capabilities to work and learn in space and provide us a gateway to future space goals.

Our friends and allies have been invited to join us as partners in the space station effort. The response has been very exciting. We can fully expect that in less than a decade, space will shine as an outstanding area of cooperation between the free peoples of this planet.

But we expect more than inspiration from our commitment to space. Space should and will become an increasing sphere of investment and commercial activity, a center of attention for entrepreneurs and businessmen. Already, many companies see great potential in using space as a new environment for industrial research and product development. As free enterprise expands into space, not only will innovative ways be discovered to produce the goods and services we now enjoy but new opportunities, inconceivable in the confines of Earth, will come to light. Before the end of the century, many billions of dollars of commercial activity will be taking place in and because of space.

Individual freedom and the profit motive were the engines of progress which transformed an American wilderness into an economic dynamo that provided the American people with a standard of living that is still the envy of the world. We must make certain the same incentives that worked so well in developing America's first frontier are brought to play in taming the frontier of space. Let us always remember that our space program, first and foremost, belongs to and should address the needs of the American people. Last year, I approved a national space strategy which identifies areas of high priority necessary to accomplish this.

Personally, I like space. The higher you go, the smaller the Federal Government looks. [*Laughter*] Seriously, though, to maximize our benefits, we must look beyond short-term steps to develop long-term goals for our national civilian space enterprise. I am, accordingly, happy to introduce today our appointees to the National Commission on Space, which will devise an aggressive civilian space agenda to carry America into the 21st century. The Commission, with the participation of the brightest minds in and out of the space community, will bring into focus a vision of America's future civilian opportunities and develop a set of civilian space goals to ensure America is ready for tomorrow. The members will talk with a broad sampling of Americans to keep our space efforts on target with the hopes, dreams, and aspirations of the people.

And it gives me great pleasure to announce to you that the Chairman of the National Commission on Space will be Dr. Thomas Paine, who has a long history of leadership within the space program. Would you stand up, Dr. Paine?

Now—remain right there—we have other members of the Commission with us today, and would they please stand up. [*Applause*]

I want to thank all of you for taking on this task. We have faith in your dedication, in your judgment, and your imagination. And thank you for being willing to give of yourselves this way. And you deserved that round of applause.

But while we're recognizing the people—four people—I'd just like to thank many of you in this room who are helping out with a private sector initiative dear to my heart, the Young Astronauts Program. Our space efforts are, by nature, future oriented. And I can't think of a better idea than giving young people a chance to get involved.

One fascinating aspect of space travel is, as Einstein pointed out: The faster you travel, the less you age. [*Laughter*] And now you know my real motive for supporting space exploration.

The challenge of pushing back frontiers is part of our national character. And as we face the vast expanses of space, let us recapture those stirrings in our soul that make us Americans. Space, like freedom, is a limitless, never-ending frontier on which our citizens can prove that they are indeed Americans.

Dr. Goddard once wrote a letter to H.G. Wells in which he explained: "There can be no thoughts of finishing, for aiming at the stars, both literally and figuratively, is a problem to occupy generations, so that no matter how much progress one makes, there is always the thrill of just beginning."

Well, let us hope that Americans never

lose that thrill. And thank you for letting me be with you today. And thank you for the honor you've done me. God bless you all.

Note: The President spoke at 12:55 p.m. in *the Regency Ballroom at the Shoreham Hotel. Prior to his remarks, the President was presented with the Goddard Memorial Trophy by Chuck J. Tringali and William P. Morns, president and first vice president, respectively, of the National Space Club.*

Nomination of John D. Crawford To Be a Member of the Railroad Retirement Board
March 29, 1985

The President today announced his intention to nominate John D. Crawford to be a member of the Railroad Retirement Board for the term of 5 years from August 29, 1983. He would succeed Earl Oliver.

Mr. Crawford has been with Chicago and North Western Transportation Co. and is currently serving as assistant vice president for labor relations. Previously, he was director of labor relations (1974–1984); assistant to the vice president, labor relations (1968–1974); assistant manager, labor relations (1964–1968); and labor attorney (1958–1964).

He graduated from Loyola University (A.B., 1948) and Georgetown University Law School (LL.B., 1951). He is married and resides in Glenview, IL. He was born August 9, 1924, in Chicago, IL.

Nomination of Paul A. Adams To Be Inspector General of the Department of Housing and Urban Development
March 29, 1985

The President today announced his intention to nominate Paul A. Adams to be Inspector General, Department of Housing and Urban Development. He would succeed Charles L. Dempsey.

Mr. Adams has been Deputy Inspector General at the Department of Housing and Urban Development (HUD) since 1980. From February to June 1983 and January to March 1981, he served at HUD as Acting Inspector General. Prior to this time, he held the following positions at HUD: Assistant Inspector General (1977–1980), Senior Inspector (1973–1977), supervisory investigator (1968–1973), and investigator in 1962–1968.

He graduated from Benjamin Franklin University (B.S., 1960). He is married, has one child, and resides in Crofton, MD. He was born September 14, 1937, in Lawrenceville, GA.

Appointment of Robert Dean Blackwill as United States Representative to the Mutual and Balanced Force Reduction Negotiations, and Nomination for the Rank of Ambassador
March 29, 1985

The President today announced his intention to appoint Robert Dean Blackwill, of Maryland, a career member of the Senior Foreign Service, Class of Minister-Counselor, to be the Representative of the United States of America for Mutual and Balanced Force Reductions Negotiations and his intention to nominate Mr. Blackwill for the rank of Ambassador while so serving. He would succeed Maynard W. Glitman.

Mr. Blackwill began his Foreign Service career as a Peace Corps volunteer in Malawi, Africa, 1964–1966. He was appointed a Foreign Service officer in 1967 and served as a training officer in the Bureau of Personnel in 1968–1969. He was an associate watch officer in the Department's Operations Center in 1969–1970 and at the end of 1970 took Swahili language training at the Foreign Service Institute. Mr. Blackwill was a political officer in Nairobi, Kenya, in 1970–1972. He then served as a staff officer in the Executive Secretariat of the Department in 1972–1973. In 1974 he became special assistant to the Counselor of the Department. In 1975–1978 he was political-military officer in London, England. From there he served as political counselor in Tel Aviv, Israel, in 1978–1979. In 1979 he became Director, Western European Affairs, on the National Security Council staff at the White House and from there served as the Principal Deputy Assistant Secretary for Political-Military Affairs in the Department in 1981. In 1982–1983 he was Principal Deputy Assistant Secretary for European Affairs. From 1983 to the present, he has been on sabbatical as associate dean at the John F. Kennedy School of Government at Harvard University.

Mr. Blackwill was born August 8, 1939, in Kellogg, ID. He graduated from Wichita State University (B.A., 1962). His foreign languages are French and Swahili.

Letter Accepting the Resignation of Michael A. McManus, Jr., as Assistant to the President and Deputy to the Deputy Chief of Staff
March 29, 1985

Dear Mike:

It is with regret that I accept your resignation as Assistant to the President, effective March 31, 1985.

During the past three years, you have performed a large number of important and significant jobs with great success. Well, I'm glad to have this opportunity to say thanks for all your efforts and contributions. Your role in coordinating the Williamsburg Summit and the 1984 GOP convention—to cite just two examples—demonstrated beyond a doubt that you are a superb manager and organizer. But your role in the White House has required more than just a knowledge of organizing events. You have also displayed a deep understanding of the goals you and I share for America and how to explain those goals to the people. That understanding has shone through in every project you have directed. I'm going to miss your wise counsel and advice, and I want to thank you personally for a job well done.

I guess I brought this on myself, though, by mentioning the natural desire of talented people to return to the private sector after a period of government service. You certainly are the kind of valuable public servant I had in mind. As you leave the government, Nancy joins me in sending you our best wishes for every future success and happiness.

Sincerely,

/S/RONALD REAGAN

March 25, 1985

Dear Mr. President:

With true mixed emotions, I hereby tender to you my resignation as Assistant to the President to be effective March 31, 1985. You have mentioned several times your understanding of the need for people in the Administration to return to the private sector and I find myself in that position.

It has been a great honor and privilege for me to serve as one of your Assistants. Your accomplishments have reserved for you an honored place in our history but more importantly the respect, thanks and appreciation of an American people in need of a sound economy, smaller government and peace in the world.

I have a sense of pride and personal satisfaction in having made some small contribution by reorganizing your Scheduling and Advance Offices, establishing a system for international travel, running the Summit and Convention, and reorganizing and modernizing the Communications Department.

I stand ready at any time to help you and your Administration in any way you may request. In the meantime, my thanks, best wishes and prayers go to you and Mrs. Reagan for the future.

Sincerely,

/S/MICHAEL A. MCMANUS, JR.

Note: The originals were not available for verification of the content of these letters.

Proclamation 5313—Suspension and Modification of Import Fees on Certain Sugars, Sirups and Molasses
March 29, 1985

By the President of the United States of America

A Proclamation

1. By Proclamation No. 5164 of March 19, 1984, I imposed import fees on certain sugars, sirups and molasses pursuant to Section 22 of the Agricultural Adjustment Act of 1933, as amended (7 U.S.C. 624).

2. The Secretary of Agriculture has advised me that he has reason to believe that changed circumstances require the termination of those import fees for articles described in item 956.15 of the Tariff Schedules of the United States (TSUS) and the modification of those import fees for articles described in items 956.05 and 957.15 of the TSUS.

3. I agree that there is reason for such belief by the Secretary of Agriculture, and therefore I am requesting the United States International Trade Commission to make an investigation with respect to this matter pursuant to Section 22 of the Agricultural Adjustment Act of 1933, as amended.

4. The Secretary of Agriculture has further advised me that a condition exists with regard to the importation of those certain sugars, sirups and molasses requiring emergency treatment and therefore the import fees for articles described in TSUS item 956.15 should be suspended and the import fees for articles described in TSUS items 956.05 and 957.15 should be modified without awaiting the report and recommendations of the United States International Trade Commission.

5. On the basis of the information submitted to me, I find and declare that changed circumstances require the suspension and modification of the import fees for sugars, sirups and molasses, as described below, without awaiting the report and recommendations of the United States International Trade Commission.

Now, Therefore, I, Ronald Reagan, President of the United States of America, by the authority vested in me by Section 22 of the Agricultural Adjustment Act of 1933, as amended, and the Constitution and statutes of the United States of America, do hereby proclaim as follows:

A. The application of the fees prescribed for item 956.15 and the provisions of headnote 4(c) of part 3 of the Appendix to the Tariff Schedules of the United States are suspended.

B. Items 956.05 and 957.15 of part 3 of the Appendix to the Tariff Schedules of the United States are amended by inserting "One cent per pound" in place of "An amount determined and adjusted in accordance with headnote 4(c)" in both places in which it occurs.

C. The provisions of paragraph C of Proc-

lamation No. 5164 are suspended.

D. This proclamation shall be effective as of 12:01 a.m. Eastern Standard Time April 1, 1985, and shall remain effective pending my action upon receipt of the report and recommendations of the United States International Trade Commission on this matter.

In Witness Whereof, I have hereunto set my hand this 29th day of March, in the year of our Lord nineteen hundred and eighty-five, and of the Independence of the United States of America the two hundred and ninth.

RONALD REAGAN

[*Filed with the Office of the Federal Register, 11:08 a.m., April 1, 1985*]

Letter to the Chairwoman of the United States International Trade Commission on the Suspension and Modification of Import Fees on Certain Sugars, Sirups and Molasses
March 29, 1985

Dear Madam Chairwoman:

Pursuant to Section 22 of the Agricultural Adjustment Act of 1933, as amended, I have been advised by the Secretary of Agriculture, and I agree with him, that there is reason to believe that changed circumstances require the termination of import fees for the entry of raw sugar as described in item 956.15 of part 3 of the Appendix to the Tariff Schedules of the United States (TSUS) and a modification of the import fees for TSUS items 956.05 and 957.15 from the current adjustable fees.

The United States International Trade Commission is therefore directed to make an investigation of this matter under Section 22 of the Agricultural Adjustment Act of 1933, as amended.

The Secretary of Agriculture has also de-

termined and reported to me, pursuant to Section 22(b) of the Agricultural Adjustment Act of 1933, as amended, that a condition exists requiring emergency treatment. I have, therefore, issued a proclamation suspending the import fees for TSUS item 956.15 and modifying the fees for TSUS items 956.05 and 957.15 to one cent per pound.

The suspension and modification of these fees will continue in effect pending receipt of the report and recommendations of the United States International Trade Commission and action that I may take thereon.

Sincerely,

RONALD REAGAN

[The Honorable Paula Stern, Chairwoman, United States International Trade Commission, 701 E Street, N.W., Washington, D.C. 20436]

Radio Address to the Nation on the Situation in Central America
March 30, 1985

My fellow Americans:

Before getting into my subject, I want to speak about some special people. Four years ago today, a man tried to take my life. And I wouldn't be here were it not for your prayers and the great skill of the medical team at George Washington University Hospital and the bravery of heroes like Special Agents Tim McCarthy, Jerry Parr, Police Officer Thomas Delahanty, and [Special Agent] Al Antonucci.

They, and you, continue to be in my thoughts, as is another who was injured that day—my Press Secretary, Jim Brady. Nancy and I ask for your continued prayers and support for Jim and his family and also for the family of Al Antonucci, the man who helped wrestle my assailant to the ground. Mr. Antonucci died last May. He was a proud American who never asked a thing of others, but who willingly risked his own life to save another.

Now, on another subject: This week the House joined the Senate in approving production of the MX Peacekeeper missile and sent an important signal: America *will* maintain deterrence by modernizing our strategic forces, and we *will* stand united behind our negotiating team at the arms talks in Geneva. And by strengthening deterrence, we can ensure those weapons are never used and meet a crucial challenge to our shared bipartisan responsibility for preserving peace.

But another crucial challenge must be squarely faced. It's a challenge that I and members of my administration will be presenting to you with the utmost seriousness in the days ahead, for it goes to the heart of American security. I'm talking about the Soviet-Cuban-Nicaraguan plan to destroy the fragile flower of democracy and force communism on our small Central American neighbors—a plan that could, for the first time, bring tyranny to our own borders, carrying the same specter of economic chaos, the same threat of political terrorism, the same floodtides of refugees we've seen follow every Communist takeover from Eastern Europe to Afghanistan, Laos, Vietnam, Cambodia, Ethiopia, and, now, Central America.

A key Soviet objective has long been to turn Central America into a beachhead for subversion. By tying us down in this hemisphere, by penetrating our vital sealanes and crippling our ability to meet our commitments worldwide, the Soviets will find it much easier to intimidate other nations and to expand their empire.

I know many well-intentioned people would rather not accept these facts. But we who have the responsibility for governing cannot afford to be ostriches with our heads in the sand.

Soviet Foreign Minister Gromyko described the region on our doorstep as "boiling like a cauldron" and urged revolution. We know that the Soviets turned Grenada into a warehouse of violence. They did this in the last 5 years, and they provided more military assistance to Cuba and Nicaragua than we did to all of Latin America. And we know that the support Nicaragua gets from Cuba, Bulgaria, East Germany, North Korea, Libya, the PLO, and Iran is a threat to our security, because the dictators of Cuba and Nicaragua have not only pledged to spread communism, they've been caught—forgive me—redhanded trying to do just that.

Right now Havana and Managua are waging a campaign of disinformation to cover up their deeds and reassure the American people with soft words of peace. A secret Nicaraguan memo leaked to the Wall Street Journal and reported yesterday revealed how the Communists have used propaganda to smear their opponents, tighten censorship, and confuse the outside world.

There are other examples of the regime's true intent. On March 1st, exiled Nicaraguan leaders, representing a broad pro-democracy movement, met in San José, Costa Rica, and made this offer: The freedom fighters in Nicaragua would agree to a cease-fire if the Communist regime will negotiate, permit free elections and genuine democracy. The answer came back quick, loud, and clear: Forget it.

U.S. support for the freedom fighters is morally right and intimately linked to our own security. If we refuse to help their just cause, if we pull the plug and allow the freedom fighters to be wiped out by the same helicopter gunships the Soviets are using to murder thousands of Afghans, then our ultimate price to protect peace, freedom, and our way of life will be dear indeed.

Nearly 24 years ago, President Kennedy, warning against Communist penetration in our hemisphere, said, "I want it clearly un- derstood that this government will not hesi- tate in meeting its primary obligations, which are to the security of our nation."

Well, for my part, I want it clearly under- stood today that if we fail to meet this obli- gation, then history will hold us fully ac- countable to the consequences, for we will send an unmistakable signal that the great- est power in the world is unwilling and in- capable of stopping Communist aggression in our own backyard.

Until next week, thanks for listening. And God bless you.

Note: The President spoke at 12:06 p.m. from the Oval Office at the White House.

Written Responses to Questions Submitted by Il Resto Del Carlino of Italy
March 27, 1985

U.S.-Soviet Relations and the Nuclear and Space Arms Negotiations

Q. How would you define the present state of relations between the U.S. and the U.S.S.R.?

The President. Neither the United States nor the Soviet Union can wish away the differences between our two societies and our philosophies. Our relationship is a diffi- cult and competitive one, with many prob- lems confronting our two nations. But we do have common interests, the foremost among them being to avoid war and reduce the level of arms. I am confident we can steer a course that does both.

Let me say how pleased I am that our negotiators are back in Geneva. The Ameri- can delegation has instructions from me that will let them explore every promising avenue for progress. Like free people ev- erywhere, I want these negotiations to produce agreements leading to deep reduc- tions in nuclear arms and will do my utmost to make this happen. I just hope the Soviet leadership is prepared to make the same commitment.

Cooperation and understanding and arms agreements are built on deeds, not words. Complying with agreements helps; violating them hurts. Respecting human rights helps; Afghanistan hurts. And of course, coopera- tion and understanding are very important for arms reduction negotiations. We cannot assume agreements will be honored. A his- tory of Soviet violations tells us we must be firm if our mutual security is to be strength- ened. America has long been ready for a relationship with the Soviet Union that is based on peaceful competition, constructive cooperation, and progress on arms reduc- tions. If the new Soviet leadership looks, they will find America a willing and fair partner in the search for a lasting peace.

Q. What are the chances in your view, Mr. President, of reaching a viable agree- ment with the Soviets on the reduction of the nuclear arsenals?

The President. I want the negotiations in Geneva to succeed. My instructions to our negotiators are extraordinarily flexible. The American team will be openminded, and we will do our part to make the negotia- tions successful.

But we are under no illusion that the ne- gotiations will be easy or that progress will come quickly. Both sides remain far apart on many crucial issues. And the Soviet com- pliance record with past agreements requires us to make certain that effective verification provisions are included in any future agreement.

If the Soviet Union is willing to meet us halfway, if they are willing to match our flexibility and openmindedness, then there is every reason to expect agreements leading to deep reductions in nuclear arms.

But we should also remember that the present situation—in which the threat of massive nuclear retaliation is the ultimate sanction, the key element of deterrence and, thus, the basis for security and peace—is unsatisfactory. It has kept the peace for 40 years, but the potential costs of a breakdown are immense. And because of continuing massive Soviet deployments of both offensive and defensive weapons, these potential costs are on the rise.

If we can, we must find a more reliable basis for security and for peace. That is why, 2 years ago, I directed a long-term research program to search for a defensive system that might reduce the danger of nuclear war. And because U.S. security is inextricably linked to that of our friends and allies, this Strategic Defense Initiative will not be limited solely to an exploration of technologies with potential against intercontinental ballistic missiles and submarine-launched ballistic missiles. It will also examine technologies with potential against shorter range missiles, like the Soviet SS–20's and others that are capable of striking the territory of our allies. During the next several years, we will work closely with our allies to ensure that, if such a defensive system is developed, allied as well as U.S. security would be enhanced. This is the real hope for future generations.

Europe

Q. Do you see the division of Europe in camps between East and West as a permanent thing, or do you see the possibility that Eastern Europe might move more toward Western Europe and the Soviet influence there could diminish?

The President. I don't think that any of us can believe that those countries would be subjected as they are to dominance by the Soviet Union forever. It was never part of the Yalta agreement. It wasn't part of the Helsinki final act, either. All the countries of Europe are supposed to have the right of self-determination. To me, it is unthinkable that in the future they will not demand to exercise that right; some of them are finding small ways to do so even today.

Now, the Soviets always reply that we are trying to change the boundaries of Europe or lure Soviet allies into the Western camp or threaten their security. They are trying to change the subject. The question is not one of boundaries or alliances; it is freedom. The Soviets are one of the few countries in the world who believe that freedom is a threat to their security. Our position in the West is that over the long term the denial of freedom is a much greater threat to the security of Europe as a whole.

Nicaragua

Q. About Latin America: The Secretary of State has stated that Nicaragua has fallen behind the Iron Curtain, which is true; Cuba fell behind it many years ago. The question is: Can the U.S. accept that the Iron Curtain be erected also in this part of the world?

The President. Well, as you know, last year our National Bipartisan Commission on Central America, the Kissinger commission, pointed out that the Soviet-Cuban thrust to make Central America part of their "geostrategic challenge" has turned the struggle in Central America into a real security and political problem, both for the United States and for the entire hemisphere. Neither the United States nor the other nations of the region can accept another well-armed Communist state—this time on the mainland—supported by the Soviet Union and working against the interests of the United States and its friends. And Nicaragua's harboring of Red Brigade fugitives is an example of how such a state can threaten interests outside this hemisphere.

In September 1983, in the Contadora document of objectives, Nicaragua agreed to establish a democratic system of government based on genuinely open elections. The Sandinistas acknowledged that democracy is indispensable to lasting peace in the region. The document of objectives also called for an end to support for subversion, a ban on foreign military bases, the reduction and eventual elimination of foreign military advisers, and reductions in arms and military personnel. We in the United States fully support these objectives, but Nicaragua has simply not come through on any of them.

I want to underline the fact that our goal is to foster democratic growth. America has and will continue to struggle for a lasting peace that enhances dignity for men and women everywhere. This is our highest aspiration, and it has never wavered.

Terrorism

Q. International terrorism is the newest form of international warfare. How does the U.S., along with the NATO allies, plan to react and win this war?

The President. International terrorism is indeed a form of warfare. And as I'm sure your readers are aware, European allies— and particularly Italy—have sharply increased their cooperation to combat this ugly form of warfare.

And today the allies have increased the exchange of intelligence information, broadened areas of cooperation in improving physical and personnel security, and expanded cooperation in antiterrorist training programs. A great deal has been accomplished, and we're working hard to do even more.

United States-Italian cooperation against terrorism is truly excellent. We recall, of course, Italy's brilliant rescue of General Dozier; since then our working relationship has grown even closer. Although terrorism is a difficult problem, I believe by working together and learning from Italy's courageous stand against terrorism, the allies will win the war against this insidious disease.

Middle East

Q. Would you be willing to take part in direct negotiations on the Middle East if it looked as if that would lead to peace?

The President. When the parties are ready for direct negotiations, we will be there to do our part. In the meantime, we are working with them in every way we can to get those negotiations underway.

Q. You have said that the United States will not talk to the PLO unless the PLO recognizes Israel's right to exist. What is the

rationale for that policy?

The President. In September 1982, in my initiative, I said that we base our approach squarely on the principle of an exchange of territory for peace, an exchange which is enshrined in U.N. Security Council Resolution 242. The PLO has refused to accept that principle and also refused to recognize the right of Israel even to exist. I don't see how an organization which has written off the one principle accepted by the parties and which refuses to recognize the existence of the party with whom peace must be negotiated can play a constructive role in the search for peace.

Q. The Israelis have said that they won't look very carefully at the credentials of a joint Palestinian-Jordanian delegation, which suggests that their position is flexible. Couldn't you accept a delegation on the same basis?

The President. I don't believe that we are saying anything different. They use the word Palestinian; we use the word Palestinian, also.

U.S.-Italy Relations

Q. Any particular message for the Italians?

The President. Italy's historic contribution to America's development—beginning, of course, with Columbus—is well known and much appreciated by all Americans. We are especially proud of the vast contributions so many Italian-Americans have made to the growth of our country. America, in turn, has shared with Italy during times of trouble.

But our special relationship is not a matter of the past; it is a hope for the future. Our cooperation is expanding in many ways. Italy's growing contribution to the future political and economic development of the modern world brightens the prospects for a promising future.

Your Prime Minister, Bettino Craxi, completed a most successful visit to the U.S. just several weeks ago. And I can tell you that the relations between our two countries have never been better. Ours is a warm friendship linked by shared values that run very deep.

Finally, let me say a few words about

democracy: The United States and Italy are two of the world's greatest democracies. People can reach their full potential only when they are free. Americans have watched with admiration the success of Italy's political leaders in firmly establishing for Italy a place among the world's foremost democracies. Prime Minister Craxi is the latest successor to a proud democratic legacy. And I believe that under your government's coalition leadership, Italian democracy will grow even brighter.

Note: The questions and answers were released by the Office of the Press Secretary on April 1.

Written Responses to Questions Submitted by Hürriyet of Turkey
March 29, 1985

U.S. Military Assistance for Turkey

Q. During your first term, administration officials emphasized in congressional hearings time after time that military aid to Turkey is insufficient to modernize her ancient armed forces. Two questions: Do you think Turkey is fit to fulfill her NATO duties under these circumstances? Since administration requests have always been cut by Congress, do you intend to increase aid to Turkey?

The President. The United States is committed to help Turkey modernize its armed forces as quickly as possible. We are doing our best to help ensure that a key ally has a strong defense.

In order to do this, we have more than tripled military assistance to Turkey since 1980. Last year Congress approved $700 million in military assistance. This year, recognizing the continuing need, I have requested Congress to approve nearly $800 million in military assistance, of which over 73 percent is either grant or on concessional terms.

Conflict in Cyprus

Q. What is your evaluation of Greek and Turkish attitudes during the last summit on Cyprus?

The President. As we said in January, the United States regrets the failure of the summit meeting between the leaders of the two Cypriot communities. We believe, however, that the pursuit of a negotiated political solution in Cyprus must continue and that the Cypriot parties themselves hold the key to their own future. We continue to support the Secretary-General's role under his Security Council mandate and for our part have encouraged all parties to this dispute to be flexible and forthcoming.

Q. Are you optimistic about a peaceful solution?

The President. As I said, we are still hopeful the Cypriot parties can find the will to move forward, under the guidance of the Secretary-General, to find a peaceful and lasting solution to the Cyprus question.

U.S. Military Bases in Greece

Q. Greek Prime Minister Papandreou has been hostile to NATO. Do you think it is secure to keep U.S. bases in Greece under the circumstances, or do you intend to move them to Turkey?

The President. The United States maintains its longstanding security relationship with Greece within the NATO partnership. We believe that U.S. bases in Greece are of value to Greece, the U.S., and NATO. That is why we negotiated a bilateral defense and economic cooperation agreement, and we continue to maintain this view.

Terrorism

Q. Turkey, like the U.S., faces constant international terrorist attacks. Armenian terrorist groups claim responsibility for Turkish victims. However, Congress is about to vote on an Armenian resolution—referring to the so-called genocide in 1915. Do you approve congressional action on such a sensitive issue?

The President. I know this is a deeply emotional issue, and I sympathize with all those who suffered during the tragic events of 1915. I also profoundly regret that Turks and Armenians have so far not been able to resolve their differences. Nevertheless, there is no question regarding my opposition to terrorism. On those grounds alone, my administration opposes congressional action on the kind of resolution to which you refer. We are concerned such resolutions might inadvertently encourage or reward terrorist attacks on Turks and Turkish-Americans. We also oppose them because they could harm relations with an important ally.

I hope the Turkish people understand that in our form of government the Executive can only seek to persuade the Congress and does not control congressional actions. Therefore, these resolutions, if adopted, would only express an opinion of the Congress. They would not and could not change my policy toward Turkey or my commitment to the fight against international terrorism.

Turkish Economy

Q. Turkey is following in the footsteps of U.S. economic policy. Liberal trade and conservative monetary policy are the basics of Turkish economic policy. Do you believe such measures should be used in developing countries? Do you think the measures are productive?

The President. Private capital working in an open market is the most effective engine of development. The success that Mr. Özal [1] has had, so far, in reinstituting an enviable economic growth rate through his liberalization policies demonstrates that fact. The United States strongly supports Turkey's economic program and applauds the responsible and successful manner in which Turkey has addressed its international financial obligations.

Q. Do you see Turkey as an economic as well as strategic ally of the U.S.?

The President. A healthy, growing Turkish economy is in the best interests of Turkey and the United States, and we are encouraging the development of a strong, competitive Turkish economy. In the world

---

[1]*Prime Minister Turgut Özal of Turkey.*

of trade, countries are at the same time partners and competitors. We look forward to competing with Turkish goods and services in the world marketplace and anticipate expanding our markets in Turkey as well.

Middle East

Q. Since 1948 the Middle East has not been at peace. What are your plans to bring peace to the region? Would you support an international conference like that most Arab nations favor?

The President. The achievement of a just and lasting peace between Israel and all its neighbors is a major goal of the United States. We are working with the parties to achieve, as a next step, a broadening of negotiations through direct talks between Israel and Jordan with Palestinian representatives. The United States firmly believes that the only practical path to peace in the Middle East lies in direct negotiations based upon United Nations Security Council Resolutions 242 and 338.

An international conference would inevitably produce extremist rhetoric and confrontation rather than serious and productive negotiation. This would not bring closer the peaceful settlement we seek.

In my September 1, 1982, Middle East peace initiative, which is firmly based on Resolutions 242 and 338 and the Camp David framework, I outlined positions which the United States would support in negotiations. These positions are aimed at the achievement of an equitable settlement that would reconcile Israel's legitimate security interests and the legitimate rights of the Palestinian people. Acceptance of our proposals by other parties is not a precondition for negotiations. We would expect other parties to put forward their positions.

Recent developments have spurred movement toward negotiations. This momentum must be maintained and built upon. The United States will be active in that effort.

U.S.-Soviet Relations and the Nuclear and Space Arms Negotiations

Q. How do you see future U.S.-Soviet relations? Are you optimistic about the

375

Geneva talks?

The President. It is regrettable that U.S. relations with the U.S.S.R. have been difficult in recent years, but we must face the fact that events such as the brutal Soviet war against the Afghan people, the continuing Soviet military buildup far beyond legitimate defense needs, and the deteriorating human rights situation in the U.S.S.R. complicate the task of developing more satisfactory relations.

Although issues are complex, I am hopeful that we are at a point where we and the Soviets can make progress on the major issues. My administration will take every opportunity to broaden our dialog with the U.S.S.R. and work for mutually beneficial solutions to our problems. No one can predict what the future might hold, but I can assure you that Mr. Gorbachev and his colleagues in the Soviet leadership will find America to be a willing partner in the search for true peace. We hope that the Soviet Union is equally committed.

I have no higher priority than negotiating the reduction and, eventually, the complete elimination of nuclear weapons, and I am pleased that new arms control negotiations are underway in Geneva. The issues are many and complex, and it would be unrealistic to expect quick or easy progress. Nevertheless, I am optimistic that agreement can be reached if the Soviets join us in a serious and constructive approach to the talks.

Strategic Defense Initiative

Q. Star Wars is the most controversial subject of our time. Is this just a project or a bargaining tool?

The President. The Strategic Defense Initiative is not an arms development program. SDI is a research effort and, as such, cannot be a bargaining tool. Its purpose is to explore the potential of newly emerging technologies to see whether we can find an effective defense against ballistic missiles, thereby strengthening deterrence and reducing the risk of war. The focus of the research is on nonnuclear technologies.

The 1972 antiballistic missile treaty permits research into ballistic missile defensive technologies, and both we and the Soviets recognize the impossibility of limiting re-search. Indeed, the Soviet Union has for many years conducted a vigorous research program in this area. In fact, over the last 20 years the Soviet Union has spent approximately as much on strategic defense as on its massive offensive programs and has engaged in activities, such as the construction of the Krasnoyarsk radar, that violate the ABM treaty.

We believe it is essential that we examine the feasibility of defensive technologies which, if the research bears out, will increase the incentives for future radical reductions in offensive nuclear arms. In any case, it would be imprudent for us not to continue our research as a hedge against a possible Soviet breakthrough in defense technologies or a complete Soviet breakout from the ABM treaty.

Presidential Visit to Turkey

Q. During your upcoming trip to Europe, would you include Turkey in your schedule?

The President. I'm afraid there will not be sufficient time on that trip to include Turkey, and I truly regret this.

U.S.-Turkey Relations

Q. Mr. President, you are as famous in Turkey as in the U.S. regarding popularity and your programs and your economic success story. You are very much liked by the Turkish public. What are your thoughts on the Turkish people? Is there any message you would like to convey to them before the historic visit of the Turkish Prime Minister?

The President. I have always thought of the Turkish people as particularly brave and steadfast—brave certainly in the military sense, as all the world knows, but brave also in terms of the determination they have shown in stabilizing and rebuilding their economy. In this, too, they are an outstanding example to the rest of the world. It is important that Turks explain to the American people and the world their significant progress toward greater democracy, freedom, and economic growth and the additional goals they have set for themselves.

The relationship between Turkey and the United States has grown during my administration, and I look forward to seeing that relationship further broadened and strengthened in the coming years. I particularly look forward to meeting your Prime Minister, about whom I have heard so much and with whom I share so many goals and opinions.

Note: The questions and answers were released by the Office of the Press Secretary on April 1.

Statement by Principal Deputy Press Secretary Speakes on Economic Assistance for Sudan
April 1, 1985

The President and members of his administration have had an opportunity to review with President Nimeiri recent economic policy actions undertaken by the Government of Sudan as part of a comprehensive economic reform program. The President believes that exchange rate adjustments, elimination of subsidies, and limitation on the budget deficit are highly commendable actions, worthy of international donor support. He recognizes that these are difficult steps to take, requiring sacrifice.

In support of these recent economic reforms, the President has directed that the United States Government proceed with disbursement of the balance of our FY 1984 Economic Support Funds Program in Sudan—$67 million. We are prepared to proceed immediately to work with the Government of Sudan and other donors to build a viable 1985 assistance program.

It is clear that the Government of Sudan is taking the steps that are required to bring its economy under control while it is faced with the added difficulties of drought and refugee emergencies. Prior to President Nimeiri's visit, the United States had already delivered or agreed to provide 750,000 tons of grain this year. We have now agreed to provide an additional 225,000 tons and will continue working with Sudan and other donors on its total needs. This will mean a total of 975,000 tons from the United States for this year.

Accordance of the Personal Rank of Ambassador to Dean Burch While Serving as Chairman of the United States Delegation to the World Administrative Radio Conference on Space
April 1, 1985

The President today accorded the personal rank of Ambassador to Dean Burch in his capacity as Chairman of the United States delegation to the first session of the World Administrative Radio Conference on Space of the International Telecommunication Union.

Mr. Burch served in the United States Army in 1946–1948. In 1953–1955 he was special assistant to the attorney general of Arizona and was legislative assistant, then administrative assistant, to Senator Barry Goldwater in 1955–1959. In 1959–1963 and again in 1965–1969 he was an attorney with the law firm of Dunseath, Stubbs, and Burch in Tucson, AZ. He was deputy director of the Goldwater for President Committee (1963–1964), chairman of the Republican National Committee (1964–1965), and campaign manager for Barry Goldwater (1968). In 1969 he was appointed to the Arizona Board of Regents by Gov. Jack Williams. He was Chairman of the Federal Communications Commission in Washington, DC, in 1969–1974. In 1974 (March-December) he was Counsellor to the President of the United States. Since 1975 he has been an attorney with the law firm of Pierson, Ball, and Dowd in Washington, DC. Since 1985 he has been Chairman of the United States delegation to the first session of the World Administrative Radio Conference on Space of the International Telecommunication Union.

Mr. Burch received his LL.B. in 1953 from the University of Arizona. He was born December 20, 1927, in Enid, OK.

Appointment of Robert S. Fryer as a Member of the Board of Trustees of the John F. Kennedy Center for the Performing Arts
April 1, 1985

The President today announced his intention to appoint Robert S. Fryer to be a member of the Board of Trustees of the John F. Kennedy Center for the Performing Arts, Smithsonian Institution, for the remainder of the term expiring September 1, 1992. He will succeed Cary Grant.

Mr. Fryer is presently serving as artistic director for the Center Theatre Group of Ahmanson Theatre in Los Angeles, CA. He has produced numerous Broadway shows, including California Suite (1976), Sweeney Todd (1978), The West Side Waltz (1981), Brighton Beach Memoirs and Noises Off (1983). He has also produced several feature films, including Great Expectations (1974) and The Boys From Brazil (1978).

He graduated from Western Reserve University (B.A., 1943). He was born November 19, 1920, in Washington, DC, and now resides in Los Angeles, CA.

Appointment of Edward N. Gladish as a Member of the National Advisory Committee on Oceans and Atmosphere
April 1, 1985

The President today announced his intention to appoint Edward N. Gladish to be a member of the National Advisory Committee on Oceans and Atmosphere for a term expiring July 1, 1987. This is a reappointment.

Mr. Gladish has been a member of the National Advisory Committee on Oceans and Atmosphere since March 1982. He is also regional manager for government and industry relations at Champlin Petroleum Co. in Englewood, CO. Previously he was manager for land services at Champlin Petroleum Co. in Long Beach, CA. He served as executive officer of the California State Lands Commission in 1973–1974 and on the State Advisory Board of the U.S. Bureau of Land Management in 1974.

He graduated from the University of California (B.S., 1953). He is married, has three children, and resides in Englewood, CO. He was born March 29, 1930, in Yreka, CA.

Interview With Lou Cannon, Dave Hoffman, and Lynn Downie of the Washington Post
April 1, 1985

Nicaragua

Q. Mr. President, you've often given your views of Nicaragua and called it a war machine and said it poses a threat to its neighbors and, ultimately, to our security. But the Sandinistas appear to be firmly in control, and there are a few signs that they're changing. What—looking back on your policy over the last 4 years—has it actually accomplished as far as Nicaragua is concerned?

The President. Well, yes, I think there are more people who are opposing the regime right now in Nicaragua than actually fought in the revolution against Somoza. And it seems to be growing—the unhappiness of the people. You only have to look at the flood of refugees that are escaping from Nicaragua to realize that the people of that country are not happy with that totalitarian regime.

Q. With what final result will that——

The President. Well, I know the Contadora is still trying to find an answer of that kind. The *contras,* themselves, have offered to lay down weapons and go into negotiations in an effort to have what they had fought the revolution for, and that is a democracy. And so, I think, as long as the people of Nicaragua are still striving for the goals of the revolution that they themselves fought, I think that we're obligated to try and lend them a hand.

Q. In this country, even though your popularity remains very high, on the issue of Nicaragua polls show that there are many Americans opposed to your policy there, and the Congress shows very little inclination to give you the $14 million you've asked. Do you have any new proposals or ideas that would change this view in Congress?

The President. Well, nothing that I can talk about here. But let me just say, I know this about what the polls show, and I know what happens up on the Hill. But we've been subjected in this country to a very sophisticated lobbying campaign by a totalitarian government, the Sandinistas. There has been a disinformation program that is virtually worldwide, and we know that both the Soviets and the Cubans have such a disinformation network that is beyond anything that we can match. And, of course, I don't think the people have heard the thing that we're tying to explain of what is going on.

People go down, some people, to Nicaragua and claim they come back now with views that are favorable to that totalitarian government. But why don't they go to some of the neighboring countries and talk to the thousands and thousands of refugees and ask them why they fled Nicaragua?

Q. Is there anything that you can do as President, that your administration can do, to help the *contras* and their supporters if Congress does not vote this money?

The President. I don't know. That's something I'd have to face if they do this. We're not alone in helping them. As a matter of fact, in spite of the polls, there is more and more private support for the *contras.*

Meeting With Soviet Leader Mikhail Gorbachev

Q. On another subject, sir: Have you heard back from the Soviets on your proposal for a meeting with Mr. Gorbachev?

The President. Lou, let me just say—and this, I know, will be kind of frustrating—I've had a response to my letter, but I never talk about content of communications between myself and other heads of state.

Q. Well, without putting it, then, in the context of a letter, we've heard that the Soviets have given some indication that they would like to meet with you, but they have not given a time and place. Could you——

The President. Well, again, as I say, that would be commenting, and that would be opening a door to all kinds of speculation. I wrote, and he answered, and we're in negotiations. And we'll just leave it at that.

Q. Well, do you expect that you will meet

with him sometime? Without reference to the letters, do you foresee a summit meeting or high-level meeting between you and him?

The President. Well, I'm going to continue—I made it evident, or made it plain, that I would have liked such a thing with his predecessors. But I'm going to continue——

Q. Do you expect——

The President. ——hopeful that we can have such a meeting.

Q. Has the killing of Major Nicholson[1] had any impact on these negotiations?

The President. No. There seems to be a little misunderstanding on the part of some columnists about my answer the other day to that, that it made me even more anxious for a summit meeting. Some have made it seem as if I was being an appeaser or something—not at all. This was a murder, a cold-blooded murder; and it reflects on the difference between two societies—one that has no regard for human life and one, like our own, that thinks it's the most important thing.

And, yes, I want a meeting even more so—to sit down and look someone in the eye and talk to him about what we can do to make sure nothing of this kind happens again.

Strategic Defense Initiative

Q. Mr. President, on a related subject, the Strategic Defense Initiative, you have said that the world would be a safer place if the superpowers moved to strategic defense from mutual assured destruction. But the Soviets don't agree. Does this mean that the present negotiations at Geneva are really on hold until the Soviets come around to your point of view, or is there some way that we can move now to have these talks deal with the immediate questions of medium-range and long-range missiles?

The President. Well, I don't think there's any hold on the talks over there. They're in three groups: One group is talking about space and defense weapons; one is talking

about strategic weapons; and the third one is talking about the intermediate-range weapons in Europe. And the negotiations are going forward.

The Strategic Defense Initiative is purely research. And Mr. Gromyko himself said there's no way to control that, that it's not covered by any treaty. And the plain truth of the matter is, they've been doing the same kind of research in the same areas and started it before we did.

Now, I do mean that if this research could lead to the kind of a weapon that would make one have to think twice as to whether they could be successful with the use of nuclear weapons, then it would lead to the very thing that both the late Mr. Chernenko and Gromyko have said, and that is that they would like to see the elimination of nuclear weapons; so would we. And if a defensive weapon that could be successful against them helps bring that about by making them too costly to take the chance of putting those costly things in the air only to be shot down, then we'd be further on the way toward the elimination of nuclear weapons. And we'd all be better off.

Q. Do we need an interim agreement to keep the number of missiles down while we're having these talks?

The President. Oh, yes. I've never believed that even though they said this, because my own response to Mr. Gromyko, when he indicated that same thing to me— my own response was: "Look, we can settle it right here. We're ready to go all the way on the elimination of nuclear weapons." But I didn't get an answer.

But, yes, I would think that the logical thing would be to start with the reduction of the numbers of weapons, to get them down to a lower level. My hope has been that once we start on that path, that gradually everyone would see that it makes more sense to keep on going until you've eliminated them.

Q. Would it be wise to try to achieve that sort of interim agreement about the time when the SALT II limitations would have expired, that have been generally observed by both sides?

The President. Oh, I haven't really

---

[1] *Maj. Arthur D. Nicholson, Jr., USA, who had recently been shot and killed in the German Democratic Republic.*

thought about whether that makes any difference or not. It's just that the world is living under a threat; and other people are going to try, as we know, to get missiles themselves. And some of them are less responsible than others, and they're not all superpowers. And I just think that it's a threat that humankind should not have to live under.

Terrorism

Q. On another subject, Mr. President, a British newspaper reported yesterday that the United States has warned Iran that military retaliation would take place if any of the Americans who have disappeared in Lebanon were to be put on a show trial or murdered by pro-Iranian factions. Has such a warning been issued to Iran?

The President. Well, here again, I don't think I should discuss anything of this kind. What I have said is that there is increasing evidence that some terrorists in the world are actually emissaries of sovereign governments. And if that's the case and can be established, then that business of trying to find and track down, in all the world, a few terrorist individuals for some crime—no, go to the source. And the government supports them, but——

Q. Would you put Iran in that category of a government that——

The President. Well, as I say, I can't comment on this specific question that you asked, beyond that. But we've been working as closely as we can with allied countries and friends to see if together, between us, we can't do something. And we have done something. I think we've had some measure of success. But in the exchange of information to get a handle on this widening terrorist activity—we know it's not just one group; there are a number of groups representing different interests. Sometimes they apparently collaborate, and it's a new form of warfare.

Q. Can you tell us something about the accomplishments in this area that you believe you've achieved?

The President. Well, we're making headway and have been successful in getting cooperation in trading information—intelligence information—getting agreements with other countries with regard to extradi-

tion and denying their countries a shelter for terrorists who then cross a border and have been in the past reasonably safe if they leave the country where they've been terrorizing. And there's getting to be much more mutual agreement about the need for all of us to work together.

South Africa

Q. Mr. President, on the subject of South Africa, there have been 38 fatalities in civil strikes there in the past few weeks, and the government seems to be engaging in increasing repression, banning assemblies and meetings. Isn't it time to go beyond the policy of constructive engagement and silent diplomacy in our dealings with South Africa?

The President. We think that what we're doing has the best effect and the most effect of anything that we could do. Just walking away would leave us with no ability to influence them. We think some progress has been made. We do know that there is a factionalism there. It isn't just a simple question of two groups—the government versus a group. Over in this group there is a division and there is a sector that wants violence as the answer and are even violent to the others, not to the government alone. And we think apartheid is the main problem that must be resolved, and we're going to continue doing all that we can to encourage the government in its course.

Q. Have we done anything to try and discourage that government from this violence? It seems that it's gotten worse rather than better.

The President. Except that the violence—nothing can be solved by violence, and that isn't the answer. But remember that violence is not just alone stemming from a government put-down of demonstrators. You have in the black community there—you've got rival factions, and the violence is sometimes between them, fighting each other. And we've seen evidence of that, and we've seen murders. And some of the 40 deaths have been created in among the people, without the government participating.

Q. When you mentioned that in your recent news conference, some people in this country and around the world took that as condoning the government's actions. Is that——

The President. No, it——

Q. ——wrong?

The President. ——no, and it wasn't intended to be. But it is true; I think some people—and I would have to say that some who did maybe have a political bias—but they tried to read into it that I was voicing a bias. And I wasn't; I was trying to point out just what I did here. Maybe I should have taken more time.

You know, in a press conference you feel a little pressed for time in your answers, and sometimes maybe you don't make them as full as they should be. But I was trying to point out that from this being simply people opposed to apartheid against a government that is supporting apartheid—no, it has gone beyond that. There is an element that wants an overthrow of the government by violence and is not just limiting its fighting to the government. It is fighting its own fellow citizens, and even in the same communities.

Defense Spending

Q. Mr. President, if we could change a little bit to domestic matters. I wanted to ask you a question about the budget. You said in a Saturday radio speech recently that you would not accept cuts in vital conventional or strategic weapons systems. The Senate Armed Services Committee has voted to cut 175,000 from the Defense payroll and bring down the deficit. Since you don't want to cut weapons systems, would this cut in personnel be acceptable to you?

The President. Well, that wasn't adopted by the Committee, was it? I understand they just sign in to the Committee——

Q. Well, it's part of an option directed toward zero real growth.

The President. Yes. And, no, that is the type of thing I haven't had a chance to study—since I heard that also—and see what the effect and where they're choosing these people to go. But, as I've said with regard to defense, when you start to economize, you have to look at it from the standpoint not of the number of dollars that you're hoping to save, but what can you do without. Now, I don't know whether we

can do without that many people and where they would come from and what shortages it would create in our defensive capability.

So, again, as I say, if we can find additional ways—and we have already reduced the original budget considerably—if we can find additional ways in which there could be some postponements of something or other—not weapons systems—there are a number of fairly civilian-type activities that take place in the military, also. If some of those would not, in any way, reduce our defensive capability and yet would provide some savings to help us as we try to get a handle on this budget—all right, that's one way to look. But I don't see where there could be any compromise on weapons systems that have been chosen, because we believe they're necessary to redress the imbalance between ourselves and the Soviet Union.

I've heard some spokesmen, and some who should know better, in and out of government, some of the shows on television, and sometimes in the newsprint, voicing their opinions that somehow we're on a parity—they've even used that term—with the Soviet Union. This is the most ridiculous thing I've ever heard. The Soviet Union virtually outnumbers us in any type of weapon you want to name, has consistently modernized their land-based nuclear missiles, where we're just trying to with the traumatic experience of the 21 these last few days—which is the first modernization of our land-based missiles in almost the lifetime of the men and women who are handling these weapons. They are about 3 to 1 in megatonnage, nuclear megatonnage, over us. They outnumber us in conventional weapons in almost every category. Their navy has several hundred more ships than we have.

We've been making progress. We think that we've achieved, I think, a deterrent to the effect that they'd have to think twice about taking us on. But we haven't caught up with them or surpassed them in any sense.

Japan-U.S. Trade

Q. Turning to trade with Japan, you have

expressed your sympathy with Prime Minister Nakasone's problems in trying to open up markets there. Nevertheless, it appears that the negotiations continue to be very difficult with Japan, particularly on telecommunications most recently. Are you satisfied, after the report from your special envoy, that some sort of agreement can still be reached, or do you think you're going to face an increasingly frustrated Congress on this issue?

The President. Well I'm going to place my confidence in Prime Minister Nakasone—and confidence that he wants to arrive at a solution to these trade problems as much as we do. And, of course, just as I do, he's got some political problems of his own. But our representatives came back, and they are reassured that there is no lack of intent on his part. And they're assured that he is going to continue doing his utmost to bring about some changes, evening up this trade imbalance. And, so, we just have to wait and see what he can accomplish. We have made some progress so far and some time ago with regard to citrus fruits, beef, things of that kind. And the negotiations aren't over by any means.

Q. Mr. President, for a long time you've been theoretically strongly committed to the idea of free trade. Will you make an active effort to try and oppose the protectionist legislation that now appears to be building in the Congress?

The President. Yes, I will, because protectionism, if you go back over the years—all of you have only read about it—but the Great Depression, I think the Great Depression was extended and carried on and worsened because of a tariff situation on our part, called Smoot-Hawley, that reacted unfavorably against us. It was supposed to be protectionist.

But protectionism is a two-way street. And it may be that here is an industry that is suffering from, let's say, some unfair competition. What we're trying to cure is unfair competition, to see that the markets are free to each other, both ways; that we're not competing with subsidized products, government subsidized and so forth. And all of these things we're doing our best to change.

But in normal competition and international trade, to set down here a restriction that is based on some import in our country from another, they, then, may retaliate and affect another industry of ours. So, to help one industry by protectionism when you can't help all the others that are our exporters—and what's going to happen to them at the other end?

We saw a little example or an example of that—not exactly in this sense, but—in the grain embargo. We lost a market, and we lost a recognition of us as a reliable trading partner in doing that.

Commemoration of V–E Day

Q. Mr. President, you said in your last news conference that you didn't want to visit Dachau during your upcoming European trip because of an unnecessary guilt feeling that you said has been imposed on the present-day German people. How do you respond to those American Jews who have interpreted this remark as minimizing the Holocaust and as passing up an opportunity to dramatize this idea of "never again"?

The President. Well, Lou, here again is one that maybe—well, no maybe about it—I guess I should have elaborated more in my answer. I have made it very plain and spoken publicly on a number of occasions, and will continue to say, we should never forget the Holocaust. We should never forget it in the sense that this must never happen again, to any people, for whatever reason in the world.

What I meant—and this time, to be a guest in that country at this particular time, when it is the coincident date with the end of the war, and recognizing that most of the population there—I grant you, there are some people there my age who remember the war and were participants in it on that side—but the bulk of the population, you might say everybody below 50 or 55, were either small children or not born yet.

And there's no question about their great feeling of guilt—even though they were not there to participate in it—of what their nation did. And then to take advantage of that visit, on that occasion, to go there—I just think is contrary to what I believe. We should all start recognizing the day of the end of the war as and make it more of a celebration of the fact that on that day, 40-odd years ago, began the friendship that we now know—40 years of peace between us. And at the same time, you can say: And let us keep it this way and never go back to that other way.

And it just seemed to me that it would be just out of line to emphasize that when I was there, as a visitor in their country. I am supportive of the Holocaust Museum; I've done everything I can to be supportive of that. And I will say anytime that anyone wants me say it, as publicly as I can, that, no, we must never forget that chapter in this history of humankind and our determination that it must never happen again.

Tax Reform

Q. Mr. President, on tax reform, Secretary Baker is at work, as you know, trying to come up with a revised proposal. And you have frequently talked about your desire to lower individual tax rates, yet the first Treasury plan envisioned a higher corporate tax burden. Are you willing to accept higher burdens on corporations as a tradeoff for lower burdens on individuals?

The President. Well, no, the corporate tax was going to be cut even lower than the top personal rate in their plan. What we're talking about is generally more money from the corporate sector, but by way of broadening the base—that the rates would be lower for everyone, but there would be an end to some loopholes that probably were never intended to allow large profit-making corporations to escape totally tax free for years on end. And it would simply mean that there'd be more fairness, that you'd know that your neighbor was paying a tax, too, and not getting off scot-free.

Q. So, you would envision, as a result of this effort, both lower corporate and individual rates, and all the revenue that is lost made up entirely by base-broadening efforts.

The President. Yes. There's no question the plan calls for a 33-percent top rate instead of 46 for the corporations, and then it calls 50, 25, and 15 for the—or, I mean 35, 25, and 15, instead of the 50 and other 13 tax brackets for individuals.

So, no, we don't want to penalize some taxpayer into paying a higher share by way of higher rates. We want all the rates to be lower, but, as I say, close those loopholes that have permitted this thing of very profitable businesses not paying any tax.

Q. There's——

The President. Got time for one more question?

Views on the Presidency

Q. Yes. Mr. President, you said at St. John's last week—I know you were in a lighter mood—but you said to the students that you're not a young man anymore. Now, you're a person who has always celebrated you own vitality, and I guess I wanted to ask you whether you feel yourself aging or growing any older in this job.

The President. No. Do I look older? [*Laughter*] I don't feel any older. No, I feel fine. And, no, I think maybe part of it, Lou, is that there've been a lot of people that have sat at that desk and have come from, let's say, different experiences in government—by the way of the legislature, for example.

I have to believe that 8 years as Governor of the most populous State in the Union, California, was a pretty good foundation. In other words, I didn't find things too different. I'd had 8 years of dealing with many of the same problems. Granted, we didn't have a foreign policy in California, but I think that this is part of it. For 8 years somebody handed me a piece of paper every night that told me what I was going to be doing the next day. [*Laughter*]

And when I became Governor, I had something of the same problems in California that we had here. I came in in the middle of the fiscal year—you don't quite come in in the middle here; you only come in 4 months into it; you've got 8 months to go on the other fellow's budget—but middle of the fiscal year and with already a deficit that had been piled up in California. And the difference there—and I wish I had it here—the difference there was that—but in the 6 months remaining to me in that, when I took office, of the budget—that first budget—I had to balance the budget, which was one of the reasons why, in contrast to everything I'd said in campaigning, I had to go for a tax increase, because when July 1st came, that budget had to be balanced. But I promised the people that as soon as we could, we'd give it back, and we did. You know that. Every time we got to the place where it was surpluses, not deficits; and every surplus, we gave back to the taxpayers.

Q. ——our last question, Dave or Lynn, do you have a question?

Balanced Budget

Q. Well, Mr. President, speaking of the balanced budget, you apparently or reportedly got very upset at a Congressman who said that he asked you if you want a balanced budget, why don't you submit one. Well, I'd like to ask you, what was your response to that question?

The President. That it was the most hypocritical question I'd ever heard. [*Laughter*]

Q. Why did you say that?

The President. What? Well, there's a member of a party that for 50 years, with only a couple of years' exception, 2 or 4 years' exception, has been responsible for the government spending—the Democratic Congresses of the past 50 years—and we've had deficit spending for 50 years and a trillion dollars piled up in national debt before we got here. That for someone now to suggest—when they themselves have refused

to give me the cuts I asked for—to suggest that I should have asked for so many more cuts, that we had a balanced budget all at once—no; it is hypocritical. He knows and everyone knows there's no way that you could pull the rug out from so many people by trying to balance this budget in one term, in one year. The people have become accustomed for a half a century to many of the things that government is doing. So, you've got to warn them that down the road here it's not going to be doing some of these things. And you start us on a downward path of reducing the deficits to where you can point to a time reasonably certain and say, "Here is where we can reach the balanced budget." And this is our goal.

But for him, as a member of the body that has refused to give me the cuts that I asked for ever since I've been here—if they'd given us the cuts in 1981 that we asked for, the budget deficit would be $50 billion less than it is today. And then for him to say, "Why don't you submit a balanced budget?"—Yes, I told him that, in no uncertain terms, how I felt about it.

Reporters. Thank you.

Note: The interview began at 4:05 p.m. in the Oval Office at the White House. The transcript was released by the Office of the Press Secretary on April 2.

Nomination of Charles A. Gillespie, Jr., To Be United States Ambassador to Colombia
April 2, 1985

The President today announced his intention to nominate Charles A. Gillespie, Jr., of California, a career member of the Senior Foreign Service, Class of Counselor, as Ambassador to the Republic of Colombia. He would succeed Lewis Arthur Tambs.

Mr. Gillespie began his career in the Foreign Service as regional security officer at the American Embassy in Manila, Philippines, in 1965–1966. In 1966–1968 he served in the same capacity in Brussels, Belgium, and from there he was assigned to the U.S. NATO Mission as administrative of-

ficer in 1968–1970. Mr. Gillespie became a special assistant in the Bureau of Administration in 1970. In 1972 he went to the U.S. Embassy in Mexico as general services officer and served there until 1975, when he became a student at Syracuse University in Syracuse, NY. In 1976–1978 he served as administrative officer at the U.S. Embassy in Managua, Nicaragua, and in 1978 returned to the Department to be Associate Director of Management Operations. In 1980–1981 he attended the National War College and in 1981 became executive assistant in the Bureau of Inter-American Affairs. From 1983 to the present, he has been Deputy Assistant Secretary of State for the Caribbean in the Bureau of Inter-American Affairs.

Mr. Gillespie was born March 22, 1935, in Long Beach, CA. He received his B.A. in 1958 from the University of California. His foreign languages are Spanish, French, and German. Mr. Gillespie is married to the former Vivian Havens, and they have two children.

Remarks Following Discussions With Prime Minister Turgut Özal of Turkey
April 2, 1985

The President. Mr. Prime Minister, it's been a great pleasure to welcome you to the White House and to our Nation's Capital. I'm delighted that we've had this opportunity to discuss a wide variety of issues of mutual importance to our two countries.

Prime Minister Özal's official visit, the first in more than a decade by a Turkish leader, has been an important part of a long-overdue revitalization in U.S.-Turkish relations. Our two governments can be justly proud that by working together we have made great strides in improving bilateral understanding and cooperation. The Prime Minister has brought me up to date on major changes that have recently occurred in Turkey and on his plans for Turkey's future.

Mr. Prime Minister, you and President Evren have good reason to be proud of your success in rebuilding democratic institutions and rekindling economic growth. You have brought a difficult international debt problem under control and opened your country to expanded trade and foreign investment. Turkey's economic reform program reflects your courage and vision and is testimony to the determination of the Turkish people. I understand and appreciate the sacrifices that your countrymen have made in this difficult but necessary undertaking.

With regard to NATO, Prime Minister Özal and I reaffirmed our firm commitment to increase our cooperation within the alliance. The strength and cohesiveness of NATO have assured the security of the Western democracies for more than three decades. But our past success does not mean we can become complacent. The forces opposing NATO continue to modernize, and continuing dangers face us in southwest Asia and the eastern Mediterranean. We agree that our multilateral security ties and bilateral military cooperation are more important than ever.

We also discussed the need to strengthen and broaden U.S.-Turkish relations. Until recently, most Americans have known Turkey best as a NATO ally. Well, Mr. Prime Minister, thanks to your leadership and the forward-looking policies you're pursuing, we're now getting to know your country better as a trading partner and for growing opportunities in finance and investment.

A new U.S.-Turkish trade organization is being established, and new treaties and agreements in the economic field are being concluded. The United States welcomes these important and progressive developments. Let me also assure you that the United States remains committed to high levels of security assistance for Turkey to speed the modernization of your armed forces and to support your economic reform program. And, of course, this assistance serves the interests of both our countries. I reiterated to the Prime Minister that I will continue to urge the Congress to fund my full security assistance request for Turkey in fiscal year 1986.

In our discussion of international and regional issues, we devoted particular attention to the Cyprus problem, and I expressed satisfaction with the progress made in the U.N.-sponsored proximity talks last fall and with the Turkish Government's positive role in promoting that progress. Resolution of the Cyprus problem remains a high priority for our administration. Though the January summit, held under the U.N. Secretary-General's auspices, did not succeed, we remain hopeful that a fair and lasting settlement can be achieved.

It's essential, Mr. Prime Minister, that our two governments do all we can in support of the Secretary-General's Cyprus initiative. Turkey is a land bridge between Europe and Asia and provides us with a special view. The Ottoman Empire managed East-West problems long before America was even known to Europe.

Today, as before, Turkey serves as a particularly important cultural and diplomatic bridge between East and West. I thank you, Mr. Prime Minister, for briefing me on Turkish policies and diplomacy in areas of great importance to both of us. You're a good friend and important ally, and I thank you for all that you're doing to strengthen our cooperation. Together, we're serving the cause of peace and freedom.

Mr. Prime Minister, in your visit to America and as you reach out to the American people to acquaint them better with Turkish achievements and hopes, please be assured that we'll do all we can to make our bilateral relations even closer.

Mr. Prime Minister, I know that your visit will make an important contribution to the further development of our relations. So, again, welcome to Washington, and God-speed.

The Prime Minister. I wish to thank President Reagan for the warm welcome he has extended to me. My visit to this great, friendly nation has a particular importance in view of the fact that this is the first visit for 14 years by a Turkish Prime Minister. Our talks have been extensive, open, and very constructive.

I have renewed to President Reagan the heartfelt congratulations of my government for his impressive victory at the elections. I have also expressed my congratulations for his success in expanding the American economy, which I hope will be to the bene-

fit of all of us.

I have expressed to the President my assessment of the issues which Turkey follows with utmost attention. We live in a turbulent world, and as far as Turkey is concerned, our region is at the present full of dangers. Again, on this occasion, I have realized how deep and strong are the bonds of friendship, alliance, and cooperation between Turkey and the United States.

I have particularly appreciated the consideration shown by the President and his administration for Turkey and for the development of Turkish-American relations. I consider this attention as a recognition of the steady commitment of the Turkish Government to democracy, peace, and defense.

Turkey's new economic policies, I believe, are well understood by the Reagan administration. Our exchange of views confirmed the existence of broad and encouraging convergence. Both administrations, I believe, are strongly committed to dialog as the best means to solve international problems. The basic cause of both of us remains peace and stability in the world.

We are also firmly convinced that a substantial balanced and verifiable reduction of armaments is an essential condition for a safer world. I have explained to the President our views as far as the situation in our region is concerned. I must say that we view the situation as quite dangerous and unstable.

I wish to thank President Reagan for this fruitful exchange of views. For me it was a confirmation of how much the sharing of values and aspirations in a context of long-standing friendship makes it easier to reach mutual understanding and agreements.

Thank you.

Note: The President spoke to reporters at 1:21 p.m. at the South Portico of the White House. Earlier, the President and the Prime Minister met in the Oval Office and then attended a luncheon in the Residence.

Nomination of Clayton Yeutter To Be United States Trade Representative
April 2, 1985

The President today announced his intention to nominate Clayton Yeutter to be United States Trade Representative. He would succeed William E. Brock.

Since 1978 Mr. Yeutter has been president and chief executive officer of the Chicago Mercantile Exchange. Previously he was a senior partner in the law firm of Nelson, Harding, Yeutter & Leonard in Lincoln, NE, in 1977–1978. Mr. Yeutter was Deputy Special Trade Representative in 1975–1977. Prior to that time, he served at the Department of Agriculture as Assistant Secretary for International Affairs and Commodity Programs (1974–1975); Assistant Secretary for Marketing and Consumer Services (1973–1974); and Administrator, Consumer and Marketing Service (1970–1971). He was director of the University of Nebraska Mission in Colombia in 1968–1970 and executive assistant to the Governor of

Nebraska in 1966–1968. He was a faculty member in the department of agricultural economics at the University of Nebraska in 1960–1966. From 1957 until 1975, he operated a 2,500-acre farming-ranching-cattle feeding enterprise in central Nebraska.

Mr. Yeutter serves as a member of the boards of directors of ConAgra, Inc., the U.S. Meat Export Federation, the Japan America Society of Chicago, Inc., and the Chicago-Tokyo Bank. He is a member and immediate past chairman of the board of directors of the Chicago Association of Commerce & Industry and a member of the board of trustees of Winrock, Inc., in Morrilton, AR.

He graduated from the University of Nebraska (B.S., 1952; J.D., 1963; Ph.D., 1966). He is married, has four children, and resides in Hinsdale, IL. He was born December 10, 1930, in Eustis, NE.

Remarks at a Ceremony Celebrating the 90th Birthday of John J. McCloy
April 2, 1985

The President. We are delighted to have so many distinguished guests here today as we pay tribute on his birthday to one of America's most distinguished public servants. John McCloy has had a long life—90 years—and most of it marked by unparalleled service to his country and humanity.

Beginning with Franklin Roosevelt, he has served nine Presidents in a wide variety of assignments. Let me testify personally to the wisdom of John's counsel. I'm proud to say he was a member of our 1980 transition team, and I can recall the insight and advice that he gave me on American-German relations at the time—insight and advice that is just as timely today as they were then.

In a few weeks I'll have a chance to more

formally celebrate the friendship of the German and American peoples. But let me say now what no one can question: It was the heroic work of men like John McCloy during the difficult postwar period that did much to preserve world freedom and unite our two nations in friendship.

And on this note, President von Weizsäcker, let me say how pleased we are to have you here today to celebrate this occasion. Your presence is an honor for the American people, but I think it's also a sign of the deep affection and high esteem the German people have for John McCloy.

We're also honored to have with us today the mayor of Berlin, Eberhard Diepgen. He has a special presentation to make on behalf of the people of his city—a people who gratefully remember John McCloy's extraordinary work in the aftermath of the Berlin blockade and airlift.

It would take too long to recite for you the rest of John McCloy's many important contributions to our country and to the cause of peace and freedom. From wartime intrigue and espionage to European reconstruction after World War II, to disarmament negotiations spanning more than 30 years, John McCloy's high intellect and selfish heart—selfless heart; I shouldn't have mispronounced that word above all—John McCloy's selfless heart has made a difference, an enduring difference, in the lives of millions.

So, as your President, John, I salute you today not only for myself and all the Presidents you've served so well but for all your countrymen and the millions of people around the world whose lives you helped make safer because of your devotion to duty and to the cause of humanity. And again, a very happy birthday from all of us.

And now I would like to ask President von Weizsäcker to say a few words—Mr. President.

President von Weizsäcker. Mr. President, may I join you on behalf of all my fellow Germans, both here and at home, in honoring a great man to whom both our nations owe an immense gratitude.

The Federal Republic of Germany today is one of the free and prosperous countries in the world—a democracy of tested stability, an important partner in the Atlantic alliance. This seems rather natural and obvious and not particularly noteworthy to us today, but it was by no means to be foreseen in the early postwar period in Europe.

A decisive role in making this miracle possible was played by the man we are honoring today—by John McCloy. It was his human decency in helping the beaten enemy to recover. It was his trust in freedom, his confidence in the deep roots of freedom among the Germans, that largely contributed to reestablish the free society in my country and to enable us to join the free nations in Europe and in the Atlantic community.

His realistic judgment, his vitality, and his actual influence were just as immense as were his fairness and his modesty. So, he became one of the foremost to have turned enemies into friends. The official visit which you, Mr. President, are going to pay to my country soon will reinforce the deep ties that bind us together. We share our values of freedom; we share the responsibility for peace; we share our future destiny.

So, it remains our common task to transmit this spirit to a younger generation. It is in this light that you, Mr. President, will be our most welcome guest a month from now. And it is in this mind that I have come to bring the warmest wishes of the German people and to pay tribute to John McCloy, a great statesman, a great American, and a great friend.

Now, with your permission, Mr. President, may I now ask the governing mayor of Berlin, Eberhard Diepgen, to say a few words in honoring McCloy from the Berliners.

Mayor Diepgen. Mr. President, the Bundestag President, the Berlin Senate, and the Berlin House of Representatives are today conferring upon you, Mr. McCloy, the dignity of an honorary citizen. This is the highest distinction that free Berlin can award.

As a high commissioner of an occupying power, only a few years after a terrible war, you, Mr. McCloy, helped us to rebuild the country which had been destroyed. And you helped us to attain the way of life of a free democracy.

When we Berliners speak about you, we think of the cessation of this mounting problem, the Marshall plan aid, and the rebirth of the Berlin economy. And we think of the American Memorial Library, the early years of the Free University, and the work of the Aspen Institute in our city. And we think of the unforgettable visit of President John F. Kennedy in Berlin.

That the free part of Berlin could become birthplace and symbol of membership of the free part of our country in the Western community—the community of ideas—is something which in a large extent we owe to you.

But in this hour, we do not look only back into the past with gratitude. In the spirit of the honorary citizen, in the spirit of the city of Berlin, we want to cement the German-American partnership and develop it further. Together, we must, and I'm sure we can, find the answers to the great questions of our time—war, hunger, unemployment, and the destruction of nature.

Mr. McCloy, I should like to read out the text of the document of the honorary citizen: "The Berlin Senate in agreement with the Berlin House of Representatives confers upon Mr. John J. McCloy the honorary citizenship of the state and the city of Berlin. In gratitude, we thereby honor the former High Commissioner of the United States of America in Germany and Chairman of the Board of the Ford Foundation for his outstanding services to Berlin. John McCloy is closely connected with the reconstruction and development of this city. His dedication contributed to a great extent to understanding of Berlin in the United States of America and to preservation of peace and freedom."

Mr. McCloy, I congratulate you.

Mr. McCloy. Thank you very much, indeed, Mr. Bürgermeister—[*inaudible*]. [*Laughter*]

I'll respond to that. Well, thank you very much. You're the *regierender bürgermeister* [governing mayor] of Berlin. Mr. President, thank you very much, indeed, for the comments that you made.

I'm a little sensitive about my age, Mr. President. But I think I ought to record the fact that I have served in two World Wars, and I served in World War I with a man who fought the Indians on the Plains. How short the span of American history really is. But that connotes—that particular fact— that, although I'm a little long in the tooth, the country has really got a very young life, and its great destinies are ahead of it.

I have another connotation, Mr. President, and that is that compared to me, what a spring chicken you are. [*Laughter*]

The President. John, you've made my day. [*Laughter*]

Mr. McCloy. Okay, well, this honor that I have received today—I'm very sensitive about my old age; I'm very aware of it. Someone said the other day that—to me— I'm sure he was a friend of mine—he said: "Jack, did you ever stop and think that with short of a few years, your life represents one-half of the entire life of the country?" Well, I hadn't thought of it before. It was a rather staggering statistic. But I've been thinking of it since.

Now, as for this very, very fine honor you've done me, Mr. Bürgermeister—you know, in Berlin, every time we went up there, it was very pleasant. As I got off the train or the plane—whatever it was in that period of the blockade—but as soon as I got off the plane, it was: "*Willkommen, Herr McCloy.*" We could make a lot of mistakes down in the zone, but we couldn't make any mistakes up in Berlin. They were glad to see ya. And it was really a very comforting thing—the welcome that you got up there. And I stop and think frequently how much we owe to the Berliner, the Berliner with his *geist* [spirit] and his *mut* [courage] and his civil courage guess is the word. Did I pronounce that right?

What the—not only Western city or Germany but the entire free world owes to the vigor and the strength and the spirit, the *mut* and, as I say, the civil courage of the Berliner. And we will continue for a long time to be grateful for the inspiration which he gave us because of his display of those features.

Well, I won't reminisce anymore. But I want to thank everybody here, and particularly the Secretary of State and the Vice President and this entire turnout. I see a great many people with whom I've had a good many vicissitudes. And let me just say how deeply appreciative I am of this tribute to me and how grateful I am for it.

Thank you all very much.

Note: The President spoke at 4:30 p.m. in the Rose Garden at the White House.

Appointment of Robert B. Delano as a Member of the Advisory Committee for Trade Negotiations
April 3, 1985

The President today announced his intention to appoint Robert B. Delano to be a member of the Advisory Committee for Trade Negotiations for a term of 2 years. This is a reappointment.

Since 1980 Mr. Delano has been serving as president of the American Farm Bureau Federation in Park Ridge, IL. He was vice president of the American Farm Bureau Federation in 1976–1980. He also operates a 400-acre grain farm. He has been president of the Southern Farm Bureau Life Insurance Co. since 1975.

He graduated from Virginia Polytechnic Institute and State University (B.S., 1944). He is married, has two children, and resides in Warsaw, VA. He was born July 8, 1924, in Warsaw, VA.

Nomination of Robert E. Rader, Jr., To Be a Member of the Occupational Safety and Health Review Commission
April 3, 1985

The President today announced his intention to nominate Robert E. Rader, Jr., to be a member of the Occupational Safety and Health Review Commission for the term expiring April 27, 1991. He would succeed Timothy F. Cleary.

Since 1979 Mr. Rader has been a partner in the firm of McCarty, Wilson, Rader & Mash in Ennis, TX. Previously, he was general counsel for Gibsons Discount Centers, Inc., in 1971–1979 and an associate with the law firm of Story, Armstrong & Steger in Dallas, TX (1969–1971).

He graduated from Harding College (1966) and Southern Methodist University Law School (1969). He is married, has three children, and resides in Ennis, TX. He was born September 11, 1944, in Cleveland, OH.

Nomination of Onalee McGraw To Be a Member of the National Council on Educational Research
April 3, 1985

The President today announced his intention to nominate Onalee McGraw to be a member of the National Council on Educational Research for a term expiring September 30, 1987. This is a reappointment.

Dr. McGraw is an educational consultant to the Heritage Foundation. She is also the author of three monographs published by the Heritage Foundation on education and family: Secular Humanism and the Schools: The Issue Whose Time Has Come; Family Choice in Education: The New Imperative; and The Family, Feminism and the Therapeutic State.

She graduated from Whittier College (B.A., 1961) and Georgetown University (Ph.D., 1970). She is married, has three children, and resides in McLean, VA. She was born October 4, 1939, in San Luis Obispo, CA.

Nomination of Marian North Koonce To Be a Member of the National Council on the Handicapped
April 3, 1985

The President today announced his intention to nominate Marian North Koonce to be a member of the National Council on the Handicapped for a term expiring September 23, 1987. This is a reappointment.

She is owner and manager of Willowbrook Ranch. She was secretary and treasurer of Western U.S. Construction Co. in 1966–1980 and co-owner of Adobes, a construction company, in 1959–1963. She is an active member of the Santa Barbara auxiliary of the Easter Seal Society.

Mrs. Koonce attended the University of Texas. She is married, has six children, and resides in Santa Barbara, CA. She was born August 11, 1924, in Yoakum, TX.

Remarks at a White House Meeting With a Group Concerned About Missing and Exploited Children
April 3, 1985

The President. I know the problem, of course, that brings us together—missing and exploited children. And it's a major issue, I believe, in America today and a problem that can threaten every American family, rich or poor. And the possibility of a kidnaping or abuse to a child is one of the major fears that I think parents now face. So, each of you are here today because you're integrally involved in the missing and exploited children issue.

Just last May we launched the National Center for Missing and Exploited Children to help address part of this issue. I know its success. And I'm pleased to see so many of the Board members, along with the Directors, here today. They have set up, among other things, a hotline where people can call in instantly. And, as I understand it, they've been getting about 225 calls a day.

Many of you here represent other major efforts, public and private, that can address these critical problems. But there's much more to be done, and I know that you've discussed ways of doing more.

So, I'm asking you today to form a new partnership for child safety. And this partnership can involve law enforcement organizations, school systems, community service groups, in coordination with the Attorney General and his offices at the Department of Justice. And I'd like to ask if you could report back to me in 3 weeks' time with your recommendations of how such a partnership should be structured. And I'll let you keep track of the calendar.

And it's my hope that this partnership can be launched so that every child in the country will have the opportunity to be safe and secure, and you're the people who will make it work. And you have my heartfelt thanks for what you're doing and what you continue to do.

Now, I understand we have a brief pause when the—[*inaudible*].

Reporter. Mr. President, Senator Dole said that the budget is going to be a hard sell. What are you going to do to help sell it—this compromise?

The President. What I always do—sell. [*Laughter*]

Q. Is it going to be tough?

The President. Isn't it always?

Note: The President spoke at 2:01 p.m. in the Cabinet Room at the White House.

Remarks Congratulating the Villanova University Wildcats on Winning the National Collegiate Athletic Association Basketball Championship
April 4, 1985

The President. It's a pleasure to have you all here today. We aren't able to give you a reception as enthusiastic as the one you got up in Philadelphia, but I want you to know that we welcome you with the same heartfelt admiration. And Rollie Massimino, members of the Villanova Wildcats: Well done. You not only represent sportsmen of great talent, you represent the spirit of overcoming great odds that Americans love so much.

You're being called the "Cinderella Team," but I don't see anyone around here who looks like he could fit into a glass slipper. [*Laughter*] Then, again, it wasn't magic; it was long, hard hours of preparation that enabled you to capture the championship. As Gary McLain said: "We worked so hard for this; no one in America knows how hard we worked. This is what can happen when you really work hard."

And, Rollie, you deserve a great deal of credit for that preparation and also for everything you've done to turn a group of tremendous individual players into a team that will go down in the history books.

I know that Monday night's victory was also a bittersweet one for you. A person whose life was so much a part of the history of Villanova basketball passed away that morning. Alex Severance left a long legacy with 60 years at the university.

And there's someone else here who deserves recognition: Jake Niven. And, Jake, I know how much you mean to this team and to all of the students at Villanova. This championship is a tribute to you and to Alex Severance. You've made your mark, and your personal courage has inspired greatness.

And it was greatness. It's almost hard to believe that any team managed to make 78.6 percent of their shots. I was beginning to think it was a hundred percent, the way it looked on television. That's better shooting than I used to do in one of those western movies. [*Laughter*] You never ran out of ammunition, and you could always do retakes. [*Laughter*]

But all of you did an extraordinary job. With the eyes of the Nation on you, you didn't buckle under the pressure; your hands stayed steady. One of the longest moments in sport must be during a jump shot, in that fraction of a second when you're suspended in the air, and the crowd is yelling, and you're looking for a small white cylinder that seems to be a mile away, and you have to throw the ball into that tiny net before Pat Ewing comes out of nowhere to block it.

A special word of congratulations to the winner of the tournament's Most Valuable Player Award, Ed Pinckney. And, Ed, I don't know if playing against Ewing is like playing against Tip O'Neill—[*laughter*]—but I understand exactly what it's like to be up against an awesome opponent. So, congratulations.

The game was a testimonial to the enormous talent on both sides. I think you'll all agree with me that Georgetown's team did a great job and that their sportsmanship was in the highest tradition of the game. As one of their team members said, "We went out with style." Well, they did just that. And I know all of us here today have tremendous respect for those fellows as players, as individuals, and as a team.

You've all heard the old saying that "It isn't whether you win or lose, but how you play the game." I think it may be more accurate to say that winning isn't everything, but it sure beats coming in second. [*Laughter*]

Seriously, this is your day. You know the people of Philadelphia are proud of you, your families are proud of you. And today I just want you to know that all of your countrymen join your family and friends in applauding your achievements.

So, God bless each one of you. And thank you very much for being here.

Coach Massimino. Mr. President, friends, this is really a pleasure. In fact, I'm probably more nervous than when you saw all of us running up and down that bench during the course of that Georgetown game. But even though you're a Hoya fan—[*laughter*]—we would like to make you an honorary Wildcat. [*Laughter*]

This is certainly a tremendous opportunity for all of us, our families, the players, Jake Niven, whom you brought out, and everybody else associated with the Villanova family. Again, I want to sincerely thank you. This just culminates the total dedication and all the hard work that these young men have done.

Thank you very much.

The President. Thank you, Coach.

Mr. Pinckney. I'd like to present a jacket on behalf of the Villanova coaching staff and players to the President.

The President. Thank you very much. I'm very proud to have that. Thank you. Thank you all very much.

And, Coach, I can't be a fan of anyone. [*Laughter*] I just think of you all as constituents. [*Laughter*] But I congratulate all of you, and I do thank you very much for this.

And I understand we interrupted your spring vacation. [*Laughter*] I'm sorry about that. Perhaps we should have waited.

Mr. Pinckney. It's beautiful to be here.

The President. Well, pleased to have you here.

Note: The President spoke at 10:46 a.m. in the Rose Garden at the White House.

Nomination of Edward A. Curran To Be Chairman of the National Endowment for the Humanities
April 4, 1985

The President today announced his intention to nominate Edward A. Curran to be Chairman of the National Endowment for the Humanities, National Foundation on the Arts and the Humanities, for a term of 4 years. He would succeed William J. Bennett.

Mr. Curran has been serving as Deputy Director of the Peace Corps since 1982. Previously he was Director of the National Institute of Education at the Department of Education in 1981–1982. He was an Associate Director of the Office of Presidential Personnel at the White House in 1981. He served on the education transition team, office of the President-elect, in 1980–1981. Mr. Curran was headmaster of the National Cathedral School, Washington, DC, in 1968–1980.

In 1957–1968 he was employed by St. John's School of Houston, TX, as a teacher and dean of student affairs. In 1960 he established schools for children of American national employees in Ecuador, Argentina, and Bolivia for Tennessee Gas Transmission Corp. In 1955–1957 he taught at Englewood School for Boys, Englewood, NJ, and acted as chairman of the lower school.

He graduated from Yale University (B.A., 1955) and Duke University (M.A.T., 1968). He is married, has two children, and resides in Bethesda, MD. He was born August 22, 1933, in North Adams, MA.

Nomination of Sheldon J. Krys To Be United States Ambassador to Trinidad and Tobago
April 4, 1985

The President today announced his intention to nominate Sheldon J. Krys, of Maryland, a career member of the Senior Foreign Service, Class of Minister-Counselor, as Ambassador to the Republic of Trinidad and Tobago. He would succeed Melvin Herbert Evans.

Mr. Krys began his career in radio/TV and public relations in 1955–1961. He was with KRSD radio station in South Dakota, WWDC in Washington, DC, and WGAY in Maryland. He was the owner and the director of Chris Seldon Public Relations.

He began his government career with the Federal Mediation and Conciliation Service in Washington, DC, as consultant to the Director of Public Affairs in 1961–1962. He came to the Department of State in 1962 as education and cultural affairs officer and in 1965 went to London as management officer. He served in that capacity until he became an international relations officer in London in 1967–1969. He returned to Washington and served as personnel officer in the Bureau of Inter-American Affairs in 1969–1970. In 1970–1974 he was Director of Personnel for Latin America and in October 1972 became a Foreign Service officer. In 1974 he went to Belgrade as administrative counselor and served there until he was assigned to the National War College in 1976. In 1977 he became a Foreign Service inspector. In 1979–1983 Mr. Krys was Executive Director of the Bureau of Near East and South Asian Affairs. He became Principal Deputy Director for Management Operations in 1983, where he served until 1984 when he became Executive Assistant to the Under Secretary of State for Management.

Mr. Krys attended the University of Maryland and National War College. His foreign languages are French and Serbo-Croatian. He is married to the former Doris Marie de Hemptinne, and they have three children. He was born June 15, 1934, in New York, NY.

Nomination of John C. Lawn To Be Administrator of the Drug Enforcement Administration
April 4, 1985

The President today announced his intention to nominate John C. Lawn to be Administrator of Drug Enforcement, Department of Justice. He would succeed Francis M. Mullen, Jr.

Since 1982 Mr. Lawn has been serving as Deputy Administrator of the Drug Enforcement Administration at the Department of Justice. Previously he was Acting Deputy Administrator of the Drug Enforcement Administration. He was special agent in charge of the FBI office in San Antonio, TX, in 1980–1982; section chief of the FBI headquarters in 1979–1980; assistant special agent in charge in the FBI office in Kansas City, MO, in 1977–1979; and supervisor at FBI headquarters in 1973–1977. He received the Law Enforcement Award given by the Association of Federal Investigators in 1983.

He graduated from St. Francis College of Brooklyn (B.A., 1957) and St. John's University (M.A., 1964). He is married, has four children, and resides in Fairfax Station, VA. He was born June 2, 1935, in Brooklyn, NY.

Appointment of Albert R. Brashear as Deputy Press Secretary for Domestic Affairs and Special Assistant to the President
April 4, 1985

The President today appointed Albert R. (Rusty) Brashear to be Deputy Press Secretary for Domestic Affairs and Special Assistant to the President. He will succeed Max Marlin Fitzwater.

In 1984–1985 he served as assistant to the Secretary and Director of Public Affairs at the Department of the Interior. For a brief period following that, he was Director of Public Affairs at the Environmental Protection Agency.

He was Press Director for the Environmental Protection Agency in 1982–1984 and press secretary to Congressman Robin Beard in 1979–1983. He was executive assistant to the president of the World's Fair in Knoxville, TN, in 1977–1979. He served as director of alumni programs at the University of Tennessee in 1975–1977 and news director for WBIR–TV–AM–FM in Knoxville, TN, in 1970–1974.

He graduated from the University of Tennessee (B.A., 1971). He is married, has two children, and resides in Alexandria, VA. He was born October 17, 1942, in Kingsport, TN.

Appointment of Dale A. Petroskey as Assistant Press Secretary
April 4, 1985

Dale A. Petroskey will become Assistant Press Secretary in the Office of the Press Secretary. He will succeed C. Anson Franklin. He will serve as a spokesman and manage the day-to-day operations of the Lower Press Office. In addition, he will be liaison with congressional press secretaries and Republican campaign organizations.

Since December 1981 Mr. Petroskey has been serving as administrative assistant to Congressman Bill Goodling. In November 1983 he also became press secretary to Congressman Goodling. Previously he was press secretary to Congressman Mark Siljander and before that was campaign manager and press secretary to the Siljander for Congress Committee. In 1978–1981 he was assistant press secretary to the Michigan House Republican Caucus.

Mr. Petroskey graduated from Michigan State University (B.A., 1978). He is married and resides in Alexandria, VA. He was born August 17, 1955, in Detroit, MI.

Remarks Following Discussions With President Belisario Betancur Cuartas of Colombia
April 4, 1985

President Reagan. President Betancur, it's a pleasure to have you visit us here in Washington. I, in particular, am pleased to have had this opportunity to reciprocate the hospitality that you extended to me during my visit to Bogotá in 1982.

Your present visit, Mr. President, gives us the opportunity to affirm, once again, the solid ties of friendship and good will between our two countries. As the leaders of free people, we share a commitment to the democratic ideals, which are at the heart of our societies.

Today we have renewed our mutual commitment to promoting democracy in this hemisphere, pursuing peace in Central America, and eliminating the scourge of narcotics trafficking from our societies. We have also explored areas of cooperation which can enhance the economic well-being of our peoples.

President Betancur, in trying to bring peace to Central America, you've played a key role in the Contadora process. And the United States fully supports the objectives of the Contadora process.

We join you in seeking a comprehensive and fully verifiable settlement of regional problems. And we, like you, believe peace can be achieved through national reconciliation and democracy. Colombia and El Salvador, for example, have invited talks with their opponents and encouraged them to be part of a truly democratic process. Those who seek democracy in Nicaragua have asked the Sandinistas to engage in talks as a step toward peace and democracy in Nicaragua. We hope that the Sandinistas will take that step toward reconciliation.

Later today I will be talking to the American people in greater detail about this subject. I am glad that President Betancur and I were able to discuss how the United States can best help the Contadora countries achieve all of the agreed-upon objectives for Central America, including national reconciliation in Nicaragua.

Mr. President, we admire your determination to end the strife which has plagued your country. The citizens of Colombia are indeed lucky to have a leader of vision, courage, and compassion. We wish you success and hope that those who have fought with weapons learn to work within the democratic process. It is appropriate that we praise your efforts to foster peace and brotherhood during this holy week.

Mr. President, your personal courage and dedication are also evident in your government's all-out battle against narcotics traffickers. You have my unbounded respect for what you're doing.

The production of illicit narcotics and the peddling of these drugs corrupt our societies, our children, and, with them, our future. The struggle against this unmitigated evil unites all good and decent people. We look forward to Mrs. Betancur's return

here later this month to join Nancy and other First Ladies in discussing the problem, especially as it affects our young people.

In the United States, the fight against drug use has a top priority. We're trying to help those on drugs get off, to prevent those not involved from starting. And we're doing our best to smash the trade in illegal drugs. This matter is of vital concern to us both, and in finding solutions to the problem, Colombia and the United States are full partners, as we affirm today in our joint statement on narcotics.

The illegal drug trade, as we both agree, is a cancer. Commercial trade, on the other hand, serves the interests of both our peoples. While Americans enjoy Colombian products such as coffee, cut flowers, and tropical fruits, Colombians benefit from U.S. technology and goods such as heavy machinery, chemicals, and wheat.

At a time when both our governments grapple with trade deficits in a world of many trading partners, let us build on our history of cooperation to develop trade policies which strengthen our economies, give incentive to enterprise, and encourage exchange between our peoples.

I look forward, Mr. President, to working closely with you on these and other significant matters. On behalf of the United States, I extend warm wishes to both you, President Betancur, and to the Colombian people. We bid you farewell. We wish you a safe and happy journey home and a happy Easter.

President Betancur. Mr. President, members of the Cabinet, my visit to the United States, which was planned some months ago at the invitation of President Reagan, comes to an end today in the cordial climate of the White House.

It has been a good opportunity to speak with President Reagan, with Vice President Bush, with Secretary Shultz, and with other members of this administration on several issues—some bilateral, others multilateral—which are of interest to the people of the Americas and, in particular, to our two nations.

Today, at your invitation, we have met in Washington to examine a number of multilateral and bilateral issues: among the first, the Central American crisis, the process of greater democracy in Latin America, the problems stemming from the foreign debt, the strengthening of the international coffee agreement and of multilateral lending institutions, and the international fight against the drug traffic; among the latter, the macroeconomic adjustment program, with self-discipline and economic growth, and the trade relations between Colombia and the United States.

I have also taken advantage of this visit to exchange ideas with distinguished Congressmen, with senior officials from the international financial institutions, with outstanding personalities from the academic world, and important leaders from the U.S. private sector.

Regarding the Central American issue, I was able to bring up my concern with the problems that affect that region. I insisted on the urgency of reactivating the negotiating process of Contadora and of exhausting all efforts of conviction to implement the principles, commitments, and recommendations which are part of the document of objectives of the act of Contadora.

During a recent visit to the Central American region's countries, I was able to see for myself the renewed desire on their part to provide new possibilities for a dialog and, for the countries which are a part of the Contadora group, their determination to offer whatever possibilities there may be in this same respect.

I am pleased to state that in my talks today with President Reagan I have encountered the same constructive spirit and his decision to provide propitious conditions to carry out reconciliation dialogs that will ultimately lead to the full participation of the political and social forces in the democratic process of the countries affected by violence and civil strife.

I am pleased that the U.S. Government at this critical moment is approaching the problems of Central America with an open mind. And I am certain that this attitude will prevail throughout the region.

On the subject of narcotics, we are carrying out a frontal assault in my country in this respect. I refer you to the communique that President Reagan and I have issued,

which clearly and categorically expresses the will of both countries to work together to rescue humanity from this scourge.

During the conversations with the authorities of the United States, I underscored the existing link that there is between the external debt and democracy and requested that a new round of negotiations, multilateral negotiations, be held to ease exports from developing countries. I have noted with interest that the United States looks upon the coming economic summit to be held at Bonn as a good occasion to examine this important subject.

In connection to Colombia's autonomous program of macroeconomic adjustment, I wish to place on record the positive support that we have received from the Inter-American Development Bank, from the World Bank, from the International Monetary Fund, as well as from the Government of the United States through its Federal Reserve, and from the Treasury Department. I have personally seen tangible proof of this support while on this visit.

We believe that the time has come, as I said before Congress, for the United States and Latin America to redefine the parameters of their mutual relations. We need what I would call a new treatment—a new understanding, a common doctrine—an alliance for peace, with the determination to go from mere tolerance, that has marked the relations between Latin America and the United States, to the formulation of a new scheme of open, constructive, and fruitful cooperation.

This new treatment, this alliance for peace, will not only improve economic relations in the hemisphere, but it will also mean the adoption of political objectives to defend democracy, which is the great spiritual value of American civilization. This consensus would allow us to strengthen the hemisphere's political institutions, would enhance the likelihood of peace and the possibilities of an enduring economic growth.

Finally, Mr. President and members of the Cabinet, it is not altogether possible in these brief remarks to bring out the significance that I assign to this historic visit to the United States, which has had a very tight schedule, as you know. I have made known to the authorities, candidly and without subterfuges, the totality of my ideas on issues which are of interest to us both.

I have been heard with attention and respect as befits the tradition of freedom and democracy of this great nation. I am pleased to state that it has been so and that I hope that my views and remarks will create a greater climate of understanding between the United States and Latin America—this vast, beautiful, and dynamic subcontinent that cherishes freedom and un-derstands that to maintain and strengthen it, we need justice, and we need development.

Thank you very much, Mr. President.

Note: The President spoke to reporters at 1:25 p.m. at the South Portico of the White House. President Betancur spoke in Spanish, and his remarks were translated by an interpreter. Earlier, the two Presidents met in the Oval Office and then attended a luncheon in the Residence.

Joint Columbia-United States Statement on Drug Abuse and Trafficking
April 4, 1985

During our meeting today, we discussed the drug scourge which afflicts both our nations, the Hemisphere at large, and mankind generally. We reviewed the measures our two nations are taking and will take, separately and together, to combat the production, trafficking, demand and use of illicit narcotics.

Our nations recognize the terrible effect drug abuse has on the health and well-being of individual users, as well as more generally on the economies and public morality of both societies. It is especially deplorable when the drug poisons are found among the young and even small children.

Drug trafficking is a criminal activity that has no frontiers and can only be controlled by a combined effort of all countries involved. We have shared our concern that the financial power resulting from the enormous profits of illicit narcotics trade poses a terrible threat to democracy in the Americas. Our mutual dedication to the anti-narcotics struggle is an integral part of the close relations that exist between our two nations. We both see a vital need to enlist the cooperation of other governments in this intensified effort.

We understand that the gravity of the problem is a consequence of both illegal production and distribution of drugs as well as growing demand. We also understand these factors are closely related and all efforts to suppress one without at the same time taking equally vigorous actions against the other will be fruitless. For these reasons, each government is prepared to assume its responsibilities, eliminating both illegal production and drug abuse.

The United States recognizes the effort, the commitment of resources and the sacrifices that Colombia has made in destroying crops and laboratories, seizing shipments and bringing suspected drug traffickers to justice, including the extradition of traffickers accused of narcotics crimes in the United States. For the United States' part, enforcement activities are increasing and prevention and education programs are having positive results in reducing drug abuse.

We are in entire agreement on the need to continue these intensified efforts and to ensure the closest possible collaboration in the war against narcotics. Both nations reaffirm respect for our mutual legal obligations to extradite traffickers under our existing treaty, and will remain in close contact to periodically examine and improve the framework of our legal and law enforcement cooperation as necessary to adapt to changing conditions as we learn from our experiences.

We have noted with satisfaction the beginning of new areas of cooperation against narcotics. Mrs. Reagan and Mrs. Betancur, who met earlier today at the White House, look forward to their meeting at the First Ladies' Conference on Drug Abuse, which will be held in Washington on April 24th. We are confident those meetings, in which they will play leading roles, will have a lasting impact.

Colombia renews the commitment to fight against drug trafficking at all levels in order to destroy the crops, the laboratories where drugs are processed, to interrupt the transportation to the U.S. market and to see that those responsible for the trafficking are severely punished. The United States commits itself to increasing its efforts to diminish use and demand of drugs, destroy crops and to strengthen its support for the war against narcotics.

The cost of success in the past has been high. It has included the life of a Colombian Cabinet Minister, Rodrigo Lara Bonilla, and law enforcement officers from both countries. We cannot allow such sacrifices to have been in vain. We pledge to each other to revitalize and intensify our efforts to destroy the trafficking network. Our decision is irreversible, our dedication total. Nothing will deter us from this fight.

RONALD REAGAN
BELISARIO BETANCUR

Remarks Announcing a Central American Peace Proposal and a Question-and-Answer Session With Reporters
April 4, 1985

The President. Good afternoon, and for those of the Christian and Jewish faiths, this is the eve of the most holy season, and it's a season for peace and a season for all people of good will to strive together for peace.

I want to announce today a proposal for peace in Central America that can enable liberty and democracy to prevail in this troubled region and that can protect the security of our own borders, economy, and people.

On March 1st in San José, Costa Rica, the leaders of the Nicaraguan democratic resistance met with a broad coalition of other exiled Nicaraguan democrats. They agreed upon and signed an historic proposal to restore peace and democracy in their country. The members of the democractic resistance offered a cease-fire in return for an agreement by the Nicaraguan regime to begin a dialog, mediated by the Bishops Conference of the Roman Catholic Church, with the goal of restoring democracy through honest elections. To date the Nicaraguan regime has refused this offer.

The Central American countries, including Nicaragua, have agreed that internal reconciliation is indispensable to regional peace. But we know that, unlike President Duarte of El Salvador, who seeks a dialog with his opponents, the Communists in Nicaragua have turned, at least up until now, a cold shoulder to appeals for national reconciliation from the Pope and the Nicaraguan bishops. And we know that without incentives, none of this will change.

For these reasons, great numbers of Nicaraguans are demanding change and taking up arms to fight for the stolen promise of freedom and democracy. Over 15,000 farmers, small merchants, whites, blacks, and Miskito Indians have united to struggle for a true democracy.

We supported democracy in Nicaragua before, and we support democracy today. We supported national reconciliation before, and we support it today. We believe that democracy deserves as much support in Nicaragua as it has received in El Salvador. And we're proud of the help that we've given to El Salvador.

You may recall that in 1981 we were told that the Communist guerrillas were mounting a final offensive, the government had no chance, and our approach would lead to greater American involvement. Well, our critics were wrong; democracy and freedom are winning in El Salvador. President Duarte is pulling his country together and enjoys wide support from the people. And all of this with America's help kept strictly limited.

The formula that worked in El Salvador—support for democracy, self-defense, economic development, and dialog—will work for the entire region. And we couldn't have accomplished this without bipartisan support in Congress, backed up by the National Bipartisan Commission on Central America, headed by Henry Kissinger. And that's why, after months of consulting with congressional leaders and listening carefully to their concerns, I am making the following proposal: I'm calling upon both sides to lay down their arms and accept the offer of church-mediated talks on internationally supervised elections and an end to the repression now in place against the church, the press, and individual rights.

To the members of the democratic resistance, I ask them to extend their offer of a cease-fire until June 1st.

To the Congress, I ask for immediate release of the $14 million already appropriated. While the cease-fire offer is on the table, I pledge these funds will not be used for arms or munitions. These funds will be use for food, clothing, and medicine and other support for survival. The democratic opposition cannot be a partner in negotiations without these basic necessities.

If the Sandinistas accept this peace offer, I will keep my funding restrictions in effect. But peace negotiations must not become a cover for deception and delay. If there is no agreement after 60 days of negotiations, I will lift these restrictions, unless both sides ask me not to.

I want to emphasize that consistent with the 21 goals of the Contadoran process, the United States continues to seek: One, Nicaragua's implementation of its commitment to democracy made to the Organization of American States; two, an end to Nicaragua's aggression against its neighbors; three, a removal of the thousands of Soviet bloc, Cuban, PLO, Libyan, and other military and security personnel; and four, a return of the Nicaraguan military to a level of parity with their neighbors.

Now, later today I will be meeting with Arturo Cruz, Adolpho Calero, and Alfonso Robelo to discuss my proposal.

Democracy is the road to peace. But if we abandon the brave members of the democratic resistance, we will also remove all constraints on the Communists.

Democracy can succeed in Central America. But Congress must release the funds that can create incentives for dialog and peace. If we provide too little help, our choice will be a Communist Central America with Communist subversion spreading southward and northward. We face the risk that a hundred million people, from Panama to our open southern border, could come under the control of pro-Soviet regimes and threaten the United States with violence, economic chaos, and a human tidal wave of refugees.

Central America is not condemned to that dark future of endless violence. If the United States meets its obligations to help those now striving for democracy, they can create a bright future in which peace for all Americans will be secure.

So, in the spirit of Easter, let us make this so. I look forward to working with the Congress on this important matter in the coming weeks.

Q. What's the incentive for the Nicaraguan Government, Mr. President?

The President. Well, to end the bloodshed that is going on, to end the great economic crisis that is growing ever more worse in their country because of what they've done.

Q. Mr. President, [House Speaker] Tip O'Neill says that this is a dirty trick, that you're trying to hoodwink the American public into thinking that it is humanitarian aid, but it really is a secret plan to proceed militarily.

The President. Well, I don't think he's heard this particular plan yet. There's been consultations, but if he's calling this a dirty trick, he's got a funny definition of dirty tricks.

Q. Mr. President, if Congress should turn you down——

Q. What makes you think that this will make Congress more likely——

Q. Go ahead, Andrea [Andrea Mitchell, NBC News].

Q. —— to accept your aid?

The President. Well, because Congress, in all of their efforts to hinder our continued aid to the *contras* and to democracy down there, have emphasized the need for a peaceful and political solution and a solution of the kind we've talked about here that would result from discussion between the parties.

Q. Mr. President, would you ask——

Q. Mr. President, you've made it plain that the $14 million, you think, is essential. But if Congress should turn you down, will you look for some other avenue to help the *contras,* some other way to continue your desire to see a restructuring of the Nicaraguan Government?

The President. Well, we're not going to quit and walk away from them no matter what happens.

Q. Would you contemplate any military action against Nicaragua? You seem to be offering either/or, and the threat is the $14 million. Is that really enough to overthrow the Nicaraguan Government?

The President. It isn't a case of overthrowing, it is a case of returning to the goals of the revolution that both the *contras* and the Sandinistas fought for. And as far as our making war or anything, that has never been our intention. And we've repeated that over and over again.

Q. Mr. President, if there is a cease-fire and there are talks but they don't produce anything, what does the $14 million go for, then? Is that to purchase weapons for the *contras?*

The President. I said after 60 days, if no agreement can be reached and unless both sides ask us to continue the same process, then, I would think that we could use that $14 million to help the *contras* in any way.

Q. Mr. President——

Q. Mr. President——

Q. [*Inaudible*]—was operated on today for the fifth time——

The President. What's that?

Q. President Neves of Brazil was operated on today for the fifth time. And the reports of his health are not very hopeful. Do you have any comment on that?

The President. I'm having a little trouble because I ran out of a battery. [*Laughter*]

Q. The President of Brazil is——

The President. Oh, the President of Brazil.

Q. He's been operated on for the fifth time.

The President. Oh, oh, I'm sorry I——

Q. Do you have any comment about that?

The President. ——I certainly don't want to—yes, I do. I think that this was a great forward step for Brazil. And all we can do is hope and pray for his well-being.

Q. Mr. President, in what way will consist the help that you're going to give to the Colombian Government to proceed the fight against the narco traffic?

The President. Oh, we're in great agreement. And we're greatly admiring of what has been accomplished there and what the President has done. And in our talks today we made agreement. In fact, there will be a statement released on the subject of narcotics alone that we discussed today.

Q. Mr. President——

Q. You have been agreed with him about that narco traffic? Are you going to take some new action with the Contadora group?

The President. We agree with him, and he agrees with us. Well, we both are together on the fact that not only must we continue the program that he has started with regard to intercepting and preventing the shipment of drugs but also here where the largest market is, that we continue our efforts to take the customers away from the drugs, which must complement the efforts to take the drugs away from the customers.

Q. Mr. President, in your peace offer, is it conditioned on withdrawal of Soviet-Cuban-PLO advisers from Nicaragua or only talks and the end of repression?

The President. No. We think that this is part of the agreement that must be reached. We said these are the points that were made also by the *contras,* that they must stop being a threat to their neighbors, get the foreign forces out, and return to the democratic goals which they, themselves, told the Organization of American States was what they were fighting the revolution for.

Q. Mr. President, are the *contras* aware of this proposal of yours? Have you gone over this with them or with their leaders before——

The President. We are just in the process of notifying people of this. You're among the first to hear.

Q. Mr. President, the Sandinistas have already turned down the San José offer from the *contras*. What makes you think that they would accept this?

The President. Because I think there are other things that are involved here. I don't think that they want to be alone completely in the Americas with all of their neighbors on the other side. And we believe that we'll have the support of the Contadoras on this. And we think, as I say, they are having great problems as these hostilities go on. Now, no, you.

Q. Mr. President, even though——

Principal Deputy Press Secretary Speakes. Let's let this be the last question, please.

Q. ——you will stipulate that the $14 million will not go for weapons and ammunition, but will go for humanitarian aid——

The President. That's right.

Q. ——will not that money then free the *contras* to use the money that they have been using for food to buy weapons? And then isn't the bottom line still the same?

The President. Well, I have a feeling that they are not well-fixed enough to provide any of these things for themselves. And this, again, is one of the things that we have offered, that this will be used for that purpose for as long as they're negotiating to try and have a peaceful settlement.

Q. But they are now somehow managing to survive; I mean, they're getting food and that sort of thing. So, If you give the money for food, can they not then use the money they're now using for food and buy weapons?

The President. Well, let me say I think that they are close to desperate straits. But I'm going to leave here now because I'm going to be seeing you later in the day——

Q. Got a budget?

Q. Have you got a budget agreement?

The President. Wait a minute. And is Bud here? I'm going to——

Mr. Speakes. Bud's here and ready.

The President. There's——

Q. No, not Bud, budget.

Q. You got a budget agreement? Budget agreement.

Q. Budget.

Q. One more question, if you get this would you agree to bring home all of our troops from all of the countries in Central America?

The President. Well, the only troops that we have down there now are troops that are on various maneuvers and training exercises.

Q. That's right. That's right. But they are in danger, especially some that have just gone down there to Honduras——

The President. No.

Q. ——with their flack jackets and ammunition. And they know they're in danger.

The President. No, they're——

Q. There are men and women down there, sir, who are in danger. Will you promise to bring them all home?

The President. If you'll look back through history, you'll find out that we traditionally have used among our neighbors for jungle training exercises of this kind. And they're not—as some loud voices up on the Hill have said—they're not down there as a threat to anyone. They're down there as we're training new enlistees in our Army, to have a well-trained military that can fight any place that might be required. And this has been done in Honduras repeatedly before. And that's all it is. So, we don't have any occupying forces down there. We've got 55 advisers—I think the number still remains—in El Salvador.

Q. When they left the other day to go down there—another contingent of them, especially from Texas—they said on the way they knew there was recent events that made it much more dangerous, and their lives were at stake. And they took their ammunition and their—other preparations.

The President. Well, that sounds like the kind of scuttlebutt you hear when enlisted men start talking among themselves.

Q. Well, these were officers——

The President. Officers do it.

Q. Have you got a——

Q. How about the budget, sir?

Q. Got a budget agreement?

The President. What?

Q. What about the budget?

Q. You've given——

The President. Later on today someone will be talking to you about that.

Q. You've given on defense, haven't you, sir?

The President. What?

Q. You've given a little bit on defense.

The President. You'll hear all about it later this afternoon.

Q. You're going to cut the Social Security COLA's down a little bit, too, aren't you, sir?

The President. But right now—Bud, will you get up there—[*laughter*]—and put them back in line? You were a marine once.

Q. You're going to cut the Social Security COLA's a little bit, aren't you, sir?

The President. You'll hear everything at 4 o'clock.

Q. Do you think the Sandinistas will cry "Uncle"?

Note: The President spoke to reporters at 3:07 p.m. in the Briefing Room at the White House. Following the President's remarks, Assistant to the President for National Security Affairs Robert C. McFarlane continued to answer reporters' questions.

Appointment of Clyde H. Slease as a Member of the Board of Visitors to the United States Military Academy
April 4, 1985

The President today announced his intention to appoint Clyde H. Slease to be a member of the Board of Visitors to the United States Military Academy for a term expiring December 30, 1987. This is a reappointment.

Mr. Slease is counsel to the law firm of Watt, Tieder, Killian and Hoffer in Vienna, VA. He was labor counsel, assistant to the president, and vice president and general counsel of the Dravo Corp. in Pittsburgh, PA, in 1948–1978. He was an attorney with the firm of Paul, Lawrence & Wills in 1946–1948.

He graduated from Haverford College (B.S., 1938) and the University of Pittsburgh (J.D., LL.B., 1941). He is married, has two children, and resides in Edgewater, MD. He was born July 26, 1916, in Hackensack, NJ.

Proclamation 5314—National Weather Satellite Week, 1985
April 4, 1985

By the President of the United States of America

A Proclamation

The United States' weather satellites have tracked the Earth's weather since April 1, 1960, and have brought unique benefits to the American people and to the world.

Weather satellites have proven exceptionally valuable in detecting, monitoring, and giving early warning of hurricanes, severe storms, flash floods, and other life-threatening natural hazards, on a local, national, and international basis.

The international weather satellite search-and-rescue program has saved over three hundred lives since 1982. The achievements of the scientific and aerospace communities in developing weather satellites have contributed significantly to the United States' leadership in satellite technology, international cooperation in space, and an integrated global weather forecasting system.

Weather satellites have evolved into environmental satellites that also monitor snow and ice cover, forest damage, vegetation, forest fires, volcanic eruptions, sea surface temperatures, and ocean currents.

Environmental satellite data are used for

research and for commercial purposes in meteorology, hydrology, agriculture, oceanography, forestry, and fisheries. The United States' prestige is enhanced by the direct dissemination of environmental satellite data to more than one hundred and twenty countries.

The National Aeronautics and Space Administration has been the world leader in the development of experimental and prototypical weather and environmental satellites. The National Oceanic and Atmospheric Administration of the Department of Commerce has demonstrated outstanding leadership in the management of operational weather and environmental satellite systems and programs.

The Congress, by Senate Joint Resolution 62, has designated the week of March 31, 1985 through April 6, 1985, as "National Weather Satellite Week," and authorized and requested the President to issue a proc-

lamation in observance of this event.

Now, Therefore, I, Ronald Reagan, President of the United States of America, do hereby proclaim the week beginning March 31, 1985 through April 6, 1985, as National Weather Satellite Week. In recognition of the twenty-fifth anniversary of weather satellites, I call upon the people of the United States to observe such week with appropriate ceremonies.

In Witness Whereof, I have hereunto set my hand this 4th day of April, in the year of our Lord nineteen hundred and eighty-five, and of the Independence of the United States of America the two hundred and ninth.

RONALD REAGAN

[*Filed with the Office of the Federal Register, 11:45 a.m., April 5, 1985*]

Note: The proclamation was released by the Office of the Press Secretary on April 5.

Proclamation 5315—National Child Abuse Prevention Month, 1985
April 4, 1985

By the President of the United States of America

A Proclamation

There is no more important test of a society than how it treats its children. Children are not only a joy to the parents who raise them; they also represent a society's future. It is imperative for American society to protect its children and nurture them.

More and more Americans are turning once again to strong and loving families as the best way to provide a nurturing environment for children. This is as it should be, but there are still many indications that we must do more to protect our children and show that we love each and every one of them. One of the most disturbing of these indications is the fact that more than 1.5 million children will be reported to local child protective agencies this year as suspected victims of child abuse or neglect. As a direct result of their maltreatment, many of these children will suffer diminished op-

portunity to develop physically, intellectually, emotionally, and socially, or to become fully contributing citizens.

Their loss is our Nation's loss. In the past decade, our knowledge of how to prevent and treat child abuse has grown substantially. The most important thing we have learned is that the active involvement of neighbors and friends—indeed of everyone in a community—is the key to success. Community child protection agencies cannot do the job alone but must rely on neighbors, friends, teachers, relatives, doctors, and volunteers to provide critical support, information, and guidance to families in which child maltreatment may occur.

Beyond these efforts, we should all consider every day the kind of society we want to create. Problems such as child pornography, violence on television, teenage suicide, missing children, and child abuse are all related to the strength or weakness of our society's values. We should resolve to strengthen the fundamental values of family and community on which our Nation was founded and which can alone provide it with a good future for all our children.

In recognition of our shared responsibility to reduce the occurrence of child abuse and neglect, the Congress, by House Joint Resolution 121, has designated the month of April 1985 as "National Child Abuse Prevention Month," and has authorized and requested the President to issue a proclamation in observance of this period.

Now, Therefore, I, Ronald Reagan, President of the United States of America, do hereby proclaim the month of April 1985 as National Child Abuse Prevention Month. As we observe this time, let us all consider the wholesome and secure development of our children on whom we depend to advance our national character and values.

In Witness Whereof, I have hereunto set my hand this fourth day of April, in the year of our Lord nineteen hundred and eighty-five, and of the Independence of the United States of America the two hundred and ninth.

RONALD REAGAN

[*Filed with the Office of the Federal Register, 11:46 a.m., April 5, 1985*]

Note: The proclamation was released by the Office of the Press Secretary on April 5.

Proclamation 5316—World Health Week and World Health Day, 1985
April 4, 1985

By the President of the United States of America

A Proclamation

World Health Day, which marks the founding of the World Health Organization, serves to remind us that good health is a priceless commodity, which all the world's people should have the opportunity to enjoy throughout their life span.

The theme for World Health Day, 1985, "Healthy Youth: Our Best Resource," is particularly appropriate this year, which has been selected by the United Nations as International Youth Year. Today's youth represent a tremendous potential for society. In all countries, rich and poor, this group is the healthiest age group of all and is far better educated than preceding generations. They have survived the infectious diseases of childhood, such as measles, whooping cough, and polio. But they are also the most vulnerable to lifestyle practices that threaten later adulthood—poor food habits, cigarette smoking, abuse of alcohol and drugs, and inadequate exercise. It is our responsibility as parents and teachers to educate our youth on the importance of avoiding harmful drugs, practicing good safety measures, maintaining a proper diet, and getting regular exercise.

Furthermore, on World Health Day, the United States is pleased to join its fellow members of the World Health Organization in promoting healthy growth, and in pledging our continued support for efforts to improve the health of people throughout the world.

The Congress, by Senate Joint Resolution 50, has designated the week of April 1 through April 7, 1985 as "World Health Week" and designated April 7, 1985 as "World Health Day," and authorized and requested the President to issue a proclamation in observance of these events.

Now, Therefore, I, Ronald Reagan, President of the United States of America, do hereby proclaim the week beginning April 1 through April 7, 1985, as World Health Week, and April 7, 1985 as World Health Day. I call upon all of the people of the United States to observe this week with appropriate programs, ceremonies, and activities and by practicing the lifestyles that promote good health.

In Witness Whereof, I have hereunto set

my hand this fourth day of April, in the year of our Lord nineteen hundred and eighty-five, and of the Independence of the United States of America the two hundred and ninth.

RONALD REAGAN

[*Filed with the Office of the Federal Register, 11:47 a.m., April 5, 1985*]

Note: *The proclamation was released by the Office of the Press Secretary on April 5.*

Proclamation 5317—Education Day, U.S.A., 1985
April 4, 1985

By the President of the United States of America

A Proclamation

In order to achieve its highest goals, education must be more than just a training in facts and figures, or even in basic skills, as important as they are. It must also include instruction in the deepest ethical values of our civilization.

Very few Americans have done more to promote these ethical values as the basis of civilization than Rabbi Menachem Mendel Schneerson, the leader of the worldwide Lubavitch movement. The word "Lubavitch" comes from the name of a Russian city and means city of love. That is very appropriate because, of all the ethical values which inform our civilization, none is more important than love—love of wisdom, love of our fellowman, and love of our Creator.

These are the values which Rabbi Menachem Mendel Schneerson exemplifies. And they are the values, with their roots in the Seven Noahide Laws, which have guided the Lubavitch movement throughout its history. They are the essence of education at its best, and we should be certain that we pass on this precious heritage to all young Americans.

In recognition of Rabbi Schneerson's contributions and in honor of his 83rd birthday, which falls this year on April 2, the Congress, by House Joint Resolution 186, has designated April 2, 1985, as "Education Day, U.S.A." and authorized and requested the President to issue an appropriate proclamation in observance of this event.

Now, Therefore, I, Ronald Reagan, President of the United States of America, do hereby proclaim Tuesday, April 2, 1985, as Education Day, U.S.A., and I call upon the people of the United States, and in particular our teachers and other educational leaders, to observe that day with appropriate ceremonies and activities.

In Witness Whereof, I have hereunto set my hand this fourth day of April, in the year of our Lord nineteen hundred and eighty-five, and of the Independence of the United States of America the two hundred and ninth.

RONALD REAGAN

[*Filed with the Office of the Federal Register, 11:48 a.m., April 5, 1985*]

Note: *The proclamation was released by the Office of the Press Secretary on April 5.*

Informal Exchange With Reporters
April 5, 1985

The President. I just came over because I had a question or two. [*Laughter*]

Q. Ask.

The President. No, we've had a good meeting, several of us here—the Senators with regard to the budget, and we're very optimistic and hopeful. We think we have a very good plan.

Social Security

Q. Mr. President, the Democrats say that you have reneged on your promise not to touch Social Security.

The President. Well, how is adding a 2-percent raise each year cutting it?

Q. Well, they say, sir, that your position was that unless you were faced with an overwhelming mandate from Congress—your words—you weren't going to do that. And they say that this group of small Republican leaders from the Senate is not a mandate.

The President. No, they were talking about totally canceling it; that regardless of what inflation might be, that there would be no increases in the COLA—or no COLA's at all. And we're providing a guaranteed—more than 6 percent, because it's compounded over the 3-year period regardless of what inflation is.

Q. How are you going to try to sell your budget, sir? Are you going on television? Do you have a plan to personally participate?

The President. Oh, I think we'll use all the normal methods to tell the people about it, because I think the people are most interested in it.

Q. Do you think the Democrats are going to beat up on you on that Social Security?

The President. Well, if they do, they'll be lying in their teeth, as they did in 1982.

Nicaragua

Q. What about Nicaragua, sir? The Nicaraguan officials say that what your plan is, is basically a declaration of war. How would you respond to that?

The President. Well, they were saying that before they even heard what the plan was. I can understand it; they don't want to give up the cushy spot that they've got right now. But we believe that the people of Nicaragua will be highly supportive of this because they still want the goals that they fought for in the revolution.

Q. The people in Nicaragua, sir, don't have much of a say in the government according to your view.

The President. No. That's one of the things we're complaining about. We want them to have more of a say.

Q. Well, is there any way you can get Ortega and the Nicaraguan Government to sit down, given what they've said today?

The President. Well, I think when they see the Contadora process and neighboring countries all in support of this—and the *contras* are the ones who are willing to lay down their arms, to simply ask for the right to negotiate and discuss what kind of a government this should be.

It's a curious thing that no one seems to have paid any attention that in El Salvador it was the democratic government, the elected government of the people, that asked the guerrillas there to lay down their arms, offered them amnesty and to talk about participating legitimately in the government. And it was the guerrillas that refused. In the neighboring country of Nicaragua, the *contras*—that some are calling the guerrillas and all, and I still say are freedom fighters—they were the ones that have made the offer to lay down their arms and enter into discussions about instituting democracy. And it was the government of Nicaragua, a totalitarian government, that refused.

Defense Spending

Q. Mr. President, when Secretary Weinberger and others and even words from you suggested that if you lowered your military request you would seriously begin to cut into the security of this country, why have you now agreed to lower your military request?

The President. Well, because we didn't lower it to the point that had been suggested by some. We've all been in agreement; yes, it is a compromise. There are things that I think were worthwhile that will not be done now for awhile—be delayed—but it will be an increase, continuing increase, and no weapons systems will be slowed down or cut out of the military budget; so that we can honestly say that with this our national security capability has not been reduced.

Q. Well, is 3 percent now your bottom line, though?

The President. Yep.

Q. Not to go any further?

The President. Nope.

Federal Budget

Q. How about the budget as a whole?

Q. Well, you said that——

Q. Might there be more need for compromise yet, still, Mr. President?

The President. Well, we've come up with more than $50 billion now in a reduction of the deficit with a budget, and we think that that's what our target was, and this is what we'd like to have.

Q. What did the Senators——

Q. ——chances are for a plan?

Q. What did the Senators here tell you about your chances on the budget?

The President. Well, we all know the same thing. We all agree; it's going to be a fight. It's been a fight since 1981. There are factions in there that just want to keep on spending in the Congress.

Nicaragua

Q. What are you going to do to sell your Nicaragua plan? Do you have a speech while you're out in California?

The President. There haven't been any plans on that yet.

Q. The Nicaraguan Government has said no, sir. What now?

The President. Well, I don't think they've heard from everybody, and there are going to be people——

[*At this point the President was interrupted by engine noise from Marine One.*]

Thank you. [*Laughter*]

The President. Their neighbors are going to begin leaning on them also.

Q. Happy Easter!

The President. Thank you. Happy Easter to all of you.

Note: The exchange began at 9:28 a.m. on the South Lawn of the White House as the President was leaving for a trip to Rancho del Cielo, his ranch near Santa Barbara, CA.

Statement on Signing the African Famine Relief Bill
April 5, 1985

Last January I announced the African hunger relief initiative, a program of action to provide over $1 billion to combat famine and malnutrition, which threaten the lives of over 14 million Africans. All Americans have been horrified at the unfolding human tragedy in Africa. The overwhelming response has been heartwarming and in the best tradition of American values and ideals. Through a community effort at all levels of American society, Americans have selflessly contributed resources, food, and their services to meet the needs of African famine victims. I am proud to say that America's massive response has been successful in preventing millions of Africans from dying.

Last month Vice President Bush visited Sudan, Niger, and Mali, three of the most seriously drought-affected countries, to study firsthand the dimensions of the famine problem, what we and other donors have been able to accomplish, and what still needs to be done. Though profoundly shocked by the degree of human suffering witnessed during the trip, the Vice President did see signs of hope. He saw that the tremendous amounts of U.S. food are indeed reaching famine victims with the help of private voluntary agencies and local governments.

The U.S. response has been far larger and faster than that of any other nation or institution. Yet, it is apparent to all that more needs to be done. This is the reason for the legislation that I submitted to Congress in January and have now signed. H.R. 1239 makes available an additional $1 billion to meet Africa's emergency needs—an amount which I should note substantially exceeds the administration's current estimate of need. However, this bill, as I requested, does support the U.S. objective of providing up to 50 percent of the emergency food aid

409

requirements in Africa. Moreover, there is sufficient flexibility for the administration to ensure that all food aid is used effectively. Thus, I intend to abide by the intent of Congress in ensuring that all the food and funds that the United States provides are directed efficiently at meeting real needs and that aid will not exceed logistical capacities. Misuse of assistance is particularly unacceptable when human lives are at stake. Moreover, as we continue to increase our shipments of food aid to those at risk in Africa, we also will continue to ensure that our aid does not provide a disincentive to increased local production that is critical to solving Africa's food problem in the long term. We are confident that, together with contributions from other donor nations, we now have the resources to combat the immediate crisis and that as a result further millions of lives will be saved.

I want to again thank the American people for their selfless outpouring of donations. We have once again shown the world that individual caring and giving is an American way of life.

Note: H.R. 1239, approved April 4, was assigned Public Law No. 99–10.

Nomination of Thomas R. Pickering To Be United States Ambassador to Israel
April 5, 1985

The President today announced his intention to nominate Thomas R. Pickering, of New Jersey, a career member of the Senior Foreign Service with the personal rank of Career Ambassador, to be Ambassador to Israel. He would succeed Samuel W. Lewis.

Ambassador Pickering is currently serving as Ambassador to El Salvador. He entered the Foreign Service in 1959 as intelligence research specialist in the Department of State and was political officer (test ban treaty) in Geneva on detail to the Arms Control and Disarmament Agency in 1961–1964. He attended Swahili language training at the Foreign Service Institute in 1964–1965. In 1965–1967 he was principal officer in Zanzibar, and deputy chief of mission in Dar es Salaam in 1967–1969. In the Department of State, he was deputy director of the Bureau of Politico-Military Affairs (1969–1973) and special assistant to the Secretary of State and executive secretary of the Department (1973–1974). In 1974–1978 he was Ambassador to the Hashemite Kingdom of Jordan and Assistant Secretary of State for Oceans and International Environmental and Scientific Affairs in the Department in 1978–1981. In 1981–1983 he was Ambassador to the Federal Republic of Nigeria, and from 1983 to the present, he has been our Ambassador to El Salvador.

Ambassador Pickering graduated from Bowdoin College (A.B., 1953), Fletcher School of Law (M.A., 1954), and the University of Melbourne (M.A., 1956). He served in the United States Navy in 1956–1959. He is married to the former Alice Jean Stover, and they have two children. He was born November 5, 1931, in Orange, NJ.

Appointment of Helen R. Cameron as Special Assistant to the President for Political Affairs
April 5, 1985

The President today announced his intention to appoint Helen R. Cameron to be Special Assistant to the President for Political Affairs.

Mrs. Cameron was the director of special groups for the 50th American Presidential inaugural. Previously she was director of the voter programs for Reagan-Bush '84. She served as executive assistant to Dr. Garrey Carruthers, Assistant Secretary of the Interior, in 1983 and executive assistant to Dr. John Hernandez, Deputy Director of the Environmental Protection Agency, in 1981–1983.

In 1972–1980 she served on the staff of Senator Pete V. Domenici (R–NM). In 1962–1972 she was in Albuquerque, NM, with the New Mexico State Republican Party.

She has two children and resides in Alexandria, VA. She was born November 24, 1934, in Alamogordo, NM.

Appointment of William B. Lacy as Deputy Assistant to the President and Director of the Office of Political Affairs
April 5, 1985

The President has appointed William B. Lacy to be Deputy Assistant to the President and Director, Office of Political Affairs. In this position, Mr. Lacy will coordinate White House and Republican Party activity during the 1985–1986 election cycle. He will serve as the chief political deputy to Edward J. Rollins, Assistant to the President for Political and Governmental Affairs.

Mr. Lacy served as director of political operations for the Republican National Committee in 1984–1985. He also coordinated RNC political activity with the National Republican Senatorial Committee, the National Republican Congressional Committee, and the Republican Governors' Association. In 1984 he coordinated RNC political activities with the Reagan-Bush committee. Before joining the Republican National Committee, Mr. Lacy was a senior account executive with Decision/Making/Information in McLean, VA. He served at the White House as Special Assistant to the President for Political Affairs in 1983 and Deputy Director of Political Affairs in 1982. In 1981–1982 he served as deputy campaign director and as a regional field director at the National Republican Congressional Committee.

He graduated from Vanderbilt University (B.A., 1975). He is married and resides in Annapolis, MD. He was born January 1, 1954, in Detroit, MI.

Nomination of Hershey Gold To Be a Member of the United States Advisory Commission on Public Diplomacy
April 5, 1985

The President today announced his intention to nominate Hershey Gold to be a member of the United States Advisory Commission on Public Diplomacy for a term expiring July 1, 1987. This is a reappointment.

Mr. Gold is chairman of the board of Super Yarn Mart in Los Angeles, CA. He is also a general partner with the Commercial Business Credit Co. and Shenandoah Properties. He is national vice president and member of the international board of directors of Shaare Zedek Medical Center of Jerusalem, Israel. He is past chairman of the State of Israel Bonds for the greater Los Angeles area and past chairman of the Western States/Israel Chamber of Commerce.

He is married, has two children, and resides in Beverly Hills, CA. He was born August 21, 1920, in Chicago, IL.

Radio Address to the Nation on the Federal Budget and the Central American Peace Proposal
April 6, 1985

My fellow Americans:

I'm speaking to you today from our ranch in California. And I'm happy to report that in keeping with the spirit of Passover and Easter, this week is ending on a very hopeful note. We received encouraging reaction to our peace proposal for Nicaragua, and we've reached an immensely important budget agreement that can help keep America's economic engines running full speed ahead for years to come.

Let me speak first about that budget agreement. For months, the voices of conventional wisdom told us government deficits are too high and must be brought down, but when asked how, they inevitably answered, "Slash defense and raise taxes."

Well, as I've said many times, we don't have a deficit problem because you're not taxed enough. In the last 10 years, revenues to government increased by over $400 billion, but spending by government went up over 600 billion.

Nor do we have a deficit problem because of military spending. We're spending $16 billion less in this fiscal year than Mr. Carter's last budget had projected would be spent. As a matter of fact, as a percentage of the Federal budget, we spent more on defense 15 years ago, and the world was a lot less dangerous then.

This week, the Senate Republican leadership agreed with us on the most far-reaching spending reduction plan in postwar history. If approved by the full Congress, almost $300 billion in red ink will be eliminated over the next 3 years. This agreement provides the foundation for historic progress because those deficits will be wiped out without raising taxes a nickel, without jeopardizing vital defense programs or any essential services.

What the Senate Republicans have done is bite the bullet on spending, and I believe they deserve your support and that of the other Members of Congress. Some 17 programs will be terminated, others will be thoroughly reformed, and spending on scores of other programs, including pay for government workers, will be frozen.

The Defense Department budget will increase by only 3 percent in real terms. We'll have to squeeze costs everywhere if our buildup is to go forward, but Secretary Weinberger assures me that our men and women in uniform can get this job done.

Now, you've been reading and hearing about $400 hammers and $700 wrenches and such. Well, these figures—where do you think they're getting them? They're getting them from us. That's what has been going on, and we've discovered it, and we're stopping it.

And we're guaranteeing Social Security recipients an increase of at least 2 percent each year over the next 3 years. If inflation ends up less than 3 percent this year over last, then under present law, Social Security recipients would not be entitled to any increase. Under this new proposal, they'll be guaranteed a 2-percent increase even if there is no inflation. And if Congress cooperates on spending, we can keep bringing inflation down until it is zero. Courage and leadership are crucial if we expect to bring deficits down in a manner that protects our security and permits continued strong economic growth. And that's what we'll be asking for in the days ahead when the Congress returns from recess.

Now, let me give you the encouraging news about our proposal for peace and democracy in Nicaragua. As you know, we've asked both sides—the Communists and the democratic resistance—to lay down their arms. We've endorsed the proposal made by the democratic resistance, the *contras*, that the Catholic Church serve as mediator to restore freedom and ensure internationally supervised elections. And we've asked Congress to release $14 million for those freedom fighters—aid that will go immediately for medicines, food, and clothing and other support to help these men and their families survive. We have made this proposal in a sincere effort to start a dialog aimed at true internal reconciliation, which can bring peace and liberty to Nicaragua.

You know, the Federal Government these days spends $14 million every few minutes, so we're asking Congress for just a few minutes worth of help for the democratic forces of Nicaragua—$14 million means very little to us, but it's a whole world to them.

President Betancur of Colombia has called our proposal positive and constructive. More than a dozen countries, including Nicaragua's neighbors, have already expressed their support. And President Duarte wrote me yesterday to say that we're taking the right step at the right time. And he added, "Your initiative and approach have my complete support and I

strongly urge all the friends of Central America in your Congress to give it their full support."

In this season of peace, we have put forth an olive branch. We've sought to make a new beginning in a time of hope for all who yearn for freedom. And around the world, those who support democracy are rallying to support our proposal. I ask only that the Members of our own Congress do the same.

I wish you all a happy and blessed Easter and Passover. Until next week, thanks for listening, and God bless you.

Note: The President spoke at 9:06 a.m. from Rancho del Cielo, his ranch near Santa Barbara, CA.

Announcement of the Recipients of the Presidential Medal of Freedom
April 8, 1985

The President today announced his intention to award the Presidential Medal of Freedom, the highest civilian award of our Government, at a luncheon to be held at the White House on May 23, 1985. The following individuals will be awarded this prestigious award by the President.

Mr. Count Basie, jazz pianist, (posthumous), for his contribution in the fields of entertainment and the arts.

Mr. Jacques-Yves Cousteau, marine explorer, for his contributions in the fields of education and science.

Dr. Jerome Holland, educator and Ambassador (posthumous), for his contributions in the fields of education and public service..

Professor Sidney Hook, philosopher and educator, for his contributions in the fields of education and philosophy.

Ambassador Jeane J. Kirkpatrick, political scientist, for her contributions to the security and national interests of the United States.

Dr. George M. Low, educator and NASA Administrator (posthumous), for his contributions in the fields of science and education.

Mr. Frank Reynolds, news correspondent (posthumous), for his contributions in the fields of journalism and communications.

Mr. S. Dillon Ripley, former Secretary of the Smithsonian, for his contributions in cultural and other significant public endeavors.

The Reverend Mother Teresa, nun, for her contributions in the field of humanitarianism.

Mr. Frank Sinatra, entertainer, for his contributions in the fields of the arts and entertainment and public service.

Mr. James M. Stewart, actor, for his contributions in the fields of the arts and entertainment and public service.

Gen. Albert Coady Wedemeyer, distinguished military hero, for his contributions to the security and national interests of the United States.

Gen. Charles E. Yeager, Air Force test pilot, for his contributions in the field of public service and national interests of the United States.

Appointment of Linda Chavez as Deputy Assistant to the President and Director of the Office of Public Liaison
April 9, 1985

The President today announced his intention to appoint Linda Chavez to be Deputy Assistant to the President and Director of the Office of Public Liaison.

Ms. Chavez is currently Staff Director for the United States Civil Rights Commission and a member of the Council of the Administrative Conference of the United States. She served as assistant to the president, American Federation of Teachers (AFT), AFL–CIO, and as editor of American Educator. Previously, she was a consultant for the President's reorganization project, Civil

Rights Section, Office of Management and Budget (July–September 1977); and was on the professional staff, Committee on the Judiciary, Subcommittee on Civil and Constitutional Rights, U.S. House of Representatives (1972–1974).

Ms. Chavez graduated from the University of Colorado (B.A., 1970) and attended the University of California at Los Angeles (1970–1972) and the University of Maryland (1974–1975). She is married, has three children, and resides in Bethesda, MD. She was born June 17, 1947, in Albuquerque, NM.

Appointment of Linda Lugenia Arey as Special Assistant to the President and Deputy Director of the Office of Public Liaison
April 9, 1985

The President today announced his intention to appoint Linda Lugenia Arey to be Special Assistant to the President and Deputy Director of the Office of Public Liaison.

Ms. Arey is currently Executive Secretary to the Department of Transportation. Previously, she was special assistant to the Deputy Secretary of Transportation (1983–1984); special assistant, Office of Public Affairs, Department of Justice (1982–1983); and special assistant to the Executive Secre-

tary, Department of Education (1981–1982). She served as assistant dean at the University of Richmond School of Law from 1978 to 1981 and was project director of the Mental Health Legal Studies Center at the university from 1977 to 1978.

Ms. Arey graduated from the College of William and Mary (B.A., 1966), Wake Forest University (M.A., 1975), and the University of Richmond School of Law (J.D., 1977). She was born November 25, 1944, in Savannah, GA, and resides in Washington, DC.

Remarks in an Interview With Nicholas Ashford and Charles Douglas-Home of the Times of London, Together With Written Responses to Questions
April 4, 1985

Q. And when Mrs. Thatcher was here, she mentioned in her toast that this year was the bicentenniary, not just of Anglo-American relations, but also the establishment of a venerable institution, which is my

newspaper, the Times of London. And in honor of that event, I'd just like to make a small presentation. This is our office—over a hundred years ago—I'm afraid it doesn't look like that anymore. It's all glass and steel and high technology. But—times have progressed since then.

The President. Well, thank you very much. I'm very pleased to have that.

U.S.-Soviet Relations

Q. Thank you very much for this opportunity of meeting with you. Could I take this opportunity just to ask you about—I know you can't say anything about the date or time or agreement of a summit—but if a summit were to take place with Mr. Gorbachev, would you regard this as a turning point in American and Soviet relations?

The President. I don't know whether you could say that, because there have been summit meetings before. I would look on it as an opportunity to clear the air and express our desire to have a relationship that would eliminate this great threat that seems to hang over the world. If in any way it could help in the negotiations that are going on in Geneva—and very frankly, I'd like to speak to him to clear up some things, like the kind of tragedy with our officer there in Germany.[1] Those things are so senseless; there's no need for them. But I don't know that you could see it as a turning point. After all, he has been for 4 years a member of the Politburo, 14 years a member of the party council. So, we know that the government really is a collective— the Politburo has the ultimate authority. So, I can't see that, as some speculated, there would be a great change of direction. It would only come about if that was the desire of that same Politburo.

Q. Given the nature of the Soviet system, how far can relations improve between the two nations?

The President. They could improve if we can show them that it would be to their material advantage as well as someone else's. I think about the Geneva talks that we're in right now. It's the first time in about 50 years and more than 20 arms talks with them between World War II and the present that they sit down faced with the possibility that either we join together in

reducing arms or they engage us in an arms race, which they know they can't win.

April 10, 1985

The President's Responses to Questions Submitted by the Times of London

Nicaragua

Q. You have expressed your determination to make the Sandinista government of Nicaragua change its ways. How far are you prepared to go to achieve this objective?

The President. We believe that our interests and those of Central America would best be served by the conclusion of a workable, comprehensive, and fully verifiable regional agreement based solidly on the 21 objectives of the Contadora process. We continue to support that process strongly through our diplomacy.

I want to emphasize that, consistent with the 21 goals of the Contadora process, the United States continues to seek Nicaragua's implementation of its commitment to democracy made to the OAS. We also seek an end to Nicaragua's aggression against its neighbors. We think they should remove the thousands of Soviet bloc, Cuban, PLO, Libyan, and other military and security personnel and return the Nicaraguan military to a level of parity with their neighbors.

Realistically, we recognize that there must be incentives to get the Sandinistas to change their behavior. If incentives are taken away, they will have no reason to compromise, and there will be no hope of a negotiated settlement.

That is why I proposed last week, as a step toward peace in the Western Hemisphere, that the Sandinistas make peace with their own people by means of negotiations, which result in genuine democratic elections.

The democratic opposition has proposed a peace initiative to the Communists, which is completely fair. It includes mediation by the Catholic bishops of Nicaragua, who have accepted the proposal. It agrees to recognize the current regime pending a free election. It asks for guarantees of free speech and the political opportunity for the opposition to state its case there. A key fea-

---

[1] *Maj. Arthur D. Nicholson, Jr., USA, who had recently been shot and killed in the German Democratic Republic.*

ture of the peace plan is a cease-fire by both sides and a lifting of the state of emergency.

This proposal is fully consistent with the 21 objectives of the Contadora process. It has the approval of President Betancur of Colombia, President Duarte of El Salvador, and other neighbors of Nicaragua. Why won't the Sandinistas accept this proposal from their own people? We hope they will, for the sake of peace in their own country and in Central America as a whole.

Strategic Defense Initiative and Arms Talks

Q. How concerned are you by the Soviet Union's attempt to drive a wedge between the U.S. and its NATO allies by its bitter opposition to your Strategic Defense Initiative, the SDI?

The President. As much as our military strength or the vigor of our economies, the continuing vitality and solidarity of the Atlantic alliance lies at the heart of the West's ability to protect its freedoms while preserving the peace. The very nature of our democratic and open societies ensures that there will always be diversity of opinion within the alliance. Nonetheless, it is critically important that the United States and its European partners stand united on the basis of our common efforts to protect our mutual security.

Therefore, it is not at all surprising that the Soviets are now seeking, as they have in the past in regard to other issues, to incite and exploit differences within the West as a means of undercutting alliance efforts to strengthen our defense and deterrent forces. Their propaganda tools are familiar ones, involving misrepresentation, threats, and now a call for a moratorium that would freeze the imbalance in Europe.

Though their current propaganda campaign contains little that is new, I can't help but be struck by how disingenuous it is for the Soviet Union—which possesses the world's only operational ABM system, which has been energetically pursuing an extensive research program in the area of ballistic missile defense, and which has taken actions counter to the letter and spirit of the ABM treaty—now to express such public criticism of the idea that the United States might also engage in its own research into the feasibility of strategic defense.

Our allies know the truth. We have consulted closely with them on the nature and purposes of SDI. They know that it is a research program designed to provide the technical basis that would allow a future President to decide whether to develop advanced systems to defend against ballistic missiles. They also know that limits on research activity are neither feasible nor verifiable.

The goal of SDI research is to find nonnuclear technologies which, if deployed, would strengthen stability and enhance our mutual security. Our research will be conducted in conformity with all treaties to which the U.S. is a party, including the ABM treaty.

For all these reasons, NATO governments support SDI research and have stated their support on many occasions, most recently at the March meeting of NATO's Nuclear Planning Group.

Q. Mr. President, you have said it may take longer than your 4-year term to achieve a major nuclear arms reduction agreement with the Soviet Union. If this is so, what do you think can be achieved by 1988?

The President. We are prepared to negotiate constructively with the Soviet Union with the goal of radically reducing nuclear arms and, ultimately, eliminating nuclear weapons entirely. If the Soviets approach the negotiations in the same serious fashion, it should be possible to reach agreement in the relatively short term. At the same time, we recognize fully the differences between us and the Soviets. Historically, it has often taken considerable negotiation to work out arms control agreements.

The U.S. will not make unilateral concessions in an effort to come quickly to agreement nor will we be subject to artificial deadlines before which agreement must be reached. We want to negotiate good agreements which enhance the security of the United States and our allies. We are prepared to negotiate as long as necessary to achieve this.

Strength of the U.S. Dollar Abroad

Q. The strong dollar has been causing chaos in European currency markets, forcing governments to raise interest rates. A sharp fall in its value could also be very damaging. Given the interrelationship between the U.S. and other Western economies, why doesn't the U.S. actively intervene with other governments to achieve greater currency stability?

The President. The strength of the U.S. dollar against European currencies over the past 4 years has primarily reflected the strong U.S. economic performance and prospects, particularly relative to the economic performance and prospects elsewhere in the world. The dramatic improvement in U.S. growth, employment, productivity, and profitability, coupled with a lower inflation rate, has stimulated demand for dollars relative to demand for other key currencies. Additionally, foreign confidence in the U.S. economy as a "safe haven" has contributed to the demand for dollars.

Experience indicates that government intervention in exchange markets can have only a very limited and temporary impact in the absence of changes in the underlying fundamentals. We remain prepared to intervene, to counter disorderly markets in instances where we believe it would be helpful. But policies that promote a convergence of economic performance, including those designed to increase incentives for stronger noninflationary growth, are the key to achieving greater exchange rate stability.

Budget Deficit

Q. You have stated that a reduction of the Federal budget deficit is a top priority, but many economists and businessmen on both sides of the Atlantic are skeptical that you will be able to achieve significant cuts. What is your strategy, given the opposition your proposals are already facing in the Congress?

The President. Congress and the administration have a common goal: We want to reduce the budget deficit. The administration and the Senate Republican leadership have reached agreement on a budget proposal for FY 1986 which restrains both civilian and military expenditure—without endangering our military preparedness—while cutting some $50 billion from our budget deficit. Our budget proposal would utilize expenditure restraint and expanding revenues from economic growth to yield a declining trend of deficits, both in absolute terms and as a share of GNP, in the coming fiscal years.

In some quarters in Congress there is inclination to spare domestic spending from reductions we have proposed and instead just cut defense expenditures, or raise taxes, or both. The administration is certainly willing to consider proposals from Congress, but I will not agree to defense spending cuts that weaken our national security or to tax increases. Despite our differences with some Members of Congress, I believe that our strong, shared determination to reduce the deficit will prevail; that we will get the cuts in spending our economy requires; and that later in the year, we can secure passage of an historic reform and simplification of our tax code that will strengthen incentives for vigorous and sustained economic growth.

Trade Negotiations and the International Monetary System

Q. You have proposed a new round of GATT negotiations. In what areas will the U.S. be putting proposals, and would the U.S. agree to linking international currency and dollar issues to these talks?

The President. We have ideas as to what subjects might be covered, and we are confident that the other participants have their own ideas as to priority areas for the negotiations. We are anxious to proceed to the preparatory phase of the negotiations in the GATT and to draw up an agenda for the new round, which we believe should be launched formally by early next year. We do not believe it is right to link progress on these negotiations with international monetary questions; issues in each should be addressed on their merits when they arise. For example, the international monetary system was discussed at the Williamsburg summit in 1983. As a result, the Group of Ten undertook a study of ways to improve the operation of the world monetary system, and we look forward with interest to seeing the report, which is to be examined by Finance Ministers this June.

Middle East

Q. Do you think recent developments in the Middle East, notably the accord between King Hussein of Jordan and the Palestine Liberation Organization, can lead to an early revival of your September 1982 Middle East peace initiative?

The President. When I made my proposals in September 1982, my goal was to stimulate efforts to achieve a just and durable peace in the Middle East. That goal remains the same today. My initiative outlined the positions we will support when negotiations resume. I believe that direct negotiations between the parties is the best way to achieve settlement. But the challenge at the moment is to get those negotiations underway.

The Hussein-Arafat accord and the ideas put forward by Egyptian President Mubarak and others in the region are positive developments. I have decided to send Assistant Secretary of State Richard Murphy to the area to explore the possibilities raised by these proposals and to see how the peace process can be moved forward.

Q. In view of the protracted Iran-Iraq war, how prepared are you to provide Saudi Arabia and other Gulf States with the sophisticated weaponry they are seeking?

The President. Our policy has been to help these countries develop their capabilities to defend themselves against regional threats to their security. We will complete a review of our Middle East security policy in the very near future. Meanwhile, we are

not initiating the sale of major new systems or augmentations to any country in the Middle East. We will respond to various requests for arms in light of the results of our review.

U.S.-United Kingdom Relations

Q. During your talks with Mrs. Thatcher in February you referred to the special quality of relations between the U.S. and Britain. What are these special qualities?

The President. In a few weeks, it will be the 200th anniversary of the date on which John Adams was received by King George III and diplomatic relations were established between the United Kingdom and the United States. With a few exceptions, the two centuries which followed have been marked by a growing closeness between our two countries. Our nations have been drawn together by common traditions and heritage and a common devotion to the concepts of liberty and human dignity. These bonds have been forged over the centuries as our countries have stood together to meet both the challenges of war and the opportunities of peace. Today relations between Great Britain and the United States are marked not only by cooperation and mutual respect but also by a deep and abiding friendship.

Note: At the beginning of the interview, Mr. Ashford and Mr. Douglas-Home presented the President with a facsimile of the front page of a 100-year-old edition of the Times of London. A tape was not available for verification of the content of the oral portion of this interview, which was released by the Office of the Press Secretary on April 11.

Statement on the Establishment of the Economic Policy Council and the Domestic Policy Council
April 11, 1985

Today I am announcing the creation of two Cabinet-level bodies—the Economic Policy Council and the Domestic Policy Council—to assist me in the formulation

and execution of domestic and economic policy. I will chair both Councils. These two Councils will replace the seven existing Cabinet Councils and the Senior Interagency Group-International Economic Policy. The new entities will streamline policy development and decisionmaking. Together with the National Security Council, they will serve as the primary channels for advising me on policy matters.

The Economic Policy Council will be composed of the Secretaries of State, Treasury, Agriculture, Commerce, and Labor, the Director of Office of Management and Budget, the United States Trade Representative, and the Chairman of the Council of Economic Advisers. It will provide advice to me concerning all aspects of national and international economic policy. The heads of the national security community departments and agencies and the Assistant to the President for National Security Affairs will participate in Council meetings whenever international policy or budget matters are discussed. In my absence the Secretary of the Treasury will serve as Chairman pro tempore.

The Domestic Policy Council will be composed of the Attorney General, the Secretaries of the Interior, Health and Human Services, Housing and Urban Development, Transportation, Energy, and Education, and the Director of the Office of Management and Budget. It will provide advice to me on domestic and social policy. In my absence the Attorney General will serve as Chairman pro tempore.

The heads of nonmember departments and agencies will be invited to participate in either Council's deliberations whenever matters affecting their organizations are on the agenda. The Vice President and Chief of Staff will serve as ex officio members of both Councils.

The new, streamlined decisionmaking process enhances my commitment to Cabinet government. It will provide for added accountability and efficiency in formulating and implementing policy.

Radio Address to the Nation on Tax Reform
April 13, 1985

My fellow Americans:

I want to talk today about one of the most historic reforms our administration will propose as a top priority for passage in Congress this year. Next month, we'll unveil our plan to completely overhaul our tax code, changing it from a source of confusion and contempt to a model of fairness, simplicity, and incentives for work, risk-taking, and growth.

For millions of us, this weekend marks the final countdown to April 15th, the dreaded day we must bare our financial souls, account for every nickel earned, and deliver to the IRS all taxes due. It is a legal obligation we must meet. But paying taxes is painful, nonetheless.

Not only because tax rates remain too high, which they are despite the reductions we've made, but because over the years the entire tax system has come to mirror Washington itself—a complicated, frustrating, unfair mystery of legalistic gobbledygook

and loopholes never designed, it seems, to help everyday wage earners, only those who can afford high-priced attorneys and accountants.

How many times have we heard about profitable companies paying little or no taxes, or seen advertising for sophisticated tax shelter schemes that enable individuals to avoid paying their fair share of taxes, or seen luxuries being written off that must eventually be paid for by somebody else— that somebody, of course, being you. I wonder how many Americans realize that tax deductions are available for seminars and conferences held on cruise ships. We know that our tax code is unfair. We know that it's complicated beyond belief. Millions of Americans need professional assistance just to complete their returns. And we know that it has bred another problem every bit as serious—the wasting of economic resources.

With all the special provisions in our tax

laws, too many economic decisions are being made for tax reasons alone, rather than in response to the marketplace. And that causes precious investment to be diverted from areas that could make the United States more productive and competitive in world markets.

Let me cite one example. Have you ever heard of a see-through building? Well, it's one that has no interior walls because it has no tenants. Between 1983 and 1984, only about half of the increase in available commercial office space was reflected in rentals. The other half resulted in vacancies. You see, the tax benefits for investment in some kinds of real estate deals are so generous that being able to rent space may be secondary. The result is overbuilding and high vacancy rates in many American cities. It's time for change—sweeping change. And when we return from the economic summit in May, we intend to move.

Treasury Secretary Jim Baker has been meeting with congressional leaders and authors of other tax reform plans, and we expect to advance a proposal that can win bipartisan approval this year.

Historically, tax reform has become a code word for tax increases, but our reform will not be a tax increase in disguise. And it probably won't please Washington's army of high-powered lobbyists. What our plan will do is give to the average family and every American with courage to invest in a new idea opportunities to make this economy the greatest miracle for growth and human progress the world has ever seen.

With your support, this will be the last year the American people face today's high tax barriers. We'll propose reducing sharply personal tax rates, bringing the top rate down to 35 percent or lower, and providing most Americans a tax cut.

Our plan will mark an historic commitment to American families, for we intend to increase significantly the personal exemption, which will be especially beneficial to low-income families, helping them leave welfare behind, find productive jobs, and join those now paying taxes and contributing to a bigger gross national product. We'll lower personal rates by broadening the base, in other words, eliminate the shelters that make tax avoidance legal. But long-standing provisions like deductions for your home mortgage will be maintained. As we lower rates on the people, we'll reduce corporate rates, too. In meeting concerns for fairness and neutrality, we must not jeopardize economic growth.

My goal is to keep America the premier job-creating nation on Earth, and we intend to unleash the full power of entrepreneurship. Together, we can seize this historic moment. We can create a new tax code—clean, simple, and fair. We can make ours the land of the future, offering unlimited opportunity to all Americans who dare to live for their dreams.

Until next week, thanks for listening, and God bless you.

Note: The President spoke at 9:06 a.m. from Rancho del Cielo, his ranch near Santa Barbara, CA.

Executive Order 12509—Technical Review Group on Inertial Confinement Fusion
April 14, 1985

By the authority vested in me as President by the Constitution and statutes of the United States of America, including Section 1633 of the Department of Defense Authorization Act, 1985 (Public Law 98–525), and in order to establish an advisory committee to review the inertial confinement fusion

program, it is hereby ordered as follows:

Section 1. There is established the Technical Review Group on Inertial Confinement Fusion. The Technical Review Group shall be composed of two members, the Director of the Office of Science and Technology Policy, who shall also serve as Chairman, and the Director of the Office of Energy Research of the Department of Energy.

Sec. 2. (a) The Task Force shall review thoroughly the accomplishments, management, goals, and anticipated contributions of the defense inertial confinement fusion program and shall advise the President and the Congress concerning its findings of fact and recommendations regarding priorities for future work in the inertial confinement fusion program. In conducting its review and recommendations, the Technical Review Group shall contract with an appropriate independent, nationally recognized organization of scientists to study the inertial confinement fusion program and to submit its evaluation to the Technical Review Group for consideration in preparation of its reports.

(b) The Technical Review Group shall submit an interim report to the President and the Committees on Armed Services of the Senate and the House of Representatives before June 1, 1985, and shall submit its final report before May 1, 1986.

Sec. 3. (a) The heads of Executive depart-ments and agencies shall, to the extent permitted by law, provide the Technical Review Group with such information as may be necessary for the effective performance of its functions.

(b) Members of the Technical Review Group shall serve without compensation for their work on the Group.

(c) The Director of the Office of Science and Technology Policy shall, subject to the availability of funds, provide the Technical Review Group with such administrative services, facilities, staff, and other support services as may be necessary.

Sec. 4. The Technical Review Group shall terminate upon the submission of its final report.

RONALD REAGAN

The White House,
April 14, 1985.

[*Filed with the Office of the Federal Register, 2:35 p.m., April 15, 1985*]

Note: The Executive order was released by the Office of the Press Secretary on April 15.

Remarks to Reporters on the Central American Peace Proposal
April 15, 1985

The President. I think you all recognize our visitors here this morning.

Q. Can you get closer?

Q. Closer, please. Come on right up.

The President. I've been pleased to confer with these distinguished Americans, and they agree with me that if any area of the world is of vital interest to the United States, it is neighboring countries in Central America. Former Secretary of State Kissinger also has asked me to express his continuing support for our Central American policy.

Our April 4th proposal asking for both sides to lay down their arms and enter a church-mediated dialog for peace offers new hope for the region. It could open the path to conciliation.

Our plan has been endorsed by Nicara-gua's neighbors; Presidents Duarte, Suazo, and Monge have all sent letters of strong support. Other Latin American nations view it as a positive step. El Salvador's President Duarte called it the right step at the right time and urged Members of Congress to support it.

I'm asking Congress to give this peace initiative and democracy a chance. I'm asking Congress to work with me to stem the flood of refugees, the threat of hostile forces on our borders, and the loss of faith in America's commitments around the world that could definitely result if we do not act quickly and responsibly.

I'm asking Congress to join me in the bipartisan spirit so essential to our security in providing this small amount, $14 million, for the more than 15,000 Nicaraguans who are struggling for democracy. It is so little, yet such an important symbol of our resolve, a signal to all of Central America and, yes, to those everywhere in the world who depend on us.

Our overall policy in the region has been working, but continued success depends on Congress' prompt release of aid for the Nicaraguan democratic resistance. Democracy and peace deserve a chance. The freedom-loving people of Nicaragua deserve a chance.

To accomplish this and protect our country we must stand together. These distinguished Americans know, in a very personal way, how crucial bipartisan unity is to a successful American foreign policy.

End of statement.

Q. Mr. President, how does the vote look now on Central America?

The President. In this photo opportunity, I'm not going to take any questions except to say—that one, I haven't had a count on that, having just returned.

Q. Are you confident?

The President. I'm always cautiously optimistic.

Note: The President spoke at 10:21 a.m. in the Oval Office at the White House following a meeting with Zbigniew Brzezinski, former Assistant to the President for National Security Affairs, James R. Schlesinger, former Secretary of Energy, both serving during the administration of President Carter, and Ambassador Jeane J. Kirkpatrick, former United States Representative to the United Nations.

Remarks at a Performance of the Ringling Brothers and Barnum and Bailey Circus
April 15, 1985

The Ringmaster. Mr. President, welcome to Ringling Brothers and Barnum and Bailey Circus, on behalf of our producer, Kenneth Feld, and children of all ages everywhere.

It is truly an honor to have you here at the Greatest Show on Earth. You have your official ringmaster's whistle. And now, will you honor us by starting our show?

The President. I will. And I want to say thanks to all of you and to all of the performers that we're going to see here for what they're doing for all of us. And later on I'll have a few words to say to all of you, but right now I'm not going to hold the show up. So, I think that's what the whistle is for. All right.

[*At this point, the President blew the ringmaster's whistle to begin the circus. The President then sat with students from Martin Luther King, Jr. Elementary School to watch the first half of the performance.*]

The President. Thank you all very much. But more importantly, all of you there in the stands—including myself now up here—

shall we just once let out a yell and show how much we appreciate what all these wonderful people have been doing for us here for the last hour?

Audience. [*Applause and cheers*]

The President. There it is. We really thank you. You know, this year is Ringling Brothers' 100th birthday. They're just a little older than I am. And this year they're going to do more than just entertain people. The Ringling Brothers Barnum and Bailey Circus, traveling across the country, is going to have a program that is called the Safe Kids campaign.

With all of the lost children, the problems that we're having in this country, they're going across the country; they're going to give children and parents an opportunity to obtain free educational material, identification documentation, and help keep their families safe and secure.

Earlier this month I met at the White House with a group of leaders from the communities, from law enforcement, schools, business, government to talk about what can be done to keep all children safe.

And I asked them to form a national partnership for child safety.

And now I'd like to ask all of you boys and girls who are here today to join, at least in part time, in that campaign. And I've jotted down a few things here on a card that we'd like to ask you to do and to tell you what to do and how you can help:

Number one, be sure to learn and know your full address and your home phone number.

Second, always let your parents know where you are, and learn to use the phone so that you could call them from anywhere.

And third and most important, listen carefully to all the special safety tips that your parents and your teachers tell you.

Each and every one of you is very important to all of us. I think you could see that when these wonderful people here were willing to give of their talent and their time to entertain us the way they have. And now, throughout the country, they're going to be participating in campaigns to see if we can't prevent the disappearance of children, that has been happening in our country.

That's all the time now, and I've taken too much time away from—all the beauty and the glamor is here—but just to add my thanks to all of you here in the show, to all of you for being here.

Thank you. God bless you all.

Note: The President spoke at 10:55 a.m. at the District of Columbia Armory.

Letter to the Speaker of the House and the President of the Senate on the Export-Import Bank of the United States
April 15, 1985

Dear Mr. Speaker: (Dear Mr. President:)

This report is being transmitted pursuant to Section 7(a)(2) of the Export-Import Bank Act of 1945, as amended. I have determined that the authority available to the Bank for fiscal year 1985 is more than sufficient to meet the current estimate of the needs of the Bank. This estimate was based upon the transactions already approved, applications received by the Bank, and projections of the level of business likely for the remainder of the fiscal year.

I am not seeking legislation to rescind any authority of the Bank. Estimates of demand for Export-Import Bank financing could change with continued growth in the U.S. economy and global recovery. In addition, the ability to respond to greater than anticipated demand could be a means to ease the transition from the direct loan to the interest rate subsidy program which I have proposed as an alternative. Therefore, I have concluded that the statutory fiscal year 1985 limit for Eximbank authority should be retained unchanged.

Sincerely,

RONALD REAGAN

Note: Identical letters were sent to Thomas P. O'Neill, Jr., Speaker of the House of Representatives, and George Bush, President of the Senate.

Appointment of Howard H. Baker, Jr., as a Member of the President's Foreign Intelligence Advisory Board
April 15, 1985

The President today announced his intention to appoint Howard H. Baker, Jr., to be a member of the President's Foreign Intelligence Advisory Board. This is a new position.

Senator Baker is a senior partner in the law firm of Vinson & Elkins in Washington, DC. He also serves as a partner in the firm of Baker, Worthington, Crossley, Stansberry & Woolf in Huntsville and Knoxville, TN. He served as a United States Senator from Tennessee from 1966 to 1985. He was minority leader in 1977–1981 and majority leader in 1981–1985. He was cochairman of the Senate Select Committee on Presidential Campaign Activities and a member of the Committee on Environment and Public Works, the Committee on Foreign Relations, the Committee on Rules and Administration, and the Select Committee on Intelligence.

He received the Presidential Medal of Freedom in 1984. He attended the University of the South and Tulane University. He graduated from the University of Tennessee (LL.B., 1949). He is married, has two children, and resides in Huntsville, TN. He was born November 15, 1925, in Huntsville, TN.

Nomination of Douglas W. McMinn To Be an Assistant Secretary of State
April 15, 1985

The President today announced his intention to nominate Douglas W. McMinn to be Assistant Secretary of State (Bureau of Economic and Business Affairs).

Since 1982 Mr. McMinn has been serving as Director of International Economic Affairs at the National Security Council. He was designated by the President to help guide policy preparations for the 1984 London Economic Summit and has been redesignated in preparing for this year's summit in Bonn. Previously he served at the Department of Commerce (1981–1982). From 1979 to 1981, he served as deputy chief of mission, Office of the United States Trade Representative, Geneva, Switzerland. He was special assistant to the Deputy Special Trade Representative (1977–1979) and served as an international economist at the Department of the Treasury from 1975 to 1977.

Mr. McMinn graduated from Gustavus Adolphus College (B.A., 1969), Johns Hopkins University (M.L.A., 1972), and Johns Hopkins University School of Advanced International Studies (M.A., 1975). He is married, has three children, and resides in Alexandria, VA. He was born July 18, 1947, in Salt Lake City, UT.

Appointment of George F. Moody as a Member of the Board of Governors of the American National Red Cross, and Designation as Principal Officer
April 15, 1985

The President today announced his intention to appoint George F. Moody to serve on the Board of Governors of the American National Red Cross for a term of 3 years. He will also be designated to act as the principal officer of the corporation.

Since 1980 Mr. Moody has been president, chief operating officer, and a director of both Security Pacific Corp. and Security Pacific National Bank. He is also a member of the office of the chief executive for both organizations and serves on the bank's management committee. He joined Security Pacific National Bank in 1953.

He is a director and was a member of the executive committee of the American Red Cross, Los Angeles chapter. He serves as a director and member of the executive committee of the United Way, Inc. He is a past director of the Los Angeles Area Chamber of Commerce, for which he served as president in 1980. He is also a director and past president of the Los Angeles Area Council, Boy Scouts of America.

He is married, has four children, and resides in Hacienda Heights, CA. He was born July 28, 1930, in Riverside, CA.

Appointment of Two Members of the President's Council on Physical Fitness and Sports
April 15, 1985

The President today announced his intention to appoint the following individuals to be members of the President's Council on Physical Fitness and Sports:

Robert P. Levy will succeed Dorothy Hamill. Mr. Levy is chairman and president of DRT Industries, Inc., in Philadelphia, PA. He serves on the boards of directors of Tate & Lyle, Inc., and the Philadelphia Chamber of Commerce. He is a trustee of the University of Pennsylvania. He graduated from the University of Pennsylvania (B.A., 1952). He is married, has five children, and resides in Bryn Mawr, PA. He was born March 30, 1931, in Philadelphia, PA.

Charles Luckman will succeed Roger Staubach. He is founder and partner in the Luckman Partnership, Inc., in Los Angeles, CA. He has also served as chairman of the board and chief executive officer of Luckman Management Corp. since 1973. He was chairman of the board and chief executive officer of Ogden Development Corp. in 1968–1974. He graduated from the University of Illinois (1931) and the University of Miami (LL.D., 1950). He is married, has three children, and resides in Los Angeles, CA. He was born May 16, 1909, in Kansas City, MO.

Remarks at a Reception Honoring Milton Pitts' 20 Years of Service as the Presidents' Barber
April 15, 1985

The President. Well, good evening. I just washed my hair, and I can't do a thing with it. [*Laughter*]

Now, Milt, don't reach for the scissors. [*Laughter*] I've got a speech I've got to make at another place here this evening. I didn't come in here for a haircut; I came in here—you got any ideas? [*Laughter*]

Well, we're all gathered here, and I know one thing, for a friend. And I found that, among other things, a great sense of humor—as a matter of fact, I've got one, Milt. [*Laughter*] What do you call 10 rabbits that are dancing backward? Give up, huh.

Mr. Pitts. I give up.

The President. A receding hare line. [*Laughter*]

No, because of that other engagement, I'm just going to take a minute here. I'm going to tell a story that Milt knows, and he likes it very much because it's about another barber, one in California—and it's really true; it's not just a joke—and in a place that, before Washington, I used to go get my hair cut.

And one day, there was one of the regular customers in there with his regular fellow, and told him to really, you know, do it up right because he and his wife were taking a trip to Europe. And the conversation that followed then: Question from the man that was doing the cutting, and he said, "Well, where are you going?" And he said, "Rome." "Oh?" He said, "Yeah. We're going to see all the monuments and all the historic things and the Colosseum and all of that."

"Nah," he says, "you won't like it. A lot of those things aren't around, or you can't find them, and there's nobody to show them to you." He says, "What line are you flying?" He says, "We're not. We're taking a ship. We're sailing." "Oh," he says, "that's a big mistake. The food is lousy. It isn't like you think it's going to be at all. You're going to be sick and tired and bored to death before you get halfway there."

Well, he went on that way about everything. And finally, sitting in the chair, he said, "And we've got an arrangement already. We're going to have an audience with the Pope."

"Oh," he says, "you think you're going to see the Pope." He says, "You'll probably be in a line—20,000 people. If you get within two blocks of him, you'll be lucky." And finally, getting the haircut, he said, "Look, will you stop trying to spoil the trip. We've been looking forward to this for a long time. Now, just cut my hair and be quiet."

And it was finished, and he went on the trip. A few weeks later, he's back and in the chair. And the first question was, "Well, how was your trip?" He said, "Wonderful." He said, "The boat—it was wonderful. We almost hated to get to Rome; we had so much fun on the ship. And the food was great, like the best restaurants you could ever imagine." And he said, "We saw everything in Rome, all the history of Rome. It was really wonderful. We saw all those things, and we had an audience with the Pope. Twenty minutes he gave us." And he said, "When I bent down to kiss his ring, he said to me, 'Where did you get the lousy haircut?' " [*Laughter*]

Well, Milt, I wish I could stay longer, but I know why we're all here: A friend, a gentleman, and we all do look a little better because of him. [*Laughter*] Matter of fact, a lot better—[*laughter*]—because of him. And I'm due in 2 or 3 days, too. I know it. [*Laughter*] So, brace yourself. But, Milt, it's a great pleasure to be here.

And, you know, his clientele—three Presidents, three Vice Presidents, Cabinet members, Members of the Congress, and all—they come and go, but he's here for the long stretch. The rest of us are sort of hair today and gone tomorrow. [*Laughter*]

Mr. Pitts. Thank you, Mr. President, for coming. Wonderful!

Mr. Meloy. We have a plaque for Mr. Pitts in honor of his 20 years here at the hotel. And it reads: In honor of Milton Pitts, barber to the Presidents for 20 years, dedicated to the service of the Sheraton-Carlton Hotel in Washington, DC, August [April] 15, 1985.

Congratulations, Mr. Pitts.

The President. Milt, congratulations.

Mr. Pitts. Thank you, Mr. President. It's wonderful of you to make it.

The President. And if they'd rewrite the Constitution, I'd try to be around for the next 20th. [*Laughter*]

Note: The President spoke at 6:26 p.m. in the Crystal Room at the Sheraton-Carlton Hotel. David M. Meloy, general manager of the hotel, was the master of ceremonies for the reception.

Remarks at a Fundraising Dinner for the Nicaragua Refugee Fund
April 15, 1985

I want to begin by saying that I'm honored to be in the presence of those who are here from Nicaragua and all the rest of you, too. Many of you have been driven from the land of your birth by a sad turn of history, but you've refused to forget your homeland or abandon your fellow Nicaraguans. And for this you deserve, and you have, both our high regard and our thanks.

Six years ago, many of you were part of the fight to overthrow an oppressive regime that had ruled your country for decades. You succeeded; the regime fell. And many rejoiced knowing that true freedom and true democracy would finally rise to take its place.

But the new regime became not a democracy but a dictatorship. Communism was embraced, and Nicaragua moved into the Soviet orbit. The best of the revolution, members of the original revolutionary government who had fought for high ideals, left the country. In all, more than a quarter of a million souls fled Nicaragua, and they're fleeing still. Many of the refugees are the poorest of the poor—Indians and peasants and terrified mothers and children. All of them need our help. But even more, perhaps, they need the attention of the world. After nearly 6 years, attention must be paid.

There's so much I want to discuss tonight, from the plight of the refugees to why they're fleeing. I want to talk about what is at stake in Central America, what is at issue, and what it means to all of us in this room, in this country, and in the West. I'll start with Nicaragua now—Nicaragua on April 15, 1985.

As you know, the Sandinista dictatorship has taken absolute control of the government and the armed forces. It is a Communist dictatorship. It has done what Communist dictatorships do: created a repressive state security and secret police organization assisted by Soviet, East German, and Cuban advisers; harassed, and in many cases expunged, the political opposition, and rendered the democratic freedoms of speech, press, and assembly punishable by officially sanctioned harassment and imprisonment or death.

But the Communists are not unopposed. They are facing great resistance from the people of Nicaragua, resistance from the patriots who fight for freedom and their unarmed allies from the prodemocracy movement.

There is growing evidence of Sandinista brutality. We've recently learned that 10 or 11 members of the Social Christian Party have been rounded up and jailed. The Sandinistas are trying to get them to confess to being counterrevolutionaries. And you might be interested in knowing one way the Communists are coercing these confessions. They have also arrested more than a hundred relatives of the political prisoners. And according to our most recent information, the Social Christian Party members are being held in the dark in small, overheated cells. Prisoners are served meals at irregular intervals—after 12 hours, for instance, and then the next in another 2. The purpose is to disorient them and wear them down. Where do they get that idea? This same method has been used against political prisoners in Cuba.

Now, we do not know the exact number of political prisoners in Nicaragua today, but we get an indication from the testimony of José Gonzalez, a former vice president of the Social Democratic Party. Gonzalez told Pope John Paul II there were about 8,000 political prisoners in 1981. He also told the Pope the Sandinistas practice repression and torture. Gonzalez, as you know, was arrested when he returned from Rome. He left Nicaragua and now lives in exile.

But the most compelling evidence of Sandinista brutality and of why people are fleeing is the Sandinistas' scorched-earth policy. We know the Sandinistas have ordered and are carrying out the forced relocation of tens of thousands of peasants. We have reports that 20,000 peasants have been moved in the past 2 months from their homes to relocation camps. Peasants who have escaped call themselves hostages and call the relocation camps concentration camps. The Communists themselves had admitted they're engaged in the forced resettlement of an estimated 65,000 people. Peasants and journalists tell of entire villages, homes, stores, and churches being burnt to the ground. They tell of animals slaughtered, crops burned, and villagers taken away at gunpoint in government trucks.

Why are the Communists doing this? Massed forced relocations are a common feature of modern Communist tyrannies, but there are other purposes here. For the people of many villages are actively supporting the freedom fighters, and so the Communists have decided to put more and more of the people of Nicaragua into closely guarded pens, and that way it will be easier for the regime to stalk the freedom fighters in the countryside. A Sandinista security chief has explained, "Anyone still in the hills is a guerrilla."

While all this is terrible, it can hardly come as a surprise to those who know what was done to the Miskito Indians. As you know, the Miskitos supported the Sandinistas against Somoza. But shortly after taking power, the Sandinistas attempted to indoctrinate the Miskitos in Marxist dogma, and the Indians resisted. The Sandinistas tried to put their own people in as leaders of the Miskito community, and the Indians resisted, so much that the Sandinistas labeled them "bourgeois" and, therefore, enemies of the people. They began to arrest Indian leaders. Some were murdered; some were tortured. One Miskito leader told our AFL–CIO that Thomas Borge and other leaders of the Sandinistas "came to my cell and warned me that Sandinismo would be established on the Atlantic coast even if every single Miskito Indian had to be eliminated."

Well, the Sandinistas came close. There were massacres. Eyewitnesses said some Miskitos were buried alive. Ten thousand Indians were force-marched to relocation camps. Miskito villages were burned down; they're still being burned down. Miskito villages were bombed and shelled, and they are still being bombed and shelled. In the name of humanity, these atrocities must be stopped.

Twenty thousand Indians are known to be incarcerated in relocation camps. About half are currently being held at the Tasba Pri Relocation Camps. *Tasba Pri*, by the way, means "free land." Well, above one "free land" camp, a New York Times reporter noted a sign that said, "Work that unites us is a revolutionary force."

In all, tens of thousands of Miskitos have been forced to flee Nicaragua, to free the land they lived on for over a thousand years. Many now live as refugees in Honduras.

Unfortunately, it's widely believed outside Nicaragua that the Sandinistas enjoy the support of the people inside, but you know this is completely untrue. We know this from many sources, even recently the American press.

A few months ago, The New Republic carried a report by Robert Leiken, who had long been sympathetic to the Sandinistas and who had formerly testified in Congress against aid to the *contras*. He wrote, "One of the most common means of sustaining the myth of popular support is the Sandinistas' use of the rationing system as a lever— ration cards are confiscated for nonattendance at Sandinista meetings." And talk of inflation is branded as "counterrevolutionary plot." Sympathy with the *contras*, he said, is more and more pervasive. In fact, the peasants now call them *Los Muchachos,* the affectionate term they once used exclusively for the Sandinistas. And what do they now call the Sandinistas? Well, the latest worker's chant is "the Sandinistas and Somoza are the same thing."

In spite of all this, the Sandinista government retains its defenders in this country and in the West. They look at all the evidence that the Sandinistas have instituted a Communist regime: all the pictures of dictator Ortega embracing Castro and visiting Moscow, all the Soviet-bloc advisers, and all the Sandinista votes in the U.N., such as their decision in line with the Soviet bloc to refuse the credentials of Israel. They look at this, and they say: "The Sandinistas aren't Communists, or aren't real Communists. Why, they're only nationalists, only socialists."

But these defenders admit there is a problem in Nicaragua. The problem, they say, is the freedom fighters. Well, just a few weeks ago, the whole world was treated to a so-called independent investigation of charges that the freedom fighters have committed atrocities. It spoke of these so-called atrocities in a rather riveting manner. And the report received great attention on television and in leading newspapers and publications. The report ignored Communist brutality, the murder of the Indians, and the arrest, torture, and murder of political dissidents. But we really shouldn't be surprised by that because, as our State Department discovered and Time magazine reported, this so-called independent investigation was the work of one of dictator Ortega's supporters, a sympathizer who has openly embraced Sandinismo and who was shepherded through Nicaragua by Sandinista operatives.

The truth is, there are atrocities going on in Nicaragua, but they're largely the work of the institutionalized cruelty of the Sandinista government. This cruelty is the natural expression of a Communist government, a cruelty that flows naturally from the heart of totalitarianism. The truth is Somoza was bad, but so many of the people of Nicaragua know the Sandinistas are infinitely worse.

We have here this evening many individuals who know these truths firsthand. Some of you may know of Bayardo Santaeliz. He is a 29-year-old Nicaraguan refugee and a former lay preacher of the Pentecostal Missionary Church in Nicaragua. And this is his story, a story told in sworn testimony before a Honduran civil rights commission.

A few years ago, the Sandinistas began pressuring Bayardo to stop preaching and start fighting for the revolution. And one night after holding a prayer session in a home on the slopes of the Momotombo Volcano, Bayardo went to bed. He was awakened by Sandinista soldiers who asked if he was an evangelical preacher; Bayardo said yes. The Sandinistas arrested him, accused him of counterrevolutionary activity, verbally abused him, and then tied him and two others to a pillar. Then the Sandinistas doused the house with gasoline and threw in a match. The room went up in flames, but they burned the rope that bound Bayardo, and he escaped with his clothes in flames and his body burned. He hid in the countryside and was rescued by *campesinos* who got him to a hospital, where he lied about the causes of his injuries. And not long after, he left Nicaragua.

Bayardo, I wonder if you could rise for a moment, wherever you are here in the room.

You know, I was going to ask all of you fellows with the cameras if you wouldn't kind of turn them off me and on him, but then he came up here; so I didn't ask you that. He's just one of the many who've suffered. He knows things and has experienced things that many of us in this country can barely imagine. And I think America has to see the true face of Nicaragua. Thank you, Bayardo.

Some people say this isn't America's problem. Why should we care if Nicaragua is a democracy or not? Well, we should care for a whole host of reasons.

Democracy has its own moral imperatives, as you well know, but it also has advantages that are profoundly practical. Democratic states do not attack their neighbors and destabilize regions. Democratic states do not find it easy to declare and carry out war. Democratic states are not by their nature militaristic. Democracies are traditionally reluctant to spend a great deal of money on arms. Democratic states have built-in controls on aggressive, expansionist behavior because democratic states must first marshal wide popular support before they move.

None of these characteristics applies to totalitarian states, however. And so, totalitarian Nicaragua poses a threat to us all.

The Sandinistas have been engaged for some time in spreading their Communist revolution beyond their borders. They're providing arms, training, and a headquarters to the Communist guerrillas who are attempting to overthrow the democratically elected Duarte government of El Salvador. The Sandinistas have been caught supporting similar antidemocratic movements in Honduras and Costa Rica; Guatemala, too, is threatened. If these governments fall, as Nicaragua has fallen, it will send millions of

429

refugees north, as country after country collapses.

Already, the refugee situation is building to unacceptable levels. More than a quarter of a million refugees have fled Nicaragua since the Sandinistas took control. Some weeks, a hundred Nicaraguans a day stream into Costa Rica alone. It must be noted here that many of these refugees carry no papers, register in no official camps, and wind up on no one's official list of those who've fled. They simply cross the border of one country or another and settle where they can.

And let me emphasize a very important point: These refugees are not simply people caught in the middle of a war. They're people fleeing for their lives from the Sandinista police state. They are fleeing from people who are burning down their villages, forcing them into concentration camps, and forcing their children into military service.

The refugees come into camps in Honduras with no food and no money. Many are sick with parasites and malaria. And the great tragedy is that these people are the innocents of the war—people without politics, people who had never presumed to govern or to tell the world how to turn. They are both innocents and victims.

And I want to take a moment to thank the people, you who are helping the refugees: Woody Jenkins, Diane Jenkins, and so many people in this room. While the world was turning away, you were helping. People like you are America at its best.

If the Communists continue unfettered by the weight of world opinion, there will be more victims, victims of a long march north. We've seen this before. We've seen the boat people leaving Southeast Asia in terror. We saw the streams of refugees leave East Berlin before the wall was built. We've seen these sad, lost armies fleeing in the night. We *cannot* allow it to happen again.

You know of our efforts to end the tragedy in Nicaragua. We want the killing and the bloodshed and the brutality to end. We've put forth a proposal for peace. We've asked for a cease-fire. We're asking the Sandinistas to join the democractic opposition in a church-mediated dialog. The church itself a year ago independently asked the Sandinistas for this dialog. We're asking the Sandinistas to take steps to hold truly democratic elections and restore freedom of speech, press, and assembly.

Nicaragua's neighbors, El Salvador and Honduras and Costa Rica, have embraced this proposal. President Duarte, President Suazo, President Monge have all personally written to me to express support for this peace plan. And who bears better witness to the merits of this plan than Nicaragua's own neighbors?

As part of our proposal, we've asked the Congress of the United States to release $14 million for food, medicine, and other support to help the patriots who believe in democracy survive in the hills of Nicaragua. This has been called a controversial request, and it's garnered some opposition in the Congress. I believe the reasons for this must be addressed.

Some claim that the freedom fighters are simply former Somozistas who want to reimpose a dictatorship. That is simply not true. Listen to the roll call of their leaders: Adolpho Calero, a Nicaraguan businessman who was imprisoned by Somoza; Alfonso Robelo, a member of the original Sandinista government, now leading freedom fighters in the south; Arturo Cruz, another former member of the Sandinista government who is supporting the freedom fighters; Eden Pastora, the famed Commander Zero, a hero of the anti-Somoza revolution.

These men are not putting their lives on the line to restore a dictatorship of the past; these men are fighting for freedom. Already they control large sections of the countryside. And as for their level of support, there are now three times as many freedom fighters fighting the Sandinistas as there were Sandinistas fighting Somoza.

There are those who say America's attempt to encourage freedom in Nicaragua interferes with the right of self-determination of the Nicaraguan people. Self-determination—you wonder what the ghosts of the Miskito Indians would say to that; you wonder what the journalists who cannot print the truth and the political prisoners who cannot speak it would say about self-determination and the Sandinistas. I think they would say that when a small Communist clique seizes a country, there is no self-determination and no chance of it.

I believe that a vote against this aid is more than a rejection of the freedom fighters. It is a rejection of all the forces of moderation from the church to the Contadora countries, which have called for freedom and democracy in Nicaragua.

I believe one inevitable outcome of a rejection of this aid would be that it would remove all pressure on the Sandinistas to change. And if no constraints are put on the Sandinistas, I believe the brutality and abuse they already aim at their own country and their neighbors may well be magnified a thousandfold.

I truly believe the history of this century forces me to believe that to do nothing in Central America is to give the first Communist stronghold on the North American continent a green light to spread its poison throughout this free and increasingly democratic hemisphere. [*Applause*] Thank you. I truly believe that this not only imperils the United States and its allies, but a vote against this proposal is literally a vote against peace, because it invites the conditions that will lead to more fighting, new wars, and new bloodshed.

This vote is more than an appropriation of money. Through this vote America will declare her commitment to peace. And through this aid, we will say to the free people of Central America: We will not betray you. We will not leave you. And we will not allow you to become victims of some so-called historic inevitability.

No evil is inevitable unless we make it so. We cannot have the United States walk away from one of the greatest moral challenges in postwar history. I pledge to you that we will do everything we can to win this great struggle.

And so, we're hopeful. We will fight on. We'll win this struggle for peace. Thank you for inviting me.

Viva Nicaragua libre! Thank you, and God bless you.

And now, I want to help Ambassador Davis, who I believe is going to give the first ever Nicaraguan Refugee Fund Humanitarian Award. And it goes this year to the executive director of Friends of the Americas, Diane Jenkins.

Diane, if you will come up here.

Note: The President spoke at 7:35 p.m. in the Grand Ballroom at the J.W. Marriott Hotel. In his closing remarks, the President referred to Arthur H. Davis, United States Ambassador to Paraguay.

Proclamation 5318—Pan American Day and Pan American Week, 1985
April 15, 1985

By the President of the United States of America

A Proclamation

The countries of the Western Hemisphere are bound together by their humanitarian ideals, their respect for individual liberty, and their yearning for peace and prosperity—goals eloquently expressed in the Charter of the Organization of American States. Just as our Revolution of 1776 was an inspiration for Simon Bolivar and Jose de San Martin, so we in the United States took inspiration from the struggle of our neighbors to be free from foreign domination. We continue to take courage from those great struggles for liberty today, when new forms of tyranny and modern totalitarian systems threaten the peace and security of the Hemisphere, especially in Central America.

The Organization of American States, embodying the Inter-American System, links together this diverse group of nations, with their Spanish, Portuguese, French, English, African, and Indian heritages. But whatever their creeds, languages, or cultures, the peoples of our Hemisphere are united in the common cause of ending poverty, disease, and illiteracy. The O.A.S. has played a notable role in this cause.

More and more countries of the Hemisphere are turning to democratic institutions to solve political, social, educational, and economic problems. They realize that peace, prosperity, and freedom are best served when the people, faced with a real choice of political parties, freely elect their own governments.

On this Pan American Day of 1985, the people of the United States extend warm greetings to all their neighbors in the Americas and reaffirm their active support for the Organization of American States and the principles for which it stands.

Now, Therefore, I, Ronald Reagan, President of the United States of America, do hereby proclaim Sunday, April 14, 1985, as Pan American Day, and the week begin-

ning April 14, 1985, through April 20, 1985, as Pan American Week. I urge the Governors of every State of the Union, and the Governor of the Commonwealth of Puerto Rico, and officials of the other areas under the flag of the United States of America to honor these observances with appropriate activities and ceremonies.

In Witness Whereof, I have hereunto set my hand this fifteenth day of April, in the year of our Lord nineteen hundred and eighty-five, and of the Independence of the United States of America the two hundred and ninth.

RONALD REAGAN

[*Filed with the Office of the Federal Register, 11:15 a.m., April 16, 1985*]

Note: The proclamation was released by the Office of the Press Secretary on April 16.

Proclamation 5319—Loyalty Day, 1985
April 15, 1985

By the President of the United States of America

A Proclamation

Providence has favored our land, with its abundant resources and industrious people, and the years of adversity in our history have been few. Yet even during the dark hours, the times of conflict or economic hardship, Americans have demonstrated their unwavering devotion to the noble ideals upon which this country was founded. Our faith in the principles of freedom, justice, and opportunity has sustained us. We have prevailed over every challenge and our success shines as a beacon of hope for the world, an enduring reminder that adherence to the fundamental values of liberty will overcome any obstacle.

Today these values are enjoying renewed allegiance in America and elsewhere; the advantages of our democratic way of life are winning the United States new admiration and respect around the world.

Americans' loyalty to their Nation is especially inspiring because it is freely given by

a free people. Nations that seek to compel the love or fidelity of their citizens without tolerance for their unalienable rights are inherently unstable and frequently dangerous to others. Now that the windows of communication and commerce are bringing nations into increasingly close relationships, the truths our forefathers found self-evident are becoming apparent to all: the future belongs to the free—to peoples who are free to work, to assemble, to vote, to travel and to emigrate, to print and to speak, and to worship as they choose.

Today, in this time of peace and prosperity at home, it is fitting that we reflect upon the venerable ideals that symbolize the American spirit. By remaining loyal to these ideals, we will be worthy of the trust a generous God has reposed in us. For this purpose, the Congress, by joint resolution approved July 18, 1958 (72 Stat. 369, 36 U.S.C. 162), has designated May 1 of each year as Loyalty Day, a day to renew our commitment to this grand republic and its democratic institutions.

Now, Therefore, I, Ronald Reagan, President of the United States of America, do hereby proclaim May 1, 1985, as Loyalty Day and call upon all Americans and patriotic, civic, and educational organizations to observe that day with appropriate ceremonies. I also call upon all government officials to display the flag of the United States on all government buildings and grounds on that day.

In Witness Whereof, I have hereunto set my hand this fifteenth day of April, in the year of our Lord nineteen hundred and eighty-five, and of the Independence of the United States of America the two hundred and ninth.

RONALD REAGAN

[*Filed with the Office of the Federal Register, 12:01 p.m., April 16, 1985*]

Note: The proclamation was released by the Office of the Press Secretary on April 16.

Proclamation 5320—Law Day, U.S.A., 1985
April 15, 1985

By the President of the United States of America

A Proclamation

May 1, 1985, is Law Day, U.S.A. This year's Law Day theme, "Liberty and Justice for All," reaffirms the principles upon which our Republic was founded. The guarantee of liberty and the right to seek justice emerged through law: through the Declaration of Independence, the Constitution, and the Bill of Rights. As Americans, we continue to preserve these principles through our lawmaking and judicial systems.

Each time we recite the Pledge of Allegiance, we renew our commitment to providing the benefits of liberty and the reality of justice for all.

These principles have served and continue to serve as an inspiration to everyone in this great Nation, because they represent a promise, an ideal, and an opportunity. It is the promise of liberty and justice for all that has brought millions of immigrants to American shores. It is the ideal of liberty and justice for all that has guided our government in making and enforcing our laws. It is the opportunity for liberty and justice for all that has inspired Americans from all walks of life to participate in and give life to our unique form of government.

The fact that we continue to strive to be one Nation, under God, with liberty and justice for all, is a tribute to the memory of the millions of Americans who, throughout our history, have been willing to die to secure or preserve these ideals. The great patriot Patrick Henry's impassioned plea, "Give me liberty or give me death," continues to symbolize today the fervor with which Americans treasure these freedoms.

Law Day is an important opportunity for all Americans to improve their understanding and appreciation of the contribution law makes to the preservation of liberty and justice. I urge all Americans to join with me in renewing our dedication to those principles for which so many Americans have sacrificed their lives.

Now, Therefore, I, Ronald Reagan, President of the United States of America, do hereby proclaim Wednesday, May 1, 1985, as Law Day, U.S.A. I urge the people of the United States to use this occasion to renew their commitment to the rule of law and to reaffirm our dedication to the partnership of law and liberty. I also urge the legal profession, schools, civic, service, and fraternal organizations, public bodies, libraries, the courts, the communications media, business, the clergy, and all interested individuals and organizations to join in efforts to focus attention on the need for the rule of law. I also call upon all public officials to display the flag of the United States on all government buildings open on Law Day, May 1, 1985.

In Witness Whereof, I have hereunto set my hand this 15th day of April, in the year of our Lord nineteen hundred and eighty-five, and of the Independence of the United States of America the two hundred and ninth.

RONALD REAGAN

[*Filed with the Office of the Federal Register, 12:02 p.m., April 16, 1985*]

Note: The President signed the proclamation at a ceremony in the Oval Office at the White House at 4:45 p.m. The proclamation was released by the Office of the Press Secretary on April 16.

Letter to the Speaker of the House and the Chairman of the Senate Foreign Relations Committee Reporting on the Cyprus Conflict
April 16, 1985

Dear Mr. Speaker: (Dear Mr. Chairman:)

In accordance with Public Law 95–384, I am submitting herewith a bimonthly report on progress toward a negotiated settlement of the Cyprus question.

Since my previous report, the leaders of the two Cypriot communities participated in a summit meeting in New York January 17–20 under the auspices of United Nations Secretary General Perez de Cuellar. At the outset of the meeting, the Secretary General expressed his expectation "that the parties would conclude an agreement containing the elements necessary for a comprehensive solution to the problem, aimed at establishing a Federal Republic of Cyprus." Had this effort succeeded, it would have set in motion a process that—over a period of time in which further concrete negotiations would take place—could have led to a true resolution of the Cyprus problem. Following the summit's close the Secretary General announced that the Turkish Cypriot side has "fully accepted the draft agreement" and that the Greek Cypriots had accepted the documentation "as a basis for negotiation." While he acknowledged that the failure to bridge the gap between these two positions meant that the summit had not achieved its goal, the Secretary General added that the two sides "had never been so close" and that he would continue his efforts.

The Turkish Cypriots, following the failure of the January summit, announced their intention to proceed to parliamentary elections in June 1985. The Turkish Cypriots have said the elections would not preclude their continued participation in the Secretary General's process and in an eventual federal Cypriot state. We have registered with both communities our conviction that any actions that might damage chances for the UN Secretary General's pursuit of a fair and lasting solution should be avoided. The Secretary General met with President Kyprianou in Geneva on March 11 where they discussed next steps in the pursuit of a solution.

Since my last report to you, Administration officials have met regularly with leaders of both Cypriot communities, including a meeting March 11 between Vice President Bush and President Kyprianou in Geneva and the ongoing contacts in Cyprus between Ambassador Boehm and both President Kyprianou and Mr. Denktash. We continue to work closely with the two Cypriot parties, and with the governments of Greece and Turkey, in support of the Secretary General's program. We urge flexibility by all parties, and we are encouraged that they continue to support a negotiated solution.

Sincerely,

RONALD REAGAN

Note: Identical letters were sent to Thomas P. O'Neill, Jr., Speaker of the House of Representatives, and Richard G. Lugar, chairman of the Senate Foreign Relations Committee.

Nomination of Lowell C. Kilday To Be United States Ambassador to the Dominican Republic
April 16, 1985

The President today announced his intention to nominate Lowell C. Kilday, of Virginia, a career member of the Senior Foreign Service, Class of Minister-Counselor, as Ambassador of the United States of America to the Dominican Republic. He would succeed Robert Anderson.

Mr. Kilday entered the Foreign Service in 1957. He served from 1957 to 1959 as consular officer at the American Embassy in Havana. From 1960 to 1961, he was cultural exchange officer in the Bureau of Educational and Cultural Affairs at the Department. In 1961 he became staff assistant in the Bureau of Inter-American Affairs and from there went to Recife as political officer, where he served until 1964. In 1964–1966 he was political officer in Rio de Janeiro and then Santo Domingo until 1967. From there he became the Ecuador desk officer in the Department. In 1968–1970 Mr. Kilday was senior watch officer in the Operations Center of the Department and in 1970 studied at the Foreign Service Institute.

For a while in 1971 he was Agency Director in the Bureau of International Organization Affairs before going to Vietnam as province senior adviser, CORDS, where he served until 1973. In 1973–1974 he was a student at the National War College, and from there he became Deputy Director, Office of Central American Affairs, 1975–1976. From 1976 to 1979, Mr. Kilday was deputy chief of mission at our Embassy in San José. In 1980 he became Director, Office of Brazilian Affairs, in the Department, and from 1983 to the present, he has been Deputy Assistant Secretary of State in the Bureau of Inter-American Affairs.

Mr. Kilday was born February 20, 1931, in New Hope, WI. He received his B.S. from the University of Wisconsin in 1956. His foreign languages are Spanish, Portuguese, and German. He is married to the former Gerda Dreher, and they have six children.

Nomination of John R. Silber To Be a Member of the Advisory Board for Radio Broadcasting to Cuba
April 16, 1985

The President today announced his intention to nominate John R. Silber to be a member of the Advisory Board for Radio Broadcasting to Cuba for a term of 1 year. This is a new position.

Dr. Silber has been president of Boston University since 1970. At Boston University he is university professor of philosophy and law. He is a spokesman on the maintenance of academic standards and the financing of higher education and has several publications on those subjects. He is also the author of numerous writings on ethics and the philosophy of law.

He was a professor of philosophy and university professor of arts and letters at the University of Texas at Austin, where he also served as dean of the College of Arts and Sciences. He has received four awards for distinguished teaching, including the Morris Ernst Award for excellence in teaching and the Danforth Foundation's E. Harris Harbison Award for distinguished teaching.

He graduated from Trinity University (B.A., 1947) and Yale University (M.A., 1952; Ph.D., 1956). He is married, has four children, and resides in Brookline, MA. He was born August 15, 1926, in San Antonio, TX.

Appointment of Edward E. Allison as a Member of the Advisory Committee for Trade Negotiations
April 16, 1985

The President today announced his intention to appoint Edward E. Allison to be a member of the Advisory Committee for Trade Negotiations for a term of 2 years. He will succeed William C. Turner.

Mr. Allison is a consultant to the firm of Heron, Burchette, Ruckert & Rothwell in Washington, DC. Previously he served as administrative assistant to Senator Paul Laxalt in 1979–1984. Prior to that time, he owned his own public relations firm, Allison & Associates, in Reno, NV. In 1970–1973 he was marketing director for Computer Sciences Corporation's northwest division in Richland, WA. He was administrative assistant to Governor Laxalt in 1968–1970.

He graduated from the University of Nevada at Reno (B.A. 1961). He is married, has two children, and resides in McLean, VA. He was born January 9, 1940, in Denver, CO.

Appointment of Mary Dewey Faison as a Member of the Advisory Committee on the Arts
April 16, 1985

The President today announced his intention to appoint Mary Dewey Faison to be a member of the Advisory Committee on the Arts (John F. Kennedy Center for the Performing Arts, Smithsonian Institution). This is a new appointment.

Mrs. Faison is an antique dealer in Charlotte, NC, and serves as chairman of the Mint Museum Antiques Show. She also serves on the development board of WTVI (public television) and is chairman of the Children's Little Theatre Ball.

She graduated from the University of North Carolina (B.S., 1962). She is married, has two children, and resides in Charlotte, NC. She was born January 17, 1940, in Goldsboro, NC.

Nomination of Glen A. Holden To Be a Member of the National Museum Services Board
April 16, 1985

The President today announced his intention to nominate Glen A. Holden to be a member of the National Museum Services Board, National Foundation on the Arts and the Humanities, for a term expiring December 6, 1989. He would succeed Anne Carroll Badham.

Mr. Holden has been president, chief executive officer, and chairman of the board of Security First Group in Los Angeles, CA, since 1973. Previously, he was president and director of the Variable Annuity Life Insurance Co. in Houston, TX (1964–1973), and a general agent with National Life Insurance Co. of Vermont in 1956–1963. He is a member of the Los Angeles Chamber of Commerce and the Century City Civic Council. He is a founder of the Music Center of Los Angeles County.

He graduated from the University of Oregon (B.S.). He is married, has three children, and resides in Los Angeles, CA. He was born July 2, 1927, in Boise, ID.

Statement on Signing the Bill Extending Conditional Loan Guarantee Agreements for Ethanol Fuel Production Facilities
April 16, 1985

I have signed S. 781, an amendment to the Biomass Energy and Alcohol Fuels Act of 1980, that extends for 5 months the deadline for four ethanol fuel production projects to meet the terms and conditions required for Federal loan guarantees.

Conservation and renewable energy sources are an important component of this administration's national energy policy. We support efforts by the private sector to develop alternative energy sources that are economically viable in the Nation's competitive marketplace.

To give the alcohol fuels industry an opportunity to develop into a competitive alternate energy source, the Department of Energy entered into four conditional commitments in 1981 to guarantee loans for the construction of ethanol fuel production facilities. Three of these conditional commitments have since expired, and a fourth expires on April 30, 1985. Although the sponsors of these projects have not yet been able to meet satisfactorily the terms and conditions, they believe that an extension of the conditional agreements until September 30, 1985, will enable them to complete these transactions. By passage of S. 781, the Congress has determined that they should be provided a last additional opportunity to do so.

This amendment does not grant any new loan guarantee authority or provide for any new commitments. However, the conditional agreements being extended commit the Government to a potential liability of some $250 million should the projects default. Utmost care must be taken to protect the taxpayers from a loss of this magnitude. In view of these circumstances, I have directed the Secretary of Energy to issue loan guarantees only to those projects that pass a rigorous economic analysis. The ethanol industry must ultimately stand on its own in the energy marketplace, competing fairly with other energy sources. The Nation will not attain greater energy security if the Government subsidizes energy sources that do not demonstrate their competitiveness. Therefore, we will not make any Federal commitments on behalf of projects that are not determined to be economically viable. To do otherwise would shift the burden of a high-risk business venture onto the shoulders of the American taxpayer.

Note: S. 781, approved April 16, was assigned Public Law No. 99-24.

Remarks at a Conference on Religious Liberty
April 16, 1985

I'm deeply honored to address this conference. I know that a good many of you've come a long way to be here today, and I know you've given greatly of your time and energy and concern. And I could only hope, as you do, that those now suffering around the world for their beliefs will draw renewed courage from your work.

The history of religion and its impact on civilization cannot be summarized in a few days or—never mind minutes. But one of the great shared characteristics of all religions is the distinction they draw between the temporal world and the spiritual world. All religions, in effect, echo the words of the Gospel of St. Matthew: "Render, there-

437

fore, unto Caesar the things which are Caesar's; and unto God the things that are God's." What this injunction teaches us is that the individual cannot be entirely subordinate to the state, that there exists a whole other realm, an almost mysterious realm of individual thought and action which is sacred and which is totally beyond and outside of state control. This idea has been central to the development of human rights.

Only in an intellectual climate which distinguishes between the city of God and the city of man and which explicitly affirms the independence of God's realm and forbids any infringement by the state on its prerogatives, only in such a climate could the idea of individual human rights take root, grow, and eventually flourish.

We see this climate in all democracies and in our own political tradition. The founders of our republic rooted their democratic commitment in the belief that all men are endowed by their Creator with certain inalienable rights. And so, they created a system of government whose avowed purpose was and is the protection of those God-given rights.

But as all of you know only too well, there are many political regimes today that completely reject the notion that a man or a woman can have a greater loyalty to God than to the state. Marx's central insight when he was creating his political system was that religious belief would subvert his intentions. Under the Communist system, the ruling party would claim for itself the attributes which religious faith ascribes to God alone, and the state would be final arbiter of youth—or truth, I should say, justice and morality. I guess saying youth there instead of truth was just a sort of a Freudian slip on my part. [*Laughter*]

Marx declared religion an enemy of the people, a drug, an opiate of the masses. And Lenin said: "Religion and communism are incompatible in theory as well as in practice . . . We must fight religion."

All of this illustrates a truth that, I believe, must be understood. Atheism is not an incidental element of communism, not just part of the package; it is the package. In countries which have fallen under Communist rule, it is often the church which forms the most powerful barrier against a completely totalitarian system. And so, totalitarian regimes always seek either to destroy the church or, when that is impossible, to subvert it.

In the Soviet Union the church was immediately attacked by the Communist revolution. But the Soviets, bowing to Western squeamishness about the denial of liberties, often characterize their actions as merely defensive.

In 1945 Josef Stalin met with Harry Hopkins, who had been sent by Harry Truman to discuss various East-West problems. In the middle of a talk about politics, Stalin interjected the following: In 1917, he said, the Russian Communist Party had proclaimed the right of religious freedom as part of their political program. But, he said, the churches of Russia had declared the Soviet Government anathema and had called on church members to resist the call of the Red Army. Now, what could we do, said Stalin, but declare war on the church! He assured Hopkins, however, that World War II had ended the church-state antagonism and now freedom of religion could be granted to the church. But that, as you know, never happened.

History has taught us that you can bulldoze a church, but you can't extinguish all that is good in every human heart. And so, in spite of the dangers involved, there are Christians and Jews and Muslims and others throughout the Communist world who continue to practice their faith. Some of them have been imprisoned for their courage. There's the late Valerie Marchenko who died in a Soviet prison hospital a few short months ago. He was 37 years old, a scholar, and a Christian who, at his most recent trial, spoke of his belief in God and his faith in human goodness. There's Father Gleb Yakunin, who was recently sent to Siberia for 5 years of internal exile. He's another prisoner of faith. And Bronislav Borovsky, recently sentenced for smuggling Bibles into Czechoslovakia. These are only a few of many.

Dr. Ernest Gordon, the president of an organization named CREED—Christian Rescue Effort for the Emancipation of Dissidents—noted that on a recent trip to Eastern Europe he spoke with a priest who had spent 10 years in prison. The priest asked him to deliver a message to the West: There is a war going on. It is not nuclear but spiritual. The fallout of the atheistic explosion is everywhere. But Dr. Gordon added, "Although the fallout may be everywhere, we are reminded that God, too, is everywhere, and not even tyrannies can keep Him out."

We in the United States have protested this terrible abuse of people who are nothing less than heroes of this century. Most recently when congressional leaders met in Moscow with General Secretary Gorbachev, they gave the Soviet leadership a list of Baltic and Ukrainian prisoners of conscience. And the Council on Soviet Jewry and other groups were magnificent in making sure that the congressional delegation did not leave without extensive data on repression against Jews in the Soviet Union.

Religious persecution, of course, is not confined to Europe. We see it in Iran, whose leaders have virtually declared war on the Bahais; we see it in Afghanistan, where the Soviet military has resorted to increasingly cruel measures against the Moslem people; and we see a variation on how to abuse religious freedom in the Sandinista regime of Nicaragua.

In Nicaragua, the Sandinista regime is faced with a politically active church that, although it supported the revolution, is now considered a major obstacle to complete totalitarian control. Sometime back, Nicaraguan Bishop Pablo Antonio Vega said that, "We are living with a totalitarian ideology that no one wants in this country."

The Sandinistas are actively attempting to discredit and split the church hierarchy. And there's one new area to be watched. The Sandinistas, like all Communist regimes, are injecting their ideology into the educational system and have begun widespread campaigns to indoctrinate children and adults. But the Catholic Church is fighting to maintain autonomy and keep this indoctrination out of their churches and schools. I just had a verbal message delivered to me from the Pope urging us to continue our efforts in Central America.

Well, this thing that I was mentioning has not been resolved. Cuba solved the problem by closing all private schools, including religious schools. The general state of religious liberty in Nicaragua is suggested by testimony from various sources but most vividly by those who have fled this brutal regime.

We recently learned of a pastor of the Evangelical Church in a Nicaraguan town who told the freedom fighters that the Sandinistas had threatened to send the 3,000 members of his church to relocation camps. The pastor and his church members are now hiding out in caves and temporary settlements in the countryside.

The Sandinistas also harass Jews. Two Nicaraguan refugees, Sarita and Oscar Kellermann, have told of the fire-bombing of their synagogue by the Sandinistas. The Sandinistas wrote on the synagogue the words, "What Hitler started we will finish." And they wrote on the Kellermann's home, "Jews out of Nicaragua."

May I interject here that stories like these of organized coercion and brutality and terror are the reason we're asking Congress for aid to help the freedom fighters and to help the victims of the Sandinista regime.

When I think of Nicaragua these days, it occurs to me anew that you can judge any new government, any new regime, by whether or not it allows religion to flourish. If it doesn't, you can be sure it's an enemy of mankind, for it's attempting to ban what is most beautiful in the human heart.

But we mustn't feel despair, because it's not appropriate to the times. We're living in a dramatic age. Throughout the world the machinery of the state is being used as never before against religious freedom. But at the same time, throughout the world new groups of believers keep springing up. Points of light flash out in the darkness, and God is honored once again.

Perhaps this is the greatest irony of the Communist experiment. The very pressure they apply seems to create the force, friction, and heat that allow deep belief to once again burst into flame.

I believe that the most essential element of our defense of freedom is our insistence on speaking out for the cause of religious liberty. I would like to see this country rededicate itself wholeheartedly to this cause. I join you in your desire that the Protestant

439

Churches of America, the Catholic Church, and the Jewish organizations remember the members of their flock who are in prison or in jeopardy in other countries. We are our brothers' keepers, all of us. And I hope the message will go forth from this conference: To prisoners of conscience throughout the world, take heart; you have not been forgotten. We, your brothers and sisters in God, have made your cause our cause, and we vow never to relent until you have regained the freedom that is your birthright as a child of God.

Now, let me turn to an issue, if I could for just a moment, that has provoked a storm of controversy: my decision to visit the war cemetery at Bitburg and my decision, on the state visit to Germany, not to visit the site of the concentration camp at Dachau. It was and remains my purpose and that of Chancellor Kohl to use this visit to Germany on the 40th anniversary of the war's end in Europe to commemorate not simply the military victory of 40 years ago but the liberation of Europe, the rebirth of German freedom, and the reconciliation of our two countries.

My purpose was and remains not to reemphasize the crimes of the Third Reich in 12 years of power, but to celebrate the tremendous accomplishments of the German people in 40 years of liberty, freedom, democracy, and peace. It was to remind the world that since the close of that terrible war, the United States and the Federal Republic have established an historic relationship, not of superpower to satellite but of sister republics bounded together by common ideals and alliance and partnership. It is to cement the 40 years of friendship between a free Germany and the United States, between the German people and the American people, that Chancellor Kohl and I agreed together to lay a wreath at the cemetery for the German war dead. That's why I accepted the invitation to Bitburg, and that's why I'm going to Bitburg.

As for the decision not to go to Dachau, one of the sites of the great moral obscenity of that era, it was taken because of my mistaken impression that such a visit was outside the official agenda. Chancellor Kohl's recent letter to me, however, has made it plain that my invitation to visit a concentration camp was, indeed, a part of his planned itinerary. So, I have now accepted that invitation, and my staff is in Germany exploring a site that will fit into our schedule there.

For years I've said it, and I'll say it again today, and I will say it again on that occasion: We must never forget the Holocaust, nor should we ever permit such an atrocity to happen ever again. Never again.

Thank you. God bless all of you.

Note: The President spoke at 1:32 p.m. in Room 450 of the Old Executive Office Building.

Remarks at a White House Meeting with the Deficit Reduction Coalition
April 16, 1985

Thank you and good afternoon and welcome to the White House, or has someone said that already?

Well, first, let me thank Red Cavaney for the outstanding work that he's doing as chairman of the Deficit Reduction Coalition. And I want to thank all of you here today. With your help, we're making tremendous progress. And now we have before us, I think, an historic opportunity: the chance to finally get control of the budget behemoth and make government once again the servant of the people, rather than the other way around.

And I think Bob Dole deserves special thanks and appreciation for his leadership role on this issue. We couldn't have come this far without him.

It used to be that talk of deficits was all doom and gloom. As a matter of fact, I did some of that talking out on the mashed-potato circuit years ago. But without the political will in Congress to reform its big-spending impulses, our economy was thrust into a position of peril, caught between the devil of higher taxes and the bottomless sea of growing deficits.

Now we can see that even our greatest problems are, as Henry Kaiser once said, simply opportunities in workclothes. To-gether with the Senate Republican leader-ship, we've fashioned a compromise budget plan that will virtually eliminate the deficit by the end of the decade. And just as im-portant, we'll begin the long-overdue work of reforming Federal spending.

Passage of this bill would be a decisive break with our spendthrift past, an achieve-ment of comparable importance to the his-toric tax cuts of 1981. Instead of a budget for the special interests, we've proposed a budget for the public interest. It'll be intro-duced as an amendment to Senate Concur-rent Resolution 32, but I just like to call it the taxpayers' protection plan.

There are, of course, some up on the Hill who aren't happy with budget reform. They are the ones who still secretly are hoping to raise taxes. Their last hope is to sabotage budget reform, so endangering the econo-my that Congress will be panicked into taking desperate measures, which they hope would be a tax increase.

The tax-increasers are like those soldiers after World War II out on some of those Pacific islands who didn't know the war had ended. They've lost the fight, and they're now reduced to hit-and-run attacks on budget reform. I have this to say to those tax-increasers huddled away up on the Hill. If I were talking to them, I would say: You're fighting a lost cause. Throw down your tax hikes and come on out into the sunlight with the rest of the American people. Get on the taxpayers' protection plan and join us in celebrating the return to fiscal sanity and a strong, healthy economy.

Let me also say that the budget freeze that some are suggesting is the wrong medi-cine at the wrong time. Why should we continue to fund wasteful, unnecessary pro-grams at their present high levels while lim-iting those programs that are truly worthy? We also know that if we leave the pork

barrels intact, the same political pressure groups will be back next year trying to fill them with pork. Every time an Amtrak—well, no, I'm getting ahead of myself there. I shouldn't.

Our proposal is for a leaner, healthier, and firmer budget that cuts what should be cut and keeps what should be kept. Special provisions have been made to protect the poor, elderly, and disabled. Full inflation adjustments will be given to those receiving Supplemental Security Income, increasing benefits from between 10, 15 dollars monthly, and food stamps, AFDC, WIC, other safety net programs will stay fully funded.

But some programs whose costs far out-weigh their benefits have been eliminated entirely. And now I'll say it—Amtrak, for instance. It's a perfect example of how gov-ernment spending gets out of hand. Origi-nally authorized for only a 2-year trial, Am-trak's proponents assured the American people that the railroad would soon be making a profit. Well, instead, Amtrak has cost taxpayers billions of dollars. That shouldn't have surprised us, because in World War I we had an experience with the Government running the railroads, and it was a disaster. Every time an Amtrak train leaves the station, it costs the taxpay-ers $35 for each passenger. In some cases it would be cheaper, actually, just to hand those passengers a free plane ticket to their destination.

Or let's take the Job Corps. It's estimated that each job created through that program costs the taxpayers $15,200. That's almost equal to sending a student to Harvard for 1 year. Maybe the result's the same, too. [*Laughter*] I won't look at Don Regan. [*Laughter*] As a graduate of good old Eureka College, I couldn't resist. [*Laughter*]

The youth employment opportunity wage would cost the Government nothing and, we believe, would create countless jobs, new jobs, for young people.

The Small Business Administration is an-other example of government poking its nose into areas where it has no business, if you'll excuse the pun. Since the tax cuts took hold, this country has become the un-disputed world leader for business creation.

Over 600,000 businesses were incorporated in 1983, an all-time record. And it looks like 1984 will turn out to have been another record year.

Just two-tenths of 1 percent of all U.S. businesses in fiscal year 1984 received subsidized credit from that program, and most of those loans went to restaurants, bars, and car dealerships, where ample private credit is available.

Other major programs in the taxpayers' protection plan have been reformed on the theory that it isn't fair to have people with low incomes subsidize special programs for the well-to-do. College student aid, for instance, will still be provided to low- and middle-income families, and this aid will cover the full cost of attending public colleges, but aid to the well-to-do will be scaled back. As the law stands now, low-income taxpayers, who may not be able to afford college for their own children, are helping subsidize the education of children whose families make as much as $100,000 a year. Now, unlike the current law, our bill would guarantee at least a 2-percent increase in Social Security benefits, more if inflation picks up, while the low-income elderly and disabled will receive full—as I said before—cost-of-living adjustments.

Throughout the budget process, defense spending has been the favorite scapegoat of those unwilling to make necessary reforms. The compromise defense appropriations of the taxpayers' protection plan allows us to keep the vital work of building up our defenses on track. We can feel secure with these spending levels, but I think it's clear that any further cuts could derail our defense program, cause expensive delays and inefficiencies, and very likely undermine our national security.

After almost two decades in which it seemed that Congress had lost control of spending, the taxpayers' protection plan is the first step to regaining that control and earning the respect of the American people. It's a model of what the democratic process can achieve. The result of intensive negotiation and compromise, it addresses a serious problem fairly and protects our national security and makes special allowance for the poor and needy. Most important, it breaks apart the congressional spending ma-

chine. And when combined with tax reform and substantial tax rate reductions, it will open the door to a growing, prosperous economy through the end of the decade and beyond.

We couldn't have gotten this far without your help. And as I've said before, if we can't make Congress see the light, we'll make them feel the heat.

I have another issue, but before I take that one up, I just want to tell you that yesterday two young Congressmen came into my office—one of them a freshman Congressman—and they handed me a letter. It contained 146 signatures and a promise—exactly the number of signatures were on that letter which promised to uphold a veto of any tax increase that I might make. They did make my day. [*Laughter*]

Well, I'd like to take a minute and ask your support on another issue today, an issue that I believe touches on the very heart and soul of what it means to be an American. In a few days, Congress will vote on whether or not to support our proposal to help put Nicaragua on a path toward peace and democracy. Recently I proposed a plan for peace and democracy in Nicaragua, an immediate cease-fire to be followed by church-mediated negotiations leading to free and honest elections and Congress supporting this peace initiative with humanitarian aid.

Few votes will ever be so important. Either way it's decided, Congress will send a signal. A "yes" vote would signal new hope for peace and a return to the original democratic promise of the Nicaraguan revolution. But if Congress votes "no," if they in essence wash their hands of our responsibility to support peaceful development and democracy in this hemisphere, they'll be sending a message of desertion, a clear statement that the greatest democracy on Earth doesn't care if communism snuffs out the freedom of our neighbors and endangers our own security. Democracies and freedom-loving people throughout the world must be amazed and I would think deeply concerned.

The Soviet-bloc and terrorist nations flood Nicaragua with arms and personnel, sparing no expense in support of the totalitarian Sandinista regime, while the U.S. Congress remains paralyzed over a mere $14 million in humanitarian aid, less than the cost of the deadly Hind helicopters the Soviets have given the Communists to use against the resistance, the freedom fighters.

Meanwhile, the Sandinistas and some misguided sympathizers in this country are waging a sophisticated disinformation campaign designed to sway public opinion. A short while ago, front pages across the country blazed the reports—the news of a new report alleging human rights abuses by the freedom fighters. Now Time magazine has learned that the report was bought and paid for by the Sandinistas. It seems that the Sandinistas think they have more to gain by lobbying Congress than negotiating with the democratic opposition. As a recent article in the New York Times reported, the Sandinistas are, quote, "pinning their hopes on the U.S. Congress."

Well, please let Congress know that there's another side, that Americans don't want the creation of another Cuba, a warehouse of subversion on the American mainland; that they don't want Libyans, the PLO, and the followers of Khomeini bunkered down just 2 hours from our southern border. Let's not let the Sandinistas be the only ones lobbying our Congress. Tell them not to sabotage our efforts for democracy in Nicaragua and peace in our hemisphere.

So, we have two major votes coming up in Congress. One will directly determine our economic security throughout the end of the decade, and the other could influence our national security throughout the end of the century. So, I feel free to ask you this because America needs your help on both of these.

And thank you, and God bless you all.

Note: The President spoke at 4 p.m. in Room 450 of the Old Executive Office Building.

Remarks at the Welcoming Ceremony for President Chadli Bendjedid of Algeria
April 17, 1985

President Reagan. Mr. President, it's a great pleasure to welcome you and Madame Bendjedid to Washington today. Yours is the first state visit to the United States by an Algerian President.

As the head of Africa's second largest nation and an acknowledged leader in the Arab, African, and nonaligned nations, your views on a wide range of issues carry great importance.

Our mutual concerns about Middle East peace, North African stability, and African economic development and political process—or progress, I should say, are among items which I look forward to discussing with you. Through these discussions we seek understanding and progress. We seek to enhance the cooperation of our governments and improve the well-being of our peoples.

The ties between our two peoples and

governments have grown over the past few years. We Americans particularly welcome the return of cordial relations, which existed in the early days of your independence. Your visit gives us an opportunity to further strengthen our bilateral ties.

In this respect, I note with satisfaction that we will sign tomorrow an agreement to establish a joint economic commission and will shortly conclude an accord on cultural exchanges. These achievements are tangible signs that the relations between the United States and Algeria are moving in a positive direction. And they're only two of the areas in which our interests coincide and are growing.

Your visit should serve as a catalyst for further friendship-building activities between our peoples and governments. The United States is already one of Algeria's major trading partners. We buy hydrocarbons from you and market American goods, services, and technology in your country. And this exchange benefits both our peoples. Let us continue to explore ways of encouraging this commerce and equalizing our balance of trade so we can invigorate both our economies.

I'm aware, Mr. President, of your particular interest in American agriculture, especially our irrigation methods and farmer technology. Your trip to California, after your visit with us in Washington, should be most enlightening, and we're delighted you're going. There in my home State, you'll have the opportunity to see American know-how put to use in producing food and fiber and to visit firms which already are working with Algeria.

This is even more appropriate, Mr. President, because of the similarity in climate between California and Algeria. And that similarity gives me a good idea of just how wonderful your country really is.

Americans are proud of our past participation in Algerian development projects, and we hope to build upon what has already been accomplished. Your material resources in Algeria are vast, Mr. President, but I'm sure you'll agree that the Algerian people are your greatest treasure.

We're gratified that at this time Algerian students are studying at American universities and technical institutes. The knowledge they gain will enable them to contribute to Algeria's progress and to help create a more prosperous future for your country. They will also serve as a human bridge of friendship between our peoples. This is the kind of technology transfer that we can all be proud of. American educational institutions are open and will remain open to those who would master the keys to development. In doing so, we seek to build a more prosperous world and to establish with you relations based on good will and mutual respect.

Mr. President, again, I give to you my good wishes and those of the American people. And in closing, I want to express our collective gratitude for the role which you and your government played in obtaining release of our Tehran hostages in 1981. It was a gallant effort and was in keeping with Algerian tradition. The records show

that your great national hero, Abd Al-Qadr Al-Jaza'iri, personally saved Americans and others from similar danger in Damascus in 1860. And we're grateful that you're following in his proud footsteps.

I look forward to spending this time with you in our discussions on matters of importance to both of us.

Mr. President, we greet you as a friend.

President Bendjedid. Mr. President, thank you for your warm welcome and for the quality of the reception given to both my delegation and myself upon our arrival. I should also like to express the pleasure I feel coming for the first time to this rich land that has brought together people from all lands into one great nation.

We are here to bring a message of friendship and respect from the Algerian people to the American people. The Algerian people have a strong sense of communion with the principles that animated and guided the American Revolution, which represented one of the turning points in the history of the quest for freedom. They also recall the ties that our two nations developed very soon after the independence of the United States of America.

It is only natural that once it had regained its sovereignty, Algeria dedicated itself to restoring a dialog with your country. I can say that through the years this dialog allowed us to know each other better, to define our perceptions, and to better understand our respective approaches toward the challenges of our times.

This visit will be an opportunity to enhance our communication with regard to bilateral as well as international issues that are of common interest. Through cooperation and trade, the United States and Algeria have undoubtedly experienced benefits to both our economies. It is undeniable that there is room for development of a dynamic cooperation that respects the interests of both partners.

Mr. President, my country is strongly committed to the ideals of the goal of the United Nations to achieve peace and development for all the nations of this world. It is an established fact in this context that progress and peace should maintain an intimate and interacting relationship. The objective of the interdependent prosperity called for by the nonaligned countries is founded on the principle of mutual interdependence and upon a quest for a world of peace and progress.

While crises accumulate and areas of tension multiply, there is, more than ever, an urgent need for the international community to combine its efforts, to summon up its collective imagination, and to take the actions necessary to bring about an era of peace, security, and worldwide development. Algeria believes that man is endowed with limitless abilities that can benefit the collective work of peace and progress. And

as long as these capabilities are shared in order to achieve the most important task, human destiny will take a course other than that of dissension and poverty.

Thank you, Mr. President.

Note: President Reagan spoke at 10:12 a.m. at the South Portico of the White House, where President Bendjedid was accorded a formal welcome with full military honors. President Bendjedid spoke in Arabic, and his remarks were translated by an interpreter. Following the ceremony, the two Presidents met in the Oval Office.

Announcement of the Recipients of the National Medal of Arts
April 17, 1985

The President today announced the following recipients of the National Medal of Arts. They will be honored at a White House luncheon on April 23, 1985. This is the first time that the award will be presented.

Elliot Carter, of New York, is a composer and the winner of two Pulitzer Prizes for music. His compositions include Piano Sonata (1946), Double Concerto for Piano and Harpsichord (1961), Piano Concerto (1965), and Night Fantasies (1980).

Ralph (Waldo) Ellison, of New York, wrote "The Invisible Man" in 1952, a book called the most distinguished American novel of the postwar period by Book Week. His latest published work is a collection of essays, "Shadow and Act," an autobiography of the spirit and intellect, which was published in 1964.

Jose Vicente Ferrer, of New York, has been a stage and screen actor since 1935. His stage and screen portrayal of Cyrano has won him acclaim and awards. He is also a director and has many roles on television.

Martha Graham, of New York, is a dancer, teacher, choreographer, and directs her own dance company. Since 1926 Miss Graham has been a leading force in American dance and is known throughout the world for her work.

Louise Nevelson, of New York, originated environmental sculpture by assembling bits of materials in what she called a "unified whole." Her work is displayed in many major museums,

and she has used wood, plaster, terra cotta, stone, bronze, aluminum, and other materials in her own sculptures.

Leontyne Price, of New York, first debuted on television but since 1955 has gone on to sing leading roles with the major opera companies of the world. She is famous for her performances in operas by Giuseppe Verdi.

Georgia O'Keeffe, of Albuquerque, began her career as an advertising artist but now is world famous for her bleached animal skulls and giant flower blossoms. She has been honored by many restrospective shows, and her work is displayed in leading museums.

Hallmark Cards, Inc., of Kansas City, has been the sponsor of the Hallmark Hall of Fame for 34 years, during which it has received 49 Emmy Awards. This giant corporation also supports a number of local arts institutions in towns and cities where it maintains facilities.

Dorothy Buffum Chandler, of Los Angeles, is credited with the major effort behind the conception and construction of the Music Center of Los Angeles. The Dorothy Chandler Pavilion, a part of that performing center, is named for her in recognition of that effort.

Lincoln Kirstein, of New York, established the School of American Ballet and the New York City Ballet because he believed the United States should have its own classical ballet style. He has published many works on dance and continues to guide the school and the City Ballet.

Paul Mellon, of Washington, DC, was instrumental in creating and endowing the National Gallery of Art. His collection of art, including prime examples of English art, has been donated to the Yale Center for British Art at Yale University.

Alice Tully, of New York, studied music and debuted in 1927 before becoming a patron of the arts. Her major gift to Lincoln Center resulted in the dedication of the Alice Tully Hall in 1969.

Executive Order 12510—Non-Foreign Area Cost-of-Living Allowances
April 17, 1985

By the authority vested in me as President by the Constitution of the United States of America and section 5941 of title 5 of the United States Code, it is hereby ordered as follows:

Section 1. Section 205 of Executive Order No. 10000 of September 16, 1948, as amended, is further amended to provide as follows:

"Sec. 205. Additional living cost compensation.

"(a) The Office of Personnel Management shall from time to time, subject to applicable law, (1) designate places in non-foreign areas eligible to receive additional compensation by virtue of living costs that are substantially higher than in the Washington, D.C., area, (2) fix for each place so designated an additional rate or rates of compensation by reason of such higher living costs, and (3) prescribe by regulation such additional policies or procedures as may be necessary to administer such compensation. Additional compensation under this section is referred to as a 'non-foreign area cost-of-living allowance'.

"(b) In fixing the non-foreign area cost-of-living allowances, the Office of Personnel Management shall make appropriate deductions when quarters or subsistence, or commissary or other purchasing privileges are furnished as a result of Federal civilian employment at a cost substantially lower than the prevailing costs in the allowance area concerned."

Sec. 2. (a) Section 201 of Executive Order No. 10000, as amended, is further amended by deleting "the word 'Territories' means Alaska, Hawaii, the" and inserting in its place "the term 'non-foreign areas' includes Alaska, Hawaii, the territories and".

(b) Executive Order No. 10000, as amended, is further amended by deleting "Territorial" and "Territories" wherever they appear and inserting in their place "non-foreign area" and "non-foreign areas", respectively.

Sec. 3. Executive Order No. 12070 of June 30, 1978, is hereby superseded.

Sec. 4. This Order shall be effective upon publication in the *Federal Register.*

RONALD REAGAN

The White House,
April 17, 1985.

[*Filed with the Office of the Federal Register, 11:26 a.m., April 18, 1985*]

Nomination of Roger William Jepsen To Be a Member of the National Credit Union Administration Board, and Designation as Chairman
April 17, 1985

The President today announced his intention to nominate Roger William Jepsen to be a member of the National Credit Union Administration Board for the remainder of the term expiring August 2, 1987. He would succeed Edgar F. Callahan. Upon his confirmation, the President intends to designate him Chairman.

Senator Jepsen (R–IA) served in the United States Senate from 1979 to 1984, where he was a member of the Committee on Agriculture, Nutrition, and Forestry; the Committee on Armed Services; and the Joint Economic Committee. He served as chairman of the Joint Economic Committee (1983–1984), chairman of the Subcommittee on Soil and Water Conservation (1981–1984), and chairman of the Subcommittee on Manpower and Personnel (1981–1984).

In addition to his congressional experi-ence, Senator Jepsen has an extensive business background. From 1976 to 1978, he was president of the H.E.P. Marketing Co. of Davenport, IA. From 1973 to 1976, he was executive vice president of the Agridustrial Electronics Co. of Davenport, IA. Prior to 1973, Senator Jepsen was branch manager of Connecticut General Life Insurance Co. in Davenport, IA. Senator Jepsen served as State senator and as Lieutenant Governor of the State of Iowa prior to being elected to the United States Senate.

Senator Jepsen graduated from Arizona State University (B.S., 1950; M.A., 1953). He is married to Dee Ann Jepsen. He was born December 23, 1928, in Cedar Falls, IA.

Toasts at the State Dinner for President Chadli Bendjedid of Algeria
April 17, 1985

President Reagan. Mr. President, Madame Bendjedid, distinguished guests: Welcome to the White House. It's our pleasure to have as our guests friends from a distant land. And today we've worked and, I might add, succeeded in bringing our nations and the leaders of our nations closer together.

Mr. President, we're proud that the United States was among the first to recognize Algeria's independence in 1962. In the years which have passed since that time, we've not always seen political issues in the same light, but total agreement is not the basis of friendship; instead it's based on respect and forthrightness. And if this be the case, Algerians and Americans should and ought to be friends.

I enjoyed our conversations today, Mr. President. They were productive, and the spirit was positive. These talks have reinforced the ties between our two governments and our peoples. In the course of our discussions, we covered a wide area—trade and economic planning, humanitarian efforts in Africa, and cultural exchanges. And I believe that the steps forward we made will be followed by many more. And we look forward to that progress.

After getting to know you, Mr. President,

I'm certain you agree that nothing would better serve the joint interests of our peoples than peace and stability in the Middle East. We're aware of your particular concerns, ties, and friendships in the region, as you're aware of ours. Let us, Mr. President, use our influence toward positive ends. Let us urge our friends toward peaceful resolution of disputes. Let us encourage them to build and to create and to do those things that make for a better life.

Americans have had a challenging Middle Eastern role for almost four decades. We've done our best to create new opportunities for peace. And we'll continue our efforts, but peace depends on all those of good will in the region, on all sides of the conflict, taking the initiative.

For our part, we continue to believe Middle East peace must emerge from direct negotiations between the parties based on U.N. Security Council Resolution 242. As you so eloquently have noted, a solution to this complex problem must address the legitimate rights of the Palestinians and provide security for all in the region, including Israel.

Algeria lies at the northern edge of a continent beset by drought and famine. Mr.

President, we applaud your government's humanitarian efforts to help your less fortunate neighbors, both by donating funds to supplement food and shelter for the people of the Sahel and by accepting and caring for thousands of refugees from the famine. Algeria has been a leader in African self-help efforts in this crisis and a shining example to others.

President and Madame Bendjedid, your visit to the United States is a new high point in Algerian and American relations, and we're honored to have you here. I'm happy to have the opportunity to get to know you as a leader of a great people and as a man of vision and strength.

To His Excellency, the President of the Democratic and Popular Republic of Algeria, and Mrs. Bendjedid. And we thank you.

President Bendjedid. Mr. President, first of all, I appreciate your kind words to me and in speaking of the Algerian people. I take great pleasure in expressing to you and through you to the American people, the sentiments of respect and friendship felt for you by the Algerian people.

Mr. President, Mr. Vice President, Excellencies, ladies and gentlemen, in this hospitable city that carries the prestigious name of one of the Founding Fathers of your great nation, allow me to evoke the deep historical roots of the relationship between our two countries, illustrated by the treaty of peace and friendship signed on the 5th of September 1795.

It equally pleases me to point out the similarity between the resistance of our two peoples to colonial occupation. Perhaps the best testimony to that is the foundation in 1846 of the city of Elkader—or in Arabic, [*different pronunciation*] Elkader—in the State of Iowa in memory of the Amir Abdel Kader Al Jaza'iri and of the Algerian national resistance. There is certainly in that symbol that our two people share the ideals of liberty and independence, as confirmed during our struggle for national independence.

It is thanks to your invitation, Mr. President, that I am here with you today at this important time in the development of our relations. I took personal pleasure in meeting you at Cancún. I also learned from Vice President Bush during his visit to Algeria the personal interest that you attach to a dialog between our two countries. It is indeed satisfying to observe that under your Presidency, exchanges between our two countries have been greatly reinforced and that many members of your Cabinet have contributed to that process.

Mr. President, beyond existing trade relations there is, in the development of our national economy, considerable potential for multifaceted cooperation between our countries. The genius of the American people has enabled man to conquer nature. Algeria aspires to enter an era of scientific and technical progress that will lead to the acquisition and mastery of advanced technology in various fields in order to spur our national development. This is another field for fruitful cooperation. On the whole, cooperation between our two countries has produced appreciable results. The expansion of these ties is both possible and desirable.

Confronted with the demands of peace, security, and development, nations known for their power and prosperity should make an even more substantial contribution. But whether the matter concerns reversal of the arms race, disarmament, or improving international political atmosphere through crises reduction and the elimination of tensions, or establishing more equitable economic relations and eradicating world hunger, the challenge is to create a better world for all.

The course of nonalignment, which inspires and guides the international policies of Algeria, seeks to promote harmony between all peoples, whatever the path they have chosen. The African Continent has witnessed the cumulative anguish of institutionalized racism, of desertification, of drought, and of famine. A universal outcry is necessary to achieve the dismantling of apartheid, the achievement of Namibian independence, and bring peace in southern Africa.

In the Middle East, it is Algeria's conviction that the Palestinian problem is at the heart of the crisis in that region. Therefore, Mr. President, recognition of the inalienable national rights of the Palestinian people is the only path to a just and durable peace in that region.

In the Maghreb, Algeria will never cease to work in the interest of regional stability. An effort must be made to find a negotiated solution based on an African and international consensus over the question of the Western Sahara.

In regard to the conflict between Iraq and Iran, Algeria will spare no efforts to achieve a reasonable peace and good relations between these two neighbors.

Mr. President, the dialog that we profoundly desire between Algeria and the United States is nourished by the need for greater understanding, agreement, and cooperation between nations.

In thanking you once again, Mr. Presi-

dent, for your kind invitation and for your courtesies to me and my delegation during our stay, I would like to propose a toast to friendship between the American and Algerian peoples; to understanding, agreement, and universal cooperation; to the health of Mrs. Reagan and yourself; to the health of Mrs. Bush and Vice President Bush; to the health of all the friends gathered here this evening.

And thank you very much.

Note: President Reagan spoke at 9:44 p.m. in the State Dining Room at the White House. President Bendjedid spoke in Arabic, and his remarks were translated by an interpreter.

Telephone Conversation With the Astronauts on Board the Space Shuttle *Discovery*
April 18, 1985

The President. Commander Bobko—Commander Bobko? Greetings. We've——

Commander Bobko. Good morning, Mr. President.

The President. Ah, thank you. I thought maybe I might have missed you. Well, listen we know you've had some frustrations up there. But overall, I think we can all be proud of the fourth mission of the *Discovery* and all that you've accomplished.

We've been watching down here, and I mean all of America. And I want you to know that we're rooting for you all. We saw a lot of human ingenuity at work, making the flyswatter-like tool. And as we watched Jeff Hoffman and Dave Griggs install it on the *Discovery's* arm, we had to acknowledge that was great work. And we're calling all of you up there now the "SWAT Team."

I want to congratulate astronauts Bobko and Williams on the maneuvers you've been putting the shuttle through. This is the 16th shuttle to go up. And we're learning more about its versatility every trip.

I've seen you playing—excuse me—I mean demonstrating with balls and jacks and yo-yos and even a slinky toy in the zero-gravity of space. And now, I know

you're doing this to make some education videotapes for students learning about the laws of physics. That's really the best thing about our space program—the inspiration and challenge that it gives our young people.

You've been conducting extensive tests on the human body's blood flow and digestion. And I want to ask astronaut-physician Rhea Seddon, how are these tests working out? And, Rhea, I'd also like to commend you on your dexterity on hitting that pin on the side of the satellite. If you don't mind, I could think of a job on a ranch in California that you might be interested in. [*Laughter*]

But, Senator Garn, I know that you're taking part in the health experiments. And, Jake, how are you doing? You're doing a fine job up there, but I could use your help down here right now in getting the Federal budget under control and arranging assistance for some people fighting for their freedom in Central America. So, don't stay up there too long. You know, Jake, maybe in around——

Senator Garn. Well, Mr. President, I'm doing just great. I've missed you, but I'll be back on Tuesday. I'm well aware of the

449

vote on the Nicaraguan aid on Tuesday night. And I'll be voting just the way you'd like me to when I get back.

The President. Well, God bless you. And you know, Jake, maybe in around 4 years or so you could use your influence with NASA to get a certain retired politician a ride on the space shuttle.

Well, I just want all of you to know how proud we are of you. Good luck, and God be with all of you.

Anyone up there want to——

Commander Bobko. Thank you very much, Mr. President. We certainly enjoy being here. And I'm sure you realize that we're just the people in space, who are the working edge of the great team that's on the ground supporting us. Thanks again.

The President. Well, you're a great team up there. And we're all very proud of you. God bless you.

Note: The President spoke at 10:04 a.m. from the Oval Office at the White House to the Discovery's *crew: astronauts Karol J. Bobko, Donald E. Williams, M. Rhea Seddon, Jeffrey A. Hoffman, S. David Griggs, Charles D. Walker, and Senator Jake Garn of Utah.*

Statement on the Festival of India
April 18, 1985

I am pleased to announce that Prime Minister Rajiv Gandhi will inaugurate the 1985–1986 Festival of India during his official visit to the United States in June. The Festival is an unprecedented, nationwide celebration which will include exhibitions, performance programs, symposia, and other educational projects in 37 States and more than 80 cities. The idea for this Year of India grew out of the visit in 1982 to Washington of Mr. Gandhi's mother, the late Prime Minister Indira Gandhi. At that time, Mrs. Gandhi and I agreed that the Festival would be an excellent vehicle for the people of the United States to learn of one of the world's most ancient and vibrant civilizations.

We would like to commend the participating institutions, sponsoring corporations, foundations and agencies of both our government and the Government of India, which are making it possible. We welcome this unique opportunity to learn more of India's culture, society, and scientific achievements.

Recalling Mrs. Gandhi's vision for India and her devotion to the arts, it is appropriate that we dedicate this Festival of India to her memory. The Festival will comprise an affirmation of the universal value of the fascinating and richly varied civilization which was her personal heritage, as well as of the vitality of the great democracy to which she devoted her life.

Nomination of Joseph F. Salgado To Be Under Secretary of Energy
April 18, 1985

The President today announced his intention to nominate Joseph F. Salgado to be Under Secretary of Energy. He would succeed William Patrick Collins.

Until February, Mr. Salgado had been an Associate Director of Presidential Personnel at the White House, where he was responsi-

ble for energy, international, and national security areas. Previously he worked with the Department of Justice in the Immigration and Naturalization Service as the Associate Commissioner for Enforcement (January 1982 to August 1983).

Before joining the administration, Mr. Sal-

Overleaf: With King Juan Carlos and Queen Sofia at Prado Palace Madrid, Spain, May 9. *Left:* Viewing an exhibit by former White House photographer Micha Evans at the Corcoran Gallery of Art, January 14. *Below:* With Canadian Prime Minister Brian Mulroney in Quebec City, Canad March 17. *Right:* With Cameron, Ashley Marie, and Michael Reaga in the Rose Garden, January 19. *Below right:* Greeting Naval Academy graduates in Annapolis, MD, May 22.

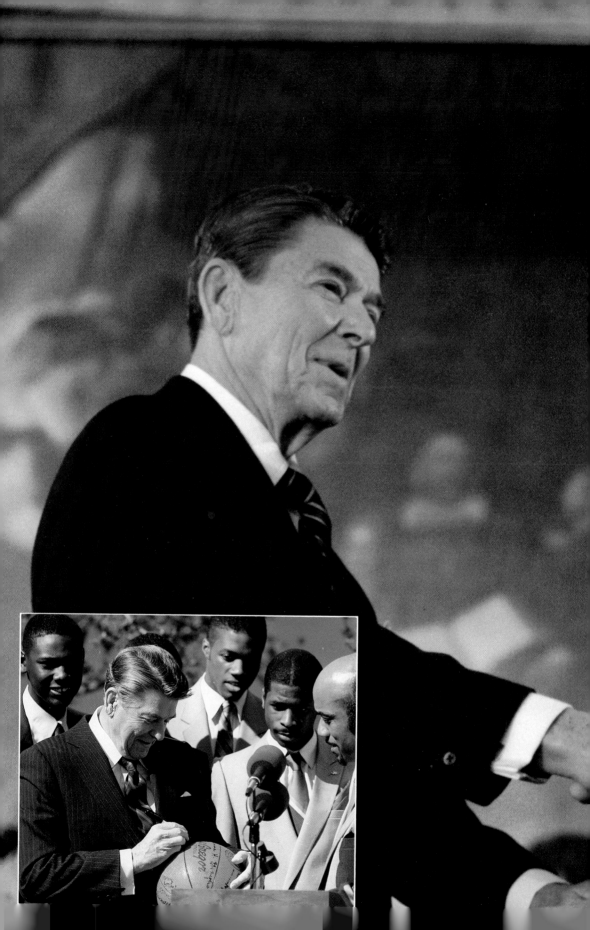

Below: Being sworn in for a second term by Supreme Court Chief Justice Warren E. Burger in the Capitol Rotunda, January 22. **Below left:** Meeting with the Spingarn High School basketball team in the Rose Garden, March 15. **Below right:** At Rancho del Cielo, CA, April 8.

Above: With President and Mrs. Chun Doo Hwan of the Republic of Korea on the South Lawn, April 26. *Left:* Leaving the Oval Office with congressional leaders after a briefing on the fiscal year 1986 budget, February 4. ***Right:*** Attending the Ringling Brothers, Barnum and Bailey Circus at the D.C. Armory, April 15. ***Overleaf:*** Addressing a special session of the European Parliament in Strasbourg, France, May 8.

gado served as deputy district attorney and senior trial attorney (1973–1981) for the Alameda County district attorney's office in California.

While a sergeant of police with the Oakland Police Department (1966–1973), Mr. Salgado graduated from San Francisco Law School (J.D., 1972) and received his bachelor of science degree from the University of San Francisco in 1968.

Mr. Salgado was born January 10, 1943, in San Diego, CA, and now resides in Alexandria, VA.

Nomination of John C. Whitehead To Be Deputy Secretary of State
April 18, 1985

The President today announced his intention to nominate John C. Whitehead as Deputy Secretary of State. He would succeed Kenneth W. Dam.

Mr. Whitehead recently retired after a 37-year career with the international investment banking firm of Goldman, Sachs & Co., where he served as senior partner and cochairman. Since his retirement as senior partner, he has continued to serve as chairman of the firm's international advisory board. He has also been a director of many leading American corporations.

Mr. Whitehead has served as president of the International Rescue Committee and as a member of the Council on Foreign Relations and the Georgetown Center for Strategic and International Studies. He is a trustee of Haverford College and the Carnegie Corp., and a Commissioner of the President's Commission on Executive Exchange.

He graduated from Haverford College (A.B., 1943) and Harvard University (M.B.A., 1947). He served in the United States Navy from 1943 until 1946. He was born April 2, 1922, in Evanston, IL, and now resides in Essex Fells, NJ.

Remarks and a Question-and-Answer Session With Regional Editors and Broadcasters
April 18, 1985

The President. Well, everybody seems to be in place. Thank you all, and welcome to the White House. I'm always pleased to be able to meet with you who operate in the business in which every minute counts, where everyone struggles to maintain the highest quality while, at the same time, fighting against an ever-approaching deadline. Making a decision under pressure of a deadline can be helpful.

America is facing a deadline, of sorts, in the form of an ever-increasing national debt. Under the pressure building to come to grips with this problem, we have an opportunity to make real progress cutting spending, progress that should have been made a long time ago.

Now, it's not going to be easy. We went the extra mile to reach an agreement with the Republican leadership of the Senate, and I agreed to compromise concerning defense and domestic spending issues. Now, it may be hard to do, but it's about time that everybody in government gritted their teeth and started being part of the solution, rather than part of the problem.

The choice is not, as some would have us believe, between cutting spending and raising taxes. The public doesn't want a tax increase, and more to the point, tax increases will not lower the level of deficit spending. Tax increases will not reduce government's demand on the private economy, which is the core of the problem. Tax increases would only serve to kick us back into recession, leading to higher deficits.

When it comes to taxes, what we need is simplification and reform, not increases. I think we can and will simplify the system and significantly reduce personal and corporate tax rates. We can lay the foundation for lower deficits and a vigorous expanding economy.

I see a consensus building on the idea of tax simplification. And the last few days' news should really make that build fast. If we can also agree on reasonable cuts in spending, there's every reason for optimism about America's economic future.

For years, we've known that we must get our fiscal house in order. Now, we have a proposal to do so that will encourage strong and steady growth without raising taxes, without jeopardizing assistance to the needy, and without endangering our security.

You know, when John F. Kennedy said to us 24 years ago, "Ask not what your country can do for you," the Federal Government wasn't doing nearly as much as it's doing today. And that's why it's time, here in 1985, to remember the second part of what J.F.K. said, "Ask what you can do for your country." And in doing that, support this fair and responsible proposal to get spending under control.

The news media is a vital part of decisions like this. That's why I'm talking about it here. Through you, people are made aware of the issues at hand and the alternatives and the consequences. Your function is vital to the viability of democracy. Without a free press democracy won't work, and all of our other rights would be in jeopardy.

Thomas Jefferson is often quoted at gatherings such as this as saying, "Were it left to me to decide whether we should have a government without newspapers, or newspapers without a government, I should not hesitate a moment to prefer the latter." Of course, he said that before he was President. [*Laughter*]

One of the first institutions to be attacked by tyrants, whether they're dictators of the left or right, is the press. We've seen this happen far too often, and it's happening in Nicaragua today. It shouldn't be forgotten that the one incident that precipitated the uprising against the Somoza dictatorship was the assassination of Pedro Joaquin Chamorro, editor of La Prensa, the nation's largest and fiercely independent newspaper. Yet control of the press under the Somoza dictatorship, which was decried by the Sandinistas, was miniscule compared to the ironfisted censorship now endured today by Nicaraguan journalists.

Humberto Belli, former editorial page editor of La Prensa, details this tragedy in his book, "Nicaragua, Christians Under Fire." It describes attacks by Sandinista mobs, official closings, the censorship of the news, the kidnaping and beating of reporters. It should be on the reading list of every journalist.

Pedro Joaquin Chamorro, Jr., who took his father's place as editor of La Prensa, watched the insidious destruction of press freedom and the suppression of other fundamental human rights by the Communist regime, and he fled the country.

Today news in Nicaragua is as controlled as that in any Eastern European state. Even a broadcast of religious services has been interfered with. The papers are filled with what the Communists consider to be good news. And as Senator Pat Moynihan once observed, countries with newspapers filled with good news are likely to have jails filled with good people.

And the jails are being filled with good people. Recently, we learned that 10 or 11 members of the Social Christian Party were rounded up and imprisoned. To force them to confess to being counterrevolutionaries, more than a hundred family members of these political prisoners were also arrested. And that's the kind of country the Sandinistas are building.

The other night, I told of what was happening to those 10 or 11 prisoners. And it was straight out of the Cuban handbook. They're put in overheated, dark cells. Then they are fed at varying intervals, like 12 hours between 2 meals, but giving you the next meal 2 hours later and so forth. All of it to create a disorientation and make it easier to break them down.

This pattern, as I say, we've seen before. Bigger jails are being built, and they're called relocation camps. Refugees are pouring out of the country. What we're witnessing in Nicaragua is the imposition, with ever-increasing intensity, of a pro-Soviet dictatorship, serving as a base camp for the spread of communism in our hemisphere.

Several years ago, there was honest disagreement over the nature of the Sandinista regime. That regime had been obscuring its true goals, deceiving its own supporters, and using a reformist cover to lull the press and potential adversaries. But by now there have been too many incautious statements, leaked memos, and secretly recorded speeches to deny the violent character and intent of this dictatorship.

The Miami Herald, which only 8 months ago had not come to this conclusion, recently editorialized that the Sandinistas are indeed trying to establish another Cuba and that this is a severe threat to Central America and to our own national security.

If we permit the Soviets, using the Sandinistas, to establish a beachhead on the American mainland and to spread their subversion, the free world will face a major challenge to the geopolitical balance of power. Economic instability, political subversion, and terrorism and a flood of refugees will likely be the price of our paralysis. We could turn around one day and find a string of pro-Soviet dictatorships in Central America and a threat to our southern border.

Congress had better come to grips with just how high the stakes are if Central America is lost. I'm asking Congress to work with me to support our peace proposal and not to desert those who are struggling for democracy against the Communists. Together, we can prevent a crisis from happening.

And I'd like to request something of you, as well. I'm not asking for stories in support of my program in Central America. I only hope that the news media takes the time and effort to present both sides.

The Communist disinformation machine is hard at work. We have reason for concern in this account about charges against the freedom fighters. For example, the falsehood that the democratic resistance is mainly composed of ex-backers of Somoza, and this is patently untrue. Yet when voiced by apologists for the Sandinista

regime, that charge often goes unchallenged.

Last week, a major publication disclosed that in handling the story of alleged crimes committed by the Nicaraguan democratic resistance, it relied on information thought to be from an independent investigation. As it turned out, the supposed investigation had been carried out by people closely aligned with the Sandinistas and was done in close collaboration with that regime.

One national publication had the courage to admit the mistake of giving credence to the report. How many other broadcast and print journalists didn't bother to correct the record and just shrugged off the whole incident?

Accurate information about what is happening in Central America is essential. And I know that your readers and your listeners can count on you. That's what freedom is all about.

And again, I'm most grateful for your being here. And I'm going to quit doing a monolog now and figure on a dialog. All right.

Nicaragua

Q. Mr. President, we all know about the situation in Nicaragua and the threat it represents for this country and the hemisphere, but yet, don't you think that the people of the United States have gotten used to having, 90 miles away in Cuba, a Communist dictatorship, a sworn enemy?

The President. Do I think that they have become used to it, you say? I've never thought about that before, but this could be possible, that they've kind of wiped it out of their minds. I don't think, in government, we can afford to.

Q. But yet it's the source.

The President. Yes, it is the source of the subversion that is taking place. And it's not alone in Nicaragua; there it's proceeded to the point of a revolutionary government, the Sandinistas. But we do know that throughout all of Latin America, under various names, there are guerrilla groups. And invariably, they have received their training, and they received their support and encouragement from Cuba. And they are assailing the duly elected governments in many of the democracies there in Latin America.

Vietnam

Q. Mr. President, to change the subject briefly, this is the month that marks the 10th anniversary of American disengagement from Vietnam. I wondered if you could give us a single recollection that you have, a vivid recollection of that time. And also, sir, tell us what lesson you believe that we've learned as a result of that experience.

The President. I hope we've learned some lessons. My recollections—I was Governor at the time when that was going on. I was burned in effigy on every campus in California. Things have changed since then.

Oh, there are many memories. And one of the first would have to be that with all that was going on and with all the propaganda here in our own country and the forces that were rising up in opposition to that war was the unselfish heroism of the young men and women in our military who were over there and giving their lives and fighting and who believed in the cause they were fighting for.

I think if I had to come out with one thing learned, I would have to say that never again must a government of the United States ask young men to go out and fight and die for a cause that we're unwilling to win. And that was the great tragedy—that was the great disgrace, to me, of Vietnam—that they were fed into this meatgrinder, and yet, no one had any intention of allowing victory.

Well, the truth of the matter is, we did have victory. And incidentally, could I just say, one complaint that I have: We continue to talk about losing that war. We didn't lose that war. We won virtually every engagement. The Tet offensive was distorted back here in the reporting. That was a victory for our side.

But what happened? We signed the peace accords, having built up the South Vietnamese Army to where we thought that with our equipment and all, they could defend themselves. And we made a pledge to them that if the North Vietnamese violated the cease-fire, the peace accords, and attacked, that we would supply the fuel for the tanks and the helicopters that we'd left

there; we would supply the ammunition for the guns and all for them to defend themselves. And when the North Vietnamese did violate the agreement and the blitz started toward the south and the then administration in Washington asked the Congress for the appropriations to keep our word, the Congress refused. We broke our pledge as a government on that basis.

And so, we didn't lose the war. When the war was all over and we'd come home— that's when the war was lost.

Nicaragua

Q. How much progress has been made today on fashioning a compromise over having the Congress approve the aid for the Nicaraguan *contras*? Do you feel that this has to be a showdown vote next Tuesday, in some fashion, that pits the personality of the President against the Speaker in some fashion? Or do you want to see this worked out this afternoon?

The President. Well, I have met and am meeting all the time with Congressmen of both parties. And the plea that I'm making is that this is another one of those things where, historically, in our tradition of closing ranks at the water's edge—we shouldn't be dealing with this as Democrats and Republicans. We should be dealing with it as Americans that have a problem involving our own national security and our relationship with friends and allies.

And frankly, I'm sorry that it's coming to a vote on Tuesday, and I think that was deliberate on the part of the leadership in the House of Representatives.

Q. To embarrass you, sir?

The President. To bring that vote up before we could really sit down and go at all the places where we had agreement and disagreement.

Now, many of the people that I've been meeting with are basically supportive of the plan, except they feel that there are others that are wavering one way or the other, that if we could make some alterations in the plan, keep basically the agreement or the arrangement that we have and the goal, but that there are places here and there and timing and so forth. And I have made it plain to all of them, we'd love to talk to them about that. My feet aren't in concrete on this. Yes, there's leeway. We're flexible as to the details of this program. But how much time do you have? It's Thursday, and they've said the vote must be Tuesday. I think it's immoral to demand that vote that quickly.

Q. Mr. President, in light of that, do you intend to try to seek a meeting with the Speaker, and if so, what would you tell him?

The President. Well, as I say, we've been meeting, and I don't know that I would have a meeting with him, but I've been meeting with chairmen of committees. I've been meeting with groups. I've been meeting with individuals on all of this and have heard some of the proposals and have sent by them my word that this, this, and this in the plan—yes, we're prepared to be flexible. Yes, we'd like to listen to alternate suggestions.

The young lady over there.

Q. What kind of a compromise would you be willing to accept on that?

The President. What's that?

Q. What kind of compromise would you be willing to accept on your proposal for Nicaraguan aid?

The President. Well, one that basically leaves the goal that what we're trying to get, in contrast to the propaganda of the Sandinistas that we're waiting with an upraised club to clobber them, that we want what the *contras* themselves asked for several weeks ago—the laying down of arms, a cease-fire, and then the coming together in a peaceful negotiation as to how they can restore the original goals of the revolution.

And we've asked for this in connection with the Contadora countries and their participation. We're in total agreement with the 21 points that have been adopted by the Contadora countries. I have called personally and met with the leaders of the neighboring countries—Honduras, Costa Rica, Guatemala, El Salvador. President Duarte has said this program of ours is the right idea at the right time. I have called Alfonsin, the President of Argentina, as a matter of fact, the President [Prime Minister] of Spain. And I've found widespread support among all of them for this plan.

But within the plan—for example, the

timing, we've said that the negotiations— we want the church to mediate, so there can be no question about somebody trying to pull undercover tricks. And we've set a period here for negotiation and then a checkpoint at which, if there is no evidence that the one group is trying to negotiate seriously, that then there is a trigger there that opens up more aid from us to the *contras.*

Now, some have suggested that maybe that period should be longer. I'm very pleased—I'd be very willing to sit down and discuss that with them as to whether it be longer, things to do with the fencing of the money and so forth, things to do with the assurance that the money would go to food and clothing and shelter, medicine for the families of the *contras.*

Farm Credit Situation

Q. Mr. President, with regard to your budget program, I'd like to ask what response you have to the farmers in the Midwest who say that your program is going to cripple the American family farmer.

The President. Well, we have spent more on farming, I guess, than has ever been spent before in history. And we will be spending some $15 billion this year on that.

We know that there are some unusual problems that have come about basically through the credit situation with farmers and the fact that farmland was one of the great inflationary items that went up as a hedge against inflation and borrowing was done on that inflated value of the land. And now with the reduction of inflation, which I think is of value to all of us, that land price has gone down, and they find themselves unable to borrow or burdened with debts that no longer have the proper collateral surrounding them.

We've put together a program. I don't say that it can resolve everyone's problem or save everyone. But we have put together a program with regard to emergency loans that amounts to $650 million. So far, we've been amazed at the low call on that. There wasn't any great rush to that money.

But I think we have to face one thing: The overall situation of the American farmer is due to government's interference in the first place. The two-thirds of farming that is out there not participant in any of the government regulation or subsidy programs does not have these economic problems and has been knowing an ever-increasing per capita consumption of its produce compared to the farms that are overly regulated with the Government.

Q. One more question?

The President. I had to take his question because he's from WHO, Des Moines. [*Laughter*]

Amtrak

Q. President Reagan, you say on the budget—it's going to take a lot of giving on a lot of people's part. Well, something near and dear to a lot of people who live along the Northeast corridor is Amtrak. No hope for Amtrak?

The President. Well, see, I'm old enough to remember that in World War I the Federal Government took over the railroads and ran them, and it was a complete disaster, and people at that time said never again.

Well, the Government has taken over the railroads again. We now have a sizable offer for Conrail, and I hope that the Congress will let us accept that offer, and we'll put freight back in the private sector, and we'll get a pretty good chunk of money. And the second, with Amtrak and the passenger traffic, I was told by the president of one of our leading rail lines that if the Government, in the beginning, had allowed the railroads to operate under the same rules and regulations that they applied to Amtrak, they wouldn't have had to give up the passenger traffic. They could have run that at a profit.

But now Amtrak is so subsidized that you have to wonder why people should be taxed to pay $35 for every passenger that gets on an Amtrak train in addition to the fare that that passenger's paying. And I gave one example here about a train in the Midwest that takes passengers in the winter down to Florida for the winter vacations, and I was given some figures that indicated that the Government could buy every one of the passengers on that train a roundtrip airline ticket and give them $100 spending money and be money ahead, instead of taking

them down on Amtrak. I think it's time for us to admit we don't know how to run a railroad.

Q. Thank you, Mr. President.

Q. Just one question——

The President. Oh, I'm sorry. Yes?

President's Trip to West Germany

Q. Regarding the upcoming trip to West Germany—53 Senators have signed a letter requesting that you drop the trip to the cemetery. In light of this and the wave of other opposition, would it damage German-American relations to seek some other gesture of reconciliation and drop that visit? And secondly, would you say that it was a failure of political analysis to realize the fallout that resulted from the itinerary as it was scheduled?

The President. The failure that I will admit to—and I realize now I should have listened to you—[*laughter*]—the failure that I will admit to is in the press conference—I didn't completely answer the question as to why I have said no to an invitation to visit Dachau. And I realize now that I'd given those who were questioning me credit for knowing more than they knew about the situation.

Helmut Kohl, sometime ago, back, I guess, when we were celebrating or observing the Normandy landings last June, he and President Mitterrand went to a military cemetery together in Verdôme. Now, here were the representatives of the two countries that have been at odds for the war of 1870, the First World War, the Second World War. The impact on all of Europe was so great to see them standing together at this ceremony that Helmut Kohl told me about this and told me how deeply he felt about it.

Now, the summit places us in Bonn in Germany close to the time of the anniversary. And he invited me to accept an invitation to be a state visitor following the summit meeting. And he suggested to me this visit, as he had done with Mitterrand, to a cemetery there. The cemetery that was picked, Bitburg, was picked because at the same time, also, there has been a church service with our military at Bitburg—we have a base there and our Americans—and

I'm going there and go to church with them and have lunch with them. And the Kohls will be with us, also.

When the invitation to visit a concentration camp was offered, whether it was my confusion or the way in which it was done, I thought that the suggestion had come from an individual and was not a part of the state visit. And I thought there was no way that I, as the guest of the government at that point, could on my own take off and go someplace and, then, run the risk of appearing as if I was trying to say to the Germans, "Look what you did," and all of this when most of the people in Germany today weren't alive or were very small children when this was happening.

And I know the feeling they have. And I know this government that for 40 years— what he'd asked me to do in the cemetery was that we should start this day now, observing this day as the day that 40 years ago the world took a sharp turn, an end to the hatred, an end to the obscenities of the persecution and all that took place. And today, after 40 years of peace, here we are—our staunchest allies in that summit are the countries that were our enemies in World War II. Now, their leaders have come here and visited Arlington, leaders from Germany, from Italy, from Japan. And this cemetery—we only found out later, someone dug up the fact that there are about 30 graves of SS troops. These were the villains, as we know, that conducted the persecutions and all. But there are 2,000 graves there. And most of those—the average age is about 18. These were those young teenagers that were conscripted, forced into military service in the closing days of the Third Reich, when they were short of manpower, And we're the victor, and they're there. And it seemed to me that this could be symbolic, also, of saying—what I said about—what this day should be. And let's resolve, in their presence, as well as in the presence of our own troops, that this must never happen again.

Well, when the furor erupted and got as far as Germany, Helmut Kohl sent me a cable. And the cable informed me that there was a mistake, that the Dachau was a part of the state itinerary, the planned trip. Well, I immediately communicated and said, "Fine, that's fine with me. If it is you, the government, that is inviting me to do this, I am more than happy to do it, because I have said repeatedly, and I would like on that occasion to say again, the Holocaust must never be forgotten by any of us. And in not forgetting it, we should make it clear that we're determined the Holocaust must never take place again." And——

Q. Does that mean you're still going to Bitburg?

The President. I think that it would be very hurtful and all it would do is leave me looking as if I caved in in the face of some unfavorable attention. I think that there's nothing wrong with visiting that cemetery, where those young men are victims of nazism also, even though they were fighting in the German uniform, drafted into service to carry out the hateful wishes of the Nazis. They were victims, just as surely as the victims in the concentration camps. And I feel that there is much to be gained from this, in strengthening our relationship with the German people, who, believe me, live in constant penance, all these who have come along in these later years for what their predecessors did and for which they're very ashamed.

No, I can't take any more. I'm told that I've run out of time. I've got those Congressmen waiting for me.

Thank you all very much.

Note: The President spoke at 1:07 p.m. at a luncheon for the editors and broadcasters in the State Dining Room at the White House.

Remarks at a White House Ceremony Honoring National Teacher of the Year Theresa K. Dozier
April 18, 1985

Welcome to the White House. I want to thank Good Housekeeping magazine, the Encyclopaedia Britannica companies, and the Council of Chief State School Officers for sponsoring the Teacher of the Year Award. We're very happy to welcome a contingent of aspiring teachers today, and we're delighted to welcome the family members and associates of our most distinguished guest. We appreciate your coming all the way from South Carolina just to chaperone Mrs. Dozier—[*laughter*]—and make sure she doesn't get into any trouble here in Washington.

All of us are here to honor a very special American. She and her colleagues are day by day, in their quiet, unsung way, probably more important to the survival and the success of our freedom than anyone else in this nation. And that's how much teachers mean to America.

Good teachers must be so many different people: our child's third parent and lifelong friend; the person who makes hard things seem easy; who teaches us to think apart, yet act together; and who conveys the meaning of ideas and, through personal example, the nobility of ideals.

Sometimes, when targets of others' rudeness and abuse, teachers must feel a little like an American dartboard, but they're tough, resilient, and pretty and clever, too. [*Laughter*] They can be funny or cross, but they stick to their challenge, whether it's with math, English, or history or teaching about word processors, which incidentally still leave me at a total loss. I haven't even mastered a pocket calculator yet. [*Laughter*]

And most of all, good teachers care. They care very much about what they teach, about the curiosity they instill, about how well their students learn, and where their lives will lead. So, we look to teachers, and we look up to teachers. We count on their conscience, their courage, and their concern. We count on them being the hero that Emily Dickinson once described: "If I

can stop one heart from breaking . . . If I can ease one life the aching or cool one pain . . . I shall not live in vain."

Each gifted instructor, each leader helping restore excellence in education today is a vessel of hope for America—hope that ignorance may be cast away; hope that young minds may be awakened to new discovery; and yes, hope that we may always be free, for with freedom, our guiding star, America's future will never be a burden dragging us down but a great soaring adventure of creativity, powered by the deepest treasures of the human mind and heart—wisdom, faith, and love.

We have such an individual with us today. Born in Vietnam, orphaned as a young girl, then adopted by U.S. Army Warrant Officer Lawrence Knecht stationed in Saigon, Mrs. Therese Knecht Dozier enjoys a dual honor: She and her brother are believed to be among the first Vietnamese children adopted by an American couple. And as a 32-year-old high school history teacher in Columbia, South Carolina, Terry Dozier is America's 1985 Teacher of the Year.

She's said, "I've always been very conscious of having been given a chance to make something of myself. I want to give that chance to others and to share the excitement of learning that I've always felt. Teaching is a way of repaying that debt."

And she has. Terry is a teacher of world history who provides students with perspective and the ability to make sound judgments. "She makes history exciting," one of her students said. Terry, I'm told your account of Louis XVI's ride to the guillotine was so packed with suspense that you had your students sitting on the edge of their seats. [*laughter*]

Her teaching is a reflection of her own experiences, a statement that there is no certainty our values will survive, that everything depends on us, and that no one should take America for granted.

I strongly believe, and I know that Secretary Bennett agrees, that our actions must reflect an awareness of history and human nature if mankind is to avoid repeating the tragedies of the past. By helping young people acquire such knowledge, Mrs. Dozier is contributing directly to the health and vitality of this country and to its freedom.

Mrs. Dozier, for all that you do so well, not only teaching but coordinating homecoming half-time activities, cheerleading in the student-faculty basketball game, and even dressing up for Punk Rock Day— [*laughter*]—we salute you.

Let me just say for the entire country, what your family, your fellow members of the faculty, and your students at Irmo High already know, you are Teacher of the Year because you've taught so many, so much, and so well, and even more, because your gift has given them joy and love of learning. And I don't think I'm speaking out of school when I add, the love they share for learning is a love they share for you.

Mrs. Terry Dozier, today, America honors you, but in truth, it's you who honors America every day of the year.

Thank you. God bless you always.

And now, I'm going to present Mrs. Dozier with a Golden Apple.

Note: The President spoke at 1:54 p.m. in the Rose Garden at the White House.

Remarks on Presenting the Congressional Gold Medal to Elie Wiesel and on Signing the Jewish Heritage Week Proclamation
April 19, 1985

The President. I'm pleased that each of you could be with us today to celebrate Jewish Heritage Week. We recall today the great accomplishments in science, philosophy, literature, art, and music made throughout history by the Jewish people. And we remember that it is the spiritual and moral values of Judaism which encompass the dream of peace and human dignity that has enabled the Jewish people—and ennobled the Jewish people, I should say, and through them, their fellow men.

Throughout the world, the Jewish people have just finished celebrating Passover, the holiday that marks the exodus from Egypt, the deliverance from slavery.

But this week, we commemorate a nondeliverance, a time when exodus was refused, when the doors of refuge were closed, and in their place came death. In the Passover narrative, the Haggadah, there is the phrase, "In every generation, they rise up against us to annihilate us." In the generation of the Holocaust, that annihilation nearly succeeded in Europe; 6 million murdered, among them, over a million children.

How does life continue in the face of this crime against humanity? The survivors swore their oath: Never again. And the American people also made that pledge: Never again. And we've kept it. We kept it when we supported the establishment of the state of Israel, the refuge that the Jewish people lacked during the Holocaust, the dream of generations, the sure sign of God's hand in history. America will never waver in our support for that nation to which our ties of faith are unbreakable.

To say "never again," however, is not enough. When, with Israel, the United States reached out to help save Ethiopian Jewry, we were also fulfilling our pledge. This was truly God's work.

Today we work on and on to help Soviet Jewry, which suffers from persecution, intimidation, and imprisonment within Soviet borders. We will never relinquish our hope for their freedom, and we will never cease to work for it. If the Soviet Union truly wants peace, truly wants friendship, then let them release Anatoly Shcharanskiy and free Soviet Jewry.

But our pledge was more than "Never again." It was also "Never forget." And we've kept that pledge, too. We kept that pledge when we established the Holocaust Memorial Commission and set the cornerstone for its museum. We keep that pledge when, in our colleges and universities, we teach each new generation of Americans the story of the Holocaust. And in our lives, we keep that pledge when we privately, in our own families and in our hearts, remember.

From the ashes of the Holocaust emerged the miracle of Israel and another miracle, that the survivors began life again. They came to new lands, many to Israel and many, thank God, to America. They built new families and with each child gave us the greatest symbol of this faith in the future. They brought to us the eloquence of a people who, in surviving such suffering, asked only for the right to remember and be remembered, a people who did not permit themselves to descend into the pits and quagmires of hatred but lifted themselves instead—and with them all of humankind—out of darkness up toward a time when hatred is no more and all nations and all people are as one.

We who had not suffered the tragedy of the Holocaust directly shared their grief and mourned for their victims. We, too, prayed for a better future and a better world, where all peoples and all nations would come together in peace and defense of humanity.

Today, there is a spirit of reconciliation between the peoples of the allied nations and the people of Germany and even between the soldiers who fought each other on the battlefields of Europe. That spirit must grow and be strengthened.

As the people of Europe rebuilt their shattered lands, the survivors rebuilt their shattered lives, and they did so despite the searing pain. And we who are their fellow citizens have taken up their memories and tried to learn from them what we must do. No one has taught us more than Elie Wiesel. His life stands as a symbol; his life is testimony that the human spirit endures and prevails. Memory can fail us, for it can fade as the generations change. But Elie Wiesel has helped make the memory of the Holocaust eternal by preserving the story of the 6 million Jews in his works. Like the Prophets whose words guide to this day, his

works will teach humanity timeless lessons. He teaches about despair but also about hope. He teaches about our capacity to do evil but also about the possibility of courage and resistance and about our capacity to sacrifice for a higher good. He teaches about death. But in the end, he teaches about life.

Elie, we present you with this medal as an expression of our gratitude for your life's work.

[At this point, the President presented Elie Wiesel with the Congressional Gold Medal.]

In honoring Elie Wiesel, we thank him for a life that's dedicated to others. We pledge that he will never forget—or that we will never forget that in many places of the world, the cancer of anti-Semitism still exists. Beyond our fervent hopes and our anguished remembrance, we must not forget our duty to those who perished, our duty to bring justice to those who perpetrated unspeakable deeds. And we must take action to root out the vestiges of anti-Semitism in America, to quash the violence-prone or hate groups even before they can spread their venom and destruction. And let all of us, Jew and non-Jew alike, pledge ourselves today to the life of the Jewish dream: to a time when war is no more, when all nations live in peace, when each man, woman, and child lives in the dignity that God intended.

On behalf of your fellow citizens, now let me sign this proclamation commemorating Jewish Heritage Week.

Mr. Wiesel. First, give this medal to my son.

Mr. President, Mr. Vice President, Secretary Bennett, Mr. Agresto, Mr. Regan, very distinguished members of the Senate, my friends—and of the House:

Mr. President, speaking of reconciliation, I was very pleased that we met before so a stage of reconciliation has been set in motion between us. But then we were never on two sides; we were on the same side. We were always on the side of justice, always on the side of memory, against the SS, and against what they represent.

It was good talking to you, and I'm grateful to you for the medal. But this medal is not mine alone. It belongs to all those who remember what SS killers have done to their victims. It was given to me by the American people for my writings, teaching, and for my testimony.

When I write, I feel my invisible teachers standing over my shoulders, reading my words and judging their veracity. And while I feel responsible for the living, I feel equally responsible to the dead. Their memory dwells in my memory.

Forty years ago, a young man awoke, and he found himself an orphan in an orphaned world. What have I learned in the last 40 years—small things. I learned the perils of language and those of silence. I learned that in extreme situations when human lives and dignity are at stake, neutrality is a sin. It helps the killers not the victims. I learned the meaning of solitude, Mr. President. We were alone, desperately alone. Today is April 19th, and April 19, 1943, the Warsaw Ghetto rose in arms against the onslaught of the Nazis. They were so few and so young and so helpless, and nobody came to their help. And they had to fight what was then the mightiest legion in Europe. Every underground received help, except the Jewish underground. And yet, they managed to fight and resist and push back those Nazis and their accomplices for 6 weeks.

And yet, the leaders of the free world, Mr. President, knew everything and did so little or nothing or at least nothing specifically to save Jewish children from death.

You spoke of Jewish children, Mr. President; one million Jewish children perished. If I spent my entire life reciting their names, I would die before finishing the task. Mr. President, I have seen children—I have seen them being thrown in the flames alive. Words—they die on my lips.

So, I have learned. I have learned, I have learned the fragility of the human condition. And I'm reminded of a great moral essayist, the gentle and forceful Abe Rosenthal, having visited Auschwitz once wrote an extraordinary reportage about the persecution of Jews, and he called it, "Forgive them not Father, for they knew what they did."

I have learned that the Holocaust was a unique and uniquely Jewish event, albeit with universal implications. Not all victims were Jews, but all Jews were victims. I have learned the danger of indifference, the crime of indifference. For the opposite of love, I have learned, is not hate but indifference. Jews were killed by the enemy but betrayed by their so-called allies who found political reasons to justify their indifference or passivity.

But I've also learned that suffering confers no privileges. It all depends what one does with it. And this is why survivors of whom you spoke, Mr. President, have tried to teach their contemporaries how to build on ruins, how to invent hope in a world that offers none, how to proclaim faith to a generation that has seen it shamed and mutilated. And I believe, we believe, that memory is the answer—perhaps the only answer.

A few days ago on the anniversary of the liberation of Buchenwald, all of us Americans watched with dismay and anger as the Soviet Union and East Germany distorted both past and present history. Mr. President, I was there; I was there when American liberators arrived, and they gave us back our lives. And what I felt for them then nourishes me to the end of my days, and will do so. If you only knew what we tried to do with them then, we who were so weak that we couldn't carry our own lives— we tried to carry them in triumph!

Mr. President, we are grateful to the American Army for liberating us. We are grateful to this country—the greatest democracy in the world, the freest nation in the world, the moral nation, the authority in the world. And we are grateful especially to this country for having offered haven and refuge and grateful to its leadership for being so friendly to Israel.

Mr. President, do you know that the Ambassador of Israel, who sits next to you, who is my friend and has been for so many years, is himself a survivor? And if you knew all the causes we fought together for the last 30 years, you could be prouder of him. And we are proud of him.

And we are grateful, of course, to Israel; we are eternally grateful to Israel for existing. We needed Israel in 1948 as we need it now. And we are grateful to Congress for its continuous philosophy of humanism and compassion for the underprivileged.

And as for yourself, Mr. President, we are so grateful to you for being a friend of the Jewish people, for trying to help the oppressed Jews in the Soviet Union and to do whatever we can to save Shcharanskiy and Abe Stolyar and Iosif Begun and Sakharov and all the dissidents who need freedom. And of course, we thank you for your support of the Jewish state of Israel.

But, Mr. President, I wouldn't be the person I am, and you wouldn't respect me for what I am, if I were not to tell you also of the sadness that is in my heart for what happened during the last week. And I am sure that you, too, are sad for the same reasons. What can I do? I belong to a traumatized generation. And to us, as to you, symbols are important. And furthermore, following our ancient tradition—and we are speaking about Jewish heritage—our tradition commands us, quote: "to speak truth to power."

So may I speak to you, Mr. President, with respect and admiration, of the events that happened. We have met four or five times, and each time I came away enriched, for I know of your commitment to humanity. And, therefore, I am convinced, as you have told us earlier when we spoke that you were not aware of the presence of SS graves in the Bitburg cemetery. Of course, you didn't know. But now we all are aware. May I, Mr. President, if it's possible at all, implore you to do something else, to find a way, to find another way, another site. That place, Mr. President, is not your place. Your place is with the victims of the SS.

Oh, we know there are political and strategic reasons, but this issue, as all issues related to that awesome event, transcends politics and diplomacy. The issue here is not politics but good and evil. And we must never confuse them, for I have seen the SS at work, and I have seen their victims. They were my friends. They were my parents. Mr. President, there was a degree of suffering and loneliness in the concentration camps that defies imagination. Cut off from the world with no refuge anywhere; sons watched helplessly their fathers being beaten to death; mothers watched their children die of hunger. And then there was Mengele and his selections, terror, fear, isolation, torture, gas chambers, flames— flames rising to the heavens.

But, Mr. President, I know and I understand, we all do, that you seek reconciliation. So do I. So do we. And I, too, wish to attain true reconciliation with the German people. I do not believe in collective guilt, nor in collective responsibility; only the killers were guilty. Their sons and daughters are not. And I believe, Mr. President, that we can and we must work together with them and with all people. And we must work to bring peace and understanding to a tormented world that, as you know, is still awaiting redemption.

I thank you, Mr. President.

Note: The President spoke at 11:32 a.m. in the Roosevelt Room at the White House.

Proclamation 5321—Jewish Heritage Week, 1985
April 19, 1985

By the President of the United States of America

A Proclamation

Those who set out to describe Jewish contributions to Western Civilization soon learn how enormous is their task. The Jewish people have contributed to the West its fundamental spiritual values. They introduced the world to monotheism and to the high ethical principles expressed in the Ten Commandments and the writings of the Prophets. The other great religions of the West—Christianity and Islam—can recognize their roots in Judaism. Western literature owes many of its most inspiring themes and allusions to the Hebrew Bible. Great Jewish thinkers—from Philo of Alexandria, to Maimonides and Saadya Gaon, to Spinoza and Martin Buber—have engaged in powerful symbiotic dialogue with Christian and Muslim writers to add vital insights to the Western philosophical tradition. In addition, individual Jews have made extraordinary contributions to the arts, literature, sciences, and humanities.

Yet throughout history the Jewish people have endured countless bloody massacres from the Inquisition to pogroms throughout Europe. None of these remotely approaches the genocidal undertaking of the Nazis who planned the wholesale destruction of European Jewry. In our own time this plan was conceived and, before we could stop it, it had taken the lives of six million Jewish men, women, and children.

Even as we herald the glory of the Jewish heritage, we commemorate as well Jewish suffering in this era. It is up to us to show the way out of this shameful cycle. We must remember the sins of the past and rededicate ourselves to shaping a future marked by tolerance, respect, and compassion. We must rededicate ourselves to the proposition that the Holocaust will remain a solitary horror and that its like will never be repeated.

Jews throughout the world have just celebrated Passover, the holiday that marks the Exodus from Egypt and the deliverance from slavery. The Jewish people came forth from the house of bondage and flowered with an abundance of creativity which has maintained itself until the present day. We learn from this that the emergence from slavery to freedom can release powers hidden within the human spirit, as the

Jewish people have once again shown since the end of the Nazi terror. The faith in God and in the Jewish people which sustained them through these tribulations has infused new life into the Jewish communities in America and the State of Israel.

In recognition of the special significance of this time of year for America's Jews, in tribute to the contributions they have made to American life, and in an effort to foster understanding and appreciation of the cultural diversity that has made America a unique society, the Congress, by Senate Joint Resolution 17, has designated April 21 through April 28, 1985, as "Jewish Heritage Week" and authorized and requested the President to issue a proclamation in observance of this event.

Now, Therefore, I, Ronald Reagan, President of the United States of America, do hereby proclaim April 21 through April 28, 1985, as Jewish Heritage Week. I call upon the people of the United States, Federal, State, and local government officials, and interested organizations to observe that week with appropriate ceremonies and activities.

In Witness Whereof, I have hereunto set my hand this 19th day of April, in the year of our Lord nineteen hundred and eighty-five, and of the Independence of the United States of America the two hundred and ninth.

RONALD REAGAN

[*Filed with the Office of the Federal Register, 4:26 p.m., April 19, 1985*]

Remarks on Signing the Victims of Crime Week Proclamation
April 19, 1985

Well, it is a pleasure to welcome you all here today to the White House, if that has not already been done—Attorney General Meese, Members of the Congress, and our very special guests here.

Since our first days in office the problem of crime has been a major concern of this administration, even while we had to act

immediately to deal with the twin crises of a declining economy and a jeopardized national defense. Making our homes and streets safe again remained among our highest priorities. At the time we took office, government was bloated and had taken on responsibilities in areas where it was neither competent nor needed. Yet, at the same time government was failing in its most legitimate and important functions, particularly preserving domestic order and protecting society from those who would prey on the innocent.

In the past few years we've seen a return to the values that are the basis for a free and a just society: the belief that right and wrong matters, that individuals are responsible for their actions, and that punishment must be swift and sure for those who transgress against the rights of their fellow citizens. It was such values and beliefs that guided us when we took office.

In the early years of this administration we launched a massive attack on the illegal drug trade and on the infrastructure of organized crime, achieving a leap in the number of prosecuters and agents who are assigned to these cases, in the number of drug cases filed, and in the number of drug convictions. We appointed judges who understood that the innocent members of society have a right to be protected from criminal offenders. We achieved some of the most significant anticrime legislation in our history, accomplishing desperately needed reforms in parole and sentencing procedures and in a wide variety of other areas, reforms that will make life tougher for career criminals and easier for the law-abiding. Indeed, we need to make life tough for many criminals, as is illustrated in the fact that the median time served for the crime of murder is 5 years, 3 months and for rape, 2 years, 9 months. This is intolerable.

At the local and State level, too, the voice of the people was heard. States passed tough new sentencing requirements; judges or prosecutors who were lax in their duty were held up to public scrutiny, and communities and neighborhoods began a new era of cooperation with law enforcement to protect lives and liberty.

And the outcome of all this is now clear. As you've already heard, crime is down significantly, and for the first time, it's down for 3 successive years—the first time that has ever happened.

I know there are some who claim this is merely a reflection of demographic trends, that there's less crime now because there are fewer members of our society who are in the crime-prone age group. But a coincidence is not a causation.

For example, during the 1960's crime rose at a much faster rate than did the crime-prone age group. Between the years 1976 and 1981, the number in the crime-prone age group rose by less than 1 percent; yet violent crime rose by over 35 percent. A critical reason for the rise in crime in past years was a failure to administer prompt and sure justice.

During the 1960's the likelihood of being imprisoned if arrested for a serious crime fell by 75 percent. In recent years these figures have turned around. The likelihood of going to prison now is almost twice as high as it was in 1970.

It's a fact that many thousands more career criminals are being imprisoned today than in 1970. That fact must be acknowledged and its meaning understood. It's happening because our criminal justice system is responding to the public outcry over crime. It's happening because we're doing more to protect the innocent and punish the guilty. And that's why, today, our homes, our families, and our societies are safer.

The real explanation then for the decline in crime can be found right where the credit for America's social progress can usually be found—the resolve of the American people to speak out, to make their voices heard, to demand justice. There's no better example of this resolve than the work of those we honor here today, who have worked with their fellow citizens to bring public attention to the plight of the victims of crime.

I'm proud that this administration led the way in passing new legislation and new programs for the victims of crime. But most of all, I share the pride of all Americans today in honoring those who have, through their work for the victims of crime, turned anguish and fear into constructive action.

I want to salute Theresa Saldana, Carole DeLuca, Caren Robinson, Cecile Laurinitis, Patti Linebaugh, and Sharon Komlos. Each of you rose above the fear and the frustration that all victims of crime must face. You turned terrible moments in your lives into something beneficial and helpful to your fellow Americans. You used your suffering so that others would suffer less. This was a noble thing to do, and for this our nation owes you all a "thanks." On behalf of the American people, I want to extend to each of you our gratitude for your patriotism and your selflessness.

And now, I would like to sign the Victims of Crime Week proclamation.

Note: The President spoke at 1:37 p.m. in the Rose Garden at the White House.

Proclamation 5322—Victims of Crime Week, 1985
April 19, 1985

By the President of the United States of America

A Proclamation

The primary function of a government is to ensure that its citizens can live safely in their communities. Yet each year millions of our citizens face the reality of violent crime, and their lives are forever changed by these acts. Many are afraid to leave their homes after dark. Others are barricaded inside with multiple locks on their doors and steel bars on their windows.

The strength of our justice system depends, in large part, upon the willingness of the innocent victims of crime to cooperate with it. Unless victims participate in the judicial process, society cannot punish criminals and prevent them from committing more crimes. While we need the help of innocent victims, they in turn deserve our support. They do not ask for pity. They ask only for our support as they recover from an unexpected, unwanted, and undeserved trauma.

After decades when most concern was focused on the rights of criminals, the public has recognized that the victims of criminals have rights also. Guided by the recommendations of the President's Task Force on Victims of Crime, my Administration is striving to ensure fair treatment for innocent victims. We are working with national organizations, as well as State and local agencies, to help people whose lives have been shattered through no fault of their own.

One of the most encouraging developments in this regard was the passage of the Victims of Crime Act of 1984, which offers unprecedented assistance to States to meet some of the needs of the targets of violent behavior. We have examined in particular the plight of people who are assaulted by people they know and trust, and we have proposed reforms to assure them the full protection of the law. It is the nature of the crime, not the relationship of the victim to the offender, that should guide the actions of the justice system.

We may reduce the frequency of violent crime, but we will never eliminate it. Every year millions of our fellow citizens will face it for the first time, and millions more will continue to face the daily challenge of lives forever changed by it. As citizens of a Nation promising justice for all, they must be treated with respect and compassion.

Now, Therefore, I, Ronald Reagan, President of the United States of America, do hereby proclaim the week beginning April 14, 1985, as Victims of Crime Week. I commend those innocent victims who have turned their anguish into action to protect their fellow citizens. I urge officials at all levels of government to give special attention to the burdens crime victims face. I ask that all Americans listen and respond to the needs of crime victims, who urgently require and deserve our support.

In Witness Whereof, I have hereunto set my hand this 19th day of April, in the year of our Lord nineteen hundred and eighty-five, and of the Independence of the United States of America the two hundred and ninth.

RONALD REAGAN

[*Filed with the Office of the Federal Register, 4:27 p.m., April 19, 1985*]

Message on the Observance of National Volunteer Week, April 22–28, 1985
April 19, 1985

Our American tradition of neighbor helping neighbor has always been one of our greatest strengths and most noble traditions. American ingenuity, coupled with organizational know-how, has provided the basis for innovative approaches to meeting the needs of our communities.

The spirit of voluntarism and compassion for others is a vital part of our national character. Each year close to a hundred million Americans help their neighbors through voluntary service. Citizens from every walk of life volunteer their time, energy and resources to help those less fortunate than themselves. We can never fully measure the positive effects that each kind word or deed has upon this great and wonderful land of ours.

One of the chief aims of my Administration has been to emphasize the vital contributions which individuals, families and private organizations make to our community life. Every day we are learning about successful Private Sector Initiatives which are the result of people caring about other people. It is my hope that during National Volunteer Week, American volunteers both at home and around the world, will receive the recognition they deserve for their generosity. It is also my hope that still more Americans will be inspired to join these volunteers who are the backbone of our community life.

And so I hail the spirit of compassionate patriotic enterprise that National Volunteer Week is meant to strengthen. I ask my fellow Americans to exercise their right and responsibility to take an active role in their neighborhoods, town, cities and their nation.

I can only repeat what I have said many times before: volunteers make a difference. May God bless each and every one of you.

RONALD REAGAN

Message on the Observance of Secretaries Week, April 21–27, 1985
April 19, 1985

Secretaries Week offers us a yearly occasion to recognize the indispensable part played by secretaries not only in our nation's commerce and industry but in other activities essential to society, such as government and the professions.

In many cases the order and smooth functioning of an enterprise hinge on the efficiency and alertness of secretaries. Their attention to detail is well known. Communications would be cumbersome without them. It is no exaggeration to say that their work is essential.

With the rapid progress of technology, new challenges face secretaries. To maintain current standards they must often master new techniques of communication, and of the storage and retrieval of information. Constantly advancing systems of administration make the work of secretaries more efficient but at the same time make it more demanding. Secretaries often bear the heaviest responsibilities for adapting to new techniques.

I am happy to call attention to the important role of secretaries in our national life, and to the demands that their responsibilities place upon them. Nancy joins me in saluting the indispensable role they play in our nation's life.

RONALD REAGAN

Appointment of Ronald H. Walker as a Special Consultant to the Office of Presidential Personnel
April 19, 1985

The President today announced that Ronald H. Walker has become a special consultant to the Office of Presidential Personnel.

Mr. Walker is the managing director of the Washington, DC, office of Korn/Ferry International. Prior to joining Korn/Ferry International in 1979, he was president of his own management consulting firm in Dallas. He was formerly associate director of World Championship Tennis. During 1975 Mr. Walker was a consultant to the Kingdom of Saudi Arabia in their establishment of a national park system. From 1972 to 1975, he served as Director of the National Park Service. From 1969 to 1972, Mr. Walker was a Special Assistant to President Nixon, responsible for coordinating and planning the President's historic trips to the People's Republic of China and to the Union of Soviet Socialist Republics, as well as to 22 other countries and every State in the Union. Mr. Walker most recently served as chairman and chief executive officer of the 50th American Presidential Inaugural Committee. He was also manager of the 1984 Republican National Convention in Dallas.

Mr. Walker is a graduate of the University of Arizona and served as a captain in the U.S. Army. Mr. Walker resides in Potomac, MD, with his wife Anne Collins Walker and their three daughters.

Radio Address to the Nation on the Central American Peace Proposal
April 20, 1985

In a few days, Congress will vote on whether or not to support our proposal to help restore peace and democracy in Nicaragua. Few votes will ever be so important to the survival of democracy in Latin America and the Caribbean. Few votes will ever be so important to the national security of the United States.

On March 1st, the leaders of the democratic resistance of Nicaragua, the so-called *contras*, sent a peace proposal to the Communists, who've taken over their country. The proposal called for a cease-fire and church-mediated negotiations that would lead to free and honest elections.

We've asked the democratic resistance to extend their offer until June 1st, and we're asking Congress to show its support for peace negotiations by releasing humanitarian aid to the democratic resistance. This support is crucial.

Negotiations would be our best and possibly last opportunity to steer the Sandinista Communists away from their present brutal course and back toward the democratic and peaceful promises of their revolution.

The responsibility now rests squarely on the shoulders of Congress. A vote for humanitarian aid to the democratic resistance will signal the United States' resolve on this issue. And courage and resolve are the only way to convince the Sandinista Communists to come to the negotiating table.

A vote against our proposal, however, could mean the beginning of the end to all hopes of peace and democracy in Central America. Already, the followers of Qadhafi and the Ayatollah Khomeini are in Nicaragua—about 2 hours by air from United States borders. And just this week, we confirmed the presence of Russian military personnel in the battle zones of northern Nicaragua.

The Soviet terrorist-bloc nations know what is at stake in Nicaragua. That's why, in the 7 months since Congress cut off aid to the democratic resistance, they've been pouring in weapons and personnel to their Communist allies, hoping to wipe out the democratic forces while they're most vulnerable.

And that's why, rather than negotiate with the democratic resistance, the Communists are still betting that the United States will abandon its friends. A recent article in the New York Times reported that the "Sandinistas pin hopes on Congress." You heard me right. The Sandinista Communists are lobbying your Senators and Representatives. Together with the misguided sympathizers in this country, they've been running a sophisticated disinformation campaign of lies and distortion.

And now we're told that in a cynical attempt to manipulate public opinion and our Congress, the Communists may put forth an 11th hour so-called peace proposal, a proposal aimed at blocking aid to the democratic resistance and giving the Communists a free hand to tighten their grip on the Nicaraguan people. The Communists know that if they can persuade Congress to cut off aid, they'll never have to negotiate with the democratic opposition. And they believe if they can stop aid to the democratic resistance, nothing can stop them.

Unfortunately, some are using this issue to play partisan politics. Before we'd even announced our peace plan, the Speaker of the House called our peace offer a dirty trick. How could church-mediated peace negotiations be a dirty trick? Do they really think the church would ever cooperate in a trick?

The opponents of our plan in the House have announced a formula for turning the democratic resistance into homeless refugees. Their alternative to a plan for peace and democracy would only provide assistance to the democratic forces if they abandon their struggle to liberate Nicaragua—in other words, surrender to communism. They would, in fact, aid the Soviet-Cuban-Sandinista effort to get rid of the democratic resistance.

We're asking Congress to be consistent and support those who are fighting communism in Nicaragua, just as we support the democratic resistance in Afghanistan and Cambodia.

Let me speak plainly. Any proposal that abandons over 15,000 members of a democratic resistance to Communists is not a compromise; it's a shameful surrender. If Congress ever approves such a proposal, it would hasten the consolidation of Nicaragua as a Communist-terrorist arsenal. And it would give a green light to Soviet-sponsored aggression throughout the American mainland, ultimately threatening our own security.

But Congress can prevent a crisis by supporting peace negotiations now. Don't let the Sandinista Communists and their sympathizers be the only voices heard. Let our Members of Congress and Senators hear the voices of you who love liberty and democracy, too. Let's give peace a chance in Nicaragua and in all of Central America.

Until next week, thanks for listening, and God bless you.

Note: The President spoke at 12:06 p.m. from Camp David, MD.

Letter to the Presidents of Colombia, Mexico, Panama, and Venezuela on the Central American Peace Proposal
April 4, 1985

Dear Mr. President:

In the efforts of the Contadora group to resolve the conflict in Central America, one key objective has been to achieve national reconciliation in those countries rent by internal conflict. In El Salvador, President Duarte has taken the initiative in launching a dialogue with the guerrilla forces seeking to overthrow that country's democratic government; in Guatemala, which has been the scene of decades of strife, hope for national reconciliation has been kindled by the interest of a broad spectrum of parties in participating in elections later this year.

Only in Nicaragua have we seen efforts to promote national reconciliation frustrated by the government's negative response. I believe we now have an important new opportunity to promote peace and reconciliation in Nicaragua.

As you are aware, the principal leaders of Nicaragua's democratic opposition groups signed a declaration on March 1, 1985, in San Jose, Costa Rica, in which they offered a ceasefire in return for agreement by the Nicaraguan Government to a dialogue mediated by the Bishops Conference of the Roman Catholic church. This offer represents a bold and important initiative which I believe the United States and the Contadora countries should work together to promote.

My government intends to take action designed to strengthen Nicaragua's democratic resistance forces while encouraging the Sandinista regime to agree to Church-mediated dialogue. I have asked Congress to make available $14 million for the Nicaraguan democratic resistance forces. On Thursday, April 4, I plan to announce to the American people that I will use these funds only for humanitarian assistance while the democratic opposition's March 1 call for dialogue remains in effect. I will ask the democratic opposition to extend their offer

until June 1. If the Nicaraguan government accepts the offer of dialogue with the opposition, then my government's assistance will remain limited to humanitarian purposes for a sufficient period to allow a serious dialogue to achieve progress. If the Sandinistas do not respond positively to the March 1 offer or, if 60 days after the offer of dialogue is accepted no agreement has resulted, I will lift this restriction on U.S. assistance unless both parties ask me to keep it in effect.

Mr. President, I am informing you of my actions before I announce them to the American people because I know the importance you attach to obtaining a negotiated settlement of the conflict in Central America on the basis of verified implementation of all of the twenty-one Contadora objectives. I believe this proposal for peace and democracy in Nicaragua can contribute toward achieving the key objective of national reconciliation in that country.

Sincerely,

/S/ RONALD REAGAN

Note: Identical letters were sent to Presidents Belisario Betancur Cuartas of Colombia, Miguel De la Madrid Hurtado of Mexico, Jorge Enrique Illueca Sibauste of Panama, and Jaime Lusinchi of Venezuela. The original was not available for verification of the content of the letter, which was released by the Office of the Press Secretary on April 22.

Remarks at the President's Volunteer Action Awards Luncheon
April 22, 1985

Thank you very much, but it's you who deserve the applause.

Today we kick off a week of activities that are honoring the spirit of voluntarism, a spirit which we can see by you gathered in this room is very much alive and still growing in America. It's no overstatement to say that America is a nation of volunteers.

I think philosophers might want to contemplate the question: Why is the freest

nation on Earth also the one in which it is so common to see people from every walk of life—rich and poor, young and old—rolling up their sleeves and pitching in to help others? Maybe it's just that we want to say thank you to the Lord who blessed our country with freedom. And the best way to do that is to care for our fellow human beings. And maybe that's why polls say that most Americans agree that no matter how big and powerful government gets and how many services it provides, it can never take the place of volunteers.

This is the fourth year that we've been giving these awards, and I thought you might be interested to hear some current news of those who've been honored in the past. Like America's volunteer spirit, their activities continue to grow, reaching out to help more and more people.

Two years ago, a group of concerned mothers received an award for their efforts to combat drunk driving. Since then, Mothers Against Drunk Driving, or MADD, as they're known, has tripled in size, and now it has chapters in almost every State of the Union. I don't think there's any question that it has been largely their energy and determination there that has helped bring about a significant drop in fatalities due to drunk driving.

The Sunshine Foundation, which grants special wishes to terminally ill children, is today helping over four times as many children as when they received the award in 1982.

And Children of the Night, a program that works with teenage prostitutes in Hollywood, is now raising funds to build a permanent shelter for these children in crisis.

The Americares Foundation, which won an award last year, has sent a shipment of vitamins to Mother Theresa in India, brought several Afghan freedom fighters to the United States for medical treatment, and just recently made its first airlift of food to the Sudan.

These are just a few examples of how volunteers make a difference. But these generous people are not alone. Recently it seemed as if all of America volunteered to help feed the starving in Africa. The plight on that unfortunate continent inspired some of the most generous giving in history, with private donations from Americans topping $100 million. I guess it's true that if you tap any American deeply enough, you'll find a volunteer.

We're going to be giving out only 18 Volunteer Action Awards today and 44 citations. The difficult part was singling out those relative few from the thousands upon thousands of worthy Americans. But in honoring you, we honor them and the best in every American—that selfless giving spirit

of voluntarism, which lends a helping hand in brotherhood and neighborliness to those in need.

So, to you all, my heartfelt congratulations. And now, with the assistance of Donna Alvarado and Governor Romney, I'll have the pleasure of handing out the awards. If you will come up here.

[*At this point, Donna Alvarado, Director of ACTION, announced the 1985 award recipients and read the citations accompanying the awards. Recipients included Sun City Prides, Sun City, AZ; Rev. Hezekiah David Stewart, College Station, AR; Dr. Kelsey J. Caplinger III, Little Rock, AR; the volunteer corps of the 1984 Olympic Games, Los Angeles, CA; Parents Anonymous, Torrance, CA; Delmarva Power & Light, Wilmington, DE; Amanda the Panda Volunteers, Fort Lauderdale, FL; Allstate Insurance Co., Northbrook, IL; Henrietta Aladjem, Watertown, MA; Missouri Speleological Survey, Inc., Eldon, MO; Vernon E. Falkenhain, Rolla, MO; Morris Pesin, Jersey City, NJ; Greensboro Symphony Guild, Greensboro, NC; Concerned Black Men, Philadelphia, PA; Les Cory, Tiverton, RI; Texas Youth Commission, Dallas House, Dallas, TX; National Court Appointed Special Advocates Association, Seattle, WA; and 19 unions cooperating in the Disaster Coastline Project, Washington, DC. The President then resumed speaking.*]

Now, before we go, there's one more special award that I'd like to present. It's to Donna Stone Pesch, who passed away just 2 months ago at the age of 49.

In 1972 she founded the National Committee for Prevention of Child Abuse, a volunteer organization that became a catalyst in heightening international awareness of child abuse. It's estimated that, while only 1 in 10 people were concerned with child abuse in 1972, today nearly 90 percent know about it, are aware and concerned, and want to help with this problem.

Clem Stone, would you please come up here to accept this award for your daughter, Donna. The good work that she did will live on in the organization that she founded and in the hearts and minds of the children that she helped from abuse and tragedy.

Congratulations to you and yours.

I thank you all again. God bless all of you for what you continue to do. And now, I guess all I can do is what the little girl told me to do that wrote me the letter. When she finished, she said, "Now, get back over to the Oval Office and go to work." [*Laughter*]

Thank you all very much.

Note: The President spoke at 1:13 p.m. in the State Dining Room at the White House. Former Governor George Romney of Michigan was chairman of VOLUNTEER: The National Center for Citizen Involvement.

Message to President José Sarney of Brazil on the Death of President-elect Tancredo de Almeida Neves
April 22, 1985

I was profoundly saddened to learn of the untimely demise of President-elect Neves. It is a tragic event for his family and for Brazil. In my meeting with him last February, I was deeply impressed by both his human warmth and his intellectual insight. He was indeed a man for the time and his country, and will be sorely missed.

Brazil will be well-served by the heirs of Tancredo's legacy. I am confident that you and the members of his cabinet, inspired by

his memory, will provide the leadership Brazil needs at this critical hour.

I would like to express my most profound condolences to you and the people of Brazil, at your great loss. My prayers, and those of Brazil's many friends in the United States, are with you as you take up your new responsibilities.

Sincerely,

RONALD REAGAN

Nomination of Douglas A. Riggs To Be General Counsel of the Department of Commerce
April 22, 1985

The President today announced his intention to nominate Douglas A. Riggs to be General Counsel of the Department of Commerce. He would succeed Irving P. Margulies.

Since 1983 Mr. Riggs has been serving at the White House as Special Assistant to the President for Public Liaison. Previously he was a practicing lawyer in Anchorage, AK, and a partner in the Seattle, WA, law firm of Bogle & Gates. In 1980 he opened the

Anchorage office of Bogle & Gates. He served as special counsel and administrative assistant to the Governor of Alaska.

He received his undergraduate degree from Brigham Young University (1966), a master's degree in labor relations from West Virginia University (1967), and a law degree from Cornell University (1973). He was born August 20, 1944, in Rigby, ID, and now resides in Washington, DC.

Nomination of Gary L. Bauer To Be Under Secretary of Education
April 22, 1985

The President today announced his intention to nominate Gary L. Bauer to be Under Secretary of Education. He would succeed Gary L. Jones.

Since 1982 Mr. Bauer has been Deputy Under Secretary of Education for Planning, Budget, and Evaluation. Previously, he was in the White House Office of Policy Development as Deputy Assistant Director for Legal Policy and Policy Adviser (1982) and Policy Analyst (1981–1982). He served on the staff of the Reagan-Bush campaign and the Office of the President-elect in 1980–1981. Prior to that time, he was director (1976–1980) and deputy director (1973–1976) of government relations for the Direct Mail/Marketing Association.

He graduated from Georgetown College (B.A., 1968) and Georgetown Law School (J.D., 1973). He is married, has two children, and resides in Falls Church, VA. He was born May 4, 1946, in Covington, KY.

Appointment of James F. Kuhn as Special Assistant to the President
April 22, 1985

The President today announced the appointment of James F. Kuhn to be Special Assistant to the President. Mr. Kuhn will serve as the President's personal aide.

Since 1981 Mr. Kuhn has been serving as a staff assistant in the Presidential Advance Office. In that capacity, he coordinated the development and execution of Presidential events at and away from the White House.

Prior to joining the White House staff, Mr. Kuhn served on the staff of President-elect Reagan, establishing the transition office in Los Angeles and coordinating the President-elect's schedule from Election Day 1980 to Inauguration Day 1981. During the 1980 Presidential campaign, he served as an advance representative of candidate Reagan. Before joining the campaign, Mr. Kuhn served as assistant to the vice president and group manager at IPS Industries, an industrial manufacturers representative firm, in Canton, OH.

Mr. Kuhn graduated from Kent State University (B.A., 1974). He is married to the former Carole McGlone. They have one daughter, Caitlin Marie, and reside in Alexandria, VA. Mr. Kuhn was born February 26, 1952, in Tiffin, OH.

Message to the Congress Reporting on the National Emergency With Respect to Iran
April 22, 1985

To the Congress of the United States:

Pursuant to Section 204(c) of the International Emergency Economic Powers Act (IEEPA), 50 U.S.C. Section 1703(c), I hereby report to the Congress on developments since my last report of October 31, 1984, concerning the national emergency with respect to Iran that was declared in Executive Order No. 12170 of November 14, 1979.

1. The Iran-United States Claims Tribunal, established at The Hague pursuant to the Claims Settlement Agreement of January 19, 1981 (the "Algiers Accords"), continues to make progress in arbitrating the claims before it. Since my last report, the Tribunal has rendered 18 more decisions for a total of 169 final decisions. Of these,

125 have been awards in favor of American claimants; 89 were awards on agreed terms, authorizing and approving payment of settlements negotiated by the parties; and 36 were adjudicated decisions. As of March 31, 1984, total payments to successful American claimants from the Security Account stood at over $337 million. Of the remaining 44 decisions, 22 dismissed claims for lack of jurisdiction, 3 partially dismissed claims for lack of jurisdiction, 13 dismissed claims on the merits, one approved the withdrawal of a claim, four were awards in favor of the Government of Iran, and one was an award in favor of the United States Government.

2. In the past six months, there have been significant changes in the composition of the Tribunal. As I noted in my last report, Professor Karl-Heinz Bockstiegel of the Federal Republic of Germany was selected to replace President Gunnar Lagergren, who resigned effective October 1, 1984. On December 1, 1984, Professor Bockstiegel was designated President of the Tribunal, in addition to his duties as Chairman of Chamber One. On November 29, 1984, the Government of Iran appointed two new arbitrators to replace Judges Mahmoud M. Kashani and Shafei Shafeiei, whose qualifications had been challenged by the United States following their unprecedented attack on one of the third-party arbitrators, Judge Mangard, in September 1984. The two new Iranian arbitrators, Hamid Bahrami Ahmadi and Seyed Mohsen Mostafavi Tafreshi, assumed their duties on January 15, 1985. In addition, the Chairman of Chamber Two, Willem Riphagen, submitted his resignation for health reasons, effective April 1, 1985, and the Chairman of Chamber Three, Nils Mangard, has submitted his resignation for personal reasons, effective no later than July 1, 1985. Swiss lawyer Robert Briner and French law professor Michel Virally have recently accepted invitations from the U.S. and Iranian arbitrators to join the Tribunal in place of Chairmen Riphagen and Mangard.

3. In spite of the disruptions that I described in my last report, the Tribunal made some progress in arbitrating the claims of U.S. nationals for $250,000 or more. The Special Chamber, which was established to consider requests for withdraw-als or terminations of claims and for awards on agreed terms, rendered 13 awards on agreed terms prior to its dissolution on January 15, 1985. With the arrival of the two new Iranian arbitrators, the Chambers have once again begun hearing and deciding cases. On March 1, the Tribunal awarded R. J. Reynolds Tobacco Co. an additional $12 million in interest on its claim, the decision in which was described in my last report. In total, more than 35 percent of the claims for over $250,000 have now been disposed of through adjudication, settlement, or voluntary withdrawal, leaving 344 such claims on the docket.

4. The Tribunal has continued with the arbitration of the claims of U.S. nationals against Iran of less than $250,000 each. In addition to 18 test cases, the Tribunal has selected 100 other claims for active arbitration. In 62 of these claims, the Department of State has submitted Supplemental Statements of Claim, containing more than 16,000 pages of text and evidence. Additional pleadings are being filed weekly. Although Iran repeatedly seeks extensions of time within which to file its responsive pleadings to these claims, the Tribunal has continued to press for their resolution. At the Tribunal, three senior legal officers and a law clerk work exclusively on these claims. Finally, since my last report, another seven of these claimants have received awards on agreed terms, bringing the total to ten.

5. The Department of State continues to coordinate the efforts of concerned governmental agencies in presenting U.S. claims against Iran as well as responses by the U.S. Government to claims brought against it by Iran. Since my last report, the Department has filed pleadings in seven government-to-government claims based on contracts for the provision of goods and services. These claims include a claim on behalf of the Agency for International Development for over $38 million based on outstanding developmental loans to the Government of Iran. In addition, the Department of State, working together with the Department of the Treasury and the Department of Justice, filed responsive pleadings in two major interpretive disputes. One related to Iran's

claim to over $400 million remaining from funds transferred pursuant to the Algiers Accords for payment of Iran's syndicated debt. The other was in response to Iran's allegations that the United States breached its obligation under the Algiers Accords to terminate litigation against Iran. The Department of State also filed pleadings in four other interpretive disputes. The Tribunal held one hearing in an interpretive dispute on whether the Tribunal has jurisdiction to arbitrate approximately 111 claims brought by Iran directly against U.S. banks which do not involve standby letters of credit. Finally, two of the Tribunal's chambers have confirmed that action will be taken on or about May 20 to strike or otherwise dispose of 248 claims brought by Iran against U.S. banks based on standby letters of credit.

6. The Algiers Accords also provided for direct negotiations between U.S. banks and Bank Markazi Iran concerning the payment of nonsyndicated debt claims of U.S. banks against Iran from Dollar Account No. 2 (the interest-bearing escrow account established at the Bank of England in January 1981 with the deposit of $1.418 billion of previously blocked Iranian funds). As of April 10, 1985, three additional settlements had been reached since my last report between Iran and U.S. banks. The three settling banks, Irving Trust Company, Morgan Guaranty Trust Company, and Banker's Trust Company, received a total of $81.91 million from Dollar Account No. 2 in payment of their claims against Iran. From this amount, $73.595 million was subsequently paid by these banks to Iran in settlement of Iran's claims against them, primarily for interest on Iran's domestic deposits with these banks. (One of these banks paid Iran an additional $8.45 million from other funds.) Thus, as of April 10, 1985, there have been 29 bank settlements resulting in payments to the settling banks of approximately $1.5 billion from Dollar Account No. 2. From

that amount, the banks have paid approximately $693 million to Iran in settlement of Iran's claims against them. About 17 banks have yet to settle their claims. In addition, attorneys from the Department of the Treasury and the Federal Reserve Bank of New York have been negotiating an "Agreed Clarification" with Bank Markazi to allow the payment from Dollar Account No. 2 of certain amounts still owing on Iran's syndicated debt.

7. There have been no changes in the Iranian Assets Control Regulations since my last report.

8. Although the attack on Judge Mangard in September seriously disrupted and delayed proceedings for three months, the Tribunal resumed full operation in January of this year and the two Iranian arbitrators who committed the attack were removed by the Government of Iran. Since that time, the Tribunal has actively pursued the arbitration of both private and government claims. Prehearing conferences and hearings that had been cancelled are being rescheduled. The Tribunal has made provision for the issuance of awards in cases heard prior to the removal of the two Iranian arbitrators and the resignations of President Lagergren and Chairmen Riphagen and Mangard. This resumption of Tribunal activities provides reason to expect that more progress will be made in the coming months.

9. Financial and diplomatic aspects of the relationship with Iran continue to present an unusual challenge to the national security and foreign policy of the United States. I shall continue to exercise the powers at my disposal to deal with these problems and will continue to report periodically to the Congress on significant developments.

RONALD REAGAN

The White House,
April 22, 1985.

Proclamation 5323—World Trade Week, 1985
April 22, 1985

By the President of the United States of America

A Proclamation

Each year, through World Trade Week, we celebrate the many ways in which international trade strengthens our country and enriches our lives.

Increased trade strengthens our own economy, as well as helping to sustain and spread world economic growth. American exports help create new growth opportunities for our businesses and new opportunities for employment for our workers. To the American consumer, freer and fairer trade has meant better products in greater variety and at lower prices.

Through contact with other societies, we receive new ideas and gain a better understanding of our traditional values. We reinforce our ties of amity and peace with other countries through strong bonds of commercial interest and mutual respect.

We Americans are used to a role of responsible leadership in world affairs. It is a role we value, and it has won us the respect of other nations. We know that more jobs, greater prosperity, and dynamic economies are based on freer and fairer trade. Other countries take courage from our confidence and competitive spirit.

Despite stronger competition for world markets, record trade deficits, and a grow-

ing threat of protectionism abroad, the United States has resisted the temptation to adopt self-defeating protectionist measures of its own. We have called upon other countries to open their markets to fair competition. We are working with our trading partners to launch a new round of multilateral trade negotiations by early next year aimed at opening markets worldwide.

Americans can be proud that economic growth in the United States has helped fuel the recovery of our trading partners who can now afford to buy more of our goods and services. Americans can be proud of the U.S. commitment to policies promoting unrestricted trade and investment consistent with our security interests.

Now, Therefore, I Ronald Reagan, President of the United States of America, do hereby proclaim the week beginning May 19, 1985, as World Trade Week, and I request all Federal, State, and local officials to cooperate in its observance.

In Witness Whereof, I have hereunto set my hand this twenty-second day of April, in the year of our Lord nineteen hundred and eighty-five, and of the Independence of the United States of America the two hundred and ninth.

RONALD REAGAN

[*Filed with the Office of the Federal Register, 4:46 p.m., April 22, 1985*]

Statement on the Israel-United States Free Trade Area Agreement
April 22, 1985

I and friends of Israel everywhere take great pleasure in congratulating Ambassador Brock and Minister of Industry and Trade Sharon on the U.S.-Israeli Free Trade Area Agreement. The signing of this historic agreement caps nearly 1½ years of intensive and highly productive discussions. These talks have deepened our understanding of each other's economies and trading

systems. And this agreement adds a new dimension to the special relationship between our countries.

The Free Trade Area Agreement is the first such agreement entered into by the United States. It fully meets the international rules regarding free trade areas contained in the GATT. When fully implemented in January 1995, the agreement will eliminate restrictions on all trade between the United States and Israel—trade which in 1984 amounted to $3.6 billion. The agreement also contains unprecedented recognition of the increasing importance of trade in services and investment, which will serve to further liberalize our bilateral economic relations.

This agreement opens up new prospects for the United States and Israel. Both our countries will derive substantial benefits through the unrestricted access it provides to each other's markets. More broadly, however, the agreement is an important milestone in our efforts to liberalize trade. We hope that it also will serve to encourage greater liberalization of the multilateral trading system and that it will help us move ahead in our continued attempts to expand world trade. I want to thank the chief negotiators, Danny Halperin from Israel and Doral Cooper from the United States, and their respective teams for a job well done.

The United States has a basic commitment to Israel's economic well-being, and we have pledged to continue to help Israel fulfill its great potential. In my discussions with Prime Minister Peres last fall, we explored ways to address Israel's pressing economic problems. We agreed that the Free Trade Area will be instrumental in helping Israel put its economy back on a foundation of vigorous, self-sustaining growth. I am confident that as this agreement is implemented, the U.S.-Israel Free Trade Area will prove to be one of the cornerstones of Israel's future economic development program.

The Free Trade Area Agreement symbolizes once again our two countries' deep community of interest and our shared values and aspirations for a better future. It underscores the importance of Israel to the United States as an ally, as a trading partner, and as a friend, and it underscores the U.S commitment to Israel's security and prosperity.

Proclamation 5324—National Organ Donation Awareness Week, 1985
April 22, 1985

By the President of the United States of America

A Proclamation

The most precious gift that one human being can bestow upon another is the gift of life. It can be given simply by making arrangements to donate our organs or those of our loved ones after death. Donation of our corneas would give others the gift of sight; donation of our kidneys, hearts, lungs, livers, and pancreata could save the lives of many people who might otherwise die.

On several recent occasions, I have asked the American people to be aware of the opportunities to donate their organs, and I have made special pleas for young children in need of liver transplants. The response proved to be overwhelming. Tragically, however, many desperately ill persons, including young children, have died while

awaiting a suitable organ.

The need for organs far surpasses the number donated each year. To increase the availability of organs for transplantation, I signed the National Organ Transplant Act on October 19, 1984. This law created an Office of Organ Transplantation in the Public Health Service and authorized a Task Force on Organ Transplantation.

It is appropriate that we as a Nation encourage organ donation and increase public awareness of the need for such donations. We also should recognize the many contributions of private organizations, including the American Council on Transplantation, to this effort. By filling out a uniform donor card and carrying it, and by making our wishes of donation known to our families, we may give the gift of life to people who so desperately need organs for transplantation.

Americans are a caring and giving people. I have heard from many Americans who have lost their loved ones in tragic accidents, but who have found solace in knowing that through their loss other lives were saved.

The Congress, by Senate Joint Resolution 35, has authorized and requested the President to issue a proclamation designating the week beginning April 21 through April 27, 1985, as "National Organ Donation Awareness Week."

Now, Therefore, I, Ronald Reagan, President of the United States of America, do hereby designate April 21 through April 27, 1985, as National Organ Donation Awareness Week. I urge all health care profession-

als, educators, the media, public and private organizations concerned with organ donation and transplantation, and all Americans to join me in supporting this humanitarian action.

In Witness Whereof, I have hereunto set my hand this twenty-second day of April, in the year of our Lord nineteen hundred and eighty-five, and of the Independence of the United States of America the two hundred and ninth.

RONALD REAGAN

[Filed with the Office of the Federal Register, 12:12 p.m., April 23, 1985]

Note: The proclamation was released by the Office of the Press Secretary on April 23.

Proclamation 5325—Asian/Pacific American Heritage Week, 1985
April 22, 1985

By the President of the United States of America

A Proclamation

The Pacific Ocean today is ringed by a large number of successful developed and developing nations. So rapid has the progress of this area been that many scholars are beginning to speak of an emerging Pacific Civilization similar to the Mediterranean Civilization of the ancient world or the Atlantic Civilization of modern times. America is well-placed to play a major role in this emerging civilization not only because of its geographic position but also because many of its citizens are themselves of Asian and Pacific ancestry.

Americans of Asian and Pacific ancestry are a diverse group, representing as many different ethnic allegiances as Americans of European ancestry, but certain common values characterize them all. Whether as immigrants to our country or as native inhabitants in the islands of the Pacific Ocean, they have retained a strong sense of traditional values emphasizing vital family and communal bonds. These values remain strong today and play an important role in the success achieved by these proud Americans.

Asian and Pacific Americans have been successful in virtually every field of endeavor. Through their achievements in many areas, they have enriched the lives of all Americans. By sharing their cultures with other Americans, they have increased our Nation's rich cultural vitality. Asian and Pacific Americans have truly helped the United States to fulfill its most cherished ideals.

Now, Therefore, I, Ronald Reagan, President of the United States of America, do hereby proclaim the week beginning May 5, 1985, as Asian/Pacific American Heritage Week and call upon all Americans to observe this week with appropriate ceremonies and activities.

In Witness Whereof, I have hereunto set my hand this twenty-second day of April, in the year of our Lord nineteen hundred and eighty-five, and of the Independence of the United States of America the two hundred and ninth.

RONALD REAGAN

[Filed with the Office of the Federal Register, 12:18 p.m., April 23, 1985]

Note: The proclamation was released by the Office of the Press Secretary on April 23.

Remarks at the Midyear Conference of the National Association of Realtors
April 23, 1985

The President. Thank you, David Roberts, Clark Wallace, distinguished guests, and all of you. I appreciate this opportunity to be with you today. Ever since my days as Governor of California, I've felt a special bond with realtors. When the fundamental issues were being decided and the political lines were drawn, I consistently found realtors as my strong and energetic allies.

And this morning, I enjoyed reading the Washington Post for the first time in a long time.[1] [*Laughter*]

But as to your being allies, this has been no mere coincidence. There are few industries in this country that reflect the free market ideals, the respect for property ownership, and the vigorous devotion to individual freedom as yours. We share a philosophy of freedom that has served our country well.

But no one ever claimed that preserving freedom would be easy. I want you to know that I'm personally grateful for the time and effort that you commit to keeping government on track, and I mean Federal, State, and local government.

Your community activism is on top of working long, hard hours at your job. And I understand that making a living in real estate is no easy proposition. [*Laughter*] You know, I'd like to tell a story. If you've heard it before, if I've told it before, just remember that after age 40 you have a tendency to tell the same stories over and over again. [*Laughter*]

But this is the story of a realtor who was out driving on a back road on his way to look at some property and suddenly noticed

down beside him was a chicken keeping pace with him, and he was doing 60 miles an hour. [*Laughter*] And suddenly, the chicken spurted out ahead of him, and it looked to him as if the chicken had three legs. And then it turned and went down a side road and into a barnyard. And the driver turned down that lane, drove into the barnyard.

There was a farmer there, and he asked him, "Did you see a chicken go by here?" And the farmer said, "Yep." He says, "Did it have three legs?" And the farmer says, "Yep. I raise them that way. I breed 'em." He says, "You do? How come?" "Well," he said, "I just love the drumstick, and Ma always liked the drumstick, and now Junior's come along, and he likes it, and we just got tired of fighting over it. So, I've been breeding three-legged chickens." [*Laughter*]

And the driver said, "Well, how do they taste?" He says, "I don't know. I haven't been able to catch one yet." [*Laughter*]

Seriously though, in these last 4½ years together, we've accomplished much. And unlike that farmer with the three-legged chicken, the American people, I think, are enjoying the rewards of our efforts. The economy we inherited was anemic and faltering. The American people were being bled white by inflation and ever-increasing taxes. And today, thanks to you and the other involved citizens who made it possible, the American people continue to reap the benefits of a healthy economy, low inflation, and stable taxes.

There's especially good news about housing. Housing starts, after a slump in February, bounced back 16 percent in March to an annual rate of almost 2 million—1.895 million to be exact. They're now 11 percent above their level in March of 1984. Permits are also doing well. They're at their highest

---

[1] *The President was referring to the National Association of Realtors' advertisement urging support of the budget plan proposed by the President and Senate Republican leaders.*

level since June of last year.

The Employee Relocation Council says that 48 percent of their member companies experienced a higher transfer volume in 1984 over the previous year, and they expect that trend to continue in 1985. For people who sell houses for a living, that's great news, as is the level of sales on existing family homes. They're off to their best start in 5 years.

Now, all of this reflects a fundamental change in the direction of the American economy. We've moved away from collectivist schemes that emphasized control, consumption, and redistribution. Instead, we set our sights on encouraging investment, production, and growth. We relaxed or eliminated controls and reduced the growth in Federal spending. And we increased incentives by lowering the people's tax rates.

In the first term, we turned a crisis situation around. In the second term, we have the opportunity to set our country on a course for a decade of unparalleled prosperity. I'll do my utmost, but I need to know that you're still with me. And let me ask you: Can I count on your help? [*Applause*] Well, that was kind of a silly question, then, wasn't it? [*Laughter*]

Well, thank you. There is much to do. And let's not kid ourselves, it isn't going to be easy. The first order of business is to come to grips with Federal spending. We hear a lot about the deficit, but what really is being talked about is deficit spending. And the way to reduce that is to reduce spending.

There are, of course, different approaches to this task. Some would have us freeze every item in the Federal budget across the board. But, now, while that may seem appealing, it doesn't get the job done. It's the wrong medicine at the wrong time. Instead, we should use this opportunity to trim programs that are wasteful, ineffective, and unnecessary—many of which never should have been funded with Federal tax dollars in the first place. To keep pouring your tax dollars into these unworthy programs at the current levels while at the same time limiting worthwhile, efficient, and absolutely necessary programs would be a travesty. A freeze is a decision not to make a decision, a retreat in the face of special interest pressure.

Our proposal, which was worked out after long, hard negotiations with the Republican leadership of the Senate, calls for a leaner, healthier budget, trimmed of much of its deadwood but ready and able to do those essential tasks which the Federal Government must do. We would protect the poor, elderly, and disabled. Full inflation adjustments will be given to those receiving supplemental security income, and also there will be an increase in monthly benefits of $10 for an individual and $15 for a couple. The food stamp, AFDC, WIC, and other safety net programs will stay intact.

Keeping the safety net intact, an increasingly expensive proposition, is a moral imperative. As far as other projects, we can no longer afford to finance everything. As a people, we must set priorities. Those programs whose costs outweigh their benefits should be terminated.

The Job Corps is one good example. It costs taxpayers about $15,200 a year. For that kind of money, we could be sending them to Harvard for a year. The price tag is high, and only one-third of those trained get jobs. And let's remember, while the Government has been doing this, the private economy has produced 8 million new jobs in the last 2 years.

If we're concerned about young people, a youth employment opportunity wage would cost the Government nothing, yet would provide employment opportunities to so many kids who are not [now] frozen out of those summer, part-time, weekend, after-school jobs.

And then there's Amtrak. When Amtrak leaves the station, they're being fueled by $35 in subsidies for every passenger. They just keep shoveling in those tax dollars, but it's you, the people, who are getting railroaded. What theoretically started out to be only a 2-year trial period, which was supposed to have provided Amtrak time to become self-sufficient, ended up as a mobile Federal money-burning machine. We can't afford it anymore. Amtrak and other programs like it are taking us on a one-way trip to the poorhouse.

Another area where savings have been achieved is in defense. Once again we've

479

agreed to lower defense spending, recently reducing our projected request by $119 billion over the next 3 years. This means that increases in defense will be limited to only 3 percent per year. I must tell you that this is the rockbottom level needed to sustain and follow through with the defense improvements we've initiated over the past 4 years. We can no longer afford to use defense spending as a whipping boy for the failure of Congress to make the necessary reductions in our domestic spending.

Incidentally, just add some of those $400 hammers and things that you've been reading about—well, those are our figures. That's what's been going on, and that's what we've found out and are stopping.

Now, these and other budget cuts, as vital as they are to the economic health of the country, will not be easy to get through the political process. It's been said that any government that robs Peter to pay Paul is bound to have the support of Paul. [*Laughter*] I think it's time we noticed that we can't rob Peter anymore. He went bankrupt a long time ago. [*Laughter*] The interest groups are out in force. They and the elected representatives with whom they've formed a symbiotic relationship are pushing not to decrease Federal spending but instead to increase taxes.

Now, you come from all over this country. Let me ask you a couple of questions. Do you think the American people want their taxes increased?

Audience. No-o-o!

The President. Well, do you think Congress should stop making excuses and start showing some backbone and leadership?

Audience. Yes!

The President. You're makin' my day. [*Laughter*] If the last election proved anything, it is the American people overwhelmingly oppose upping the tax load. But laying the opposition of the people aside, let's look at the practical argument. Raising taxes will not lower the deficit; raising taxes

will simply drain more money from the private sector, kick us back into recession, and in the end increase deficit spending. For this reason, let me pledge to you: I will not be a party to a tax increase.

We should do something about taxes, and it isn't increase them. What we need to do is to reform and simplify the system—cut out the loopholes, bring the rates down for everybody. But let me pledge something else to you: I will not be a party to a so-called tax reform if it is a disguised tax increase or if it eliminates the deduction families need for their home mortgage.

Now, if you hear a sound in the distance, it might well be the groan of the big spenders and the big taxers. They know you're in town. [*Laughter*]

I just have one more question to ask you: Are you going to pay them a visit and give them the message you just gave me?

Audience. Yes!

The President. All right.

I've said so often, we don't have to make them see the light, just feel the heat. [*Laughter*] But what we are doing is more than just deciding economic policy; we're charting the future of this country. We have it within our power to build a new era of good feeling.

Last year it became clear that a change had occurred in America. The uncertainty and pessimism of the 1970's had been left behind. The new patriotism, a positive spirit which unites all of us of every race and religion, was front-cover material for major magazines. That's the kind of America—proud, strong, and united—that we are trying to build, and it is up to us. And I am happy that, as always, we are on the same team—America's team.

Thank you. God bless you all.

Note: The President spoke at 9:50 a.m. in the International Ballroom at the Washington Hilton Hotel.

Remarks at a Ceremony Honoring Peace Corps Volunteers for Africa
April 23, 1985

Today, I think it's America that is cheering you. As we send you off to Africa on your mission of aid and good will, you make us proud to be Americans.

This is the second day of National Volunteer Week. And I've been meeting here in the White House with men, women, and children from across our country who are outstanding examples of the volunteer spirit. But I've come to realize that even if we celebrated Volunteer Week every week, all year long, it wouldn't be enough time to honor all the remarkable, selfless Americans who give their time, money, labor, and love to help their neighbor. Even if, as in your case, the neighbor lives across an ocean on another continent.

The French chronicler of American life, Alexis de Tocqueville, remarked on the spirit of voluntarism in this country 150 years ago. I was only a small boy then. I didn't hear him—[*laughter*]—but I remember well. He said, "Americans are forever forming associations." "No sooner do they see a need," he observed, "than they rush to meet it."

Well, the tide of giving and concern that has risen in response to the plight of millions in Africa is one of the latest and proudest examples of that quality in the American character that makes us rush to volunteer. New private sector initiatives are developing at unprecedented rates to find innovative ways to help those in need. Americans of every age, from every city and region, have pitched in to do their part.

In Portland, Oregon, Sarah Kreinberg is just 7 years old, suffering from cancer, has donated over $2,200 that she earned selling tree ornaments and other handcrafted items to friends and neighbors because she wanted to help other suffering children in Ethiopia. Her parents, by the way, were Peace Corps volunteers in South America.

When the First Baptist Church of Belfry, Kentucky, received an unexpected gift of $125,000, the congregation unanimously voted to send $100,000 of that to Ethiopian relief. Their generosity set off, as a member described it, "one miracle after another of giving."

Last February the all-star players of the National Basketball Association donated their prize money, and the NBA matched the players' contributions for a total of $100,000.

Today, every few minutes on the radio, you can hear the stars of rock, soul, and country music who came together as "USA for Africa," singing the chorus of "We Are the World," America's recent number-one song hit. Every time a record is sold, more money is raised for African famine relief.

Since we first learned of the crisis in Africa, private donations have been flooding in, and they now total over $100 million. With our recently approved supplemental for humanitarian assistance, the United States will have committed over a billion dollars to African famine relief.

But as we see here today, America is giving more than money. Last January Peace Corps Director Loret Miller Ruppe announced a recruitment drive for agricultural volunteers for Africa. In the following weeks the Peace Corps was besieged by responses. All across America there were people rushing to volunteer, willing to interrupt their lives and devote the next 2 years to meeting the emergency.

And you are a cross section of America. Now, some of you are first generation Americans; some of you are naturalized citizens. You come from all across the country, from Honolulu, Hawaii, to Madawaska, Maine, and you represent a wide range of ages. I'm told that one retired couple, the Bells, is following their son into service in the Peace Corps.

Soon you'll be in Africa, where you'll be a vital part of the relief aid to help the millions suffering from malnutrition and starvation. You'll be living in some of the most impoverished countries of the world, working in food production, soil conservation, fisheries production, forest preservation,

481

and water supply development. By bringing your training and skills to bear on the underlying problems of agricultural and economic development, you can help your host nations make the difficult but vital journey from dependence on short-term aid to self-sufficiency.

Last month, when Vice President Bush returned from his trip to the famine-stricken regions of Africa, he gave me a personal account of the heartbreaking conditions in that land. While there, he visited one Peace Corps project, and he told me of the outstanding work of the Peace Corps volunteers. The crisis in Africa is severe and the problems deeply rooted, but relief efforts are already making a great difference.

Today we also honor three outstanding individuals who are making a difference around the world and have been selected as Peace Corps Volunteers of the Year. Kathy Lynn Gilchrist of Salem, Oregon, established a seaweed farm in Micronesia, providing a new food source and employment opportunities. Mr. Lynn Blaylock of Minne-apolis, Minnesota, is working with dairy farmers and sheepherders on the Caribbean island of Barbados to increase and improve livestock feeds. And Phil Heilman of Gibsonia, Pennsylvania, is working with school-age children in the west African nation of Burkina Faso to start home and school gardens and raise small animals to increase food availability. All three of these Volunteers of the Year deserve our warmest thanks for their untiring commitment to the peoples of the host nations.

In the chorus of the song, "We Are the World," they sing, "We are the ones to make a brighter day, so let's start giving." Well, you have answered that call to make a brighter day. We are proud of you; we are grateful. Good luck, Godspeed, and God bless you.

And, George, let's now start meeting and shaking hands with these young people.

Note: The President spoke at 11:12 a.m. in the Rose Garden at the White House. In his closing remarks, the President referred to the Vice President.

Nomination of John Arthur Ferch To Be United States Ambassador to Honduras
April 23, 1985

The President today announced his intention to nominate John Arthur Ferch, of Ohio, a career member of the Senior Foreign Service, Class of Minister-Counselor, as Ambassador to the Republic of Honduras. He would succeed John Dimitri Negroponte.

Mr. Ferch entered the Foreign Service in 1958. He began with language training at the Foreign Service Institute, where he studied until 1959. In 1959–1961 he was vice consul/economics officer at our Embassy in Buenos Aires, Argentina. From there he became an international relations officer at the U.S. Mission to the Organization of American States in Washington, DC, in 1961–1963. In 1963–1964 he was on detail to the University of Michigan for advanced economics training. He became an econom-ics officer in Bogotá, Colombia, 1964–1967. In 1967–1969 he served as principal officer in Santiago de los Caballeros, Dominican Republic. In 1969 he was chief of the economic section in San Salvador, El Salvador, until 1971, when he went to Guatemala to serve in the same capacity until 1975. In 1975–1976 he attended the National War College. In 1976 he became Director, Office of Food Policies and Programs, in the Department until 1978, when he went to Mexico to serve as deputy chief of mission. From 1982 to the present, he has been Chief of the U.S. Interests Section in Havana, Cuba.

Mr. Ferch received his B.A. in 1958 from Princeton University and later attended George Washington University and the University of Michigan. His foreign language is

Spanish. Mr. Ferch is married to the former Sue Ann McMurray, and they have four children. He was born February 6, 1936, in Toledo, OH.

Appointment of Frederick Elliot Hart as a Member of the Commission of Fine Arts
April 23, 1985

The President today announced his intention to appoint Frederick Elliot Hart to be a member of the Commission of Fine Arts for a term of 4 years. He would succeed Walter A. Netsch.

Mr. Hart is a sculptor in Washington, DC. His works include the Vietnam Veterans Memorial and the west facade sculptures for the National Cathedral, both in Washington, DC. In 1975 he founded the firm of Hytla & Hart, Ltd., a design and production company specializing in architectural sculpture and traditional decorative elements for restoration projects as well as new construction.

He is a member of the National Sculpture Society and the Sacred Arts Commission. He attended the University of South Carolina, American University, and the Corcoran School of Art.

He is married, has two children, and resides in Washington, DC. He was born November 3, 1943, in Atlanta, GA.

Statement by Principal Deputy Press Secretary Speakes on the Death of Major Arthur D. Nicholson, Jr., in the German Democratic Republic
April 23, 1985

The statement provided by the Soviet Embassy on April 22 concerning the murder of Maj. Arthur Nicholson is a distortion of the facts and unacceptable to us.

On April 22, Soviet Embassy Chargé d' Affaires Sokolov called on Assistant Secretary of State Burt to present a statement on the Soviet Union's assessment of the April 12 meeting between Generals Otis and Zaytsev. Mr. Burt informed Mr. Sokolov that he found the Soviet statement totally unacceptable. After reviewing the Soviet statement with Secretary Shultz and other senior officials, Acting Assistant Secretary Kelly, in Mr. Burt's absence, called Mr. Sokolov into the Department that afternoon and reiterated in the Secretary's name that we found the Soviet statement totally unacceptable. We understand that prior to that meeting the Soviet Embassy had released the substance of its statement to the press, although Mr. Sokolov did not mention this fact at the meeting.

The description of Major Nicholson's killing released by the Department of State is accurate. The Soviet attempt to excuse the killing by stating that Major Nicholson was an "unknown intruder who did not comply with the warnings of the sentry" is not at all acceptable.

Major Nicholson was acting in accordance with procedures and practices which have been completely normal and accepted for many years. He was acting in accordance with the spirit and letter of the Huebner-Malinin Agreement of 1947, which governs the activities of the military liaison missions (MLM) on both sides. Soviet military missions operating in the Federal Republic of Germany under this agreement function in exactly the same way. That is an essential point, which the Soviet account unacceptably distorts.

While performing the normal and accepted duties of a member of our military liaison mission, using a clearly identified MLM vehicle and wearing an insignia clearly identifying him as a member of the U.S. military liaison mission, Major Nicholson was shot and killed by a Soviet sentry. No verbal warning was issued. The shot or shots which the sentry fired before killing him did not constitute warning in any accepted or acceptable sense of the word.

The Soviet military at the scene prevented Sergeant Schatz, Major Nicholson's driver, from providing first aid and left Major Nicholson lying without medical aid for approximately an hour. We do not know why they did this. We cannot imagine that they did it in keeping with the instructions of the "military manual" referred to in the Soviet statement. Like the shooting itself, it was and remains unacceptable to us.

There is another essential point: What we find appalling about the Soviet statement of April 22 is the apparent inability of Soviet officials to understand the human issue involved in Major Nicholson's death. In the wake of this tragedy, we agreed to discuss changes in procedures to ensure that such a tragedy could never happen again. We note that yesterday's Soviet statement reiterates this commitment on the Soviet side. But by again repeating their restrictive interpretation of the procedures in force at the time, the Soviet authorities demonstrate that they do not grasp the unacceptability of continued use of force and violence as a first reaction against even the most minor issue.

Major Nicholson constituted no threat either to Soviet forces or to the security of the Soviet Union. He was unarmed, as all military liaison mission members are unarmed. The task of the U.S. military mission is to build confidence by openly observing the placement of Soviet forces. The use of lethal force against a member of a military mission was contrary to the practices for dealing with respective military missions which have been in effect for over 35 years. We have not used and will not use lethal force in dealing with such practices on the part of Soviet MLM personnel in the Federal Republic of Germany. Members of the U.S. forces in Germany have written instructions to this effect. The use of lethal force against Major Nicholson was not only a violation of normal practice under an agreement in force, it was an outrage.

Major Nicholson's death was a senseless, unnecessary act which raises serious questions about orders provided to Soviet military personnel throughout the world. The Soviet statement again expresses regret. We believe that this is not enough. What is needed is some sense that they recognize the enormity of this outrage.

It is for this reason that we have from the beginning expressed our belief that the Soviets owe us and Major Nicholson's family an apology and compensation for Major Nicholson's widow and for his child. In his meeting with General Zaytsev, General Otis set forth these considerations fully and clearly. General Zaytsev did not accept them. Instead, he referred them to higher authority as was accurately stated in our account of the meeting. The Soviets subsequently have so far refused to respond to these requests. For our part, we will continue to point out that they are matters of elementary justice. Continued Soviet refusal to address this matter in a responsible and reciprocal fashion can not fail to have adverse consequences on future relations.

Note: Larry M. Speakes read the statement to reporters in the Briefing Room at the White House during his daily press briefing, which began at 12:15 p.m.

Remarks at a Luncheon for Recipients of the National Medal of Arts
April 23, 1985

The President. Well, thank you, all of you, for being here. It's a great pleasure and an honor for Nancy and me to welcome you to the White House today.

This is an historic occasion. Two years ago, I asked Frank Hodsoll to work with Congress to establish a National Medal of the Arts. And last year Congress passed this legislation, and today we award the first medals.

Before we do, there's some thanks in order to those who worked to make this ceremony possible. I want to thank the Committee on the Arts and Humanities and its Chairman, Andrew Heiskell. Thanks are due also to Senators Robert Stafford, Claiborne Pell, and Paul Simon and Congressman Tom Coleman for their leadership in enacting this legislation. And thanks also to Frank Hodsoll, the National Council of the Arts, and Robert Graham, the artist who designed the medal that we're about to award today. And finally, thanks to Ambassador Terra for that wonderful reception last night. So, thanks to you all.

Now, that was the serious part; now to the fun part. We award today for the first time in our history the National Medal of Arts. The purpose of this medal is to recognize both individuals and groups who have made outstanding contributions to the excellence and availability of the arts in the United States. And through this medal, we recognize both the artist and the patron, both the creator of art and the supporter and encourager of the creator of art. The one needs the other, and the United States needs both.

In recognizing those who create and those who make creation possible, we celebrate freedom. No one realizes the importance of freedom more than the artist, for only in the atmosphere of freedom can the arts flourish. Artists have to be brave; they live in the realm of idea and expression, and their ideas will often be provocative and unusual. Artists stretch the limits of understanding. They express ideas that are sometimes unpopular. In an atmosphere of liberty, artists and patrons are free to think the unthinkable and create the audacious; they are free to make both horrendous mistakes and glorious celebrations. Where there's liberty, art succeeds.

In societies that are not free, art dies. In the totalitarian societies of the world, all art is officially approved. It's the expression not of the soul but of the state. And this state-sanctioned art is usually, as a rule, 99 percent of the time, utterly banal, utterly common. It is lowest common denominator art. In fact, it is not art at all; for art is an expression of creativity, and creativity, as I've said, is born in freedom—which is not to suggest that great artists who love the truth of art cannot be found in totalitarian states. They're there. Visit a prison, you'll find a number of them. Their garrets are jail cells; their crime is that they refused to put their minds in chains and their souls in solitary. Some artists are forced to the fringes of society. Their work is repressed. These artists may be unpersons, but all of them are heroes.

I know you feel solidarity with them; I know you often think of your brother and sister artists throughout the world. And I hope you continue to pay tribute to them by celebrating freedom in your work and in your lives.

I happen to think, though, that to be an artist is always difficult, even in free societies. Expressing the truth in ideas requires risk—risk for the artist and risk for the patron. There's no way of knowing in advance how society will receive a new idea. Ralph Waldo Emerson said, "To be great is to be misunderstood." It's my hope that this medal today will go some way to telling the great artists here in this room that I think we finally understand you.

We celebrate today the courage, talent, and commitment of the American artists here assembled. We celebrate also the courage, generosity, and far-sightedness of the patrons who have helped bring American art to broad audiences and to preserve great works for the future. We thank all of you for your great work. You've done honor to your nation.

And now, Nancy will help me announce the honorees.

Mrs. Reagan. Hallmark Cards is represented today by Donald Hall, chairman of the board and chief executive officer. Hallmark is an outstanding example of enlightened corporate support of arts, nationally and locally. Hallmark supports ballet, opera, symphonic music, and theater. It's brought the arts to the children of Kansas City and has won 49 Emmies for its production, "The Hallmark Hall of Fame." And last night, it added to its awards by being given the TV Academy's Hall of Fame Award. So, we're just adding our own to that.

Louise Nevelson is a distinguished artist who has made a significant contribution to the art of the 20th century. She's one of a handful of truly original and major artists in America. As a young woman, she studied painting, sculpture, drawing, voice, acting, and modern dance. She developed her personal approach to sculpture by using wood in a unique way to create environments. She's won many awards and honors. And we're happy today to add to those. She says she's used to carrying heavy things. [*Laughter*]

Jose Ferrer was born in Puerto Rico. He made his debut on the New York stage in 1935, a recipient of three Tony Awards for acting and directing. He's most remembered for performances on film, stage, and on television as Cyrano de Bergerac. Mr. Ferrer has certainly enriched the art of stagecraft. He became the general director of the New York City Theater Company in 1948. And he, too, has won innumerable awards, and his credits are too long to go into. We'd be here all day. Jose.

Georgia O'Keeffe was born in Sun Prairie, Wisconsin. She worked in her early years as a commercial artist and art supervisor in public schools. For 30 years, she resided in New Mexico painting landscapes, flowers, stones, and skeletons with singular vision. She's turned ordinary objects into fascinating subjects. Her giant-sized, single flower blossoms are recognized around the world. Mrs. O'Keeffe's contribution to painting is now part of the American heritage. She's unable to be with us today, but accepting her medal will be Carter Brown, Director of the National Gallery of Art, who

just last week visited her in New Mexico.

Lincoln Kirstein was born in Rochester, New York. Mr. Kirstein devoted his life to the patronage and development of American ballet. It was his dream to start a ballet company. He preserved, and out of his collaboration with George Balanchine grew both the School of American Ballet and the New York City Ballet. A poet, art critic, and writer on dance, he founded the dance index and the dance archives of the Museum of Modern Art. Mr. Kirstein's imprint on ballet is truly indelible.

Leontyne Price was born in Laurel, Mississippi. And she's one of our greatest opera singers. She made her debut with the San Francisco and Metropolitan Operas in 1961. She's appeared abroad with numerous companies but has spent the major part of her career in the United States doing opera, concerts, recitals, and recordings. Through recordings, Ms. Price's artistry will live on for future generations as one of the greatest opera artists of our time.

Paul Mellon has devoted a lifetime to the enrichment of the arts. He began by accumulating books and paintings on sports, and this eventually extended to other fields. His generosity has supplied a variety of cities with museum structures and collections of European art. All of us are familiar with the magnificent Mellon treasures at the National Gallery of Art, where Mr. Mellon's leadership as Trustee and Chairman of the Board has been extraordinary. Mr. Mellon has truly enriched our Capital and the Nation.

Alice Tully was born in Corning, New York. Ms. Tully is a leading patron of music in New York and throughout the Nation. She's also an artist. And after studying voice in Paris and giving concerts, she gave up performance and devoted herself to philanthropy. Her major gift was the chamber music hall at Lincoln Center, which was dedicated to her in 1969. She's been a board member of Juilliard School of Music and the New School of Music in Philadelphia and helped organize the Chamber Music of Lincoln Center. Ms. Tully's generosity has enhanced the field of music and brought excellent music to millions.

Ralph Ellison is an author and educator

whose academic career has included positions at Bard College, UCLA, the University of Chicago, Rutgers, Yale, and New York University. The recipient of many awards, here and abroad, he's best known for his collection of essays and the very distinguished American novel of the postwar period, "Invisible Man." Mr. Ellison's contribution to American society certainly will not be forgotten.

Dorothy Buffum Chandler—Buffie—is a great patron and civic leader for the arts in Los Angeles. She conceived and organized the funding of the Los Angeles Music Center, which in 1964 opened the Dorothy Chandler Pavilion. More than 35 million people have attended events at this center. Enriching the lives of the people of Los Angeles with theater, classical music, ballet, the Center stimulated the flowering of the performing arts throughout Los Angeles County. Buff Chandler's represented here by her daughter, Camilla Chandler Frost.

Elliott Carter is a distinguished composer who studied at Harvard and later in Paris with the famous Nadia Boulanger. He's taught at St. John's University, Columbia, Yale, Cornell, and the Juilliard School of Music. He's a recipient of numerous awards, including two Pulitzer Prizes for music. Mr. Carter.

Martha Graham was born in Pittsburgh, Pennsylvania. She's dominated the field of dance as a teacher, performer, choreographer, and director. She's invented new forms and movements and influenced generations. So many of our best dancers owe their beginnings to this great lady. Nearly 60 years later, she is still creating and still giving. Miss Graham.

The President. Well, thank you, Nancy. [*Laughter*] We're proud to be associated with all of you. And we thank you for what you've done to make America a better place.

It's fitting that these first National Medals of Art are being presented on the 20th anniversary of the National Endowment of the Arts. I congratulate the Endowment and

the honorary chairwoman of the 20th Anniversary Committee, who also happens to be my most generous patron, my roommate— [*laughter*]—and also my friend, Charlton Heston, the chairman of the committee.

For two decades now the National Endowment has been doing wonderful work. Most recently, they've been involved in a great endeavor to preserve and protect our rich heritage of film and television and the dance. And they've been building endowments for fine art institutions and helping struggling young artists find an audience. And the members of the Endowment would all be the first to say that none of their great work would have succeeded without the generous financial help and support of the American people, of unknown, unsung citizens who each day volunteer their time and money to encourage the arts.

Just last week, as a matter of fact, the New Orleans Symphony was too low on funds to continue their performances. The city rallied round the group in a new private sector initiative called Proud Citizens for Our Culture. In just 4 days, $445,000 was raised by the volunteers. And I am told that hundreds of thousands of dollars will be forthcoming from the business community. Now, this is quite a tribute to the performing arts.

And today we celebrate the people of New Orleans and the people from all over our country who've made contributions such as this. And so, again, a thank you to all of you—artists and patrons and recipients and encouragers—thank you for being what you are and doing the great work that you do. And thank you for honoring your nation.

God bless you all.

Note: The President spoke at 1:06 p.m. in the State Dining Room at the White House. In his remarks, the President referred to United States Ambassador at Large for Cultural Affairs Daniel J. Terra.

Proclamation 5326—National Defense Transportation Day and National Transportation Week, 1985
April 23, 1985

By the President of the United States of America

A Proclamation

Our Nation's history can be traced through the development and growth of transportation in America. Our country has grown as transportation has given us access to new geographic, economic, and technical frontiers.

During colonial days, Americans were dependent on the river systems and ocean ports still used in commerce today. President Thomas Jefferson commissioned Lewis and Clark to explore the West through our rivers, providing new opportunities for trade and commerce. In 1825, the Erie Canal, connecting Buffalo to New York, opened the Great Lakes for settlement and industry.

Pioneers broke new ground to the West by way of the Cumberland Road in 1811. Other highways were soon developed to move people and goods across the wilderness. Completion of the first transcontinental railroad in 1869 joined East to West, ushering in a new era of transportation, strengthening American commerce.

Aviation history was made at Kitty Hawk in 1903, launching an aviation system now serving over 300 million passengers a year. Today, we are witnessing the beginning of a new era in space transportation with the development of commercial space vehicles.

As our cities grew, transit systems evolved to provide affordable, convenient urban transportation. The 20th Century brought the automobile, truck, intercity bus, rapid rail systems, and an expanded road system that now includes thousands of miles of interstate highways.

As has been true throughout our history, transportation today is critical to our economy and necessary to our defense. America's transportation systems have made our society the most mobile on earth. A diverse transportation network has assured the rapid, safe, and dependable movement of people and goods throughout the country and around the world.

In recognition of transportation's importance, and to honor the millions of Americans who serve and supply our transportation needs, the Congress, by joint resolution approved May 16, 1957, has requested that the third Friday in May of each year be designated as National Defense Transportation Day; and by joint resolution approved May 14, 1962, that the week in which that Friday falls be proclaimed National Transportation Week.

Now, Therefore, I, Ronald Reagan, President of the United States of America, do hereby designate Friday, May 17, 1985, as National Defense Transportation Day and the week beginning May 12, 1985, through May 18, 1985, as National Transportation Week. I urge the people of the United States to observe these occasions with appropriate ceremonies that will give full recognition to the importance of our transportation system to this country.

In Witness Whereof, I have hereunto set my hand this twenty-third day of April, in the year of our Lord nineteen hundred and eighty-five, and of the Independence of the United States of America the two hundred and ninth.

RONALD REAGAN

[Filed with the Office of the Federal Register, 11:33 a.m., April 24, 1985]

Statement on Senate Approval of United States Assistance for the Nicaraguan Democratic Resistance
April 23, 1985

Tonight the Senate cast an historic vote for freedom and democracy in Central America. A clear majority has spoken in favor of a consistent and effective policy that is true both to our principles and to our interests.

To reach this result the White House and Senators of both parties worked together to find common agreement; and we now stand upon common ground. Support for the Nicaraguan democratic resistance is a crucial component of the proposal approved by the Senate. Our hemisphere will not be a safe place if the United States ceases to stand by its friends.

Today's vote will contribute toward bringing both peace and democracy close to the people of Nicaragua. That vote demonstrates that a direct bipartisan consensus on this critical issue remains possible. I urge Members of the House to lend their support.

Letter to Senate Majority Leader Dole on the Central American Peace Proposal and United States Assistance for the Nicaraguan Democratic Resistance
April 23, 1985

Dear Senator Dole:

I announced on April 4 a proposal to promote peace in Central America by fostering a dialogue between the Government of Nicaragua and the democratic resistance, accompanied by a ceasefire in the conflict between them. My proposal was intended, in the words of the Contadora Document of Objectives agreed to by Nicaragua and its neighbors, "to promote national reconciliation efforts . . ., with a view to fostering participation in democratic political processes in accordance with the law."

Since April 4, I have had the benefit of many fruitful discussions with Latin American leaders and with members of the Congress. I have been encouraged by these discussions, which have shown that a broad consensus exists on the need for reconciliation in Nicaragua, based on democratic principles, as an essential aspect of achieving peace in Central America.

Today the Senate will vote on a resolution, S.J. Res. 106, the text of which is required by a law enacted last October. That text purports to release appropriated funds and free the Executive Branch from restrictions against the support of military or paramilitary action in Nicaragua. However, my intentions are founded on a different approach. Accordingly, I want to make clear to the Senate, as it approaches this important vote, how I will proceed in pursuit of peace if S.J. Res. 106 is enacted.

First, I will provide assistance to the democratic resistance only for food, medicine, clothing, and other assistance for their survival and well-being—and not for arms, ammunition, and weapons of war. Second, I will not use more than the $14 million already appropriated during the current fiscal year for such assistance. No other U.S. Government funds would be spent for such material assistance to the armed democratic resistance. I will personally establish thorough procedures for the detailed management and accountability of the program in order to assure that these limitations on both the nature and amount of U.S. assistance are scrupulously observed.

I recognize the importance some Senators have attached to bilateral talks between the United States and Nicaragua and the establishment of a ceasefire. I have considered these views and believe that such steps could help to promote the internal reconciliation called for by Contadora and endorsed by so many Latin American leaders.

Therefore, I intend to resume bilateral talks with the Government of Nicaragua and will instruct our representatives in those talks to press for a ceasefire as well as a church-mediated dialogue between the contending Nicaraguan factions. I must emphasize, however, that such bilateral talks must be in support of the Contadora process and the internal dialogue and cannot become a substitute for these efforts to achieve a comprehensive, verifiable agreement among all the nations of Central America. Also, as I said on April 4, peace negotiations must not become a cover for deception and delay. If the Sandinista government shows bad faith by seeking to gain unilateral advantage, for example through a further arms buildup during a ceasefire or intransigence in negotiations, I would feel obligated to respond accordingly in our diplomatic efforts and would not expect the democratic resistance to continue to observe a ceasefire which was unfairly working to their disadvantage.

I will report to the Congress no later than September 1, 1985, on the progress made in achieving a verifiable peace and reconciliation in Nicaragua based on democratic principles. Such report shall also include an accounting for the funds obligated or expended under this joint resolution and may include such recommendations as I deem appropriate with respect for Nicaragua. I shall expect any recommendations for additional legislation for further assistance or sanctions to receive expedited handling.

While economic sanctions are unlikely by themselves to create sufficient pressure to change Nicaragua's behavior, the Sandinistas should not benefit from their present access to the U.S. market while continuing their intransigence on issues affecting our national security. The Administration will favorably consider economic sanctions against the Government of Nicaragua and will undertake multilateral consultations with other Central American states in this regard.

The U.S. condemns atrocities by either side in the strongest possible terms. We will use our assistance to help ensure against wrongful acts by those who seek our help and we will urge them to take steps to investigate allegations of such acts and take appropriate actions against those found to be guilty.

The United States now stands at a moment of judgment. Experience has shown that a policy of support for democracy, economic opportunity, and security will best serve the people of Central America and the national interests of the United States. If we show consistency of purpose, if we are firm in our conviction that the promising developments over the past year in El Salvador, Honduras, Costa Rica, and Guatemala also show the way for a better future for Nicaragua, then over time we can help the democratic center prevail over tyrants of the left or the right. But if we abandon democracy in Nicaragua, if we tolerate the consolidation of a surrogate state in Central America, responsive to Cuba and the Soviet Union, we will see the progress that has been achieved begin to unravel under the strain of continuing conflict, attempts at subversion, and loss of confidence in our support.

There can be a more democratic, more prosperous, and more peaceful Central America. I am prepared to devote my energies toward that end. But, I also need the support of the Congress. I hope that you will give me your support today.

Sincerely,

/s/RONALD REAGAN

[The Honorable Robert Dole, Majority Leader, United States Senate, Washington, D.C. 20510]

Note: The original was not available for verification of the content of this letter, which was released by the Office of the Press Secretary on April 24.

Nomination of Abraham D. Sofaer To Be Legal Adviser of the Department of State
April 24, 1985

The President today announced his intention to nominate Abraham D. Sofaer to be Legal Adviser of the Department of State. He would succeed Davis Rowland Robinson.

Judge Sofaer is currently United States District Judge for the Southern District of New York. Previously, he was professor of law, Columbia University (1969–1979); hearing officer, New York State Department of Environmental Conservation (1975–1976);

Assistant United States Attorney, Southern District of New York (1967–1969); and law clerk to the Honorable William J. Brennan, Jr., United States Supreme Court (1966–1967).

Judge Sofaer graduated from Yeshiva College (B.A., 1962) and New York University School of Law (LL.B., 1965). He is married, has four children, and resides in New York City. He was born May 6, 1938, in Bombay, India.

Designation of Roger B. Porter as Executive Secretary of the Economic Policy Council
April 24, 1985

The President today announced he was designating Roger B. Porter to be Executive Secretary of the Economic Policy Council.

Mr. Porter is Deputy Assistant to the President for Policy Development and Director of the White House Office of Policy Development. He served as Executive Secretary of the Cabinet Council on Economic Affairs from 1981 to 1985. He was on the faculty of the School of Government at Harvard University from 1977 to 1981. He is the author of several books and articles, including "Presidential Decision Making."

Mr. Porter was a White House fellow from 1974 to 1975. He was appointed Special Assistant to the President and served as Executive Secretary of the President's Economic Policy Board from 1974 to 1977. He was assistant dean and tutor in politics at

Queen's College, Oxford University, from 1971 to 1972. He served as associate director of the Utah Local Government Modernization Study in 1972 and has been actively involved in State constitutional revision efforts. He was selected as one of the Ten Outstanding Young Men in America for 1981 by the United States Jaycees.

A native of Utah, Mr. Porter received his B.A. degree from Brigham Young University in 1969 and was selected as a Rhodes scholar and as a Woodrow Wilson fellow, receiving his bachelor of philosophy degree from Oxford University in 1971. He received his M.A. and Ph.D. degrees from Harvard University in 1978.

He is married to the former Ann Robinson, has three children, and resides in McLean, VA. He was born on June 19, 1946.

Appointment of Haley Barbour as Special Assistant to the President for Political Affairs
April 24, 1985

The President today announced the appointment of Haley Barbour to be Special Assistant to the President for Political Affairs.

He has been a partner in the law firm of Henry, Barbour & DeCell and is also a director of the Deposit Guaranty Corp. He is on the board of the Deposit Guaranty National Bank. From 1973 to 1976, he served as the executive director of the Mississippi Republican Party and of the Southern Association of Republican State Chairmen. He was the Republican nominee in the 1982 Mississippi Senate race against Senator John Stennis.

He graduated from the University of Mississippi (J.D., 1973). He is married, has two children, and resides in Crystal City, VA. He was born October 22, 1947, in Yazoo City, MS.

Address to the Nation on the Federal Budget and Deficit Reduction
April 24, 1985

My fellow Americans:

I must speak to you tonight about a serious problem that demands your immediate attention. I need your help.

Today the United States Senate began a rendezvous with history. The threads of our past, present, and future as a nation will soon converge on the single overriding question before that body: Can we at last, after decades of drift, neglect, and excess, put our fiscal house in order? Can we assure a strong and prosperous future for ourselves, our children, and their children by adopting a plan that will compel the Federal Government to end the dangerous addiction to deficit spending and finally live within its means?

Throughout our history, we Americans have been willing to meet great challenges and do what is right when our destiny demanded it. Just 4 years ago this week, I asked your support for our bipartisan recovery program. That was the program the spenders said wouldn't work, and they called it Reaganomics. You might remember April 1981: a time when our defenses were weak, inflation still in double digits, and economic growth almost dead from a government that taxed too much and spent even more than it taxed.

We knew it would take a great effort to turn that around. We knew that letting you keep more of your earnings to get our economy moving again would be resisted by the old guard in Washington. But we also knew the answer to a government that's too fat is to stop feeding its growth. We wanted America to rediscover opportunity. We asked for your help then, and you gave it to us.

You turned America around—turned around her confidence, turned around her economy, turned around over a decade of one national nightmare after another. We're into our 29th straight month of economic growth, with inflation staying down and more of us working than ever before—that's 8 million new jobs. Now that our program is working, you may have noticed they're not calling it Reaganomics anymore.

Once again, the United States is the flagship economy for the world. A new generation of entrepreneurs is coming up, pointing us toward a 21st century full of amazing change and vast new opportunities.

We must seize this historic moment to shape America's future—to completely overhaul our tax code, changing it from a source of confusion and contempt to a model of fairness and simplicity, with strong, new incentives for even greater growth.

So many good things lie ahead for America. And yet all our progress, all the good we've accomplished so far, and all our dreams for the future could be wrecked if we do not overcome our one giant obstacle.

The simple truth is: No matter how hard you work, no matter how strong this economy grows, no matter how much more tax money comes to Washington, it won't amount to a hill of beans if government won't curb its endless appetite to spend. Overspending is the subject we must now address—how budgets got so far out of balance and, yes, what together we can and must do to correct this.

You know, sometimes the big spenders in Congress talk as if all that money they spend just kind of magically appears on their doorstep, a gift from the Internal Revenue Service. They talk as if spending were all giving and no taking.

Well, there is no magic money machine. Every dollar the government spends comes out of your pockets. Every dollar the government gives to someone has to first be taken away from someone else. So, it's our moral duty to make sure that we can justify every one of your tax dollars, that we spend them wisely and carefully and, just as important, fairly.

Unfortunately, hardly anyone could honestly call Federal budgets wise, careful, or fair. Is it fair to ask one small business to help subsidize its competitors? Is it fair to ask workers in the private economy to pay for civil service pensions that are much more generous than the retirement benefits they receive? Is it fair to ask low-income families to help pay for the college education of children from families with incomes as high as $100,000 a year? Is it fair to ask taxpayers to help pay billions for export subsidies to a handful of America's biggest corporations?

Well, it isn't fair, and you know it. But that's the law of the land right now, just part of the legacy of 50 years of trying to do good things for all by treating your earnings like government property.

The time has come to decide what benefits we can properly expect from the Federal Government for ourselves, our neighbors, and those in need; and what government can take from us in taxes without making everyone worse off, including those who need our help. The one thing we cannot do is stay on the immoral, dead-end course of deficit spending.

Today our national debt amounts to nearly $8,000 for every man, woman, and child in America, and it's increasing by about $1,000 per person each and every year. Just to cover the interest on that debt, the Federal Government will spend $155 billion this year alone. That's more than its entire budget as recently as 1966.

Despite your worries and all the warnings, the trend has continued year after year. We've had only one balanced budget in the last quarter century. As a nation, our debt has grown and grown and grown until now it totals $1.7 trillion—a number so big that it's nearly unimaginable. A single billion is 1,000 millions. A trillion is a million millions.

Now, this is not just my problem. This is not just Congress' problem. This is our problem, and we must solve it together as Americans.

Tonight, I'm asking all of you—Democrats, Republicans, and independents—to give me your help to put our financial house in order so that our tax, spending, and monetary policies will not hinder growth, but encourage it; not send inflation and interest rates shooting back up, but keep them heading down; and not drown us under a tidal wave of debt, but protect us in the safe harbor of financial stability, with a sound and powerful economy.

Not surprisingly, some still want to raise your taxes. They say we cut your taxes too much in 1981, when we ended years of bracket creep and lowered rates for every American taxpayer. Well, this is simply untrue. And it implies government has a right to take from you all that it needs to satisfy the demands of special interest groups.

Surely, there's no faster way to see our prosperity vanish than to yoke the decent, hard-working, taxpaying citizens of this great nation to an automatic spending machine in Washington, DC. Government should tax to meet government's needs, not government's wants.

Nine days ago I received a very welcome

gift—a letter with 146 signatures. One hundred and forty-six Members of Congress have pledged to uphold what I repeat tonight will be my certain veto of any tax increase Congress sends me, no matter how cleverly it's disguised.

Is it too much to ask the spoilers to give up their hidden agenda to increase taxes, which would only slow the economy, throw people out of work, and, yes, make the deficit worse? Do they still not understand how generous you've been, paying heavy taxes to defend freedom around the world, ease starvation in distant nations, and help the needy, the elderly, and the sick and handicapped here at home?

Well, as you can see [*referring to televised graphics*], the rising blue bar shows that the taxes you paid in the last 20 years increased by over $620 billion. And if you think that's a staggering sum, well, you're right. But look at this rising red bar showing government spending. In that same 20-year period, the red bar went up even more. It went up by over $840 billion. Government spending—that's the real Washington monument.

Taxes are too high, but spending is even higher. During the 20 years when inflation, steep Federal income tax rates, and rising State, county, and local taxes were pushing you into tax brackets once reserved for the wealthy, Congress was writing checks and spending your money even faster than you could spend it.

What went wrong? Where has all the money gone? Well, during the strong, prosperous Eisenhower years in the 1950's and through the Kennedy years, we kept spending in check. During those Kennedy years there was a tax cut proposed similar to our cut. It was enacted in 1964, and the economy grew then as it has grown now.

But others in government did not take the next logical step and say: Look, freedom and incentives are working. So, let's reduce tax rates further. Let's transform our ghettos into havens for enterprise, give families new incentives to save for their children's education—let's make every citizen a shareholder in America's future.

Government did the opposite. Government began to take over America. In the name of the Great Society, it began doing things never before felt possible or desirable. Government took over passenger railroads. It began contributing billions to 39,000 local government budgets. Its spending on agriculture subsidies soared to a level higher than the total net income from every farm in America.

Let me interject something here, and I'll state it plainly and simply: The enormous weight of Federal spending and runaway deficits has gone far toward placing in jeopardy one of every seven family farms in the United States. This is not simply an economic statistic. It is a great social tragedy that should command the concern of every American. Control of this runaway engine of Federal spending has become crucial to the survival of the family farm in the United States.

The new programs started after 1964. They cost $16 billion by 1966, $78 billion by 1975, and $148 billion per year by 1981.

Today government puts a dime into the fare box every time somebody boards a local bus or transit line. Today government subsidizes loans for every imaginable purpose—from education to aircraft exporters to luxury waterfront developments and hotels—so that government's lending business is bigger than Chase Manhattan and the Bank of America's combined. And the spending line keeps going up.

To be sure, much good has been done. In health, education, and food assistance, we're spending more than ever before in our history. But in many areas, we're spending where we should not be and spending what we can no longer afford. And so much of what we spend goes not to the individuals needing help, but to thousands upon thousands of bureaucrats, researchers, planners, managers, and professional advocates who earn their living from the great growth industry of government. It's no accident that some of the wealthiest communities in America are the communities surrounding the Federal Government in Washington, DC.

My fellow citizens, the time has come for government to make the same hard choices your families and businesses do. The time has come for your public servants to bring spending down into line with tax revenues.

Accomplishing this, bringing the spending line down to our incomes is the heart of our deficit reduction plan that we put together with Senator Dole and his colleagues. We call it the taxpayers' protection plan, and that's just what it is. It will reduce deficits by $300 billion over 3 years, bringing us within reach of a balanced budget by 1990. And it will do this not by raising your taxes, but by reversing 20 years of overspending.

Our plan attacks excessive spending across the board. No part of the budget is spared, and a shared effort will be asked of all. But unlike a spending freeze, which would not reduce deficits nearly enough and which would make no distinction between worthy and wasteful programs, our plan recognizes that all spending is not created equal. Some programs are vital to our national security and domestic welfare and must be given first priority. Others are no longer affordable or were not proper Federal responsibilities to begin with.

Our plan establishes clear national priorities. It keeps what should be kept and cuts what should be cut. Our first priority must always be our national security. The Soviets are far more dangerous today than during the fifties and sixties, periods in which we devoted far more to our defense. And they continue arming well beyond the defense needs of their country. Because of that threat, we must maintain modest but steady growth each year. Three percent is the rockbottom level that we must maintain for effective deterrence to protect our security.

As I've said, even with this small increase, we'll spend a smaller share of our budget on defense than we did 20 years ago. Cuts we've proposed in projected defense spending will contribute a hundred billion dollars, a full one-third of our proposed budget savings for the next 3 years. Now, this will require canceling some programs; some nonessential military bases may be closed or cut back. But mainly, we will continue to identify and eliminate waste and crack down harder on excesses in contract costs.

Waste in the Department of Defense must and is being eliminated, as is fraud in defense contracts. The stories you've been reading and hearing about $400 hammers and such are things that we've discovered

were going on before and that we're correcting.

Padding of expense accounts, overcharging for weapons, profiteering at the expense of the public—these should be and will be prosecuted to the full extent of the law. Men who illegally line their pockets with dollars the American people have contributed to our defense are stealing from the arsenal of democracy the very weapons our young men need to defend freedom. And our tolerance of this selfish behavior was long ago exhausted.

The Senate will face demands to cut defense even more, but here we must draw the line. Federal overspending is not caused by meeting vital security needs, and even our critics know that further reductions would jeopardize our security. Our strategic programs, our 600-ship navy, our conventional weapons modernization, and our readiness programs must go forward.

Our plan will freeze the defense-spending share of our gross national product at 6.4 percent for the next 3 years. That is a share well below the 8 or 9 percent at the time of the Eisenhower and Kennedy. The remaining two-thirds of our deficit reduction can and must come from other parts of the budget—from domestic programs that are no longer necessary or in need of basic reform.

Let me give some examples of the sort of programs we intend to cut back. When Amtrak was begun in 1971 for a 2-year trial run, we were told it would soon turn a profit. Well, 14 years and nearly $9 billion later, Amtrak is still running on taxpayers' subsidies. Every time a train leaves the station, it costs taxpayers $35 for each passenger on board. In some cases, it would be cheaper just to hand them plane tickets. Eliminating Amtrak will save $8 billion over the next decade.

We'll also save billions by eliminating taxpayer subsidies to some of America's biggest corporations through Export-Import Bank loans and by abolishing the Small Business Administration's lending programs, which are not only costly and unfair but unneeded in an economy creating over 600,000 new businesses and corporations a year.

Supporters of programs like these always

ignore the big hidden costs all of us eventually have to pay. If programs like these can't be cut, we might as well give up hope of ever getting government spending under control. If Congress can't bring itself to do what's right, well, they should at least give me what 43 Governors already have—a line-item veto. Then I'll make the cuts; I'll take the responsibility and the heat, and I'll enjoy it.

One area we will not touch, however, is the safety net for needy Americans. Programs that provide income, food, housing, and medical aid for the neediest Americans were reformed in 1981 and are now targeted to genuine need. But these programs only make up 8 percent of the budget, so we need everyone's help to get spending under control.

The burden will not be great if all of us help carry the load. We're asking the 46 million Americans who receive a retirement, veterans, or Social Security check to accept a guaranteed 2-percent increase over the next 3 years in place of the existing cost-of-living adjustment. If, however, inflation should rise above 4 percent, the amount above 4 percent would be added to the 2 percent.

Now, these programs now total nearly $250 billion per year—25 percent of our entire budget. They cost 30 times more than they did just three decades ago. Our veterans, disabled workers, and retired citizens have earned their benefits. They deserve an adequate and dignified standard of living, and we will never renege on that pledge.

All of us together have a shared interest in a healthy, expanding economy. It means jobs, opportunities, and rising incomes for our younger citizens and a steady flow of tax payments into the funds that support our retired citizens.

A small effort now will mean big gains for all Americans later. If we can keep our economy on track, 16 million more Americans will be working in 1988 than were employed at the end of 1982. With that much growth, with that many new jobs, there will never be any doubt: The retirement checks that 46 million Americans depend on will be secure; the economic base that supports them will be strong; and the tax payments that fund them will be abundant.

If we want to continue trying to make these the best years of our lives, if we want to protect our retired and disabled, boost small business, create jobs, strengthen our farm economy, our exports, improve our cities, and help your families send your children to college, there is one sure-fire way to do it: We're all going to have to pitch in together. But if we refuse, if we go back to the old pattern of business as usual, then let there be no mistake: Business as usual will eventually destroy our prosperity and all the blessings it has given us.

My fellow citizens, you remember the words of young John Kennedy, words of challenge to America in 1961: "Ask not what your country can do for you—ask what you can do for your country." In those days Federal spending was only a fraction of what it is today. Since then government programs have grown to the point where they touch almost half the families in America.

Today his question is more relevant than before. All of us are being challenged again to ask what we can do for our country, challenged to work together—237 million strong—to build a secure and lasting foundation for the American dream.

Even with all our cuts and reforms, our plan still provides $560 billion for nondefense programs next year—the highest level in history. Congress has before it a budget that doesn't mortgage our future to higher taxes and expanding debt. It is a fair program; it is a balanced program; it will protect the neediest among us; it will stop the worst abuses of overspending; and it not only deserves your support, it must have your support to pass.

So, let me stress as strongly as I can, this shared effort we're asking you to make now will be our best assurance of avoiding painful hardship down the road.

We stand at a crossroads. The hour is late, the task is large, and the stakes are momentous. I ask you to join us in making your voices heard in the Senate this week and later in the House. Please tell your Senators and Representatives by phone, wire, or mailgram that our future hangs in the balance, that this is no time for partisanship, and that our future is too precious to permit this crucial effort to be picked apart piece by piece by the special interest groups. We've got to put the public interest first.

My fellow Americans, I hope history says of us that we were worthy of our past, worthy of our heritage. We can seize the moment; we can do our best for America to keep our future strong, secure, and free. Our children will thank us, and that's all the thanks we'll ever need.

Thank you, God bless you, and good night.

Note: The President spoke at 8 p.m. from the Oval Office at the White House. His address was broadcast live on nationwide radio and television.

Statement on House of Representatives Disapproval of United States Assistance for the Nicaraguan Democratic Resistance
April 24, 1985

I am deeply disappointed by the House defeat of the bipartisan consensus reached yesterday in the Senate. This kind of action damages national security and foreign policy goals.

Today's votes in the House are not the final actions on this issue. The House of Representatives should reverse its mistake and develop a responsible approach that assists those fighting for democracy and free-dom in Central America.

Notwithstanding today's votes, I intend to return to the Congress again and again to seek a policy that supports peace and de-mocracy in Nicaragua. The United States will continue to work for these goals.

Our friends in Central America look to us for help against totalitarianism. We must continue to support the fight for freedom in Nicaragua.

Written Responses to Questions Submitted by ABC of Spain
April 18, 1985

The Nation's Economy

Q. Mr. President, you are going to Europe to take part in the economic summit. Europe is not in its best shape eco-nomically, contrary to the United States. Do you think that the recipe you used so suc-cessfully in your country will work for the rest of the world?

The President. We have been pleased at the pace of the U.S. recovery, especially our record in job creation. It has required some difficult choices, but we continue to move in the direction of a freer, more competi-tive economy. We are already reaping the benefits in many sectors. U.S. businesses, for example, have enjoyed a substantial rise in the real rate of return to investment, and this has further contributed to the recovery.

Our European allies are now entering a recovery phase, although their rates of growth and job creation remain below their potential. Some European governments have stated that they consider structural ri-gidities, especially in labor markets, to be the major obstacle to improved growth and job creation, and they are looking at new alternatives. Every country must choose its own path, but I hope our success in Amer-ica might serve as an example.

We will be discussing economic strategies at the Bonn Economic Summit. I look for-ward to the exchange of views. While each country has a different resource base, differ-ent needs, and approaches, there is much to be learned from this sharing of national ex-periences.

497

Strategic Defense Initiative

Q. There is a certain concern in Europe about the Strategic Defense Initiative. Some fear that it will accelerate the arms race, while others suspect that it will only defend American cities. Do you find these fears justified?

The President. Secretary of State Shultz and Foreign Minister Gromyko agreed in Geneva in January that the new set of arms control negotiations should aim to prevent an arms race in space and to terminate it on Earth, to limit and reduce nuclear arms, and to strengthen strategic stability. The Strategic Defense Initiative, or SDI, is a research program whose goals are completely consistent with this.

SDI is examining technologies which may make possible nonnuclear defenses against ballistic missiles. If these technologies prove themselves, they would enhance deterrence and stability by discouraging any aggressor from contemplating a first strike. If successful, our efforts will direct resources of both sides away from offense to defenses, and thus pave the way for further reductions in offensive nuclear arsenals. Over the long run, new defensive technologies may make possible the elimination of nuclear weapons.

Our security is inextricably linked to that of our allies, and SDI is an investment in our mutual security. SDI research is designed to examine technologies with applicability not only to intercontinental-range ballistic missiles but also to shorter range missiles. So, I think that the concerns you mention are not valid, that SDI research is an important part of the search for peace and stability in the world.

Eastern Europe

Q. Your visit will also coincide with the 40th anniversary of the end of World War II, which meant the end of fascism and the division of Europe. Everything indicates that fascism does not have a chance to reappear. Do you think that the division of Europe is also an irrevocable fact?

The President. We would hope that the division of Europe is temporary and not a permanent fact. That division is a constant reminder of promises, which the Soviets have not kept. Half the people of Europe are still denied the freedoms pledged to them 40 years ago.

And let me add that those who claim boundaries are the issue in Europe do not want to face up to the real issue, which is independence, democracy, and freedom, including free elections.

We will continue our efforts to promote basic rights in Eastern Europe, confident that the peoples' desire for freedom will eventually triumph.

Spain

Q. Mr. President, your trip to Europe will bring you to Spain. Is this your first visit to our country?

The President. No, I visited Madrid in July of 1972, when I was Governor of California, our most populous State, and one with a great Spanish heritage. I'm delighted to be coming back to Spain, this time representing the entire American people. Also, you know, during my first term as President, I was privileged to be the host to King Juan Carlos in 1981 and to Prime Minister Gonzalez in 1983. It is an honor for me to return these visits with one of my own. I can't tell you how much Nancy and I are looking forward to the visit; we are very excited about it.

Q. How would you describe the present state of U.S.-Spanish relations?

The President. I think they are excellent. We have a good working relationship with Prime Minister Gonzalez. Our two governments consult closely on a variety of subjects, just as we do with other friends and allies. And aside from the official part of the relationship, there is a constant exchange in trade, culture, and education that helps cement the traditional ties of friendship between our two countries. Of course, the many Americans of Spanish descent make us feel especially close to Spain. We've been very interested in Spain's progress as a democracy—the form of government we believe in and one which is now the trend in Central and South America.

Q. It has been said that you go to Madrid to help Prime Minister Gonzalez to keep Spain in NATO. Would you please define the attitude of your administration toward the issue of Spain in the Western alliance?

The President. The purpose of my trip is to underline the strong ties that bind our two democracies together.

My views on NATO are well known: A strong Western alliance is the best guarantee of peace. NATO is the real peace movement of our time and has kept the peace in Europe for the past 36 years.

So, I think the security of the entire Western World is enhanced by the participation of each member of the NATO alliance. But, as with every other country in NATO, it is up to Spain to decide how best to meet its own security requirements.

Q. I am sure you are aware that the extreme left will do everything possible to disturb your Madrid visit. How do you plan to deal with it, sir, if it is not a secret?

The President. One of the real strengths of a democracy is that people are free to express their views. Our Constitution guarantees the right of the people peacefully to assemble, and they do. Democracy implies a marketplace of ideas, some conflicting ones, but an opportunity for everyone to look, examine, and then choose. But it's good to remember that to interfere with the representation of ideas is not democratic. Of course, it's pointless to speculate about what extremists might or might not do, either in Spain or elsewhere. I am sure that the traditional warmth, friendly hospitality, and courtesy that have been hallmarks of the Spanish people will be the things we remember after this visit.

Q. Mr. President, as you know, Spain has a special relationship with Latin America. How do you see the situation there, including Cuba, Chile, and Nicaragua, especially considering that the Sandinistas have asked Mr. Gonzalez to act as a mediator between them and your administration?

The President. Well, we value Spain's counsel on Latin America as on a wide variety of other subjects. I think the U.S. and Spain agree on what we would like in Latin America—democratic governments, economic progress, and regional peace and stability. Each of those goals reinforces the others. Progress has been made, but there is a lot more we all have to do.

In that connection, Spain is playing an important role in fostering democracy in Latin America, above all by virtue of the example it has set over the past decade. We, too, are trying to promote democracy, as well as equitable economic growth through development assistance programs and private sector investment.

As far as peace and stability in Central America are concerned, we are working on several fronts. One is to find a regional solution through the Contadora process. We want to prevent a crisis in Central America and to encourage democracy, which is the real path to both peace and economic progress.

Hispanic Americans

Q. The Hispanos represent the fastest growing minority in the United States. How do you see them, their role, and their future in this country?

The President. One of the greatest strengths of our nation is the rich mixture of people from various cultural backgrounds, and few groups have contributed more to our nation than Americans of Hispanic heritage. In many communities across the land, Hispanics are a vital element in fostering America's achievements in the arts and industry, in agriculture and education, in religion and business, in science and politics, and in every other aspect of American life.

Hispanic Americans were among the first settlers in the New World, some arriving in America long before the United States became an independent nation. They came in search of a better life for themselves and their children, and they have helped to create a richer life for all of us.

In our international relations, Hispanic Americans also contribute to our nation's identity—our own perception of who we are and our role in the world, as well as others' perception of us. The strong family and cultural ties which bind Hispanics in the United States with our nearest neighbors and with Spain are an important element of the strength of the Western Hemisphere and the world. We Americans seek economic progress and justice for mutual benefit throughout the hemisphere and throughout the world, and we look to Americans of Hispanic heritage for leadership as we work together toward these goals.

Views on the Presidency

Q. Mr. President, you are in your second term, which does not seem to be dull at all—contrary to some predictions—but it will be the last one. How would you like history to remember you?

The President. Well, I'd better leave it to history to be the judge of that. But our basic goals are pretty straightforward: at home, to keep the economy growing while reducing the burden of taxes; and in the

world, to keep the peace and preserve freedom, while fostering economic prosperity.

I think we've made a lot of progress in these areas, but I'm the first to recognize that the job is far from finished. The secret to achieving all these goals is individual freedom—releasing the creative energies of the human spirit. I hope history will say that we moved in that direction during my time.

Note: The questions and answers were released by the Office of the Press Secretary on April 25.

Remarks at a Ceremony Honoring Youth Volunteers
April 25, 1985

The President. I want to tell all of you how much I've looked forward to having you here today—please, sit down—and saluting your efforts as youth volunteers.

Since our first days in office, encouraging the kind of volunteer work you do has been one of our highest priorities. Now, this doesn't stem from any pride of authorship. Believe me, nobody in this administration thinks that we invented voluntarism. From the foundation of our Republic to the taming of the frontier, right up to modern times and your wonderful work, voluntarism, the idea of neighbor helping neighbor, has been one of the distinguishing marks of the American experience and one of the primary causes of our nation's greatness.

I don't think many of us realize how very unique we are in this country. There aren't very many countries where it's done this way. I'm sure many of you've heard or read about the works of a Frenchman named de Tocqueville. He was very famous. He wrote remarkably accurate accounts of America back in the mid-1800's in a book called "Democracy in America." He had come here especially from France to see what was the reason for this great miracle of the United States. And one of the things that truly astonished him was the extraordinary capacity that Americans have for identifying a social problem, forming a self-help group of a fraternal, religious, or charitable

nature, and then pitching in to solve the problem. So, voluntarism was hardly our idea. It's always been a great American tradition.

But what motivated our efforts to revitalize voluntarism and stimulate private sector initiatives was the lack of emphasis put on it during much of the 1960's and 1970's. You see, back then the idea grew that government, rather than free people working in a free economy and society—that government was somehow the principal engine of social progress. And this point of view was, of course, at great variance with the wisdom of our Founding Fathers, who understood the danger to liberty and creativity caused by intrusive government.

And sure enough, it wasn't long before the proliferation of bureaucracy began to suffocate that voluntary spirit which had always been a hallmark of the American people. Sometimes it seemed as though a social problem couldn't be addressed without a government grant, a roomful of highly paid consultants, and an office staff with lots of Ph.D.'s and impressive titles.

I remember when I was Governor back in California, we were one of the first to question this outlook. And at the time, we were helped by the publication of a remarkable book called "Reclaiming the American Dream" by Richard Cornell, a book that questioned the role of big government and showed how voluntarism could work in America. Well, we adopted many of its ideas in our California administration, and we're continuing them here in Washington today.

And I remember another experience from those California days that I think has meaning for all of you. It was one of those nights in the storm season, and down at Newport Beach, those homes, those beach homes all along the waterfront were being destroyed by an unusually high tide and the high waves that went with it. And they were hitting those homes. And they were crumbling and being washed away into the ocean.

TV was down there covering the rescue operation all night long. And I remember at 2 o'clock in the morning, I was still watching the efforts of the people who were loading sandbags—picking up the sand from the beach into bags and trying to build sandbag parapets there to save the homes, to break the waves.

And I should mention to those of you who may not know, it gets cold at night in California, even in the summertime. Matter of fact, California is the only place in the world, I've often said, where you can fall asleep under a rosebush in full bloom and freeze to death. [*Laughter*]

Well, anyway, watching them—there was one young fellow there, dripping wet, in swimming trunks. He had to be cold—but back and forth, lugging those sandbags, building those parapets. And suddenly, one of the TV reporters grabbed him and asked him if he lived in one of those houses. And, no, he didn't live down at the beach at all. And finally, the question came: Well, then—been working all night in just a pair of trunks, wet, cold, out there—why? Why was he doing this? And the answer was so poignant. I think it will sound familiar to us. But I thought at the time, it ought to be put up on a billboard because he said: "Well, I guess it's the first time any of us"—meaning young people—"had ever thought we were needed."

Well, I'm here to say you are needed. And there's no limit to what you can do.

Perhaps many of you here saw the television special last night. It told another in-

credible story of what young Americans who feel needed are doing to help the less fortunate. The children of New York's public schools put their own private sector initiative together to help fight the tragic famine in Ethiopia. In a program called Children for Children, the students in every public school in New York worked together to raise money for food and supplies for the sick and the starving in Africa. These American children, many of whom were from the poorest areas of New York City, gave generously of their time and money to help other children in Africa. They raised over $150,000. And on Valentine's Day, an airplane loaded with grain and food supplies arrived in Africa to help save the lives of the sick and dying children in Ethiopia.

I think today it's fitting to salute this heroic act of generosity by the children of New York. They, just as all of you here today, show us why we should work hard to encourage voluntary action in America. We're particularly honored to have with us each of you who have gone out and done so much to recover this great American tradition.

All of you and thousands of your friends in nationwide organizations like the Scouts, 4-H, Boys and Girls Clubs, Future Farmers of America, Future Homemakers of America, Camp Fire, and winners of the Congressional Medal—Congressional Award, I should say—all have made our country a much better place in which to live.

Others of you are involved in private sector initiatives like Crime Stoppers, who steer youngsters away from trouble and toward self-reliance; Junior Safety Officers, who teach younger children about "stranger danger"; Friend-to-Friend Volunteers, who help handicapped youth; the Red Cross Clown Corps, who bring laughter and fun to those who need it so badly.

In the Touch America Project, over 10,000 young people helped to improve the public lands by blazing trails, stabilizing streams, and cleaning mudslide damage during the first year of operation. Pyramid Communications volunteers research, write, produce, and market their own radio and television programs.

And voluntarism is a terrific way to acquire new skills. Youth with the Anacostia Unlimited Skills Program learn technical skills and then go on to train their peers. Volunteers for Aunt Martha's Youth Services donate their time and talents in alcohol and drug prevention programs and as counselors in crisis intervention.

The Voluntary Action Center serves as a youth volunteer clearinghouse in Montgomery, Alabama, that recruits and places hundreds of youth volunteers in a variety of positions. The Student Volunteer Work Project in New York helps disadvantaged students learn marketable skills through the special work they do.

Hundreds of Magic Me volunteers brought great happiness to many elderly people in Baltimore last year. And Super Volunteers are springing up all over the country to spread the good news about how much fun it really is to get involved with people who need you.

Your pep and energy are astounding. How am I supposed to keep up with you? [*Laughter*] Someone once said that when you do the common things of life in an uncommon way, you'll command the attention of the world.

Well, today I have some young friends here with me who exemplify that sentiment, and at this time I would like to present each of you with a Presidential commendation for the outstanding work that you've done.

Monica Perez, of Washington, DC. This fourth grader from Nativity Catholic Elementary School conducts a summer school in her home for neighborhood children to teach them basic reading and writing skills.

Lucy Theodore, of Brooklyn, New York. Lucy, the daughter of Haitian immigrants, volunteers in her high school at a counseling center, on a local French language radio station, in a hospital in the patients' screening area, and tutors students in a local college. While on vacation with her family in Haiti, she did extensive volunteer work in the poor sections with doctors.

Jason Hardman, of Elsinore, Utah. Discovering that his rural hometown of Elsinore had no public library, 10-year-old Jason Hardman located a basement room at the town hall and stocked the shelves with over 1,000 books. For the last 5 years, Jason has continued to run the Elsinore library that now contains over 17,000 volumes.

Ann Tweedy, of Moorestown, New Jersey. During Christmas of 1983, Ann spearheaded a drive to write over 1,000 Christmas letters to the soldiers in Lebanon. Since then she has singlehandedly begun a toy drive for the Salvation Army and started school-based fundraising drives for the Statue of Liberty by collecting Kellogg cereal boxtops.

Petra Mastenbroek, of Seattle, Washington. After attending a Chemical People meeting in 1983, Petra organized a group called FOCUS—Friends Offering Care, Understanding and Support. She has developed a number of programs that teach youth how to stand up and say no to drugs.

Mark Perry, of Little Rock, Arkansas. This 20-year-old has been doing volunteer work since he was 14. He has done considerable work with patients at the children's hospital in Arkansas, and he also conducts a job search program for young teens.

Trevor Ferrell, of Philadelphia, Pennsylvania. Trevor's campaign began in December 1983, when after seeing a TV report, he started taking blankets to street people sleeping on steam vents in downtown Philadelphia. Since that time, hundreds of volunteers have rallied around Trevor to help distribute food and clothing and to refurbish a house for the street people, known as Trevor's Place.

Well, congratulations to all of you. As you leave us today and grow older in this world, may all your dreams come true. God Bless you all. And now I'm going to go down and see that you get those certificates.

Trevor Ferrell. Thank you very much, Mr. President. I'd like to thank everybody for all the help, and I'd like to thank Mr. President for the certificate. And I'm accepting it for all the volunteers who give and do, not because they're paid to do it.

And there's this one little paragraph I memorized:

"I am only one, but still I am one. I cannot do everything, but still I can do something. And because I cannot do everything, I will not refuse to do something that I can do."

Oh yes, I'd like to thank you for the Inaugural money that your fund gave to each of us.

The President. Well, thank you. Thank you very much.

[*At this point, Mr. Ferrell presented the President with a plaque.*]

And thank you all again. Nancy would be here to join me in saying her thanks, but she has 17 First Ladies from 17 other countries with her. And they're down in Atlanta on a youth drug program today. So, she

couldn't be here.

God bless you all. Thank you all very much.

Reporter. Mr. President, Senator Dole says your visit to Bitburg will be less than appropriate, sir. Are you considering changing your plans?

The President. I'm just considering putting this on my desk.

Note: The President spoke at 11:40 a.m. in the Rose Garden at the White House.

Proclamation 5327—National DES Awareness Week, 1985
April 25, 1985

By the President of the United States of America

A Proclamation

Between 1941 and 1971, a number of pregnant women in the United States were prescribed DES (diethylstilbestrol) to prevent miscarriage. This powerful synthetic hormone was used not only in problem pregnancies but also in some normal pregnancies. As a result, some three million children were exposed to DES while in the womb.

Many scientists fear that exposure to DES may be linked to some forms of cancer. This fear is enough to call attention to the possible health threats faced by past users of DES and their children. Many of the cancers that may be related to DES can be effectively treated if detected at an early, localized stage. Awareness of the threats posed by past DES use should result in increased attention to regular checkups, the first step to effective detection and treatment.

To increase the public understanding of

DES exposure, the Congress of the United States, by Senate Joint Resolution 63, has designated the week of April 21 through April 27, 1985, as "National DES Awareness Week" and authorized and requested the President to issue a proclamation calling for observance of this week.

Now, Therefore, I, Ronald Reagan, President of the United States of America, do hereby proclaim the week of April 21 through April 27, 1985, as National DES Awareness Week. I call upon all government agencies and the people of the United States to observe this week with appropriate activities.

In Witness Whereof, I have hereunto set my hand this 25th day of April, in the year of our Lord nineteen hundred and eighty-five, and of the Independence of the United States of America the two hundred and ninth.

RONALD REAGAN

[*Filed with the Office of the Federal Register, 4:36 p.m., April 25, 1985*]

Proclamation 5328—Older Americans Month, 1985
April 25, 1985

By the President of the United States of America

A Proclamation

Within recent years, older Americans have achieved economic parity with the rest of our Nation's population. This welcome development has meant a true sense of independence for most older Americans.

The tremendous strides that we as a Nation have made in our standard of living and health care have also meant that each succeeding generation of older Americans is proving to be more vigorous and self-sufficient than were its forebears at comparable ages. This translates into a real increase in independence for our Nation's older people.

In the years ahead, we can enhance our personal independence even further by pursuing lifestyles designed to protect our health; by thoughtful planning for our retirement years; and by maintaining strong and close ties with our families, neighbors, and friends.

Our rich heritage of neighbor assisting neighbor continues to thrive not only in its original form, but also as manifested in the emergence of a variety of private helping organizations at the community level. For those older Americans who need outside support to maintain the independence we cherish, it is reassuring to know that assistance is available through a nationwide network of State and area agencies and also private agencies who devote services to the elderly.

Each of us can enrich the lives of others—and ennoble our own lives—by volunteering in whatever way we can to help older Americans in need of assistance. Age is no barrier to this effort, which should involve families, neighbors, and friends, as we help others continue to realize the dream of independence.

When we—each in our own way—strive to maintain our independence and help others to do the same, we will be fulfilling the theme of this year's Older Americans Month, "Help Yourself to Independence."

Now, Therefore, I, Ronald Reagan, President of the United States of America, do hereby proclaim the month of May 1985 as Older Americans Month. I ask public officials at all levels, community agencies, educators, the communications media, and the American people to take this opportunity to honor older Americans and to encourage them to do everything they can to make their health last a lifetime.

In Witness Whereof, I have hereunto set my hand this twenty-fifth day of April, in the year of our Lord nineteen hundred and eighty-five, and of the Independence of the United States of America the two hundred and ninth.

RONALD REAGAN

[*Filed with the Office of the Federal Register, 4:37 p.m., April 25, 1985*]

Nomination of Francis S. Blake To Be an Assistant Administrator of the Environmental Protection Agency
April 25, 1985

The President today announced his intention to nominate Francis S. Blake to be an Assistant Administrator (General Counsel) of the Environmental Protection Agency. He would succeed A. James Barnes.

Mr. Blake is currently a partner with the law firm of Swidler, Berlin & Strelow, Chtd. Previously, he was Deputy Counsel to Vice President Bush and Deputy Counsel to the Presidential Task Force on Regulatory Relief (1981–1983); associate with Leva, Hawes, Symington, Martin & Oppenheimer

(1978–1981); law clerk to Justice John Paul Stevens, U.S. Supreme Court (1977–1978); and law clerk to Judge Wilfred Feinberg, U.S. Court of Appeals for the Second Circuit (1976–1977).

Mr. Blake graduated from Harvard College (B.A., 1971) and Columbia Law School (J.D., 1976). He is married, has two children, and resides in Bethesda, MD. He was born July 30, 1949, in Boston, MA.

Designation of Lynn S. Wyatt as a Member of the Board of Visitors to the United States Naval Academy
April 25, 1985

The President today announced his intention to designate Lynn S. Wyatt to be a member of the Board of Visitors to the United States Naval Academy for the term expiring December 30, 1986. She will succeed Lando William Zech.

Mrs. Wyatt is actively involved in community and charity projects. She serves as vice chairman of the Houston Grand Opera and as a trustee of the Museum of Fine Arts in Houston. She is chairman of the St. Joseph's Hospital Foundation and a board member of Children's Mental Health Services, both in Houston. Mrs. Wyatt is a founding member of the Princess Grace Foundation and chaired its first inaugural gala in Washington, DC.

Mrs. Wyatt attended Bennington College in Vermont. She is married, has four children, and resides in Houston, TX. She was born July 16, 1935, in Houston.

Appointment of Joe L. Allbritton as a Member of the Board of Trustees of the John F. Kennedy Center for the Performing Arts
April 25, 1985

The President today announced his intention to appoint Joe L. Allbritton to be a member of the Board of Trustees of the John F. Kennedy Center for the Performing Arts, Smithsonian Institution, for the remainder of the term expiring September 1, 1986. He will succeed Delores Hope.

Mr. Allbritton is chairman and chief executive officer of the Riggs National Bank in Washington, DC. He also serves as chairman of the board of the following corporations: University Bancshares, Inc., in Houston, TX; Allbritton Communications Co. in Washington, DC, which owns five network-affiliated stations, including WJLA, and five daily newspapers; Houston Financial Services, Ltd., in London, England; the Perpetual Corp. in Houston, TX; and Pierce National Life Insurance Co. in Los Angeles, CA.

He serves as a member of the Greater Washington Board of Trade and as a trustee of the Federal City Council of Washington. He is a member of the Council on Foreign Relations and the National Corporate Cabinet of the American Heart Association. He is former chairman of the Baylor College of Medicine in Houston.

Mr. Allbritton received an LL.B. from Baylor University in 1949. He served in the United States Navy in 1943–1946. He is married, has one child, and resides in Washington, DC. He was born December 29, 1924.

Proclamation 5329—Fair Housing Month, 1985
April 25, 1985

By the President of the United States of America

A Proclamation

1985 marks the seventeenth anniversary of the passage of Title VIII of the Civil Rights Act of 1968, commonly referred to as the Federal Fair Housing Act. That law declared it to be a national policy to provide, within constitutional limits, for fair housing throughout the United States. In particular, that Act prohibits discrimination in housing on the basis of race, color, religion, sex, or national origin.

Fairness is the foundation of our way of life and reflects the best of our traditional American values. Invidious, discriminatory housing practices undermine the strength and vitality of America and her people. In this seventeenth year since the passage of the Fair Housing Act, let us work together to strengthen enforcement of fair housing laws for all Americans so as to make the idea of nondiscriminatory housing a reality.

The Congress, by Senate Joint Resolution 79, has designated the month of April 1985 as "Fair Housing Month" and authorized and requested the President to issue an appropriate proclamation in observance of this event.

Now, Therefore, I, Ronald Reagan, President of the United States of America, do hereby proclaim the month of April 1985 as Fair Housing Month, and I invite the Governors of the several States, the chief officials of local governments, and the people of the United States to observe this month with appropriate ceremonies and activities.

In Witness Whereof, I have hereunto set my hand this 25th day of April, in the year of our Lord nineteen hundred and eighty-five, and of the Independence of the United States of America the two hundred and ninth.

RONALD REAGAN

[*Filed with the Office of the Federal Register, 11:38 a.m., April 26, 1985*]

Note: The President signed the proclamation at a ceremony in the Oval Office at the White House at 4:45 p.m. Among those participating in the ceremony were Secretary of Housing and Urban Development Samuel R. Pierce, Jr., Attorney General Edwin Meese III, and several Members of Congress.

Proclamation 5330—Prayer for Peace, Memorial Day, May 27, 1985
April 26, 1985

By the President of the United States of America

A Proclamation

Memorial Day is the one day we set aside each year for a special observance of the sacrifices Americans have made throughout our history for the ideals of peace, freedom, and justice for all. It is fitting upon this occasion that we look forward with hope to the future and also back with remembrance to the commitment and bravery of previous generations of Americans.

This year, we observe the fortieth anniversary of the end of the most destructive war the world has ever known—a war the United States did not want but nevertheless fought with total commitment to protect the most cherished human ideals. Throughout that war, and in our foreign relations afterward, we have sought to achieve true and lasting peace for all the people of the world.

Today, our desire for peace is equally great. In our observances this Memorial Day, we honor the brave Americans whc paid the highest price for their commitment to the ideals of peace, freedom, and justice. Our debt to them can be paid only by our own recommitment to preserving those same ideals. But our recommitment cannot be for ourselves alone. It must also be for our children, and for the generations yet to come. Peace, freedom, and justice are not things that were won for us two hundred years ago or forty years ago; they must be won again and again by each successive generation.

And so today, let us pray for peace; and let us remember those who gave so much for peace that the ideals of the West may survive.

In recognition of those Americans to whom we pay tribute today, the Congress, by joint resolution of May 11, 1950 (64 Stat. 158), has requested the President to issue a proclamation calling upon the people of the United States to observe each Memorial Day as a day of prayer for permanent peace and designating a period on that day when the people of the United States might unite in prayer.

Now, Therefore, I, Ronald Reagan, President of the United States of America, do hereby designate Memorial Day, Monday, May 27, 1985, as a day of prayer for permanent peace, and I designate the hour beginning in each locality at 11 o'clock in the morning of that day as a time to unite in prayer. I urge the press, radio, television, and all other information media to cooperate in this observance.

I also request the Governors of the United States and the Commonwealth of Puerto Rico, and the appropriate officials of all local units of government, to direct that the flag be flown at half-staff during this Memorial Day on all buildings, grounds, and naval vessels throughout the United States and in all areas under its jurisdiction and control, and I request the people of the United States to display the flag at half-staff from their homes for the customary forenoon period.

In Witness Whereof, I have hereunto set my hand this twenty-sixth day of April, in the year of our Lord nineteen hundred and eighty-five, and of the Independence of the United States of America the two hundred and ninth.

RONALD REAGAN

[*Filed with the Office of the Federal Register, 3:59 p.m., April 26, 1985*]

Message to the Congress Proposing Additions to the National Wild and Scenic Rivers and National Wilderness Preservation Systems
April 26, 1985

To the Congress of the United States:

Balancing the development of our Nation's many natural resources with the need to preserve our national treasures is a formidable challenge. Continued economic growth depends in part upon prudent use of our natural resources. At the same time, we must protect wilderness areas and wild, free-flowing rivers for this and future generations to enjoy in their natural, undeveloped state.

To further this effort and pursuant to the Wilderness Act of 1964 and the Wild and Scenic Rivers Act of 1965, I am today proposing, at the recommendation of the Secretary of the Interior and the Secretary of Agriculture, four additions to the National Wilderness Preservation System and three additions to the National Wild and Scenic Rivers System. These additions total over 382,000 acres of wilderness and nearly 174 river miles.

Briefly described, the proposed additions to the Wilderness System are:

(1) The Powderhorn area, in Gunnison and Hinsdale Counties, Colorado— 43,311 acres of unique subalpine and alpine tundra, most of which is currently managed as the Powderhorn Primitive Area. This area offers exceptional

opportunities for primitive and unconfined recreation.

(2) The Great Rift area in Blaine, Butte, Minidoka, and Power Counties, Idaho— 322,450 acres of desert lava flows. This area, part of which is within the Great Rift National Natural Landmark, is an outstanding example of basaltic volcanism.

(3) The Humbug Spires area in Silver Bow County, Montana—8,791 acres characterized by awesome granite spires and domes. Much of this area was designated as a Primitive Area in 1982.

(4) The Scab Creek area in Sublette County, Wyoming—7,636 acres of highly scenic rocky bluffs interspersed with small stands of timber and small meadows. This area, in the foothills of the Wind River Range, was designated as a Primitive Area in 1975.

In addition, I am transmitting three legislative proposals to designate the following additions to the National Wild and Scenic Rivers System:

(1) The North Fork Kern River in Tulare County, California—60.7 miles of the river in the Inyo National Forest and the Sequoia National Park.

(2) The Cache la Poudre River in Larimer County, Colorado—two segments totalling 62 miles of the river in the Roosevelt National Forest and the Rocky Mountain National Park.

(3) The Manistee River in Manistee, Wexford, and Lake Counties, Michigan— two segments totalling 51 miles of the river in the Manistee National Forest.

Pursuant to existing law, the Secretary of the Interior and the Secretary of Agriculture have also concluded that certain areas studied are not suitable for wilderness designation or for inclusion into the national rivers system.

I concur in all of these recommendations, and I am transmitting to the Congress today letters and reports from the Secretaries of the Interior and Agriculture regarding all of these wilderness and rivers proposals. I applaud the Congress for responding to my last wilderness and rivers transmittal in September 1982 by designating the Aravaipa Canyon Wilderness in Arizona, the Paddy Creek Wilderness in Missouri, the Verde Wild and Scenic River in Arizona, and the AuSable Wild and Scenic River in Michigan. I reaffirm my support for the rest of the wilderness and river designations included in my September 1982 transmittal, and urge the Congress to act expeditiously and favorably on those designations as well as the legislative proposals I am transmitting today, so that these precious and irreplaceable resources may be protected and preserved.

RONALD REAGAN

The White House,
April 26, 1985.

Message to the Congress Transmitting a Report on United States Participation in the United Nations
April 26, 1985

To the Congress of the United States:

In accordance with the provisions of Section 116 to Public Law 98–164, I am pleased to report on the costs and benefits of United States participation in the United Nations.

The United Nations is an important body and one that deserves our most serious attention. At the same time, as the legislation that gives rise to this report suggests, it is generally recognized that the United Nations as it now functions does not fulfill many of the aspirations of its founders. The central question for the United States, then, is whether the United Nations can be made a more effective institution for the solution of international conflicts, for the promotion of national independence, democracy, and economic and social development—in short, whether the United Nations can renew its dedication to the ideals enshrined 40 years ago in its Charter.

After the tragedy of the Second World War, the United States called upon the nations of the world to create an international institution in order, in the words of the Preamble to the United Nations Charter, "to save succeeding generations from the scourge of war, which twice in our lifetime has brought untold sorrow to mankind." All too soon, however, it became apparent that this vision, in which the territorial integrity and political independence of each state were universally acknowledged, did not inspire universal respect.

The United Nations, acting through the Security Council—the U.N. organ vested with primary responsibility for ensuring international peace and security—has had some notable successes in keeping the peace. But as U.N. Secretary General Perez de Cuellar has pointed out, the Security Council has in recent decades proved increasingly ineffective in fulfilling this most critical obligation. I share the Secretary General's desire to make the United Nations a positive force in the maintenance of world peace. This report, like the legislation under which it is submitted, reflects our commitment to that greater goal. I hope this review will be a significant contribution to the reexamination and reassessment that the Congress contemplates.

RONALD REAGAN

The White House,
April 26, 1985.

Note: The 59-page report was entitled "Report Reviewing United States Participation in the United Nations."

Remarks at a White House Ceremony Honoring Participants in the Retired Senior Volunteer Program
April 26, 1985

The President. Welcome to the White House. Since Monday, we've been observing National Volunteer Week. And in the past few days, it's been my pleasure to meet different groups of volunteers. Yesterday, it was over a hundred fifty youngsters. It was enjoyable, but I have to admit I've been looking forward to today. Now I get a chance to meet some kids of my own age. [*Laughter*]

Allow me to begin with a story; and it's a true story. This past February in New Mexico, a school bus in the Navajo Head Start program got stuck in the mud. Inside were the driver, Willie Castillo, a woman who often served as a volunteer, and 10 preschool children. As Willie tried to free the vehicle, he smelled smoke. And a moment later, he saw flames. Willie shouted at the children and began to clear them from the bus. The volunteer remained calm and helped Willie carry to safety several of the smallest children, including one little girl who was sound asleep.

As the flames spread, Willie returned to the bus to make a final check and found a 3-year-old boy who couldn't unfasten his seatbelt. Willie freed the belt, scooped the boy up in his arms, threw him from the bus, then jumped clear himself. In an instant, the gas tank exploded, and the bus was engulfed by flames.

Willie and the volunteer had saved the lives of 10 children. The volunteer had also proved that heroes need not be young. You see, she was Willie's grandmother. Her name is Mae Chee Castillo, and she happens to be 72 years old.

Since my Navajo is a little rough, I'm sticking to English, and Mae is supposed to be listening to me through an interpreter.

Willie and Mae Castillo, thank you both for being so brave. And, Mae, thanks for showing that folks at our age still have plenty of spunk. [*Laughter*]

But the voluntarism that Mae Castillo and each of you represents has deep roots in American history. Daniel Boorstin, the Librarian of Congress, discusses the topic in his book, "The Americans, The National Experience." "Groups moving westward," he writes, "organized into communities in order to conquer the great distances, to help one another. They dared not wait for government to establish its machinery. If the services that elsewhere were performed by governments were to be performed at all, it would have to be by private initiative."

Helping out became an American habit. Americans helped to rebuild a neighbor's barn when it burned down and then formed a volunteer fire department so it wouldn't burn down again.

I have to interject here, one of my favorite stories, back in an earlier day, when we began—all of us who came or our ancestors from someplace else—revisiting the motherlands of all of us, there was an elderly couple visiting in Italy, and they were looking at that great volcano there, and the guide was telling them of the terrible power that it had and the great heat that it generated and everything else. And the old boy said to his wife, "Hell, we've got a volunteer fire department at home, put that thing out in 15 minutes." [*Laughter*]

But in that early day, those people harvested the next fellow's crops when he was ill. They raised school funds at quilting bees and church socials. After earthquakes and floods, we took it for granted that our neighbors would be there.

At the end of World War II, however, our volunteer efforts began to wane. Government was growing, and step by step, it took over tasks that used to be performed by towns, churches and synagogues, neighbors and families.

Why should I get involved?—people asked. Let the government handle it. Well, this growth of government began to undermine our sense of self-reliance and erode our individual rights. No one understood this better than President John F. Kennedy.

Only by doing the work ourselves, he reminded us, can we hope to maintain the authority of the people over the state to ensure that the people remain the master and the state the servant.

"Everytime we try to lift a problem from our own shoulders," he said, "and shift it to the government, to that same extent, we are sacrificing the liberties of the people."

One of the chief aims of our administration has been to reemphasize the vital contributions which individuals, families, and private organizations make to our community life. As we've done so, we've begun to see a rebirth of the volunteer spirit. Today thousands of new private sector initiatives are making life better for millions.

According to a Gallup Poll, the number of Americans who volunteer their time has reached 92 million—well over half our adult population. As volunteer efforts multiply, older Americans are playing a central role. Perhaps the most significant volunteer work by older Americans is that represented by the group to which each of you belongs—the Retired Senior Volunteer Program, RSVP.

Founded in 1969, RSVP today has more than 700 projects coordinating the volunteer efforts of some 350,000 older Americans. RSVP projects are community-planned, controlled, and supported. And the RSVP program itself generates more than $7 worth of services for every Federal dollar that is spent.

Let me tell you about a few of the RSVP members with us today—people who demonstrate the kind of volunteer work that our senior citizens are providing across the country.

Chester Turner, 77, lives in Charlottesville, Virginia. Chester is deaf, but that doesn't stop him; not by a longshot. Each week, Chester visits the residents of a nursing home and those of a home for mentally retarded and handicapped children. In his own home, a senior citizen highrise, Chester acts as a handyman. Chester Turner, for making such a difference in the lives of so many, I thank you.

In Jamestown, New York, Dorothy Brooks is a professional pianist. Once a week Dorothy puts on a vaudeville show at a nursing home, a psychiatric center for the local VA hospital, where she has been volunteering for 41 years. Dorothy happens to be 82, and that makes her one of the few people around who can call me "Sonny." [*Laughter*]

Dorothy Brooks, thank you and may you

keep your show on the road for many years to come.

Fred Bonanno, 74, lives in Deerfield Beach, Florida, and volunteers nearly full time as a counselor at the Fort Lauderdale Vietnam Veterans Hospital. Fred has a particular bond with the veterans of the war in Vietnam—his son was killed there. With immense courage, Fred has transformed his grief into gifts of kindness and understanding, helping Vietnam veterans come to grips with their lives a decade after the war itself came to an end. Fred, no President can pay you higher honor than to simply say: Your son would have been proud of you.

One member of RSVP has a national reputation. His name is Harry Morgan, and he is in his seventies. And Harry has been acting for decades on stage, screen, and television. Harry, you've been well known to all of us over the years, first in "December Bride" and then in "Pete and Gladys" and then in "Dragnet," but it's for your "M*A*S*H" performance as Colonel Potter—irascible, lovable Colonel Potter—for which I suspect you will be best remembered.

And, Harry, you volunteered for the John Meekum Microsurgery Institute, served as a spokesman for the National Arthritis Foundation, and used your M*A*S*H role to draw attention to veterans' needs, making public service announcements and speaking at benefits and charities. Recently you were named honorary chairman of RSVP, a new and challenging role. And, Harry, I want to present you with a certificate of appreciation for accepting the honorary chairmanship and offer you my personal congratulations.

Mr. Morgan. Thank you, Mr. President. I will just put that down there and hope it doesn't break.

Thank you, Mr. President. That's a very great honor, and I am going to do my best to live up to it.

Now, I am going to spring a little teaser on you. You are probably not used to these. I have been in the Oval Office many, many more times than just this morning. And I once lived in the White House for 4 days in the Presidential quarters. Well, before I get arrested, I had better tell you that NBC did a sort of a maxiseries called "Backstairs at the White House," and I played President Truman. [*Laughter*] But you've got a better set than we had, and we didn't have a Rose Garden. But then they never promised us a rose garden.

Now, if I could just take a few minutes to establish my credentials as a senior citizen by way of, I think, kind of a cute story. Years ago—and not so many years ago—when Prince Charles was visiting America—of course, eventually he came to Hollywood, and they had a big luncheon for him in the commissary at Twentieth Century Fox. Well, practically every star in Hollywood was there, including Henry Fonda, who was an old friend of mine going back to summer stock days, and we hadn't seen one another in a long time, so we had a lot to talk about.

Well, in the commissary the people were seated at a U-shaped table, and Fonda and I were down here like this, and Shirley Fonda was seated next to Charlton Heston, some distance away, and she saw Fonda and me talking animatedly and she said to Heston, "Harry was in Henry's first picture." And Heston said to Shirley, "Harry was in everybody's first picture." [*Laughter*] Which wasn't really true.

You know, President Reagan, you and I did a picture together. Thirty-four years ago, in 1954, the President and I were in a picture called "Prisoner of War," which was about some American soldiers who had been captured by the North Koreans and put in a prison camp. It wasn't the President's first picture, and it wasn't my first picture. It could have been our last. [*Laughter*] It wasn't, but even if it had been, it wouldn't have mattered because at least one of us would have found something else to do. [*Laughter*]

Just to finish this up, maybe on a little more serious note, which is what this is all about, after all: I was in M*A*S*H for 8 years, and I think that that is probably the reason that I am standing here. I've often said that being in M*A*S*H made me a better actor, but that's not very important. Something else it did, it made me a better human being, and I think maybe a little of

Colonel Potter rubbed off on me. Thank you.

I have one very delightful task to perform. Mrs. Castillo and her son—her grandson—I beg your pardon—Willie have a little presentation to make to the President.

Mrs. Castillo. Mr. President, I am honored and grateful to be here at this recognition ceremony. My grandson Willie and I were very fortunate to remove these children from the bus before it burst into flames. I risked my life to save these children because the children are the future of the Navajo Nation. I have traveled a great distance to be with you today. I see these children as my own children, and I want the best educational opportunities for them. Likewise, as an elderly, I see the many unmet needs of other Native American elderly, who do not have the basic necessities of life such as food, housing, electricity, water, and health care. I plead with you to recognize the needs of Native American children and elderly. Among the many needs we have are educational facilities, hospitals, senior citizen services, and policies for the aged.

We need to continue current levels of economic benefits such as Social Security, since many, many Native American elderly depend on this support for their only source of income.

We need funds for these services that I have mentioned because in the Indian country there is little or no private sector. I ask for your support and understanding, Mr. President.

We have no roads. The roads where I live are not paved. In your position, please help us. In appreciation for your recognition of my grandson, my tribe, and I, I am honored to present this robe to you to show my respect and heartfelt thanks.

The President. Thank you very much. And, Mrs. Castillo, I would like to say that I think most of those things that you were talking about here, those problems, come under what we have called the safety net and which we intend to continue. Even with regard to our battles to lower the deficit, these things will not be done away with or reduced. I thank you, and I'm very proud to have this Navajo blanket.

And to each of you out there, you're heroes of selflessness, making America better and warmer by allowing others to benefit from the wisdom of your lifetimes. So, on behalf of all Americans, thank you, and God bless you.

Note: The President spoke at 10:45 a.m. in the Rose Garden at the White House. Mrs. Castillo spoke in Navajo, and her remarks were translated by an interpreter.

Nomination of Harry George Barnes, Jr., To Be United States Ambassador to Chile
April 26, 1985

The President today announced his intention to nominate Harry George Barnes, Jr., of Maryland, a career member of the Senior Foreign Service, Class of Career Minister, as Ambassador to the Republic of Chile. He would succeed James Daniel Theberge.

In 1951 Mr. Barnes entered the Foreign Service as consular officer in Bombay and was head of the consular section in Prague in 1953–1955. He attended Russian language training in Oberammergau, Germany, in 1955–1956. He was publications procurement officer in Moscow in 1957–1959.

In 1959–1962 he was political officer of the Office of Soviet Affairs in the Department. He attended the National War College in 1962–1963. In 1963–1967 he was deputy chief of mission in Katmandu. He attended Romanian language training at the Foreign Service Institute in 1967–1968 and was deputy chief of mission in Bucharest in 1968–1971. In the Department he was supervisory personnel officer (1971–1972) and Deputy Executive Secretary (1972–1974). In 1974–1977 he was Ambassador to Romania. In 1977–1981 he was Director General of the Foreign Service and Director of Personnel in the Department. He was appointed Ambassador to India in 1981.

Mr. Barnes was born June 5, 1926, in St. Paul, MN. He graduated (B.A., summa cum laude, 1949) from Amherst College and received his M.A. in 1968 from Columbia University. He served in the United States Army in 1944–1946. His foreign languages are Romanian, Russian, Nepali, French, Hindi, Spanish, and German. He is married to the former Elizabeth Ann Sibley, and they have four children.

Nomination of William Andreas Brown To Be United States Ambassador to Thailand
April 26, 1985

The President today announced his intention to nominate William Andreas Brown, of New Hampshire, a career member of the Senior Foreign Service, Class of Minister-Counselor, as Ambassador to the Kingdom of Thailand. He would succeed John Gunther Dean.

In 1956 Mr. Brown entered on duty in the Department of State. He served as consular and commercial officer in Hong Kong in 1957–1959. In 1959–1961 he was a language student in Taichung, Taiwan. In 1961–1964 he served as political officer in Singapore, followed by a tour in Kuching, Sarawak, as principal officer until 1965. He then studied the Russian language at the Foreign Service Institute in 1965–1966. From there he went to Moscow as political officer in 1966–1968. In 1968–1970 he was political officer in New Delhi. In 1970 he became Deputy Director, Office of Asian Communist Affairs, and in 1972 went to the National War College. In 1972–1973 he studied Mongolian at Leeds, England. Mr. Brown was detailed to the Environmental Protection Agency, where he served as special assistant to the Administrator in 1974–1976. In 1977 he went to Moscow as political counselor, where he served until 1978 when he departed for Taipei as deputy chief of mission, Chargé, and First Acting Director. He became Director of the American Institute, Taiwan, in Tel Aviv, where he served as deputy chief of mission in 1979–1982. In 1982–1983 he was visiting professor at the University of New Hampshire. And from 1983 to the present, he has been Principal Deputy Assistant Secretary of State for East Asian and Pacific Affairs.

Mr. Brown was born September 7, 1930, in Winchester, MA. He graduated from Harvard College (B.A., 1952) and Harvard University Graduate School (M.A., 1955; Ph.D., 1963). He served in the U.S. Marine Corps in 1952–1954 and U.S. Marine Corps Reserve in 1954–1960. His foreign languages are Malay, Russian, Mongolian, French, and Japanese. He is married to the former Helen Melpomene Coutchavlis, and they have four children.

Nomination of David George Newton To Be United States Ambassador to Iraq
April 26, 1985

The President today announced his intention to nominate David George Newton, of Virginia, a career member of the Senior Foreign Service, Class of Counselor, as Ambassador to the Republic of Iraq. He would be our first Ambassador to Iraq since resumption of diplomatic relations on November 26, 1984.

Mr. Newton began his career with Bell Telephone Co. in 1957–1958. In 1962 he entered the Foreign Service Institute for training and from there served as vice consul, American consulate general, Zurich, Switzerland, until 1964. In 1964–1966 he took Arabic language training at the Foreign Service Institute in Beirut, Lebanon. Following this he became economic officer at the American Embassy in Sanaa, Yemen, until 1967. In 1967–1969 he returned to the Department as economic officer in the Bureau of Near Eastern and South Asian Affairs (Lebanon, Jordan, Syrian Arab Republic, and Iraq desks). In 1970–1973, he served as political officer in Jedda, Saudi Arabia. From there he returned to Sanaa as deputy chief of mission until 1975. Mr. Newton then became Division Chief of Near Eastern Affairs in the Bureau of Intelligence and Research in the Department in 1975–1977. In 1978–1981 he served as deputy chief of mission in Damascus, Syria, and in 1981–1984 as political counselor at the U.S. Interests Section in Baghdad, Iraq. From 1984 to the present, he has been Chargé d'Affaires at the Embassy in Baghdad.

Mr. Newton was born November 13, 1935, in Boston, MA. He graduated from Harvard College (A.B., 1957) and the University of Michigan (M.A., 1970). His foreign languages are Arabic, German, and French. Mr. Newton served in the United States Army in 1958–1961. He is married to the former Margarete Rathay, and they have two children.

Remarks Following Discussions With President Chun Doo Hwan of the Republic of Korea
April 26, 1985

President Reagan. President Chun was the first head of state to visit during my Presidency. And it was my pleasure to meet with him again today for a useful discussion of international and bilateral issues.

The ties linking the Republic of Korea and the United States are many and strong. Our security ties, which I reaffirm today, remain a linchpin of peace in Northeast Asia.

I vividly recall standing at the Korean demilitarized zone 17 months ago. Perhaps nowhere in the world is the contrast between our shared democratic values and communism clearer than it is there on the DMZ. And nowhere is it clearer that strength is the surest path to peace.

In reference to his country's security, President Chun and I shared concern about the continuing forward deployment of North Korean forces toward the demilitarized zone. We agreed that this deployment heightens the need for vigilance on our part.

The two Koreas today stand apart. But this may not always be so, and we pray it will not be. I expressed support to President Chun for the Republic of Korea's creative approach in engaging North Korea in direct talks. We share the conviction that the key to reducing tension lies in a direct dialog between the parties.

The Republic of Korea is a growing economic power, and President Chun and I discussed the contribution that economic development makes to stability and security on the Korean Peninsula.

President Chun and I agreed on the need to defend and expand the free market in our own relationship, and multilaterally. I expressed appreciation for the steps Korea has already taken in this regard. And we agreed to intensify the close consultations between our governments.

President Chun explained the steps his government has taken to further promote freedom and democracy. I welcomed the considerable progress that has already been made and expressed continuing support for such steps, which are contributing to the attainment of political progress. I reiterated our support for President Chun's commitment to a peaceful transfer of power at the end of his term in 1988.

President Chun also discussed another event of momentous importance, which is coming to Korea in 1988, the Seoul Olympics. I expressed our complete support for Seoul as the Olympic site and offered to share our experience from the 1984 Olympics to help make it the best ever.

The United States and Korea enjoy an especially warm relationship, and that was reflected in our talks today. We agreed that in addition to the annual U.S.-Korean security consultative meeting, the two governments should intensify their consultations on political matters in Northeast Asia.

The President and Mrs. Chun will be stopping in Hawaii on their way back to Korea. Nancy and I wish them a safe and a pleasant journey home. And we send with them the greetings of all of us to our friends, the Korean people.

President Chun. Mr. President, I deeply appreciated the opportunity today to discuss with you matters of significance to our two countries. First let me say that the reaffirmation by the President of the United States of the importance of continued endeavors to further develop and strengthen the existing ties between Korea and the United States will be wholeheartedly welcomed by the people of the Republic of Korea. It is my great pleasure to convey to the great people of the United States of America the expression of unswerving friendship of the Korean people along with my own, and I transmit their high respect to you for your excellency, President Reagan, as the leader of the free world.

I'm satisfied with the results of the very good talks that I had with you today. The talks demonstrate the solid foundation on which the traditional strong ties between our two countries rest. We pledge our continued effort to further consolidate the partnership between our two countries. We face the year 2000 with a sure feeling of confidence and hope.

President Reagan and I have shared the understanding of the present situation on the Korean Peninsula. I am convinced that the firm determination of the United States, in close cooperation with Korea, will resolutely cope with any military adventurism

or terrorist attacks of North Korea against the peace of this region and that such efforts will greatly contribute to peace and stability of our region.

The next few years will be a crucial period for the prevention of another war on the Korean Peninsula and to establish a permanent peace on the Korean Peninsula. It is most reassuring therefore that the President of the United States has reaffirmed the firm commitment of the United States to the defense of Korea.

We also shared views that the endeavor to resolve the Korean question through direct dialog between South and North Korea are more important now than ever before. At the same time we exchanged views on a wide range of diplomatic cooperation with a view to maintaining and strengthening peace on the Korean Peninsula. The Korean Government is making, in good faith, efforts through direct dialog to do something about the antagonism and mutual distrust that have been allowed to accumulate over the years. We must ultimately achieve peaceful reunification of the divided land through democratic means. I believe that the cooperation of our friends, as well as other countries concerned, is of importance to the success of such peace efforts. In this connection, Mr. President, I appreciate your understanding and support for the efforts aimed at stability and peace of Korea and the region.

President Reagan and I also agreed that the expansion of trade, based on the principles of free trade, is important to the development of the world economy and that we will continue to strengthen our efforts to this end. Recognizing the steady increase of bilateral economic exchange, including trade, would contribute to the interest and common prosperity of both Korea and the United States. President Reagan and I have pledged our efforts to further enhance the economic partnership between our two countries. In particular, we discussed ways to achieve a balanced expansion of our bilateral trade and to strengthen mutual cooperation in the fields of energy, technology, and joint ventures in third countries. We agreed to further develop the framework for economic consultation between our two countries, including the annual Korea-U.S. economic consultations. In this regard, I stress that sustained growth of the Korean economy is essential to the security of the Korean Peninsula and thus to the stability of Northeast Asia. President Reagan also shares this view.

In addition, the President and I agreed to further promote bilateral exchanges in many areas, including social, cultural, educational, and sports fields, with a view to establishing a solid foundation for a deepened mutual understanding and friendship between our two countries.

Korea continues its efforts to build an open society on the basis of stability as we march toward a bright future of a democratic society with greater benefits for all, ensuring abundance and freedom for all citizens. Based on such development, Korea will be able to make ever more valuable contributions to the stability and prosperity of Northeast Asia and to further strengthen

regional cooperation among the Pacific Rim countries.

At this particular juncture, the talks which I had today with President Reagan have indeed been most significant and timely.

Before closing my remarks, I would like to express my greatest respect and continued support for the unwavering and dedicated efforts of President Reagan to safeguard world peace and promote democracy everywhere. I wish to extend my sincere appreciation to His Excellency Ronald Reagan and Mrs. Reagan for the warm hospitality that has been accorded to us. I thank you very much indeed.

Note: President Reagan spoke at 1:29 p.m. at the South Portico of the White House. President Chun spoke in Korean, and his remarks were translated by an interpreter. Earlier, the two Presidents met in the Oval Office and then attended a luncheon in the Residence.

Written Responses to Questions Submitted by La Vanguardia of Spain
April 25, 1985

Strategic Defense Initiative

Q. What do you answer to those critics who say that the SDI, Strategic Defense Initiative, is dangerous and violates the spirit of the ABM treaty? What is the logic behind SDI?

The President. SDI is a research program. Its purpose is to investigate technologies that might lead to a more stable and reliable strategic balance.

What we are talking about is simply a research program to determine the feasibility of effective defenses against ballistic missiles. The object of the program is to provide a technical basis for a decision, sometime in the next decade, on whether to develop mainly nonnuclear systems to defend the United States and our allies against ballistic missile attack. We believe a deterrent balance incorporating greater reliance on defense would provide a sounder basis for a

stable strategic relationship.

SDI has been structured so as to remain fully in compliance with all U.S. treaty commitments, including the ABM treaty. There is no question that the ABM treaty permits such research. Indeed, the Soviets are energetically pursuing a program of research into many of the same technologies being investigated in SDI.

As the communique of NATO's Nuclear Planning Group meeting in March shows, our allies support the SDI research program. The communique reflects our common belief that it is in our mutual interest as an alliance to examine technologies which have the potential to enhance deterrence and stability. The allies are well aware that the Soviets have for several years been pursuing a large-scale program of research into advanced defensive systems. It would be folly to allow Moscow to hold a monopoly on these technologies.

The security of the U.S. is inextricably linked to that of our allies. The SDI program is examining technologies with potential against not only ballistic missiles of intercontinental range but also those of shorter range. Because SDI seeks to strengthen allied security as well as our own, it is entirely appropriate that allied nations should be able to participate in SDI research. We welcome such participation.

Nuclear and Space Arms Negotiations

Q. What are your expectations for the Geneva talks? If the Russians have violated other agreements, what will prevent that from happening again? Are there any guarantees of verification?

The President. To take the last part of your question first: Effective verifiability is one of the most important factors by which we will judge any arms control agreement.

In Geneva we will work for a verifiable agreement on deep reductions in nuclear arms, both strategic and intermediate range, with the objective of strengthening strategic stability. We also seek to reverse the erosion of the ABM treaty, which has occurred as a result of Soviet activities inconsistent with its letter and spirit. Finally, we hope to engage the Soviets in a constructive dialog about the possibilities for a mutual transition to a world in which defensive systems, complemented by further reductions in offensive nuclear weapons, might lay the foundation for a safer and more stable deterrent balance.

Our negotiators have great flexibility in pursuing these goals, but we have no illusions; the talks may be long and complex. They will demand great patience and fortitude from us. However, we are well prepared, and I am optimistic that we are in a good position to negotiate an equitable agreement.

Terrorism

Q. What can be done, in your judgment, to combat international terrorism? Do you see a possibility of more coordination between NATO governments in this area?

The President. The upsurge in terrorist attacks has heightened awareness of the threat in Europe and elsewhere. The new phenomenon we have seen of the use of terrorism as an instrument of state policy demands new approaches from us. It must be halted. The resources being given to terrorist groups and movements by certain nations is a serious threat to democracy.

NATO Foreign Ministers, in their December communique, expressed determination to prevent and suppress terrorism. Bilateral, technical cooperation among a number of NATO members has been intensified, such as that recently announced by France and the Federal Republic of Germany, and European governments have announced other initiatives in the European Community framework. The economic summit partners have also focused attention on the need to combat terrorism.

The U.S. is committed to consult and work closely with its European partners to combat terrorism on a bilateral or multilateral basis. In short, we are united in our commitment that international terrorism must be stopped.

Spanish Membership in NATO

Q. Would NATO be stronger if Spain becomes a full member of the alliance?

The President. Spain is a valued member of NATO, a fact which already strengthens the alliance and thus enhances the prospects of preserving the peace. The principal issue at the moment—and it is for Spain itself to decide—is whether it wishes to remain in the alliance.

We of course support continued Spanish membership, as do the other allies. NATO is a free alliance of free peoples; that is the real source of its strength. The choice is up to the people of Spain. We respect that.

Central America

Q. Do you see any possibility of U.S. intervention in Central America to protect Western interests?

The President. Well, if you mean military intervention, certainly not. But we will do all we can to support democracy in the region. For the United States, genuine democracy is the best defense the Western Hemisphere can have against the threat of Communist expansion, and we are committed to support our democratic friends. The establishment of a dictatorial pro-Soviet regime in Central America would constitute a serious threat to the freedom of the people of Central America and to the security of the United States.

The United States is pursuing a policy in Central America based on assisting the Central Americans in several areas. We will help the development of democratic societies and the consolidation of democratic institutions, the promotion of economic growth, and the pursuit of diplomatic discussions aimed at resolving differences among the countries of the region, particularly the Contadora process.

In addition, we will help our friends defend themselves against armed attack and subversion. Just as democracy cannot flourish in an atmosphere of chronic underdevelopment, neither can democratization, development, and diplomatic dialog be pursued in an atmosphere of military intimidation. And for these same reasons, I have supported the offer of the democratic resistance in Nicaragua for a cease-fire and for negotiations with the Sandinistas there. We want to see the original promises of that country's revolution against the Somoza dictatorship kept—promises of democracy, freedom for the church, a free press, and free elections. These are our goals everywhere in Central America.

Contadora Process

Q. Do you perceive any possibility of success in the Contadora process?

The President. Most definitely. The Contadora countries—Venezuela, Colombia, Mexico, and Panama—have narrowed the differences of the Central American countries considerably. For a long time the Government of Nicaragua did not deal seriously in Contadora, insisting that the problems of the region should be settled on a bilateral basis. The other countries persisted, however, and some progress has been made. The problems that exist in Central America have been a long time in the making, and they will not be resolved overnight. The Contadora process has been functioning for a little more than 2 years, which is not a long time for a complex international discussion. We should take heart in the progress that has been made and support the Contadora countries in their efforts to reach a comprehensive and fully verifiable agreement.

All nine Contadora participants have formally agreed that reconciliation within the countries experiencing internal conflict and the establishment of democratic governments are indispensable for any regional agreement. El Salvador under President Duarte is pursuing a policy of internal reconciliation which includes reforms, a general opening of the political system, and dialog with its armed opposition. The Sandinista regime in Nicaragua should follow his example and move to reconcile its differences with the armed and unarmed democratic opposition. This would be an extraordinarily positive development as far as the Contadora process is concerned.

Note: The questions and answers were released by the Office of the Press Secretary on April 27.

Interview With Foreign Journalists
April 25, 1985

Worldwide Economic Recovery and the Bonn Economic Summit

Q. Mr. President, thank you very much for having us in this very famous Oval Office. When our group discussed the framework of this interview, it was very hard to achieve a consensus regarding the priority of questions. We hope there will be no such problem at the summit meeting in Bonn, which is, of course, the main purpose of your visit to Europe.

The world is faced with the problem of if the economic momentum can be sustained and secured after the great locomotive seems to be slowing. How do you see the economic scenario in America and globally? And what would be, in your view, the best outcome in Bonn? What should be done at the summit meeting?

The President. I'm not going to attempt to set an agenda for it. I know that we will be talking about political problems, we will be talking about this economic situation, and I know that our economic recovery did get out ahead of the others. I think one of the things that is of great importance that we want to be talking about is another round of trade talks, to resist the protectionism that raises its head every once in awhile and to see if we can't come more and more to open trade between ourselves and other industrial countries. That will be, I am quite sure, prominent on the agenda.

I know that in the last two summits we've also exchanged ideas about what we all can do to help in the recovery, and I am glad to see recovery beginning to take hold in those other countries. It will, hopefully, equalize the currency values and so forth.

I know that just as one country, our own, can export inflation and economic problems, it can also export prosperity and help to the recovery, and I think that we are having a hand in that.

Q. Especially for Western Europe you recommended recently at the New York Stock Exchange, I remember, to follow your recovery program of '81 by cutting taxes, spending, and overregulation and throwing off the weight of government. What kind of tax cuts did you mean? Lesser income taxes or only incentives for investments and innovations?

The President. High tax rates do not necessarily mean high revenues for government. As a matter of fact, this, we think, was responsible for our recent recession—our government was taking too big of a share of the private sector. And I think that other countries—some of our allies and friends—are looking at themselves to see if this is the same situation. When we reduced the rates there was an increase, a surge in the overall revenues because of the economic expansion that resulted. Incentive, whether it's for business and industry or for individuals, does result in higher earnings. There was an Arab philosopher about 1,400 years ago by the name of ibn-Khaldun who

said that in the beginning of the empire the rates were low, and the revenues were great. And he said at the end of the empire the rates were great, and the revenues were low.

U.S. Dollar and the International Monetary System

Q. Mr. President, I wanted to ask you something about the dollar and the international monetary system. The dollar has lost in the past month about 20 percent of its value and before then, in a matter of a few weeks went very, very high, reaching high records against the Deutschmark and other currency. The monetary system, it's unstable and volatile. Your Secretary of the Treasury said that he was willing to do something about it, and it seems that something should be done. How strong is your commitment for a high-level monetary meeting, that should be hosted in Washington, and what concrete steps are you willing to take to improve this shaky system?

The President. Well, I'm afraid your question is too specific for the answers that I have available at this time. Two years ago at the Williamsburg summit we all agreed upon embarking on a study—the European Ten, ourselves and others, our trading partners—and that study has been going on for 2 years. The study will be, and the report will come in in June, after the summit conference in Bonn. And I think when we get that report and see the recommendations and what has been proposed, then it can be determined whether a meeting of the kind that has been suggested is warranted and what the agenda would be, as that meeting would then take up the report of this 2-year study. So, until then I can't comment on an agenda.

Q. So, are you backing off from the statement of Mr. Baker [1] that said that Washington will host a——

The President. Oh, no. No, I think that this is also what he was trying to say—that we are perfectly willing, but we feel that we should wait and see what's the result of that study, what are we going to be hearing

---

[1] *Secretary of the Treasury James A. Baker III.*

and seeing as a result of that.

And of course, to the preface to your question there about the dollar declining, we think that that part could be attributed to the economic recovery of our trading partners.

We think also that some of the fluctuation has to do with speculators, those people who read all the economic signs and then go running out and either buy or sell other currencies or our own. And that this can, on a simple buy-and-sell market, result in changes. Frankly, we were very pleased with the decline in value.

U.S. Trade Relations

Q. Let me ask a question with regard to trade, Mr. President. How are you going to deal with the trade conflicts between Japan and the United States, and do you think that you have to berate Mr. Nakasone for his inability, even at the meeting of the Bonn summit?

The President. Well, we think we've been making great progress in the bilateral meetings that we've been having. I can tell you that Prime Minister Nakasone, I think, himself, is committed to a belief in more open and free trade between nations. I realize that, just as all heads of state do, he has some political problems, too, in opposition to some moves he might want to make. The same would be true of me here in our own country.

But we have made great progress, and I think we'll continue to make progress in opening up markets to open trade between allies. And I have a great admiration for what he is doing and what he has set out to do.

Q. Mr. President, in recent years your trade policy officials have made much of their efforts to promote the multilateral trade system. At the same time, they've used the possibility of bilateral deals with individual countries as something of a lever to bring other trading partners to the bargaining table. There are experts who suggest that subjecting a fifth or a quarter of your trade of the United States, external trade, to a deal, perhaps with Canada, could weaken the multilateral trading system. I'm wondering: A, how you feel about that; secondly, what happens if there is a new

GATT round? What happens to the bilateral deals at that point?

The President. Well, because of the direction the bilateral is taking between us and Canada, we've been, for each other, we've been the greatest of trading partners. Here we are with a very unique border that extends for several thousand miles with no guards or forts along that border. We have a pretty common heritage in this country. It's been reflected in trade, and sometimes there have been efforts here and there in particular areas to curb trade. Just as we're meeting with Prime Minister Nakasone, we have been meeting with Canada to eliminate some of the problems that, in reality, are peculiar to our two countries.

And I don't think that that in any way does anything but even strengthen or add to our multilateral efforts. It just demonstrates that countries can mutually benefit from free and open trade.

Strategic Defense Initiative

Q. Mr. President, I imagine that there'll be a number of leaders in Bonn who would like to discuss with you your Strategic Defense Initiative during your visit there. The question I wanted to ask was that the British Foreign Secretary recently raised some concerns about your initiative. He warned that there would be no advantage in creating a new Maginot Line, which could be outflanked by simpler countermeasures, and he also suggested that the huge research program might acquire an unstoppable momentum of its own.

I wonder what your reaction would be to those two points?

The President. Well, I think that's in a sense borrowing trouble. We're embarked on a research program. We don't have something ready for deployment; we're not talking about deploying. What we're researching to see is if there is an answer to the nuclear threat to all the world.

We have a situation now between the major powers where we have a deterrent based totally on offensive weapons, and in our own country, it's called the MAD policy, and what it stands for is mutual assured destruction, meaning that—and to me, there's always been something a little immoral about that—that our deterrent is if you try to blow our people up, we'll blow yours up.

Now, in the whole history of the world, every offensive weapon has always led to a defensive weapon. We're doing a re-search—if we would come up with a de-fense that would, in effect, make nuclear weapons obsolete, I think it would aid in what we're doing in Geneva with our arms reduction talks: an effort to reduce greatly the number of such weapons in the world to the point that we don't leave as a heri-tage to our children this threat of destruc-tion, literally of the world, if some madman comes along someday in one country or the other and decides to take that action.

And I've made it perfectly plain that if our research—while I have any claim to it—is successful in any way, before there would ever be deployment, I would want to sit down with our allies and discuss this totally and share. And I haven't even ruled out sharing with our potential adversaries. If we could substitute for simply an exchange of offensive threats, either totally defense or a combination of the two, so that we weren't just living under this total threat that threatens even the rest of the world who might not even be participants—except in the destruction.

Q. Still on this subject, Mr. President, President Mitterrand of France has invited other European countries to joint efforts to create European technological cooperation. I was wondering what you think of this ini-tiative and if you don't think that SDI has set the stage for a technological confronta-tion between Europe and United States?

The President. I don't know that I can answer that. I imagine that I'll be hearing about that at the summit, and I'll be looking forward to the discussion of it. The only restriction we've ever wanted to place on technology is letting or giving that technol-ogy to a potential adversary, who then could use it to an advantage over us mili-tarily. And that's been the result of COCOM, which we have with our allies in our restraint on providing such technology to the other country.

I know that we, on SDI, have invited all of our allies to come in and compete for contracts on the research and to participate

in the research on that weapon.

I think on that previous question, I left out something or other there that I should have said in addition, and that is that on SDI, also, that in the meantime—no, we support France and England in going for-ward on their own nuclear weapons. I think it's been made necessary. We are, as you know, going forward with ours—with the MX, with the B–1 bomber and even a bomber beyond that, and with the Trident submarine—because that—to use one of our own expressions, "that's the only game in town."

Now, did I finish with yours?

Q. Well—no—*[laughter]*—we'll just go on to—just to make——

NATO

Q. Mr. President, NATO is today much stronger than it was in '81, when you as-sumed the Presidency, thanks to the United States.

The President. Well, thank you.

Q. But is NATO in these days strong enough?

The President. Is it strong enough? I think basically—for a deterrent, yes. There is no question we do not match the Soviet Union in its military buildup, either in the strate-gic or in the conventional. But I think in the sense of a deterrent that a war, trying to take advantage of their superior forces, they would face more damage than they would want to accept. So, I think that from a deterrent standpoint—yes.

Q. You stopped the stationing of the Per-shing II in Germany. Is that only for techni-cal reasons, or has it something to do with the——

The President. Yes, we——

Q. ——Geneva——

The President. ——yes, we've not——

Q. ——arms control talks?

The President. ——we've not stopped that on a basis of changing a policy—no. We're going forward with that plan. Those coun-tries requested those weapons of us, and the Soviets have continued to augment their in-termediate-range weapons that are targeted on European targets.

No, we would like, in the talks going on at Geneva, we would like something that would indicate that they were willing to reduce those. You know, our original proposal on the intermediate-range weapons was total elimination, zero-zero. Well, we gained half our point. The Soviets agreed to zero for us, but not zero for them. But we're going to continue.

Incidentally, I want you to know also that SDI and the research that's going forward is not just aimed at strategic weapons, such as a protection for ourselves. It would be very definitely a factor with regard to those SS–20's, those Soviet intermediate-range weapons, for protection of the allies.

Italian Elections

Q. Yes, Mr. President, we are going to have very soon in Italy local elections, and the Communist Party has said that if it should win those local elections, it would give them a political, national meaning. And they would want to be in charge of the government, to put a crisis on the Craxi government and have a new government headed by Communists. How would you feel about that? They were talking about NATO and all of this. How would you feel about the Communists taking the leadership in Italy?

The President. Well, if you look at any country in the world that is run by a Communist government, you see that the people are denied all the democratic rights that we and our societies have come to believe are democracy and are the rights of the people. I can't quite believe that the Italian people, with their love of independence and freedom, would settle for what the Communist government would mean to them and would take away from them.

So, I hope it doesn't happen. But if it does, from what I know of your people, I would think the Communists might get a rude surprise when they started to implement their ideology.

European Unity

Q. And just one second about Europe, Mr. President. It seems that Europe is at a balance. You have asked Europe to take responsibility on the economic side, and it's also a quite balanced point of equilibrium from the political side. How strong do you feel that Europe should be united political-

ly? And how do you feel about a unified European monetary system to balance the general equilibrium?

The President. Oh, I don't know that I want to get into things that are purely——

Q. Just your opinion.

The President. ——yes, between those countries. But it seems to me that, as you so graciously said about the alliance and its closeness now, it seems to me that there is a greater bond—certainly in Western Europe, which is all we can talk about—a bond, between the countries than I can remember in my rather long lifetime, a friendship, and now with the Congress that I will be addressing there that represents all the countries of Europe, elected directly by all the people of Europe, and the European Community—all of these things I think represent great progress.

Q. And the monetary system?

The President. Now, you're suggesting a single monetary——

Q. European monetary system.

The President. European. I just don't feel that I could comment on that. I haven't done any study on my own of what that could mean or what the problems might be. I just hesitate to comment.

U.S. Trade Negotiations

Q. Well, let me throw out my question on trade. Do you think that the Bonn summit would be able to set early 1986 as a target for starting a new round of multilateral trade talks?

The President. Well, that's what we're going to ask for, that the trade round begin early in 1986. And I have a feeling that we're not going to be alone in that. I think there are others that want to see another trade round. So, I'm hopeful that will be an outcome of this summit.

Q. Are you really optimistic about this result, outcome of Bonn?

The President. Well, so far everything has shown progress. There haven't been very many setbacks in the sense of countries adopting more protectionist measures. My own feeling is that protectionism just leads to a restraint in trade and a lowering of prosperity for everyone involved.

And I know in our own Great Depression

back in the early thirties, I believe that depression was worsened and was maintained over a longer period of time than need be because our country turned to a thing called the Smoot-Hawley tariff. And I think that was a great factor in our decline.

So, no, I think that all the signs—maybe the progress hasn't been as fast as we'd all like, but it has been progress.

Q. Just on that same point, Mr. President, if there is no agreement for a 1986 start to the GATT round, is it your feeling that another Smoot-Hawley can surface quickly, and it will be beyond your control? Is that what you're saying to the world?

The President. No, because I know that there are factions in our country, as there are in every country, who want protectionism. But I think the progress we've made so far and the economic recovery we're having, I believe we can defeat those protectionist factions.

Now, what could happen if others suddenly adopted protectionism and strengthened the hand thereby of those people in our own country; I don't know. But I don't see any threat of that right now.

Q. The less-developed countries, of course, aren't at the table in Bonn. They have a special interest in what takes place. Of course, their debt problems we all know about. Will you be pushing your fellow summiteers to perhaps drop their own protectionist policies with regard to the Third World? Textiles comes to mind, sugar quotas.

The President. I think it could help those countries. We've all expressed a desire to help the lesser developed countries. And too much of the time that has taken the form of just economic aid, handouts.

I think that we should be directing ourselves more to helping them help themselves. And in that connection, I have to say, our own country, this country, has purchased more of the production, particularly manufactured goods, of the lesser developed countries than all of the rest of the world put together. And I don't think it's hurt us; our recovery continues.

Q. But your Caribbean Initiative, for example, explicitly excludes textiles. Why not include it?

The President. We have had a setup on

textiles with regard to growth because—and this, I think, every country agrees on—that here and there, when an industry is faced with a crisis, a temporary situation, to help rather than let them go down to destruction. Yes, we've all done that, and we have done it.

We have a steel program in our country that is only invoked in the event of unfair competition first, but also if it is leading to a disaster. And then we have temporarily invoked some regulations to help them get on their feet again.

U.S.-Soviet Relations

Q. Mr. President, when Mr. Gorbachev took over as Soviet leader, Mr. Shultz greeted the event as a moment of opportunity for an across-the-board improvement in relations. Do you think that the killing of the U.S. major in East Germany and Mr. Gorbachev's latest accusations about the Geneva negotiations mean that we're now in for another rough period of East-West relations?

The President. Well, I think it was in keeping with what has been the Soviet attitude on other things of that kind, including the shooting down of the Korean airliner. We certainly, out in the Western World, I don't think can quite understand that kind of attitude.

I think they missed a great opportunity to achieve some stature in the world by not admitting that this was a most regrettable thing and a tragic thing and extending an apology to the widow and child of the major and, yes, offering some compensation.

Q. Mr. President, it's been announced from Moscow that Mr. Gorbachev will come to New York for the United Nations session next September. Could you tell us today if you will meet him at that time?

The President. I'd be very willing to. I've expressed the belief that we should have a meeting, and his letter to me acknowledged that and said that he felt the same way. Now, I don't know what his schedule—he will be coming here for the United Nations—whatever it is, if that should be the time. I certainly could arrange mine to accommodate and have that meeting. And one of the reasons why I think such a meeting should take place is that I've always believed that people get in trouble when they're talking about each other instead of when they're talking to each other.

Q. And what will you tell him—to Gorbachev?

The President. What?

Q. What will you tell him when he comes?

The President. Well, I think that when we meet there should be some open discussion about some of these differences, some of the things that cause us all to be suspicious of each other, and see if we can't get some things out in the open on the table so that we understand each other better.

Message to the German People

Q. Thank you very much, Mr. President, for granting us this interview. Please allow me this last question. We Germans hope your heart is not too heavy after all these misunderstandings regarding your visit.

Forty years after the Second World War, what message would you have for the people of the Federal Republic?

The President. The message that I would have for them, and particularly in this anniversary situation that is coming up, is one of recognition that for 40 years we have been friends. The summit meeting consists of the heads of state of countries that were 40

years ago bitter enemies. We're friends; we have been at peace. I would extend my own admiration for the democracy that the people of Germany have created in these 40 years, for their dedication to democratic ideals, and that would observe this particular time as one of recognition of the reconciliation that has taken place between onetime enemies and which we are more than reconciled—we have become close friends and allies.

Q. You will not comment on Bitburg, I guess.

The President. No, no. I am going to be a guest of your government, I'm looking forward to the entire trip.

Q. The German people would like to welcome you very much.

The President. I'm looking forward to it.

Q. Thank you.

Note: The interview began at 2:37 p.m. in the Oval Office at the White House. Participants included Horst-Alexander Siebert, Die Welt, Bonn; Mario Calvo-Platero, Il Sole 24 Ore, Italy; Toshikaka Yoshida, Nihon Keizai Shimbun, Japan; Fred Harrison, Financial Post, Canada; Michel Faure, Liberation, France; and Richard Beeston, Daily Telegraph, London. The transcript of the interview was released by the Office of the Press Secretary on April 27.

Radio Address to the Nation on the Bonn Economic Summit and the Federal Budget
April 27, 1985

My fellow Americans:

On Tuesday Nancy and I will be on our way to Bonn, West Germany, where I'll be meeting with the leaders of our most important trading partners. This is another in a series of meetings designed to enhance the economic cooperation between the free people of the world. By working together with our allies, we hope to ensure that the engines of growth and progress keep running with efficiency. We want to make certain that the fruits of open and free exchange are enjoyed by all and that free trade is a two-way proposition.

In meetings like this, one can't help but be struck by the vitality of the Western alliance—clear evidence of the relationship between freedom and economic progress.

One of the purposes of this trip to Europe will be to commemorate the 40th anniversary of the end of the Second World War, the monumental catastrophe that inflicted death and destruction as mankind had never before witnessed. I think it's also fitting for us to commemorate this as an anniversary of peace and the beginning of a new relationship with former enemies, to take stock of all that's been accomplished in these 40 years of friendship.

In these last four decades, the rise in the living conditions of people in the Western democracies has been nothing short of a miracle. The abundance we enjoy should lay to rest the lie that freedom must be sacrificed for progress to be made. Freedom not only is right; freedom works. It builds societies that are humane and positive in spirit.

Citizens of democratic countries enjoy opportunity and well-being far beyond anything available to those forced to endure tyranny. A lack of faith in freedom often stems from the belief that people are not capable of making the tough decisions necessary for a country's security and economic health.

Americans have proven these cynics wrong time and again. It wasn't that long ago we faced monstrously high inflation and economic stagnation here in the United States. As a people we stood at a crossroads, and instead of fearing our challenge Americans pushed forward with confidence and enthusiasm. Together, we cut the rate of inflation and brought back healthy growth. Our economy has produced 8 million new jobs in the last 28 months. Some of our European friends are calling it the American miracle.

Well, it wasn't a miracle. By working together and making some needed changes, we turned a bad situation around. Now it's time for the next step—tackling some fundamental problems and laying the foundation for a decade of economic growth.

Last Wednesday night I went on television to explain to you the budget decisions we must make. Our greatest challenge is bringing down deficit spending and doing it in a way which will keep our economy vigorous and expanding.

I worked out with Senator Dole and the Republican leadership of the Senate a proposal that will bring us within reach of a balanced budget by the end of the decade.

It is a balanced effort of holding down the cost of defense and domestic programs while cutting from the Federal budget nonessential programs that are wasteful, inefficient, and, in more than a few cases, should never have been financed with your tax dollars in the first place. Many of these programs were brought on line at a time when Congress was acting like there was no limit to how much of your money they could spend. Today we know better, and it's time to trim the deadwood from the Federal budget.

Many of our opponents in Congress are advocating a freeze in Federal spending and an increase in taxes. The across-the-board freeze they advocate would limit worthwhile and absolutely needed programs while at the same time freeze in wasteful and inefficient ones. A freeze is really a decision not to make a decision. It is a retreat in front of special interest pressure.

Raising taxes is also no alternative. First, the American people don't want their taxes increased. You demonstrated that overwhelmingly in the last election. Second, raising taxes carries the risk that it'll kick us back into recession, which would end up increasing the deficit. Third, raising taxes will simply make it more likely that Congress will increase spending.

Slogans and easy answers, like a freeze or raising taxes, are not the way to go. The answer is responsible reduction of Federal spending. It will work if we have the courage to say no to the special interest groups.

I hope you'll let your elected representatives know how you feel, that you support our efforts to trim wasteful programs and to put our economic house in order. When I'm meeing with our friends and allies in Europe this coming week, I'll do so with confidence because ultimately I know you'll make the right decision. Our free society is based on faith in the people.

Until next week, thanks for listening, and God bless you.

Note: The President spoke at 12:06 p.m. from the Oval Office at the White House.

Letter to the Speaker of the House and the President of the Senate on the Designation of Least-Developed Beneficiary Developing Countries
April 29, 1985

Dear Mr. Speaker: (Dear Mr. President:)

Pursuant to section 504(c)(6)(B)(ii) of Title V of the Trade Act of 1974, as amended (the Act), I wish to inform you of my intent to designate the following 32 countries as least-developed beneficiary developing countries for the purposes of the Generalized System of Preferences Program (GSP):

Bangladesh	Lesotho
Benin	Malawi
Bhutan	Maldives
Botswana	Mali
Burkina Faso	Nepal
Burundi	Niger
Cape Verde	Rwanda
Central African	Sao Tome and Principe
Republic	Sierra Leone
Chad	Somalia
Comoros	Sudan
Djibouti	Tanzania
Equatorial Guinea	Togo
Gambia	Uganda
Guinea	Western Samoa
Guinea-Bissau	Yemen Arab Republic
Haiti	(Sanaa)

GSP beneficiary countries that are designated as least-developed beneficiary developing countries are exempt from competitive need limits imposed under section 504(c) of the Act.

Section 504(c)(6)(B)(i) of the Act requires that on or before July 4, 1985, and periodically thereafter, the President make a determination based on the considerations listed in sections 501 and 502(c) of the Act, as to which current GSP beneficiary countries qualify as least-developed beneficiary countries. Among the considerations listed in sections 501 and 502(c) is the level of economic development of a beneficiary as indicated by per capita GNP, the general living standard of its inhabitants and other economic factors that the President deems appropriate. Section 504(c)(6)(B)(ii) of the Act requires that the President notify Congress of his intent to designate a beneficiary country as a least-developed beneficiary country at least 60 days before such determination becomes final.

I have determined that the 32 countries listed above qualify as least-developed nations. The list includes all those countries now eligible for GSP under the U.S. program and recognized by the United Nations as least-developed countries.

In order to insure that Congress has a full 60-day period in which to review this decision prior to its implementation, the designation with respect to the 32 GSP beneficiary countries will not become effective until the statutory deadline of July 4, 1985, contained in section 504(c)(6)(B)(ii) of the Act.

Sincerely,

RONALD REAGAN

Note: Identical letters were sent to Thomas P. O'Neill, Jr., Speaker of the House of Representatives, and George Bush, President of the Senate.

Message to the Congress Transmitting the Israel-United States Free Trade Area Agreement
April 29, 1985

To the Congress of the United States:

I am pleased to transmit to you, pursuant to section 102 of the Trade Act of 1974 (19 U.S.C. 2112(e)(2)), the text of the Agreement on the Establishment of a Free Trade Area between the Government of the United States of America and the Government of Israel entered into in Washington on April 22, 1985.

This historic Agreement was negotiated under the terms of Title IV of the Trade and Tariff Act of 1984 (P.L. 98–573) and provides for the creation of a Free Trade Area between the United States and Israel in order to strengthen and develop the two nations' economic relations and to further the friendship between them.

With the Agreement I am transmitting the proposed United States-Israel Free Trade Area Implementation Act to be considered by the Congress in accordance with the procedures of section 151 of the Trade Act of 1974; and a statement of administrative action that is proposed to implement the Agreement. Section 102 also requires a statement of reasons, first, as to how the Agreement serves the interest of United States commerce, and second, as to why the implementing bill and proposed administrative action is required or appropriate to carry it out. The second of these requirements is met by the statement of administrative action. This letter shall meet the first.

The signing of this Agreement on April 22, 1985 marked the end of lengthy negotiations with Israel. The passage of the pro-

posed implementing legislation, I believe, will mark the beginning of a strong new trading relationship with our friends in Israel. This Agreement, the first of its kind for the United States, provides for the elimination of substantially all the trade barriers between the United States and Israel and will be instrumental in the development of bilateral trade for our mutual benefit.

This Agreement serves the interests of United States commerce because it will create significant expansion of our trade with Israel. For the United States, the Agreement will provide duty free access to an $8 billion market in which we currently face relatively high duties and certain non-tariff barriers and in which we face a tariff disparity resulting from an Israeli agreement with the European Community. This Agreement will ensure that American firms can compete fairly and competitively in the Israeli market.

I would like, in closing, to express my appreciation for the close cooperation between the Congress and the Administration that has been the hallmark of our joint effort to make the U.S.-Israel Free Trade Area a reality. Our success in this undertaking should be a matter of pride for us all and a model for future trade initiatives.

RONALD REAGAN

The White House,
April 29, 1985.

Remarks on Signing the Proclamation and Executive Order on Child Safety
April 29, 1985

Attorney General Meese, Governor Martin, Congressman Lewis, Senator Thurmond, Senator Hawkins, and ladies and gentlemen, welcome once again to the White House. I saw many of you just a few weeks ago. This time I ordered some good weather for this happy day. [*Laughter*]

I've read your plan for a public-private partnership to encourage child safety, and I concur with your proposals. And I am here

today to sign both the proclamation for National Child Safety Awareness Month and the Executive order concerning the Child Safety Partnership. And I'd just like to say, before I put my name on these papers, that Nancy and I have been so moved, so touched by the recent efforts of the citizens of our nation in response to the sad problem of missing children, kidnaped children, exploited and abused children. There's a wonderful thing about Americans: They discover a problem; they publicize it; they talk about it; and they come up with plans to deal with it. And they always succeed.

Last year I challenged the private sector to assist us in combating the problem of missing children. Within a few short weeks the Trailways Corporation formed a partnership with the International Association of Chiefs of Police. They started a program called Operation Home Free. In less than a year over 3,500 children have been reunited with their families, and this was only the beginning.

Innovative private sector initiatives are surging up all over the country. As you can see from this wonderful display behind us here, there's no limit to what can be done to combat the problem of missing and exploited children.

The Woolworth Company is producing and posting pictures of missing children in their stores. K-Mart and the Guardian Corporation will put pictures in over 43 million photo-finishing bags each year. Pictures of missing children will appear on over 4 million tollway tickets in New York and on milk cartons around the Nation. And the Mobil Corporation is working to display photographs in their stations in the Washington, DC, area.

These efforts have been valuable in locating thousands of children. Safeway supermarkets have been putting pictures of missing children on their grocery bags. Last month two children were located within 2 days because of that effort.

Now, all of these companies are just part of a larger effort. Each week we find more and more organizations coming up with creative programs using their resources.

Recently I was able to visit the Ringling Brothers Barnum and Bailey Circus, and there we launched one of the first Safe Kids Clubs that will now be found all along the route of the circus. All club members are fingerprinted and photographed and receive safety tips to follow.

The media has also become involved, not only to report on these programs but to participate. WVUE in New Orleans, for instance, just launched their child video print program, which will video tape any children in the New Orleans area.

It's important to note here that the Federal Government, too, is involved. The Department of Health and Human Services administers programs to prevent and treat child abuse and neglect as well as provide services to runaway and homeless youth. And the National Center on Child Abuse and Neglect continues to work on this problem, with much cooperation from the private sector.

As a result of their good works, I believe that the public awareness campaign that is being waged will bring us that much closer to ending the scourge of child abuse and child sexual abuse. I could go on with what has and has not been happening. These private sector initiatives are tremendous. But it just occurs to me that even though the abuse and exploitation of children is a big problem, it is simply no match for the heart and the commitment of the American people—of the people, you here in this garden today.

So, God bless you all. And I'm proud and happy to be here to sign the proclamation for National Child Safety Awareness Month of 1985 and the Executive order. And now I'll write instead of talk. [*Laughter*]

[*At this point, the President signed the proclamation and the Executive order.*]

There. Some days are happier than others. Thank you all very much.

Note: The President spoke at 10:57 a.m. in the Rose Garden at the White House.

Proclamation 5331—National Child Safety Awareness Month, 1985
April 29, 1985

By the President of the United States of America

A Proclamation

May has been designated as National Child Safety Awareness Month this year, but for a mother or father who has suffered the tragedy of a missing child, the nightmare is not confined to one day, one week, or one month. It stays with them until their child is found. For all too many parents, it stays with them forever.

More than 1,500,000 children have been reported missing in the United States, but until recently there was little concerted action to deal with this problem. Today, however, a new spirit of activism is bringing together parents, law enforcement officials, and community agencies in an energetic drive to increase public awareness of the need to protect our Nation's children.

One of the most encouraging developments in this regard was the establishment of the National Center for Missing and Exploited Children. This Center disseminates educational material about child safety, offers information about voluntary identification procedures for young people, and maintains a toll-free hotline to help locate missing children. It is providing a needed focus for our Nation's efforts to stem this serious problem.

The safety of our children is everyone's responsibility, and by working together we can make a difference. It is important for parents to instruct their children at an early age and ensure that they know their complete name, address, and how to dial their telephone number. The public and private sectors can provide the assistance that is needed by children who are victims of abuse, including safe and secure shelter for runaway and homeless youth to protect them from the dangers they might encounter on the streets. Corporations can be help-ful by publicizing the plight of missing children to facilitate their identification and return home.

The most important thing we can all do, however, is to create a society in which our children are respected, loved, and cherished. The family is the natural place for demonstrating this love and respect, but the spirit of respect for family values should be spread widely throughout society. Activities such as child pornography should be straightforwardly condemned as inconsistent with a society that truly loves its childhood and respects the integrity of the childhood years. By speaking up and making their voices heard, concerned Americans can make a big difference in the kind of society our children will grow up in and, even more, in their ability to grow up with the love and security that should be every child's birthright.

The Congress, by House Joint Resolution 33, has designated the month of May 1985 as "National Child Safety Awareness Month" and has authorized and requested the President to issue a proclamation in observance of this event.

Now, Therefore, I, Ronald Reagan, President of the United States of America, do hereby proclaim May 1985 as National Child Safety Awareness Month. I call on all Americans to join the effort to protect our children to ensure a healthy and productive generation of Americans as our contribution to the future.

In Witness Whereof, I have hereunto set my hand this 29th day of April, in the year of our Lord nineteen hundred and eighty-five, and of the Independence of the United States of America the two hundred and ninth.

RONALD REAGAN

[*Filed with the Office of the Federal Register, 4:25 p.m., April 29, 1985*]

Executive Order 12511—President's Child Safety Partnership
April 29, 1985

By the authority vested in me as President by the Constitution and laws of the United States of America, including the Federal Advisory Committee Act, as amended (5 U.S.C. App. II), and in order to establish an advisory committee to recommend initiatives by which the private and public sectors may cooperate in promoting the safety of children, it is hereby ordered as follows:

Section 1. Establishment. (a) There is established the President's Child Safety Partnership.

(b) The Partnership shall be composed of not more than 26 members designated or appointed by the President from among citizens of the United States, and shall include the Attorney General, the Secretary of Health and Human Services, and the Secretary of Education. The President shall designate a Chairman from among the members of the Partnership.

Sec. 2. Functions. (a) The Partnership shall examine issues and make recommendations to the President on preventing the victimization and promoting the safety of children in the United States.

(b) The Partnership may conduct such studies, inquiries, hearings, and meetings as may be necessary to carry out its functions. The focus of the Partnership's inquiries and reports shall be on recommendations for public-private cooperation to encourage and facilitate private sector involvement in child safety efforts, including activities appropriate for action by service organizations, schools, businesses, charitable organizations, and public safety organizations.

(c) The Partnership shall report to the President from time to time as requested and shall submit its final report by April 29, 1987.

Sec. 3. Administration. (a) The heads of Executive agencies shall, to the extent permitted by law, provide the Partnership such information as it may require to carry out its functions.

(b) Members of the partnership shall serve without compensation for their work on the Partnership. However, members appointed from among private citizens, including employees from State and local government, may, subject to the availability of funds, be allowed travel expenses, including per diem in lieu of subsistence, as authorized by law for persons serving intermittently in the government service (5 U.S.C. 5701–5707).

(c) The Attorney General shall, to the extent permitted by law, provide the Partnership with such administrative services, funds, facilities, staff, and other support services as may be necessary for the performance of its functions.

Sec. 4. General. (a) The Departments of Justice, Health and Human Services, and Education are directed to join with the Partnership to encourage the development of public/private sector initiatives to prevent and respond to the victimization of children.

(b) Notwithstanding any other Executive order, the functions of the President under the Federal Advisory Committee Act, as amended, except that of reporting to the Congress, which are applicable to the Partnership, shall be performed by the Attorney General, in accordance with guidelines and procedures established by the Administrator of General Services.

(c) The Partnership shall terminate on April 29, 1987, or 60 days after submitting its final report, whichever is earlier.

RONALD REAGAN

The White House,
April 29, 1985.

[*Filed with the Office of the Federal Register, 4:28 p.m., April 29, 1985*]

Remarks at the Annual Meeting of the Chamber of Commerce of the United States
April 29, 1985

George, it's always a pleasure to share a platform with you—*[laughter]*—but I get a little worried when I see you here like this. *[Laughter]* With both of us here, who's minding the store? *[Laughter]* Well, I know that you've made George feel appreciated, and I don't mind telling you that I, too, appreciate George Bush very much.

Ladies and gentlemen of the United States Chamber of Commerce, it's an honor to join you for your annual meeting. No organization has done more to foster the spirit of enterprise in America. And you have my heartfelt thanks for your support as our administration has worked to push back government and restore to our country its rightful economic freedom and vigor.

Van Smith, as chairman you deserve a particular note of thanks. It's been hard work, I know, but your time and skill have been deeply appreciated.

There's another person here today who gives this annual meeting special meaning, and this is the 10th anniversary of his leadership. And in that time, I know, he's transformed this organization into not just a dynamic voice in America but one of the premier voices for economic freedom throughout the world. He and the chamber's board of directors have brought about a revolutionary change in the effectiveness of the federation. So, Dick Lesher, president of the U.S. Chamber, would you mind standing up so I can personally——*[applause]*. Congratulations. Congratulations, and I'm glad now that all of us had a chance to salute you.

Now, I know that you're all too busy to get in the game of golf. But that was just a sneaky way of indicating that I got a little story about golf I'd like to tell you. *[Laughter]*

Seems there was a fellow who had a little trouble connecting with the ball. And on one tee, he happened to put the ball next to an anthill. And when he took his first swing, he missed the ball and hit the anthill—sent a few hundred of them into orbit.

Then he took a second swing, and again he missed and hit the anthill. As he wound up for a third try, one ant said to the other: "You know, it's about time we got on the ball." *[Laughter]*

And that was just a sneaky way for me to say that it's time we got on the ball—as I said in my address to the Nation on Wednesday night—got on the ball with regard to the budget. And permit me to say a few words about the budget to you now.

We came to office in 1981. With your assistance, we took the first steps in decades to restrain the growth and the power of government and to bring to an end its encroachment on American enterprise. We cut the growth of spending and regulations, supported a sound monetary policy, put in place new incentives for business investment, and enacted a personal income tax rate cut of nearly 25 percent.

Our reasoning on the tax cut was simple. Throughout the seventies, effective tax rates had risen relentlessly, eroding economic incentives, and thereby driving millions to choose leisure over work, conformity over innovation, and immediate gratification over saving and investment. The impact of inflation on outdated depreciation schedules, meanwhile, was undermining capital investment. We believed that a tax cut would reverse the process, producing wide and lasting economic growth.

At the time, you'll remember, our policies were received with something less than universal acclaim. In October 1982 John Kenneth Galbraith stated, "We have . . . an unprecedented experiment in economic policy, and it has failed."

Well, Mr. Galbraith was correct that it was an experiment. He simply should have waited for the results. As of this April, the economy has been growing for 29 straight months. The recovery of business investment has been the strongest in 35 years. Productivity has risen, bringing to an end the stagnation that characterized the ending of the last decade. Inflation is at the lowest rate in almost two decades, and the economy has been creating new jobs at the rate of nearly 300,000 each month.

My friends, forgive me, but I still believe that with all of us pitching in together, you ain't seen nothin' yet. And you know, I said this before, but I'm going to repeat it, I was certain our program was working when they stopped calling it Reaganomics. [*Laughter*]

As for government revenues—despite the impression that many have to the contrary—they're actually on the rise. In 1984 Federal receipts increased 11 percent—a healthy gain of 7 percent even after accounting for inflation. This fiscal year that remarkable pace is being sustained.

The effects of our tax cut are now, by now, unmistakable. The American people have rising incomes and new opportunities. Business is growing, and government is actually watching its revenues rise.

John Kenneth Galbraith, where art thou now? [*Laughter*]

Our tax cut program has worked so well that next month I will unveil our plan to go farther. This plan will simplify the tax code, broaden the tax base, and cut both personal and corporate tax rates. And by adding to tax incentives, or the incentives our first tax cuts provided, the new plan could widen the economic expansion.

When I announce our new proposal next month, I hope you'll study it carefully; judge it in its entirety; ask whether it will make our economy as a whole still stronger, our tax code fairer, and whether it will provide new incentives that will foster economic growth in which all of us can share. My friends, I can assure you the answer will be yes.

The promise of our economic future is great, and the achievements of recent years have been historic. But both have been cast in shadow by a problem that could wipe them out—the Federal deficit. It's important to be clear about the source of the deficit. It has not arisen as a result of the tax cut. On the contrary, as I have said, government revenues are actually on the rise. The deficit problem is a problem of spending—spending without direction or discipline, spending that in the past 20 years has burgeoned absolutely out of control. In 1966 Great Society programs cost $16 billion; by 1975 that figure had risen to $78 billion; by 1981 to a staggering $148 billion.

Now, this cannot go on. We must reduce the deficit, and do so at once. According to some, there are four options for doing so.

Option one is a tax increase. This would squander our progress by placing a new damper on economic activity. Over time, it might even increase the deficit by cutting government revenues. My friends, I have a feeling you and I agree about the next sentence I'm about to speak. A tax increase, any tax increase, is out. Matter of fact, the only way they'll pass a tax increase is over my dead body. [*Laughter*] Not that I want of give my opponents any ideas. [*Laughter*]

Option two is to make radical cuts in defense spending. In consultation with the Senate leadership, we have agreed to cut our proposed increase in defense spending down to 3 percent. But we've concluded that it be cut no further. The military might of the Soviets is growing. We simply cannot afford to break off our program to modernize our forces, and we dare not place in jeopardy weapons systems that are central to American security. Keeping our country secure is government's first job, and as long as I'm President, I intend to see that job gets done.

Option three is to shrink the safety net for the needy. Yet it's the duty of the government to care for those in genuine need. In 1981, moreover, programs that provide income, food, housing, medical aid were reformed and are now targeted only at those who need them. Shrinking the safety net is out.

And that brings us to option four: cuts in a vast number of subsidies and entitlements that are out of date, serve only special interest groups, result from bureaucratic attempts at redistribution and social engineering or give funds to those who do not need them.

As George Bush told you, it's here that the Senate leadership and our administration decided we must concentrate our cuts. In brief, we went after the fat. As I mentioned on television last Wednesday night, our taxpayers' protection plan will reduce deficits by $300 billion over 3 years and bring us within reach of a balanced budget by 1990. It asks fundamental questions and acts on the conclusions.

Is it fair to force all taxpayers to subsidize the travel of a few? Of course not. So, our plan will cut Federal subsidies to Amtrak, which at present costs taxpayers $35 per passenger every time a train leaves the station.

I know this might strike a little close to home, but is it fair to force small businesses to subsidize their competitors or to force taxpayers to subsidize our biggest corporations? No, it is not. So, our plan will deal with both those inequities.

The need for our plan is obvious, but you can count on it to run into stiff opposition. It cuts across an array of special interests. It'll cause many to make difficult adjustments by paring back middle class entitlements and curtailing subsidies to business.

Indeed, many of you may find that the rollback in business subsidies will affect the enterprises that you lead, and yet we're calling for sacrifices at a time when they can be most easily borne. As I said earlier, the economy is healthy and growing. When we put our plan into effect, it is certain to grow still stronger.

While Churchill may have had nothing to offer but blood, sweat, toil, and tears, what we have to offer is, in a word, prosperity. But I need your help to knock some sense into the spenders. Can I count on you? [*Applause*]

Thank you. You've made my day. To put our plan into effect, we'll have to let the opposition know that the American people have had enough. The budget this year is more than a matter of balance sheets; it'll decide whether spending will make us all government servants or whether the American people can once again master the governmental process. In a fundamental sense, what is at stake is nothing less than our democracy itself.

Now, I know the chamber has already been hard at work getting out the word, and I thank you from the bottom of my heart. By the way, I'm a little surprised that Dick Lesher was able to get off the phone long enough to be here. Dick, when this is over, you can make up for it by skipping lunch. [*Laughter*]

This week will prove crucial. Critical votes will take place in the Senate, and there'll be long days and late nights. It so happens that while all this is taking place, I will be away in Europe.

Now, Dick and ladies and gentlemen, would you please hold a few feet to the fire for me? And like the Gipper said: Wherever I am, I'll know about it, and I'll be happy. [*Laughter*]

It's been a pleasure to join you this morning to talk about the budget and, in a wider sense, the cause that unites us—economic growth. Growth is what we have already fostered. Growth is what we continue to seek, and growth, I'm confident to say, is what together we shall achieve.

Thank you. God bless you all.

Note: The President spoke at 11:27 a.m. at DAR Constitution Hall.

Proclamation 5332—Mother's Day, 1985
April 29, 1985

By the President of the United States of America

A Proclamation

For most of this century, we have set aside the second Sunday in May as a special day when we honor our mothers. It is very appropriate that we do so because from the earliest days of our country, mothers have played a major role in building America into a great Nation. The fortitude, courage, and love of family and country shown by these brave pioneer women lives on in mothers today.

It is especially important that we honor mothers today, because we are more aware than ever before of the importance of the family unit, in which mothers play so central a role. Families are truly the foundation of society, and mothers the vital foundation of the life of the family. Their influence on the training and education of our youth is so deep and pervasive that it is impossible to measure.

When we honor mothers, therefore, we honor the women who shape our Nation's future. Their collective effect on the America our children will inherit is greater than that of any act of Congress or any Presidential decision. I am happy, therefore, to have this chance once a year to pay them tribute.

In recognition of the contributions of all mothers to their families and to the Nation, the Congress, by a joint resolution approved May 8, 1914 (38 Stat. 770), has designated the second Sunday in May each year as Mother's Day and requested the President to call for its appropriate observance.

Now, Therefore, I, Ronald Reagan, President of the United States of America, do hereby request that Sunday, May 12, 1985, be observed as Mother's Day. I direct government officials to display the flag of the United States on all Federal government buildings, and I urge all citizens to display the flag at their homes and other suitable places on that day.

In Witness Whereof, I have hereunto set my hand this twenty-ninth day of April, in the year of our Lord nineteen hundred and eighty-five, and of the Independence of the United States of America the two hundred and ninth.

RONALD REAGAN

[*Filed with the Office of the Federal Register, 4:26 p.m., April 29, 1985*]

Interview With Foreign Journalists
April 29, 1985

President's Trip to Germany

Q. Mr. President, thank you very much for giving us the opportunity to talk to you before your trip to Europe. My name is Fritz Pleitgen. I'm with German Television. May I introduce to you my colleagues.

Here to my left, Gerard Saint-Paul, TF–1, France. Jon Snow, ITN, Great Britain. Toyohiro Akiyama, TBS, Japan. Sergio Telmon, RAI, Italy. And last, not least, Joseph Schlesinger, CBC, Canada.

And now, my first question. The controversy over your intended Bitburg cemetery visit is sharpening, and it overshadows the economic summit, and it spoils your idea of reconciliation. The Congress urge you not to go. The veterans urge you not to go. And the Holocaust victims urge you not to go. And the majority of the American people are against this visit. Mr. President, how does this turmoil of emotions affect you personally and politically and has the final word been spoken on Bitburg?

The President. The final word has been spoken as far as I'm concerned. I think it is morally right to do what I'm doing, and I'm not going to change my mind about that.

I don't believe it actually has affected a majority of the people here. As a matter of fact, some of our own people have done polls and surveys and reveal that this is not of that great a concern.

Now, I can understand how some of the people feel, because very frankly I don't believe that many of your American colleagues—in that sense, I mean in the press—have been quite fair about this. I think they've gotten a hold of something, and, like a dog worrying a bone, they're going to keep on chewing on it. But this all came about out of a very sincere desire of Chancellor Kohl and myself to recognize this 40th anniversary of the war's end—and incidentally it's the 30th anniversary of our relationship as allies at NATO—that shouldn't we look at this and recognize that the unusual thing that has happened—that in these 40 years since the end of that war, the end of that tragedy of the Holocaust, we have become the friends that we are, and use this occasion to make it plain that never again must we find ourselves enemy, and never again must there be anything like the Holocaust.

And if that is what we can bring out of these observances and the trip that has been planned, then I think everything we're doing is very worthwhile.

Q. But there have been made mistakes in Bonn and in Washington, and isn't it yours and Chancellor Kohl's obligation to correct these mistakes and solve this crisis?

The President. Well, I'm not sure that I agree about mistakes. There have been mistakes with regard to information that was given on the various locales. Let me just point out one place in which I think the whole distortion started. And it started with me, perhaps in answering, incompletely, a question.

When the invitation came to a state visit—and for the purpose that I've mentioned, because the Chancellor and I had talked about this, that there's no longer, after 40 years, a time when we should be out shooting off fireworks and celebrating a victory or commiserating a victory or a defeat.

This is a time to recognize that after years and years, centuries, indeed, of wars being settled in such a way that they planted the seeds of the next war and left hatreds that grew and grew until there would be another war, that the miracle that has happened, that has brought 40 years of peace and 40 years of alliance, that those countries that were of the Axis and the countries of the allies—we're sitting down together in the summit—and do this every year—and we're friends and allies, that this was the thing that we were seeking to do.

But the distortion came when I received what seemed to be a private invitation to go to one of the concentration camps, and I didn't see any way that I, as a guest of the state and of the Government of Germany, could take off on my own and go, and that might then look as if I was trying to do something different than the purpose that we had in mind. And I received a cable from Chancellor Kohl that no, such a visit to—and it will be Bergen-Belsen—was included in the trip, and I immediately accepted. I thought it was appropriate in that

way.

The thing I thought was inappropriate, when it seemed that someone else was asking me to simply step away from the plans that were being made for me as a guest and go off on my own, and other than that mistake, I think that what has been planned is all in the spirit of recognizing what has been achieved. Your country now has the most democratic government it has ever had in its existence. You are, and have been for 30 years, one of the principal allies in the NATO defense for Western Europe and of the United States. And this is what we're seeking to recognize.

But at the same time, I think I'm free to say, just as your own people have said, and that is that we all must never forget what did take place and be pledged to the fact it must never take place again.

Q. Mr. President, sorry to insist on that, but the news report published in the New York Times says that some SS buried in Bitburg maybe participated in a massacre in Oradour. Oradour is a village in the south of France. And there were altogether 642 victims. Did you know that? How would you comment on that?

The President. Yes, I know all the bad things that happened in that war. I was in uniform for 4 years myself. And again, all of those—you're asking with reference to people who are in the cemetery, who are buried there. Well, I've said to some of my friends about that, all of those in that cemetery have long since met the supreme judge of right and wrong. And whatever punishment or justice was needed has been rendered by one who is above us all.

And it isn't going there to honor anyone. It's going there simply to, in that surrounding, more visibly bring to the people an awareness of the great reconciliation that has taken place and, as I've said before—too many times, I guess—the need to remember in the sense of being pledged to never letting it happen again.

Q. So, we go back to the Bonn summit, Mr. President. This summit could be a contribution to Western unity.

The President. Yes.

Strategic Defense Initiative

Q. But SDI, your strategic initiative of defense, does not provoke unanimity. For instance, President Mitterrand of France said yesterday in my TV station that the SDI technology is very interesting, but the strategy is maybe wrong. What do you answer to that?

The President. Well, perhaps at the summit if that subject comes up, perhaps I can clarify things for him so he'll understand what it is that we have in mind.

First of all, let us be perfectly aware that the Soviet Union has, over a longer period of time, has already embarked on that kind of research. And what would be the plight of all of us if the Soviet Union, which has the most and greatest nuclear weapons arsenal in the world, also had with it a defense against nuclear weapons and the rest of the world didn't?

Now, what I think President Mitterrand needs to know is that all we're embarking on is research to see if there is the potential for a defensive weapon. And if there is, before any deployment took place, we would join with our allies—you, the countries that are represented here—with regard to any deployment and what our strategy regarding the use of that weapon should be.

But as it stands now, the world is faced with a threat in which our only deterrent against nuclear attack is to threaten retaliation so that in a sense we're saying if you wipe out millions of our people, we'll wipe out millions of yours. And it seems to me that if there is the possibility of having a deterrent that is more based on defensive weapons, which don't kill people but only kill weapons, that then we should be moving in that direction at the same time that we continue our effort to get the reduction between us of nuclear weapons.

May I also say I know that President Mitterrand as well as Prime Minister Thatcher have problems in their own countries with regard to the support for your own nuclear arsenals. And because we're just going into a research and we don't know how long this is going to take, I am in full support of England and France continuing to go forward with their own programs of nuclear defense, nuclear deterrent.

Q. Mr. President, you suggested that this was a good moment to explain to anyone who wasn't certain—to President Mitterrand and others—the benefits of SDI. Yet wouldn't it perhaps have been a better idea to explain all this and talk it out with the allies before you announced it? Isn't there a sense in this, perhaps mirroring our first issue which was that of how to celebrate 40 years of peace, isn't there a sense in which you have announced moves and only afterwards had to get the allies agreement?

The President. Well, I can't remember the exact context of how an announcement was made or whether it was simply contained in our request going to our own legislature for the funding of such research. But as quickly as we could, we did go—and at the military level and at a higher level—we sent representatives over to brief all of the heads of your seven states as well as deal with your own military and our military leadership on this.

Nicaragua Peace Proposal

Q. Your aides say that you're very upbeat as you move towards this summit. Yet it's not been a good week for the person we've come to know as the Great Communicator. Is there any sense, particularly thinking of the *contra* vote and the confusion about Bitburg, is there any sense in which you feel something's happened to the Great Communicator in the last 10 days or so?

The President. No. I've had 4 years of fighting with the recognition that one House of our legislature is of the opposing party, as a majority of the opposing party. And your parliamentary systems—you don't have such things; the party and the individual are the same. But then, I had the experience of 7 out of 8 years as Governor of California having a hostile legislature, and yet we managed to accomplish a great many things. I have not given up on *contra.* Our position and the problem in Nicaragua, the vote up there and the debate, whether they admitted it or not, is simply: Do they want another totalitarian Marxist-Leninist government, like Cuba's, now on the mainland of the Americas, or do they want the people of Nicaragua to have the democracy that they're willing to fight for and that they did fight for in overthrowing the Somoza dictatorship?

And whatever way they may want to frame it, the opponents in the Congress of ours, who have opposed our trying to continue helping those people, they really are voting to have a totalitarian Marxist-Leninist government here in the Americas, and there's no way for them to disguise it. So, we're not going to give up.

As for the budget, we've just started that fight, and I'm determined that we're going to carry through with a plan that puts us back on a course that ends deficit spending.

But no, I don't feel I've been destroyed.

U.S. Trade Negotiations

Q. Mr. President, let me change the subject. You have indicated your intention beginning a new round of trade talks. Given that some European countries may need some encouragement or some incentives to start talking early 1986, what would you do at the summit to try to encourage them?

The President. Well, I think that this is one of the subjects—it always has been—at the summits that we talk about, is the opposing of the forces in each of our countries who want increased protectionism in trade. Protectionism has never been successful, and it usually ends up creating great economic problems for everyone.

We have had some fine bilateral discussions with your own Prime Minister, Prime Minister Nakasone. We've made great progress there in ridding ourselves of obstructions to back-and-forth trade, and so with our allies. We're all somewhat guilty, even though we profess we want free trade, and we all really know down in our hearts that it is the best way to go, there still are elements of protectionism that all of us practice.

So, what we feel is, it's time to have another round of discussions to see how we can further liberalize and open up our markets to each other.

Q. But in connection with that kind of trade talk, I think most Europeans will probably want to gang up on the Japanese, on that other so-called Japan program. How would you do it?

The President. Well, we'll try to see that no one gangs up on anyone else because, as I said, everyone is guilty. They've all got some elements of protectionism. And we need to get it all out on the table and see how, together, we can end those things that do bring about, well, trade measures that are unfair.

Meeting With Soviet Leader Mikhail Gorbachev

Q. Mr. President, your attitude after the nomination of Mr. Gorbachev at the Kremlin has been welcomed in Europe, your idea of having a meeting with him. I think that Mr. Gorbachev has taken a hard line, and do you still want to meet him, and what kind of meeting do you want?

The President. Well, yes I'd like to meet him. I've always believed that you only get in trouble when you're talking about each other instead of when you're talking to each other. And some people in my own country—again, some of your colleagues—have taken the tone that my expressing a desire to meet with him somehow is soft or not looking at reality. No, I think it's looking at reality.

And I think that until we sit down and face each other, look each other in the eyes as you and I are now, and try to eliminate some of the mutual suspicions and express our own objections to some of the practices that have been going on, such as the recent, terribly tragic case of the murder of our Major Nicholson there—the only way to settle this is not standing here several thousand miles apart saying things about each other. It's to express ourselves to each other and express ourselves as to what is needed if we're going to ever end these hostilities or at least reduce them. And so, yes, I look forward to a meeting.

Nicaragua

Q. In the meantime, Mr. Gorbachev is helping Ortega. What is the position of the United States vis-a-vis Nicaragua at the present? Do you rule out the use of force, the use of American troops——

The President. Yes.

Q. ——in the area?

The President. I've never considered it. What we have in Nicaragua is a revolution that was fought—and literally with our approval. The United States—I wasn't here then during the fighting of that revolution, but the United States stayed back. And anytime there's a revolution there are various factions, all of whom were opposed to the government that they're rebelling against, and they joined together.

They promised all the other countries in the Americas—Canada, the United States, all the Latin American countries—they promised that their goal was a democratic government, with free elections, pluralism, free labor unions, human rights observed, freedom of speech and religion, and so forth.

When the revolution was over, this country, under the previous administration, immediately went with aid—more financial aid to the new government of Nicaragua than had been given in 40 years to the previous government of Nicaragua—but then saw them do exactly what Castro did in Cuba after his people won the revolution. The one faction, the Sandinistas—that faction eliminated all the other participants in the revolution.

Some were exiled; some had to flee the country; many were jailed. And they drove them out, and then they made it plain, as Castro did in 1959, that they intended a Marxist-Leninist state. And they violated every promise they'd made to the Organization of American States.

Now, the people that are so-called *contras,* that are fighting against this, are veterans of the revolution. They are not remnants of the previous government trying to get a dictatorship back in power. These are the people, many of them were imprisoned themselves by the previous dictator. And they're demanding a restoration of the democratic goals of the revolution. And we feel obligated to give them support.

But the plan that we've asked the Congress to adopt is one in which those *contras,* themselves, have volunteered to lay down their weapons and ask them to be allowed to negotiate with their former companions in the revolution, the Sandinista government—negotiate how to restore the democratic goals. And they've asked that it be mediated by the church.

Well, we have advanced that plan here

and have said to the Congress that we will use whatever money is appropriated for food and medicines and so forth, not for military weapons. And we have the support of their allies—I mean, of their neighbors, Honduras and Costa Rica and Guatemala and El Salvador. The President of El Salvador has said that this is the right idea at the right time. And this is what we've asked of our own Congress, and it's what we want.

We're not even seeking an overthrow of the present government. As a matter of fact, our plan says that while these negotiations go on, the present government stays in power. But it is simply for them to adopt the principles for which they said they were fighting in the first place.

U.S.-Canada Relations

Q. Mr. President, we've been talking about free trade or freer trade. At Quebec City in March, you and Prime Minister Mulroney pledged yourself to trying to eliminate trade barriers between our two countries. But we in Canada feel that there is a rise of protectionism in the United States, and certainly in the U.S. Congress. Now, I know you say there's a bit of protectionism in all of us; and there is.

Now, there's also a report coming out in September. But I know, because I remember your campaign in 1980, when you talked about a North American common market, given the fact that you've been President now for 4 years, what sort of trade relationship would you envisage? What sort of new trade relationship would you envisage between Canada and the United States?

The President. Well, as free as possible. And of course, Canada and the United States, we are each other's largest trading partner. These two countries here and that several-thousand-mile border without so much as one fortification or one armed sentry along that border, we're very unique. We have everything in common, including our heritage and background and language and all. And it is true that here and there, there have come about those specific trade barriers or restraints. And what we've authorized on both sides is for our people at the ministerial level to get together and do the best we can to eliminate those barriers.

And we, too, have made great progress, as I said earlier, with another country, with Japan. We've made great progress and some of the things that we celebrated there on this recent visit, the signing of some very basic agreements. So, I'm quite optimistic about what's going to take place and how we can free up our border and rid it on both sides of these restrictions.

Q. You know, sir, in many ways, we in Canada feel like we're caught between a rock and a hard place. On the one hand, the Canadian dollar has gone down vis-a-vis the U.S. dollar. And all sorts of American producers are complaining that the competition in lumber, let's say, is unfair. On the other hand, in trying to seek new markets, we're up against the fact that the Canadian dollar is perhaps overvalued vis-a-vis overseas currencies.

The question really is: How would you respond if Congress went ahead and put restrictions, let's say, on lumber trade and other sectors if trades or imports are being hurt?

The President. Well, I'm opposed to it. And that is what I've had to tell our trading partners—Prime Minister Mulroney and Prime Minister Nakasone and the others—is to tell them that pressure is coming from elements in Congress who, for whatever their own reasons are, are trying to pass. And that's why it's beholden on us to make progress in eliminating these barriers before they try to have their way.

Now, I'm opposed to those protectionist proposals in the Congress. And of course, I ultimately do have some power, that of veto, for measures that might be passed. But we have to recognize it, just as I think that the Prime Minister in your country, just as Prime Minister Nakasone in his, I think are being pressed from the bureaucracy of their governments and from the legislatures as to restricting in how far they can go. So, between us, we just have to carry on the fight. And if we make enough progress in getting equal agreements between us, we take away the ammunition of those who are trying to force protectionism on us.

Nuclear and Space Arms Negotiations

Q. Unfortunately the time is running out. We have just 3 minutes to go. A question— Soviet leader Gorbachev has just offered deep strategic arms cuts. Do you think it's a good proposal, or do you feel that he just wants to put you on the defensive?

The President. Well, if he's trying to put me on the defensive by asking for deep nuclear weapons cuts, I won't be on the defensive, because I won't defend against that.

I was very optimistic before the talks started, when the late Chernenko and Foreign Minister Gromyko both publicly stated that they would like to see the elimination of nuclear offensive weapons.

Well, I told Gromyko over in the Oval Office when he was here we could sign something right then, that that was our ultimate goal and that I was more than pleased to hear them say that it was theirs.

Now, I recognize that that would probably have to be brought about by various stages of reductions in numbers of weapons; and we're very willing; and we have faced them there with proposals that make that evident, that we will join in real reductions of offensive nuclear weapons.

Minister Gromyko said to me at one time: "How long are we going to sit here on these mountains, ever getting higher, of such weapons?" And I asked him then, I said: "Well, we have it between us the ability to lower those mountains, and as long as we're equal at whatever level we stop, then we have a legitimate deterrent that would indicate that they'll never be used."

European Unity

Q. Mr. President, are you in favor of strong European unification, which of course is the thing of Europe itself, and do you intend to support it in your Strasbourg speech?

The President. Well, I don't know how far I should go in attempting to or appearing to be interfering in a problem that involves purely the European countries. I am gratified, and I think the world should be pleased, to see how the unity of Western Europe has—as far as it has come now.

You know, 200 years ago, our first President, George Washington, in his farewell address to the Nation, urged them not to get involved in European affairs because of the rivalries and the enmities that existed between them. And here today that's no longer true. Here today we are all allied, and there is this spirit of unity, so I just would hesitate to voice an opinion as to how far they would go with a union of Europe. That, I think—I don't want the United States to sound as if we're interfering.

Q. Thank you very much, Mr. President. I wish you a pleasant and a good and a successful trip to Europe.

The President. Thank you very much. I'm looking forward to it.

Note: The interview began at 2:33 p.m. in the State Dining Room at the White House.

Proclamation 5333—National Tourism Week, 1985
April 29, 1985

By the President of the United States of America

A Proclamation

Travel has long been recommended as a way to broaden the mind and refresh the spirit. But in previous ages, travel was often hazardous and difficult. The rewards of a romantic adventure could sometimes be more than overbalanced by the dangers a traveler might encounter along the way.

Today, the travel and tourism sector of our economy constitutes the second largest retail industry in the United States. The benefits of travel remain as enticing as ever, but the hazards and dangers have largely disappeared. Americans who want to travel abroad can experience the tremendous diversity of the world's cultures on group excursions or on individually designed tours.

Many Americans, however, are choosing to remain near home and explore the natural beauties and historic monuments of our own Nation. And many citizens of foreign lands are joining them in discovering that America's rich history and scenic wonders make it an excellent place to take a vacation.

The Congress, by Public Law 98–424 of September 25, 1984, has designated the week beginning May 19, 1985, as "National Tourism Week" and has authorized and requested the President to issue a proclamation in observance of this event.

Now, Therefore, I, Ronald Reagan, President of the United States of America, do hereby proclaim the week beginning May 19, 1985, as National Tourism Week. I call upon the people of the United States to observe this week with appropriate ceremonies and activities.

In Witness Whereof, I have hereunto set my hand this twenty-ninth day of April, in the year of our Lord nineteen hundred and eighty-five, and of the Independence of the United States of America the two hundred and ninth.

RONALD REAGAN

[*Filed with the Office of the Federal Register, 10:57 a.m., April 30, 1985*]

Executive Order 12512—Federal Real Property Management
April 29, 1985

By the authority vested in me as President by the Constitution and laws of the United States of America, including section 486(a) of title 40 of the United States Code, and in order to ensure that Federal real property resources are treated in accordance with their value as national assets and in the best interests of the Nation's taxpayers, it is hereby ordered as follows:

Section 1. General Requirements. To ensure the effective and economical use of America's real property and public land assets, establish a focal point for the enunciation of clear and consistent Federal policies regarding the acquisition, management, and disposal of properties, and assure management accountability for implementing Federal real property management reforms, all Executive departments and agencies shall take immediate action to recognize the importance of such resources through increased management attention, establishment of clear goals and objectives, improved policies and levels of accountability, and other appropriate actions. Specifically:

(a) The Domestic Policy Council shall serve as the forum for approving government-wide real property management policies;

(b) All Executive departments and agencies shall establish internal policies and systems of accountability that ensure effective use of real property in support of mission-related activities, consistent with Federal policies regarding the acquisition, management, and disposal of such assets. All such agencies shall periodically review their real property holdings and conduct surveys of such property in accordance with standards and procedures determined by the Administrator of General Services. All such agencies shall also develop annual real property management improvement plans that include clear and concise goals and objectives related to all aspects of real property management, and identify sales, work space management, productivity, and excess property targets;

(c) The Director of the Office of Management and Budget shall review, through the management and budget review processes, the efforts of departments and agencies toward achieving the government-wide property management policies established pursuant to this Order. Savings achieved as a result of improved management shall be applied to reduce Federal spending and to support program delivery;

(d) The Office of Management and Budget and the General Services Administration shall, in consultation with the land managing agencies, develop legislative initiatives that seek to improve Federal real property management through the adoption of appropriate private sector management techniques; the elimination of duplication of effort among agencies; and the establishment of managerial accountability for implementing effective and efficient real property management practices; and

(e) The President's Council on Management Improvement, subject to the policy direction of the Domestic Policy Council, shall conduct such additional studies as are necessary to improve Federal real property management by appropriate agencies and groups.

Sec. 2. Real Property. The Administrator of General Services shall, to the extent permitted by law, provide government-wide policy oversight and guidance for Federal real property management; manage selected properties for agencies; conduct surveys; delegate operational responsibility to agencies where feasible and economical; and provide leadership in the development and maintenance of needed property management information systems.

Sec. 3. Public Lands. In order to ensure that Federally owned lands, other than the real property covered by Section 2 of this Order, are managed in the most effective and economic manner, the Departments of Agriculture and the Interior shall take such steps as are appropriate to improve their management of public lands and National Forest System lands and shall develop appropriate legislative proposals necessary to facilitate that result.

Sec. 4. Executive Order No. 12348 of February 25, 1982, is hereby revoked.

RONALD REAGAN

The White House,
April 29, 1985.

[Filed with the Office of the Federal Register, 10:58 a.m., April 30, 1985]

Proclamation 5334—Helsinki Human Rights Day, 1985
April 30, 1985

By the President of the United States of America

A Proclamation

May 7, 1985, marks the opening session in Ottawa of the Human Rights Experts Meeting of the Conference on Security and Cooperation in Europe. This meeting is mandated to deal with questions concerning the record of all 35 CSCE states in protecting human rights and fundamental freedoms, in all their aspects, as embodied in the Final Act. This is the first CSCE meeting that has ever been devoted exclusively to human rights issues. It visibly manifests the success of joint U.S.-West European efforts to utilize CSCE as a major forum for discussions on human rights.

The United States delegation will work tirelessly to achieve meaningful results at this assembly, which discusses an issue of great concern to this Nation.

Human rights and fundamental freedoms lie at the heart of the commitments made in the Helsinki Accords of 1975 and in the Madrid Concluding Document of 1983. These documents set forth a clear code of conduct, not only for relations among sovereign states, but also for relations between states and their citizens. They hold out a beacon of hope for those in the East who seek a freer, more just, and more secure life. We and the other Atlantic democracies will not waver in our efforts to see that these commitments are someday fully honored in all of Europe.

Let us as Americans look once again to our commitment to implement fully the human rights and humanitarian provisions of the Helsinki Accords, because these freedoms are fundamental to our way of life. Let us pledge ourselves once again to do everything in our power so that all men and women may enjoy them in peace. In doing so, we call on all 35 CSCE states to dedicate themselves to upholding these humane principles.

The Congress, by Senate Joint Resolution 15, has designated May 7, 1985, as "Helsinki Human Rights Day" and authorized and requested the President to issue a proclamation reasserting our commitment to the Helsinki Accords.

Now, Therefore, I, Ronald Reagan, President of the United States of America, do hereby proclaim May 7, 1985, as Helsinki Human Rights Day and call upon all Americans to observe this day with appropriate observances that reflect our continuing dedication to full implementation of the commitment to human rights and fundamental freedoms made in the Helsinki Accords.

In Witness Whereof, I have hereunto set my hand this thirtieth day of April, in the year of our Lord nineteen hundred and eighty-five, and of the Independence of the United States of America the two hundred and ninth.

RONALD REAGAN

[*Filed with the Office of the Federal Register, 4:13 p.m., April 30, 1985*]

Message to the Congress Transmitting a Report on POW's and MIA's in Southeast Asia
April 30, 1985

To the Congress of the United States:

In accordance with Section 1525 of the Department of Defense Authorization Act of 1985, I am submitting the attached report detailing actions taken by the United States Government in pursuit of our national goal of returning any servicemen who may still be held captive in Southeast Asia;

the fullest possible accounting of those still missing; and the repatriation of all recoverable remains of those who died serving our Nation.

In doing so, I would like to reemphasize my personal dedication to this great national effort and my confidence that the actions of those involved throughout the Executive branch of Government in the resolution of this issue reflect this same dedication. In this effort, there can be no partisan or parochial views or any special interests, but only the interest of the entire American people to see to it that all of us do our duty toward those who served this Nation so well in time of war and their families who look to us to help secure the answers they so rightfully seek and deserve.

RONALD REAGAN

The White House,
April 30, 1985.

Message to the Congress Transmitting the Annual Report of the National Science Foundation
April 30, 1985

To the Congress of the United States:

I am pleased to send to you the annual report of the National Science Foundation for Fiscal Year 1984. This report describes research supported by the Foundation in the mathematical, physical, biological, social, behavioral, and information sciences; in engineering; and in education in those fields.

Achievements such as the ones described in this report are the basis for much of our Nation's strength—its economic growth, military security, and the overall well-being of our people.

We face challenges in science, engineering, and technology, but I am confident about our ability to meet those challenges. The National Science Foundation has been and will remain a key part of the national effort to keep vital our great capabilities in research and productivity and to stay ahead of world competition through innovation and new discoveries.

RONALD REAGAN

The White House,
April 30, 1985.

Statement on the Soviet-United States Nuclear and Space Arms Negotiations
April 30, 1985

I have just met with our three senior negotiators in the Geneva talks. Ambassadors Kampelman, Tower, and Glitman briefed me on developments in the first round which has just ended. We also had an initial discussion of our preparations for the next round.

These negotiations are among the most complicated and difficult ever undertaken, and it is clear that they will take time. But we find ourselves in the best position to achieve meaningful arms limitations that has existed in a generation. With patience, strength, and Western solidarity, we will succeed.

My administration is committed to achieving verifiable and equitable agreements substantially reducing U.S. and Soviet nuclear arsenals. This is one of the most important and urgent tasks facing the international community, and we will not waver in our determination to achieve this goal. With our skilled and dedicated negotiating team we are doing our part, and, as long as the Soviet Union is similarly committed, there are grounds for optimism that agreement can be reached.

I am leaving later today for Europe, where I will take part in the economic summit in Bonn and meet with some of our allied leaders both there and in bilateral visits to Germany, Spain, and Portugal. In addition to the major economic issues which are on the summit agenda, my private discussions with these allied leaders will also cover security issues, including developments in Geneva. Our commitment, and that of our friends and allies, to our twin goals of peace and prosperity remains steadfast.

Nomination of Robert L. Pugh To Be United States Ambassador to Mauritania
April 30, 1985

The President today announced his intention to nominate Robert L. Pugh, a career member of the Senior Foreign Service, Class of Counselor, as Ambassador to the Islamic Republic of Mauritania. He would succeed Edward Lionel Peck.

Mr. Pugh began his career in the Foreign Service in 1961. He studied at the Foreign Service Institute and then served as an international economist in the Department from 1961 to 1963. He then went back to the Institute for further study from 1963 to 1964. In 1964 he became political/military officer at the U.S. Embassy in Ankara, Turkey, where he served until 1967 when he went to Isfahan as principal officer of the American consulate. From 1969 to 1972, he was political officer in the Office of Turkish Affairs, Bureau of Near Eastern and South Asian Affairs, in the Department.

In 1972 he went to Athens, Greece, to serve as political/military officer until 1976. From there he returned to Washington as congressional relations officer until 1977. From 1977 to 1979, he was political adviser to CINCUSNAVEUR in London. In 1979 he served as Deputy Director of the Office of Southern European Affairs in the Bureau of European Affairs. From 1981 to 1982, he was a personnel placement officer in the Bureau of Personnel. In 1982 he went to the U.S. Embassy in Beirut as deputy chief of mission, where he served until 1984. Since then he has been attending the Executive Seminar in National and International Affairs at the Foreign Service Institute.

Mr. Pugh graduated from the University of Washington (B.A., 1954). His foreign languages are French, Turkish, and Persian. He is married and has two children. He was born October 27, 1921, in Clinton, PA.

Nomination of Rose Marie Monk To Be a Commissioner of the Copyright Royalty Tribunal
April 30, 1985

The President today announced his intention to nominate Rose Marie Monk to be a Commissioner of the Copyright Royalty Tribunal for the term of 7 years from September 27, 1984. She would succeed Thomas C. Brennan.

Ms. Monk is currently executive assistant with Nofziger Communications, Inc. Previously she served as special assistant to the Honorable Milan D. Bish, Ambassador to Barbados and the Eastern Caribbean (1982–1983). She served as executive assistant to Lyn Nofziger (Assistant to the President for

Political Affairs) at the White House (1981–1982) and at the Reagan for President Committee, where Mr. Nofziger served as Press Secretary (1980). Ms. Monk also was executive assistant to Mr. Nofziger at the Lyn Nofziger Co. in Los Angeles (1979–1980) and at Citizens for the Republic (1977–1979).

Ms. Monk graduated from the University of Texas (B.A., 1964). She was born May 12, 1942, in McAllen, TX, and now resides in Washington, DC.

Nomination of Patti Birge Tyson To Be a Commissioner of the Postal Rate Commission
April 30, 1985

The President today announced his intention to nominate Patti Birge Tyson to be a Commissioner of the Postal Rate Commission for the term expiring November 22, 1990. She would succeed James H. Duffy.

Ms. Tyson is currently Executive Assistant to the Secretary of Health and Human Services. Previously, she was chief counsel and staff director, Subcommittee on the Legislative Process, House Committee on Rules (1977–1983); administrative assistant to Congressman Gillis Long (D–LA) in 1975–1976; assistant to the division director, Bureau of Quality Assurance (1974–1975); and executive assistant to Congresswoman Margaret Heckler (R–MA) in 1968–1972.

Ms. Tyson graduated from the University of Texas (A.B.) and the National Law Center, George Washington University (J.D.). She was born October 3, 1939, in Sherman, TX, and now resides in Washington, DC.

Appointment of Stanley S. Scott as a Member of the President's Commission on White House Fellowships
April 30, 1985

The President today announced his intention to appoint Stanley S. Scott to be a member of the President's Commission on White House Fellowships. This is an initial appointment.

Mr. Scott has been with Philip Morris since 1977 serving as assistant director, corporate relations and communications (1977); director, corporate public affairs (1977–1979); and vice president, public affairs (1979–1984). He was elected a vice president of Philip Morris, Inc., on August 29, 1984, and was appointed director, corporate affairs, in July of 1984. Previously, Mr. Scott served as Assistant Administrator of AID (1975–1977); Special Assistant to the President, the White House (1973–1975); and assistant to the Director of Communications for the executive branch, the White House (1971–1973).

Mr. Scott graduated from Lincoln University (B.S., 1959). He is married, has three children, and resides in Dobbs Ferry, NY. He was born July 2, 1933, in Bolivar, TN.

Nomination of Elliott Abrams To Be an Assistant Secretary of State
April 30, 1985

The President today announced his intention to nominate Elliott Abrams as Assistant Secretary of State for Inter-American Affairs. He would succeed Langhorne A. Motley. Ambassador Motley was Ambassador to Brazil from September 1981 to June 1983, and has served as Assistant Secretary of State for Inter-American Affairs since then.

Mr. Abrams has been serving as Assistant Secretary of State for Human Rights and Humanitarian Affairs since November 1981. Previously he was Assistant Secretary of State for International Organizations. Before assuming his post at the State Department, he was an attorney with the law firm of Verner, Lipfert, Bernhard and McPherson of Washington, DC, in 1979–1981. He was special counsel to Senator Daniel Moynihan (D–NY) in 1977–1979. In 1973–1975 he was an attorney with the firm of Breed, Abbott and Morgan of Boston, MA.

Mr. Abrams graduated from Harvard University (B.A., 1969), the London School of Economics (M.Sc., 1970), and Harvard Law School (J.D., 1973). He was born January 24, 1948, in New York, NY. He is married and resides in Washington, DC.

Statement on Senate Action on the Budget Resolution
April 30, 1985

A short time ago the Senate took an important step toward putting our nation's fiscal house in order. The vote today on the $300 billion taxpayers' protection plan demonstrated foresight and responsible leadership. Majority Leader Dole and his colleagues are to be commended.

This step, though crucial, was just the first on a long and difficult road. To carry the taxpayers' protection plan through to final passage, the Senators who voted for the plan today will have to stand fast against a long list of amendments—amendments that would weaken the package, split the coalition of Senators who support the package, and ultimately do grave damage to our economy. I am confident, however, that if a majority of the Senate remains true to the spirit of unity and determination so apparent today, then the taxpayers' protection plan will become law, and the American economy will continue to expand with vigor.

Remarks on Departure for Europe
April 30, 1985

Nancy and I leave tonight for the economic summit in Bonn and our state visits to the Federal Republic of Germany, Spain, and Portugal. And I'll also have the opportunity to speak to the Parliament in Strasbourg, France, to mark the 40th anniversary of the end of the Second World War in Europe and the beginning of an unprecedented period of peace and prosperity.

Forty years ago, World War II was nearing its end, much of Europe lay in ruins. The destruction and terrible human losses were matched by fear and doubt about an uncertain future.

We leave tonight for a Europe that is rebuilt from the disaster of war and morally restored from the despair of 1945. The strong, confident alliance of free people who've done this can take satisfaction in their achievements and look to the future with confidence. So, we leave on this journey infused with pride and hope. We are proud of our Atlantic partnership that anchors the freedom and democracy which our nations have created from the rubble of 40 years ago.

Our hopes for the future are high. Despite the hectic pace of change in today's world, we know that by allowing the freest expression of individual human aspirations, we can surmount our challenges and build a more secure and peaceful future. We know this because of a simple truth which makes our societies strong: Freedom works.

The economic summit conference, now an annual event, spans the free world from the Federal Republic of Germany to Japan, providing the clearest possible symbol of our modern economic interdependence. At this year's summit, we will strive for agreement to meet the challenge of greater growth on which our good fortunes depend. In doing so we will work to ensure cooperation among our economies. We approach this challenge with vigor, vision, and optimism.

We visit Europe determined to carry forward the spirit of peace and reconciliation among old adversaries and the power of our democratic ideals. The friendship between the American and German peoples—a great blessing that has grown rich and strong over our three centuries of shared national experience—is dramatic proof of how former enemies can be brought together again.

What better example of the success of democracy could we find than the strong new democratic systems in Spain and Portugal? We're pleased to salute the accomplishments of these countries, whose contribution to the New World was so great. The partnerships that we've built in Europe, the Atlantic community, and across the Pacific are the underlying foundation for the freedom that protects peace and security and strengthens the prosperity for hundreds of millions of people across this planet.

So, we leave tonight, eager to see again our European and Japanese friends and confident that, together, we can meet the challenge of expanding freedom and of preserving the blessings of the peace that we share.

Note: The President spoke to administration officials and members of the White House staff at 9:37 p.m. at the South Portico of the White House.

Executive Order 12513—Prohibiting Trade and Certain Other Transactions Involving Nicaragua
May 1, 1985

By the authority vested in me as President by the Constitution and laws of the United States of America, including the International Emergency Economic Powers Act (50 U.S.C. 1701 *et seq.*), the National Emergencies Act (50 U.S.C. 1601 *et seq.*), chapter 12 of Title 50 of the United States Code (50 U.S.C. 191 *et seq.*), and section 301 of Title 3 of the United States Code,

I, Ronald Reagan, President of the United States of America, find that the policies and actions of the Government of Nicaragua constitute an unusual and extraordinary threat to the national security and foreign policy of the United States and hereby declare a national emergency to deal with that threat.

I hereby prohibit all imports into the United States of goods and services of Nicaraguan origin; all exports from the United States of goods to or destined for Nicaragua, except those destined for the organized democratic resistance, and transactions relating thereto.

I hereby prohibit Nicaraguan air carriers from engaging in air transportation to or from points in the United States, and transactions relating thereto.

In addition, I hereby prohibit vessels of Nicaraguan registry from entering into United States ports, and transactions relating thereto.

The Secretary of the Treasury is delegated and authorized to employ all powers granted to me by the International Emergency Economic Powers Act to carry out the purposes of this Order.

The prohibitions set forth in this Order shall be effective as of 12:01 a.m., Eastern Daylight Time, May 7, 1985, and shall be transmitted to the Congress and published in the *Federal Register*.

RONALD REAGAN

The White House,
May 1, 1985.

[*Filed with the Office of the Federal Register, 10:48 a.m., May 1, 1985*]

Message to the Congress on Economic Sanctions Against Nicaragua
May 1, 1985

To the Congress of the United States:

Pursuant to section 204(b) of the International Emergency Economic Powers Act, 50 U.S.C. 1703, I hereby report to the Congress that I have exercised my statutory authority to declare a national emergency and to prohibit: (1) all imports into the United States of goods and services of Nicaraguan origin; (2) all exports from the United States of goods to or destined for Nicaragua except those destined for the organized democratic resistance; (3) Nicaraguan air carriers from engaging in air transportation to or from points in the United States; and (4) vessels of Nicaraguan registry from entering into United States ports.

These prohibitions will become effective as of 12:01 a.m., Eastern Daylight Time, May 7, 1985.

I am enclosing a copy of the Executive Order that I have issued making this declaration and exercising these authorities.

1. I have authorized these steps in response to the emergency situation created by the Nicaraguan Government's aggressive activities in Central America. Nicaragua's continuing efforts to subvert its neighbors, its rapid and destabilizing military buildup, its close military and security ties to Cuba and the Soviet Union and its imposition of Communist totalitarian internal rule have been described fully in the past several weeks. The current visit by Nicaraguan President Ortega to Moscow underscores this disturbing trend. The recent rejection by Nicaragua of my peace initiative, viewed in the light of the constantly rising pressure that Nicaragua's military buildup places on the democratic nations of the region, makes clear the urgent threat that Nicaragua's activities represent to the security of the region and, therefore, to the security and foreign policy of the United States. The activities of Nicaragua, supported by the Soviet Union and its allies, are incompatible with normal commercial relations.

2. In taking these steps, I note that during this month's debate on U.S. policy toward Nicaragua, many Members of Congress, both supporters and opponents of my proposals, called for the early application of economic sanctions.

3. I have long made clear that changes in Sandinista behavior must occur if peace is to be achieved in Central America. At this time, I again call on the Government of Nicaragua:
- to halt its export of armed insurrection, terrorism, and subversion in neighboring countries;
- to end its extensive military relationship with Cuba and the Soviet Bloc and remove their military and security personnel;
- to stop its massive arms buildup and help restore the regional military balance; and
- to respect, in law and in practice,

democratic pluralism and observance of full political and human rights in Nicaragua.

4. U.S. application of these sanctions should be seen by the Government of Nicaragua, and by those who abet it, as unmistakable evidence that we take seriously the obligation to protect our security interests and those of our friends. I ask the Government of Nicaragua to address seriously the concerns of its neighbors and its own opposition and to honor its solemn commitments to non-interference, non-alignment, respect for democracy, and peace. Failure to do so will only diminish the prospects for a peaceful settlement in Central America.

RONALD REAGAN

The White House,
May 1, 1985.

Statement by Principal Deputy Press Secretary Speakes on Economic Sanctions Against Nicaragua
May 1, 1985

The President has ordered the imposition by the United States of economic sanctions against the Government of Nicaragua under authority granted by the International Emergency Economic Powers Act and other authorities. The sanctions include a total embargo on trade with Nicaragua, notification of U.S. intent to terminate its Treaty of Friendship, Commerce, and Navigation with Nicaragua, and the suspension of service to the United States by Nicaraguan airlines and Nicarguan flag vessels. A report on these actions is being sent today to the Congress.

The President authorized these steps in response to the emergency situation created by the Nicaraguan Government's aggressive activities in Central America. Nicaragua's continuing efforts to subvert its neighbors, its rapid and destabilizing military buildup, its close military and security ties to Cuba and the Soviet Union, and its imposition of Communist totalitarian internal rule have been described fully in the past several weeks. Since the House of Representatives failed to act on the President's peace initiative, there have been further indications of this disturbing trend:

—the new ties between Nicaragua and the Soviet Union announced by TASS in connection with Daniel Ortega's current trip to Moscow;

—the recent apprehension in Honduras of several agents of the Nicaraguan state security service, who admitted that they have traveled to Honduras from Nicaragua in order to aid and assist Honduran insurgents;

—delivery last week to Nicaragua by the Soviet Union of additional MI–8/17 helicopters;

—the delivery last week by East Germany of a large shipment of military transport equipment to Nicaragua; and

—the rejection by Nicaraguan leaders of any possible church-mediated dialog with the democratic opposition of Nicaragua.

These events and the recent Nicaraguan rejection of the President's peace initiative, viewed in the light of the constantly rising pressure that Nicaragua's military buildup places on the democratic nations of the region, makes clear the urgent threat that Nicaragua's activities represent to the security of the region and, therefore, to the security and foreign policy of the United States. The activities of Nicaragua, supported by the Soviet Union and its allies, are incompatible with normal commerical relations.

During the month-long debate on U.S. policy toward Nicaragua, many Members of Congress, both supporters and opponents of the administration's proposals, called for the early application of economic sanctions. It should be understood, however, that the President does not consider the imposition of these sanctions to be a substitute for U.S. assistance to the unified democratic opposition.

The administration has long made clear that changes in Sandinista behavior must occur if peace is to be achieved in Central America. In making this announcement, the President again calls on the Government of Nicaragua:

—to halt its export of armed insurrection, terrorism, and subversion in neighboring countries;

—to end its extensive military relationship with Cuba and the Soviet bloc and remove their military personnel;

—to stop its massive arms buildup and help restore the regional military balance; and

—to respect, in law and in practice, democratic pluralism and observance of full political and human rights in Nicaragua.

The administration has repeatedly urged the Government of Nicaragua to respect its 1979 commitments to the OAS and more recently to the 1983 Contadora document of objectives, whose terms closely parallel our own basic objectives. Heretofore the Sandinistas have ignored or rejected all such appeals.

The American Embassy in Managua has just renewed with the Government of Nicaragua the President's strong endorsement for internal dialog and reiterated his firm intention to pursue U.S. interests and national objectives in Central America. In this regard, it should be noted that the measures being instituted by the President are easily rescinded if Nicaragua acts to relieve our concerns.

The President remains convinced that the church-mediated dialog between the Government of Nicaragua and the unified democratic opposition, as called for by the resistance on March 1 and in the President's April 4 peace proposal, could make a major contribution to resolution of conflict in the region. The President continues to believe that direct pressure presents the only effective means of moderating Nicaraguan behavior and is using the means available to him toward that end. He urges all Members of the Congress to support future requests for assistance to the Nicaraguan democratic resistance. He has also made it clear that the embargo does not apply to those goods destined for the organized democratic resistance nor will it apply to donations of articles such as food, clothing, and medicine intended to be used to relieve human suffering.

In the meantime, U.S. application of these measures should be seen by the Government of Nicaragua and by those who abet it as unmistakable evidence that we take seriously the obligation to protect our security interests and those of our friends. The President calls again on the Government of Nicaragua to address seriously the concerns of its neighbors and its own democratic opposition and to honor its solemn commitments to noninterference, nonalignment, respect for democracy, and peace. Failure to do so will only diminish the prospects for a peaceful settlement in Central America.

Bonn Economic Summit Political Declaration on the 40th Anniversary of the End of the Second World War
May 3, 1985

The Heads of State or Government of Canada, the French Republic, the Federal Republic of Germany, the Republic of Italy, Japan, the United Kingdom and the United States, with the President of the Commission of the European Community, meeting together in Bonn on the eve of the fortieth anniversary of the end of the Second World War, remember in grief all those who lost their lives in that time, whether by acts of war or as victims of inhumanity, repression and tyranny. We acknowledge the duty we owe to their memories, and to all those who follow after them, to uphold peace, freedom and justice in our countries and in the world.

We have learned the lessons of history. The end of the war marked a new beginning. As the sounds of battle ceased, we tackled the tasks of moral and spiritual renewal and physical reconstruction. Transcending the hostilities which had once divided us we initiated on the basis of common values a process for reconciliation and cooperation amongst us. Today, linked in a peaceful, secure and lasting friendship, we share in all our countries a commitment to freedom, democratic principles and human rights. We are proud that the Governments of our countries owe their legitimacy to the will of our people, expressed in free elections. We are proud that our people are free to say and write what they will, to practise the religions they profess, and to travel where they will. We are committed to assuring the maintenance of societies in which individual initiative and enterprise may flourish and the ideals of social justice, obligations and rights may be pursued.

We recognise that we can secure those aims, and meet both the opportunities and the challenges presented by technological and industrial change, more effectively in partnership than on our own. In Europe, the Community, the embodiment of reconciliation and common purpose, is growing in membership, strength and prosperity. The nations of the dynamic Pacific region are drawing ever closer together. The partnership of North America, Europe and Japan is a guarantee of peace and stability in the world.

Other nations that shared with ours in the agonies of the Second World War are divided from us by fundamental differences of political systems. We deplore the division of Europe. In our commitment to the ideals of peace, freedom and democracy we seek by peaceful means to lower the barriers that have arisen within Europe. We believe that the CSCE process with its promise of enhancing human rights provides an opportunity to increase confidence, cooperation and security in Europe. Considering the climate of peace and friendship we have reached amongst ourselves 40 years after the end of the war, we look forward to a state of peace in Europe in which the German people will regain its unity through free self-determination and in Asia we earnestly hope that a political environment will be created which permits the parties to overcome the division of the Korean peninsula in freedom.

As recognized in the Charter of the United Nations all countries have a joint responsibility to maintain international peace and security and to this end refrain from the threat and the use of force. We for our part share a determination to preserve the peace while protecting our democratic freedoms. To that end, each of us will work to maintain and strengthen a stable military balance at the lowest possible levels of forces, neither seeking superiority for ourselves nor neglecting our defenses. We are prepared to pursue a high-level dialogue to deal with the profound differences dividing East and West. We strongly support endeavours to strengthen the peace and enhance deterrence through the negotiation of meaningful reductions in existing levels of nuclear arms, limitations on conventional arms, the banning of chemical weapons and lessening the risks of conflict. We welcome the opening of negotiations in Geneva. We appreciate the positive proposals of the United States of America. We urge the Soviet Union to act positively and constructively in order to achieve significant agreements there.

We shall continue to seek to work with the developing countries, so as to help them to fight hunger and disease, to build free and prosperous societies, and to take their part in the community of nations committed to peace and freedom. We respect genuine nonalignment as an important contribution to international security and peace.

So, as we look back to the terrible suffering of the Second World War and the common experience of 40 years of peace and freedom, we dedicate ourselves and our countries anew to the creation of a world in which all peoples enjoy the blessings of peace, of justice, and of freedom from oppression, want and fear; a world in which individuals are able to fulfill their responsibilities for themselves, to their families and to their communities; a world in which all nations, large and small, combine to work together for a better future for all mankind.

Bonn Economic Summit Declaration on Sustained Growth and Higher Employment
May 4, 1985

1. Conscious of the responsibility which we bear, together with other Governments, for the future of the world economy and the preservation of natural resources, we, the Heads of State or Government of seven major industrial nations and the President of the Commission of the European Communities, meeting in Bonn from 2 to 4 May 1985, have discussed the economic outlook, problems, and prospects for our countries and the world.

2. World economic conditions are better than they have been for a considerable time. Since we last met, further progress has been achieved in bringing down inflation and strengthening the basis for growth. The recovery in the industrial countries has begun to spread to the developing world. The debt problems of developing countries, though far from solved, are being flexibly and effectively addressed.

3. Nevertheless, our countries still face important challenges. Above all, we need:
—to strengthen the ability of our economies to respond to new developments;
—to increase job opportunities;
—to reduce social inequalities;
—to correct persistent economic imbalances;
—to halt protectionism; and
—to improve the stability of the world monetary system.

4. Our discussions of these challenges have led us to the following conclusions:

(a) The best contribution we can make to a lasting new prosperity in which all nations can share is unremittingly to pursue, individually in our own countries and co-operatively together, policies conducive to sustained growth and higher employment.

(b) The prosperity of developed and developing countries has become increasingly linked. We will continue to work with the developing countries in a spirit of true partnership.

(c) Open multilateral trade is essential to global prosperity and we urge an early and substantial reduction of barriers to trade.

(d) We seek also to make the functioning of the world monetary system more stable and more effective.

(e) Economic progress and the preservation of the natural environment are necessary and mutually supportive goals. Effective environmental protection is a central element in our national and international policies.

I. Growth and Employment

5. In order to sustain non-inflationary growth and higher employment, we have agreed that:
—We will consolidate and enhance the progress made in bringing down inflation.
—We will follow prudent, and where necessary strengthened monetary and budgetary policies with a view to stable prices, lower interest rates and more productive investment. Each of our countries will exercise firm control over public spending in order to reduce budget deficits, when excessive, and, where necessary, the share of public spending in Gross National Product.
—We will work to remove obstacles to growth and encourage initiative and enterprise so as to release the creative energies of our peoples, while maintaining appropriate social policies for those in need.
—We will promote greater adaptability and responsiveness in all markets, particularly the labour market.
—We will encourage training to improve occupational skills, particularly for the young.
—We will exploit to the full the opportunities for prosperity and the creation of permanent jobs, provided by economic change and technological progress.

6. Building on these common principles, each of us has indicated the specific priorities for national policies.
—The President of the United States considers it essential to achieve a rapid and

appreciable cut in public expenditures and thus a substantial reduction in the budget deficit. He stresses also the need for further deregulation and for a reform of the tax system aimed at encouraging the efficient use of resources and stimulating new saving and investment.

—The President of the French Republic stresses the need to continue bringing down inflation, to modernize the means of production and to improve employment, to control public spending and to combat social inequality. In that context he attaches high priority to education, research and investment in high technologies with a view to sustained growth.

—The Government of the United Kingdom will continue to work to reduce inflation and to create the conditions for sustained growth. It will continue to keep public spending under strict control and maintain monetary discipline. It will promote the development of small and medium-sized businesses and advanced technological industries, and encourage initiative and enterprise and the creation of new job oppportunities.

—The Government of the Federal Republic of Germany attaches high priority to strengthening the flexibility and vigour of the economy in order to achieve a lasting improvement in growth and to create new jobs. Small and medium-sized businesses should be especially encouraged as well as high technologies. It will continue to reduce the claims of the public sector on the economy, the budget deficit and the burden of taxation.

—The Government of Japan considers it essential to persevere with its policy of budgetary discipline and strengthening market functions, particularly with a view to fostering investment. It intends to achieve further progress in deregulating financial markets, promoting the international role of the Yen, facilitating access to markets and encouraging growth in imports.

—The Italian Government gives priority to the further reduction of inflation and of the public deficit, while sustaining growth and investment. Particular emphasis will be put on incentives to create small and medium-sized industries, especially in the field of high technology, and to promote employment, especially for young people.

—The Government of Canada will focus on promoting investment and creating jobs in the private sector, on removing obstacles to sustained non-inflationary growth, on reducing the budget deficit and on restraining government expenditure. It will encourage entrepreneurial activities, with emphasis on the small and medium-sized business sectors.

—The Commission of the European Communities attaches high priority to completing a genuine internal market without barriers, which will eliminate rigidities and generate fresh economic growth on a Community-wide scale. A strengthened European Monetary System and closer economic convergence will further serve this end.

By pursuing these policies we will not only address our domestic problems, but at the same time contribute to an enduring growth of the world economy and a more balanced expansion of international trade.

II. Relations with Developing Countries

7. Sustained growth in world trade, lower interest rates, open markets and continued financing in amounts and on terms appropriate to each individual case are essential to enable developing countries to achieve sound growth and overcome their economic and financial difficulties. Flows of resources, including official development assistance, should be maintained and, wherever possible, increased, especially to the poorer countries. In particular, more stable long-term finance, such as direct investment from industrial countries, should be encouraged. We welcome longer-term debt restructuring agreements between debtor countries and commercial banks. We continue to stand ready, where appropriate, to negotiate further multi-year reschedulings of debts to governments and government agencies.

8. We continue to encourage the constructive dialogue with the developing

countries in the existing international institutions with a view to promoting their economic development and thereby their social and political stability. We emphasize the crucial role of, and the improved cooperation between, the International Monetary Fund and the World Bank Group in supporting policies by debtor countries necessary to strengthen the confidence of domestic and foreign creditors and investors, to mobilize domestic savings and to ensure efficient use of resources and sound long-term development. We agree to work to ensure that these institutions are equipped with the necessary resources and instruments, and we stand ready to discuss an increase in the resources available to the World Bank which may be necessary in the coming years. We remain concerned over the particular problems facing a number of developing countries that are neither among the poorest nor foremost among the group of major debtors. We agree that consideration should be given to easing the financial constraints of these countries on a case-by-case basis.

9. We are deeply concerned about the plight of African peoples who are suffering from famine and drought. We welcome the positive response from our citizens and from private organizations, as well as the substantial assistance provided by the governments of many countries and the establishment by the World Bank of the Special Facility for Subsahara Africa. We shall continue to supply emergency food aid. In addition, we shall intensify our co-operation with African countries to help them develop their economic potential and a long-term food strategy, based on their own agricultural programmes. We are prepared to promote increases in food production by supplying agricultural inputs such as seed, pesticides and fertilizers, within the framework of agricultural development projects. We agree upon the need to improve the existing early warning systems and improve transportation arrangements. Political obstacles in the countries concerned should not be allowed to stand in the way of the delivery of food to the hungry. We emphasize the need to examine the establishment of a research network on dry zone grains. We shall strengthen our co-operation with Afri-

can countries in fighting against desertification. Countinued efforts are needed by all countries in a position to contribute to any or all of this work. We call upon the Soviet Union and other Communist countries to assume their responsibilities in this regard. We have set up an expert group to prepare proposals for follow-up measures to be reported to Foreign Ministers by September 1985.

III. Multilateral Trading System and International Monetary System

10. Protectionism does not solve problems; it creates them. Further tangible progress in relaxing and dismantling existing trade restrictions is essential. We need new initiatives for strengthening the open multilateral trading system. We strongly endorse the agreement reached by the OECD Ministerial Council that a new GATT round should begin as soon as possible. Most of us think that this should be in 1986. We agree that it would be useful that a preparatory meeting of senior officials should take place in the GATT before the end of the summer to reach a broad consensus on subject matter and modalities for such negotiations. We also agree that active participation of a significant number of developed and developing countries in such negotiations is essential. We are looking to a balanced package for negotiation.

11. It is also essential to improve the functioning of the international monetary system. We take note that the Finance Ministers of the Group of Ten, at their meeting in Tokyo in June, intend to complete their current work on ways to improve the functioning of the monetary system and to put forward proposals, to be discussed at the next meeting of the Interim Committee of the International Monetary Fund in Seoul in October, with a view to making the international monetary system more stable and more effective.

IV. Environmental Policies

12. New approaches and strengthened international co-operation are essential to anticipate and prevent damage to the environment, which knows no national frontiers. We shall co-operate in order to solve

pressing environmental problems such as acid deposition and air pollution from motor vehicles and all other significant sources. We shall also address other concerns such as climatic change, the protection of the ozone layer and the management of toxic chemicals and hazardous wastes. The protection of soils, fresh water and the sea, in particular of regional seas, must be strengthened.

13. We shall harness both the mechanisms of governmental vigilance and the disciplines of the market to solve environmental problems. We shall develop and apply the "polluter pays" principle more widely. Science and technology must contribute to reconciling environmental protection and economic growth.

14. Improved and internationally harmonized techniques of environmental measurement are essential. We invite the environmental experts of the Technology, Growth and Employment Working Group to consult with the appropriate international bodies about the most efficient ways for achieving progress in this field.

15. We welcome the contribution made by the Environment Ministers to closer international co-operation on environmental concerns. We shall focus our co-operation within existing international bodies, especially the OECD. We shall work with developing countries for the avoidance of environmental damage and disasters worldwide.

V. Co-operation in Science and Technology

16. We are convinced that international co-operation in research and technology in major projects should be enhanced to make maximum use of our scientific potential. We recognize that such projects require appropriately shared participation and responsibility as well as adequate rules concerning access to the results achieved, the transfer of technology and the use of technologies involved.

17. We welcome the positive responses of the Member States of the European Space

Agency (ESA), Canada and Japan to the invitation of the President of the United States to co-operate in the United States Manned Space Station Programme on the basis of a genuine partnership and a fair and appropriate exchange of information, experience and technologies. Discussions on intergovernmental co-operation in development and utilization of permanently manned space stations will begin promptly. We also welcome the conclusions of the ESA Council on the need for Europe to maintain and expand its autonomous capability in space activity, and on the long-term European Space Plan and its objectives.

18. We welcome the report from the Technology, Growth and Employment Working Group on the work done in the eighteen areas of co-operation and invite the Group to complete its review by the end of the year. We welcome the positive contribution which the Ministerial Conference on "Technological Development and Employment" held in Venice has made towards wider acceptance of the role of technological change in promoting growth and employment. We also welcome the results of the Rambouillet Conference on Bioethics and thank the Federal Republic of Germany for its willingness to host a symposium on neurobiology in 1986.

19. We have agreed to meet again next year and have accepted the Japanese Prime Minister's invitation to meet in Japan.

Note: Chancellor Helmut Kohl of the Federal Republic of Germany read the declaration at 3:45 p.m. at the Bundestag. Also present for the reading were President Reagan, President François Mitterrand of France, Prime Minister Margaret Thatcher of the United Kingdom, Prime Minister Brian Mulroney of Canada, Prime Minister Yasuhiro Nakasone of Japan, Prime Minister Bettino Craxi of Italy, and Jacques Delors, President of the Commission of the European Communities.

Radio Address to the Nation on the Bonn Economic Summit
May 4, 1985

My fellow Americans:

Greetings from Europe. I'm speaking to you from Bonn, West Germany. It's 6 o'clock in the evening here, and we've just completed the 11th annual economic summit among the world's 7 major industrial democracies, together with the European Commission.

This year's summit is winding up on the eve of the 40th anniversary of the end of World War II. As is fitting, we celebrate the remarkable achievements of the world's family of free nations during these last four decades: peace has flourished; our economies have prospered, and technological advances have revolutionized our lives.

The friendly atmosphere of our meetings made it difficult to imagine that the United States, France, Britain, and Canada were pitted against countries which today are among freedom's staunchest supporters—the Federal Republic of Germany, Japan, and Italy. We celebrate our shared success, and we take heart that former enemies have been reconciled and are now partners and friends.

All of us are looking to the future to what could and should be the next 40 years of growth—growth of our economies and our freedom, growth of human progress in our own countries and around the world.

I was encouraged that the leaders present acknowledged how together we can sustain a future in which the freedom of our people can fully flourish in a world at peace.

On the economic front, I reviewed the progress America has enjoyed from reducing tax rates and increasing personal incentives. We all looked ahead to new and more vigorous efforts to reduce the heavy drag of government on our economies. I spoke of our own plans for a radical overhaul of our tax system, making it more simple and fair and bringing personal tax rates further down to strengthen the promise of growth well into the 1990's.

One great challenge all our countries face is government overspending leading to dangerous deficits, which, if left unchecked, will mortgage our future and impoverish our children. Few people realize that America's deficit, as a percentage of our total economy, is about the same as or less than most other summit countries. All of us must work harder to cut wasteful, unnecessary government spending.

On the trade front, it was clear that almost all of my summit partners want a 1986 target date to begin a new round of trade negotiations. These negotiations would be aimed at freer trade, more open markets, and greater competition worldwide. I'm heartened by the progress on this issue since last year's summit. Everyone now recognizes new negotiations are needed soon. We're pleased that plans for these negotiations, so important to world prosperity, have gained momentum.

In the area of security, we reaffirmed our determination to remain vigilant while working for progress in the Geneva arms control talks with the Soviets. The Soviet Union continues to be the major source of aggression in the world, building up its military forces far beyond any defensive needs and, through those forces and those of its satellites, promoting violence and repression across the globe, from Afghanistan to Cambodia to Nicaragua. So, we the democratic nations must continue to maintain our strength and keep the peace to enhance deterrence while striving, through negotiations, to achieve equitable and verifiable reductions in nuclear arsenals. The West will receive no gifts from the Soviets. Allied unity and resolve is the only message we can expect them to respect and respond to in a constructive way.

We also discussed our research on a nonnuclear defense, a defense not to harm people, but to prevent nuclear missiles from reaching our soil. I explained that this research will not produce results overnight and is no substitute for allied strategic modernization, but that over time, if our research proves out, we could lessen the threat of nuclear attack and begin to get rid of these dangerous weapons. Our host, Chancellor Kohl, welcomes SDI research, and other summit leaders said they'll examine how they might participate in this immensely hopeful undertaking.

One unexpected but encouraging development in the meetings here in Bonn was the real interest expressed by all the leaders in cracking down on international drug trafficking. Recognizing the terrible scourge of drugs and the danger they pose to our youth, we all agreed to intensify our efforts to tackle this problem. As a matter of fact, Nancy has just returned from Rome, where she had a private audience to discuss this great social problem with His Holiness Pope John Paul II, who has also spoken out

against this terrible evil.

The Bonn summit made clear that 40 years after defeating fascism, freedom continues to shower us with infinite blessings. But as long as another system drives relentlessly to expand and control, we must be freedom's protector. If we are, if we remain as strong and true as we must be, these next 40 years will truly be the golden age of democracy.

Until next week, thanks for listening, and God bless you.

Note: The President spoke at 6:06 p.m. from Schloss Gymnich in Bonn, Federal Republic of Germany.

Written Responses to Questions Submitted by Cambio 16 of Spain
April 25, 1985

Spanish Membership in NATO

Q. The relations between the United States and Spain are in an excellent moment now. However, there are four subjects that could disturb this relationship, the first of which is: What is your opinion about the promise of Prime Minister Felipe González to hold a referendum about whether Spain remains in NATO?

The President. Well, first let me talk about the purposes of my trip to Europe.

I am going to Europe for the Economic Summit of Industrialized Nations in Bonn and for state visits to Spain, Portugal, and the Federal Republic of Germany. It's a very important trip for me. I'll be working with the leaders of other countries to make progress on economic and political issues and to strengthen the ties between good friends. But I will be asking for European help and support in the greatest moral challenge of our time. I am going to ask help in encouraging freedom throughout the world.

Americans and Europeans have many great challenges ahead of us. There are some who say the West lacks energy—the moral and spiritual energy to carry forth our great hopes and plans, but that is just not true. Europe, including Spain, is greater

than ever in history. Europe is the treasury of centuries of thought and culture. As the leader of an allied country and friend, I value the ties between the United States and Europe; and the United States and Spain have never been closer.

One of the longstanding ties between Europe and the United States is a new one insofar as Spain is concerned. I am talking about the linkage to NATO. The position of the United States on NATO is very clear: Peace is strengthened whenever NATO is strengthened. Having Spain as a member strengthens NATO; I believe it also adds to Spain's own security.

And I am pleased, too, that Spain and Portugal are entering the European Economic Community. That is also something the United States has consistently supported.

Whether Spain stays in NATO is clearly a decision for Spain to make, as was the decision to seek partnership in the Economic Community. We respect the right of the Spanish people to make their own decision on this.

U.S. Military Bases in Spain

Q. In Spain there are big sectors that are

for the elimination of the North American bases in our country. Mr. González said that he would like a reduction in the amount of American soldiers. Has your administration plans to eliminate any base or to reduce the amount of military presence in Spain?

The President. The United States and Spain work together closely in the military field in accordance with the 1982 agreement on friendship, defense, and cooperation. We will continue to do so. The only plans we have are to do our best to carry out all our obligations under the terms of that agreement.

U.S. Deployment of Nuclear Weapons in Spain

Q. Last January this correspondent wrote about the Pentagon's plans to deploy nuclear weapons in eight Western countries, among them Spain. Was the Government of Spain aware of these plans? Which political steps would have been necessary for the Defense Department to carry out this nuclear weapons policy?

The President. There has been a lot of misunderstanding about this question. The 1982 agreement between the U.S. and Spain is unambiguous: No nuclear weapons can be stored or installed in Spain without the agreement of the Spanish Government. I stand by that agreement fully and completely.

United States-Spain Relations

Q. The fourth problem is: How do you explain that a friendly country like the United States, which has a treaty signed with Spain, sent two American diplomats to take pictures of the residence of Prime Minister González?

The President. I wouldn't comment on a report like that.

Q. My last question would be: As one of the principal leaders of the West of conservative ideology, what is your opinion, Mr. President, of Felipe González, one of the younger Socialist leaders in Western Europe?

The President. I was very impressed by Prime Minister González when he visited Washington in 1983, and I look forward to meeting with him again on my visit. I think we have an excellent working relationship, and we consult frequently on a range of issues. We both want to maintain the ties of friendship that are key to the relations between our two countries. As a Californian, I am particularly aware of the Spanish heritage that is a part of America. I will work with your Prime Minister to maintain and expand on the strong and cordial relations between our peoples.

Note: The questions and answers were released by the Office of the Press Secretary on May 5.

Written Responses to Questions Submitted by El Pais of Spain
April 29, 1985

Spanish Membership in NATO

Q. Soon you will be officially visiting Spain, where a large part of public opinion still thinks that the country should not be a part of NATO. How important for your administration, which already has secured continued access to military bases in Spain, is the permanence of Spain in NATO?

The President. For 37 years there has been a consensus in the United States and in Western Europe that a strong NATO is the best way to prevent another war from ever starting. In the United States NATO

enjoys the strong support of both our political parties. And the concept of collective security, which NATO so ably represents, is a belief that also transcends the lines of nearly all political parties in Europe.

Spain strengthens NATO, which in turn means that Spain's membership helps strengthen peace. But NATO is a free alliance of free nations, and whether Spain wishes to remain a member of NATO is clearly for Spain to decide.

Q. Is the announced referendum to decide on Spanish membership in NATO a point of concern in the relations between the two countries, and during your visit to Madrid will you try to get assurances from the Spanish Government about the permanence of Spain in the Atlantic alliance?

The President. I will be telling the people of Spain and my government hosts that the United States welcomes Spain as a NATO member and sees benefits to Spain, Europe, and the world from its membership in this peaceful alliance. But as I said in my previous answer, NATO is a free alliance. It is clearly up to Spain to decide whether it wishes to remain a member.

U.S. Military Bases in Spain

Q. Will your administration accept a reduction of the United States military presence in Spain or the closure of some bases in our country, as has been suggested by the Spanish Prime Minister, Mr. Felipe González, as a kind of political token to pay for maintaining Spain in NATO?

The President. The U.S. presence in Spain is an important element of the U.S. contribution to NATO and Western security. Granting access to U.S. forces is a contribution on the part of Spain.

The U.S. and Spain work together closely in the military field in accordance with the 1982 agreement on friendship, defense, and cooperation; we will continue to do so. The only plans we have are to do our best to carry out all our obligations under the terms of that agreement.

U.S. Deployment of Nuclear Weapons in Spain

Q. Important sectors of Spanish public opinion were worried when they heard recently that the United States had contingency plans to store nuclear warheads in Spanish territory. May your government guarantee that in the future nuclear weapons won't be deployed or stored in Spain without the consent of the Spanish people and that our country is not a part of the actual American contingency plans?

The President. The 1982 agreement on friendship, defense, and cooperation between our two countries specifically states that no nuclear weapons can be stored or installed in Spain without the agreement of the Spanish Government. The United States honors its obligations under that agreement fully and completely and will continue to do so.

Nicaragua

Q. As you know, the crisis in Central America is perceived in a quite different way in Europe and in the U.S. This perception is even more different in Spain. You have just announced a new proposal for peace in Nicaragua. Will you ask for the support of Mr. González for your plan, and do you think that Spain may help in some practical way to find a political solution to the crisis in the region?

The President. Sometimes people tend to overemphasize areas where there may be different points of view and overlook the much broader areas of agreement. In Central America, the U.S. and Spain both would like to see personal liberty, democratic governments, economic progress, and regional peace and stability.

One of the most important contributions Spain makes in fostering democracy is the example it has set over the past decade. Let me note, by the way, that when I took office 4 years ago only one of the five countries in Central America was a democracy. Now there are three democracies and one country well on the way back to democratic government.

In Nicaragua, we want to facilitate an internal dialog between the Communist Sandinistas and the democratic opposition. This would be an important adjunct to the efforts of the Contadora countries to find a regional solution, which we support.

Freedom works in Central America, as it does in other parts of the world. We want the Sandinistas to give their people freedom and their neighbors peace. I don't think that's too much to ask.

Note: The questions and answers were released by the Office of the Press Secretary on May 5.

Written Responses to Questions Submitted by EFE of Spain
April 29, 1985

Spanish Membership in NATO

Q. The most recent polls show that a majority of Spaniards are against the continued membership of Spain in NATO. If Spain withdrew from NATO or refused to join the military structure of the alliance, what could be, in your opinion, the implications and consequences for the United States, the European allies, Spain itself, and the future of U.S.-Spanish military cooperation? What incentives, if any, would you be willing to give Spain so as to facilitate its full membership in the alliance?

The President. Well, let's not start by getting into hypothetical questions of what might or might not happen. The main point I want to make is that NATO is the real peace movement. A strong Western alliance is the single surest guarantee of peace in Europe.

We believe that Spain's membership and eventual full participation in NATO strengthens NATO and strengthens Spain. But NATO is a free alliance of free peoples. We respect the right of the Spanish people to decide what they want to do.

United States-Spain Relations

Q. In the light of the moderate and pro-Western policies of the Spanish Socialist Government, have there been any changes in your initial attitude with regard to Socialist regimes in Western Europe? How would you characterize the state of U.S.-Spanish relations now, and what do you expect from your official visit to Madrid and talks with Spanish leaders?

The President. For me, the most important factor about a government is whether it believes in individual freedom and acts on that belief. The people of any democratic country render the final judgment on their government.

I think relations between the U.S. and Spain are very positive. Our two governments have an excellent working relationship in a range of areas, including security. In addition, we have developed close ties in trade, culture, and education.

During the visit, Secretary of State Shultz and Foreign Minister Morán will preside over a meeting of the U.S.-Spain Joint Council, the principal mechanism for implementing our 1982 agreement on friendship, defense, and cooperation. I will have important meetings with Spain's leaders. I expect that all aspects of this visit will further strengthen the ties between our peoples.

Q. The trade balance between the United States and Spain is still favorable to the United States. Which steps is your government prepared to take to reduce the imbalance. And in which way will bilateral trade relations be affected by Spain's membership in the European Economic Community?

The President. Trade is, of course, of major interest to both our countries. First, let's look at a few of the facts. Spanish exports to the United States have tripled over the last decade. They did so well in 1984—they went up by 60 percent—that the U.S. trade surplus with Spain was 10 times smaller that year than the year before. So, even though trade is not in perfect balance, it is heading in that direction.

In part, this shows how the sustained U.S. economic recovery is benefiting all our trading partners. I expect this trend to continue. What we all have to do now is act to ensure noninflationary growth and to keep our markets open to each other. I am committed to both goals.

I think it's a bit too early to predict all the economic pluses and minuses that will arise from Spain and Portugal joining the European Community. Let me just say that the United States has consistently supported their joining the Community and is pleased that negotiations on entry terms have been successfully concluded.

Nicaragua

Q. The Sandinistas have rejected your proposal for talks with the Nicaraguan rebels. Which options are you considering to keep the pressure on Nicaragua? Do they include the breakup of diplomatic relations, economic sanctions or a blockade, a collective military action through the Organization of American States or even a direct military action by the United States?

The President. Well, we are reviewing our relationship with the Communist Sandinista government, and we are not taking the Sandinistas' response to their democratic resistance forces as a legitimate one. We urge them to consider very carefully the proposal from their own people who are in opposition to them. It represents an opportunity to achieve the national reconciliation which is indispensable for peace in Nicaragua and in Central America. I know that many other governments, especially in Latin America and Europe, are urging the Sandinistas to reconsider their initial response. But the evidence of the last 5 years is that the Sandinistas only show flexibility when incentives are maintained.

The freedom fighters represent a critical element in this situation, because they truly represent the aspirations of the people of Nicaragua.

For our part, the United States will continue to work for peace, freedom, and democracy in Nicaragua and throughout Central America. We've seen great progress in El Salvador and other Central American countries in the past few years. There is no reason for the countries of the region to have their progress toward democracy subverted by the Sandinistas.

We believe a peaceful solution through the Contadora process and through reconciliation between the Sandinistas and their opposition within Nicaragua is still possible. That is what we are working toward. The problem in Nicaragua is the Communist Sandinistas; they are the ones who are depriving their own people of the freedom they seek.

Latin America

Q. Given the renewed American emphasis on promoting democracy and stability in Latin America, what concrete steps are you prepared to take to foster the return of democracy to Chile and Paraguay and to help the debt-ridden countries of the region to solve their economic plight? Would you favor a moratorium on debt payments and/or an international conference as the Latin American leaders have been calling for?

The President. Our interests in Chile and Paraguay are the same as elsewhere in Latin America—to promote personal liberty, democracy, peace, and economic development. In Chile we are working to promote national reconciliation and dialog; through these efforts we hope to see an early return to democracy there.

United States economic growth has already contributed greatly to the recovery of Latin American economies by providing an expanding market for their exports. Latin American and Caribbean exports to the U.S. rose 15 percent in 1984.

Beyond that, the U.S. Government is taking a variety of steps to help Latin American economies. We provide trade credits and guarantees. We participate in the so-called Paris Club restructurings to provide relief on official debt.

I should stress, though, that sound economic policies by the debtor nations themselves are also essential. Together, all these efforts should lead to improved conditions for growth and private investment, so that the Latin American nations can achieve sustainable economic growth. We favor continued dialog on debt-related issues and problems, both bilaterally and in appropriate multilateral fora. However, like the major debtor countries themselves, we do not think that a debt moratorium would advance the long-term interests of the countries involved.

The countries of Central and South America and our neighbor to the north, Canada, are vitally important to the United States. We seek a Western Hemisphere that lives in peace, democracy, freedom, and prosperity. And I have to say I believe we are making great strides in those directions.

Note: The questions and answers were released by the Office of the Press Secretary on May 5.

Written Responses to Questions Submitted by Diario De Noticias of Portugal
April 29, 1985

U.S. Deployment of Nuclear Weapons

Q. The American press recently published a report on U.S. plans to deploy nuclear weapons in various strategic points in Europe, including the Azores, in case of an emergency. The Portuguese Government claims never to have been contacted on the subject. Does this plan exist? Has the U.S. considered such a possibility?

The President. These press reports are very misleading. Both Portugal and the United States are members of the NATO alliance, and NATO's policy with regard to nuclear weapons—a policy to which the U.S. strictly adheres—was set out by the NATO heads of government in the 1957 Paris agreement. There it was agreed that deployments of nuclear warheads and missiles would take place only by agreement of the NATO states directly involved. We stand by that agreement fully and completely.

U.S. Military Bases in Portugal

Q. Would it be correct to say in light of international political developments that the strategic importance of Lajes base in the Azores has increased in recent years?

The President. Lajes has been important to Western defense ever since World War II. At that time it played a significant role in protecting the Atlantic sealanes. Lajes continues to play that role today. The core of Atlantic security remains the defense of the territorial integrity of the NATO member states. In that respect Lajes' role as part of the air bridge between the U.S. and Europe is also an important element of collective security.

Q. Given the strategic geographical position of mainland Portugal, does the administration intend to negotiate in the near future for the installation of new military bases in Portugal?

The President. We value the close cooperation which exists between Portugal and the United States in defense matters. We are working to assist Portugal's military modernization effort so that Portugal can fulfill its desire to play a more active role in the defense of the West through NATO. While we have no new negotiations ongoing at present, our defense cooperation was recently strengthened by the agreements in December 1983 and March 1984 regarding our continued access to the Portuguese base at Lajes and the installation of a satellite tracking station in southern Portugal. There are, however, ongoing discussions implementing the agreement on the satellite tracking station.

U.S.-Portugal Relations

Q. Given the political differences between President Eanes and Prime Minister Mário Soares—a phenomenon of Portuguese internal politics generally called a "conflict between organs of sovereignty"—has this, in your view, caused difficulties in the bilateral relations between the U.S. and Portugal?

The President. The premise of your question concerns Portuguese internal politics and that is not a matter for me to discuss. The point to be remembered is that relations between the United States and Portugal are excellent. Areas of cooperation have expanded substantially over the past 10 years as our two countries have found, in a common commitment to democracy, a broader and firmer basis for our traditional friendship as peoples and allies. Defense cooperation is certainly an important and constructive part of our relationship.

But it would be a mistake to overlook the many other ways in which our two countries and peoples are linked together. There are rich human ties between Portugal and the many Americans who are Portuguese by birth or descent. The flow of our peoples back and forth across the Atlantic is growing, particularly as more and more Americans discover the beauties of your country and visit Portugal as tourists. The United States has sought to assist Portugal's development and infrastructure in a number of ways, both through technical and financial assistance and in the construction of schools, health centers, and other facilities.

Trade between our two countries is substantial and the U.S. represents a good market—which is largely untapped, but rapidly expanding—for Portuguese exports. In 1984 U.S. merchandise imports rose over 25 percent, helping Portugal's overall exports to the U.S. increase by 70 percent. United States firms are increasingly looking at investment opportunities as Portugal takes steps to improve the climate for foreign investment, particularly in the private sector. In addition, Portugal's creation of the Luso-American Foundation will provide an important new vehicle for cooperation between us in a number of economic, technical, and other areas.

International Trade

Q. The American economic miracle has had negative effects on the smaller economies, such as the Portuguese, and especially in the countries of the Third World, becoming ever more backward and impoverished. What do you judge to be the best measures that could be adopted to improve the commercial balance with Portugal, unbalanced heavily in favor of the U.S.? What do you think could be done to close the ever-growing gap between industrial countries and those still developing?

The President. The sustained recovery and growth of the U.S. economy has had beneficial effects on the international economy. About one-quarter of our economic growth has spilled over to other countries, helping to promote recovery abroad, both by our OECD trading partners, such as Portugal, and elsewhere. Furthermore, the strong U.S. dollar has given a competitive advantage to foreign producers, including those of Portugal. So, in 1984 alone, Portugal's overall exports to the U.S. increased by 70 percent.

The best thing we can do at this point is to keep our markets open to ensure that growth continues and strengthens. I am committed to doing that and to fighting protectionism. The best thing the developing countries can do for themselves, it seems to me, is to maintain market-related economic policies that will assure that they

share in the benefits of worldwide economic growth. All our trading partners, both the developed and developing countries, should work together to resolve specific trade problems as they occur and to obtain agreement to the commencement of a new round of trade negotiations early next year.

U.S. Relations With Angola and Mozambique

Q. What conditions need to be met for the normalization of relations between the U.S. and the Portuguese-speaking countries of Africa, namely Angola and Mozambique? What role could Portugal play in this process?

The President. Our relations with Mozambique have developed rapidly in the recent past, and I would not characterize them as being anything other than normal today. We maintain accredited Ambassadors in each other's capitals. We and the Mozambican Government are working together to implement programs of U.S. economic development assistance. The U.S. also has made major contributions of food to relieve the serious shortages created by drought conditions in Mozambique.

We also have been in frequent direct contact with the Angolan Government in an effort to facilitate a negotiated solution to the conflict between South Africa and Angola and to secure the implementation of United Nations Resolution 435, calling for the independence of Namibia. It has been the policy of the last three administrations, however, that formal diplomatic relations with Angola could not be considered until the issue of Cuban troops there has been resolved.

With regard to Portugal's role, we value its experience and knowledge of Africa. Portugal has played a constructive role in the process leading to the recent expansion of relations between Mozambique and the West, including specifically the United States. We have and will continue to consult closely with your government as we address the issues of the region, including those involving Mozambique and Angola.

Note: The questions and answers were released by the Office of the Press Secretary on May 5.

563

Remarks at a Commemorative Ceremony at Bergen-Belsen Concentration Camp in the Federal Republic of Germany
May 5, 1985

Chancellor Kohl and honored guests, this painful walk into the past has done much more than remind us of the war that consumed the European Continent. What we have seen makes unforgettably clear that no one of the rest of us can fully understand the enormity of the feelings carried by the victims of these camps. The survivors carry a memory beyond anything that we can comprehend. The awful evil started by one man, an evil that victimized all the world with its destruction, was uniquely destructive of the millions forced into the grim abyss of these camps.

Here lie people—Jews—whose death was inflicted for no reason other than their very existence. Their pain was borne only because of who they were and because of the God in their prayers. Alongside them lay many Christians—Catholics and Protestants.

For year after year, until that man and his evil were destroyed, hell yawned forth its awful contents. People were brought here for no other purpose but to suffer and die—to go unfed when hungry, uncared for when sick, tortured when the whim struck, and left to have misery consume them when all there was around them was misery.

I'm sure we all share similar first thoughts, and that is: What of the youngsters who died at this dark stalag? All was gone for them forever—not to feel again the warmth of life's sunshine and promise, not the laughter and the splendid ache of growing up, nor the consoling embrace of a family. Try to think of being young and never having a day without searing emotional and physical pain—desolate, unrelieved pain.

Today, we've been grimly reminded why the commandant of this camp was named "the Beast of Belsen." Above all, we're struck by the horror of it all—the monstrous, incomprehensible horror. And that's what we've seen but is what we can never understand as the victims did. Nor with all our compassion can we feel what the survivors feel to this day and what they will feel as long as they live. What we've felt and are expressing with words cannot convey the suffering that they endured. That is why history will forever brand what happened as the Holocaust.

Here, death ruled, but we've learned something as well. Because of what happened, we found that death cannot rule forever, and that's why we're here today. We're here because humanity refuses to accept that freedom of the spirit of man can ever be extinguished. We're here to commemorate that life triumphed over the tragedy and the death of the Holocaust—overcame the suffering, the sickness, the testing and, yes, the gassings. We're here today to confirm that the horror cannot outlast hope, and that even from the worst of all things, the best may come forth. Therefore, even out of this overwhelming sadness, there must be some purpose, and there is. It comes to us through the transforming love of God.

We learn from the Talmud that: "It was only through suffering that the children of Israel obtained three priceless and coveted gifts: The Torah, the Land of Israel, and the World to Come." Yes, out of this sickness—as crushing and cruel as it was—there was hope for the world as well as for the world to come. Out of the ashes—hope, and from all the pain—promise.

So much of this is symbolized today by the fact that most of the leadership of free Germany is represented here today. Chancellor Kohl, you and your countrymen have made real the renewal that had to happen. Your nation and the German people have been strong and resolute in your willingness to confront and condemn the acts of a hated regime of the past. This reflects the courage of your people and their devotion to freedom and justice since the war. Think how far we've come from that time when despair made these tragic victims wonder if anything could survive.

As we flew here from Hanover, low over

the greening farms and the emerging springtime of the lovely German countryside, I reflected, and there must have been a time when the prisoners at Bergen-Belsen and those of every other camp must have felt the springtime was gone forever from their lives. Surely we can understand that when we see what is around us—all these children of God under bleak and lifeless mounds, the plainness of which does not even hint at the unspeakable acts that created them. Here they lie, never to hope, never to pray, never to love, never to heal, never to laugh, never to cry.

And too many of them knew that this was their fate, but that was not the end. Through it all was their faith and a spirit that moved their faith.

Nothing illustrates this better than the story of a young girl who died here at Bergen-Belsen. For more than 2 years Anne Frank and her family had hidden from the Nazis in a confined annex in Holland where she kept a remarkably profound diary. Betrayed by an informant, Anne and her family were sent by freight car first to Auschwitz and finally here to Bergen-Belsen.

Just 3 weeks before her capture, young Anne wrote these words: "It's really a wonder that I haven't dropped all my ideals because they seem so absurd and impossible to carry out. Yet I keep them because in spite of everything I still believe that people are good at heart. I simply can't

build up my hopes on a foundation consisting of confusion, misery, and death. I see the world gradually being turned into a wilderness. I hear the ever approaching thunder which will destroy us too; I can feel the suffering of millions and yet, if I looked up into the heavens I think that it will all come right, that this cruelty too will end and that peace and tranquility will return again." Eight months later, this sparkling young life ended here at Bergen-Belsen. Somewhere here lies Anne Frank.

Everywhere here are memories—pulling us, touching us, making us understand that they can never be erased. Such memories take us where God intended His children to go—toward learning, toward healing, and, above all, toward redemption. They beckon us through the endless stretches of our heart to the knowing commitment that the life of each individual can change the world and make it better.

We're all witnesses; we share the glistening hope that rests in every human soul. Hope leads us, if we're prepared to trust it, toward what our President Lincoln called the better angels of our nature. And then, rising above all this cruelty, out of this tragic and nightmarish time, beyond the anguish, the pain and the suffering for all time, we can and must pledge: Never again.

Note: The President spoke at 12:10 p.m. after laying a wreath at a camp memorial. Following his remarks, the President and Chancellor Kohl traveled to Bitburg.

Remarks at a Joint German-American Military Ceremony at Bitburg Air Base in the Federal Republic of Germany
May 5, 1985

Thank you very much. I have just come from the cemetery where German war dead lay at rest. No one could visit there without deep and conflicting emotions. I felt great sadness that history could be filled with such waste, destruction, and evil, but my heart was also lifted by the knowledge that from the ashes has come hope and that from the terrors of the past we have built

40 years of peace, freedom, and reconciliation among our nations.

This visit has stirred many emotions in the American and German people, too. I've received many letters since first deciding to come to Bitburg cemetery; some supportive, others deeply concerned and questioning, and others opposed. Some old wounds have been reopened, and this I regret very much because this should be a time of healing.

To the veterans and families of American servicemen who still carry the scars and feel the painful losses of that war, our gesture of reconciliation with the German people today in no way minimizes our love and honor for those who fought and died for our country. They gave their lives to rescue freedom in its darkest hour. The alliance of democratic nations that guards the freedom of millions in Europe and America today stands as living testimony that their noble sacrifice was not in vain.

No, their sacrifice was not in vain. I have to tell you that nothing will ever fill me with greater hope than the sight of two former war heroes who met today at the Bitburg ceremony; each among the bravest of the brave; each an enemy of the other 40 years ago; each a witness to the horrors of war. But today they came together, American and German, General Matthew B. Ridgway and General Johanner Steinhoff, reconciled and united for freedom. They reached over the graves to one another like brothers and grasped their hands in peace.

To the survivors of the Holocaust: Your terrible suffering has made you ever vigilant against evil. Many of your are worried that reconciliation means forgetting. Well, I promise you, we will never forget. I have just come this morning from Bergen-Belsen, where the horror of that terrible crime, the Holocaust, was forever burned upon my memory. No, we will never forget, and we say with the victims of that Holocaust: Never again.

The war against one man's totalitarian dictatorship was not like other wars. The evil war of nazism turned all values upside down. Nevertheless, we can mourn the German war dead today as human beings crushed by a vicious ideology.

There are over 2,000 buried in Bitburg cemetery. Among them are 48 members of the SS—the crimes of the SS must rank among the most heinous in human history— but others buried there were simply soldiers in the German Army. How many were fanatical followers of a dictator and willfully carried out his cruel orders? And how many were conscripts, forced into service during the death throes of the Nazi war

machine? We do not know. Many, however, we know from the dates on their tombstones, were only teenagers at the time. There is one boy buried there who died a week before his 16th birthday.

There were thousands of such soldiers to whom nazism meant no more than a brutal end to a short life. We do not believe in collective guilt. Only God can look into the human heart, and all these men have now met their supreme judge, and they have been judged by Him as we shall all be judged.

Our duty today is to mourn the human wreckage of totalitarianism, and today in Bitburg cemetery we commemorated the potential good in humanity that was consumed back then, 40 years ago. Perhaps if that 15-year-old soldier had lived, he would have joined his fellow countrymen in building this new democratic Federal Republic of Germany, devoted to human dignity and the defense of freedom that we celebrate today. Or perhaps his children or his grandchildren might be among you here today at the Bitburg Air Base, where new generations of Germans and Americans join together in friendship and common cause, dedicating their lives to preserving peace and guarding the security of the free world.

Too often in the past each war only planted the seeds of the next. We celebrate today the reconciliation between our two nations that has liberated us from that cycle of destruction. Look at what together we've accomplished. We who were enemies are now friends; we who were bitter adversaries are now the strongest of allies.

In the place of fear we've sown trust, and out of the ruins of war has blossomed an enduring peace. Tens of thousands of Americans have served in this town over the years. As the mayor of Bitburg has said, in that time there have been some 6,000 marriages between Germans and Americans, and many thousands of children have come from these unions. This is the real symbol of our future together, a future to be filled with hope, friendship, and freedom.

The hope that we see now could sometimes even be glimpsed in the darkest days of the war. I'm thinking of one special story—that of a mother and her young son living alone in a modest cottage in the middle of the woods. And one night as the Battle of the Bulge exploded not far away, and around them, three young American soldiers arrived at their door—they were standing there in the snow, lost behind enemy lines. All were frostbitten; one was badly wounded. Even though sheltering the enemy was punishable by death, she took them in and made them a supper with some of her last food. Then, they heard another knock at the door. And this time four German soldiers stood there. The woman was afraid, but she quickly said with a firm voice, "There will be no shooting here." She made all the soldiers lay down their weapons, and they all joined in the makeshift meal. Heinz and Willi, it turned out, were only 16; the corporal was the oldest at 23. Their natural suspicion dissolved in the warmth and the comfort of the cottage. One of the Germans, a former medical student, tended the wounded American.

But now, listen to the rest of the story through the eyes of one who was there, now a grown man, but that young lad that had been her son. He said: "The Mother said grace. I noticed that there were tears in her eyes as she said the old, familiar words, 'Komm, Herr Jesus. Be our guest.' And as I looked around the table, I saw tears, too, in the eyes of the battle-weary soldiers, boys again, some from America, some from Germany, all far from home."

That night—as the storm of war tossed the world—they had their own private armistice. And the next morning, the German corporal showed the Americans how to get back behind their own lines. And they all shook hands and went their separate ways. That happened to be Christmas Day, 40 years ago.

Those boys reconciled briefly in the midst of war. Surely we allies in peacetime should honor the reconciliation of the last 40 years.

To the people of Bitburg, our hosts and the hosts of our servicemen, like that generous woman 40 years ago, you make us feel very welcome. *Vielen dank.* [Many thanks.]

And to the men and women of Bitburg Air Base, I just want to say that we know that even with such wonderful hosts, your job is not an easy one. You serve around the clock far from home, always ready to defend freedom. We're grateful, and we're very proud of you.

Four decades ago we waged a great war to lift the darkness of evil from the world, to let men and women in this country and in every country live in the sunshine of liberty. Our victory was great, and the Federal Republic, Italy, and Japan are now in the community of free nations. But the struggle for freedom is not complete, for today much of the world is still cast in totalitarian darkness.

Twenty-two years ago President John F. Kennedy went to the Berlin Wall and proclaimed that he, too, was a Berliner. Well, today freedom-loving people around the world must say: I am a Berliner. I am a Jew in a world still threatened by anti-Semitism. I am an Afghan, and I am a prisoner of the Gulag. I am a refugee in a crowded boat foundering off the coast of Vietnam. I am a Laotian, a Cambodian, a Cuban, and a Miskito Indian in Nicaragua. I, too, am a potential victim of totalitarianism.

The one lesson of World War II, the one lesson of nazism, is that freedom must always be stronger than totalitarianism and that good must always be stronger than evil. The moral measure of our two nations will be found in the resolve we show to preserve liberty, to protect life, and to honor and cherish all God's children.

That is why the free, democratic Federal Republic of Germany is such a profound and hopeful testament to the human spirit. We cannot undo the crimes and wars of yesterday nor call back the millions back to life, but we can give meaning to the past by learning its lessons and making a better future. We can let our pain drive us to greater efforts to heal humanity's suffering.

Today I've traveled 220 miles from Bergen-Belsen, and, I feel, 40 years in time. With the lessons of the past firmly in our minds, we've turned a new, brighter page in history.

One of the many who wrote me about this visit was a young woman who had recently been bas mitzvahed. She urged me to lay the wreath at Bitburg cemetery in honor of the future of Germany. And that is what we've done.

On this 40th anniversary of World War II, we mark the day when the hate, the evil, and the obscenities ended, and we commemorate the rekindling of the democratic spirit in Germany.

There's much to make us hopeful on this historic anniversary. One of the symbols of that hate—that could have been that hope, a little while ago, when we heard a German band playing the American National Anthem and an American band playing the German National Anthem. While much of the world still huddles in the darkness of oppression, we can see a new dawn of freedom sweeping the globe. And we can see in the new democracies of Latin America, in the new economic freedoms and prosperity in Asia, in the slow movement toward peace in the Middle East, and in the strengthening alliance of democratic nations in Europe and America that the light from that dawn is growing stronger.

Together, let us gather in that light and walk out of the shadow. Let us live in peace.

Thank you, and God bless you all.

Note: The President spoke at 3:33 p.m. after laying a wreath in a nearby military cemetery in Bitburg. He was accompanied by Chancellor Kohl. Following the ceremony, the President returned to Schloss Gymnich in Bonn, where he stayed during his visit to Germany.

Toast at the State Dinner in Bonn, Federal Republic of Germany
May 5, 1985

President and Mrs. von Weizsäcker, Chancellor and Mrs. Kohl, honored guests, Nancy and I want to thank you for your warm and gracious hospitality. Our visit to the Federal Republic of Germany has been a wonderful and enriching experience. Today was especially moving. We cannot fully understand the long road we've all traveled since 1945 unless we remember the beginnings. By standing before mass graves at a spot such as Bergen-Belsen, we could begin—but only begin—to feel the suffering of so many innocent people and to sense the horror which confronted our leaders 40 years ago. And by joining Chancellor Kohl in Bitburg, we could better understand the price paid by the German people for the crimes of the Third Reich.

Today, as 40 years ago, the thought uppermost in our minds must remain: Never again. You, Mr. President, embody the values which we're working to protect today. Your distinguished career in business and politics, your engagement in church affairs, are exemplary. Over the years, Americans have been especially moved by our ability to articulate the soul of the German nation. You have been eloquent in your message of sorrow over Germany's historic burdens. You've been inspiring in your offer of hope. I remember so vividly my visit to the great city of Berlin in 1982. Your achievement in restoring confidence and hope to democracy's city was a service to the entire West.

The camaraderie of this evening, the good will that we've enjoyed, reflect the deep and abiding friendship between our two peoples, an affection that overcame the bitterness of war. The passage penned by Schiller in "Wilhelm Tell" says, "What's old collapses, times change and new life blossoms in the ruins." Forty years ago, our friendship blossomed in the ruins. Today the bond between us is a powerful force for good, improving the material well-being of our peoples, helping keep us at peace, and protecting our freedom. In this year, studded with anniversaries, let us remember to celebrate the beginning of friendship as well as the end of war.

You, Mr. President, and Chancellor Kohl have been among the most thoughtful spokesmen for the spirit of the Federal Republic. Through you we've experienced the warmth and depth of German-American solidarity. By working together as friends and allies we have accomplished more than any visionary could have predicted.

Europe has enjoyed 40 years of peace. This did not just happen by chance. Peace has been the outcome of decisions made by individuals with the wisdom to see what was needed and the courage to do it. Chancellor Kohl, I understand and appreciate how difficult it was for you to stand firm and refuse to back away from the decision to modernize NATO's nuclear deterrent. By moving forward we balanced off the threat created by the massive Soviet buildup of the last decade and gave substance to our arms reduction talks in Geneva.

What we seek in Geneva is an agreement which will permit us to reduce significantly the size of nuclear arsenals. For too long we have lived in the shadow of nuclear destruction. The United States is now moving forward with a research program which could offer a way to diminish the threat of nuclear annihilation. I hope that the Federal Republic will join us in this effort to find ways to enhance deterrence based on protection instead of retaliation, on systems capable of destroying attacking missiles but incapable of threatening people.

Today, very appropriately, marks the 30th anniversary of the Federal Republic's entry into NATO. As always, our collective effort will be founded on one simple truth: NATO threatens no one; NATO protects the peace.

It's especially fitting that on this the anniversary of the end of a worldwide conflagration that the leaders of the seven great industrial democracies met here in the Federal Republic to exchange ideas on economic issues and matters of state. As individuals elected by the people to represent their values as well as their interests, our good will and cooperation reflect the highest aspirations of the free people of this planet. The freedom our peoples have enjoyed in these last four decades has opened the door to a future in which our potential will be limited only by our imagination. The free people of the world, especially here in the Federal Republic and in the United States, stand together on the edge of this new era, a time of space stations, conquering diseases, and great leaps in the standard of living for all mankind.

Ahead of us may be a time when the artificial barriers that divide Germany, and indeed all Europe, are cast away, a time when there will be no need for weapons or barbed wire or walls in Berlin.

These are not dreams. I believe from the bottom of my heart we have every reason for confidence. The future is on the side of the free. The Federal Republic and the United States have proven that. Our 40 years of friendship are reason enough to rejoice, but let us look to the next 40 years, to the freedom and peace our children and their children will enjoy, to the boundless progress they will make, and to the friendship between Germany and the United States, which will serve them well just as it has served us.

Let me then offer a toast to the many friends gathered here tonight and especially to our shared future. To the President, to Germany, to America, and to freedom throughout Europe.

Note: President Reagan spoke at 9:25 p.m. at Schloss Augustusburg in response to a toast by President von Weizsäcker.

Remarks to Citizens in Hambach, Federal Republic of Germany
May 6, 1985

Chancellor Kohl, honored guests, and my young friends of Germany and Europe, *danke schon.* [thank you]. Nancy and I are very happy to be with you and to see that the ideals of the first Hambach Fest live on today. To join you at this site so rich in history makes this a very special day.

Already, you have given us a gift of hope and beauty from the site of this sturdy old castle in the spirit of your youth and the spirit of Germany's future and, yes, from the warmth that we feel in German hearts.

I may not say it well, but I can truly say, *wir fuellen ganz hier zu hause* [we feel completely at home here].

In welcoming us, you honor the 237 million Americans that I'm privileged to represent. I might add that, as you've been told, more Americans trace their roots to this land, these towns, and your families than to almost any other place or people in the world.

It's fitting that we meet where so much that is good and worthy of our two nations began. From here in the Rhineland-Palatinate, thousands left to cross a mighty ocean, to push back America's frontiers and to help us win a great struggle for independence. You have been told that, yes, one regiment came from Zweibrücken, led by Count Christian and Viscount Wilhelm von Frobach. They fought by our side. They were with us the day we won the historic battle of Yorktown, the day the American Revolution triumphed.

And it was from this hill on this good soil that freedom was proclaimed and the dream of democracy and national unity came alive in the German soul.

I am only a visitor to your country, but I am proud to stand with you today by these walls of Schloss Hambach. They are walls of time that cradle the glorious past and that reach toward the promise of a future written for eternity across this wide open sky. Think back to that first Festival of Freedom that was held here in 1832. What noble vision it was that inspired and emboldened your first patriots—not violence, not destruction of society, and not some far-flung utopian scheme. No, their vision and cry were revolutionary in the truest sense of that word. Those first patriots cried out for a free, democratic, and united Germany, and we do so again today. They cried out for solidarity with freedom fighters in Poland, and we do so again today. And they waved the colors of black, red, and gold to announce rebirth of human spirit and dignity, and those colors wave proudly here today.

The dream was voiced by many that year. But there was one student, and I am told that his name was Karl Heinrich Bruggemann, whose passion and eloquence echo with us still. "All Germanic peoples," Karl said, "will and must acquire greater dignity; the times of tyranny have passed. Free states will flourish, patriotic nations will in future celebrate the New Europe."

The new Europe. One hundred fifty-three years have come and gone, bringing great change and progress. But the new Europe is yet to be complete. Why is this so? We know the answer. It is not that freedom has not worked for the European people, but that too many Europeans have been forbidden to work for freedom. It's not that democracy was tried and found wanting, but that some forbid democracy to be tried because they knew it would succeed.

Europe today—divided by concrete walls, by electrified barbed wire, and by mined and manicured fields, killing fields—it is a living portrait of the most compelling truth of our time: The future belongs to the free.

You are living in the springtime of your lives. The world needs your idealism, your courage, and your good works. From one whose own life spans many years—my critics in America would tell you too many years—[*laughter*]—permit me to offer you some observations about the future, about the creative future that can be ours if only we apply our wisdom and will to heed the lessons of history. Let me speak to you for a moment about your responsibilities and your opportunities.

In many ways, the challenges of 1832, when thousands of young Germans came here to protest repression, were similar to those you face today. By that year of 1832, Germany was changing rapidly. The Industrial Revolution was sweeping across Europe. But in dealing with these new problems, strong forces inside and outside Germany resisted democracy and national unity.

The great hopes that arose in 1832 and again in 1848 were set back. But despite the difficulties of democratic movements, we know for sure that totalitarianism, by whatever name, will never fulfill German aspirations within a united Europe.

The cause of German unity is bound up with the cause of democracy. As Chancellor Kohl said in his state of the nation address last February, "Europe is divided because part of Europe is not free; Germany is divided because part of Germany is not free." And democracy will only be complete, Europe will only be united, when all Germans and all Europeans are finally free.

But even if national unity cannot be achieved immediately, you, the youth of Germany, you who are Germany's future, can show the power of democratic ideals by committing yourselves to the cause of freedom here in Europe and everywhere.

You know some may not like to hear it, but history is not on the side of those who manipulate the meaning of words like revolution, freedom, and peace. History is on the side of those struggling for a true revolution of peace with freedom all across the world.

Nothing could make our hearts more glad than to see the day when there will be no more walls, no more guns to keep loved ones apart. Nothing could bring greater happiness than to reach an agreement that will rid the Earth of nuclear weapons forever, and we will never stop praying, never stop working, never stop striving one moment to bring that day closer.

But my young friends, I must also plead for realism, for unless and until there's a changing by the other side, the United States must fulfill a commitment of its own—to the survival of liberty. The first frontier of European liberty begins in Berlin, and I assure you that America will stand by you in Europe, and America will stand by you in Berlin.

Understanding the true nature of totalitarianism will be worth as much to us as any weapons system in preserving peace. Realism is the beginning of wisdom, and where there's wisdom and courage, there will be safety and security, and they will be yours.

Your future awaits you, so take up your responsibilities and embrace your opportunities with enthusiasm and pride in Germany's strength. Understand that there are no limits to how high each of you can climb. Unlike your cousins on the other side of the wall, your future is in your hands—you're free to follow your dreams to the stars. And, you know, we have something so precious if we'll just remember: The eternal youngness of freedom makes it irresistible to people everywhere.

And we who live in this great cathedral of freedom need to remind ourselves that we can see our future shining, we can see new freedom spires rising, and yes, we can see the times of tyranny passing if we will just believe in our own greatest strengths— our courage, our worthiness, our unlimited capacity for love.

Let us ask ourselves: What is at the heart of freedom? In the answer lies the deepest hope for the future of mankind and the reason there can be no walls around those who are determined to be free. Each of us, each of you, is made in the most enduring, powerful image of Western civilization. We're made in the image of God, the image of God, the Creator.

This is our power, and this our freedom. This is our future. And through this power—not drugs, not materialism nor any other "ism"—can we find brotherhood. And you can create the new Europe—a Europe democratic, a Europe united east and west, a Europe at long last completely free.

Now, we hear it said by some that Europe may be glum about her future, that Europe dares no more. Well, forgive me, but I think this kind of talk is nonsense. And I hope you think it's nonsense, too. It is you, Germany, and you, Europe, that gave the values and vitality of Judeo-Christian civilization to America and to the world. It is Europe that has known more tragedy and triumph than any place in history. Each time you suffered, you sprang back like giants—the giants, Adenauer and Schuman, Churchill and Monnet.

Today, only 40 years after the most devastating war known to man, Western Europe has risen in glory from its ruins. Today Europe stands like Schloss Hambach, a magnificent monument to the indomitable spirit of free people.

No country in the world has been more creative than Germany, and no other can better help create our future. We have already seen one miracle, your *Wirtschaftswunder*. The experts expected it would be decades before Germany's economy regained its prewar level. You did it in less than one. The experts said the Federal Republic could not absorb millions of refugees, establish a democracy on the ashes of nazism, and be reconciled with your neighbors. You did all three.

Germany's success showed that our future must not depend on experts or on government plans, but on the treasures of the human mind and spirit—imagination, intellect, courage, and faith. We remembered Ludwig Erhard's secret, how he blazed Germany's path with freedom by creating opportunity and lowering tax rates, to reward every man and woman who dared to dream and to create the future—your farmers, labor leaders, carpenters, and engineers—every German hero who helped to put the pieces of a broken society back together.

I want to encourage you today to consider joining with your friends now or in the future to start up your own business, become part of a great new movement for progress—the age of the entrepreneur. Small businesses will be the biggest job creators for the future.

Human faith and skill discovered oil where once there was only sand. Today we're discovering a new world of computers, microchips, and biotechnology. The new technologies can bring opportunities, create more jobs, produce medical breakthroughs, make our world cleaner and more humane, and provide better means of communication to bring the people of the world closer together. One top American computer firm was actually started by two college students in a garage behind their house.

Technology developed in the Federal Republic can make your air and water more pure, preserve the environment for your children. And because you're free, because you live in a democracy, you can help make all these things happen. You can make your voices heard so that technology works for us, not against us. My young friends, you can not only control your lives, you can help invent the future.

New technologies may someday enable us to develop far safer defenses—a nonnuclear defense not to harm people, but to prevent missiles from reaching our soil; a nonnuclear defense not to militarize space, but to demilitarize the arsenals of Earth. For now we must rely on a system based on the threat of nuclear retaliation called mutual assured destruction. But someday, your children may be protected and war could be avoided by a system we would call mutual assured survival. Someday, technology developed by your generation could render nuclear weapons obsolete.

Working together in space—as we've done with your fine astronaut, Ulf Merbold—we can create the future together. We've learned enough from our shuttle flights to believe that we'll be able to manufacture in space rare crystals and medicines in far greater quantities, medicines to treat diseases that afflict millions of us. In the zerogravity of space, we could make medicines to treat victims of heart attack and manufacture factor 8, a rare and expensive medicine used to treat hemophiliacs. We could study the beta cell, which produces insulin and which could give us mankind's first permanent cure for diabetes. We know from one of our flights this is possible in space. In your lifetime, men and women will be living and working in space.

We're going to make the extraordinary commonplace—this is freedom's way. And those secrets for our future belong not just to us in Europe and America, but to all people, in all places, in all time. Look at Singapore, Hong Kong, Taiwan—tiny specks on the globe, densely populated, and with few natural resources. But today they are stunning success stories—mighty little engines of growth and progress, pulling the world forward, thanks to their dynamic policies of incentives that reward innovation, risk-taking, and hard work.

The future awaits your creation. From your ranks can come a new Bach, Beethoven, Goethe, and Otto Hahn for Germany's future. Your future will be a way station further along that same journey in time begun by the great patriots at Hambach 153 years ago—a journey that began in a dream of the human heart; a journey that will not be complete until the dream is real, until the times of tyranny have passed, until the fear of political torture is no more, until the pain of poverty has been lifted from every person in the world forever. This is freedom's vision, and it's good. And you must go out from here and help make it come true.

My young friends, believe me, this is a wonderful time to be alive and to be free. Remember that in your hearts are the stars of your fate; remember that everything depends on you; and remember not to let one moment slip away, for as Schiller has told us, "He who has done his best for his own time has lived for all times."

I'd like to insert something here that isn't in the scripts that you may have. [*Laughter*] There is a poem in our country, born of a story of ours, in which the words are, "breathe there a man with soul so dead who never to himself hath said, this is my own, my native land."

Thank you. Thank you for welcoming us. Thank you for your warmth and your kindness. Thank you for this very wonderful day. I will always remember it, and I'll always remember you.

Mein herz ist mit ihnen. [My heart is with you.] *Gottes segen.* [God bless.] Thank you very much.

Note: The President spoke at 12:42 p.m. at Hambach Castle. Following his remarks, the President traveled to Madrid, Spain.

Proclamation 5335—Dr. Jonas E. Salk Day, 1985
May 6, 1985

By the President of the United States of America

A Proclamation

One of the greatest challenges to mankind always has been eradicating the presence of debilitating disease. Until just thirty years ago poliomyelitis occurred in the United States and throughout the world in epidemic proportions, striking tens of thousands and killing thousands in our own country each year.

Dr. Jonas E. Salk changed all that. This year we observe the 30th anniversary of the licensing and manufacturing of the vaccine discovered by this great American. Even before another successful vaccine was discovered, Dr. Salk's discovery had reduced polio and its effects by 97 percent. Today, polio is not a familiar disease to younger Americans, and many have difficulty appreciating the magnitude of the disorder that the Salk vaccine virtually wiped from the face of the earth.

Jonas E. Salk always had a passion for science. It was because of this that he finally chose medicine over law as his career goal. Even after his great discovery, he continued to undertake vital studies and medical research to benefit his fellowman. Under his vision and leadership, the Salk Institute for Biological Studies has been in the forefront of basic biological research, reaping further benefits for mankind and medical science.

In recognition of his tremendous contributions to society, particularly for his role in the epochal discovery of the first licensed vaccine for poliomyelitis, and in celebration of the thirtieth anniversary of its mass distribution, the Congress, by House Joint Resolution 258, has designated May 6, 1985, as "Dr. Jonas E. Salk Day" and authorized and requested the President to issue a proclamation in observance of this event.

Now, Therefore, I, Ronald Reagan, President of the United States of America, do hereby proclaim May 6, 1985, as Dr. Jonas E. Salk Day. I urge the people of the United States to observe the day with appropriate tributes, ceremonies, and activities throughout the Nation and by paying honor, at all times, to this outstanding physician and to his life's work.

In Witness Whereof, I have hereunto set my hand this sixth day of May, in the year of our Lord nineteen hundred and eighty-five, and of the Independence of the United States of America the two hundred and ninth.

RONALD REAGAN

[*Filed with the Office of the Federal Register, 3:16 p.m., May 7, 1985*]

Note: The proclamation was released by the Office of the Press Secretary on May 7.

Proclamation 5336—Vietnam Veterans Recognition Day, 1985
May 7, 1985

By the President of the United States of America

A Proclamation

As President and Commander in Chief, I have been pleased to witness a new and abiding recognition of those brave Americans who answered their country's call and served in the defense of freedom in the Republic of South Vietnam. That recognition, figured in the Memorial the Federal government accepted last November as a permanent sign of our determination to keep faith with those who served in that conflict, is both the result and the cause of a new unity among our people. Ten years after American personnel left Vietnam, we honor and remember the deeds of a group of veterans who served as selflessly and fought as courageously as any in our history.

Together we have come through a decade of disillusionment and doubt and reached a new consensus born of conviction—that, however long the wisdom and merits of U.S. policy in the Vietnam era may be debated, no one can withhold from those who wore our country's uniform in Southeast Asia the homage that is their due. Their cause was our cause, and it is the cause that animates all of our experience as a Nation. Americans have never believed that freedom was the sole prerogative of a few, a grant of governmental power, or a title of wealth or nobility. We have always believed that freedom was the birthright of all peoples, and our Vietnam-era veterans pledged their lives—and almost 60,000 lost them—in pursuit of that ideal, not for themselves, but for a suffering people half a world away.

On this day, we recall these sacrifices and say again to our Vietnam veterans: Your cause is our cause. We have not forgotten you. We will not forget you. To those who were killed in Vietnam we say: Your names are inscribed not only on the walls of black granite on the Mall in our Nation's Capital,

but in the hearts of your fellow Americans. To those still listed as missing in action in Southeast Asia: We have raised the fullest possible accounting of your fate to one of highest national priority. To those who returned and resumed their daily lives in our Nation's cities, towns, and farms: We will continue to meet our commitment to compensation and health care programs for the more than 300,000 service-disabled Vietnam veterans and to programs to aid in Vietnam veterans' readjustment.

To all of our Vietnam-era veterans, we rededicate ourselves on this day to offer our continuing praise and thanks for your courage and patriotism. We pledge that our Nation will never forget the men and women who gave so much of themselves on behalf of the highest of human ideals.

The Congress, by Senate Joint Resolution 128, has designated May 7, 1985, as "Vietnam Veterans Recognition Day" and authorized and requested the President to issue a proclamation commemorating this important observance.

Now, Therefore, I, Ronald Reagan, President of the United States of America, do hereby proclaim May 7, 1985, as Vietnam Veterans Recognition Day. I urge all citizens, community leaders, interested organizations, and government officials to observe this day with programs, ceremonies, and activities that commemorate the service and sacrifices of the more than 3 million brave men and women who served in Vietnam.

In Witness Whereof, I have hereunto set my hand this seventh day of May, in the year of our Lord nineteen hundred and eighty-five, and of the Independence of the United States of America the two hundred and ninth.

RONALD REAGAN

[*Filed with the Office of the Federal Register, 11:21 a.m., May 14, 1985*]

Remarks to Community Leaders in Madrid, Spain
May 7, 1985

Thank you, Mr. Boada, and thank you all. Your Majesty, ladies and gentlemen, it's a great honor to be with you today. I've been wanting to revisit Spain since I first became President, and I'm delighted that we were finally able to make it here this year. After all, it's already been almost five centuries since your first delegation visited our country.

We have much to celebrate as we approach the 500th anniversary of the voyage of Christopher Columbus. And it's no exaggeration to say that we stand at the outset of a new golden age—a golden age of freedom that is sweeping across both the old world and the new. I'm convinced that historians will look back on Iberia's peaceful and joyful embrace of democracy as a decisive turning point. They will see it as the moment when freedom ended a long retreat and began a broad, new advance that has spread from Spain and Portugal to the Americas and has, in one short decade, brought over 225 million people into the family of free nations.

Freedom, we see, is contagious, and the force of your example has inspired a continent. When I first became President a little over 4 years ago, the map of our hemisphere was shadowed by dictatorships. But in country after country, the dictators have given way to the democratic aspirations of their people. Today, for the first time ever, the exceptions to the democratic tide in Spanish-speaking America can be counted on the fingers of one hand. They number four. Two, Paraguay and Chile, have entrenched military rule; the two others, Cuba and Nicaragua, are Communist tyrannies.

Sometimes the courage and character of one man can shape the course of history. Throughout the last decade, King Juan Carlos has set a moral example to this country and to the world, and in the storm of events, he has been like an anchor holding fast to the principles of democracy and freedom. Your Majesty, you are a true representative of the democratic aspirations of the Spanish people. All true democrats, all freedom-loving people everywhere salute you.

We salute, too, the remarkable achievement of the people of this land. Any visitor here can see that freedom is flourishing. For democracy to succeed, its roots must grow deep and wide. This means social cooperation, national unity, and a willingness to share power—in short *convivencia*, a wonderful word to describe the culture of democracy.

Spain's proud achievements rank among the foremost contributions to Western civilization. But for too long this great nation was excluded from the community of Western democracies, and we were all diminished by your absence. Now Spain is an important partner in the free alliance of European democracies, the North Atlantic Treaty Organization that has protected our liberties and kept the peace for almost 40 years—the longest period of peace Europe has known since the Roman Empire. And we need Spain.

Soon Spain will take its rightful place as a full member in the European Community, the largest free economic union in the world, larger even than that other economic union and free trade zone, the United States. Your accession into the European Economic Community will create opportunities for both our countries, and we have consistently backed and applaud Spanish and Portuguese membership in the EC.

Today we've come to understand that all the nations of the Earth are part of one global economy, our economic fates interwoven in a tapestry of a million connecting threads. We understand that we break those ties only at our peril, for if too many of them are severed, our prosperity will begin to unravel.

I am old enough to remember the dark days of the Great Depression when short-sighted national interest and beggar-thy-neighbor economic policies ended up turning us all into beggars and plunged the world into a totalitarian nightmare from which we did not escape until the end of a long and bloody World War.

With that lesson fresh in their minds, the leaders of democratic Europe, the United States, and other free nations met after World War II and agreed to demolish the trade barriers that had done so much evil. Their agreement, called the General Agreement on Tariffs and Trade, knocked tariff barriers down to their lowest level in modern history and contributed to an unrivaled period of world economic expansion that helped to rebuild the war-ravaged European Continent and gave the free nations a standard of living that would once have been thought unattainable.

Trade continues to fuel the global economy today. Over one-quarter of the world's output is traded internationally—more than twice as much as in 1970. But these gains are increasingly threatened by demands for protectionism. Protectionism is the wrong word; we should call it by its real name—destructionism. We will continue to resist these destructive pressures, but to succeed, all our governments must cooperate. The nations at the Bonn Economic Summit took an important step forward in calling for another round of trade negotiations. Soon we will realize that in a global economy all markets are common markets and that we will advance most quickly down the road of progress when we walk together.

Let's also keep in mind the enormous contribution made by the free movement of capital and respect for property rights. Spain has been attracting an increasing amount of foreign investment, reflecting a growing confidence in Spain's economic future and the stability of her institutions—a confidence I fully share.

Like the global economy, our national economies benefit from freedom and suffer in its absence. The fifties and sixties were boom years for the West, and Europe achieved an unprecedented level of pros-

perity. But come the seventies, the secret seemed to have been lost throughout the Western industrialized nations. Growth sputtered and almost died out. Inflation raged out of control. More and more people lost their jobs. Innovation and productivity lagged. Instead of building the future, we seemed to be slipping remorselessly back into the past.

As pessimism replaced progress, voices were raised saying that our decline was inevitable. Our world, they said, was rapidly running out of resources, and we must rely on government to distribute fairly our dwindling economic wealth. People began to lose faith in freedom, and it became fashionable to talk of a convergence between the free, democratic countries and the totalitarian dictatorships.

I know that Spain had its own share of these problems; moreover, you had to face them while confronting the demands of your historic transition to democracy. You have a starkly descriptive word for the human costs of economic malaise—*paro.*

Every nation is different, and solutions must take those differences into account. But I believe strongly that there are certain basic principles which, applied wisely, can benefit all. From your introduction, Mr. Boada, I would guess that these principles enjoy widespread support among members of the APD. That is one of the reasons that I am particularly pleased to hear.

In the United States we rejected pessimism. We came to believe that government was more the problem than the solution, that the massive growth of government spending was weighing down the private sector, and that huge increases in taxes and regulations were stifling individual initiative and destroying opportunity for our people. In our country we've always held it as an article of faith that freedom works, and I came into office determined to give freedom a chance.

So, in the United States we began by cutting taxes, bringing the top rate down dramatically and lowering tax rates across the board by about nearly one quarter. By reducing unnecessary regulations, we limited the role of government and set enterprise free without endangering the essential protections that a compassionate society must provide.

Many economists schooled in the old policies of government control predicted disaster. Instead, as the recovery took hold, inflation and interest rates dropped, new businesses began incorporating at the astounding rate of over 600,000 a year, and employment took off—up about 8 million new jobs. And in 1984 we enjoyed the strongest economic growth in three decades.

We've decided that freedom works so well in creating jobs and opportunity for the American people, that we want even more of it. When I return to the United States, I will be presenting an historic tax reform proposal to our legislature that will not only cut tax rates even further but make them less progressive. We believe that there's nothing progressive about tax rates that discourage people from climbing up the ladder of success.

Some point to our budget deficits as the source of our economic expansion. But if that were true, why did a decade of deficit spending in the seventies fail to revitalize our lagging economy? The fact is that many of the Western industrialized nations have larger deficits, as a percentage of their gross national product, than the United States, and yet their recoveries have been sluggish. Deficits slow growth; they don't create it. And we're committed to a program that will cut government overspending and bring our budget into balance by the end of the decade. But at the same time, we found that the greatest barriers to risk-taking, investment, and a strong, growing economy are steep, progressive tax rates.

Our experience has shown us that government alone cannot stimulate economic progress, but it can set it free. The Western developed nations have led the world in creating a higher standard of living for their citizens through the growth of personal freedom, the same freedom that is the soul of human happiness and spiritual fulfillment.

Nevertheless, some governments try to control their economies. They've taken over many industries and subsidized others; they've subsidized exports and protected themselves against imports; they've sent their immigrants home in order to relieve unemployment, and they've passed strict job laws that restrict the movement of labor. But as controls multiplied, investment lagged, growth slowed, and employment declined.

The one measure not taken is the one that has proven, time and time again, to be most effective—cutting marginal personal income tax rates. The historical record is clear—tax cuts work. Germany lifted itself out of the ashes of World War II in the late 1940's when Ludwig Erhard reduced that country's tax rates. Starting in 1950, over 20 years of tax cutting did the same for the Japanese, catapulting them out of underdevelopment and into the front ranks of world economic powers. Between 1973 and 1975, Austria gave itself the largest tax cut in recent European history, making her economy more vibrant among democratic-Socialist nations.

In my own country we have had three major rounds of tax cuts—in the twenties, the sixties, and the eighties—setting off three of the most prosperous periods in our history. Each time critics said we were giving huge breaks to the wealthy at the expense of the poor; but each time after taxes were cut the wealthy ended up paying a larger share of total tax burden, as lower rates attracted more money into productive investment instead of into sterile areas of tax avoidance.

Tax cuts, a boon to the industrialized countries, are a necessity to the nations of the Third World, where tax rates often rise faster, higher, and steeper, blocking economic growth and locking them into underdevelopment. Throughout Africa and Latin America, we see that, where markets are relatively free and tax rates are lower, there is a faster rise in the people's standard of living. And in Asia economic freedom has really taken hold, fueling the meteoric rise of the Pacific Basin nations, boosting the ASEAN countries, and even giving Communist China a helpful push toward prosperity. Soon we may see an economic revolution in India, where Rajiv Gandhi is reducing regulations, lowering tariffs, and slashing taxes.

In our country a whole new generation of entrepreneurs has emerged. Men and women with new ideas and the tenacity to make them happen have sparked a renaissance of innovation, making new breakthroughs every day in such 21st century technologies as bioengineering, microchips, and fiber optics.

It's been individuals—small businessmen and entrepreneurs—who have fueled America's economic boom. It is estimated that 7 out of 10 of all of our new jobs have come from small, new, and growing firms. One of the largest, most successful personal computer firms in America was started by two college students in the garage behind their house.

That's one reason why we believe special tax breaks and subsidies for existing big businesses won't do the trick. Many nations have lower corporate taxes and much more generous investment credits and tax write-offs for business than we do in America. But the most fertile and rapidly growing sector of any economy is that part that exists right now only as a dream in someone's head or an inspiration in his or her heart. No one can ever predict where change will come from or foresee the industries of the future; no government would ever target those two young men working through the night, making dreams come true in their garage.

If we put our trust in experts and rely on their knowledge to shape our destiny, then we condemn ourselves to live in the past. For how can they be experts in what hasn't been invented yet, what doesn't yet exist? In 1899 the head of the United States Patent Bureau advised our then President to abolish that office because, he said, "Everything that can be invented has been invented." Well, at one point, Thomas Watson, the man behind IBM, which is today one of the largest manufacturers of computers in the world, is reported to have said, quote: "I think there is a world market for about five computers."

Well, 500 years ago there lived a man who didn't believe in the accepted wisdom. His stubborn adherence to his vision made him an exile from his own land and brought him seeking financial backing to Spain. George Santayana, a son of Spain, wrote a poem of him:

Columbus found a world, and had no chart,
Save one that faith deciphered in the skies;
To trust the soul's invincible surmise
Was all his science and his only art.

Christopher Columbus was one of the original entrepreneurs. Like many who would come after him, he didn't discover what he had set out to find, but his discovery quite literally changed the shape of the known world, turned it upside down, and began a whole new chapter in the history of man.

In the seventies some said we had reached, quote: "the limits to growth." But we decided they were telling us the Earth was flat when it really is round. We decided to discover a new world not subject to such pessimistic constraints, a new world of hope and opportunity where our tomorrows are as limitless as the horizon.

A half-millennium after Columbus, wouldn't this be the best way to celebrate: for the people of the new and the old worlds to join with each other on a new voyage of exploration and discovery, and together stake our claim on the future.

Thank you, God bless you, and God bless the lasting friendship between our two nations.

Note: The President spoke at 10:40 a.m. at the Juan March Foundation. He was introduced by Claudio Boada, president of Banco Hispano Americano.

Remarks Following Discussions With Prime Minister Felipe González Márquez in Madrid, Spain
May 7, 1985

I want to thank President González for our very productive discussions today and for his wonderful Spanish hospitality.

I also want to say how at home a Californian like me feels in these lovely surroundings. We owe so much to the history and the heritage of Spain.

The United States and Spain have long been friends and close allies. Our discussions today demonstrated a broad degree of agreement on the kind of world that our two democracies want to help bring about. Where there were differences, I think we both profited from the particular perspectives that we bring to the challenges we face.

Spain is making an important contribution to Western security through NATO and our bilateral agreement. We appreciate Spain's support for our efforts to negotiate deep reductions in offensive nuclear arsenals. And we agree on the pressing need to strengthen peace and security in Europe and throughout the world.

I expressed my congratulations to President González for the successful conclusion of the negotiations on Spain's entry into the European Community. I know that Spain was worked hard for years to achieve this goal, and we have supported you throughout.

We noted that further efforts are needed to strengthen peace, democracy, and economic progress in Central and South America. And I know this is a region of special interest to Spain as it is to the United States.

And I also expressed to the President, and want to emphasize again to the Spanish people, how deeply the people of the United States admire what Spain has accomplished in one short decade.

Mr. President, Spain's example has made spirits soar everywhere that people strive for democracy. Many nations, especially in Latin America, are following your lead.

So, it's an honor to be here, to benefit from your views and to give you and all Spaniards the very deepest wishes of the people of the United States for continued success.

Note: The President spoke to reporters at 3:18 p.m. in the garden at Moncloa Palace. Earlier, the President and the Prime Minister met privately and then attended an expanded meeting and a working luncheon at the Palace.

Toast at the State Dinner in Madrid, Spain
May 7, 1985

Your Majesties, 1985 is a year laden with anniversaries of great historical significance. It was 500 years ago that Christopher Columbus and his son Diego came to Spain seeking support for a voyage of exploration. Much will be said about this as we prepare to celebrate 7 years from now, the quincentennial discovery of the Americas. Yet it's not so much the voyage but rather the decision to make the voyage that we should commemorate.

The skills of the captains and sailors, although vital to success, were less significant than the genius of Columbus and the vision of Queen Isabella. Though beseiged with serious challenges, the Spanish throne overcame the doubters and cynics and thus opened a golden age for Spain and a new chapter in human history.

It gives me great pleasure to be with you this evening to applaud another decision of courage and vision, the decision to chart for Spain a course to democracy. The Spanish Crown played a significant role in this historic turning point as well. Your dedication and ideals, Your Majesties, have earned the respect and gratitude of freedom-loving peoples everywhere.

And since your national journey to freedom began, talented leaders have emerged, and the Spanish people have nobly risen to this occasion. Your Majesty, we know that the President and the other leaders of Spain in and out of government have brought Spain peacefully and, yes, gracefully into the family of democratic nations. The American people admire you, and they admire your great achievements. Having been a republic for 200 years we Americans know full well that the road of freedom is not always easy, yet there is every reason to be optimistic. As Sancho proclaimed in Cervantes' "Don Quixote," "A stout heart breaks bad luck." After seeing your nation make dramatic and fundamental change, remaining ever true to the humane values at the core of representative government, no one can doubt that Spain indeed has a stout heart and that because of it your luck will be good.

Because of the efforts of your generation, Spain is no longer isolated on the Iberia Peninsula but is now a vital and growing influence among the free nations of the world. New doors of opportunity are opening, especially in the area of trade and international investment. During these last 40 years, the Western nations have enjoyed tremendous benefit from a relatively free and open trading system. That's why I'm pleased to see Spain becoming a full partner in the European Community, moving to further open the door of economic cooperation with other free countries.

Your Majesty, we would like to work with Spain to keep international trade open and fair. America believes in free people, free markets, and free trade. Increasing the level of exchange between countries serves the interest of all. Trade and investment create a healthy interdependence between free peoples and expand opportunity and unleash new potential. The benefits of trade have been particularly clear as we've seen a vigorous American economy help serve as an engine for progress, pulling the economies of Europe into better times.

Of course, ultimately, whether a country prospers will depend on its domestic policies. Each nation must follow its own path, but I hope the progress that we've made in the United States might encourage others. Instead of trying to redistribute existing wealth, we've tried to produce more. Instead of imposing more controls and regulations, we've sought to free our peoples entrepreneurial spirit. Instead of channeling more of our resources into bureaucracy, we've sought to expand private investment.

The result has been solid growth and low inflation. Almost 8 million new jobs have been created in the United States in the last 2 years.

Your Majesties, the United States has much for which to be grateful to Spain. Our Southwest was settled by pioneers from your country, and a rich Hispanic heritage is still part of our way of life in my adopted home State of California. Today, as Spain takes its place with the democratic nations, I predict the relationship between our peoples will grow and bear fruit as never before.

One of the reasons for my visit to the European Continent is to commemorate the end of the Second World War, that monstrous conflagration that engulfed much of the world. It would be easy to talk in times like this of the heroism of battle and the sacrifice of those who died. Well, instead I've tried to mark this as an anniversary of the beginning of 40 years of peace. For free people, peace is the most precious possession, second only to the preservation of their own liberty. Peace magnifies the joys and meaning of life; it permits the resources of a country to be directed to those productive endeavors that add to well-being and happiness. Everyone is better off when the blessings of peace are enjoyed by a free people. As Cervantes said, "When God sends the dawn, He sends it for all."

But peace doesn't happen on its own. All free people share the responsibility of maturing it, nurturing it, investing in it, taking careful thought, and doing what is necessary to preserve it.

As is fitting, the choice about Spain's contribution to Western security is wholly in Spain's hands. Your decision will be respected. I would say only that the people of the United States would be proud to have the people of Spain continue to stand beside us and the other members of the alliance in our collective, noble effort to preserve the peace and protect human liberty. We believe the peace can and will be preserved by the collective strength of the Western democracies. And if we're strong, we need not be afraid to negotiate with any potential adversary.

The United States is now engaged in arms talks in Geneva. We're seeking not just arms control but an actual reduction in the level of nuclear arsenals. I'm pleased to note that Spain is part of the Western efforts in Stockholm to negotiate a lessening of the tensions between East and West.

The United States is also moving forward on a research project that could use new technologies to diminish the threat of nuclear missiles and lead mankind into a happier and safer time. Our Strategic Defense Initiative is aimed at finding new means for deterring war. It's not based on the threat of nuclear retaliation, but on the contribution of a nonnuclear defense system that would be capable of destroying missiles and incapable of threatening people. By making missiles less of a threat, we hope to make them easier to give up and thus make arms reduction agreements more likely.

Ortega y Gasset once wrote, "Nations are formed and are kept alive by the fact that they have a program for tomorrow." Well, the program for the future of the Western democracies is peace, progress, and freedom.

Today Spain is moving forward in a voyage of freedom and democracy, every bit as courageous as that of Columbus. Spain can be confident of the outcome because the future is on the side of the free. Things that are today beyond the imagination of dictators and tyrants will be conceived of and made reality by free men and women. This we can count on. It is when people can speak and pray, work for themselves, live without fear of repression that the most potent force on this planet is energized—the genius and power of free people under God.

Your Majesties, today let us be grateful for that love of liberty deeply rooted in the soul of our people. Yes, its fire will light the way to a future more glorious than the golden age of yesteryear. We're building a new world of peace, progress, and freedom.

And I now ask all of you to join me in a toast to His Majesty the King and to the people of Spain, all champions of democracy.

Note: The President spoke at 10:48 p.m. at the Royal Palace in response to a toast by King Juan Carlos I. The following day, the President traveled to Strasbourg, France.

Address to a Special Session of the European Parliament in Strasbourg, France
May 8, 1985

The President. Thank you, ladies and gentlemen. It is an honor to be with you on this day.

We mark today the anniversary of the liberation of Europe from tyrants who had seized this continent and plunged it into a terrible war. Forty years ago today, the guns were stilled and peace began, a peace that has become the longest of this century.

On this day 40 years ago, they swarmed onto the boulevards of Paris, rallied under the Arc de Triomphe and sang the Marseillaise. They were out there in the open and free air. And now, on this day 40 years ago, Winston Churchill walked out onto a balcony in Whitehall and said to the people of Britain, "This is your victory." And the crowd yelled back, in an unforgettable moment of love and gratitude, "No, it is yours." Londoners tore the blackout curtains from their windows, put floodlights on the great symbols of English history. And for the first time in nearly 6 years, Big Ben, Buckingham Palace, and St. Paul's Cathedral were illuminated against the sky.

Across the ocean, a half a million New Yorkers flooded Times Square and laughed and posed for the cameras. In Washington, our new President Harry Truman called reporters into his office and said, "The flags of freedom fly all over Europe."

On that day 40 years ago, I was at my post in an Army Air Corps installation in Culver City, California. Passing a radio, I heard the words, "Ladies and gentlemen, the war in Europe is over." I felt a chill, as if a gust of cold wind had just swept past, and even though for America there was still a war in the Pacific front, I realized I would never forget that moment.

This day can't help but be emotional, for in it we feel the long tug of memory. We're reminded of shared joy and shared pain. A few weeks ago in California, an old soldier with tears in his eyes said: "It was such a different world then. It's almost impossible to describe it to someone who wasn't there. But when they finally turned the lights on in the cities again, it was like being reborn."

If it is hard to communicate the happiness of those days, it is even harder to communicate, to those who did not share it, the depth of Europe's agony. So much of it lay in ruins. Whole cities had been destroyed. Children played in the rubble and begged for food.

And by this day 40 years ago, over 40 million lay dead, and the survivors—they composed a continent of victims. And to this day we wonder: How did this happen? How did civilization take such a terrible turn? After all the books and documentaries, after all the histories and studies, we still wonder: How?

Hannah Arendt spoke of the "banality of evil"—the banality of the little men who did the terrible deeds. We know they were totalitarians who used the state, which they had elevated to the level of a god, to inflict war on peaceful nations and genocide on innocent peoples. We know of the existence of evil in the human heart, and we know that in Nazi Germany that evil was institutionalized, given power and direction by the state and those who did its bidding. We

also know that early attempts to placate the totalitarians did not save us from war. They didn't save us from war; in fact they guaranteed war. There are lessons to be learned in this and never forgotten.

But there is a lesson, too, in another thing we saw in those days, perhaps we can call it the commoness of virtue. The common men and women who somehow dug greatness from within their souls, the people who sang to the children during the Blitz, who joined the resistance and said no to tyranny, the people who had the courage to hide and save the Jews and the dissidents, the people who became for a moment the repositories of all the courage of the West— from a child named Anne Frank to a hero named Raoul Wallenberg. These names shine. They give us heart forever. The glow of their memories lit Europe in her darkest days.

Who can forget the hard days after the war? We can't help but look back and think life was so vivid then. There was the sense of purpose, the joy of shared effort, and later the impossible joy of our triumph. Those were the days when the West rolled up its sleeves and repaired the damage that had been done, the days when Europe rose in glory from the ruins. Old enemies were reconciled with the European family. Together, America and Western Europe created and put into place the Marshall plan to rebuild from the rubble. And together we created an Atlantic alliance, which proceeded not from transient interests of state, but from shared ideals. Together we created the North Atlantic Treaty Organization, a partnership aimed at seeing that the kind of tyrants that had tormented Europe would never torment her again.

NATO was a triumph of organization and effort, but is was also something very new and very different. For NATO derived its strength directly from the moral values of the people it represented, from their high ideals, their love of liberty, and their commitment to peace. But perhaps the greatest triumph of all was not in the realm of a sound defense or material achievement. No, the greatest triumph after the war is that in spite of all of the chaos, poverty, sickness, and misfortune that plagued this continent, the people of Western Europe resisted the call of new tyrants and the lure of their seductive ideologies. Your nations did not become the breeding ground for new extremist philosophies. You resisted the totalitarian temptation. Your people embraced democracy, the dream the Fascists could not kill. They chose freedom.

And today we celebrate the leaders who led the way—Churchill and Monnet, Adenauer and Schuman, De Gasperi and Spaak, Truman and Marshall. And we celebrate, too, the free political parties that contributed their share of greatness—the Liberals and the Christian Democrats, the Social Democrats and Labour and the Conservatives. Together they tugged at the same oar, and the great and mighty ship of Europe moved on.

If any doubt their success, let them look at you. In this room are those who fought on opposite sides 40 years ago and their sons and daughters. Now you work together to lead Europe democratically; you buried animosity and hatred in the rubble. There is no greater testament to reconciliation and to the peaceful unity of Europe than the men and women in this chamber.

In the decades after the war, Europe knew great growth and power, amazing vitality in every area of life—from fine arts to fashion, from manufacturing to science to the world of ideas. Europe was robust and alive, and none of this was an accident. It was the natural result of freedom, the natural fruit of the democratic ideal. We in America looked at Europe and called her what she was—an economic miracle.

And we could hardly be surprised. When we Americans think about our European heritage, we tend to think of your cultural influences and the rich ethnic heritage you gave us. But the Industrial Revolution that transformed the American economy came from Europe. The guiding intellectual lights of our democratic system—Locke, Montesquieu, and Adam Smith—came from Europe. And the geniuses who ushered in the modern industrial-technological age came from—well, I think you know, but two examples will suffice: Alexander Graham Bell, whose great invention maddens every American parent whose child insists on phoning his European pen pal

rather than writing to him—and he was a Scotsman—[*laughter*]—and Guglielmo Marconi, who invented the radio, thereby providing a living for a young man from Dixon, Illinois, who later went into politics. I guess I should explain: That's me. Blame Marconi. [*Laughter*] And Marconi, as you know, was born in Italy.

Tomorrow will mark the 35th anniversary of the Schuman plan, which led to the European Coal and Steel Community, the first block in the creation of a united Europe. The purpose was to tie French and German and European industrial production so tightly together that war between them "becomes not merely unthinkable, but materially impossible." Those are the words of Robert Schuman; the Coal and Steel Community was the child of his genius. I believe if he were here today, I believe he would say: We have only just begun!

I'm here to tell you that America remains, as she was 40 years ago, dedicated to the unity of Europe. We continue to see a strong and unified Europe not as a rival but as an even stronger partner. Indeed, John F. Kennedy, in his ringing declaration of interdependence in the Freedom Bell city of Philadelphia 23 years ago, explicitly made this objective a key tenet of postwar American policy; that policy saw the New World and the Old as twin pillars of a larger democratic community. We Americans still see European unity as a vital force in that historic process. We favor the expansion of the European Community; we welcome the entrance of Spain and Portugal into that Community, for their presence makes for a stronger Europe, and a stronger Europe is a stronger West.

Yet despite Europe's economic miracle, which brought so much prosperity to so many, despite the visionary ideas of the European leaders, despite the enlargement of democracy's frontiers within the European Community itself, I'm told that a more doubting mood is upon Europe today. I hear words like "Europessimism" and "Europaralysis." I'm told that Europe seems to have lost that sense of confidence that dominated that postwar era. Well, if there is something of a lost quality these days, is it connected to the fact that some in the past few years have begun to question the ideals and philosophies that have guided the West for centuries, that some have even come to question the moral and intellectual worth of the West?

I wish to speak, in part, to that questioning today. And there is no better place to do it than Strasbourg—where Goethe studied, where Pasteur taught, where Hugo knew inspiration. This has been a lucky city for questioning and finding valid answers. It is also a city for which some of us feel a very sweet affection. You know that our Statue of Liberty was a gift from France, and its sculptor, Auguste Bartholdi, was a son of France. I don't know if you've ever studied the face of the statue, but immigrants entering New York Harbor used to strain to see it, as if it would tell them something about their new world. It's a strong, kind face. It is the face of Bartholdi's mother, a woman of Alsace. And so, among the many things we Americans thank you for, we thank you for her.

The Statue of Liberty—made in Europe, erected in America—helps remind us not only of past ties but present realities. It is to those realities we must look in order to dispel whatever doubts may exist about the course of history and the place of free men and women within it. We live in a complex, dangerous, divided world; yet a world which can provide all of the good things we require—spiritual and material—if we but have the confidence and courage to face history's challenge.

We in the West have much to be thankful for—peace, prosperity, and freedom. If we are to preserve these for our children and for theirs, today's leaders must demonstrate the same resolve and sense of vision which inspired Churchill, Adenauer, De Gasperi, and Schuman. The challenge was to rebuild a democratic Europe under the shadow of Soviet power. Our task, in some ways even more daunting, is to keep the peace with an ever more powerful Soviet Union, to introduce greater stability in our relationship with it, and to live together in a world in which our values can prosper.

The leaders and people of postwar Europe had learned the lessons of their history from the failures of their predecessors. They learned that aggression feeds on ap-

peasement and that weakness itself can be provocative. We, for our part, can learn from the success of our predecessors. We know that both conflict and aggression can be deterred, that democratic nations are capable of the resolve, the sacrifices, and the consistency of policy needed to sustain such deterrence.

From the creation of NATO in 1949 through the early 1970's, Soviet aggression was effectively deterred. The strength of Western economies, the vitality of our societies, the wisdom of our diplomacy all contributed to Soviet restraint; but certainly the decisive factor must have been the countervailing power—ultimately, military, and above all, nuclear power, which the West was capable of bringing to bear in the defense of its interests.

It was in the early 1970's that the United States lost that superiority over the Soviet Union in strategic nuclear weapons, which had characterized the postwar era. In Europe the effect of this loss was not quickly perceptible, but seen globally, Soviet conduct changed markedly and dangerously. First in Angola in 1975, then when the West failed to respond, in Ethiopia, in South Yemen, in Kampuchea, and ultimately in Afghanistan, the Soviet Union began courting more risks and expanding its influence through the indirect and direct application of military power. Today we see similar Soviet efforts to profit from and stimulate regional conflicts in Central America.

Audience members. Boo-o-o!

The President. They haven't been there. I have.

The ineffectual Western response to Soviet adventurism of the late 1970's had many roots, not least the crisis of self-confidence within the American body politic wrought by the Vietnam experience. But just as Soviet decisionmaking in the earlier postwar era had taken place against a background of overwhelming American strategic power, so the decisions of the late seventies were taken in Moscow, as in Washington and throughout Europe, against a background of growing Soviet and stagnating Western nuclear strength.

One might draw the conclusion from

these events that the West should reassert that nuclear superiority over the Soviet Union upon which our security and our strategy rested through the postwar era. That is not my view. We cannot and should not seek to build our peace and freedom perpetually upon the basis of expanding nuclear arsenals.

In the short run, we have no alternative but to compete with the Soviet Union in this field, not in the pursuit of superiority but merely of balance. It is thus essential that the United States maintain a modern and survivable nuclear capability in each leg of the strategic triad—sea, land, and air-based. It is similarly important that France and Britain maintain and modernize their independent strategic capabilities.

Now, the Soviet Union, however, does not share our view of what constitutes a stable nuclear balance. It has chosen instead to build nuclear forces clearly designed to strike first and thus disarm their adversary. The Soviet Union is now moving toward deployment of new mobile MIRV'ed missiles which have these capabilities plus the potential to avoid detection, monitoring, or arms control verification. In doing this the Soviet Union is undermining stability and the basis for mutual deterrence.

One can imagine several possible responses to the continued Soviet buildup of nuclear forces. On the one hand, we can ask the Soviet Union to reduce its offensive systems through equitable, verifiable arms control measures. We are pressing that case in Geneva. Thus far, however, we've heard nothing new from the other side.

A second possibility would be for the West to step up our current modernization effort to keep up with constantly accelerating Soviet deployments, not to regain superiority but merely to keep up with Soviet deployments. But is this really an acceptable alternative? Even if this course could be sustained by the West, it would produce a less stable strategic balance than the one we have today. Must we accept an endless process of nuclear arms competition? I don't think so. We need a better guarantee of peace than that.

And fortunately, there is a third possibility. It is to offset the continued Soviet offensive buildup in destabilizing weapons by developing defenses against these weapons. In 1983 I launched a new research program—the Strategic Defense Initiative.

The state of modern technology may soon make possible, for the first time, the ability to use nonnuclear systems to defeat ballistic missiles. The Soviets themselves have long recognized the value of defensive systems and have invested heavily in them. Indeed, they have spent as much on defensive systems as they have on offensive systems for more than 20 years.

Now, this research program will take time. As we proceed with it, we will remain within existing treaty constraints. We will also consult in the closest possible fashion with our allies. And when the time for decisions on the possible production and deployment of such systems comes, we must and will discuss and negotiate these issues with the Soviet Union.

Both for the short- and the long-term I'm confident that the West can maintain effective military deterrence. But surely we can aspire to more than maintaining a state of highly armed truce in international politics.

During the 1970's we went to great lengths to restrain unilaterally our strategic weapons programs out of the conviction that the Soviet Union would adhere to certain rules in its conduct—rules such as neither side seeking to gain unilateral advantage at the expense of the other. Those efforts of the early 1970's resulted in some improvements in Europe, the Berlin Quadripartite Agreement being the best example. But the hopes for a broader and lasting moderation of the East-West competition foundered in Angola, Ethiopia, Afghanistan, and Nicaragua.

The question before us today is whether we have learned from those mistakes, and can we undertake a stable and peaceful relationship with the Soviet Union based upon effective deterrence and the reduction of tensions. I believe we can. I believe we've learned that fruitful cooperation with the Soviet Union must be accompanied by successful competition in areas, particularly Third World areas where the Soviets are not yet prepared to act with restraint.

[*At this point, some members of the audience walked out.*]

You know, I've learned something useful. Maybe if I talk long enough in my own Congress, some of those will walk out.

But let me talk about the reflections which have molded our policy toward the Soviet Union. That policy embodies the following basic elements:

While we maintain deterrence to preserve the peace, the United States will make a steady, sustained effort to reduce tensions and solve problems in its relations with the Soviet Union.

The United States is prepared to conclude fair, equitable, verifiable agreements for arms reduction, above all with regard to offensive nuclear weapons.

The United States will insist upon compliance with past agreements, both for their own sake and to strengthen confidence in the possibility of future accords.

The United States seeks no unilateral advantages and, of course, can accept none on the Soviet side.

The United States will proceed in full consultation with its allies, recognizing that our fates are intertwined and we must act in unity.

The United States does not seek to undermine or change the Soviet system nor to impinge upon the security of the Soviet Union. At the same time it will resist attempts by the Soviet Union to use or threaten force against others or to impose its system on others by force.

Ultimately, I hope the leaders of the Soviet Union will come to understand that they have nothing to gain from attempts to achieve military superiority or to spread their dominance by force but have much to gain from joining the West in mutual arms reduction and expanding cooperation.

I have directed the Secretary of State to engage with the Soviet Union on an extended agenda of problem solving. Yet even as we embark upon new efforts to sustain a productive dialog with the Soviet Union, we're reminded of the obstacles posed by our so fundamentally different concepts of humanity, of human rights, of the value of human life. The murder of Major Nicholson by a Soviet soldier in East Germany and the Soviet Union's refusal to accept responsibility for this act is only the latest reminder.

If we're to succeed in reducing East-West tensions, we must find means to ensure against the arbitrary use of lethal force in the future, whether against individuals like Major Nicholson or against groups such as the passengers on a jumbo jet.

It is for that reason that I would like to outline for you today what I believe would be a useful way to proceed. I propose that the United States and the Soviet Union take four practical steps.

First, that our two countries make a regular practice of exchanging military observers at military exercises and locations. We now follow this practice with many other nations, to the equal benefit of all parties.

Second, as I believe it is desirable for the leaders of the United States and Soviet Union to meet and tackle problems, I am also convinced that the military leaders of our nations could benefit from more contact. I therefore propose that we institute regular, high-level contacts between Soviet and American military leaders to develop better understanding and to prevent potential tragedies from occurring.

Third, I urge that the Conference on Disarmament in Europe act promptly and agree on the concrete confidence-building measures proposed by the NATO countries. The United States is prepared to discuss the Soviet proposal on nonuse of force in the context of Soviet agreement to concrete confidence-building measures.

Fourth, I believe a permanent military-to-military communications link could serve a useful purpose in this important area of our relationship. It could be the channel for exchanging notifications and other information regarding routine military activities, thereby reducing the chances of misunderstanding and misinterpretation. And over time, it might evolve into a risk-reduction mechanism for rapid communication and exchange of data in times of crisis.

These proposals are not cure-alls for our current problems. They will not compensate for the deaths which have occurred. But as terrible as past events have been, it would be more tragic if we were to make no attempt to prevent even larger tragedies from occurring through lack of contact and communication.

We in the West have much to do, and we

must do it together. We must remain unified in the face of attempts to divide us and strong in spite of attempts to weaken us. And we must remember that our unity and strength are not a mere impulse of like-minded allies, but the natural result of our shared love for liberty.

Surely we have no illusions that convergence of the Communist system and the free societies of the West is likely. We're in for an extended period of competition of ideas. It is up to us in the West to answer whether or not we will make available the resources, ideas, and assistance necessary to compete with the Soviet Union in the Third World. We have much in our favor, not least the experience of those states which have tried Marxism and are looking for an alternative.

We do not aspire to impose our system on anyone, nor do we have pat answers for all the world's ills. But our ideals of freedom and democracy——

Audience members. Nicaragua! Nicaragua!

The President. Is there an echo in here? [*Laughter*]

Our ideals of freedom and democracy and our economic systems have proven their ability to meet the needs of our people. Our adversaries can offer their people only economic stagnation and the corrupt hand of a state and party bureaucracy which ultimately satisfy neither material nor spiritual needs.

I want to reaffirm to the people of Europe the constancy of the American purpose. We were at your side through two great wars; we have been at your side through 40 years of a sometimes painful peace. We're at your side today, because, like you, we have not veered from the ideals of the West—the ideals of freedom, liberty, and peace. Let no one—no one—doubt our purpose.

The United States is committed not only to the security of Europe, we're committed to the re-creation of a larger and more genuinely European Europe. The United States is committed not only to a partnership with Europe, the United States is committed to an end to the artificial division of Europe.

We do not deny any nation's legitimate interest in security. We share the basic aspirations of all of the peoples of Europe—freedom, prosperity, and peace. But when families are divided and people are not allowed to maintain normal human and cultural contacts, this creates international tension. Only in a system in which all feel secure and sovereign can there be a lasting and secure peace.

For this reason we will support and will encourage movement toward the social, humanitarian, and democratic ideals shared in Europe. The issue is not one of state boundaries but of ensuring the right of all nations to conduct their affairs as their peoples desire. The problem of a divided Europe, like others, must be solved by peaceful means. Let us rededicate ourselves to the full implementation of the Helsinki final act in all its aspects.

As we seek to encourage democracy, we must remember that each country must struggle for democracy within its own culture. Emerging democracies have special problems and require special help. Those nations whose democratic institutions are newly emerged and whose confidence in the process is not yet deeply rooted need our help. They should have an established community of their peers, other democratic countries to whom they can turn for support or just advice.

In my address to the British Parliament in 1982, I spoke of the need for democratic governments to spread the message of democracy throughout the world. I expressed my support for the Council of Europe's effort to bring together delegates from many nations for this purpose. I am encouraged by the product of that conference—the Strasbourg initiative.

We in our country have launched a major effort to strengthen and promote democratic ideals and institutions. Following a pattern first started in the Federal Republic of Germany, the United States Congress approved the National Endowment for Democracy. This organization subsequently established institutes of labor, business, and political parties dedicated to programs of cooperation with democratic forces around the world. I hope other democracies will join in this effort and contribute their wisdom and talents to this cause.

Here in Western Europe you have created a multinational democratic community in which there is a free flow of people, of information, of goods, and of culture. West Europeans move frequently and freely in all directions, sharing and partaking of each other's ideas and culture. It is my hope that in the 21st century, which is only 15 years away, all Europeans, from Moscow to Lisbon, will be able to travel without a passport; and the free flow of people and ideas will include the other half of Europe. It is my fervent wish that in the next century there will be one free Europe.

I do not believe those who say the people of Europe today are paralyzed and pessimistic. And I would say to those who think this, Europe, beloved Europe, you are greater than you know. You are the treasury of centuries of Western thought and Western culture; you are the father of Western ideals and the mother of Western faith. Europe, you have been the power and the glory of the West, and you are a moral success. In the horrors after World War II, you rejected totalitarianism; you rejected the lure of the new superman and a new Communist man; you proved that you were and are a moral triumph.

You in the West are a Europe without illusions, a Europe firmly grounded in the ideals and traditions that made her greatness, a Europe unbound and unfettered by a bankrupt ideology. You are today a new Europe on the brink of a new century, a democratic community with much to be proud of.

We have so much to do. The work ahead is not unlike the building of a great cathedral. The work is slow, complicated, and painstaking. It's passed on with pride from generation to generation. It's the work not only of leaders but of ordinary people. The cathedral evolves as it is created, with each generation adding its own vision. But the initial ideal remains constant, and the faith that drives the vision persists. The results may be slow to see, but our children and their children will trace in the air the emerging arches and spires and know the faith and dedication and love that produced them. My friends, Europe is the cathedral, and it is illuminated still.

And if you doubt your will and your spirit and your strength to stand for something, think of those people 40 years ago who wept in the rubble, who laughed in the streets, who paraded across Europe, who cheered Churchill with love and devotion, who sang the "Marseillaise" down the boulevards. Spirit like that does not disappear; it cannot perish; it will not go. There is too much left unsung within it.

I would like to just conclude with one line, if I could, and say we've seen evidence here of your faith in democracy, in the ability of some to speak up freely as they preferred to speak. And yet I can't help but remind all of us that some who take advantage of that right of democracy seem unaware that if the government that they would advocate became reality, no one would have that freedom to speak up again.

Thank you all for your graciousness on this great day. Thank you, and God bless you all. Thank you.

Note: The President spoke at 2:35 p.m. in the assembly chamber at the Palais de l'Europe. He was introduced by Pierre Pflimlin, President of the European Parliament. Following his address, the President met briefly with Marcelino Oreja, Secretary General of the Council of Europe. He then traveled to Lisbon, Portugal.

Letter to General Secretary Mikhail Gorbachev of the Soviet Union on the 40th Anniversary of the End of the Second World War
May 8, 1985

Dear Mr. General Secretary:

The 40th anniversary of the victory in Europe is an occasion for both our countries to remember the sacrifice of those men and women everywhere who gave the last full measure of devotion to the cause of fighting tyranny. Together with our other allies, our two countries played a full part in that long struggle. We demonstrated that despite our differences we can join together in successful common efforts.

I believe we should also see this solemn occasion as an opportunity to look forward to the future with vision and hope. I would like our countries to join in rededication to the task of overcoming the differences and resolving the problems between us, and in renewed progress toward the goals of making peace more stable and eliminating nuclear weapons from the face of the earth. By pursuing those goals, we will truly honor those whose memory we commemorate today.

Sincerely,

/S/RONALD REAGAN

Note: The original was not available for verification of the content of this letter.

Remarks Following Discussions With Prime Minister Mário Soares in Lisbon, Portugal
May 9, 1985

It's a special pleasure to visit this green and beautiful country, and I am particularly delighted to have had an opportunity to review important international questions with my good friend, Mário Soares.

I fondly recall my previous meetings with him and remember so well his central role in bringing democracy to Portugal and in promoting freedom throughout the world.

This morning we had a friendly and very useful exchange of views with the Prime Minister, Vice Prime Minister Machete, and other members of the Portuguese Government. There was a feeling of sadness as well as we reflected on the sudden death of former Vice Prime Minister Professor Mota Pinto. He was a man dedicated to the ideals of individual freedom and political democracy, and he was a champion of the Atlantic alliance.

I agree with the Prime Minister that the state of Portuguese-American relations is excellent. I am pleased by the degree of mutual respect and the spirit of cooperation which exists between our two nations and which characterized our talks today.

Portugal is a steadfast and valued ally, and I came to Lisbon knowing that I would consult not only with partners but with friends. Our meetings gave us a valuable opportunity to review our bilateral relations, both in the security field and in the economic area. We reviewed the significant steps recently taken toward expanding our economic cooperation and strengthening the ties between our economies. And as the Prime Minister noted, we addressed a number of international issues of mutual concern.

Our discussions were characterized by a close similarity of viewpoints. I profited greatly from hearing the views and insights of the Portuguese Government. Our talks ranged broadly both over East-West matters and Third World questions. I would note in particular the attention given to southern Africa, which reflects Portugal's special knowledge and expertise in this region, and our ongoing close consultations on the problems of the area.

I also took the opportunity to applaud Portugal's pending entry into the European Community. We have long supported Portuguese entry, and as I told Prime Minister Soares, we view the recent accord both as a major step forward for Portugal and as a contribution to European unity.

And now, if you will permit me, following a little translation, we have an important date to keep just across the garden.

Thank you.

Note: The President spoke to reporters at 11:50 a.m. at the Palace of Sao Bento. Earlier, the President and the Prime Minister met privately and then attended an expanded meeting with their senior aides at the Palace.

Address Before the Assembly of the Republic of Portugal in Lisbon
May 9, 1985

I'm sorry that some of the chairs on the left seem to be uncomfortable. [*Laughter*]

[*The President was referring to a walkout by Communist Party Assembly members prior to his address.*]

I'm deeply honored to be with you distinguished ladies and gentlemen here in this assembly that is so rich in history, where the voice of the Portuguese people is heard.

For us, a long journey is ending now, but one fruitful in results and rich in memory. World leaders in summit conference, the youth of modern Germany, warm welcomes at the European Parliament and in Spain— all these things we have seen and been grateful for. We have seen, too, memorials to the devastation of the past, to the memory of war, and to the cruelty of totalitarian rule. Yet we have also seen the prospering cities and nations of the modern Europe and experienced the warmth of her free people. Let there be no doubt that these things too are monuments, monuments to the future and to the human spirit—its capacity for hope and change, its passion for peace and freedom.

And now, at last, we have the honor of coming here to Portugal, a particularly fitting place for an American to make farewells as well as bring greetings. For as the history books of America's schoolchildren teach them, it was from these shores that the first maritime explorers departed, the scientists and adventurers whose skill and courage would lead someday to the discovery of a new world and a new nation.

And I hope, by the way, that you'll not think it impertinent of me to mention that anyone who's had the two careers I've had—in Hollywood and in Sacramento, the capital of California—owes the Portuguese people a special debt. It was, after all, your countryman of five centuries ago, João Rodrigues Cabrilho, who discovered a very long stretch along the North American coastline that came to be known as California. In fact, some in my country claim I've been around so long that my ranch in the Santa Ynez Mountains was originally sold to me by Cabrilho himself. [*Laughter*]

But I know it's customary for Presidents and statesmen to talk of your nation's great maritime discoveries, to speak of your past. And it's certainly no surprise that, gazing back across time, many look with wonder at a small nation in the 15th century that refused to go the way of other war-ravaged European nations—that spurned conflict and turned its talents instead to exploration, to adventuring into new realms, to daring to dream, to believe in themselves and in the future. And this vision eventually doubled the size of the known world and is rightly thought of as a signal event in human history.

So, this old and glorious heritage of your country forms a distant yet close bond between our lands and fills any American who comes here with humble gratitude and admiration for all the achievements of your people. Although I'm not sure we would catch every allusion to Greco-Roman mythology, I do know that most Americans— not a few of them Portuguese-Americans—

would share the sentiment of your epic, "The Lusiadas:" "Let us hear no more then of Ulysses and Aeneas and their long journeying, no more of Alexander and Trajan and their famous victories. My theme is the daring and renown of the Portuguese . . ."

But we must do more than today celebrate the daring and renown of the Portuguese past. For the events of the last decade suggest that you're once again embarked on an adventure, a great adventure that all the world is watching closely. Once again you're charting a new course, not just for Portugal but for all others, especially those peoples of the Third World with whom your long-established ties permit you to speak with a special trust, wisdom, and candor.

In little more than a decade, your nation has moved rapidly through stages of development that illustrate the history of this century—from far-flung empire and dictatorship to a confrontation with totalitarian ideology to a decisive turn to democratic self-rule. While it's always hard to distinguish between the ripples of daily events and the great tides of history, I will still venture a prediction.

Future historians will recognize in Portugal's journey the journey of our time, the journey of our century. For you, the people of Portugal, have chosen freedom. You have elected to embark on a great adventure in democracy. And let me assure you today that 237 million of my countrymen and many millions more who will find in your example their own way to freedom salute your decision and celebrate again in the words of "The Lusiadas," your "daring and renown."

Your adventure is important to our century, a century of so much promise and so much tragedy. I must state it that starkly. I have come from seeing places that remind us of the havoc and wrong that human hatred can cause. But here in the new Portugal and throughout Europe, we see our century's promise, a promise not just of material progress—a time when mankind's age-old enemies of hunger and disease and poverty are things of the past—but also the promise of progress in the human spirit as well. A progress toward the day when each man, woman, and child on Earth will live in freedom and have a right to a voice in their own destiny.

So, in these final miles of our journey across Europe, a journey into the future as well as well as the past, let me tell you what I think we've discovered. Whether one regards it as revealed truth or only as a great story, we learn in Genesis of a moment when humankind lived in harmony with itself and with God. Some have said the meaning of history is found in the unfolding story of our return to such a time, a journey painfully and frequently broken by heartbreak and suffering. Well, for now, I will leave such thoughts to the theologians and the historians. But this much I do know— I've seen in these past days reminders of the tragedy and the grandeur of our time. I've heard the voice of the 20th century; it is humanity's voice, heard in every century, every time. And the words are unmistakable. They call out to us in anguish, but also in hope: Let the nations live in peace among themselves. Let all peoples abide in the fellowship that God intends.

But tragically, this great longing felt by every people in every time has not always been shared by their governments, especially those modern governments whose leaders and ideologies glorify the state and make a cult of personal power. At the end of the last World War, Europe and all the world hoped that we'd at last seen an end to conflict and armaments. It wasn't to be so. But at least we didn't repeat the mistake of an earlier time, the mistake that eventually led to world war, the mistake of believing it is enough only to wish for peace. Instead we accepted reality. We took seriously those who threatened to end the independence of our nations and our peoples, and we did what peoples who value their freedom must do—we joined together in a great alliance. And we rearmed, but we did so only so that never again would we be forced under the weight of our betrayed illusions to resort to violence.

No one knows better than the people of Portugal, who have with Great Britain the oldest mutual defense treaty in European history, the value of such alliances and such readiness in preventing aggression and war. And so, we've labored together—Old World

591

and New World, Europe and America, Portuguese and American. And NATO has worked; we have kept the peace for 40 years. Let us keep the peace another 40 years and another after that.

Today Portugal's contribution to the Western alliance remains of critical importance. Your geographic location is strategically vital, your armed forces are modernizing to expand their role in NATO—all of this further testimony that martial skill and a love of national independence are more than just parts of the Portuguese past.

Yet even your contributions to the alliance are superseded by the example of what you're doing now. Yes, democratic Portugal has faced political problems and social problems and economic problems, and, no, democracy, particularly in its earlier years, does not always go smoothly.

But this is true of any nation and especially any democracy. In my country, we've learned over and over again that democracy can only work when it is judged not in the short run but over the long term, when we keep in mind the principles upon which it is based and remember how right Winston Churchill was to remind us that democracy truly is the worst form of government, except for all the others.

The essential truth at the heart of Portuguese and American democracy is our belief that governments exist for the sake of the people and not the other way around. And this belief is based on an essential insight of our civilization—the dignity of man, the value of the individual. My own nation's forefathers justified our revolution with these words in the Declaration of Independence: ". . . all men are created equal, that they are endowed by their Creator with certain unalienable Rights, that among these are Life, Liberty and the pursuit of Happiness."

Well, it is this trust in the individual—the right to speak, to assemble, to publish, and to vote, even to walk out—that is the meaning of democracy. Our democratic governments are not built on the proposition that the people are always right; indeed, within the structure of our governments there are safeguards against the whims or passions of the majority. But democratic government is built on the proposition that there resides in the common people an uncommon wisdom, that over the long run the people and their right to political self-expression are the best protection against freedom's oldest and most powerful enemy—the unchecked growth and abuse of the power of the state.

Now, this belief is not always easy to preserve, especially when the ship of state is buffeted by storms. There will always be those who lose faith and preach panic; you've sometimes heard their voices. But I believe that here in the nation of navigators there is a respect for the wisdom of holding fast to the course that has been charted. We know there will always be answers if we trust in the people, if we go to them, give them the facts, and rely on them to make the right decisions.

In my own country we have learned this lesson many times. No one had more right to question this belief than one of our great Presidents and founders of my own political party, Abraham Lincoln. Even facing a civil war and powerful voices that told him that people could not be trusted with such momentous issues, Lincoln, with his typical backwoods wisdom, eloquently explained why over the long run democracy is the most pragmatic form of government. He said, and every American knows the words: "You can fool some of the people all of the time, and all of the people some of the time. But you cannot fool all of the people all of the time."

Portugal and her people are moving forward. You have handled during the past few years enormous problems, yet your democracy is strong and intact. You are embracing the free market; you are entering the Common Market; you are beginning to grow economically; you believe, as we do, that freedom works.

This democratic experience and economic development go hand in hand. History shows a strong, unbreakable link between political freedom and economic growth, between democracy and social progress. And in our own time—a great revolution is underway in the world, a great longing for personal freedom and democratic self-rule that surfaces again and again, even in Communist countries. At the start of this century there were only a handful of democracies, but today more than 50 countries— one-third of the world's population—are living under democratic rule. One of the engines of this progress is the desire for economic development, the realization that it is free nations that prosper and free peoples who create better lives for themselves and their children. This realization is growing throughout the world, and in some nations it's causing conflict and disorder. In a sense, then, Marx was right; economic progress is leading to clashes with old entrenched political orders. But Marx was wrong about where all this would occur, for it is the democratic world that is flexible, vibrant, and growing—bringing its peoples higher and higher standards of living even as freedom grows and deepens. It is in the collectivist world that economies stagnate, that technology is lagging, and that the people are oppressed and unhappy with their lives.

So, everywhere we turn, there is an uprising of mind and will against the old cliches of collectivism. Throughout the world the old cries of "power to the state" are being replaced by cries of "power to the people." Throughout the world we can see movement toward a time when totalitarian rule and the terrible suffering that it causes is only a sad and distant memory. That's why what you are doing in your country is so important. First at the British Parliament in 1982 and then again in Strasbourg yesterday, we've called for concerted action—for a global campaign for freedom, an international strategy for democratic development.

I can think of no more fitting place to renew that call to the world than here in Portugal, and I can think of no people better equipped to advance the cause of democratic development and human freedom than the Portuguese. Let Portugal again lead the world, and let the Portuguese again cross small seas and great ones bearing news of science and discovery, the new science of democracy, the discovery of freedom—that it works, that it prospers, and that it endures.

And I hasten to add that freedom can guarantee peace. Let us never forget that aggression and war are rarely the work of a nation's people, for it is the people who must bear the brunt and endure the worst of war. No, war and aggression in our century have almost always been the work of governments, one of the militarists and idealogues who may control them. And that is why war and aggression have a tiny constituency. Let democracy spread, let the people's voice be heard, and the warmongers will be made outcasts and pariahs. Let us not be afraid that in our crusade for freedom to proclaim to the world that the cause of democratic government is also the cause of peace.

This pursuit of peace has occupied much of our efforts on this journey and in our broader diplomatic efforts. Important negotiations are now underway in Geneva, negotiations that can lessen the chance of war by producing verifiable agreements and the first real reduction in nuclear weapons. So, too, the United States is moving forward with technological research that we hope someday will lessen the chance of war by reducing dependence on a strategy based on the threat of nuclear retaliation.

I know you share my hopes that our efforts to reach negotiated solutions will succeed. And I know, too, that you understand working toward this goal means remaining strong in our alliance and in our resolve to protect our nation's freedom and independence. Our agreement on this point is why we can be hopeful that a century that has seen so much tragedy can also be a century of hope. In the United States and here in Portugal, in Europe and throughout the world, we have rediscovered the preciousness of freedom, its importance to the cause of peace and to restoring to humanity the dignity to which it is entitled.

This belief in human dignity suggests the final truth upon which democracy is based—a belief that human beings are not just another part of the material universe, not just mere bundles of atoms. We believe in another dimension—a spiritual side to man. We find a transcendent source for our claims to human freedom, our suggestion that inalienable rights come from one greater than ourselves.

No one has done more to remind the world of the truth of human dignity, as well as the truth that peace and justice begins with each of us, than the special man who came to Portugal a few years ago after a terrible attempt on his life. He came here to Fatima, the site of your great religious shrine, to fulfill his special devotion to Mary, to plead for forgiveness and compassion among men, to pray for peace and the recognition of human dignity throughout the world.

When I met Pope John Paul II a year ago in Alaska, I thanked him for his life and his apostolate. And I dared to suggest to him the example of men like himself and in the prayers of simple people everywhere, simple people like the children of Fatima, there resides more power than in all the great armies and statesmen of the world.

This, too, is something the Portugese can teach the world. For your nation's greatness, like that of any nation, is found in your people. It can be seen in their daily lives, in their communities and towns, and especially in those simple churches that dot your countryside and speak of a faith that justifies all of humanity's claims to dignity, to freedom.

I would suggest to you that here is power, here is the final realization of life's meaning and history's purpose, and here is the foundation for a revolutionary idea—the idea that human beings have a right to determine their own destiny.

I hope you'll forgive me if I leave you with one story about our early days as a democracy. At a critical moment in our history when disunity and discord prevailed on every side, a man celebrated as an inventor and scientist interrupted the proceedings of the Constitutional Convention, trying at the time to formulate the Constitution of the United States. It was Benjamin Franklin who rose to say to his fellow delegates that

he had lived a long time and that he had learned above all that not the smallest bird falls from the heavens without the knowledge of God. It is said that he then knelt and asked the delegates to kneel with him and seek a guidance greater than their own. And from then on, every constitutional meeting opened with prayer.

A great democracy was born after those words, just as a great democracy was born in Portugal. It was born because the Portuguese are a people who love freedom and peace, who are willing to sacrifice for a better life for their children. But most of all it was born because the Portuguese are unafraid to acknowledge a higher law that operates in the affairs of mankind, that higher law dictates human freedom and dignity.

There is a word in your language I remember using in a speech during my first year in office, a very useful word evoking the remembrance of things past—I hope I get it right—*saudades*. Even in the short time Nancy and I have been with you in Portugal, we've developed a deeper appreciation for that word's meaning. We shall miss you; we shall miss Portugal. And we hope someday you will permit us to return, to visit with you again, and, as you say, *muitas saudades*.

Until then, on behalf of the American people, we extend our warmest wishes—we look with hope toward your future and ours, a future we know will be one of democracy and freedom. One in which we also know the Portuguese people will write another great and inspiring chapter in history.

Thank you, and God bless you all.

Note: The President spoke at 12:30 p.m. in the Assembly chamber.

Toast at a Luncheon Hosted by Prime Minister Mário Soares in Lisbon, Portugal
May 9, 1985

Prime Minister Soares and distinguished guests, thank you. The warmth of your welcome is much appreciated as is the beauty

of this land. Nancy and I are especially grateful for your invitation to come here to Sintra, this green and enchanting place that

Lord Byron called the "glorious Eden." We can now sense what he felt when he penned those words.

But the magnificence of Portugal is not merely found in the grandeur of landscape and scenery. Overriding the loveliness we see the sculpture of your land as the soul and spirit of the Portuguese people. Mr. Prime Minister, we Americans take great pride in our frontier heritage and in our love of liberty. And when it comes to pushing back frontiers and to the commitment to human freedom, our two peoples are as one family.

Five centuries ago, the Portuguese were the pathfinders who led the way to a new era in the history of mankind. Like Americans, seeking new horizons is so much a part of your national character.

Portugal's many experiences or achievements during the Age of Discovery are a great source of pride. Today you have equal reason to be proud of what you've overcome in order to ensure that future generations will continue to enjoy the fruits of democracy and freedom. It has taken enormous energy and commitment. With courage and tenacity you cast off the chains of a dictatorship, defeated those who would have subverted your cause, and have built a government based on the popular vote and a respect for human rights.

I'm pleased to have this opportunity to salute your personal courage and leadership, Mr. Prime Minister, and to applaud what you and the people of Portugal have accomplished together. I also want to extend my thanks for Portugal's continuing contribution to the Western alliance. This is even more meaningful now that you have proudly joined the ranks of the democratic nations.

The ever-more apparent failure of communism, wherever it has been tried, makes it increasingly important for the free people of the world to stand together. John Dos Passos, an American writer who, like so many of our fellow citizens, had family roots in Portugal, wrote late in his life: "Marxism has not only failed to promote human freedom. It has failed to produce food."

History is on the side of the free because freedom is right and because freedom works. Only in democratic countries is the individual free to create and dream without fear; to profit from the product of one's labor on investment or investment; to organize unions and cooperative efforts with like minded peoples; to peacefully try to change what is into something totally new and different.

Under freedom, innovation and ideas are unleashed that otherwise would be smothered by oppression and control. Free people are not afraid of change. In market economies, change becomes a means of creating new wealth by meeting the needs and wants of others and by doing it cheaper and better.

Mr. Prime Minister, we're aware of the economic challenges that you face. It wasn't that long ago when we in the United States found ourselves with similar economic difficulties. We decided to shun regulatory and redistribution schemes and, instead, put in place incentives for our people to work and produce and invest, freeing our economy to grow. Evey country must find its own way, but I would hope that our experience and the success that we've enjoyed might provide encouragement for others.

We want Portugal to succeed and your people to prosper. A recent investment mission here by American firms was sponsored by our two governments. This is the type of private sector activity which serves the interests of both our peoples.

Our cooperation in educational endeavors, as we're doing in the Fulbright Program, will also reap many rewards in the future. Let us see to it that these positive steps are only the first of many. The recent establishment of the Luso-American Foundation bodes well for the relations between our governments and our peoples.

Today we are laying the foundation for the progress and freedom our children will enjoy. What we do today is for them tomorrow. They'll stand on our shoulders, and we must give them strong backs so they may see well into the future. And it will be people like you, Mr. Prime Minister, to whom future generations will be most grateful. You can be especially proud of your strong leadership in bringing democracy to Portugal.

So, all, please join me in a toast to Prime Minister Soares and the Portuguese people, building a future of freedom and progress.

Note: The President spoke at 3:14 p.m. at *Sintra Palace. He spoke in response to a toast by Prime Minister Soares. Following his remarks, the President returned to Queluz Palace, where he stayed during his visit to Portugal.*

Toast at the State Dinner in Lisbon, Portugal
May 9, 1985

President Eanes, Mrs. Eanes, ladies and gentlemen, in 1983 Nancy and I welcomed President and Mrs. Eanes, as you've been told, to the White House on a state visit. And while in Washington, the Eanes's told us a great deal about the history of Portugal. Last month, Mrs. Eanes returned to the White House to attend a conference of First Ladies that Nancy had organized, and once again we heard about the glories of Portugal—the magnificent climate, the alluring beauty of your coast, the splendor of your architecture, and most important the renowned friendliness and energetic talent of the Portuguese people. Well, that did it, and here we are.

Mr. President and Mrs. Eanes, it is an honor for us to join you. For your warmth, your kindness, and your hospitality we thank you from our hearts. We're delighted to be here in one of the oldest states in Europe, a country that traces her independence to 1140 and her present-day boundaries to 1249. As you noted in Washington, Mr. President, during her eight centuries of independence, Portugal has been a major participant in the long and complex effort that created the Europe that we know today.

Still more significant, Portugal contributed to our conception of the world itself. It was your country, smaller than many others and situated on the extreme western edge of the continent, that became a keystone by which Europe was joined with Africa, Asia, and America, integrating for the first time the four corners of the Earth.

Young students in America, and I would imagine in all lands, will forever be fascinated by the dreams and skill and courage of the Portuguese, who gave the world some of the greatest adventures in human history. Portuguese ships reaching the Canary Islands as early as 1337; then, supported by Prince Henry the Navigator and John II, exploring further to the Congo, southern Africa, and around the Cape of Good Hope; and in 1499, Vasco da Gama's miraculous return from India, an epic event that stirred all Europe and formed the basis for one of the great literary works of Western civilization, the poem "The Lusiadas."

By the early 1500's your flag was flying in the Americas, and by 1542 João Cabrilho discovered California, and that happens to be one discovery, if I may say so, for which Nancy and I will always be particularly grateful.

In these years man's sense of the possible was expanded. The unknown world yielded to reason and daring. The known world was celebrated and adorned. It was a time of intellectual and cultural excitement, a time when the Portuguese were reaching for the new and the unexplored and when the greatness of the human spirit was given expression in greatness of deed and art.

Today, Mr. President, we who have studied and been so stirred by the feats of Portugal's past, see your nation setting off on am ambitious new voyage into the future. Your democracy is just a decade old. Already, it has been threatened, but you overcame those threats. You've suffered economic disruptions and slow growth, but you're facing these problems forthrightly, and I believe you will overcome them as well. In doing so you bring honor to democratic ideals; and you are, once again, expanding the limits of the possible. Portuguese democracy is no longer a risky experiment but a solidly established fact. The spirit of daring is thriving again.

Mr. President, your personal leadership in helping to shepherd the Portuguese renewal has been strong, constant, and decisive. You have defended democratic freedoms and civil liberties. You have become a symbol of your country's commitment to liberty, helping Portugal herself become an example for all the world, showing those who still thirst for freedom that totalitarianism can be rebuffed and representative government established in its place. And for all this, Mr. President, we heartily salute you.

I'm pleased that since our last meeting our two nations have strengthened the bonds that unite us. We have completed agreements on military assistance and cooperation. Portugal has created the Luso-American Foundation, which will prove an important instrument for cooperation in economic, technical, and other spheres. American banks have placed branches here in Lisbon, and recently a delegation of American business leaders visited Portugal to consider further investments in this country and joint undertakings with Portuguese enterprises. American business leaders know that Portugal now offers freedom and stability in economic life; these are precious seeds of opportunity that can blossom into great enterprises yielding greater abundance for tomorrow.

The friendship and trust between Portugal and the United States runs deep. We serve proudly together as members of the NATO alliance, defending the West. We consult widely on other foreign policy matters, and we in the United States value the perspective that your long involvement with Africa has given you on that continent.

I believe that the stars of our progress are bright. And as travel between our countries increases and Portugal takes up its membership in the European Community—an important step for Portugal and all of Europe—they will shine brighter still. We look forward to the work that Portugal and the United States will do together—improving the lives of our people, defending the free world, and by our example extending comfort to the downtrodden and hope to the oppressed everywhere.

At the close of the "The Lusiadas," the poet addresses King Sebastião and, in a wider sense, Portugal herself. He speaks of the John I and Pedro the Just, two of Portugal's monarchs on the eve of the Age of Discovery:

Yet thou, Sebastião, thou, my king, attend;
Behold what glories on thy throne descend!
Oh, be it thine these glories to renew,
And John's bold path and Pedro's course pursue.

Mr. President, it is in our own time that Portugal is truly taking up the poet's challenge. Today the ancient glories are being renewed in freedom, and the bold path has a very special name—*democracia.*

Ladies and gentlemen, please join me in a toast to you, Mr. President, to Portugal, and to the success of Portugal's future of freedom, democracy, and peace.

Note: President Reagan spoke at 10:14 p.m. in the Throne Room at Ajuda Palace. He spoke in response to a toast by President Eanes.

The President's News Conference
May 10, 1985

The President's Trip to Europe

The President. Ladies and gentlemen, I wanted to share with you this morning some of the more significant results of this trip and to take a few of your questions before we leave for home.

The journey to Europe has involved many highs and, yes, some anguishing moments. It took us to one of Europe's youngest capitals and two of its oldest and to a city which symbolizes the continuing quest for European unity. And at every stop I emphasized that our European friends can count on the United States to be their partner, to help them grow, to support their democratic aspirations, and to stand with them to protect the peace.

We are leaving today with our Atlantic ties strengthened, and we're returning home mission accomplished.

Let me summarize what I believe to be our lasting achievements.

First, our visit to the Federal Republic has strengthened U.S.-German relations and the prospects for continuing peace in Europe. The German leadership characterized our visit as opening a new page in German history. I believe that our partnership and friendship have never been greater or stronger. At the Bonn Economic Summit we agreed to a common strategy to ensure continued economic prosperity and job creation. We also moved closer to our goal of launching a new multilateral trade round to eliminate barriers to free trade. All the summit countries have agreed to the need for a new round; all but one agreed that it should begin early next year.

We were pleased that our partners endorsed U.S. efforts in Geneva to achieve significant reductions in nuclear arms. We also reached agreement for intensified cooperation against international drug trafficking.

Next, at the European Parliament in Strasbourg, we set forth a sensible framework for improved U.S.-Soviet relations based on strength, realism, peaceful competition, and negotiations. I conveyed to the Soviet Union once again America's heartfelt desire for peace. The constructive, commonsense initiatives we proposed to reduce tensions between us deserve a serious Soviet response.

In Spain and Portugal, we further enhanced our ties with two close friends and valued partners. It was heartening to see firsthand the strides these two courageous democracies have made, both politically and economically.

It's been a long, historic, and thoroughly worthwhile trip. Issues of major significance were dealt with openly, vigorously, and in depth. From our meetings came a strongly shared commitment to freedom, democracy, growth, and European unity.

And now, I don't think that I've left anything unanswered, but you probably want to ask some questions anyway.

All right, Andrea [Andrea Mitchell, NBC News].

Defense Spending and Social Security

Q. Mr. President, a week ago, you said it would be an irresponsible act if anyone agreed to zero growth on defense. Now you have accepted that, and you've also accepted a freeze on all COLA's, including Social Security. Can you explain about your campaign promise and why you've changed your mind?

The President. Well, let's take the defense matter first. The zero growth is for 1 year, the first year, and then the growth rate that we had asked for for the next 2 years is included in this but at the same time. And just a little while ago—somewhere around 4 o'clock in the morning in Washington—I had the assurance of the Senators that this is done with the proviso that if at any time the zero growth reveals in the coming year that it is going to in any way reduce our national security or harm it in any way, I will be back asking for a supplemental to overcome that.

Now, the second thing that you asked about was——

Q. Social Security.

The President. Social Security. Well, first of all, I never felt when I was answering the accusations that were made in a somewhat demagogic way in the campaign that I was going to cut the benefits, reduce them for the recipients. And I was denying that I had any such idea or would ever have any such idea. I didn't have in my mind that we were talking about any potential or possible increases. But it was interpreted that way, so, okay, I live with that. The thing that has been agreed to actually will amount to about the same benefits as the 2, 2, and 2, which I proposed.

Now, we have found that the 2, 2, and 2 that I had proposed—that most people aren't aware of all of the terms of that. And this is particularly true of the Social Security recipients. Most of them were not aware or did not recall that if inflation drops below 3 percent, there is no COLA. And most of them were not aware that our 2, 2, and 2 was 2, plus any percentage of increase in inflation above 4 percent. And when this was pointed out to them in surveys, roughly around 70 percent of the people preferred that and said that they would take that.

Now, as I say, we have—all right, so we have held for 1 year a freeze in this and then return to the normal COLA process. And as I say, for 3 years that comes out about even to the 2, 2, 2.

So, the other thing that I did say was that unless I was faced with a mandate—and I would suggest that I was faced with a mandate when 79 percent of the Senators, which means pretty much half and half Democrat and Republican, demanded that we have some curbing of the COLA's.

Helen [Helen Thomas, United Press International]?

Meeting with Soviet Leader Gorbachev

Q. Do you plan to go to the U.N. in the fall with the possibility of meeting Gorbachev? And why is it that you can preach reconciliation to the Germans, who committed so many horrors, and not say the same thing to the Soviet Union on this trip?

The President. Well, I thought that I had said some things. I told about the changes that we felt in this unifying of Europe should take place, but I also emphasized that it must take place peacefully, that I was not suggesting any hostile action.

With regard to going to the U.N., no, we have no confirmation yet that Mr. Gorbachev is coming. The word probable is about the best way to describe it. But it did not—that statement did not come from him.

I then extended an invitation that if he was going to be here, the door was open for a meeting between us. And that still goes. So, the ball is in his court, first, to decide whether he's coming here. And then, second, as to time and place for such a meeting, if he is willing.

Eastern Europe

Q. Mr. President, in the past you've drawn a distinction between dictatorships on the right and Marxist dictatorships, saying those on the right can evolve into democracies, but Communist dictatorships

never do. Yet here in Europe, you have talked about the changes you want to see in Eastern Europe, where Communist dictatorships are most deeply entrenched. How do you see those changes taking place and what is your role in those changes?

The President. Well, we've said that we would be most helpful to anyone who wants to make this modification. We have seen enough examples, in the Americas alone, of military dictatorships or just outright dictatorships and pressure from the people in the democratic process changing those to the point that today south of our border, roughly 90 percent of the people in what we call Latin America are now living in democracies or in countries that are moving toward democracy. And the only two totalitarian powers in our hemisphere are Nicaragua and Cuba. So, it is true that there is evidence that right-wing governments or dictatorships—well, we're standing in one that has gone from dictatorship to democracy. The same was true in Spain, when we were there.

But it is true that what has been called the Brezhnev doctrine has been predominant, that once they get their grip in a country, it doesn't change. There are evidences that that isn't true. Well, as a matter of fact, that, too, happened here because— in addition to dictatorial tradition—there was a time when communism seemed to be moving in here. And again, the people of Portugal made that change.

Bill [Bill Plante, CBS News]. And then I'll take you.

SALT Agreements

Q. Mr. President, a few days ago, an official of your government, Richard Perle, in the Defense Department, said that it was his opinion that it was time for the United States to start violating or stop observing the SALT agreements.

First of all, sir, what do you think of him offering that opinion? And second, what do you think about it? Is it time to stop observing the SALT agreement?

The President. Well, first of all, you know, in the country of ours, everyone's got a right to express their opinion, and he was doing no more than that—something that I know is very precious to all of you. But I would—I'm trying to think of how I want to answer this question. Maybe you'd better reframe that last part again so I can get my mind switched from whether he had a right to or not.

Q. Well, let me put it this way, sir: What do you think? Is it time for the United States to stop observing the SALT treaty, which, of course, we've never ratified?

The President. All right, yes. We have tried on what seemed to be a verbal agreement between ourselves and the Soviet Union for some time that, even though we had not ratified that treaty, it had been signed by the negotiators, that we would both seek to abide by the terms. There's considerable evidence now that that has been rather one-sided. And if it has been, then there's no need for us to continue.

But whether we do or not, that's a decision to be made down the road. Actually, we have not come to a point in which we, in any way, in our own buildup are violating or going beyond the terms of that treaty. It is possible with regard to one system of weapons that we might come to such a point. And we'll make that decision then. And if we do, we'll do it openly, and we will do it with full knowledge of the Soviet Union.

Nicaragua

Q. Yes, sir. Almost everywhere that you went in Europe, the foreign leaders opposed the Nicaraguan trade embargo, and we now hear that Costa Rica has opposed it. Why is it, sir, that some of your closest allies don't back you on this and don't seem to feel that Ortega and the Sandinistas are the threat that you think he is?

The President. I don't think there's any question, Chris [Chris Wallace, NBC News], that they don't agree with us about the threat—they do. They know what Nicaragua is. On the other hand, we're running into a kind of a philosophical difference here, I think with regard to sanctions. We did a lot of soul searching about it ourselves. There are a number of people, certainly a number of governments, who just don't believe in that as a legitimate weapon.

On the other hand, when we were trying to get aid for the people of Nicaragua in their struggle for democracy and against totalitarianism, many of our own people in the Congress brought up the fact of how could we be doing this at the same time that we continued to maintain relations. Well, we had continued to maintain relations, and even including trade relations, with them as a refutation of their charge that we were seeking their overthrow.

All we have ever sought is that they, as one faction—when I say "they," I mean the Sandinista government. That Sandinista government has never been legitimized by the people. It is one faction of a revolution that overthrew a dictator. And they stole that revolution away from the other factions which we now call the *contras*. And the leaders of the *contras* were leaders in that revolution also.

And in doing that, we have felt that what we are seeking and trying to pressure them to do is to come together again in discussion and negotiations to restore the promises they, themselves, had made as to what the goals of the revolution were. And in doing that—and as I say, to refute their charges that we were somehow threatening them with aggression, and if you'll remember, there was a time when Mr. Ortega had us, every other week, landing the marines in Nicaragua, and we never had any intention to do such a thing. So, we maintained our embassy there, we continued our trade to show what we really wanted to do.

And then, in this recent vote in the Congress, we found many Congressmen justifying their position on the grounds that how could we still be doing business and yet wanting to aid this other faction of the revolution. And we have decided that pressure is needed to bring them to the realization that they should restore the original goals of their revolution.

Meeting With Soviet Leader Gorbachev

Q. Mr. President, in recent days, Mr. Gorbachev has had some rather harsh things to say about the United States and about you. If there is a summit meeting, what would you have to talk about, and what do you think that such a meeting could reasonably produce in the current climate?

The President. Oh, I think there would be a lot to talk about, and I just happen to believe, that it's time we started talking to each other instead of about each other. And with regard to the harsh things that he's had to say about me, what's new about that. That, I think, has been consistent not only with me but with every other American President. It's just their way of doing things.

Defense Spending

Q. Mr. President, a few days ago—I'd like to go back to the defense budget—a few days ago you told us it would be an irresponsible act to freeze it. This morning you seem to say it's okay to freeze it, but if you discover in the future that it is irresponsible, you'll go back to Congress. Doesn't that suggest, sir, that you don't really have a firm view of what figure is needed? And doesn't it open you up in the House of Representatives to the House taking more out of the defense budget?

The President. Not one penny more should be taken out of that budget than has been given now. And, as I've said, we're talking about the year of 1986, and I have the agreement of the Senate that if this represents—and I, in my own mind, feel that it does represent a cut in spending beyond which we should go—that they recognize that I will be returning for a supplemental appropriation.

On the other hand, I have to point out to you that in this we have gotten more than 90 percent of what we have asked for in the budget. It will amount to some $56 billion this year—almost $300 billion, which was our goal over the first 3 years. And there's no questioning the importance of sending a signal, not only to the world but to our own business and financial communities that we are determined to deal with a deficit problem that has been a Democratic heritage for the last 50 years of deficit spending, continued deficit spending. And once and for all, we're going to try to get hold of it. Yes, Lesley [Lesley Stahl, CBS News].

Q. Mr. President, as you probably well know, you've been called the Teflon President now for almost 5 years. You, in this Senate vote on the budget, asked for a 6-percent increase in defense and no cuts in

Social Security. Why shouldn't this be interpreted as a cave-in on your part, and do you think that the Teflon has begun to peel?

The President. No, I have always believed from all my past experiences as a negotiator that you recognize that the other fellow is probably going to offer less than whatever you ask. And I've always kind of believed in leaving a cushion there for dealing. But this time things have changed. This was a deal—I don't like the word "deal"—this was a working out—*[laughter]*—of a budget that was acceptable to the Senate, as well as to ourselves. And I think that the first one we presented was a very sound budget. But I recognize that, in the give and take that must take place in a system such as ours, to attain more than 90 percent of what we asked for means that, all right, we can do some giving along the line also.

Q. Teflon?

Q. Mr. President, Mike Deaver says the Portuguese President is waiting.

The President. Oh, I have a President waiting for me here. Can I take one more, or——

Q. You can if you want to.

The President. All right, one more. I'm sorry——

Tax Increase

Q. Mr. President, since you've shown a willingness to compromise on the budget on defense and some of the spending programs, would you also be willing to compromise on your tax reform program as a price of getting that, or 90 percent of it, to accept, perhaps, a temporary tax increase or a surcharge?

The President. No. You've now come down to what was part of our success in getting what we have. They all know that I absolutely will not accept a proposal for a tax increase. I think it is the worst kind of economic practice to do that. I think it would endanger our recovery, and they know that I will veto any proposal that comes to me for a tax increase. They also know that I have a signed letter, signed by 146 Representatives, which is enough to sustain a veto—that, I have that in my pocket also.

So, they tell me I have to go—that your President is waiting.

The President's Visit to Portugal

Q. ——Portuguese television. One quick question, Mr. President. Would you compare to the reception you have here in Portugal with those in other countries in Europe—would you compare your reception here in Portugal?

The President. Well, may I say to you that every place I've been in Europe, I have been impressed by the warmth of the people, by their open hospitality and welcome to me and that has held true here, as much as in any other country, and I have been greatly heartened by the reception of the people. Now, if in your minds you are thinking in terms of certain demonstrations, well, I'd have that in my own country. There is a faction wherever you go that's on the other side, and it happens to be a faction that kind of goes out of its way to be rude and nasty in expressing its opinion. But I've just come to accept that as part of the way of life. And as Harry Truman said, "If you can't stand the heat, stay out of the kitchen."

So, I just have to tell you, I'm most gratified. I think I leave with sound friendships with the people of your government, personal friendships, as well as alliances between us or agreements between us. And I'm very pleased.

Michael K. Deaver

Let me just say one thing and then I have to go back here. Since there's been a lot of discussion about some members of my administration, and one in particular this being Mike Deaver's last day—I just want to say to you that I consider Mike's leaving in the nature of an amputation, and it is me that is suffering the amputation. He has been with us a number of years. I have never found fault with anything that he's doing, with his loyalty, with his friendship, and with the common sense that he has always used. And that extends to the arrangements for this trip and the part that he has played in the arranging of the trip. And while it was very difficult, I know that most of you are totally exhausted; some of us managed to survive a little better— [*laughter*]—if so, it's because we had Mike working in our behalf, particularly. And he's going to be greatly missed.

All right. Thank you all.

Note: The President's 30th news conference began at 9:40 a.m. at Queluz Palace in Lisbon, Portugal. Michael K. Deaver was Deputy Chief of Staff and Assistant to the President. Following the news conference, the President returned to Washington, DC.

Remarks Upon Return From Europe
May 10, 1985

Well, Vice President Bush, members of the Cabinet, members of the diplomatic corps, to each and all of you who are here, Nancy and I thank you from the bottoms of our heart for coming out to give us a warm welcome home. We've had a fine trip, a full and challenging trip, and as I said this morning, a successful trip, and we think we're returning home "mission accomplished."

We return with warm memories of European friendship for America. The European people know the United States is working hard for freedom, democracy, and peace, and believe me they appreciate our efforts, as we do theirs.

I know you've heard that because there were a few demonstrations, some things might have been going wrong. But you know every time I noticed who was demonstrating, I felt reassured that we were saying and doing the right things.

I don't mind telling you there's a very special person who does a wonderful job on these trips, also. Whether meeting with leaders and parents concerned about drugs in Bonn, Lisbon, or with the Holy Father at the Vatican, or doing a pretty fair flamenco in Madrid, I think Nancy's one of the best ambassadors America's ever had. And I look at the press she got, I'm taking flamenco lessons myself. [*Laughter*]

Well, we feel good about what's been done, and after every summit leader agreed that steady economic growth means each government getting spending under control, how sweet it is to return with a 50–49 Senate victory for spending restraint and no tax increase.

And thank you, George Bush, for flying all the way back here from the West and casting the tie-breaking vote.

And our thanks to Bob Dole and Pete Dominici, the Republican leadership of the Senate, their colleagues, and Senator Pete Wilson for the grit that he showed in coming back when we needed him the most.

So, I thank them all for a budget resolution that moves Congress toward real spending restraint and significantly lower deficits. This was a courageous and a politically difficult action.

During these discussions with our economic allies, concern was voiced that projected budget deficits threaten world economic growth. Well, this Senate budget resolution represents a savings of almost $300 billion over the next 3 years, and it reflects the Senate's willingness to bite the bullet to help sustain our economic expansion.

It's easy for some to attack individual elements of the Senate package, but I'm convinced that this was the only serious deficit reduction package that could pass the Senate.

Our commitment to America's security is determined by the threat posed by our adversaries. If we conclude that our national security is jeopardized, I will not hesitate to request, and the Senate leaders have assured me that they will consider, supplemental funding for fiscal year '86.

I know Americans agree with us that we must restrain the growth of this Federal Establishment. The Senate has made an important commitment to cut excessive spending. Now it's up to the House to do as good a job reducing the deficit by cutting spending and not raising taxes. And we urge the House to pass a responsible budget resolution as soon as possible. We're committed to reducing excessive government spending and urge bipartisan support in both Houses of the Congress to help us in that effort.

And now, it's time to say goodbye again. This time I don't mind because we're just going upstairs, and we'll see you all very soon.

Thank you all again. God bless you all. Thank you.

Note: The President spoke to administration officials and members of the White House staff at 2:05 p.m. at the South Portico of the White House.

Letter Accepting the Resignation of Michael K. Deaver as Assistant to the President and Deputy Chief of Staff
May 10, 1985

Dear Mike:

You know I've accepted your resignation orally but I suppose I have to put something down on paper—after all, this is Washington. The only place I haven't accepted it is in my heart, and there I never will.

I've come to the conclusion that Nancy and I will both agree you will bodily leave the West Wing. You will no longer bear a government title. You will not actually handle such things as schedule, trips, etc., but that's as far as we go. You will continue to be a part of our lives. We will have concern—one for the other, and refuse surgery that would in any way remove you from a relationship that is part of our life-support system. In return, we will continue to be eternally grateful.

Sincerely,

/s/RON

Dear Mr. President:

It is with sincere mixed emotions that I write this letter of resignation as Deputy Chief of Staff of the White House.

During these four and one half years I've experienced the most personally rewarding and satisfying time of my life.

Probably the most exciting part of this experience for me has been the thrill of seeing you, Mr. President, rise to the great challenges under difficult circumstances and achieve success.

To say I'm grateful for this opportunity falls way short of my true feelings. I'll always remember these years with fondness and pride.

Please remember, I'm always there if either you or Nancy need me.

God bless you both.

Sincerely,

/s/MIKE

Note: The originals were not available for verification of the content of these letters.

Proclamation 5337—National Correctional Officers Week, 1985
May 10, 1985

By the President of the United States of America

A Proclamation

Correctional officers occupy a vital role in our Nation's criminal justice systems. They are called upon to ensure the custody, safety, and well-being of the over 680,000 inmates in prisons and jails. Without these officers performing demanding and often dangerous assignments, it would be impossible to carry out the primary law enforcement mission of protecting the law-abiding citizens of this country.

In a time of rapidly growing inmate populations, the demands upon correctional officers are many. As the backbone of our correctional systems, they work hard to maintain the high professional standards necessary to ensure the safe and orderly running of our Nation's prisons and jails. The dedication exhibited by these officers in the daily performance of their duties deserves our greatest respect and appreciation.

In recognition of the contributions of correctional officers to our Nation, the Congress, by Senate Joint Resolution 64, has designated the week beginning May 5, 1985, as "National Correctional Officers Week" and authorized and requested the President to issue an appropriate proclamation in commemoration of the observance.

Now, Therefore, I, Ronald Reagan, President of the United States of America, do hereby proclaim the week beginning May 5, 1985, as National Correctional Officers Week. I call upon officials of State and local governments and the people of the United States to observe this week with appropriate ceremonies and activities.

In Witness Whereof, I have hereunto set my hand this tenth day of May, in the year of our Lord nineteen hundred and eighty-five, and of the Independence of the United States of America the two hundred and ninth.

RONALD REAGAN

[*Filed with the Office of the Federal Register, 11:22 a.m., May 14, 1985*]

Note: The proclamation was released by the Office of the Press Secretary on May 11.

Proclamation 5338—National Asthma and Allergy Awareness Week, 1985
May 10, 1985

By the President of the United States of America

A Proclamation

Asthma and allergic diseases are among the Nation's most common and costly health problems. More than 35 million Americans suffer from these diseases—about one out of every six persons. The American public pays approximately $4 billion per year in medical bills directly related to the treatment and diagnosis of asthma and allergic diseases, and another $2 billion per year in indirect social costs. Absenteeism in the schools and in the work place resulting from these diseases has an enormous effect on the Nation.

Although modern medical treatments of asthma and allergic disorders have reduced the danger of death considerably, thousands of individuals still die each year from asthma—a disease that affects children more often than adults.

In order to improve the quality of life for those who suffer from asthma and allergic diseases, research scientists supported by the National Institutes of Health (NIH) are acquiring vital knowledge of these disorders. These scientists are optimistic that information gained through their research will provide means to develop new techniques for diagnosing, treating, and possibly preventing these debilitating diseases.

In addition, the NIH works closely with the Asthma and Allergy Foundation of America, as well as with other volunteer and professional health groups, to bring to the attention of health care professionals and the public current research results that can be translated into improved health care.

To focus public and professional attention on the seriousness of asthma and allergic diseases, the Congress, by Senate Joint Resolution 83, has designated the week of May 5, 1985, through May 11, 1985, as "National Asthma and Allergy Awareness Week" and authorized and requested the President to issue a proclamation in observance of that week.

Now, Therefore, I, Ronald Reagan, President of the United States of America, do hereby proclaim the week beginning May 5, 1985, through May 11, 1985, as National Asthma and Allergy Awareness Week. I call upon all government agencies, health organizations, communications media, and the people of the United States to observe this week with appropriate ceremonies and activities.

In Witness Whereof, I have hereunto set my hand this tenth day of May, in the year of our Lord nineteen hundred and eighty-five, and of the Independence of the United States of America the two hundred and ninth.

RONALD REAGAN

[*Filed with the Office of the Federal Register, 11:23 a.m., May 14, 1985*]

Note: The proclamation was released by the Office of the Press Secretary on May 11.

Radio Address to the Nation on the Trip to Europe and Mother's Day
May 11, 1985

My fellow Americans:

I've just completed an extraordinary 10-day visit to Europe, where I attended the Bonn Economic Summit and helped mark with European leaders the 40th anniversary of V–E Day. It was an exciting trip and a demanding one, and it left Nancy and me with a number of unforgettable memories.

But sometimes the most memorable moment is something you notice by chance, that hits your heart and yields an unforgettable image. For me it was the sight of an elderly woman standing among the onlookers as we drove through the streets of Strasbourg, France, on the way to the European Parliament to help mark the 40th anniversary of V–E Day.

Most of the onlookers waved and smiled, but the elderly woman who had stepped off the sidewalk and onto the street was waving a handkerchief in the air and smiling and yelling "Hello." She looked just like the young French women who waved their handkerchiefs 40 years ago as the American convoys drove through the newly freed nation of France, and then I realized, maybe she was one of those young women. And as we drove by her, I thought perhaps she knows better than all of us what the anniversary of V–E Day is all about.

It was a wonderful trip, but it's good to be home. And it's especially good to be home this weekend because tomorrow is a holiday very close to our hearts—it's Mother's Day.

Mothers are the creators of the family, and the family is the center of society. It's no accident that America chose to honor all mothers with a special holiday. After all, mothers have made a unique contribution to our country. They're the main communicators of the values by which our nation has flourished for more than 200 years—the values of honesty, responsibility, decency, and personal effort. By imparting these and other values to our children, the mothers of America quite literally shape the future.

Mother's Day takes on a special significance this year for a number of reasons. One is the extraordinary phenomenon of the mothers of America joining together to press for much needed change in our society. There's Mothers Against Drunk Driving, the remarkable group started by a woman whose daughter was killed several years ago by a drunk driver. MADD, as it is called, has been responsible for helping bring tougher laws against drunk drivers in many States. The group has also heightened public awareness of the problem of drunk driving and made our children more aware of its hazards.

There is also the growing number of women who've joined in the fight against drug abuse. Recently in Washington there was a very important conference for the wives of 17 heads of state and government leaders on how they can strengthen families and help combat the epidemic of drug addiction among our children. That meeting was conceived and chaired by another Reagan named Nancy. I'm deeply proud of her involvement in this crusade, proud of her heartfelt commitment and the sacrifices she's made to help children in their struggle against drug addiction. Nancy, like any mother, feels pain when she sees and hears the cry of a child. So, I hope you don't mind my taking this moment to say thanks Nancy and happy Mother's Day.

And like all of you, I find my thoughts turning to my own mother, Nelle Reagan. She was truly a remarkable woman—ever so strong in her determination yet always tender, always giving of herself to others. She never found time in her life to complain; she was too busy living those values she sought to impart in my brother and myself. She was the greatest influence on my life, and as I think of her this weekend I remember the words of Lincoln, "All that I am, or hope to be, I owe to my mother."

There's a group of mothers I'd like to mention, whose lives aren't remarked upon enough, but who should be given special mention today. That is the group of mothers who've made an extraordinary personal commitment by adopting children with special needs. These are mothers who have adopted older children, often foster children, and mothers who have taken in children who are unwell, either emotionally or physically, or who need special care of one sort or another. No one knows the heartaches and joys these mothers go through helping those who are most in need of a parent's loving concern.

Finally, one other group deserves special honors, it's the largest of all—the working mothers of America. Some devote their full time to raising families, others combine that responsibility with jobs in the marketplace. Some are breadwinners; others are not. But all deserve our respect and thanks. All of these mothers work hard; in fact, they must be the hardest working people in America. Happy Mother's Day to these and all other mothers.

Until next week, thanks for listening, and God bless you.

Note: The President spoke at 12:06 p.m. from the Oval Office at the White House.

Statement on the Conference on Confidence and Security Building Measures and Disarmament in Europe
May 13, 1985

Tomorrow, May 14, the Stockholm Conference on Confidence and Security Building Measures and Disarmament in Europe (CDE) enters its sixth round. The Conference includes all the NATO, Warsaw Pact, and European neutral countries and is thus in a unique position to play a major role in improving East-West relations. I attach great importance to this Conference.

The NATO countries have worked together at Stockholm to introduce a series of concrete confidence-building measures designed to make European military activities more predictable and more stable and to ensure that no weapons of any kind are ever used. These measures would require the mandatory notification and observation of all military activities above a certain level, together with appropriate verification measures, such as information exchange and on-site inspection. They are designed to reduce the risk of war by miscalculation and misunderstanding, guard against a surprise attack, and increase significantly the political cost to any state which would use the threat of force to intimidate another.

This ambitious program has the full sup-

port of all the nations of NATO as well as bipartisan political support here at home. The neutral and nonaligned countries of Europe also support the general principles outlined in the NATO proposal.

In my address to the European Parliament last week, I urged once again that the Stockholm Conference reach prompt agreement on this package of measures proposed by the NATO countries. And I reiterated our pledge that the United States is prepared to discuss the Soviet proposal on nonuse of force in the context of Soviet agreement to concrete confidence-building measures. We hope the Soviet Union will give this serious consideration.

In Stockholm we have an opportunity to work in practical ways to reduce tension in Europe. The Conference is now at a point where it could move into a more intense negotiating phase, if the Soviet Union is prepared to join the rest of the Conference in negotiating meaningful confidence-building measures which go well beyond existing arrangements. In seeking this goal, Ambassador James E. Goodby, my representative to the Stockholm Conference, has my full confidence and support.

Nomination of Russell F. Miller To Be Deputy Inspector General of the United States Synthetic Fuels Corporation
May 13, 1985

The President today announced his intention to nominate Russell F. Miller to be Deputy Inspector General of the United States Synthetic Fuels Corporation for a

term of 7 years. He would succeed Robert Gambino.

Mr. Miller is currently Director of Investigations, U.S. Synthetic Fuels Corporation.

Previously, he was a consultant on the staff of the assistant to the Chairman of the Board of Directors for Inspections and Internal Audit at the U.S. Synthetic Fuels Corporation (1981–1982) and was engaged in residential real estate sales work in 1979–1980. He retired in 1979 as a senior officer after 29 years in the Central Intelligence Agency, where he served as chief of field units abroad, responsible to the U.S. Ambas-sador and to CIA headquarters in Washington.

Mr. Miller graduated from the University of Iowa (B.A., 1943) and Drake University College of Law (LL.B., 1950). He attended the Georgetown University School of Foreign Service (1946). He is married, has four children, and resides in Potomac, MD. He was born October 25, 1921, in Panora, IA.

Appointment of A. Freeman Holmer as a Member of the National Council on Public Works
May 13, 1985

The President today announced his intention to appoint A. Freeman Holmer to be a member of the National Council on Public Works. This is a new position.

Mr. Holmer is currently coordinator for government affairs for the Eugene, Oregon, Chamber of Commerce. Previously, he was with the State of Oregon as director of finance and administration and vice chancellor for administration, higher education; with the State of Wisconsin as director of environmental protection; and with the Council of State Governments as associate director in Washington, DC.

Mr. Holmer graduated from Concordia College (B.A., 1938) and the University of Oregon (M.A., 1946). He is married, has two children, and resides in Eugene, OR. He was born November 3, 1917, in St. Paul, MN.

Appointment of Theodore C. Barreaux as a Member of the Board of Trustees of the Woodrow Wilson International Center for Scholars
May 13, 1985

The President today announced his intention to appoint Theodore C. Barreaux to be a member of the Board of Trustees of the Woodrow Wilson International Center for Scholars, Smithsonian Institution, for a term expiring October 23, 1990. This is a reappointment.

Mr. Barreaux is currently vice president, American Institute of Certified Public Accountants. Previously, he was Director of Congressional Relations, Office of the Chairman, U.S. Securities and Exchange Commission (1972–1976); senior consultant, Development Alternatives, Inc. (1971–1972); vice chairman and senior adviser, Planning and Review Commission, Office of the Director, Office of Economic Opportunity, Executive Office of the President (1970–1971); and special assistant to the Federal Cochairman of the Four Corners Regional Commission, U.S. Department of Commerce (1969–1970).

Mr. Barreaux attended the University of the City of New York. He resides in Washington, DC, and was born September 12, 1943, in New York City.

Nomination of Edward Joseph Perkins To Be United States Ambassador to Liberia
May 13, 1985

The President today announced his intention to nominate Edward Joseph Perkins, of Oregon, a career member of the Senior Foreign Service, Class of Minister-Counselor, as Ambassador to the Republic of Liberia. He would succeed William Lacy Swing.

Mr. Perkins began his government career in 1958 as Chief of Personnel, Army and Air Force Exchange Service, in Taipei, Taiwan. In 1962 he became Deputy Chief of Personnel and Administration, Army and Air Force Exchange Service, in Okinawa and in 1964 was made Chief of Personnel and Administration, where he served until 1966. In 1966–1967 he was assistant general services officer in the Far East Bureau of the Agency for International Development. In 1967 he went to Bangkok as assistant general services officer at the United States Operations Mission to Thailand. In 1969 he served as management analyst and in 1970 assistant director for management at the mission, where he served until 1972. In 1972 he returned to the Department of State in Washington to become staff assistant in the Office of the Director General of the Foreign Service. From 1972 to 1974, Mr. Perkins was personnel officer in the Director General's office. In 1974–1975 he served as administrative officer in the Bureau of Near Eastern and South Asian Affairs and from there became a management analysis officer in the Office of Management Operations. From 1978 to 1981, Mr. Perkins was counselor for political affairs at our Embassy in Accra, Ghana. In 1981–1983 he was deputy chief of mission in Monrovia, Liberia. In 1983 he studied French at the Foreign Service Institute. From 1983 to the present, he has been Director, Office of West African Affairs, in the Bureau of African Affairs.

Mr. Perkins studied at the University of California and Lewis and Clark College. He graduated from the University of Maryland (B.A., 1967) and the University of Southern California (M.P.A., 1972; D.P.A., 1978). His foreign languages are Thai, French, and Japanese. He was born June 8, 1928, in Sterlington, LA. He is married to the former Lucy Liu, and they have two daughters.

Appointment of Three Members of the National Commission for Employment Policy
May 13, 1985

The President today announced his intention to appoint the following individuals to be members of the National Commission for Employment Policy for terms expiring March 20, 1988. These are reappointments.

Walton E. Burdick is currently vice president of personnel for the IBM Corp. He graduated from Cornell University (B.S., 1955). He is married, has five children, and resides in Mount Kisco, NY. He was born May 16, 1932, in Scranton, PA.

Max L. Rowe is currently an attorney with the law firm of Kirkland & Ellis in Chicago, IL. He graduated from the University of Illinois (A.B., 1943; J.D., 1946) and the University of Chicago (M.B.A., 1952). He is married, has four children, and resides in Wilmette, IL. He was born August 14, 1921, in Dallas City, IL.

Paula V. Smith is currently Missouri director of labor and industrial relations in Jefferson City, MO. She graduated from Washington University (B.S., 1972) and St. Louis University (M.B.A., 1977). She is married, has three children, and resides in St. Louis, MO.

Message on the Observance of National Nursing Home Week, May 12–18, 1985
May 13, 1985

During National Nursing Home Week, I urge all Americans to remember the contributions our older citizens have made in building America. These men and women are an important link with traditional American values for our young people today. Continued contact between older and younger Americans helps to strengthen these values for our future.

I support the goals of the nursing home industry to provide the highest standards of medical and social services for the elderly, but institutional care is not enough. We must also encourage everyone to include the elderly in their lives. Wisdom, memory and life experience can help us all to better understand this complex and changing world.

Throughout the year let us visit our elderly relatives and friends in nursing homes to share our love and caring. We owe them our help, understanding and, above all, respect. In return, they will give us their experience and sense of continuity. Together we can enrich all of our lives.

RONALD REAGAN

Message on the Observance of Police Week and Police Officers' Memorial Day, May, 1985
May 13, 1985

At this time each year we stop a moment to remember those law enforcement officers who have given their lives in the line of duty.

Few of us take the time to consider how much we rely on these individuals who defend the principles of law and order that uphold our nation. Our police officers preserve our rights while protecting us from those who would abuse them.

Every year, tragically, some among the ranks of these brave men and women sacrifice their lives in the performance of their jobs. The giving of this most precious possession, life itself, is a dramatic demonstration of the intense dedication and selfless service of those who keep the peace and safeguard our lives and property each and every day. Let us resolve to do all in our power as citizens of these United States to support our law enforcement officers in their work and pray that no more of them are taken from their families and those they so ably serve. In this way, those who have laid down their lives for their fellowman will not have died in vain.

RONALD REAGAN

Nomination of Lewis Arthur Tambs To Be United States Ambassador to Costa Rica
May 14, 1985

The President today announced his intention to nominate Lewis Arthur Tambs to be Ambassador of the United States of America to the Republic of Costa Rica. He would succeed Curtin Winsor, Jr.

Mr. Tambs served in the United States Army in 1945–1947 and in 1950–1951. In 1953–1954 he was an assistant plant engineer at Standard Brands, Inc., in San Francisco, CA. He was in Venezuela as pipeline engineer at Creole Petroleum (1954–1957) and general manager of CACYP-Instalaciones Petroleras (1957–1959). In 1960–1961 he was cryogenic small piping designer at Air Reduction Corp. in San Francisco. He was teaching and research assistant at the University of California at Berkeley (1961–1964) and instructor, then assistant professor of history, at Creighton University in Omaha, NE (1965–1969). In 1969–1982 he was with Arizona State University in Tempe, AZ, as assistant professor (1975–1982). Mr. Tambs was a lecturer in Brazilian history, American Graduate School of International Management, at Thunderbird Campus in Glendale, AZ, in 1973–1979; visiting professor of Latin American history at

the University of Arizona summer school in Guadalajara, Mexico, in 1974–1976, and lecturer, 18th annual Institute for the Study of Comparative Politics and Ideologies at the University of Colorado in Boulder, 1982. In 1972–1975 he was also director of the Center for Latin American Studies. He was a consultant to the National Security Council at the White House in 1982–1983 and from 1983 to the present has been our Ambassador to the Republic of Colombia.

He graduated from the University of California at Berkeley (B.S.I.E., 1953) and the University of California at Santa Barbara (M.A., 1962; Ph.D., 1967). His foreign languages are Spanish and Portuguese. He is married to the former Phyllis Greer and has five daughters.

Nomination of Lannon Walker To Be United States Ambassador to Senegal
May 14, 1985

The President today announced his intention to nominate Lannon Walker, of Maryland, a career member of the Senior Foreign Service, Class of Minister-Counselor, to be Ambassador of the United States of America to the Republic of Senegal. He would succeed Charles W. Bray III.

Mr. Walker entered on duty in the Department of State in 1961 and attended Western Arabic language school in 1962. In 1962–1964 he served as political officer at the U.S. Embassy in Rabat, Morocco. In 1964 he became principal officer at the American consulate in Constantine, Algeria. He returned to the Department in 1966 as a staff officer in the Executive Secretariat and then became Deputy Director. In 1969 he took economic training at the Foreign Service Institute. In 1970–1971 Mr. Walker was economic counselor at the U.S. Embassy in Tripoli, Libya. He then became deputy chief of mission at the U.S. Embassy in Yaounde, Cameroon, in 1971–1973. From

there he served as administrative counselor at the U.S. Embassy in Saigon, Vietnam, 1973–1974. In 1974 he went to the U.S. Embassy in Kinshasa, Zaire, first as economic counselor and then deputy chief of mission, where he served until 1977. He returned to the Department as office director for Central Africa and then became Assistant Secretary in the Bureau of African Affairs in 1977–1982. In 1982–1983 he took a leave of absence from the Department and became president, Joint Services Group, in Washington, DC. He returned to the Department in 1983 as senior adviser in the Bureau of African Affairs and from 1984 to the present has been Acting Deputy Inspector General.

Mr. Walker was born January 17, 1936, in Los Angeles, CA. He received his B.S.F.S. in 1961 from Georgetown University School of Foreign Service. His languages are French, Western Arabic, and Spanish. He is married to the former Arlette Daguet, and they have two daughters.

Nomination of Marvin L. Stone To Be Deputy Director of the United States Information Agency
May 14, 1985

The President today announced his intention to nominate Marvin L. Stone to be Deputy Director of the United States Information Agency. He would succeed Leslie Lenkowsky.

Mr. Stone served as editor of U.S. News & World Report from April 1976 until April 1985. He joined U.S. News & World Report in 1960 as Pentagon correspondent and shortly thereafter became associate editor for military and scientific affairs. He became executive director of the magazine in February 1973. Prior to joining U.S. News & World Report he studied science writing on a Sloan Foundation fellowship at Columbia University (1958–1959) and was special assistant to the chief of Army research and development at the Pentagon in 1959–1960. In 1949–1958 he was with the International News Service and served an 8-year tour as a war and foreign correspondent. He is on the executive committee of the American Society of Magazine Editors, a director of the National Press Foundation, and on the National Advisory Board of American University. He is past chairman of the U.S. Navy Memorial Foundation, past president of the Foreign Correspondents' Club of Japan and of the Columbia Journalism Alumni (Region South). He has received numerous awards for his work in the field of journalism.

He graduated from Marshall University in Huntington, WV, and the Columbia Graduate School of Journalism (1949), where he won a Pulitzer traveling fellowship. He is married, has three children, and resides in Falls Church, VA. He was born February 26, 1924, in Burlington, VT.

Appointment of Juan Rangel as a Member of the National Commission for Employment Policy
May 14, 1985

The President today announced his intention to appoint Juan Rangel to be a member of the National Commission for Employment Policy for the term expiring March 20, 1988. This is a reappointment.

Mr. Rangel is president and chief executive officer of MedCentre Bank, National Association, in San Antonio, TX. Previously he was president and chief executive officer of Commerce Bank, NA, in Laredo, TX. He was also secretary/treasurer and director of International Bancshares Corp. in Laredo, TX. In 1978–1981 he was senior vice president of the International Bank of Commerce in Laredo. He was vice president of Union National Bank (1975–1978) and national bank examiner for the Comptroller of the Currency in 1969–1975.

He graduated from St. Mary's University (B.B.A., 1971) and the University of Wisconsin Banking Graduate School (1978). He is married, has three children, and resides in San Antonio, TX. He was born May 23, 1948, in Castroville, TX.

Appointment of Naomi Zeavin as a Member of the Advisory Committee on the Arts of the John F. Kennedy Center for the Performing Arts
May 14, 1985

The President today announced his intention to appoint Naomi Zeavin to be a member of the Advisory Committee on the Arts (John F. Kennedy Center for the Performing Arts). This is an initial appointment.

Mrs. Zeavin is president of UR Unique, a marketing and public relations firm, in Falls Church, VA. She is a former author, actress, producer, and director and has worked for JBS Productions. She served as a member of the American Federation of Television and Radio Artists (AFTRA), Screen Actors Guild, Women in Film, and Women's Committee in AFTRA. She produced, wrote, and directed the film "Journey to Augustow" in Poland for PBS. In 1980–1984 she was appointed by Governor Dalton to serve on the board of visitors for the two deaf and blind schools of Virginia.

She attended Emerson College in Boston, MA. She is married, has four children, and resides in Falls Church, VA. She was born March 12, 1933, in New Britain, CT.

Nomination of Barbara Jean Mahone To Be Chairman of the Special Panel on Appeals
May 14, 1985

The President today announced his intention to nominate Barbara Jean Mahone to be Chairman of the Special Panel on Appeals for a term of 6 years. This is a new position established by P.L. 95–454.

Since 1983 Ms. Mahone has been Chairman of the Federal Labor Relations Authority. Previously, she was with the General Motors Corp. in 1973–1983, serving as manager of industrial relations for the Packard electric division (1982–1983); director of personnel administration for the Rochester products division (1978–1982); manager of career planning in human resources management (1974–1977); senior staff assistant of the personnel analysis group (1974); and staff assistant of the employee benefits section in 1973–1974.

She graduated from Ohio State University (B.S., 1968), the University of Michigan (M.B.A., 1972), and Harvard Business School (P.M.D., 1981). She was born April 19, 1946, in Nostagula, AL, and now resides in Washington, DC.

Executive Order 12514—Prescribing the Order of Succession of Officers To Act as Secretary of Defense, Secretary of the Army, Secretary of the Navy, and Secretary of the Air Force
May 14, 1985

By the authority vested in me as President by the Constitution and laws of the United States of America, including section 3347 of title 5, United States Code, it is hereby ordered as follows:

Part I. Succession to the Position of Secretary of Defense.

In the event of the death, disability, or

absence of the Secretary of Defense, the incumbents in the Department of Defense positions listed below shall succeed to the position of, and act as, Secretary of Defense in the order indicated:

1. Deputy Secretary of Defense.
2. Secretary of the Army.
3. Secretary of the Navy.
4. Secretary of the Air Force.
5. Under Secretary of Defense for Policy.
6. Under Secretary of Defense for Research and Engineering.
7. Assistant Secretaries of Defense and the General Counsel of the Department of Defense, in the order fixed by their length of service as such.
8. Under Secretaries of the Army, the Navy, and the Air Force, in the order fixed by their length of service as such.
9. Assistant Secretaries of the Army, the Navy, and the Air Force, in the order fixed by their length of service as such.

Precedence within a particular group between or among two or more officers having the same date of appointment shall be as determined by the Secretary of Defense at the time of appointment.

Part II. Succession to the Position of Secretary of the Army.

In the event of the death, disability, or absence of the Secretary of the Army, the officers designated below shall succeed to the position of, and act as, Secretary of the Army in the order indicated:

1. Under Secretary of the Army.
2. Assistant Secretaries of the Army, in the order fixed by their length of service as such.
3. Chief of Staff, United States Army.
4. Vice Chief of Staff, United States Army.
5. Commanding General, U.S. Army Forces Command.

Part III. Succession to the Position of Secretary of the Navy.

In the event of the death, disability, or absence of the Secretary of the Navy, the officers designated below shall succeed to the position of, and act as, Secretary of the Navy in the order indicated:

1. Under Secretary of the Navy.
2. Assistant Secretaries of the Navy, in the

order prescribed by the Secretary of the Navy, or if no order is prescribed by the Secretary, then in the order fixed by their length of service as such.

3. Chief of Naval Operations.
4. Vice Chief of Naval Operations.

Part IV. Succession to the Position of Secretary of the Air Force.

In the event of the death, disability, or absence of the Secretary of the Air Force, the officers designated below shall succeed to the position of, and act as, Secretary of the Air Force in the order indicated:

1. Under Secretary of the Air Force.
2. Assistant Secretaries of the Air Force, in the order fixed by their length of service as such.
3. Chief of Staff, United States Air Force.
4. Vice Chief of Staff, United States Air Force.
5. The senior Deputy Chief of Staff who is not absent or disabled.
6. The Commander, Air University.

Part V. Variations in the Order of Succession.

Without regard to any other part of this Order, except Part VI, the President, or the person acting as President under section 19 of title 3, United States Code, may, in the event of the death, disability, or absence of the Secretary of Defense, appoint any officer designated in Part I of this Order to succeed to the position of, and act as, Secretary of Defense; and that person may, in the event of the death, disability, or absence of the Secretary of a Military Department, appoint any officer designated in the part of this Order that relates to the order to succession in the Department concerned to succeed to the position of, and act as, the Secretary of that Department.

Part VI. Temporary Nature of Succession/ Acting Capacity.

Succession to office pursuant to this Order shall be on a temporary or interim basis and shall not have the effect of vacating the statutory position held by the successor. An officer shall not succeed to any position under this order if the position that he occupies entitling him so to succeed is held by him in an acting capacity only.

Part VII. Revocation of Prior Executive Order.

Executive Order No. 10820 of May 18, 1959, is hereby revoked.

RONALD REAGAN

The White House,
May 14, 1985.

[Filed with the Office of the Federal Register, 10:29 a.m., May 15, 1985]

Executive Order 12515—Generalized System of Preferences
May 14, 1985

By virtue of the authority vested in me by the Constitution and statutes of the United States of America, including Title V of the Trade Act of 1974 (19 U.S.C. 2461 *et seq.*), as amended, section 604 of the Trade Act of 1974 (19 U.S.C. 2483), and section 503(a)(2)(A) of the Trade Agreements Act of 1979 (93 Stat. 251), and as President of the United States of America, in order to provide for the continuation, to the greatest extent possible, of preferential treatment under the Generalized System of Preferences (GSP) for articles that are currently eligible for such treatment and that are imported from countries designated as beneficiary developing countries, consistent with the changes to the Tariff Schedules of the United States (TSUS) (19 U.S.C. 1202), which have resulted from the recent enactment of the Trade and Tariff Act of 1984 (Public Law 98–573), it is hereby ordered as follows:

Section 1. In order to take into account the changes made by the Trade and Tariff Act of 1984, Annex II of Executive Order No. 11888 of November 24, 1975, as amended, listing articles that are eligible for benefits of the GSP when imported from any designated beneficiary developing country, is further amended as set forth in Annex 1 to this Order.

Sec. 2. Annex III of Executive Order No. 11888, as amended, listing articles that are eligible for benefits of the GSP when im-

ported from all designated beneficiary countries except those specified in general headnote 3(c)(iii) of the TSUS, is further amended as set forth in Annex II to this Order.

Sec. 3. General headnote 3(c)(iii) of the TSUS, listing articles that are eligible for benefits of the GSP except when imported from the beneficiary countries listed opposite those articles, is modified as set forth in Annex III to this Order.

Sec. 4. (a) The amendments made by the paragraphs numbered (b) in Annex I, Annex II, and Annex III to this Order shall be effective with respect to articles both: (1) imported on or after January 1, 1976, and (2) entered, or withdrawn from warehouse for consumption, on or after January 1, 1985.

(b) The remaining amendments made by this Order shall be effective with respect to articles both: (1) imported on or after January 1, 1976, and (2) entered, or withdrawn from warehouse for consumption, on or after November 14, 1984.

RONALD REAGAN

The White House,
May 14, 1985.

[Filed with the Office of the Federal Register, 10:41 a.m., May 15, 1985]

Note: The annexes were printed in the Federal Register *of May 16.*

Proclamation 5339—National Science Week, 1985
May 14, 1985

By the President of the United States of America

A Proclamation

We live in an age when rapidly changing science and technology are transforming our economy and our way of life. But this is nothing new for Americans, because we have always been inventors and explorers who looked to science as a way of achieving a better future.

Today the pace of scientific discovery has accelerated, and its effects are being felt worldwide. No nation or group of nations has a monopoly on the world's scientific talent, so no nation can take for granted that it will remain in the forefront of technological change just because it has been in the past. America must continually strive to undertake basic research in science as well as to develop new technological applications of scientific ideas.

In order to do this, it is particularly important that we provide our young people with good scientific education. Even those who do not pursue careers in science should understand the scientific method and appreciate the contributions science and technology make to our way of life.

Americans are coming together to meet the challenges that the rapid advance of scientific knowledge creates for us. As we have so many times before in our history, we see these challenges as opportunities. Our businesses, universities, and State and local governments are working in partnership with the Federal government to meet our needs through research and education.

As these cooperative relationships develop, we can look forward with confidence to an era of scientific discovery and technological innovation unimagined only a few years ago.

In recognition of the importance of science, technology, and science education, and to draw public attention to the great works being accomplished in these fields, the Congress, by Senate Joint Resolution 59, has designated the period from May 12 through May 18, 1985, as "National Science Week" and has authorized and requested the President to issue a proclamation in observance of this event.

Now, Therefore, I, Ronald Reagan, President of the United States of America, do hereby proclaim the week of May 12 through May 18, 1985, as National Science Week. I urge the people of the United States to observe this week and participate in the many activities planned by universities, businesses, State and local governments, and the Federal government during this period.

In Witness Whereof, I have hereunto set my hand this fourteenth day of May, in the year of our Lord nineteen hundred and eighty-five, and of the Independence of the United States of America the two hundred and ninth.

RONALD REAGAN

[*Filed with the Office of the Federal Register, 9:16 a.m., May 16, 1985*]

Note: The proclamation was released by the Office of the Press Secretary on May 15.

Message to the Senate Transmitting the International Telecommunication Convention
May 15, 1985

To the Senate of the United States:

With a view to receiving the advice and consent of the Senate to ratification, I transmit herewith the International Telecommunication Convention, with annexes, and a Final Protocol, signed at Nairobi on November 6, 1982.

I transmit also, for the information of the Senate, the report of the Department of State with respect to the Convention.

The International Telecommunication Convention (Nairobi, 1982) abrogates and replaces, in relations between Contracting Governments, the International Telecommunication Convention (Malaga-Torremolinos, 1973) to which the United States is a party.

The International Telecommunication Convention is the basic instrument of the International Telecommunication Union, which provides the framework for the orderly conduct of international telecommunications. It is in the public and commercial interest of the United States to continue to play an active role within this framework.

The International Telecommunication Convention entered into force on January 1, 1984, for governments that have deposited their instrument of ratification or accession, by diplomatic channel through the intermediary of the Government of Switzerland, with the Secretary General of the International Telecommunication Union.

I believe that the United States should become a party to the International Telecommunication Convention (Nairobi, 1982), and it is my hope that the Senate will take timely action on this matter and give its advice and consent to ratification.

RONALD REAGAN

The White House,
May 15, 1985.

Appointment of Two Members of the Advisory Committee for Trade Negotiations
May 15, 1985

The President today announced his intention to appoint the following individuals to be members of the Advisory Committee for Trade Negotiations for a term of 2 years:

Tatiana Brandt Copeland is a reappointment. Since 1980 she has been president of Tebec Associates Limited, a consulting firm in the field of national and international taxation, in Wilmington, DE. Previously she was employed with E.I. DuPont de Nemours as manager of the international department (1975–1980). She graduated from the University of California at Los Angeles (B.S., 1964) and the University of California at Berkeley (M.B.A., 1966). She is married and resides in Greenville, DE. She was born February 23, 1941, in Dresden, Germany.

Donald E. Petersen will succeed Philip Caldwell. He has been president and chief operating officer of Ford Motor Co. since 1980. He has been a member of the company's board of directors since September 1977. Prior to his present position, he was executive vice president, Ford international automotive operations. He joined Ford Motor Co. in 1949. He graduated from the University of Washington (B.A., 1946) and Stanford University (M.B.A., 1949). He is married and resides in Bloomfield Hills, MI. He was born September 4, 1926, in Pipestone, MN.

Statement on the Exile of Andrei Sakharov and Human Rights in the Soviet Union
May 15, 1985

Two years ago I signed the proclamation designating May 21 as National Andrei Sakharov Day. Recalling that Dr. Sakharov's Nobel Peace Prize cited him as a "spokesman for the conscience of mankind," I said that we who value freedom and human dignity must do all in our power to prevent him from being silenced.

As we honor Dr. Sakharov today and re-dedicate ourselves to the values of peace, freedom, and justice that he represents, we do so with solemn awareness that for more than 1 year, he and his brave wife, Yelena Bonner, have been cut off from all direct contact with family or friends in the West. A year ago this month, Dr. Sakharov embarked on a hunger strike to protest the refusal of Soviet authorities to permit his wife to travel abroad for urgently needed medical treatment. Soviet authorities have turned a deaf ear to the outpouring of international outrage over the treatment of one of the Soviet Union's most distinguished citizens and of his courageous wife, who is a decorated veteran of World War II.

In recognizing the courage and ideals that Dr. Sakharov embodies, let us also remember the many thousands of his countrymen who likewise suffer the denial of basic human rights. Today the human rights situation in the Soviet Union remains bleak. Soviet authorities have succeeded in eliminating the main vehicle for human rights activism—the Helsinki monitors movement. Anatoly Shcharanskiy, Yuriy Orlov, and other monitors are now serving long terms of imprisonment or exile. Religious groups have become a major target of persecution, and Baptists, Catholics, Ukrainian Uniates,

Pentecostalists, and other groups have been subjected to arrest and harassment. The crackdown on Hebrew teachers and Jewish cultural activists which began in July 1984 continues. Jewish emigration last year reached a 10-year low.

In exiling Dr. Sakharov to Gorky, the Soviet Government has attempted to silence and remove him from international attention, but their efforts will ultimately fail. Americans and others around the world who have drawn inspiration from his courage understand their obligation to carry his message to all and to redouble their efforts in pursuit of world peace and respect for human rights. I am appreciative for the efforts undertaken by the Andrei Sakharov Institute, and I recognize the many concerned citizens around the world who have been inspired by Dr. Sakharov and who support his goals and ideals. We must act on his behalf, ensuring that his message of hope and freedom will never be silenced.

Today we renew our call to the new Soviet leadership to end the isolation of Dr. Sakharov and his wife and to permit Yelena Bonner to travel abroad for needed medical care. Let all who cherish Dr. Sakharov's noble values, both governments and individuals, continue to press the Soviets for information about the Sakharovs and for an end to Soviet persecution of two of its most distinguished citizens.

Memorandum on Social Security for Federal Employees
May 15, 1985

Memorandum for the Heads of Executive Departments and Agencies

Subject: Coordination of Determinations on Social Security for Federal Personnel

Under the Social Security Amendments of 1983, Federal employees hired on or after January 1, 1984, as well as certain other Federal officers and employees, will be fully covered under the Social Security system. Under section 205(p) of the Social Security Act (42 U.S.C. 405(p)) and section 3122 of the Internal Revenue Code (26 U.S.C.

3122), the head of each Executive department or agency is vested with the responsibility for determining which personnel of the department or agency are employees covered by Social Security and what amounts of their remuneration are subject to withholding of Social Security tax.

In order to ensure that Social Security coverage and taxation will be consistently and efficiently applied within the Executive branch in conformance with the Social Security Act and the Internal Revenue Code, I am hereby directing that the Internal

Revenue Service and the Social Security Administration provide guidance to Executive departments and agencies concerning Social Security coverage and taxation for Federal personnel, including applicable regulations and published rulings and proce-

dures. I ask the heads of Executive departments and agencies to follow such guidance in making their determinations under the aforementioned sections 205(p) and 3122.

RONALD REAGAN

Remarks Following Discussions With President José Napoleón Duarte of El Salvador
May 16, 1985

President Reagan. Well, it's always a pleasure to welcome President Duarte, a close friend. He and his people are struggling against great adversity to consolidate their democratic institutions, and we're honored to be doing what we can to help.

They're striving to build a society that guarantees free exercise of religion and speech, that does not tolerate human rights abuses, that offers its people the benefits of a growing economy. And those who question our efforts in Central America should take note of the heartwarming progress that President Duarte has made.

The people of El Salvador had another free election in March; economic reforms are continuing; and Communist guerrillas are losing ground. And none of this would have been possible without the economic assistance and military training and equipment that we provided, and yet that assistance passed in the House by a very slim margin.

If there's to be peace and democracy in the region, if our neighbors are to be spared the tragedy that comes from every Communist dictatorship, we must have the courage to help all our friends in Central America.

In his efforts to bring peace to his land, President Duarte has initiated a church-mediated dialog with those fighting against his government. He has gone the extra mile to seek genuine reconciliation and to ensure his enemies the right to participate in the democratic process. He did not dictate who could represent the opposition. He met with both armed and unarmed opponents. His sincere efforts should serve as a model

for all of Central America, especially those in Nicaragua who have not permitted free and fair elections, have refused to participate in a church-mediated internal dialog, and have not followed peaceful policies toward their neighbors.

President Duarte has much to be proud of. The recent successful election and the indisputable improvement in the human rights climate in El Salvador are due in no small part to his efforts. I deeply appreciate his courageous support of my Nicaraguan peace initiative of last April and of our trade embargo against Nicaragua. And I assured him that we will continue our efforts to thwart Communist aggression and subversion in the region.

Peace will not be possible in Central America until Nicaragua ceases to support the subversion of its neighbors and itself achieves national reconciliation through democratic elections. The United States will continue working with President Duarte to build peace, prosperity, and freedom in his own land and to bring stability throughout Central America. It's been a great pleasure to exchange views with him today.

President Duarte. It is always a fruitful experience to visit with my good friend, President Ronald Reagan. We have today addressed most of the underlying problems of mutual concern and agreed that peace is obtainable in Central America as we draw the line on Marxist totalitarianism.

We have come far in El Salvador but have yet a long, difficult road to travel. The March election reaffirmed the commitment of my people to a peaceful, democratic solution of our problems. I fully share that commitment. But the need to curb foreign intervention is paramount in our purposes.

Later this week and next, I shall meet with congressional, business, and labor leaders of the United States. I will reassure them all of my unwavering support to democratic, peaceful changes based on a strong and healthy economy, which we will work to build in close partnership with private enterprise.

Of the two Central American revolutions of 1979, ours has succeeded as Nicaragua's has been betrayed. We have fulfilled our commitment and kept our promises, while the Marxist Sandinista regime has not. Our press is free to say and publish what it wants. La Prensa in Nicaragua is censored every day down to a few lines.

I have assured President Reagan of our support of his purpose to stop the spread of foreign ideologies and thank him for his continuing and stimulating acknowledge of our efforts.

Note: President Reagan spoke to reporters at 11:56 a.m. at the South Portico of the White House following a meeting with President Duarte in the Oval Office.

Message to the Congress Reporting Budget Rescissions and Deferrals
May 16, 1985

To the Congress of the United States:

In accordance with the Impoundment Control Act of 1974, I herewith report two new rescission proposals totaling $37,401,818, two new deferrals totaling $24,000,000, and a revised deferral now totaling $32,300,000. The rescissions affect programs in the Department of Energy and the Corporation for Public Broadcasting. The deferrals affect programs in the Department of Energy and the Tennessee Valley Authority.

The details of these rescissions and deferrals are contained in the attached report.

RONALD REAGAN

The White House,
May 16, 1985.

Note: The attachment detailing the proposed rescissions and deferrals was printed in the Federal Register *of May 21.*

Nomination of Glenn R. Wilson, Jr., To Be President of the Government National Mortgage Association
May 16, 1985

The President today announced his intention to nominate Glenn R. Wilson, Jr., to be President of the Government National Mortgage Association, Department of Housing and Urban Development. He would succeed Robert W. Karpe.

Since 1975 Mr. Wilson has been president and owner of Mid-Continent Enterprises, Inc., in Grand Island, NE. Previously, he was executive director of the Nebraska Republican State Central Committee in 1971–1975; executive director of the Young Republican National Federation in 1970–1971; and district sales representative with the Masonite Corp. in 1968–1969.

He was a member of the Multi-Family Committee of the National Association of Home Builders in 1984. He served as president of the Home Owners Warranty Corp. of Nebraska and of the Nebraska State

Home Builders Association in 1979–1980.

He is married, has four children, and re-

sides in Grand Island, NE. He was born February 20, 1938, in Pittsburgh, PA.

Nomination of Antonio Navarro To Be a Member of the Advisory Board for Radio Broadcasting to Cuba
May 16, 1985

The President today announced his intention to nominate Antonio Navarro to be a member of the Advisory Board for Radio Broadcasting to Cuba for a term of 3 years. This is a new position.

Mr. Navarro is a senior vice president of W.R. Grace & Co. He joined the company in 1961 and in 1971 was appointed vice president of Grace's Natural Resources Group, general manager of the industrial complex in Paramonga, Peru, and manager of Grace's Peruvian chemical division. In 1973 he became vice president of the corporate communications division and was

based in New York. He was elected a corporate vice president in 1978 and named to his present position in February 1982.

He serves on the advisory board of the Council of the Americas, is a member of the North American-Chilean Chamber of Commerce, and is a member of the Pan-American Society of the United States.

He graduated from the Georgia Institute of Technology (B.S., 1944). He is married, has three children, and resides in New York, NY. He was born September 26, 1922, in Havana, Cuba.

Appointment of Matthew J. Guglielmo as a Member of the President's Committee on Mental Retardation
May 16, 1985

The President today announced his intention to appoint Matthew J. Guglielmo to be a member of the President's Committee on Mental Retardation for a term expiring May 11, 1988. He will succeed Lawrence A. Kane, Jr.

Mr. Guglielmo is vice president, corporate merchandise programs, for Carter Hawley Hale Stores, Inc., in Los Angeles, CA. He is a member of the executive committee of the California Association State Hospitals Parent Council for the Retarded. He is a member of the executive committee and chairman of the East Los Angeles Regional Center for the Developmentally Disabled.

He has been recognized for his efforts to

improve the care and well-being of the mentally retarded and the developmentally disabled. His honors include the United States Congressional Achievement Award and the Community Service Award for his outstanding contribution to the State of California. As a tribute to Mr. Guglielmo's work, the Matthew J. Guglielmo Biology Research Fellowship was established at the City of Hope in 1974 and the Matthew J. Guglielmo Chair in Mental Retardation was established in perpetuity at California State University, Los Angeles, in 1981.

He is married, has three children, and resides in San Marino, CA. He was born January 5, 1920, in New York, NY.

Remarks at the Annual Republican Senate/House Fundraising Dinner
May 16, 1985

Thank you, John. I thank you all very much, all of you, for this wonderful evening and the privilege of being here. I must say that I was a little disturbed—nostalgia had seized me with the presence of Bob Hope here, and, then, when Drew Lewis introduced him, instead of me doing it—you see, back in Hollywood, when you did many benefits for worthy causes, if you didn't sing or dance and you were asked to appear at one of those, you'd always say, "Well, what can I do?" and someone would always say, "You can introduce someone else." [*Laughter*]

So, that was a function of mine; I've done it many times. As a matter of fact, I remember one night when there were seven of us standing there and lined up to introduce Nelson Eddy, singing "Shortnin' Bread." [*Laughter*]

But all I can say is, it's great to be back in the United States of America. Now, if you see me glancing over in this direction a lot, it's because after my experience at Strasbourg I keep expecting the left side of the room to walk out. [*Laughter*] The truth is I never realized I had such a moving effect on leftwingers. [*Laughter*]

But I want to set the record straight and say now that there's absolutely no truth to the rumor that Bob Dole and Bob Michel have asked me to speak before a special session of Congress.

This may be called the President's Dinner, but it's really your dinner. For the second year in a row, you've made this the most successful fundraising event in the history of the Republican Party, as you've been told. And to all of you here tonight who've given so generously, you have my deepest gratitude. Your continued support is essential if we're going to keep America on the right track, growing stronger, braver, and freer every year.

A lot of you know Ed Rollins, and many of you will be working closely with him in the coming months. And I just want to take this opportunity to say what an outstanding job Ed has done over the years working to make our hopes and ideals a political reality.

Ted Welch, Drew Lewis, and Jack McDonald, you've done a superb job making this event possible. To the Members of the House and Senate who are here tonight, don't think I don't appreciate what it's like out there in the trenches. It's gotten to the point where you can't even have an operation in peace any more without Bob Dole calling you in for a vote. [*Laughter*]

Special thanks should go to Bob Dole and Bob Michel for their outstanding leadership on the Hill. We saw an example of that leadership last week when, as John told you, the Senate passed an historic bill to turn the tide of runaway congressional spending.

And now, Bob Michel has a somewhat different situation to contend with. I understand now that House proceedings are televised. Tip O'Neill is getting to be known as the J.R. Ewing of Washington, DC. [*Laughter*]

Maybe the House Democrats have been in power so long they've forgotten the basic courtesies due their opponents in a democracy. Suppose we just teach them a few manners in 1986. [*Laughter*]

But we're up against a tough challenge in this next election. Being right doesn't automatically or immediately translate into political might, without a lot of hard work. We are bucking an historical trend in midterm elections, but that's nothing new to us. For the last 4½ years, we've been bucking the historical trend, and we've been winning with spending and tax cuts, tax reform, strengthened defenses, and support for democracy around the world.

But then we were bucking a 4-year trend when we came into office, just by feeling good about America. They said these things couldn't be done, but we're doing them. And that's the main reason, I believe, that in 1986 we're not only going to keep control of the Senate but build a winning coalition that will break the liberals' paralyzing grip on the House.

The American people will see that they have a choice between the party of action and the party of stagnation, between a party of doers and a party of do-nothings. Take the budget, for instance. The budget debate has been completely revolutionized. The question isn't any longer: Can government spending be cut? Today the only question is: How much and where?

Have you ever stopped to think that this is really about the first time that you have ever seen the two parties, and today the only difference between them is the argument about what should be cut, but both agreed that government spending should be cut.

The Republican-controlled Senate has passed a budget that will shrink the deficit, prepare the way for tax reform, and help put our economy on a growth path through the end of the decade. The Senate Republicans have shown that they have the right stuff to make tough political choices by doing what everybody agrees has to be done—cutting spending. By putting the needs of the country above any short-term political interest, our Senate Republicans have shown courage and leadership, and the country will thank them for it.

It awaits to be seen whether the Democrats in the House are up to this challenge. Will they shrink from this great moment and retreat into excuses and partisan politics? The Democrats have been talking about deficits for years. The coming budget vote in the House will be the measure of their sincerity. It'll signal to the country whether they'll cooperate in the business of running this country or if they're determined to reduce themselves to the role of spoilers, detractors, and negativists.

If the Democrats in the House can't bring themselves to cut wasteful Federal spending, there's always another option: Give me what 43 Governors already have—a line-item veto. I'll take the political heat; in fact, I'll enjoy it.

Some Democrats, in their effort to torpedo any constructive budget compromise, are proposing drastic cuts in defense that would seriously threaten our country's national security and tax increases that could strangle our economic prosperity. We had a referendum on that idea last November. The American people overwhelmingly rejected it. We've already compromised greatly on defense by agreeing to freeze spending at last year's levels with only an adjustment for inflation. Now, this was not an easy decision. There's no question about it, this will temporarily slow down our vitally needed defense buildup at a time when the Soviet Union is pouring unprecedented amounts of resources into their offensive military arsenals. But I've been assured that if I feel our national security is imperiled, I can come back to Congress for supplemental appropriations. Our leaders in the Senate have assured me of that. And if the Congress persists in making further reductions which could jeopardize our negotiating position in Geneva, I may take them up on that offer.

As I said, there are still a few people, also, who want to raise your taxes. There are also a few people who still claim the Earth is flat. [*Laughter*] As far as we're concerned, those questions were answered a long time ago—both of them. In case the taxaholics have any doubts left, however, I want to show them this. This is a letter given to me by Representatives Connie Mack of Florida and Beau Boulter of Texas, with the signatures of 146 Republican Representatives who have pledged to support a veto of any tax increase, no matter how cleverly it's disguised. I carry this letter all the time. [*Laughter*] I sleep with it under my pillow. [*Laughter*] Whenever the job gets a little tough, I take it out and read it. And it really does make my day. [*Laughter*]

I'm determined that 1985 is going to go down in history as the year of tax reform and further rate reductions. This will be the year when that colossus of waste, unfairness, and inefficiency known as our tax code will finally be cleaned up.

We stand at the threshold of a new golden age of economic achievement and technological discovery. But a complicated and tangled tax code, along with unproductively high income tax rates, keep the door to progress partially closed. That's why we will be very soon announcing our tax reform plan to lower income tax rates, make our tax system fairer and simpler, and ensure that America is the sunrise industrial power of the 21st century.

Everywhere I went on our recent trip to Europe, I repeated one simple yet profound message: Freedom works. Except for a few people on the far left-hand side of the aisle, the response was extremely enthusiastic, especially among young people. Of course every time I started talking about individual freedom and human dignity, the Communists stood up and walked out of the room. I suppose they were just rushing off to greet Daniel Ortega, who seemed to be following me in most of the countries where we were.

And I notice that many in our House of Representatives had second thoughts about their vote to block aid to the freedom fighters when Mr. Ortega immediately flew off to Moscow for what looked like a victory celebration. Mr. Ortega, of course, was looking for another installment on that almost $2 billion in military and economic assistance the Soviets and their friends have been pouring into Nicaragua to prop up the brutal Communist regime there.

Sooner or later we are all forced to shed whatever illusions we may have had about the nature of Communist regimes. Let's only hope that this time it isn't too late for those brave Nicaraguans who are battling to bring freedom to their suffering country.

I hope Congress will change its mind. I still think that we can together rise above partisanship and do what we know is right, and I think every American knows in his heart that supporting freedom and democracy is right. I'm convinced that last month's vote against the freedom fighters in Nicaragua will be remembered as only a short, shameful episode—an exception to our great country's historic allegiance to the cause of freedom and human rights.

So, our agenda these next few months is full. I am reminded of a story about Winston Churchill near the close of the Second World War. He was visited by a delegation from the Temperance League and chastised by one woman who said, "Mr. Prime Minister, I've heard that if all the whiskey you have drunk since the war began were poured into this room, it would come all the way up to your waist." Churchill looked dolefully at the floor, then at his waist, then up to the ceiling. And he said: "Ah, yes, madam. So much accomplished; so very much more left to do." [*Laughter*]

Yes, we have much left to do and with your help we are going to make it happen. We have begun no less than the renewal of the American dream, and we are not going to stop until that dream of hope, faith, and opportunity becomes a living reality for every American. That's the vision that guides us; that is the vision that the Republican Party is working toward. And to paraphrase John Paul Jones, we have only just begun to fight.

Thank you. Thank you all from the bottom of an awful lot of hearts in this room—those Representatives and Senators that you've met, myself, Nancy, George, and all of us. We are deeply indebted to you.

Thank you, and God bless you.

Note: The President spoke at 9:45 p.m. in Hall A at the Washington, DC, Convention Center. He was introduced by Senator John Heinz of Pennsylvania.

Remarks at the Convention of the National Republican Heritage Groups Council
May 17, 1985

Thank you very much, and good afternoon. You know, I've been an after-lunch speaker many times, but I really am after lunch this time, aren't I. [*Laughter*]

Well, greetings to your chairman, Michael Sotirhos, your executive director, Radi Slavoff, your honorary chairman, and to your convention chairman, Dr. Theodore Perros. The work of all of you has meant a very great deal to me personally and to our party and to our cause. And I'm delighted to have this opportunity to be with you, at least for a short time today.

A few years ago, most of us had a great aching in our hearts about America. As we picked up the morning papers, there was never any telling what new setbacks or international humiliation awaited us. And that's not even to mention what was happening here at home—economic decline, endless increases in crime, and a deepening social discontent stemming from overly intrusive government, the loss of basic values, and stifled economic opportunity.

Well, together, you and I offered the American people a way out of all of this. And just as we always knew they would, they took us up on the offer. Now we've turned away from the days of defeatism and malaise; America's back where she belongs—the champion of peace and freedom throughout the world.

I can think of few Americans who've made a more vital contribution to this effort than those of you who are in this room today. The story of America's economic, social, and spiritual recovery can be traced in great part to the resurgence of both Republican principles and the organizational strength of our party. And it hasn't been too many years that we've been able to talk about that. But it's there now, and you've contributed mightily to that resurgence. You're here today because of your dedication to your party and your country and your desire to give as well as to receive—to do something for America in return for all that she's done for you and your families. In that quest, let me assure you that you've succeeded. And so, I wanted to come by today just to thank and salute you.

As you know, I've just returned from Europe, where I had an opportunity to see as well as speak about the new energy and dynamism that is sparking the cause of democracy and personal freedom throughout the world. There just isn't any question in my mind that people everywhere seek now to fulfill one of the oldest and deepest aspirations of the human spirit—the right to self-expression, to democratic self-rule, to representative government in every land.

You know, when I first began speaking a few years ago about expanding the frontiers of freedom throughout the world, some people asked whether, in preaching this forward strategy for freedom, I was calling for what was known in the 1950's as a rollback—the end of totalitarian rule in other countries.

Well, you see, I always thought the question was misstated. The very word "rollback" suggests that somehow we who are promoting freedom are attempting to stop or roll back the inevitable and that history was actually on the side of those who prescribed totalitarian rule.

Well, it's true that in our century totalitarian ideologies, by holding out the false hope of utopia and promising an end to poverty and war, caught certain historical tides at their height and then flooded some of the lowlands of Western civilization and culture. But now everywhere we look today there is evidence this tide has spent itself and is receding, leaving behind only a totalitarian wasteland.

Look around the world at the growing insurgencies against repressive rule in totalitarian countries, the revolt of intellectuals against the stale cliches and bogus prophecies of Marxism-Leninism, the steady growth of the power and especially the number of nations that are turning to democracy. They all point to one powerful, undeniable truth: That bright, shining crest on the horizon is no mirage but the distant tip of a tidal wave called freedom, a tidal wave that will soon roll and crash its way across the desert that is 20th century totalitarianism.

So you see, it's the other way around. The events of this century are making possible the realization of the age-old aspirations of mankind for freedom. And those who would stand in its way are really the ones seeking to roll back history.

Now, don't mistake me, history has no inevitable outcome; it's still the work of free men and women; so, it's still up to you and me. So, if the cause of freedom is to continue to prosper, the United States must remain strong militarily and economically. We have to continue to strengthen institutions like Radio Free Europe and Radio Liberty. And we have to continue helping the resistance in Afghanistan and especially in Nicaragua.

A few people who voted the other way with regard to Nicaragua in the Congress are doing a little rethinking since Mr. Ortega went on his Moscow tour.

And yes, we have to continue to state in public the crucial moral distinctions between democratic government and the totalitarian state. And much of this will depend on how the Republican Party fares in the next few years. And once again I think the prognosis—but only with your help—is an optimistic one. Our party has been unstinting in its support of democratic development and the struggle against totalitarianism. We've led the way in supporting the resistance movements in Nicaragua and Afghanistan. And we can be proud that in supporting a strong defense, Radio Liberty, Radio Free Europe, and in being realistic about Soviet intentions, our party, the Republican Party, has led the way.

Now, I mentioned defense there, and we're talking about how to cure some great misconceptions that are the result of a drumbeat of ceaseless propaganda that's been prevalent in the land with regard to national defense. Just give you one line about it. That $436 hammer—we never bought that. We're the ones that found out that that's what they'd been asking for; then we didn't buy it. And that's true of all those other horror stories. The truth is they're success stories. We are the ones who have been uncovering all that trash and doing something about it.

You know, I've been encouraged by many of those in the Democratic Party who are wondering about a burden that some in their party would have them take on. Already many are asking if they really want to be remembered as the party that couldn't support vital weapons programs or the party that, at a critical turning point in the struggle between totalitarianism and freedom, did not aid those struggling to save freedom in their own countries—countries like Nicaragua—from totalitarian rule.

And that's why bringing home the meaning of the Republican Party is so vital. We have already seen—and I think more than I can remember in any previous time—people who've decided to change the "D" after their name here in government to an "R." I talked to one of those the other day, and I told him—having been one of those who quite some time ago changed that letter—I told him that if he was having any qualms to remember that a fellow named Winston Churchill once changed parties. And Winston gave as the reason—and I think it fits the situation today—he said: "Some men change principle for party. And some men change party for principle."

We need more Members of the House and Senate here in Washington who think as we do on these issues. Now, many of them maybe won't change that letter, but there are some who find that when it comes time to pull the voting lever they like the things that we're trying to do, rather than the objectionism and obstructionism that is coming from the leadership of their own party.

I want to encourage you to keep building the party. Believe me, bringing more ethnic Americans into our fold is the key to the positive realignment that we are beginning to see take shape. And if asked why they should become Republican, talk to them about some of the things that I've just said, and tell them about freedom. They might be interested in that. Believe me, in the coming years, freedom and foreign policy are going to be the issues that move the voter, even as they move the world.

These are exciting times—the cause of freedom is on the move everywhere in the world—times when all of us can be grateful for the special chance that we have to help light the way toward a future of peace and freedom.

So, let me leave you here with a few last words from Teddy Roosevelt: "We, here in America, hold in our hands the hope of the world, the fate of the coming years; and shame and disgrace will be ours if in our eyes the light of high resolve is dimmed if we trail in the dust the golden hopes of mankind."

Well, that light of high resolve is not dimmed in America; I have seen it so many times on so many thousands of faces all across this land; I can see it in your eyes. And just last week I was seeing it in the eyes of 10,000 young people, young Germans, in their teens. And I talked to them about freedom and that they should be proud of the 40 years now of democracy and freedom that their country has known since the days of Hitler. And when I finished speaking, I had a tennis ball in my throat because the band started playing our national anthem, and I saw 10,000 young German students singing our national anthem in English.

These golden hopes of mankind are here for us to protect and preserve. Let us resolve to pass that sacred heritage on to other generations of Americans and to make it someday, we hope and pray, the birthright of all the peoples of the world.

Thank you for letting me come in here and talk to you. Thank you, and God bless you.

Note: The President spoke at 1:02 p.m. in the main ballroom at the Shoreham Hotel.

Nomination of L. Craig Johnstone To Be United States Ambassador to Algeria
May 17, 1985

The President today announced his intention to nominate L. Craig Johnstone, a career member of the Senior Foreign Service, Class of Minister-Counselor, to be Ambassador of the United States of America to the Democratic and Popular Republic of Algeria. He would succeed Michael H. Newlin.

Mr. Johnstone began his career in 1965 as an intern at the International Institute for Education, USAID contract, in Vietnam. He served in 1965–1966 in Vietnam with the Agency for International Development and in 1966–1970 with the Department of State on detail to USAID in Vietnam.

In 1970–1971 Mr. Johnstone was at the Council on Foreign Relations in New York and the Institute of Politics at Harvard University. In 1971 he became political/military officer at our Embassy in Ottawa, Canada. In 1973–1974 he was on leave without pay status at Capitol Hill. In 1974 he returned to the Department as Deputy Director of the Executive Secretariat in the Office of the Secretary of State, where he served until 1976. In 1976 he went on detail to the U.S. Sinai Support Mission. In 1976–1977 he was chief of the economic section at our Embassy in Jamaica. Mr. Johnstone took French language training in 1978 and then went to our Embassy in France as political/military officer. In 1981–1983 he was Chief of the Office of Central American Affairs and from 1983 to present has been a Deputy Assistant Secretary of State for Inter-American Affairs.

Mr. Johnstone was born September 1, 1942, in Seattle, WA. He received his B.A. in 1964 from the University of Maryland, did graduate studies there in 1965, and graduate studies at Harvard in 1971. He was on the faculty at the Institute of Politics at Harvard in 1971–1972. His foreign languages are Vietnamese, French, and Spanish. Mr. Johnstone is married to the former Janet Gail Buechel, and they have three children.

Nomination of Edward Morgan Rowell To Be United States Ambassador to Bolivia
May 17, 1985

The President today announced his intention to nominate Edward Morgan Rowell, a career member of the Senior Foreign Service, Class of Minister-Counselor, to be Ambassador of the United States of America to the Republic of Bolivia. He would succeed Edwin Gharst Corr.

Mr. Rowell was with Woodward & Lothrop in Washington, DC, in 1955–1956. In 1956 he began his career in the Foreign Service in training assignments, first as a management analyst and then as a budget examiner. He served as vice consul and economic/commercial officer in Recife, Brazil, in 1958. He then went to Curitiba, Brazil, as consul and principal officer in 1958–1961. In 1961 he returned to the Department as Special Assistant to the Deputy Assistant Secretary for Inter-American Affairs. In 1962–1964 he was officer in charge of Honduran affairs for the Department and the Agency for International Development. In 1964–1965 he was detailed to Stanford University for Latin American studies. In 1965 he served as political officer and deputy chief of section at the U.S. Embassy in Buenos Aires, Argentina. He then became chief of the political section of the U.S. Embassy in Tegucigalpa, Honduras, where he served until 1970. In 1970 he returned to the Stanford University graduate school of business for senior training. Mr. Rowell then served as a Foreign Service inspector in the Department in 1971–1974. In 1974–1975 he was Deputy Director/Economic Officer in the Office of Iberian Affairs. In 1975 he became Deputy Director, Office of West European Affairs, and then Director. In 1978 he went to Lisbon, Portugal, as deputy chief of mission and from 1983 to present has been a Deputy Assistant Secretary for Consular Affairs.

Mr. Rowell was born October 13, 1931, in Oakland, CA. He received his B.A. from Yale University in 1953 and attended Stanford University in 1964–1965 and the graduate school of business at Stanford in 1970–1971. He served in the United States Army in 1953–1955. His foreign languages are Spanish, Portuguese, and French. Mr. Rowell is married to the former Le Wood, and they have three children.

Nomination of Nicholas Ruwe To Be United States Ambassador to Iceland
May 17, 1985

The President today announced his intention to nominate Nicholas Ruwe to be Ambassador of the United States of America to the Republic of Iceland. He would succeed Marshall Brement.

Mr. Ruwe was with Petroleum Consultants Training Program in Houston, TX, in 1956–1960. In 1960 he joined the Volunteers for Nixon/Lodge in their Presidential campaign. In 1961–1964 he worked on numerous campaigns, i.e., Tower for Senate in Houston, TX; Goode for Congress, San Antonio, TX; Bailey for Mayor, Houston, TX, and Percy for Governor, Chicago, IL. Mr. Ruwe worked in 1965–1967 as a stockbroker with Clark & Dodge in New York City and Detroit. In 1968 he returned to the campaign trail in New York for Nixon for President. In 1969 Mr. Ruwe came to the Department of State as an Assistant Chief of Protocol, where he served until 1975. In 1975–1977 he was vice president of Pathfinder Corp., in Washington, DC. He then campaigned for Reagan for President in Washington, DC, and California in 1979–1980. In 1980–1984 he was chief of staff for

Richard Nixon, General Services Administration, New York City. From 1984 to the present, Mr. Ruwe worked with the President's Inaugural Committee.

Mr. Ruwe was born September 22, 1933, in Detroit, MI. He received his B.A. in 1955 from Brown University and attended the University of Michigan graduate school of business administration in 1955–1956. His foreign language is French. Mr. Ruwe is married to the former Nancy Lammerding.

Proclamation 5340—Modification of Import Quotas on Certain Sugar Containing Articles
May 17, 1985

By the President of the United States of America

A Proclamation

1. By Proclamation No. 5294 of January 28, 1985, I imposed, on an emergency basis, import quotas on certain sugar containing articles pursuant to Section 22 of the Agricultural Adjustment Act of 1933, as amended (7 U.S.C. 624) ("Section 22"). These quotas were to remain in effect pending investigation by the United States International Trade Commission (the "Commission") and Presidential action on the report and recommendations of the Commission.

2. The Secretary of Agriculture has advised me that, due to unexpected circumstances, it is appropriate to modify those import quotas, pending the investigation, report, and recommendations of the Commission, to permit the entry of certain articles currently excluded by those quotas.

3. I agree that it is appropriate to modify those quotas immediately while awaiting the investigation, report, and recommendations of the Commission.

Now, Therefore, I, Ronald Reagan, President of the United States of America, by the authority vested in me by Section 22 of the Agricultural Adjustment Act of 1933, as amended, and the Constitution and statutes of the United States of America, do hereby proclaim as follows:

A. Part 3 of the Appendix to the Tariff Schedules of the United States is amended by:

(1) inserting in the superior heading for items 958.16 through 958.18—

(a) "(Proclamation No. 5294, effective January 29, 1985)" after "on the effective date of this proclamation";

(b) "over 10 percent by dry weight of" immediately after "Articles containing"; and

(c) the words "(a) articles not principally of crystalline structure or not in dry amorphous form that are prepared for marketing to the retail consumers in the identical form and package in which imported, or (b)" immediately after "except";

(2) deleting—

(a) the column heading "Effective Period" above the superior heading for items 958.16 through 958.18;

(b) "Until 10/1/85" for each of items 958.16 through 958.18; and

(c) items 958.20, 958.25, and 958.30 together with their superior headings;

(3) inserting in item 958.18 the words, "except cake decorations and similar products to be used in the same condition as imported without any further processing other than the direct application to individual pastries or confections; finely ground or masticated coconut meat or juice thereof mixed with those sugars; and minced seafood preparations within the scope of item 183.05 containing 20 percent or less by dry weight of those sugars" immediately after "183.05"; and

(4) effective on October 1, 1985—

(a) the superior heading to items 958.16 through 958.18 is modified by striking out the words "During the period beginning on the effective date of this proclamation (Proclamation No. 5294, effective January 29, 1985) through September 30, 1985, if" and inserting in their place "Whenever, in any 12-month period beginning October 1 in any year,"; and

(b) by striking out the quota quantities "1,000 short tons", "2,500 short tons", and "28,000 short tons" from items 958.16, 958.17, and 958.18, respectively, and inserting in their place "3,000 short tons", "7,000 short tons", and "84,000 short tons", respectively.

B. This proclamation shall be effective as of 12:01 a.m. Eastern Daylight Time on the second day following the date of signing.

C. The quotas for items 958.16 through 958.18 shall terminate upon the filing of a notice in the *Federal Register* by the Secretary of Agriculture that the Department of Agriculture is no longer conducting a price support program for sugar cane and sugar beets.

In Witness Whereof, I have hereunto set my hand this 17th day of May, in the year of our Lord nineteen hundred and eighty-five, and of the Independence of the United States of America the two hundred and ninth.

RONALD REAGAN

[*Filed with the Office of the Federal Register, 4:25 p.m., May 17, 1985*]

Letter to the Chairwoman of the United States International Trade Commission on the Modification of Import Quotas on Certain Sugar Containing Articles
May 17, 1985

Dear Madam Chairwoman:

This is to inform you that, pursuant to Section 22 of the Agricultural Adjustment Act of 1933, as amended, I have modified, on an emergency basis, the description of the articles covered by the quotas established in Proclamation No. 5294 to permit the entry of:

—articles containing 10 percent or less by dry weight of sugar and,

—articles containing over 10 percent by dry weight of sugar if they are:

(a) not principally of crystalline structure or not in dry amorphous form that are prepared for marketing to the retail consumers in the identical form and package in which imported;

(b) within the scope of item 183.05, contain not over 65 percent by dry weight of sugar, and are cake decorations and similar products to be used in the same condition as imported without any further processing other than the direct application to individual pastries or confections;

(c) within the scope of item 183.05, contain not over 65 percent by dry weight of sugar, and are finely ground or masticated coconut meat or juice mixed with sugar; or

(d) within the scope of item 183.0505, contain 20 percent or less by dry weight of sugar.

An unexpectedly large volume of imports of these sugar-containing articles has caused the quotas for these articles to be closed or nearly closed for this fiscal year. This early closing of these quotas was unanticipated and is working or is expected to work severe hardship on importers and users of a number of articles containing relatively small amounts of sugar.

I believe it is appropriate not to cause such hardship in connection with these articles in the context of emergency action, but rather to permit their entry pending the investigation by the United States International Trade Commission.

Therefore, I have issued this day a proclamation modifying the description of the articles covered by the quotas established in

Proclamation No. 5294 to permit the entry of articles as indicated above.

Sincerely,

RONALD REAGAN

[The Honorable Paula Stern, Chairwoman, United States International Trade Commission, 701 E Street, N.W., Washington, DC 20536]

Proclamation 5341—Senior Center Week, 1985
May 17, 1985

By the President of the United States of America

A Proclamation

Older Americans are as diverse and fascinating as America itself. The memories they carry with them constitute a living treasury of knowledge about the history of our times. But older Americans are far more than just a repository of knowledge about the past. They are living active lives today and contributing greatly to enriching the lives of their families, friends, and communities.

One of the objectives of the Older Americans Act is to help older Americans secure the full enjoyment of their freedom to participate in our Nation's life. Senior centers play a very important role in achieving this goal by tapping older people's experience, skills, and knowledge and providing a focus for their energies. These centers are helping to realize the theme of this year's Older Americans Month, which is now in progress: "Help Yourself to Independence."

The activities sponsored by senior centers are as various and interesting as the citizens who make use of them. Courses on art and literature, discussions of current events, and training sessions on how to use a computer are among the wide variety of events that occur in senior centers. The staffs of these

centers are to be commended for their spirit of innovation and their dedication to enhancing the lives of older Americans. Once again, Americans are showing that anything is possible if we have the faith, the will, and the heart.

The Congress, by Senate Joint Resolution 60, has designated the week beginning May 12, 1985, through May 18, 1985, as "Senior Center Week" and authorized and requested the President to issue a proclamation in observance of this event.

Now, Therefore, I, Ronald Reagan, President of the United States of America, do hereby proclaim the week of May 12, 1985, as Senior Center Week, and I call upon the people of the United States to honor older Americans and those local organizations that bring together activities and services for their benefit.

In Witness Whereof, I have hereunto set my hand this seventeenth day of May, in the year of our Lord nineteen hundred and eighty-five, and of the Independence of the United States of America the two hundred and ninth.

RONALD REAGAN

[Filed with the Office of the Federal Register, 11:02 a.m., May 20, 1985]

Note: The proclamation was released by the Office of the Press Secretary on May 18.

Proclamation 5342—National Digestive Diseases Awareness Week, 1985
May 17, 1985

By the President of the United States of America

A Proclamation

Digestive diseases rank third in contributing to the total economic burden of illness in the United States. In terms of human discomfort and pain, mortality, and impact on the Nation's economy, they represent one of our most serious health problems. Digestive diseases are the leading cause of hospitalization and surgery in this country, and each day some 200,000 people miss work because of digestive problems. Twenty million Americans are treated for some type of chronic digestive disorder each year, and almost half of the United States population suffers an occasional digestive disorder, creating a yearly expenditure of approximately $17 billion in direct health care costs and a total economic burden of $50 billion.

Research into the causes, cures, prevention, and clinical treatment of digestive diseases and related nutrition problems is a national concern. The week of May 12, 1985, marks the second anniversary of the initiation of a national digestive diseases education program. Its goals are to involve the digestive diseases community, including the Coalition of Digestive Disease Organizations, the Federation of Digestive Disease Societies, the National Digestive Diseases Advisory Board, the National Digestive Diseases Education and Information Clearinghouse, and the National Institute of Arthritis, Diabetes, and Digestive and Kidney Diseases, in educating the public and health care practitioners to the seriousness of these diseases and the methods available to prevent, treat, and control them.

In recognition of these important efforts to combat digestive diseases, the Congress, by Senate Joint Resolution 94, has designated the week beginning May 12, 1985, as "National Digestive Diseases Awareness Week" and has authorized and requested the President to issue a proclamation calling for observance of this week.

Now, Therefore, I, Ronald Reagan, President of the United States of America, do hereby proclaim the week of May 12, 1985, as National Digestive Diseases Awareness Week. I urge the people of the United States and educational, philanthropic, scientific, medical, and health care organizations and professionals to participate in appropriate ceremonies to encourage further research into the causes and cures of all types of digestive disorders so as to alleviate the suffering of their victims.

In Witness Whereof, I have hereunto set my hand this seventeenth day of May, in the year of our Lord nineteen hundred and eighty-five, and of the Independence of the United States of America the two hundred and ninth.

RONALD REAGAN

[*Filed with the Office of the Federal Register, 11:03 a.m., May 20, 1985*]

Note: The proclamation was released by the Office of the Press Secretary on May 18.

Radio Address to the Nation on Armed Forces Day and Defense Spending
May 18, 1985

My fellow Americans:

Not too long ago one of our Ambassadors visited an American armored cavalry regiment stationed on the NATO line in Germany. As he returned to his helicopter, he was followed by a young 19-year-old trooper. The trooper asked him if he could get a message to the President. Well, the Ambassador said that sometimes getting messages to the President was part of his job. And the young trooper then said, "Will you tell him we're proud to be here, and we ain't scared of nothin."

Well, not long ago the Ambassador was in Washington and told me the sequel to that incident. I'd repeated a story in a talk that was carried on our Voice of America radio program, and there in that base in Germany the young trooper heard the broadcast and knew that I'd received his message. His commanding officer said that he ran down the company street yelling: "The system works! The system works!"

Well, the system does work, but not just because Ambassadors can get messages from a 19-year-old trooper to the President. Our system—this way of life we call democracy and freedom—really works because of the dedicated Americans like that GI in Germany, who've always been willing to defend our way of life from foreign aggressors—from those who do not love freedom and seek to destroy it.

Today is Armed Forces Day, a day we set aside to remember and thank those Americans who wear our country's uniform and who serve our nation in so many places around the globe. Many are far from home, and things you and I take for granted—family, friends, all the good things that go with life in our hometowns—they've given all these things up for the sake of a challenge and to answer a call. The challenge is the task of defending freedom, and the call they've answered is summarized in three words: duty, honor, country.

So, on Armed Forces Day, let's remember the debt we owe those in uniform. News of this broadcast will be carried on the Armed Forces Network, and I know I speak for all Americans when I say to our soldiers, sailors, airmen, marines, and coast guardsmen: We thank you for the job you're doing and the sacrifices you're making for all of us at home. And we're grateful and proud of you for your devotion to country and to the cause of freedom.

Now, remembering to say thank you is very important, but we here at home have a greater responsibility. As you know, since my first day in office, restoring respect for America's military and rebuilding our nation's defenses has been one of my highest priorities. It remains so today.

I'm sure you've read about the discussions going on in the Congress on military spending. I'll reserve comment on them until the Congress has completed its current work, but I do want to say this much: One of the things that has most deeply disturbed Americans during the past decade, even though it isn't always talked about as much as other political issues, was the expansion of Soviet influence beyond their borders—Angola, Ethiopia, Cambodia, Afghanistan, and Nicaragua are cases in point. This trend was of natural concern to the American people, especially right here on the continent.

The tendency of some leaders to shut their eyes to the real world, their lack of realism about our foreign adversaries and communism's unrelenting assault on human freedom requires that we face up to the need to restore effective deterrence and help our friends.

Americans don't want to take chances with our national security. It's just one of the strongest impulses in our body politic. Americans know an act of Congress can repeal vital military expenditures. They also know what an act of Congress can't repeal: the aggressive tendencies and intentions of our adversaries.

So, I want to say today I'll be conferring with the Congress and with Secretary of

Defense Caspar Weinberger on the military budget. And believe me, our attack on waste and fraud in procurement—like discovering that $436 hammer—is going to continue, but we must have adequate military appropriations. As President Kennedy said: "There is no discount on defense."

My first responsibility as President is the safety and security of the American people. So, if a suitable compromise can't be worked out, I won't hesitate to put our case before the American people and ask for your support. On this Armed Forces Day let's say thanks to all Americans in uniform, but let's make sure we give them the tools they need to do their job.

Until next week, thanks for listening, and God bless you.

Note: The President spoke at 12:06 p.m. from Camp David, MD.

Remarks at a White House Ceremony Launching the Summer Jobs for Youth Program
May 20, 1985

Secretary Brock and distinguished guests, ladies and gentlemen, good morning, and welcome to the White House.

I know one young person that isn't lacking for a summer job. As a matter of fact, she has a permanent job daily on her radio station. Kelly is a sports announcer.

These past couple of months, as the trees have begun to leaf out and the flowers to blossom, spring has come to America—an America that is in good economic health. For more than 2 years our economy has been growing steadily. And this morning at 8:30 a.m. the Commerce Department released some additional figures that indicate that very definitely.

Our basic industries have achieved new productivity while technological breakthroughs involving the computer and the microchip have produced entirely new fields of services and goods. And nearly 8 million jobs have been created and more than 200,000 last month alone.

As summer follows spring, inflation will remain low and our economy will continue to grow, creating still more jobs. Yet even in these good economic times, thousands of young Americans, as Bill has told you, have trouble finding summer jobs. Many live in parts of our inner cities where there are few employers. Some are black or Hispanic and suffer from higher rates of unemployment than other young Americans.

Ironically, the very young people who will find it hardest to get work will be the ones who need jobs the most. To them, a summer job means a chance to escape poverty and disadvantage, a chance to get the work experience that would enable them to climb the economic ladder.

I think many of us here remember summer jobs. I remember they taught me a great deal about the satisfactions of good, honest work. I was 14 when I got my first summer job. Before that summer was over, I was laying hardwood floor; I was shingling roof, painting, and using a pick and shovel to dig for foundation in house construction. I have to confess that pick and shovel work got a little heavy at times.

One day I was hard at it, swinging a pick, and I had that pick right up over my shoulder for another blow when the noon whistle blew. And I just said, "That's it." And I didn't complete the swing, I just dropped the pick behind me and stepped out from under it. And then I heard a rather profane and angry voice behind me—[*laughter*]—and I turned around, and there stood the boss with the pick imbedded in the ground right between his feet. [*Laughter*] So, ever since that, I've kept in mind a simple lesson: If you start swinging, finish. [*Laughter*]

But I can't help thinking that those summer jobs might have been impossible for me to get if certain laws in place today had been in effect back then. And maybe in our effort to do good, maybe we haven't been as successful as we thought we were when we passed some of those laws.

Under the current minimum wage law, for example, many young people have been priced out of the labor market. To put these young Americans back in the market, we have proposed the youth employment opportunity wage—legislation that would allow employers to hire young people at a lower minimum wage during the summer months. Our bill would increase summer employment opportunities, yet provide explicit safeguards to protect permanent employees and the young people themselves.

The youth employment opportunity wage has wide support, including the endorsement of the National Conference of Black Mayors. For thousands of young Americans, it would represent breakthrough legislation. Let's hope that Congress will act soon.

In the meantime, our administration will continue its work to provide summer jobs for young Americans. We firmly believe that the surest source of the real work, not make-work, is in the private sector. So, at the center of our efforts lies a partnership between the Government and the private sector.

As part of our Job Training Partnership Act this year, our summer youth employment program includes nearly $825 million in funding for State and local governments. And these governments have available some $100 million left over from the 825 million granted them last year for summer employment. So, these levels of government can use this over $900 million this summer to work with other nonprofit concerns as they provide work experience for more than 850,000 young people.

Private efforts in the summer jobs program can offer still more opportunities. Last summer, for example, television stations like WDAF in Kansas City aired summer job-a-thons. Newspapers like the Atlanta Journal/Constitution permitted youngsters to run a "Jobs Wanted" ads for free. Corporations like Walt Disney Productions hired thousands of young people and enterprises like Chevron, Sun Company, and Hewlett-Packard contributed facilities, personnel, and hundreds of thousands of dollars.

This summer, as in years past, the White House Office of Private Sector Initiatives will receive help in overseeing the summer jobs program from the National Alliance of Business. Bill Kolberg and the other executives at the NAB have my deepest thanks.

This year's spokesmen for the summer jobs program will be the members of the American Sportscasters Association. Vin Scully, as representative of that association, you have my gratitude, and Vin, coming from somebody who used to do a little sports announcing himself, I'd like to say: You're one of the very best.

Finally, to the 170 representatives of corporations and private industry councils who have received summer jobs awards—many present today—our congratulations. You've already done much for young Americans, and I know that this summer, you'll do still more.

Together, we can provide summer jobs for hundreds of thousands of our young people. In so doing, we'll help to teach them the spirit of enterprise and to give them the most important kind of capital, not the kind that accumulates in banks, but that which, through actual work experience is stored up in the heart and mind.

Thank you, God bless you.

Note: The President spoke at 11:42 a.m. in the Rose Garden at the White House.

Nomination of Paul J. Hare To Be United States Ambassador to Zambia
May 20, 1985

The President today announced his intention to nominate Paul J. Hare, a career member of the Senior Foreign Service, Class of Minister-Counselor, as Ambassador

Extraordinary and Plenipotentiary of the United States of America to the Republic of Zambia. He would succeed Nicholas Platt.

Mr. Hare entered the Foreign Service in 1960. In 1961–1963 he served as administrative officer at our Embassy in Kuwait. Thereafter he became consular officer at the U.S. Embassy in Tunisia. In 1964–1968 he was on assignment to the Agency for International Development (CORDS and the U.S. Embassy in Saigon and several provinces in Vietnam). He returned to the Department in 1969 as Vietnam desk officer for awhile and then served as Moroccan desk officer until 1971. In 1971–1972 he was Deputy Director of Policy Planning in the African Bureau. In 1972 he became press officer then Deputy Director, Office

of Press Relations, until 1975. In 1975 he went to Brisbane, Australia, as consul of the American consulate. In 1977–1979 he became Peace Corps Director in Morocco. He then returned to the Department as Director of the Office of Southern African Affairs, where he served until 1981 when he went to Israel as counselor for political affairs, and where he has been serving to the present time.

Mr. Hare was born December 8, 1937, in Alexandria, VA. He received his B.A. in 1959 from Swarthmore College and attended the University of Chicago from 1959 to 1960. His foreign language is French. He is married to Robbie Anna, and they have two children.

Nomination of Alice Wright Algood To Be a Member of the National Museum Services Board
May 20, 1985

The President today announced his intention to nominate Alice Wright Algood to be a member of the National Museum Services Board, National Foundation on the Arts and the Humanities, for a term expiring December 6, 1989. This is a reappointment.

Mrs. Algood is a board member and former chairman of the Tennessee State Museum Association. She is a member, past

chapter president, and past State president of the Association for the Preservation of Tennessee Antiquities. She also serves as legislative chairman of the American Legion Auxiliary.

She attended Louisiana State University. She is married, has two children, and resides in Columbia, TN. She was born March 11, 1926, in Columbia, TN.

Letter to the Speaker of the House and the President of the Senate on the Activities of United Nations Member Countries
May 20, 1985

Dear Mr. Speaker: *(Dear Mr. President:)*

Pursuant to Public Law 98–151, I am transmitting herewith the report on the activities of countries within the United Nations and its specialized agencies.

This report assesses the degree of support of United States foreign policy in the United Nations context by the governments of countries which are members of the

United Nations.

In addition, this report includes the report required of the Secretary of State under Section 117 of Public Law 98–164 on the performance of UN member countries in international organizations.

Sincerely,

RONALD REAGAN

Note: Identical letters were sent to Thomas P. O'Neill, Jr., Speaker of the House of Representatives, and George Bush, President of the Senate.

Proclamation 5343—National Maritime Day, 1985
May 21, 1985

By the President of the United States of America

A Proclamation

The restructuring of the Nation's maritime policy and regulations to create an environment in which our shipping industry can prosper is of great importance to the United States.

Since its birth as a Nation, the United States has relied on the oceans for commerce and as avenues for the protection of national interests. The United States is truly a maritime power by necessity.

Maritime power has two principal components. One component, the Navy and the Coast Guard, guards America's free use of the seas while the other component, the Merchant Marine, supports trade with nations and, in an emergency, becomes a part of our military establishment—integral with our military forces.

This role of our civilian mariners is not new. In World War II, virtually every serviceman who saw action against the enemy was transported overseas by ship. In Vietnam, more than 90 percent of the war material utilized in that conflict went by sea.

Our brave merchant seamen took their place alongside the fighting men of our armed services in combat against a determined enemy. In World War II, from December 1941 to August 1945, the United States lost 5,638 merchant seamen aboard 733 ships sunk by submarines. Through the first part of 1943, the casualty rate among U.S. merchant seamen was greater than in all the armed services.

To maintain America's maritime power this Administration has advocated that a number of steps be taken by government, industry, and labor:

—Maintenance of a superior Navy, Marine Corps, and a highly capable Coast Guard. A superior Navy is required to protect merchant ships in time of emergency, in recognition of the critical nature of their military and economic cargoes.

—An economically independent United States flag merchant marine of not less than its current capabilities.

—An adequate shipyard mobilization base. The construction of the 600-ship Navy is helping to maintain the shipyard mobilization base.

—Continued emphasis on merchant vessel security agreements between the United States and its allies, such as the NATO ship-sharing agreement.

The enactment of the Shipping Act of 1984 was a major step toward regaining a prominent position on the world's trade routes for our country. It diminished or streamlined outdated regulations that governed the ocean liner industry, and it has helped rekindle the spirit of American maritime enterprise. American-flag liner companies are now in the forefront of developments that are providing shippers with more efficient, extensive, and innovative intermodal services.

Our Merchant Marine is being bolstered by the replacement of obsolete ships with new, efficient, and highly competitive vessels. With the cooperation of seafaring labor, these new fleet additions are being operated with small crews that increase their productivity and competitiveness.

These healthy trends should be encouraged. We must work to continue to develop the strong American merchant marine to serve our Nation's peacetime trade and support our Armed Forces.

In recognition of the importance of the American merchant marine, the Congress, by joint resolution approved May 20, 1933, designated May 22 of each year as "National Maritime Day" and authorized and requested the President to issue annually a proclamation calling for its appropriate observance. This date was chosen to commemorate the day in 1819 when the SS SAVANNAH departed Savannah, Georgia, on the first transatlantic steamship voyage.

Now, Therefore, I, Ronald Reagan, President of the United States of America, do hereby proclaim May 22, 1985, as National Maritime Day, and I urge the people of the United States to observe this day by displaying the flag of the United States at their homes and other suitable places, and I request that all ships sailing under the American flag dress ship on that day.

In Witness Whereof, I have hereunto set my hand this twenty-first day of May, in the year of our Lord nineteen hundred and eighty-five, and of the Independence of the United States of America the two hundred and ninth.

RONALD REAGAN

[*Filed with the Office of the Federal Register, 2:18 p.m., May 21, 1985*]

Message to the Congress Transmitting the Finland-United States Agreement on Nuclear Energy
May 21, 1985

To the Congress of the United States:

I am pleased to transmit to the Congress, pursuant to section 123 d. of the Atomic Energy Act of 1954, as amended (42 U.S.C. 2153(d)), the text of the proposed Agreement for Cooperation Between the Government of the United States of America and the Government of the Republic of Finland Concerning Peaceful Uses of Nuclear Energy and accompanying annexes and agreed minute; my written approval, authorization and determination concerning the agreement; and the memorandum of the Director of the United States Arms Control and Disarmament Agency with the Nuclear Proliferation Assessment Statement concerning the agreement. The joint memorandum submitted to me by the Secretaries of State and Energy, which includes a summary of the provisions of the agreement, and the views and recommendations of the Members of the Nuclear Regulatory Commission and the Director of the United States Arms Control and Disarmament Agency are also enclosed.

The proposed revised agreement with Finland has been negotiated in accordance with the Nuclear Non-Proliferation Act, which sets forth certain requirements for new agreements for peaceful nuclear cooperation with other countries. In my judgment, the proposed agreement for cooperation between the United States and Finland, together with its accompanying agreed minute, meets all statutory requirements.

The proposed agreement reflects the desire of the Government of the United States and the Government of Finland to confirm and refine a framework for peaceful nuclear cooperation between our two countries in a manner which recognizes both the shared non-proliferation objectives and the friendly and harmonious relations between the United States and Finland. The agreement will in my view further the non-proliferation and foreign policy interests of the United States.

I have considered the views and recommendations of the interested agencies in reviewing the proposed agreement and have determined that its performance will promote, and will not constitute an unreasonable risk to, the common defense and security. Accordingly, I have approved the agreement and authorized its execution.

Under current law, this agreement may be brought into force upon the completion of 60 days of continuous session of the Congress. However, the pending Export Administration Act reauthorization bill would revise the procedures in sections 123 and 130 of the Atomic Energy Act for bringing the agreement into force. If these amendments are enacted in their current form before the completion of the 60-day period provided for in current law, this agreement will not be brought into force until an additional 30 days of continuous session has passed, in keeping with the intent of the proposed amendments. In that case, this submittal shall constitute a submittal for purposes of both section 123 d. of the Atomic Energy Act and section 123 b. as it is proposed to be amended. The Administration is prepared to begin consultation with the Senate Foreign Relations and House Foreign Affairs Committees on the proposed agreement immediately.

RONALD REAGAN

The White House,
May 21, 1985.

Statement by Principal Deputy Press Secretary Speakes on the Mutual and Balanced Force Reduction Negotiations
May 21, 1985

Today the President met with Ambassador Robert Blackwill, who will serve as the new U.S. Representative to the Mutual and Balanced Force Reductions (MBFR) talks in Vienna, which reconvene this week. The U.S. delegation in Vienna together with those of our NATO allies are seeking to reach an equitable and verifiable agreement with the Warsaw Pact on the reduction to equal levels of conventional force manpower in central Europe. Such an agreement would enhance stability and security, reduce the risk of war, and promote mutual confidence in Europe. The President expressed his continuing interest in and support for efforts in the MBFR negotiations.

Ambassador Blackwill's work in Vienna will go hand in hand with U.S. participation in other negotiations that seek to promote security and stability. In Geneva, the United States next week will return for a second round of negotiations with the Soviet Union on nuclear and space arms in an effort to enhance stability and eliminate entirely the risk of nuclear war. Also in Geneva, the United States has submitted to the 40-nation Disarmament Conference a draft treaty for the complete and verifiable prohibition of chemical weapons. And in Stockholm at the Conference on Confidence and Security Building Measures and Disarmament in Europe (CDE), the NATO alliance is actively seeking agreement on concrete measures to reduce the risks of surprise attack in Europe.

The President urged Ambassador Blackwill, together with his Western colleagues in Vienna, to probe for all possible areas of agreement in order to achieve concrete results, noting that if the Soviet Union and its partners show a similar degree of willingness to find mutually acceptable solutions to the difficult issues on the table, progress in MBFR will be possible.

Informal Exchange With Reporters Prior to a Meeting Between President Reagan and President Roberto Suazo Córdova of Honduras
May 21, 1985

Q. I hear you've been pounding the table on Nicaraguan aid.

President Reagan. Oh, just kind of slapped it. [*Laughter*]

Q. They think you mean business.

President Reagan. Then I'm happy.

Q. President Suazo, are you prepared to lift restrictions on the *contras* if Congress approves new aid to them?

President Suazo. What kind of restrictions?

Q. Well, forcing them to go beyond the borders into Nicaragua, not allowing them to operate out of Honduras.

President Suazo. The Congress is the one that has to decide what it wants to do. It's their business.

What the American Congress and the American people should remember is that 24 hours after this request by President Ronald Reagan was rejected by the Congress, President Daniel Ortega was in Moscow saying hello to Chairman Gorbachev of the Soviet Communist Party.

I think that everybody recognizes that this vote in the Congress of the United States in which they rejected the request of President Reagan for humanitarian assistance for the *contras* was a victory for President Daniel Ortega and for the Communist Party, and I think that it's not my business, but the Congress of the United States decides—the thing was lost by two votes and I can't interfere in domestic American politics. But, although I'm not an American, I think that you should feel proud in the United States that the United States has recovered its leadership position in the world under a great leader named Ronald Reagan.

And so, we in Central America are fighting for the establishment of democratic regimes that represent the will of the people freely expressed. We're fighting for liberty; we're fighting for justice. We strongly support the Contadora process; their meetings continue.

The five Central American countries that participate in that process—the one that places the most obstacles in the path of a peaceful solution within a global framework for the entire region is precisely the regime in Nicaragua.

I've told journalists that have visited Honduras that they should try going to Cuba, Afghanistan, and Moscow and speak as freely as they do in the United States and in Honduras and see what would happen under these Communist governments. They'd wind up in jail or who knows what.

Q. President Reagan, are you encouraged by what you heard from your GOP leadership today about the chances for new aid?

President Reagan. I've been encouraged by what I've just been hearing here. [*Laughter*]

Q. You didn't put him up to it, did you?

President Reagan. We just met a few seconds before you came in here. We haven't seen each other.

President Suazo. I'd like to remind you that the shield of Honduras says, "A free, sovereign, and independent . . . ." What I've said represents my beliefs. I believe that President Reagan has recovered the position of leadership that the United States had been losing. And all of us who believe in democracy have regained our faith and our trust in this leadership; our faith and trust have been reborn.

I think he's a man who makes vigorous decisions, and I think the American people should think about this and pray to the Lord God Almighty that He illuminate the President in the decisions that he makes.

But I have not been coached. I haven't been put up to this. [*Laughter*] I came here accepting the very kind invitation issued to me by President Reagan.

And furthermore, President Reagan is not an executioner. He is not a dictator by any matter of means. And he's always been a strong believer in democracy, and he never has imposed any kind of restrictions on a free, sovereign and independent country like Honduras.

Q. Thank you very much.

Q. Are you content to have the *contras* stay in Honduras then?

President Suazo. No more.

Q. Thank you.

Note: The exchange began at 11:30 in the Oval Office at the White House. President Suazo spoke in Spanish, and his remarks were translated by an interpreter.

Remarks Following Discussions With President Roberto Suazo Córdova of Honduras
May 21, 1985

President Reagan. It's been a privilege to have President Suazo of Honduras, a friend of the United States and a friend of democracy, here for a visit.

We've had very useful discussions during which both of us expressed our satisfaction with the positive relationship that our two countries enjoy. We're in full agreement that the growth of democracy and economic opportunity is essential to peace and security in Central America.

We reviewed the accomplishments of the U.S.-Honduran joint commission established last year to promote the closest possible cooperation between our two governments. The joint commission is an excellent example of how friends can work together in a framework of mutual respect and cooperation.

I expressed to President Suazo my personal appreciation for his government's strong support for our policies in Central America. Our two governments share serious concern over the threat to the entire region posed by the Communist Sandinista regime in Nicaragua and its Cuban and Soviet supporters. President Suazo and I renewed our commitment to face this challenge together and to counter aggression and subversion.

I also expressed today my continued support for peace efforts through the Contadora process. Honduras and the United States both back a comprehensive solution based on full, verifiable implementation of the Contadora document of objectives, including dialog to achieve national reconciliation through democratic elections.

President Suazo and I are today issuing a joint statement that sums up the state of relations between our two countries. In it, the American commitment to the sovereignty and territorial integrity of Honduras is restated in clear and firm terms.

Honduras is a friendly nation facing a serious threat of Communist aggression and subversion. There should be no doubt that we will fulfill our mutual defense obligation under the Rio treaty and the OAS Charter.

Finally, it was a great personal pleasure to meet again with President Suazo. Honduras is on the path to democracy—a course which will in the long run ensure its people the fruits of freedom and prosperity.

I and the people of the United States look forward to continued close friendship and cooperation with President Suazo and the people of Honduras.

President Suazo. Mr. President, this is the fourth meeting between us since I became President of my country as a result of the freely expressed will of the Honduran people.

This visit takes place a scant 6 months prior to general elections in Honduras. And for the first time in 50 years, a civilian will have the great privilege of handing over the reins of government to another civilian elected in free and honest elections.

Our emerging democracy has been subjected to the worst economic crisis of the century and exposed to the most severe international threats. These circumstances have made our task more difficult. Not everything I would have liked to have done has been possible. However, I will hand over to my legitimate successor a nation enjoying complete freedom, ready to face the challenges of the future with faith in its capacity for progress and with a deep-rooted conviction of justice.

Honduras, which has honored friendship and solidarity with other democracies, also needs it friends. It requires a clear expression of support in order to continue its development in peace, security, and with justice and liberty for all.

My visit to this beautiful country underlines the beginning of a new relationship between Honduras and the United States, a new relationship which is based on mutual respect and cooperation with interdependency. A new relationship takes into account our differences and our common interests, our needs, and our potential.

As a result of high-level negotiations between our countries over the past 6 months, President Reagan and I have today committed ourselves to a more solid friendship and to closer cooperation based on mutual respect of our own dignity.

Thus, we have reaffirmed the general principles of a new relationship in economic as well as security matters. We have decided to continue to maintain on a permanent basis the high-level commissions which have been meeting to deal with these matters and to have systematic consultations between the Secretary of State and the Foreign Minister of Honduras.

President Reagan, with great sensitivity, has understood the urgent need to cooperate with the Honduran people in order to stabilize and reactivate our economy. We have reached a mutually satisfactory agreement for the disbursement of aid programs for this year. And talks have been initiated to project economic and technical cooperation over the coming years. This dialog will allow us to give proper attention to the renewed efforts which will have to be made in order to speed up a process of economic, social, and administrative reform. The success of democracy in Honduras will depend on carrying out these efforts.

Even though social justice, the sustained development of our economy, and political participation should be the basis of our national security, President Reagan and I have evaluated the international dangers faced by Honduras, the Central American region, and the United States itself. Our countries will not fail to provide assistance to each other in order to face these threats. In the case of Honduras, we have received security guarantees from the United States.

Honduras does not have aggressive designs on any country. In the crisis faced by Central America, we shall continue our efforts to reach a negotiated agreement within the Contadora peace initiative. We look forward to a full and verifiable regional peace and cooperation agreement based on the 21 objectives set forth by the five Central American states.

Mr. President, our talks have proven to be very helpful in promoting excellent links of friendship and cooperation between our peoples and governments, as well as for the peace and security of the Central American region. I shall return to Honduras having reaffirmed my admiration for the American people, my faith in the understanding of its legislators, and my confidence that the leadership, which you undoubtedly exert, will always be present to serve the ideals that make this nation great, ideals which were shared by the founding fathers of our respective nations when they were searching for independence, democracy, and liberty.

Thank you very much.

Q. Mr. President, we understand you've pounded the table in frustration over Nicaragua. Is that right, sir?

President Reagan. I was slapping a fly. [*Laughter*]

Q. Are you going to get aid to the *contras* through now, sir?

President Reagan. Well, we'll see. We are going to try.

Q. Are you optimistic about it?

President Reagan. I'm always optimistic.

Q. Did you really pound the table, though?

President Reagan. I killed a fly.

Q. Does it have to go through the CIA to be acceptable to you?

President Reagan. I am not going to give any details.

Q. Would you like to disband Congress? Be truthful, now.

Note: President Reagan spoke to reporters at 1:34 p.m. at the South Portico of the White House. President Suazo spoke in Spanish, and his remarks were translated by an interpreter. Earlier, the two Presidents met in the Oval Office and then attended a luncheon in the Residence.

Joint Honduras-United States Communique
May 21, 1985

The Presidents of the United States of America and the Republic of Honduras, meeting in Washington, D.C., on May 21, 1985, with full commitment of their Governments to the ideals of justice, liberty and democracy that the people of the Western Hemisphere seek, and recognizing the critical situation in which these values are being tested in Central America today as well as the urgent obligation to safeguard them, issue this communique:

The two Presidents noted with satisfaction the warm, cooperative ties between the two nations, including the very close security relationship which contributes to peace and stability in the Central American region and strengthens the independence and sovereignty of their respective nations. Both Presidents expressed great satisfaction with the work of the Joint Commission on U.S.-Honduran relations that was formed in Washington in November 1984 to promote, on the basis of sovereign equality and mutual respect, sustained economic and social development and enhanced security.

The Presidents reviewed the results of recent discussions on economic matters within the Joint Commission, in particular the program for economic revitalization being developed by the Government of Honduras and the support of that program by the United States through economic assistance funds. They reaffirmed the agreements reached by the Joint Commission for the disbursement during 1985 of $147.5 million in Economic Support Funds. The two Presidents expressed approval of the objectives of the Honduran economic program to achieve sustained, non-inflationary economic growth through measures to control fiscal and balance of payments deficits.

They endorsed the mutual efforts to encourage expansion of the productive and exporting sectors of the Honduran economy. They agreed that their governments will cooperate closely and will seek increasing levels of bilateral and multilateral economic assistance to support economic stability, growth, and development to improve the living standard of the people of Honduras.

The Presidents reviewed the work on security issues of the Joint Commission, including the ongoing review of the Military Assistance Agreement between the United States and Honduras of 1954. They expressed approval for modification of that Agreement and associated documents with respect to the following:

—the exercise of criminal jurisdiction over United States Department of Defense personnel present in Honduras;

—the sharing of maintenance and repair costs at specified Honduran airfields;

—the establishment of standard procedures for settling claims associated with United States military activity in Honduras; and

—the establishment of a joint political-military administrative group to review and facilitate appropriate administrative issues.

They further expressed satisfaction with the substantive progress made in the Joint Commission's review of the following areas of mutual interest: operating procedures related to the scheduling and planning of combined military exercises; counter-terrorism training; U.S. use of Honduran military facilities and airspace; and continued joint consultations and security threat analysis to facilitate Honduran planning of minimum force and force modernization requirements.

In the context of their review of the security relationship, the two Presidents reaffirmed their governments' intention to continue to work closely together to confront the serious threats to the peace and security of both countries through mutual assistance and the development of defensive capabilities. To this end, the Government of the United States will continue to cooperate, as necessary and appropriate, in the strengthening of Honduras' defenses and the modernization of its armed forces.

The Government of the United States further reiterated its firm and unwavering commitment to cooperate in the defense of the sovereignty and territorial integrity of Honduras in accordance with the reciprocal rights and obligations relating to individual and collective self defense and the use of armed force, as expressed in the Inter-American Treaty of Reciprocal Assistance, the Charter of the United Nations and the Charter of the Organization of American States.

In view of the very close and cooperative nature of the two countries' political and security relationships and the very serious security threats that exist in Central America, the Governments of the United States and Honduras reaffirm the rights and obligations in these three agreements, including Article 3 of the Inter-American Treaty of Reciprocal Assistance, Article 51 of the Charter of the United Nations and Article 21 of the Charter of the Organization of American States. In case of an armed attack against Honduras, the United States will take appropriate measures, consistent with the rights and obligations cited above, to consult with and support in a timely and effective manner the Government of Honduras in its efforts to defend its sovereignty and territorial integrity against communist aggression.

To ensure the success of these cooperative efforts, the two Presidents agreed that the Governments will maintain close working relations through the continued work of the Joint Commission, and periodic consultations of their foreign ministers and other governmental officials on matters of mutual interest or concern.

Lastly, the two Presidents reiterated their conviction that the development of the Central American people can be fulfilled only in a climate of peace and liberty. In this sense, they expressed their firm support for a verifiable and comprehensive implementation of the Contadora Document of Objectives including, in particular, dialogue to achieve national reconciliation in the democratic framework.

Proclamation 5344—National Osteoporosis Awareness Week, 1985
May 21, 1985

By the President of the United States of America

A Proclamation

Osteoporosis is a condition in which bone mass decreases, causing bones to be more susceptible to fracture. It may develop without warning. A fall, blow, or lifting action that would not strain the average person can easily cause one or more bones to break in a person with severe osteoporosis.

Some 15 to 20 million Americans are afflicted with osteoporosis. The risk of developing the disease increases with age and is higher in women than in men. It is estimated that 25 percent of postmenopausal women in the United States will develop osteoporosis. Among people who live to be age 90, 32 percent of women and 17 percent of men will suffer a hip fracture, mostly due to osteoporosis. More than 50,000 older women and many older men die each year in the United States as a result of such complications. It is estimated that national health costs related to osteoporosis are at least $3.8 billion annually.

As scientific knowledge about the disease continues to grow, there is reason for hope. New research findings and new approaches to prevention, diagnosis, and treatment are being developed. The Federal government and private voluntary organizations have created a strong and enduring partnership committed to research on osteoporosis. Working together, our objective must be to uncover the cause and cure for this major public health problem.

The Congress, by Senate Joint Resolution 61, has designated the week beginning May 20, 1985, through May 26, 1985, as "National Osteoporosis Awareness Week" and authorized and requested the President to issue a proclamation in observance of this event.

Now, Therefore, I, Ronald Reagan, President of the United States of America, do hereby proclaim May 20, 1985, through May 26, 1985, as National Osteoporosis Awareness Week. I urge the people of the United States and educational, philanthropic, scientific, medical, and health care organizations and professionals to observe this week with appropriate ceremonies and activities.

In Witness Whereof, I have hereunto set my hand this twenty-first day of May, in the year of our Lord nineteen hundred and eighty-five, and of the Independence of the United States of America the two hundred and ninth.

RONALD REAGAN

[*Filed with the Office of the Federal Register, 10:49 a.m., May 22, 1985*]

Proclamation 5345—National Medical Transcriptionist Week, 1985
May 21, 1985

By the President of the United States of America

A Proclamation

Record-keeping is a vital function in our society, and one of the most important records for every American is the medical record. That record, including reports prepared and edited by a medical transcriptionist from physician dictation, is the permanent history of a patient's medical care.

A century ago, physicians knew many of their patients from birth, knew all their ailments, and provided all their medical care. Today, with medical specialization and greater mobility among people, many skilled physicians may treat the average American during a lifetime. Using transcribed medical reports, each physician can easily and quickly review a patient's medical history even if the physician has never seen that patient before. Because of the work done by trained medical transcriptionists, patients can be assured that the history of their medical care is portrayed accurately and legibly. Medical transcriptionists have therefore become a vital link between the physician and the patient.

It is appropriate for our Nation to recognize the contributions of medical transcriptionists. We should encourage hospitals, allied health education programs, and community colleges to provide appropriate courses of instruction recognizing the high standards that must be met by medical transcriptionists and the vital function they perform.

In recognition of the need for medical transcriptionists in today's society, the Congress, by Public Law 98–609, has designated the week beginning May 20, 1985, as "National Medical Transcriptionist Week" and authorized and requested the President to issue a proclamation in observance of this event.

Now, Therefore, I, Ronald Reagan, President of the United States of America, do hereby designate the week of May 20 through May 26, 1985, as National Medical Transcriptionist Week, and I urge all Americans to participate in appropriate ceremonies in observance of this event.

In Witness Whereof, I have hereunto set my hand this twenty-first day of May, in the year of our Lord nineteen hundred and eighty-five, and of the Independence of the United States of America the two hundred and ninth.

RONALD REAGAN

[*Filed with the Office of the Federal Register, 10:50 a.m., May 22, 1985*]

Remarks at the Annual Conference of the Council of the Americas
May 21, 1985

It's a pleasure to have you all here today. And a special word of thanks to your chairman, David Rockefeller, for all he's done for many years to strengthen political and economic relations with our friends and neighbors in Latin America.

Four-and-a-half years ago when we picked up the mantle, I fully understood that if our southern neighbors were to live in peace and be spared the tragedy of Communist dictatorship, we must have a balanced policy on Latin America. Our strategy's been based on four mutually reinforcing elements. We've been seeking to help bolster the development of democratic institutions, to improve the living conditions of the people and restore economic growth, to provide security assistance and thwart Communist-supported subversion and aggression, to find realistic diplomatic solutions to conflict in the region.

No strategy is worth the paper it's written on unless it's backed up with the hard work of loyal and talented individuals, and I'd like to take this opportunity to recognize a man that I've relied on heavily. Bill Middendorf, would you please stand up? I want to tell you how much I personally appreciate your service. You've done a terrific job at the Organization of American States during a very trying time. And having just returned from Europe, I can tell you that your next job, representing us to the European Communities, will also be a major challenge. [*Laughter*]

And I'd also like to introduce Elliott Abrams, whom I've asked to serve as Assistant Secretary of State for Inter-American Affairs. Elliott has been an articulate spokesman for our country in the field of human rights. And I'm looking forward to working even more closely with you. Now, just make sure you get all the phone numbers of everybody in the room before they leave today. [*Laughter*] Seriously, I hope you'll give Elliott your strong support.

With the energy and the creative talents of people like Bill Middendorf, Elliott Abrams, all of you here today, much has been accomplished in Central America. The people there, with the regrettable exception of Nicaragua, are enjoying the rising democratic tide.

One of the most damaging lies of our era is the falsehood that people must give up freedom to enjoy economic progress, which makes me think of a story—everything makes me think of a story—[*laughter*]—about three dogs, an American dog and a Polish dog and a Russian dog. And they were all having a visit, and the American dog was telling them about how things were in this country. He said, "You know, you bark, and if you have to, you bark long enough, and then somebody comes along and gives you some meat." And the Polish dog said, "What's meat?" [*Laughter*] The Russian dog says, "What's bark?" [*Laughter*]

I have to interrupt right here and tell you that on one of my visits—I won't name him; I don't want to embarrass him—but one of the heads of state that I met with on this visit, he gave me one while I was on the way. He told me the story about the two fellows in the Soviet Union who were walking down the street, and the one of them says, "Have we really achieved full communism? Is this it? Is this now full communism?" And the other one said, "Oh, hell no, things are going to get a lot worse." [*Laughter*]

Well, developing countries are discovering that the only things produced by communism are oppression and deprivation. The political freedom now emerging in Latin America gives us reason to be optimistic about the changes for economic progress. We're doing all we can to work with the new democracies in Central America, our neighbors in the Caribbean, and other countries in the hemisphere to strengthen their democratic institutions and to invigorate their domestic economies.

In Central America the downward economic spiral, by and large, has been halted. Excluding Nicaragua, the regional gross domestic product was up 1.2 percent in 1984. This year we expect regional growth, again excluding Nicaragua, of 2½ percent.

We recognize this economic growth is fragile, and sustaining it will require a long-term process of prudent economic reforms. Consistent with the findings of the bipartisan Kissinger commission, we're moving forward with a wide-ranging economic and security assistance effort in Central America called the Jackson plan, named, of course, after the late Senator Henry "Scoop" Jackson.

Throughout Latin America, we've committed considerable resources to human development. We're spending hundreds of millions of dollars in health initiatives, housing and infrastructure programs, food and agricultural assistance also, and employment projects and educational opportunities, including scholarships permitting young people in the region—many of them from poor families—to study here in the United States. Now, more can and will be done in each of these areas.

In the Caribbean our Caribbean Basin Initiative went into effect January 1, 1984. It's just beginning to take hold. Companies are starting to respond to new incentives that provide for manufacturers of most goods 12 years of duty-free commerce with the United States. This should encourage domestic and foreign investment. Already, some 250 to 300 new export-oriented investments in the region have created over 30,000 jobs.

In 1984 CBI-eligible imports to the United States increased by about 17 percent over the 1983 level, and that's a $555 million increase. And for the first time since 1981, our exports to the region also showed growth last year.

Our administration has stressed the necessity of strong private sector involvement if economic progress is to be made in Latin America. The single most important reform any government can make is to lower its peoples' personal income tax. Government spending programs—but what I should say, not just income tax—I'm sorry, I've been just coming from a session having to do with our own income tax—lowered personal tax rates in those countries. Government spending programs aimed at building the infrastructure will not do the job.

The efficiency, the ingenuity, and vitality

of private enterprise and free people must be brought into play. I'd like to express my appreciation for the courage and foresight of those American companies who, during a time of economic uncertainty, invested in the future of Latin America.

I think we've turned the corner, and better times are ahead for our neighbors to the south. Our own economic growth has helped and continues to help stimulate growth in Latin America. And as their economies come around, their prosperity will add to ours.

I'd also like to thank Puerto Rico's Governor, Rafael Hernandez Colon, with us today, for the support that you've given to help us promote democracy and economic progress in the entire Caribbean region.

Now, last week I met with President Duarte of El Salvador, a country that is turning around a desperate economic situation and making great progress in its efforts to develop the institutions of democracy. I couldn't help but remember how close the House vote was last year on the crucial issue of military assistance to his government. A loss would likely have undermined everything that President Duarte was trying to accomplish.

Recently a top Salvadoran guerrilla leader surrendered. And according to press reports, this commandant confirmed, as have other defectors, what we've been trying to tell some of the doubting Members of Congress: Nicaragua supplies and supports the Communist insurgency in El Salvador. The former Salvadoran guerrilla leader reportedly confirmed they'd been getting 20,000 to 30,000 rounds of ammunition and 5,000 sticks of TNT from Nicaragua every month, and he asserts they get 70 percent of their arms from Nicaragua. One encouraging thing we can say is that this does reflect something of a decline in what has been normal over the recent years; so possibly we're having some success in intercepting those shipments.

With that, the Communists have been conducting military operations, kidnaping and murdering village mayors, and destroying El Salvador's economic infrastructure—blowing up bridges, power lines, and more. This is aggression, pure and simple. Those who willfully ignore this aggression endanger freedom in Central America and, in the long run, the security of the United States.

I might point something out here that's rather of interest. Our Bud McFarlane was in Central America not too long ago, and he was talking to the *contra* leaders there. And he asked them—he said, apropos of what the guerrillas are doing in El Salvador and the attacks that they're making on these vital structures—he said, "Why, if you're trying to put pressure on your government here—why don't you attack some of these vital, strategic targets?" And to show you the difference between the *contras* and the guerrillas, the *contras* said, "No, that would hurt the people, and we're of the people. We're not going to do that." I think they deserve our support.

Let there be no mistake, helping those who fight for freedom and supplying security assistance for our democratic friends in Central America are vital to the future of that region and to our national security as well.

We have it within our grasp to build a new unity of purpose in this hemisphere, to recapture the spirit of freedom and enterprise that brought many of our forebears from the Old World to the New.

The challenge is great, but I know we'll meet our responsibility. As I told the people of Europe during my recent trip, the future is on the side of the free.

I thank each of you for what you're doing to make the dream of the Americas come true from one end of the hemisphere to the other. I need your active help to inform your fellow citizens and the Congress of how vital it is for us to see our southern neighbors through this time of economic uncertainty and Communist subversion. Together we can work with the people of Latin America to build a freer, more prosperous future. And I know I can count on you.

Thank you, and God bless you.

Note: The President spoke at 4:31 p.m. in Room 450 of the Old Executive Office Building. In his remarks, the President referred to Ambassador J. William Middendorf II, Permanent United States Representative to the Organization of American States.

Executive Order 12516—President's Commission on Executive Exchange
May 21, 1985

By the authority vested in me as President by the Constitution and statutes of the United States of America, it is hereby ordered that Executive Order No. 12493 of December 5, 1984, is amended by substituting for subsection (a)(2) of section 2 thereof the following:

"(2) career Federal Executives, who are members of the Senior Executive Service, or equivalent level, or are candidates for the Senior Executive Service, or are of outstanding qualification and are serving at an equivalent level to a Senior Executive Service candidate, provided that such level is not lower than level 15 of the General Schedule, will be selected as Presidential Exchange Executives and assigned for one year to positions in the private sector offering significant challenge, responsibility and regular and continuing contact with senior private sector officials."

RONALD REAGAN

The White House,
May 21, 1985.

[*Filed with the Office of the Federal Register, 8:56 a.m., May 23, 1985*]

Note: The Executive order was released by the Office of the Press Secretary on May 22.

Address at the United States Naval Academy Commencement Exercises in Annapolis, Maryland
May 22, 1985

Congresswoman Holt, Secretary Lehman, Admiral Watkins, General Davis, Admiral Larson, distinguished guests, members of the class of 1985, ladies and gentlemen: I am so proud and honored to be here and to have a 22-gun salute. [*Laughter*]

But it's an honor for any President to commemorate the graduation of new officers from our service academies, but today is a special privilege for me. I was reminded on the way up here that we have a lot in common. You were the first class to enter the Naval Academy during my term in office, and you might say we've finished a 4-year course together. Now we're both about ready for the real stuff. [*Laughter*] One thing bothers me, though. I still seem to be climbing that greased monument and you only had to do it once, 3 years ago.[1] [*Laughter*]

Well, looking out over your faces in this inspiring and historic setting gives reason for confidence in our nation's future. These last 4 years have been spent preparing you to assume responsibility for the protection of our country and all that we stand for. You're part of a noble tradition.

America's independence and freedom, since we were but 13 Colonies huddled along the Atlantic coast, have relied on the bravery, the good sense, and leadership of her officer corps. We've leaned heavily on men of the sea, on our Navy and Marine Corps. Your careers will be no less significant to future generations of Americans than those of past naval heroes.

You will hear during your career, as I've heard during times in my life, that maintaining the military at peak readiness—keeping our forces trained and supplied with the best weapons and equipment—is too costly. Well, I say it is too costly for America not to be prepared. As Presidents

---

[1] *The President was referring to the Herndon Monument, an obelisk which freshmen must scale on the first afternoon of Commissioning Week.*

since Washington have noted: The way to prevent war is to be prepared for it.

And as obvious as that is, it's not always appreciated. There's a story about John Paul Jones' chief gunners mate. It was during the gore and thunder of that most historic battle. He was loading and firing cannon and carrying the wounded to the medical officer, cutting away the tangled rigging. And apparently in the midst of that first fight, John Paul Jones went below momentarily and changed into a new uniform. And as he emerged on deck a voice rang out through the smoke and fire—it was the British captain asking, "Have you struck your colors?" And the gunners mate, sweat and blood dripping from his body, turned and saw Jones now in his fresh uniform reply: "I have not yet begun to fight." And the gunners mate said, "There's always somebody who didn't get the word." [*Laughter*]

Now, my chief of staff, Don Regan, is a marine, and he keeps telling me that story's incorrect—that it was a marine in the rigging and not the gunners mate that said that. [*Laughter*]

Well, today as throughout our history, it is strength not weakness, resolve not vacillation, that will keep the peace. It's about time that those who place their faith in wishful thinking and good intentions get the word.

During the 1930's I saw America, disillusioned by the First World War, permit our military power to decline. The lack of will on the part of the Western democracies encouraged the totalitarians of that day. Churchill called what followed the most avoidable of all wars, and it turned out to be the most costly of all wars, both in terms of resources and in terms of human suffering.

Americans were spared much of the direct ravages of the Second World War due to geography, the grace of God, and the incredible skill and unmatched courage of our Armed Forces in the desperate months after Pearl Harbor. Fighting a delaying action, often against overwhelming odds, they bought the time needed to build our forces. Coral Sea, Midway, Guadalcanal are names that have gone down in the annals of truly historic battles. I couldn't help but see those names up there on the stadium. Many good men gave their lives in the 1940's for America's unwillingness to prepare in the 1930's. Let me promise you: As long as I'm President that will not happen again.

Since the end of the Second World War, American military might has been an immensely positive force in the world. We used our economic resources to help rebuild the devastated homelands of our allies and of our former enemies as well. Those people, wherever they are in this world, who've enjoyed the rights to speak and to pray and to direct the course of their government through democratic elections owe their freedom to one degree or another to the protection of the United States military. It doesn't take much imagination to know how different things would be had the Soviet Union, not the United States, militarily and economically dominated the world after 1945.

There are some who analyze world events who operate under the assumption that the United States and the Soviet Union are morally equivalent. This reasoning does a great disservice to our forefathers and all the brave individuals throughout our history who have fought and died to keep this country free. The United States is a democratic nation of free people. We are a far more moral and decent land than any totalitarian state, and we should be proud of it.

During the last decade, perhaps as a result of confusion stemming from the Vietnam war, America again permitted its military strength to decline. For the Navy this meant going from almost 1,000 ships in the late 1980's—or 1960's, I should say—to under 500 by 1980. In real terms, our overall military spending dropped by 20 percent in the 1970's.

And how did the Soviets seize this historic opportunity for better relations? They raced forward with the largest peacetime military expansion in history. They built almost three times as many ships as we did in the 1970's, turning what had once been a navy aimed at coastal defense into an offensively designed, blue-water navy—a formidable threat to peace and stability throughout out the world. The Soviet's Pacific fleet alone now has more than 500 vessels, including two aircraft carriers and more than 130 submarines.

There had been theories that Soviet belligerence would wane as their relative strength to the United States increased. Those theories went by the wayside in the late 1970's as Soviet advisers and military equipment, along with thousands of Cuban surrogate troops, poured into Africa; Soviet tanks invaded Afghanistan. A weaker America did not mean a more peaceful world. That's about as likely as Army stealing the statue of Tecumseh. [*Laughter*]

Four years ago, when you were entering Annapolis, we were putting in place a program to rebuild America's weakened defenses, and I'm proud to say that much progress has been made. I know you're ready for the Navy, and I can tell you the Navy is now much more ready for you. And thanks to Secretary of the Navy John Lehman's aggressive leadership, we now have 532 battleforce ships in commission. In 1984 alone, the Navy took delivery of 25 ships. We currently have 102 battleforce ships under construction or conversion in 21 shipyards. By the end of the decade, we'll realize our goal of a 600-ship Navy, which will include 15 deployable aircraft carriers.

And we've taken the steps necessary to make certain that our ships are in fighting trim and able to accomplish their mission. We've moved forward to ferret out waste and inefficiency. And by the way, that's why you hear those stories about outrageously expensive hammers or bolts and things of that kind. We're finding the waste and cutting it out. Those press stories are actually success stories, because by and large they represent our efforts to make the best use of our defense dollar. To make sure our military is ready, we've purchased spare parts, ammunition, better and more efficient equipment, and top-of-the-line weapons systems. Most important, we've got the best darn bunch of officers and crews this Navy or any navy has ever had.

By the end of the 1970's many of our military personnel were demoralized. The purchasing power of their pay had eroded, as had public recognition of their service. Enlisting quality personnel was increasingly difficult, and the reenlistment rates plummeted. We had ships that couldn't leave port for lack of a full crew.

Today that situation has been dramatically reversed. We've not only been meeting our recruitment goals but we're bringing in individuals fully capable of handling the sophisticated equipment and high-tech weapons systems of the modern Navy. Reenlistment rates are up in all of the services. And testing among our sailors and marines suggests that drug use, once a major problem, has dropped more than anyone would have predicted possible. And I've heard of your excellent record in this area, and I commend you for it.

Although I'm an old horse cavalryman myself, I've always had a soft spot in my heart for the Navy. Back in my former profession, I played a naval officer in "Hellcats of the Navy." And Nancy was a Navy nurse in the same picture. [*Laughter*] Now, speaking for myself only, if they should send me another script, it probably would be for "Old Man and the Sea." [*Laughter*]

"Hellcats" was about the submarine force, and I had an experience down in San Diego where we made most of that picture. The submarine training base down there taught me a little about the Navy. It seems that just about the same time we were making the picture, the flyboys over there at the naval air station came over and invited the officers, the submariners, to come over and kind of learn a little about their occupation.

And having gotten them there and then strapped in, they took them up and gave them the works, the whole load. Well, this group of somewhat upset officers—[*laughter*]—returned to the naval base. And then they thought they should return the favor, so they invited the flyboys to come over and learn something about the submarine service.

And they took them out in the submarine, and they were below, and they dived. And then all of a sudden, bells began ringing, and sirens sounding, and fellows were running back and forth, and there were red lights flashing. And it seemed that there was a dial there that said that they were not coming out of their dive. They were going on down. And worriedly they pointed out to these flyers what this meant—that if it passed that red point on the dial, that was below the ability of the submarine to withstand the pressure.

And then in the midst of all of that excitement, and as it got closer and closer to that red line, one fellow just climbed the ladder into the conning tower and opened the hatch. [*Laughter*] They were still tied to the dock. [*Laughter*]

Well, that was just a movie, but the job you'll do is as vital as at any time in the history of our Republic. Our economy is run on fuel and resources from far away countries brought to us by way of the oceans. Even many of our own resources, the oil in Alaska for example, are transported by sea.

And the great democratic nations of the world are tied by shared values and a reliance on the sealanes. Our treaty commitments mean little without access to the Atlantic, the Pacific, the Caribbean, the Mediterranean, the Indian Ocean, the Persian Gulf—all the great bodies of water.

The challenge is great. Our Navy is meeting a heavier responsibility than we had in the sixties and meeting it with fewer ships. And that means the officers and crew of every vessel must work harder, carry a heavier load, and endure longer, more strenuous cruises. The *Ticonderoga*, our first Aegis-equipped, guided-missile cruiser, spent over 80 percent of her time underway during a 6½ month maiden cruise in 1984. That same year the aircraft carrier *Ranger* and her battle group set a record for sustained continuous operations for conventional-powered carrier battle groups—121 days, steaming more than 50,000 miles.

Men and women on these and other ships are under great stress, handling advanced weapons systems and sophisticated equipment. And that's all the more reason to salute them after setting a new record for aircraft safety last year. Many who served could easily have better paying civilian jobs. Sailors on the carriers are away from their families 70 percent of the time; yet 60 percent of these fine young people reenlist.

Then there's the *New Jersey*. In mid-1983 she left Long Beach on what was to have been a 2½ month shakedown cruise in the western Pacific. After traveling to Thailand and the Philippines, she was ordered to Central America. After a few weeks there, she went through the Panama Canal and at high speed proceeded to Beirut, where she remained until May of 1984. She spent 322 days under way, with only three port visits on a voyage that covered 76,000 miles. The only relief for her crew was given by the magnificent contribution of 349 volunteers from the Ready Reserves. With 3-week shifts aboard the battleship, they permitted much of the *New Jersey's* crew to rotate home for leave.

In today's Navy, as with the other services, the Reserves are playing an increasingly important role. Who are they? Citizens concerned about the future of this country and determined to do their part. They share their time, energy, and talent to keep America strong, safe, and free.

Sometimes it's hard to find the words to express my heartfelt gratitude for those who serve on active duty and in the Reserves. But it isn't difficult to find the words to explain why they do what they do. It only takes one word—patriotism. And as Commander in Chief, I am overwhelmed at times by their dedication and courage.

I see this every day. We've enlisted the talent of some Naval Academy graduates at the White House. Robert McFarlane, my national security adviser, his deputy, Admiral John Poindexter, graduated in 1959 and 1958 respectively, and I'm proud to note that their sons are following in their footsteps here at the Academy.

One man who sat where you do now and graduated from the Naval Academy in 1968 is another member of our administration—Assistant Secretary of Defense James Webb, the most decorated member of his class. James' gallantry as a marine officer in Vietnam won him the Navy Cross and other decorations, including two Purple Hearts. James wrote several books about American service men and women. In his book, "A Sense of Honor," he describes the life that you have chosen. He wrote:

"Servicemen are always in motion, in the air at more than the speed of sound, underwater at depths whales could only dream of, on the surface of the water cruising at 30 miles an hour through crashing seas with another ship almost touching theirs . . . replenishing their oil supplies. Or they are on the ground, in the dirt, testing and training weapons that may someday kill others but today may deal them that same irony. The smallest margin of error separates a live man from a dead man. And in war, of course, they are the first and usually the only ones to pay. The President and the Congress may suffer bad news stories. The military man suffers the deaths of his friends, early and often." End quote.

I want each of you to know that this President understands and appreciates the job that you will be doing. Your lives are precious. You are putting yourselves in harm's way for America's sake, and I will do everything in my power to make certain the country gives you the tools and equipment you need to do your job and to come home safely.

There's a new appreciation for our men and women in military service. One manifestation of this is the effort now going forth to build a Navy memorial in the Nation's Capital, a living tribute to you and all those in the United States Navy, officers and enlisted, who have gone before you.

Whether we remain at peace, whether we remain free, will depend on you—on your character, your decisions, your leadership. Our ships are in a state of forward deployment, adding both to our deterrence and to our flexibility in dealing with any potential crisis. The theory of deterrence means more than preventing nuclear war. That certainly is an aspect of deterrence, an important one in which the Navy, with her fleet of Poseidon and Trident submarines, is a leading player. Those men who stay submerged for months at a time, foregoing home and family, are the ultimate guarantees against nuclear attack.

But the spectrum of conflict ranges from terrorism and guerrilla warfare through conventional and nuclear confrontation. The Navy is an intricate part of a wide-ranging strategy of deterrence across this spectrum. We hope to dissuade hostile action at any level by persuading potential aggressors that whatever their target they'll lose more than they will gain. The Navy and Marine Corps' power and forward deployment puts them on the front lines of deterrence. The leadership and judgment of naval officers, serving in the far reaches of the globe, are critical to our success as a nation.

So, let me leave you with these thoughts. Your countrymen have faith in you and expect you to make decisions. The issues will not be black and white, otherwise there would be no decision to make. Do not be afraid to admit and consider your doubts, but don't be paralyzed by them. Be brave. Make your judgment and then move forward with confidence, knowing that although there's never 100-percent certainty, you have honestly chosen what you believe to be, as you have been told by the Admiral, the right course. Do this, and the Amer-

ican people will always back you up.

You're joining the officer ranks of the United States Navy and Marine Corps. You're part of a proud tradition. John Paul Jones, entombed here at Annapolis and enshrined in the hearts of all Americans once said, "I hoisted with my own hands the flag of freedom . . . and I have attended it ever since with veneration on the ocean."

As you go forth in your career, the flag will be in your hands. Carry it and yourselves with pride.

Good luck. God bless you, and I wish you fair winds and following seas.

Note: The President spoke at 10:35 a.m. at the Navy Marine Corps Stadium. In his opening remarks, the President referred to Adm. James D. Watkins, Chief of Naval Operations, Gen. J.K. Davis, Assistant Commandant of the Marine Corps, and Adm. Charles R. Larson, Superintendent of the Naval Academy. Following his address, the President returned to the White House.

Nomination of Robert M. Kimmitt To Be General Counsel of the Department of the Treasury
May 22, 1985

The President today announced his intention to nominate Robert M. Kimmitt to be General Counsel of the Department of the Treasury. He would succeed Peter J. Wallison.

Mr. Kimmitt has been serving at the White House since 1983 as Deputy Assistant to the President for National Security Affairs and Executive Secretary and General Counsel of the National Security Council.

After being commissioned as a Regular Army officer in 1969 at West Point, Mr. Kimmitt completed field artillery, airborne, and ranger schools. He then served a 17-month combat tour with the 173d Airborne Brigade in Vietnam (1970–1971) and was subsequently assigned to the 101st Airborne Division at Fort Campbell, KY (1972–1974). He attended Georgetown University Law School from 1974 to 1977, during which

time he also served as a legislative counsel to the Army's Chief of Legislative Liaison (summer 1975) and then as an NSC staff member specializing in arms sales policy (1976–1977). Upon graduation from law school, he served as a law clerk to Judge Edward Allen Tamm of the U.S. Court of Appeals for the District of Columbia Circuit (1977–1978). He returned to the NSC staff in 1978, serving both as legal counsel and arms sales policy officer until early 1982, when he left active military service to join the senior staff of the NSC. In 1982–1983 he served as General Counsel and Director of Legislative Affairs and Security Assistance for the NSC.

Mr. Kimmitt graduated from the United States Military Academy at West Point (B.S., 1969) and Georgetown University Law Center (J.D., 1977). He is married to the former Holly Sutherland. They have four children and reside in Arlington, VA. He was born December 19, 1947, in Logan, UT.

Appointment of the 1985–1986 White House Fellows
May 22, 1985

The President today announced the appointments of the 1985–1986 White House fellows. This is the 21st class of fellows since the program began in 1964.

The 14 fellows were chosen from among 1,139 applicants and screened by 11 regional panels. The President's Commission on White House Fellowships, chaired by Vice Adm. James B. Stockdale, USN (Ret.), interviewed the 34 national finalists before recommending the 14 persons to the President. Their year of government service will begin September 1, 1985.

Fellows serve for 1 year as special assistants to the Vice President, members of the Cabinet, and the President's principal staff. In addition to the work assignments, the fellowship includes an education program which parallels and broadens the unique experience of working at the highest levels of the Federal Government.

The program is open to U.S. citizens in the early stages of their careers and from all occupations and professions. Federal Government employees are not eligible, with the exception of career Armed Forces personnel.

Leadership, character, intellectual and professional ability, and commitment to community and nation are the principal criteria employed in the selection of fellows.

Applications for the 1986–1987 program are available from the President's Commission on White House Fellowships, 712 Jackson Place NW., Washington, DC 20503.

The 1985–1986 fellows are:

John L. Barry, 33, of Norfolk, VA, is currently a student at the Armed Forces Staff College and a major in the United States Air Force.

Thomas E. Bennett, Jr., 34, of Stillwater, OK, is currently executive vice president of Stillwater National Bank and Trust Co.

Alexander Dimitrief, 26, of Cambridge, MA, is currently a student at Harvard Law School. He is also managing editor of the Harvard Law Review.

Jeri A. Eckhart, 30, of Boston, MA, is currently manager of the Boston Consulting Group.

Karen M. Galatz, 30, of Carson City, NV, is currently the Governor of Nevada's executive aide and news secretary.

Charles R. Kubic, 34, of New York, NY, is currently a lieutenant commander in the United States Navy and assistant officer in charge of construction in the Mediterranean.

Jerrold T. Lundquist, 35, of Stamford, CT, is currently a consultant with McKinsey and Co.

Mark T. Parris, 28, of Dallas, TX, is currently executive director of the Baylor Institute for Rehabilitation.

Kien D. Pham, 27, of Stanford, CA, is currently an M.B.A. student at the Graduate School of Business at Stanford University.

Ronald Z. Quincy, 34, of Lansing, MI, is currently executive director of the Michigan department of civil rights.

Charlene C. Quinn, 30, of Baltimore, MD, is currently professor, School of Nursing, at the University of Maryland.

Arnold I. Rachlis, 36, of Evanston, IL, is currently a rabbi at the Jewish Reconstruction Congregation.

Ann E. Rondeau, 33, of Washington, DC, is currently a lieutenant commander in the United States Navy in the Office of the Assistant Secretary of Defense, International Security Affairs, at the Pentagon.

Richard P. Sybert, 32, of Los Angeles, CA, is currently a partner with Sheppard, Mullin, Richter & Hampton.

Message to the Congress Transmitting the Annual Report on Federal Advisory Committees
May 23, 1985

To the Congress of the United States:

As provided by the Federal Advisory Committee Act, I am pleased to transmit the Thirteenth Annual Report on Federal Advisory Committees.

Federal advisory committees have been referred to variously as the fourth arm of government or as a public-private partnership. Known by many names and descriptions, these committees play an important role in determining public policy and contribute to our Nation's security, economic vitality, scientific achievements, and quality of life.

In fiscal year 1984, over 25,000 private citizens representing nearly every occupation and geographical area exemplified our great American tradition of civic service by participating as members of Federal advisory committees. These individuals devoted countless thousands of hours of talent and expertise to developing and offering recommendations affecting almost every Federal program.

Because most advisory committees have low operating costs and the great majority of committee members serve on a noncompensated basis, the Federal government receives tremendous benefit for a modest in-

vestment. However, committee productivity is not uniform as some committees have outlived their usefulness while others receive insufficient support and attention from their sponsoring agencies. In the interest of good management I have directed all executive departments and agencies to undertake a thorough review of their committees to eliminate those that are unnecessary and to strengthen management and oversight of those that remain. A task force of senior agency personnel from several agencies chaired by the General Services Administration has been commissioned to carry out this initiative during fiscal year 1985.

We shall work in cooperation with the Congress to assure the American people that advisory committee expenditures are a wise investment and that committee service is a noble and worthy endeavor.

RONALD REAGAN

The White House,
May 23, 1985.

Note: The 131-page report was entitled "Federal Advisory Committees: Thirteenth Annual Report of the President—Fiscal Year 1984."

Message to the Congress Transmitting the Annual Report of the Federal Council on the Aging
May 23, 1985

To the Congress of the United States:

In accordance with Section 204(f) of the Older Americans Act of 1965, as amended, I hereby transmit the Annual Report for 1984 of the Federal Council on the Aging. The report reflects the Council's views in its role of examining programs serving older Americans.

It should be noted that the 1985 Annual Report of the Medicare Board of Trustees indicates that projected annual revenues from payroll taxes are expected to be sufficient to pay annual enrollee benefits for Medicare Part A through the first part of the next decade, and reserves in the Hospital Insurance Trust Fund are likely to be sufficient to cover annual shortfalls for an additional five years. Data from the 1985 Trustees Report should be used to update statements made on page 21 of the Annual Report of the Federal Council on the Aging.

RONALD REAGAN

The White House,
May 23, 1985.

Remarks at the Presentation Ceremony for the Presidential Medal of Freedom
May 23, 1985

From my days on the dinner circuit and in Hollywood, I can remember when associations holding a dinner and wanted someone prominent in public life to attend their annual dinner they would notify the individual that he or she had recently won the society's highest award, an award that they could collect if they showed up. And if they didn't, they would pick somebody else to give the honor to.

Well, a couple of months ago an invitation for lunch at the White House was sent to some of the individuals gathered in this room today, an invitation that also notified them they were recipients of this country's highest civilian honor. But I want to assure you that as flattered as Nancy and I are to have you here, this was not some conspiracy on our part to get this distinguished and talented group over to the house for lunch. Because, you see, the invitation really did not come from us at all. It comes from an entire nation, from all of America.

For your achievements in diplomacy, entertainment, government, politics, learning, culture, and science, the American people honor you today. Each of you has achieved that hardest of all things to achieve in his life—something that will last and endure and take on life of its own.

My guess is that probably as long as this nation lasts, your descendants will speak with pride of the day you attended a White House ceremony and received this, the Medal of Freedom—America's highest civilian honor. And 50 years from now, a century from now, historians will know your names and your achievements. You've left humanity a legacy, and on behalf of the American people, Nancy and I want to congratulate you.

You know, one of our medal winners today once made a film with Frank Capra about a man who took his own life for granted and was saddened by how little impact he seemed to have had on the world. But then a benevolent angel gave him the opportunity to see how different his hometown would have been had he not lived. And the man was astonished to discover how much good he had done without knowing it—how many people he had touched and how many lives he had made richer and happier.

Well, more than you will ever know, this world would have been much poorer and a dimmer place without each of you. In a million countless ways you've inspired and uplifted your fellow men and women, and we want you never to forget that. And we are grateful to you for it, also.

It's a wonderful day for you and your families and for Nancy and myself, and I was just thinking, sometimes it's fun to be President. [*Laughter*]

But I'm about to present the medals, but I want each of you to know that it comes with the heartfelt thanks, the admiration and pride of the some 238 million Americans who couldn't be here for lunch, but are, believe me, here in spirit.

[*As the President called each name, the recipient or the person accepting for the recipient went to the podium to receive the medal and remained standing behind the President. The President read the citations which accompany the medals. The texts of the citations are printed below.*]

So, now, the first Medal of Freedom goes to Count Basie, and it will be received by his son, Aaron Woodward. Aaron.

For more than half a century, William "Count" Basie enraptured the people of America with his brilliant and innovative work in the field of jazz. In the 1930's and 40's, the Count became part of the fabric of American life as the leader of one of the greatest bands of the Big Band Era. His songs, from "April in Paris" to "One O'Clock Jump," are American classics. Count Basie cut a notch in musical history and found a place in our hearts forever. Among the royalty of American arts and entertainment, there is no one more honored and more beloved than the Count.

And now—there's a middle name here that's bothering me—I hadn't used it before myself, but—Captain Jacques-Yves Cousteau. Did I get it right?

For decades, Captain Jacques-Yves Cousteau has been a celebrated undersea explorer. His journeys aboard the Calypso have become known to millions through his books and films. His manned, undersea colonies yielded wealths of research and data and made important technical advances. His aqualung has made underwater diving available to all. Captain Cousteau perhaps has done more than any other individual to reveal the mysteries of the oceans that cover more than two-thirds of the surface of our planet. It is, therefore, likely that he will be remembered not only as a pioneer in his time but as a dominant figure in world history.

And Dr. Jerome Holland to receive—and his wife, Mrs. Laura Holland.

Dr. Jerome Hartwell Holland, one of thirteen children in a small-town family in New York State, rose from poverty to become a leading educator, civil rights activist, author and diplomat. Dr. Holland dedicated his career to improving the lives of others, particularly his fellow black Americans, and to working for peace. A man of vigor and wisdom, Dr. Holland led a life of service, the memory of which today serves as an inspiration to millions.

Sidney Hook:

Scholar, philosopher, and thinker—Sidney Hook stands as one of the most eminent intellectual forces of our time. His commitment to rational thought and civil discourse has made him an eloquent spokesman for fair play in public life. His devotion to freedom made him one of the first to warn the intellectual world of its moral obligations and personal stake in the struggle between freedom and totalitarianism. A man of truth, a man of action, Sidney Hook's life and work make him one of America's greatest scholars, patriots, and lovers of liberty.

Jeane Kirkpatrick:

For four years as the Representative of the United States to the United Nations, Ambassador Jeane Kirkpatrick held high the flag of our country with courage and wisdom. She is an endlessly articulate spokeswoman for the moral and practical benefits of freedom and a tireless defender of the decency of the West. Jeane Kirkpatrick is a patriot, and there is no honor more appropriate for her than one entitled, "The Presidential Medal of Freedom." It's bestowed this day by a nation that knows Jeane Kirkpatrick's work has only just begun.

Dr. George M. Low. This will be received by his wife, Mrs. Mary Low.

During his distinguished public service at NASA, Dr. George M. Low helped lead this nation's space program to its greatest achievements, directing the first manned landing on the moon and planning the shuttle program. As President of Rensselaer Polytechnic Institute, he continued to make his mark on the future, improving academic excellence and launching a program to spur technological innovation. Our nation will be reaping the benefits of his wisdom and vision for years to come.

Frank Reynolds, to be received by Mrs. Henrietta Reynolds.

Reporter and anchorman, family man and a patriot, Frank Reynolds' life exemplified the highest standards of his profession. His commitment to the truth, his unfailing sense of fairness, his long experience as both witness and participant in the great events of our time earned him the respect of his colleagues and the trust and admiration of the American people. We honor his memory for his aggressive but fair-minded reporting and devotion to profession, to family, and to country.

S. Dillon Ripley:

Upon becoming Secretary of the Smithsonian Institution, S. Dillon Ripley ordered the statue of Joseph Henry turned so that it faced not inward toward the castle but outward toward the Mall, thereby signaling his intentions to open the Institution to the world. During the next 20 years, S. Dillon Ripley did just that, opening eight museums and doubling the number of visitors to the Institution. With dedication and tireless effort, S. Dillon Ripley made the Smithsonian one of the greatest museums and centers of learning on Earth.

Frank Sinatra:

For nearly 50 years, Americans have been putting their dreams away and letting one man take their place in our hearts. Singer, actor, humanitarian, patron of art and mentor of artists, Francis Albert Sinatra and his impact on America's popular culture are without peer. His love of country, his generosity toward those less fortunate, his distinctive art, and his winning and passionate persona make him one of our most remarkable and distinguished Americans, and one who truly did it "His Way."

James M. Stewart:

James Maitland Stewart arrived in Hollywood in 1935, and today, half a century later, his credits include more than 70 pictures, including such classics as "Mr. Smith Goes to Washington," "The Philadelphia Story," and "It's a Wonderful Life." A patriot, Mr. Stewart served with distinction as a pilot during World War II, rising to the rank of colonel in the Eighth Air Force. His typically American characters—boyish, honest and kind— mirror the Jimmy Stewart in real life—an American boy who grew to a glorious manhood, but never lost his sense of wonder or his innocence.

Lieutenant General Albert C. Wedemeyer:

As one of America's most distinguished soldiers and patriots, Albert C. Wedemeyer has earned the gratitude of his country and the admiration

of his countrymen. In the face of crisis and controversy, his integrity and his opposition to totalitarianism remained unshakeable. For his resolute defense of liberty and his abiding sense of personal honor, Albert C. Wedemeyer has earned the thanks and the deep affection of all who struggle for the cause of human freedom.

Chuck Yeager:

A hero in war and peace, Charles Yeager has served his country with dedication and courage beyond ordinary measure. On October 14, 1947, in a rocket plane which he named "Glamorous Glynnis" after his wife, Chuck Yeager became the first human being to travel faster than the speed of sound, and in doing so, showed to the world the real meaning of "The Right Stuff."

Well, that concludes our presentation. And congratulations to all of you who've made all of our lives richer.

Thank you. God bless you all.

Note: The President spoke at 1:26 p.m. in the East Room at the White House following a luncheon for the recipients and their guests.

Proclamation 5346—National Farm Safety Week, 1985
May 23, 1985

By the President of the United States of America

A Proclamation

From the beginning of our Nation's history, agriculture has been one of the major elements of the American success story. Since this country was founded, when over 90 percent of its labor force was on the farm, it has excelled at growing food and other agricultural products. This success was achieved long before we became a leader in industry, technology, science, and commerce.

Today, technological advances have made possible productivity undreamed of in the days when Cyrus McCormack designed and built the first horse-drawn reaper. The United States now supplies food to millions of people around the world, and our productive capabilities grow still greater every year.

But the farmer's life is still difficult and dangerous. While the new technology that makes such bounty possible has brought advances in safety, it also carries its own risks, and requires knowledge and care in its use. Incidents of accidental death, injury, and job-related illnesses are still tragically numerous on the farms, in the homes, and on the roads of rural America. But with increased education about the need for farm safety, and with ongoing improvements in product design, there is hope that we can make real progress in protecting America's farmers and their families from accidents and injuries.

Now, Therefore, I, Ronald Reagan, President of the United States of America, do hereby proclaim the week of September 15 through September 21, 1985, as National Farm Safety Week. I urge all those Americans engaged in agriculture or its related services, and especially those training inexperienced or young workers, to establish and follow safety procedures and instill dedication and commitment to safety and health care in all those who can be influenced by their example.

In Witness Whereof, I have hereunto set my hand this twenty-third day of May, in the year of our Lord nineteen hundred and eighty-five, and of the Independence of the United States of America the two hundred and ninth.

RONALD REAGAN

[*Filed with the Office of the Federal Register, 2:30 p.m., May 24, 1985*]

Note: The proclamation was released by the Office of the Press Secretary on May 24.

Remarks at the Signing Ceremony for the Internal Revenue Code Amendments Bill
May 24, 1985

The President. I am delighted to have you here for this signing of H.R. 1869. It repeals a requirement for a very extensive regulation—an unnecessary one, I think, on people who use business vehicles for private purposes also. And I am glad to have you here, and it is just a part of what I hope will be a larger tax reform later, so we can all be together for another signing. But more about that next week.

Q. We are looking forward to it, Mr. President.

Q. I hope the rest of the tax reform is as easy as this one was. I somehow doubt it.

The President. You and me both.

[*At this point, the President signed the bill.*]

This will gladden the hearts of many Americans, and I know that you had there the public support in this.

Q. Thank you. We appreciate you doing this, sir.

The President. It is the least that I can do.

Q. We are glad that you did that for the American working man and woman. That is what that is all about.

Q. Particularly in my district. Thank you, Mr. President.

Q. It is great for the people.

The President. And, as I say, I think we can remove a few more regulations.

Q. Mr. President, how would you like to give one of those pens to Jim Abdnor. It was his bill on the Senate side there.

Senator Abdnor. Thank you, Mr. President.

The President. All right.

Q. Can another one of those pens be given away or one has to go to the Archives? [*Laughter*]

Q. You mean the one in Nebraska?

Q. Thank you, Mr. President. It shows common sense and logic prevail.

The President. God bless you all.

Q. Thank you.

Q. The first stage in tax reform—that is what I told Mr. Baker when he testified.

Q. That was the up-end.

Q. That was the downturn. [*Laughter*]

Q. I wish all our battles on deregulation were this easy.

The President. Yes, I do, too. I think we have got a lot more to go.

Reporter. Mr. President, did you know this was in the bill last year? Didn't you know this provision was in the bill last year? Why did you sign it last year with this onerous provision in it?

The President. Because I didn't have line-item veto.

Q. Mr. President, do you think the House version of the budget is really going to hurt national security?

The President. I think I am going to wait and express my opinion when it gets to Congress.

Q. You are concerned about it?

The President. Yes, I am concerned.

Q. Thank you very much, Mr. President.

Note: The President spoke at 1:03 p.m. in the Oval Office at the White House. Among those attending the ceremony were Secretary of the Treasury James A. Baker III, *Senate Majority Leader Robert Dole, Senator James S. Abdnor of South Dakota, and Senator John Heinz of Pennsylvania. A tape was not available for verification of the content of these remarks. H.R. 1869 was assigned Public Law No. 99-44.*

Nomination of Thomas Gale Moore To Be a Member of the Council of Economic Advisers
May 24, 1985

The President today announced his intention to nominate Thomas Gale Moore to be a member of the Council of Economic Advisers. He would succeed William A. Niskanen, Jr.

Dr. Moore is a senior fellow at the Hoover Institution and director of its domestic studies program. He has also been a lecturer in economics at Stanford's Graduate School of Business and at UCLA. Previously he was on the faculty of Michigan State University as professor of economics (1969–1974) and associate professor of economics (1965–1968). In 1968–1970 he served at the White House as senior staff economist to the Council of Economic Advisers. He was assistant professor of economics at Carnegie Institute of Technology in 1961–1965.

He has published extensively in economic, political, and law journals and has organized and chaired numerous conferences on regulation, antitrust, health care, conscription, and income redistribution at the Hoover Institution and elsewhere. His publications include: "The Economics of the American Theater" (1968), "Freight Transportation" (1972), "Trucking Regulation: Lessons from Europe" (1976), and "Uranium Enrichment and Public Policy" (1978).

Dr. Moore graduated from George Washington University (A.B., 1957) and the University of Chicago (A.M., 1959; Ph.D., 1961). He is married, has two children, and resides in Palo Alto, CA. He was born November 6, 1930, in Washington, DC.

Nomination of Anne E. Brunsdale To Be a Member of the United States International Trade Commission
May 24, 1985

The President today announced his intention to nominate Anne E. Brunsdale to be a member of the United States International Trade Commission for a term expiring June 16, 1993. She would succeed Veronica Haggart.

Ms. Brunsdale is a resident fellow of the American Enterprise Institute for Public Policy Research (AEI) and serves as managing editor of Regulation, a bimonthly magazine. She served at AEI as director of publications (1970–1977) and as research associate in 1967–1970. In 1966–1967 she was associate director of publications for the Free Society Association in Washington, DC. In 1957–1965 she was with Craig-Hallum Corp. in Minneapolis, MN, as investment analyst then vice president for research of a regional investment firm.

She graduated from the University of Minnesota (B.A., 1945; M.A., 1946) and Yale University (M.A., 1949). She was born October 1, 1923, in Minneapolis, MN, and now resides in Washington, DC.

Accordance of the Personal Rank of Ambassador to Lewis A. Dunn While Serving as United States Coordinator and Alternate Representative to the 1985 Nuclear Non-Proliferation Treaty Review Conference
May 24, 1985

The President today accorded the personal rank of Ambassador to Lewis A. Dunn, of Virginia, in his capacity as coordinator of United States preparations for the 1985 Nuclear Non-Proliferation Treaty (NPT) Review Conference and Alternate United States Representative to the Review Conference.

Mr. Dunn is presently an Assistant Director in the U.S. Arms Control and Disarmament Agency, where he has been serving since 1983. In 1982–1983 he was counselor to Ambassador at Large Richard T. Kennedy, and in 1981–1982 he was Special Assistant for Nuclear Affairs to the Under Secretary of State for Management. Prior to his government service, Mr. Dunn was on the senior professional staff and project leader at Hudson Institute in New York in 1976–1981. In 1974–1976 he was a member of the professional staff at Hudson Institute. In 1971–1974 he was assistant professor of political science at Kenyon College, and in 1969–1971 he was an instructor of political science at Kenyon College.

Mr. Dunn graduated from Cornell University (A.B., 1965) and the University of Chicago (Ph.D., 1973). He was born January 7, 1944, in New York, NY. He is married to the former Roberta Baltz.

Accordance of the Personal Rank of Ambassador to Warren Zimmermann While Serving as Deputy to the Head of the United States Delegation to the Nuclear and Space Arms Negotiations With the Soviet Union
May 24, 1985

The President today accorded the personal rank of Ambassador to Warren Zimmermann, of Virginia, a career member of the Senior Foreign Service, Class of Minister-Counselor, in his capacity as deputy to the head of the United States delegation to the arms reduction negotiations in Geneva.

Mr. Zimmermann has been a career Foreign Service officer since he began his career in 1962–1964 in Caracas, Venezuela. In 1964 he was assigned to the Foreign Service Institute to study Serbo-Croatian. From there in 1965–1968 he served as political officer in Belgrade, Yugoslavia. He returned in 1968–1970 to the Bureau of Intelligence and Research as a Soviet policy analyst. In 1970–1973 he served as a special assistant to the Secretary of State in the Office of the Counselor. In 1973 he studied Russian at the Foreign Service Institute and from there became Deputy Counselor of the U.S. Embassy for politico-military affairs in Moscow. In 1975–1977 he returned to the Bureau of European and Canadian Affairs, where he was assigned as Special Assistant for Policy Planning. In 1977–1980 Mr. Zimmermann was counselor of the U.S. Embassy for political affairs in Paris, France. In 1980–1981 he was Deputy Chairman of the U.S. delegation to the Commission on Security and Cooperation in Europe Conference (CSCE) in Madrid, Spain, and in 1981 became deputy chief of mission at our Embassy in Moscow.

Mr. Zimmermann graduated from Yale University (B.A., 1956) and Cambridge University (M.A., 1958). His foreign languages are Russian, Serbo-Croatian, Spanish, and

French. He was born November 16, 1934, in Philadelphia, PA. He is married to the former Corinne Chubb, and they have three children.

Accordance of the Personal Rank of Ambassador to Henry F. Cooper While Serving as a Deputy United States Negotiator at the Nuclear and Space Arms Negotiations With the Soviet Union
May 24, 1985

The President today accorded the personal rank of Ambassador to Henry F. Cooper, of Virginia, in his capacity as Deputy United States Negotiator for Defense and Arms, arms reduction negotiations in Geneva.

Dr. Cooper began his career as an engineer/technician at the Savannah River Plant in Aiken, SC, in 1956–1958, where he was employed during the summer months. In 1958–1960 he was an instructor in engineering mechanics at Clemson University. He then became a member of the technical staff, Bell Telephone Laboratories, where he conducted independent scientific and technical research in 1960–1964. In 1972–1980 he was a member of the senior technical staff and program manager, R&D Associates, and then became deputy director, nuclear effects division, of R&D Associates in 1982–1983. He entered government service in 1980 as Deputy to the Assistant Secretary of the Air Force for Research, Development, and Logistics. In 1983–1985 he was Assistant Director for Strategic Programs, U.S. Arms Control and Disarmament Agency.

Dr. Cooper graduated from Clemson University (B.S., 1958; M.S., 1960) and New York University (Ph.D., 1964). He served in the United States Air Force in 1964–1972. He is married to the former Barbara Kays, and they have three children. He was born November 8, 1936, in Augusta, GA.

Accordance of the Personal Rank of Ambassador to Ronald F. Lehman II While Serving as a Deputy United States Negotiator at the Nuclear and Space Arms Negotiations With the Soviet Union
May 24, 1985

The President today accorded the personal rank of Ambassador to Ronald F. Lehman II, of Virginia, in his capacity as Deputy United States Negotiator for Strategic Nuclear Arms, arms reduction negotiations in Geneva.

Dr. Lehman began his career as legislative assistant for the Armed Services Committee in 1976–1978. He then served as professional staff member of the Committee on Armed Services, United States Senate, 1978–1981. In 1982–1983 he served as Deputy Assistant Secretary of Defense for Strategic Forces Policy. In 1983 he became Special Assistant to the President for National Security Affairs and Senior Director for Defense Programs and Arms Control on the National Security Council staff, where he continues to serve. He has recently been named Deputy United States Negotiator for Strategic Nuclear Arms, United States delegation to the arms reduction negotiations in Geneva.

Dr. Lehman graduated from Claremont Men's College (B.A., 1968) and Claremont Graduate School (Ph.D., 1975). He holds the rank of major in the United States Army Reserve. His foreign languages are Vietnamese and German. He is married to Susan Elizabeth Lehman. He was born in Napa, CA, in 1946.

Accordance of the Personal Rank of Ambassador to John A. Woodworth While Serving as a Deputy United States Negotiator at the Nuclear and Space Arms Negotiations With the Soviet Union
May 24, 1985

The President today accorded the personal rank of Ambassador to John A. Woodworth, of Virginia, in his capacity as Deputy United States Negotiator for Intermediate-Range Nuclear Forces, arms reduction negotiations in Geneva.

Mr. Woodworth began his career as an OSD management intern in 1965–1967, followed by plans analyst, Military Assistant Division, in the Office of the Assistant Secretary of Defense, in 1967–1968. He was an instructor of history and international politics at the University of South Carolina in 1968–1969. In 1969 he became a defense planner in the Office of the Assistant Secretary of Defense. He then was appointed an OSD fellow in public affairs, Woodrow Wilson School, Princeton University, 1972–1973. In 1973–1978 he served as a nuclear defense planner at the U.S. Mission to NATO in Brussels, Belgium. Mr. Woodworth then became Deputy Director, Office of Theater Nuclear Forces Policy, in the Office of the Assistant Secretary of Defense, 1978–1981. In 1980–1981 he was also

Assistant Deputy Director, Department of Defense SALT task force. In 1981 he served as Director, Office of Theater Nuclear Forces Policy, in the Office of the Assistant Secretary of Defense, and then in 1982 became the Secretary of Defense representative of the U.S. delegation to the U.S.-Soviet negotiations on intermediate-range nuclear forces. In 1984 he served as Secretary of Defense Representative on the U.S. delegations to the CSCE Conference on Disarmament in Europe (Switzerland) and to the United Nations Conference on Disarmament (Geneva). He presently serves as Deputy Negotiator for Intermediate-Range Nuclear Forces, U.S. delegation to the arms reduction negotiations in Geneva.

Mr. Woodworth graduated from Duke University (B.A., 1963) and Georgetown University (M.S., 1966). He served in the United States Air Force in 1968–1969. His foreign language is French. He is married to the former Laura Carver, and they have three children. He was born July 5, 1941, in University Heights, OH.

Appointment of Walter G. Sellers as a Member of the National Afro-American History and Culture Commission
May 24, 1985

The President today announced his intention to appoint Walter G. Sellers to be a member of the National Afro-American History and Culture Commission for a term expiring January 18, 1986. He would succeed Douglas Russell.

Since 1951 Mr. Sellers has been with Central State University in Wilberforce, OH, serving in various administrative posi-

tions. He is currently director of alumni and community affairs for the university. He is past president of the Ohio Association of College Admissions Counselors, the Council of Admissions Officers of the State-assisted Colleges and Universities, and the Southwest Ohio School Boards Association. He is currently president of the Ohio School Boards Association.

Mr. Sellers graduated from Central State University (B.S.). He is married, has three children, and resides in Wilberforce, OH. He was born July 21, 1925, in Daxley, GA.

Remarks at the Annual Meeting of the National Association of Manufacturers
May 24, 1985

It's indeed an honor for me to be able to speak to you, the representatives of some 13,500 manufacturing enterprises across our country.

For 90 years, the National Association of Manufacturers has given able voice to the concerns of American industry. And I'm very happy to be anyplace with something that's older than I am. [*Laughter*]

In recent years, as our administration has fought to halt the growth of government and expand the freedom in the marketplace, your association has given valuable support. I owe each of you a deep debt of gratitude. And I'd like to take this opportunity to give particular thanks to your chairman, Stan Pace, your president, Sandy Trowbridge, and your vice chairman, Bob Dee.

You know, I remember an old story that's appropriate as we consider the challenges now before our nation. Most things make me think of a story, and I'm just remembering the many times that I've addressed you before that I haven't told it to you. [*Laughter*] If I have, be polite and—[*laughter*]. It has to do with an old farmer that took over some creek land down there in a creek bottom, never had been farmed before, covered with rocks and brush. And he worked and he worked and he cleared away the brush and he had the rocks hauled away and he fertilized and he cultivated and he planted. And he really created a gardenspot. And he was so proud of that that one day at church he asked the preacher if he wouldn't come out and see what he'd accomplished.

Well, the preacher went out there, and he took one look, and he said, "Oh, this" he said, "I've never seen anything like it." He said, "These melons, these are the biggest melons I've ever seen. The Lord certainly has blessed this land." And he went on—the tallest corn that he'd ever seen and the squash and the tomatoes and the string beans, everything. And every time he was praising the Lord for all of this. And the old boy was getting pretty fidgety. And finally he couldn't stand it anymore, and he said, "Reverend, I wish you could have seen this when the Lord was doing it by himself." [*Laughter*]

And so it is with our nation. We've been blessed with a vast and beautiful land and with an energetic and enterprising people. Yet it's up to us to keep our nation prosperous, strong, and free. We must examine our problems, decide upon the solutions, and then forcefully and without hesitation take action.

Secretary of State Shultz has just spoken to you, and yesterday you heard from President José Napoleon Duarte about Central America, an area where the principle of forthright action unmistakably applies. My remarks today will focus on the budget and tax reform, but permit me to say a few words first about this region I've just mentioned.

Our policy in Central America is straightforward. We intend, first, to offer support to the free nations of the region, to those that have already achieved democracy, and to those that are working toward it in good faith. Democracy in the region has achieved a firm foothold. Costa Rica has long been a healthy democracy. Honduras is making strides, and now, under the leadership of President Duarte and in the face of attacks by Communist guerrillas, El Salvador, too, is making progress. Just last week the New York Times carried a front page story on El Salvador that reported human rights violations at a 5-year low, new successes in countering the Communist guerrillas, and a rising international confidence in El Salvador itself.

We are also determined to prevent the Communist regime in Nicaragua from exporting revolution. Since taking power in 1979 that regime has established regular censorship of the press, harassed the church, driven the Jewish community out of the country, and practiced virtual genocide against the Miskito Indians. They have expanded their military forces from 5,000 troops to regular forces of more than 60,000; from a handful of tanks and aircraft to more than 350 armored vehicles and tanks and an air force of 30 helicopters and 45 fixed-wing aircraft.

Nicaragua is another pawn in the Soviet grand strategy of expansion—a direct challenge to America just 700 miles from our territory. Already more than 250,000 Nicaraguans have fled, many flooding into Costa Rica and Honduras. If the Sandinistas, the Communists, are allowed to export their violence, the flood will grow and our Southern States could become virtual refugee camps for hundreds of thousands—even millions—of the dispossessed.

Our administration firmly believes that the United States should provide aid to the Nicaraguan freedom fighters struggling for the democratic ideals that the Sandinista revolution has betrayed. So far, the House of Representatives has blocked this aid, but we are going to come back again and again until the House fulfills its responsibilities to protect freedom and our own security.

Permit me now to turn to the Federal budget and tax reform. And first, the budget.

With your assistance, when we came to office in 1981, we took the first steps in decades to restrain the growth and power of government and to create incentives for American enterprise.

The results have been dramatic. The economy has shown solid growth for the last nine quarters. The recovery of business investment has been the strongest in some three decades. Productivity has risen, bringing an end to stagnation that characterized the close of the last decade. Inflation is at the lowest level in more than a decade, and the economy has been creating new jobs at the rate of hundreds of thousands each

month. Just this week the Dow Jones Industrial Average broke 1,300, a new record, and the New York Daily News carried a headline that I will always cherish, it simply read, "Zippity Doo Dow." [*Laughter*]

As for government revenues, despite a widespread impression to the contrary, they're actually on the rise. In 1984 Federal receipts increased 11 percent, a healthy gain of 7 percent, even after accounting for inflation. This fiscal year that remarkable pace is being sustained.

I had to believe it was working when they stopped calling it Reaganomics. [*Laughter*] Sadly, however, the historic achievements of recent years have been cast in shadow by a menace that could wipe them out—the Federal deficit.

It's important to be clear about the source of the problem. This deficit has not arisen as a result of the tax cuts. On the contrary, as I've said, government revenues are actually on the rise even though we've reduced the rates. Instead the deficit problem is a problem of spending, spending without discipline or direction, spending that in recent decades has burgeoned absolutely out of control.

Sometimes I think that government is like that old definition of a baby: an enormous appetite at one end and no sense of responsibility at the other. [*Laughter*]

To begin to bring deficit spending under control, we've worked with the Senate to put together a package of spending cuts that would trim $56 billion from the budget next year and some $300 billion over 3 years. While, like all budget resolutions, it has its imperfections, the Senate resolution is historic, a major effort to control government spending. It will prepare the way for tax reform and help put our economy on a growth path through the end of the decade.

Yesterday the House passed its own budget resolution. It is, frankly, unacceptable—unacceptable to me and to the American people. House sponsors claim that their plan will save some $56 billion—in fact, billions of those savings would come from what could only be charitably described as phantom cuts. Even worse, the House plan fails adequately to address the fundamental problem of unbridled domestic spending.

Instead it goes easy on the fat in domestic programs and turns instead to our Armed Forces, freezing the budget for our national defense at last year's level—in real terms, a deep cut.

Yet such a further cut in defense spending would undermine our negotiating position in Geneva and put the defense of our nation at risk. My friends, the Senate has shown the way. We can cut the deficit while protecting our security. I want to thank you from the bottom of my heart for all the help that you provided during the Senate budget process. Now, we must work together to make certain that those Senate efforts are reflected in the final budget resolution. Can I count on you? [*Applause*] Thank you.

Next Tuesday I will address the Nation about a dramatic proposal to reform our system of taxation, the first comprehensive plan to modernize the system since the income tax code was enacted some 70 years ago. It is a proposal that will affect Americans of all ages and occupations and touch every aspect of the economic life of our country. Details of the proposal will have to wait until the address on Tuesday, but I would like to discuss with you the principles upon which our plan is based and the outlines of the plan itself.

Already the momentum of public support is building to the point that what was once thought impossible is now considered all but inevitable. Tax reform's time has come.

We propose to replace a tax system that is almost universally regarded as needlessly complicated and unfair and replace it with a simpler, fairer, more streamlined model. Today almost half of all taxpaying Americans seek professional advice on filling out their forms, and there are probably a lot more every year who end up wishing they did. Tax reform will mean that you will not have to have an advanced degree in accounting to get your taxes right. Most people will be able to fill out their tax forms without paying for help and in a fraction of the time that they take now.

With simplicity will come fairness. The complexity of the current tax code makes it ripe for abuse. Today you can see advertisements for tax shelters and tax avoidance schemes with little or no economic justifica-

tion, from credits for investments in windmills to deductions for so-called educational cruises on oceanliners. Well, the American people know that such waste doesn't come free. And that for everyone who finds a shelter, someone else is left out in the cold; that for everyone who avoids paying his fair share, someone else has to make up the shortfall by paying a heavier tax burden.

Just as important as the unfairness of all this is the tremendous waste of time, energy, resources that the present system entails. Instead of inventing a better mousetrap, our entrepreneurs and businessmen have to spend their time avoiding the tax trap. Steeply rising income tax rates punish success, discourage hard work and initiative, and cut into savings. And meanwhile, tax loopholes and shelters divert investment away from the productive economy and into areas that are often economically stagnant.

Now, this is what happens when the Government tries to run the economy through the tax code. Tax considerations become paramount in business decisions, and the rationale and efficient allocation of resources by the market is distorted out of all recognition. Our economy becomes enmeshed in a bureaucracy instead of energized by opportunity. And economic growth slows, and with it, the creation of new jobs and businesses.

Well, we have a better idea. Let's remove government obstacles to growth, lower rates, close loopholes, and put this country on an ascending spiral of business formation, job creation, and technological innovation.

We've seen what the first tax cuts achieved in revitalizing our economy and setting it firmly on a path of healthy noninflationary growth. Tax reform is the necessary next step, truly returning us to the free market principles that made the United States the land of opportunity and the greatest economic power in the world.

As in the past, on so many of our initiatives, we'll be looking for your help. And I know that on this vital issue I can depend on your support. And, in advance, from the bottom of my heart, I thank you.

Two centuries ago, America was born in a

rebellion against unfair taxation. Today another revolution is quietly growing, a peaceful revolution to restore this country to its original promise, to strike a blow for fairness, to break the last economic shackles from the land of the free and the home of the brave and propel America into a future of almost limitless possibilities.

My friends, it's been an honor and a pleasure to talk to you on this, the eve of the second American revolution. And we will make you safe in your books and records.

Thank you, and God bless you all.

Note: The President spoke at 2:15 p.m. in the Grand Ballroom at the J.W. Marriott Hotel.

Written Responses to Questions Submitted by Il Tempo of Italy
May 23, 1985

The President's Trip to Europe

Q. You have just completed what many press accounts see as a highly controversial trip to Europe, marked by an uproar over your decision to visit a German military cemetery and by failure to obtain French agreement for a 1986 round of trade liberalization negotiations. How do you personally assess your European trip?

The President. Well, I think the headlines sometimes obscure the most significant events in public life and that history has a way of clarifying genuine achievement. Personally, I am very heartened by the results of my trip. I am confident that they do add up to real achievements and represent a success for the Western partnership as a whole. That is why I reported "mission accomplished" to the American people and Congress. For example, the visit definitely strengthened U.S.-German relations and the prospects for continuing peace in Europe— twin accomplishments which have major importance for every country in Europe, not least of all Italy.

At the Bonn Economic Summit we agreed to a common strategy aimed at continued economic growth and job creation— again, an accomplishment which vitally affects every country in Europe. And while it is true that one country out of the seven summit participants did not join the rest of us in agreeing on a date to begin multilateral trade talks, we did move much closer to our goal of launching those talks. I was also heartened by the across-the-board support for our arms control efforts positions in

Geneva.

In my speech to the European Parliament, we set forth a framework for improved U.S.-Soviet relations, spelling out a number of constructive, commonsense, confidence-building measures aimed at lowering tensions. Here, too, we were dealing with the crucial issue of war and peace as well as the shape of Europe during the rest of this century and on into the next. And in that context I should mention my stops in Spain and Portugal, Europe's newest democracies. There, we saw heartening proof that freedom works.

Finally, let me add how much I appreciate the very special flavor which your country provided to my trip. In the first place it was pleasant, as always, to have the company of your Prime Minister, representing his democratic coalition government, during the economic summit in Bonn. Mr. Craxi's vigor, poise, and intelligence tangibly contributed to the value of our discussions and the positive statements we produced. And, of course, I was very personally pleased by Nancy's program in Rome and the marvelous hospitality she found there. I hope it's not too presumptuous for a proud husband to note that Nancy's work on drug abuse interested all of my colleagues and was a constructive accompaniment to our summit agreement for intensified cooperation against international drug trafficking.

Strategic Defense Initiative

Q. Mr. President, from your discussions in Bonn with your European partners and allies did you get a sense that they are ready to cooperate with the United States in the research program for the Strategic Defense Initiative, even if the Soviets and other critics of the program will protest that SDI runs counter to the ABM treaty?

The President. There is no question that all of our key allies—and that of course includes Italy—are extremely interested in our Stategic Defense Initiative. During the Bonn Economic Summit, I was delighted to see that all of our partners support our SDI research program as prudent and necessary. Whether they choose to participate in our research effort is, of course, for them to decide. We know there are a number of questions, but I wish to emphasize that we would welcome participation by our allies.

As for Soviet protests that such research runs counter to the ABM treaty, I can only say that such protests are factually wrong and proceed from cynical efforts to distort the meaining of the ABM treaty. The truth is, we are and will remain in full compliance with our ABM treaty obligations.

It is also important to know that the Soviets themselves obviously understand the value of defensive systems. The Soviets are spending as much on defense as offense, and of course they have the only operational ABM and antisatellite systems deployed by anyone in the world. Given their actions, it's only reasonable that we proceed with our research program.

Q. What was your response to those Europeans who say that SDI may precipitate a deadlock in Geneva that would plunge European governments into another debate over the nature of their security ties with the United States?

The President. I believe that it is far too early in this extraordinarily complex set of negotiations—which address strategic nuclear weapons, intermediate-range nuclear weapons, and space weapons—to speak of deadlock. In any event, we firmly oppose the idea that progress in any one area of the negotiations should or must be held hostage to progress in any other area. Rigid insistence on such a self-defeating formula would violate both common sense and mankind's genuine interest in achieving the widest possible agreement on arms reductions. I believe that it is very much in the

Soviets' own interests to avoid placing purely artificial impediments in the way of achievement, and I am hopeful that they will join with us in working for a safer, more stable, and more peaceful international community.

Nuclear and Space Arms Negotiations

Q. The first phase of the Geneva talks was relatively unproductive, by admission of your own administration. In part, this has been attributed to the Soviet desire to see if they could get anything from the U.S. without bargaining. Are you hopeful that some real bargaining may now begin in Geneva? And in which one of the three baskets of negotiations?

The President. My ardent desire is that through patient and serious and realistic negotiations we can make significant progress in all three of the baskets, as you call them. Obviously, I do not underestimate the difficulties of our task. After all, these negotiations affect our vital security interests. But because they do entail issues that are literally matters of life and death, it is imperative that we stick with them and not let ourselves be discouraged by either the slow pace of progress or by the tactics which the Soviets themselves might from time to time adopt in the hope that these will weaken Western cohesion and resolve.

Meeting With Soviet Leader Mikhail Gorbachev

Q. In your judgement, which are the areas that potentially are more suited to an improvement of relations with the Soviet Union and in which you could achieve some progress in a summit meeting with Mr. Gorbachev?

The President. Well, I am not really sure it would be helpful for me to speculate at this point on what areas of improved relations might come out of an eventual meeting with Mr. Gorbachev. I might note that while I have publicly expressed my interest in such a meeting and my willingness to meet with Mr. Gorbachev, he himself has not yet officially indicated when—or for that matter where—he thinks a meeting should take place. In general, however, I would emphasize to you a view I have often voiced in the past: It is always much better to be talking to a person than about him. And if and when Mr. Gorbachev and I get together—which I hope will be soon—you can be sure, for the American part, that it will be in the spirit of good will, seriousness, and a determination to explore whatever avenue may be open toward better understanding, reduced tensions, and peace. I must underline, however, that meetings do not in and of themselves guarantee progress—it is the overall relationship between our countries that counts, and this relationship is not enhanced when expectations about any one meeting are too high.

East-West Relations

Q. Are you concerned that a strong push by the Europeans for a summit conference, and possibly in the direction of a new détente, may create a situation in which the tactics of the summit may be more important than the substance of the discussions? What are your bottom-line conditions in requesting a well-prepared summit?

The President. If nothing else, my most recent discussions with our allies and part-

ners at the Bonn Economic Summit further convinced me that European leaders attach far more importance to the substance of East-West relations than to what you call tactics. Their stakes in a genuinely improved East-West climate are as strong—perhaps even stronger than our own, and they do not want such a critical relationship built on illusion, ambiguity, or misunderstanding. Despite what the Soviets themselves may be hoping or saying for propaganda purposes, the Western track record is impressive when it comes to sizing up our adversary and taking joint action in response. Allied firmness on commitment to the two-track NATO decision on intermediate-range missiles is eloquent proof of that. So, yes, we will be well prepared on our side for a summit meeting, and the bottom line for us means, as I earlier indicated, a meeting based on a spirit of good will, seriousness, and a sincere effort to address and, if possible, improve the core concerns of our relationship.

Note: The questions and answers were released by the Office of the Press Secretary on May 25.

Radio Address to the Nation on Tax Reform
May 25, 1985

My fellow Americans:

If you were tuned in to the radio one Saturday in the middle of April, you may have heard me speak about one of the most compelling issues of our time—tax simplification.

It was April 13th then, and I'm sure many of you were approaching those final moments before your tax forms were due with a rising sense of frustration, even anger. Nobody's ever going to enjoy paying taxes; it just isn't human nature. But I also know that the American people wouldn't find the whole process so aggravating if they didn't feel our tax system was shot through with unfairness, inequality, and waste.

The American people are always willing, even eager, to do their duty. But you quite naturally resent it when you see others shirking theirs. It rankles to know that your tax rates are so high because others who can afford high-priced lawyers and tax consultants are able to manipulate the system to avoid paying their fair share. And it simply adds insult to injury when, on top of a large tax bill to the IRS, you have to pay a professional to tell you how much you owe.

The United States tax code is so mammoth, so incredibly complex that even experts can't agree on what it says. We've seen the damage an unfair tax system can do to our economy, our pocketbooks, our faith in American justice, and to our confidence in government institutions.

Well, that's all going to change. Next

Tuesday we'll announce an historic change in the tax laws to remove the dark cloud of unfairness from our tax system. We're going to overhaul the whole rickety, jerry-rigged tax code and come out with a newer, sleeker model that will not only be fairer and simpler but will significantly reduce taxes for the majority of all Americans.

Starting today we're declaring the 1040 tax form an endangered species. Our plan is to make the paying of your taxes so easy that many Americans won't even have to fill out a form. We're going to do away with the inequities and the economically unjustifiable tax breaks, things like deductions for windmills and so-called educational cruises on luxury oceanliners.

By closing such loopholes, we'll be able to lower taxes and begin to flatten the present steeply rising system of tax brackets so that you can keep more of each additional dollar you earn. We want to knock down the barriers on the road to success so that all Americans can go as far as their hard work, skill, imagination, and creativity will take them. Closing wasteful business loopholes will also allow us to lower tax rates on America's businesses and entrepreneurs.

We stand today on the threshold of a new technological age that is already beginning to revolutionize our lives for the better and open the way to a future of almost unlimited possibility. By lowering rates, we can unleash an entrepreneurial explosion of business formation, job growth, and technological innovation that will rival even our most optimistic dreams. Our plan will also recognize the central role of the American family in preserving and protecting our nation's values. Raising a family has always involved hardship and sacrifice along with the love and the joy. But for most of these last four decades, the Government hasn't been making it any easier.

Since 1948 the personal exemption, which allows breadwinners to deduct a certain amount from their taxable income for every man, woman, and child who is dependent on them, has dwindled to a mere fraction of its original value. The result—a tax increase of immense proportions that struck directly at the pocketbook of America's families. In effect, it's been families that have borne the burden of the explosive growth in government and domestic spending these last four decades.

Well, it's time families got a little help, and that's what we propose to do. By greatly expanding the personal exemption, raising the standard deduction, lowering rates, and retaining the home mortgage interest deduction on principal residences, we're going to make it a lot easier for struggling lower-income households and for the working-poor families to climb up the ladder of success.

This must be a priority of a profamily, pro-opportunity society. The timid, the cynical, and the special interests will combine to say that what we want—fairness, hope, and opportunity—is impossible. Well, they'll be wrong; they've been wrong so many times in these last 4½ years. Nothing can stop America when it hears the call to justice. No one can stop America from doing what it knows is right.

On Tuesday night I will be announcing the details of this historic tax package on nationwide TV. I hope you'll tune in and listen to what I have to say. This could be the single most important step we'll take in this decade to fulfill the American dream of hope and opportunity for us and for future generations.

Until next week, thanks for listening, and God bless you.

Note: The President spoke at 12:06 p.m. from the Oval Office at the White House.

Remarks to Participants in the President's Inaugural Bands Parade at Walt Disney's EPCOT Center Near Orlando, Florida
May 27, 1985

Please all be seated, and I want to thank all of you, Senator Paula Hawkins, Congressman Ireland, Congressman Connie Mack—McCollum, the distinguished people here, and Mr. and Mrs. Eisner, all of you ladies and gentlemen, and these wonderful young people.

We have come here—our first stop this morning on this Decoration Day was at Arlington Cemetery—and I just wonder if because of the special character of this day, Memorial Day, if we couldn't perhaps bow our heads for a few seconds in silent prayer for those who have given their lives that we might live in liberty. [*A silent prayer was observed.*] Amen.

Well, indeed it is an honor for me to be here today to receive a magnificent gift that I received on a second and very much warmer Inauguration Day. I understand that in preparing for this event more than 2,500 young people worked with sponsors in the private sector who donated food, transportation, and lodging. And each of you who helped to make this private sector initiative possible has my heartfelt thanks.

Tomorrow evening I will address the Nation about a dramatic proposal to reform our tax system. It's a proposal intended to launch a new American revolution and to give to you young people, as you come of age, a nation of ever-greater freedom and vitality and strength.

You know, today we're enjoying a standard of living that, when I was your age, could not even have been imagined. Buoyed by medical breakthroughs and rising standards of living, the life expectancy of Americans has been increasing steadily for 50 years. I've already surpassed my own life expectancy at my birth by 20 years. Now, there are a lot of people that find that a source of annoyance, but I appreciate it very much.

Today we take for granted so many inventions that inspired wonder not long ago—the polio vaccines of Dr. Jonas Salk and Dr. Albert Sabin; television, first in black and white and now in vivid color; drought-resistant seeds and cold-resistant grains; computers in the workplace and the home; spacecraft that can orbit the Earth for days and then land gently on a desert runway. Despite the predictions so many made during the Great Depression when I was a young man, life in America today is not worse—it's far better. And let us ask, then, what made it so? Was it government directing our daily lives?

During these past five decades the Government has indeed provided vital services and helped improve life for many people. No one doubts the necessity of a strong national defense or the role our military has played in keeping us free. Likewise no one doubts the importance of the government safety net for those in genuine need.

Yet our national experience shows that when government grows beyond these two limited duties, when government lays claim to more and more of our resources and begins, through massive regulation and high taxation, to impinge on our individual freedoms, then our economy grows not more prosperous but less so.

Throughout the 1970's, for example, government's growth was unbridled, yet our economy stagnated. By 1980 the gross national product registered zero growth. If it was not the Government that spurred our economic growth was it perhaps our natural resources? Our vast land has always been blessed by a mighty multitude of resources—broad plains, powerful rivers, and rich deposits of minerals. Yet in a sense, the primary reality of a resource exists not in the earth but in the minds of the men and women who give it usefulness and value.

Consider oil. A century ago oil was nothing but a thick, foul, and useless liquid. It was the invention of the internal combustion engine that gave oil its function. Or think of sand, sand that used to be nothing but the stuff that deserts are made of. The development of the silicon microchip has given sand a vital function. And today we use it to make chips that give home computers their intelligence, monitor functions on aircraft, and guide our satellites through the dark reaches of space. No, it's not been so much our resources or our government that have given us our enduring vibrancy and growth but the initiative and enterprise of individual Americans.

Air travel, for example, has become commonplace because test pilots like Lindbergh had daring, and engineers like Boeing and Douglas had the wits and determination. The Government might have wished it could simply decree a polio vaccine, but it took years of unremitting effort and dedication by Doctors Salk and Sabin to make the vaccines a reality.

In this setting, one story of a private initiative is particularly appropriate. Back in Missouri in the early 1900's there lived a farmboy who discovered that he had a knack for drawing barnyard animals. As an adult, he began to put his animals into cartoons, and he became convinced that he could entertain people by telling stories about a little creature with a high voice, red trousers, and yellow shoes and white gloves.

Professionals in the field made fun of the idea, and to produce his first cartoons the young man had to sell or pawn virtually everything he owned. But today, 57 years later, this man and his creation have become permanently fixed in the history of our popular culture. His name was Walt Disney; his little creature was Mickey Mouse.

The determination that each of these heroes of progress demonstrated came from within. Yet in each case it was crucial to the success of their efforts that they were operating in a climate of economic liberty—in a free market where they could make use of pooled resources, experiment with new techniques and products, and submit their plans and hypotheses to the test of practical experience.

This aspect of freedom, economic freedom, is one of the distinctive characteristics of life in our nation, as interwoven into the American legacy as freedom of speech and press. It has enabled our people to make our nation into a marvel of economic progress, and, as with all the freedoms that we enjoy, it's our duty to cherish and protect it.

Just as the American people rebelled against oppressive taxation some two centuries ago, the reform that I will announce tomorrow will represent a dramatic effort to make our tax code more simple, efficient, and fair and place more resources into the hands of your families and, ultimately, you yourselves. It'll expand our economic freedom and clear the way for even greater economic vitality than that which we enjoy today.

Nor will the benefits be economic alone. With more resources at their disposal, the American people will be able to provide greater support to the institutions that they themselves value—our schools, universities, the arts, our churches and synagogues. As our economy grows they, too, will flourish.

John Marshall said, "The power to tax involves the power to destroy." If so, then the power to cut taxes must surely be the power to create—the power to force government to stand back and let the people themselves give expression to the spirit of enterprise—building and imagining; giving to you, our sons and daughters, a nation of ever-greater prosperity and freedom.

My friends, thank you again for the gift of this magnificent inaugural parade. May you enjoy all the blessings of a free and bountiful nation, and on this, the eve of the second American revolution, may you always remember the enduring truth that our tax plan seeks to embody and that Americans have cherished through the ages—God made man for liberty.

Thank you all, God bless you, and now, let the parade begin.

Note: The President spoke at 12:41 p.m. from a reviewing stand near the American Adventure Showcase. In his opening remarks, the President referred to Mr. and Mrs. Michael Eisner. Mr. Eisner was chairman of the board and chief executive officer of Walt Disney Productions. Participating in the parade were the bands scheduled to perform in the 1985 Inaugural Parade, which was cancelled due to extremely cold weather. Following his remarks, the President traveled to Miami.

Remarks at a Fundraising Dinner for Senator Paula Hawkins in Miami, Florida
May 27, 1985

I just have to say, I'm either the latest after lunch speaker or the earliest dinner speaker—[*laughter*]—that I know of.

Senator Hawkins—and I know that here with us, because they came down with us—are Congressmen Ireland and Connie Mack and Jeannie Austin and Jeb Bush.[1] I thank you all. Thank all of you.

It's an honor for me to be with you today in support of a Member of the United States Senate who has been absolutely indispensable to the cause of a strong America—Senator Paula Hawkins.

Now, if you want to do me a favor and if you want to do the country a favor, just make sure that she goes back to the Senate for 6 more years. [*Applause*] I guess I can count on you. I thought you'd indicate your pleasure at that. But it's always a treat for me to visit Florida. Wasn't the Fountain of Youth somewhere around here? [*Laughter*]

I'd like to express my thanks to all of you today who've done so much over the years—the precincts you've walked, the stamps you've licked, the contributions you've made, have all made a difference. People like Jim McLamore and Tibor Hollo[2] have given new meaning to the term "committed."

You have more than your share of people committed to the cause. There's Jorge Mas and his team from the Cuban-American Foundation. And then there's Carlos Perez, the Cuban firecracker, and his Concerned Citizens for Democracy. And I know I speak for Senator Hawkins when I say thanks for all that you've done.

Pardon my borrowing a line, but when it comes to your support, I wouldn't leave home without it. [*Laughter*]

---

[1] *State chairman of the Florida Republican Party and chairman of the Dade County Republican Party, respectively.*

[2] *Cofounder and chairman emeritus of Burger King Corp. and chairman of the fundraising dinner for Senator Hawkins, respectively.*

We Republicans have been blessed with grassroots supporters who are committed to the ideals of individual freedom, family values, free enterprise, and a strong America. While the other party has tried to build a coalition by segmenting America into warring factions over the past years—pitting white against black, women against men, young against old—we've taken a more positive path. The Republican Party has sought to unite our citizens by building on those fundamental beliefs that made America the great land that she is.

As Andy Ireland keeps emphasizing, the door to our party is wide open, the welcome mat is out, and our agenda is opportunity and freedom for all. We don't promise quota systems and giveaway programs. We promise to do what's right for America and for all Americans.

Senator Hawkins is herself a great example of how our party works. She's one of two Republicans in the United States Senate who happen to be women. That's two more than the opposition have. Now, throughout the country hundreds of Republican women hold elected office, and last year there was a net gain of 95 Republican women elected to State and Federal legislative bodies—the biggest jump in the history of either party.

It will take all of us working together to meet the serious challenges that America faces. And what we do will determine if our country remains the free and decent place that we want it to be.

Senator Hawkins has been an articulate champion of our cause. She's been a leading figure, for example, in the fight against drug trafficking—a menace to every family in America. She has been working within the legislative process to support those countries that are battling the drug traffickers and penalize those that are not. She's made it her business to expose the Cuban-Nicaraguan drug connection. High-level officials of these governments have been personally implicated and, in some cases, indicted.

673

I have a message for Fidel Castro about the drug trade. He can tell America's television network people anything he wants, but nobody in his regime is going to get away with this dirty drug business.

We're moving forward on a broad front to attack the use of illegal drugs. Working with private and charitable organizations, with schools, family groups, and others, we're encouraging people, especially young people, not to get involved with drugs and to help those already on drugs to get off. I happen to be very personally, very proud that Nancy has taken the personal interest that she has in this positive initiative to win the drug war. When I come home from the office and open the door and say, "I'm home," if there's no answer, well, I know where she is and what she's doing. [*Laughter*]

But another part of our strategy is a strong law enforcement/interdiction campaign aimed at stopping the drug flow before it reaches the customers. It's a complicated and frustrating job, but our commitment sends a message to every youngster in this country: Drug use is a threat, an ugly, life-destroying vice. And it's wrong. And I'm pleased that the message seems to be getting through. Young people in America are turning away from drugs.

Let me be partisan and add something here—one thing more and more young people are turning to is the Republican Party. Nothing gave me greater joy than the multitude of young faces evident everywhere we stopped during the 1984 campaign.

What we do—our efforts to make America a better country—is for them. Illegal drugs are only part of the crime epidemic. For far too long our legal system has resembled a jigsaw puzzle of complicated roadblocks through which our law enforcers have been forced to maneuver in order to do their job. In 1984, with a Republican majority in the Senate, we passed a comprehensive crime control act—a major step toward reestablishment of the balance to the criminal justice system. It's about time our criminal justice system gets back to serving the cause of justice and not the interests of criminals.

Paula Hawkins is a Senator of accomplishment. She has authored 32 bills and amendments which have passed the Senate and have gone on to become law. Now, that's an amazing record for any Senator, much less a freshman. We can expect even more from her during her second term, and she's earned a second term.

Of course, all this effort means little if our country is not secure. During these last 4 years, we've been moving forward to rebuild America's military strength, which was neglected during the 1970's. I can't tell you how vital Republican control of the Senate has been in this effort. The opposition often acts like a weaker America is a safer America.

Well, like it or not, that's the kind of bizarre logic that will carry the day if the other party regains control of the Senate. But with a Republican majority, we can count on common sense and courage to rule the day. Republicans know it is strength, not weakness, that will ensure the peace. We are fully aware of the threat communism poses to human freedom. And don't let anyone tell you we're morally equivalent with the Soviet Union. I have heard that term used in places. This is a democratic country of free people, a democratic country where all people enjoy the right to speak, to worship God as they choose, and live without fear. We are morally superior, not equivalent, to any totalitarian regime, and we should be darn proud of it.

In Central America today our ideals are being put to the test. The freedom of our friends and neighbors to the south is at stake, as is the security of the United States. And I'm happy to say that Paula Hawkins is one elected official who didn't have to wait until Daniel Ortega went to Moscow yet again before she realized that he's a Communist.

Many of those opposing our efforts have steadfastly refused to acknowledge that the rulers of the regime in Managua are, by their own admission, hardcore Communists and consider themselves part of the international Communist movement. Many of our own elected officials act as if they don't believe the Sandinista regime is playing a significant role in the Communist insurgency in El Salvador. Incidentally, I think some of our people get confused—they're not that familiar with Central America—when we talk Sandinista government and *contras* or the freedom fighters. I'm going to quit using both terms and start calling them what they are—it's the freedom fighters against the Communists.

Now, this role that they're playing in the insurgency in El Salvador—this despite the fact that top defectors from the El Salvadoran guerrillas have been telling us they receive guidance, training, funds, and vast amounts of arms and ammunition from their Communist friends in Nicaragua. Nicaragua today equals aggression, pure and simple. For the sake of peace in Central America, for the security of our own country, we cannot permit these Communists to succeed.

Closing our eyes and making a wish, which seems to be about the only course of action our opponents will support, won't make this threat go away. We need to assist those governments targeted by the Communists, and it's imperative that we support those brave individuals who are putting their lives on the line to bring democracy to Nicaragua.

The freedom fighters are a shield for Nicaragua's democratic neighbors, preventing the Communist regime from focusing its full strength on subversion and aggression. The freedom fighters are the best hope for democracy in that troubled country. Those who would have us abandon them and the people of Nicaragua are cutting off our chances to avoid a major crisis in Central America.

Lincoln's words ring as true today as they did over a hundred years ago: "Our defense," he said, "is in the preservation of the spirit which prized liberty as the heritage of all men, in all lands everywhere. Destroy this spirit and you have planted the seeds of despotism at your own doors."

And let's recognize the truth that Fidel Castro is behind much of the trouble in Central America. His consuming hatred of America and his ideological commitment to Communist tyranny has impoverished his country and oppressed its people. Thomas Jefferson once wrote, "Enlighten the people

generally, and tyranny and oppressions of body and mind will vanish like evil spirits at the dawn of day." Well, the Communists understand this, and that's why they're deathly afraid of the free flow of information. And that's why I'm especially proud that, at long last, Radio Marti is on the air. Now, there's a certain fellow with a beard who isn't so happy about Radio Marti—[*laughter*]—but at least for now Radio Marti's signal is getting through.

I firmly believe the tide of history is moving away from communism and into the warm sunlight of human freedom. To win this struggle, to preserve our way of life, to maintain the peace, we must be strong and true to our ideals. And together we can meet the challenge. Future generations, not only in the United States but throughout the hemisphere, will be grateful for what we do today. We're passing to them the most precious gift of all—liberty.

Now, I know a moment ago when I mentioned our defense buildup—I know the wave of propaganda, the drumbeat that is going on through this country with regard to our defense spending program. And one of the things that's the hardest and most frustrating to bear is the fact that our very success has been adding to the feeling that something is wrong with what we are doing. That is, every time we find one of those $400 hammers or something like that, it is added to the thought that, well, something is wrong and wasteful in the Defense Department.

Those are success stories. I don't know how long $400 hammers have been going on, but I know that in these 4 years we've been finding them and not buying them. [*Laughter*]

Now, you know, I know that the defense budget is large, you count this in the number of dollars and so forth, and where we're trying to balance the budget, erase the deficit. But I would just like to give you some comparative figures from the past. In the fifties, defense spending averaged 46 percent or better of the total budget. In the sixties, it averaged almost 40 percent, 39½ percent. It averages now only 29 percent of our budget. So, when we set out to cut spending, we think that it makes a lot of sense to cut where the bulk of the spending is, which is in domestic spending for a lot of things that government shouldn't have been doing in the first place.

And again, I come back down to this fact: None of what we're doing could have been done if we didn't control one House of the Senate [Congress]. You know that for about 42 out of 46 years our opponents held both Houses of the Congress. And finally, 4 years ago, we got control of this one House. It is absolutely essential if we are to succeed in what we have started to do. And to just give you one idea of how much has been accomplished, Republicans—for most of those 40-odd years I'm talking about—Republicans continually had to fight in the Congress a rearguard action against further government spending and increased government spending.

The debate that is raging in the Congress today shows what's been accomplished with that Republican Senate and with Senators like Paula Hawkins in that the debate is over how to go about cutting the spending. No one's talking about increasing it, they're only talking about cutting it.

We'll keep on until pretty soon more and more of them will find out that there is a wide open door to our party, and they can come on over and straighten up and fly right. [*Laughter*] But in the meantime, please send Paula back. We need her very much.

Thank you very much. God bless you.

Note: The President spoke at 4:44 p.m. in the International Ballroom at the Omni International Hotel. Prior to his remarks, the President attended a reception in the Florida Ballroom at the hotel for major donors to Senator Hawkins' campaign. Following his remarks, the President returned to Washington, DC.

Nomination of John Douglas Scanlan to be United States Ambassador to Yugoslavia
May 28, 1985

The President today announced his intention to nominate John Douglas Scanlan, of Hawaii, a career member of the Senior Foreign Service, Class of Minister-Counselor, as Ambassador to the Socialist Federal Republic of Yugoslavia. He would succeed David Anderson.

Mr. Scanlan served in the United States Navy in 1945–1946 and was an instructor at the University of Minnesota in 1955. In 1956 he entered the Foreign Service as intelligence research officer in the Department. In 1958–1960 he was general services officer in Moscow. He attended Polish language training at the Foreign Service Institute in 1960–1961. He was consular officer, then political officer in Warsaw (1961–1965), political officer in Montevideo (1965–1967), and principal officer in Poznan (1967–1969). In 1969–1971 he was senior State Department representative, NMCC, JCS, at the Pentagon and officer in charge of U.S.–U.S.S.R. bilateral affairs in the De-

partment in 1971–1973. He was counselor for political affairs in Warsaw in 1973–1975 and was a member of the Executive Seminar in National and International Affairs at the Foreign Service Institute in 1975–1976. In the Department he was special assistant to the Director General of the Foreign Service in 1976–1977 and on detail to the United States Information Agency as Deputy Director for Europe in 1977–1979. In 1979–1981 he was deputy chief of mission in Belgrade. In 1981–1982 he was Deputy Assistant Secretary of State for European Affairs in the Department, and in 1983–1984 he was a foreign affairs fellow at the Fletcher School of Law and Diplomacy, Tufts University, in Medford, MA. In 1984 he became Chairman of the United States delegation to the Conference on Security and Cooperation in Europe (CSCE) Cultural Forum Preparatory Conference. Since 1985 he has been in the Bureau of European Affairs.

Mr. Scanlan graduated from the University of Minnesota (B.A., 1952; M.A., 1955). His foreign languages are Polish, Russian, Serbo-Croatian, Spanish, and French. He was born December 20, 1927, in Thief River Falls, MN. He is married to the former Margaret Anne Calvi, and they have four children.

Nomination of Thomas B. Day To Be a Member of the National Science Board
May 28, 1985

The President today announced his intention to nominate Thomas B. Day to be a member of the National Science Board, National Science Foundation, for a term expiring May 10, 1990. He would succeed Michael Kasha.

Since 1978 Dr. Day has been president of San Diego State University in California. Previously, he was at the University of Maryland as acting vice chancellor for academic affairs (1977–1978); special assistant to the chancellor (1977); and vice chancellor for academic planning and policy (1970–1977). He was a member of the faculty of the University of Maryland in 1957–1965 as a research associate and professor.

He graduated from the University of Notre Dame (B.S., 1952) and Cornell University (Ph.D., 1957). He is married, has nine children, and resides in San Diego, CA. He was born March 7, 1932, in New York, NY.

Proclamation 5347—Minority Enterprise Development Week, 1985
May 28, 1985

By the President of the United States of America

A Proclamation

The greatest strength of our economic system is the opportunity it affords to every American to prosper according to his or her own talents and efforts. No other nation in history has so boldly set individual opportunity as its leading goal or come so close to achieving it.

This emphasis on opportunity works to the benefit of all Americans, but it especially helps Americans who are members of minority groups. In the past, these minority entrepreneurs were subject to laws and regulations that prevented them from competing freely in the marketplace. But those laws contradicted the spirit of freedom that animates our democracy, and today they are only an historical memory, a reminder of the need to be forever vigilant in defense of individual freedom.

Minority enterprises today form a significant proportion of all the Nation's businesses, and their number is continuing to grow. The talents, insights, and hard work of minority Americans are adding to our Nation's technological prowess, providing us with new solutions for important problems and creating jobs in many industries, some of which did not even exist only a few years ago. This is the genius of economic freedom, and we should do everything in our power to preserve this freedom and expand it so that opportunity for all will continue to be the defining characteristic of our society.

Now, Therefore, I, Ronald Reagan, President of the United States of America, do hereby proclaim the week of October 6 through October 12, 1985, as Minority Enterprise Development Week, and I call upon all Americans to join together with minority business enterprises across the country in appropriate observances.

In Witness Whereof, I have hereunto set my hand this twenty-eighth day of May, in the year of our Lord nineteen hundred and eighty-five, and of the Independence of the United States of America the two hundred and ninth.

RONALD REAGAN

[*Filed with the Office of the Federal Register, 4:20 p.m., May 28, 1985*]

Address to the Nation on Tax Reform
May 28, 1985

My fellow citizens:

I'd like to speak to you tonight about our future, about a great historic effort to give the words "freedom," "fairness," and "hope" new meaning and power for every man and women in America.

Specifically, I want to talk about taxes, about what we must do as a nation this year to transform a system that's become an endless source of confusion and resentment into one that is clear, simple, and fair for all—a tax code that no longer runs roughshod over Main Street America but ensures your families and firms incentives and rewards for hard work and risk-taking in an American future of strong economic growth.

No other issue goes so directly to the heart of our economic life. No other issue will have more lasting impact on the well-being of your families and your future.

In 1981 our critics charged that letting you keep more of your earnings would trigger an inflationary explosion, send interest rates soaring, and destroy our economy. Well, we cut your tax rates anyway by nearly 25 percent. And what that helped trigger was falling inflation, falling interest rates, and the strongest economic expansion in 30 years.

We have made one great dramatic step together. We owe it to ourselves now to take another. For the sake of fairness, simplicity, and growth, we must radically change the structure of a tax system that still treats our earnings as the personal property of the Internal Revenue Service; radically change a system that still treats people's earnings, similar incomes, much differently regarding the tax that they pay; and, yes, radically change a system that still causes some to invest their money, not to make a better mousetrap but simply to avoid a tax trap.

Over the course of this century, our tax system has been modified dozens of times and in hundreds of ways, yet most of those changes didn't improve the system. They made it more like Washington itself—complicated, unfair, cluttered with gobbledygook and loopholes designed for those with the power and influence to hire high-priced legal and tax advisers.

But there's more to it than that. Some years ago an historian, I believe, said that every time in the past when a government began taxing above a certain level of the people's earnings, trust in government began to erode. He said it would begin with efforts to avoid paying the full tax. This would become outright cheating and, eventually, a distrust and contempt of government itself until there would be a breakdown in law and order.

Well, how many times have we heard people brag about clever schemes to avoid paying taxes or watched luxuries casually written off to be paid for by somebody else—that somebody being you. I believe that, in both spirit and substance, our tax system has come to be un-American.

Death and taxes may be inevitable, but unjust taxes are not. The first American Revolution was sparked by an unshakable conviction—taxation without representation is tyranny. Two centuries later, a second American revolution for hope and opportunity is gathering force again—a peaceful revolution, but born of popular resentment against a tax system that is unwise, unwanted, and unfair.

I've spoken with and received letters from thousands of you—Republicans, Democrats, and Independents. I know how hungry you are for change. Make no mistake, we—the sons and daughters of those first brave souls who came to this land to give birth to a new life in liberty—we can change America. We can change America forever. So, let's get started. Let's change the tax code to make it fairer and change tax rates so they're lower.

The proposal I'm putting forth tonight for America's future will free us from the grip of special interests and create a binding commitment to the only special interest that counts—you, the people who pay America's bills. It will create millions of new jobs for working people, and it will replace the politics of envy with a spirit of partnership—the opportunity for everyone to hitch their wagon to a star and set out to reach the American dream.

I'll start by answering one question on your minds: Will our proposal help you? You bet it will. We call it America's tax plan because it will reduce tax burdens on the working people of this country, close loopholes that benefit a privileged few, simplify a code so complex even Albert Einstein reportedly needed help on his 1040 Form, and lead us into a future of greater growth and opportunity for all.

We want to cut taxes not opportunity. As you can see, the percentage of income tax owed would come down, way down, for those earning less than $15,000, down for earnings between $15,000 and $30,000, down for earnings between $30,000 and $50,000, and down for those earning more than $50,000.

How would the proposal work? The present tax system has 14 different brackets of tax rates ranging from 11 to 50 percent. We would take a giant step toward an ideal system by replacing all that with a simple three-bracket system—with tax rates of 15, 25, and 35 percent.

Now, let me point out right here that under our plan, by taking the basic deductions, the average family earning up to $12,000 or any blind or elderly American living at or below the poverty level would be dropped completely from the tax rolls—not one penny of tax to pay.

After taking the basic deductions, the first tax rate of 15 percent would apply to each dollar of taxable income up to $29,000 on a joint return. The second rate, 25 percent, would apply—and only apply—to taxable income above $29,000 up to a maximum of $70,000. The same principle applies throughout. Only taxable income above $70,000 would be taxed at the third and highest rate of 35 percent. Then no matter how much more you earned, you would pay 35 cents on any dollar to Uncle Sam. That's the top—35 percent—down from 50 percent today.

By lowering everyone's tax rates all the way up the income scale, each of us will have a greater incentive to climb higher, to excel, to help America grow.

I believe the worth of any economic policy must be measured by the strength of its commitment to American families, the bedrock of our society. There is no instrument of hard work, savings, and job creation as effective as the family. There is no cultural institution as ennobling as family life. And there is no superior, indeed no equal, means to rear the young, protect the weak, or attend the elderly. None.

Yet past government policies betrayed families and family values. They permitted inflation to push families relentlessly into higher and higher tax brackets. And not only did the personal exemption fail to keep pace with inflation; in real dollars its actual value dropped dramatically over the last 30 years.

The power to tax is the power to destroy. For three decades families have paid the freight for the special interests. Now families are in trouble. As one man from Memphis, Tennessee, recently wrote: "The taxes that are taken out of my check is money that I need, not extra play money. Please do all that you can to make the tax system more equitable toward the family." Well, sir, that's just what we intend to do—to pass the strongest profamily initiative in postwar history.

In addition to lowering your tax rates further, we'll virtually double the personal exemption, raising it by next year to $2,000 for every taxpayer and every dependent. And that $2,000 exemption will be indexed to protect against inflation. Further, we will increase the standard deduction, raising it to $4,000 for joint returns.

Beyond this, we intend to strengthen families' incentives to save through individual retirement accounts, IRA's, by nearly doubling—to $4,000—the amount all couples can deduct from their taxable income. From now on, each spouse could put up to $2,000 a year into his or her IRA and invest the money however they want, and the value of the IRA would not be taxable until they approach retirement.

Some families could save more, others less; but whether it's $400 or $4,000, every dollar saved up to $4,000 each year would be fully deductible from taxable earnings. Let me add that we would also raise by nearly a full third the special tax credit for low-income working Americans. That special incentive—a credit to reduce the tax they owe—would be raised from the present $550 to a maximum level of over $700.

Now, let's look at some examples of families in different income groups to illustrate how dramatically these incentives could help you to better your lives.

Take a family of four, struggling at a poverty-level existence, with an annual income of $12,000. By nearly doubling the personal exemption and raising the standard deduction, we will, as I said before, guarantee that that family pays no income tax at all.

But what if, being industrious, they go out and earn more, say $5,000 more, how much tax would they pay? Only 15 cents on each dollar of the additional $5,000. They would thus pay a total tax of only $750 on $17,000 of earnings; that's less than 5 percent on their total income.

We're offering a ladder of opportunity for every family that feels trapped, a ladder of opportunity to grab hold of and to climb out of poverty forever.

Now, let's take a larger working family— husband, wife, and four children—earning an income of $26,000 a year. Right away, under our plan, the value of that family's personal exemptions would be $12,000. Add to this the new higher standard deduction, and if they save a single IRA, this family could reduce the amount of income subject to tax by $18,000. On earnings of $26,000,

they would pay only $1,200 tax, again an effective tax rate of less than 5 percent. And now they could earn $17,000 more, and it would be taxed at only 15 cents on the dollar.

Higher income couples would also see their effective tax rates lowered. A young married couple earning $40,000 and taking deductions could find themselves paying an effective tax rate of barely 10 percent.

The power of these incentives would send one simple, straightforward message to an entire nation: America, go for it!

We're reducing tax rates by simplifying the complex system of special provisions that favor some at the expense of others. Restoring confidence in our tax system means restoring and respecting the principle of fairness for all. This means curtailing some business deductions now being written off; it means ending several personal deductions, including the State and local tax deduction, which actually provides a special subsidy for high-income individuals, especially in a few high-tax States.

Two-thirds of Americans don't even itemize, so they receive no benefit from the State and local tax deduction. But they're being forced to subsidize the high-tax policies of a handful of States. This is truly taxation without representation.

But other deductions widely used, deductions central to American values, will be maintained. The mortgage interest deduction on your home would be fully retained. And on top of that, no less than $5,000 in other interest expenses would still be deductible. The itemized deductions for your charitable contributions will remain intact. The deductions for your medical expenses will be protected and preserved. Deductions for casualty losses would be continued; so, too, would the current preferential treatment of Social Security. Military allowances will not be taxed. And veterans' disability payments will remain totally exempt from Federal taxation. These American veterans have already paid their dues.

The number of taxpayers who need to itemize would be reduced to 1 in 4. We envision a system where more than half of us would not even have to fill out a return. We call it the return-free system, and it would be totally voluntary. If you decided to participate, you would automatically receive your refund or a letter explaining any additional tax you owe. Should you disagree with this figure, you would be free to fill out your taxes using the regular form. We believe most Americans would go from the long form or the short form to no form.

Comparing the distance between the present system and our proposal is like comparing the distance between a Model T and the space shuttle. And I should know—I've seen both.

I've spoken of our proposed changes to help individuals and families. Let me explain how we would complement them with proposals for business—proposals to ensure fairness by eliminating or modifying special privileges that are economically unjustifiable and to strengthen growth by preserving incentives for investment, research, and development.

We begin with a basic recognition: The greatest innovations for new jobs, technologies, and economic vigor today come from a small but growing circle of heroes, the small business people, American entrepreneurs, the men and women of faith, intellect, and daring who take great risks to invest in and invent our future. The majority of the 8 million new jobs created over the last 2½ years were created by small enterprises—enterprises often born in the dream of one human heart.

To young Americans wondering tonight, where will I go, what will I do with my future, I have a suggestion: Why not set out with your friends on the path of adventure and try to start up your own business? Follow in the footsteps of those two college students who launched one of America's great computer firms from the garage behind their house. You, too, can help us unlock the doors to a golden future. You, too, can become leaders in this great new era of progress—the age of the entrepreneur.

My goal is an America bursting with opportunity, an America that celebrates freedom every day by giving every citizen an equal chance, an America that is once again the youngest nation on Earth—her spirit unleashed and breaking free. For starters, lowering personal tax rates will give a hefty boost to the nearly 15 million small businesses which are individual proprietorships or partnerships.

To further promote business formation, we propose to reduce the maximum corporate tax rate—now 46 percent—to 33 percent, and most small corporations would pay even lower rates. So, with lower rates, small business can lead the way in creating jobs for all who want to work.

To these incentives we would add another—a reduction in the tax on capital gains. Since the capital gains tax rates were cut in 1978 and 1981, capital raised for new ventures has increased by over one hundredfold. That old tired economy, wheezing from neglect in the 1970's, has been swept aside by a young, powerful locomotive of progress carrying a trainload of new jobs, higher incomes, and opportunities for more and more Americans of average means.

So, to marshal more venture capital for more new industries—the kind of efforts that begin with a couple of partners setting out to create and develop a new product—we intend to lower the maximum capital gains tax rate to 17½ percent.

Under our new tax proposal the oil and gas industry will be asked to pick up a larger share of the national tax burden. The old oil depletion allowance will be dropped from the tax code except for wells producing less than 10 barrels a day. By eliminating this special preference, we'll go a long way toward ensuring that those that earn their wealth in the oil industry will be subject to the same taxes as the rest of us. This is only fair. To continue our drive for energy independence, the current treatment of the costs of exploring and drilling for new oil will be maintained.

We're determined to cut back on special preferences that have too long favored some industries at the expense of others. We would repeal the investment tax credit and reform the depreciation system. Incentives for research and experimentation, however, would be preserved.

There is one group of losers in our tax plan—those individuals and corporations who are not paying their fair share or, for that matter, any share. These abuses cannot be tolerated. From now on, they shall pay a minimum tax. The free rides are over.

This, then, is our plan—America's tax plan, a revolutionary first for fairness in our future, a long overdue commitment to help working Americans and their families, and a challenge to our entire nation to excel—a challenge to give the U.S.A. the lowest overall marginal rates of taxation of any major industrial democracy, and yes, a challenge to lift us into a future of unlimited promise, an endless horizon lit by the star of freedom, guiding America to supremacy in jobs, productivity, growth, and human progress.

The tax system is crucial, not just to our personal, material well-being and our nation's economic well-being; it must also reflect and support our deeper values and highest aspirations. It must promote opportunity, lift up the weak, strengthen the family, and perhaps most importantly it must be rooted in that unique American quality, our special commitment to fairness. It must be an expression of both America's eternal frontier spirit and all the virtues from the heart and soul of a good and decent people—those virtues held high by the Statue of Liberty standing proudly in New York Harbor.

A great national debate now begins. It should not be a partisan debate for the authors of tax reform come from both parties, and all of us want greater fairness, incentives, and simplicity in taxation. I'm heartened by the cooperation and serious interest already shown by key congressional leaders, including the chairman of the Senate Finance Committee, Republican

Bob Packwood, and the chairman of the House Ways and Means Committee, Democrat Dan Rostenkowski.

The pessimists will give a hundred reasons why this historic proposal won't pass and can't work. Well, they've been opposing progress and predicting disaster for 4 years now. Yet here we are tonight a stronger, more united, more confident nation than at any time in recent memory.

Remember, there are no limits to growth and human progress when men and women are free to follow their dreams. The American dream belongs to you; it lives in millions of different hearts; it can be fulfilled in millions of different ways. And with you by our side, we're not going to stop moving and shaking this town until that dream is real for every American, from the sidewalks of Harlem to the mountaintops of Hawaii.

My fellow citizens, let's not let this magnificent moment slip away. Tax relief is in sight. Let's make it a reality. Let's not let prisoners of mediocrity wear us down. Let's not let the special interest raids of the few rob us of all our dreams.

In these last 4 years, we've made a fresh start together. In these next 4, we can begin a new chapter in our history—freedom's finest hour. We can do it. And if you help, we will do it this year.

Thank you. God bless you, and good night.

Note: The President spoke at 8 p.m. from the Oval Office at the White House. His remarks were broadcast live on nationwide radio and television.

Message to the Congress Transmitting Proposed Tax Reform Legislation
May 29, 1985

To the Congress of the United States:

We face an historic challenge: to change our present tax system into a model of fairness, simplicity, efficiency, and compassion, to remove the obstacles to growth and unlock the door to a future of unparalleled

innovation and achievement.

For too long our tax code has been a source of ridicule and resentment, violating our Nation's most fundamental principles of justice and fair play. While most Americans labor under excessively high tax rates that discourage work and cut drastically into savings, many are able to exploit the tangled mass of loopholes that has grown up around our tax code to avoid paying their fair share—sometimes to avoid paying any taxes at all.

The American people want change and for very good reason. Our present tax code is not only unfair, it slows economic growth and job creation, and hinders technological advancement by interfering with free markets and diverting productive investment into tax shelters and tax avoidance schemes. In 1981, we made the first necessary, historic step by cutting tax rates and opening the way to vibrant economic growth and expanding opportunity for all Americans. Now is the time to build on our success, to redesign the basic structure of our tax system in order to discourage non-productive eco-

nomic activity, to encourage greater compliance and to liberate incentives still further.

Accordingly, I hereby submit my proposal to overhaul our tax code based on the principles of simplicity and fairness, opening the way to a generation of growth. This is a tax proposal we can be proud of, a proposal that will help fulfill America's commitment to fairness, hope, and opportunity for all its citizens.

I urge your prompt enactment of this historic program for redesigning the tax code, and I look forward to working with you toward that end.

RONALD REAGAN

The White House,
May 29, 1985.

Remarks and a Question-and-Answer Session With Reporters Following Discussions With King Hussein I of Jordan
May 29, 1985

The President. I have just concluded a very useful meeting and lunch with King Hussein. We all recognize that the positive atmosphere which has developed in the Middle East recently can be credited in great measure to His Majesty King Hussein. Steps he's taken over the last year gave new momentum to the search for peace.

Our discussions today have provided further evidence of Jordan's commitment to a peaceful resolution of the Middle East conflicts, which should prompt a sense of gratitude from men of good will everywhere.

The United States has long played a central role in the Middle East peace process. We're proud of what we've helped accomplish, and we look forward to continuing to make meaningful contributions. But we hope that His Majesty's courageous steps forward can lead to direct negotiations between the parties, based on United Nations Security Council Resolutions 242 and 338, by the end of this year. And we'll do our part to help bring this about.

Our goal remains a just, lasting, and comprehensive peace which will satisfy the le-

gitimate rights of the Palestinian people and provide for the security of all states in the region, including Israel.

We recognize Jordan's economic and security needs. And in the spirit of working together, I have told the King that we will be able to count on the United States for assistance in addressing problems which Jordan may face in those areas.

We're pleased and proud to have had His Majesty here with us today.

The King. Thank you very much, indeed, Mr. President, for your kind words.

Ladies and gentlemen, I have had a full, friendly, and useful discussion with the President on all issues of mutual concern.

Regarding the prospects of peace in our area, I have told the President that a just, comprehensive, and durable peace in the Middle East should secure the legitimate rights of the Palestinian people, including their right of self-determination within the context of a Jordanian-Palestinian confederation.

I have also assured the President that on the basis of the Jordan-PLO accord of 11th

February and as a result of my recent talks with the PLO and in view of our genuine desire for peace, we are willing to negotiate, within the context of an international conference, a peaceful settlement on the basis of the pertinent United Nations resolutions, including Security Council Resolutions 242 and 338.

We are offering a unique opportunity for peace which might not be with us for long. I hope the United States, under the courageous and dedicated leadership of President Reagan, will find a way to seize this opportunity and respond positively to our peace efforts. The active and balanced role of the United States is an essential element for the success of the peace process.

I should like to thank the President for his hospitality and kind words and wish him continued good health and every success.

Q. Your Majesty, a question, please.

The King. Go ahead.

Q. If you can hear me, sir, can you explain, please, why Jordan needs an international conference in order to negotiate with Israel? Couldn't it do it directly? Could you elaborate a little on what your thinking is?

The King. In that regard, it is our hope that an international conference would enable the parties to the conflict to negotiate the establishment of a just and durable peace in the Middle East.

We need the international umbrella to offer us the opportunity to negotiate. And when I speak of negotiations, I obviously mean negotiations amongst the party to the conflict—in other words, negotiations between the Arab side, in this case a Jordanian-Palestinian delegation, with Israel on the other side.

Q. Mr. President, would the United States participate?

The President. Would we what?

Q. What is your view of such an international conference?

The President. This is under discussion, and we have not resolved some differences that we have in views on this. But we're going to certainly continue in these discussions.

Q. Well, what are the objections, Mr. President——

Q. What are the problems that remain, the definitions of Palestinian representation

in the delegation? Have you agreed on the Palestinian representation in the delegation, especially Jordan said PLO should be represented?

The President. We have made it very plain heretofore, and nothing has changed, with regard to those conditions under which we would meet with the PLO.

Q. Your Majesty, if I may ask, whether it's an umbrella of an international conference or not, you would be negotiating directly with Israel for the first time, would you not?

The King. Well, I can cite an example of the international conference of 1973. We met, and negotiations were carried out between the Arab side and Israel.

Q. So, you're saying this is not new. This is not a different form of direct negotiation?

The King. This is, I believe, a last chance for peace. We are approaching it, as I've explained, determined to do all we could for the establishment of a just and durable peace in our area. And obviously, when we speak of negotiations, we speak of them within the context of an international conference, but negotiations amongst the parties to the conflict.

Q. On a nonbelligerent basis?

The King. Well, we certainly are approaching the whole issue not in a belligerent fashion. I'm almost sure of that.

Q. Your Majesty, has the PLO agreed to this framework, sir? Has the PLO agreed to this framework?

The King. What I have said in my statement is the result of my discussions with the PLO, yes.

Q. Your Majesty, are you committed to going forward with this this year?

Q. Talks can take place this year?

The King. I am certainly hoping very, very much indeed that we will see some progress this year, yes.

Q. Mr. President, have they come up with a Palestinian delegation acceptable to you?

The President. This is all being worked on right now with us—or together. This is what we're discussing.

Q. Mr. President, the King has said that this opportunity will only be with us for a short time. In view of the situation in Lebanon, is there not something that the United States can do immediately to speed this process?

The President. Who's he asking? Which one of us——

Q. Mr. President, the King has said that the opportunity for peace may be a very short one. In view of the situation in Lebanon, is there not something the United States can do to speed the process—and do something immediately?

The President. We think that the situation in Lebanon with regard to the peace process will be resolved completely when Israel has made its complete withdrawal from Lebanon.

Q. Mr. President, do you want——

Q. But what about the Soviets?

The President. Wait a minute, there's a young lady over here's been trying for——

Q. Mr. President, do you feel the need to send a new envoy to the area to be able to continue all these negotiations between the different parties?

The President. Well, no. The people we have working there are going to continue.

Q. What about the Soviets?

Q. Mr. President, do you want to involve the Soviets at this point, at this preliminary point in this quest for a peace agreement? Do you think that would help or hinder the process?

The President. Well, I'm not going to respond to that question because, as I say, we're still discussing this whole matter, and I'm not going to get into any great details—things of that kind.

Q. Is that one of the problems, Mr. President? Is that one of the problems—Soviet participation?

The President. As I say, just generally, we're discussing and hopeful at arriving at a solution.

Q. Your Majesty, does your proposal include Soviet participation?

The King. I've spoken of an international conference of the five permanent members of the Security Council.

Q. So, the Soviets would be included?

The King. Well, that's what we're all working on, as the President has said.

Q. Well, Your Majesty, when you talk about 242 as being a governing principle, are the Palestinians agreed on that? Are

you telling us——

The King. Yes, sir. I am saying that.

Q. ——that the Palestinians agree that 242 and 338 are the governing resolutions?

The King. Every word I've made in my statement is a result of agreement between us and the PLO.

Q. Arafat, the PLO.

The King. PLO, yes.

Q. Okay.

Q. Mr. President——

Q. Your Majesty, did you just——

The President. Wait, wait, wait. One second. Wait.

Q. Will you recognize the PLO if they accepted 242 and 338?

The President. Now, what?

Q. Would you recognize the PLO if they accepted 242 and 338?

The President. His Majesty has said that they've discussed this and, yes, that this——

Q. I'm asking if you would recognize—the United States would recognize the PLO if they accept 242 and 338 explicitly?

The President. Well, as I've said, our terms have been made very plain for quite some time as to what is necessary for us to negotiate with the PLO, and they remain unchanged.

Q. Your Majesty, did you discuss the sale of Hawk missiles by the U.S. to Jordan?

The King. I think we've said enough, sir.

Q. Why did you say it was the last chance?

Q. Mr. President——

Q. Did we get all the points you asked us to ask about?

The President. Well, because—oh, I will answer then this word that this was the last chance, and then this is the last we're going to take.

The last chance—I think that the conditions have never been more right than they are now to pursue this peace. And who knows whether those conditions will ever come as close together again as they have now. So, that's why I think the term "last chance." And I think we ought to keep that in mind that perhaps it is the last chance.

And now, we're not going to take any more questions. And I feel a few drops of rain, and it doesn't bother His Majesty or me, but we don't want any of you to get wet, so—[laughter]——

Note: The President spoke at 1:31 p.m. in the Rose Garden at the White House. Earlier, the President and King Hussein met in the Oval Office and then attended an expanded meeting with U.S. and Jordanian officials in the Cabinet Room. Following the meetings, the President and King Hussein attended a luncheon in the Residence.

Remarks on Tax Reform to Concerned Citizens
May 29, 1985

Good afternoon, and welcome to the White House. I'm glad you could be here so that we can celebrate the day together.

I don't know if you happened to be watching TV last night, but the networks were kind enough to give me a few minutes to speak about a subject that's very close to my heart and close to your wallets. I'm talking about our historical—or historic proposal to completely overhaul that old jalopy of our tax system, replace it with a fairer, simpler, sleeker, more compassionate model—an all-American tax plan providing new freedom, fairness, and hope for all.

Short of sending the IRS, the Internal Revenue Service, on a permanent holiday, this historic reform will give the long-suffering American taxpayers the most relief they've had since, well, at least since our historic 23-percent tax cut of 1981.

They say that as you grow older you get set in your ways and that certain habits become ingrown. I guess when it comes to cutting taxes, I'd have to plead guilty to that. But I gave them fair warning. After those first dramatic tax rate cuts passed, catapulting our economy out of malaise and putting American industry on the cutting edge of progress, I told them, "You ain't seen nothin' yet!" [Laughter]

Our proposal is not a tax increase, and it will not increase the deficit. It will mean lower taxes for a majority of Americans, with expanded opportunities to save and invest. We want to do away with the trials and tribulations of filling out your tax forms for as many people as possible. Eventually, as many as half of all the taxpayers won't have to worry about 1040 Forms. They won't have to fill out any tax form at all. We're thinking of calling this one the zero form.

We're replacing the present steeply graded system of 14 different tax rates with a flatter, simpler, 3-step design that will allow you to keep more of each individual dollar that you earn. That means you'll get to save more of that raise that you earned, or if you go out there and work extra hard, you know that you're doing it for yourself and your family, not just to line the pockets of the Federal Government. It's our belief that the tax system should no longer be an obstacle course on the road to success.

What does America's tax plan mean for the average family? Well, I enjoy talking statistics, so let's talk a few. Of those who file and pay taxes, 7 in 10 will pay at a maximum rate of 15 percent, and fully 97 percent of all taxpayers will pay no more than 25 cents on the very last dollar they earn. Only 3 percent of America's families will have to pay at the highest rate, which will be 35 percent.

We're also going to give the American family a long overdue break by virtually doubling the personal exemption to a full $2,000. [Applause] Well, after that I guess I don't have to explain to you—that's $2,000 for every man, woman, and child. We're also increasing the standard deduction to $4,000 for a joint return. That means a family of four wouldn't pay a cent in income taxes on the first $12,000 of income earned.

Our plan will also mean an historic correction of a problem we've let go on too long—the increasing tax burden on low- and fixed-income Americans that's been knocking the bottom rungs off the ladder of opportunity. A compassionate, profamily opportunity society should give a break as well to those Americans struggling to get by and move up. And that's exactly what we intend to do.

By hiking the earned income tax credit, indexing it for inflation, and practically doubling the personal exemption, we can make sure that the working families do not suffer under the burden of Federal taxation. Giving a leg up to those struggling to move up is what America is all about. And that's a top priority of our tax proposal.

We're also going to make some other chances to help families—or changes, I should say, not chances. Right now our tax system discriminates against homemakers, making IRA's fully available only to spouses who work outside the home. We're going to change that. Believe me, the work of the homemaker deserves to be treated with as much dignity and worth as that of any other worker. Well, it's a pretty hare-brained social policy that punishes spouses who decide to stay home and take care of the children. So, now every husband and wife will each have full access to an IRA tax-deductible savings account up to $4,000 a couple every year.

I think you can begin to see that making ends meet is going to be a lot easier for a lot of people under our plan, especially those of low and modest incomes who find it difficult to cope under the existing unfair code.

We're making many changes. But while we're throwing out the bad in the old tax law, we're being sure to keep the good, with special attention to those provisions that protect our families. The home mortgage interest deduction will be kept in full for principal residences, and no less than $5,000 will still be deductible for other interest expenses, which could include a second residence.

Deductions for charitable giving, medical bills, and casualty losses and the current preferential treatment of Social Security and the exclusion of veterans' disability payments will be maintained.

Now, you may have noticed that I haven't mentioned some tax deductions which are currently on the books—tax loopholes for things like windmills and so-called educational cruises on oceanliners. But we're eliminating or drastically curtailing these

sort of tax dodges, which are really no more than windfalls to a privileged few, loopholes that everyone else ends up paying for through higher tax rates.

Also, in the interest of fairness, we're removing the reduction—or the deduction for State and local taxes, which has until now been one of the major pressures pushing up the tax rates of the American people. I don't believe that we can justify a system that forces taxpayers in low-tax States to subsidize the big-spending policies of a few high-tax States. That really is taxation without representation. And contrary to what some have been saying, lower rates, doubling the personal exemption, and raising the standard deduction will more than make up for the loss of State and local tax deductions for most taxpayers.

On the corporate side, we're streamlining the present ad hoc system of deductions in order to set the stage for an entrepreneurial renaissance of business formation, job creation, and technological advancement. By lowering the overall tax rates that affect corporations but making sure that every profitable corporation pays some tax, we will be untangling our economy from a bureaucratic tax code that has been distorting our free markets and slowing economic growth.

Together with a lower top rate on personal and corporate income, these changes will immediately open up new horizons to America's entrepreneurs, unlocking the full potential of American industry, and creating jobs and opportunity for all Americans, including those in our hard-pressed cities.

It's been remarked that there are three stages of reaction to a new idea like our tax proposal. First stage is: "It's crazy. It'll never work. Don't waste my time." The second: "It's possible, but it's not worth doing." And finally: "I've always said it was a good idea. I'm glad I thought of it." [*Laughter*] Well, we're rapidly sweeping up on that third stage. [*Laughter*]

Even those in this town who are still reluctant are being lifted up and carried forward by the momentum of public support for a fundamental change in our tax laws. And once called impossible, tax fairness and simplification are now all but inevitable.

687

Congressman Rostenkowski and Senator Packwood have committed themselves to move ahead on tax simplification. Sure, there are those who still have the special interest fever, and they're going to do everything they possibly can to torpedo our program for economic freedom. But with your help and all those cards and letters flooding into Rosty—[*laughter*]—signaling support of tax simplification, we have only one thing to say: America, go for it!

I'm going to paraphrase a statement by Admiral Farragut—cleaned up just a little: Blast the torpedos! Full speed ahead! [*Laughter*] For too long we've lived with a tax system that is a blot, a stain on the shining mantle of our democratic government. We've quietly tolerated a tax code which we know is an outrage, one riddled through with special privileges and inequities that violates our most fundamental American values of justice and fair play.

As I said last night—and I bet a lot of you here today would agree with me—in its very spirit and substance our tax system could only be described as un-American. Well, there are two things we can do about it. We can either declare April 15th a day of national mourning—[*laughter*]—or we can change the system. And I don't think Americans can recognize an injustice without trying to change it.

Now, that's how this great country got started. Our forefathers rebelled against the injustice of oppressive taxation. In place of King George's despotism, they created a government of, by, and for the people—a new democratic nation in which all men were created equal.

Today we're undertaking another great adventure in freedom—a second American revolution, a peaceful revolution of hope and opportunity. And one of its first orders of business is to toss our present moldy tax code overboard and get a new one.

It's my most profound hope that this effort will be a bipartisan one, that forward-looking Members from both sides of the aisle in Congress will join us in this great endeavor. If I get up to Boston in the near future, I'm going to invite Tip O'Neill over for tea to discuss a—[*laughter*]—tax proposal. It makes sense, the two of us having our own Boston tea party. [*Laughter*]

But for the sake of our traditions and for the sake of our present well-being and future happiness, we must take this next vital step toward freedom. It'll be good for our economy; it'll be good for individuals; it will be fairer and more just. But most of all, it will help strengthen America's most important institution—the family. As I said last night, this is the single, strongest, profamily initiative in postwar history.

The family is the moral core of our society, the repository of our values, and the preserver of our traditions. The family's like a tree with its roots in the experience of past generations and its branches reaching boldly out into the future. Our families are the safe haven where we're taught charity, generosity, and love and from which spring our most cherished concepts of human dignity and the worth of each individual life. It's there that we learn to nourish the young and care for the elderly.

In our contemporary society, we find so many of our fundamental values have come under attack, but I believe the moral vision of family life is still carried in America's heart. And we know that the underlying truth of that vision is what keeps us good and strong and makes our nation the land of the free and the home of the brave.

In raising the next generation of Americans, the tired breadwinner and the exhausted homemaker are doing the essential work of our society.

You know, every once in a while I've heard people say we don't have any heroes anymore. They haven't looked around their own neighborhood. You see them getting up, sending the kids off to school, going to work every morning, supporting their church and their charity and all the good things in this society. You bet they're heroes. It's through their sweat, toil, and tears that the foundations of our society are built, and America's tax plan will simply give them a little help.

We've come too far down the road of progress to turn back now. I don't believe that having tasted the success of these last 4 years, we still shrink from the challenge to make that success complete. Together we can make 1985 one of the milestone years in history, a date that future generations will look back on as marking a crucial step in the steady ascent of human freedom. We can do it. And if you help, we'll do it this year.

My friends, it's been an honor and a pleasure to talk to you on this, the dawn of the second American revolution.

I'd just like to tell you one line that a Senator spoke back around 1913 when they were debating the income tax amendment.

And on the floor of the House this gentleman said, "We don't need this tax for government's needs. We must have it for government's wants." Well, they've had long enough for their wants. We're going to get them back to their needs.

Thank you. God bless you all.

Note: The President spoke at 2:32 p.m. in the East Room at the White House.

Designation of L.E. Thomas as a Member of the Board of Visitors to the United States Naval Academy
May 29, 1985

The President today announced his intention to designate L.E. (Tommy) Thomas to be a member of the Board of Visitors to the United States Naval Academy for the term expiring December 30, 1987. He would succeed Bernard E. Smith, Jr.

Mr. Thomas has been in the car dealership business since 1951 and currently is the owner of Tommy Thomas Chevrolet in Panama City, FL. He has served as president of the Alabama Automobile Dealers Association (1962); president, Birmingham Sales Executives Club (1963); and president of the Oneonta Chamber of Commerce (1964). He was awarded the Silver Knight award by the National Management Association for his efforts on behalf of the free enterprise system.

Mr. Thomas graduated from Aviation Mechanics and Aerial Gunnery School at Jacksonville Naval Air Station (1943). He served in the U.S. Marines (1943–1945) and in the Reserves (1947–1950). He is married, has three children, and resides in Panama City, FL. He was born July 7, 1925, in Elmira, NY.

Executive Order 12517—Delegation Concerning the United States-India Fund for Cultural, Educational, and Scientific Cooperation
May 29, 1985

By the authority vested in me as President by the Constitution and statutes of the United States of America, including section 301 of Title 3 of the United States Code, and in order to delegate certain functions concerning the United States-India Fund for Cultural, Educational, and Scientific Cooperation to the Secretary of State, it is hereby ordered as follows:

Section 1. All functions vested in the President by the United States-India Fund for Cultural, Educational, and Scientific Cooperation Act (Title IX of Public Law 98–164, 97 Stat. 1051; "the Act") are delegated to the Secretary of State.

Sec. 2. India rupees provided to the President for purposes of Title IX of the Act and under Title III of the Departments of Commerce, Justice, and State, the Judiciary, and Related Agencies Appropriation Act, 1985 (Public Law 98–411, 98 Stat. 1545) are allocated to the Secretary of the Treasury for investment to generate earnings for purposes ot Title IX of the Act.

RONALD REAGAN

The White House,
May 29, 1985.

[*Filed with the Office of the Federal Register, 11:05 a.m., May 30, 1985*]

Proclamation 5348—Very Special Arts U.S.A. Month, 1985
May 29, 1985

By the President of the United States of America

A Proclamation

Art is one of the most important forms of human expression. Whether as creators or as spectators, Americans participate in the arts in some form almost every day, and their lives are made richer by this activity. Art also brings us into contact with the rich aesthetic tradition of our civilization, while the art of other cultures can be one of the best introductions available for those who want to learn more about them.

The importance of art makes it essential that all Americans be able to make use of this unique resource. The National Committee, Arts with the Handicapped, is an educational affiliate of the John F. Kennedy Center for the Performing Arts. During the past eleven years, it has served as the coordinating agency for arts programs for disabled children, youth, and adults. The Very Special Arts Program that it sponsors provides ongoing arts programs for many Americans with disabilities.

The Very Special Arts Program makes it possible for disabled Americans to participate in the arts and enrich their lives in the same way as all other Americans. Through it, they can gain the opportunity for self-expression within the context of our rich cultural tradition. This program deserves the support and assistance of all Americans.

In recognition of the importance of arts education in the lives of everyone, including those with disabilities, and in celebration of Very Special Arts Programs throughout the country, the Congress, by Senate Joint Resolution 103, has designated the month of May 1985 as "Very Special Arts U.S.A. Month" and authorized and requested the President to issue a proclamation in observance of this event.

Now, Therefore, I, Ronald Reagan, President of the United States of America, do hereby proclaim the month of May 1985 as Very Special Arts U.S.A. Month. I encourage the people of the United States to observe this month with appropriate ceremonies, programs, and activities.

In Witness Whereof, I have hereunto set my hand this twenty-ninth day of May, in the year of our Lord nineteen hundred and eighty-five, and of the Independence of the United States of America the two hundred and ninth.

RONALD REAGAN

[*Filed with the Office of the Federal Register, 2:21 p.m., May 30, 1985*]

Note: The proclamation was released by the Office of the Press Secretary on May 30.

Remarks at the "Prelude to Independence" Celebration in Williamsburg, Virginia
May 30, 1985

Thank you, ladies and gentlemen, Governor Robb, Senator Trible, Mayor Walker, and distinguished members here of the Williamsburg Foundation, the officials of that organization, and you ladies and gentlemen.

It is very good to return to this city which is so closely associated with the birth of the American Republic. Boston is called the

Cradle of Liberty, Philadelphia is where the Liberty Bell first rang, but Williamsburg, too, has an honored place in our history and our hearts. Because, as you have been told, here a practical plan for American self-government and a declaration which became the basis for the Bill of Rights of our Constitution were written, endorsed, and sent out to the world by the Virginia Legislature.

Here the arguments against unjust taxation rang out like a firebell in the night, and the chief arguer, Patrick Henry, gave our movement for independence the one thing it needed to become a revolution—he gave it passion.

And here, through long hours of great debate in the capitol behind me, the people of the colony evolved irresistibly from British subjects to American patriots.

And so, I'm happy and honored to speak in Williamsburg today. For I, too, mean to speak of liberty and a practical plan to increase its measure in our country. I wish to speak also of the philosophical underpinnings of that plan, for whatever happens to it, I mean for it to be understood.

Two nights ago I unveiled our proposal to revolutionize the Federal tax code. I spoke of the system as it is now, and as we wish it to be. But just for a moment today I want to note how our modern tax system evolved from a modest attempt to raise modest revenues to the behemoth to which we are currently beholden.

The Federal income tax only began in 1913. At that time some strange things happened. When it was being debated in the Congress one man spoke prophetically—or I should say, very honestly when he said, "We don't need this tax for government's needs. We need it for government's wants." And he was pretty prophetic, but there was another man that was almost laughed out of public life and public office, a Senator who said, "If we pass this amendment, we may very well see the day when the government could think it could take as much as 10 percent of a person's earnings." [*Laughter*] They thought that was a pretty ridiculous statement.

Well, this income tax was instituted because the Federal Government needed more money to operate because there was a widespread feeling that the rich ought to contribute to the system that made their riches possible. It was a system aimed almost exclusively at the wealthy, a class tax, as opposed to a mass tax.

The first tax rates were low. The 1913 income tax imposed a top personal rate of 6 percent. And you had to report an income of more than a half a million dollars a year to pay it. The poor and the middle class paid nothing. The personal exemption was $3,000. Now you know why they're called "the good old days." [*Laughter*]

During the First World War tax rates were increased, but they were relaxed again during the 1920's. Right up until the eve of World War II, the Federal income tax was still a tax limited to the wealthy. It affected only 4 or 5 million people, and their taxes yielded, in all, less than 20 percent of the Nation's revenues.

But during and after the war a great change came—tax rates were increased, exemptions were reduced, and inflation brought more people into the tax structure. Withholding was introduced for the first time, and suddenly just about every working American was paying the Federal income tax. And the tax suddenly was the largest single component of government revenues.

What followed, we know too well—the tax system began to grow and grow, rates were pushed higher, more and more people found themselves paying more and more money. Ironies abounded. As the tax system grew bigger and more powerful, it also grew more incompetent. And as it demanded more to pay for programs to better our lives, it became more heartless.

Seventy-two years after its inception, what is our Federal tax system? It's a system that yields great amounts of revenue, yes, but even greater amounts of discontent, disorder, and disobedience. It's a system in which the top personal tax rate rose to 94 percent. And it only came down from those heights when a young man named John Kennedy decided some time back that while it's all right for the Federal Government to be your partner, it's not quite fair that he be your boss.

It's a system from which no full-time wage earner is exempt. Now, almost everyone, no matter what their circumstances or their special needs, must pay. In fact, so many pay so much that someone has figured out that it takes the average taxpayer until almost May every year before he starts working for himself. Up till then, he's working for the government.

It's a system that allows an exemption of barely over $1,000 a year for each child born into a family, an exemption so utterly out of touch with the realities of everyday life that it serves as a metaphor for exactly how ridiculous the entire structure is.

It's a system that increasingly treats our earnings as if they were the personal property of the Government, with decent citizens called before the Internal Revenue Service to answer for their income and expenditures and show their papers and their proof in a drama that is as common as it is demeaning. Wasn't there a line a couple of hundred years ago about being safe in your books and your records?

Well, it's a system so utterly complex and ultimately inexplicable that half the time the tax professionals themselves aren't sure what the rules are—a system that even Albert Einstein is said to have admitted he couldn't begin to fathom. You know, it's said that his hair didn't look that way until after he experienced his first tax form. [*Laughter*]

It's a system that is antigrowth and antiproductive for it discourages the very virtues that make a man and woman valued contributors to society. You know this if you've ever worked overtime to pay for your child's braces. The money you earn is taxed at so high a rate as to render your extra efforts almost totally without point or profit.

It is, finally, a system whose most serious sin may be its most subtle for it seems so rigged, so unfair, that it corrupts otherwise honest people by encouraging them to cheat.

Thirty and forty years ago you didn't hear people brag at social get-togethers about how they got their tax bill down by exploiting this loophole and engineering that credit. But now you do. And it's not considered bad behavior. After all, goes this thinking, what's immoral about cheating a system that is itself a cheat? That isn't a sin,

it's a duty.

Our Federal tax system is, in short, utterly impossible, utterly unjust, and completely counterproductive. It's earned a rebellion, and it's time we rebelled.

We must move and move now for all the reasons I've named and more. The current system just doesn't work anymore. The underground economy and the cult of cheating prove that this is so. What to do? Well, we took our first step toward a second American revolution in 1981 when we lowered tax rates for every individual in this country. This increased our economic freedom and sparked one of the greatest economic expansions in our nation's history.

But now is the time to take the second step, the historic step for America's tax plan. Now is the time to turn our tax system around once and for all and make it more just, more equitable, more comprehensible. Now is the time to create a tax system that will encourage and not penalize the creation of wealth and jobs. Now is the time, in short, to get the Federal Government off our backs and out of our way.

You're familiar with our plan. We propose to simplify the rate structure down to just three rates—15, 25, and 35 percent. We propose to increase the personal exemption by almost a hundred percent, from just over $1,000 to $2,000 for every taxpayer and dependent with a provision to increase it still more if inflation occurs. We propose to end unproductive tax shelters so that no one will be able to hide in the havens that privilege builds. But we will retain those few tax advantages that speak directly to how Americans live their lives and how the American economy operates. For instance, the mortgage interest deduction stays for the house that you own and live in, and along with that, no less than $5,000 in other interest expenses would still be deductible.

We propose to lower the top corporate income tax rate from the current 46 percent to 33 percent, and we've proposed a new minimum tax to deal with those corporations and individuals that have managed not to pay any tax at all.

Now, you might see the present tax structure as a hornet's nest. Our plan is an attempt to burn away the webs and the nest and let the Sun shine in to start new, start clean, and start over. Is this long overdue reform revolutionary? I believe it is, but we conservatives don't launch revolutions lightly. There must be a clear and compelling need, and the reform that's proposed must bear within it the promise to better the lives of all of our citizens, and the reform must be achievable.

Well, our tax reform plan of 1985 satisfies those requirements. Beyond that, it will go a long way towards satisfying America's hunger for justice, thirst for opportunity, and search for freedom. By lowering the highest tax rates on individuals and businesses, we encourage the growth of our economy. Lower tax rates, of course, increase the after tax wages for additional work. And so, people will be able to profit once again from working overtime or at a second job. Lower tax rates will also increase the aftertax return on savings and investment. And so, people will tend to save and invest more. This will provide the money the economy needs to build additional factories or buy more machinery.

These are not just economic facts. What I am speaking about is a profound public good. For when a society has high levels of economic growth, most everyone benefits, especially the poor. More jobs are created, there's more money to spend on medical care and education, the standard of living increases, and all of this enhances the quality of life.

By simplifying the rate structure itself and by eliminating the devices by which the powerful evade their responsibilities, we ensure that people in the same circumstances will pay the same levels of tax. We'll ensure that those now earning lower incomes will not find themselves paying a greater percentage of their income in taxes than those earning higher incomes. We'll ensure that from the hard streets of the cities to the soft green hills of the suburbs the people of America will pay their fair share and no more.

So, I believe the virtues of our proposal are clear. You'll know that your neighbor is paying roughly what you are, that no one will be able to rig the system to his benefit. You'll know that the tax rates themselves won't creep up and mug you just as you

start to succeed in the world. And we'll all know that those least able to pay will pay little or nothing.

But what is the broader purpose of our tax proposal? Well, I'm glad to be standing in front of the House of Burgesses as I address that question. The members who spoke in this capital said no to taxes because they loved freedom. They argued, "Why should the fruits of our labors go to the Crown across the sea?" Well, in the same sense, we ask today: Why should the fruits of our labors go to that Capitol across the river?

You know, we have a saying among some of us there in Washington: We're going to stick to it. If I sound like I'm talking about government as something else, I am. When we who are now there start talking about government as "we" instead of "they" we've been there too long. [*Laughter*]

When you read our tax code you realize that somehow we got lost along the way. Somewhere along the line, we stopped understanding that people worked not for the government, but for themselves; that they get up every morning and go out into the world to earn their bread, not to support a government, but to support their families. We, the citizens of the United States, have got to get public law back in line with private imperatives.

I see all of you out here and I'm sure that most of you have a wallet in your pocket or your purse. Just think of what you have in that wallet, how you earned it, and what you want to spend it on. That's your money. That's your effort. That's your freedom there. The disposition of that money belongs, by rights, to you.

I want a tax system that keeps as much of that money in your wallet as possible. The primary reason is moral. It's your money, after all. But the secondary reason is practical. You'll do more for the economy with it, and you'll do more to benefit your fellow citizen with it than the government will.

Now, I'm going to be speaking a great deal about tax reform over the next few weeks and months. And I expect it to be challenging. It's a shrewd turn of the American people that, when you announce a plan to help them, they stand back and scrutinize it and approach with a question: Now, how are you going to hurt me this time? [*Laughter*] Well, this is not an unreasonable question. So many times the American people have been promised better and been delivered worse. But I tell you from the bottom of my being, this is a plan that's going to help our country by helping every individual in it.

Our tax proposal will not increase the deficit; it is revenue neutral. It is not a tax increase; in fact, it's designed to be the first step toward lower tax rates in the future. When you simplify a thing, make its lines clear and clean, you make it much less vulnerable to quiet mischief and selfish tinkering. So, if some Congress of the future gets it in its head to increase taxes—to raise the lowest personal tax rate from 15 percent to something higher—the public will immediately see what is happening and understand what is happening. And they will rise up and resist, and they will be heard.

In a way what I'm trying to say is an unclean, unsound structure is vulnerable to mischief. When the house is a mess and everything's chaos, you're not likely to notice when something is missing. But when the house is clean and designed with balance you tend to notice if somebody tries to cart off the furniture. [*Laughter*]

Our forefathers fought a revolution for two reasons: to give liberty to a naturally independent people and to secure, in the words of a Burgess who met here, ". . . Prosperity in the Community and Security to Individuals." The idea of freedom impelled them; it intoxicated them. And it's freedom that impels us still.

History's not a static thing. History moves; it never stops. And the American Revolution continues as we continue to push back the barriers to freedom. We, like the patriots of yesterday, are struggling to increase the measure of liberty enjoyed by out fellow citizens. We're struggling, like them, for self-government—self-government for the family, self-government for the individual and the small business and the corporation.

And so, we offer this tax proposal of 1985 in the name of growth and fairness. We offer it to ensure generations of economic power for the citizens of this free and vital nation. We're doing it in the name of our children, and we're doing it in the memory of those towering souls who walked these streets and met in this capitol and together wrested justice from the heart of oppression. We offer this plan in memory of the patriots who took a handful of demoralized little colonies and invented a nation. We're doing it to continue their work.

I ask for your help. Without it, nothing can be accomplished; but with it, everything is possible. And so, in the truest sense, this great effort—America's tax plan—is in your hands. And for that I'm truly thankful. And I can only urge: America, go for it!

Thank you. Thank you, and God bless you. And thank you for inviting me. It's been wonderful to be here.

Thank you very much.

Note: The President spoke at 10:36 a.m. at the Colonial Capitol Building. The Colonial Williamsburg Foundation sponsored the celebration.

Remarks on Arrival in Oshkosh, Wisconsin
May 30, 1985

The President. Well, listen, this is really a welcome, and I want to thank you very much. If you didn't recognize him, that gentleman coming down the steps with me was your Senator Kasten from Wisconsin. And this is quite a welcome.

I saw a sign out there—"Where's Nancy?"

Well, I have to tell you a little about First Ladies. They don't really—not supposed to work for the Government. They're not on salary or anything. But they find out that they do have a lot of things that they have to do. And that's true of her. And, you know, she's been working very hard on the drug programs to make sure that more young people in our country don't become victims of drugs. And I'm very proud of her for doing that. So, I'll have to say hello for her.

There aren't any words to tell you how much I appreciate your all coming out here for a welcome of this kind. I know you'd rather be in school.

Audience. No–o–o!

The President. [*Laughter*] You wouldn't? [*Laughter*]

Audience. No–o–o!

The President. All right.

Well, I understand now that some of your folks are waiting downtown for me to make a speech down there, and I'll have to get going.

Audience. No!

The President. But I also want to tell you something that I'll have to tell them again, too, when I get down there. When I was your size, your age, one of the things I wore most of all were some bib overalls that said, "Oshkosh, B'gosh."

Audience. Yea!

The President. So, now, finally, I'm going to be in the place where they came from— those overalls.

Audience. Yea!

The President. But I was very happy in those days—in wearing them.

And, again, I just want to thank you all. It's great to see you, and wish we could spend more time here, but the Senator and I have to go downtown now.

Thank you all. God bless you.

Audience. Yea!

Note: The President spoke at 1:18 p.m. to schoolchildren gathered at Wittman Field.

Remarks to Citizens in Oshkosh, Wisconsin
May 30, 1985

The President. Thank you. Now, don't go too far away with those. I won't wait till the ranch. Every once in a while I see on my schedule that I am having a working breakfast with the congressional leadership. As long as I am working, I'll wear those. [*Laughter*] It might impress them enough that we will get things done.

I thank you all. It's good to be in Oshkosh, B'gosh! A lot of your schoolchildren were out at the airport when we came in, and I told them that when I was their age and their size I was wearing them, and at that time, though, they had it on and as a kind of a trademark in stripes where it said "Oshkosh, B'gosh" on the overalls.

But it's an honor to be here with your outstanding Senator Bob Kasten and your superb Members of the Congress, Tom Petri and Toby Roth. Each of them is serving the people of Wisconsin and our nation with high distinction. And Bob Kasten has long been a leader for the kind of reform that I would like to talk to you about now.

The night before last, television networks were kind enough to give me a few minutes to talk about our system of taxation. I announced our plan to put more resources into the hands of the American people by making our tax code more simple, fair, and efficient and the most sweeping change in our tax laws it would be in more than 70 years. I knew we were on the right track when the high-priced tax attorneys started shedding tears after I spoke.

And now that I've come to Main Street America, and now that I have seen a smile on the face of Oshkosh, I know we said the right thing. [*Applause*]

Thank you. I'm delighted to be with you and to join in the fun. And, my friends, if you will permit me, I would like to begin by conducting a little poll using an impartial and scientifically selected sample—you. Would you mind answering some questions? For example, do the people of Oshkosh want our tax system to be complicated and unfair?

Audience. No!

The President. Well, do you want steeply

rising tax brackets that punish achievement and hurt the American family?

Audience. No!

The President. Or would you like a dramatic simplification that eliminates loopholes and makes our tax system straightforward, fair for all?

Audience. Yes!

The President. And would you like to see a tax plan that increases personal exemptions, brings tax rates further down, and reduces the tax burden on working Americans and their families?

Audience. Yes!

The President. Well, that's the tax plan that, with your help, we can and will pass this year.

You know, I've been asking people informally about tax reform everywhere I go. And the answers are just the same everyplace I know of except for one city—Washington, DC. Sometimes folks back there are a little slow to catch on. I may need some help getting it through to them that the American people consider it high time for a change in our tax laws. Can I count on you to give me a hand?

Audience. Yes!

The President. All right. Our tax proposal is a true first. It's a plan for fairness, incentives, rewards, and simplicity in taxation. It won't raise taxes or increase the deficit. In fact, we call it America's tax plan because it will lower taxes and expand opportunities. Do you remember about 6 weeks or so ago, the last tax day, April 15th, how you felt, how you prepared to sign that complicated document that turned over a big chunk of your income to bureaucrats you'd never even met? Remember what your kitchen or dining room table looked like with the forms and the receipts and the tax tables spread out across it?

Well, under our tax proposal most of you, if you choose, will never have to go through anything like that again. Form 1040 will be shortened and more than half of all Americans won't have to fill out a tax form at all. It will be just that easy.

Let me tell you how it will work. And don't worry, I can keep it short and simple because it is short and simple. To begin with, we intend to replace the present steeply rising system of 14 different tax brackets with a flatter, three-step design that will allow you to keep more of each additional dollar that you earn. Currently, tax rates range all the way up to 50 percent, 14 brackets. Under our proposal there will be only three tax rates—15, 25, and 35 percent, period.

For families, the lowest rate of 15 percent would apply to each dollar of taxable income up to $29,000. The next tax rate, 25 percent, would apply to each dollar of taxable income from $29,000 to $70,000. And the top rate, 35 percent, would take effect on taxable income over $70,000. Now, no matter how much you earned after that, Uncle Sam would never get more than 35 cents of each dollar that you earn.

What does America's tax plan mean for the average family? Well, of those who file and pay taxes, 7 in 10 will pay at a maximum rate of 15 percent. And fully 97 percent of all taxpayers will pay no more than 25 cents on the very last dollar they earn. Only 3 percent of America's families will have to pay at the highest rate, 35 percent.

The next part of our plan will further help the American family. You may remember that back in 1948 the personal exemption was set at $600. Today, 37 years later, after inflation during the 1970's eroded the value of the dollar and made it so much more expensive to raise children or care for elderly parents, the personal exemption has risen all the way to, well, just to $1,040. And frankly, my friends, I think that's a little ridiculous.

To give your families the break they've so long deserved, we intend to increase the standard deduction to $4,000 and to nearly double the personal exemption for every taxpayer and dependent to $2,000. And we're going to raise it, right away, starting January 1st, 1986. You know that sounds so good, even to me, I'm going to say it again. We intend to double the personal exemption to $2,000, effective next year. And by the way, that $2,000 would also be indexed to protect against any rise in inflation.

Suppose your family wants to save some extra money and invest it in an IRA. Right now our tax system limits—you know what those are, those revenue accounts where you can put money in a savings account and you don't have to pay tax on it for having done that—right now, our system limits IRA's to $2,250 per household. Again, my friends, that makes no sense. Homemakers should have the same rights to IRA's as wage earners. In economic terms, homemakers produce goods and services that are invaluable. And by nurturing our children, caring for us when we get sick, and looking after the elderly, they—perhaps more than any others—give our country its strength and heart.

And here's where we get the next part of our tax plan, also designed to help the family. Under our proposal, every husband and wife will have the same access to IRA accounts—up to $4,000 a year for each couple.

Now, you can begin to see how much easier that'll make it for families here in Oshkosh and around the country to make ends meet. Consider a Wisconsin family of four struggling at the poverty line with an income of $12,000. By raising the level at which people begin to pay taxes and by doubling the personal exemption, our plan would ensure that the family would pay no Federal income tax at all—none.

Or consider a larger working family of six, one that lives right here in Oshkosh, earning the median income—that's at the half-way mark of all earnings, $26,000. By taking advantage of our proposal, including the new IRA provisions, that Oshkosh working family could reduce its taxable income to only $8,000 and pay 15 percent of that $8,000, just $1,200 for an effective tax rate of less than 5 percent.

Now, I want you to know that I've got a little holdout. There's a little group over there—I'm going to raise their taxes. But seriously, all the way up and down the income scale, the overwhelming majority of American families will find themselves with more resources to devote to their children, to pay for their home, and, perhaps here in Oshkosh, to buy a boat, and to put away for retirement. That sounds pretty good to me. Does it sound good to you, too? [*Applause*]

Well, all right. You know, they may have heard you all the way to the Congress in Washington.

But another problem with the tax system as it stands now is that it looks like Swiss cheese. Now, Wisconsin is famous cheese country, so you know what I'm talking about—big holes no matter how you slice it. Well, under our proposal, tax breaks for things like windmills and so-called educational ocean cruises will all be eliminated or drastically reduced.

We want to do away with a tax code that reflects years of lobbying efforts by powerful special interests. Instead, we want a tax code for Main Street America—one that will help people like the worker at Oshkosh Truck Corporation and his family, the youngster who's just graduated from Oshkosh West High and is—[*applause*]—and maybe is starting work here in town as a clerk at Kline's—[*laughter*]—the teller at the First Wisconsin National Bank and her children.

But as we throw out the bad in the old tax system, we'll be sure to keep the good. The home mortgage interest deduction reflects our nation's historic commitment to the value of homeownership. For principal homes it's a deduction that we intend to keep. Likewise we will retain preferential treatment for Social Security and veterans' disability payments and keep in place the current itemized deductions for charitable contributions.

On the business side, our tax plan will be just as sweeping, one that will clear the way for surging business formation, job creation, and the technological innovation that fosters so much of our economic growth. The tax plan for business includes a reduction in the maximum corporate tax rate, down from 46 to just 33 percent. The institution of a minimum tax to make certain that all corporations pay a fair share and a reduction in the maximum tax on capital gains.

Now, many of you'll remember the late Congressman from Wisconsin, our dear friend, Bill Steiger. Bill's father, Carl, is on the dais here today. I would like to have him stand. Carl, take a bow.

Well, back in 1978 Bill Steiger engineered a cut in the maximum capital gains tax from 49 to 28 percent. Almost instantly the amount of venture capital available in our country rose sharply, making it possible to expand existing companies and to form new ones, creating new jobs in the process.

The very next year scores of new companies were formed in California's Silicon Valley alone. And in the years since, we've seen capital raised for new ventures increase by over a hundredfold.

Is there someone there that needs some help? We've got a doctor here, I know. If they could get backstage, I know we have got a doctor back here. All right.

Building on Bill Steiger's achievement, in 1981 we cut the top capital gains tax down to 20 percent. And now we want to cut it again down to 17½ percent. This new cut will foster still more growth and job creation, a renaissance of American entrepreneurship.

America was born in the midst of a great revolution sparked by oppressive taxation. There was something about the American character—open, hard-working, and honest—that rebelled at the very thought of taxes that were not only heavy but unfair.

Today the proud American character remains unchanged. But slowly and subtly, surrendering first to this political pressure and then to that, our system of taxation has turned into something completely foreign to our nature—something complicated, unfair, and in a fundamental sense, un-American. Well, my friends, the time has come for a second American revolution.

From Oshkosh to Miami to Santa Fe, we, the people, must unite. Those who have been elected to positions of public trust must show true leadership and political courage. For the sake of our traditions of liberty, for the sake of our strength and prosperity as a nation, but most of all for the sake of our families, we must take this next step toward freedom. Let us resolve here today, during this dawn of the second American revolution, that this great task shall be accomplished. We can do it, and if you help, we will do it this year. America, go for it!

You know, back in 1913—I just say this in closing—back in 1913 when they were discussing having an income tax and having an amendment to the Constitution to make it possible, there was one Senator who rose on the floor of the Senate, and he said something at the time that was very prophetic. He said, "We must have this tax not for government's needs, but for government's wants." Well, I think for the last 70 years government has been wanting too much, and let's get it back to where we pay for what it needs and no more.

I just told some people back in Williamsburg, Virginia, this morning, that some of us who are there now in Washington—we keep talking about ourselves as "we" when we talk about government—or I should say "they" when we talk about government. And I've told our people, when we start talking about government as "we" instead of "they," we have been there too long. I think I outlasted them.

So, I thank you all. God bless you all and God bless this wonderful city of Oshkosh. Thank you all very much.

Note: The President spoke at 1:40 p.m. at the Winnebago County Courthouse.

Nomination of Dennis R. Patrick To Be a Member of the Federal Communications Commission
May 30, 1985

The President today announced his intention to nominate Dennis R. Patrick to be a member of the Federal Communications Commission for a term of 7 years from July 1, 1985. This is a reappointment.

Mr. Patrick has been a Commissioner on the Federal Communications Commission since 1983. Previously, he was a special assistant to the Assistant Secretary of Commerce for Communications and Information, Department of Commerce (1983); Associate Director for Legal and Regulatory Agencies, Office of Presidential Personnel, the White House (1982–1983); and an attorney with the law office of Adams, Duque & Hazeltine in Los Angeles, CA.

Mr. Patrick graduated from Occidental College (A.B., 1973) and the University of California at Los Angeles (J.D., 1976). He was born June 1, 1951, in Los Angeles, CA, and now resides in Washington, DC.

Remarks at the Great Valley Corporate Center in Malvern, Pennsylvania
May 31, 1985

The President. Governor Thornburgh, ladies and gentlemen here on the dais, and all of you: I thank you very much. It's great to be here at the Valley Corporate Center, the workplace of the future. Here in the Route 202 corridor, America is truly on a high-tech highway, rolling full speed ahead, and there ain't no stopping us now.

Let me tell you, it's also great to leave Washington once in awhile and see what the real America is up to. I've heard that some of the advanced-technology companies up here are working on what they call very large integrated systems. Now, that's nothing new to me. Most of the time in Washington I feel like I'm working with a very large disintegrating system. [*Laughter*]

Although, I have to confess I'm not very up to date on all this new high-tech computer lingo. I thought hacking meant what the Congress has been trying to do lately to the defense budget. [*Laughter*]

But we do have a new tax plan that I think the high-techers—in fact, all Americans will like. Last Tuesday night, I addressed the Nation on our proposal to totally revamp our nation's Rube Goldberg tax system and turn it into a model of efficiency and fairness that works for the new age of silicon chips, CAD/CAM, bioengineering, robotics, and all the other marvels of this new technological era.

We call it America's tax plan because it will mean tax relief for American families, individuals, and businesses. It'll mean less redtape and lower rates for the majority of Americans. It will not be a tax increase; it will not expand the deficit. It will increase incentives to work, save, and invest. And it will mean that American technology can shoot ahead, and it will help America outproduce and outcompete anybody, anywhere in the world.

Our tax cuts in 1981 lifted our economy out of—you've heard the word back then—"malaise" and into an almost 2½ years of growth. If those tax cuts could take a sick economy suffering from runaway inflation, skyrocketing interest rates, declining investments, sinking morale, and slumping initiative and turn it into the strongest, most dynamic and innovative economy in the world, think what America's tax plan can do today. We can build success on top of success. We can ignite the second stage of our booster rockets and blast this economy to new heights of achievement. We can do it, and we will do it.

With your help and the leadership of Pennsylvania's finest—Governor Dick Thornburgh, Senator Arlen Specter, Congressmen Dick Schulze, Bob Walker, and Larry Coughlin, and others like Senator Heinz who aren't here today—we're going to go the distance.

For too long our tax code has been a damper on the economy. Steeply rising tax rates punish success, while tangled and needlessly complicated rules of compliance can boobytrap any new enterprise that can't afford high-priced lawyers and tax consultants to protect itself from the tax man.

April 15th wasn't so long ago. And I'm sure many still remember that mounting feeling of frustration and resentment as you worked late into the night trying to make sense of the maze of bureaucratic rules and regulations. Nearly half of all Americans threw up their hands in dismay and went to get professional help on their taxes this year. Well, paying someone to figure out how much you owe the Government in taxes just adds insult to injury. Don't you think America's had enough?

Well, we're going to break apart the shackles and liberate America from tax bondage. We're going to dramatically simplify the whole process of paying taxes. Eventually, as many as half of you won't have to worry about the 1040 Form. In fact, you won't have to fill out a tax form at all. That's how I spell relief. [*Laughter*]

We're going to replace the present obstacle course of some 14 different brackets with a flatter, simpler, three-step design that will allow you to keep more of each additional dollar you earn. The present tax structure locks Americans into a future of ever-climbing tax rates. Even though our tax system is indexed for inflation, as real incomes increase the tax bite grows larger and larger. America's tax plan is a dynamic model for the future that gives Americans the freedom to get ahead, move up, and succeed. This means that if you work overtime or get a raise, if you're promoted to a better job, if you're able to save some money and invest it, then fewer of those dollars will go into Uncle Sam's pockets and more will end up in your wallets, where they belong.

We think that the Federal Government should get out of the business of punishing people for hard work and success with high tax rates. Instead, we want to encourage all Americans to follow their dreams, to go as far as their courage, initiative, and creativity will take them. We think that's what America is all about, and that's why we're saying: America, go for it.

Now, this——

Audience. [*Inaudible*]

The President. Hey! That's why. Well, that's where I got the idea. [*Laughter*]

Well, this proposal will be a first for the American family—as I said on Tuesday, the single strongest profamily initiative in postwar history. Raising a family in this modern age isn't always easy, and the Federal Government hasn't been helping much. Since 1948 the personal exemption has been declining in value to the point where it's now only a fraction of its original worth, due to inflation. But we're going to turn that around by virtually doubling the personal exemption to a full $2,000. That's $2,000 for every taxpayer and dependent in the

family. Together with our hike in the standard deduction of up to $4,000 for joint returns, our tax proposal would mean that a Pennsylvania family of four wouldn't pay a penny in Federal income taxes on the first $12,000 of income earned. And with the lower marginal rates of our new design, they'd pay only 15 cents on each dollar of taxable income from there on up to $29,000.

In helping America's families, we know that we have right on our side. Our proposal also would provide equal access to IRA's for homeowners—or homemakers—I'm sorry—homemakers. And that's as much as $4,000 of tax-deductible IRA savings funds per couple each year. And we're keeping those deductions in the present code on which our families depend, such as home mortgage interest deductions on principal residences and at least $5,000 in other interest payments which could include a second residence. Deductions for charitable giving, medical bills and casualty losses, the current preferential treatment of Social Security and the exclusion of veterans' disability benefits will be maintained.

This is one tax proposal that America can be proud of. It promotes all our nation's most basic values. It's profamily and profairness, pro-opportunity, and most of all profuture. I bet a lot of people here can remember the bad old days of the seventies when punitively high tax rates on capital gains were squeezing the life out of our venture capital markets and putting the lid on innovation. Since then, two dramatic cuts in the capital gains tax have produced a renaissance of entrepreneurship and catapulted America to the cutting edge of high-tech.

Venture capital—that's the capital that funds the new, adventurous, high-risk industries like many of these here in the Great Valley Corporate Center. It is thriving. From a disastrous low of $39 million in the depths of 1977, the total of venture capital in this country—it exploded to $4.2 billion last year.

High-tech is spreading across the country like wildfire. Silicon Valley is being joined by Silicon Bayou in Louisiana, Silicon Mountain in Colorado and, as some have called it, the Silicon Valley of the East—right here in the Route 202 corridor.

Well, we've got good news for our silicon cities. We're going to feed the fires of technological invention by lowering the capital gains tax once again, giving it a top rate of 17½ percent. We're going to make sure that American technology wins the race to the 21st Century.

There's been an evolution in thinking on this issue in Congress. About a year ago, the then-Senator from Massachusetts, Paul Tsongas, confessed that he had voted against the first capital gains tax cut for the very simple reason, to him—he said that it was probusiness, while most House Democrats were reflexively antibusiness. Senator Tsongas had a change of heart though after the measure was passed. And to quote the Senator, he said: "That bill, which I did not support, did more for the economy of my State than anything I did as a Congressman."

Well, today we can see that many more Democrats in the Congress have had a change of heart, and that we're building strong bipartisan support for a progrowth policy.

I hope you all saw Rosty on TV last Tuesday night after my speech. "Rosty" is short for Dan Rostenkowski, the Democratic chairman of the House Ways and Means Committee. He's all for tax fairness and simplification, too. And he asked the American people to write in and tell all of us in Washington where they stand. Well, we've gotten a tidal wave of mail telling us, quite simply, to go for it. So, keep those cards and letters coming in. [*Laughter*]

By streamlining our tax code, we'll speed our progress. Our present tax code diverts too many of our precious resources into wasteful loopholes and tax dodges like jojoba bean shelters, windmills, racehorse writeoffs, and Cayman Island trusts. These shelters are not only economically unjustifiable, they're unfair to the vast majority of unsheltered taxpayers who have to make up the difference with higher tax rates. It's about time that we pulled our investment money out of foreign tax havens and put it back into fueling America's economic growth.

By closing these loopholes we'll be able to put the three tax rates that most directly

affect America's—or cut the three tax rates, I should say—that directly affect America's entrepreneurs. Not only will we lower the capital gains tax and give venture capital another shot in the arm, we'll also cut the corporate tax, continue graduated tax rates for small corporations, and bring the top personal income tax rate down to its lowest level in more than five decades. In addition, we're preserving incentives for research and experimentation that are so important to investment in techological innovation. As I said last Tuesday night, it's our ambition to make these next decades of American history the age of the entrepreneur.

Every day America's inventing a better future—new miracle medicines to cure disease and prolong life, and ingenious new mechanical organs that can duplicate the work of nature; silicon chips, tinier than your thumbnail, are able to process more information than a whole computer used to; new metals and plastics that strengthen our defenses and would extend man's habitat into space by the end of the century; new disease- and insect-resistant grains that will help feed a hungry world. Maybe even someday high-tech will invent a cure for the bureaucracy down in Washington. [*Laughter*]

Right now the army of lobbyists and special interests are dug in around the Capitol Building, firing every weapon in their arsenal in an attempt to shoot down our proposal for tax fairness and tax simplification. They're allied with the Washington sophisticates and so-called experts who tell us that tax simplification will never pass, that it challenges too many of those interests and takes away the special privileges of a powerful few who like the present tax code just fine. But I think the sophisticates and the lobbyists and the experts have forgotten one thing—they've forgotten about you.

They've forgotten about the rest of America that exists beyond the shores of the Potomac. So, I think it's about time that we reminded them. Let's make them hear what America thinks. And remember, Washington is a few miles off, so you're going to have to speak up if you want Pennsylvania to be heard.

Do the people of Pennsylvania want a tax

system that's needlessly complicated and unfair?

Audience. No!

The President. I can hear you, but the walls of that Capitol Building are pretty thick.

Do the people of Pennsylvania want a tax system that discourages entrepreneurship and puts a lid on innovation?

Audience. No–o–o!

The President. Do you want a tax system of, by, and for the tax lawyers?

Audience. No–o–o!

The President. You're doing just fine. [*Laughter*]

Or do you want a tax plan that is fairer and simpler, that lowers tax rates for your families, and that gives high-tech a boost?

Audience. Yes!

The President. Thank you. [*Laughter*] You just made my day. [*Laughter*]

Hope and optimism are what drive the American people, and if they set their minds on something, you can bet it'll happen. We're a can-do nation, with little patience for the voices of resignation and the status quo. Two centuries ago, not far from where we stand today, General Washington and his army of patriots endured terrible suffering in the snows of Valley Forge because they knew that their winter of hardship would be followed sooner or later by a springtime of liberty. Those were the times that tried men's souls. These are the times that challenge our hearts and minds.

It's time to take another step in that long march of freedom, to make our future big and adventurous and worthy of our past. Now is the time to inaugurate the second American revolution of hope and opportunity, to declare our independence once again, and to commit ourselves to the ideals that have always kept us strong and free and true. We can do it.

Thank you, and God bless you all, and let's get in out of the rain.

Note: The President spoke at 12:11 p.m. to an outdoor gathering of center employees and their families. Following his remarks, the President had lunch with a group of chief executive officers of area companies. He then traveled to Camp David, MD.

Nomination of Chester Evans Finn, Jr., To Be an Assistant Secretary of Education
May 31, 1985

The President today announced his intention to nominate Chester Evans Finn, Jr., to be Assistant Secretary for Educational Research and Improvement, Department of Education. He would succeed Donald J. Senese.

Since 1981 he has been a professor of education and public policy, lecturer in political science, and codirector of the Center for Education Policy at Vanderbilt University. He was legislative director in the office of Senator Daniel Patrick Moynihan in 1977–1981; research associate in governmental studies at the Brookings Institution in 1974–1977; Counsel to the American Ambassador to India in 1973–1974; special assistant to the Governor for education, Commonwealth of Massachusetts in 1972–1973.

He was director of policy analysis at the University of Massachusetts in 1971–1972 and Staff Assistant to the President at the White House in 1969–1971.

He graduated from Harvard University (B.A., 1965; M.A., 1967; Ph.D., 1970). He is married, has two children, and resides in Nashville, TN. He was born August 3, 1944, in Columbus, OH.

Nomination of Robert K. Dawson To Be an Assistant Secretary of the Army
May 31, 1985

The President today announced his intention to nominate Robert K. Dawson to be an Assistant Secretary of the Army (Civil Works). He would succeed William R. Gianelli.

Since 1984 Mr. Dawson has been serving as Acting Assistant Secretary of the Army (Civil Works). Previously, he was Principal Deputy Assistant Secretary of the Army (Civil Works) in 1981–1984; administrator of the Committee on Public Works and Transportation, U.S. House of Representatives in 1974–1981; and legislative assistant to U.S. Representative Jack Edwards in 1972–1974.

He graduated from Tulane University (B.S., 1968) and Cumberland School of Law, Samford University (J.D., 1971). He is married, has two children, and resides in Alexandria, VA. He was born January 22, 1946, in Scottsboro, AL.

Nomination of James Johnson Duderstadt To Be a Member of the National Science Foundation
May 31, 1985

The President today announced his intention to nominate James Johnson Duderstadt to be a member of the National Science Foundation for a term expiring May 10, 1990. He would succeed Edwin Ernest Salpeter.

Mr. Duderstadt has been with the University of Michigan since 1969 serving as assistant professor (nuclear engineering) (1969–1972); associate professor (1972–1976); professor (1976–1981); and dean of the college of engineering (1981–present).

He has served as a consultant to NASA Lewis Research Center (1972), the U.S. Army Missile Command (1973–1975), and the Argonne National Laboratory (1975–1979).

Mr. Duderstadt graduated from Yale University (B.A., 1964) and the California Institute of Technology (M.S., 1965; Ph.D., 1967). He is married, has two children, and resides in Ann Arbor, MI. He was born December 5, 1942, in Fort Madison, IA.

Appointment of Bettye Collier-Thomas as a Member of the National Afro-American History and Cultural Commission
May 31, 1985

The President today announced his intention to appoint Bettye Collier-Thomas to be a member of the National Afro-American History and Culture Commission for a term expiring January 18, 1986. She would succeed Alexis M. Herman.

Dr. Collier-Thomas is currently executive director of Bethune Museum-Archives, Inc.

Previously, she was a lecturer at Howard University (1982–1983); a special consultant to the National Endowment for the Humanities (1977–1981); and a consultant to the National Council of Negro Women at the National Endowment for the Humanities (1977).

Dr. Collier-Thomas graduated from Allen University (B.A., 1963), Atlanta University

(M.A., 1966), and the George Washington University (Ph.D., 1974). She is married and resides in Washington, DC. She was born February 18, 1941, in Macon, GA.

Message to the Congress Reporting on the Whaling Activities of the Soviet Union
May 31, 1985

To the Congress of the United States:

Pursuant to the provisions of subsection (b) of the Pelly Amendment to the Fishermen's Protective Act of 1967, as amended (22 U.S.C. 1978(b)), I am reporting to you following certification by the Secretary of Commerce that the Soviet Union has conducted whaling activities that diminished the effectiveness of the International Whaling Commission conservation program.

Under the Pelly Amendment, when the Secretary of Commerce determines that a foreign country is conducting a fishing operation that diminishes the effectiveness of an international fishery conservation program, he will certify this determination to the President. After receiving a certification, the President may direct the Secretary of the Treasury to embargo the offending country's fishery products to the limits of the General Agreement on Tariffs and Trade. Within 60 days following the certification, the President is required to notify the Congress of any action taken under the certification.

On April 1, 1985, Secretary of Commerce Malcolm Baldrige certified the Soviet Union for whaling that diminished the effectiveness of the International Whaling Commission (IWC) conservation program. Secretary Baldrige based his determination on: (1) the Soviet harvest of Southern Hemisphere minke whales was greater than the level the United States considered the U.S.S.R.'s traditional share; (2) the 1984–85 IWC quota for Southern Hemisphere minke whales was exceeded due to Soviet harvest; and (3) there had been no indication that the Soviets intended to comply with IWC standards.

Southern Hemisphere minke whales are taken by the Soviet Union, Japan, and Brazil. The quota for these minke whales is divided into six areas. Brazil harvests whales from a land-based operation in Area Two, and Japan and the Soviet Union then divide the quota for the remaining five areas.

The Soviet Union, Japan, and Brazil have objected to the IWC Southern Hemisphere minke whale quota and, consequently, are not bound by the quota under international law. Even though the objections release the governments from any treaty obligation to observe the IWC limit, the taking of more minke whales than established by quota is inconsistent with this international conservation standard and, in the absence of any indication of compliance with IWC standards, diminishes the effectiveness of the Commission and its conservation program.

For the 1984–85 whaling season, Japan and the Soviet Union agreed not to exceed their 1983–84 harvest levels of 3027 and 3028, respectively, of Southern Hemisphere minke whales. These levels, if met, would exceed the 1984–85 IWC quota of 4224. Based on past allocations, the United States indicated that Japan and the Soviet Union could each take 1941 minke whales and remain consistent with the IWC limit. Japan has observed this limit, but the Soviet Union has not. We have taken a number of steps to resolve the Soviet whaling problem.

The trade sanctions authorized by the Pelly Amendment against Soviet fish products will not aid other Administration efforts to change the Soviet whaling policy. Under the Packwood-Magnuson Amendment, we cut in half Soviet-directed fishing allocations in our exclusive economic zone. We have also encouraged the Japanese to refrain from importing Soviet whale products taken contrary to the IWC conservation program, and Cabinet-level officials have met with Soviet officials to resolve the problem. These actions are designed to encourage the Soviet Union to observe the IWC program. A Pelly Amendment embargo, however, will have a negligible effect on the Soviet Union, as most of the products imported into the United States, such as king crab, are highly marketable elsewhere.

In addition, United States fishing interests could be seriously harmed by such a sanction. An embargo imposed in 1985 could cost the United States 90,000 metric tons of expected joint-venture catch and over $12 million. An embargo could result in the permanent dissolution of the U.S.-U.S.S.R. joint-venture company, which provides markets for underutilized species and fish that might solely be harvested by foreign vessels. Unemployment of U.S. fishermen and other related workers could also result from the loss of this joint-venture company.

In light of this assessment of the effect of an embargo on Soviet fishery products, I have not taken any action against the U.S.S.R. under the Pelly Amendment. If the Soviet Union makes no progress towards complying with the IWC program, I intend to reassess my position and take necessary action. I will send you a supplemental report at that time.

RONALD REAGAN

The White House,
May 31, 1985.

Radio Address to the Nation on Tax Reform
June 1, 1985

My fellow Americans:

I wonder how many of you know about the Quaker whose patience was sorely tried when the cow he was trying to milk kept kicking the milkpail over. Finally, he got up from the milking stool, faced the cow, and said, "Thou knowest I cannot strike thee. Thou knowest I cannot even curse thee. But doest thou knowest I can sell thee to someone who will?"

It's been a busy week here in Washington. We've made a proposal for merging tax reforms. It's also been a week in which we tried to bring a little Quaker wisdom here, too. And let me explain why the two go together.

You see, Washington doesn't take to change very well. Special interest groups set up offices here, hire some energetic staff members, make it a point to get to know the right people, and then use their influence to win special treatment. The accumulation of all these special privileges—and the tax code is the best example—frequently leads to a tangle of confusing laws and chaotic regulations. It's the public interest that suffers. And the ones who have to try and make sense of all the rules and regulations, not to mention footing the bill for the special privileges, are Americans like you who can't afford to hire a lobbyist in Washington.

Well, that's where the President comes in. The whole idea of the Presidency is having somebody in the Oval Office who can try to get above the bickering and buttonholing in the cloakrooms and corridors and say, "Look, enough of this. Let's just get something done for a change that will help the people."

You see, the President and the Vice President are the only ones in Washington elected by all the people. In a way then, the President should be the people's lobbyist, your lobbyist. And any President who wants to succeed should remember his first obligation is to the people. They elected him, and only they can give him the support he needs to get things done.

Well, that's certainly been the case in the last 4 years. The victories we've won belong to the people. You made them happen by writing, telegramming, or speaking personally to your Representatives and Senators. You made your voice heard here in Washington, a voice strong enough to make the politicians do what was right, not for the special interests but for America.

So, this week, once again, I've been trying to do my job by giving you the facts

705

and asking for your help. I won't spend a lot of time right now telling you about the current problems with our tax code. Each of you has had to face that nightmare every April 15th. So, that's why I proposed a sweeping new reform that will reduce the 14 tax brackets we now have to only 3—a reform that will reduce the many special tax privileges. If our plan goes through, making out your taxes each year will be more simple, and it will reduce all those feelings of unfairness and injustice that so many Americans rightly harbor about our current tax code.

In addition to bringing simplicity and fairness, our plan is also profamily. By raising your standard deduction, boosting exemptions to $2,000 for each taxpayer and dependent, and by expanding the IRA's to include spouses staying at home, our plan is progrowth. And, too, most people would pay lower taxes.

And should you decide to work overtime or put more into your savings, the Government would take less away than it does now. And needy families—those at the poverty line or near it—would no longer have to pay Federal income taxes at all. New incentives in the tax code would help them rely less on welfare and public assistance. We'd also be giving small business a hand, the companies largely responsible for providing most of the new jobs in America.

Our tax reform package has many other advantages. Believe me, I could go on. There isn't time for that because I need to get back to that Quaker and his cow. You see, here in Washington the special interests are trying to pick apart our tax reform package. Just as it has opposed so many of the other good things we've tried to do for the American people, much of official Washington is going to oppose this tax reform, too.

That's where all of you and a little Quaker wisdom come in. Just like that Quaker's cow, many in official Washington make a habit of kicking over the American people's milkpail. And as my chief of staff Don Regan said recently, we're going to need the people to go talk to the cow and maybe ask him a few questions about how he or she likes it here on the farm.

So, yes, we very much need your support, especially those of you who've never written before to your Representatives or Senators. Please make your views known, and remind official Washington that you expect to be listened to. Tell them the time for America's tax plan is long overdue. And tell them it's time they stopped letting the entrenched interests and special privileges kick over the milkpail.

Until next week, thanks for listening, and God bless you.

Note: The President spoke at 12:06 p.m. from Camp David, MD.

Nomination of John William Bode To Be an Assistant Secretary of Agriculture
June 3, 1985

The President today announced his intention to nominate John William Bode to be an Assistant Secretary of Agriculture (Food and Consumer Services). He would succeed Mary Claiborne Jarratt.

Since 1981 he has been serving as Deputy Assistant Secretary at the Department of Agriculture. Previously he was special assistant to the Assistant Secretary for Food and Consumer Services, Department of Agriculture. In 1979–1981 he was a congressional aide on the U.S. Senate Committee on Agriculture, Nutrition, and Forestry.

Mr. Bode graduated from the University of Oklahoma (B.A., 1977) and George Mason University School of Law (J.D., 1983). He is married, has one child, and resides in Alexandria, VA. He was born January 24, 1955, in Oklahoma City, OK.

Appointment of Frieda K. Wallison as a Member of the National Council on Public Works Improvement
June 3, 1985

The President today announced his intention to appoint Frieda K. Wallison to be a member of the National Council on Public Works Improvement. This is a new position.

Mrs. Wallison is an attorney and partner in the law firm of Jones, Day, Reavis & Pogue in Washington, DC. Previously, she was a partner in the firm of Rogers & Wells in 1978–1983; executive director and general counsel of the Municipal Securities Rulemaking Board in 1975–1978; a special counsel in the Division of Market Regulation at the Securities and Exchange Commission in 1975; and was with the firm of Carter, Ledyard & Milburn in New York City in 1966–1975.

She graduated from Smith College (A.B., 1963) and Harvard Law School (LL.B., 1966). She is married, has three children, and resides in Bethesda, MD. She was born January 15, 1943, in New York, NY.

Appointment of Mildred Lois Nichols Teas as a Member of the Library of Congress Trust Fund Board
June 3, 1985

The President today announced his intention to appoint Mildred Lois Nichols Teas to be a member of the Library of Congress Trust Fund Board for the term of 5 years from March 9, 1985. She will succeed Mrs. Charles W. Engelhard.

Mrs. Teas is a member of the Kent Waldrep International Spinal Cord Research Foundation. She serves on the executive committee of Texans for the Republic and as a member of the Dallas Historical Society.

She is married, has one child, and resides in Dallas, TX. She was born October 8, 1935, in Cisco, TX.

Executive Order 12518—Trade in Services
June 3, 1985

By the authority vested in me by the International Investment and Trade in Services Survey Act (Public Law 94–472, as amended by Section 306 of Public Law 98–573), and in order to assure that information necessary for developing, formulating and implementing United States policy concerning trade in services is collected, analyzed and disseminated, it is hereby ordered that Executive Order No. 11961 of January 19, 1977, as amended, is redesignated "International Investment and Trade in Services" and is further amended by (1) substituting "International Investment and Trade in Services Survey Act" for "International Investment Survey Act of 1976" wherever it appears; (2) substituting "(5)" for "(4)" in Section 2; (3) adding "and trade in services" after "investment" in Section 3; and (4) adding ", (5)" after "(4)" in Section 3.

RONALD REAGAN

The White House,
June 3, 1985.

[Filed with the Office of the Federal Register, 10:15 a.m., June 4, 1985]

Message to the Congress on Trade With Hungary, China, and Romania
June 3, 1985

To the Congress of the United States:

I hereby transmit the documents referred to in subsection 402 (d) (5) of the Trade Act of 1974 with respect to a further 12-month extension of the authority to waive subsection (a) and (b) of section 402 of the Act. These documents constitute my decision to continue in effect this waiver authority for a further 12-month period.

I include as part of these documents my determination that further extension of the waiver authority will substantially promote the objectives of section 402. I also include my determination that continuation of the waivers applicable to the Hungarian People's Republic, the People's Republic of China, and the Socialist Republic of Romania will substantially promote the objectives of section 402. The attached documents also include my reasons for extension of the waiver authority; and for my determination that continuation of the waivers currently in effect for the Hungarian People's Republic, the People's Republic of China and the Socialist Republic of Romania will substantially promote the objectives of section 402.

RONALD REAGAN

The White House,
June 3, 1985.

REPORT TO CONGRESS CONCERNING
EXTENSION OF WAIVER AUTHORITY

Pursuant to subsection 402(d)(5) of the Trade Act of 1974 ("The Act") I have today determined that further extension of the waiver authority granted by subsection 402(c) of the Act for twelve months will substantially promote the objectives of section 402, and that continuation of the waivers currently applicable to the Hungarian People's Republic, the People's Republic of China, and the Socialist Republic of Romania will also substantially promote the objectives of section 402 of the Act. My determination is attached and is incorporated herein.

The general waiver authority conferred by section 402(c) of the Act is an important means for the strengthening of mutually beneficial relations between the United States and certain countries of Eastern Europe and the People's Republic of China. The waiver authority has permitted us to conclude and maintain in force bilateral trade agreements with Hungary, the People's Republic of China, and Romania. These agreements continue to be fundamental elements in our political and economic relations with those countries, including our important, productive exchanges on human rights and emigration matters. Moreover, continuation of the waiver authority might permit future expansion of our bilateral relations with other countries now subject to subsections 402 (a) and (b) of the Act, should circumstances clearly warrant this renewal of the general waiver authority.

I continue to believe that extending the current waivers applicable to Hungary, the People's Republic of China, and Romania will substantially promote the objectives of section 402 of the Act.

Hungary.—Hungary has continued to take a relatively positive and constructive approach to emigration matters. Although three new emigration cases were recorded during the past year, all of them are on the way to being resolved. The number of Hungarian citizens who apply to leave Hungary remains small, and emigration permission is granted without undue difficulty. No sanctions are imposed on those who seek to emigrate, nor do emigration procedures appear excessive.

People's Republic of China.—China continued its relatively open emigration policy throughout the past year. In fiscal year 1984, our Embassy and Consulates in China issued nearly 13,000 immigrant visas, 30 percent more than the 10,000 issued in the previous fiscal year. The number of immigrant visas issued has increased every year since the U.S. normalized relations with China in 1979. In addition, our posts in

China issued 24,000 non-immigrant visas during FY–1984, compared with 16,000 the previous year, to Chinese who wished to study, conduct business, or visit relatives in the United States. Other Western countries have also experienced increases in Chinese travel and emigration.

Romania.—Emigration from Romania to all countries has more than tripled since 1975, the first year Romania enjoyed MFN status, and emigration to the United States was five times higher in 1984 than in 1975. In 1984, over 4,500 people departed Romania for the U.S., ethnic German departures for the FRG set another all-time high of nearly 15,000, and 1,908 Romanian Jews left for Israel, the highest annual figure since 1976. So far this year, departures for Israel have been running behind last year's peak levels, and there has been an upturn in ethnic German emigration following a reduced level of departures during the winter months of 1984–85. The Administration is continuing to seek improvements in Romanian emigration procedures, and will continue closely to monitor Jewish emigra-tion to Israel.

The Romanian government has continued to honor its assurances, which I received from President Ceausescu in June 1983, that Romania would not require reimbursement of education costs as a precondition to emigration.

While many problems remain in the emigration area, Romania's performance has continued to improve over the last year in respect to the numbers of people receiving exit documentation and time required to process their applications. On the basis of Romania's performance and the progress it has made in the area of emigration since last year, I believe that continuation of the waiver applicable to Romania will substantially promote the objectives of the Act.

For the above reasons, I have determined that continuation of the waivers for Hungary, the People's Republic of China and Romania will substantially promote the objectives of the Act.

Note: The message was released by the Office of the Press Secretary on June 4.

Memorandum on Trade With Hungary, China, and Romania
June 3, 1985

Memorandum for the Secretary of State

Subject: Determination under Subsection 402(d) (5) of the Trade Act of 1974—Continuation of Waiver Authority

Pursuant to the authority vested in me under the Trade Act of 1974 (Public Law 93–618), January 3, 1975 (88 Stat. 1978) (hereinafter "the Act"), I determine, pursuant to subsection (d) 402 (5) of the Act, that the further extension of the waiver authority granted by subsection 402 (c) of the Act will substantially promote the objectives of section 402 of the Act. I further determine

that the continuation of the waivers applicable to the Hungarian People's Republic, the People's Republic of China and the Socialist Republic of Romania will substantially promote the objectives of section 402 of the Act.

This determination shall be published in the *Federal Register*.

RONALD REAGAN

Note: The memorandum was released by the Office of the Press Secretary on June 4.

Nomination of Allie C. Felder, Jr., To Be a Member of the Board of Directors of the Overseas Private Investment Corporation
June 4, 1985

The President today announced his intention to nominate Allie C. Felder, Jr., to be a member of the Board of Directors of the Overseas Private Investment Corporation, United States International Development Cooperation Agency, for a term expiring December 17, 1987. This is a reappointment.

Dr. Felder is senior vice president of the Cooperative League of the U.S.A. in Washington, DC. He has been a member of the Overseas Private Investment Corporation since 1971. He taught at the International Cooperative Training Center at the University of Wisconsin and was an associate professor of agricultural economics at Hampton Institute. He spent 13 years in India as a consultant to the American International Association and for the Cooperative League of the U.S.A.

He graduated from Hampton Institute (B.S., 1943), the University of Illinois (M.S.C., 1947), and Ohio State University (Ph.D., 1952). He is married, has two children, and resides in Washington, DC. He was born August 12, 1921, in Durham, NC.

Nomination of Dwight A. Ink To Be an Assistant Administrator of the Agency for International Development
June 4, 1985

The President today announced his intention to nominate Dwight A. Ink to be an Assistant Administrator (Bureau for Latin America and the Caribbean) of the Agency for International Development, United States International Development Cooperation Agency. He would succeed Victor M. Rivera.

He has been Acting Director of the General Services Administration since March 1985. Previously he was a consultant to McManus Associates and the Agency for International Development for mission management and staff utilization. He chaired the U.S. delegation to Mexico for the U.S.-Mexico Exchange on Administrative Reform in May 1985. He was Vice President for Administration of the U.S. Synthetic Fuels Corporation in 1981–1984.

He was Director of the Community Services Administration from May to September 1981 and prior to that was Vice President for Management, National Consumer Cooperative Bank. In 1976–1980 he was director, Office of Sponsored Research and Continuing Education, the American University. He was Deputy Administrator of the General Services Administration in 1973–1976; first Assistant Secretary for Administration, Department of Housing and Urban Development, in 1966–1969; Assistant General Manager, U.S. Atomic Energy Commission, in 1959–1966.

He served as assistant to the Chairman of the AEC in 1958–1959; management assistant in 1955–1958; chief, Reports and Statistics Branch, Savannah River Operations Office, in 1952–1955; and program analyst, Office of Community Affairs, Oak Ridge Operations Office, in 1951–1952.

He graduated from Iowa State University (B.S.) and the University of Minnesota (M.A.). In 1942–1946 he served in the United States Air Force. He is married, has five children, and resides in Rockville, MD. He was born September 9, 1922, in Des Moines, IA.

Nomination of S. Bruce Smart, Jr., To Be an Under Secretary of Commerce
June 4, 1985

The President today announced his intention to nominate S. Bruce Smart, Jr., to be Under Secretary of Commerce for International Trade. He would succeed Lionel H. Olmer.

Mr. Smart has been with the Continental Group, Inc., since 1953, serving in various sales and general management positions (1953–1968) and as executive vice president, forest products operations (1969–1973); vice chairman, U.S. operations (1973–1975); and president and chief operating officer (1975–1980). He has served as chairman and chief executive officer of the Continental Group, Inc., since 1981.

Mr. Smart graduated from Harvard College (A.B., 1945) and the Massachusetts Institute of Technology (S.M., 1947). He is married, has four children, and resides in Fairfield, CT. He was born February 7, 1923, in New York, NY.

Remarks on Tax Reform at a Meeting With Corporate Leaders
June 4, 1985

The President. Well, I can handle what Jim has just said. I know that you've been up on the Hill testifying, and I'd like to add my thanks, and my thanks for your coming down here. Maybe you haven't had time to study our tax reform proposal, but I'm sure you have familiarized yourself to quite an extent with it.

It isn't perfect, as Jim has said, but we believe that it'll work and that we can surpass it. I add to that, having been out on the road for a few days in addition to the polls that we have seen, the people obviously do support this, and I'll be on my way again tomorrow morning.

We all know the shortcomings of the present system. It's unfair; it's hindered technological investment; it impedes economic growth; it does all the things that we've been blaming it for. You supported our efforts in '81 when we reduced taxes. And while we didn't reverse the spending increase of the government, at least we cut back on the rate of increase in spending, and certainly we reduced considerably the paperwork and the regulations that government was imposing on everyone. And the results speak for themselves.

For over 30 months now, at the present rate of growth in the economy, we've had a higher percentage of the working pool employed than any time in our previous history, low inflation rates, interest rates falling. And all our trading partners and their allies and even some of our unfriendly types out there have become envious of what we've done.

And now, thanks to your efforts, maybe we'll have an opportunity to finish the job of providing and securing economic good health for America. But there's an army of lobbyists—maybe you saw some of them up there on the Hill—and special interests that are dug in, and they're firing every weapon they own. But I think maybe you've shown them that there are loyal soldiers on the right side who can fire a few salvos themselves.

Together we can brighten the future for our children and our grandchildren. And I'm glad and proud that the American business community has statesmen like yourselves who are willing to come up here and do what you've done in support of this.

And now, as I said, I'm supposed to leave you and turn you back over to Jim and to Don Regan and discuss some, well, the specific provisions that directly concern you. And again, I'll say thanks to you for coming up here.

Reporter. Mr. President, some of the 1981 tax proposals which you just talked about are repealed in this new proposal. How do you justify that?

The President. Well, I think that that would simply mean that we did what we could at that particular time, knowing that there was more really that should be done. And this just shows that we're continuing to improve.

Q. How are you going to sell this in the Rust Belt, Mr. President?

Principal Deputy Press Secretary Speakes. Bob, I'm sorry. That's all.

Q. Thank you.

Note: The President spoke at 3:05 p.m. in the Roosevelt Room at the White House. In his remarks, the President referred to James A. Baker III, Secretary of the Treasury, and Donald T. Regan, Chief of Staff and Assistant to the President.

Proclamation 5349—Youth Suicide Prevention Month, 1985
June 4, 1985

By the President of the United States of America

A Proclamation

During the past 20 years, the suicide rate has tripled among young people aged 15–24. In fact, suicide has become the third leading cause of death in this age group. Last year alone, over 5,000 young Americans took their own lives, and many more attempted to do so.

When a young person commits suicide, it is a personal tragedy as well as a source of deep anguish for family, friends, and neighbors. But it is also a tragedy for society, which must cope not only with the loss of human potential that is the result of the death of any individual, but also with its responsibility to identify the causes of suicide and develop strategies to reduce its incidence. Although the issues involved in each case are complex and unique, we can draw encouragement from the fact that suicide is no longer a silent subject but a recognized public health problem that can and must be addressed.

Because the root causes of suicide involve so many different psychological, physical, social, and spiritual dimensions, successful preventive action requires the combined efforts of individuals, families, communities, organizations, and governments at all levels. Young people and families who have a member who may be contemplating suicide need to know that there are indeed places to turn for advice and assistance. People who come into contact with youth—educators, counselors, coaches, ministers, health care providers—can play a key role in helping a despondent young person by identifying the existence of a problem or contributing factors like drug abuse and family break-up. Government can assist through research and policies which strengthen the family unit and foster a sense of individual self-worth. In short, all of us have the opportunity and responsibility to help deal with this growing problem.

In recognition of the increase in suicide among America's youth and its consequences for our society, the Congress, by Senate Joint Resolution 53, has designated the month of June 1985 as "Youth Suicide Prevention Month" and authorized and requested the President to issue a proclamation in observance of this month.

Now, Therefore, I, Ronald Reagan, President of the United States of America, do hereby proclaim the month of June 1985 as Youth Suicide Prevention Month. I call upon the Governors of the several States, the chief officials of local governments, all health care providers, educators, the media, public and private organizations, and the people of the United States to observe this month with appropriate programs and activities.

In Witness Whereof, I have hereunto set my hand this fourth day of June, in the year of our Lord nineteen hundred and eighty-five, and of the Independence of the United

States of America the two hundred and ninth.

RONALD REAGAN

[*Filed with the Office of the Federal Register, 10:59 a.m., June 5, 1985*]

Note: The proclamation was released by the Office of the Press Secretary on June 5.

Remarks at the AT&T Technologies Plant in Oklahoma City, Oklahoma
June 5, 1985

The President. Thank you Chairman Brown, Governor Nigh, Senator and Mrs. Nickles, Congressman Mickey Edwards, all of you. You've made me so at home, I've begun to feel like a genuine Sooner. Come to think of it, the Sooner the better.

Well, I'm proud to be in the home of your champions, the Oklahoma City 89'ers. I'm proud to stand with all of you here on the grounds of this showcase industry for American technology; here on the frontlines where America is charging forward in the battle for international competitive success.

We want to help, so, I'd like to speak about our proposal to leave more earnings in the hands of you, the people, by making our tax code more simple and fair—the most sweeping change in our tax laws in more than 70 years. I seem to remember saying in my television speech that the power of these new incentives would send one message to an entire nation: America, go for it!

Well, within minutes of that speech, the telegrams began coming in. From North Bergen, New Jersey; Jacksonville, Florida; from Lake Oswego in Oregon—the voice of America was coming through loud and clear: Yes, let's go for it!

And I'm ready to do all I can, but I need your help. Are you with me? Can I count on you?

Audience. Yes!

The President. Thank you. We call our proposal America's tax plan because it means fairness for taxpayers and prosperity for our nation.

On the business side, the present tax code has a top corporate tax rate of 46 percent. That's too high. But it also provides loopholes that are big enough for a 747 to slide through. Well, you know, in recent years some of our biggest corporations paid no taxes whatsoever, while everyday working people have been taxed up to their eyeballs.

Audience. Yes!

The President. Well, I have a feeling you agree with me that enough is enough, and those days are over. From now on, all will pay their fair share.

Our tax plan would ensure that all corporations that earn sufficient income pay a minimum tax. We would also clear the way for more jobs, new products, and technologies by reducing the corporate tax rate from 46 percent to 33 percent. We would cut the maximum tax on capital gains from 20 percent to 17½ percent, because when we cut capital gains in 1978 and again in 1981, venture capital increased a hundredfold, producing new jobs, higher incomes, and more and more opportunities for Americans.

Now, good as that is, it still isn't good enough. Just like your company shot ahead of the pack, we won't be satisfied until the United States of America can outproduce, outcompete, and outsell anybody anywhere in the world.

Now, I'm delighted to see so many families here today, because when it comes to the income tax you pay, our plan represents the most important profamily proposal in postwar history. We would replace the present system of 14 different brackets with a simple 3-bracket system that will allow you to keep more of each additional dollar you earn. Right now, individual tax rates go all the way up to 50 percent. And you know

713

what that means when you work overtime, right? Yes, it's like Uncle Sam holding a giant stop sign, putting the brakes on your initiative and on progress.

Well, under America's tax plan, the three new rates would be 15, 25, and 35 percent, period. It'll give you the freedom to get ahead, to move up, to succeed. If you work overtime or get a raise, if you're promoted to a better job, if you're able to save some money and invest it, then few of those dollars—or fewer will go to line Uncle Sam's pockets and more will end up in your wallets, where they belong.

Sixty-nine percent of all taxpayers will pay the lowest rate of 15 percent; 28 percent will pay the middle rate of 25 percent; and only 3 percent of American taxpayers will pay the 35 percent top rate. And we're going to make the tax system so simple, so straightforward that at least half of all Americans, if they choose, won't even have to fill out a tax form.

That sounds pretty good to me, and I think you've made it evident it sounds pretty good to you, too.

There's more help on the way for families here in Oklahoma City and throughout America. To give your families the tax relief they deserve, we intend to raise the standard deduction for joint returns to $4,000. We would nearly double the personal exemption for every taxpayer and dependent to $2,000. And we would do this right away on January 1st, 1986.

Now, just in case you couldn't hear me all the way in the back there, I'm going to say it again. We intend to nearly double your personal exemption all the way up to $2,000 effective next year. I said that again; I know you heard me. I said it because I just like saying it. And that $2,000 would be indexed to protect against inflation.

We want to help your family save by expanding the limits also for individual retirement accounts, the things we call IRA's. Our present tax system limits IRA's to $2,250 when one spouse works in the home. You know, that means you can put the money in a retirement account, and you don't have to pay tax on it. I don't think this makes any sense to you, and we didn't think it makes any sense. We happen to think that the homemakers should have the

same rights to IRA's as wage earners. After all, our homemakers produce goods and services that, even in strictly economic terms, are invaluable. And by nurturing our children, caring for our ill, and looking after our elderly, homemakers give America its strength and heart.

Under our proposal, husbands and wives will have the same access to IRA accounts, and we'll put this change into effect by raising the IRA per household limit from $2,250 a year up to $4,000 for every household.

Now, as we put more resources into your hands, we intend to close the loopholes that benefit the few at the expense of the many. It's about time that we do away with tax breaks for windmills and so-called educational cruises on oceanliners and tax dodges like Cayman Island trusts. It's about time we pulled our money out of foreign tax havens and put it back into investments for you and the future of America.

Now, deductions——

Audience member. We love you, Reagan!

The President. Thank you. Deductions for State and local taxes will also be dropped. Two-thirds of Americans don't even itemize, so they receive no benefit from the State and local tax deduction. Yet it is this majority that is now subsidizing a handful of the high-tax States.

My friends, some State governments outside Oklahoma have not yet learned to say no to special interest groups and higher taxes. I just don't believe the good people of Oklahoma or other low-tax States like Texas, Montana, or New Hampshire should be forced to pay for their lack of resolve. Do you?

Audience. No!

The President. Now, every State has its right to manage its own affairs. But they do not have the right to make all of you carry the burden of their decisions. They do not have the right to make you pay the freight. We could, however, suggest another option to them—restrain spending and go for growth by enacting tax cuts of your own.

And as we eliminate some deductions for a favored few, we're going to keep others that are important to all of you. The home mortgage interest deduction, for example, reflects America's historic commitment to the value of home ownership. For principal homes, it's a deduction that we intend to keep. You'll also be able to deduct up to $5,000 in other interest payments that you may make, which could be used for a second residence, if you so chose. Those military allowances and veterans' disability payments that are exempt from Federal tax will remain so. American veterans have paid their dues.

And I think you can begin to see how much easier our new tax plan will make it for families, here in Oklahoma City and across the country, to make ends meet. Consider an Oklahoma family of four struggling near the poverty level with an income of $12,000. By raising the level at which people begin to pay taxes, by doubling the personal exemption, and increasing the standard deduction, our plan would ensure that the family would pay no income tax at all on those earnings—none.

Or consider a family of six, in which the wage earner works right here at your AT&T plant. Say he earns an income of $26,000 a year. By taking advantage of our proposal, including the new IRA provisions, that Oklahoma City working family could reduce its taxable income to only $6,000. They would pay 15 percent on that $6,000, which is just $900, which would mean an effective tax rate on their total income of less than 3½ percent.

Now, all the way up and down the income scale, American families would have more resources to devote to their children, to pay for your homes, to put away for retirement, and perhaps here in Oklahoma to buy a boat to use on Grand Lake or Lake Eufaula.

What we're talking about is revolutionary change—a plan that is progrowth, profairness, profamily, and profuture. This is your plan, and you can make it happen this year if you'll just tell those in Washington to get on board. And if they refuse, please tell them something else—tell them to stand aside and get out of the way.

You know, sometimes these days—I know you've heard it, I have—people, you read here and there, they say we have no more heroes. Well, they just haven't looked in their own neighborhoods.

Audience member. Bless you, Ronnie!

The President. We see heroes every day. They're the ones getting up every morning, they get the kids off to school, go to work 5 days a week—many right here in the Oklahoma City Works—support our churches and schools. On weekends, they spend extra time with the kids and teach them the enduring values of work, faith, freedom, and love.

And for too long, our tax code has discouraged us, not helped us. It's undermined work and cut into savings. Its unfairness has made our people sick at heart. The time's come for a second American revolution, a revolution in the name of our families and of you, the true American heroes. We can do it, and with your help, we will do it this year.

You know, I just have to interject something here. Back when I was Governor of California and we had a big surplus one year. And my finance director wanted to know what plan did I have for spending that. And I said, "I've got a plan. Let's give it back." It amounted to $850 million. And we figured out you could just give that back to the people by way of a reduction in their income tax for that year; we'd make it up with the surplus.

But to tell you what happens to some people if they're around government too long—after I made the announcement we were going to do this, one State senator stomped into my office one day and said, "I consider that an unnecessary expenditure of public funds." [*Laughter*] He'd forgotten where that money comes from. [*Laughter*] You haven't.

Well, I've been honored to join you and your families in Oklahoma as you celebrate this 25th anniversary, your silver anniversary of the dedication of the AT&T Oklahoma City Works. You've made me feel very welcome, and I shall always be grateful. I have to leave now, but before I do, there's just one more thing I want to say and that is: America, let's go for it!

And then I'm going to just tell you a little thing that—I hope I have not violated a lesson—that I learned here in Oklahoma from an Oklahoman, the Reverend Bill Alexander—God rest his soul.

Bill Alexander heard me make a speech, and he then told me the story of his first sermon. And I always figured it was a connection between my speech and his story. He said that he worked for weeks on that sermon. And the first sermon he was to preach, he'd been asked to preach at a little country church out there in the countryside. And he went out for an evening service, stood up on the pulpit, and the church was empty except for one lone little man sitting out there.

Well, Bill went down, and he said, "My friend, I'm just a young preacher getting started, and you seem to be the only member of the congregation that showed up. Should I go through with it?" The fellow said, "Well, I wouldn't know about that sort of thing. I'm a little old cowpoke out here in Oklahoma. But I do know this: If I loaded up a truckload of hay, took it out in the prairie and only one cow showed up, I'd feed her." [*Laughter*]

Well, Bill told me he figured that as a cue and got back up on the pulpit; and an hour and a half later said, "Amen." [*Laughter*] Went down, and he said, "My friend, you seem to have stuck with me. And like I told you, I'm a young preacher getting started—what did you think?" "Well," he said, "like I told you, I don't know about that sort of thing. But I do know this: If I loaded up a truckload of hay, took it out in the prairie, and only one cow showed up, I sure wouldn't give her the whole load." [*Laughter*]

So, I'll just thank you all—hope I haven't given you the whole load. Thank you, and God bless Oklahoma.

Note: The President spoke to plant employees and their families at 12:19 p.m. He was introduced by Charles L. Brown, chairman of the board of AT&T. Following his remarks, the President toured the automated computer division of the plant.

Remarks at a Fundraising Luncheon for Senator Don Nickles in Oklahoma City, Oklahoma
June 5, 1985

The President. Senator, Mrs. Nickles, Congressman Mickey Edwards, and all of you very distinguished ladies and gentlemen. I was hoping I would hear the finish of that story about Bartlesville. [*Laughter*] But I thank you for a very warm welcome, and thank you for welcoming me to one of the most industrious, energetic, best all-around success stories in America today. You're doing fine, Oklahoma; Oklahoma's okay!

I'll have to be careful or I might get carried away and start singing "Boomer Sooner." Or should I have said, "Ride 'em Cowboys"?

But I always get a thrill out of coming back to the home of the National Cowboy Hall of Fame. I seem to remember a famous country and western song warning mothers not to let their babies grow up to be cowboys. [*Laughter*] The song forgot to say that cowboys can sometimes grow up and be President. [*Laughter*]

Well, there's one cowboy who has been around almost as long as your State. [*Laughter*] It's a privilege to come and speak for a fellow member of the youth generation—[*laughter*]—the youngest Member of the United States Senate, your own Don Nickles. When I mention that Don is the youngest, let me add he's also one of the brightest and the best. That's why I ask you right now, please send Don Nickles back to the United States Senate for 6 more years.

Oklahoma needs him, I need him, and believe me, America needs Don Nickles, too. He's carrying on in the fine tradition of Dewey Bartlett and Henry Bellmon, who were two other great Sooners. I enjoy your accent here in the Southwest—your accent on opportunity. And I have to believe that your young Senator and this State—still brand new, with plenty of heart and plenty of hope—were a match made for each other.

You elected Don Nickles as one of the members of that Republican posse that rode into the Senate in 1981 to help rescue a nation besieged. You elected a man of integrity, a man of deep courage and conviction, who has been a champion for freedom at home and abroad.

Don Nickles has not been afraid to stand up for the taxpayers of Oklahoma against the Federal Establishment in Washington, DC. He's been a firm defender and a firm voice for the rights of the family.

He has a keen understanding of the great truths of our age. He understands that freedom is among the greatest of all blessings and that freedom is a gift of God. He understands that communism poses a grave and mortal threat to human liberty. And he understands that we can't preserve peace by appeasing the Communist bloc; we must preserve peace by blocking communism.

And because he has stood for these things, because he has not bowed to prevailing pressures to get along by going along, Don Nickles has done his job well. When it comes to getting credit for helping break the back of runaway prices or helping bring down interest rates or creating some 8 million new jobs, Don, you've not only earned your spurs, you're a member of the "A-Team." You've earned Oklahoma's support.

Don is one of the strongest advocates for energy independence in the United States Congress. So, when I say that you've earned your Oklahoma support, I don't mind adding you have my support for the deregulation of natural gas.

Senator Nickles. Thank you.

The President. That posse I mentioned not only helped rescue us from economic danger, they're leading us on a fast gallop toward a wide-open future of opportunity, progress, and strength for America. We must hold on to our Republican majority.

Your Senator and I agree on a good many things. We agreed that the Federal Government is not our greatest national resource; it's no great gusher of black gold. The Federal Government is the single greatest obstacle to our success. And the last thing we need is another politician telling us we have big deficits because you're not taxed

enough. Those deficits ballooned from 50 years of government taxing and spending too much.

Some people have labored so long to make government bigger that they've developed a knee-jerk addiction to tax increases, and every time their knee jerks, we get kicked. [*Laughter*]

We need Senator Nickles because he's one of those pushing hardest for a solution to overspending—a constitutional amendment mandating government may spend no more than government takes in. And he's pushing hardest for a reform that Oklahoma's constitution, your State constitution contains—our's did in California—but that the President of the United States still does not have authority to line-item veto individual items out of a bloated spending in appropriation bills.

Now, I don't question others' good intentions. I've simply noticed there's a well-known road that's paved with good intentions, but no one wants to go where it would take you. [*Laughter*]

You know, I've become convinced over the years that the distinguish between right and left—the distinction, I should say, is false. There is no real right or left. There's only an up or down—up to the ultimate in individual freedom consistent with an orderly society or down through statism and the welfare state to the darkness of totalitarian tyranny and human misery.

If you take the two classic examples of left and right back in our modern history—Stalin and Adolph Hitler. Follow them. Follow to the right—they're given as the examples of the extreme right and the extreme left. Well, follow that extreme right and that extreme left, and you come full circle to where the two join, and there isn't any difference, not a dime's worth, between them. The answer is to resist the invasion of our freedoms even though they tell us it's in a worthy cause to give up a freedom for this or that program. And as I say, to keep going up where the Founding Fathers intended we should go—the ultimate in human freedom.

The tax system is perhaps our most acute barometer of how free we are—the degree to which society rewards or suppresses our thrift and risk-taking and hard work. For too many years, we sat back and allowed the hand of Goliath to sweep away more and more from our national table, leaving us with crumbs from the food we ourselves produced.

Do you know that once upon a time, 1913, when they were talking about the income tax amendment, there was a Congressman that got laughed out of public life, a Senator, because he stood up on the floor protesting this amendment. And in doing that, he said: "Do you realize that if we pass this, some day the government might even take 10 percent of a person's earnings?" [*Laughter*] And they thought he was so ridiculous for saying that that they wouldn't elect him anymore.

But as our tax system grew worse, we began to change—cheating became commonplace, industries retreated from frontiers of competition to safe havens of subsidies, and a fever of envy, suspicion, and strife arose among a once united people.

Don Nickles and I went to Washington to try to begin changing all that—to build with you a new future of freedom, fairness, and hope. We took our first step in 1981 by lowering tax rates for every individual. And still, we're not home yet. I may be getting up there in years—as a matter of fact, I've been 39 for 35 years now—[*laughter*]—but I promise you today, I'm not turning back until we can pass on to Don's generation, and hopefully, he and his generation will pass on to the next, a government and tax system of, by, and for the people, and not the other way around.

Well, like a surrey with the fringe on top, our tax system has seen its day. We need a plan for America's future. And that's what America's tax plan is—fairness, opportunity, and hope for our future for every person and every family. And make no mistake, a plan that changes a 14-bracket system into a 3-bracket system; drops the personal rate to 35 percent from 70 percent just 5 years ago; cuts tax burdens for every income group; cuts corporate rates from 46 to 33 percent, with lower rates than that for many small corporations; cuts the top capital gains rate to 17½ percent; provides relief from double taxation of dividends; nearly doubles the personal exemption;

nearly doubles the limits on IRA's for many couples; removes or curtails some 65 categories of preferential tax treatment; and insists that every individual in business pay their fair share—that plan will be a second American revolution that changes this nation for the better and changes it forever.

A revolution for fairness, because everybody will have to put their shoulder to the wheel; for opportunity, because lower tax rates will encourage capital formation, overtime work, savings, and risk-taking in new ventures; and yes, a revolution for hope, because a more productive, competitive, dynamic economy will mean lower inflation, stronger growth, and more jobs for all Americans in the 1990's and on into the 21st century.

I want to see America's economy breaking free. I want to see American technology win that race into the 21st century. And that's why I want to see our tax plan pass this year. Can we count on your support? [*Applause*] Thank you. I kind of figured that that's how you'd respond. But mark my words, if we pass this plan, America's tax plan, we can ignite this economy. And yes, we can outproduce, outcompete, and outsell anybody, anywhere in the world.

I had a big kick at the recent economic summit when some of our good friends and allies from those other countries—they haven't caught up with us yet. And they were kind of asking how we did it. Some of our press had said that they were going to constantly assail me about our high interest rates and so forth—they didn't at all. And I was able to point out, they've all got higher taxes than we have, and they've all got more restrictions on free enterprise than we have. And when I heard one President of a European country talking about they had to get busy and have some more entrepreneurship in their countries, I thought, well, we've got some disciples. [*Laughter*]

Well, America's going to run up a score for growth like Oklahoma's teams run up the score with touchdowns on a Saturday afternoon. And having been a sports announcer, I know something about that.

As we work together to strengthen our economic future, we're determined to move forward with our defense rebuilding program. A weaker America will not be a safer America; our program is peace through strength.

Peace through strength rests on a secure foundation of values. Don't let anyone tell you that we're morally equivalent to the Soviet Union. This is a democratic country of free people. A democratic country where all of us enjoy the right to speak, to worship God as we please, and to live without fear. We're not equivalent—we're far superior to any totalitarian regime, and we should be darn proud of it.

Just south of our border we face a major challenge to democracy and our own security from Soviet-sponsored subversion and aggression. I'm happy to report that Don Nickles is one Senator who didn't have to wait until the dictator of Nicaragua went to Moscow before he knew he was a Communist.

Congress can no longer ignore the obvious: The Soviet-bloc nations and their terrorist allies are pouring in weapons and ammunition to establish a beachhead on our own doorstep. Top defectors from the El Salvadoran guerrillas have given us detailed information about the guidance, the training, the funds, and the ammunition that they receive from the Communists in Nicaragua to overthrow the El Salvadoran democratic government that they have finally achieved. It was a dark day for freedom when, after the Soviet Union spent $500 million to impose communism in Nicaragua, the United States Congress could not support a meager $14 million for the freedom fighters in Nicaragua who were opposed to that totalitarian government.

Those who put their lives on the line for democracy look to us as their last, best hope. We failed them once; we dare not fail them again. Lincoln's words ring as true today as they did over a hundred years ago, when he said, "Our defense is in the spirit which prized liberty as the heritage of all men, in all lands everywhere. Destroy this spirit and you have planted the seeds of despotism at your own doors."

Well, everything we do is a fragment of history, a passing moment in time. The time is now to understand that history will not wait upon a passive America. The time is now to understand that communism has

already made its choice. It's an aggressive, implacable foe of freedom. The little dictator who went to Moscow in his green fatigues to receive a bear hug didn't foresake the doctrine of Lenin when he returned to the West and appeared in a two-piece suit. He made his choice long ago.

History will not wait on us. Soon, the United States Congress must also make a crucial choice for our future, and we'd better hope that this time they choose wisely. We'd better hope they remember one simple truth: Freedom isn't free, and if freedom is taken from our neighbors, freedom will be taken from you and from me.

Like it or not, freedom depends on us. Like it or not, peace in Central America ultimately depends on our commitment, our courage, and our faith. Help America and her friends meet this challenge. Stick with us in this noble effort, and future generations will thank us for the most precious gift of all—the gift of life in lands of liberty.

Little or none of what we've accomplished in these 4½ years would have been possible if we had not had a majority in the United States Senate. We must hold that majority. So, you send Don Nickles back to the Senate for all our sakes.

I'm just going to interject something here before I close. A few moments ago, I mentioned strength and the need for our defense and so forth. I know that today there is a great misconception held by a great many people in this country as the result of a drumbeat of propaganda that would have us believe that the Defense Department is engaged in loading the guns with money, and we hear about $400 hammers and so forth and so on. I don't know how many years that sort of thing had been going on, but I just want you to know—and we're trying to find a way to let all America know—we're not buying those $400 hammers, we're the ones that are finding them and doing away with that kind of thing.

Thank you for your very warm and wonderful welcome. I know I can't stay and eat. I've got to move on. Atlanta, Georgia, is next. [*Laughter*]

God bless you all. Thank you very much.

Note: The President spoke at 1:16 p.m. in

the Grand Ballroom at the Skirvin Hotel. Following his remarks, the President attended a private reception at the hotel for major donors to Senator Nickles' campaign. He then traveled to Atlanta, GA.

Remarks at a Fundraising Dinner for Senator Mack Mattingly in Atlanta, Georgia
June 5, 1985

Thank you very much. You know, years and years ago, in another life of mine—[*laughter*]—I was in some pictures where you were the crusading newspaperman, and I remember there was always a line you never had to learn, because it was the same line. And that was, there would be a scene where you came rushing in, grabbed the phone, and you said, "Give me the city desk, I got a story that'll crack this town wide open."

So, I hope you won't mind if I take a moment to give you a news flash, because it's a strong vote of confidence in America's future. We've just learned—and I have just been informed before I came down here—that interest rates have dropped to their lowest level since 1978, and the stock market today closed at its highest level ever, a little over 1,320.

Our short-term bonds—the interest rate now, for the first time since I told you, is just below seven points as of today—and that reminds me that in 1981 when we got to Washington, they were 16—[*laughter*]—and the long-term, 30 years, notes are 10¼, and that's also a low since 1978.

Well, now to get on with the business at hand. It's always a pleasure for me to lend my support to elected officials who've done a good job and have been helpful in accomplishing administration goals. But I've come to do more than that today. Today I'm here to tell you that Mack Mattingly is not just a good Senator, he's a great Senator. He's not just helpful; he's been indispensable in our efforts to invigorate the economy, get Federal spending and taxing under control, and to strengthen America's defenses. And I want to thank all of you for sending him to Washington. And I want to ask one favor of you. Can I count on you to send him back

for another vote?

I have a special place in my heart for Mack. We both came to Washington in 1981, so you might say we're both in the same class, we were freshmen together. And we both came for the same purpose: Our country was plagued by serious problems and government, as usual, was not the answer. The type of fundamental changes needed to turn the situation around required a team effort. And Mack's not just been a member of the team, he'd been a star player.

On our way here in Air Force One, I was looking down over your countryside out here because most of the way from Oklahoma I was looking down at clouds. And I could say that it reminded me of a story, but actually, I wanted to tell the story whether anything reminded me or not. [*Laughter*]

It was about a fellow that was driving down a country road, and all of a sudden he looked out and there beside him was a chicken—he was doing about 45 and the chicken was running alongside. [*Laughter*] So he stepped on the gas, he got it up to about 60, and the chicken caught up with him and was right beside him again, and then he thought, as he was looking at him, that the chicken had three legs. But before he could really make up his mind for sure, the chicken took off out in front of him at 60 miles an hour and turned down a lane into a barnyard. Well, he made a quick turn and went down into the barnyard, too, and there was a farmer standing there, and he asked him, he said, "Did a chicken come past you?" And he said, "Yeah." Well, he said, "Am I crazy or did the chicken have three legs?" He says, "Yep, it's mine." He says, "I breed three-legged chickens."

[*Laughter*] And the fellow said, "For heaven sakes, why?" Well, he says, "I like the drumstick, and Ma likes the drumstick, and now the kid likes the drumstick, and we just got tired of fighting for it." [*Laughter*] And the driver said, "Well, how does it taste?" He says, "I don't know. I've never been able to catch one." [*Laughter*]

Well, seriously, since coming to Washington, as Mack told you, we've made some changes, and unlike that farmer who raised the three-legged chicken, we are getting the benefit, and the American people are getting the benefit of the things that we changed. And I hope you'll remind all your fellow Georgians that Senator Mack Mattingly was a star player on the team that licked inflation. We can't let people forget those bad old days when prices were shooting through the roof. They say that money talks. Well, a few years ago the only thing it said was goodbye. [*Laughter*]

But with Senators like Mack in the majority we averted an economic catastrophe. It took all of us working together to overcome entrenched, irresponsible spending, taxing, and regulatory policies. And I'd like to take this opportunity to thank also Congressmen Newt Gingrich and Pat Swindall for all that they've done in this effort as well.

And when I say all of us working together, I don't just mean those of us in public office. I know State chairman of the 1984 Reagan-Bush campaign, Macon's Mayor George Israel, is here. And so is Republican State chairman and State Senator Paul Coverdell. They and all of you are essential to our success in Washington. With you behind us, we don't have to make the opposition see the light. They've just felt the heat.

Together we represent a new force in this country. I think what we're witnessing is a realignment of southern politics. A new coalition is being built, a coalition dedicated to the ideals of individual freedom, family values, free enterprise, and a strong America. And we're reaching out to Americans of every race and religion. The doors are open, the welcome mat is out, our agenda is opportunity and freedom for all.

More and more of our Democrat friends and neighbors are recognizing that old political labels no longer apply. I think it's a sign of the times when a political pro like State Senator Frank Albert from Augusta can switch labels and be backed up by the voters. We have to reach out to all people who share our vision of the future.

And today we're on the cutting edge of change. Joined by concerned members of the other party, we're laying the foundation for a new era of prosperity and good will. Now, getting there's going to take some doing.

Last week I spoke to the Nation, as Mack has told you, about taxes. And I hope you agree with me that an overhaul of the tax system in this country is long overdue.

Our taxes are too high, unfair, and overly complicated. The tax code works against the best interests of working people, families, and a healthy economy. It distorts the decisions of businessmen and investors, often encouraging them to direct resources into useless tax dodges rather than encouraging them to invest in the future. It stifles incentive and promotes nonproductive investment. It is time for a change, and as I said the other night, I think America should go for it.

Now, our proposal would cut down—or cut out complications and bring down the rates. And the core of the idea is to reduce the number of tax rates from 14 to 3—15 percent, 25 percent, and 35 percent. The majority of Americans would be paying at a lower tax rate than they do now. The complex system of itemized deductions, exclusions, and special credits would go through a major simplification and reform. Average Americans will end up with a lower tax burden. And in the new system, they won't have to hire a tax lawyer to do it.

Yes, a few will pay more. Some of these will be individuals and corporations who've been manipulating the system and using loopholes to avoid paying their fair share. This can no longer be tolerated. Teddy Roosevelt once said: "The first requisite of a good citizen in this Republic of ours is that he shall be able and willing to pull his own weight."

We're not judging those who've used every legal means to reduce their tax obligation, but we are plugging up some of the holes. The days of the free ride are over. But let me say, however, it's only right to do this if, at the same time, we eliminate the unfair punishment the tax has been imposing on all of us.

We've included in our plan elements designed to help the American family and our less fortunate citizens as well. It lowers the top rate on capital gains from 20 to 17½ percent to encourage investment. It contains incentives for new businesses to get off the ground and create jobs.

It's a plan to help all of us better our lives and our future, and that's why we call it America's tax plan. Now, there are cynics, as Mack said, who suggest that democracy has become so partisan that such fundamental reform is impossible. Well, we've all heard that before. Pardon me for bringing back a line, but I have a message for those naysayers: You ain't seen nothin' yet.

A tax overhaul will help, but we must keep making progress on the spending side as well. Senator Mattingly has been in the forefront of much of what we've accomplished already, but he'll tell you there's still a long way to go.

One reform that would help is that change that he's been long advocating: The Chief Executive of the United States should have the same tool to control spending as 43 Governors have today in this land. It'll provide leverage against pork-barreling at the taxpayers' expense. The only ones threatened by it are the big spenders and the special interests. The line-item veto is long overdue.

While we're at it—and I know Mack supports this as well—let's pass a constitutional amendment requiring the government to do exactly what each and every family in America has to do—balance its budget.

What we are doing will determine the kind of land that our children will inherit. A major commitment of this administration, which again has had more than full support from Mack, has been our war against drug abuse. I'd like to thank Mack for what he's done and also his wife, Carolyn, for her marvelous support. Nancy's taken such an active role in the fight against drug abuse, and she tells me that Carolyn is a real trooper.

In 1984, with a Republican majority in the Senate, we passed legislation that will go a long way to help in the battle against drug peddlers and other criminals. The Comprehensive Crime Control Act was a big step in the right direction. It's about time our criminal justice system returns to serving as a pathway to justice instead of a roadblock to removing criminals from our streets.

Now, these are not Republican issues or Democrat issues. The security of the family and the security of our country should not be the focus of partisan debate. I'd like to thank Mack and other responsible elected representatives that you've sent to Washington, from both parties, who've supported our efforts to rebuild America's defenses and keep our country strong, safe, and at peace.

If our country's not secure, nothing else has any meaning. Today, we as a nation face a challenge to our south. If we have the courage to do what is right, we can avoid a crisis. Inaction and lack of resolve are not the answer. The Soviet Union has poured hundreds of millions of dollars in military arms and equipment down there. We must assist those friendly governments under attack and help them defend themselves. And we must lend our support to those freedom fighters struggling for democracy in Nicaragua.

This is a matter of the freedom of our friends and neighbors and the security of our country. We cannot and will not permit the Communists to impose their will on the people of Central America.

People all over the world look to us for leadership. If we falter, they know there's no hope. Five years ago America seemed to be faltering. People were believing those naysayers that I spoke about a few minutes ago. For the first time in my life, I heard people talking about our country as if we were a nation in decline.

Well, in 1981, thanks to all of you, a new team arrived in Washington. And I think that Mack and I and the other members of the team understand the puzzle palace on the Potomac a bit more now than we did, but we're just as optimistic about what can be accomplished. Once America's made up its mind, there's nothing we can't do. I told the people of Europe during my recent visit—and I firmly believe—the future is on the side of the free. And with God's help and the support of good people like yourselves, we'll keep America the land of the free and the home of the brave.

I just want to interject something here that I said this morning in Oklahoma, I want to say it again to you. I have mentioned keeping us strong; I have mentioned strengthening our defenses. I know that throughout the country today, there is a great deal of concern—there's been a drumbeat of propaganda, you've heard it all—$400 hammers, $700 wrenches or whatever, and so forth—and a great feeling that maybe the Defense Department is just standing there throwing money down the gunbarrel.

Well, I don't know how long, how many years that sort of thing—the $400 hammers and so forth—has been going on. But what I do know—and we're looking for a way to make the people of this country understand—is, we're not buying those $400 hammers. We're the ones who, for the first

time, are finding out about them and cutting them off.

Your tax dollars have brought us a defense that—I can quote the words of a general of the Chiefs of Staff who was given, in World War II on the beach at Anzio, a battlefield commission and rose to become Chairman of the Joint Chiefs of Staff. And he says that the military we have now is the best that he has seen in 45 years.

Thank you all for letting me be here today and be a part of this. And let me just close and say, I don't want to go back to Washington without him or without her. Send them both back there with us.

Thank you all very much. God bless you. Thank you.

Note: The President spoke at 6:45 p.m. in the Grand Ballroom at the Waverly Hotel. Prior to his remarks, the President attended a private reception at the hotel for major donors to Senator Mattingly's campaign. The President remained overnight at the hotel.

Remarks at Northside High School in Atlanta, Georgia
June 6, 1985

The President. Thank you all very much. One of the prerequisites of the office I hold is that I am Commander in Chief. And in military regulations and custom, the commanding general dictates the uniform of the day. [*Laughter*] There. That's better, isn't it?

Thank you, Pamela, and thank you, Billy Densmore, for that fine show, and thank all of you. It's wonderful to be here. May I interject something right now and tell you that I will feel very comfortable with those gifts that you have given me, particularly that jersey, because a few years ago, playing football for Dixon High School, I, too, wore a purple and white jersey.

I guess I should tell you how all this came about. For some time, I've been hearing about a school in Atlanta that's made a big comeback. About 10 years ago it was in academic trouble. But now the SAT scores

of its students keep going up and up; in fact, they've been going up for 8 years. And the school is now rated one of the best educational establishments in the Nation.

I've been told that 7 years ago the school has so much trouble getting students involved in student activities that they held a big school dance with no admission charge, and only one student showed up. [*Laughter*]

But now, school spirit has returned and getting involved again, and the school has a performing arts program that I can see for myself rivals the TV show, "Fame."

Eight years ago the school could barely get anyone to go out for sports. But in 1982 this school graduated a young man named Sam Graddy, who helped America win the gold in the 400-meter relay at the 1984 Olympics.

I've been thinking that this school in Atlanta is a kind of metaphor for the whole country, because Northside High is back and standing tall.

One of the nicest things about my job is that now and then it allows me to speak on behalf of the entire Nation. And so, I've come here today to say to you, on behalf of the people of our country: Well done!

And allow me to thank you for the kindness with which you greeted a very special lady in my life when she visited here last October. Nancy told me all about you, and I heard she got into a little trouble. Someone asked her if she came to Atlanta for political reasons, and she said, "No, I'm here for drugs." [*Laughter*] I can't tell you what confusion that caused. [*Laughter*] But Nancy was very impressed by what you've done to combat drug abuse, to get the word out that using drugs is dumb and dangerous. And I want you to know that when she came back to the White House, she told me about your school band and the chorus and the troupe of dancers. And then she showed me what she was proudest of—the permanent hall pass. [*Laughter*] Can I have one too? [*Laughter*]

You make us all very proud. And the most impressive thing about what you've done to turn around Northside High is that *you* did it. You and an American hero named Bill Rudolph. You know, in some schools you're taking a chance when you invite students to applaud their principal. But I knew you'd come through. Your teachers helped, your faculty helped, serious committed teachers such as Ray Lamb, who last year won a Presidential Award for Excellence in the teaching of math. And your parents did it; your parents turned around Northside High. You know better than I how they joined together to help you get drugs out of Northside. And I'd like to mention also Families in Action, a group that has achieved tremendous results in the area of drug education. Together all these individuals and groups helped create an environment where, as Bill Rudolph puts it, "each student may reach his maximum level in achievement in an environment of mutual respect."

You are a triumphant example of private sector initiative, a triumph of community spirit, and you're proof that no force on

Earth can stop individuals from achieving great goals when they have the will and the heart to pull together and work together.

All around the country, we're seeing a massive movement at the grassroots level where the private sector and schools are forming partnerships in education. At the White House we've adopted a school, the Martin Luther King, Jr. School, in Washington. I even got to take part with my pen pal, who's a second grader there.

And remarkable things are happening everywhere. During the last few years, we've seen how a school in Chicago, called Providence-St. Mel's, prevented their doors from closing because of the private donations that came to their aid.

And now, I'm here today at Northside High because the students, faculty, and private sector groups have formed creative partnerships to make your school stronger and better than ever.

And now, while all of you were trying to fix what was wrong with your school, we were trying, and still are, back in Washington, to fix the things that are wrong with America. And you've been so successful here, I figured I'd come down and ask for your help. [*Laughter*]

We've already come a long way. Just 5 years ago, when some of you were in junior high, America was in bad shape, mostly bad economic shape. Rising prices were making it harder for your parents to buy essentials like food and clothing, and unemployment was rising; there were no jobs for seniors in high school and college to graduate into. It was as if opportunity had just dried up, and people weren't feeling the old hope Americans had always felt. And that was terrible because hope was always the fuel that kept America going and kept our society together.

Just a few years later everything's changed. You and your parents are finally getting a breather from inflation. And if you graduate and go out into the work force in June, there will be jobs waiting for you. Hope has returned, and America's working again.

Now, you know how all this came about, how we cut tax rates and trimmed Federal spending and got interest rates down. But what's really important is what inspired us to do these things. What's really important is the philosophy that guided us. The whole thing could be boiled down to a few words—freedom, freedom, and more freedom. It's a philosophy that isn't limited to guiding government policy. It's a philosophy you can live by; in fact, I hope you do.

I mentioned in that paragraph there about interest rates coming down. Just yesterday we got an announcement that government short-term bonds—the interest rates for the first time since 1978 have dropped below 7 percent.

So, now, I'll go on after announcing that. And, as you know, that last week I unveiled our proposal to make the Federal tax system fairer, clearer, and less burdensome for all Americans. Now, someone might say it's odd to talk about tax policy with young people in their teens. But I don't think so. You not only understand what taxes are, what effect they have in the average person's life, but if you don't understand, you will pretty soon when you get your first job. I know some of you already have part-time jobs, and I know you keep your eye on the part of the check that shows what Uncle Sam is taking out.

What we're trying to do is change some of those numbers. We want the part of your check that shows Federal withholding to have fewer digits on it. And we want the part that shows your salary to have more digits on it. We're trying to take less money from you and less from your parents.

And whatever you and they do with this additional money will not only help you, it will help the whole country by making our entire economy stronger. Maybe you'll take some of the money and put it in the bank. Fine. You'll earn interest on your savings, and you'll also make more money available for others to borrow, to expand their business, or improve their home. Maybe you'll spend it. And that's fine, too, although I hope you don't spend it all. But what you spend will increase demand for various products. And that will help create jobs. But whatever you do with it, you'll be the one who's doing the doing. You'll make the decisions. You'll have the autonomy. And that's what freedom is.

When taxes are lowered, economic growth follows. And economic growth is good for just about everyone, especially the poor. It gives them a ladder they can use to climb out of poverty. And for those who aren't poor, but who are by no means rich—and that's most of the people in America—economic growth gives them options they never had before. When you and your parents and friends are allowed to keep more of the fruits of your labors, a whole new world of options will open up for you.

You'll be better situated to pay for college. You'll be able to save and pool your money with friends and maybe even start a small local business. I knew a fellow who once bought into a little hamburger stand out west. He was just a regular guy, but he worked hard and advertised, and the little stand prospered. You may have heard of it. It's called McDonald's. I was thinking about Ray Kroc recently and how the jingle that he uses applies to our tax program: "You deserve a break today." And tomorrow, too, and for the rest of your life.

And we're trying to give a break, a much-deserved, long-overdue break, to the American family. I'll tell you how strange America's current tax laws are. They allow a deduction of only slightly more than $1,000 for every dependent person in your family. Now, if you think about what it costs for your parents to put food on the table and buy you everything from books to braces, you know that $1,000 doesn't even make a dent in it. We're going to virtually double that exemption to $2,000 with increases if inflation occurs. But it'll go a long way toward encouraging families again and giving your parents the break they deserve.

We're going to close the unproductive tax loopholes that have allowed some of the truly wealthy to avoid paying their fair share. In theory, some of those loopholes were understandable, but in practice they sometimes made it possible for millionaires to pay nothing, while a bus driver was paying 10 percent of his salary, and that's crazy. It's time we stopped it.

And the way I see it, if our current tax structure were a TV show, it would either be "Foul-ups, Bleeps, and Blunders," or "Gimme a Break." If it were a record album, it would be "Gimme Shelter." If it were a movie, it would be "Revenge of the Nerds" or maybe "Take the Money and Run." And if the IRS, Internal Revenue Service, ever wants a theme song, maybe they'll get Sting to do, "Every breath you take, every move you make, I'll be watching you."

What we're trying to move against is institutionalized unfairness. We want to see that everyone pays their fair share, and no one gets a free ride. Our reasons? It's good for society when we all know that no one is manipulating the system to their advantage because they're rich and powerful. But it's also good for society when everyone pays something, that everyone makes a contribution.

After all, we're all citizens, equal in the eyes of the law, and equal in the eyes of God. You're given a lot of benefits when you're born in the U.S.A, but you're given a responsibility, too, a responsibility to do your part and become a contributing member of the American family and an equal partner in America, Incorporated. When you pay your taxes, you buy your shares. And every year you get to vote on who should be on the board of directors.

Now, you'll be hearing more about our tax proposals over the next few weeks. A great debate has begun, and there will be much talk, pro and con. And that's good, that's what America's all about.

But the heartening thing is that no one in Washington is standing up and saying, "Leave the tax system as it is, it's wonderful, we love it." Just about everyone admits it has to be changed. The only disagreements now are over the specifics. And no one, or just about no one, is saying we ought to raise taxes and take more of the people's money. Actually, I think it would be fun if some politician would say that. I haven't seen anyone run out of town on a rail in years. [*Laughter*]

I'm going to leave you today with some questions that I hope you'll think about, but I need you to answer them.

Tell me, do you think your hard-working parents ought to be able to start holding on to more of their paychecks or less?

Audience. More!

The President. Do you think the million-

aire ought to pay more in taxes than the bus driver or less?

Audience. More!

The President. Do you think America needs more economic growth or less?

Audience. More!

The President. Do you think we need more jobs created and more business started or less?

Audience. More!

The President. Well, if, like young Oliver Twist, you've concluded that the answer is more, and you apparently have—you're the future. You'll soon have the vote. And you already have a voice. Make it heard. Write a letter to the editor or to your Congressman or Congresswoman, talk to your parents and the neighbors, get all the facts. And if you can help us, do.

After I made my speech the other night we received hundreds of phone calls and telegrams, and more than 9 out of 10 supported our ideas to change the tax system. And a lot of those telegrams bore just three words. They said, "Go for it!"

Well, not a bad way of expressing our hopes for you—Go for it! Reach those heights, excel, push yourself to the limits, strive for excellence. Enjoy your freedom, breathe it in, use it to create the most important and moving thing a man or woman can create—a decent and meaningful life.

I look at all of you, and I think: You're free to be anything. You're free to be whatever you want to be with no one and nothing stopping you. In a free society, you're free to invent yourself—to turn yourself into a great teacher, a racecar driver, a minister, or a movie star, or a grower and seller of flowers. You can be anything. It's your invention. And there's nothing to stop you.

We want an America that's economically strong and economically free. But a caution here—that's the nice thing about getting older, you know, you get to caution people. Not that I'm getting older but—[*laughter*]. We want to remember that while the creation of wealth is good—wealth, after all, generates jobs and prosperity—we must not let the creation of wealth become a preoccupation with material things.

We've made so much economic progress

in our country, but it will mean very little if your children look back at your days as a time of materialism and selfishness and looking out for number one. The people you're sitting with right now, they're your brothers and sisters. Someday you'll have a home or an apartment, and your neighbors will be your brothers and sisters then. And it's up to us, as members of the American family, to take care of each other and love each other.

There's an old American tradition called houseraising, the pioneers out West would get together and build each other's houses. That was a long time ago, but it's still going on. Every time someone helps a lonely old man or woman in a shelter for the poor, that's a houseraising. Every time someone volunteers their time or money to raise funds for the local library, that's a houseraising. Every time a community gets together and says something like, "We're going to turn Northside High into one of the greatest schools in Georgia," that's houseraising.

I wish you a nation of strength and wealth and power. But more than that, I wish you a nation where the houseraising continues. And somehow, looking out at all of you, I suspect we have nothing to worry

about. I have this feeling the helping and houseraising will continue.

I thank you all, all of you, for this wonderful day. And I thank you in behalf of Nancy, too. They had her scheduled someplace else or she'd have been here with me. And she remembers you and speaks of you often with great pride and great enthusiasm.

And I have to tell you that when you were singing earlier here, just about one more song of the kind I heard and I'd have had a lump so big in my throat—I told Bill Rudolph—that I wouldn't be able to talk. Maybe that would have been a break for all of you. [*Laughter*]

But thank all of you for this very wonderful start of a day, and God bless you all.

Note: The President spoke at 10:36 a.m. in the gymnasium. In his remarks, the President referred to Pamela Gold, covaledictorian of the class of 1985, who introduced the President; and William Densmore, director and founder of the School of Performing Arts at the high school. Following his remarks, the President attended a reception for school leaders. He then traveled to Birmingham, AL.

Remarks at a Fundraising Luncheon for Senator Jeremiah Denton in Birmingham, Alabama
June 6, 1985

Mr. Chairman, Mr. Mayor, Senator Denton, Mrs. Denton, all of you, thank you all very much. You know, listening to Jerry, I was reminded of what a great general of ours said when he was asked about any secret weapons we might possess in World War II. And he said that our secret weapon was just the best darned kids in the world. Well, whenever I'm with Jerry, I see that one of the best darned kids grew up into one of the best darned officers and now is one of the best darned Senators in the United States Congress.

Jerry and I came into office in the same year, 1981, and for the last 4½ years, he's been a pillar of support for our efforts to

keep America strong and free and true. He's been rated the most conservative Senator by the National Journal. That's my kind of Senator. His voting record has been rated 100 percent by the American Conservative Union, the U.S. Chamber of Commerce, the Conservatives Against Liberal Legislation— I like the name of that one—the National Alliance of Senior Citizens, the Christian Voters Victory Fund, and some others. The magazine, Conservative Digest, took a poll of its readers, and Jerry Denton was their second most admired Senator. Now, knowing Jerry, he's probably wondering where he slipped up. But that's all right because we're going to make sure that you have at least another 6 years to make number one.

He's more than one voice and one vote in the Senate. He's one of the most persuasive leaders on the Hill. And he's also one of the most effective spokesmen I know for the interests of his State, this proud and growing State of Alabama, which, as he says so well, is marching confidently into the future.

One example of Jerry's abilities in looking out for Alabama is the Tenn-Tom Waterway, which, due in great part to his support and leadership, was completed ahead of schedule.

We're also joined tonight with three very able State leaders—State Republican Chairman Emory Folmar, who also did a tremendous job for us as his finance chairman in the campaign, and from the Republican National Committee, Perry Hooper and Jean Sullivan. I also want to recognize the job that's being done by Congressman Bill Dickinson and Sonny Callahan. I don't know if Sonny claims any relation to Harry Callahan, but after all he's done, he really makes my day. [*Laughter*]

Jerry's been telling me about the progress of Operation Open Door, the program that's been set up to bring Democrats into the Republican fold. So, let me pause right here and congratulate all of you. Welcome on board. And those of you made the decision in the Grand Old Party. Nowadays, we also call it the Great Opportunity Party. Switching to the Republican Party is rapidly becoming a venerable tradition—Sonny and Emory are both Republican converts and, well, so is the President of the United States. [*Laughter*]

I know from personal experience how hard it can be to make the change from Democrat to Republican. I also know that there comes a time when you look in your heart and realize that it may be hard to change, but it's just something that you've got to do. Party loyalty can be mighty fierce, though.

We all know that story about way back when—probably one of the first Republicans was running here in the South for office, out soliciting votes, and he was rejected by one gentleman who said to him, "I'm a Democrat, always been a Democrat, my pappy was a Democrat, and my grand-

pappy was a Democrat." And the candidates made the mistake of saying, "Well, if your pappy was a jackass and your grandpappy was a jackass, what would that make you?" And he says, "A Republican." [*Laughter*]

But I think all that's changing. While a lot of Democrats have stood fast by their principles, the party has been pulled out from under their feet by a kind of left-wing leadership. I know it's what made me change, and I found the answer and will suggest it to others who maybe are considering it. As I say, I know the pain. It was like changing your religion. And I was converted in principle before I could still bring myself to make that change in party. And then I heard the words of another man who had changed party, Winston Churchill. And Winston said, "Some men change principle for party and some change party for principle."

A lot of Democrats supported Senator Denton and me in 1980, and we're very grateful. And we just want to say to any registered Democrats out there who might not be so happy about the direction their party is heading: If you're looking for a new home the Republican Party has a welcome mat out, and the doors are wide open. Come on over. And I can tell you, if you really look back—and I look back to that first vote that I cast in 1932 as a Democrat and others that I cast subsequently—and I remember what I voted for, not who. And then the time came when I realized that what I had voted for there—reduction of the Federal Government in cost, elimination of useless boards and commissions, States rights—not protectionism, but free trade. The leadership of the Democratic Party today does not represent those things, but millions of rank-and-file patriotic Democrats throughout the Nation represent those things, and I believe that we're trying to represent them in the leadership of the Republican Party. So, you're welcome.

Well, today, June 6th is a double anniversary. It marks the day, 41 years ago, that the allies won Normandy beach and the day, 39 years ago, that Jerry won his lovely bride, Jane, and convinced her to marry him. Happy anniversary. Congratulations to you both.

That coincidence kind of makes you think how closely intertwined our families, our faith, and our communities are with the freedom that we cherish. The family is the guardian of our most treasured possessions—our values of loyalty, chastity, and love and our belief in human dignity and the incalculable worth of each individual life—and through the family, each generation passes these values on to the next as a sacred inheritance. It's the family that civilizes us, that keeps us human, and ensures that our future will be humane.

Totalitarian ideologies, in their drive to subvert human nature, will always be hostile to the family and its transcendent loyalties. We have seen that today in Russian totalitarianism; the taking over of the children by the state, the virtual elimination of family control. But free and democratic nations must be sure to honor, protect, and nourish their families as if their very survival depended on it, because in truth it does.

In his 4½ years in the Senate, Jerry's been an untiring advocate of the family, and I might say his seven children and eight grandchildren attest to the fact that he practices what he preaches. [*Laughter*]

Jerry established and chairs the Senate Caucus on the Family. He's been a leader in the fight against child abuse, and his adolescent family life act has been on the books since 1981, helping to combat the tragedy of adolescent pregnancy. And Jerry knows that families don't hand over to the State all rights to their children when they walk through the front door on their way to school. I know there's been a strong push here in Birmingham to help restore voluntary prayer in public schools. As this week's Supreme Court decision shows, we still have an uphill battle before us. So, I hope we can also count on the support of Alabama's entire congressional delegation for our prayer amendment, because it is time it was adopted.

Last year with the passage of the Equal Access Act, Jerry made sure that student religious groups have the same rights as other student groups. Thomas Jefferson said, "The God who gave us life gave us liberty." Well, thanks to Jerry's determined efforts, Alabama schoolchildren now have a

little more liberty to thank their God for both these great gifts.

Last week I announced our plan to completely overhaul our nation's tax structure and replace it with one that's fairer, simpler, more compassionate, and most importantly, one that gives the American family a long-overdue break. As I said then, our proposal is the strongest profamily initiative in postwar history. First, it will take the tax lid off our economy and make America an engine of economic growth and job creation. We've called it America's tax plan, and I'm convinced that it is quite simply the most effective jobs creation bill that ever came before the United States Congress. We're not going to rest until every American who wants a job has a job, until the doors of opportunity are open so wide that everyone from the inner cities to the countryside can walk right on through.

We're also going to give immediate tax relief to America's families by nearly doubling the personal exemption, raising the standard deduction, lowering income tax rates, and making tax-deductible IRA accounts fully available to homemakers, so that spouses that choose to stay home and take care of the children are no longer penalized. Through our plan, a family of four wouldn't pay a cent in Federal income tax on the first $12,000 of income and only 15 cents on the dollar up to $29,000 of taxable income.

Our tax proposal will right the injustices in the old system, help families, and increase economic opportunity. There are two things that our tax plan will not do, however. It will not expand the deficit, and it will not raise taxes. Now, I'm glad that some forward-looking Democrats in Congress have decided to join hands with us and work alongside their Republican colleagues to remold our tax system along the lines of fairness, simplicity, and economic growth. Since Rosty [1] and I went on TV urging tax change, Washington has been deluged under a mountain of letters and telegrams, most with one very simple message: America, go for it! Well, all I have to

---

[1] *Representative Dan Rostenkowski of Illinois.*

say is, keep those cards and letters coming, folks.

I can only hope that this emerging spirit of bipartisanship will also transfer to the transcendent moral issue of our time—the support and protection of freedom from the assault of communism. Sooner or later, we're all forced to shed any illusions we may have had about Communist regimes. Jeremiah Denton knows from experience what communism means. He wrote about it graphically in a book called, "When Hell was in Session." And we're all seeing that communism has become synonymous with starvation, terror, brutality, and prison camps.

Some would like to ignore Nicaragua's connection to the international terrorist network, the PLO, Libya, and the followers of the Ayatollah Khomeini, who now—thanks to the Sandinista Communists—have a foothold in Central America, just 2 hours by air from our southern border. Some would like to ignore the incontrovertible evidence of the Communist religious persecution of Catholics, Jews, and fundamentalists; of their campaign of virtual genocide against the Miskito Indians; of their attempted subversion of their free, democratic neighbors.

When it comes to the Communists in Nicaragua, some have adopted a see no, hear no evil, speak no evil attitude. But as the refugees come flooding out of Nicaragua, it becomes harder and harder not to hear their cries of anguish, not to see the suffering of their shattered lives. And it becomes all but impossible not to speak out against the tragedy the Communists are inflicting on their country.

I remember in Washington a few weeks back meeting a young man who was a fundamentalist preacher in Nicaragua. His face was simply a gargoyle. He had prayed, and they came in the night, the military, with the Sandinistas, and took him out, tied him to a pillar of the house where he was sleeping and then threw gasoline in the house and set it on fire. Well, fortunately, the fires burned the ropes before they could kill him. But he, with his clothing in flames and his body in flames, fled. Campesinos found him, took him to a hospital. He had to hide who he was and how this had happened, or they would have caught him again. And he was in Washington, there, still speaking out for what he believes in. And what was his sin in the eyes of the Sandinista government? He'd prayed and prayed with some of the people, the citizens there who still wanted to have religion.

When it comes to the Communists and what they're doing to their country, well, Daniel Ortega's money-run to the Soviet Union should have come as no surprise. Still, for many, it took this last trip to dispel their final illusions and to make it clear that the Nicaraguan Communists are no more and no less than agents of Soviet expansionism and the sworn enemies of freedom.

But still, in spite of what some keep saying, we remain committed to a peaceful solution. And so do the democratic opposition in Nicaragua. But while they're waiting for their own government to talk to them, they must survive. And that's what our assistance is designed to do—to give peace a chance and to keep alive the goal of freedom in Nicaragua.

Congress is now reconsidering its aid cutoff to the freedom fighters. In fact, the Senate vote comes up today. So, I'm afraid Jerry and I are going to have to do a quick disappearing act after my speech to get him up there in time to cast his vote to give freedom a chance in Nicaragua.

If aid to the freedom fighters passes the Senate, which I have faith it will, then it'll be up to the Democratically controlled House to show the Sandinista Communists that they're not fooling anybody; that when it comes to supporting freedom and reconciliation in Nicaragua, the United States can be counted on. America stands as one.

This, as I mentioned, is a day of anniversaries, proud and happy ones. But a few weeks ago on the other side of the globe, another terrible and bitter anniversary was noted—the 10th anniversary of the fall of South Vietnam to the Communists. Today the Vietnamese Communists can celebrate the transformation of their nation into one of the poorest countries on Earth. They can celebrate the creation of new Vietnamese gulags, 10 years of torture and forced relocations, and the flight of nearly a million refugees and boat people.

Americans visiting Vietnam have been surprised to find out how warmly they're received, to see people rushing up to them with smiles of joy, and to hear the Vietnamese use all the English at their command to say, "America, number one."

Well, 10 years later, after a prolonged season in hell, the memory of freedom still survives. The young children may have known only the darkness of Communist tyranny, but even they have parents and older relatives who tell them of South Vietnam before the fall and bring a ray of hope into their lives. The Vietnamese people say that America is number one because America tried to give freedom a chance in Vietnam. And 10 years later, the people for whom our brave American soldiers fought and died and sacrificed are still profoundly grateful.

The Vietnamese Government says they also want us back. They want to normalize relations with the United States. But we have made it clear there is only one way this can take place. The American people demand the fullest possible accounting for our POW's and MIA's. This and a peaceful resolution of their brutal occupation of Cambodia would help bring Vietnam out of international isolation.

For almost 8 years, Jeremiah Denton endured the inhuman trials and tortures of North Vietnamese prison camps, but his faith and the love of his family and country not only gave him the courage to survive but to alert the world of the horrors of the Vietnamese gulag. He became in those 8 years not only a great hero to his country but a hero to the cause of human freedom. He learned then that the struggle for liberty is the struggle for life, itself. And he learned that Abraham Lincoln's words were never truer—that the United States is still the ". . . last, best hope of earth."

I think Jeremiah Denton said it best when, after almost 8 years of unimaginable suffering and hardship, he stepped from that plane and onto his home soil. And I remember seeing that early in the morning in Sacramento on television, without any knowledge that we would ever be standing here in this particular situation. And I think we can all say with him today what those of us who were watching saw him say then— the simplest, truest words ever spoken— "God bless America."

Thank you, thank you all. God bless you all, and God bless America. Thank you.

Note: The President spoke at 12:48 p.m. in the main hall at the Birmingham-Jefferson Civic Center. Prior to his remarks, the President attended a reception at the civic center for donors to Senator Denton's campaign. Following his remarks, the President returned to Washington, DC.

Nomination of Thomas Morgan Roberts To Be a Member of the Nuclear Regulatory Commission
June 6, 1985

The President today announced his intention to nominate Thomas Morgan Roberts to be a member of the Nuclear Regulatory Commission for the term of 5 years expiring June 30, 1990. This is a reappointment.

Mr. Roberts is currently a member of the Nuclear Regulatory Commission. He was with Southern Boiler & Tank Works, Inc., from 1962 to 1978 and served as president and chief executive officer from 1969 to 1978. Previously he was an underwriting member of Lloyd's of London and director of Boyle Investment Co. in Memphis, TN.

Mr. Roberts graduated from the Georgia Institute of Technology (B.S., 1959). He served as an officer in the United States Navy from 1959 to 1962. He is married and has three children. He was born April 14, 1937, in Memphis, TN.

Appointment of Peter H. Dailey as United States National Chairman for United Nations Day, 1985
June 6, 1985

The President today announced his intention to appoint Peter H. Dailey to be the United States National Chairman for United Nations Day, 1985. He would succeed Theodore Burtis.

Mr. Dailey is currently chairman of Enniskerry Financial Co. and president of the World Business Council. Previously, he was United States Ambassador to Ireland (1982–1984) and chairman, president, and chief executive officer of Dailey International Group, in Los Angeles (1968–1982). He was

senior vice president and director, Western and Far Eastern Regions, of Campbell Ewald Co. in 1964–1968. He served as vice president of Foote, Cone and Belding, in 1963–1964.

Mr. Dailey served in the United States Navy in 1954–1956. He graduated from the University of California (B.S., 1954). He is married, has five children, and resides in Los Angeles, CA. He was born May 1, 1930, in New Orleans, LA.

Nomination of George Cranwell Montgomery To Be United States Ambassador to Oman
June 7, 1985

The President today announced his intention to nominate George Cranwell Montgomery, of Tennessee, to be Ambassador to the Sultanate of Oman. He would succeed John R. Countryman.

Mr. Montgomery served on the legislative staff of the Honorable Howard Baker in 1975–1980. He then became special counsel to the Senate Majority Leader in 1980–1985. Mr. Montgomery was in the United States Navy in 1966–1972, when he resigned as a lieutenant. Since 1972 he has been serving in the United States Naval Re-

serve, where he has attained rank of commander. His memberships include the Court of Appeals for the District of Columbia, the American Bar Association, and the District of Columbia Bar Association.

Mr. Montgomery graduated from the University of Virginia (B.A., 1966) and Vanderbilt University (J.D., 1975). His foreign languages are Latin and German. He has one child and resides in Davidsonville, MD. He was born August 24, 1944, in Chattanooga, TN.

Nomination of Perry L. Adkisson To Be a Member of the National Science Board
June 7, 1985

The President today announced his intention to nominate Perry L. Adkisson to be a member of the National Science Board, National Science Foundation, for a term expiring May 10, 1990. He would succeed Lewis M. Branscomb.

He is currently deputy chancellor of Texas A&M University system in College Station, TX. He has been with Texas A&M since 1953, serving as associate professor (1958–1963); professor (1963–1979); head of the department of entomology (1967–1978);

distinguished professor of entomology (1979–present); vice president for agriculture and renewable resources (1978–1980); and deputy chancellor for agriculture (1980–1982). He served as a consultant to the International Atomic Energy Agency in Vienna, Austria, in 1969 and as a consultant to the U.S. Environmental Protection Agency, Hazardous Materials Advisory Committee, in 1971.

He graduated from the University of Arkansas (B.S., 1950; M.S., 1954) and Kansas State University (Ph.D., 1956). He is married, has one child, and resides in Bryan, TX. He was born March 11, 1929, in Hickman, AR.

Remarks and a Question-and-Answer Session With Economic Editors During a White House Briefing on Tax Reform
June 7, 1985

The President. I know that Secretary Baker has already briefed you, and Don Regan will be talking to you after I finish. These CEO's always want to have the last word. [*Laughter*] But I'm going to speak for a few minutes and then take some questions, time permitting.

People all across the country are embracing our tax plan, America's tax plan, because they rightly see it as fairer and simpler—something they've been waiting for for a long, long time. All the indications are favorable. Polls show a ground swell of popular support, and a rising stock market and dropping interest rates suggest that the financial markets are very comfortable with America's tax plan.

Our tax overhaul will begin with major tax relief for families who've seen their personal exemptions whittled away by inflation and who've shouldered a huge increase in the tax load. Our family relief plan would raise the standard deduction, practically double the personal exemption, lower marginal income tax rates significantly, and give homemakers equal access to tax deductible IRA's.

Now, I know that I may be saying things that Jim Baker's already said to you, but we're also expanding the earned-income tax credit for low-income wage earners and indexing it to inflation. And the result will be that families will have an easier time making ends meet, and those at the bottom end of the ladder will be virtually exempt from taxation.

Opportunity is key to the promise to the American dream, but high tax rates have transformed that difficult but rewarding climb up the ladder of success into a bitter and exhausting enslavement on the tax treadmill, and that's all going to change.

The tax system must no longer be poverty's accomplice. An American opportunity society begins with an expanding, healthy economy, and that's where our progrowth initiatives come in.

First, we're cutting marginal income tax rates by an average of 19 percent; there's no surer way of getting more economic growth. We saw it happen in Germany after World War II, when Ludwig Erhard's tax cuts helped revitalize their economy; in Japan, when 20 years of continuous tax cutting was instrumental in catapulting that nation into the front ranks of the world's economic leaders.

And here at home, we've had three dramatic examples of lower marginal rates liberating growth—Andrew Mellon's tax cuts in the twenties, John Kennedy's in the sixties, and our almost 25-percent across-the-board tax cut that helped lift the American economy out of malaise and into a surging economic growth in 1981.

America's tax plan will give us just about the lowest tax rates of any country in the industrialized world. And that, along with our vibrant economy, will make us the investment capital of the world.

Some, I know, are concerned about the elimination of the investment tax credit and the restructured depreciation system. We feel our plan would stimulate new economic growth. One of the important ways our proposed depreciation system would be superior to the accelerated system that we had is that it would be indexed to inflation. So, businesses wouldn't have to worry about a decline in the real value of their writeoffs. It would also reduce the distortions in economic efficiency caused by the investment tax credit and other provisions so that the market, not the Government, would determine the flow of capital.

As part of our growth agenda, we're also cutting the capital gains tax. The two previous capital gains cuts in 1978 and '81 probably saved the life of the American economy. Excessively high capital gains had almost strangled the technological revolution at its birth. Venture capital, the high-powered money to finance the riskiest and most daring projects, had all but dried up to a mere $39 million in commitments in 1977. But after cutting capital gains, venture capital shot to all-time high, increasing over a hundredfold to $4.2 billion in 1984 alone.

We're pulling ahead of the competition. Cutting capital gains again, we'll make sure that we stay there. We're closing the door on unjustifiable tax shelters so that we can open the door for innovation, opportunity, and growth. It's time that we pulled our investment money out of the tax shelters and reinvested it in America's future.

We've also pared down deductions for business entertainment expenses. It just doesn't seem right for a wage earner carrying his tuna fish sandwich to work to subsidize exorbitant business lunches at luxury restaurants.

We'd still allow for legitimate expenses. But to those who complain they can't live quite so high off the corporate account, we can only ask: "Well, why not 'brown bag it' once in a while? Why not find smarter ways to put our money to work than investing so heavily in executive lunches?"

We're keeping the provision for writeoffs of intangible drilling costs. Today we import more than a fourth of our oil from abroad. And the money we spent on those imports last year represented half our total trade deficit—scuttling the IDC deductions, which slow oil exploration in this country and reduce our output by as much as half a

billion barrels a day. I don't believe we want to increase our energy dependence on foreign imports or give the ailing OPEC cartel a shot in the arm. We must ensure reliable, secure energy sources here at home.

Also key to a fairer, simpler tax code is elimination of the deduction for State and local taxes. The current deduction benefits wealthy citizens at the expense of those less fortunate. About two-thirds of all Americans and an even greater majority of low- and middle-income taxpayers do not itemize and get no benefit from the State and local tax deduction. The simple fact is low- and middle-income taxpayers are being cheated, because whatever State they're in, high or low tax, the present system forces them to pay the bill for the wealthy few who use the State and local deduction. And that's the injustice. Perhaps if the high-tax States didn't have this Federal crutch to prop up their big spending, they might have to cut taxes to stay competitive.

Some of the elected representatives from the high-tax States don't seem to like that idea much, but maybe they should take a poll of their constituents to see if their people think a tax cut is such a bad idea.

We should get out of the habit of thinking of our economy as static and frozen in place. Our tax proposal is a dynamic model for the future. Any change of such scope and magnitude's going to require some adjustments. For the great majority of Americans, it'll be a very pleasant adjustment to lower rates and new and more plentiful opportunities—a growing, expanding, superenergized economy, an economy of hope and opportunity that just won't quit. I don't think we should settle for less.

And now, I've got time for a few questions here.

Q. Mr. President, are you comfortable with the 24-percent increase in the tax-take from corporations in the short term in the new tax plan?

The President. I believe that what we've done with regard to corporations is aimed more at corporations that, in all good faith, have taken advantage of the present tax structure to make a profit, and at the same time, many of them avoid paying any tax whatsoever or certainly reducing it greatly.

What we think we've done—and by reducing the rate from 46 percent to 33 percent—is actually make the tax structure more fair for business and industry. But also, we have plugged that loophole or series of loopholes by which a number were not paying at all. And that's where the increase would come.

Q. Can we follow up? It also would be knocking the supports out from under some of the basic industries that have enjoyed those benefits—steel—heavy type of capital intensives industries. Is that your aim?

The President. No. But we also don't think that the compensating factor of the reduction in the rates, from 46 to 33, and then some of the other advantages that will be as a part of this plan, we don't believe that we're knocking the props out from under anyone.

Q. Mr. President, there are proposals on the Hill for a fourth tax bracket, perhaps a 40 percent, for those in the upper income levels. Would you consider that? Might you go along with that proposal?

The President. No. As a matter of fact, I think that'd be contrary to what we're doing. Right now, I feel like I'm standing against a cellophane wall getting shot at from both sides, because there are also some people up there on the Hill that want to reduce that top tax from 35 to 30. So, the 40-percenters will be shooting and so will the 30-percenters, and we think that the bracket we've chosen is a fair one.

Q. Mr. President, as you know, the deductions for State and local taxes, along with interest deductions, have been with us since the first income tax in 1913 when the top rate, as I'm told, was about 7 percent. So——

The President. If you were making a half a million dollars a year——

Q. Well, I wasn't. [*Laughter*]

The President. ——back in 1913. [*Laughter*]

Q. I'm not—not now either. [*Laughter*] And of course that's been around a long time, and you want to get rid of it. So, the question obviously is, considering what's happening on the Hill: Just how open to negotiation are you on this tax program?

The President. You mean on the——

Q. Not just on that, but on the whole plan.

The President. Well, we think that we've worked out a pretty good plan. We've made some changes from the Treasury One proposal that we think were justified and should be made. We think that this one is balanced.

But if they start nibbling at some of the specific proposals there on the Hill, as they undoubtedly will, there's one thing that they're going to have to be able to answer for any change they want to make. And that is: Where are they going to get the replacement revenue? For example, the deductibility of State and local taxes is a tremendous part of the revenue proposal, and I don't know where they would get the money that would be eliminated if they did away with that.

Q. Mr. President, you have always been an advocate of federalism and of having decisions on taxes and spending made as close to the local taxpayer as possible. Aren't you in this proposal trying to force certain States to cut their taxes and thereby cut their programs also?

The President. We just said that if this kind of subsidy is taken away from them, they might take a look to see if they haven't just been sort of inspired to raise their taxes because of the deductibility feature. And no one, no level of government should be taxing more than is absolutely necessary. We should be taxing to meet government's real needs, not government's wants.

And we think that the overall tax reduction that we're giving the people in a way does something that I also have advocated for a great many years and that is that the Federal Government, beginning back in the Depression days, gradually preempted so much taxing authority that local and State governments found it impossible to go to the people for a tax increase that they might actually need for something necessary.

And by doing what we did in '81 and doing what we're now doing with this proposal, we are reducing the share that the Federal Government is taking and opening up the fact that some local level of government or State level with a real need now can find that there's more leeway out there.

Back when I was casting my first vote, the total amount of money that governments were taking in this country was about 10 cents out of every dollar earned and of that two-thirds was going to local and State governments, only less than one-third to the Federal Government. Now we're taking up there somewhere around 35 cents for all—total governments. And of that amount, three-fifths is taken by the Federal Government and only two-fifths left for the State and local. So, we're in a sense redressing this back to where there'll be more availability out there in the earnings of the people.

Ms. Mathis. One more question.

The President. Now, I'm—all right.

Q. Yes. I think that there is considerable concern in Congress about the distribution benefits, the fairness issue. And one way of figuring it is that the people in the bracket of $20,000 to $50,000, they would get an average tax cut of about $200. But people over $200,000 would actually get a tax cut of about $10,000. Do you think that that's fair or should that be altered?

The President. Well, I don't know that the figures are completely accurate on this other, but I do know that the brackets and the percentages—it is still a progressive tax, and we have not come down to proportionate tax, as some of the flat tax people would have us do.

I think we have to recognize that that tiny percentage of people up there at that top level, roughly about 3 percent of the taxpayers—yes, if you go dollar-wise, they're going to get tremendous amounts of dollars back. But they're also going to be paying a tremendously greater, much greater tax out of those earnings.

But when you start talking about people—like now, some of the salaries that are so loosely thrown around of a million dollars or more a year, obviously, they're going to get a bigger bundle of dollars, as I've said. But at the same time, proportionately, they're going to be paying hundreds of times more tax than the individuals that you mentioned. But I believe that that middle-income group is also going to be doing better than that tax that's been proposed.

Ms. Mathis. Thank you very much.

The President. You won't let me take any more? Can't I take the lady's question? *[Laughter]* If I don't, you'll have to.

Yes.

Q. Thank you, Mr. President. Education for the handicapped has been proven to be an investment rather than an expense. For instance, at Cal State Northridge in Los Angeles, the masters program produces graduates who are able to earn up to $45,000 to $60,000 a year—thanks to the program for deaf-mainstreamed education there—at the cost to the taxpayer of $6,200 a year. May I ask, what is the proposal in the tax plan at the moment to maintain such programs to help these people to be able to find employment and so relieve the Government of the tax burden of supporting them?

The President. I don't think I heard—you're talking about our aid to college students now?

Q. To the handicapped students, the deaf students, particularly.

The President. Well, now—I should have let him answer this to begin with—*[laughter]*—because I don't think that we're having that much of a——

Secretary Baker. She's—I think that's a budget question, if I may say so. You've proposed a budget question, not a tax question.

The President. Yes.

Q. Well, we were hoping that it would be part of the tax plan, to incorporate it as a peripheral for the budget.

The President. I think that what we're talking about is the whole general thing in the educational funds of the Federal Government. And I think that they have been misread, also, and are not taking into consideration a number of programs in which we have changed from a specific program—where we found the administrative overhead when the Federal Government dictated it was very high—that we have switched to incorporate things in block grants, where the local entity can utilize that in the way that they think meets their priorities, because they're not the same wherever we go. And I think you'll find that we have provided—that we're not actually cutting into those funds.

I can just give you one example. We have in 1 block grant, we reduced—or one series of 10 block grants—we incorporated some 62 categorical grants, Federal grants, and in so doing found that we had reduced the regulations and the redtape on local levels of government from 801 pages of regulations down to 30 pages of regulations, by incorporating it into the block grant.

So, having been a Governor and knowing what some of those redtape restrictions did

to us when we started implementing the programs, I think that we've made an improvement there overall.

But I'm going to have to turn it over to the CEO now. Thank you all very much.

Note: The President spoke at 1:33 p.m. in Room 450 of the Old Executive Office Building. Susan K. Mathis was Deputy Director of Media Relations.

Radio Address to the Nation on United States Assistance for the Nicaraguan Democratic Resistance
June 8, 1985

My fellow Americans:

Today I want to give you some encouraging news about the opportunities for liberty, democracy, and peace in Central America, particularly in Nicaragua. This hope is based on a renewed chance for the United States to provide support to those who struggle against totalitarian communism on the mainland of this hemisphere.

We're being given something very precious—a second chance to do what is right. Recently, on April 4th, I met here in Washington with Adolfo Calero, Arturo Cruz, and Alfonso Robelo, the three principal leaders of the Nicaraguan democratic opposition. I asked these three brave men to extend their offer of a cease-fire and a church-mediated dialog with the Sandinista regime in Managua.

Those exiled patriots and their followers made this proposal in San José, Costa Rica, on March 1 in a declaration of unity, common cause, and democratic purpose. Unfortunately, their proposal was immediately rejected by the Sandinista Communists who similarly rebuffed our April 4th endorsement of this realistic peace proposal.

Shortly thereafter, our House of Representatives voted not to provide assistance to the Nicaraguan freedom fighters. The Sandinistas and their cohorts believed the way was clear for the consolidation of their Communist regime. Nicaragua's dictator

raced to Moscow and the bloc capitals of Eastern Europe to seal closer relations with these Communist tyrannies.

And now the Nicaraguans are not only continuing to import offensive weapons, they have stepped up their attacks on neighboring Honduras and unarmed Costa Rica. But as I said, we have a second chance to do what is right. On Thursday the United States Senate, in a show of bipartisan support, voted to aid the freedom fighters struggling for liberty and democracy in Nicaragua. The Senate has seen that their struggle is ours, that they need and deserve our help.

In the House some claim that the U.S. plans to become militarily involved in Central America. Well, no such plan exists. That charge is simply a distraction from the two paramount questions that must be faced by every Member: Will you support those struggling for democracy? Will you resist the Soviets' brazen attempt to impose communism on our doorstep or won't you?

There's a bipartisan proposal in the House to keep alive the dream of freedom and peace in Nicaragua. It'll be put forward next Wednesday by Republicans Bob Michel of Illinois and Joe McDade of Pennsylvania and Democrat Dave McCurdy of Oklahoma. It is essential that this bipartisan amendment be passed without any weakening of its provisions in order for us to have a hope for peace, democracy, and reconciliation in Nicaragua.

The legislation will provide $27 million worth of assistance to the freedom fighters, and that's not much compared to the hundreds of millions the Communists are spending to prop up their Nicaraguan dictatorship.

The solution to the tragedy in Nicaragua is the very same the Congress has supported in El Salvador—liberty, democracy, and reconciliation. In El Salvador we've worked with Congress and stood firmly behind President Duarte and the democratic forces. We seek the same goals in Nicaragua. As in El Salvador, the United States stands with the democratic Senator—Senate, I should say, against the enemies of liberty on both left and right. And the freedom fighters share our goals for democracy.

One of their leaders, Adolfo Calero, said this week, "We of the Nicaraguan democratic resistance believe that true peace can only come with democracy and that democracy is a precondition for peace—not the other way around."

To seize this opportunity before us, to seize this second chance now offered, the Congress and the executive branch must embark on a bipartisan course for a negotiated political settlement, national reconciliation, democracy, and genuine self-deter-

mination for the people of Nicaragua.

Just 6 years ago, the people of Nicaragua—students, labor unions, businessmen, and the church—fought for a democratic revolution, only to see it betrayed by a handful of Soviet-backed Communists. We must not sit by while the Nicaraguan people are saddled with a Communist dictatorship that threatens this entire hemisphere. A House vote for humanitarian aid to the freedom fighters will send a strong bipartisan message that we will not tolerate the evolution of Nicaragua into another Cuba nor will we remain with our heads in the sand while Nicaragua becomes a Soviet client state with military installations constructed for use by the Soviet bloc.

A Soviet base in Nicaragua would give the Russians a foothold on the American mainland. America's proudest moments have come when Democrats and Republicans united for the cause of democracy. That is the path which is succeeding in El Salvador, and that is the path that will succeed in Nicaragua, too, if we support the bipartisan proposal to aid the freedom fighters.

Until next week, thanks for listening, and God bless you.

Note: The President spoke at 12:06 p.m. from Camp David, MD.

Remarks at a White House Reception for New Republicans
June 10, 1985

The President. I know you've made Ed Rollins very happy—*[laughter]*—and I can tell you that George and I are very happy also.

The Vice President. Yes, we are.

The President. Can't tell you how happy.

Welcome here to the White House. You've already met a few converts from the other two branches of government. I'm very excited today because Ed Rollins is allowing me to speak for the executive branch. *[Laughter]*

Welcome to the Republican Party. Welcome to the party of the open door. We're

happy to have you, and we're richer, very much so, for your presence. You have our admiration also.

Many of you hold public office, and you were longtime Democrats, and you changed parties at considerable risk. It was an act of courage and an act of conscience. When Winston Churchill did what you did in his country, he said, "Some men change principle for party, and some change party for principle." He was one of the latter, as you are. And you have our thanks.

I was thinking this morning about political independence, and I remember the story of President Kennedy and how he asked an aide how he planned to vote in an important election back there in Massachusetts. And the aide hesitated; he didn't want to admit he just couldn't, in good conscience, vote for the Democratic candidate. And Kennedy said, "Say it. Of course, you're going to vote for the Republican. Sometimes party loyalty asks too much." [*Laughter*] Well, sometimes it does.

You know what you've left and why, and I'm not going to use this forum to run down the other party. They have enough troubles—[*laughter*]—and we don't want to add to them, well, maybe later. [*Laughter*] But as a fellow convert, let me tell you what, in my view, you've joined. You've joined the party of ideas, a party that has positive and coherent programs to deal with the great problems of our time. You've joined the party of the working man and woman.

Let the other party have the entrenched interests and the powerbrokers and special interest politics; we don't have any of that. We just have the people—and more and more people who won't be held down by any government plans but who are going to break free to follow their dreams—and that's the great opportunity party that we're building together.

You've joined the party that can speak of and glory in the best of American tradition and American culture because it believes in those traditions and that culture. You've joined a party that looks at our vast and imperfect nation and sees that it's precious and to be protected, a party that still feels the old tug of the immigrants' love for America—the pure, unalloyed love of those who have experienced less free places and who adored America for giving them freedom and opportunity.

You've also joined the party of the young. I don't mean to brag but 59 percent of those aged 18 to 24 voted for the Republican national ticket in 1984; many people see this as a trend. There is a rumor that our young people just kind of related to the youthfulness of the top of our ticket. [*Laughter*] I not only heard that rumor; I spread it. [*Laughter*]

You've joined a party that was once rather sedate. That party was—or that was until the current leaders and shapers of the GOP started lobbing around intellectual handgrenades and insisting that America stop talking about economic justice and start creating the conditions that make it possible and stopped ignoring or just talking about ways to deal with the greater foreign policy challenge of our time—the militarist, expansionist intentions of communism—and start doing something about it.

And the supply-siders, the "Neocons," the New Right, the new Republican majority—whatever you call them—they took the Grand Old Party and made it the grand new party, with great new power—the GNP—speaking of which, we also turned the economy around.

You've joined a robust and rambunctious party that is rich in diversity and full of variety, a party that is black and white and brown and yellow, old and young and rich and poor.

You're not joining a perfect party. We began in greatness more than 100 years ago, and we've known considerable greatness since. And, yes, we've made our mistakes. There've been good ideas that we embraced too slowly and movements that we rejected outright when, at their core, there was really some good.

And I have to tell you that I know what you've gone through and what you feel, because it's still—I find it a little strange when I keep going on here saying "we" so much. For a long time I was saying "they" about the Republican Party.

But more often than not, we've been on the right side and fought the good fight, and it's wonderful to see our new recruits. And it's wonderful to be fighting for a second American revolution of hope and opportunity for all the American people.

Now, members of the press in the back there and many others are interested to know who the new Republicans are. Well, they're Judge Berlaind Brashear, a lifelong Democrat who switched parties, because in his words, "I feel many black leaders have lost faith in our two-party system, but I have faith in the people." The judge is one of the first black Texas Republican elected officials since Reconstruction.

And there's an Italian immigrant who taught himself English, earned a college degree in America, and was a loyal Democrat all his life. But after being elected to his State assembly, he switched parties and became a Republican—all that in the year 1984, in the State of New York, and with the name "Ferraro." [*Laughter*] We welcome Arnaldo J.A. Ferraro to the Republican Party.

Then there is Dexter Lehtinen, a member of the Florida State Legislature and a decorated Vietnam veteran who was wounded in action. He, too, was a longtime Democrat, but he became a Republican in March. He told us, "I grew weary of trying to convince the Democrats that crime should not pay and that crime victims matter."

Well, you know, I have to tell you when I was Governor of California and had a majority of the Democrats in both houses of the legislature, and then through a couple of special elections and coincidences we wound up with a one-vote majority in the legislature, and in that year, with that one vote in each house which allowed us to put the majority on the committees and appoint the chairman of the committees, we passed 41 anticrime bills, every one of which had been in the legislature for quite a period of time and buried in the committees until they became Republican committees.

Well, these that I've named are just a few. You're not isolated cases. You're part of a great national change, a national movement that is sweeping the electorate. You're representative of something that's going on across the country—the millions of grassroot Democrats and Independents who have been voting for the Republican Party because they feel it represents what they believe about America and the future.

You and people such as Andy Ireland, Bob Stump, and Phil Gramm are part of a change that is sweeping the country. You're familiar with all the polls; the most recent was in the New York Times last Wednesday. I don't normally read the New York Times for fun—[*laughter*]—but there it was on the front page: "About the same number of people now identify themselves as Republicans as call themselves Democrats." Remember when they called us the minority party? How sweet it is! [*Laughter*]

I just want to add one thing—not for those in this room, but for those who may listen later—it's that in America a lot of people are sort of born into a political party. Their families belong to the same party for generation after generation. And it seems like heresy or a renunciation of who you are and where you're from to switch. Well, this kind of fidelity to traditions and old ties is good; Americans are a faithful people. But the thing is, all of you have demonstrated when the party you were born into changes, when the party you were born into no longer represents the hopes and aspirations of the people you came from, well, then that party left you— you didn't leave it. And that has happened.

I cast my first vote as a Democrat in 1932. And the Democratic Party platform in that year called for a 25-percent reduction in government spending; it called for the elimination of needless bureaus and agencies and departments of government; it called for a return to States and local communities the authority and autonomy they said had been unjustly seized by the Federal Government. And I think you're evidence today that there is a different party today that runs on that platform, and that is the Republican Party.

You went to a new party, becoming a faithful member of that party, and doing that as a reaffirmation of what you are and where you're from. As I've said, it's a reaffirmation of the dreams that your parents and grandparents dreamed. It's a reaffirmation of your tradition, your culture, your ethnic loyalties, and your Americanism. And let me add that if we ever let you down, you don't owe us your undying loyalty. If we ever leave you, you'll be right to leave us.

We're richer for your presence, and the future of this party is in your hands and the hands of your friends and relatives and fellow Republicans, which leaves me, as I look at you, very optimistic about the future of the GOP and very optimistic about the future of America.

I just have one little personal thing I have to say here talking about my own conversion. I campaigned for awhile as a Democrat for Republican candidates. And finally I was pretty much accepted as a Republican and was speaking at a Republican fundraiser, and right in the middle of my speech a woman stood up out in the middle of the audience, and she said, "Have you reregistered yet?" [*Laughter*] And I said, "No, but I'm going to." She said, "I'm a registrar." And she came right down the middle—[*laughter*]—put it there on the podium, and I signed up and then said, "Now, where was

I?" [*Laughter*]

Well, welcome aboard, welcome home, and thank you, and God bless you all. Thank you very much.

And converts make the best kind. Thank you very much.

Note: The President spoke at 12:02 p.m. in the State Dining Room at the White House.

Remarks to the Los Angeles Lakers, the National Basketball Association Champions
June 10, 1985

The President. Well, I thank you all very much for that greeting, but believe me these are the ones that deserve the applause. And it is we who today will say, "Hail to the Lakers."

It was a great pleasure to welcome all of you to the White House. Your entire championship series down to yesterday's great win was an inspiration. And all of you showed America what pride, determination, and guts can accomplish when they're combined with some of the best talent on the floor.

Yesterday afternoon, it really was showtime in the Boston Garden. And your victory is all the greater because you won it from another truly great team. When you went to the Garden, you knew that the next two games were going to decide the championship either way, and you knew that even though you were playing in Boston it wasn't going to be any tea party. [*Laughter*]

Kareem says that yesterday's victory was just like the Brooklyn Dodgers' breakthrough against the Yankees in the 1955 World Series. Well, Kareem, I remember that series, so I think you may be, as they sometimes say of me, showing your experience. [*Laughter*]

But yesterday all you showed was why you've been voted the most valuable player of the series. As so many said, you're 38, but you played like you were 25. And that 14-foot sky hook with only 61 seconds left in the game was truly a thing of beauty. All I can say is we're all looking forward to seeing you defend the Lakers' championship title next year.

And then there was your teammate, Magic Johnson, who put in a magnificent performance. Magic, you ended the series with 84 assists, breaking the record for a 6-game championship series by an awesome 24. Does America believe in Magic? You bet we do. [*Laughter*]

Some may have thought the Celtics' title was an immovable object, but yesterday they came up against an irresistible force by the name of James Worthy. I don't know what all those sirens are doing; we're all here. [*Laughter*] But the Celtics' head coach said that one of the reasons his team lost was they just couldn't stop James Worthy. And, James, if you're ever thinking of a career after basketball, we've got some lobbying work up on Capitol Hill—[*laughter*]—that we could use you for.

Kurt Rambis and Mitch Kupchak also get great credit for their tenacious and aggressive play. And I think Kurt ought to win an etiquette award for the player with the best manners. [*Laughter*] It's not everybody who knows what to say when he dives over the sidelines and into a lady's lap. [*Laughter*]

Everyone on the Lakers' team deserves praise, and there's certainly enough credit to go around. Though you've got your full complement of stars, it's teamplay that made you great. And for that, for the training, the strategy, and the never-say-die encouragement that went into making you

741

number one, we have your great coach, Pat Riley, to thank.

And I understand that the Lakers' family has not only been an example for young people on the court but also off the court. Lakers' wives have taken on drug abuse prevention as their special project. And I want you to know how grateful both Nancy and I are for your important work in this area.

Well, the Lakers are no longer simply L.A.'s heroes; today you belong to the whole country; you're America's champions. And we're mighty proud of you. So, congratulations, and well done, and God bless you all.

Commissioner Stern. Mr. President, thank you for your kind invitation and gracious remarks. Because of basketball's purely domestic origins, we're proud to be called America's game.

The NBA championship series confirmed that description, Mr. President—a diverse group of players and coaches from all parts of this great country once again demonstrated that sacrifice, hard work, and teamplay lead to success.

It is my honor as commissioner of the NBA to present to you the 1985 NBA Champion Los Angeles Lakers, who will be represented at the podium by the captain, Kareem Abdul-Jabbar, the irrepressible Magic Johnson, and the head coach, Pat Riley.

Kareem Abdul-Jabbar. I was telling the President that I'm not a Republican, but I am one of his constituents, and because of that, I figured we should suit him up the right way.

The President. Thank you very much.

Kareem Abdul-Jabbar. Just so we know who's number one here. [*Laughter*]

The President. Thank you very much. I'm very proud to have this.

Kareem Abdul-Jabbar. My pleasure. Thank you.

Magic Johnson. I guess I'm next. [*Laughter*] This is just another one of our gifts to say thank you for having us here and—what more can I say? I think Kareem said it all. And this is just great being here, being with the President and all you good people. So, here it is, to you.

The President. Well, thank you. Thanks very much.

Coach Riley. Mr. President, on behalf of the players and the entire Laker organization, we would like to express our appreciation and gratitude for this honor, for being able to come to the White House, because we know that there's only one other place other than Los Angeles that there's a winner, and that's here. So, we appreciate that, Mr. President.

And we also know that, occasionally, you like to head west and—the ranch out there—and when you hit that Arizona-California border, we want you to be a little casual with the 1985 championship hat and a championship shirt.

The President. Thank you very much. Thank you.

I just have to explain something. The reason that they had to bend over to reach the microphone was because if I'd put it up at their height, there's no way I could stretch that high, but they could always bend down a little bit. I appreciate your doing that.

Thank you all very much. God bless you.

Note: The President spoke at 2:12 p.m. in the Rose Garden at the White House. During the ceremony, the President received a jersey, a cap, and an autographed basketball.

Statement on Soviet and United States Compliance With Arms Control Agreements
June 10, 1985

In 1982, on the eve of the strategic arms reductions talks (START), I decided that the United States would not undercut the expired SALT I agreement or the unratified SALT II agreement as long as the Soviet Union exercised equal restraint. Despite my serious reservations about the inequities of the SALT I agreement and the serious flaws of the SALT II agreement, I took this action in order to foster an atmosphere of mutual restraint conducive to serious negotiation as we entered START.

Since then the United States has not taken any actions which would undercut existing arms control agreements. The United States has fully kept its part of the bargain, however, the Soviets have not. They have failed to comply with several provisions of SALT II, and we have serious concerns regarding their compliance with the provisions of other accords.

The pattern of Soviet violations, if left uncorrected, undercuts the integrity and viability of arms control as an instrument to assist in ensuring a secure and stable future world. The United States will continue to pursue vigorously with the Soviet Union the resolution of our concerns over Soviet noncompliance. We cannot impose upon ourselves a double standard that amounts to unilateral treaty compliance.

We remain determined to pursue a productive dialog with the Soviet Union aimed at reducing the risk of war through the adoption of meaningful measures which improve security, stability, and predictability. Therefore, I have reached the judgment that, despite the Soviet record over the last years, it remains in our interest to establish an interim framework of truly mutual restraint on strategic offensive arms as we pursue with renewed vigor our goal of real reductions in the size of existing nuclear arsenals in the ongoing negotiations in Geneva. Obtaining such reductions remains my highest priority.

The U.S. cannot establish such a framework alone. It will require the Soviet Union to take the positive, concrete steps to correct its noncompliance, resolve our other compliance concerns, and reverse its unparalleled and unwarranted military buildup. So far, the Soviet Union has not chosen to move in this direction. However, in the interest of ensuring that every opportunity to establish the secure, stable future we seek is fully explored, I am prepared to go the extra mile in seeking an interim framework of truly mutual restraint.

Therefore, to provide the Soviets the opportunity to join us in establishing such a framework which could support ongoing negotiations, I have decided that the United States will continue to refrain from undercutting existing strategic arms agreements to the extent that the Soviet Union exercises comparable restraint and provided that the Soviet Union actively pursues arms reduction agreements in the currently ongoing nuclear and space talks in Geneva.

As an integral part of this policy, we will also take those steps required to assure the national security of the United States and our allies which were made necessary by Soviet noncompliance. Appropriate and proportionate responses to Soviet noncompliance are called for to ensure our security, to provide incentives to the Soviets to correct their noncompliance, and to make it clear to Moscow that violations of arms control obligations entail real costs.

Certain Soviet violations are, by their very nature, irreversible. Such is the case with respect to the Soviet Union's flight-testing and steps towards deployment of the SS–X–25 missile, a second new type of ICBM prohibited by the unratified SALT II agreement. Since the noncompliance associated with the development of this missile cannot be corrected by the Soviet Union, the United States reserves the right to respond in a proportionate manner at the appropriate time. The Midgetman small ICBM program is particularly relevant in this regard.

Other Soviet activities involving noncompliance may be reversible and can be corrected by Soviet action. In these instances, we will provide the Soviet Union additional time to take such required corrective action. As we monitor Soviet actions for evidence of the positive, concrete steps needed on their part to correct these activities, I have directed the Department of Defense to conduct a comprehensive assessment aimed at identifying specific actions which the United States could take to augment as necessary the U.S. strategic modernization program as a proportionate response to, and as a hedge against the military consequences of, those Soviet violations of existing arms agreements which the Soviets fail to correct.

To provide adequate time for the Soviets to demonstrate by their actions a commitment to join us in an interim framework of true mutual restraint, we will plan to deactivate and dismantle according to agreed procedures an existing Poseidon SSBN as the seventh U.S. Ohio-class submarine puts to sea later this year. However, the United States will keep open all programmatic options for handling such milestones as they occur in the future. As these later milestones are reached, I will assess the overall

situation in light of Soviet actions correcting their noncompliance and promoting progress in Geneva and make a final determination of the U.S. course of action on a case-by-case basis.

I firmly believe that if we are to put the arms reduction process on a firm and lasting foundation and obtain real reductions, our focus must remain on making best use of the promise provided by the currently ongoing negotiations in Geneva. Our policy, involving the establishment of an interim framework for truly mutual restraint and proportionate U.S. response to uncorrected Soviet noncompliance, is specifically designed to go the extra mile in giving the Soviet Union the opportunity to join us in this endeavor.

My hope is that if the Soviets will do so, we will be able jointly to make progress in framing equitable and verifiable agreements involving real reductions in the size of existing nuclear arsenals in the Geneva negotiations. Such an achievement would not only provide the best and most permanent constraint on the growth of nuclear arsenals, but it would take a major step towards reducing the size of these arsenals and creating a safer future for all nations.

Message to the Congress Transmitting a Report on Soviet and United States Compliance With Arms Control Agreements
June 10, 1985

To the Congress of the United States:

The attached classified report responds to a requirement in the FY–85 Department of Defense Authorization Act (Section 1110 of P.L. 98–525) requesting a report that:

(A) describes the implications of the United States Ship Alaska's sea trials, both with and without the concurrent dismantling of older launchers of missiles with multiple independently targeted reentry vehicles, for the current United States no-undercut policy on strategic arms and United States security interests more generally;

(B) assesses possible Soviet political, mili-

tary, and negotiating responses to the termination of the United States no-undercut policy;

(C) reviews and assesses Soviet activities with respect to existing strategic offensive arms agreements; and

(D) makes recommendations regarding the future of United States interim restraint policy.

In accordance with our prior interim restraint policy, the United States has scrupulously lived within the SALT I and II agreements governing strategic offensive arms. The United States has fully kept its part of the bargain. By contrast, we have found and reported to the Congress that the

Soviet Union has violated major arms control obligations, as fully documented in comprehensive reports to the Congress on this subject in January 1984 and February 1985. Multiple Soviet violations of the SALT II Treaty and of other agreements were fundamental considerations in assessing a future United States interim restraint policy.

The basic United States strategic goals remain unchanged. In the years ahead, the United States objective is a radical reduction in the levels and the power of existing and planned offensive nuclear arms, as well as on stabilization of the relationship between nuclear offensive and defensive arms, whether on earth or in space.

I firmly believe that if we are to put the arms reduction process on a firm and lasting foundation, our focus must remain on making best use of the promise provided by the current negotiations in Geneva. The policy outlined in my report, involving the establishment of an interim framework for truly mutual restraint and proportionate United States responses to uncorrected Soviet noncompliance, is specifically designed to go the extra mile in giving the Soviet Union the opportunity to join us in this vital endeavor.

I believe that this policy, addressed in the classified report and the unclassified fact sheet, both recognizes the recent views of the Congress and serves as a basis for bipartisan support.

RONALD REAGAN

The White House,
June 10, 1985.

Nomination of Bruce Chapman To Be United States Representative to the United Nations Vienna Office and Deputy United States Representative to the International Atomic Energy Agency
June 10, 1985

The President today announced his intention to nominate Bruce Chapman to be the Representative of the United States of America to the Vienna Office of the United Nations and Deputy Representative of the United States of America to the International Atomic Energy Agency, with the rank of Ambassador. He would succeed Richard Salisbury Williamson.

Mr. Chapman has been serving as Deputy Assistant to the President and Director of the Office of Planning and Evaluation since 1983. In 1981–1983 he was Director, Bureau of the Census. Mr. Chapman was secretary of state for the State of Washington in Seattle. In 1960–1971, he was publisher for Advance magazine; a writer for the New York Herald Tribune; and was self-employed as a consultant and writer.

During the years 1968–1981, he served on the Washington Commission on the Causes and Prevention of Civil Disorders; the Governor's Urban Affairs Council (a Washington State study commission); U.S. Commission on Civil Rights for Washington State; the President's Advisory Council on Historic Preservation; and the University of Washington visiting committee for the school of international studies.

Mr. Chapman graduated from Harvard College (B.A., 1962). He is married to the former Sarah Gilmore Williams, they have two children and reside in Washington, DC. He was born December 1, 1940, in Evanston, IL.

Appointment of Eugene B. Burroughs as a Member of the Advisory Committee to the Pension Benefit Guaranty Corporation
June 10, 1985

The President today announced his intention to appoint Eugene B. Burroughs to be a member of the Advisory Committee to the Pension Benefit Guaranty Corporation for a term expiring February 19, 1988. He would succeed Joseph Lydon.

Mr. Burroughs is currently director of the investment department of the International Brotherhood of Teamsters in Washington, DC. Previously he was chief accountant for the International Brotherhood of Teamsters (1963–1969). He was appointed by President Ford as a member of the Advisory Committee to the Pension Benefit Guaranty Corporation and served as chairman of the Investment Policy Panel. He is past president of the Washington Society of Investments Analysts and is general chairman of the 1985 annual conference of the Financial Analysts Federation. He is a member of the board of directors of the Financial Analysts Federation and Potomac Asset Management Co. in Washington, DC.

Mr. Burroughs graduated from Benjamin Franklin University (B.S., 1955). He is married, has two children, and resides in McLean, VA. He was born August 22, 1931, in Washington, DC.

Appointment of Charles R. Work as a Member of the District of Columbia Commission on Judicial Disabilities and Tenure
June 10, 1985

The President today announced his intention to appoint Charles R. Work to be a member of the District of Columbia Commission on Judicial Disabilities and Tenure for a term expiring March 18, 1990. He would succeed Vincent Hamilton Cohen.

Mr. Work is currently a partner with the law firm of McDermott, Will & Emery in Washington, DC. Previously, he was a partner with Peabody, Lambert & Meyers (1975–1982); Deputy Administrator, Law Enforcement Assistance Administration, U.S. Department of Justice (1973–1975); Deputy Chief and Chief, Superior Court Division, Office of the U.S. Attorney for the District of Columbia (1969–1973); and Assistant United States Attorney (criminal trial section) (1966–1969).

Mr. Work graduated from Wesleyan University (B.A., 1962), the University of Chicago Law School (J.D., 1965), and the Georgetown University Law Center (LL.M., 1966). He is married, has three children, and resides in Washington, DC. He was born June 21, 1940, in Glendale, CA.

Appointment of William F. Martin as Executive Secretary of the National Security Council
June 11, 1985

The President today announced his intention to appoint William F. Martin as Executive Secretary of the National Security Council. He will succeed Robert M. Kimmitt.

Mr. Martin has served on the National

Security Council staff since 1982 as Director of International Economic Affairs, Deputy Executive Secretary, and Special Assistant to the President for National Security Affairs (Coordination). In his new capacity, Mr. Martin will retain the title of Special Assistant to the President for National Security Affairs.

Prior to joining the National Security Council sB'aff, Mr. Martin was special assistant to the Under Secretary of State for Economic Affairs. In 1979–1981 he served in the International Energy Agency in Paris as special assistant to the Executive Director and was responsible for overall coordination of International Energy Agency ministerial meetings. Before that he was a program officer of the Workshop on Alternative Energy Strategies based at the Massachusetts Institute of Technology.

He graduated from the University of Pennsylvania (B.S., 1972) and the Massachusetts Institute of Technology (S.M., 1974). He is married to the former Jill Wheaton, and they have two sons. He was born October 4, 1950, in Tulsa, OK.

Nomination of Rozanne L. Ridgway To Be an Assistant Secretary of State
June 11, 1985

The President today announced his intention to nominate Rozanne L. Ridgway to be an Assistant Secretary of State (European and Canadian Affairs). She would succeed Richard R. Burt.

Since 1982 she has been serving as U.S. Ambassador to the German Democratic Republic, Berlin. Previously, she was special assistant to the Secretary of State in 1981–1982; Counselor of the Department of State in 1980–1981; Ambassador to Finland in 1977–1980; Deputy Assistant Secretary of State for Oceans and Fisheries Affairs, with the rank of Ambassador, in 1975–1977; and deputy chief of mission in Nassau in 1973–1975. Prior to that time, she served in the Department as Deputy Director, Policy Planning and Coordination, in the Bureau of Inter-American Affairs (1972–1973) and desk officer for Ecuadorean affairs in 1970–1972.

Ambassador Ridgway was political officer in Oslo (1967–1970) and served in the Department as international relations officer in the Bureau of European Affairs (1964–1967). She was visa officer in Palermo in 1962–1964, personnel officer in Manila in 1959–1962, and information specialist at the Department in 1957–1959.

She graduated from Hamline University (B.A., 1957). She was born August 22, 1935, in St. Paul, MN.

Appointment of William R. Jackson as a Member of the Council of the Administrative Conference of the United States
June 11, 1985

The President today announced his intention to appoint William R. Jackson to be a member of the Council of the Administrative Conference of the United States for a term of 3 years. He will succeed Michael R. Gardner.

Mr. Jackson is a partner in the law firm of Jackson, Bolton and Gomes in Tustin, CA. Previously, he was a partner in the law firm of Brill & Hunt in Los Angeles, CA (1979–1982); a partner in the firm of Kendig, Stockwell & Gleason in Beverly Hills, CA (1976–1979); an attorney in the firm of Long & Levit in Los Angeles (1972–1976); and president of Jackson-Nolen, Inc. (general contractors), in 1966–1972.

He graduated from Brigham Young University (B.S., 1960) and the University of California at Los Angeles (J.D., 1965). He is married, has five children, and resides in Tustin, CA. He was born March 26, 1937, in Los Angeles, CA.

Appointment of Portia Scott as a Member of the National Afro-American History and Culture Commission
June 11, 1985

The President today announced his intention to appoint Portia Scott to be a member of the National Afro-American History and Culture Commission for a term expiring January 18, 1986. She will succeed Margaret Burroughs.

She is the assistant to the general manager of the Atlanta Daily World. Previously she was with the Atlanta Daily World and the Birmingham World as a reporter, editor, and assistant production manager. She was an instructor of journalism at Clark College in Atlanta, GA, in 1972–1976.

Ms. Scott was organizer and president of the new Atlanta section, National Council of Negro Women, Inc. (1975–1978), and served as a member of the Governor's Commission on the Status of Women (1975–1977). In 1978 she was appointed to a 4-year term on the State Commission (Georgia) on Physical Fitness.

She graduated from Howard University (B.A., 1964) and Atlanta University (M.A., 1971). She has one child and resides in Atlanta, GA. She was born June 9, 1943, in Atlanta, GA.

Statement on Signing the United States-Israel Free Trade Area Implementation Act of 1985
June 11, 1985

I have signed today H.R. 2268, the United States-Israel Free Trade Area Implementation Act of 1985, that approves and provides the necessary authority to implement the Free Trade Area Agreement between the United States and Israel.

The signing of this act is the culmination of an effort that began in November 1983 when former Israeli Prime Minister Shamir and I agreed to begin discussions toward the establishment of a bilateral free trade area between our countries. On October 30, 1984, I signed into law the Trade and Tariff Act of 1984 that, among other things, authorized the negotiation of an agreement with Israel. On April 22, 1985, after completion of negotiations, the Agreement on the Establishment of a Free Trade Area between the Government of the United States of America and the Government of Israel was signed in Washington by Ambassador William E. Brock and Minister of Industry and Trade Ariel Sharon. Today this act provides congressional approval of that agreement and provides the necessary legal authority to implement all of its terms.

The passage of this act and the approval of the agreement that underlies it is of great significance for three reasons:

First, the establishment of the U.S.-Israel Free Trade Area will stand as a model of the close cooperation between the administration and the Congress that can bring about a result benefiting all Americans. This was a bipartisan accomplishment. I especially wish to recommend the leadership of Senate Majority Leader Dole, Chairman Packwood and Senator Danforth of the Senate Committee on Finance, and Chairman Rostenkowski and Representatives Sam Gibbons and Bill Frenzel of the House

Committee on Ways and Means for their efforts in making the U.S.-Israel free trade area a reality.

Second, the new free trade area between the United States and Israel represents an important milestone in this administration's efforts to liberalize trade. We hope that it will also serve to encourage greater liberalization of the multilateral trading system and that it will help us move ahead in our continued attempts to expand world trade.

Third, and finally, I believe this new eco-nomic relationship with our friends in Israel will further our historic friendship, strengthen both of our economies, and provide for new opportunities between our peoples for communication and commerce. Nothing better demonstrates the shared community of aspirations between our nations than our promotion of free and harmonious trade for our mutual benefit.

Note: H.R. 2268, approved June 11, was assigned Public Law No. 99–47.

Remarks at the Welcoming Ceremony for Prime Minister Rajiv Gandhi of India
June 12, 1985

The President. Mr. Prime Minister, Nancy and I take great pleasure in welcoming you and Mrs. Gandhi to the White House today.

In 1949 your grandfather, Prime Minister Nehru, visited the United States on what he termed a voyage of discovery. He said that, "Though we may know the history and something of the culture of our respective countries, what is required is a true understanding and appreciation of each other." Well, Prime Minister, your visit marks a continuation of that process of mutual discovery.

Today we celebrate the depth and vitality of the ties between our nations. We Americans place great value on India's friendship. Our shared democratic ideals serve as a bridge between us. Our cultural differences enrich our relationship. Our mutual commitment to the freedom and dignity of man set us on a different road, a higher road than governments which deny the human rights so cherished by our peoples.

Mr. Prime Minister, on this, your own voyage of discovery, you will find a deep well of affection and respect for India and its people. You will sense America's admiration for India's strength in overcoming adversities and a heartfelt sympathy for the tragedy that you've personally suffered. You will also discover that the United States remains steadfastly dedicated to India's unity and that we firmly oppose those who would undermine it.

Mr. Prime Minister, you'll find that we respect India's nonalignment and recognize the pivotal role your country plays in south Asia. We're supportive of your efforts and those of others in south Asia to overcome past animosities in seeking stability, security, and cooperation in the region.

Mr. Prime Minister, our peoples have much to gain from one another. Enthusiasm for the growing potential of our commercial and economic relations is evident here. Expanding cultural, scientific, and educational exchanges will also be a great boon to both our peoples.

Our countries have areas of disagreement, yet these are opportunities to prove our mutual good will by discussing our differences forthrightly. We do so with confidence because we're convinced that our fundamental areas of agreement far outweigh the differences of the moment.

This understanding gives us reason for optimism about the future of our relations. Your stay with us will also provide us a better understanding of you, Mr. Prime Minister. Americans are impressed with what they've seen; your leadership and your idealism are inspiring. We're eager to learn more of your vision for India's future.

I've been impressed with your efforts to invigorate India's economy. In much of the developing world, people are moving away

749

from redistribution and state control—methods that have brought only a scarcity and suffering. New and more successful models for development focus on incentives rather than controls; on production rather than redistribution. And here in the United States, we found that reducing tax rates has been the most important factor in the progress we've made. And we have every reason to look to the future with confidence and optimism.

Just as current technology overcame past problems, new technologies will provide solutions to maladies which today seem insurmountable. Free people, free minds, and free markets will develop innovations which will ensure a more prosperous and peaceful tomorrow. The people of the United States look forward to working with India in building a better tomorrow.

Three years ago, when the late Prime Minister Indira Gandhi and I met here, we agreed that a Festival of India would advance America's knowledge of India's heritage and achievements. You will inaugurate that festival, now dedicated to your mother's memory, during your visit here this week. This is an auspicious year for such a festival. As you know, it has been dubbed the Year of India in recognition of a resurgent American interest in India's culture and history.

I look forward to our talks, for I'm sure that, as with our predecessors, we, too, will be enriched by the exchange. This is an opportunity to broaden the understanding and deepen the cooperation between our countries and to advance the cause of peace in your region and in the world.

Mr. Prime Minister, on behalf of all Americans, welcome to the United States.

The Prime Minister. Mr. President, Sonia and I are honored and delighted to be here. I bring you, to Mrs. Reagan, and to the warm-hearted people of the United States the Indian peoples' greetings and friendship. Millions of Indian eyes are focused on this spot today, leaping over oceans and continents.

Three years ago, welcoming Indira Gandhi, my predecessor, my mother, on this very stretch of green, you remarked so truly that our two people, with all their differences, have much in common. Yes,

there are differences, but rising above them are the beliefs we share in common—in the supremacy of freedom, in the necessity of equality, in the sovereignty of the people's will.

As I flew in here I saw, in passing, the memorial to Thomas Jefferson, who proclaimed in simple and stirring words that all men are created equal and independent. Behind me is a house which has been the home of eminent men who have symbolized your nation's dreams and its drive to greatness. One of them, Abraham Lincoln, said that a nation cannot be half slave and half free and that a house divided against itself cannot stand. The best minds of our age tell us that a world divided against itself cannot endure.

It should be the task of all of us who hold responsibility for other people's lives to recognize what life and its continuance demand in this hate-filled, violence-prone world of ours. The inevitability of coexistence must propel us towards the imperative of cooperation.

The United States and India have been developing a tradition of working together. If my visit strengthens that tradition, it will have given further substance to what is in any case one of the most important and one of the most pleasantly rewarding of journeys. I look forward, in particular, to my talks with you, Mr. President. We know of your lifelong feeling for India and look forward to welcoming you there.

From this week, a Festival of India opens here in Washington; several other cities will soon join in it. The Festival portrays India's aspirations, achievements, and ancient living heritage. I hope that it will enable the people of the United States to understand what we are, why we are so, and how the Indian civilization has endured for 5,000 years. The purpose of the Festival is to secure greater understanding and, with it, greater friendship from the American people, who have, themselves, built a dynamic civilization.

It was a great act of imagination and constructiveness when you and our late Prime Minister decided we should try to develop a better grasp of each other through the medium of culture. I am sure it will provide a story for developing an understanding and cooperation in other fields.

Thank you again, Mr. President, for your welcome and for the opportunity for this renewal of our dialog.

Note: The President spoke at 10:08 a.m. at the South Portico of the White House, where the Prime Minister was accorded a formal welcome with full military honors. Following the ceremony, the President and the Prime Minister met in the Oval Office.

Nomination of Jennifer Ann Hillings To Be an Assistant Secretary of Transportation
June 12, 1985

The President today announced his intention to nominate Jennifer Ann Hillings to be an Assistant Secretary of Transportation (Public Affairs). She would succeed Mari Maseng.

Ms. Hillings is currently media coordinator for the Western United States for the Department of the Interior. Previously, she was Deputy Director, Public Affairs, Department of Commerce (1983–1984); press secretary, Conference on Productivity (1983); and press secretary, Republican National Committee (1981–1982).

Ms. Hillings graduated from the University of Southern California (B.A., 1976). She was born October 7, 1954, in Washington, DC, and resides in Sacramento, CA.

Nomination of Henry M. Ventura To Be Deputy Director of ACTION
June 12, 1985

The President today announced his intention to nominate Henry M. Ventura to be Deputy Director of the ACTION agency. He would succeed Betty H. Brake.

Mr. Ventura is currently executive director of the National Advisory Council on Adult Education. Previously, he was director of development, University of California, San Diego (1981–1982); program director, Brakeley, John Price Jones, Inc., Los Angeles (1980–1981); director of development, special programs (1973–1979) and director of planning, university lmbraries (1973–1979), University of Southern California, Los Angeles; and assistant dean of student affairs, Whittier College (1970–1973).

Mr. Ventura graduated from Los Angeles City College (A.A., 1966) and California State University (B.A., 1968; M.A., 1970). He is married, has one child, and resides in Bethesda, MD. He was born September 4, 1945, in Los Angeles, CA.

Appointment of 22 Members of the Christopher Columbus Quincentenary Jubilee Commission
June 12, 1985

The President today announced his intention to appoint the following individuals to be members of the Christopher Columbus Quincentenary Jubilee Commission. These are new positions.

Lee Collins is currently vice president of Bank Hapoalim in Los Angeles, CA. He was born February 16, 1917, in Kearny, NJ, and resides in Beverly Hills, CA.

Virgil C. Dechant is currently the chief executive officer of the Knights of Columbus. He was born September 24, 1930, in Antonino, KS, and resides in Hamden, CT.

Daniel M. DiCarlo, Jr., is currently president of Area Lighting Research. He was born September 14, 1938, in New Castle, PA, and resides in Hackettstown, NJ.

John N. Goudie is currently president of Goudie & Associates Realty. He was born October 8, 1945, in Havana, Cuba, and resides in Miami, FL.

Herbert Cameron Haight is currently an insurance agent with Lutheran Mutual Life. He was born October 23, 1932, in San Francisco, CA, and resides in Spokane, WA.

William Hardy McNeill is currently the Robert A. Milliken Distinguished Service Professor of History at the University of Chicago. He was born October 31, 1917, in Vancouver, Canada, and resides in Chicago, IL.

James J. O'Connor is chairman, president, and chief executive officer of Commonwealth Edison Co. He was born March 15, 1937, in Chicago, IL, and resides in Evanston, IL.

Venrendo S. Sequenzia is currently publisher of the Florida Italian Bulletin and the Connecticut Italian Bulletin. He was born August 3, 1917, in Sortino, Italy, and resides in Fort Lauderdale, FL.

Arthur E. Teele, Jr., is currently president of the National Business League in Washington, DC, and is a partner with the law firm of Sparber, Shevin, Shapo and Heilbronner in Miami, FL. He was born May 14, 1946, in Washington, DC, and resides there.

Upon the recommendation of the majority leader of the Senate, in consultation with the minority leader of the Senate:

Mary Jane Checchi is currently a freelance consultant. She was born December 10, 1945, in Calais, ME, and resides in Washington, DC.

Luis A. Ferre is currently State chairman of the Republican Party of Puerto Rico, president of the Luis A. Ferre Foundation, and founder and trustee of the Ponce Museum of Art. He was born February 17, 1904, in Ponce, PR, and resides in San Juan.

Jayne H. Plank is currently Director for Intergovernmental Affairs, Office of Legislative and Intergovernmental Affairs, U.S. Department of State. She was born March 10, 1933, in Washington, DC, and resides in Washington.

Charles William Polzer is currently an ethnohistorian at the Arizona State Museum. He was born December 1, 1930, in San Diego, CA, and resides in Tucson, AZ.

Peter F. Secchia is currently chairman of the board of Universal Companies. He was born April 15, 1937, in Tenafly, NJ, and resides in Grand Rapids, MI.

Michael A. Valerio is currently the owner and chairman of the board of Papa Gino's of America, Inc. He was born August 1, 1931, in Villa Latina, Italy, and resides in Framingham, MA.

Upon the recommendation of the Speaker of the House of Representatives, in consultation with the minority leader of the House of Representatives:

Mario Cuomo is currently the Governor of the State of New York. He was born June 15, 1932, in Queens, NY, and resides in Holliswood, NY.

Aldo Annuzzio DeAngelis is currently an Illinois State senator and assistant minority leader. He was born March 25, 1931, in Chicago Heights, IL, and resides in Olympia Fields, IL.

Eugene C. D'Angelo, Jr., is currently president of WBNS and WTHR Television. He was born July 31, 1928, in Columbus, OH, and resides in Dublin, OH.

Arthur J. Decio is currently chairman of the board and chief executive officer of Skyline Corp. He was born October 19, 1930, in Elkhart, IN, and resides in Elkhart.

Jane Lee Garcia is currently president of the Bronx Museum of the Arts. She was born November 8, 1940, in Colorado Springs, CO, and resides in the Bronx, NY.

Charles N. Ginoli is currently president of Ginoli & Co., Ltd. He was born June 7, 1918, in Spring Valley, IL, and resides in Peoria.

Henry Raymont is currently president of Mondus Novus Foundation, Inc. He was born April 21, 1927, in Koenigsberg, Germany, and resides in Washington, DC.

Nomination of Edwin G. Corr To Be United States Ambassador to El Salvador
June 12, 1985

The President today announced his intention to nominate Edwin G. Corr, of Oklahoma, a career member of the Senior Foreign Service, Class of Minister-Counselor, as Ambassador to the Republic of El Salvador. He would succeed Thomas R. Pickering.

Mr. Corr served in the United States Marine Corps in 1957–1960 and was a teaching assistant at the University of Oklahoma in 1960–1961. He entered the Foreign Service in 1961 as a trainee at the Foreign Service Institute. In 1962 he was international affairs officer in the Office of Mexican and Caribbean Affairs in the Department. He served as a junior officer in Mexico, then administrative assistant to the Ambassador in Mexico City (1962–1966). He was regional Peace Corps director in Cali, Colombia, in 1966–1968. He attended the Institute for Latin American Studies at the University of Texas in 1968–1969. In 1969–1971 he was desk officer in the Office of Panamanian Affairs in the Department and program officer at the Inter-American Foundation in 1971–1972. He was executive assistant to the Ambassador in Bangkok, Thailand (1972–1975); counselor for political affairs in Quito, Ecuador (1975–1976), followed by deputy chief of mission in Quito (1976–1978). In 1978–1980 he was Deputy Assistant Secretary of State for International Narcotics Matters in the Department. He then served as Ambassador to Peru in 1980–1981 and Ambassador to Bolivia from 1981 to the present.

Mr. Corr was born August 6, 1934, in Edmond, OK. He graduated from the University of Oklahoma (B.S., 1957; M.A., 1961). His foreign language is Spanish. He is married to the former Susanne Springer, and they have three daughters.

Statement on House of Representatives Approval of United States Assistance for the Nicaraguan Democratic Resistance
June 12, 1985

Today the House of Representatives took an historic vote to support democracy and liberty in Central America. A clear bipartisan majority has shown that our nation stands with those who are determined to pursue a political solution and seek a democratic outcome to the crisis in Nicaragua.

Members of the House, on both sides of the aisle, have voted to help bring about the internal reconciliation in Nicaragua essential to peace and a democratic future for all Central America.

Up until now the Communist Sandinistas, backed by Havana and Moscow, have stridently rejected national reconciliation through a church-mediated dialog as proposed by the unified Nicaraguan opposition.

Today's vote in the House complements the Senate's vote last week to support, with humanitarian assistance, those risking their lives for democracy. Both houses and both sides of the aisle have now demonstrated American resolve to safeguard our own national interests and to advance the rights of the people of Central America. This vote will strengthen the democratic center in Nicaragua against the extremes of the left and the right—just as has occurred in El Salvador.

It is my hope that, in this same spirit, the House and Senate will now act quickly to send me a bill making effective support available through appropriate mechanisms to those who so critically need it.

Toasts at the State Dinner for Prime Minister Rajiv Gandhi of India
June 12, 1985

The President. Good evening, and welcome to the White House.

Prime Minister and Mrs. Gandhi and other distinguished guests from India, it's a pleasure to have you here. Yours is among the most ancient of cultures and ours is one of the youngest. Ours is, however, the oldest constitutional democracy and yours is relatively new—38 years of age. Although young, Indian democracy has achieved strength and maturity, and today I have found that's also true of India's Prime Minister, who's just 3 years older than independent India.

And, Mr. Prime Minister, I'm happy to report to all present this evening that although a few years separate us—just a few—[*laughter*]—we hit it off, and just as with relations between our countries, I predict good things ahead.

Mr. Prime Minister, you were recently quoted as saying about our two countries that basically we stand for the same things—freedom, democracy, independence. And I'm sure that our meetings today reinforce that observation. To paraphrase Tolstoy, undemocratic societies are all undemocratic in their own way, but democratic societies are all alike. And so it is with India and the United States; we are ultimately so similar. And yet like family members, we often find it hard to communicate. Today we opened up personal channels of communication that will serve our countries well.

India and the United States, Mr. Prime Minister, have enormous strengths on which we can draw in seeking to improve our relations. Democracies have valuable experience in reconciling differing points of view within their own national societies. This is particularly true in our great nations, both mosaics of diverse cultures, religions, and languages. And the key to our success domestically is dialog—the quality of careful listening and serious speaking one to another. Dialog can be the key to better understanding between our nations as well.

Our meetings this week build upon the working relationship established by your late mother. Mr. Prime Minister, India and the United States have just begun to write the history of our relations. As the magnificent Festival of India will illuminate, you have enriched the world with beauty, culture, science, and philosophy. Perhaps your most precious gift to us has been the many Indians who have become proud citizens of our country. Some are here tonight, and they embody the human bond that is between us.

Being the Year of India in America, your visit and the Festival of India couldn't have been better timed. We have today set out an agenda for deepening our cooperation across a broad spectrum of issues ranging from political to economic and scientific.

This afternoon our two nations agreed to extend by an additional 3 years the very successful science and technology initiative launched as a result of my meetings with the late Prime Minister Indira Gandhi in 1982. This is one example, an important example, of the kind of cooperation that bodes well for the future of Indo-U.S. relations.

So, let us move forward together. And with the greatest of admiration for you and the great nation you lead, I propose a toast to Indo-American friendship.

The Prime Minister. Mr. President, First Lady, ladies and gentlemen, I feel privileged to be in this historic house once again. My wife and I are grateful for the warm and generous words you have spoken about India and about your meeting with my mother.

I recall the esteem that she had for you. I recall, also, the last time she was here, a wish that you had then expressed about holding a Festival of India has come true. It is good of you to dedicate that festival to Indira Gandhi's memory. We appreciate the special interest Mrs. Reagan has taken in it as patron of the U.S. national committee.

Every encounter between the peoples of the United States and India is an essay in understanding. It provides an opportunity for the reaffirmation of our commitment to personal liberty, to the rule of law, and to free expression. We both are rather outspoken people, not known for keeping quiet about what we feel and what we believe. But being candid with each other is a measure of the stability of our relationship. Both of us are animated by that capricious tolerance which marks the democratic spirit. It is one of the reasons why, in spite of some differences on policies and particulars, a firm people-to-people relationship endures between us.

It is in that spirit that we had our conversation today, at which we discussed our assessments and concerns; you have referred to some. I mentioned to you about our apprehensions at the growing militarism around the region around India, which is increasing our burdens. We have always been against outside presences and pressures, which can lead to instability. To reduce tensions in south Asia, India has taken several initiatives with its neighbors. But the success of our efforts depends very much upon what the big powers do in our region in pursuit of interests. A stable, united, peaceful India, I should think is in everyone's interest.

That is the India we are engaged in developing. For that purpose, we need peace in our neighborhood; we need peace in the world. We desire a global partnership for socioeconomic development, for the satisfaction of human needs, for the promotion of mutual understanding, and for the prevention of war.

Development and peace are closely linked. If disarmament is important for developed countries, it is even more relevant for the developing. We are appalled at the destructive fire that men have built over the years. We are concerned about the new dimensions in the arms race. The very survival of mankind today rests in the hands of a very few countries, leaving mankind to wait in fear and hope.

Six nations, including India, recently issued an appeal for disarmament. Any positive steps taken towards disarmament will be acclaimed and supported by India, the nonaligned community, and by peoples all over the world.

We welcome the negotiations between the United States and the Soviet Union at Geneva and hope that their deliberations will lead to positive results. Nonalignment has been a positive force for peace; it stands for friendship and cooperation with all. Any nation's independence must include the option to steer clear of bloc identification. One friendship need not be at the cost of another. We want to enlarge cooperation between our two countries in numerous fields.

India today is poised for greater growth. We have taken up plans and policies to generate new employment in our rural areas and to harness the productive energies of our young. We want the nation to benefit from the enterprise latent in our people. Growth has to be carefully calibrated so that in enlarging national production, it redresses regional imbalances and ensures social justice. This is indeed the basis of planning within our democratic system.

In three decades we have tried to catch up with what others have achieved in a century or more. We have narrowed the industrial and technological gap. Our seventh plan envisages an investment of $150 billion. We need new technology in a big way. A good part of it we will develop ourselves, but we must necessarily acquire the most advanced knowledge wherever it is generated.

The United States is preeminently the land of high technology. Recently, our two countries have reached an understanding on transfer of high technology; these arrangements must be worked out with great speed.

Mr. President, one of your great predecessors, Franklin Roosevelt, had said, "The only limit to our realization of tomorrow will be our doubts of today." These words bring out the spirit of striving which marks America. Each generation must reestablish freedom and justice; each generation must respond to new situations. There is just enough time to dip in time's refreshing river. Situations change, peoples change, good ideas become dull and unexciting; sometimes they undergo distortion.

The great personalities who created modern India—Mahatma Gandhi, Jawarahal Nehru, Indira Gandhi—have taught us to be humble and firm and to persist. Our ancient book, the Bhagavad-Gita, told us, "You have a right only to do your duty, not to the fruits thereof." In that spirit, we shall strive.

Mr. President, I thank you again for your warm welcome and generous hospitality. We hope that you will give us the pleasure of welcoming you and Mrs. Reagan in India.

I now request you to join me in a toast to the health of President and Mrs. Reagan, to the prosperity of the American people, and to growing cooperation between our two countries in the interest of our two peoples and in the cause of a better world.

Note: The President spoke at 9:45 p.m. in the State Dining Room at the White House.

Nomination of John R. Wall To Be a Member of the Occupational Safety and Health Review Commission
June 13, 1985

The President today announced his intention to nominate John R. Wall to be a member of the Occupational Safety and Health Review Commission for the remainder of the term expiring April 27, 1987. He would succeed Robert A. Rowland.

Mr. Wall has been retired since 1982. Prior to his retirement, from 1956 to 1982, he was with Republic Steel Corp., serving as assistant general traffic manager, director of personnel—labor relations, and as vice president—labor relations.

Mr. Wall graduated from Georgetown University (B.S., 1939) and the Georgetown University Law Center (LL.D., 1942). He is married, has two children, and resides in Bratenahl, OH. He was born November 6, 1917, in Lynchburg, VA.

Remarks to Citizens in Bloomfield, New Jersey
June 13, 1985

Thank you, Governor Tom Kean, and thank you Mayor Kinder. You know, I think New Jersey is very lucky to have Tom Kean as its Governor. He is one of the ablest State executives in the country; he happens to be one of my favorite Governors.

He calls me now and then, and I'll ask him, "Well, Tom, what should I do about the budget?" And he says, "Come to New Jersey." And then I say "Tom, what should I do about taxes?" And he says, "Come to New Jersey." He's a great booster of your State, and I've been here four times in the past year alone, so you can see I take his advice seriously. I'm also delighted to be here with two of our finest Members of Congress, Congressmen Dean Gallo and Matt Rinaldo.

It's great to be back in New Jersey. I've been in Hammonton, Elizabeth, Hacken-

sack, Hoboken, and Oradell in the past 12 months, and I am very happy to meet the people of Bloomfield.

You know, I've been traveling across the country the past few weeks talking about tax reform—why we need it, what it is, and how it will affect us all. And I brought my message here today because we cannot make a change this great without the help of all the people in America. We especially need the help of the most committed and hardest working citizens in the country, which means we need the support of the people of the Garden State.

Now occasionally, I get into a sort of a dialog with the audience when I'm speaking. It's kind of my way of gauging public opinion. I call it the Reagan poll. Well, frequently, I do it somewhere near the end of my talk, but today I'm going to do it at the beginning.

And here goes. Now, listen carefully. If you really, truly love our current Federal tax system, the one we have now that you just had to deal with a couple of months ago, how about a big cheer for it?

Audience. Boo-o-o!

The President. Now, I didn't really ask for laughter, I just asked for a cheer.

Now, how about this? If you even like our current Federal income tax system, how about a big cheer?

Audience. Boo-o-o!

The President. Well, not even one cheer. There must not be anyone from the IRS here.

All right now. It wasn't completely silence, but the sounds you did make was as good as silence. I think it demonstrates a fact with which we're all familiar: Our current Federal tax system is neither admired nor respected. It encourages cheating; it is inherently unjust; it has created a vast and unproductive underground economy; it is tottering on an unsound foundation; and it's time we simply tore it down and built a better one.

Our current tax system is ready for the ash heap of history. And having decided that, now comes the difficult business of creating a new tax system that is fair and easy to comprehend. A new tax system that will allow people to get ahead, that won't keep holding them down, a new tax system that will finally put the family at center stage and the special interests way high up in the back of the balcony where they belong.

Now, I believe that we have created such a system in the proposal that we put forth 2 weeks ago. I know you're familiar with the particulars. You've been reading about them in the magazines and the newspapers and listening to debates, and I hope you've had some time to sit down at the kitchen table and figure out what you would pay under our proposals. Because if you have, then, you know that our proposals will very likely speed tax relief for you and your family.

I did some research the other day, and I found that, according to the most recent statistics, the typical income for a family of four in the State of New Jersey is $36,450.

Now, what would our tax plan do for the family, and how would it affect it? To start with, under our plan the personal exemption for each taxpayer and dependent in the family is almost doubled to $2,000. So, the family will immediately deduct $8,000 from its taxable income. Then it will subtract the standard deduction—for a joint return it's $4,000. Now, you have $12,000 that's not taxable. And let's say you decide to save for the future by investing in what we call the IRA, individual retirement account, for $2,000 of savings. That $2,000 is not taxed. And now, you're up to $14,000 on which you won't pay a penny of Federal tax.

On the remaining $22,450, you'll pay a tax rate of 15 percent, which means you pay an effective tax rate on the whole $36,450 of less than 10 percent. Now, you realize I haven't tried to estimate the other deductions such as interest on your home mortgage or charitable deductions and so forth.

But that family, that New Jersey family, will do a lot better under our system than the current one. How much better? Well, under the current system, they'd pay $4,635 a year if they just took that $14,000 deduction, not counting any others, in Federal income tax. And under our proposal, they'd pay more than $650 less.

And for the first time in years in our country, the man and woman at the head of the family will be able to work overtime or take a second job without seeing those new wages eaten up by high marginal tax rates as you go up in those 14 brackets that we presently have.

The poor will benefit from our tax proposals because most of them won't pay any Federal income tax at all. Middle-income earners will benefit from lower tax rates and the increases in the personal exemption, the standard deduction, and in the IRA's. In fact, 58 percent of all American families will pay lower taxes under our plan. Over 21—or another 21 percent, I should say, will probably pay the same as they pay now—no more. And all of us will benefit from the economic growth that will follow the lowering of taxes, just as you found it brought about the lowering of taxes here in your State brought about increased economic recovery and prosperity and productivity in this State.

So, what I'm talking about is a good deal for the American people. And that's why tax reform has garnered such support across the country. And that's why my friends in the other party support it.

One of them, your senior Senator, is a pioneer of the tax reform movement. We admire Bill Bradley; we're glad he's on the team, and his leadership is indispensable to victory.

But tax reform is not without its foes. There are those who won't oppose it outright, but who'll try to nickel and dime it to death. Others will use any false argument they can, any scare tactic to cloud the truth and raise confusion.

There are those who say that our tax plan will benefit some States and hurt others. They say that when we eliminate the deduction for State and local taxes, we'll hurt the people who pay those taxes in the high-tax States. Well, again, it's simply not true.

First off, two-thirds of the people who live in such States don't itemize and don't deduct their State and local taxes to begin with. So, the current State tax deduction is of absolutely no use to two-thirds of the households in the high-tax States.

And let me add here that I don't consider New Jersey to be a high-tax State. For instance, New Yorkers have to pay top income tax rates that are more than four times as high as New Jersey's. And your Governor, Tom Kean, by the way, I happen to know he's spoken about what he's done, but I know he's trying to cut your State income taxes even further. And I'm for him.

Now, my second point: Most of the lucky one-third who do itemize will, under our plan, get a Federal tax cut to help lower their tax bill. As an example, here's a New Jersey family of four that's making almost $42,000 a year. They live in Bloomfield. They're very happy here. They love Mayor Kinder, as who doesn't. Now, this family itemizes on the deductions for a joint return from New Jersey. They take the average estimated amount. And under the current tax system, that family would pay a Federal income tax of $4,948. Under our

plan, the new plan, they'll pay some $600 less. Now, that's $600 a year in savings for a family that itemizes. And I haven't even begun to calculate what they'll save on accountants and tax lawyers.

Finally, our third point: Because our tax plan will encourage economic growth, it will broaden the tax base in every city, town, and State in the country. Now, Bloomfield has a vibrant local economy. When the people of this town are allowed to keep more of their hard-earned money and are allowed to spend it, save it, and invest it; well, then the business community of Bloomfield will really bloom.

But there's a greater point, and let me put it more clearly. When you've got a tax plan that's progrowth, profamily, and pro-fairness, then you've got a tax plan that's pro-New Mexico, pro-New York, pro-New Jersey—it's a tax plan that is pro-American; it's America's tax plan.

Now, we're not favoring one State over another. We're favoring every taxpayer in America by creating greater fairness, greater justice, and lower tax rates. Our tax plan will close the loopholes that are manipulated by some to avoid paying taxes. The truth is everyone should pay their fair share.

And no one, no matter how powerful or privileged, should be able to use tax shelters to keep from paying taxes when the middle class, with no place to hide and no protection from clever accountants, bear more than their share of the load.

Now, our plan will not increase the deficit nor will it be used to raise revenue. You know, some people are talking about turning tax reform into a tax increase. Well, let me tell you, anyone who tries that, I have a veto pen ready for them.

Our tax program is designed to ensure the growth of the American economy in our time and in our children's time. It's aimed at creating investment and jobs and personal wealth. We're not just talking about a better deal for now—we're talking about the future. And we're not just predicting economic growth, we're promising it. We know it will happen.

So much is ahead of us; more important, so much is ahead for our children. You know, it's the oldest cliche, only because it's true: The fuel that has kept America going, that made every tired breadwinner get up every morning and go to work, the thing that's made every one of our families hold together and pull at the same oar, the fuel that kept all that going was the hope that the kids in their day would have it better.

It was the hope that our children would have more than we did, that they'd live richer lives in terms of experience, opportunity, and wealth. We're a nation that got up every morning for the children, and we still do. And when I talk about economic growth, I don't mean more wealth for now—we're doing all right. I mean creating a whole world of real and tangible opportunities and possibilities for our children.

If I could jog your memory a little bit, there was a time not too long ago—just a few years ago—when America was being told that we were living in an age of limits; that things had changed; that we'd gone about as far as we could go, and from here on it was going to be all downhill, and we'll just have to get used to being second rate. You remember those words about a malaise that we were suffering. And America, being an openminded and realistic country listened and pondered and considered, and then America made a decision. It told the pessimists to take a hike.

I'm not optimistic about the future of America because I have a sunny disposition. I'm not optimistic because I don't know the realities. I'm optimistic because I do know them. I'm optimistic because I have witnessed the American experience for more than seven decades, and I know that the American people can do anything.

In the past 5 years, the American people—not the politicians, not the elites, not the heavy-browed intellectuals, but the American people—singlehandedly turned our country around. And all we in Washington did was try to get the Government out of your way.

Reforming our tax structure is the next step—and as your Governor told you—in

the second American revolution. And I need your help. The sharks are circling our tax plan and trying to take a bite. We happen to have a foolproof shark repellent in the will of the American people. But your voice must be heard.

Can you help us? Will you help us?

Audience. Yes!

The President. All right. Will you write your Representatives? You don't have to write the two here, they've already heard you. [*Laughter*] Write your Representatives, your Senators, and tell them how you feel. It really does mean something in Washington to hear from you—the mail and the telegrams and the phone calls. Tell them how you feel. And that's great because without you, nothing can be accomplished; but with you, everything is possible.

And if you get pessimistic or think your contribution won't make a difference, just think of those young soldiers that you were told about of two centuries ago, who, during another revolution, trained on the Green, held together, and marched New Jersey and America into freedom.

You know, speaking of this, I just want to say one last thing, too. If you feel like adding a P.S. to your letter, I've talked about tax reform, but there's another vital thing lying before the Congress today. Add a P.S. that yes, let's go forward with that budget we've proposed that will reduce the total of government spending.

We've been spending too much for too long, and it's time to put government, the Federal Government, on a diet, just as your Governor's doing here in your own State.

Well, it's been wonderful to be here. I hate to go, but I'll be talking to Governor Kean again, which means I'll be back. So, I'll see you then. Good luck, God bless you, and by the way, I love New Jersey!

Thank you very much.

Note: The President spoke at 12:10 p.m. from the steps of the Municipal Building.

Message to the Congress Transmitting the Final Report of the Chemical Warfare Review Commission
June 13, 1985

To the Congress of the United States:

Section 1511 of Public Law 98–525, the Department of Defense Authorization Act, 1985, required establishment of a bipartisan commission to "review the overall adequacy of the chemical warfare posture of the United States with particular emphasis on the question of whether the United States should produce binary chemical munitions."

Pursuant to this legislation, Executive Order 12502 established the Chemical Warfare Review Commission on January 28, 1985. Eight distinguished citizens have served on the Commission. It met for two months and heard testimony from more than 75 persons in developing its report. The Commissioners have traveled to Europe to talk with our commanders and Allies there and to examine our defenses against chemical attack at first hand.

The Commission has now reached a consensus on the points it was asked to consider and has submitted its findings. I am conveying these in the attached report for the consideration of the Congress as it deliberates the question of this Nation's posture for deterrence of chemical warfare.

The Commission has found that the United States must have a credible retaliatory capability to deter attack, that the present United States stockpile of agents and munitions does not constitute an effective retaliatory capability, and that the projected binary munitions program offers a much safer and more credible deterrent. Also, this program, far from impeding arms control, will provide an essential assist to our negotiating efforts.

The report of this distinguished Commission has strengthened my own very real concern for our country's chemical deterrence posture. I urge the Congress to authorize funding for the binary munitions program as expeditiously as possible.

RONALD REAGAN

The White House,
June 13, 1985.

Executive Order 12519—Amending the Generalized System of Preferences
June 13, 1985

By virtue of the authority vested in me by the Constitution and statutes of the United States of America, including Title V of the Trade Act of 1974 (the Trade Act) (19 U.S.C. 2461 *et seq.*), as amended, section 604 of the Trade Act (19 U.S.C. 2483), and section 503(a)(2)(A) of the Trade Agreements Act of 1979 (93 Stat. 251), in order to modify, as provided by sections 504 (a) and (c) of the Trade Act (19 U.S.C. 2464 (a) and (c)), the limitations on preferential treatment for eligible articles from countries designated as beneficiary developing countries; and to adjust the original designation of eligible articles after taking into account information and advice received in fulfillment of sections 131–134 and 503(a) of the Trade Act (19 U.S.C. 2151–2154, 2463), it is hereby ordered as follows:

Section 1. In order to subdivide and amend the nomenclature of existing items for purposes of the Generalized System of Preferences (GSP), the Tariff Schedules of the United States (TSUS) (19 U.S.C. 1202) are modifed as provided in Annex I to this Order.

Sec. 2. Annex II of Executive Order No. 11888, as amended, listing articles that are eligible for benefits of the GSP when imported from any designated beneficiary developing country, is amended as set forth in Annex II to this Order.

Sec. 3. Annex III of Executive Order No. 11888, as amended, listing articles that are eligible for benefits of the GSP when imported from all designated beneficiary countries except those specified in General Headnote 3(c)(iii) of the TSUS, is amended as set forth in Annex III to this Order.

Sec. 4. General Headnote 3(c)(iii) of the TSUS, listing articles that are eligible for benefits of the GSP except when imported from the beneficiary countries listed opposite those articles, is modified as set forth in Annex IV to this Order.

Sec. 5. In order to provide staged reductions in the rates of duty for those new TSUS items created by Annex I to this Order, Annex III to Proclamation 4707 and Annex III to Proclamation 4768 are amended as set forth in Annex V to this Order.

Sec. 6. Whenever the column 1 rate of duty in the TSUS for any item specified in Annex I to this Order is reduced to the same level as, or to a lower level than, the corresponding rate of duty in the column entitled "LDDC" by Annex I to this Order, the rate of duty in the column entitled "LDDC" for such item shall be deleted from the TSUS.

Sec. 7. Annexes III and IV of Proclamation 4707 and Annexes II, III, and IV of Proclamation 4768 are superseded to the extent inconsistent with this Order.

Sec. 8. General Headnote 3(c)(i) of the TSUS, listing the designated beneficiary developing countries for purposes of the GSP, is modified as provided in Annex VI to this Order.

Sec. 9(a). The amendments made by the sections designated "A" in the Annexes to this Order, by section C of Annex I, by section B of Annex V, and by Annex VI shall be effective with respect to articles both: (1) imported on or after January 1, 1976, and (2) entered, or withdrawn from warehouse for consumption, on and after the date that is fifteen days after the date of publication of this Order in the *Federal Register.*

(b) Unless otherwise specified, the remaining amendments made by this Order shall be effective with respect to articles both: (1) imported on or after January 1, 1976, and (2) entered, or withdrawn from warehouse for consumption, on or after July 1, 1985.

RONALD REAGAN

The White House,
June 13, 1985.

[*Filed with the Office of the Federal Register, 4:02 p.m., June 13, 1985*]

Note: The annexes were printed in the Federal Register *of June 17.*

Nomination of John S. Erthein To Be a Member of the National Council on the Handicapped
June 13, 1985

The President today announced his intention to nominate John S. Erthein to be a member of the National Council on the Handicapped for a term expiring September 17, 1987. This is a reappointment.

Mr. Erthein has served as a member of the National Council on the Handicapped since 1982. He is also president of Erthein and Associates in Washington, DC. Previously, he was vice president of marketing for Greeting Card Publishing (1974–1978) and a management consultant for Fry Consultants, Inc., in Chicago, IL (1970–1974).

Mr. Erthein graduated from Columbia College (B.A., 1964) and Columbia University School of Business (M.B.A., 1966). He is married and resides in Los Angeles, CA. He was born March 9, 1944, in New York, NY.

Proclamation 5350—Father's Day, 1985
June 13, 1985

By the President of the United States of America

A Proclamation

By tradition, the third Sunday in June is celebrated as Father's Day, a day on which we honor our Nation's fathers.

In honoring fathers, we honor families. Families are the bedrock of our Nation's strength, and fathers play an indispensable role in forming vital, whole families. They serve as models and guides for their sons and daughters and help to pass on to the next generation the heritage of our civilization.

Being a good father is an art that cannot be taught in schools. The main ingredient for success is simply a caring attitude. Fathers who love their families can never completely fail, and children will always remember the influence of a father who tries to do his best. For many children, the memory of a loving father will be the most important influence in their lives.

The love a father feels for his children can take many forms. The only constant is that he shares their lives in a special and irreplaceable way. He feels their hurts as well as their joys, their pains as well as their triumphs. In this way, he plays an indispensable role in their moral development, and they return to him a love and satisfaction that cannot be found anywhere else.

On Father's Day, we pay tribute to all in our society who have taken on the responsibilities and joys of fatherhood. Whether our fathers are near at hand or a continent away, with their families or watching from the light of eternity, we take this day to remember them, to say our thanks for the years they have given us, and to ask that they receive God's blessings.

Now, Therefore, I, Ronald Reagan, President of the United States of America, in accordance with the joint resolution of the Congress (36 U.S.C. 142a), do hereby proclaim Sunday, June 16, 1985, as Father's Day. I invite the States and communities and the people of the United States to observe that day with appropriate ceremonies as a mark of gratitude and abiding affection for their fathers. I direct government officials to display the flag of the United States on all Federal government buildings, and I urge all Americans to display the flag at their homes and other suitable places on that day.

In Witness Whereof, I have hereunto set my hand this thirteenth day of June, in the year of our Lord nineteen hundred and eighty-five, and of the Independence of the United States of America the two hundred and ninth.

RONALD REAGAN

[*Filed with the Office of the Federal Register, 10:21 a.m., June 14, 1985*]

Nomination of Thomas Anthony Nassif To Be United States Ambassador to Morocco
June 14, 1985

The President today announced his intention to nominate Thomas Anthony Nassif, of Virginia, as Ambassador to the Kingdom of Morocco. He would succeed Joseph Verner Reed, Jr.

Mr. Nassif began his career in personnel with Southern Pacific Railroad in Los Angeles, CA, from 1963 to 1965. Following his graduation from law school he became a law clerk with Masry & David in Los Angeles from 1968 to 1969. From 1969 to 1972, he was a partner/attorney with Sands & Nassif in El Centro, CA. In 1972 he had his own law practice in El Centro. In 1973–

1979 he was partner/lawyer with the firm of Byrd, Sturdevant, Nassif & Pinney in El Centro, and from 1980 to 1981, he was a partner/lawyer with Gray, Cary, Ames & Frye in El Centro. Mr. Nassif was appointed Deputy Chief of Protocol in the Department of State in 1981, where he served for 2 years. From 1983 to the present, he has been a Deputy Assistant Secretary in the Bureau of Near Eastern and South Asian Affairs in the Department.

Mr. Nassif was born on July 22, 1941, in Cedar Rapids, IA. He received his B.S. in 1965 from California State University at Los Angeles and his J.D. in 1968 from California Western University school of law in San Diego. Mr. Nassif served in 1960 with the U.S. Army National Guard and continued in the Reserve until 1968. His foreign language is French. He is married to the former Zinetta Marie Meherg, and they have two children.

Appointment of William Eugene Baumgaertner as a Member of the National Capital Planning Commission
June 14, 1985

The President today announced his intention to appoint William Eugene Baumgaertner to be a member of the National Capital Planning Commission for the term expiring January 1, 1991. He would succeed Helen M. Scharf.

Mr. Baumgaertner is currently department head for traffic and planning with Greenhorne & O'Mara, Inc., in Greenbelt, MD. Previously, he was project manager (senior traffic engineer) with Hennington,

Durham & Richardson, Inc., in Atlanta, GA (1980–1982); chief, traffic engineering division, Anne Arundel County, MD (1979–1980); and project engineer (senior traffic engineer), Hennington, Durham & Richardson, Inc., Chevy Chase, MD (1978–1979).

Mr. Baumgaertner graduated from the University of Maryland (B.S., 1971; M.S., 1978). He is married and resides in Annapolis, MD. He was born March 9, 1947, in Louisville, KY.

Appointment of Five Members of the President's Committee on Mental Retardation
June 14, 1985

The President today announced his intention to appoint the following individuals to be members of the President's Committee on Mental Retardation for terms expiring May 11, 1988.

Dorothy Corbin Clark is currently a registered nurse in Provo, UT. She graduated from the University of Utah (R.N.) and Brigham Young University (B.S.). She is married, has three children, and resides in Provo, UT. She was born October 8, 1924, in Moab, UT. This is a reappointment.

Martha Lois Eargle is currently owner of Eargle & Thurman Realty Marketing & Associates. She is married, has four children, and resides in

Conway, SC. She was born June 24, 1936, in Sumter, SC. She would succeed Lila Thompson.

Madeline B. Harwood is currently a lobbyist for the Vermont State Medical Society. She graduated from the Mary Fletcher Hospital School of Nursing (R.N.). She is married, has four children, and resides in Manchester Center, VT. She was born July 7, 1914, in Newbury, VT. This is a reappointment.

William Kerby Hummer is currently a physician in Santa Monica, CA. He graduated from the University of Iowa (B.A., M.D.) and the University of Minnesota (M.S.). He is married, has one child, and resides in Los Angeles. He was born February 17, 1937, in Davenport, IA. He would succeed Richard E. Blanton.

U. Yun Ryo is currently associate professor of radiology and medicine at the University of Chicago. He graduated from Kyungbook Na-

tional University (M.S.). He is married and resides in Chicago, IL. He was born August 2, 1935, in Kyungbook, Korea. He would succeed Timothy J. O'Brien.

Remarks at the Presentation Ceremony for the "C" Flag Awards
June 14, 1985

Secretary Pierce and ladies and gentlemen, we're delighted to have all of you here today because this is the last formal event involving the Advisory Council on Private Sector Initiatives.

And I want to begin by expressing my deep personal gratitude to each of you for being a part of this tremendously important, history-making event. And a special word of thanks is in order to Bob Galvin, the Advisory Council Chairman; to Bill Taylor and the citation program sponsors who made these awards—or this awards program possible; and to John Phelan from the New York Stock Exchange.

I know words like "historymaking" or "historic" get thrown around a lot in this city, but let me assure you that in this case those words are more than just Washington puffery.

Some of you've heard me talk about de Tocqueville's reflections on 19th century America and his astonishment at the extent to which Americans made their society work—not by relying on government but by helping each other. You all know that this tradition—one of the driving engines of social progress in our country—was in serious jeopardy some years ago when the idea took hold that the only way to handle a social problem was a huge new Federal spending program, an army of functionaries and consultants to administer it.

And it was very successful for the bureaucrats. Government bureaucracy reached gargantuan size. And because nothing stifles initiative and imagination like bureaucracy, America's self-help tradition lost much of its force and energy.

But any modern-day de Tocqueville looking over America would see a return now to that tradition and a revival of the idea, which all of you embody, that compassion

with ingenuity works, that the American people are anxious and ready to help each other. They just need to be asked.

I hope you'll forgive me if I tell a little story that I think has a special pertinence about some of these things. Back in my early days in radio, every studio had a sound-effects man. And he had a kind of a wagon there on wheels he'd bring in for dramatic presentations and so forth.

And he had experimented with all the things that you could do to make sounds that otherwise you couldn't get on radio. For example, he had, I know, in our own studio half coconut shells with which he would beat on his chest, and you would have a horse galloping. [*Laughter*] And, then, he had plenty of cellophane that he could crackle and crinkle, and that was a raging fire while the things were going on.

Well, one day we had a play that called for water falling on a board, and he got to work, the headphones on, and to listen and all during the rehearsals, he was working. He tried rice on a drum; he tried dried peas on a piece of cardboard; I recall. He tried everything, and nothing would give him the sound of water on a board.

And then, you know what? He tried water on a board—[*laughter*]—and it sounded just like water on a board. [*Laughter*] Well, in a way, then, that's what all of you have done—the simple and obvious thing that somehow had been forgotten. You just went to people; you asked them to lend a hand. And you discovered that that's just the question they needed to hear. And because you did, you've helped change America.

Your projects have ranged from child-safety awareness to food banks, job training, neighborhood revitalization, and scores of other programs in art, ecology, and education and services for the elderly. I like that last one particularly. [*Laughter*]

There is a grassroots movement out there that just can't be stopped. Earlier this week, Tom Evans and his education committee sponsored a symposium on partnerships in education. Close to 500 people came to Washington to talk about creative ways for business and schools to work together. And because of your efforts, the New York Stock Exchange has identified private sector initiatives as an issue of great importance to corporate America and cohosted this morning's symposium on excellence in private sector initiatives.

In addition to being here today for this awards program, there is special significance in that it is Flag Day. And later I'll be out at Fort McHenry to salute the Stars and Stripes.

Flags have always symbolized important characteristics of the American people—the Stars and Stripes for independence and the World War II "E" Flag for excellence. And now, as you look around here, in the Rose Garden you see the "C" Flag—a symbol of private sector initiative that says, "We can, and we care."

Thousands of these flags are flying around the country, reflecting the ingenuity and compassion of people in organizations that are putting something back into their communities. That's the reason we have three mikes; every time they see me come out here, one of them flies over.[1] [*Laughter*]

I want to thank each of the winners for their enormous commitment and dedication and patriotism. I think you all know that I could go on at some length about your achievements.

Safeway stores put pictures of missing children on their shopping bags, and within two weeks two of the eight children were found.

Last year over 5,600 hours of instruction time were donated to the schools that ARCO employees have adopted.

B. Dalton Bookseller has launched a 4-year national literacy initiative, already involving 375 communities and 30,000 volunteers.

Through LISC, the Local Initiative Support Corporation, BankAmerica Foundation has financed 27 different rehabilitation projects in distressed areas.

Last year the members of the South Shore Chamber of Commerce provided jobs for over 1,000 juvenile offenders that earned over $350,000 that was paid back to victims in restitution.

And through its youth leadership program, Westinghouse Broadcasting and Cable, Incorporated, recognize outstanding high school seniors who exemplify the innate will to win.

And the list goes on. I wish there were time to mention the contributions of everyone. I couldn't possibly do that, but what I can do is thank you, not just for myself, but as President for the millions of Americans who, if they had the chance, would want to personally express their gratitude to you.

You have made a difference for your country and for millions of your countrymen. You have helped renew and enrich America by awakening one of her oldest and most noble traditions. And now, given this marvelous start, I cannot help but feel that our work has just begun. The challenge is before us to make better use of all our resources. We can only do this by working together. No one sector can do it alone.

The crystal tetrahedrons that I am awarding today symbolize how the fusion on the private, public, and nonprivate sectors can form a solid base. Only by working together and finding some private solutions to public problems can we restore the strong balance needed for the future health of our Nation.

Our country is great because it is built on principles of self-reliance, opportunity, innovation, and compassion for the others. Private sector initiatives embody this spirit and are a vital part of the Nation's character.

To each of you here today who have taken a leadership role in helping to meet our challenge, I thank you, and all of America thanks you. God bless you all.

---

[1] *The President was referring to the noise of an airplane flying overhead.*

Note: The President spoke at 11:05 a.m. in the Rose Garden at the White House. The

President awarded citations to 100 business-es and associations for their outstanding private sector initiatives. The top 30 of this group received a special private sector initiative award. R. William Taylor, president of the American Society of Association Executives, was the Chairman of the Awards Committee for the President's Private Sector Initiatives Citation Program.

Presidential Findings on United States-Canadian Crude Oil Transfers
June 14, 1985

On March 18, 1985, at the Quebec Summit, I joined Prime Minister Mulroney in endorsing a Trade Declaration with the objective of liberalizing energy trade, including crude oil, between the United States and Canada. Both Governments recognized the substantial benefits that would ensue from broadened crude oil transfers and exchanges between these two historic trading partners and allies. These benefits would include the increased availability of reliable energy sources, economic efficiencies, and material enhancements to the energy security of both countries. Following this Declaration, Canada declared that it would permit Canadian crude oil to be freely exported to the United States effective June 1, 1985.

Before crude oil exports to Canada can be authorized, I must make certain findings and determinations under statutes that restrict exports of crude oil. I have decided to make the necessary findings and determinations under the following statutes: Section 103 of the Energy Policy and Conservation Act (42 U.S.C. 6212); section 28 of the Mineral Lands Leasing Act of 1920, as amended by the Trans-Alaska Pipeline Authorization Act of 1973 (30 U.S.C. 185); and section 28 of the Outer Continental Shelf Lands Act (43 U.S.C. 1354) (crude oil transported over the Trans-Alaska Pipeline or derived from the Naval Petroleum Reserves is excluded).

I hereby find and determine that exports of crude oil under these statutes are in the U.S. national interest, and I further find and determine that such U.S. crude oil exports to Canada—

• will not diminish the total quantity or quality of petroleum available to the United States;

• will not increase reliance on imported oil;

• are in accord with provisions of the Export Administration Act of 1979; and

• are consistent with the purposes of the Energy policy and Conservation Act.

Therefore, such domestic crude oil may be exported to Canada for consumption or use therein.

These findings and determinations shall be published in the *Federal Register*. I direct the Secretary of Commerce to take all other necessary and proper action to expeditiously implement this decision.

RONALD REAGAN

The White House,
June 14, 1985.

[*Filed with the Office of the Federal Register, 9:35 a.m., June 17, 1985*]

Message to the Congress Transmitting the Presidential Findings on United States-Canadian Crude Oil Transfers
June 14, 1985

To the Congress of the United States:

I hereby transmit the requisite findings and determinations to permit the export of non-Alaskan North Slope crude oil to Canada. These findings and determinations are made pursuant to section 28 of the Outer Continental Shelf Lands Act (43 U.S.C. 1354), section 28(u) of the Mineral

Lands Leasing Act (30 U.S.C. 185(u)), and section 103 of the Energy Policy and Conservation Act (42 U.S.C. 6212).

RONALD REAGAN

The White House,
June 14, 1985.

Proclamation 5351—Family Reunion Month, 1985
June 14, 1985

By the President of the United States of America

A Proclamation

Family reunions are occasions that renew the feelings of love, pride, and support that nurture our lives. There is no more joyous and poignant family reunion than the return to the family of a child who has run away from home.

The number of young people between the ages of 10 and 17 who ran away from home last year is estimated at more than one million. The heartache of such a breakdown in family relationships is incalculable. But for many thousands of families, the joy of reunion was realized with the return of a son or daughter and a resolution of the conditions that precipitated the flight of the child.

In all likelihood, the return was aided by one of the professionals and volunteers who staff runaway shelters throughout the country. Last year alone, some 200,000 young Americans and their families received counseling aimed at resolving family conflicts and pressures. Almost half the young people who sought help were returned safely to their homes.

Much remains to be done, and all of us can play a role. Volunteers are needed to help staff crisis intervention programs. Parents themselves must recognize the importance of keeping open lines of communica-

tions with their children and strive to strengthen family relationships.

Families are the cornerstone of America. All of America's families should be encouraged to continue strengthening their ties through gatherings and activities such as family reunions that involve as many members as possible.

The Congress, by House Joint Resolution 64, has designated the period between Mother's Day, May 12, and Father's Day, June 16, 1985, as "Family Reunion Month" and authorized and requested the President to issue a proclamation in observance of this period.

Now, Therefore, I, Ronald Reagan, President of the United States of America, do hereby proclaim the period between May 12 and June 16, 1985, as Family Reunion Month. I call upon all Americans to celebrate this period with appropriate ceremonies and activities and recognition of the resources available to help strengthen families.

In Witness Whereof, I have hereunto set my hand this fourteenth day of June, in the year of our Lord nineteen hundred and eighty-five, and of the Independence of the United States of America the two hundred and ninth.

RONALD REAGAN

[*Filed with the Office of the Federal Register, 10:55 a.m., June 17, 1985*]

Proclamation 5352—Baltic Freedom Day, 1985
June 14, 1985

By the President of the United States of America

A Proclamation

This year marks the 45th anniversary of the United States non-recognition policy by which our government refuses to recognize the forcible Soviet occupation of Estonia, Latvia, and Lithuania. It has been 45 years since the dark year of 1940 when invading Soviet armies, in collusion with the Nazi regime, overran these three independent Baltic Republics.

The atrocious character of the Soviet oppression was shockingly illustrated by the imprisonment, deportation, and murder of close to 100,000 Balts during a four-day reign of terror June 14–17, 1941. The suffering of this brutal period was made even worse when Nazi forces struck back through these three states at the beginning of the Nazi-Soviet war and instituted a civil administration under control of the nefarious Gestapo. Due to Soviet and Nazi tyranny, by the end of World War II, the Baltic nations had lost twenty percent of their total population.

Today, suppression and persecution are the daily burdens of the Estonian, Latvian, and Lithuanian people. Soviet policies are specifically targeted toward the very ethnic life and historical heritage of the Baltic nations. Russification takes place under many guises: forced relocation, expanded colonization by Russian immigrants, and heavy pressure against the indigenous religious, cultural, and social traditions.

Yet despite this crushing system, the Baltic peoples courageously continue to resist amalgamation by pressing for their national, political, and religious rights. Peaceful expression of demands through the underground press, petitions to government officials, demonstrations, the activities of the Catholic Church and other religious denominations, Helsinki monitoring groups, and committees to defend the rights of religious believers command the admiration of everyone who loves and honors freedom.

Significantly, the defense of national and personal rights is led not by those who grew up during the years of independence, but by a new generation born and raised under the Soviet system. The message of these heroes, both young and old, is: "You, our free brothers and sisters, are our voice to the free world. You must not cease to inform the world of what is being inflicted upon us here behind the Iron Curtain, for it is from your efforts that we get our strength to survive."

All the people of the United States of America share the aspirations of the Baltic nations for national independence. The United States upholds their rights to determine their own national destiny, free of foreign interference. For 45 years, the United States has not recognized the forcible incorporation of the Baltic States into the Soviet Union, and it will not do so in the future.

The Congress of the United States, by Senate Joint Resolution 66, has authorized and requested the President to issue a proclamation for the observance of June 14, 1985, as "Baltic Freedom Day."

Now, Therefore, I, Ronald Reagan, President of the United States of America, do hereby proclaim June 14, 1985, as Baltic Freedom Day. I call upon the people of the United States to observe this day with appropriate ceremonies and to reaffirm their commitment to the principles of liberty and freedom for all oppressed people.

In Witness Whereof, I have hereunto set my hand this fourteenth day of June, in the year of our Lord nineteen hundred and eighty-five, and of the Independence of the United States of America the two hundred and ninth.

RONALD REAGAN

[*Filed with the Office of the Federal Register, 10:56 a.m., June 17, 1985*]

Remarks at a Flag Day Ceremony in Baltimore, Maryland
June 14, 1985

Thank you all for that welcome, and thank you, Senator Mathias. Governor Hughes, Mayor Schaefer, and Members of the Congress who are here, I appreciate their warm welcome, and Don Schaefer, I know you're the mayor, but I understand that just the other day the Earl of Baltimore returned to the city. [*Laughter*] It is great to be here in the home of the Baltimore Orioles.

I don't know about you, but I always get a chill up and down my spine when I say that Pledge of Allegiance, and I hope that everyone here will join us and Americans all across the country when we pause for that pledge tonight. You've been given the time in which we will all do that across the Nation—reaffirm our thankfulness, our love, and our loyalty to our blessed and beautiful land.

This flag that we salute today is a replica of one that flew through the night, as you know, 171 years ago during the bombardment of Fort McHenry signaling defiance to the British and hope and inspiration to Francis Scott Key. Some historians have called the War of 1812 the second war of independence, the crucial test of our young republic as it fought for its life against what was then the strongest nation on Earth. By the end of the summer of 1814, the British had already taken our capital and burned the White House as the Senator told you. Baltimore was the next target in their grand design to divide our forces and crush this newly independent nation of upstart colonies. All that stood between the British and Baltimore, all that stood between America and defeat, was this fort and its guns blocking their entry into Baltimore Harbor.

The British fleet of warships moved within 2 miles of the fort and began a bombardment that was to last for 25 hours. Through the dark hours of the night, the rockets fired and the bombs exploded and a young American patriot named Key, held captive aboard a British ship, watched anxiously for some proof, some sign, that liberty would prevail.

You can imagine his joy when the next morning, in the dawn's early light, he looked out and saw the banner still flying—a little tattered and torn and worse for wear, but still flying proudly above the ramparts. Fort McHenry and the brave men manning it had withstood the assault. Baltimore was saved. The United States, this great experiment in human freedom, as George Washington described it, would endure.

Thinking back to those times, one realizes that our democracy is so strong because it was forged in the fires of adversity. In those dark days of the war it must have been easy to give in to despair. It truly was a perilous night for our new nation. But our forefathers were motivated by something bigger than themselves. From the harsh winter of Valley Forge to the blazing night above Fort McHenry, those patriot soldiers were sustained by the ideal of human freedom.

Through the hardships and the setbacks, they kept their eyes on that ideal and that purpose, just as through the smoke of battle they kept a lookout for the flag. But with the birth of our nation, the cause of human freedom had become forever tied to that flag and its survival.

As the American Republic grew and prospered and new stars were added to the flag, the ideal of freedom grew and prospered. As our country spread across the continent, millions of the dispossessed, the persecuted, the tired, the hungry, and poor flocked to our shores. And the human energies unleashed in this land of liberty were like those never before seen in this world.

From the mountains of Kentucky to the shores of California to the Sea of Tranquility on the Moon, our pioneers carried our flag before them, a symbol of the indomitable spirit of a free people. And let us never forget that in honoring our flag, we honor the American men and women who have courageously fought and died for it over the last 200 years—patriots who set an ideal above any consideration of self and who suffered for it the greatest hardships. Our flag flies free today because of their sacrifice.

And today we mark the 100th anniversary of the first Flag Day ceremony. It was a small and modest ceremony honoring the anniversary of the creation of our flag, a "Flag Birthday," as they called it, conducted by a young schoolteacher and his students at the Stony Hill School in Wisconsin. The teacher's name was Bernard Cigrand, and through his subsequent efforts, he helped establish the national observance of Flag Day. His granddaughter, Mrs. Elroya Cigrand Brown, is with us today to help us celebrate. Congratulations, Mrs. Brown.

We have a few other distinguished relatives with us today—the great-great-great-granddaughter of Francis Scott Key, Mrs. Elizabeth Blunt Wainwright, and her two sons, Andrew and Peter. Mrs. Wainwright, it's been many years since your ancestor wrote the stirring poem that's become our national anthem. Now, with that same spirit of self-reliance, a private sector initiative called the Patriots of Fort McHenry has been formed to refurbish this historic monument. I commend the ingenuity and patriotism of the business and civic leaders that are undertaking this important event.

As we mark the 100th "Flag Birthday," the ideals for which our flag stands still challenge our nation. And today, as before, we strive to reach the full potential of freedom, to put things right, and open wide the door of the American opportunity society so that all of our citizens can walk through.

The great American experiment in freedom and democracy has really just begun. Celebrations such as this remind us of the terrible hardships our forefathers willingly endured for their beliefs. And they challenge us to match that greatness of spirit in our own time.

These anniversaries remind us that freedom is not a resting place, but a constant goal spurring us on to ever-greater achieve-

ments. America has always recognized our historic responsibility to lead the march of freedom. Since our revolution, the first democratic revolution, and the founding of our republic, America has been a hope and inspiration to the oppressed and tyrannized the world over.

In the storm-tossed history of our globe, the United States has been a strong and steady rudder, holding the world fast to the course of democratic progress. That progress hasn't always been easy, and there have been many setbacks along the way. In my lifetime, the world has suffered the agony of the twin inhuman ideologies of nazism and communism. But today freedom is rising. Around the globe, freedom is taking root and growing strong. Over 90 percent of the people in the countries to our south now live in democracies or countries that are confidently moving in that direction. El Salvador, beset by terrorists, supportive of the Communist regime in Nicaragua, has come securely through its own perilous night, and its democratic flag still flies proudly over a free land.

The democratic nations of Costa Rica and Honduras have also suffered from years of armed Communist subversion and recently from outright military attacks by Nicaragua. But the Communist bullying tactics have only bolstered the determination of the democratic Central American nations to defend their freedom. Freedom is the wave of the future.

In those countries around the world where the tyrants still hold sway, new resistance movements are gaining momentum. In Nicaragua, Angola, Afghanistan, and Cambodia, the freedom fighters now fight for their freedom and for human rights. They fight for the same ideals that inspired our forefathers, though the tyrants they battle are incomparably more ruthless. Still, the power and justice of their cause is such that, even despite sometimes overwhelming odds, many of the rebel movements continue to gain recruits and grow in strength.

So, freedom's story is still being written. The brave defense of Fort McHenry by our patriot army was one of its first chapters. But the story will continue as long as there are tyrants and dictators who would deny their people their unalienable rights to life, liberty, and the pursuit of happines.

I would interject here, right now—I have a letter which I treasure very much. It is a full letter. It is on a slip of paper only 2½ inches long and just under an inch in height. But on that is penned a letter, which can only be read with a magnifying glass, and then, in my case, had to be translated, and there are 10 names affixed in signature to that tiny letter. It was smuggled out of a labor camp in the Soviet Union. It was signed by 10 women in that camp who have gone through hunger strikes in their desire for freedom. And the reason they wrote me was to tell me that we, in the United States, represented to them the hope that one day there would be freedom throughout the world. I'm going to keep that letter for as long as I live.

You know, the story, as I say, will continue. Every time we place our hand over our heart and pledge allegiance to the flag, we'll be reminded that our most precious inheritance is freedom and that history has bestowed on our nation the unique respon-sibility for its protection.

When the commanding officer of Fort McHenry commissioned the original Star-Spangled Banner, the one that was later to bring so much hope to Francis Scott Key, he ordered one that would be, in his words, "so large that the British will have no diffi-culty in seeing it from a distance." Today the flag we so proudly hail still sends a mes-sage to any distance that the spirit of a free people is unconquerable and that our democratic nation will always remain "the land of the free and the home of the brave."

Thank you all for what you're doing. God bless you, and God bless America.

Thank you.

Note: The President spoke at 2:49 p.m. to participants in the "Pause for the Pledge of Allegiance" program at Fort McHenry, which was sponsored by the National Flag Day Foundation. In his opening remarks, the President referred to Earl Weaver, who was returning as the manager of the Balti-more Orioles baseball team.

Proclamation 5353—Flag Day and National Flag Week, 1985
June 14, 1985

By the President of the United States of America

A Proclamation

The history of the flag of the United States presents in capsule form the history of our Nation. Although there was a great variety of colorful and interesting flags during the Colonial period, it was not until June 14, 1777, two years after the Battle of Bunker Hill, that the delegates at the Conti-nental Congress adopted the familiar design we know today. They voted "that the flag of the thirteen United States be thirteen stripes, alternate red and white; that the union be thirteen stars, white in a blue field representing a new constellation."

Since 1777, the flag of our Nation has been redesigned periodically to reflect the admission of new States. It has flown over our public buildings, our town squares, and many private homes. It has been carried proudly into battle, and our national an-them gives a dramatic account of the hope and inspiration it has given to many Ameri-cans. Today, it is the leading symbol of the Nation we love and an emblem recognized around the world as a sign of our unity and devotion to freedom.

To commemorate the adoption of our flag, the Congress, by a joint resolution ap-proved August 3, 1949 (63 Stat. 492), desig-nated June 14 of each year as Flag Day and requested the President to issue an annual proclamation calling for its observance and the display of the flag of the United States on all government buildings. The Congress also requested the President, by a joint res-olution of June 9, 1966 (80 Stat. 194), to issue annually a proclamation designating the week in which June 14 occurs as National Flag Week and calling upon all citizens of the United States to display the flag during that week.

Now, Therefore, I, Ronald Reagan, President of the United States of America, do hereby proclaim June 14, 1985, as Flag Day and the week beginning June 9, 1985, as National Flag Week, and I direct the appropriate officials of the government to display the flag on all government buildings during that week. I urge all Americans to observe Flag Day, June 14, and Flag Week by flying the Stars and Stripes from their homes and other suitable places.

I also urge the American people to cele-

brate those days from Flag Day through Independence Day, set aside by Congress as a time to honor America (89 Stat. 211), by having public gatherings and activities at which they can honor their country in an appropriate manner.

In Witness Whereof, I have hereunto set my hand this 14th day of June, in the year of our Lord nineteen hundred and eighty-five, and of the Independence of the United States of America the two hundred and ninth.

RONALD REAGAN

[*Filed with the Office of the Federal Register, 11:16 a.m., June 17, 1985*]

Appointment of David C. Fischer as United States Commissioner on the International Boundary Commission, United States and Canada
June 14, 1985

The President today announced his intention to appoint David C. Fischer to be Commissioner on the part of the United States on the International Boundary Commission, United States and Canada. He would succeed Frank A. Whetstone.

Mr. Fischer is currently senior vice president and chief administrative officer for Huntsman Chemical Corp. in Salt Lake City, UT. Previously, he was Special Assistant to the President at the White House

(1981–1985); a member of the staff of Deaver and Hannaford Co. in Los Angeles (1978–1980); and executive assistant to Governor Reagan and director of advance operations, Reagan for President (1980–1981).

Mr. Fischer graduated from California State Polytechnic University (B.S., 1969) and Brigham Young University (J.D., 1976). He is married, has three children, and resides in Farmington, UT.

Radio Address to the Nation on Civil Rights
June 15, 1985

My fellow Americans:

In less than 3 weeks we'll be celebrating the greatest blow ever struck for the cause of freedom—the Declaration of Independence. "We hold these truths to be self-evident," our Founding Fathers proclaimed, "that all men are created equal, that they are endowed by their Creator with certain Unalienable Rights."

That declaration inspired our nation to reach new heights of human freedom, but

its promise wasn't complete until we abolished the shame of slavery from our land and, in the lifetime of many of us, wrote the civil rights statutes that outlawed discrimination by race, religion, gender, or national origin.

Discrimination is still not yet a thing of the past, unfortunately; and for the last 4½ years, this administration has acted vigorously to defend and extend every American's fundamental right to equal treatment.

The Justice Department has worked energetically to end discrimination in employment, voting, housing—in all the areas covered by law. Our record on enforcing minority voting rights is at the top of the list. And we've increased to an all-time high the number of criminal civil rights cases filed. We have a proud record on civil rights.

The principle that guides us and the principle embodied in the law is one of nondiscrimination. I'm sure that you have all seen the statue representing justice that presides in many of our courtrooms—the woman with the blindfold covering her eyes. Her eyes are covered because true justice should never depend on whether you're rich or poor, or black or white, or if you're Hispanic or Asian, or if your ancestors came from Italy, Poland, Latvia, or any other country, including Ireland, where some of my family's from.

Equal treatment and equality before the law—these are the foundations on which a just and free society is built. But there are some today who, in the name of equality, would have us practice discrimination. They have turned our civil rights laws on their head, claiming they mean exactly the opposite of what they say. These people tell us that the Government should enforce discrimination in favor of some groups through hiring quotas, under which people get or lose particular jobs or promotions solely because of their race or sex. Some bluntly assert that our civil rights laws only apply to special groups and were never intended to protect every American.

Well, they couldn't be more wrong. When the Civil Rights Act of 1964 was being debated in the Congress, Senator Hubert Humphrey, one of its leading advocates, said he'd start eating the pages of the act if it contained any language which provides that an employer will have to hire on the basis of percentage or quota. But I think if Senator Humphrey saw how some people today are interpreting that act, he'd get a severe case of indigestion.

The truth is, quotas deny jobs to many who would have gotten them otherwise, but who weren't born a specified race or sex. That's discrimination pure and simple and is exactly what the civil rights laws were designed to stop. Quotas also cast a shadow on the real achievements of minorities, which makes quotas a double tragedy.

In 1980 and 1984 I ran for President and told you I was opposed to quotas. In response to your mandate, our administration has worked to return the civil rights laws to their original meaning—to prevent discrimination against any and all Americans.

William Bradford Reynolds, the Assistant Attorney General for Civil Rights, has played a key role in that effort. Brad Reynolds is not only a tireless fighter against discrimination, he's a brilliant and dedicated lawyer. Recently, I nominated Brad Reynolds to be Associate Attorney General—the number three job in the Justice Department. He deserves that promotion, but his nomination is being opposed by some who don't agree with us about civil rights, by some who favor the discrimination of quotas.

Brad Reynolds' qualifications and character are impeccable. Indeed everyone knows Brad Reynolds is a man of integrity and strong ideals, that he's firmly committed to the same vision of a just society that I am. I've nominated Brad Reynolds to carry out my policies, the policies for which you elected me, the policies that reflect our best principles as a nation. I'm confident that the Senate will confirm him.

Twenty-two years ago Martin Luther King proclaimed his dream of a society rid of discrimination and prejudice, a society where people would be judged on the content of their character, not by the color of their skin. That's the vision our entire administration is committed to—a society that keeps faith with the promise of our Declaration of Independence, a proud society in which all men and women truly are created free and equal under God.

Until next week, thanks for listening, and God bless you.

Note: The President spoke at 12:05 p.m. from Camp David, MD.

Informal Exchange With Reporters on the Trans World Airlines Hijacking Incident
June 16, 1985

Q. Mr. President——

Q. ——trying to help the hostages?

Q. What about the hostages?

The President. Now——

Q. What can you do to help the hostage situation?

Q. ——to help the hostages?

The President. Well, we're doing everything we can do, but I'm not going to talk about details. I don't think that would be proper.

Q. Are you ruling out U.S. military response, sir?

The President. I'm not going to comment on anything of that kind.

Q. What do you know about the rumors or the—not rumors, but the fact that they've taken several hostages off in Beirut, six hostages, we believe—people with what they said were Jewish-sounding names.

The President. Yes, and I think that's been made public, yes.

Q. What can we——

Q. Have we been able to talk to the Government in Lebanon or whoever's in charge over there about that?

The President. Yes, we're very much concerned about those hostages also.

Q. Do you have any idea where those people are being held?

Q. Mr. President, do you see any encouraging signs, sir?

The President. I just don't want to comment on anything of that kind.

Q. Are we going to negotiate——

The President. The very fact that it has gone on this long without any of their threats of violence or that general destruction and massacre have not been carried out, naturally, is encouraging.

Q. Well, sir, can this be negotiated? Can it be worked out?

Q. Would you like to see Israel return some of those Shiite prisoners, sir?

The President. This is a decision for them to make, and the decision isn't so simple as just trading prisoners. The decision is at what point can you pay off the terrorists

without endangering people from here on out once they find out that their tactics succeed.

Q. Are you still opposed then? Are you still opposed to negotiating with terrorists?

The President. This has always been a position of ours, yes.

Q. Sir, how might this be worked out, then?

The President. Well, again, I can't——

Q. Give us your thoughts on a way.

The President. No, I can't comment. I think that we're going to continue doing the things that we're doing and just hope that they themselves will see that—for their own safety—that they'd better turn these people loose.

Q. Thank you, Mr. President.

Q. Sir, have you talked to any governments this morning, and have you carried any requests to the Israelis, the Syrians?

The President. We've been in contact with the Governments of Lebanon and Syria and Israel, but again, I can't go any further in any details.

Q. Why did you decide to cut short your weekend, sir? We'd been told that you were going to stay for the full time.

The President. Well, I decided with this third trip to Beirut now and the activity that is going on that I'd rather be here, face to face, than dealing on the telephone.

Q. What will you do this afternoon?

Q. What are you going to do now that you're here? What would you do?

Q. What are you going to do this afternoon?

The President. Well, we're going to continue consulting and keeping up to date on the bulletins for any openings that may come.

Q. Do you think there's a way to end this peacefully, sir?

The President. I have to believe that.

Q. What were you suggesting when you said that for their own safety they should turn these people loose?

The President. Well, there have been instances in which hijackers have found that action was taken that resulted in their death or capture so——

Q. Would action be taken in this case?

The President. Again, I would be comenting on the details, and I've said I won't comment.

Q. Thank you.

Note: The exchange began at 11:15 a.m. on the South Lawn of the White House as the President was returning from a weekend stay at Camp David, MD.

Remarks Announcing the Establishment of the Blue Ribbon Commission on Defense Management
June 17, 1985

Ladies and gentlemen, during the past 4 years we have made great progress in rebuilding our national defense and in confronting the challenge of effective defense management. Credit rightly goes to our civilian defense leadership, particularly Defense Secretary Caspar Weinberger. It also goes to our men and women in uniform and to the American people for their support in our efforts.

We've accomplished a great deal, and we have much to be proud of, but there's still a great deal left to do. When our administration began its activities, the problem of defense management we knew would be demanding and difficult, almost as difficult as I had getting that sentence out. [*Laughter*] There were various barriers to efficient management, including legislative barriers, that stubbornly defied our efforts to remove them. And that's why I appointed an individual with unmatched management credentials when I appointed Cap Weinberger. And while overseeing our much-needed buildup of our defensive strength, Cap has done a tremendous job at ferreting out waste and fraud. That's one of the reasons why you hear about it in the news.

But a public misconception has developed from all of this, a misconception born, at least in part, of a drumbeat of propaganda and demagoguery that denies the real accomplishment of these last 4 years. The situation reminds me of the old saying, "Don't clean the skeletons out of the closet. They'll accuse you of murder."

Well, we've ignored that advice in this administration. When Secretary Weinberger came to the Defense Department he pledged, with my full and continuing support, to improve the efficiency and effectiveness of defense management. And he went straight for the skeletons in the closet, and there were many. Cap has put in place many management reforms, and more proposals are being considered, both by the Department and Congress.

I think all of the reforms and all of the new proposals should at this time be evaluated and reviewed. And, so, today I've decided, at the recommendation of Secretary Weinberger and in consultations with Congress, to appoint an independent, bipartisan, Blue Ribbon Commission on Defense Management. They will review the progress already made in improving management and procurement. And we've also asked them to look at the organization and decisionmaking procedures at Defense and give us their recommendations.

In addition, the Commission will study and report on the congressional oversight process as it relates to the Defense Department. It's my expectation that the Commission will send us an eventual blueprint for action that will provide for continuing improvement in the Department of Defense's peacetime and combative effectiveness.

This is an important task, and, so, I've asked David Packard to serve as Chairman of the Commission. He is a former Deputy Secretary of Defense, as you know, with an impeccable record that includes wide experience in and knowledge of our defense system, the defense industry, and government. I will soon ask a number of other leaders in the business, legal, and academic communities to join us in this effort.

And may I point out here that few things are more important to me than the work that this commission will do. Waste and fraud by corporate contractors are more than a ripoff of the taxpayer—they're a blow to the security of our nation. And this the American people cannot and should not tolerate.

I want to thank Bill Dickinson of Alabama and Bill Roth of Delaware, who have been working on this issue in the House and Senate. They and many other Members of the Congress have given us sound advice on the creation of this commission.

I hope that Congress as a whole will support this effort and that together all of us— the administration, the Commission, the Congress—will be able to establish the bipartisan support needed to ensure a strong defense for America and its allies.

I thank you, and now, Mr. Packard.

Note: The President spoke at 2:10 p.m. in the Rose Garden at the White House. Prior to the announcement, the President met with David Packard and Secretary Weinberger in the Oval Office. They were then joined by members of the House and Senate Armed Services Committees.

Nomination of Richard R. Burt To Be United States Ambassador to the Federal Republic of Germany
June 17, 1985

The President today announced his intention to nominate Richard R. Burt, of the District of Columbia, as Ambassador to the Federal Republic of Germany. He would succceed Arthur F. Burns.

Mr. Burt began his career in 1971 as a copy editor for the Boston Globe in Massachusetts. In 1973 he served as a consultant for the Rand Corp.; Hudson Institute; Stanford Research Institute; European-American Institute for Security Research; and the House Republican Wednesday Group. He was a research associate in 1973–1975 at the International Institute for Strategic Studies in London, England, and in 1975

became assistant director. In 1977–1980 he was a correspondent with the New York Times in Washington, DC.

In 1972 Mr. Burt was a senior research associate at the United States Naval War College. He was appointed in 1981 as Director of the Bureau of Politico-Military Affairs in the Department of State, where he served for a year. He has served as Assistant Secretary of State for European and Canadian Affairs since 1983.

Mr. Burt graduated from Cornell University (B.A., 1969) and the Fletcher School of Law and Diplomacy (M.A., 1972). He is married to the former Gahl Lee Hodges.

Remarks Following Discussions With President Habib Bourguiba of Tunisia
June 18, 1985

President Reagan. President Bourguiba and distinguished guests and ladies and gentlemen, I've enjoyed this opportunity to exchange views with one of the great liberators of modern day Africa. President Bourguiba of Tunisia is a statesman whose influ-

ence extends far beyond the boundaries of his own country, a man of dignity and honor. And today he and I discussed issues of particular concern to our two governments and peoples, including developments in the Maghreb and the situation in the

Middle East.

The United States and Tunisia share common interests and common values, including a belief that international relations should be based on mutual respect, reason, and cooperation, not subversion and coercion.

The United States remains firmly committed to the sanctity of Tunisia's territorial integrity and to the principle of noninterference in its internal affairs. We welcome the evolution of closer relations between the states of the Maghreb within such a framework.

President Bourguiba and I also discussed the present state of affairs in the Middle East and the efforts to maintain momentum toward a regional peace.

Historically, Mr. President, you have supported a constructive approach to ending the turmoil that has plagued the region for decades. We hope you will again use your influence to support those who are taking the steps necessary for direct negotiations based on United Nations Security Council Resolutions 242 and 338.

As you know, the goal of this administration remains a just, lasting, and comprehensive peace which will address the legitimate rights of the Palestinian people and provide for the security of all states in the region, including Israel.

Mr. President, your visit reaffirms the underlying strength of the bond between us and the warmth of our friendship. It has been a great pleasure to review with you our past exemplary ties. We're confident that the good will between us will flourish in the years to come. Tunisia can rely on the continuing support and friendship of the United States of America.

Mrs. Reagan and I wish you and Mrs. Bourguiba Godspeed on your journey home and on the great endeavors in which you will continue to lead Tunisia. Thank you, and God bless you all.

President Bourguiba. I should like, first of all, to tell you how happy I am to be once again in the United States, this great nation, friend of Tunisia.

My visit, at the invitation of President Reagan, has deep significance for me since it stresses, once again, the exemplary nature of the friendly relations between Tunisia

and the United States that have been between us for so long.

I should like to express my heartfelt thanks to President Reagan, as well as to his administration of the American people, for the extremely warm and friendly welcome extended to myself and to my delegation since we arrived in Washington. I am deeply touched by this exceptionally friendly greeting and welcome, and I am very impressed, also, to find the President so fit. I am also very impressed by his very sharp and acute analyses and perceptions.

Together we carried out a review of bilateral relations between us. We are gratified by the positive trend of those relations. We are agreed upon the ways and means to give them more impetus and greater diversification.

Together, also, we have carried out a survey of international and regional problems of interest to our two countries; more specifically, we have looked into the situation in the Maghreb, the Middle East, Africa, and the Mediterranean area. More specifically, President Reagan and I took up the evolution of the Israel-Palestinian conflict.

Since in 1965 I had first called upon parties concerned to show realism and to accept the United Nations legal framework as a basis for settlement, 20 years later I remain convinced that this approach remains the only honorable one for all, and 20 years later the Arabs are sorry that they did not accept this approach. At the Fez summit, the Arab community had the great merit to give its support to this approach, and now it remains for the other party—Israel—to resolve to choosing a realistic and peaceful policy.

It remains, nevertheless, that true to our policy of noninterference in the internal affairs of other countries and respectful of the free choice of the Palestinian people, Tunisia will bring her support to any initiative of peace that the Palestinians themselves will deem the most appropriate to recover their legitimate rights and set into motion a just and durable peace in the region.

In this connection, may I stress how close our views are, and I'm personally very gratified that President Reagan's and my views are so close on these issues. I'm also happy to observe that President Reagan is motivated by a sincere will to work for relaxation of tensions, peace, and security in the world.

I also use this opportunity to recall to President Reagan what are the essential and permanent principles of the foreign policy of Tunisia—based upon dialog and peaceful coexistence among states, strengthening of peace and stability in the world, and supporting all just causes.

And finally, I should like to express to President Reagan my best wishes for his personal happiness and health and ask him to convey to the American people a message of friendship and esteem from the Tunisian people.

Note: President Reagan spoke to reporters at 1:22 p.m at the South Portico of the White House. President Bourguiba spoke in French, and his remarks were translated by an interpreter. Earlier, the two Presidents met in the Oval Office and then attended a luncheon in the Residence.

Nomination of Bernard Kalb To Be an Assistant Secretary of State
June 18, 1985

The President today announced his intention to nominate Bernard Kalb to be an Assistant Secretary of State (Public Affairs). He would succeed Robert John Hughes.

Mr. Kalb has been serving as spokesman for the Department of State since January 1985. Previously, he was chief diplomatic correspondent for NBC News (1980–1985); CBS diplomatic correspondent, Washington (1963–1980); Washington anchor for the CBS Morning News with John Hart (1970–1972); and CBS correspondent, Moscow (1960–1963). In 1946 he joined the New York Times and served over the next 15 years as a writer for the Times radio station WQXR, city reporter, reporter in the United Nations bureau, chief of the Southeast Asia and India bureau, and reporter in the Washington bureau. He served as press attaché at the American Embassy in Moscow from 1956 to 1957.

Mr. Kalb graduated from City College of New York (B.S.S., 1951) and Harvard College (M.A., 1953). He served in the United States Army from 1942 to 1944. He is married, has four children, and resides in Rockville, MD. He was born February 4, 1922, in New York City.

The President's News Conference
June 18, 1985

Trans World Airlines Hijacking Incident

The President. I have a statement. One hour ago the body of a young American hero Navy diver, Robert Dean Stethem, was returned to his native soil in a coffin after being beaten and shot at pointblank range.

His murder and the fate of the other American hostages still being held in Beirut underscore an inescapable fact: The United States is tonight a nation being attacked by international terrorists who wantonly kill and who seize our innocent citizens as their prisoners.

In response to this situation, I am directing that the following steps be taken. I have directed the Secretary of Transportation, in cooperation with the Secretary of State, to explore immediately an expansion of our armed sky marshal program aboard international flights of U.S. air carriers for better protection of passengers.

I have directed the Secretary of State to issue an immediate travel advisory for U.S.

citizens traveling through the Athens International Airport warning them of dangers.

This warning shall remain in effect until the Greek Government has improved the security situation there and until it has demonstrated a willingness to comply with the security provisions of the U.S.-Greek civil aviation agreement and the Tokyo, Montreal, and Hague conventions regarding prosecution and punishment of air pirates.

I've asked for a full explanation of the events surrounding the takeover of the aircraft in Athens. I have appealed through the Department of Transportation and the Federal Aviation Administration for all U.S. air carriers to review the wisdom of continuing any flights into Athens until the security situation there improves.

And further, I have asked Secretaries Shultz and Dole to report to me on whether we should terminate the service of foreign air carriers whose governments do not honor appropriate international conventions or provide adequate security at their airports.

I'm calling upon all allied and friendly governments to redouble their efforts to improve airport security and take other measures to prevent the hijacking of aircraft.

I will also be asking them to take steps to prevent travel to places where lawlessness is rampant and innocent passengers are unprotected. And I'm urging that no American enter any Middle Eastern country that does not publicly condemn and disassociate itself from this atrocity and call for the immediate safe release of our citizens.

Let me further make it plain to the assassins in Beirut and their accomplices, wherever they may be, that America will never make concessions to terrorists—to do so would only invite more terrorism—nor will we ask nor pressure any other government to do so. Once we head down that path there would be no end to it, no end to the suffering of innocent people, no end to the bloody ransom all civilized nations must pay.

This act of terrorism is a stain on Lebanon and particularly on those Lebanese in whose name it has been done. Those in Lebanon who commit these acts damage their country and their cause, and we hold them accountable.

I call upon those holding our people to release them without condition. I call upon the leaders of Lebanon, political and religious, to meet their responsibilities and to do all that is necessary to end this crime now in the name of the God they worship. And I call on other governments to speak out and use their influence as well.

This attack is an attack on all citizens of the world who seek to live free from the fear and scourge of terrorism. My thoughts and prayers are, as are those of all Americans, with the prisoners now being held in Lebanon and with their families.

Let me conclude by stating the obvious: We're in the midst of a dangerous and volatile situation. Before taking your questions, I must stress that speculation tonight over what steps we might or might not take in hypothetical circumstances can only lead terrorists to work harder. Consequently, there are many questions to which I should not and cannot respond. I think I have, in this statement, covered virtually all the points that I can safely discuss, and I'm sure that you would understand the reason for that.

And so, that said, Mike Putzel, Associated Press, has the first question.

Q. Good evening, Mr. President. The world's attention is focused tonight on the victims of TWA Flight 847. But as you know, there are seven other Americans who were kidnaped earlier and have spent 3 months to a year in captivity——

The President. Yes.

Q. ——in Lebanon. Will you accept a solution to the current crisis in Beirut that leaves any Americans still in captivity, either from the airplane or those kidnaped earlier?

The President. We certainly include those in every conversation we have with regard to our people there. And this has gone on—the instance of one of them—for a considerable period of time. And we have used every effort to see if we can locate who has them, where they are, whether they're together or separated, and where they might be, because we cannot give up on them. And I hope that they have confidence in that.

And yet, as you can imagine, it is an extremely difficult, seemingly impossible task in that area, with all the factions there, to know whether they are being moved about and what we can do. But no, we haven't given up on them, and we include them in all of our conversations about the present hijack victims.

Q. If I may follow up, sir. Can you tell us, sir, what happened to the policy of swift and effective retribution that you announced 4½ years ago to deal with international terrorism such as that that we've seen——

The President. Well, when I was speaking about that I was talking about a situation in which a government on the other side was involved—so there was a direct source there for the evil. I would have to tell you—and I can't go farther than this in telling you—that the problem is the who in perpetrating these deeds—who their accomplices are, where they are located—because retaliation in some peoples' minds might just entail striking a blow in a general direction, and the result would be a terrorist act in itself and the killing and victimizing of innocent people.

Now, as far as I can go is to tell you that we have used our utmost capacity and intelligence gathering to try and find these people and these places that I'm talking about. And I can only say that we have gathered a considerable body of evidence, but I'm not going beyond that.

Q. Mr. President, do you think that any of the U.S. policies, past and present, have contributed to the rise of radicalism and anti-Americanism in the Middle East? And I'd like to follow up.

The President. Helen [Helen Thomas, United Press International], no, I don't believe that we have. Possibly when we had a peacekeeping force there in connection with our allies—the other countries that had forces in there—we realize that as they began to succeed in keeping some semblance of order in that turmoil, terrorism rose up to strike at all of us that were there in an effort to make our job impossible. And that's why the international force withdrew.

We seem to be a target, also, I'm quite sure, because of our friendship and support of Israel. It just seems there is an anti-Americanism that is rampant there on the part of those who don't want peace with Israel and who have consistently over the years committed terrorist acts against the Israelis.

Q. Mr. President, they wonder why you don't lean on Israel a little bit since the U.S. says that the holding of the Shiite prisoners is against international law—that's our position.

The President. Yes.

Q. Israel has said she is willing to, so why don't you promote it?

The President. Helen, because the linkage that has been created makes it impossible for them and for us. There was no question but that they were going to in stages; they already had started releasing. But it has now been tied to where such a movement would be, in effect, giving in to the terrorists. And then, as I say, who is safe? That's all terrorists have to know is that they can succeed and get what they want. It's the same as the customs in single kidnapings—crimes in our country here in which we know that, if possible, you try to resolve the situation without paying the ransom.

Q. Mr. President, many Americans are very frustrated tonight and feel powerless and feel that they want to strike back somehow at these people who have kidnaped our citizens, murdered some of our citizens. What do you say to those who feel that there's somehow a perception that America is weakened by these acts of terrorism and that we can no longer protect our citizens abroad?

The President. Those people, I think, that do are jumping to conclusions and don't realize what the situation is. But I'm as frustrated as anyone. I've pounded a few walls myself, when I'm alone, about this. It is frustrating. But as I say, you have to be able to pinpoint the enemy. You can't just start shooting without having someone in your gunsights.

Q. Well, sir, have there been things that you've learned about the limits of American power in these sorts of situations, things that you've learned since 4 years, 5 years ago that have perhaps changed your mind about the criticism during the 1980 campaign?

The President. No. Again, I have to say

that when you think in terms of, for example, immediate force, you have to say, "Wait a minute. The people we're dealing with have no hesitation about murder." As a matter of fact, most of them even approve of suicide. How do you attack without finding that, yes, you may have punished, before you're through, the guilty; but in the meantime, the victims are dead. And that's the great hazard in this. How, for example, in the several times that the plane was in Algeria and subsequently then in Beirut, with a dozen hijackers onboard armed with submachine guns—how could you possibly attempt anything without knowing that those guns would be turned first on the victims within the plane, the so-called hostages.

Let me take Bill Plante [CBS News] here first and get——

Q. Mr. President, you spoke of frustration in your inability to deal with this. I spoke today to the wife of one of the hostages who had a very simple and straightforward question which I want to relay to you. She said,"What would you do, sir, if your wife or one of your children were aboard that flight?"

The President. I would still have to think of the safety of all of them. Strangely enough, I just heard someone on one of your networks tonight asking the same question of Al Haig.[1] It would be a horrible situation, yes, and yet it isn't any more horrible just because it would be me than it is for those people that are presently waiting for some reply. But you can't, as I say, give in to the terrorists without knowing that you're then sentencing someone else to go through the same agony and other people to also be victimized.

Q. But, sir, can you say tonight that there is something that the United States can do, some arrangement that we can possibly make?

The President. Now, you're getting beyond that point. So far these questions you've asked have been questions that I thought it was safe to answer. You're now getting into that area that I said—and I

---

[1] *Former Secretary of State and Supreme Allied Commander in Europe.*

hope you understand—that I can't talk about.

Sam [Sam Donaldson, ABC News]?

Q. Mr. President, is the safe return of the hostages your primary goal, and how does that fit in with the other considerations that you as President—some of which you've talked about tonight—are going to have to take into account?

The President. That is the goal—the safe return. And yet, as I say, in a manner that does not reward the hostages for the crime that they have committed, because that gang would be out next week for another try. And this is the thing we must recognize, that it is a cowardly crime in that they hold all the cards once they have these people in their power. And we have to consider their safety. Yes, I could get mad enough now to think of a couple of things we could do to retaliate, but I would probably be sentencing a number of Americans to death if I did it.

Q. Well, sir, that brings up another question, then. In 1980, in your frustration, as every American felt about that hostage crisis, you said in April, "This should have gone on 6 days, let alone 6 months." Is there, therefore, a point in time at which you'll believe that the national interest requires action?

The President. The thing that I always felt about that one, as I say, it was much different than what we have here; you had a government committing that crime. I don't know what measures were looked at as to what you could do with regard to another government. But there it was not this crime of unidentified people—no connection that you can pin on them as to someone in charge, that you can go to that person. That was a different situation than what we're having now with carbombs and hijackings, and this kind of crime. Remember, for example, in the carbombings, the perpetrator of that crime is no longer with us; they are willing to go up themselves.

Ralph [Ralph Harris, Reuters], welcome back. Did you have your hand up there?

Meeting with Soviet Leader Mikhail Gorbachev

Q. Yes, thank you, Mr. President. If I can

change the subject just for a moment—you've invited Mr. Gorbachev to meet you in Washington. And 6 weeks ago you were asked about the invitation. You said, "The ball is in his court." Have there been any developments since then? Do you think there will be a summit this year?

The President. I have to be optimistic and think there will. All I know is that I, feeling that it was our turn, issued the invitation for such a meeting. And there has been, evidently, expressions that—willing to have such a meeting, and discussions are going on with regard to time and place. But I can't give you any report on where those negotiations have taken us.

Now——

TWA Hijacking Incident

Q. Mr. President, if I can come back to the situation in Lebanon—you've made a distinction between unidentified terrorists and the state terrorism. Is not Mr. Berri representing the Government of Lebanon? And does that not create a situation where he is, in fact, identifiable?

The President. Well, now, he's in the position of supposedly having taken the hostages away from the hijackers. But to say that because he holds a post, a so-called Cabinet post, in the Government of Lebanon, that this now involves the Government of Lebanon, I think, is to give the Government of Lebanon a cohesiveness it doesn't have. He is acting as an individual, and he's acting less as a Minister in the Cabinet and acting in his own position as the head of the Amal, one of the factions of the Shiite Muslims there. He has his own militia, and he has his own army. So, it isn't that simple that you can say this is the Government of Lebanon.

Q. If I may follow up, please, sir, on the roles here in that case is Mr. Berri part of the problem or part of the solution, and is he the only solution to this problem?

The President. Now, you're getting into the area of questions that I can't answer on this. But he could be the solution [*snapping his fingers*] that quickly.

Q. Mr. President, so far this evening you've given us a rather somber assessment of what's going on in Lebanon. What is your own estimate as to how long this crisis may

go on? Do you expect a fairly short resolution, or could this drag on for awhile?

The President. You're asking one of those questions I can't answer. I can't discuss that or any of the things that we are doing.

Q. Could I follow up? In terms of your own assessment of American power in the world and how it relates to this episode—in 1984 when you were running for reelection, you told American voters that America is standing tall——

The President. Yes.

Q. ——again, comparing it with the supposed weakness under your predecessor. Is America standing tall today?

The President. Yes, I think we are.

Q. Despite the——

The President. I can't recall in my lifetime any time when it's been used to such an extent as it is now. And the very fact that the terrorists are not all from one source. If they could be linked to a country, if you knew the source and what they were trying to do—but we've got a variety of terrorist organizations. And sometimes, recently, we've found that here and there a couple of them claim that they've cooperated in some terrorist act.

But again, the situation is one that can't be talked about because the first priority is the safety of those victims.

Wait a minute, I think I had better go—Candy [Candy Crowley, Associated Press Radio]?

Q. Mr. President, if I could get back to an earlier question. In the speech in which you talked about swift and effective retribution in 1981, you also said, let it be known that there are limits to our patience. Are there limits to your patience on this issue, or are you willing to wait it out for as long as it takes?

The President. I have to wait it out as long as those people are there and threatened and alive, and we have a possibility of bringing them home—I'm going to say a probability of bringing them home.

Q. If I could follow up, sir. I wonder if you think that perhaps that's how former President Carter felt about the Iranian hostages and what the difference is here, that he said many times that he wanted to bring them home safe and that was his goal.

The President. Yes.

Q. How is this different?

The President. Well, as I say, I did not openly criticize him, and as a matter of fact, in the closing days of the campaign when it appeared that we were getting them home, I didn't say any word or make any comment on the situation because I didn't want to endanger what was going on.

I just felt, as I say, that there were two governments, and it just seems to me that you have a great many more opportunities then to find vulnerabilities in another government and things that you can say in return, that you can offer as a trade. All right.

Q. Mr. President, do you think that the Israelis are holding the 700 to 800 Shiite prisoners in violation of international law, as the State Department said on April 4th? And if so, have you got any assurances from them that they would release those prisoners if we got the hostages back?

The President. We have not dealt with him on that. As I say, we have not interfered in any way with them and what they're doing. With regard to the international law, it's my understanding that taking them across a border from their own country and into another country is a violation of the Geneva accords and—what?

Q. I'm sorry, if I could follow up, sir, has the International Red Cross been dealing with them for us on that issue, dealing with the Israelis on that issue?

The President. Again, we're getting into areas that I can't talk about. I covered it— all I can mainly talk about. I can't resist, because I know you've probably got to get that red coat back in the morning. [*Laughter*]

Q. No, no, that belongs to WWDB in Philadelphia. More than 500 American flyers were rescued by General Mikhailovitch of Yugoslavia in 1944, and they want to erect a memorial on Federal property, which the Senate approved twice and Mr. Derwinsky supported repeatedly, while President Truman gave the general the Legion of Merit. Why, Mr. President, since it's very important to rescue Americans, are you allowing your State Department to stop this in its tracks?

The President. I will have to tell you, Lester [Lester Kinsolving, Globe Syndicate], that this is the first that I've heard about it, and so you've given me a question to ask when I leave here tonight, to find out about that.

Q. I salute you.

The President. All right. Let me—all right.

Q. Mr. President, since Nabih Berri has joined the terrorists in their call for Israel to release the Shiite prisoners is he not now part of their effort?

The President. Again, this is too delicate for me to comment or give an answer to that question. I'm not going to do it.

Q. If I may follow up, he said today that if the United States does not ask Israel to release the Shiite prisoners that he would give the hostages back to the terrorists. In that case would you hold him responsible?

The President. Yes. I would.

No, Robert [Robert M. Ellison, Sheridan Broadcasting Network], yes. No, no. Here, you, yes.

South Africa

Q. To change the subject again, Mr. President. Yesterday South Africans saw the new government in Namibia, which the United Nations condemned. Last week South Africa raided neighboring Botswana, killing 12 people. And last month a South African commando unit tried to blow up oil tanks partly owned by a U.S. company. In view of these events, do you plan any changes, alterations, modifications in your policy of constructive engagement with South Africa?

The President. Well, as you know, we brought our Ambassador home for consultations. All I can tell you is that we think we have been successful in getting some concessions there and some changes in their policy of apartheid, which we all find repugnant. And we're going to continue doing that.

The raid across the border was perhaps the kind of incident that I've just been talking about here in our own situation. There is no question about the violence of the ANC [African National Congress] and their striking and their attacks on people and their murdering and so forth. But again, was the strike back at the people that were guilty, or was it just a retaliation in a general direction? So, we don't know about that, but we are very concerned about it.

Q. If I may, then you do not consider these recent events to be a setback in your policy with South Africa?

The President. Well, they're certainly not something that we heartily approve of, but whether they're something to make us break off relations with another government, I don't think that, either.

All right.

MX Missile

Q. Mr. President, would you be willing to accept 40 MX missiles instead of 50 if Congress gave you an extra $200 million for the Midgetman and accelerated the development of that program?

The President. Well, you've asked one here that I think we'd have to look at that very seriously to see whether there was an advantage in that or not or whether even their giving that money could accelerate the Midgetman program. I don't know that it could. But I do know that the debates that are going on about the MX, I think are a lot of wasted rhetoric, and we ought to get on with it.

It is most vital to us that we modernize our land-based missiles, and that is the missile that is on hand and available now. It has a hard-target capacity and an accuracy that is virtually unequaled anywhere. We need it.

Terrorism

Q. Mr. President, you've said repeatedly during your administration, as you've said tonight, that you can't give in to terrorism. But each time that we've had one of these incidents, such as the case of the marines who died in Beirut, there had been a lot of talk from the administration but no action. Is there any danger that terrorists in the Middle East might get the feeling that the U.S. bark is worse than its bite and that they can do these things with impunity knowing we won't retaliate?

The President. Well, I hope not. But again, let me just point out to you in that incident, a man who committed the crime—or men—I don't know how many

were in the truck—they're gone. This is one of the horrifying things of some of these terrorist acts is you have a group of people who think their ticket to heaven is to do this and to take some others with them. So, when it was over, the truck and the people in it—or person in it—were gone, and the same was true of the Embassy bombing.

Now, how do you establish a connection between them and someone else? Was there someone else that set them on their way—you have no way of knowing. So, again, as I say, you're left with only one form of retaliation and that is if you just aim in the general direction and kill some people, well, then, you're a terrorist, too.

MX Missile

Q. Back to the MX, Mr. President. Do you have a new basing plan, because that was the condition, wasn't it, on the Senate cap—that they could above 50 if you had a new basing plan, and Mr. Weinberger indicated that you do want more MX's——

The President. One thing right now, we do know from the research that we've done and the experimenting that we've done, we can vastly harden a silo to the extent that we think that it would take a very direct hit to do away with those—or to eliminate those missiles.

Helen I think said——

Ms. Thomas. You have 5 more minutes.

The President. Oh, well. Your watch was off there?

Tax Reform

Q. Mr. President, you've been spending a lot of time monitoring the situation in Beirut on the hijacking. I was wondering, how much time are you devoting to domestic issues during your day, particularly the tax effort on the Hill?

The President. That's one thing I have to tell you, you can't just aim yourself at this tragedy, great as it is. I don't think that I neglect it in any way, because there is a limit to what you can do or what can be reported in the times between. Yes, we're very serious about both the budget and tomorrow morning I will be making another appearance in connection with the tax reform.

Q. I was wondering, as a followup, sir, efforts are underway to enact a tax increase either in tandem with the tax reform or separately. Are you in touch with that——

The President. Oh, a tax increase? I don't have to spend any time at all on that. [*Laughter*] No, because there just ain't gonna be none.

Let me go way into the back here to—

Middle East Peace Efforts

Q. [*Inaudible*] from Yugoslav Television. Do you think that this tragic accident might in any way influence the ongoing process of solving the Middle East problem through Palestinian-Jordan-Israeli talks?

The President. I don't really see that they have been—they're certainly not a setback to us with regard to the peace talks. And I know that King Hussein, when he was here, made it plain that he is not retreating from the effort that he is making. And I have to commend him for his courage and his willingness to do what he's doing in trying to bring about direct negotiations between the Arab States and Israel and the Palestinians to try to get a peace, a lasting peace, in the Middle East. So, we are doing everything we can, also, to be of help to him.

There's another red coat behind you, Larry.

Views on the Presidency

Q. Mr. President, so far this year, you've seen your defense budget request slashed on the Hill, you've had very difficult battles on the Hill with the MX and with a number of other issues, you've had to endure the Bitburg controversy, and now this hostage crisis. Do you feel that the Teflon that's covered your Presidency has slipped off? Is your luck running out?

The President. I never thought there was any Teflon on me anyplace. But we seem to have reversed the course with regard to the *contras.* And with regard to Bitburg, in spite of the efforts of some of you, from the very first, I felt it was the morally right thing to do. And I'm pleased that I did it. And it was a worthwhile experience over

there. And I began to get my reward when I spoke to 10,000 young teenage Germans and at the end of that heard 10,000 young Germans sing our national anthem in our language. I think it was a recognition.

Those that indicated that in some way I might be suggesting that we forget the Holocaust—no, in no way. Nor are the Germans trying to forget the Holocaust. I was amazed—in this 40 years now of friendship that has followed all of that hatred and the evil of the Holocaust and of nazism—to learn that the Germans, not only have they preserved the horrible camps and maintained museums with the photos all blown up of the worst and most despicable things that happened there, but they bring their schoolchildren every year and show them and say that this must never happen again.

I have never suggested in going there that this was a forgive-and-forget thing. It's up to someone else to forgive—not us—if there is any forgiveness, and certainly we must never forget. And so, if there is any Teflon, I didn't think that I lost any on doing that. But now, as I say, we've reversed the thing on the *contra* aid.

We only have a conference to go, and either way it turns out I think is going to be a plus and be more than we originally asked for. The MX battle is on. And of course, now, in the budgeting battle, I do believe that one version of a budget that has been proposed is no way to eliminate the deficit. I think that the Senate plan, with its $56 billion savings in the first year, is the answer to eliminating the deficit and eventually going to work on the national debt.

So, I don't think I've suffered too much.

Ms. Thomas. Thank you, Mr. President.

The President. There, you did it, Helen.

Q. Your watch has stopped.

The President. My watch says you gave me 5 extra minutes.

Note: The President's 31st news conference began at 8 p.m. in the East Room at the White House. It was broadcast live on nationwide radio and television.

Remarks and a Question-and-Answer Session With Members of the Chamber of Commerce in Mooresville, Indiana
June 19, 1985

The President. You may have heard about our proposal to overhaul the tax code, make it fairer and simpler and more compassionate. And I wanted to bring the message directly to you in America's heartland. I've been traveling all over the country; the enthusiasm, I must say, for America's tax plan is overwhelming.

I call it America's tax plan because it will take the load off the back of the long-suffering American taxpayer. It'll take the low-income wage earner and the retired elderly off the tax rolls entirely, and it'll remove the tax distortions that I think are holding the American economy back from reaching its full potential.

Mac's Restaurant sums up our message in two words when they say, "Treat yourself." Our proposal makes the system fairer. By closing loopholes and ensuring that all big businesses and individuals pay their fair share, we think we can lower the tax burden on everyone. And one of the best things about our tax proposal is the boost it'll give to America's mainstream.

We're cutting tax rates for small and entrepreneurial businesses. We're cutting top rate on personal income tax to 35 percent, on corporations from 46 to 33 percent, while keeping the graduated scale for small corporations. The tax rate—or the capital gains tax rate again will be cut, this time to 17½ percent. The objective is to create a small business renaissance in America, to make this decade the age of the entrepreneur.

I read in the news that Bill Seashols said one of the strengths of Mooresville is that people still believe in the work ethic here and they emphasize the importance of family. Well, that's what America's tax plan is all about, too. It'll set our economy humming and be the best jobs creation bill, we think, that we've ever had.

And, second, it will give families and wage earners some long-overdue relief by increasing the standard deduction and practically doubling the personal exemption to $2,000. By lowering marginal rates, we'll allow the people to keep more of each extra dollar they earn. If you work overtime or get a raise or save some money and invest it, more of that extra income will end where it belongs: in your cash registers and pockets and not in Uncle Sam's wallet. By removing low-income earners from tax rolls, the climb up the ladder of success I think will be easier for everyone.

I'm excited about all the good things this plan will do for America. And if you're excited, too, and if you all think that our plan is good for America, maybe you could let those people there in the back of the room know.

Well, that's enough of the monolog from me. I think we're slated for something of a dialog, and I'd like to hear what you feel about our plan.

[*At this point, several members of the business community spoke.*]

Q. As a physician, many of my patients are older Americans, and they wanted me to ask you how your new tax plan was going to affect them as older Americans.

The President. Well, I think first of all that a great many elderly people will be at an income level—in a retirement income level in which they won't pay any tax at all. They will benefit to the same extent that everyone else will with the reduced rates.

For example, today there are people at the poverty level that find themselves paying an income tax. In ours, let's say a family of four—a husband and wife and two children—at $12,000, they won't pay any tax. And then it starts at a 15-percent bracket and goes to the 25 and finally the 35.

I think that they'll find that there are many provisions in this plan that will be of help to them. Certainly they will not be penalized in any way.

Q. Thank you, Mr. President. My name is Bruce Marine, and my question is: Does the proposed tax reform shift the tax burden from the individuals to the business or from middle income to higher income?

The President. No, as a matter of fact it just, I think, treats everyone squarely. The one thing that is being done in business—now, we're lowering the rate in the corporations. But also, we're taking away some so-called loopholes and some things that some businesses, based on the nature of their business, could take advantage of the present tax system to the point that even making a substantial profit, major corporations have not paid any tax at all because of some of the provisions of the present tax code.

We're changing that; we think that everybody ought to share and pay a fair share. As I pointed out, in small corporations, some of your businesses have incorporated. Well, in those the maximum tax, of course, is 33 percent, but for the smaller businesses, it'll be graduated. It'll be a progressive tax, so that before you get to the 33-percent bracket, there will be a lower tax that will be beneficial there.

Now, most of you, however, in small business pay on a personal income tax rate. So, you'll be benefiting also in that. And incidentally, while I'm here let me—you said thanks to me—let me say thanks to you. Do you know that in the last 2½ years, we have created some 8 million new jobs in the United States. We have averaged for these 2½ years 300,000 people a month finding work and going to work in this country. And the bulk of those are produced by small business not by the major corporations.

That's why at the recent economic summit I sat there kind of glowing inside as some of my colleagues—the Prime Ministers and the heads of state and Presidents of the other European countries that were our trading partners and allies—were telling me that they believe the answer to some of their problems—because they haven't created a new job in Europe in 10 years. They have the same number of jobs that they had 10 years ago. And they were telling me that they believe entrepreneurship is probably the answer to their problem. [*Laughter*] I said I thought it might be. [*Laughter*]

Q. Mr. President, my name is Tim Currens. My question to you is: What effect do you believe the proposed tax plan will have on business growth, and are there any built-in incentives for business within the proposed tax plan?

The President. Yes, I believe the incentives that we have there are—the whole thing is aimed toward growth and encouraging growth. Part of that is the reduction, again, of the capital gains tax, which we found—you know, the capital gains tax is—there's been some demagoguery around that that's a tax for rich people that can sell something for a profit and so forth. We found that with the two reductions in recent years—the one in 1978 in the rate of that tax and then the reduction that we made in 1981—in both instances, the revenue from capital gains for the Government went up tremendously.

In 1977—or was it 1979, Don? I think it was '79—the pool of capital available, risk capital, for backing someone that wanted to start a business, as you did, was down to $39 million. By 1984, it was up to 4½ billion, and we think that a large part of that had to do with the tax change in capital gains.

Q. Mr. President, my name is George Smith. How do you see your tax program affecting interest rates on and the availability of money for single and multifamily development?

The President. Well, I think what the example I just gave—I think is some of the answer to that. And I think it will. As to interest rates, as you know, yesterday the prime came down to the lowest it has been since 1978—down to 9½ percent. We think there are going to be further dips in that.

We have some of our short-term government paper now that is out at an interest rate of under 7, and that also is the lowest that it has been since 1978.

Incidentally, in answering both yours and the other question, too, I should have mentioned that I think that the very fact that we're going to be putting—that the average individual is going to have more money in their pockets and take away from some of what they're giving to government—it's going to make them better customers for all of you and be a stimulant to business just in that way alone.

Q. Bill Cherry, Mr. President, Plainfield Chamber of Commerce. I'd like to ask you, besides the deduction and the number of tax brackets, how else—what other parts of your plan is going to simplify the system for most of us?

The President. Wow! You know, I may turn my head here to Don Regan again. If you haven't met him, Don Regan was Secretary of the Treasury when this plan was being created and is now the Chief of Staff. For me to try and off the top of my head bring up some of the other benefits—now wait a minute. Again, you asked——

Q. ——simplification.

Q. ——down to three.

The President. Yes, it's 14 tax brackets; it's really down to four.

Q. Okay.

The President. There's one at zero.

Q. All right. Yes. [*Laughter*]

Q. ——some other points. Are there any other that you think might——

The President. In the simplifying of it? Yes, I believe we have—in return for these grants coming down—we have eliminated a number of deductions. And yet, for example, the deduction that has been taken and now will be eliminated—of deducting local and State taxes from your income tax—we discovered that two-thirds or more of the people in this country do not itemize, so they weren't getting that deduction anyway. And you only got that deduction when you got into the upper brackets. But we've also found out that—as against the reduction in rates—everybody still gets a tax cut even without that deduction.

We think it can be simplified at this extent—and Don, you just interrupt me if I miss something here. We believe we're going to try something· else in this that will be optional with the people and the nonitemizers—that a person, if they decide to, can provide to their employer what things they have like interest on a home mortgage and so forth, and then the employer will simply direct to the IRS in Washington. Instead of sending you the form that tells you how much salary you got, they will simply send that plus your other figures to Washington, and you will receive direct from Washington without filling out any kind of a form—you'll either receive a bill for tax if you owe some, or you'll receive the refund if, out of your withholding, you have a refund coming. You won't have to even fill out or sign a tax form, just send in the check or get the check. [*Laughter*]

And this we think—now, again, as I say, that is optional. If someone mistrusts IRS and decides they want to take a look themselves, they're free to do that. The nonitemizers, of course, that will be very simple for them. We have left—even though a recommendation was made earlier that we should eliminate the deduction for charitable contributions. We believe that in this country, which is so unique in all the world in voluntarism—this country supports many worthwhile cultural activities by private contributions—like symphony orchestras and so forth—than all the rest of the world put together. And we thought we don't want to discourage in any way something that is so typically American.

It's believed there are some 95 million adult Americans today that are actually engaged in some kind of volunteer work, whether in their church or their community or the school board or whatever, in this country. And we think that's a much greater force for good than even government. So, we've left that.

But the number of reductions—or deductions that have been eliminated, the increasing of the personal exemption—almost doubling that—then almost doubling the—for each dependent, increasing the earned income tax credit, those things—and then pretty much it's just a simple goal from there.

Q. Mr. President, we just have time for one short question.

The President. Well—[*laughter*]——

Q. I shook hands with you earlier.

The President. Yes.

Q. I'd like to ask you the question here if anyone will pay more taxes?

The President. The only people that we can see that will pay more taxes are those that presently are unfairly not paying their share, those that have been taking advantage of so-called tax shelters and those, as I said, for example, at the major corporate level where they have found that they can earn a profit and escape paying any tax whatsoever.

But I tried one because, you know, some people have been throwing around the fact that this favors the rich. You might be interested to know that only 3 percent of the earners in America will be in the 35-percent bracket—the top bracket. They will pay 14 percent of the total amount of tax revenue that the Government receives. So, it is not benefiting them, and yet they, too, will get a reduction—the very fact that the more they earn, they get 65 cents out of every dollar. I remember back in those "if" days in Hollywood when I was only getting 10 cents out of every dollar. [*Laughter*] And I said no to a lot of parts I'd have liked to played, but I just wasn't about to work for a dime—[*laughter*]—on the dollar.

But the same is true with the middle class. And I did a little—some pen-and-ink work myself one day. I had some figures for a town in New Jersey where I was speaking that I'd used in there about someone at about a middle-income range of $42,000 of income, family of four, and what the tax would be for them. And I got very curious. So, I multiplied by 10 on income to see about this benefiting the rich. And it is a progressive tax. And that has been the tradition since the income tax started, virtually, of—that you not only pay—you know, the Lord in the Bible says that tithing—the Lord's share—is a tenth. And He says if He profits you 10 times as much, you give 10 times as much. Well, under the income tax, when you start computing Caesar's share—[*laughter*]—with the progressive tax, it doesn't come out that way. It isn't proportioned.

So, I was very interested, with my figures, to take this family here, and then take this one over here that earned 10 times as much, and this one over here would be paying 30 times as much in tax as this middle class family here. So, that worked out pretty well.

Incidentally, there's another feature, too, in helping here. You know that right now the IRA's—these independent retirement accounts where you can take $2,000 of your salary and put it in a bank account for retirement, and you don't have to pay income

tax on that $2,000—and this has been true for male employees, female employees. And then we come to the husband and wife team where the wife is the housekeeper, and I think she's allowed about $250, isn't it? The man could take out $250 for her and so deposit $2,250.

Well, we happen to think that the housewife is very well employed, and from now on they'll be able to take out $4,000 and put it aside.

Well, I don't know if——

Q. Thank you very much, Mr. President. We appreciate—this community filled and bursting with voluntarism—before you go, I want to give you two gifts. And the first— Mooresville is the home of the Indiana State flag. And Mooresville goes back to 1824. And Paul Hadley designed this flag, and we would like to give this to you on behalf of visiting Mooresville as the home of the State flag.

The President. Well, thank you.

Q. And, secondly, this is a gift. And I think probably I can probably begin by saying that on behalf of the 8 million new jobs—this is made by the 35 people that are in new jobs created because of Indiana Uniform. They wanted to give you a work shirt—[*laughter*]—which is a symbol of industry. [*Laughter*] And on the back, we want to tell you about your tax plan.

The President. "America's Tax Plan of the Future. Go for it." [*Laughter*]

Q. Thank you, sir.

The President. Thank you. Thank you all very much. And I see I have a pin here that was also given to me. It's of your flag.

Q. Yes, thank you.

The President. And before I get to that national convention of the Jaycees that I'm going to speak to now in Indianapolis, I think I'll put this on so that they'll know where we are. [*Laughter*]

I thank you all very much. Are we supposed to just get on our way now?

Q. Yes, sir.

The President. Well, this is a case of just eat and run.

———

Reporter. Mr. President——

Q. Mr. President, there are two people

being held hostage from Indiana. Can you report any progress since last night to the people of this State and the rest of the country?

The President. Not since last night, no. There have been few if any changes. There have been some reports, unconfirmed as yet, to the fact that something to do with how the hijackers got on the plane, and we haven't been able to confirm those yet.

We also know—from one strange interview that was done this morning that was allowed by the hijackers—that the answer to who is still in the plane is the crew—the three-member crew is still on the plane, and the captain was allowed to do an interview through the pilot's window this morning.

Q. Is Nabih Berri still in control of these people? Does he still have them?

The President. Yes. And we're doing—as I said last night, there are things I just can't talk about. We're doing everything we can——

Q. Mr. President——

The President. ——to put the pressure on to bring those people home safely.

Q. Does the Red Cross have any role?

The President. I——

Q. ——international organization like that have any role in something like this?

The President. Again, Sam [Sam Donaldson, ABC News], this is one that I can't—I just won't speak to, and I can't speak to and—anymore than I would speak of others that could or could not be involved in trying to help us in this.

To the families of those here from your own State, I think we all are praying—that's all—I've been praying ceaselessly for them and for their safety.

Q. Will you meet—*[inaudible]*—Mr. President?

The President. I don't know whether I'll have an opportunity because I'm due back in Washington this afternoon.

Q. We couldn't hear you.

Q. Can't you?

Q. What did you say?

Q. Thank you, Mr. President.

The President. They turned out the lights. That tells me I can't talk anymore.

Q. Thank you, sir.

Note: The President spoke at 12:37 p.m. in the meeting room at Mac's Family Restaurant.

Remarks Following the Meeting With the Chamber of Commerce in Mooresville, Indiana
June 19, 1985

The President. I understand that you were hearing out here what was going on inside.

Audience. Yea!

The President. Well, I hope we answered all of your questions on the tax bill. And if you feel like writing letters to people in Congress to tell them how you feel about the bill, it'd sure be helpful—or a wire, mailgram.

But thank you all. We've got to go down now and speak to the convention in Indianapolis, but thank you all for being out here. It's been wonderful to be back in the heart of America.

Thank you all.

Note: The President spoke at 1:09 p.m. outside of Mac's Family Restaurant.

Remarks at the Annual Convention of the United States Jaycees in Indianapolis, Indiana
June 19, 1985

Audience. [*Chanting*] U.S.A.! U.S.A.! U.S.A.!

The President. Thank you all very much. Thank you, President Tommy Todd, Doris Gosnell, Governor Orr, Mayor Hudnut of Indianapolis, Lieutenant Governor Mutz, Congressman John Myers, and all of you members of this great and growing organization.

Listening to that warm introduction, feeling your enthusiasm shake this hall, I could only think, I've found it; I'm in Hoosier Heaven. You know, I grew up not too far from here hearing the song about Indiana's Wabash Cannonball, but I'd say I've just heard the sound of an all-American cannonball.

Well, I'm happy to be with you here today, for my heart is with you every day of the year. I remember addressing a group just about 4 years ago at this time, down in San Antonio, Texas, and I asked for their help to put the pieces of a broken economy back together. They were and are a very special group of people. They're heroes who live in the frontiers of American life. They're people who behold in the dawn each day a dream far away, to strive for and win. They're men and women who laugh at folly and fear and who see setbacks not as excuses to quit but as spurs to struggle and sweat even harder to carry on. They are the Jaycees. They stand for opportunity, and they're leading the economic comeback of the United States of America.

But before I go on with my remarks for today, let me speak to a concern that I know is on all your minds—our American prisoners in Beirut. We're continuing to do everything that we can to bring all credible influence to bear, to get our people freed and returned home safe and sound. But let me say we must not yield to the terrorist demands that invite more terrorism. We cannot reward their grisly deeds. We will not cave in.

Audience. [*Chanting*] U.S.A.! U.S.A.! U.S.A.!

The President. Thank you very much.

Well, now, to get on with our visit here today, in 6,500 chapters, 270,000 members strong, you are leaders in your communities, movers and shakers in get-out-the-vote drives, in raising funds for muscular dystrophy—as you've just been told—in helping to locate missing children, and problem solving of every sort. An organization for men only, you opened your doors to more than 30,000 women members, and today we salute all of your new Jaycee members.

Four years ago, I came before you to say, If you think you're better off with the high taxes and runaway monster government of the past, then go ahead and oppose our new program, but if you're ready to try something new, if you're ready to tell Washington, DC, "No more business as usual, because we're going to make America great again," then lend us your help and commit your lives, and you did that.

You joined us and gave your all because we believe in America, not the America of special interests, bureaucrats, or the elite, powerful, and well connected, but the America of hard-working families who sustain their communities, who abide by the law, who not only pay their own bills but every cent spent by government as well. Jefferson's vision of unalienable rights of life, liberty, and the pursuit of happiness, of government's responsibility to grow, not for its own sake but to provide the ultimate in individual freedom—that is the commitment of this administration.

So, we set out together to give the words "freedom," "incentives," and "growth" new life. And what have we accomplished? Well, not all that we want, by no means. But while the sourpusses predicted failure, inflation went from 12.4 percent to 4 percent; the prime rate from over 20 percent to 9½ percent as of yesterday—[*applause*]—that's the lowest level in 6½ years for that. Government stopped engorging itself with the people's earnings. Nearly 8 million new jobs were created, more jobs per month than

Europe created in the last 10 years; 635,000 new business incorporations last year; zero growth turned into 30 straight months of economic expansion and sent consumer confidence to its highest levels since 1966.

My friends, thanks to you, a no-hit, no-run, no-win team is working its way back to championship form. And you know something? Winning is just the beginning, because momentum creates more momentum. We're not turning back to that failed, unhappy past. This is the moment to push forward together, to get the job done right, to change our lives for the better and change America forever.

So, like in 1981, I've come to ask a simple but crucial question for our future: Are you with us, can we count on your support again? [*Applause*] Well, thank you very much.

I hope you agree that a Congress serious about cutting deficits will pass the budget savings that we've asked for and will give this President the same authority that 43 Governors already have—authority to line-item veto budget-busting items in appropriation bills.

And if we're ever going to handcuff the big-spenders, we can't stop with a line-item veto; we must go all the way and pass a constitutional amendment mandating government may spend no more than government takes in.

Now, I've come today to speak to you on another subject; I've come to speak about our tax system. I pray that this won't send shudders through the hall. But then I wouldn't be surprised. A system with 14 different tax brackets that stifle hard work and success; a system that has singled out families for cruel and unusual punishment; a system that caters to the powerful few with loopholes galore, but lets working people take it on the chin—that system is unfair at its core. It has become public enemy number one. It's earned a revolt, and it's time we tore it down.

Trying to tackle the great challenges of our future with today's outdated tax system—that's a little like trying to win the Indianapolis 500 on a bicycle. [*Laughter*] We're proposing a plan that will say, if I may paraphrase the start of that race: America, start your engines! We're propos-

ing a plan that will tell 238 million Americans—go for it!

We would get rid of the current 14-bracket system and replace it with a simple 3-bracket system of 15, 25, and 35 percent. Those brackets would apply to your taxable income, not to your gross income. And these lower rates would mean you could keep more of each additional dollar that you earn or save. We call it America's tax plan because it will mean fairness and tax relief for the majority of families, individuals, and businesses in every region of the country.

Families are the bedrock of our society, and they're going to receive long-overdue relief. It's a national scandal that Washington sat back for over three decades and let the value of the personal exemption collapse. Well, we're putting an end to benign neglect. Of immense importance to working and middle class families, we will nearly double—to $2,000—the personal exemption for every taxpayer and dependent. The exemption will be indexed to inflation to prevent any erosion.

We would raise the standard reduction [deduction] for joint returns to $4,000. And to end unjust discrimination against homemakers, we would nearly double—to $4,000—the amount every couple can put into individual retirement accounts and deduct from their taxable income. We're not promoting one kind of family over another; we just want all families treated the same.

I think you know who gets the lion's share of the credit for creating nearly 8 million new jobs in the last 2½ years. When it comes to producing jobs, American small business is king, and small businesses will remain king because America's tax plan is the biggest jobs creation bill in history.

Reducing personal tax rates will give a shot in the arm to small businesses which aren't incorporated; so will reducing the maximum corporate tax rate—now 46 percent—to 33 percent, with most small corporations paying lower corporate tax rates which will be progressive from 15 percent to 33 percent. And reducing the top tax rate on capital gains will fuel the high-risk ventures that can pay off with great leaps in productivity and new jobs and technologies.

We want every man and woman to have their chance to stand among the new heroes of our age—the American entrepreneurs. Entrepreneur—you know, that's such a nice word. That's a French word—it means Jaycees.

As we open the windows of opportunity for all, we're going to start shutting the doors on special privileges that enable some to avoid paying their fair share. I don't think we need to keep subsidizing $100 lunches to stay competitive in world markets. I don't think the great majority of taxpayers should have to subsidize the State and local deduction for the wealthy few in a handful of high-tax States. And I don't think the loopholes like jojoba bean shelters, windmills, racehorse writeoffs, and Cayman Island trusts are the foundation for a lean and mean America in the eighties and nineties and 21st century.

These shelters aren't justified. They cheat the great majority of unsheltered taxpayers who must make up the difference with higher tax rates. And it's about time that we pulled our investment money out of unfair subsidies, out of shelters, out of foreign tax havens, and invested that money in America's future. It's time that we all pulled on the same oar so we could all go forward together, and nobody gets left behind.

I know the special interests and their lobbyists are regrouping. They're already swarming like ants into every nook and cranny in Congress. But the American people have their lobbyist, too—you're looking at him.

Our plan will not increase the deficit. It is not a tax increase nor will I ever permit it to become a tax increase. I will veto any tax increase the Congress sends me, and I don't usually threaten vetoes. I say I'll wait until I see what comes before me on my desk. As for a tax increase—I know what that is, I'll veto it already.

But America's tax plan will mean that every income group's tax burden will fall. Every group in every region will be better off. And I predict that after all is said and done, the Congress will pass this historic plan because it is profairness, profamily, progrowth, and most important, it is profuture.

Too many pundits haven't calculated what America's tax plan will mean for our future. In a word, lower tax rates mean new opportunity, a whole world of opportunity for people. If you earn more, if you're promoted to a better job, if you're able to save some money and invest it, then fewer of those dollars will go to line Uncle Sam's pockets and more will end up in your wallets where they belong. That's the key difference from the tax system we have now. And when you see that bright green light telling you, go ahead, take a risk, shoot for your dreams and do more with your lives, it'll be America that gains the most, America that becomes more competitive, and yes, America that lights up the sky with economic fireworks that spell "U.S.A. Number One." I've often said and believe it must always remain our goal: We cannot be satisfied until the United States can outproduce, outcompete, and outsell anybody, anywhere in the world.

Well, America's tax plan will enable us to do just that. Tax rates are like prices for producing, saving, and investment. And history shows that in the case of two countries, A and B, and the tax rates are cut in B, then capital will flow from A to B. By bringing down our prices, by making them cheaper, well, than virtually anywhere in the world, we're going to create powerful incentives for people to invest, produce, and save in America. We're going to create powerful incentives for people all over the world to do their shopping and create jobs in America's stores ahead of any other store.

We're going to contribute to another surge of venture capital and entrepreneurial activity. We're going to make it possible for tomorrow's industrial giants to be born in America, born in a small business that may begin in the dream of one Jaycee.

This is the future that we can invent and create together. And we shouldn't settle for less; our dreams can be real. I'm convinced that getting this program passed will be the best thing we can ever do for ourselves. Help us get it passed by Thanksgiving, and then we'll give America the best Christmas present we've ever had.

Now, some people, and I don't question their intentions, are already fixing to pick our plan apart. For example, some say that to make it even fairer, we must raise the top tax rate higher than 35 percent so the rich pay more. But that argument misses the central point of what we're doing. We're not lowering the top tax rate to 35 percent so the rich will do better; we're lowering the top rate to 35 percent so that every working American will have a better chance to get rich.

There's something else they forget. Nearly 15 million small businesses pay their taxes by the personal rates, so raising the top tax rate is a tax-increase-in-waiting for every one of them. I think the Congress should hear what you think about this, but you're going to have to speak up because they're 600 miles away.

A potential tax increase on millions of American small businesses—now, is that your idea of fairness?

Audience. No-o-o!

The President. I'm sorry, your answer didn't quite reach DC. You said what? Is it——

Audience. No-o-o!

The President. Is a tax increase on small business your idea of strengthening growth and our future?

Audience. No-o-o!

The President. Well, then maybe you'd like to tell Congress you support our plan—you want it passed. America should unite and America should go for it!

There's no limit to the good we can do, for there's no limit to the goodness in America's heart and spirit. You know this; you're the ones who show us every day in places like Anderson, South Carolina, where Jaycees built a Vietnam war memorial to the 28 young men who gave their last full measure of devotion in that war; in Stevens Point, Wisconsin, where they've bought a computer that is helping cerebral palsy victim Don Zivney to speak after 22 years of silence.

You remind us what I recently told a talented group of students in Atlanta, Georgia. As important as the creation of wealth is to generate jobs and a brighter future, we don't want our children to grow up believing wealth and material comforts should be their main goals in life. It isn't looking out for number one that counts most; it's loving our neighbor, and we have that on pretty good authority.

This is America's tradition from our first days when the pioneers would get together and build each other's houses. They called it houseraising. Well, that was long ago, but it's still going on.

Every time someone helps a friend down and out, helps a lonely stranger hungry and cold, that's a houseraising. Every time someone gives time or money to support their local police, help the handicapped, or improve their library or school, that's a houseraising, too. And every time a group of people get together and vow, don't tell us how big the problem is, the Jaycees can solve it, that's a houseraising.

I thank you for this wonderful time that we spent together. I wish you an America rich in success, rich in our kindness and love for each other. And if I must say goodbye, and I do—because saying goodbye to the Jaycees is pretty hard to do—then I'll do it by leaving you some words I almost feel were written for you—they're from a very noted poet in our background. He said:

> Believe in your mission, Greet life with a cheer;
> There's big work to do, and that's why you're here;
> Let the world be better for you, and at last, when you die;
> Let this be your cry, Come on my soul, carry on.

Thank you for the miracles you do every day. God bless you all, and God bless America.

Note: The President spoke at 1:53 p.m. at the Indiana Convention Center. In his opening remarks, the President referred to Tommy Todd, president of the U.S. Jaycees, and Doris Gosnell, president of the U.S. Jaycees Women.

Nomination of Rebecca Gernhardt Range To Be an Assistant Secretary of Transportation
June 19, 1985

The President today announced his intention to nominate Rebecca Gernhardt Range to be an Assistant Secretary of Transportation (Governmental Affairs). She would succeed Charles G. Hardin.

Mrs. Range is currently Counselor to the Secretary of the Department of Transportation. She was in the office of Senator Ted Stevens from 1977 to 1984, serving as leadership assistant (1977), legislative correspondent (1977–1978), legislative assistant (1978–1981), and chief of staff (1981–1984).

Mrs. Range graduated from DePauw University (B.A., 1976) and Columbus School of Law at Catholic University (J.D., 1982). She is married, has two children, and resides in Washington, DC. She was born October 23, 1954, in Mansfield, OH.

Appointment of Theodore Schwinden as a Member of the Advisory Commission on Intergovernmental Relations
June 19, 1985

The President today announced his intention to appoint Gov. Theodore Schwinden, of Montana, to be a member of the Advisory Commission on Intergovernmental Relations for a term of 2 years. He would succeed Scott M. Matheson.

Governor Schwinden has been Governor of the State of Montana since 1981. Previously, he was Lieutenant Governor (1977–1981); commissioner of State lands (1969–1976); a representative for the United States, selected by U.S. Secretary of Agriculture Orville Freeman, on a wheat trade mission in Asia (1968); and president of the Montana Grain Growers Association (1965–1967). In 1958 he was elected to the Montana House of Representatives. He was named to the Legislative Council in 1959 and 1961 and served as house minority whip during the 1961 session.

Governor Schwinden graduated from the University of Montana (B.S., 1949; M.S., 1950). He served in the United States Army from 1943 to 1946. He is married, has three children, and resides in Helena, MT. He was born August 31, 1925, in Wolf Point, MT.

Executive Order 12520—Quarters Allowance to Department of Defense Employees In Panama
June 19, 1985

By the authority vested in me as President by the Constitution and the laws of the United States of America, including section 1217a of the Panama Canal Act of 1979 (22 U.S.C. 3657a), it is hereby ordered as follows:

Section 1. The Secretary of Defense is authorized to prescribe the regulations referred to in section 1217a of the Panama Canal Act of 1979, relating to quarters allowances.

Sec. 2. The regulations prescribed under Section 1 shall be consistent with Article VII(4) of the Agreement in Implementation of Article IV of the Panama Canal Treaty and with all other relevant provisions of the

Panama Canal Treaty and related agreements.

RONALD REAGAN

The White House,
June 19, 1985.

[*Filed with the Office of the Federal Register, 10:03 a.m., June 20, 1985*]

Note: The Executive order was released by the Office of the Press Secretary on June 20.

Message to the Congress Reporting Budget Deferrals
June 20, 1985

To the Congress of the United States:

In accordance with the Impoundment Control Act of 1974, I herewith report three new deferrals of budget authority for 1985 totaling $278,500,000 and two revised deferrals now totaling $8,792,615. The deferrals affect programs in the Departments of Agriculture and Energy, the Agency for International Development, and the United States Information Agency.

The details of these deferrals are contained in the attached report.

RONALD REAGAN

The White House,
June 20, 1985.

Note: The attachment detailing the deferrals was printed in the Federal Register *of June 26.*

Memorandum on Pasta Product Exports From the European Economic Community
June 20, 1985

Memorandum for the United States Trade Representative

Subject: Determination Under Section 301 of the Trade Act of 1974

Pursuant to Section 301(a) of the Trade Act of 1974, as amended (19 U.S.C. 2411(a)), I have determined that the preferential tariffs granted by the European Economic Community (EEC) on imports of lemons and oranges from certain Mediterranean countries deny benefits to the United States arising under the General Agreement on Tariffs and Trade (GATT), are unreasonable and discriminatory, and constitute a burden and restriction on U.S. commerce. I have further determined that the appropriate course of action to respond to such practices is the withdrawal of equivalent concessions with respect to imports from the EEC. I will therefore proclaim an increase in duties on pasta products classified in items

182.35 and 182.36 of the Tariff Schedules of the United States imported from the EEC. This action has been necessitated by the unwillingness of the EEC to negotiate a mutually acceptable resolution of this issue. At such time as the United States Trade Representative makes a determination that a mutually acceptable resolution has been reached, I would be prepared to rescind this measure.

Reasons for Determination

Based on petitions filed by the Florida Citrus Commission, the California-Arizona Citrus League, the Texas Citrus Mutual and the Texas Citrus Exchange, the United States Trade Representative initiated an investigation in November, 1976 concerning the EEC's preferential tariff treatment with respect to citrus imports from certain Mediterranean countries. The petitions alleged that these discriminatory tariffs, which are granted in the context of broader trade agreements with the Mediterranean countries, are inconsistent with the most-favored-nation principle of the GATT and placed U.S. exporters at a competitive disadvantage in the EEC market. Similar complaints had been filed by the U.S. industry in 1970 and 1972 under Section 252 of the Trade Expansion Act of 1962.

As a result of this investigation, we have found that since the 1960's, the EEC has levied a higher duty on imports of citrus from the United States than that levied on imports from certain Mediterranean countries. The level of discrimination is significant. In some cases the United States pays a duty five times greater than that paid by other suppliers. This discriminatory tariff treatment has impaired the ability of U.S. citrus exporters to market their fruits in the EEC and is, in the view of the United States, inconsistent with the EEC's obligations under the GATT.

Nevertheless, recognizing the political importance of these preferential tariffs to the EEC, the United States made extensive efforts over the course of a number of years to resolve the matter through bilateral consultations rather than mount a legal challenge against the EEC in the GATT. The United States also tried to resolve this issue in the context of tariff concessions granted during the Tokyo Round of Multilateral Trade Negotiations. With the exception of a few minor tariff reductions resulting from the Tokyo Round, these efforts were without success. Following the conclusion of the Tokyo Round, the United States initiated consultations under the provisions of the GATT, but the EEC again rebuffed all efforts to reach a compromise solution.

With any possibility of a negotiated settlement thus ruled out, the United States invoked the dispute settlement procedures of the GATT as the only alternative means of seeking a redress of our complaint. In 1983, a panel was established to review the U.S. complaint. Throughout this procedure, the United States has continued to demonstrate its willingness to seek a mutually acceptable solution to this problem. For example, the United States agreed to the unusual step of allowing the Director-General of GATT to attempt to arbitrate the dispute before

pressing its request for formation of a dispute settlement panel. Unfortunately, the attempt failed. The EEC rejected all efforts at compromise.

In December, 1984, based on a voluminous record, the panel found unanimously that the EEC preferences nullified and impaired U.S. benefits arising under the GATT with respect to U.S. exports of oranges and lemons, two of the eight categories of U.S. citrus exports affected by the tariff preferences. The panel recommended that the EEC reduce its MFN rate of duty on fresh oranges and lemons no later than October 15, 1985.

Although the panel did not rule on this issue, the United States continues to believe that the EEC citrus preferences are inconsistent with the most-favored-nation principle of the GATT, and thus nullify or impair U.S. benefits with respect to exports of the other citrus items as well as lemons and oranges. Nevertheless, the United States has been willing to accept the panel's more limited recommendation for the following reasons. The sole interest of the United States in bringing this issue to the GATT has been to obtain the elimination or reduction of a barrier to U.S. citrus exports. While the panel's recommendation does not call for the elimination of the barriers, we believe its implementation by the EEC would significantly increase access for key U.S. citrus exports to that market. Moreover, the panel's recommendation does not require the EEC to take action inconsistent with its preferential trading arrangements; indeed it would result in lower tariffs for the preference receiving countries as well.

The EEC, however, has been unwilling to accept either the panel's findings or recommendation and has effectively prevented a resolution of this issue in the GATT. Thus, U.S. attempts to resolve this problem at the bilateral or multilateral level have not succeeded.

In light of the results of the USTR's investigation, I believe we must recognize that the level of trade concessions between the United States and EEC is no longer in balance. We estimate that the value of annual U.S. exports of oranges and lemons would increase by more than $48 million if the

EEC had implemented the panel's recommendation.

The EEC's unwillingness to implement the panel's finding or to otherwise provide adequate compensation to the United States requires us to re-balance the level of concessions in U.S.-EEC trade. Increasing the duty on pasta imports from the EEC is a reasonable and appropriate means by which to achieve this.

This determination shall be published in the *Federal Register.*

RONALD REAGAN

[*Filed with the Office of the Federal Register, 10:04 a.m., June 20, 1985*]

Remarks at the Awards Presentation Ceremony for the Presidential Scholars
June 20, 1985

Secretary Bennett and ladies and gentlemen, good afternoon, and welcome to the White House. It's an honor to welcome to this historic house so many young Americans who have already shown just how much they have to offer our country.

In 1964 President Johnson established awards to honor academic excellence among our high school students, and in 1979 the program was expanded to include achievements in the arts. This year, as always, the Commission on Presidential Scholars has worked hard to make the final choices.

Chairman Beverly White, I want to thank you and all of the Commission members for your fine efforts. Twenty students have been selected for superior achievements in the arts. In the academic category, fifteen scholars have been selected at large, while one young man and one young woman have been chosen from each of the 50 States, the District of Columbia, Puerto Rico, and American families living abroad. It all adds up to 141 of our country's finest students—young Americans who can inspire us all.

That inspiration is of particular importance now that we're involved in a national effort to improve American education. Just 2 years ago, the Department of Education report entitled "A Nation at Risk" concluded that if a foreign power had attempted to impose on America the mediocre educational performance that then existed, we might well have viewed it as an act of war.

Since then we've made dramatic progress. All 50 States now have task forces on education, while 43 have made their graduation requirements more demanding. Perhaps most telling, Scholastic Aptitude Test scores have risen in 2 of the last 3 years, and that's for the first time in 20 years.

But we still have more to do, much more. Secretary Bennett has done a great deal to direct our efforts by focusing on what he calls the three C's: content, character, and choice. Just as we're guided by those faithful old three R's—reading, 'riting, and 'rithmetic—the three C's can help us understand the fundamental aspects of good education.

And when I looked over your award citations, I realized that the 141 of you here today provide a beautiful illustration of the three C's in practice.

The first C is content, and in recent years many of our schools have placed too little emphasis on the actual knowledge that our students acquire. Well, today we must go forward with the basics, making certain that all American students learn to read, write, and speak clearly, develop an ability to work with numbers, acquaint themselves with the fundamentals of American history, and come to understand the core values of Western civilization. Content, in other words, means seeing to it that every American student masters a specific body of knowledge.

Each of you has done just that. Kenneth

Berryman, for example, will spend this summer working the jet propulsion laboratory in Pasadena studying orbital mechanics. Now, I'm not a scientist myself, but I believe that means that Kenneth knows a thing or two about mathematics. Or consider ballerina Yolanda Jordan. Yolanda has mastered the arduous and demanding technique of classical ballet.

As for the second C, in achieving these awards, each of you has demonstrated one crucial element of character—the ability to work hard and to stick with it. Greg Johnson of Kentucky grew up in a housing project, the son of a single mother who works at a second job cleaning a bank at night to support her family. He started school in a readiness class for children not quite prepared for first grade. This spring Greg graduated as the first black valedictorian in the history of his high school.

Others among you have demonstrated that you understand the importance of giving of yourselves to others. Hannah Joyner, of South Carolina, for instance, will spend this summer working with children who have learning disabilities. Then there's Shannon Holliday, of Alabama, who's long been active in her community's drug abuse program. Together, you show that education is not a matter of knowledge alone but of things like honesty, kindness, and loyalty.

And the final C is choice. A large part of the problem today is that too often schools cannot be held accountable. Accountability is improved when parents are able to choose between a variety of schools, and again this principle is evident here today. Many of the artists among you attended schools designed for talented young performers. One of you, Monty Greek, of Nebraska, spent his early years in the kind of school that, until today, I thought only people my age remembered—a one room schoolhouse.

In case after case, your group demonstrates that schools that are in some way unique, that offer parents a different choice, can help to foster excellence. And

there we have it—the three C's of content, character, and choice as illustrated by 141 remarkable young Americans.

Many of your parents are here today. They are the ones with the ear-to-ear smiles. [*Laughter*] And as your first and most influential teachers, they merit a good part of the praise. You just made their day. [*Laughter*]

Many of your teachers are also present, and they deserve special gratitude. Their efforts have given you the greatest gift that one person can give to another—a well-trained and perceptive mind. I know you'll—well, you already have joined me in thanks to your teachers.

But the main honors go to you. You've given your studies your best efforts for so many years, and you've set a wonderful example for all American students to follow. So, on behalf of a grateful nation, I commend you.

You know, sometimes there are pleasant tasks in this job of mine, like this one this morning. But sometimes, also, there are responsibilities that get very irksome, like the one that I now face in which, without getting a chance to meet each of you individually, I have to turn you over to Secretary Bennett, and I have to hasten back to the Oval Office.

And I have that on good authority that that's what I need to do because early in my administration, a metropolitan newspaper asked children—young people—to write in and tell them what advice they would give to the newly elected President—me. And I have never forgotten one of them—from an 11-year-old girl. She told me a number of things that I should do, and then she wrote, "Now, get back to the Oval Office and get to work." [*Laughter*] So, I'll do that.

Thank you all. Congratulations to all of you young people. God bless you all. Thank you.

Note: The President spoke at 11:32 a.m. on the South Lawn of the White House.

Statement Announcing Actions Against Terrorism
June 20, 1985

Last night senseless terrorism again took its toll on Americans, this time in El Salvador. Of the 15 killed and 13 wounded, 2 were U.S. businessmen and 4 were unarmed, off-duty marines not in uniform. They also killed 9 and injured 13 other innocent Salvadoran and Guatemalan men and women. This atrocity, like the bombing earlier yesterday in Frankfurt, Germany, is further evidence that the war which terrorists are waging is not only directed against the United States, it is a war against all of civilized society. This is a war in which innocent civilians are targets. This is a war in which innocent civilians are intentional victims, and our servicemen have become specific targets. This cannot continue.

We must act against those who have so little regard for human life and the values we cherish. And we must do so in concert with other nations who share our democratic institutions and basic disdain for violence and the use of force. We of the Western World must act together, as we once did over a century ago to wipe piracy from the seas and as we did 45 years ago against the threat of tyranny.

In response to the death of our marines and private citizens in El Salvador, I have directed the Secretary of State and Secretary of Defense, with the help of our intelligence services, to immediately provide whatever assistance is necessary to President Duarte's government in order to find and punish the terrorists who perpetrated this act.

To this end, I have today directed that we expedite the delivery of security assistance items on order by the Salvadoran Government and am prepared to use my emergency authorities to furnish the Salvadoran Armed Forces with additional military assets which will help them prosecute their campaign against the Communist guerrillas. Their hope that terrorism will weaken our resolve or support for the revitalization of democracy in El Salvador is futile. If other U.S. military assets can be effective in this regard, then I shall provide them.

I expect our Congress to support these measures and will be consulting with the appropriate legislative committees of the Congress on what additional steps can be taken in El Salvador and elsewhere to end the external support the Salvadoran terrorists receive from Nicaragua and the Communist bloc.

I have also today appointed Vice President Bush to take the lead within the U.S. Government and with our allies to determine what actions, military and otherwise, we and our similarly threatened friends can take to end this increasingly violent and indiscriminate but purposeful affront to humanity. As a first priority, I have asked the Vice President to focus on this matter during his visit to European capitals next week. Upon his return, he is to convene a governmentwide task force to develop recommendations for my decision on how all available U.S. resources can best be brought to bear in dealing with this problem.

Finally, I want you, the American people, to know that what we do in these circumstances must not be done in pointless anger. These events call for reasoned responses to lawless actions by those who do not abide by the norms of civilized society. As your President, I believe that our actions must be appropriate and proportionate to the criminal acts which have been taken against our citizens. Those who are responsible for such lawlessness and those who support it must know that the consequences of their actions will never be capitulation to terrorist demands.

We are both a nation of peace and a people of justice. By our very nature, we are slow to anger and magnanimous in helping those in less fortunate circumstances. No nation on Earth has been more generous to others in need, but we also have our limits—and our limits have been reached. We cannot allow our people to be placed at risk simply because they are blessed in being citizens of this great republic.

Note: Larry M. Speakes, Principal Deputy Press Secretary to the President, read the President's statement to reporters in the

Briefing Room at the White House during his daily press briefing, which began at 12:35 p.m.

Nomination of Constance Horner To Be Director of the Office of Personnel Management
June 20, 1985

The President today announced his intention to nominate Constance Horner to be Director of the Office of Personnel Management.

Since May 1983 Mrs. Horner has served as Associate Director for Economics and Government in the Office of Management and Budget. Previously she was Director of VISTA and Acting Associate Director of ACTION (1981–1983). She also served in 1981 as Deputy Assistant Director of ACTION for Policy and Planning. She was a member of the Department of Education transition group in the office of the President-elect (1980–1981). She has contributed articles on public policy for the Wall Street Journal, the New York Times, the American Spectator, and other publications. She has also taught at secondary schools in the United States and at universities abroad.

Mrs. Horner is a graduate of the University of Pennsylvania and holds a master of arts degree from the University of Chicago. She is married, has two children, and resides in Washington, DC. She was born February 24, 1942, in Summit, NJ.

Designation of Ralph C. Bledsoe as Executive Secretary of the Domestic Policy Council
June 20, 1985

The President today announced he was designating Ralph C. Bledsoe to be Executive Secretary of the Domestic Policy Council.

Mr. Bledsoe, a Special Assistant to the President and Assistant Director for Management and Administration of the Office of Policy Development, has served as Executive Secretary of the Cabinet Council on Management and Administration from 1982 to 1985 and as Executive Director of the Federal Property Review Board from 1984 to 1985. He was Associate Director of the White House Office of Planning Evaluation from 1981 to 1982.

Mr. Bledsoe was a senior faculty member at the Federal Executive Institute in Charlottesville, VA, from 1973 to 1980 and was director of the Emergency Management Institute at Emmitsburg, MD, from 1980 to early 1981. He was a member of the faculty and first director of the University of Southern California School of Public Administration Sacramento program from 1971 to 1873.

He was with the System Development Corp. between 1958 and 1971, 3 years of which were as manager of its public safety systems department. In 1972 he was appointed to the board of directors of the California Crime Technologies Research Foundation and in 1984 was elected to the National Academy of Public Administration. Mr. Bledsoe served in the U.S. Air Force between 1955 and 1958.

A native of Waco, TX, Mr. Bledsoe received a bachelor of business administration degree from Texas A&M College in 1955, an M.B.A. degree from the University of California at Los Angeles in 1962, and master and doctor of public administration degrees from the University of Southern California in 1968 and 1971, respectively.

He is married to the former RoseMarie Frechette. They have four daughters and reside in Great Falls, VA. He was born on October 10, 1933.

Remarks on Presenting the Presidential Medal of Freedom to Mother Teresa
June 20, 1985

The President. This great house receives many great visitors, but none more special or more revered than our beloved guest today. A month ago, we awarded the Medal of Freedom to 13 heroes who have done their country proud. Only one of the recipients could not attend because she had work to do—not special work, not unusual work for her, but everyday work which is both special and urgent in its own right. Mother Teresa was busy, as usual, saving the world. And I mean that quite literally. And so we rather appreciated her priorities, and we're very happy, indeed, that she could come to America this week.

Now, a moment ago, I said we'd awarded the Medal of Freedom to heroes who've done our country proud. And I believe Mother Teresa might point out here that she is most certainly not an American but a daughter of Yugoslavia, and she has not spent her adult life in this country but in India. However, it simply occurred to us when we wanted to honor her that the goodness in some hearts transcends all borders and all narrow nationalistic considerations.

Some people, some very few people are, in the truest sense, citizens of the world; Mother Teresa is. And we love her so much we asked her to accept our tribute, and she graciously accepted. And I will now read the citation.

Most of us talk about kindness and compassion, but Mother Teresa, the saint of the gutters, lives it. As a teenager, she went to India to teach young girls. In time, Mother Teresa began to work among the poor and the dying of Calcutta. Her order of the Missionaries of Charity has spread throughout the world, serving the poorest of the poor.

Mother Teresa is a heroine of our times.

And to the many honors she has received, including the Nobel Peace Prize, we add, with deep affection and endless respect, the Presidential Medal of Freedom.

[*At this point, the President presented the award to Mother Teresa.*]

May I say that this is the first time I've given the Medal of Freedom with the intuition that the recipient might take it home, melt it down and turn it into something that can be sold to help the poor. [*Laughter*]

And I want to thank you for something, Mother Teresa. Your great work and your life have inspired so many Americans to become personally involved, themselves, in helping the poor. So many men and women in every area of life, in government and the private sector, have been led by the light of your love, and they have given greatly of themselves. And we thank you for your radiant example.

Mother Teresa. I am most unworthy of this generous gift of our President, Mr. Reagan, and his wife and you people of United States. But I accept it for the greater glory of God and in the name of the millions of poor people that this gift, in spirit and in love, will penetrate the hearts of the people. For in giving it to me, you are giving it to them, to my hands, with your great love and concern.

I've never realized that you loved the people so tenderly. I had the experience, I was last time here, a sister from Ethiopia found me and said, "Our people are dying. Our children are dying. Mother, do something." And the only person that came in my mind while she was talking, it was the President. And immediately I wrote to him, and I said, "I don't know, but this is what happened to me." And next day it was that immediately he arranged to bring food to our people. And I can tell you the gift that has come from your people, from your country, has brought life—new life—to our suffering people in Ethiopia.

I also want to thank the families here in United States for their continual and delicate love that they have given, and they have shown, by leaving their children to become sisters and to serve the poor throughout the world. We are now over the world and trying to bring the tenderness and the love of Jesus.

And you, you cannot go where we go. You cannot do what we do. But together, we are doing something beautiful for God. And my gratitude to you, President, and your family and to your people. It's my prayer for you that you may grow in holiness to this tender love for the poorest of the poor. But this love begins at home, in your own family, and it begins by praying together. Prayer gives a clean heart, and a clean heart can see God. And if you see God in each other, you will have love, peace, joy together. And works of love are works of peace. And love begins at home.

So, my sisters, brothers, and fathers, you are going—and all our poor people, thousands and thousands of thouands of people that we deal with, I bring their gratitude to you. And keep the joy of loving. Love them, and begin in your own family first. And that love will penetrate right through the furthest place where no one has ever been—there is that tenderness and love of Christ.

And remember that whatever you do to the least, you do it to Him, Jesus said. You did it to me. What a wonderful opportunity for each one of us to be 24 hours with Jesus. And in doing what we are doing, as he said, if you receive a little child in my name, you receive me. If you give a glass of water in my name, you give it to me. What a wonderful and beautiful tenderness and love of Christ for each one of us.

So, once more, I want to thank you for this beautiful gift, which I am sure it will bring great joy to our people by sharing it with them.

God bless you and keep you in his heart.

Note: The President spoke at 3:01 p.m. in the Rose Garden at the White House.

Remarks at the Annual Convention of the Lions Club International in Dallas, Texas
June 21, 1985

Thank you, Bert Mason, my fellow Lions, Congressman Armey. I always enjoy visiting Texas. It's a big State with a big heart.

A member of my staff was visiting not long ago and asked the cab driver about the scooped out top on the Texas Stadium here in Dallas. And the cabbie, in keeping with typical Texas modesty, simply replied, "That's so God can watch."

Well, it's a pleasure to be with you today. I know that every Lion, wherever you are from, has a Texas-sized heart, and I'd like to welcome especially those many Lions who are here from other countries. All I can tell you is that, as Lions, you are associated with some of the best darn Americans this country has to offer.

There are few citizens who so well reflect the heart and soul of our country as do the Lions. Our forefathers and mothers were fiercely independent and proud of their freedom. Yet the spirit of neighbor helping neighbor is an essential part of the legacy they left us.

The idea of a humanitarian service organization that Melvin Jones set in motion in 1917 was totally consistent with the American character. His dream quickly spread throughout this country, was carried to distant lands, and you are now, as Bert told you, the largest service club organization on the face of the Earth. Who says that one individual can't make a difference?

Melvin Jones knew that good deeds benefit the giver and the receiver, that one who gives of himself is spiritually enriched. Today we also understand that government cannot assume the responsibility for all good works without destroying the spirit of benevolence and sense of community so important to the well-being of any free society.

Government, even with the best of intentions, sometimes does more harm than good. But, you know, sometimes these government programs are a bit like the story of the country preacher who called on a town about a hundred miles away. He'd been invited there to speak; went there for this revival meeting. And on the way to church, he noticed on the main street of that town, sitting on the porch of a little country store, was a man from his own hometown, an individual who happened to be known for his excessive drinking.

And the minister stopped and went up to him, asked what he was doing so far from home. And he said, "Well, reverend, the beer is 5 cents a bottle cheaper here." [*Laughter*] Well, the reverend told him that didn't make much sense, the expense of traveling all that way and back, the price of lodging all the time he was there. And the drinker just watched him and then said, "Reverend, I'm not stupid. I just sit here and drink until I show a profit." [*Laughter*]

That was the kind of logic that fit some of the Federal programs of the last 20 years. [*Laughter*]

Excessive government spending, taxing, and regulating—no matter how well intended—is a formula for disaster. And that's exactly where this country was headed and why we changed course 4½ years ago. The American people decided once again to give freedom a chance. It was time to put this country back on the path to lower taxes, individual responsibility, and economic growth. I'm proud of what we accomplished during our first term. We started rebuilding our defensive strength, we beat down inflation, and we got our country moving again.

The foundation was laid during the first term. Now it's time to finish the job. And the first order of business is a complete overhaul of America's antiquated, unfair, and overly complicated tax system. The cur-

rent tax code is the Federal Government's version of Rubik's Cube. [*Laughter*] It's a game that most of us never figure out and few of us win.

I like to think of our proposal as a fair share tax, because it will mean greater fairness and new opportunity for every income group in every region of America. It will, when enacted, cut out complications and bring down the rates. It'll reduce the number of rates from 14 to 3—15, 25, and 35 percent. The mind-boggling system of itemized deductions, special credits, and exclusions will go through a major simplification and reform. The result will be a simpler and fairer system that will enable out economy to grow more competitive and our people to prosper.

Now, today the tax code is so voluminous and complex even the Internal Revenue Service has trouble understanding it. Do you remember not too long ago they had to warn taxpayers not to depend too much on their own employees because they didn't understand it either? Well, fairly enforcing such a mishmash of ever-changing rules and regulations is a Herculean effort. And if you get the feeling that some people aren't paying their fair share, while others are getting soaked, you're right. And that's got to stop.

Let me just add in here—when the income tax amendment was passed back in 1913, it consisted of 16 words. Today I've been told that over at the Treasury Department, the books of regulations and rules and explanations of the income tax make a line of books 57 feet long. The simpler system we're proposing will be easier to enforce. It also will be more difficult for special interests without the cover of an incomprehensible tax code to have tailormade tax breaks written into the system. It's about time a tax code is written for the general interest instead of the special interests.

As for the amount of taxes paid, the fact is most Americans will end up with lower tax burdens when our plan is adopted. Taxes for the poor and elderly will be less or eliminated altogether. Some people, generally those who've legally manipulated the current system, will pay more. But in the end, everyone will benefit because our tax program is designed to keep our economy vigorous and growing—the key to a better tomorrow.

The old system has been a drag on the most productive members of our society. Our plan is future oriented, a blueprint for progress and better times. Today the Government taxes away one of every two dollars of those in the top bracket. Well, our plan will take only about one in three dollars. Today the Government takes away one of every three dollars of millions of middle-income families. Our plan will make that only one in four dollars. Today those who want to take more money home spend their time trying to find tax dodges and shelters. Our system will encourage them to be more efficient, to increase their investments, to work harder, which benefits everyone.

Our plan encourages entrepreneurs to get new businesses off the ground. And such small businesses are the source of most new jobs in the mainspring of innovation and creativity in the business world.

And just as for individuals, by bringing down the rates and reducing the number of deductions and complications, we will ensure that American business remains a shining light of enterprise and productivity that can and will lead the world to better times.

By lowering the tax rates, cutting regulation, getting control of spending, we broke out of the quagmire of inflation and recession. The growth we've enjoyed has astounded our friends abroad and confounded our adversaries. I'll never forget sitting down with our allies at the last three international economic summits and being asked by my colleagues from those other countries how our economy was producing so many new jobs. In the last 30 months nearly 8 million new jobs were created in America. In virtually all of Europe they told me not one new job has been created in the last 10 years.

The American people aren't the only ones who've benefited, however. As our economy picked up, Americans began spending and investing money in other countries. Our own prosperity has been and continues to be a mighty engine for economic progress, pulling along even stag-nant, over-regulated, and over-taxed economies.

I hope those of you who are here from other countries will carry this message back to your people: Americans want you to succeed and to prosper. We have no desire to live as an island of plenty. We don't want jobs and higher standards of living just for our people. We don't want prosperity just at home. We'll be satisfied with nothing less than a worldwide recovery.

Now, we fully recognize that all free people, with their diverse cultures and customs, must choose their own course, their own way. Nevertheless, we hope that our friends will learn from our experience.

Free men, free minds, and free markets can and will make this a better world. It's only when people are free to challenge what exists and offer something new that mankind is able to step forward; only when people are free to dream and discuss untried ideas that a society remains vibrant; only when people are free in the marketplace to meet the needs of others as best they can that innovation and opportunity can become the order of the day.

Such freedom serves as a ladder of social and economic advancement for all people, step by step improving the lot of every individual from top to bottom. Ingenuity, imagination, and creativity—these are the forces unleashed by human freedom; these are the forces that built America. And if given a chance, they can reshape the face of this planet.

Critics of freedom would have us believe that liberty is at odds with the spirit of brotherhood. Well, you are living proof of the good will and humane values that are generated by freedom. Today there's a new recognition of the principles advocated by Melvin Jones. Individual commitment is alive and well. The latest statistics on private sector initiatives show that 92 million people in the United States volunteer a portion of their time—this is an increase of 8 million between 1981 and 1983. Most volunteers donate 1 to 3 hours a week; the next largest percentage donates more than 5 hours weekly.

And in 1984 there was a record rise in giving to charitable causes, up 11.1 percent over 1983. The amount given voluntarily by Americans is greater than the entire national budgets of two-thirds of the nations of the world, more than $74 billion last year. Now, that is just the assets donated. Time and in-kind contributions if calculated in dollars would double or triple that amount.

These are the kind of statistics that underscore the true strength of our country. And much of this philanthropy, in keeping with our traditions, is aimed at helping the less fortunate in other countries. When famine raised its ugly head in Ethiopia, Americans rushed to aid those in need. So far this year the United States has donated 425,000 tons of food. This compares to a paltry 2,500 tons donated by Communist Ethiopia's closest ally, the Soviet Union. It seems with all their sloganeering about the only things Communist countries produce in quantity are misery, weapons, and aggression. The record of humanitarian assistance provided by the Soviet bloc governments, even to their own allies, is a disgrace, and the world, especially the developing world, should know about it. Of course, Communist countries have trouble producing even enough food for their own populations.

You know, there's a story—I kind of collect stories that I understand and I can conver—I mean, I can convince myself are true that are being told among the Russian people to each other, and this one has to do with a commissar who visited a collective farm, grabbed the first fellow that was walking by, and said, "How are things going? Are there any complaints?" And the farmer he grabbed says, "Oh, comrade commissar, I've never heard anyone complain." And the commissar said, "Well, how are the crops?" "Oh, sir, they've never been better." "How about potatoes?" He said, "Comrade commissar, if the potatoes were put in one pile, they would reach the foot of God." And the commissar said, "Just a minute. This is the Soviet Union; there is no God." And the worker said, "That's all right. There are no potatoes." [*Laughter*]

Seriously though, the outpouring of love and support by the free people of the world to the hungry of the world is something we can all be proud of. And as usual, Lions are doing their share as we see in your efforts to get food and supplies into remote areas in Ethiopia. I also am aware of your campaign against blindness in the industrialized and developing countries. And you deserve everyone's deepest admiration for these projects and for your many other humanitarian endeavors.

On the domestic front, last year you reached out to feed America's needy during National Care and Share Day. You're involved in community projects throughout the country.

And I'd like to take this opportunity to thank you for all you're doing to fight drug abuse. Nancy told me all about your convention last year. And she was gratified to be honored by you, but when she got home, she said she felt like she should have been giving you the award and not the other way around.

Your efforts and those of other concerned Americans outside the structure of government are absolutely vital to the success of this all-important campaign. With the help of the Quest National Center and [entertainer] Bill Cosby, you're teaching kids to say no to drugs. We're trying to deter young people from getting involved and to help those using drugs to stop. And we'll be satisfied with nothing less than a drug-free America. Together we're going to cut the legs out from under the drug dealers, by eliminating the demand for their goods. It's the Lions versus the drug dealers, and I'm betting on the Lions.

The other half of the law—or the war, I should say, is a strong law enforcement and drug interdiction campaign to stop the flow of illegal drugs before it reaches the customers. Now, this is a complicated and frustrating job, but it lets every youngster in this country know we're serious. It sends the message that drug use is a threat; an ugly, life-destroying vice; and that it is wrong. I'm pleased to report that the message is getting through. Young people are turning away from drugs. Today fewer young people are smoking marijuana, cocaine use is leveling off. A new sense of responsibility is emerging in the entertainment industry. The trends are in the right direction, and this is cause for rejoicing. But please, don't let up.

Illegal drugs, of course, are only one part of a crime epidemic that spread across our country in the sixties and seventies. Well-intentioned liberals cut the muscle out of our criminal justice system and then acted surprised when the criminal element took the offensive. Law enforcers have been operating under bizarre rules that serve as roadblocks to the conviction of the guilty, but do little to protect the innocent.

Well, last year we passed a Comprehensive Crime Control Act, a first step toward reestablishing a balance to the criminal justice system. Let me assure you Attorney General Meese is going to keep pushing for further reforms until every American neighborhood is safe. I hope we can count on your support, because we're taking the streets back for the good and decent people of this country.

In the last few days, it has become even more clear that the criminal threat to civilization is no mere domestic problem. Wednesday night in El Salvador four young marines in civilian clothes, along with civilians from America and several other countries, were gunned down in a sidewalk cafe. This event was preceded by the wanton bombing of an air terminal in Frankfurt, Germany; the hijacking of one of our airliners; and the seizure of a Jordanian aircraft. The killers in El Salvador are no different than those other perpetrators of inhumane acts.

I can promise all of them this: They will never succeed in weakening our resolve to resist terrorism. We consider these murders, hijackings, and abductions an attack on all Western civilization by uncivilized barbarians. We will continue to act with appropriate restraint. But let no one doubt our resolve. Those who commit such crimes should be aware of the truth of President Theodore Roosevelt's observation, "The American people," he said, "are slow to wrath, but once their wrath is kindled, it burns like a consuming flame."

Well, like our forefathers, we have the courage to protect our rights, and we're proud of our freedom. We're working hard to improve our own lot, to contribute to the less fortunate, and to improve our communities and neighborhoods.

The truth is, it is only under freedom that a true fellowship of the spirit can exist. Love is not something that can be mandated by law or enforced by bureaucracy. It is when people voluntarily help one another, giving of themselves freely, that they receive the blessings of the soul which God has promised. This is an important part of freedom, the shining light which is a beacon to all who live in the darkness in tyranny—the fundamental truth that free people do indeed love and care for one another.

Thank you, Lions. You're holding the torch for all the world to see. Fellow Lions, God bless you all.

Note: The President spoke at 11:59 a.m. in the Reunion Arena. He was introduced by Bert Mason, international president of the organization. Prior to his remarks, the President met in the arena with families of the hostages in the TWA hijacking incident.

Nomination of William P. Horn To Be an Assistant Secretary of the Interior
June 21, 1985

The President today announced his intention to nominate William P. Horn to be Assistant Secretary for Fish and Wildlife, Department of the Interior. He would succeed G. Ray Arnett.

Mr. Horn is currently Deputy Under Secretary, Department of the Interior. Previously, he was minority consultant, Committee on Interior and Insular Affairs, U.S. House of Representatives (1977–1981); special assistant to the Assistant Secretary for Land and Water Resources, U.S. Department of the Interior (1976–1977); special assistant to the Secretary of Commerce

(1975–1976); and acting executive director, House Republican Conference, U.S. Congress (1972–1975).

Mr. Horn graduated from the American University (B.A., 1972) and Washington College of Law (at the American University) (J.D., 1983). He is married, has two children, and resides in McLean, VA. He was born December 16, 1950, in Dover, DE.

Appointment of Thomas N. Tripp as a Member of the Advisory Committee for Trade Negotiations
June 21, 1985

The President today announced his intention to appoint Thomas N. Tripp to be a member of the Advisory Committee for Trade Negotiations for a term of 2 years. He would succeed George B. Cook.

Mr. Tripp is currently an attorney in the private practice of law in Columbus, OH. He is also owner-founder, Black Sheep Enterprises, and a political consultant and campaign manager for candidates for public office in Ohio, Minnesota, Illinois, and Pennsylvania.

Mr. Tripp graduated from Michigan State University (B.S., 1964) and the George Washington University (J.D., 1967). He is married, has three children, and resides in Gahanna, OH. He was born June 19, 1942, in Evanston, IL.

Appointment of Gopal S. Pal as a Member of the President's Committee on the National Medal of Science
June 21, 1985

The President today announced his intention to appoint Gopal S. Pal to be a member of the President's Committee on the National Medal of Science, for a term expiring December 31, 1987. He would succeed Naomi J. McAfee.

Dr. Pal has been a dentist in Annandale, VA, since 1974. He was associate professor in the department of pedodontics at Howard University School of Dentistry (1978–1981); a member of the staff of the Fairfax County Department of Health Dental Clinic (1969–1974); clinical instructor, Georgetown University Dental School, department of pedodontics (1968–1969); and in the private practice of dentistry in Trivandrum, India (1962–1966).

Mr. Pal graduated from the University of Calcutta (B.D.S., 1962), the University of Bombay (M.D.S., 1966), and the University of Iowa (M.S., 1968). He is married, has two children, and resides in McLean, VA. He was born March 24, 1939, in Trivandrum, India.

Proclamation 5354—Increase in the Rates of Duty for Certain Pasta Articles From the European Economic Community
June 21, 1985

By the President of the United States of America

A Proclamation

1. On June 20, 1985, I determined pursuant to section 301(a) of the Trade Act of 1974, as amended (the Act) (19 U.S.C. 2411(a)), that the preferential tariffs granted by the European Economic Community (EEC) on imports of lemons and oranges from certain Mediterranean countries deny benefits to the United States arising under the General Agreement on Tariffs and Trade (GATT) (61 Stat. (pts. 5 and 6)), are unreasonable and discriminatory, and constitute a burden or restriction on U.S. commerce. I have further determined, pursuant to section 301(b) of the Act (19 U.S.C. 2411(b)), that the appropriate course of action to respond to such practices is to withdraw concessions with respect to imports from the EEC.

2. Section 301(a) of the Act authorizes the President to take all appropriate and feasible action to obtain the elimination of an act, policy, or practice of a foreign government or instrumentality that 1) is inconsistent with the provisions of, or otherwise denies benefits to the United States under, any trade agreement; or 2) is unjustifiable, unreasonable, or discriminatory and burdens or restricts U.S. commerce. Section 301(b) of the Act also authorizes the President to suspend, withdraw, or prevent the application of benefits of trade agreement concessions with respect to, and to impose duties or other import restrictions on the products of, such foreign government or instrumentality. Pursuant to section 301(a) of the Act, such actions can be taken on a nondiscriminatory basis or solely against the foreign government or instrumentality involved.

3. I have decided, pursuant to section 301(a)(2) and (b) of the Act, to increase the U.S. import duties on the pasta articles provided for in items 182.35 and 182.36 of the Tariff Schedules of the United States (TSUS) (19 U.S.C. 1202) which are the product of any member country of the EEC.

Now, Therefore, I, Ronald Reagan, President of the United States of America, acting under the authority vested in me by the Constitution and the statutes of the United States, including but not limited to sections 301(a)(2) and (b) and section 604 of the Trade Act of 1974, do proclaim that:

1. Subpart B of part 2 of the Appendix to the TSUS is modified as follows:
   (a) The heading is amended by adding after 1962 "or Section 301 of the Trade Act of 1974".
   (b) The following new items and superior heading, set forth in columnar form, are inserted in the columns designated "Item", "Articles", and "Rates of Duty 1", respectively, following TSUS item 945.69:

"Macaroni, noodles, vermicelli, and similar alimentary pastes (provided for in items 182.35 and 182.36, part 15B, schedule 1) if the product of any member country of the EEC:		
945.80	Not containing egg or egg products	40% ad val.
945.82	Containing egg or egg products	25% ad val."

2. If, in the opinion of the United States Trade Representative, a mutually acceptable resolution of this issue has been reached with the EEC, he shall so advise the President, together with a recommendation concerning the modification or termination of this action. A decision by the President to modify or terminate this action shall be published in the *Federal Register*.

3. This proclamation shall be effective

with respect to articles entered, or withdrawn from warehouse for consumption, on or after the date which is 15 days after the date on which this proclamation is signed.

In Witness Whereof, I have hereunto set my hand this 21st day of June, in the year of our Lord nineteen hundred and eighty-five, and of the Independence of the United States of America the two hundred and ninth.

RONALD REAGAN

[*Filed with the Office of the Federal Register, 10:49 a.m., June 24, 1985*]

Note: The proclamation was released by the Office of the Press Secretary on June 22.

Radio Address to the Nation on the Federal Budget
June 22, 1985

My fellow Americans:

Later today, Nancy and I will be going to Andrews Air Force Base to be with the families and friends of four American marines, four young men whose bodies are being returned after they were murdered by Communist guerrillas in El Salvador last Wednesday night. We will carry with us all of the grief and sorrow and rising anger of a nation whose patience has been stretched to its limit.

I will speak to the country and to the loved ones of those brave men who defended our freedom. But before we go, I must also speak to you about important deliberations that are now taking place in Congress.

We've made considerable progress this year in achieving the spending reductions needed to bring down the budget deficit and keep our economy growing and producing new jobs. The Senate has passed a plan for $56 billion of budget savings, which would also allow us to keep most of our defense-rebuilding program on track. We all owe a debt of gratitude to the Senate for their courage.

Unfortunately, we cannot say the same about the plan passed by the House. It is not a true budget savings plan. Many of its so-called savings are simply phantom cuts. Further, the House makes no meaningful effort to shrink this gargantuan Federal spending machine that gobbles up your taxes and divvies them out to a multitude of special interests.

Unlike the Senate, which has proposed real, substantial, and permanent reforms, the cuts of the House budgeteers are not enough and certainly not permanent. The freezes and other one-time measures the House proposes are not solutions that would permit us to get a handle on Federal overspending, they would only postpone the inevitable. And what's even worse in these perilous times, the House budget would send a signal of weakness by cutting purchasing power for vital defense needs.

All of us know that there's been waste in defense spending. But after years of others closing their eyes to this problem, it's our administration that has begun uncovering and rooting out that waste and going after the defense contractors who shamelessly cheat America. And this is why we've taken an additional step.

This week I appointed a special bipartisan blue ribbon commission to review defense management and procurement. So, yes, we can and must eliminate waste. But it is sheer folly to blindly weaken ourselves when our adversaries are conspiring and working so hard to bleed and cripple America. It is time to stop treating our Defense Establishment and intelligence agencies like enemies and concentrate our attention and anger on the true enemies of freedom and democracy in the world.

For the past 2 weeks, the House and Senate have been meeting in a conference committee trying to come up with a final budget for the next fiscal year. I'm sorry to report that they haven't made much progress. So far, the House has turned away from realism on defense and refused to accept the many program reforms and permanent savings in domestic spending that are proposed in the Senate version.

And, as is predictable, whenever sufficient will is lacking to make the tough decisions on spending, calls are raised for tax increases. Well, if I must, I'll repeat it until I'm blue in the face: I will veto any tax increase the Congress sends me. And I'm pleased to say I have been promised the votes to sustain that veto.

All of us have a great deal at stake in the outcome of these Senate-House negotiations for the sake of both our national security and our economic well-being. If the conference committee reports a budget that achieves substantial and permanent changes, it will pave the way for continuing the low inflation and falling interest rates that will keep our economy growing and keep Americans working.

If, on the other hand, the process breaks down and the Congress can't do what's right on defense or on controlling domestic spending, then the consequences will be very bad. America will be seen as too weak to respond to threats, and all the progress we've made in our economy will be placed at risk.

I'm asking for your support to make Congress understand this is a moment in our history when all of us should pull together and put our national interest above partisan politics. The challenges we face are big, but not too big if we Republicans and Democrats unite for a stronger and safer America. We still have time. So, let's get started.

Until next week, thanks for listening, and God bless you.

Note: The President spoke at 12:06 p.m. from Camp David, MD.

Remarks to the Families of the United States Marines Slain in El Salvador
June 22, 1985

Ladies and gentlemen, we are here today to receive, in the name of our country, the remains of four United States marines killed in the line of duty in a country far away. They were victims of vicious evil. And we grieve for their loss and for the other innocent victims of that vicious attack.

When a nation is a family, and ours is, no death is impersonal, no death is discreet, no death is in and of itself. Each death is a tear in the fabric, a break in the whole. But when a serviceman dies, we feel a special anguish. A serviceman's life is a hard life, a life of sacrifice and risk. And we're never good enough to them. We're never as good as we should be, because that's not possible. No one can treat such men and women as they deserve, because what they give us is beyond our powers to repay.

And so, when they're taken from us, when they're taken because they wore our uniform with love and pride, when they're killed because they put themselves in harm's way for our sake, then we feel an anguish that cuts at the heart and cannot forget.

Gregory Weber was 22 years old, and he went to guard the American Embassy because, as he told his father, "Dad, they need a few good men down there."

Thomas Handwork was 24 and a 5-year veteran of the corps. It wasn't a job to him; it was a calling. He'd wanted to be a marine from the first days he could walk and talk. He dreamt about the corps. It was all he wanted.

Bobby Dickson was 27 years old and a southerner, raised in a tradition of manly honor. He feared nothing.

And Patrick Kwiatkowski was the youngest of the four, only 20 years old. His 21st birthday was yesterday. A volunteer from Wausau, Wisconsin.

They were all volunteers. They were four young men who chose to follow an honored and ancestral path. And so they swung the bag over their shoulders, kissed their parents goodby, and went off to serve their country. They chose to follow the life of service and selflessness and courage. They did it for love and honor—*Semper Fi.*

To those who love them and who will take them to their rest, we know that no words can console. But we thank you for your sons and daughters and your brothers. We thank you for these fine young men. No words can console, but we know of the promise in the Bible, "Blessed are they that mourn, for they shall be comforted. Blessed are the peacemakers, for they shall be called the children of God."

As we mourn these children of God, we remember another promise, "Blessed are they which do hunger and thirst after righteousness, for they shall be filled."

They say the men who murdered these sons of America escaped and disappeared into the city streets. But I pledge to you today, they will not evade justice on Earth any more than they can escape the judgment of God. We and the Salvadoran leaders will move any mountain and ford any river to find the jackals and bring them and their colleagues in terror to justice.

And now, today, we grieve for four young men taken from us too soon. And we receive them in death as they were on the last night of their lives, together and following a radiant light—following it toward heaven, toward home. And if we reach—or when we reach heaven's scenes, we truly will find it guarded by United States marines.

Note: The President spoke at 4:11 p.m. at Andrews Air Force Base, MD.

Informal Exchange With Reporters on the Trans World Airlines Hijacking Incident
June 23, 1985

The President. Are you all saying the same thing, because I cannot sort you out.

Q. [Inaudible]

The President. Well, Berri seems to be the only one, then, that is making a linkage between that and our hostages. That is not a linkage; that is a matter of Israeli law. It is a problem of their own, and under their law those 31 people are being released. It has nothing to do with our hostages.

Q. Wouldn't this break the ice, sir?

The President. What?

Q. Wouldn't this break the ice?

The President. I don't believe that there's any linkage.

Q. Are you pleased that Israel released the prisoners?

The President. I'm not going to comment one way or the other on that because we have avoided any idea of linkage there. There is none.

Q. Can you report any progress on getting the hostages home, sir?

The President. I'm not going to speculate.

I'm just going to say that we are doing everything that can be done.

Q. Are we talking to the Shiites about a swap plan between the hostages and the Shiites?

The President. All I know is that there are a number of countries that I appreciate that have volunteered to be of help if they can, and that's all that I can say about it.

Q. What's the plan?

The President. You know that I couldn't answer that question or tell you. I don't think that we could make things like that public.

Q. Are you ruling out military deterrence, sir?

The President. Yes.

Reporters. Thank you.

Note: The exchange began at 2:22 p.m. on the South Lawn of the White House as the President was returning from a weekend stay at Camp David, MD. The remarks were released by the Office of the Press Secretary on June 24.

Nomination of Donald Alden Hicks To Be an Under Secretary of Defense
June 24, 1985

The President today announced his intention to nominate Donald Alden Hicks to be Under Secretary of Defense for Research and Engineering. He would succeed Richard D. DeLauer.

Mr. Hicks has been with Northrop Corp. since 1963, serving as vice president for engineering, Ventura division (1963–1966); vice president and manager, applied research department (1966–1971); vice president and manager, Northrop Corporate Laboratories (1971–1974) and senior vice president (1974–present). Previously, he was a chief in the applied physics section for Boeing Co. (1956–1961) and a research physicist for Lawrence Radiation Laboratories (1953–1956).

Mr. Hicks graduated from Olympic Junior College (A.A., 1948) and the University of California at Berkeley (A.B., 1950; M.S., 1954; Ph.D., 1956). He is married, has two children, and resides in Beverly Hills, CA. He was born February 20, 1925, in Ely, NV.

Executive Order 12521—Offsets in Military-Related Exports
June 24, 1985

By the authority vested in me as President by the Constitution and the laws of the United States of America, including the Defense Production Act of 1950, (50 U.S.C. App. 2061 *et seq.*), as amended by Public Law 98–265, and in order to provide for the performance of certain reporting functions with respect to the effect of offsets on international trade, it is hereby ordered that Section 602 of Executive Order No. 10480 of August 14, 1953, as amended, is further amended by adding the following new subsection:

"(d) (1) The functions conferred upon the President by Section 309 of the Defense Production Act, as amended, with respect to the preparation and submission of reports to the Congress concerning offsets shall be performed by the Director of the Office of Management and Budget (OMB). The Director may further delegate to the heads of Executive departments and agencies responsibility for preparing and submitting for his review particular sections of such reports. The heads of Executive departments and agencies shall, to the extent provided by law, provide the Director with such information as may be necessary for the effective performance of these functions.

"(2) In order to ensure that information gathered purusant to this authority shall be subject to appropriate confidentiality protections, the United States International Trade Commission, which previously has been designated a 'central collection agency' in gathering this information under 44 U.S.C. 3509, is authorized, pursuant to Section 705 of the Defense Production Act, as amended, to collect the information required for compilation of the data base to be used in the preparation of the first such report to the Congress.".

RONALD REAGAN

The White House,
June 24, 1985.

[*Filed with the Office of the Federal Register, 4:29 p.m., June 24, 1985*]

Executive Order 12522—Reimbursement of Federal Employee Relocation Expenses
June 24, 1985

By the authority vested in me as President by the laws of the United States of America, including Public Law 98–473 and Section 301 of Title 3 of the United States Code, it is hereby ordered as follows:

Section 1. Executive Order No. 11609 of July 22, 1971, as amended, is further amended by revising the present text of Section 1(7)(c) to read as follows:

"(c) The authority of the President under 5 U.S.C. 5724c to prescribe the regulations provided for therein pursuant to which each agency shall carry out its responsibilities under 5 U.S.C. 5724c; *provided,* that the Director of Central Intelligence, after consultation with the Administrator of General Services, shall prescribe such regulations for the Central Intelligence Agency".

Sec. 2. This Order shall be effective as of October 12, 1984.

RONALD REAGAN

The White House,
June 24, 1985.

[Filed with the Office of the Federal Register, 4:30 p.m., June 24, 1985]

Remarks at a Fundraising Reception for the John F. Kennedy Library Foundation
June 24, 1985

I was very pleased a few months ago when Caroline and John came to see me and to ask for our support in helping the library. I thought afterwards what fine young people they are and what a fine testament they are to their mother and father.

It was obvious to me that they care deeply about their father and his memory. But I was also struck by how much they care about history. They felt strongly that all of us must take care to preserve it, protect it, and hand it

They're right, of course. History has its claims, and there's nothing so invigorating as the truth. In this case, a good deal of truth resides in a strikingly sculpted library that contains the accumulated documents, recollections, diaries, and oral histories of the New Frontier. But I must confess that ever since Caroline and John came by, I've found myself thinking not so much about the John F. Kennedy Library as about the man himself and what his life meant to our country and our times, particularly to the history of this century.

It always seemed to me that he was a man of the most interesting contradictions, very American contradictions. We know from his many friends and colleagues, we know in part from the testimony available at the library, that he was self-deprecating yet proud, ironic yet easily moved, highly literary yet utterly at home with the common speech of the ordinary man. He was a writer who could expound with ease on the moral forces that shaped John Calhoun's political philosophy. On the other hand, he possessed a most delicate and refined appreciation for Boston's political wards and the characters who inhabited it. He could cuss a blue streak—but then, he'd been a sailor.

He loved history and approached it as both romantic and realist. He could quote Stephen Vincent Benét on General Lee's army: "The aide de camp knew certain lines of Greek and other such unnecessary things that are good for peace, but are not deemed so serviceable for war . . ."

And he could sum up a current statesman with an earthy epithet that would leave his audience weak with laughter. One sensed that he loved mankind as it was, in spite of itself, and that he had little patience with those who would perfect what was not really meant to be perfect.

As a leader, as a President, he seemed to have a good, hard, unillusioned understanding of man and his political choices. He had written a book as a very young man about why the world slept as Hitler marched on. And he understood the tension between good and evil in the history of man; understood, indeed, that much of the history of man can be seen in the constant working out of that tension. He knew that the United States had adversaries, real adversaries, and they weren't about to be put off by soft reason and good intentions. He tried always to be strong with them and shrewd. He wanted our defense system to be unsurpassed. He cared that his country could be safe.

He was a patriot who summoned patriotism from the heart of a sated country. It is a matter of pride to me that so many men and women who were inspired by his bracing vision and moved by his call to "ask not," serve now in the White House doing the business of government. Which is not to say I supported John Kennedy when he ran for President; I didn't. I was for the other fellow. But you know, it's true, when the battle's over and the ground is cooled, well, it's then that you see the opposing general's valor.

He would have understood. He was fiercely, happily partisan. And his political fights were tough—no quarter asked, none given. But he gave as good as he got. And you could see that he loved the battle.

Everything we saw him do seemed to betray a huge enjoyment of life. He seemed to grasp from the beginning that life is one fast-moving train, and you have to jump aboard and hold on to your hat and relish the sweep of the wind as it rushes by. You have to enjoy the journey; it's unthankful not to.

I think that's how his country remembers him, in his joy—and it was a joy he knew how to communicate. He knew that life is rich with possibilities, and he believed in opportunity, growth, and action.

And when he died, when that comet disappeared over the continent, a whole nation grieved and would not forget. A tailor in New York put up a sign on the door: "Closed because of a death in the family." The sadness was not confined to us. "They cried the rain down that night," said a journalist in Europe. They put his picture up in huts in Brazil and tents in the Congo, in offices in Dublin and Warsaw. That was some of what he did for his country, for when they honored him they were honoring someone essentially, quintessentially, completely American. When they honored John Kennedy, they honored the Nation whose virtues, genius, and contradictions he so fully reflected.

Many men are great, but few capture the imagination and the spirit of the times. The ones who do are unforgettable. Four administrations have passed since John Kennedy's death; five Presidents have occupied the Oval Office, and I feel sure that each of them thought of John Kennedy now and then and his thousand days in the White House.

And sometimes I want to say to those who are still in school and who sometimes think that history is a dry thing that lives in a book: Nothing is ever lost in that great house; some music plays on.

I've even been told that late at night when the clouds are still and the Moon is high, you can just about hear the sound of certain memories brushing by. You can almost hear, if you listen close, the whir of a wheelchair rolling by and the sound of a voice calling out, "And another thing, Eleanor!" Turn down a hall and you hear the brisk strut of a fellow saying, "Bully! Absolutely ripping!" Walk softly, now, and you're drawn to the soft notes of a piano and a brilliant gathering in the East Room where a crowd surrounds a bright young President who is full of hope and laughter.

I don't know if this is true, but it's a story I've been told. And it's not a bad one because it reminds us that history is a living thing that never dies. A life given in service to one's country is a living thing that never dies—a life given in service, yes.

History is not only made by people; it is people. And so, history is, as young John Kennedy demonstrated, as heroic as you want it to be, as heroic as you are.

And that's where I'll end my remarks on this lovely evening, except to add that I know the John F. Kennedy Library is the only Presidential library without a full endowment. Nancy and I salute you, Caroline and John, in your efforts to permanently endow the library. You have our support and admiration for what you're doing.

Thank you, and God bless you all.

Note: The President spoke at 8:10 p.m. at the home of Senator Edward M. Kennedy in McLean, VA.

Appointment of 17 Members of the Commission on the Bicentennial of the United States Constitution, and Designation of the Chairman
June 25, 1985

The President today announced his intention to appoint the following individuals to be members of the Commission on the Bicentennial of the United States Constitution. The President also intends to designate Chief Justice Warren E. Burger as Chairman, who is a member by law.

Frederick K. Biebel is executive vice president and treasurer of the International Republican Cooperation Fund in Washington, DC. He was born April 5, 1926, in Bridgeport, CT, and now resides in Stratford, CT.

Betty Southard Murphy is partner in the law firm of Baker & Hostetler in Washington, DC. She was born March 1, 1928, in East Orange, NJ, and now resides in Alexandria, VA.

Phyllis Schlafly is president of Eagle Forum in Washington, DC. She was born August 15, 1924, in St. Louis, MO, and now resides in Alton, IL.

Bernard H. Siegan is distinguished professor of law at the University of San Diego. He was born July 28, 1924, in Chicago, IL, and now resides in La Jolla, CA.

Ronald H. Walker is managing director and partner of Korn/Ferry International in Washington, DC. He was born July 25, 1937, in Bryan, TX, and now resides in Potomac, MD.

Charles Alan Wright is professor of law at the University of Texas at Austin. He was born September 3, 1927, in Philadelphia, PA, and now resides in Austin, TX.

Upon the recommendation of Warren E. Burger, Chief Justice of the United States:

Herbert Brownell is currently of counsel with the law firm of Lord, Day and Lord in New York City. He was born February 20, 1904, in Peru, NE, and now resides in New York City.

Cornelia G. Kennedy is currently U.S. Circuit Judge for the Sixth Circuit. She was born August 4, 1923, in Detroit, MI, and now resides in Grosse Pointe Woods, MI.

Obert Clark Tanner is founder and chairman of the board of OC Tanner & Co. He was born September 20, 1904, in Farmington, UT, and now resides in Salt Lake City, UT.

Charles Edward Wiggins is currently U.S. Circuit Judge for the Ninth Circuit. He was born December 3, 1927, in El Monte, CA, and now resides in San Francisco, CA.

Upon the recommendation of the President pro tempore of the Senate in consultation with the majority leader and minority leader of the Senate:

Harry McKinley Lightsey, Jr., is dean, University of South Carolina School of Law. He was born December 27, 1931, in Columbia, SC, and now resides in West Columbia, SC.

Edward P. Morgan is owner of the law firm of Welch & Morgan of Washington, DC. He was born May 28, 1913, in St. Louis, MO, and now resides in Bethesda, MD.

Theodore Fulton Stevens is a U.S. Senator for the State of Alaska. He was born November 18, 1923, in Indianapolis, IN, and now resides in Chevy Chase, MD.

Upon the recommendation of the Speaker of the House of Representatives, in consultation with the minority leader of the House of Representatives:

Lynne Anne Vincent Cheney is currently senior editor of the Washingtonian magazine. She was born January 14, 1941, in Casper, WY, and now resides in Washington, DC.

Philip M. Crane is U.S. Representative for the

12th District of Illinois. He was born November 3, 1930, in Chicago, IL, and now resides in Washington, DC.

William Joseph Green is an attorney with the firm of Wolf, Block, Schorr & Solis-Cohen of Philadelphia. He was born June 6, 1938, in Philadelphia, PA, and still resides there.

Thomas Henry O'Connor is a professor of history at Boston College. He was born December 9, 1922, in Boston, MA, and resides in Braintree, MA.

Nomination of Elliott Abrams To Be a Member of the Board of Directors of the Inter-American Foundation
June 25, 1985

The President today announced his intention to nominate Elliott Abrams to be a member of the Board of Directors of the Inter-American Foundation for a term expiring September 20, 1990. He would succeed Langhorne A. Motley.

He is an Assistant Secretary of State-designate (Bureau of Inter-American Affairs). He has been serving as Assistant Secretary of State for Human Rights and Humanitarian Affairs since 1981. Previously he was Assistant Secretary of State for International Organizations. Before assuming his post at the State Department, he was an attorney with the law firm of Verner, Lipfert, Bernhard and McPherson of Washington, DC, in 1979–1981. He was special counsel to Senator Daniel Moynihan (D–NY) in 1977–1979. In 1973–1975 he was an attorney with the firm of Breed, Abbott and Morgan of Boston, MA.

Mr. Abrams graduated from Harvard University (B.A., 1969), the London School of Economics (M.Sc., 1970), and Harvard Law School (J.D., 1973). He is married and resides in Washington, DC. He was born January 24, 1948, in New York, NY.

Appointment of David McLean Walters as a Commissioner of the Franklin Delano Roosevelt Memorial Commission
June 25, 1985

The President today announced his intention to appoint David McLean Walters to be a Commissioner of the Franklin Delano Roosevelt Memorial Commission. He will succeed James H. Rowe, Jr.

He is chairman and president of the Miami Children's Fund in Coral Gables, FL. Mr. Walters is also currently a fellow at Boston University Medical School.

He graduated from the Cleveland School of Law (B.A., LL.B.) and the University of Miami Law School (J.D., 1950). He is of counsel to the firm of Walters, Costanzo, Miller, Russell, Heller and Dittmar. In 1977–1978 he was the Presidential representative to the Vatican and Holy See with the rank of Ambassador.

He has one child and resides in Miami, FL. He was born April 4, 1917, in Cleveland, OH.

Appointment of James L. Hooley as Special Assistant to the President and Director of Presidential Advance
June 25, 1985

The President has announced the appointment of James L. Hooley as Special Assistant to the President and Director of Presidential Advance.

Since November 1983, Mr. Hooley has been Deputy Director of Presidential Advance and has been Acting Director since June 3 of this year. He joined the White House staff as a member of the Advance Office in September 1982.

Mr. Hooley resigned from the White House staff following the 1984 Republican National Convention to work on the Reagan-Bush reelection campaign. At Reagan-Bush he acted as director of advance for Presidential appearances. He rejoined the White House staff following the November election and was detailed to the 50th American Presidential Inauguration, where he was appointed group director for Presidential events. In this position, he was responsible for inaugural activities involving the President and Mrs. Reagan, as well as the youth-related events.

Prior to his White House service, Mr. Hooley served in the Senior Executive Service as Director of Intergovernmental Affairs for the U.S. Department of Labor. From February until September 1981, he was executive assistant and counselor to the Secretary of Labor.

He has been working for Ronald Reagan since May 1978, serving as an advanceman and organization consultant until the 1980 election. Prior to that time he had served in several national and statewide campaigns as a political consultant.

Mr. Hooley is a graduate of the American University in Washington, DC. He was born May 9, 1951, in Albany, NY, and currently resides in Alexandria, VA.

Interview With Arab Journalist Nasser Eddin Nashashibi
June 11, 1985

Middle East Peace Efforts

Q. Why is the U.S. Government hesitant to initiate a revival of a Middle East peace plan?

The President. My initiative, which I outlined in my speech of September 1, 1982, is still on the table, and we continue to believe it represents the most promising proposal for progress toward peace yet presented. We have not hesitated to urge the parties to the conflict to work on ways to move the peace process forward. There is now momentum within the region, and we will do what is appropriate to sustain it, but we must recognize that peace can only be achieved when the parties are willing to negotiate directly.

Q. How do you evaluate the recent visit to Washington of King Hussein of Jordan?

The President. I think we understand each other very well, and I admire the King's courage and sincerity. The recent steps by King Hussein and others in the region have given a new impetus to the process of peacemaking. King Hussein in Washington made clear his desire and that of his Palestinian partners for a peaceful settlement through negotiations, with a Jordanian-Palestinian delegation on one side and Israel on the other, in a supportive international context. The King seeks a peaceful settlement on the basis of United Nations Security Council Resolutions 242 and 338. The visit afforded us an opportunity to reaffirm our view that a just and durable peace must address the legitimate rights of the Palestinian people as well as the security of all states in the region.

The King confirmed our joint commitment to move promptly "this year," as he said, toward direct negotiations among the parties. We hope to be able to help the parties build upon the outcome of these meetings. I am convinced events are moving in the right direction.

Q. Would a process of mixing the Fahd "Fez" plan, the Reagan initiative, the recent resolution between Jordan and the PLO, the Resolution 242, lead to a new peace effort, taking into consideration the Israeli reservations?

The President. I think a new and increasingly realistic attitude toward peace is developing. It is based on a number of contributions, including the ones you have cited. U.N. Security Council Resolution 242 remains the essential foundation for negotiations. I am not going to predict the final outcome, but I am confident that when peace is achieved you will be able to look back and say many of these contributions played an important role.

It is also important to recognize that my own proposals were an outline of the positions the U.S. would support in negotiations. We have not asked others to subscribe to our positions. Each of the parties is free to bring its own views to the table, and we would expect them to do so. The important thing is to begin direct negotiations since it is through the process of such give and take that differences will be worked out and a just and lasting peace can be achieved.

Q. Now that we are heading towards negotiations between the Arabs and Israel, what do you expect the Arabs and Israelis to do before they sit down and negotiate?

The President. We are trying to keep away from anything that sounds like we are imposing solutions to the problems here. All that we are trying to do is help get them together. It seems that solutions are going to involve one side giving up territory in return for defensible borders where peace is guaranteed. The Arab States must recognize that Israel *does* have the right to exist as a nation and that peace will provide security for the Arabs as well.

Q. And what do you hope, Mr. President, that the Arabs will do in their turn from now until the beginning of the coming negotiations?

The President. I hope that the Arabs will show more approval and support of King Hussein, instead of leaving him alone by himself.

Q. This point is very important, Mr. President.

The President. King Hussein is entitled to know that the Arabs are supporting him in what he is trying to do.

Q. Is there anything you wish from the Israelis in these days?

The President. The Israelis, as Mr. Peres said, are looking forward to sitting down to negotiate.

Q. Recent visits by King Fahd and President Mubarak have left them feeling a lack of interest by the Reagan administration to seek a comprehensive solution to the problems of the Middle East. Does this lack of interest, coupled with the devastation of Lebanon, not warrant a superpower such as the U.S. to get hold of all parties in the Middle East conflict and dictate to them a solution which is just for all concerned?

The President. I can't agree with your statement. I do not believe King Fahd or President Mubarak perceive a lack of interest in Middle East peace on the part of the United States. Nothing could be further from the truth. The United States has a deep and lasting interest in seeing a comprehensive peace settlement in the Middle East, and we have consistently communicated that fact to all our friends in the region.

I do not believe, however, that a settlement imposed by any outside power is possible or even desired by the parties. The reality is that peace can only be achieved through a willingness of the parties to sit down and negotiate their differences. My September 1 initiative outlined the positions the U.S. would support in such negotiations, but a real peace can only be achieved by the parties themselves through direct negotiation.

Q. How long will the U.S. tolerate the loss of innocent lives in Lebanon, in Iraq, in Iran, in Israel, and in the West Bank? Is this worth the anti-American feelings that we are witnessing in this area?

The President. The United States is deeply concerned about the suffering of the peoples in the Middle East brought about through the many conflicts existing in that region. The effort to seek solutions to those

819

problems has remained among the highest priorities of the past eight administrations, and it is worth noting that the cost in American lives, effort, and resources has also been high. We will not flag in this effort, but the reality remains that solutions will only be found when the parties to the conflicts have made their own decision to seek a peaceful way to resolve their differences. Negotiations bring results. Egypt and Israel have clearly demonstrated this, and we are actively working to support the process of negotiations in resolving other disputes in the region.

It is important to remember that Americans and the peoples of the Middle East share a great reservoir of common interests and values. This is a reservoir which is being added to every day through trade relations, scholarly activities, and joint scientific endeavors. The participation of a Saudi astronaut in the launching of ARAB-SAT is an event which illustrates the great Arab scientific and mathematical strides made long before the New World was discovered. And it will remind us all how closely our futures are linked.

U.S. Assistance for Sudan

Q. We read everywhere that Sudan could be the breadbasket of the world and not only provide food for the area and Egypt but also for Ethiopia and the starving masses there. Can't the U.S. Government pull together all its resources and potentialities to airlift individuals and equipment into the Sudan and work side by side with the locals to save the situation?

The President. As you know, this year Sudan, like its neighbors, is in the grip of the worst drought in a hundred years. The failure of the rains has resulted in a huge deficit of grains and millions of hungry people. The U.S. has responded to this catastrophe by shipping more than 1 million tons of food. This assistance involves a massive effort to overcome distances and transportation problems. I understand that one out of six Sudanese is dependent on U.S. food aid. Sudan has assumed an additional burden by welcoming hundreds of thousands of drought victims fleeing famine and war in neighboring countries.

The U.S. has responded generously to various appeals issued by the Sudanese Government and the United Nations to assist these refugees, which now number more than 1 million. Despite the ravages of drought, we fully recognize Sudan's long-term agricultural potential. Our development assistance emphasizes the promotion of technology and institutions to make better use of the many millions of arable acres which now lie idle. Along with other donors and international agencies, we are turning to the problem of rehabilitation of agriculture from the drought. This will require a great effort by Sudan, and we stand ready to help.

Soviet Role in the Middle East

Q. Are you not fearful of the Soviets regaining their position and influence in the Middle East to offset the West?

The President. I believe the Soviet Union's influence in the Middle East should be commensurate with its willingness to play a constructive role in solving the problems of the region. But the Soviets have been anything but constructive, a fact often noted by the leaders of the region.

U.S. Policy in the Mediterranean

Q. We understand that the proximity of Central and South America are important to the United States. Do you not give equal importance to the Mediterranean, especially Turkey, Greece, and Cyprus?

The President. Both the Western Hemisphere and the Mediterranean are critical areas for the security of the United States. Turkey and Greece are important partners in NATO and are essential to preserving stability in that strategic part of the world. We also have a close and friendly relationship with the Government of Cyprus.

U.S.-Morocco Relations

Q. Why hasn't the Reagan administration reacted to the new relationship between Libya and Morocco?

The President. The Government of Morocco and we have had a number of intense and thorough discussions regarding the effect of the Morocco-Libyan treaty of union on U.S.-Moroccan relations. Morocco realizes our opposition to the treaty, but we are satisfied that the treaty has not been implemented in such a way as to affect our bilateral relations with Morocco. We will, however, continue to monitor the implementation.

The U.S. values highly our relations with Morocco, and we expect our relationship to remain strong. King Hassan has reiterated the reasons for this treaty, indicating that it is directed at Libya's previous support for the Polisario. Our view of the reprehensible nature of the Libyan regime is well known. We will not alter our position with regard to Libya unless and until Colonel Qadhafi's support for international terrorism and his subversion of governments ceases.

Q. What is the solution to the Sahara war between Morocco and the Polisario?

The President. The United States supports efforts to achieve a negotiated settlement through a cease-fire and subsequent referendum. The U.S. believes that a political solution is the only way to end the conflict.

U.S. Policy in the Middle East

Q. Couldn't the Reagan administration look at the area as four distinct groups: (1) North African countries; (2) Sudan and Egypt; (3) the Arabian Peninsula; and (4) the Fertile Crescent, which includes Jordan, Syria, Lebanon, Israel, and, hopefully, Palestine? Looking from a geopolitical point of view, perhaps the problems could be easily tackled rather than considering the entire region as one big problem. Maybe four smaller problems could be handled more easily than one major problem?

The President. There is no easy answer to your question. We see the Middle East as a greatly diverse region with many commonalities. We deal with it as a region, but also note the individual countries have separate problems and interests. There are clearly some instances of interaction between separate events and problems, but not in all cases. Depending on the issue, we approach subjects both bilaterally and multilaterally.

U.S.-Libya Relations

Q. How do you define—in common terms—the present U.S.-Libyan relationship, if any?

The President. Our relationship is minimal. In fact, we have no official representation in Libya, and we will not have any

until Libya changes its behavior. Again, we are prepared to improve our relationship with Libya *if and only if* there is a complete and lasting reversal of Qadhafi's support for international terrorism and his subversion of governments.

Middle East Peace Efforts

Q. Former administrations came very close, at least, to an attempt at resolving the Middle East dilemma. Now that you are secure in office, could you not bring the conflicting groups to your ranch at Santa Barbara as Carter did at Camp David?

The President. Look, the real need is to get negotiations underway. Location is not the problem.

Q. We have seen that you were able to bring—in the most diplomatic fashion and against all odds—the Soviets to the table. I cannot believe that you cannot do the same with the Middle East today. Why?

The President. The parallel with arms negotiations is interesting. I sincerely wish that the parties to the conflict in the Middle East would sit down together at a table and negotiate, and I believe that we are moving in that direction. The most important point in your parallel is that both we and the Soviets agreed that arms control negotiations should be face to face. We know that we don't agree in our positions, and we are not sure of the outcome, but we are convinced of the value in trying to work toward an agreement by talking directly. The need in the Middle East is for the parties to decide for themselves that they wish to pursue a just and lasting peace through direct negotiations.

Q. Why do you oppose the participation of the Soviets in an international conference for the Middle East, as already suggested by many Arab countries and by the Soviet Union?

The President. This is really two separate questions. The first is: Why do we feel an international conference will not contribute to a peaceful settlement? Our view is that, as a practical matter, an international conference will result only in political theater and would not contribute to solutions. Only direct negotiations can achieve real results. We understand Jordan's need for a supportive international context in which to begin direct negotiations. We will continue our discussions with both Jordan and Israel in order to ascertain how such a context can best be provided.

The second question relates to the willingness of the Soviets to contribute to solutions to problems in the Middle East. We have indicated on any number of occasions that we would welcome a constructive approach by the Soviet Union to the problems of the region. We have also made clear what kind of activities we believe would be constructive. So far, however, their approach has been anything but helpful, and we see no indications their approach will change.

U.S.-Soviet Relations

Q. Do you think that the new leadership in the Soviet Union would be more forthcoming in cooperating with the U.S. toward world peace and security, especially in Africa and the Middle East?

The President. That is a question for Mr. Gorbachev to answer. For our part, we believe that our two countries should seek to contribute to the peaceful resolution of disputes in crucial regions rather than making them more dangerous. We also believe that we should seek to avoid confrontations over these issues. That is why I proposed periodic consultations between our respective experts on some of these problems. Our hope is that such talks can help prevent misunderstandings that might result in confrontation. We have had such discussions on southern Africa and the Middle East. While these talks have been useful, they have not yet revealed any greater willingness on the Soviets' part to promote rather than impede peaceful solutions.

Iran-Iraq War

Q. How do you see the end of the Iraq-Iran war? Once again, are we to believe that those regional wars are necessary for Western economies as we were taught in our economics classes in Western universities?

The President. Any contention that regional wars somehow serve Western economic interests in Marxist nonsense having no role in U.S. foreign policy.

We have a compelling humanitarian interest in the earliest end to the bloodshed. Moreover, the security and economic interests of the U.S., our Western allies, and friends in the region also would be best served by an immediate end to the war that leaves both countries independent and able to continue national development.

Middle East and NATO

Q. Do you not think that the continuation of disturbance and wars in the Middle East affects the safety of the back door of the NATO alliance?

The President. Yes, I do, and this is an issue of great concern. The world cannot ignore the consequences of instability in any part of the globe, and we must all join together in the effort to achieve solutions to regional problems.

Persian Gulf

Q. Are you satisfied with the safety of the Gulf States from any external danger?

The President. No, I am not satisfied with the current situation. As long as the Iran-Iraq war continues, and as long as Iran pursues its policy of supporting terrorism and declines to resume a responsible role in the family of nations, the stability and security of the Gulf States will be at risk. The United States has a vital interest in maintaining freedom of navigation in the Gulf and stability in the region generally, and we have worked with our friends in the area, including Saudi Arabia and the other members of the Gulf Cooperation Council, to support their legitimate defensive needs and to encourage their collective security efforts. These countries are now in a better position to defend, with their own resources, their sovereignty and territorial integrity against potential adversaries, but more remains to be done. We agree with the Gulf States that the only way to end the Iran-Iraq war is through peaceful negotiations, and we have supported their efforts in the U.N. and elsewhere to bring this about. We also support the position of Kuwait and other Gulf States that the only way to eradicate terrorism is to refuse to give in to demands and provocations and to work with other concerned members of the international community to find ways to end this scourge once and for all.

Soviet Occupation of Afghanistan

Q. Do you anticipate any solutions for the situation in Afghanistan?

The President. The war in Afghanistan is the result of the presence of over 115,000 Soviet troops who are trying to subjugate the Afghan people. There is only one solution to the problem—the complete withdrawal of Soviet troops. A negotiated political settlement remains the goal of U.S. policy.

The Soviet forces at their present levels cannot defeat the Afghan resistance, but the resistance cannot hope to expel the Soviet Army from Afghanistan. What is needed is to move from the battlefield to the negotiating table. We fully support the Government of Pakistan's strong resistance to cross-border intimidation.

We are encouraged that the United Nations has announced another round of indirect or proximity talks on Afghanistan for late June in Geneva. It is our hope that progress can be made there toward a settlement although the recent increase in Soviet military activity does not lead to optimism. In contacts with the Soviets at various levels, we have stressed our support for a negotiated political settlement. We will certainly continue to make the point in our future discussions with Soviet officials.

Middle East Peace Efforts

Q. Forgetting your official position as leader of the free world, and frankly between us as human beings, how would you go about resolving the Middle East situation?

The President. Forgetting my position as President of the United States is not something I am permitted to do under the U.S. Constitution. Nevertheless, I do believe that the positions I outlined on September 1, 1982, represent the most viable approach to taking the next step to resolve the Arab-Israeli conflict. It is important to note, however, that I gave them as the positions the U.S. would support in negotiations. We do not ask others to subscribe to them in advance; in fact, we fully expect others to bring their own positions to the table. That is what negotiations are all about—reconciling opposing positions. The important thing is to get those negotiations underway and for the parties to work out their differences directly in a peaceful fashion.

Q. Allow me to thank you again, Mr. President, as a great man of peace. We are all transit passengers in this life, and what counts is the good memory and the historical judgment afterwards. History will judge you as a great crusader for peace and justice. God bless you.

The President. I promise we shall keep trying. I am pleased to have you here. God bless you, too.

Note: A tape was not available for verification of the content of this interview, which was released by the Office of the Press Secretary on June 26.

Message to the Senate Transmitting an Amendment to the Statute of the International Atomic Energy Agency
June 26, 1985

To the Senate of the United States:

I transmit herewith, for Senate advice and consent to acceptance, an amendment to Article VI, paragraph A.1 of the Statute of the International Atomic Energy Agency, as amended. The amendment was recommended unanimously by the Board of Governors of the Agency on June 6, 1984, and approved by the Agency's General Conference on September 27, 1984. I also transmit the report of the Department of State on the amendment.

The amendment, if approved by two-thirds of the members of the Agency, will increase from nine to ten the members of the Agency designated for a seat on the

Board of Governors by virtue of their status as most advanced in the technology of atomic energy without regard to geographical distribution. This expansion will accommodate the entry of the People's Republic of China into the organization, which occurred on January 1, 1984. Under the amendment, the People's Republic of China will be able to occupy a seat on the Board of Governors without displacing any of the other designated members (currently these are Australia, Belgium, Brazil, Canada, Egypt, France, the Federal Republic of Germany, India, Japan, the USSR, the United Kingdom, and the United States).

I recommend that the Senate give early and favorable consideration to this matter, and give advice and consent to acceptance by the United States of the amendment to Article VI, paragraph A.1 of the Statute, as amended.

RONALD REAGAN

The White House,
June 26, 1985.

Nomination of Charles A. Trabandt To Be a Member of the Federal Energy Regulatory Commission
June 26, 1985

The President today announced his intention to nominate Charles A. Trabandt to be a member of the Federal Energy Regulatory Commission, Department of Energy, for a term expiring October 20, 1988. He would succeed Georgiana H. Sheldon.

Mr. Trabandt is Counsellor to the Controller at the Department of the Interior. He joined the Department of the Interior in 1984 as executive assistant to the Secretary. Previously he was on the staff of the U.S. Senate Committee on Energy and Natural Resources, serving as chief counsel (1981–1984) and minority staff counsel (1977–1981). He was minority counsel for the Energy Research and Development Subcommittee, Committee on Science and Technology, in 1975–1977. He was program manager for Tetra Tech, Inc., in Arlington, VA, (1972–1975) and at the Central Intelligence Agency in 1969–1972.

He graduated from the U.S. Naval Academy (B.S., 1963) and Georgetown University Law Center (J.D., 1975). He is married, has four children, and resides in Arlington, VA. He was born November 26, 1941, in Baltimore, MD.

Remarks to the Finalists in the Teacher in Space Project
June 26, 1985

The President. Class will come to order. [*Laughter*] Well, good afternoon, and welcome to the White House, if no one has said that to you yet.

First, let me congratulate you all. The fact that you've come this far in the selection process is testimony to your abilities and the respect of your colleagues. And I'm sure that you've made your schools and communities and your students very proud. I also want to tell you that your shuttle doesn't blast off for a while yet, so there's still time to back out. [*Laughter*]

I suppose that we all have a few special teachers that we remember with particular affection and gratitude. One such teacher for me was Esther Barton, back in Dixon, Illinois. I sometimes wonder what she would have made of our Teacher in Space Project. But I have a hunch, remembering some of my escapades, that if she were here today, she'd tell you this won't be the first time I've sent a teacher into orbit. [*Laughter*]

But I remember one story that she told us about how, when the British were marching toward Washington in the War of 1812, Dolly Madison had time only to save a few precious personal possessions and one portrait of George Washington. Right there. A few hours after she escaped by wagon, the British looted and burned the White House, destroying everything but that one portrait of the father of our country that Dolly Madison saved from the flames.

Well, in that same way, America's teachers are the preservers and protectors of our heritage. You save our past from being consumed by forgetfulness and our future from being engulfed in ignorance.

Every new class is a generation to whom you must transmit the treasures of our civilization. Every new year for the schoolteacher is like a new age of enlightenment in which young minds become awakened to the truths that we hold to be self-evident. You teach your students math and science and literature and history—a variety of subjects. You give them many facts and much knowledge. But your task is greater than that because with the facts, you must impart the values that give them meaning and context—our most sacred values of human dignity and the worth of the individual. You teach an understanding of liberty with respect for the law and help show the way of freedom under God while guiding our youth into the constructive paths of self-fulfillment.

In the hands of America's teachers rests the formidable responsibility of molding and inspiring tomorrow's heroes—the medical scientists who will invent cures for disease, the businessmen who will found whole new industries, the writers, artists, doctors—who knows, maybe even a politician or two. [*Laughter*]

All Americans who strive to excel, not because they are in competition with anyone else, but because they're in competition with their own imagination to be the very best possible in whatever job they have.

I have some warm memories of another teacher, too, in Dixon, Illinois—this time at high school level—B.J. Frazier. I remember

one day, he not only taught English, but—and I don't know whether principals still do this today or not—but he taught English, but was also principal. And I was in his office—[*laughter*]—it wasn't exactly a social call—[*laughter*]—and I remember the conversation that he said to me that it didn't matter to him what I thought of him at that time, that what he was concerned about was what would I think of him 15 years from now.

And I must say, before he departed this Earth and 15 or more years had passed, I'm grateful that I had the opportunity to tell him what I thought of him, which was what he had meant to me, and as the years went by, I had come to realize how much he had meant.

A journalist named Clark Mollenhoff has written a poem about teachers and says it better than I can. The title of the poem is "Teacher." I don't know whether any of you are familiar with it or not. He was a White House correspondent for quite some time before I got here. But his poem reads:

You are the molders of their dreams—the gods who build or crush their young beliefs in right or wrong.
You are the spark that sets aflame a poet's hand, or lights the flame in some great singer's song.
You are the gods of the young—the very young.
You are their idols by profession set apart.
You are the guardians of a million dreams.
Your every smile or frown can heal or pierce a heart.
Yours are 100 lives, 1,000 lives.
Yours is the pride of loving them, the sorrow too.
Your patient work, your touch, make you the gods of hope that fills their souls with dreams and make those dreams come true.

Emerson said that men love to wonder, and that's the seed of our science. Well, it's also wonder that opens the doors of possibility to young minds, that leads to the avenues of hope and opportunity.

When one of you blasts off from Cape Kennedy next January, you will be representing that hope and opportunity and possibility—you'll be the emissary to the next generation of American heroes. And your message will be that our progress, impressive as it is, is only just a beginning; that our achievements, as great as they are, are only a launching pad into the future. Flying up above the atmosphere, you'll be able to truly say that our horizons are not our limits, only new frontiers to be explored.

Speaking of limits, you might be interested that what you're about to do was not so long ago considered completely impossible by the best authorities on the subject. In 1955, about 2 years before sputnik, Dr. Wooley, Britain's royal astronomer, said conclusively, "Space travel is utterly bilge." [*Laughter*] Now, whichever one of you is chosen might also want to take under consideration the opinion of another expert, "The acceleration which must result from the use of rockets," he said, "inevitably would damage the brain." [*Laughter*] So, consider yourself forewarned. [*Laughter*]

But seriously, I wish you all the best of luck, and I hope your mission is as successful as the one that we've just completed. I'm glad it's not me who'll have to make the final selection of the first teacher astronaut because each one of you is eminently

qualified. For the lucky one who does go up in the shuttle, I have only one assignment: Take notes. There will be a quiz after you land. [*Laughter*]

So, thank you, and God bless you all, and may I ask though, in their being here, is there a possibility that on the schedule is a view of that movie that we saw the other night? Well, then, to those of you who don't make it—have you seen it yet?

Audience. Yes!

The President. Oh, well, then you know already what I was going to say. [*Laughter*] It's just about as close to being in space as I think you can be and still have your feet on the ground. I was really carried away with that. We never had anything like that in the horse cavalry when I was—[*laughter*]——

But again, I say thank you, and God bless you all. And as I understand now, down at the other end of the hall in the dining room there are refreshments—I can't join you there; I've got to get back to the Oval Office. [*Laughter*]

Thanks very much.

Note: The President spoke to the elementary and high school teachers at 2 p.m. in the East Room at the White House.

Appointment of Mark S. Fowler as a Member of the Council of the Administrative Conference of the United States, and Redesignation as Vice Chairman
June 26, 1985

The President today announced his intention to appoint Mark S. Fowler, Chairman of the Federal Communications Commission, to be a member of the Council of the Administrative Conference of the United States for a term of 3 years. This is a reappointment. Upon his reappointment, the President also intends to redesignate him as Vice Chairman.

Since 1981 Mr. Fowler has been serving as Chairman of the Federal Communications Commission. He has been a member of the Administrative Conference of the

United States since November 1981 and has served as Vice Chairman since June 1983. Previously, he was a partner in the firm of Fowler & Myers in Washington, DC (1975–1981), and an associate in the law firm of Smith & Pepper in Washington, DC, in 1970–1975.

He graduated from the University of Florida (B.A., 1966; J.D., 1969). He is married, has two children, and resides in McLean, VA. He was born October 6, 1941, in Toronto, Canada.

Appointment of General B.A. Schriever as a Member of the National Commission on Space
June 26, 1985

The President today announced his intention to appoint Gen. B.A. Schriever, U.S. Air Force, retired, to be a member of the National Commission on Space. This is a new position.

In September 1966, after over 34 years of service, General Schriever retired as commander, Air Force Systems Command. His assignments during his military career included chief, Maintenance and Engineering Division and chief of staff of the 5th Air Force Command (1942–1944); chief of staff of the Headquarters of the Far East Service Command (1944); commanding officer, Advanced Headquarters Far East Air Service Command (1944–1946); chief, Scientific Li-

aison Branch, deputy chief of staff, Materiel (1946–1949); assistant for development planning, Office of the Deputy Chief of Staff, Headquarters U.S. Air Force (1951–1954); assistant to the commander, Air Research and Development Command (ARDC), in 1954–1957; deputy commander for ballistic missiles, ARDC (1958–1959), and commander of ARDC in 1959–1961.

General Schriever graduated from Texas A&M University (B.S., 1931) and the National War College (1950). He is married, has four children, and resides in Washington, DC. He was born September 14, 1910, in Bremen, Germany.

Proclamation 5355—Helen Keller Deaf-Blind Awareness Week, 1985
June 26, 1985

By the President of the United States of America

A Proclamation

The sights and sounds of the world around us are among the gifts we cherish most. But for approximately 40,000 Americans who are both deaf and blind, seeing and hearing exist only as dreams. Through an accident of birth or illness, these men and women may never gaze at the splendor of a spring garden or listen to the voices of their loved ones. Cut off from what most of us take for granted, people who can neither see nor hear live in a kind of solitary confinement.

This month marks the 102nd anniversary of the birth of an American who found herself in such a prison—and broke out of it. At the age of 19 months, Helen Keller lost her sight, hearing, and speech, and her formative years were spent in utter isolation. But she had two powerful forces on her side: an absolute determination to overcome her

handicaps, and the devotion of one person, Annie Sullivan, who recognized the child's innate abilities and helped her construct a bridge to the world at large.

Today, the scientific and medical communities are showing great determination to build more bridges for deaf-and-blind individuals. Research on disorders that cause deaf-blindness is being conducted and supported on several fronts: by the Federal government through the National Institute of Neurological and Communicative Disorders and Stroke, and the National Eye Institute; by universities and other institutions of higher learning; and by voluntary health agencies and numerous groups in the private sector.

America can ill afford to lose the contributions of her deaf-and-blind citizens. Helen Keller became renowned for her writings and her civic spirit at a time when the study of deaf-blindness was in its infancy. Scientific progress will enable the deaf-

827

and-blind to utilize their talents and ideas, and expand their educational and employment opportunities, thereby increasing their contributions to our society.

To focus public attention on deaf-blindness and the hope through research of someday averting this tragedy, the Congress, by Senate Joint Resolution 125, has designated the week of June 23 through 29, 1985, as "Helen Keller Deaf-Blind Awareness Week" and authorized and requested the President to issue a proclamation to observe this week.

Now, Therefore, I, Ronald Reagan, President of the United States of America, do hereby proclaim the week of June 23 through June 29, 1985, as Helen Keller Deaf-Blind Awareness Week. I call upon all government agencies, health organizations, communications media, and the people of the United States to observe this week with appropriate ceremonies and activities.

In Witness Whereof, I have hereunto set my hand this twenty-sixth day of June, in the year of our Lord nineteen hundred and eighty-five, and of the Independence of the United States of America the two hundred and ninth.

RONALD REAGAN

[*Filed with the Office of the Federal Register, 12:09 p.m., June 27, 1985*]

Remarks to State and Local Officials During a White House Briefing on Tax Reform
June 27, 1985

Well, thank you very much, and, unless someone has already said it here, welcome to the White House. I always enjoy saying that over here because it's just one of those Washington oddities that the Executive Office Building, one of the oldest government buildings here, is always called the White House. I haven't eaten a meal here but—[*laughter*]——

Well, it's an honor to welcome all of you here today, so many State legislators, mayors, and local officials. Sometimes I can't help thinking of people like you as emissaries from the real world—that great land that lies beyond the Potomac—where a special interest is a hobby like fishing, and a lobbyist is someone who hangs around a hotel. [*Laughter*]

But now, I know that you've already been briefed on a number of specific aspects of our proposal for all Americans to pay their fair share of taxes and no more. Permit me then to give you an overview, if I can, of why I believe this plan is so important and how it'll affect you in those very difficult jobs that you have to perform in your States and localities.

When the income tax first became law back in 1913, the tax code amounted to just 15 pages. Today it runs 4 volumes, and the number of pages adds up to more than 4,000. The complexity alone is staggering, but worse is the unfairness, the simple injustice that such complexity engenders. You just know that with a tax code that complicated, there are going to be accountants and lawyers who know how to make it work to their advantage and to the advantage of their clients—and that ordinary Americans who can't afford such high-paid professional help will end up paying for it with higher taxes. When it comes to taxes, one man's loophole is another man's noose.

Many Americans, individuals and families, paid a higher tax rate last year than the gigantic corporations that they work for. And well-to-do individuals are able to take so-called educational ocean luxury cruises or buy sky boxes at sporting events and write it all off as business expense. Now, I'm certainly not against big business or businessmen. These are the people who provide many of our jobs and create much of America's wealth. What I am against is the unfair tax system that allows them to take perfectly legal deductions, deductions that by virtually any standards of fairness are ludicrous.

The key idea in our proposal is that by ironing out the complexities and closing unfair loopholes, by making everyone pay their fair share, we can make the system more equitable and dramatically lower marginal tax rates without a loss in revenue. Lower marginal rates for both individuals and corporations will mean a greater reward for work, saving, and risk-taking, more efficient use of scarce capital, and a stronger and healthy economy. In other words, our fair share plan is also a progrowth tax plan.

Another key component of our proposal is to provide America's families with a long overdue break by practically doubling the personal exemption. Indeed, our plan would drop virtually every poor family in America off the tax rolls entirely. And a working family with two or three children would pay less than a 10 percent income tax on its earnings well into the $25,000 to $30,000 range.

Now, I know that many are concerned about our proposed elimination of the State and local tax deduction. Well, the first point to make here is an argument for fairness—and I have a hunch that maybe somebody here's already made this argument—but only about one in three itemize their deductions and get the benefit of that deduction. There can be no justification for a preference that gives the wealthiest—one taxpayer in three—a rebate on local taxes while its less fortunate members—or neighbors pay a full dollar locally plus higher Federal taxes in order to fund that rebate.

Recently, too, I heard some good news from my home State of California. Now,

California is generally considered one of the high-tax States and so, according to the prevailing wisdom, would have the most to lose from the loss of deductibility. The Los Angeles Times has reported, however, that the State Franchise Tax Board has completed a study, finding that Californians would dramatically benefit under our new plan.

In the end, all America will benefit from this fairer, progrowth tax plan. In the words of Democratic Governor Michael Dukakis of Massachusetts, "If my taxpayers are better off, particularly my middle-income taxpayers are better off under this plan, that's really the issue, isn't it?"

Well, lower tax rates, doubling the personal exemption, an end to loopholes—it all adds up to fairness, more growth, more jobs, and renewed hope for our future. My friends, isn't that why we are all in government in the first place?

So, I'm going to get back over to the Oval Office and turn you back to these people here for your questions. And again, I thank you all for coming here and for letting us tell you about this.

You know, for as many years as I can remember it, there have been voices raised in Washington about the ever-increasing complexity and difficulty of the tax and saying that we should have tax reform. And finally, for the first time, I think it's within reach. It's been talked about; it's never been attempted. Well, here it is, and we've got a chance to go at it. And then just think, even Einstein will be able to fill out his 1040, which he couldn't do himself. [*Laughter*]

Thank you all. God bless you.

Note: The President spoke at 11:32 a.m. in Room 450 of the Old Executive Office Building.

Nomination of J. Winston Porter To Be an Assistant Administrator of the Environmental Protection Agency
June 27, 1985

The President today announced his intention to nominate J. Winston Porter to be Assistant Administrator, Office of Solid Waste, of the Environmental Protection Agency. He would succeed Lee M. Thomas.

Mr. Porter is president and owner of J.

Winston Porter and Associates, a management and engineering firm, in Leesburg, VA. Previously, he was with the Bechtel Co. as vice president and manager of services for Saudi Arabian Bechtel Co. in Al-Khobar, Saudi Arabia (1975–1976); vice president of International Bechtel, Inc. (1974–1975); manager of the environmental services department in San Francisco (1972–1974); senior engineer and later supervisor in the scientific development operation (1966–

1972). He was chairman of the chemistry department of the University of Petroleum and Minerals in Dhahran, Saudi Arabia (1965–1966).

He graduated from the University of Texas at Austin (B.S., 1960) and the University of California at Berkeley (Ph.D., 1965). He is married, has two children, and resides in Leesburg, VA. He was born November 14, 1937, in Houston, TX.

Statement on Senate Action on the Nomination of William Bradford Reynolds To Be Associate Attorney General
June 27, 1985

I am deeply disappointed by the action of the Senate Judiciary Committee this morning. That some members of the committee chose to use the confirmation process to conduct an ideological assault on so superbly qualified a candidate was unjust and deeply wrong.

Let me emphasize that Mr. Reynolds' civil rights views reflect my own. The policies he pursued are the policies of this administration, and they will remain our policies as long as I am President.

Mr. Reynolds retains my full faith and confidence.

Appointment of Three Members of the Architectural and Transportation Barriers Compliance Board
June 27, 1985

The President today announced his intention to appoint the following individuals to be members of the Architectural and Transportation Barriers Compliance Board:

Steven A. Diaz, for the term expiring December 3, 1987. He will succeed David H. Welch. Since 1974 Mr. Diaz has been deputy city attorney for the city and county of San Francisco, CA. He graduated from the University of Santa Clara (J.D., 1973). He was born May 2, 1948, in Brooklyn, NY, and now resides in San Francisco, CA.

Norman Hughes, for the term expiring December 3, 1987. He will succeed Mary Alice Ford.

He is assistant to the Assistant Secretary for Conservation and Renewable Energy at the Department of Energy. He graduated from the Lawrence Institute of Technology (B.S.). He was born February 10, 1943, in Detroit, MI, and now resides in Metamora, MI.

William J. Tangye, for the remainder of the term expiring December 3, 1986. He will succeed Nackey Scripps Loeb. Mr. Tangye is executive director of the Southern Building Code Congress International in Birmingham, AL. He graduated from California State Polytechnic University (B.S.C.E., 1967). He was born March 27, 1945, in Oakland, CA, and now resides in Birmingham, AL.

Proclamation 5356—National P.O.W./M.I.A. Recognition Day, 1985
June 27, 1985

By the President of the United States of America

A Proclamation

Since the Revolutionary War, America's men and women have made unselfish sacrifices to defend freedom. In each of America's wars, America's prisoners of war have faced extraordinary hardships and overcome them through extraordinary sacrifices. The bravery, suffering, and profound devotion to duty of our P.O.W.s and M.I.A.s have earned them a preeminent place in the hearts of all Americans. Their heroism is a beacon to follow forever. Their spirit of hope and commitment to the defense of freedom reflects the basic tenets of our Nation.

This country deeply appreciates the pain and suffering endured by families whose fathers, sons, husbands, or brothers are today still missing or unaccounted for. These families are an example of the strength and patriotism of all Americans. We as a people are united in supporting efforts to return the captive, recover the missing, resolve the accounting, and relieve the suffering of the families who wait. We accept our continuing obligation to these missing servicemen. Until the P.O.W./M.I.A. issue is resolved, it will continue to be a matter of the highest national priority. As a symbol of this national commitment, the P.O.W./M.I.A. Flag will fly over the White House, the Departments of State and Defense, the Veterans' Administration, and the Vietnam Veterans Memorial on July 19, 1985, and over the Vietnam Veterans Memorial on Memorial Day and Veterans Day.

By Senate Joint Resolution 87, the Congress has designated July 19, 1985, as "National P.O.W./M.I.A. Recognition Day." On this day, we recognize the special debt all Americans owe to our fellow citizens who gave up their freedom in the service of our country; we owe no less to their families.

Now, Therefore, I, Ronald Reagan, President of the United States of America, do hereby proclaim Friday, July 19, 1985, as National P.O.W./M.I.A. Recognition Day. I call on all Americans to join in honoring all former American prisoners of war, those still missing, and their families who have endured and still suffer extraordinary sacrifices on behalf of this country. I also call upon State and local officials and private organizations to observe this day with appropriate ceremonies and activities.

In Witness Whereof, I have hereunto set my hand this 27th day of June, in the year of our Lord nineteen hundred and eighty-five, and of the Independence of the United States of America the two hundred and ninth.

RONALD REAGAN

[*Filed with the Office of the Federal Register, 10:40 a.m., June 28, 1985*]

Executive Order 12523—National White House Conference on Small Business
June 27, 1985

By the authority vested in me as President by the Constitution and laws of the United States of America, and in order to implement the White House Conference on Small Business Authorization Act (Public Law 98–276), it is hereby ordered as follows:

Notwithstanding the provisions of any other Executive order, the functions of the President under the Federal Advisory Committee Act applicable to the White House Conference on Small Business Authorization Act, except that of reporting annually to the Congress, shall be performed by the Administrator of the Small Business Administration in accordance with the guidelines and procedures established by the Administrator of General Services.

RONALD REAGAN

The White House,
June 27, 1985.

[*Filed with the Office of the Federal Register, 10:41 a.m., June 28, 1985*]

Remarks at a Luncheon With Community Leaders in Chicago Heights, Illinois
June 28, 1985

The President. When we speak up, people speak up. With what we believe, we can defeat the armies of lobbyists in Washington. And I've come here to enlist your support in our efforts to push our profamily, profairness tax plan past the lobbyists and special interests and through the Congress.

And—stepping outside for a few minutes, that's why my schedule is pretty short here. And I wanted to have this opportunity to appeal to you, the community leaders, directly—you want to be—[*inaudible*]—leaders in the community, the battle for tax fairness can only be won out here in America's heartland by community leaders like you. The people you represent, the people you cherish—grassroots heritage, values of family and faith and neighborhood and work that our tax must—[*inaudible*].

We need to mobilize nationwide—every town and community—so that we can make sure the American people win this one. If we live up to—or leave it up to the special interests, I should say, in Washington, that's the last we'll hear about tax fairness, and we're writing the epitaph. We have to make our voices loud and clear and make them heard in Washington.

I think America wants tax fairness and wants it now. We have—it made me think when I was talking about the epitaph, is some years ago when I was Governor of California, I was on a trip to Castlereagh, Ireland, where St. Patrick erected the first cross. And a young Irish guard was showing us through the old ruins of the cathedral and then the old ancient ceremony on

Castlereagh. And he took us to one tomb, and there inscribed on the tomb was this epitaph: "Remember me as you pass by—or as—as you are so once was I. As I am, you, too, will be. So, be content to follow me."

And that had proven too much for some Irishmen who had scratched underneath: "To follow you I am content. I wish I knew which way you went." [*Laughter*]

Reporter. Mr. President, the spokesman for the hostages said that the American people should raise hell to get Israel to release those prisoners. He said that this morning.

The President. I'm not going to comment on that or anything else. I only know that none of us, any country, can afford to pay off terrorists for the crimes that they're committing because that will only lead to more crimes.

Q. Will that be a payoff, sir? Israel releases the prisoners?

The President. I have commented several times on that, Chris [Chris Wallace, NBC News]. Israel had always intended to release them and had made that very clear. So, a linkage that has tied it to our hostages is something that never should have happened.

Q. Sir, David Stockman says that——

The President. I've only got a few minutes to eat spaghetti——

Q. Sir, David Stockman says——

The President. ——and I know that's what you all came in for—you're hoping I'll spill it. [*Laughter*]

Q. David Stockman says that raising taxes is the only fiscal responsible way to go.

The President. He didn't say it. We know what he said. And the story is fallacious.

Q. He said the Times said, sir, that he said that some of the people in the administration on Capitol Hill had been using these phony numbers and probably ought to be in jail.

The President. No. We have the speech. We know exactly what he said, and it is a definite and deliberate misquote. And I'm not going to answer any more questions. Let me eat spaghetti.

Q. Are you going to keep him as budget director?

Q. Sir, as I always get to say, maybe just one more about the linkage of the 7 to the 39. Conwell also said he thought that was a terrible mistake to link the 7 hostages to the 39.

The President. I don't think anything that attempts to get people back who have been kidnaped by thugs and murderers and barbarians is wrong to do. And we are going to do everything that we can to get all of the Americans back that are held in that way.

Q. Are you making progress, Mr. President?

The President. I am not going to speculate. You know me—I am superstitious. I

never talk about a no-hitter if you're pitching one. [*Laughter*]

Q. Then you won't make a deal? Is that it? You won't make a deal?

The President. I am taking the spaghetti here. And I am asking Jim Thompson——

Q. Do you like spaghetti?

The President. I am asking Governor Jim Thompson to apply executive order—he will declare—because this is a working lunch, I understand—answers and all. [*Laughter*] I am going to ask him to declare that it is all right to talk with your mouth full. [*Laughter*]

Q. Okay, then, does that mean——

Q. You won't ask the Israelis under any condition——

Principal Deputy Press Secretary Speakes. That is the end of it. The President says no more questions. So, let's scoot right out. Just turn right and go right out.

Q. Bon appétit.

Reporters. Thank you.

Note: The President spoke at 11:25 a.m. in the teachers lunchroom at Bloom High School. During the informal exchange at the end of the remarks, reporters referred to David A. Stockman, Director of the Office of Management and Budget, and Allyn Conwell, a hostage in the TWA hijacking incident. A tape was not available for verification of the content of these remarks.

Remarks to Citizens in Chicago Heights, Illinois
June 28, 1985

Thank you, Governor Jim Thompson and Mayor Panici. It's great to be here with your senior Senator, Alan Dixon, with three of Illinois' finest Representatives—your own George O'Brien, John Grotberg, Phil Crane, State Senator DeAngelis.

I came to talk about tax fairness and simplification. But first, I want to say a few words about a subject that I know is on all our minds: the outrage of international terrorism.

When terrorism strikes, civilization itself is under attack; no nation is immune. There's no safety in silence or neutrality. If

we permit terrorism to succeed anywhere, it will spread like a cancer, eating away at civilized societies and sowing fear and chaos everywhere. This barbarism is abhorrent, and all of those who support it, encourage it, and profit from it are abhorrent. They are barbarians.

In a different age, the civilized world faced the bloody scourge of piracy. It was a long fight against a great but diffuse evil. But it was won in the end because civilized nations refused to succumb and missed no opportunity to stamp it out. The United

States can be proud of the role that it played in that struggle, a role our marines still sing about in the marine anthem.

In our time, it's terrorism that must be overcome. We cannot accept these repeated and vicious attacks against our nation and its citizens. Terrorists, and those who support them, must and will be held to account.

But now, onto a happier and brighter subject, one that is very close to your families and America's future—that's our plan to completely overhaul our tax system. We're going to junk the present code with its loopholes and shelters and special interest provisions and replace it with a fairer, simpler plan, written with the average American in mind—a plan that rewards hard work, supports our families, protects the old and the poor, and gives the U.S. economy a powerful boost ahead in world competition.

Today I'm bringing you a message of hope and opportunity and a call to action. America is the greatest country on this Earth, but our tax system is a disgrace. It is unworthy of us. Ours is a government of the people, but our tax code seems designed of, by, and for the tax lawyers. The time for excuses has past. Let's turn the years of bitterness, frustration, and anger at paying unfair and wasteful taxes into a ground swell of support for change.

Now, I know some people are skeptical—too often before they've seen America's hopes for tax fairness shot down by the special interests. Well, the lobbyists are out in force again; they've dug in around the Capitol building in Washington, trying to keep the special interests in and the people's interests out. But they've forgotten one thing—this time they're going to have to contend with the allied forces of the President and Chicago's own Dan Rostenkowski, chairman of the House Ways and Means Committee. And if they think that things have been hot so far, Ron and Rosty have got news for them—[*laughter*]—you ain't seen nothin' yet.

Now, this issue goes beyond Democrat or Republican—it's simply a matter of doing what's right for America. And if we work together with good faith and determination, the people can win this time, and they will win.

In the past, positive change has been daunted by the sheet size and complexity of the tax code. Ordinary people couldn't even hope to understand it, so taxes became the specialty of the high-priced tax consultants, who spend their whole lives mastering its intricacies and manipulating the code for the benefit of their intricacies and manipulating the code for the benefit of their privileged clients. The result is that workers sometimes find themselves paying higher taxes than the giant corporations they work for, and hardworking families have to struggle under a growing tax burden while the special interests get a free ride. Now, we're not against big corporations—they provide many of the jobs, goods, and services that keep America strong. It's the system that's unfair, and that's what we're going to change.

Just a few moments ago, I told some people inside the building here of a letter that I just received the day before yesterday. It's a letter from a man out here in the country, an executive who's earning in six figures—well above $100,000 a year. He wrote me in support of the tax plan because he said, "I am legally able to take advantage of the present tax code—nothing dishonest, doing what the law prescribes—and wind up paying a smaller salary than my secretary gets—or I mean, paying a smaller—I'm sorry, paying a smaller tax than my secretary pays." And he wrote me the letter to tell me he'd like to come to Washington and testify before Congress as to how that's possible for him to do and why it is wrong. So, this is the kind of spirit that is going on throughout the country.

It stands to reason that the more complex our tax code is, the more open it is to abuse. So, we're making it simple to make it fair. America's tax plan will do away with special breaks for a few so we can lower the tax rates for all. Our simpler, three-bracket design will assure that no American pays one penny more than his fair share.

Since we unveiled our plan, I've received a lot of mail from people who—even though they presently make use of the special breaks in the tax code, as this instance I just gave you—support change for fairness. One man who works in the advertising business wrote, "We can no longer go on asking middle America to finance special interest tax shelters." Another wrote and said—he described himself as one of the favored few who has the financial resources to take advantage of the tax laws—but he said, "It is wrong for this country to subsidize those of us who are truly wealthy and pay no Federal income tax." When it comes to making our tax system fairer, he said, "right is right," and "I put on my American citizen hat and set aside my partisan position."

Well, right is right, and fair is fair, and it's time for all of us to put on our American citizen hats and do the right thing for America. By closing the loopholes, we can bring tax rates down for the vast majority of Americans. Our tax proposal is the opposite of trickle down; it's bubble up.

Most important of all, America's long suffering families will get dramatic tax relief. The fair share plan gives all of America's families a much-needed break by lowering the tax rates, increasing the standard deduction, making tax deductible IRA's equally available to homemakers, and best of all, nearly doubling the personal exemption so that you can deduct $2,000 for yourself and every one of your dependents.

And we propose indexing that so that if inflation continues to make that $2,000 not worth as much as it was when we started, we'll increase the $2,000 exemption. In our view, nearly doubling the personal exemption makes our tax proposal twice as good.

I've often said that those people who say there are no more heroes just don't know where to look. You see them in communities like this one every day—the wage earner, checking in at sunrise at the factory gate; the homemaker, doing the work of 10 to keep the house running; the parents who save and sacrifice and do without so that they can provide their children with the things they need. It's their hard work, dedication, and faith that keep the American dream alive. Are we profamily? You bet we are. In fact, you might say that the family is the one shelter we approve of. We are also completely exempting the low-income elderly from taxation. We think they've worked hard enough all their lives, and they shouldn't have to carry the IRS on

their backs into retirement. And we're dropping the struggling low-income families from the tax rolls altogether. Giving a leg up on the ladder—that's what America is all about.

This is a tax plan for a growing, dynamic America. Lower, flatter tax rates will give Americans more confidence in the future. It'll mean if you work overtime or get a raise or a promotion or if you have a small business and are able to turn a profit, more of that extra income will end up where it belongs—in your wallets, not in Uncle Sam's pockets.

With lower personal and corporate rates and another capital gains tax cut, small and entrepreneurial businesses will take off. Americans will have an open field to test their dreams and challenge their imaginations, and the next decade will become known as the age of opportunity. American industry will benefit, too, because the billions that are presently being squandered on the loopholes—things like jojoba bean shelters, racehorse writeoffs, windmill farms, and luxury lunches for business executives—will be reinvested in the productive economy, where it will build new factories and businesses, create new jobs, and finance the new inventions that will keep America number one in the world market.

The economic misuse of the real estate provisions in our tax code alone is mind-boggling. Some business districts look more like ghost towns, with building after building constructed primarily for tax reasons and never occupied. Tax waste, we should call it. It's huge, reaching into the multibillions, and you, the American people are paying for it with higher taxes and lower economic growth. It's time we pulled our money out of the tax shelters and invested it in America's future.

Now, you can get a feeling for how good our tax proposal will be for our economy. In the month since we announced it, the financial markets have been smiling, interest rates have been falling, the stock market has been rising—to a new record, as a matter of fact, both signs of confidence in the future—and inflation still lies dormant. From that double-digit figure of a couple of years ago, it is down now to 3.7 percent for the last 12 months. I'm not going to be happy until it isn't even seven-tenths of 1 percent.

But in that time we've also seen the special interests fire their first volley to shoot down America's fair share plan—so far they haven't made a dent. Our tax plan is strong and solid because it's fair, and we're going to make sure it stays that way.

The opponents of our fair share plan have one strategy—to filibuster it to death, to delay, put off, procrastinate. They'll think of a million excuses for inaction. They'll study and debate and meet in committee—they'll nibble at it all summer and then try to bury it deep in the bowels of the next session of Congress. But if we wait, if we let them delay, then we might as well kiss tax fairness goodbye. That's why we've got to set a date—a vote up or down on the fair share plan this year—in 1985.

Now, that means we have to start putting a grassroots coalition together now so that we make sure that Congress will hear the voice of the people over the pleadings of the special interests. We have to be ready to move out this fall with a people's crusade for our profamily, profairness, profuture tax plan. When Congress gets back to town after summer vacation, I'm heading out into the country—I'm going to campaign all across this nation throughout the fall for tax fairness. We're going to take it to the people, and we're going to win one for America.

And I'm going to look to Alan Dixon and

George O'Brien, and Phil Crane and John Grotberg to help us marshall the profairness, progrowth forces in the Congress. I didn't tell them I was going to say that. [*Laughter*] If we make the commitment now, if we can work together to get the fairness bill through the House and the Senate, we can do it by Thanksgiving. And we're going to keep this historic reform above politics so that it will truly be an American victory. And then when our nation comes together to celebrate Thanksgiving, we'll have something extra special to be thankful for.

Then there will be one more step—for the House and the Senate to agree on the final version in conference, and that'll be the best Christmas present that America has ever had.

We're asking for your help—keep those cards and letters coming in, start building those grassroots organizations, stand up and be counted, and join the people's crusade to make 1985 the year that the people won a big one for fairness and justice. In other words: America, go for it!

Thank you. This is my kind of town, and you're my kind of people—Dixon, Illinois, isn't too far from here.

God bless you all. Thank you.

Note: The President spoke at 12:47 p.m. from the front steps of Bloom High School. Prior to his remarks, the President met in the school library with families of the hostages in the TWA hijacking incident.

Nomination of Richard F. Hohlt To Be a Member of the Board of Directors of the Overseas Private Investment Corporation
June 28, 1985

The President today announced his intention to nominate Richard F. Hohlt to be a member of the Board of Directors of the Overseas Private Investment Corporation, United States International Development Cooperation Agency, for a term expiring December 17, 1987. He would succeed William G. Simpson.

Since 1980 Mr. Hohlt has been with the U.S. League of Savings Institutions and is currently serving as senior vice president for government affairs. Previously, he was vice president for government affairs (1982–1984) and assistant vice president for government affairs (1980–1982). He was Executive Assistant to U.S. Senator Richard G.

Lugar in 1977–1980; deputy campaign manager for Dick Lugar for Senate Committee in 1976–1977; and assistant to Mayor Richard G. Lugar of Indianapolis in 1975–1976. Prior to that time, he was assistant to the Marion County treasurer in Indianapolis and was the city controller's internal auditor/systems analyst.

Mr. Hohlt graduated from Millikin University (B.S., 1970). He was born December 4, 1947, in Indianapolis, IN, and now resides in Alexandria, VA.

Appendix A—Digest of Other White House Announcements

The following list includes the President's public schedule and other items of general interest announced by the Office of the Press Secretary and not included elsewhere in this book.

January 1

The President met at the home of Walter and Leonore Annenberg in Palm Springs, CA, with Secretary of State George P. Shultz, Secretary of Defense Caspar W. Weinberger, and Robert C. McFarlane, Assistant to the President for National Security Affairs, to discuss the upcoming U.S.-Soviet arms control talks in Geneva, Switzerland.

January 2

The President left Palm Springs and traveled to Los Angeles for a meeting with Prime Minister Yasuhiro Nakasone of Japan. Prior to his meeting with the Prime Minister, the President met at the Century Plaza Hotel with Secretary of State George P. Shultz and Robert C. McFarlane, Assistant to the President for National Security Affairs. Following the meeting with Prime Minister Nakasone, the President left Los Angeles and returned to Washington, DC.

January 3

The President met throughout the day at the White House with members of the White House staff. In the afternoon, he met with representatives of several Federal departments to discuss their budgets.

January 4

The President met at the White House with:
—bipartisan congressional leaders, to discuss the upcoming U.S.-Soviet arms control talks in Geneva, Switzerland;
—the Vice President, for a luncheon meeting;
—Secretary of State George P. Shultz;
—representatives of several Federal departments, to discuss their budgets.

The White House announced that the President has invited Prime Minister Turgut Özal of Turkey to make an official working visit to Washington. Prime Minister Özal has accepted the invitation and will meet with the President at the White House on April 2.

The President designated Lee M. Thomas, Assistant Administrator of the Environmental Protection Agency (Solid Waste and Emergency Response), to be Acting Administrator of the Environmental Protection Agency, effective January 6.

The President designated Albert James Barnes, Assistant Administrator of the Environmental Protection Agency (General Counsel), to be Acting Deputy Administrator of the Environmental Protection Agency, effective January 6.

The President announced his intention to nominate Richard H. Hughes to be a member of the Board of Directors of the Export-Import Bank of the United States for a term expiring January 20, 1987. This is a reappointment.

The President announced his intention to nominate Rosalie Gaull Silberman to be a member of the Equal Employment Opportunity Commission for a term expiring July 1, 1990. This is a reappointment.

The President transmitted to the Congress the sixth annual report of the Department of Energy.

In the afternoon, the President left the White House for a weekend stay at Camp David, MD.

January 6

The President returned to the White House from Camp David, MD.

January 7

The President met at the White House with:
—members of the White House staff;
—former government officials who are serving as members of the organizing committee for a national campaign in behalf of a single 6-year term for a U.S. President.

January 8

The President met at the White House with members of his staff.

In an Oval Office ceremony, the President received the official Presidential medallion commemorating the 40th President and 43d Vice President. Among those participating in the ceremony were Senator Mark O. Hatfield of Oregon, chairman of the Presidential Inaugural Medals Committee, and Michael K. Deaver, general chairman of the Committee for the 50th American Presidential Inaugural.

The President spoke by telephone with Secretary of State George P. Shultz and Robert C. McFarlane, Assistant to the President for National Security Affairs, to discuss the U.S.-Soviet arms control talks in Geneva, Switzerland.

The President transmitted to the Congress the following reports:
- —the second biennial report on coastal zone management;
- —the seventh annual report on Federal energy conservation programs covering fiscal year 1983;
- —the third annual report on Alaska's mineral resources, covering calendar year 1984.

The White House announced that the President has invited President Mohammed Hosni Mubarak of Egypt to make an official working visit to the United States. President Mubarak has accepted the invitation and will meet with the President at the White House on March 12.

January 9

The President met at the White House with:
- —members of the White House staff;
- —the Vice President, for a luncheon meeting;
- —the Vice President and Secretary of State George P. Shultz, who reported on his discussions with Soviet Minister of Foreign Affairs Andrey A. Gromyko in Geneva, Switzerland.

The President transmitted to the Congress:
- —the 1983 annual report of the Federal Prevailing Rate Advisory Committee;
- —the annual report of the Rehabilitation Services Administration, which covers activities supported under the act in fiscal year 1983.

January 10

The President met at the White House with:
- —members of the White House staff;
- —the Cabinet, to discuss government reorganization in the areas of trade, energy, and education, and to review the U.S.-Soviet arms control talks in Geneva, Switzerland.

The President attended a reception in the Roosevelt Room at the White House for William D. Ruckelshaus, who has resigned as Administrator of the Environmental Protection Agency.

January 11

The President met at the White House with members of his staff.

The President left the White House for a weekend stay at Camp David, MD.

January 13

The President returned to the White House following a weekend stay at Camp David, MD.

January 14

The President met at the White House with members of the White House staff.

The President participated in a photo session at the White House for Glamour magazine's article on its selection of the Outstanding Young Working Women of 1985.

January 15

The President met at the White House with:
- —members of the White House staff;
- —members of the Council for a Black Economic Agenda;
- —representatives of the business community, including the American Business Conference, the Business Roundtable, the Chamber of Commerce of the United States, the National Association of Manufacturers, the National Association of Wholesale Distributors, and the National Federation of Independent Business, to discuss the budget deficit;
- —the Cabinet, for a general discussion of government agency reorganization initiatives for the second term.

In an Oval Office ceremony, the President received diplomatic credentials from Ambassadors Francis Joseph Saemala of the Solomon Islands, Rodrigo Lloreda of Colombia, Emmanuel Jacquin de la Margerie of France, and Tolo Beavogui of Guinea.

The President transmitted to the Congress the 13th annual report on the Administration of the Federal Railroad Safety Act of 1970.

In the evening, the President went to the Corcoran Gallery of Art to attend a reception hosted by the Hoover Institution.

January 16

The President met at the White House with:
- —members of the White House staff;
- —members of the Committee for the Next Agenda, a group of public policy experts from several associations, institutes, and foundations, to discuss the committee's report on suggested Presidential initiatives in the areas of management and domestic and foreign policies during his second term.

The President met in Room 450 of the Old Executive Office Building with a group of Republican mayors who were in Washington for a meeting of the U.S. Conference of Mayors.

The White House announced that the President sent a message to Tancredo de Almeida Neves following his election, by a special electoral college, as President of Brazil. The message extended the President's "warmest congratulations" on the President-elect's victory.

The President declared a major disaster for the State of Arizona as a result of strong winds and heavy rainfall beginning on or about July 12, 1984, which caused extensive property damage.

January 17

The President met at the White House with:
- —members of the White House staff;
- —the Vice President, for a luncheon meeting;

—the Cabinet, for a report on the current status of the budget and a report on accident rates among Federal employees.

Late in the afternoon, the President attended a reception in the Blue Room for Citizens for America.

The White House announced that the President has invited Prime Minister Margaret Thatcher of Great Britain to make an official working visit to the United States. Prime Minister Thatcher has accepted the invitation and will meet with the President at the White House on February 20.

January 18

The President met at the White House with:
—members of the White House staff;
—Secretary of State George P. Shultz.

The White House announced that the President has invited His Majesty Fahd bin Abd al-Aziz Al Saud to make a state visit to the United States. The King has accepted the invitation and will meet with the President at the White House on February 11.

The President declared a major disaster for the State of New Mexico as a result of severe snowstorms and rainstorms that began on December 18, 1984, which caused extensive property damage.

In the evening, the President and Mrs. Reagan attended the Prelude Pageant to the 50th American Presidential Inaugural on the Ellipse.

January 19

The President and Mrs. Reagan attended a private luncheon, hosted by a small group of their friends, at Blair House.

In the afternoon, the President and Mrs. Reagan hosted a reception on the State Floor at the White House for members of the Inaugural Trust, major contributors to the Committee for the 50th American Presidential Inaugural.

In the evening, the President and Mrs. Reagan went to the District of Columbia Convention Center to attend the 50th American Presidential Inaugural Gala.

January 20

The President and Mrs. Reagan began the day with breakfast at the White House. They then went to the Washington Cathedral to attend the National Prayer Service of Thanksgiving, an interfaith, nonsectarian religious service.

Following the swearing-in ceremony at the White House, the President and Mrs. Reagan attended a reception in the State Dining Room for Reagan and Bush family members, congressional leaders, Cabinet members, and other invited guests. Later in the afternoon, the President and Mrs. Reagan hosted a reception on the State Floor for entertainers who participated in the Inaugural Gala at the Washington Convention Center.

January 21

The President and Mrs. Reagan began the day with breakfast at the White House. They then attended services at St. John's Episcopal Church where an Inauguration homily was given by the Reverend John C. Harper, D.D., rector of the church. Upon their return to the White House, the President and Mrs. Reagan had coffee in the Blue Room with members of the joint congressional escort committee before traveling to the Capitol.

In the evening, the President and Mrs. Reagan attended a series of Inaugural Balls at various locations throughout the city: the DC Starplex Armory (the Inaugural Ball for Young Americans); the National Air and Space Museum; the Pension Building; the District of Columbia Convention Center (two separate balls); the John F. Kennedy Center for the Performing Arts; the Sheraton Washington Hotel; the Shoreham Hotel; the Washington Hilton Hotel (two separate balls). They also attended the American Legion's "Salute to Heroes" ball, honoring 200 Congressional Medal of Honor recipients, at the Capital Hilton Hotel.

January 22

The President met at the White House with:
—members of the White House staff;
—the bipartisan congressional leadership, to discuss budget and arms control issues;
—a group of leaders of prolife organizations.

The President hosted a reception on the State Floor for members of the Inaugural Committee staff.

The White House announced that on January 21, the President recess appointed the following individuals:
—John A. Bohn, Jr., as a First Vice President of the Export-Import Bank of the United States for a term expiring January 20, 1989. This is a reappointment.
—Richard H. Hughes, as a member of the Board of Directors of the Export-Import Bank of the United States for a term expiring January 20, 1987. This is a reappointment.

January 23

The President met at the White House with:
—members of the White House staff;
—Directors of the Committee for the 50th American Presidential Inaugural;
—Sharlene Wells, of Utah, the current Miss America;
—Vice President Bush, Secretary of State George P. Shultz, Secretary of the Treasury

Donald T. Regan, and other White House and administration officials, for an overview of economic objectives for the Bonn Economic Summit meeting, which was given by Under Secretary of State for Economic Affairs W. Allen Wallis, as well as a presentation on the current international economic situation by Assistant Secretary of the Treasury for International Affairs David C. Mulford.

The President transmitted to the Congress the first annual report of the National Endowment for Democracy.

January 24

The President met at the White House with:
—members of the White House staff;
—Giovanni Spadolini, Italian Minister of Defense;
—the Vice President, for a luncheon meeting;
—the Cabinet Council on Commerce and Trade, to discuss the report of the President's Commission on Industrial Competitiveness.

In a White House ceremony, 12-year-old Lisa Marcks, a Special Olympian from Nazareth, PA, presented the President with a copy of a commemorative book on the 1984 Olympics held in Los Angeles. The CIGNA Foundation is providing marketing support for the sale of the book as part of a fundraising effort for the Special Olympics.

January 25

The President met throughout the day at the White House with members of the White House staff.

January 26

In the evening, the President attended the Alfalfa Club dinner at the Capital Hilton Hotel.

January 28

The President met at the White House with:
—members of the White House staff;
—representatives of financial institutions and the housing industry, to discuss the Federal budget deficit;
—Republican members of the Senate Finance Committee and the House Ways and Means Committee, to discuss tax reform;
—members of the House Republican Whip organization, to discuss upcoming legislation.

The White House announced that Chancellor Helmut Kohl has invited the President to extend his stay in the Federal Republic of Germany following the Bonn Economic Summit. The President has accepted the invitation and will make a state visit on May 5–8. The President's itinerary is still being discussed with the Government of the Federal Republic of Germany.

The White House announced that at the invitation of the Government of Spain, the President will pay a state visit to Spain on May 8–10. The President's itinerary during his visit to Spain is under discussion between the two governments.

The White House announced that the President has invited Dr. Raul Alfonsin, President of the Argentine Republic, to make a state visit to the United States. President Alfonsin has accepted the invitation and will meet with the President at the White House on March 19.

January 29

The President met at the White House with:
—members of the White House staff;
—Clarence M. Pendleton, Jr., Morris B. Abram, and Linda Chavez of the Commission on Civil Rights, to discuss the work of the Commission;
—the Cabinet, to discuss the farm debt situation and Federal Government management and efficiency issues.

In the evening, the President attended a dinner for freshman Members of Congress in the State Dining Room at the White House.

The White House announced that at the invitation of President Antonio dos Santos Ramalho Eanes, the President will pay a state visit to Portugal on May 10–12. The President's itinerary during his visit to Portugal is under discussion between the two governments.

January 30

The President met at the White House with:
—members of the White House staff;
—Defense Minister Yitzhak Rabin of Israel;
—members of the House Appropriations Committee, to discuss defense issues, including the MX missile;
—U.S. Representative to the United Nations Jeane J. Kirkpatrick.

In the morning, the President made a telephone call to the U.S. Savings Bond Leadership Conference at the Mayflower Hotel and spoke with Kent M. Black, chairman and president of the conference.

In a ceremony in the Indian Treaty Room of the Old Executive Office Building, the President presented the first Presidential Awards for Design Excellence. The program, sponsored by the National Endowment for the Arts, provides national recognition for Federal design excellence.

The White House announced that the administration will submit a request for $1.8 billion in military assistance funds for Israel as part of the President's budget for fiscal year 1986. This was discussed by the President and Israeli Minister of Defense Yitzhak Rabin in their meeting this morning. This amount, which would be in the form of grant assistance, would be an increase over the level of U.S. military assistance to Israel for fiscal year 1985 by $400 million. The administration is requesting this amount to help Israel meet its security requirements for the coming fiscal year and to assure that it maintains its qualitative military edge. This decision reflects the longstanding and unwavering commitment by the United States to Israel's security.

The White House announced that Richard P. Riley, currently Special Assistant to the Secretary of the Treasury, will become Special Assistant to the Chief of Staff at the White House.

The President announced his intention to designate John E. Bennett as Vice Chairman of the National Advisory Committee on Oceans and Atmosphere. He would succeed S. Fred Singer. Mr. Bennett has been serving as a member of the committee since July 9, 1984.

January 31

The President met at the White House with:
—members of the White House staff;
—members of the House Armed Services Committee, to discuss defense issues, including the MX missile;
—the Vice President, for a luncheon meeting;
—Senator Mack Mattingly of Georgia, to discuss the line-item veto.

February 1

The President met at the White House with:
—members of the White House staff;
—Tancredo de Almeida Neves, President-elect of Brazil;
—a group of authors, educators, and researchers, who discussed their work with the President at a luncheon meeting.

The White House announced that the President has invited President Chun Doo Hwan of the Republic of Korea to make an official working visit to the United States. President Chun has accepted the invitation and will meet with the President at the White House in April 1985. The exact dates of the visit will be announced later.

In the afternoon, the President left the White House for a weekend stay at Camp David, MD.

February 3

The President returned to the White House from a weekend stay at Camp David, MD.

February 4

The President met at the White House with:
—members of the White House staff;
—Zulu Chief Gatsha Buthelezi of South Africa, president of the national cultural liberation movement Inkatha, to discuss the situation in South Africa.

February 5

The President met at the White House with:
—members of the White House staff;
—Minister of External Relations Roland Dumas of France;
—the National Security Council;
—a group of leaders of new high-technology industries, to discuss the Federal budget;
—the Cabinet, to discuss the Economic Report of the President and the Federal Government management report.

February 6

The President met at the White House with:
—members of the White House staff;
—the Republican congressional leadership, to discuss the State of the Union Address.

February 7

The President met at the White House with:
—members of the White House staff;
—U.S. Ambassador to the Philippines Stephen Warren Bosworth, to discuss the situation in the Philippines;
—Clara Hale, the founder and proprietor of the Hale House for Children in New York, NY, a home for drug-addicted infants, whom the President introduced during his State of the Union Address.

In the morning, the President attended the swearing-in ceremony in the Oval Office for William J. Bennett as Secretary of Education, John S. Herrington as Secretary of Energy, and Donald Paul Hodel as Secretary of the Interior. They were sworn in by Attorney General William French Smith.

The President announced his intention to appoint the following individuals to be members of the Commission on the Ukraine Famine. These are new positions:

C. Everett Koop, Surgeon General of the Public Health Service, Department of Health and Human Services;

Gary L. Bauer, Deputy Under Secretary for Policy Planning and Budget, Department of Education; and

Howard Eugene Douglas, United States Coordinator for Refugee Affairs and Ambassador at Large, Department of State.

February 8

The President met at the White House with:
—members of the White House staff;
—M. Peter McPherson, Administrator of the Agency for International Development, and Senator Pete V. Domenici of New Mexico, to discuss the Central American energy and mineral development program;
—Mayor Dana G. (Buck) Rinehart of Columbus, OH, to discuss the contingency plan prepared by the Columbus city government to

deal with proposed reductions in Federal funding to the city;

—Secretary of the Treasury James A. Baker III and his family;

—Assistant to the President and Chief of Staff Donald T. Regan and his family.

The President transmitted to the Congress a report on the National Defense Stockpile, pursuant to the Department of Defense Authorization Act, 1985.

The President announced his intention to nominate Mark L. Edelman, an Assistant Administrator of the Agency for International Development (Bureau for African Affairs), to be a member of the Board of Directors of the African Development Foundation for the remainder of a term expiring September 22, 1985. He would succeed Francis Stephen Ruddy.

In the afternoon, the President left the White House for a weekend stay at Camp David, MD.

February 10

The President returned to the White House from a weekend stay at Camp David, MD.

February 11

The President met at the White House with members of the White House staff.

The White House announced that the President has invited President Chadli Bendjedid of Algeria to make a state visit to the United States. President Bendjedid has accepted the invitation and will meet with the President at the White House on April 17.

February 12

The President met at the White House with:

—members of the White House staff;

—Cabinet Council on Natural Resources and Environment, to discuss proposed Superfund reauthorization legislation.

In the afternoon, the President presented the Presidential Citizens Medal to John F.W. Rogers in the Oval Office. He was awarded the medal for his work, while Assistant to the President for Management and Administration, on the refurbishing of the White House and the Old Executive Office Building.

February 13

In the morning, the President left the White House for a trip to Rancho del Cielo, his ranch near Santa Barbara, CA.

February 14

The White House announced that the President has asked Secretary of State George P. Shultz to represent him at the forthcoming inauguration of Julio Mario Sanguinetti as President of Uruguay. This event will mark the return of democracy to Uruguay, and we are pleased to participate in this historic celebration. Inauguration ceremonies are scheduled for March 1–2 in Montevideo.

The White House announced that at the invitation of President Pierre Pfimlin of the European Parliament, President Reagan will address the European Parliament in Strasbourg, France, on May 8. In order to accommodate the invitation from President Pfimlin, the United States and the Federal Republic of Germany have agreed to change the dates of the President's state visit to the Federal Republic to May 5–6. The President's schedule for the remainder of his European trip is currently being discussed with the countries concerned, Spain and Portugal.

February 16

The President spoke by telephone with President Hafiz al-Assad of Syria, thanking him for Syria's assistance in the return of former hostage Jeremy Levin, Beirut bureau chief of the Cable News Network.

February 17

The President returned to Washington, DC, following his trip to Rancho del Cielo, his ranch near Santa Barbara, CA.

February 18

The President telephoned Jeff Keith, a cancer victim who had lost his leg, to congratulate him on completing his coast-to-coast run, which was sponsored by the American Cancer Society. The run began in Boston, MA, and ended in Los Angeles, CA.

February 19

The President met at the White House with:

—members of the White House staff;

—freshmen Members of the 99th Congress.

The White House announced that at the request of the President, Vice President Bush, accompanied by Mrs. Bush, will travel to Sudan, Niger, and Mali, African countries affected by drought and famine, between March 3 and 10. The Vice President will then travel to Geneva, Switzerland, where he will address the United Nations Donors Pledging Conference on March 11. The Vice President's trip will help direct international attention to the magnitude of the current African drought and famine crisis and, along with his visit to Geneva, focus world attention on the need for increased long-term humanitarian assistance through agricultural research, land management, training programs, and policy reform. In addition, the Vice President will address the National Press Club on February 25 concerning the drought and famine crisis in Africa.

The President telephoned Jeremy Levin, Beirut bureau chief of the Cable News Network, upon his return after being held captive by terrorists in Lebanon.

The White House announced that in accordance with section 446 of the District of Columbia Self-Government and Governmental Reorganization Act of 1973, the President transmitted to the Congress the fiscal year 1985 District of Columbia request for supplemental appropriations that would provide an increase of $39 million for the General Fund, an increase of $15.2 million for the Capital Projects Fund, and $2.3 million for inaugural expenses. These requests are for District of Columbia funds and do not affect the Federal budget.

The President transmitted to the Congress the 1983 annual report of the National Advisory Council on Adult Education.

February 20
The President met at the White House with members of the White House staff.

The White House announced that at the request of the President, Vice President Bush will lead the U.S. delegation to the inauguration of Tancredo de Almeida Neves as President of Brazil on March 15. Other members of the U.S. delegation will be U.S. Ambassador to Brazil Diego Asencio and Assistant Secretary of State for Inter-American Affairs Langhorne A. Motley. While en route to Brazil, the Vice President will pay a brief visit to Grenada on March 14 and will also pay a brief visit to Honduras on his return trip to Washington on March 16. The Vice President's attendance at the inauguration of Brazil's newly elected President, as well as his visits with members of Grenada's new democratically elected government and with members of the democratic Government of Honduras, underscore the United States' continuing strong support and encouragement for democratic governments in the Western Hemisphere.

The President announced his intention to nominate Secretary of the Treasury James A. Baker III to be the United States Governor of the International Monetary Fund for a term of 5 years; United States Governor of the International Bank for Reconstruction and Development for a term of 5 years; United States Governor of the Inter-American Development Bank for a term of 5 years; United States Governor of the African Development Bank for a term of 5 years; United States Governor of the Asian Development Bank; and United States Governor of the African Development Fund.

February 21
The President met at the White House with:
—members of the White House staff;

—the Vice President, for lunch.
The President met in Room 450 of the Old Executive Office Building with the leadership of the National Conference of State Legislatures.

February 22
The President met at the White House with:
—members of the White House staff;
—Minister of Foreign Affairs Abdellatif Filali of Morocco.
The President attended a farewell reception for Attorney General William French Smith in the Roosevelt Room.

The White House announced that the President has invited Prime Minister Rajiv Gandhi of India to make an official working visit to the United States. Prime Minister Gandhi has accepted the invitation and will meet with the President at the White House on June 12.

In the afternoon, the President left the White House for a weekend stay at Camp David, MD.

February 24
The President returned to the White House from a weekend stay at Camp David, MD.

February 25
The President met at the White House with members of the White House staff.

In the morning, the President attended the swearing-in ceremony in the Oval Office for Edwin Meese III as Attorney General of the United States. Mr. Meese was sworn in by Deputy Executive Clerk Daniel J. Marks.

The President transmitted to the Congress the third annual report of the Tourism Policy Council, covering fiscal year 1984.

February 26
The President met at the White House with:
—members of the White House staff;
—the Republican congressional leadership, to discuss the farm situation, the budget, and the MX missile;
—Secretary of Education William J. Bennett and David P. Gardner, Chairman of the National Commission on Excellence in Education, for a luncheon meeting to discuss the future of American education;
—the Cabinet, to discuss the farm credit program, the Middle East, and Central America;
—the Senate Armed Services and Appropriations Committees, to discuss the MX missile.

February 27
The President met at the White House with:
—the Senate Republican class of 1980, for a breakfast meeting to discuss the MX missile, the budget, and farm credit;
—members of the White House staff;

—Jerry S. Parr, Special Agent in Charge of the Presidential Protective Division, U.S. Secret Service, who is retiring after 22 years of service.

The President hosted a farewell reception for Counsellor to the President Edwin Meese III in the Roosevelt Room. Mr. Meese will be assuming his new position as Attorney General.

February 28

The President met at the White House with:
—members of the White House staff;
—Gen. Paul Gorman, Commanding General, U.S. Southern Command, who was presented with the Defense Distinguished Service Medal by the President upon retiring after 35 years of service;
—Senator Don Nickles and Representative Mickey Edwards of Oklahoma, to discuss proposed provisions in the Treasury Department tax plan affecting independent oil producers;
—Gov. Terry Branstad of Iowa, to discuss the farm situation in his State.

The President attended a farewell reception for Secretary of the Interior William P. Clark.

March 1

The President met at the White House with:
—members of the White House staff;
—Arab-American leaders.

In the afternoon, the President met for a short time in the East Room with senior Presidential appointees, who were being briefed by administration officials on the budget and other issues.

The President transmitted to the Congress the 19th annual report of the Department of Housing and Urban Development, covering calendar year 1983.

In the evening, the President attended the 12th annual Conservative Political Action Conference dinner at the Sheraton Washington Hotel.

March 4

The President met at the White House with:
—members of the White House staff;
—Jean-Claude Paye, Secretary General of the Organization for Economic Cooperation and Development (OECD), to express appreciation for the organization's activities on major economic issues affecting the industrialized countries and to discuss the strength of the U.S. economy and the April ministerial meeting of OECD, with particular attention to the need for a new round of trade talks beginning in 1986;
—the National Security Council;
—Mrs. Reagan, for lunch.

March 5

The President met at the White House with:

—Republican Members of the House of Representatives, to discuss the MX missile and defense spending;
—members of the White House staff;
—former Gov. Edmund G. Brown of California.

In an Oval Office ceremony, the President received diplomatic credentials from Ambassadors Nizar Hamdoon of Iraq, Joaquim Rafael Branco of Sao Tome and Principe, Sir Wallace Rowling of New Zealand, Eduardo Palomo of Guatemala, and Edmund Richard Mashoko Garwe of Zimbabwe.

The White House announced that the President has invited President Belisario Betancur Cuartas of the Republic of Colombia to make an official working visit to the United States. President Betancur has accepted the invitation and will meet with President Reagan at the White House on April 4.

March 6

The President met at the White House with:
—Democratic Members of the House of Representatives, for a breakfast meeting to discuss the MX missile;
—members of the White House staff;
—the bipartisan congressional leadership, Secretary of State George P. Shultz, Senator John Tower of Texas, and Ambassadors Maynard W. Glitman and Max M. Kampelman, the head negotiators of each of three groups making up the U.S. delegation to the U.S.-Soviet negotiations on nuclear and space arms, for a general review of arms control issues.

March 7

The President met at the White House with:
—Members of Congress, for a breakfast meeting to discuss defense spending, farm legislation, and various other issues;
—members of the White House staff;
—Speaker of the House of Representatives Thomas P. O'Neill, Jr., for a luncheon meeting;
—the Cabinet Council on Management and Administration, to discuss Federal employee pay comparability and the disposal of surplus Federal property;
—Vladimir Vasil'yevich Shcherbitskiy, member of the Soviet Politburo, to discuss U.S.-Soviet relations.

In an Oval Office ceremony, the President met with 7-year-old Danielle Newman, of Alsip, IL, the 1985 National Easter Seal Child. Other participants in the ceremony included entertainer Pat Boone and his wife Shirley, who participated in the Easter Seal Telethon, members of Danielle's family, and representatives of the National Easter Seal Society.

In the evening, the President telephoned the family of Enrique Camarena Salazar, a Drug Enforcement Administration agent who was killed in Mexico.

March 8

The President met at the White House with:
—the congressional delegation to the U.S.-Soviet negotiations on nuclear and space arms;
—members of the White House staff;
—student winners of the Voice of Democracy Program.

In the afternoon, the President went to Bethesda Naval Hospital for his annual physical examination. Following his examination, the President went to Camp David, MD, for a weekend stay.

March 10

The President returned to the White House from Camp David, MD.

In the evening, the President spoke by telephone with Robert C. McFarlane, Assistant to the President for National Security Affairs, concerning the announcement by the Soviet Government of the death of President Konstantin U. Chernenko.

March 11

The President met at the White House with:
—members of the White House staff;
—his foreign policy advisers, to discuss the U.S. delegation to funeral services for Soviet President Konstantin U. Chernenko;
—Japanese Ambassador to the United States Yoshio Okawara, who is leaving his post, to discuss improvements in U.S. trade with Japan.

In the afternoon, the President met in Room 450 of the Old Executive Office Building with members of the American Legislative Exchange Council, who were being briefed by other administration officials.

The White House announced that the President has designated the Vice President, Secretary of State George P. Shultz, and Ambassador Arthur A. Hartman, U.S. Ambassador to the Soviet Union, to serve as the delegation to the funeral of Soviet President Konstantin U. Chernenko in Moscow. The Vice President will also be carrying a personal letter from the President to Mikhail Gorbachev, the General Secretary of the Communist Party.

In the evening, the President went to the Soviet Embassy to sign the book of condolences on the death of Konstantin U. Chernenko.

Later in the evening, the President and Mrs. Reagan hosted a private dinner for Queen Sirikit of Thailand in the Residence.

March 12

The President met at the White House with members of the White House staff.

March 13

The President met at the White House with:
—members of the White House staff;
—Dr. Henry A. Kissinger, former Secretary of State, for a luncheon meeting to discuss foreign policy issues and the MX missile.

March 14

The President met at the White House with:
—members of the White House staff;
—Collin Boatwright, a 14-year-old Detroit News newspaper carrier.

March 15

The President met at the White House with:
—members of the White House staff;
—Secretary of State George P. Shultz, who reported on his recent trip to the Soviet Union and his meeting with Mikhail Gorbachev, General Secretary of the Communist Party;
—Secretary of Labor Raymond J. Donovan.

The President announced the members of the official delegation to the funeral of Prime Minister J.M.G. Adams of Barbados. The delegation will be departing today for the funeral, which will be held March 16 in Barbados. Secretary of Agriculture John R. Block will head the delegation. Other members will be:

Thomas H. Anderson, Jr., U.S. Ambassador to Barbados;
CINCLANT Adm. Wesley L. McDonald; and
Charles A. Gillespie, Deputy Assistant Secretary of State for Caribbean Affairs.

The President signed H.R. 1093, which implements the treaty between the United States and Canada concerning Pacific salmon, signed at Ottawa on January 28.

March 17

In the afternoon, the President left the White House for a trip to Quebec City, Canada.

March 18

In the evening, the President returned to the White House from a trip to Canada.

The White House announced that the President has declared a major disaster for the State of Florida because of the impact of severe freezing temperatures on the State's agricultural industry and the resultant unemployment in agriculture and related industries.

March 19

The President met at the White House with members of the White House staff.

During the morning and afternoon, the President met at the White House with Members of Congress to discuss the MX missile.

March 20

The President met at the White House with:
—members of the White House staff;
—American rabbinical representatives.

Throughout the morning, the President met at the White House with Members of the House of Representatives to discuss the upcoming vote in the House on the MX missile.

The White House announced that the President has declared a major disaster for the State of New York as a result of severe storms and flooding during the period of December 29–30, 1984, which caused extensive property damage. The President's action will permit the use of Federal funds in relief and recovery efforts in the designated areas of Lewis and Oswego Counties for public assistance only.

March 21

The President met at the White House with:
—members of the White House staff;
—the Vice President, for lunch.

The White House announced that the President and Mrs. Reagan have invited Prince Charles and Lady Diana of Wales to attend a dinner at the White House on November 9. The Prince and Princess have accepted the invitation. As patrons of the Treasure Houses of Britain exhibition at the National Gallery, their Royal Highnesses will be visiting Washington on November 8–12.

March 22

The President met at the White House with:
—members of the White House staff;
—the Joint Chiefs of Staff;
—Republican Senators, for a luncheon meeting to discuss the budget;
—Members of Congress, to discuss the MX missile.

The President transmitted to the Congress the fiscal year 1984 annual report of the National Endowment for the Arts and the National Council on the Arts.

The President declared a major disaster for the State of New York as a result of severe storms and flooding which began on February 23 and caused extensive property damage.

March 23

In the evening, the President attended the annual Gridiron Dinner at the Capital Hilton Hotel.

March 25

The President met at the White House with:
—the Godfrey Sperling Group, for a breakfast meeting with the reporters;
—members of the White House staff;
—Ambassador Max M. Kampelman, head negotiator for arms reductions at the U.S.-Soviet negotiations on nuclear and space arms in Geneva.

March 26

In the morning, the President telephoned Mrs. Karen Nicholson to express his condolences on the death of her husband, Maj. Arthur D. Nicholson, Jr., USA, who was killed in the German Democratic Republic.

The President met at the White House with:
—members of the White House staff;
—U.S. Ambassador to Greece Monteagle Stearns, to discuss the current political situation in Greece;
—Members of Congress, to discuss the MX missile.

In an Oval Office ceremony, the President presented the Congressional Gold Medal to Margaret Truman Daniel in honor of her father, the late President Harry S. Truman. The medal is presented by Congress in recognition of outstanding public service to the United States. Members of the Truman family and members of the Missouri congressional delegation were present for the ceremony.

In the evening, the President attended a reception for the Victory '84 Committee on the State Floor of the White House.

March 27

The President met at the White House with:
—members of the White House staff;
—Chinese Ambassador to the United States Zhang Wenjin, to discuss U.S.-China relations;
—U.S. Representative to the United Nations Jeane J. Kirkpatrick;
—the Cabinet, to discuss medical assistance concerning a liver transplant for 14-month-old Ryan Osterblom of Indialantic, FL, and drug interdiction and enforcement efforts;
—a group of innovators from high-technology industries, for a luncheon meeting.

March 29

The President met at the White House with members of the White House staff.

In the afternoon, the President briefly attended a farewell reception for Adm. Daniel J. Murphy, USN (ret.), Chief of Staff for the Vice President.

The White House announced that the President has declared a major disaster for the State of

Illinois as a result of severe storms and flooding beginning on February 23, which caused extensive property damage.

Later in the afternoon, the President left the White House for a weekend stay at Camp David, MD.

March 31

The President returned to the White House from a weekend stay at Camp David, MD.

April 1

The President met at the White House with:
—members of the White House staff;
—Gaston J. Sigur, Jr., Special Assistant to the President for National Security Affairs, and Lionel Olmer, Under Secretary of Commerce for International Trade, to report on their recent trip to Japan to discuss the status of U.S.-Japan trade negotiations;
—President Gaafar Mohamed Nimeiri of Sudan.

In the evening, the President hosted a farewell reception for U.S. Representative to the United Nations Jeane J. Kirkpatrick in the Roosevelt Room.

The President transmitted a report to the Speaker of the House and the chairman of the Senate Foreign Relations Committee concerning the late transmittals of certain international agreements.

April 2

The President met at the White House with members of the White House staff.

In an Oval Office ceremony, the President received diplomatic credentials from Ambassador Nobuo Matsunaga of Japan.

The President met in Room 450 of the Old Executive Office Building with local and national leaders of the Associated General Contractors of America.

The President hosted a reception for Presidential Trust members in the Residence.

In the evening, the President went to the Mayflower Hotel to attend the Republican Eagles dinner.

April 3

The President met at the White House with:
—members of the White House staff;
—the Republican congressional leadership, to discuss the budget and tax reform;
—Lord Carrington, Secretary General of NATO;
—Speaker of the House of Representatives Thomas P. O'Neill, Jr., and Minority Leader Robert H. Michel, to discuss the upcoming congressional trip to the Soviet Union.

April 4

The President met at the White House with:
—members of the White House staff;
—U.S. Ambassador to Japan Michael J. Mansfield, to discuss the current trade situation with Japan
—Premier John W.D. Swan of Bermuda;
—Jeff Keith, a cancer victim who completed a fundraising coast-to-coast run from Boston, MA, to Los Angeles, CA, and is the recipient of an award from the American Cancer Society;
—Nicaraguan democratic resistance leaders Arturo Cruz, Adolfo Calero, and Alfonso Robelo, to discuss the President's Central American peace proposal.

April 5

The President met at the White House with Senate Majority Leader Robert Dole and Senator Pete Domenici, to discuss the budget.

Later in the morning, the President left the White House for a trip to Rancho del Cielo, his ranch near Santa Barbara, CA.

April 9

The White House reannounced that dates are being set for a visit of President Chun Doo Hwan of the Republic of Korea. It was announced on February 1 that President Chun would be making a visit to Washington on April 25–27 and meeting with the President at the White House on April 26.

April 15

The President met at the White House with:
—President Luis Alberto Monge Alvarez of Costa Rica, who presented the President with a letter supporting the Central American peace proposal;
—the Cabinet, to discuss Central America and the budget;
—Norman Wymbs, chairman of the Ronald Reagan Boyhood Home Preservation Foundation.

In the evening, the President attended a reception for the President's Committee of Citizens for the Republic at the Phillips Collection.

The President transmitted to the Congress the fiscal year 1986 budget of the District of Columbia.

The President requested the Congress to provide $4.3 million in fiscal year 1985 and $6.1 million in fiscal year 1986 to the Arms Control and Disarmament Agency to provide for the expenses of the new round of arms negotiations in Geneva. The President also requested $331,000 in fiscal year 1985 and $775,000 in fiscal year 1986 to establish and operate the Commission on the Bicentennial of the United States Constitution. In addition, routine appropriation language changes for various agencies were also requested.

April 16
The President met at the White House with:
—members of the White House staff;
—the Republican congressional leadership;
—President Abdou Diouf of Senegal, to discuss ongoing economic reform programs in that country;
—the Vice President, for lunch;
—Speaker of the House of Representatives Thomas P. O'Neill, Jr., and Minority Leader Robert H. Michel, who reported on their recent trip to the Soviet Union.

Later in the afternoon, the President presented the Congressional Gold Medal to Danny Thomas in the Roosevelt Room. He was awarded the medal for his humanitarian efforts and outstanding work as a American, particularly his work for St. Jude's Children's Research Hospital in Memphis, TN.

April 17
The President met at the White House with members of the White House staff.

The President transmitted to the Congress the 19th annual report of the National Endowment for the Humanities, covering the year 1984.

April 18
The President met at the White House with members of the White House staff.

The President attended a luncheon hosted by Robert C. McFarlane, Assistant to the President for National Security Affairs, in the Roosevelt Room. Also attending the luncheon was a delegation of European leaders who presented the President with a petition to the U.S. Congress supporting restoration of aid to the Nicaraguan freedom fighters.

Throughout the day, the President met with Members of the Senate to discuss the situation in Central America.

April 19
The President met at the White House with:
—members of the White House staff;
—Jewish leaders.

In the morning, the President conferred by telephone with Chancellor Helmut Kohl of the Federal Republic of Germany, discussing the President's upcoming state visit.

The White House announced that based on further consultations between the United States Government and the Government of the Federal Republic of Germany and a visit to possible sites by a White House team headed by Michael K. Deaver and assisted by the Chancellor's staff, the President and Chancellor Kohl have decided to participate jointly in a commemorative ceremony

at the Bergen-Belsen Concentration Camp on Sunday, May 5. The ceremony will honor the victims of nazism.

April 21
The President returned to the White House from a weekend stay at Camp David, MD.

April 22
The President met at the White House with:
—members of the White House staff;
—the Economic Policy Advisory Board.

Throughout the day, the President met with Members of Congress to discuss the Central American peace proposal.

In the evening, the President hosted a reception for the Republican Congressional Leadership Council in the Residence.

April 23
The President met at the White House with:
—members of the White House staff;
—Jacques Delors, President of the European Communities Commission, to discuss the upcoming economic summit and other issues.

Throughout the day, the President met with Members of the House of Representatives to discuss the Central American peace proposal.

The President announced his intention to appoint James C. Miller III, Chairman of the Federal Trade Commission, to be a member of the Council of the Administrative Conference of the United States for a term of 3 years. This is a reappointment.

April 24
The President met at the White House with members of the White House staff.

In the morning, the President greeted participants in the First Ladies Conference on Drug Abuse in the Blue Room.

In the afternoon, the President participated in the swearing-in ceremony in the Oval Office for Faith Ryan Whittlesey as U.S. Ambassador to Switzerland.

In the evening, the President attended a dinner given by Senator Paul Laxalt of Nevada at the Georgetown Club.

April 25
The President met at the White House with:
—members of the White House staff;
—the Cabinet and members of the White House staff, for lunch to discuss the upcoming economic summit;
—Anne Christa Cordrey, the 1985 Poster Kid for the Allergy and Asthma Foundation of America.

April 26

The President met at the White House with members of the White House staff.

April 27

In the evening, the President attended the White House Correspondents Association's annual dinner at the Washington Hilton Hotel.

April 29

The President met at the White House with:

—members of the White House staff;

—the Cabinet and members of the White House staff, for a luncheon meeting to discuss the upcoming economic summit.

In the afternoon, the President attended the swearing-in ceremony in the Roosevelt Room for William E. Brock as Secretary of Labor. Mr. Brock was sworn in by the Vice President.

The White House announced that President Reagan has invited President Habib Bourguiba of the Republic of Tunisia to make an official working visit to the United States. President Bourguiba has accepted the invitation and will meet with President Reagan at the White House on June 18.

April 30

The President met at the White House with:

—members of the White House staff;

—Senator John Tower of Texas and Ambassadors Maynard W. Glitman and Max M. Kampelman, the head negotiators of each of three groups making up the U.S. delegation to the U.S.-Soviet negotiations on nuclear and space arms, to report on the first round of negotiations.

The White House announced that the President has designated Mr. and Mrs. Fess E. Parker, Jr., of Santa Barbara, CA, to be official U.S. representatives to the celebration in Australia of Australian-American Friendship (Coral Sea) Week. This annual event commemorates the May 1942 Battle of the Coral Sea, an important turning point in World War II. The event celebrates Australian-American friendship and the solidarity which evolved from that significant victory in the common defense of Australia. This year's observance will be held in various locations in Australia on May 3–10. Mr. Parker, a U.S. Navy veteran of the World War II Pacific Theater, and his wife, will be guests of the Australian Government and will participate in major events in Sydney, Melbourne, Adelaide, and Canberra.

In the evening, the President left the White House for a 10-day trip to Europe.

May 1

The President arrived at Cologne/Bonn airport and proceeded to Schloss Gymnich, his residence during his stay in the Federal Republic of Germany.

May 2

The President met in the morning at Schloss Gymnich with administration officials and members of the White House staff.

The President went to Villa Hammerschmidt, the official residence of West German President Richard von Weizsäcker, for the formal arrival ceremony for his state visit. President Reagan then met with President Weizsäcker at Villa Hammerschmidt and later with Chancellor Helmut Kohl at the Federal Chancellery.

In the afternoon, the President attended a plenary session with summit leaders at the Federal Chancellery. He then went to the residence of William M. Woessner, Deputy Chief of the U.S. Mission, for bilateral meetings with Prime Minister Yasuhiro Nakasone of Japan and President François Mitterrand of France.

In the evening, the President met at Schloss Gymnich with Prime Minister Margaret Thatcher of the United Kingdom.

Later, he attended a reception hosted by Chancellor Kohl at Schloss Augustusburg and a dinner for summit leaders at Schloss Falkenlust. He then returned to Schloss Gymnich.

May 3

The President met in the morning at Schloss Gymnich with administration officials and members of the White House staff.

The President began the first full day of meetings of the Bonn Economic Summit by attending a morning working session with summit leaders at Palais Schaumburg. After a working luncheon at Palais Schaumburg, he participated in an afternoon plenary session with summit leaders at the Federal Chancellery.

In the evening, the President attended a dinner at Palais Schaumburg hosted by Chancellor Kohl for summit leaders. He then returned to Schloss Gymnich.

May 4

The President met in the morning at Schloss Gymnich with administration officials and members of the White House staff.

The President went to the Federal Chancellery for a morning plenary session in the NATO Room, followed by a plenary luncheon.

In the evening, the President attended a dinner at Villa Hammerschmidt hosted by President von Weizsäcker for summit leaders. He then returned to Schloss Gymnich.

May 6

In the afternoon, upon arriving in Madrid, Spain, the President attended a formal arrival ceremony at Pardo Palace, his residence during his stay.

In the evening, the President received a courtesy call from Spanish Prime Minister Márquez Felipe González at Pardo Palace. Later, the President and Mrs. Reagan dined with King Juan Carlos and Queen Sofia at Zarzuela Palace, their Majesties' residence. The President and Mrs. Reagan then returned to Pardo Palace.

May 7

In the afternoon, the President met with Manuel Fraga, leader of the opposition party, in the Tapestry Room at Pardo Palace.

May 8

After a brief arrival ceremony at Strasbourg airport, the President proceeded to Chateau des Rohan, where he attended a luncheon hosted by Pierre Pflimlin, President of the European Parliament.

In the evening, following his arrival in Lisbon, Portugal, the President attended an official welcoming ceremony at Jeronimos Monastery, where he also placed a wreath at the tomb of Luis Camoes, a Portuguese poet.

Later, the President met privately with President Antonio dos Santos Ramalho Eanes of Portugal and then held an expanded meeting with U.S. and Portuguese officials at Queluz Palace. He remained at the Palace overnight.

May 9

In the afternoon, the President met with Dr. Lucas Pires, president of the Centro Democratico Social Party, at Queluz Palace.

May 10

In the morning, the President reviewed an exhibition of Lusitanian horses in the garden at Queluz Palace. The President then returned to Washington, DC.

May 11

In the morning, the President left the White House for a weekend stay at Camp David, MD.

May 13

In the afternoon, the President returned to the White House from Camp David, MD.

The White House announced that the President has invited His Majesty King Hussein I of the Hashemite Kingdom of Jordan to make an official working visit to the United States. His Majesty has accepted the invitation and will meet with the President at the White House on May 29.

The President transmitted to the Congress the fiscal year 1984 annual report of the Commodity Credit Corporation.

The President transmitted to the Congress the fourth annual report on the state of small business.

May 14

The President met at the White House with:
—members of the White House staff;
—the bipartisan congressional leadership, to discuss the President's trip to Europe;
—the Cabinet, for a report on the budget from David A. Stockman, Director of the Office of Management and Budget, Secretary of the Treasury James A. Baker III, and Donald T. Regan, Chief of Staff and Assistant to the President, and to discuss the President's trip to Europe.

May 15

The President met at the White House with:
—Secretary of the Treasury James A. Baker III, Donald T. Regan, Chief of Staff and Assistant to the President, and other members of the White House staff;
—a tax reform group;
—the board of directors of the Ronald Reagan Presidential Foundation;
—the Old Dominion University women's basketball team, the National Collegiate Athletic Association champions;
—Bill Lucas, a Wayne County, MI, executive who recently became a Republican.

The White House announced that the President has invited President Roberto Suazo Cordova of the Republic of Honduras to make an official working visit to the United States. President Suazo has accepted the invitation and will meet with President Reagan at the White House on May 21.

The President requested the Congress to appropriate $2 billion in fiscal year 1985 and $1.2 billion in fiscal year 1986 for international security assistance. This request would provide $1.5 billion to Israel and $500 million to Egypt in fiscal year 1985 to assist these countries through their economic difficulties and $1.2 billion in fiscal year 1986 to help Israel meet its short-term foreign exchange requirements. This assistance would be accompanied by economic reforms in both countries. In addition, $8 million is requested in 1985 for various programs on the West Bank and in Gaza.

May 16

The President met at the White House with:
—members of the White House staff;
—Secretary of State George P. Shultz and Robert C. McFarlane, Assistant to the President for National Security Affairs, to report on the Secretary's trip to the Middle East and the U.S.-Soviet arms control negotiations;

—the Vice President, for lunch;
—the Economic Policy Council, to discuss pending trade legislation.

The President transmitted to the Congress the sixth annual report as required by the Powerplant and Industrial Fuel Use Act of 1978.

May 17

The President met at the White House with members of the White House staff.

The White House announced that the President today requested the Congress to provide the following:

—Appropriation language in fiscal year 1985 that would remove the earmarking of funds for population activities for the Agency for International Development.

—Fiscal year 1986 amended budget requests providing a net reduction of $56.2 million for the Department of Energy. This reduction is primarily the result of reduced funding requirements of the Southeastern Power Administration and the availability of prior year fund balances to help provide for energy supply research and development activities.

—$3.4 million in fiscal year 1985 for the Department of the Treasury to consolidate the headquarters operations of the Financial Management Service (FMS). This proposal also reflects reductions of $2.6 million in fiscal year 1985 and $3.5 million in fiscal year 1986 made possible by reduced postage costs of the FMS.

The President also transmitted appropriations requests totaling $4.0 million in fiscal year 1985 and $17.6 million in fiscal year 1986 for the legislative branch and the judiciary and a fiscal year 1985 appropriation language change for the Federal Home Loan Bank Board.

In the afternoon, the President left the White House for a weekend stay at Camp David, MD.

May 19

The President returned to the White House from a weekend stay at Camp David, MD.

May 20

The President met at the White House with members of the White House staff.

In the evening, the President attended a farewell reception for Michael K. Deaver, Deputy Chief of Staff and Assistant to the President, in the Rose Garden.

May 21

The President met at the White House with:
—members of the White House staff;
—the Republican congressional leadership.

May 22

The President met at the White House with:

—members of the White House staff;
—members of the Scottish Rite of Freemasonry.

In an Oval Office ceremony, the President received diplomatic credentials from Ambassadors Gabriel de la Guardia of Panama, Nicolae Gavrilescu of Romania, Han Xu of the People's Republic of China, and Mohammed Kamal of the Hashemite Kingdom of Jordan.

The President requested the Congress to provide the following:

—$113 million in 1985 for the Department of Agriculture to enable the Federal Crop Insurance Corporation to meet its obligations through fiscal year 1985. The Corporation has experienced greater than anticipated losses due to severe weather conditions during 1984 and the early part of 1985.

—$75 million in 1985 and $50 million in 1986 to initiate the commercialization of the civil land remote sensing satellite system (LANDSAT). These funds would enable a private corporation to take over the LANDSAT system.

—A reduction of $44.2 million in 1985 for the Veterans Administration. This reduction is possible because the number of recipients receiving readjustment benefits and the amounts being paid these recipients is less than had been anticipated.

The President also transmitted an appropriation request for $5 million in fiscal year 1985 for the legislative branch and requests totaling $3 million in fiscal year 1985 and a reduction of $395,000 in fiscal year 1986 for the Department of State.

May 23

The President met at the White House with:
—members of the White House staff;
—Lindsey Joffe, of Williamsville, NY, the National Arthritis Foundation poster child, and her family;
—Danny Ferry of DeMatha High School in Washington, DC, the Nation's most outstanding high school basketball player;
—Carol Gearhart, of Oxnard, CA, the Multiple Sclerosis Mother of the Year, and John Grout, of San Diego, CA, the Multiple Sclerosis Father of the Year.

May 24

The President met at the White House with:
—members of the White House staff;
—Secretary of Commerce Malcolm Baldrige and Lionel Olmer, Under Secretary of Commerce for International Trade, who reported on their trip to India, China, and the Soviet Union;

—Dith Prahn, presently a photographer for the New York Times, whose ordeal under the Khmer Rouge and eventual escape from Cambodia are portrayed in the film "The Killing Fields," and Hang Ngor, the actor who portrayed Mr. Prahn in the film.

May 25

In the evening, the President attended a tennis tournament benefit for the Nancy Reagan Drug Abuse Fund on the South Lawn of the White House. The tournament was sponsored by the Community Foundation of Greater Washington, Inc. Following the tournament, a reception for the participants was held in the East Room.

May 27

In the morning, the President visited Arlington National Cemetery and placed a wreath at the Tomb of the Unknown Soldier. He then left for a trip to Florida.

May 28

The President met at the White House with:
—members of the White House staff;
—Ambassador Max M. Kampelman, to discuss the upcoming second round of the U.S.-Soviet arms control negotiations;
—the Cabinet; Dwight A. Ink, Acting Administrator of General Services; James C. Sanders, Administrator, Small Business Administration; James M. Beggs, Administrator, National Aeronautics and Space Administration; Harry N. Walters, Administrator of Veterans Affairs; and senior White House staff members, to review the President's tax reform proposal;
—senior administration officials, to discuss the tax reform proposal.

May 29

The President met at the White House with:
—members of the White House staff;
—Mrs. Geneva Camarena Salazar and her family. She is the widow of Enrique Camarena Salazar, a Drug Enforcement Administration agent who was killed in Mexico.

The President transmitted to the Congress the annual report of the Corporation for Public Broadcasting for fiscal year 1984.

May 31

The President met at the White House with:
—members of the White House staff;
—Prime Minister Milka Planinc of Yugoslavia.

In the afternoon, after speaking at the Great Valley Corporate Center in Malvern, PA, the President traveled to Camp David, MD, for a weekend stay.

The President declared a major disaster for the Commonwealth of Puerto Rico as a result of severe storms, landslides, mudslides, and flooding beginning on May 16, which caused extensive property damage.

June 1

The President telephoned Brigitte Gerney, who was injured in a New York City construction-site accident, to express his encouragement and support.

June 2

The President returned to the White House from a weekend stay at Camp David, MD.

In the evening, the President and Mrs. Reagan attended a gala performance at Ford's Theatre.

June 3

The President met at the White House with:
—members of the White House staff;
—the National Security Council, to review SALT II restrictions;
—David Owen, leader of the Social Democratic Party in the United Kingdom, to discuss East-West relations.

The President declared a major disaster for the State of Ohio as a result of severe storms and tornadoes beginning on May 31, which caused extensive property damage.

The President declared a major disaster for the Commonwealth of Pennsylvania as a result of severe storms and tornadoes beginning on May 31, which caused extensive property damage.

The President announced his intention to appoint the following individuals to be members of the Board of Directors of the Federal Finance Bank:

Richard G. Darman, Deputy Secretary of the Treasury; and

Carole Jones Dineen, Fiscal Assistant Secretary of the Treasury.

June 4

The President met at the White House with:
—members of the White House staff;
—the Republican congressional leadership, to discuss tax reform and aid to the *contras;*
—Senator Jake Garn of Utah and space shuttle astronauts.

The President announced his intention to nominate the following individuals to be members of the Board of Directors of the Commodity Credit Corporation:

John R. Norton III, Deputy Secretary of Agriculture, will succeed Richard E. Lyng; and

Robert L. Thompson, Assistant Secretary of Agriculture (Economics), will succeed William Gene Lesher.

The President announced his intention to appoint the following individuals to be members of the National Commission on Agricultural Trade and Export Policy:

John R. Norton III, Deputy Secretary of Agriculture, will succeed Richard E. Lyng; and

Robert L. Thompson, Assistant Secretary of Agriculture (Economics), will succeed William Gene Lesher.

June 6

The President announced his intention to appoint the following individuals to be members of the Advisory Commission on Intergovernmental Relations for terms of 2 years:

Edwin Meese III, Attorney General. He would succeed William P. Clark.

William Emerson Brock III, Secretary of Labor. He would succeed Raymond J. Donovan.

Mitchell E. Daniels, Jr., Deputy Assistant to the President and Director, Office of Intergovernmental Affairs. He would succeed Lee L. Verstandig.

Gilbert M. Barrett, county commissioner of Dougherty County, GA. This is a reappointment.

James S. Dwight, partner, Deloitte, Haskins & Sells. This is a reappointment.

Gov. John Carlin of Kansas. He would succeed Governor Bruce Babbitt of Arizona.

June 7

The President met at the White House with:
—members of the White House staff;
—the Vice President, for lunch.

The President transmitted to the Congress the eighth annual report of the National Institute of Building Sciences.

The President requested the Congress to provide the following for fiscal year 1985:
—$76.4 million for the Department of Agriculture's special supplemental food program.
—$2.5 million for the Department of Commerce to pay additional claims against the Fishermen's Guaranty Fund.
—$15 million in transfer authority to cover additional pay costs for the Federal Aviation Administration.

The President also transmitted appropriations requests totaling $3.5 million in fiscal year 1985 and $4.9 million in fiscal year 1986 for the legislative branch and a request by the judiciary for $5.5 million in fiscal year 1985 to build a new office building on the grounds of the U.S. Capitol.

In the afternoon, the President left the White House for a weekend stay at Camp David, MD.

June 9

The President returned to the White House from Camp David, MD.

In the evening, the President telephoned his support to participants of an Americans Against Abortion rally in Los Angeles, CA.

June 10

The President met at the White House with:
—members of the White House staff;

—President Nicolas Ardito Barletta of Panama, to discuss Central American policy and U.S.-Panama issues.

June 11

The President met at the White House with:
—members of the White House staff;
—a bipartisan group of Members of the House of Representatives, to discuss the vote on aid to the Nicaraguan democratic resistance;
—a group of space scientists, for lunch.

The White House announced that the President has asked the Vice President to undertake a foreign policy mission later this month to consult with allied leaders on national security and trade issues. Accordingly, the Vice President, accompanied by Mrs. Bush, will visit Rome, Bonn, The Hague, Brussels, Geneva, Paris, and London between June 23 and July 3 for meetings with government leaders in those capitals. The President has asked the Vice President to follow up on the discussions of the Bonn summit and consult with national leaders, as well as the NATO and European Community leadership, on a full range of issues, including intermediate-range nuclear force (INF) deployment, interim restraints related to the SALT II treaty, arms control, the Strategic Defense Initiative, and international trade.

June 12

The President met at the White House with:
—members of the White House staff;
—the Vice President, for lunch;
—the Senate Steering Committee, to discuss legislative matters.

The White House announced that during the President's visit to China last year, he invited President Li Xiannian to make a state visit to the United States. President Li has accepted the invitation and will meet with President Reagan at the White House on July 23.

June 13

The President met at the White House with members of the White House staff.

In the afternoon, the President participated in a ceremony honoring Gen. Jimmy Doolittle, formally presenting the general with his fourth star. Also present were active and retired four-star generals of the Air Force.

The President requested the Congress to provide $250 million in fiscal year 1985 for economic assistance to the Government of Jordan.

June 14

The President met at the White House with members of the White House staff.

After his remarks at Fort McHenry in Baltimore, MD, the President traveled to Camp David for a weekend stay.

June 16

The President returned to the White House from a weekend stay at Camp David, MD.

The President telephoned C.E. Meyer, Jr., president and chief executive officer of Trans World Airlines, to discuss the hijacking of TWA flight 847.

June 17

The President met at the White House with:
—members of the White House staff;
—the National Security Council, for an update on the situation in the Middle East;
—the Economic Policy Council, to review trade issues;
—small business leaders, to discuss tax reform;
—Senators Howell T. Heflin and Jeremiah Denton of Alabama and Mack Mattingly of Georgia, to discuss restrictions on textile and apparel imports;
—the Chemical Warfare Review Commission, a group of Members of the House of Representatives, and Donald S. Lowitz, Ambassador to the Conference on Disarmament, to receive the Commission's report and to discuss binary chemical weapons.

June 18

The President met at the White House with:
—members of the White House staff;
—the cochairmen of a tax reform coalition.

In the afternoon, the President telephoned the family of Robert D. Stethem, the navy serviceman killed in Beirut during the hijacking of Trans World Airlines flight 847, to extend his and Mrs. Reagan's condolences.

June 19

The President met at the White House with members of the White House staff.

In the evening, the President and Mrs. Reagan attended the premiere of the film "The Dream is Alive" at the National Air and Space Museum.

June 20

The President met at the White House with:
—members of the White House staff;
—the Vice President, for lunch;
—Alexandre Hay, president of the International Committee of the Red Cross.

The White House announced that the President has invited Prime Minister Poul Schlüter of Denmark to make an official visit to the United States. Prime Minister Schlüter has accepted the invitation and will meet with the President at the White House on September 10.

June 21

After his remarks in Dallas, TX, the President traveled to Camp David, MD, for a weekend stay.

June 23

The President returned to the White House from a weekend stay at Camp David, MD.

June 24

The President met at the White House with:
—members of the White House staff;
—Governors Bruce Babbitt of Arizona, Dick Thornburgh of Pennsylvania, Lamar Alexander of Tennessee, Robert D. Orr of Indiana, Joseph E. Brennan of Maine, John H. Sununu of New Hampshire, James Martin of North Carolina, Charles S. Robb of Virginia, and Arch A. Moore, Jr., of West Virginia, to discuss tax reform;
—Armand Hammer, Chairman of the President's Cancer Panel.

June 25

The President met at the White House with:
—members of the White House staff;
—the bipartisan congressional leadership, for a luncheon meeting to discuss the hijacking of Trans World Airlines flight 847, the current legislative agenda, and tax reform;
—Andy North, the U.S. Open golf champion.

June 26

The President met at the White House with:
—the House Ways and Means Committee, to discuss passage of the tax reform plan;
—members of the White House staff.

The President requested the Congress to provide the following:
—$300,000 in fiscal year 1985 for the Department of the Treasury, to cover activities related to U.S. participation in the International Police Organization (INTERPOL).
—$3.3 million in fiscal year 1986 for the Department of Energy, to cover operations of the Alaska Power Administration.
—Appropriation language for the Department of the Treasury and the Environmental Protection Agency.

June 27

The President met at the White House with:
—members of the White House staff;
—racecar driver Richard Petty, who was accompanied by Senator Jesse Helms of North Carolina.

Appendix B—Nominations Submitted to the Senate

The following list does not include promotions of members of the Uniformed Services, nominations to the Service Academies, or nominations of Foreign Service officers.

Submitted January 3

Edwin Meese III,
of California, to be Attorney General.

Ronald Alan Pearlman,
of Missouri, to be an Assistant Secretary of the Treasury, vice John E. Chapoton, resigned.

Jose Manuel Casanova,
of Florida, to be United States Executive Director of the Inter-American Development Bank for a term of 3 years (reappointment).

Frank H. Conway,
of Massachusetts, to be a member of the Foreign Claims Settlement Commission of the United States for the term expiring September 30, 1987 (reappointment).

Michael Huffington,
of Texas, to be an Assistant Secretary of Commerce, vice Lawrence J. Brady, resigned.

Alfred Clinton Moran,
of Illinois, to be an Assistant Secretary of Housing and Urban Development, vice Stephen J. Bollinger, deceased.

Richard H. Francis,
of Virginia, to be President of the Solar Energy and Energy Conservation Bank, vice Joseph S. Bracewell.

Marge Bodwell,
of New Mexico, to be a member of the National Advisory Council on Women's Educational Programs for a term expiring May 8, 1986 (reappointment).

Naomi Brummond,
of Nebraska, to be a member of the National Advisory Council on Women's Educational Programs for a term expiring May 8, 1986, vice Mary Jo Arndt, term expired.

Judith D. Moss,
of Ohio, to be a member of the National Advisory Council on Women's Educational Programs for a term expiring May 8, 1987 (reappointment).

Submitted January 3—Continued

Helen J. Valerio,
of Massachusetts, to be a member of the National Advisory Council on Women's Educational Programs for a term expiring May 8, 1987 (reappointment).

J. Floyd Hall,
of South Carolina, to be a member of the National Council on Educational Research for a term expiring September 30, 1986 (reappointment).

Donna Helene Hearne,
of Missouri, to be a member of the National Council on Educational Research for a term expiring September 30, 1986 (reappointment).

George Charles Roche III,
of Michigan, to be a member of the National Council on Educational Research for a term expiring September 30, 1986 (reappointment).

Carl W. Salser,
of Oregon, to be a member of the National Council on Educational Research for a term expiring September 30, 1986 (reappointment).

Reese H. Taylor, Jr.,
of Nevada, to be a member of the Interstate Commerce Commission for a term expiring December 31, 1985 (reappointment).

Wanda L. Forbes,
of South Carolina, to be a member of the National Commission on Libraries and Information Science for a term expiring July 19, 1988, vice Francis Keppel, term expired.

Margaret Phelan,
of Kansas, to be a member of the National Commission on Libraries and Information Science for a term expiring July 19, 1988, vice Philip A. Sprague, term expired.

Patricia Barbour,
of Michigan, to be a member of the National Commission on Libraries and Information Science for a term expiring July 19, 1989, vice Carlos A. Cuadra, term expired.

Daniel W. Casey,
of New York, to be a member of the National Commission on Libraries and Information Sci-

Submitted January 3—Continued

ence for a term expiring July 19, 1989, vice Helmut A. Alpers, term expired.

Walter C. Wallace,
of New York, to be a member of the National Mediation Board for the term expiring July 1, 1987 (reappointment).

Annelise Graebner Anderson,
of California, to be a member of the National Science Board, National Science Foundation, for a term expiring May 10, 1990, vice Walter Eugene Massey, term expired.

Karen J. Lindstedt-Siva,
of California, to be a member of the National Science Board, National Science Foundation, for a term expiring May 10, 1990, vice Charles Pence Slichter, term expired.

Simon Ramo,
of California, to be a member of the National Science Board, National Science Foundation, for a term expiring May 10, 1990, vice Eugene H. Cota-Robles, term expired.

Vernon L. Grose,
of California, to be a member of the National Transportation Safety Board for the term expiring December 31, 1987, vice Francis H. McAdams, term expired.

Charles E. Courtney,
of California, to be an Associate Director of the United States Information Agency, vice W. Scott Thompson.

Ernest Eugene Pell,
of Maryland, to be an Associate Director of the United States Information Agency, vice Kenneth Y. Tomlinson.

To be members of the National Council on the Arts for terms expiring September 3, 1990:

Joseph Epstein, of Illinois, vice Thomas Patrick Bergin, term expired.

Helen Frankenthaler, of New York, vice James Rosenquist, term expired.

Margaret Eleanor Hillis, of Illinois, vice Robert Lawson Shaw, term expired.

M. Ray Kingston, of Utah, vice Bernard Blas Lopez, term expired.

Talbot LeLand MacCarthy, of Missouri, vice Rosalind W. Wyman, term expired.

Carlos Moseley, of South Carolina, vice Jacob Lawrence, term expired.

Submitted January 3—Continued

The following-named persons to the positions indicated, to which positions they were appointed during the recess of the Senate from June 29, 1984, until July 23, 1984:

Robert A. Rowland,
of Texas, to be an Assistant Secretary of Labor, vice Thorne G. Auchter, resigned.

Donald Ian Macdonald,
of Florida, to be Administrator of the Alcohol, Drug Abuse, and Mental Health Administration, vice William E. Mayer.

Carol Gene Dawson,
of Virginia, to be a Commissioner of the Consumer Product Safety Commission for the remainder of the term expiring October 26, 1985, vice Samuel D. Zagoria, resigned.

Marianne Mele Hall,
of New Jersey, to be a Commissioner of the Copyright Royalty Tribunal for the unexpired term of 7 years from September 27, 1982, vice Katherine D. Ortega, resigned.

Martha R. Seger,
of Michigan, to be a member of the Board of Governors of the Federal Reserve System for a term of 14 years from February 1, 1984, vice Nancy Hays Teeters, term expired.

To be members of the National Council on the Humanities for terms expiring January 26, 1990:

William Barclay Allen, of California, vice Charles V. Hamilton, term expired.

Mary Joseph Conrad Cresimore, of North Carolina, vice Louis J. Hector, term expired.

Leon Richard Kass, of Illinois, vice M. Carl Holman, term expired.

Kathleen S. Kilpatrick, of Connecticut, vice Harriett Morse Zimmerman, term expired.

Robert Laxalt, of Nevada, vice Sister Joel Read, term expired.

James V. Schall, of California, vice Leon Stein, term expired.

Helen Marie Taylor, of Virginia, vice Mary Beth Norton, term expired.

Lando W. Zech, Jr.,
of Virginia, to be a member of the Nuclear Regulatory Commission for the term of 5 years expiring June 30, 1989, vice Victor Gilinsky, term expired.

Submitted January 3—Continued
The following-named persons to the positions indicated, to which positions they were appointed during the last recess of the Senate:

Peter Scott Bridges,
of Louisiana, a career member of the Senior Foreign Service, Class of Minister-Counselor, to be Ambassador Extraordinary and Plenipotentiary of the United States of America to the Somali Democratic Republic.

John W. Shannon,
of Maryland, to be an Assistant Secretary of the Army (new position: P.L. 98–94 of September 24, 1983).

John D. Ward,
of Colorado, to be Director of the Office of Surface Mining Reclamation and Enforcement, vice James R. Harris.

Richard H. Jones,
of Virginia, to be Deputy Administrator of the Federal Aviation Administration, vice Michael J. Fenello, resigned.

Helmut A. Merklein,
of the District of Columbia, to be Administrator of the Energy Information Administration, vice J. Erich Evered, resigned.

Elizabeth Helms Adams,
of California, to be a member of the National Advisory Council on Women's Educational Programs for a term expiring May 8, 1987, vice Diana Powers Evans, term expired.

Peter Douglas Keisler,
of Connecticut, to be a member of the National Advisory Council on Women's Educational Programs for a term expiring May 8, 1987, vice Maria Pornaby Shuhi, term expired.

Rosalie Gaull Silberman,
of California, to be a member of the Equal Employment Opportunity Commission for the remainder of the term expiring July 1, 1985, vice Cathie A. Shattuck, resigned.

Richard H. Hughes,
of Oklahoma, to be a member of the Board of Directors of the Export-Import Bank of the United States for a term expiring January 20, 1985, vice James Ernest Yonge, resigned.

William J. McGinnis, Jr.,
of New Jersey, to be a member of the Federal Labor Relations Authority for a term of 5 years expiring July 1, 1989, vice Ronald W. Haughton, term expired.

Submitted January 3—Continued
Edward J. Philbin,
of California, to be a Federal Maritime Commissioner for the term expiring June 30, 1989, vice James V. Day, resigned.

James A. Lastowka,
of Virginia, to be a member of the Federal Mine Safety and Health Review Commission for a term of 6 years expiring August 30, 1990, vice A.E. Lawson, term expired.

Mary L. Azcuenaga,
of the District of Columbia, to be a Federal Trade Commissioner for the term of 7 years from September 26, 1984, vice Michael Pertschuk, resigned.

To be members of the Board of Directors of the Legal Services Corporation for the terms indicated:

For the remainder of the terms expiring July 13, 1986:

Hortencia Benavides, of Texas, vice Ronald B. Frankum.
Leaanne Bernstein, of Maryland, vice Albert Angrisani.

For terms expiring July 13, 1986:

Lorain Miller, of Michigan, vice Milton M. Masson, Jr., resigned.
Claude Galbreath Swafford, of Tennessee, vice Robert E. McCarthy.
Robert A. Valois, of North Carolina, vice Donald Eugene Santarelli.

For terms expiring July 13, 1987:

William Clark Durant III, of Michigan, vice William J. Olson.
Paul B. Eaglin, of North Carolina, vice Robert Sherwood Stubbs II.
Pepe J. Mendez, of Colorado, vice Peter Joseph Ferrara.
Thomas F. Smegal, Jr., of California, vice David E. Satterfield III.
Basile Joseph Uddo, of Louisiana, vice Howard H. Dana, Jr.
Michael B. Wallace, of Mississippi, vice George E. Paras.

Karen Pryor,
of Washington, to be a member of the Marine Mammal Commission for the term expiring May 13, 1986, vice Donald Kenneth MacCallum, term expired.

Robert Elsner,
of Alaska, to be a member of the Marine Mammal Commission for the term expiring May 13, 1987, vice Robert B. Weeden, term expired.

Submitted January 3—Continued
Barbara W. Schlicher,
of New Jersey, to be a member of the Board of
Directors of the National Corporation for Housing Partnerships for the term expiring October
27, 1987, vice Frank J. Donatelli, resigned.

Pauline Crowe Naftzger,
of California, to be a member of the National
Museum Services Board for a term expiring December 6, 1988, vice Neil Harris, term expired.

Rosemary M. Collyer,
of Colorado, to be General Counsel of the National Labor Relations Board for a term of 4
years, vice William A. Lubbers, term expired.

John N. Griesemer,
of Missouri, to be a Governor of the United States
Postal Service for the remainder of the term expiring December 8, 1986, vice John R. McKean.

Henrietta Fay Guiton,
of California, to be a Commissioner of the Postal
Rate Commission for the remainder of the term
expiring November 22, 1988, vice Simeon Miller
Bright.

Ralph E. Kennickell, Jr.,
of Virginia, to be Public Printer, vice Danford L.
Sawyer, Jr., resigned.

Mae Neal Peden,
of Virginia, to be an Assistant Administrator of
the Agency for International Development, vice
Elise R.W. du Pont, resigned.

Eric Reichl,
of Connecticut, to be a member of the Board of
Directors of the United States Synthetic Fuels
Corporation for the remainder of the term expiring September 14, 1986, vice C. Howard Wilkins,
resigned.

Tom Corcoran,
of Illinois, to be a member of the Board of Directors of the United States Synthetic Fuels Corporation for the term expiring August 16, 1990, vice
Milton M. Masson, Jr.

Paul Webster MacAvoy,
of New York, to be a member of the Board of
Directors of the United States Synthetic Fuels
Corporation for the term expiring September 14,
1991, vice Robert A.G. Monks, resigned.

Withdrawn January 7

Michael Huffington,
of Texas, to be an Assistant Secretary of Commerce, vice Lawrence J. Brady, resigned, which
was sent to the Senate on January 3, 1985.

Submitted January 9

The following-named persons to be members of
the National Advisory Council on Women's
Educational Programs for the terms indicated:

For terms expiring May 8, 1986:
Lilli K. Dollinger Hausenfluck, of Virginia (reappointment).
Marcilyn D. Leier, of Minnesota (reappointment).
Virginia Gillham Tinsley, of Arizona (reappointment).

For a term expiring May 8, 1987:
Mary Jo Arndt, of Illinois, vice Eleanor Knee
Rooks, resigned.

The following-named persons to be members of
the National Council on the Arts for terms
expiring September 3, 1990:
Lloyd George Richards, of New York, vice
Maureene Dees, term expired.
James Nowell Wood, of Illinois, vice Martin
Friedman, term expired.

Rosalie Gaull Silberman,
of California, to be a member of the Equal Employment Opportunity Commission for a term expiring July 1, 1990 (reappointment).

Richard H. Hughes,
of Oklahoma, to be a member of the Board of
Directors of the Export-Import Bank of the
United States for a term expiring January 20,
1987 (reappointment).

Submitted January 11

Herbert Blalock Dixon,
of the District of Columbia, to be an Associate
Judge of the Superior Court of the District of
Columbia for a term of 15 years, vice James A.
Washington, Jr., retired.

Submitted January 18

James A. Baker III,
of Texas, to be Secretary of the Treasury.

Richard G. Darman,
of Virginia, to be Deputy Secretary of the Treasury, vice R. T. McNamar.

John S. Herrington,
of California, to be Secretary of Energy.

William J. Bennett,
of North Carolina, to be Secretary of Education.

Submitted January 18—Continued

John A. Bohn, Jr.,
of Virginia, to be First Vice President of the Export-Import Bank of the United States for a term expiring January 20, 1989 (reappointment).

Submitted January 22

Donald P. Hodel,
of Virginia, to be Secretary of the Interior.

Submitted January 28

Lee M. Thomas,
of Virginia, to be Administrator of the Environmental Protection Agency, vice William D. Ruckelshaus, resigned.

Submitted February 4

Donna M. Alvarado,
of Virginia, to be Director of the ACTION agency, vice Thomas W. Pauken.

Thomas Allen Sands,
brigadier general, United States Army, to be a member and President of the Mississippi River Commission.

Robert Joseph Dacey,
brigadier general, United States Army, to be a member of the Mississippi River Commission.

Justin W. Dart, Jr.,
of Texas, to be a member of the National Council on the Handicapped for a term expiring September 17, 1987 (reappointment).

Jeremiah Milbank,
of Connecticut, to be a member of the National Council on the Handicapped for a term expiring September 17, 1986, vice Carmine R. Lavieri, deceased.

Submitted February 8

John E. Krings,
of Virginia, to be Director of Operational Test and Evaluation, Department of Defense (new position—P.L. 98–94 of September 24, 1983).

Lynda Anne Barness,
of Pennsylvania, to be a member of the Board of Directors of the Inter-American Foundation for a term expiring October 6, 1990, vice Doris B. Holleb, term expired.

Submitted February 11

Mark L. Edelman,
an Assistant Administrator of the Agency for International Development, to be a member of the Board of Directors of the African Develop-

Submitted February 11—Continued

ment Foundation for the remainder of the term expiring September 22, 1985, vice Francis Stephen Ruddy, resigned.

Daniel H. Carter,
of Texas, to be a member of the National Commission on Libraries and Information Science for a term expiring July 19, 1989, vice Margaret S. Warden, term expired.

The following-named persons to be members of the Board of Directors of the National Institute of Building Sciences for terms expiring September 7, 1987:

MacDonald G. Becket, of California (reappointment).

Kyle Clayton Boone, of North Carolina (reappointment).

Submitted February 20

James A. Baker III,
of Texas, to be United States Governor of the International Monetary Fund for a term of 5 years; United States Governor of the International Bank for Reconstruction and Development for a term of 5 years; United States Governor of the Inter-American Development Bank for a term of 5 years; United States Governor of the African Development Bank for a term of 5 years; United States Governor of the Asian Development Bank; and United States Governor of the African Development Fund.

The following-named persons to be members of the National Council on Educational Research for terms expiring September 30, 1987:

Elaine Y. Schadler, of Pennsylvania (reappointment).

Gwyneth Gayman, of California (reappointment).

The following-named persons to be members of the Advisory Board for Radio Broadcasting to Cuba for the terms indicated:

For terms of 2 years:

Anne Elizabeth Brunsdale, of the District of Columbia (new position).

Jose Luis Rodriguez, of Florida (new position).

For terms of 3 years:

Joseph Francis Glennon, of Florida (new position).

Danford L. Sawyer, Jr., of Florida (new position).

861

Submitted February 20—Continued

Roxanne S. Vierra,
of Colorado, to be a member of the National Council on the Handicapped for a term expiring September 17, 1987 (reappointment).

George D. Hart,
of California, to be a member of the National Council on the Humanities for a term expiring January 26, 1990, vice Jacob Neusner, resigned.

Submitted February 25

Max M. Kampelman,
of the District of Columbia, to be Ambassador Extraordinary and Plenipotentiary of the United States of America to the United States Office for Arms Reduction Negotiations in Geneva.

John Goodwin Tower,
of Texas, for the rank of Ambassador during his tenure of service as United States Negotiator on Strategic Nuclear Arms.

Maynard W. Glitman,
of Vermont, a career member of the Senior Foreign Service, Class of Minister-Counselor, for the rank of Ambassador during his tenure of service as United States Negotiator on Intermediate Range Nuclear Arms.

Thomas J. Aquilino, Jr.,
of New York, to be a Judge of the United States Court of International Trade, vice Frederick Landis, retired.

Frank H. Easterbrook,
of Illinois, to be United States Circuit Judge for the Seventh Circuit, vice a new position created by P.L. 98–353, approved July 10, 1984.

James F. Holderman, Jr.,
of Illinois, to be United States District Judge for the Northern District of Illinois, vice a new position created by P.L. 98–353, approved July 10, 1984.

James R. Laffoon, of California,
to be United States Marshal for the Southern District of California for the term of 4 years (reappointment).

Submitted March 4

Donald E. Shasteen,
of Maryland, to be Assistant Secretary of Labor for Veterans' Employment, vice William Coskrey Plowden, Jr.

Submitted March 4—Continued

John H. Moore,
of California, to be Deputy Director of the National Science Foundation, vice Donald Newton Langenberg, resigned.

Submitted March 5

John R. Norton III,
of Arizona, to be Deputy Secretary of Agriculture, vice Richard E. Lyng, resigned.

William Lockhart Ball III,
of Georgia, to be an Assistant Secretary of State, vice W. Tapley Bennett, Jr., resigned.

Submitted March 7

Carol Los Mansmann,
of Pennsylvania, to be United States Circuit Judge for the Third Circuit, vice a new position created by P.L. 98–353, approved July 10, 1984.

J. Thomas Greene,
of Utah, to be United States District Judge for the District of Utah, vice a new position created by P.L. 98–353, approved July 10, 1984.

Carolyn R. Dimmick,
of Washington, to be United States District Judge for the Western District of Washington, vice a new position created by P.L. 98–353, approved July 10, 1984.

George S. Rosborough, Jr.,
of Missouri, to be a member of the National Museum Services Board for a term expiring December 6, 1988, vice Douglas Dillon.

Submitted March 8

Donald J. Devine,
of Maryland, to be Director of the Office of Personnel Management for a term of 4 years (reappointment).

Jacob Neusner,
of Rhode Island, to be a member of the National Council on the Arts for a term expiring September 3, 1990, vice Jessie A. Woods, term expired.

Submitted March 12

Marshall B. Babson,
of Connecticut, to be a member of the National Labor Relations Board for a term expiring December 16, 1989, vice Don Alan Zimmerman, term expired.

Submitted March 12—Continued

Wilford W. Johansen,
of California, to be a member of the National
Labor Relations Board for a term expiring August
27, 1988, vice Howard Jenkins, Jr., resigned.

Submitted March 13

John F.W. Rogers,
of New York, to be an Assistant Secretary of the
Treasury (new position—P.L. 98–594 of October
30, 1984).

Submitted March 14

Midge Decter,
of New York, to be a member of the Advisory
Board for Radio Broadcasting to Cuba for a term
of 1 year (new position).

Submitted March 19

Fernando Enrique Rondon,
of Virginia, a career member of the Senior Foreign Service, Class of Minister-Counselor, to be
Ambassador Extraordinary and Plenipotentiary of
the United States of America to the Republic of
Ecuador.

Faith Ryan Whittlesey,
of Pennsylvania, to be Ambassador Extraordinary
and Plenipotentiary of the United States of
America to Switzerland.

Submitted March 21

Peter C. Myers,
of Missouri, to be an Assistant Secretary of Agriculture, vice John B. Crowell, Jr., resigned.

Robert L. Thompson,
of Indiana, to be an Assistant Secretary of Agriculture, vice William Gene Lesher, resigned.

A. James Barnes,
of the District of Columbia, to be Deputy Administrator of the Environmental Protection Agency,
vice Alvin L. Alm, resigned.

Terence C. Golden,
of Texas, to be Administrator of General Services,
vice Gerald P. Carmen, resigned.

Stephen L. Hammerman,
of New York, to be a Director of the Securities
Investor Protection Corporation for a term expiring December 31, 1985, vice Ralph D. DeNunzio, term expired.

Submitted March 22

Martha Graham,
of New York, to be a member of the National
Council on the Arts for the remainder of the
term expiring September 3, 1986, vice Erich
Leinsdorf.

Submitted March 25

Vernon A. Walters,
of Florida, to be the Representative of the United
States of America to the United Nations, with the
rank and status of Ambassador Extraordinary and
Plenipotentiary, and the Representative of the
United States of America in the Security Council
of the United Nations.

Submitted March 26

John Dimitri Negroponte,
of New York, a career member of the Senior
Foreign Service, Class of Minister-Counselor, to
be Assistant Secretary of State for Oceans and
International Environmental and Scientific Affairs, vice James L. Malone.

Submitted March 27

Donald S. Lowitz,
of Illinois, for the rank of Ambassador while serving as the United States Representative to the
Conference on Disarmament.

George Southall Vest,
of Maryland, a career member of the Senior Foreign Service, Class of Career Minister, to be Director General of the Foreign Service, vice
Alfred L. Atherton, Jr.

Walter K. Stapleton,
of Delaware, to be United States Circuit Judge
for the Third Circuit, vice a new position created
by P.L. 98–353, approved July 10, 1984.

Charles C. Lovell,
of Montana, to be United States District Judge for
the District of Montana, vice a new position created by P.L. 98–353, approved July 10, 1984.

Submitted March 28

Theodore J. Garrish,
of Virginia, to be an Assistant Secretary of
Energy (Congressional, Intergovernmental and
Public Affairs), vice Robert C. Odle, Jr., resigned.

J. Michael Farrell,
of the District of Columbia, to be General Counsel of the Department of Energy, vice Theodore
J. Garrish.

Submitted March 28—Continued

Susan Meredith Phillips,
of Iowa, to be a Commissioner of the Commodity Futures Trading Commission for the term expiring April 13, 1990 (reappointment).

Susan Meredith Phillips,
of Iowa, to be Chairman of the Commodity Futures Trading Commission (reappointment).

Submitted March 29

Beryl Wayne Sprinkel,
of Virginia, to be a member of the Council of Economic Advisers, vice Martin S. Feldstein, resigned.

Submitted April 1

Richard Thomas McCormack,
of Pennsylvania, to be the Representative of the United States of America to the Organization of American States, with the rank of Ambassador.

Robert Dean Blackwill,
of Maryland, a career member of the Senior Foreign Service, Class of Minister-Counselor, for the rank of Ambassador during the tenure of his service as the Representative of the United States of America for Mutual and Balanced Force Reductions Negotiations.

Kenneth F. Ripple,
of Indiana, to be United States Circuit Judge for the Seventh Circuit, vice a new position created by P.L. 98–353, approved July 10, 1984.

Paul A. Adams,
of Maryland, to be Inspector General, Department of Housing and Urban Development, vice Charles L. Dempsey, resigned.

John D. Crawford,
of Illinois, to be a member of the Railroad Retirement Board for the term of 5 years from August 29, 1983, vice Earl Oliver, term expired.

Submitted April 3

Charles A. Gillespie, Jr.,
of California, a career member of the Senior Foreign Service, Class of Counselor, to be Ambassador Extraordinary and Plenipotentiary of the United States of America to the Republic of Colombia.

Submitted April 4

Onalee McGraw,
of Virginia, to be a member of the National Council on Educational Research for a term expiring September 30, 1987 (reappointment).

Submitted April 4—Continued

Marian North Koonce,
of California, to be a member of the National Council on the Handicapped for a term expiring September 23, 1987 (reappointment).

Robert E. Rader, Jr.,
of Texas, to be a member of the Occupational Safety and Health Review Commission for the term expiring April 27, 1991, vice Timothy F. Cleary, term expiring.

Submitted April 5

Sheldon J. Krys,
of Maryland, a career member of the Senior Foreign Service, Class of Minister-Counselor, to be Ambassador Extraordinary and Plenipotentiary of the United States of America to the Republic of Trinidad and Tobago.

John C. Lawn,
of Virginia, to be Administrator of Drug Enforcement, vice Francis M. Mullen, Jr., resigned.

John P. Moore,
of Colorado, to be United States Circuit Judge for the Tenth Circuit, vice Robert H. McWilliams, Jr., retired.

Stanley Sporkin,
of Maryland, to be United States District Judge for the District of Columbia, vice June L. Green, retired.

Herbert M. Rutherford III,
of Virginia, to be United States Marshal for the District of Columbia for the term of 4 years, vice James O. Golden.

Edward A. Curran,
of Maryland, to be Chairman of the National Endowment for the Humanities for a term of 4 years, vice William J. Bennett.

Submitted April 15

Thomas R. Pickering,
of New Jersey, a career member of the Senior Foreign Service, personal rank of Career Ambassador, to be Ambassador Extraordinary and Plenipotentiary of the United States of America to Israel.

Hershey Gold,
of California, to be a member of the United States Commission on Public Diplomacy for a term expiring July 1, 1987 (reappointment).

Submitted April 16

Douglas W. McMinn,
of Virginia, to be an Assistant Secretary of State,
vice Richard T. McCormack, resigning.

Submitted April 17

William Emerson Brock III,
of Tennessee, to be Secretary of Labor.

Lowell C. Kilday,
of Virginia, a career member of the Senior Foreign Service, Class of Minister-Counselor, to be
Ambassador Extraordinary and Plenipotentiary of
the United States of America to the Dominican
Republic.

George F. Gunn, Jr.,
of Missouri, to be United States District Judge for
the Eastern District of Missouri, vice a new position created by P.L. 98–353, approved July 10,
1984.

Sam B. Hall, Jr.,
of Texas, to be United States District Judge for
the Eastern District of Texas, vice Joe J. Fisher,
retired.

William H. Opel,
of Alaska, to be United States Marshal for the
District of Alaska for the term of 4 years, vice
Robert D. Olson, Sr., resigned.

John R. Silber,
of Massachusetts, to be a member of the Advisory
Board for Radio Broadcasting to Cuba for a term
of 1 year (new position).

Glen A. Holden,
of California, to be a member of the National
Museum Services Board for a term expiring December 6, 1989, vice Anne Carroll Badham, term
expired.

Submitted April 18

Joseph F. Salgado,
of California, to be Under Secretary of Energy
vice William Patrick Collins, resigned.

Submitted April 22

Margaret DeBardeleben Tutwiler,
of Alabama, to be an Assistant Secretary of the
Treasury (new position—P.L. 98–549 of October
30, 1984).

Submitted April 23

J. Frederick Motz,
of Maryland, to be United States District Judge
for the District of Maryland, vice a new position
created by P.L. 98–353, approved July 10, 1984.

Gary L. Bauer,
of Virginia, to be Under Secretary of Education,
vice Gary L. Jones, resigned.

Douglas A. Riggs,
of Alaska, to be General Counsel of the Department of Commerce, vice Irving P. Margulies, resigned.

Submitted April 24

John Arthur Ferch,
of Ohio, a career member of the Senior Foreign
Service, Class of Minister-Counselor, to be Ambassador Extraordinary and Plenipotentiary of
the United States of America to the Republic of
Honduras.

Submitted April 25

Abraham D. Sofaer,
of New York, to be Legal Adviser of the Department of State, vice Davis Rowland Robinson, resigned.

Withdrawn April 25

John D. Ward,
of Colorado, to be Director of the Office of Surface Mining Reclamation and Enforcement, vice
James R. Harris, to which position he was appointed during the last recess of the Senate,
which was sent to the Senate on January 3, 1985.

Submitted April 26

D. Lowell Jensen,
of Virginia, to be Deputy Attorney General, vice
Carol E. Dinkins, resigned.

William Bradford Reynolds,
of Maryland, to be Associate Attorney General,
vice D. Lowell Jensen.

Francis S. Blake,
of Maryland, to be an Assistant Administrator of
the Environmental Protection Agency, vice A.
James Barnes.

Submitted April 29

Harry George Barnes, Jr.,
of Maryland, a career member of the Senior Foreign Service, Class of Career Minister, to be Ambassador Extraordinary and Plenipotentiary of

Submitted April 29—Continued
the United States of America to the Republic of
Chile.

William Andreas Brown,
of New Hampshire, a career member of the
Senior Foreign Service, Class of Minister-Counselor, to be Ambassador Extraordinary and Plenipotentiary of the United States of America to the
Kingdom of Thailand.

David George Newton,
of Virginia, a career member of the Senior Foreign Service, Class of Counselor, to be Ambassador Extraordinary and Plenipotentiary of the
United States of America to the Republic of Iraq.

Submitted April 30

Robert L. Pugh,
of Virginia, a career member of the Senior Foreign Service, Class of Counselor, to be Ambassador Extraordinary and Plenipotentiary of the
United States of America to the Islamic Republic
of Mauritania.

Samuel B. Sterrett,
of Maryland, to be a Judge of the United States
Tax Court for a term expiring 15 years after he
takes office (reappointment).

Rose Marie Monk,
of Texas, to be a Commisisoner of the Copyright
Royalty Tribunal for the term of 7 years from
September 27, 1984, vice Thomas C. Brennan,
term expired.

Patti Birge Tyson,
of Texas, to be a Commissioner of the Postal Rate
Commission for the term expiring November 22,
1990, vice James H. Duffy, term expired.

Submitted May 13

John Montague Steadman,
of the District of Columbia, to be an Associate
Judge for the District of Columbia Court of Appeals for the term of 15 years, vice John W. Kern
III, retired.

Submitted May 14

J. William Middendorf II,
of Virginia, to be the Representative of the
United States of America to the European Communities, with the rank and status of Ambassador
Extraordinary and Plenipotentiary.

Edward Joseph Perkins,
of Oregon, a career member of the Senior Foreign Service, Class of Minister-Counselor, to be
Ambassador Extraordinary and Plenipotentiary of

Submitted May 14—Continued
the United States of America to the Republic of
Liberia.

Russell F. Miller,
of Maryland, to be Deputy Inspector General of
the United States Synthetic Fuels Corporation for
a term of 7 years, vice Robert W. Gambino, resigned.

Submitted May 15

Lewis Arthur Tambs,
of Arizona, to be Ambassador Extraordinary and
Plenipotentiary of the United States of America
to the Republic of Costa Rica.

Lannon Walker,
of Maryland, a career member of the Senior Foreign Service, Class of Minister-Counselor, to be
Ambassador Extraordinary and Plenipotentiary of
the United States of America to the Republic of
Senegal.

Loren A. Smith,
of Virginia, to be a Judge of the United States
Claims Court for a term of 15 years, vice Joseph
V. Colaianni, resigned.

Robert C. Broomfield,
of Arizona, to be United States District Judge for
the District of Arizona, vice Valdemar A. Cordova.

Donald E. Walter,
of Louisiana, to be United States District Judge
for the Western District of Louisiana, vice a new
position created by P.L. 98–353, approved July
10, 1984.

Claude M. Hilton,
of Virginia, to be United States District Judge for
the Eastern District of Virginia, vice a new position created by P.L. 98–353, approved July 10,
1984.

Marvin L. Stone,
of Virginia, to be Deputy Director of the United
States Information Agency, vice Leslie Lenkowsky, resigned.

Barbara Jean Mahone,
of Ohio, to be Chairman of the Special Panel on
Appeals for a term of 6 years (new position—P.L.
95–454 of October 13, 1978).

Submitted May 20

L. Craig Johnstone,
of Washington, a career member of the Senior
Foreign Service, Class of Minister-Counselor, to
be Ambassador Extraordinary and Plenipotentia-

Submitted May 20—Continued

ry of the United States of America to the Democratic and Popular Republic of Algeria.

Edward Morgan Rowell,
of California, a career member of the Senior Foreign Service, Class of Minister-Counselor, to be Ambassador Extraordinary and Plenipotentiary of the United States of America to the Republic of Bolivia.

Nicholas Ruwe,
of the District of Columbia, to be Ambassador Extraordinary and Plenipotentiary of the United States of America to the Republic of Iceland.

Glenn R. Wilson,
of Nebraska, to be President, Government National Mortgage Association, vice Robert W. Karpe, resigned.

Antonio Navarro,
of New York, to be a member of the Advisory Board for Radio Broadcasting to Cuba for a term of 3 years (new position).

Submitted May 21

Paul Julian Hare,
of the District of Columbia, a career member of the Senior Foreign Service, Class of Minister-Counselor, to be Ambassador Extraordinary and Plenipotentiary of the United States of America to the Republic of Zambia.

Alice Wright Algood,
of Tennessee, to be a member of the National Museum Services Board for a term expiring December 6, 1989 (reappointment).

Submitted May 22

Robert Michael Kimmitt,
of Virginia, to be General Counsel for the Department of the Treasury, vice Peter J. Wallison, resigned.

Anton Ronald Valukas,
of Illinois, to be United States Attorney for the Northern District of Illinois for the term of 4 years, vice Dan K. Webb, resigned.

Richard A. Levie,
of the District of Columbia, to be an Associate Judge of the Superior Court of the District of Columbia for a term of 15 years, vice John F. Doyle, retired.

Submitted May 29

Wayne E. Alley,
of Oklahoma, to be United States District Judge for the Western District of Oklahoma, vice a new

Submitted May 29—Continued

position created by P.L. 98–353, approved July 10, 1984.

Anne E. Brunsdale,
of the District of Columbia, to be a member of the United States International Trade Commission for the term expiring June 16, 1993, vice Veronica A. Haggart, resigned.

Thomas B. Day,
of California, to be a member of the National Science Board, National Science Foundation, for a term expiring May 10, 1990, vice Michael Kasha, term expired.

Thomas Gale Moore,
of California, to be a member of the Council of Economic Advisers, vice William A. Niskanen, Jr., resigned.

John Douglas Scanlan,
of Hawaii, a career member of the Senior Foreign Service, Class of Minister-Counselor, to be Ambassador Extraordinary and Plenipotentiary of the United States of America to the Socialist Federal Republic of Yugoslavia.

Withdrawn May 29

George Charles Roche III,
of Michigan, to be a member of the National Council on Educational Research for a term expiring September 30, 1986 (reappointment), which was sent to the Senate on January 3, 1985.

Submitted May 31

Lee L. Verstandig,
of the District of Columbia, to be Under Secretary of Housing and Urban Development, vice Philip Abrams, resigned.

Dennis R. Patrick,
of the District of Columbia, to be a member of the Federal Communications Commission for a term of 7 years from July 1, 1985 (reappointment).

Withdrawn May 31

Robert A. Rowland,
of Texas, to be an Assistant Secretary of Labor, vice Thorne G. Auchter, resigned, to which position he was appointed during the recess of the Senate from June 29, 1984, until July 23, 1984, which was sent to the Senate on January 3, 1985.

Anne Elizabeth Brunsdale,
of the District of Columbia, to be a member of the Advisory Board for Radio Broadcasting to

Withdrawn May 31—Continued
Cuba for a term of 2 years (new position), which was sent to the Senate on February 20, 1985.

Submitted June 3

Robert K. Dawson,
of Virginia,
to be an Assistant Secretary of the Army, vice William R. Gianelli, resigned.

Chester Evans Finn, Jr.,
of Tennessee, to be Assistant Secretary for Educational Research and Improvement, Department of Education, vice Donald J. Senese, resigned.

James Johnson Duderstadt,
of Michigan, to be a member of the National Science Board, National Science Foundation, for a term expiring May 10, 1990, vice Edwin Ernest Salpeter, term expired.

Submitted June 5

Alex Kozinski,
of California, to be United States Circuit Judge for the Ninth Circuit, vice a new position created by P.L. 98–353, approved July 10, 1984.

James D. Todd,
of Tennessee, to be United States District Judge for the Western District of Tennessee, vice a new position created by P.L. 98–353, approved July 10, 1984.

Richard V. Wiebusch,
of New Hampshire, to be United States Attorney for the District of New Hampshire for the term of 4 years, vice W. Stephen Thayer III, resigned.

Larry James Stubbs,
of Georgia, to be United States Marshal for the Southern District of Georgia for the term of 4 years, vice M. Clifton Nettles III, deceased.

S. Bruce Smart, Jr.,
of Connecticut, to be Under Secretary of Commerce for International Trade, vice Lionel H. Olmer, resigned.

John William Bode,
of Oklahoma, to be an Assistant Secretary of Agriculture, vice Mary Claiborne Jarratt, resigning.

John R. Norton III,
of Arizona, to be a member of the Board of Directors of the Commodity Credit Corporation, vice Richard E. Lyng, resigned.

Robert L. Thompson,
of Indiana, to be a member of the Board of Directors of the Commodity Credit Corporation, vice William Gene Lesher.

Submitted June 5—Continued
Allie C. Felder, Jr.,
of the District of Columbia, to be a member of the Board of Directors of the Overseas Private Investment Corporation for a term expiring December 17, 1987 (reappointment).

Dwight A. Ink,
of Maryland, to be an Assistant Administrator of the Agency for International Development, vice Victor M. Rivera.

Submitted June 7

John C. Whitehead,
of New Jersey, to be Deputy Secretary of State, vice Kenneth W. Dam.

Thomas Morgan Roberts,
of Tennessee, to be a member of the Nuclear Regulatory Commission for the term of 5 years expiring June 30, 1990 (reappointment).

Submitted June 10

George Cranwell Montgomery,
of Tennessee, to be Ambassador Extraordinary and Plenipotentiary of the United States of America to the Sultanate of Oman.

Perry L. Adkisson,
of Texas, to be a member of the National Science Board, National Science Foundation, for a term expiring May 10, 1990, vice Lewis M. Branscomb, term expired.

Submitted June 11

Clayton Yeutter,
of Nebraska, to be United States Trade Representative, with the rank of Ambassador Extraordinary and Plenipotentiary, vice William Emerson Brock III.

Bruce Chapman,
of Washington, to be the Representative of the United States of America to the Vienna Office of the United Nations and Deputy Representative of the United States of America to the International Atomic Energy Agency, with the rank of Ambassador.

Submitted June 12

Rozanne L. Ridgway,
of the District of Columbia, a career member of the Senior Foreign Service, Class of Career Minister, to be an Assistant Secretary of State, vice Richard R. Burt.

Submitted June 12—Continued

Louis L. Stanton,
of New York, to be United States District Judge
for the Southern District of New York, vice
Henry F. Werker, deceased.

Edwin G. Corr,
of Oklahoma, a career member of the Senior Foreign Service, Class of Minister-Counselor, to be
Ambassador Extraordinary and Plenipotentiary of
the United States of America to the Republic of
El Salvador.

Submitted June 13

Jennifer Ann Hillings,
of California, to be an Assistant Secretary of
Transportation, vice Mari Maseng, resigned.

Henry M. Ventura,
of California, to be Deputy Director of the
ACTION agency, vice Betty H. Brake, resigned.

Submitted June 14

Elliott Abrams,
of the District of Columbia, to be an Assistant
Secretary of State, vice Langhorne A. Motley.

Thomas Anthony Nassif,
of Virginia, to be Ambassador Extraordinary and
Plenipotentiary of the United States of America
to the Kingdom of Morocco.

James M. Rosenbaum,
of Minnesota, to be United States District Judge
for the District of Minnesota, vice a new position
created by P.L. 98–353, approved July 10, 1984.

John S. Erthein,
of California, to be a member of the National
Council on the Handicapped for a term expiring
September 17, 1987 (reappointment).

John R. Wall,
of Ohio, to be a member of the Occupational
Safety and Health Review Commission for the
remainder of the term expiring April 27, 1987,
vice Robert A. Rowland.

Submitted June 17

Richard R. Burt,
of the District of Columbia, to be Ambassador
Extraordinary and Plenipotentiary of the United
States of America to the Federal Republic of Germany.

Submitted June 20

Bernard Kalb,
of Maryland, to be an Assistant Secretary of State,
vice Robert John Hughes, resigned.

Submitted June 20—Continued

Stanley Marcus,
of Florida, to be United States District Judge for
the Southern District of Florida, vice a new position created by P.L. 98–353, approved July 10,
1984.

Thomas E. Scott,
of Florida, to be United States District Judge for
the Southern District of Florida, vice a new position created by P.L. 98–353, approved July 10,
1984.

Submitted June 21

Rebecca Gernhardt Range,
of the District of Columbia, to be an Assistant
Secretary of Transportation, vice Charles G.
Hardin, resigned.

Joseph J. Farnan, Jr.,
of Delaware, to be United States District Judge
for the District of Delaware, vice a new position
created by P.L. 98–353, approved July 10, 1984.

Edmund V. Ludwig,
of Pennsylvania, to be United States District
Judge for the Eastern District of Pennsylvania,
vice Raymond J. Broderick, retired.

Maurice Owens Ellsworth,
of Idaho, to be United States Attorney for the
District of Idaho for the term of 4 years, vice
Guy Gordon Hurlbutt, resigned.

Submitted June 25

Donald Alden Hicks,
of California, to be Under Secretary of Defense
for Research and Engineering, vice Richard D.
DeLauer, resigned.

William P. Horn,
of Virginia, to be Assistant Secretary for Fish and
Wildlife, Department of the Interior, vice G. Ray
Arnett, resigned.

Roger J. Miner,
of New York, to be United States Circuit Judge
for the Second Circuit, vice a new position created by P.L. 98–353, approved July 10, 1984.

Roger L. Wollman,
of South Dakota, to be United States Circuit
Judge for the Eighth Circuit, vice a new position
created by P.L. 98–353, approved July 10, 1984.

Roger G. Strand,
of Arizona, to be United States District Judge for
the District of Arizona, vice Charles A. Muecke,
retired.

869

Richard H. Mills,
of Illinois, to be United States District Judge for
the Central District of Illinois, vice J. Waldo Ack-
erman, deceased.

John M. Walker, Jr.,
of New York, to be United States District Judge
for the Southern District of New York, vice
Morris E. Lasker, retired.

Charles A. Trabandt,
of Virginia, to be a member of the Federal
Energy Regulatory Commission for a term expiring October 20, 1988, vice Georgiana H. Sheldon,
term expired.

J. Winston Porter,
of Virginia, to be Assistant Administrator, Office
of Solid Waste, of the Environmental Protection
Agency, vice Lee M. Thomas.

Appendix C—Checklist of White House Press Releases

The following list contains releases of the Office of the Press Secretary which are not included in this book.

Released January 3

Announcement:
Submission of reports to the President by Presidential Emergency Boards Nos. 205 and 206 to investigate rail labor disputes

Transcript:
Press briefing on the African hunger relief initiative—by M. Peter McPherson, Administrator of the Agency for International Development

Released January 9

Statement:
Unemployment rate figures for December 1984—by Larry M. Speakes, Principal Deputy Press Secretary to the President

Released January 11

Announcement:
Nomination of Herbert Blalock Dixon, Jr., to be an Associate Judge of the Superior Court of the District of Columbia

Released January 15

Statement:
Industrial production and retail sales figures for December 1984—by Larry M. Speakes, Principal Deputy Press Secretary to the President

Announcement:
President's participation in the pregame toss of the coin for Super Bowl XIX via special hookup between Stanford Stadium in Stanford, CA, and the White House

Released January 17

Statement:
Housing starts and housing permit figures for December 1984—by Larry M. Speakes, Principal Deputy Press Secretary to the President

Released January 18

Statement:
Personal income and personal consumption ex-

Released January 18—Continued

penditure figures for November and December 1984—by Larry M. Speakes, Principal Deputy Press Secretary to the President

Transcript:
Press briefing on Soviet-U.S. nuclear and space arms negotiations—by Secretary of State George P. Shultz

Released January 21

Advance text:
Inaugural Address

Released January 22

Transcript:
Press briefing on economic statistics and trends—by Secretary of Commerce Malcolm Baldrige

Statement:
Economic statistics for 1984—by Larry M. Speakes, Principal Deputy Press Secretary to the President

Released January 23

Statement:
Consumer Price Index—by Larry M. Speakes, Principal Deputy Press Secretary to the President

Released January 25

Advance text:
Remarks to the 1985 Reagan Administration Executive Forum at DAR Constitution Hall

Released January 30

Transcript:
Press briefing following her meeting with the President—by Ambassador Jeane J. Kirkpatrick, U.S. Representative to the United Nations

Released February 4

Advance text:
Remarks at the annual convention of the National Religious Broadcasters

Released February 5

Transcript:
Press briefing on the Economic Report of the President—by William A. Niskanen, member of the Council of Economic Advisers

Transcript:
Press briefing on White House personnel changes—by Assistant to the President and Chief of Staff Donald T. Regan

Released February 6

Transcript:
Press briefing following the President's meeting with the Republican congressional leadership on the State of the Union Address—by Senate Majority Leader Robert Dole and House Minority Leader Robert H. Michel

Advance text:
Excerpts from the State of the Union Address

Advance text:
State of the Union Address

Fact sheet:
State of the Union Address

Released February 8

Transcript:
Press briefing on the Central American energy and mineral development program-by M. Peter McPherson, Administrator of the Agency for International Development and Senator Pete V. Domenici of New Mexico

Released February 11

Advance text:
Toast at the state dinner for King Fahd bin 'Abd al-'Aziz Al Sa'ud of Saudi Arabia

Released February 13

Statement:
Retail sales figures for January—by Larry M. Speakes, Principal Deputy Press Secretary to the President

Released February 19

Statement:
Housing starts and building permit figures for January—by Larry M. Speakes, Principal Deputy Press Secretary to the President

Announcement:
Submission by Presidential Emergency Board No. 207 of its report to the President concerning a dispute between the Port Authority Trans-

Released February 19—Continued
Hudson Corporation (PATH) and the Brotherhood of Railroad Signalmen

Released February 20

Advance text:
Toast at a dinner hosted by Prime Minister Margaret Thatcher of the United Kingdom at the British Embassy

Released February 25

Announcement:
Nomination of Thomas J. Aquilino, Jr., to be a Judge of the United States Court of International Trade, Frank H. Easterbrook to be United States Circuit Judge for the Seventh Circuit, James F. Holderman, Jr., to be United States District Judge for the Northern District of Illinois, and James R. Laffoon to be United States Marshal for the Southern District of California

Released February 26

Announcement:
Nomination of Melvin T. Brunetti to be United States Circuit Judge for the Ninth Circuit, R. Allan Edgar to be United States District Judge for the Eastern District of Tennessee, and Howell Cobb to be United States District Judge for the Eastern District of Texas

Transcript:
Press briefing following the President's meeting with the Republican congressional leadership to discuss the farm situation, the budget, and the MX missile—by Senate Majority Leader Robert Dole and House Minority Leader Robert H. Michel

Released February 27

Announcement:
Nomination of Edith H. Jones to be United States Circuit Judge for the Fifth Circuit, George La Plata to be United States District Judge for the Eastern District of Michigan, and Ronald E. Meredith to be United States District Judge for the Western District of Kentucky

Released February 28

Announcement:
Nomination of Joseph H. Rodriguez to be United States District Judge for the District of New Jersey, Alice M. Batchelder to be United States District Judge for the Northern District of Ohio, and Herman J. Weber to be United States District Judge for the Southern District of Ohio

Released February 28—Continued
Advance text:
Remarks at the annual meeting of the National Association of Independent Schools

Released March 1

Advance text:
Remarks at the 12th annual Conservative Political Action Conference dinner

Fact sheet:
President's Blue Ribbon Task Group on Nuclear Weapons Program Management

Released March 4

Advance text:
Remarks at the annual legislative conference of the National Association of Counties

Released March 6

Fact sheet:
H.R. 1096, farm credit and African famine relief bill

Released March 7

Announcement:
Nomination of Carol Los Mansmann to be United States Circuit Judge for the Third Circuit

Announcement:
Nomination of J. Thomas Greene to be United States District Judge for the District of Utah

Announcement:
Nomination of Carolyn R. Dimmick to be United States District Judge for the Western District of Washington

Released March 8

Statement:
Unemployment rate for February—by Larry M. Speakes, Principal Deputy Press Secretary to the President

Announcement:
Nomination of Mark L. Wolf to be United States District Judge for the District of Massachusetts

Announcement:
Nomination of William G. Young to be United States District Judge for the District of Massachusetts

Transcript:
Press briefing on Soviet-U.S. nuclear and space arms negotiations—by Robert C. McFarlane, Assistant to the President for National Security Affairs

Released March 8—Continued
Transcript:
Press briefing on the President's trip to Canada—by Assistant Secretary of State for European and Canadian Affairs Richard R. Burt

Released March 11

Announcement:
Results of the President's annual physical examination (2 releases)

Released March 12

Advance text:
Toast at a dinner honoring President Mohammed Hosni Mubarak of Egypt

Released March 13

Statement:
Retail and durable goods sales figures for February—by Larry M. Speakes, Principal Deputy Press Secretary to the President

Announcement:
Nomination of Ann C. Williams to be United States District Judge for the Northern District of Illinois

Released March 15

Announcement:
Distribution of surplus moneys from the Presidential Inaugural Fund

Released March 17

Advance text:
Remarks upon arrival at Quebec City, Canada

Released March 18

Advance text:
Toast at a luncheon with Provincial and community leaders in Quebec City, Canada

Advance text:
Remarks at the signing ceremony for documents issued at the conclusion of meetings with Prime Minister Brian Mulroney of Canada

Released March 19

Advance text:
Remarks at the Senate Republican Policy Committee luncheon

Advance text:
Toast at the state dinner for President Raúl Alfonsin of Argentina

Released March 20

Transcript:
Press briefing on his nomination to be Secretary of Labor—by William E. Brock

Released March 21

Statement:
Gross national product figures for the fourth quarter of 1984—by Larry M. Speakes, Principal Deputy Press Secretary to the President

Released March 22

Statement:
Consumer Price Index and durable goods sales figures for February—by Larry M. Speakes, Principal Deputy Press Secretary to the President

Announcement:
Nomination of John Montague Steadman to be an Associate Judge of the District of Columbia Court of Appeals

Released March 25

Fact sheet:
Proposed summer youth employment opportunity wage legislation

Released March 27

Announcement:
Nomination of Walter K. Stapleton to be United States Circuit Judge for the Third Circuit

Announcement:
Nomination of Charles C. Lovell to be United States District Judge for the District of Montana

Released March 28

Advance text:
Remarks to brokers and staff at the New York Stock Exchange

Advance text:
Remarks to the students and faculty of St. John's University in New York, NY.

Released March 29

Statement:
Leading economic indicators for February—by Larry M. Speakes, Principal Deputy Press Secretary to the President

Advance text:
Remarks at the National Space Club luncheon

Released April 1

Announcement:
Nomination of Kenneth F. Ripple to be United States Circuit Judge for the Seventh Circuit

Released April 3

Transcript:
Press briefing following the President's meeting with the Republican congressional leadership on the budget and tax reform—by Senate Majority Leader Robert Dole and House Minority Leader Robert H. Michel

Released April 4

Transcript:
Press briefing on Central America—by Robert C. McFarlane, Assistant to the President for National Security Affairs

Statement:
White House and Senate Republican leadership agreement on a budget reduction plan—by Donald T. Regan, Assistant to the President and Chief of Staff

Transcript:
Press briefing on the budget—by Donald T. Regan, Assistant to the President and Chief of Staff

Transcript:
Press briefing on the budget—by David A. Stockman, Director of the Office of Management and Budget

Statement by the President:
Central American peace proposal (as read to reporters in the Briefing Room)

Released April 5

Announcement:
Nomination of Stanley Sporkin to be United States District Judge for the District of Columbia

Announcement:
Nomination of John P. Moore to be United States Circuit Judge for the Tenth Circuit

Announcement:
Nomination of Herbert M. Rutherford III to be United States Marshal for the District of Columbia

Statement:
Employment figures for March—by Larry M. Speakers, Principal Deputy Press Secretary to the President

Released April 9

Statement:
Japan-U.S. trade relations—by Donald T. Regan, Assistant to the President and Chief of Staff

Released April 10

Transcript:
Press briefing on Soviet-U.S. relations and on Nicaragua—by Assistant to the President for National Security Affairs Robert C. McFarlane

Released April 11

Fact sheet:
Economic Policy Council and Domestic Policy Council

Released April 12

Statement:
Producer price index figures for March—by Larry M. Speakes, Principal Deputy Press Secretary to the President

Photocopy:
1984 income tax return of the President and Mrs. Reagan

Released April 15

Advance text:
Remarks at the Nicaraguan Refugee Fund dinner

Excerpts:
Quotations from the President's remarks at the Nicaraguan Refugee Fund dinner

Released April 16

Transcript:
Press briefing following the President's meeting with the Republican congressional leadership on aid to the Nicaraguan democratic resistance and the budget—by Senator Alan K. Simpson of Wyoming and House Minority Leader Robert H. Michel

Statement:
Housing starts, housing permit figures, and the Index of Industrial Production for March 1985—by Larry M. Speakes, Principal Deputy Press Secretary to the President

Released April 17

Announcement:
Nomination of George F. Gunn, Jr., to be United States District Judge for the Eastern District of Missouri

Released April 17—Continued
Announcement:
Nomination of Sam B. Hall, Jr., to be United States District Judge for the Eastern District of Texas

Announcement:
Nomination of William H. Opel to be United States Marshal for the District of Alaska

Released April 18

Statement:
First quarter gross national product figures—by Larry M. Speakes, Principal Deputy Press Secretary to the President

Released April 23

Advance text:
Remarks at the midyear conference of the National Association of Realtors

Statement:
Consumer Price Index—by Larry M. Speakes, Principal Deputy Press Secretary to the President

Announcement:
Nomination of J. Frederick Motz to be United States District Judge for the District of Maryland

Released April 24

Transcript:
Press briefing on the budget—by Donald T. Regan, Assistant to the President and Chief of Staff, and David A. Stockman, Director of the Office of Management and Budget

Excerpts:
President's address to the Nation on the Federal budget and deficit reduction

Advance text:
Address to the Nation on the Federal budget and deficit reduction

Fact sheet:
Address to the Nation on the Federal budget and deficit reduction

Released April 25

Statement:
Public response to the President's address to the Nation on the Federal budget and deficit reduction—by Larry M. Speakes, Principal Deputy Press Secretary to the President

875

Released April 29

Statement:
New home sales for March—by Larry M. Speakes, Principal Deputy Press Secretary to the President

Advance text:
Remarks to the U.S. Chamber of Commerce

Transcript:
Press briefing on the economic summit—by Secretary of the Treasury James A. Baker III

Released April 30

Statement:
Leading economic indicators for March—by Larry M. Speakes, Deputy Press Secretary to the President

Announcement:
Nomination of Samuel B. Sterrett to be a Judge of the United States Tax Court

Transcript:
Press briefing on the President's trip to Europe—by Secretary of State George P. Shultz

Advance text:
Remarks on departure for the trip to Europe

Released May 1

Fact sheet:
On the Nicaraguan economy, sugar exports, and trade with the United States

Transcript:
Interview of Donald T. Regan, Assistant to the President and Chief of Staff—by Andrea Mitchell, NBC News "Today"

Released May 2

Fact sheet:
Economic sanctions against Nicaragua

Transcript:
Interview of Secretary of State George P. Shultz by CBS News "Morning"

Transcript:
Interview of Donald T. Regan, Assistant to the President and Chief of Staff, by ABC News "Good Morning America"

Transcript:
Press briefing on the President's bilateral meetings with Bonn Economic Summit participants—by Secretary of State George P. Shultz

Released May 2—Continued
Transcript:
Interview of Secretary of the Treasury James A. Baker III by NBC News "Today"

Released May 3

Statement:
Unemployment rate for April—by Larry M. Speakes, Principal Deputy Press Secretary to the President

Transcript:
Interview of Secretary of the Treasury James A. Baker III by ABC News "Good Morning America"

Transcript:
Interview of Secretary of State George P. Shultz by NBC News "Today"

Transcript:
Press briefing on the Bonn Economic Summit—by Secretary of State George P. Shultz

Released May 4

Transcript:
Press briefing on the Bonn Economic Summit—by Secretary of the Treasury James A. Baker III

Transcript:
Press briefing on the Bonn Economic Summit—by Secretary of State George P. Shultz

Released May 5

Advance text:
Remarks at Bergen-Belsen concentration camp, Federal Republic of Germany

Advance text:
Remarks at Bitburg Air Base, Federal Republic of Germany

Biographical data:
Gen. Matthew B. Ridgway, USA (Ret.), who accompanied the President to the German military cemetery in Bitburg, Federal Republic of Germany

Biographical data:
Gen. Johanner Steinhoff, German Air Force (Ret.), who accompanied German Chancellor Helmut Kohl to the German military cemetery in Bitburg, Federal Republic of Germany

Advance text:
Toast at the state dinner in Bonn, Federal Republic of Germany

Released May 5—Continued
Transcript:
Interview of Secretary of State George P. Shultz by CBS News "Face the Nation"

Transcript:
Interview of Assistant Secretary of State Richard R. Burt and Franz-Josef Strauss, head of the Christian Social Union, by NBC News "Meet the Press"

Released May 6

Advance text:
Remarks in Hambach, Federal Republic of Germany

Transcript:
Interview of Assistant to the President for National Security Affairs Robert C. McFarlane by CBS News "Morning News"

Released May 7

Advance text:
Remarks to Spanish community leaders in Madrid, Spain

Advance text:
Toast at the state dinner in Madrid, Spain

Transcript:
Press briefing on the President's visit to Spain— by Secretary of State George P. Shultz

Transcript:
Press briefing on the President's address to a special session of the European Parliament in Strasbourg, France—by Assistant to the President for National Security Affairs Robert C. McFarlane

Transcript:
Interview of Assistant to the President for National Security Affairs Robert C. McFarlane by NBC News "Today"

Released May 8

Advance text:
Address to a special session of the European Parliament in Strasbourg, France

Fact sheet:
Address to a special session of the European Parliament in Strasbourg, France

Released May 9

Advance text:
Address to the Assembly of the Republic in Lisbon, Portugal

Released May 9—Continued
Advance text:
Toast at the state dinner in Lisbon, Portugal

Transcript:
Interview of Donald T. Regan, Assistant to the President and Chief of Staff, by CBS News "Morning News"

Transcript:
Press briefing on the President's trip to Europe— by Secretary of State George P. Shultz

Released May 10

Transcript:
Interview of Donald T. Regan, Assistant to the President and Chief of Staff, by NBC News "Today"

Statement by the President:
The trip to Europe and the fiscal year 1986 budget (as read to administration officials and members of the White House staff upon return to the White House)

Released May 14

Statement:
Retail sales figures for April—by Larry M. Speakes, Principal Deputy Press Secretary to the President

Released May 15

Announcement:
Nomination of Robert C. Broomfield to be United States District Judge for the District of Arizona

Announcement:
Nomination of Claude M. Hilton to be United States District Judge for the Eastern District of Virginia

Announcement:
Nomination of Loren A. Smith to be a Judge of the United States Claims Court

Released May 16

Statement:
Housing starts and housing permit figures for April—by Larry M. Speakes, Principal Deputy Press Secretary to the President

Released May 21

Statement:
First quarter growth of the gross national product—by Larry M. Speakes, Principal Deputy Press Secretary to the President

Released May 21—Continued

Transcript:
Press briefing following the President's meeting with the Republican congressional leadership on the budget and aid to the Nicaraguan democratic resistance—by Senate Majority Leader Robert Dole and House Minority Leader Robert H. Michel

Released May 22

Advance text:
Remarks at commencement exercises at the U.S. Naval Academy in Anapolis, MD.

Announcement:
Nomination of Richard A. Levie to be an Associate Judge of the Superior Court of the District of Columbia

Announcement:
Nomination of Anton Ronald Valukas to be the United States Attorney for the Northern District of Illinois

Announcement:
The President's visit to Arlington National Cemetery and Orlando and Miami, FL, on May 27

Released May 23

Transcript:
Press briefing on Senate approval of production of the MX missile—by Assistant to the President for National Security Affairs Robert C. McFarlane

Released May 24

Advance text:
Remarks to the National Association of Manufacturers

Released May 27

Advance text:
Remarks to participants in the President's Inaugural Bands Parade at Walt Disney's EPCOT Center near Orlando, FL

Advance text:
Remarks at a fundraising dinner for Senator Paula Hawkins in Miami, FL

Released May 28

Announcement:
Nomination of Wayne E. Alley to be United States District Judge for the Western District of Oklahoma

Advance text:
Address to the Nation on tax reform

Released May 28—Continued

Fact sheet:
Address to the Nation on tax reform

Released May 29

Transcript:
Interview of Donald T. Regan, Assistant to the President and Chief of Staff, by ABC News "Good Morning America"

Transcript:
Interview of Secretary of the Treasury James A. Baker III on NBC News "Today"

Transcript:
Interview of Secretary of the Treasury James A. Baker III on CBS News "Morning News"

Released May 30

Advance text:
Remarks at the "Prelude to Independence" celebration in Williamsburg, VA

Advance text:
Remarks to citizens of Oshkosh, WI

Fact sheet:
The President's trip to Virginia and Wisconsin

Released May 31

Advance text:
Remarks at the Great Valley Corporate Center, Malvern, PA

Released June 4

Announcement:
Nomination of James D. Todd to be United States District Judge for the Western District of Tennessee

Announcement:
Nomination of Alex Kozinski to be United States Circuit Judge for the Ninth Circuit

Announcement:
Nomination of Richard V. Wiebusch to be United States Attorney for the District of New Hampshire

Announcement:
Nomination of Larry James Stubbs to be United States Marshal for the Southern District of Georgia

Transcript:
Press briefing following the President's meeting with the Republican congressional leadership on tax reform and on aid to the Nicaraguan democratic resistance—by Senate Majority Leader

Released June 4—Continued
Robert Dole and House Minority Leader Robert
H. Michel

Released June 5

Advance text:
Remarks at the AT&T Technologies Plant in
Oklahoma City, OK

Advance text:
Remarks at a fundraising luncheon for Senator
Don Nickles in Oklahoma City, OK

Advance text:
Remarks at a fundraising dinner for Senator
Mack Mattingly in Atlanta, GA

Released June 6

Advance text:
Remarks at Northside High School in Atlanta, GA

Advance text:
Remarks at a fundraising luncheon for Senator
Jeremiah Denton in Birmingham, AL

Released June 7

Statement:
Household survey of unemployment figures for
May—by Larry M. Speakes, Principal Deputy
Press Secretary to the President

Released June 10

Transcript:
Press briefing on compliance with arms control
agreements—by Assistant to the President for
National Security Affairs Robert C. McFarlane

Fact sheet:
Building an interim framework for mutual restraint

Released June 11

Transcript:
Press briefing following the President's meeting
with a bipartisan group of Members of the House
of Representatives—by House Minority Leader
Robert H. Michel and Representatives Joseph M.
McDade of Pennsylvania, Dante B. Fascell of
Florida, and Dave McCurdy of Oklahoma

Announcement:
Nomination of Louis L. Stanton to be United
States District Judge for the Southern District of
New York

Released June 12

Announcement:
The President's Citation Program for Private
Sector Initiatives and award recipients

Released June 13

Advance text:
Remarks to citizens in Bloomfield, NJ

Released June 14

Statement:
Producer Price Index—by Larry M. Speakes,
Principal Deputy Press Secretary to the Presi-
dent

Advance text:
Remarks at the "Pause for the Pledge of Alle-
giance" program at Fort McHenry in Baltimore,
MD

Announcement:
Nomination of James M. Rosenbaum to be United
States District Judge for the District of Minnesota

Released June 16

Transcript:
Press briefing of the Trans World Airlines hijack-
ing incident—by Robert B. Sims, Deputy Press
Secretary for Foreign Affairs

Released June 18

Fact sheet:
Concerning Executive Order 12510 of April 17

Released June 19

Advance text:
Remarks at the annual national convention of the
U.S. Jaycees in Indianapolis, IN

Transcript:
Press briefing on the Vice President's upcoming
European trip—by the Vice President

Released June 20

Statement:
Gross national product second quarter growth
rate and consumer prices for May—by Larry M.
Speakes, Principal Deputy Press Secretary to the
President

Excerpts:
Letter to the President from King Hussein I of
Jordan

Released June 20—Continued

Announcement:
Nomination of Stanley Marcus to be United States District Judge for the Southern District of Florida

Announcement:
Nomination of Thomas E. Scott to be United States District Judge for the Southern District of Florida

Released June 21

Advance text:
Remarks at the annual convention of the Lions Club International in Dallas, TX

Announcement:
Nomination of Joseph J. Farnan, Jr., to be United States District Judge for the District of Delaware

Announcement:
Nomination of Edmund V. Ludwig to be United States District Judge for the Eastern District of Pennsylvania

Announcement:
Nomination of Maurice Owens Ellsworth to be United States Attorney for the District of Idaho

Released June 24

Advance text:
Remarks at a fundraising reception for the John F. Kennedy Library Foundation in McLean, VA

Released June 25

Announcement:
Nomination of Richard H. Mills to be United States District Judge for the Central District of Illinois

Announcement:
Nomination of Roger J. Miner to be United States Circuit Judge for the Second Circuit

Announcement:
Nomination of Roger G. Strand to be United States District Judge for the District of Arizona

Released June 25—Continued

Announcement:
Nomination of John M. Walker, Jr., to be United States District Judge for the Southern District of New York

Announcement:
Nomination of Roger L. Wollman to be United States Circuit Judge for the Eighth Circuit

Released June 28

Advance text:
Remarks to citizens in Chicago Heights, IL

Released June 30

Transcript:
Interview of Assistant to the President for National Security Affairs Robert C. McFarlane by ABC News

Transcript:
Interview of Assistant to the President for National Security Affairs Robert C. McFarlane by CBS News

Transcript:
Interview of Assistant to the President for National Security Affairs Robert C. McFarlane by NBC News

Transcript:
Interview of Assistant to the President for National Security Affairs Robert C. McFarlane by Cable Network News

Transcript:
Interview of Assistant to the President for National Security Affairs Robert C. McFarlane by Independent Network News

Transcript:
Press briefing on the release of American hostages in the Trans World Airlines hijacking incident—by Secretary of State George P. Shultz

Summary of events:
Trans World Airlines hijacking incident

Appendix D—Acts Approved by the President

Approved January 9

S.J. Res. 6 / Public Law 99–1
A joint resolution extending the time within which the President may transmit the Budget Message and the Economic Report to the Congress and extending the time within which the Joint Economic Committee shall file its report

Approved February 11

S.J. Res. 36 / Public Law 99–2
A joint resolution to designate the week of February 10, 1985, through February 16, 1985, as "National DECA Week"

Approved March 8

H.J. Res. 50 / Public Law 99–3
A joint resolution designating the week beginning March 3, 1985, as "Women's History Week"

Approved March 13

H.R. 1251 / Public Law 99–4
An act to apportion funds for construction of the National System of Interstate and Defense Highways for fiscal years 1985 and 1986 and substitute highway and transit projects for fiscal years 1984 and 1985

Approved March 15

H.R. 1093 / Public Law 99–5
Pacific Salmon Treaty Act of 1985

Approved March 22

H.J. Res. 85 / Public Law 99–6
A joint resolution to designate the week of March 24, 1985, through March 30, 1985, as "National Skin Cancer Prevention and Detection Week"

Approved March 27

S. 592 / Public Law 99–7
An act to provide that the chairmanship of the Commission on Security and Cooperation in Europe shall rotate between members appointed from the House of Representatives and members appointed from the Senate, and for other purposes

S. 689 / Public Law 99–8
African Famine Relief and Recovery Act of 1985

Approved April 3

H.J. Res. 134 / Public Law 99–9
A joint resolution authorizing and requesting the President to designate the week of March 10 through 16, 1985, as "National Employ-the-Older-Worker Week"

Approved April 4

H.R. 1239 / Public Law 99–10
An act making urgent supplemental appropriations for the fiscal year ending September 30, 1985, for emergency famine relief and recovery in Africa, and for other purposes

S.J. Res. 79 / Public Law 99–11
A joint resolution to designate April 1985, as "Fair Housing Month"

S.J. Res. 62 / Public Law 99–12
A joint resolution commemorating the twenty-fifth anniversary of United States weather satellites

H.J. Res. 121 / Public Law 99–13
A joint resolution to designate the month of April 1985 as "National Child Abuse Prevention Month"

H.J. Res. 160 / Public Law 99–14
A joint resolution designating March 22, 1985, as "National Energy Education Day"

H.R. 1866 / Public Law 99–15
An act to phase out the Federal supplemental compensation program

S.J. Res. 50 / Public Law 99–16
A joint resolution to designate the week of April 1, 1985, through April 7, 1985, as "World Health Week", and to designate April 7, 1985, as "World Health Day"

S.J. Res. 71 / Public Law 99–17
A joint resolution to approve the obligation of funds made available by Public Law 98–473 for the procurement of MX missiles, subject to the enactment of a second joint resolution

H.J. Res. 181 / Public Law 99–18
A joint resolution to approve the obligation and availability of prior year unobligated balances

Approved April 4—Continued
made available for fiscal year 1985 for the procurement of additional operational MX missiles

H.J. Res. 186 / Public Law 99–19
A joint resolution designating April 2, 1985, as "Education Day, U.S.A."

Approved April 14

H.J. Res. 74 / Public Law 99–20
A joint resolution to designate the week of September 8, 1985, as "National Independent Retail Grocer Week"

S.J. Res. 35 / Public Law 99–21
A joint resolution to authorize and request the President to issue a proclamation designating April 21 through April 27, 1985, as "National Organ Donation Awareness Week"

Approved April 15

H.R. 1847 / Public Law 99–22
An act to amend title 28, United States Code, with respect to the United States Sentencing Commission

H.R. 730 / Public Law 99–23
An act to declare that the United States holds in trust for the Cocopah Indian Tribe of Arizona certain land in Yuma County, Arizona

Approved April 16

S.781 / Public Law 99–24
An act to amend the Biomass Energy and Alcohol Fuels Act of 1980 to clarify the intention of section 221 of the Act

Approved April 19

H.J. Res. 236 / Public Law 99–25
A joint resolution commemorating the twenty-fourth anniversary of the Bay of Pigs invasion to liberate Cuba from Communist tyranny

S.J. Res. 17 / Public Law 99–26
A joint resolution to authorize and request the President to issue a proclamation designating April 21 through April 28, 1985, as "Jewish Heritage Week"

S.J. Res. 109 / Public Law 99–27
A joint resolution to designate the week of April 14, 1985, as "Crime Victims Week"

Approved April 25

S.J. Res. 63 / Public Law 99–28
A joint resolution to designate the week of April 21, 1985, through April 27, 1985, as "National DES Awareness Week"

Approved April 25—Continued
S.J. Res. 15 / Public Law 99–29
A joint resolution to designate May 7, 1985, as "Helsinki Human Rights Day"

Approved April 30

H.J. Res. 33 / Public Law 99–30
A joint resolution designating the month of May 1985, as "National Child Safety Awareness Month"

Approved May 14

S.J. Res. 64 / Public Law 99–31
A joint resolution to designate the week beginning May 5, 1985, as "National Correctional Officers Week"

S.J. Res. 83 / Public Law 99–32
A joint resolution designating the week beginning on May 5, 1985, as "National Asthma and Allergy Awareness Week"

H.J. Res. 258 / Public Law 99–33
A joint resolution to designate May 6, 1985, as "Dr. Jonas E. Salk Day"

H.J. Res. 195 / Public Law 99–34
A joint resolution designating May 1985 as "Older Americans Month"

S.J. Res. 128 / Public Law 99–35
A joint resolution to designate May 7, 1985, as "Vietnam Veterans Recognition Day"

Approved May 15

S. 597 / Public Law 99–36
An act to amend subtitle II of title 46, United States Code, "Shipping", making technical and conforming changes, and for other purposes

S.J. Res. 65 / Public Law 99–37
A joint resolution designating the month of November 1985 as "National Alzheimer's Disease Month"

S.J. Res. 53 / Public Law 99–38
A joint resolution to authorize and request the President to designate the month of June 1985 as "Youth Suicide Prevention Month"

S.J. Res. 94 / Public Law 99–39
A joint resolution to designate the week beginning May 12, 1985, as "National Digestive Diseases Awareness Week"

S.J. Res. 60 / Public Law 99–40
A joint resolution to designate the week of May 12, 1985, through May 18, 1985, as "Senior Center Week"

Approved May 17

S.J. Res. 59 / Public Law 99–41
A joint resolution to designate "National Science Week"

Approved May 20

S.J. Res. 61 / Public Law 99–42
A joint resolution to designate the week of May 20, 1985, through May 26, 1985, as "National Osteoporosis Awareness Week"

Approved May 21

S.J. Res. 103 / Public Law 99–43
A joint resolution to designate the month of May 1985, as "Very Special Arts U.S.A. Month"

Approved May 24

H.R. 1869 / Public Law 99–44
An act to amend the Internal Revenue Code of 1954 to repeal the contemporaneous recordkeeping requirements added by the Tax Reform Act of 1984, and for other purposes

S. 661 / Public Law 99–45
An act entitled the "George Milligan Control Tower"

S. 484 / Public Law 99–46
An act to amend the Saccharin Study and Labeling Act

Approved June 11

H.R. 2268 / Public Law 99–47
United States-Israel Free Trade Area Implementation Act of 1985

Approved June 12

S.J. Res. 93 / Public Law 99–48
A joint resolution to designate the month of May 1985 as "Better Hearing and Speech Month"

Approved June 13

S.J. Res. 66 / Public Law 99–49
A joint resolution designating June 14, 1985, as "Baltic Freedom Day"

Approved June 14

S.J. Res. 142 / Public Law 99–50
A joint resolution to designate June 12, 1985, as "Anne Frank Day"

H.J. Res. 25 / Public Law 99–51
A joint resolution to designate the week beginning June 2, 1985, as "National Theatre Week"

H.J. Res. 64 / Public Law 99–52
A joint resolution designating Mother's Day, May 12, 1985, to Father's Day, June 16, 1985, as "Family Reunion Month"

Approved June 17

H.R. 873 / Public Law 99–53
An act to amend title 5, United States Code, to provide that employee organizations which are not eligible to participate in the Federal employees health benefits program solely because of the requirement that applications for approval be filed before January 1, 1980, may apply to become so eligible, and for other purposes

Approved June 20

H.J. Res. 211 / Public Law 99–54
A joint resolution to recognize the pause for the Pledge of Allegiance as part of National Flag Day activities

Approved June 26

H.R. 14 / Public Law 99–55
An act to designate the Federal Building and United States Courthouse in Ashland, Kentucky, as the "Carl D. Perkins Federal Building and United States Courthouse"

S.J. Res. 125 / Public Law 99–56
A joint resolution designating the week of June 23, 1985, through June 29, 1985, as "Helen Keller Deaf-Blind Awareness Week"

Approved June 27

S.J. Res. 87 / Public Law 99–57
A joint resolution to provide for the designation of July 19, 1985, as "National P.O.W./M.I.A. Recognition Day"

Subject Index

Name Index

Abe, Shintaro—2–4
Abell, Richard Bender—34
Abdnor, James S.—659, 660
Abdul-Jabbar, Kareem—741
Abrams, Elliott—546, 646, 817
Adams, John—56
Adams, John Quincy—418
Adams, Paul A.—366
Adelman, Kenneth L.—63, 638
Adenauer, Konrad—571, 583, 584
Adkisson, Perry L.—732
Ahmadi, Hamid Bahrami—473
Akiyama, Toyohiro—534
Aladjem, Henrietta—470
Alberdi, Juan Bautista—311
Albert, Frank—721
Alexander III—591
Alexander, Bill—715
Alexander, Lamar—210, 211
Alfonsín, Maria Lorenzo—316
Alfonsín, Raúl—311, 313, 315, 455
Algood, Alice Wright—636
Allbritton, Joe L.—505
Allison, Edward E.—436
Alvarado, Donna M.—98, 470
Alvarez, Luis W.—362
Amdahl, Gene Myron—280
Anderson, Jack—211
Antonucci, Al—370
Arafat, Yasser—167, 332
Arendt, Hannah—582
Arey, Linda Lugenia—414
Armey, Richard—803
Armstrong, Ben—117
Armstrong, Debbie—340
Armstrong, Neil A.—362
Armstrong, William L.—314
Arndt, Mary Jo—9
Ashford, Nicholas—414, 418
Austin, Jeannie—673

Babbage, Charles—165
Babson, Marshall B.—271
Bach, Johann Sebastian—572
Bachrach, Howard L.—215
Baker, Earl—236
Baker, Howard H., Jr.—424
Baker, James A., III—15, 16, 20, 26, 30, 40, 105,
    114, 116, 131, 333, 419, 420, 519, 659, 660,
    704, 711, 712, 733, 736
Baker, William O.—185
Bakes, Philip John, Jr.—273
Baldrige, Malcolm—183, 184, 419, 704
Ball, William L., III—238
Banting, Frederick Grant—305
Barbour, Haley—492
Barnes, Albert James—322

Barnes, Harry George, Jr.—512
Barness, Lynda Anne—139
Barnett, Barney—175
Barreaux, Theodore C.—608
Barry, John L.—654
Barry, Marion—343
Bartholdi, Auguste—584
Bartlett, Dewey—716
Barton, Esther—824
Basie, William (Count)—413, 656
Bauer, Gary L.—472
Baumgaertner, William Eugene—763
Baylor, Elgin—293
Beasley, Henry R.—244
Becket, MacDonald G.—148
Beeston, Richard—524
Beethoven, Ludwig van—572
Bell, Alexander Graham—184, 583
Bell, Temple—481
Bell, Wilson—481
Belli, Humberto—452
Bellmon, Henry—716
Bello, Andres—67
Bemiss, FitzGerald—22
Benjamin, Norman L.—195
Bendjedid, Chadli—443, 445, 447–449
Bendjedid, Halima—443, 447, 448
Benét, Stephen Vincent—814
Benjamin, Normal L.—814
Bennett, Thomas E., Jr.—654
Bennett, William J.—31, 32, 71, 216, 358, 419,
    459, 798, 799
Berg, Paul—215
Bergman, Irving T.—45
Bergsma, Joel J.—170
Berri, Nabih—782, 783, 790, 812
Berryman, Kenneth—799
Best, Charles Herbert—305
Betancur, Rosa Elena Alvarez de—397
Betancur Cuartas, Belisario—396, 399, 413, 416,
    469
Biebel, Frederick K.—816
Bieber, Owen—195
Bing, Dave—293
Blackwill, Robert Dean—367, 639
Blake, Francis S.—504
Blaylock, Lynn—482
Bledsoe, Ralph C.—801
Bloch, Erich—184
Block, John R.—83, 207, 249, 369, 419
Boada, Claudio—575, 576, 758
Bobko, Karol J.—449, 450
Bockstiegel, Karl-Heinz—473
Bode, John William—706
Boehm, Richard Wood—434
Bolaños, Enrique—342